CHAUCER'S

MAJOR POETRY

CHAUCER READING TO A ROYAL AND NOBLE AUDIENCE

Corpus Christi College, Cambridge, MS 61
Reproduced by permission.

ALBERT C. BAUGH

UNIVERSITY OF PENNSYLVANIA

Editor

Chaucer's Major Poetry

PRENTICE-HALL, INC., *Englewood Cliffs, New Jersey*

ISBN: 0-13-128223-9

Library of Congress Catalog Card Number: 63-10513

19   18   17   16   15

PRENTICE-HALL INTERNATIONAL, INC., *London*
PRENTICE-HALL OF AUSTRALIA, PTY. LTD., *Sydney*
PRENTICE-HALL OF CANADA, LTD., *Toronto*
PRENTICE-HALL OF INDIA PRIVATE LIMITED, *New Delhi*
PRENTICE-HALL OF JAPAN, INC., *Tokyo*

PREFACE

THE PRESENT VOLUME offers critical texts of all of Chaucer's poetry except the *Romaunt of the Rose*, the fragmentary *Anelida and Arcite*, and a few of the short lyrics. *The Legend of Good Women* is represented by the original version of the Prologue and the legend of Cleopatra. Otherwise all texts are complete. From *The Canterbury Tales* only the two prose treatises are omitted. Information concerning the manuscripts on which the various texts are based will be found in the introductions to the separate poems.

A feature of the edition is the extensive annotation on the same page as the text. The notes gloss obsolete words and meanings, explain difficult passages, interpret allusions, and occasionally call attention to a particular source, especially when it is helpful to the understanding of a passage or enables the reader to sense the way Chaucer drew upon a memory stored with the fruits of his wide reading. Classical allusions are explained. It is hoped that those who have had sufficient Latin and Greek to put them beyond the need for such explanations will tolerate them in the interest of students to whom they will be useful. I have, moreover, not hesitated to repeat an explanation in the annotations of different texts, since it is not to be assumed that all students will read all the poems in the book or read them in sequence.

There are some notes which the teacher, or those familiar with Middle English, could dispense with, but experience has shown me how many things puzzle the student who is making his first acquaintance with the English of the fourteenth century. If I have gone too far, I can only quote in defense the words of a much greater literary commentator: "It is impossible for an expositor not to write too little for some, and too much for others . . .; how long so ever he may deliberate, [he] will at last explain many lines which the learned will think impossible to be mistaken, and omit many for which the ignorant will want his help. These are censures merely relative, and must be quietly endured." I may perhaps quote one more sentence from Dr. Johnson: "I have not passed over, with affected superiority, what is equally difficult to the reader and to myself, but where I could not instruct him, have owned my ignorance." This is perhaps no great virtue, but I should like to claim it.

My indebtedness to previous editors, especially Skeat, Manly, and Robinson, and to Root's commentary on the *Troilus*, is gratefully acknowledged. Where I have offered a different interpretation I have generally recorded previous views as well. I wish to thank Miss Rosalie B. Green, Director of the Index of Christian Art, Princeton University, who was most obliging in responding to my appeal for help. To the Master and Fellows of Corpus Christi College, Cambridge, and to Dr. Richard Vaughan, the Librarian, I am indebted for permission to reproduce the illumination which forms the frontispiece to the book. Dr. Vaughan's efforts to obtain a photograph of high quality for the reproduction went considerably beyond the call of duty. It is pleasant to record my obligation to various friends who have put their special knowledge at my service, even though more specific acknowledgment is made at the appropriate places. To my colleague Professor William Roach I am especially indebted for his constant interest and ready help in any problem involving Old French. My research assistant Lazaros Varnas has helped with the collation of the texts and the typing of the notes. It is a pleasure to record his cheerful industry, his scholarly zeal, and, above all, his accuracy. But my greatest debt is to my wife, who bravely sorted and filed upwards of 20,000 slips for the glossary, a labor which her knowledge of Middle English made possible. In addition she typed the final copy, as well as my introductions and the notes to some of the texts. Moreover she has read the proof independently and caught a number of misprints that in spite of my best effort had escaped me. Without her help the book would have been the poorer and would have been considerably delayed. Finally, I cannot omit from these acknowledgments a word of warm appreciation to Miss Ruth D. Keener of Appleton-Century-Crofts, who has seen more than one of my books through the press and whose imagination and taste have again contributed much to the physical form of the present volume.

University of Pennsylvania   A. C. B.

CONTENTS

INTRODUCTION

The Life of Chaucer

FAMILY AND NAME. The family of the poet Geoffrey Chaucer can be traced back four generations to Robert le Taverner of Ipswich, who died about 1280. Ipswich was its original home, but as far back as we know it, the family had business interests also in London. Robert the Taverner was known in London as Robert Malyn, and Malyn was probably the original family name. If so, it suggests a French origin. In the days when given names began to be further identified, the second name might be derived from an occupation, a place of residence, or a personal characteristic. Thus the same person may appear in the records with various designations. Robert's son was known as both Andrew le Taverner and Andrew de Dennington (a village near Ipswich), and his son in turn, who was the poet's grandfather, appears as Robert Malyn, Robert de Dennington, Robert the Saddler, and Robert le Chaucer. The name Chaucer (F. *chaussier*) means maker of *chausses*, a kind of footwear, and we may without violence think of it as the equivalent of Shoemaker. The family interests were clearly identified with the leather and the wine trades. Robert le Chaucer was a man of property, with considerable holdings in both Ipswich and London. His wife's name was Mary de Westhale, and thus both paternal grandparents of the poet can be identified. Chaucer's father was John Chaucer. The real key to the reconstruction of the poet's ancestry was the discovery by Furnivall in 1873 of a deed in which Geoffrey Chaucer disposed of a piece of property in London and described himself as the son of John Chaucer. The poet's mother's name, as we have more recently learned, was Agnes de Copton. John Chaucer was a vintner, and like his father, served as a deputy to the King's Butler. He was also in the king's service and accompanied Edward III on his expedition to Antwerp in 1338. He was a man of means, with property in both Ipswich and London. At his death in 1366 (or early 1367) he was about fifty-three. Concerning all these forebears of the poet many other details will be found in A. A. Kern, *The Ancestry of Chaucer* (Baltimore, 1906).

BIRTH AND EDUCATION. The world has generally noted when famous people died, but we are often uncertain about when they were born. We do not know when Chaucer was born or when his parents were married. There is no mention of any brothers or sisters. We are reduced to inferences. In a famous lawsuit in 1386 between representatives of the Scrope and the Grosvenor families, over the right to bear a certain coat of arms, Chaucer was one of the many witnesses produced by both sides. In his testimony he gave his age as forty years and upwards and said that he had borne arms for twenty-seven years. The latter statement seems to be exact and agrees with the record of his first-known military service in 1359, but the early figure is very general and tells us no more than that he was then in his forties. It has been customary to consider 1340 as the approximate year of his birth, but mainly because it is a round number. Other considerations suggest that the date is two or three years too early. The house in Thames Street which, as mentioned above, the poet disposed of in 1381, is probably where the child was born. Of his education we know nothing. That he attended a school, as did the "litel clergeon" in *The Prioress's Tale*, is most likely. Miss Rickert (*MP*, xxix. 257–74) suggested the possibility that Chaucer attended the almonry school of St. Paul's, mainly because the school had an excellent library left by various almoners in their wills, a library which contained many of the books which Chaucer later shows a knowledge of. There is nothing improbable in the suggestion. That he was ever a student at one of the Inns of Court, as some have believed, is less likely. His education was probably continued while he was a page in Lionel's household and later when a valet in that of the king. He would have learned to read and write (both French and English) and to cipher. Certainly he learned Latin, as his reading of Ovid and Virgil and numerous other Latin writers shows. He has told us in several of his poems how much he delighted in reading. He was widely read in both French and Latin. His acquaintance with Dante and certain works of Boccaccio testifies to his knowledge of Italian.

THE EARLIEST RECORDS. The earliest record that we have of Chaucer is in some fragments of the household accounts of Elizabeth, countess of Ulster, the wife of Lionel, duke of Clarence, third son of Edward III. These show modest sums paid out for articles of clothing and other necessaries for Geoffrey Chaucer in April, 1357 and at Christmas of that year, which the countess spent at Hatfield, her residence in Yorkshire. While his position is not particularized, he was evidently one of the young people in the service of the countess. Such service with families of wealth and position was one of the ways by which those with the necessary connections might provide opportunities for their children to continue their education, learn the ways of polite society, and become known to persons who might further their advancement later. John Chaucer evidently succeeded in placing his son very well. It is interesting to note that John of Gaunt spent this Christmas at Hatfield—he was not far from Chaucer's age—and that one of the young women in the countess's service was a Philippa Pan', who probably became in time the poet's wife. While Geoffrey was still in the service of Lionel and the countess he went to France in the army of Edward III (November, 1359). During the seven weeks in which Edward unsuccessfully besieged Rheims, Chaucer was taken prisoner. He was ransomed on March 1, 1360, and the king contributed £16 to his ransom. During the peace negotiations later that year he was employed as a messenger, bearing letters to England from the negotiators at Calais. We thus see him getting his start, in a humble way to be sure, as a public servant.

MARRIAGE. For six years (1360–66) Chaucer disappears from sight. During most of this time Lionel was in Ireland as the viceroy of the king, and it has been suggested that Chaucer may have been with him. It seems more likely that he was in the service of the king. At any rate, at the end of this period we find him married. When the marriage took place we do not know, but it is likely that his wife, whose name was Philippa, was the Philippa Pan' mentioned as in the service of Lionel's wife in the same document that gives us our first record of Chaucer. Following the death of Countess Elizabeth in 1363, Philippa seems to have been taken into the service of Lionel's mother, the queen, who in September, 1366, gave her an annuity of 10 marks for her good service, past and future. In the grant she is called Philippa Chaucer and later payments of the annuity were often made through her husband. Since marriages between yeomen and esquires of the king and *domicellae* of the queen were not uncommon, the sequence of the facts and assumptions sketched above is entirely plausible. We would gladly know more about the identity of Philippa Pan'. The interpretation of Pan' as *panetaria* (pantry mistress) must be given up. From a consideration of all the evidence, the detailing of which would take us too far afield, it would seem likely that she was the daughter of Sir Paon de Roet, a Hainault knight who accompanied Philippa of Hainault to England on her way to becoming the wife of Edward III. She would thus be the sister of Katherine de Swynford, who, after the death of her husband, became the mistress of John of Gaunt and ultimately his third wife. Philippa was granted several annuities by John of Gaunt, two of them jointly with her husband, besides New Year's gifts and other presents. In 1386, near the end of her life, she was admitted into "the fraternity of Lincoln cathedral" along with John of Gaunt's son (the future Henry IV), Katherine's son Sir Thomas de Swynford, and several others. She seems to have been a person of some prestige in her own right. We shall never know whether she contributed to the success of her husband's official career or whether his declining fortunes after 1387 were in any way connected with her death. In spite of the poet's playful strictures on marriage, there is no reason to think that the union was not a happy one.

DIPLOMATIC MISSIONS. In June, 1367, Chaucer received an annuity or yearly stipend of 20 marks as a *valettus* or yeoman of the king, and the following year he is listed among the esquires. His duties were not menial, though they involved close attendance upon the king, and living at the court. Esquires were frequently employed as messengers, and, as they grew in age and responsibility, were sent on a variety of diplomatic missions by the king. Chaucer was so employed. We do not always know the exact nature of a mission or its destination. In some cases the records merely tell us that Chaucer was granted letters of protection until a certain date (such as Michaelmas) because he was about to leave "for parts beyond the sea" and "on secret negotiations of the king." But fortunately, in a number of cases they are more specific. Thus, even before he received his annuity in 1367 there is evidence that he was in Spain, since in February, 1366, he was given a safe-conduct by the King of Navarre to pass through his kingdom with three companions, horses, and servants, and to return. We can hardly doubt that he was there on the business of the English king and the Black Prince, who were at the time attempting to restore Don Pedro to the throne of Castile. He was abroad again in 1368 and 1370 on unspecified missions, and throughout the 1370's we find him on various occasions sent to Flanders, France, and Italy, sometimes in the company of others of higher rank. On one of these occasions he was a member of a commission to negotiate a marriage between the young Prince Richard and a daughter of the king of France. Two of his assignments at least took him to Italy.

ITALIAN JOURNEYS. The two journeys to Italy are of special interest because of their effect on his literary work. The first, so far as now known, was in December, 1372, and covered about six months (to May 23, 1373). Its primary purpose was to arrange with the duke and citizens of Genoa for an English port where Genoese merchants might establish their headquarters in England. But he also went to Florence, perhaps, as has been suspected, to talk to those from whom Edward III had received loans. A question of some interest is whether in the course of the trip he visited Petrarch. The Clerk of Oxenford, about to relate the story of Patient Griselda (which is based on Petrarch's version) says:

> I wol yow telle a tale which that I
> Lerned at Padowe of a worthy clerk, . . .
> Fraunceys Petrak, the lauriat poete.

A meeting between the two poets would not have been impossible, but the failure of Petrarch to make any mention of it in his letters—and he was prone to mention such things—is thought to cast doubt upon it. The second journey to Italy was in 1378. It is interesting to note that on this occasion he appointed his fellow poet John Gower and one other man to act for him, if necessary, during his absence. He received money for his expenses on May 28, left presumably the same day, and returned September 19. The purpose of the mission, on which he accompanied Sir Edward Berkeley, was to discuss with Barnabo Visconti, lord of Milan, whose murder is one of the "tragedies" of *The Monk's Tale*, and with the famous Sir John Hawkwood, leader of a powerful band of mercenaries, matters touching the king's military expedition. The wording is vague, but there can be no doubt that the mission was for the purpose of securing help in the war with France. While Chaucer's stay in Italy was only for a few weeks each time, the visits gave him an opportunity to buy Italian books. On the first trip he almost certainly acquired a manuscript of Dante's *Divina Commedia* and on the second trip several long poems of Boccaccio, about which more will be said later.

CONTROLLER OF CUSTOMS. The esquires and the damoiselles lived at the court. There were married esquires, like Chaucer, but we do not know what special living arrangements, if any, were made for them. On May 10, 1374 Chaucer leased the apartment or dwelling over Aldgate, one of the stone entrances in the city wall. Chaucer and Philippa were thus able to set up housekeeping, a circumstance which marked the end of their immediate attendance upon the king and queen. Chaucer must have expected other employment. The explanation is to be found in his appointment on June 8 as Controller of the Custom and Subsidy of wools, hides, and woolfells in London. Appointments of this kind were quite normal for esquires of the king. The post to which Chaucer was named required that he keep the records with his own hand, a procedure which was regularly specified and which gives point to the eagle's remark in *The Hous of Fame* (lines 652–60). His new responsibilities, however, did not prevent him from being sent on a number of the missions mentioned in the preceding paragraph. In 1382 he was appointed to the additional post of Controller of the Petty Customs. Since the office was in a building adjoining the Wool Custom, it would not have been difficult for him to exercise the dual function. In 1385 he was given permission to perform his duties by deputy. Chaucer retained both positions until December, 1386. He was the only person in the reign of Richard II who held both offices at the same time, the only one who was permitted to exercise one of them by deputy, and his tenure of the controllership of the Wool Custom greatly exceeded that of any other controller in this period.

FINANCIAL PROSPERITY. The period of roughly twelve years during which Chaucer held the controllership of the Wool Custom was one of genuine prosperity. He had an annuity from the king of 20 marks ($£13$ $6s$ $8d$) and Philippa had one of half that amount. In addition, he had a grant of a pitcher of wine daily, which he commuted into another 20 marks yearly. The pensions to Geoffrey and Philippa from John of Gaunt, if they were paid regularly, amounted to $£40$ a year. Chaucer received $£10$ a year as controller, supplemented from time to time by a gift of 10 marks "for his diligent services." (It is supposed that he was also allowed to collect certain fees.) These items constituted his more or less regular income. But the king was in the habit of appointing his esquires to wardships, which involved looking after the heir of a tenant-in-chief during his minority and arranging his marriage. Chaucer had two such wardships, that of Edmund Stapleton, yielding him $£104$ in 1375, the other an unspecified (but smaller) amount. Moreover, in order to encourage vigilance (and honesty) the king rewarded the controller with the value of any cargo that was caught trying to leave England without paying the export tax. In 1376 Chaucer received such a reward, amounting to over $£71$. If we include only the sums which we know about, and there may well have been others of which the record has not been preserved, it is clear that during this period Chaucer and his wife had an average income of $£99$ a year. At the beginning of the present century, before the devaluation of the pound, it was customary to multiply fourteenth-century amounts by twenty or thirty in order to arrive at the equivalent purchasing value. Two world wars have made such a multiple obsolete. We now have to figure in terms of forty or fifty, and even if we use the lower of these figures we can estimate Chaucer's average income at close to $20,000. Unfortunately, leaner years were in store for the poet.

CECILIA CHAUMPAIGNE. The period of prosperity was not free from troubles, about which we have only fragmentary information. We know that in 1379 Chaucer appointed a professional attorney to represent him in a suit brought by one Thomas Stondon on a plea of "contempt and trespass." We know nothing more about it. Seemingly more serious is a deed of May 1, 1380, in which a certain Cecilia Chaumpaigne released to Chaucer all her rights of action against him "de raptu meo." The release was witnessed by Sir William Beauchamp and several other important friends of Chaucer. Two months later she gave a general release to Richard Goodchild, cutler, and John Grove, armorer, at the same time that these two released Chaucer of any action against him. Grove agreed to pay Cecilia $£10$, which he later did, and Goodchild probably paid her as well for releasing him. Cecilia has been identified as the daughter of a deceased London baker. How old she was we do not know, but she had to be of legal age. Not only does the three-cornered arrangement make the relation of the parties complicated, but we cannot be sure of the nature of the offense of which Cecilia must have claimed to be a victim. The word *raptus* meant not only the felony of rape, but was also used in charges and indictments for abduction and what we would call assault and battery. An article in the *Law Quarterly Review* (October, 1947), arguing that the offense involved was actually rape, must be pronounced inconclusive. Until more evidence is found the question remains open, and in the meantime it is best to suspend judgment.

REMOVAL TO KENT. In December, 1386, successors were appointed to Chaucer's two offices in the Customs. We do not know whether he gave up his posts voluntarily or whether his replacement was due to political pressure. It is currently the fashion to regard the latter possibility with skepticism, but it cannot be entirely dismissed. The tide of resentment against the young Richard II and his favorites was strongly on the rise. The change of controllers, however, was clearly not something sudden and unforeseen. Two months before, October 5, his apartment over Aldgate was leased to some one else. How much earlier he had given it up we do not know, but as much as a year before, October 12, 1385, he had been appointed one of the justices of the peace for Kent, to fill out the unexpired term of a justice who had died. It was an unwritten law that a justice of the peace be a resident of the county, and it would seem likely that Chaucer had taken up at least partial residence in Kent by that time. Such a change of residence would be a possible explanation of the fact that on February 17, 1385, at his request, he was allowed to appoint a permanent deputy in the Customs. He was reappointed a justice in June 1386, and in the office he was associated with sixteen others, a dozen of whom were the wealthiest and most important men in the county. In August he was elected one of the two Knights of the Shire to represent Kent in the Parliament that met the first of October. His election was pretty certainly at the king's desire, was brought about by the magnates of Kent, who were mostly of the king's party, and was for the purpose, to quote Tout, "of securing the complacency of the Commons by the infusion of a liberal sprinkling of courtiers and placement among their ranks." The experience for Chaucer could not have been a pleasant one, for during the two months that Parliament was in session Richard was forced to dismiss his chancellor and his treasurer and accept the appointment of a regency under the duke of Gloucester, the leader of the opposition. Moreover, an inquiry promptly instituted by Gloucester into the collection of the wool tax may have had something to do with Chaucer's severance from the controllership, which he had been exercising for more than a year and a half by deputy. His residence in Kent would appear to have continued for a number of years, possibly until near the end of his life. A number of indications point to Greenwich as the place where he lived. It was only a short distance down the river, a mere four miles as the crow flies from his former dwelling over Aldgate. It did not prevent him from coming to London, whether to collect his pension at the exchequer in person or for other purposes when necessary, and it must have offered an agreeable quiet for those intervals of leisure when he could work on *The Canterbury Tales*.

CLERK OF THE KING'S WORKS. The years immediately following Chaucer's brief experience in Parliament are somewhat obscure to us and seemingly were not easy ones for the poet. They were darkened by the death of his wife, probably in 1387, since the last payment on her pension was made on the 18th of June. They may have been troubled by financial problems. On May 1, 1388, he sold his annuities; at his request the king transferred them to one John Scalby. At this time Gloucester and his adherents had seized control. In the Merciless Parliament, convened on February 3 and shamelessly packed, the principal supporters of the king were charged with treason and promptly condemned. His staunch friend Sir Simon Burley, constable of Dover Castle, was beheaded on February 5; Sir Robert Tresilian, Chief Justice of the King's Bench, and Sir

Nicholas Brembre, late Mayor of London, suffered similar fates by February 20; the Earl of Oxford, the king's favorite, escaped to the Continent, but a number of lesser adherents of the king were also executed. Chaucer may have feared for the permanence of his grants. On the other hand, he may have been in need of ready money. Whatever his reasons, he gave up what had been a steady income of 40 marks a year, and he was by medieval standards approaching the period of old age. The fact that on April 16 John Churchman, one of the Collectors of the Wool Custom, claimed that Chaucer owed him 66s 8d can hardly have been a factor, since the amount was relatively small.

In May, 1389 King Richard, now in his twenty-third year, appeared in council and claimed the right to exercise the prerogatives of his position. His manner was conciliatory, his request reasonable, and the council could hardly refuse him. He showed unusual astuteness in his appointment of a new chancellor and a new treasurer, and otherwise displayed the marks of a skillful politician. For the next eight years England enjoyed a moderate and stable government. The restoration of the king to power was of immediate benefit to the poet. Within two months of Richard's appearance in council he appointed Chaucer (on July 12) Clerk of the Works at Westminster, the Tower of London, the various royal manors and lodges, and even the mews for the king's falcons at Charing Cross, looking after repairs, hiring workmen, contracting for materials and the like. It has often been pointed out in connection with *The Knight's Tale* (ll. 1881 ff.) that in 1390 he was responsible for the erection of two scaffolds in Smithfield from which the king, the queen, and other ladies could view the tournaments held there. In March, 1390, he was named with five others to survey the walls, ditches, sewers, bridges, etc., along the Thames between Greenwich and Woolwich, and to compel the owners of adjacent lands to restore these utilities where necessary. Since Chaucer's wages as Clerk of the Works were 2s. a day, or over £30 per year, his financial needs were again taken care of. Two previous incumbents of the office had come to it from positions as overseers of Eltham and other royal manors nearby, and Miss Galway (*MLR*, xxxvi. 1–36) has made a good case for supposing that when Chaucer took up his residence in Kent it was as supervisor of the favorite manors of Richard and Anne, Eltham in Kent and Shene in Surrey. Greenwich was within easy reach of both.

CHAUCER ROBBED. On September 6, 1390 Chaucer was twice robbed—the same day and by the same band of robbers—the first time of £10 and the second time of £9 3s 8d. Some of the thieves were caught, one of them turned informer, and in his testimony he gave details concerning a half-dozen other robberies that they had committed in different counties. The following January Chaucer was excused from the repayment of the loss, here stated as £20. He continued to exercise his clerkship until June 17, when his successor was appointed. This is the last specific office, so far as we know, that Chaucer held.[1] That

---

[1] In 1390–1 he was appointed a subforester of North Petherton in Somersetshire, allegedly by Roger Mortimer, earl of March, and the appointment was renewed in 1397–8 by Mortimer's widow. The statements are found in Collinson's *History . . . of Somerset* (1791), but the records on which they are based are transcripts. We do not know whether Chaucer was ever at North Petherton in person, and Russell Krauss (in *Three Chaucer Studies*, New York, 1932) has questioned whether he owed the appointment to Mortimer. The chief interest that attaches to the matter is that, according to the same authority, Thomas Chaucer was appointed to much the same post in 1416–17 (see below).

he remained in some capacity in the service of Richard is indicated by a gift of £10 from the king on July 9, 1393 "for his good service in the present year." On February 28, 1394 Richard granted him a fresh annuity of £20 for life, and on October 13, 1398 a butt of wine yearly. During these years there are a number of "loans" recorded, or advances on his annuity; some of them were so small as to suggest the need for ready money. The larger advances may have been to make sure that his semiannual instalments would be paid when they were due, since the exchequer was sometimes short of funds. In 1398 Isabella Bukholt, widow of the Keeper of the Mews at Charing Cross while Chaucer was Clerk of the Works, sued Chaucer for a debt of £14 1s 11d. His name is joined in the suit with that of John Goodale who owed her (she claimed) £12 8s. Whether these debts were entirely personal or whether Chaucer's grew out of a claim against his office we do not know. Ten days after the suit was officially entered, Chaucer was granted letters of protection, valid for two years, because he feared that he might be annoyed by plaints or suits while attending to "many arduous and urgent matters" within the kingdom to which the king had appointed him. The documents from which we catch these glimpses of Chaucer in his later years tell us a few things, but unfortunately leave us wondering much more about the circumstances that lie behind them.

LAST MONTHS. In 1397 the character of Richard's rule suddenly changed. He condemned and had put to death Gloucester and Arundel, who had deprived him of power and humiliated him ten years before. He became insanely autocratic. On a political pretext he banished Henry of Lancaster and on the death of John of Gaunt in February, 1399, confiscated the vast Lancastrian estates. Many important people became alarmed. On July 4, while Richard was conducting a punitive campaign in Ireland, Henry returned at the head of a small force and was joined by increasing numbers of the nobility while Richard's supporters melted away. On September 30, 1399, in Parliament, Richard was formally deposed and Henry of Lancaster was declared king. Two weeks later Lancaster's coronation as Henry IV took place.

There is evidence as early as 1395 that Chaucer was already in Henry's service. There is, of course, nothing incompatible in his serving both Richard and Henry at the same time, for the king and the earl were still on friendly terms. In any case, once Richard had accepted with resignation his removal from the throne, Chaucer joined the chorus that welcomed the new king. Without much delay, he dusted off the *Complaint to His Purse* (see p. 540), added an envoy, and sent it off. The reply was prompt. On the very day of Henry's coronation, October 13, an entry on the Patent Roll records a grant of 40 marks in addition to the £20 which had been granted the poet by Richard, and a week later Henry reconfirmed Richard's grants (including the butt of wine) when Chaucer appeared in Chancery and took oath that he had lost the original letters. It is pleasant to observe that in his old age, when any services that he might render were probably limited, Chaucer continued to enjoy what can only be interpreted as the warm regard of both Richard II and John of Gaunt's son.

His financial security now amply provided for, Chaucer leased, on the day before Christmas, 1399, a house in the garden of St. Mary's chapel, Westminster Abbey. The yearly rent was to be 53s 4d and the lease was for 53 years, terminable at Chaucer's death. Whether this marks his return from residence in Kent is not certain, but is possible. In any case, he had less than a year to enjoy his new home. He died October 25, 1400 and was buried in Westminster Abbey. The date of his death comes from the inscription over his tomb, erected by an admirer in 1566, but the marble tomb probably copied an earlier record or was based on an authentic tradition. There is no reason to doubt its accuracy.

CHAUCER'S CHILDREN. In the absence of family Bibles, parish registers, and other sources of information that are found useful in genealogical search at a later date, it is impossible to speak with finality about Chaucer's children. In the first third of the fifteenth century his son Thomas Chaucer, helped by a fortunate marriage, became a large landowner and held important offices. When Henry V died in 1422 his son was still an infant, and the country was ruled by a council of twenty-three, most of whom were great nobles and administrative officers. Thomas Chaucer was a member of this council. Thomas's daughter Alice, after being twice widowed, became duchess of Suffolk. Sometime after his death (in 1434) one of his Oxford friends, speaking of him, mentions that he was the poet's son. In a lawsuit of 1396 he is named "Thomas Chaucer, esquire, son of Geoffrey Chaucer, esquire" (Manly, *Times Literary Supplement*, Aug. 3, 1933). He once used the poet's seal, he held the forestership of North Petherton which Geoffrey had held, and after an interval leased the poet's house at Westminster. From the presence of the Roet arms on his tomb it seems quite certain that his mother was Philippa Chaucer, but in the light of the many favors that she received from John of Gaunt, and considering Thomas Chaucer's great success, some have suggested that Philippa may have been one of Gaunt's mistresses and that Gaunt was the real father of Thomas.[2] Some years younger was "little Lewis, my son," for whom, when he was a child of ten, Chaucer wrote *A Treatise on the Astrolabe* (1391). Lewis and Thomas were associated in 1403 in the garrison of the royal castle of Carmarthen. An Elizabeth "Chaucy" became a nun at Barking in 1381, and from the fact that John of Gaunt paid £51 8s 2d for her expenses on the occasion the same suspicion of his paternity has been expressed as in the case of Thomas. An Agnes Chaucer was one of the *domicellae*, along with Joan Swynford, at Henry IV's coronation in 1399, but whether she and Elizabeth were daughters of Geoffrey we do not know. There were apparently no descendants of the poet living after the fifteenth century.

While there is much that we would like to know, it is remarkable that we know so much about a man in the fourteenth century who was neither a member of the nobility nor an important political figure. From the time he became an esquire in Edward III's household his career was similar to that of other esquires and appears to have followed a normal and regular pattern. What we cannot explain, any more than we can of Shakespeare, is his genius.

HIS DEVELOPMENT AS A POET. It has seemed best to recount the facts of Chaucer's life without much reference to his poetry, and the full discussion of that poetry is reserved for the introductions which accompany the several poems. The following paragraphs are limited to a few points of a broader nature.

---

[2] On Thomas Chaucer's career see Martin Ruud, *Thomas Chaucer* (Minneapolis, 1926) and records published by the present writer in *PMLA*, XLVII. 461–515 and XLVIII. 328–39. John of Gaunt's paternity of Thomas Chaucer is most strongly argued by Russell Krauss, "Chaucerian Problems," in *Three Chaucer Studies*, ed. Carleton Brown (New York, 1932), pp. 1–182, and vigorously refuted by Manly (*RES*, x. 6–10).

For Chaucer literature was an avocation. He took great delight in books, as he more than once tells us, and from the many thousands of lines of verse that have come down to us—not to mention a number of works in prose—it is evident that he enjoyed writing. But most of his writing was done in the course of a busy life and was subject to many interruptions, especially during the years when he was being sent on diplomatic missions to different parts of the Continent. All of his poetry was written for courtly audiences, and we may assume that his success as a story-teller and his reputation as a poet spurred him on to further endeavors. In the early part of his career he was also an occasional poet; it is believed that some of his poems were written for particular occasions, as will be pointed out in the introductions to those poems.

In the appreciation of a poet's development it is necessary to know the order in which his poems were written and the successive influences that helped to shape them. The dates of Chaucer's more important productions have now been established within reasonable limits, and in the present volume his poems have been arranged, except for the short lyrics which are grouped together at the end, in what is believed to be their order of composition. The position of *The Canterbury Tales*, of course, reflects the date of the collective work, of which some of the tales were written earlier.

It is apparent that in the beginning Chaucer's literary tastes were formed on French models, to which whatever he learned from Virgil and Ovid was easily adapted. He seems to have been indifferent to his predecessors and contemporaries in the English tradition. In this he was reflecting the taste of the English court. There were categories of French literature, such as the *chansons de geste*, to which he seems to have been equally indifferent. His chief interest was in the allegorical love poetry that enjoyed a vogue for more than a hundred years, thanks to the *Roman de la Rose*, its source and fountain head. In spite of its great length (over 21,000 lines) Chaucer shows an intimate and detailed acquaintance with it, and in *The Legend of Good Women* Alceste, in defending the poet against the God of Love's strictures, credits him with having translated it.[3] But there were three later poets who carried on the tradition: Guillaume Machaut, Eustache Deschamps, and Jean Froissart, best known today for his famous *Chronicles*. Chaucer was well acquainted with at least some of the poetry of each of them; certain of his borrowings from them are pointed out in the introductions and notes below, especially those to *The Book of the Duchess* and *The Hous of Fame*. These two poems and *The Parlement of Foules* are often spoken of as belonging to Chaucer's French period, as representing the stage of his development when he was most strongly under the influence of French poets.

His two journeys to Italy (in 1372–3 and 1378) greatly broadened his literary outlook. To the first trip we must almost certainly credit his acquaintance with Dante's *Divine Comedy*, already apparent in *The Hous of Fame*. But even more important was the journey of 1378, for it was on this trip that he came to know the work of Boccaccio. Two of Boccaccio's longer poems, the *Teseida* and the *Filostrato*, he made the basis of his *Palamon and Arcite* (later to be made into *The Knight's Tale*) and his great love poem *Troilus and Criseyde*. He never forgot what the French poets taught him, but on this foundation

---

[3] A translation of parts of the poem, running to nearly 7700 lines, is included in editions of Chaucer's works. It falls into three fragments marked by linguistic and stylistic differences. Of these, only Fragment A (the first 1705 lines) is likely to be by Chaucer. If so, it is probably among his earliest work.

he built with new matter from Italy. The stage of his work which shows this new influence is often spoken of as his Italian period, and its hallmark is not so much Dante as Boccaccio. Its culmination is the *Troilus*.

Even in the *Troilus*, however, he has to a large extent struck out on his own, and by the time he began work on *The Canterbury Tales* he had become completely independent. Having learned all that others could teach him, having mastered his medium and acquired full confidence in his own ability, he allowed his personality free play and trusted unhesitatingly to his artistic intuitions. This stage can only be considered his English period.

The Language of Chaucer

THE LANGUAGE OF CHAUCER is that of cultivated Londoners in the last half of the fourteenth century, though doubtless modified by literary conventions. The most important difference between the language of his poetry and the ordinary speech of his day was in the use of the final -e [ə]. This remnant of the Old English inflectional system had almost certainly ceased to be pronounced by Chaucer's time, but its normal use in English poetry at an earlier date, when English had more numerous and distinctive inflectional endings, made possible its survival as a convention in Chaucer's time. He therefore uses it freely when he needs it for metrical purposes. Whether the -es of the genitive and plural forms of nouns had syllabic value in ordinary speech, and this is not unlikely, it is also an important feature of Chaucer's verse. Otherwise, as Chaucer read his poetry aloud to courtly audiences, his pronunciation would have been that of the London of his day, even to the occasional Kentish form that he uses for the sake of a rime.

To one approaching the poetry of Chaucer for the first time the language may seem strange and difficult. The strangeness is due in large part to the spelling, the difficulty to the changes in grammar and vocabulary that have taken place in the English language since the fourteenth century. A reasonably uniform spelling did not gain acceptance in England until the seventeenth century. In the time of Chaucer and, more important, the two generations after his death, when most of the existing manuscripts of his poems were copied, the spelling is a reasonable attempt to represent the sounds of words, but such representation could be achieved with a choice of symbols, was subject to regional variations, and was marked by the habits—sometimes pronounced idiosyncrasies—of the individual scribe. Scribal eccentricities can be removed in a modern edition, but considerable variation was normal—*mor, more, moore,* etc. It would be easy to regularize the spelling of most words, but the result would suggest a uniformity that does not exist at this period and is seldom seen even in the spelling of a single scribe. The reader soon gets used to the spelling varieties in the texts of Chaucer's poems—after a time he hardly notices them—and is able to pass to the reading of other texts if he wishes to pursue further the study of Middle English literature or read the works of Chaucer's contemporaries.

Once the strangeness of the spelling has become familiar, any difficulty which the student experiences in understanding Chaucer will be due to four things: (1) obsolete words; (2) words still current but which Chaucer uses in other than their modern senses; (3) a small number of Middle English idioms and syntactical constructions; and (4) a few inflectional survivals from Old English which have now disappeared. The first two of these differences are explained in the notes accompanying the text and in the glossary. The last two are briefly summarized in the following paragraphs. But in addition to understanding the language, the student should learn to read Chaucer's poetry with a reasonable approximation to fourteenth-century pronunciation. This is essential not only to an appreciation of the music of Chaucer's lines, but to the rhythm of the verse and the correctness of many rimes.

PRONUNCIATION

1. Since Chaucer lived before the Great Vowel Shift, which raised the pronunciation of English long vowels and in the case of $\bar{\imath}$ and $\bar{u}$ made them into diphthongs, his pronunciation of vowels was much like that of German, French, and Italian today. The approximate pronunciation of vowels and diphthongs is shown in the following table.

Sound	Pronunciation	Spelling	Examples
ā	like *a* in *father*	a, aa	fader, caas
a	like *a* in *what*	a	what
ē̜	like *a* in *mate*	e, ee	swete, neede
ē̜	like *e* in *there*	e, ee	bere, heeth
e	like *e* in *met*	e	hem
ə	like *a* in *about*	e	yonge
ī	like *i* in *machine*	i, y	blithe, nyce
i	like *i* in *bit*	i, y	list, nyste
ō̜	like *o* in *so*	o, oo	dom, roote
ō̜	like *o* in *cloth*	o, oo	lore, goon
o	like *o* in *or*	o	for
ū	like *oo* in *root*	ou, ow	hous, how
u	like *oo* in *book*	u, o	ful, nonne
ü	like Fr. *u* in *tu*	u	vertu
au	like *ow* in *how*	au, aw	cause, drawe
ęi	like *ay* in *day*	ai, ay, ei, ey	fair, may, feith, eyr
ęü	ę + u	ew	fewe, shewe
iu	like *ew* in *few*	eu, ew	reule, newe
ǫi	like *oy* in *boy*	oi, oy	point, joye
ou̯	like *ow* in *grow*	ou, ow	thought, knowe

2. **Open and close** *e*. The spelling **e** or **ee** represents two different sounds in Chaucer, that in ModE. *breath* [ē̜] and that in *mate* [ē̜]. For the sake of simplicity we may ignore the fact that the last-named sound is today a diphthong [ei] or [e¹]. Since the two sounds have fallen together in ModE. [i] the distinction rests upon a knowledge of their respective sources, *i.e.*, upon etymology. In some cases, such as words containing West Saxon **æ**, it is necessary to go behind the OE. vowels since the sounds so spelled were of two different origins, varied in the different dialects of Old English, and developed differently in Middle English. For some words the spelling in Modern English is a guide: those spelled with *ea* (*sea*, *beast*, etc.) have the open *e* in Middle English, those spelled *ee* (*see*,

feet) have the close *e*. For the more technical treatment of the problem the student is referred to the appendix to this section (p. xxvi).

3. Open and close *o*. The spelling **o** or **oo** likewise represents two different sounds in Chaucer, that in ModE. *broth* [ǭ] and that in *note* [ọ̄], although the latter is now followed by a *u*-glide and is really a diphthong [ou] or [oᵘ]. Here the present pronunciation is a guide, since the two sounds have been kept apart in Modern English. Those words with open *o* in Chaucer are now pronounced like *note* or *stone*, while those with close *o* are now pronounced like *mood* or (if shortened) like *good* or *cud*. It is important to remember that the spelling **oo** in Chaucer should never be pronounced like ModE. *mood*. For fuller discussion see p. xxv.

4. The indeterminate vowel or schwa [ə] is written **e**. It occurs finally and in endings such as **ed, ede, eth,** and the **es** in the genitive and the plural of nouns, but in these endings it was sometimes pronounced *id, is,* as shown by rimes like **harmed: harm hyd, werkis: derk is.**

5. The diphthong **au** (**cause, drawe**) has become [ǭ] in Modern English. The change seems to have taken place in some words or in the use of some speakers by the fifteenth century and may even have begun earlier.

6. No distinction in rime is made by Chaucer between the spellings **ei, ey** and **ai, ay.** The pronunciation is held by some scholars to be approximately like the diphthong in English *aisle*, by others to be a sound resembling that in *day*. It is given in the table as [ɛi], which indicates agreement with the latter view and is an approximate pronunciation. The first element in the diphthong may have been a low-front vowel [æ] as in *hat* or a mid-front vowel [ɛ] like the *e* in *met*. At D 2101 Chaucer rimes **reyse** (to raise) with **eyse** (ease), which is usually written **ese** and has a long open **e**.

7. Words spelled **-ew** were pronounced in two different ways, [iu] and [ɛu]. Words pronounced [iu] are frequently found together in rime: **hewe** (hue), **knewe, newe, rewe** (rue), **trewe** (representing OE. **īw, ēow**), but with these Chaucer avoids riming **fewe, hewe** (to chop), **rewe** (row), **shewe, shrewe** (representing OE. **ēaw, ǣw**).

8. A Kentish pronunciation is sometimes used for the sake of the rime. Examples are **feere** "fire" (TC 3. 978), **a-fere** "afire" (TC 1. 229), **fulfelle** "fulfill" (TC 3. 510), **kesse** "kiss" (E 1057), **keste** "kissed" (F 350). The stem vowel in these words represents OE. ȳ̆ (**fyr, fullfyllan, cyssan**). OE. ȳ̆ was a rounded vowel (pronounced with rounding of the lips), similar to the French *u* and the German *ü*. In ME. it developed differently in the different dialects. In the west and southwest it retained its original quality. In the rest of England it lost its lip-rounding and became a simple ĭ, but in Kentish this ĭ underwent an additional change and was lowered to an ĕ. The normal London form was ĭ, but the Kentish pronunciation was frequently heard in London, and after 1385 Chaucer lived for some years in Kent. Other Kentish forms (which are not frequent) are pointed out in the notes and the glossary.

9. The doubling of a vowel (**caas, moot**) is only a way of indicating length.

Consonants

10. For most consonants modern English is a sufficient guide to the pronunciation. In certain positions consonants which have since become silent were still pronounced:

k and **g** in **knyght, knowe, gnawe,** etc.

gh (a spirant like the *ch* in German *ich* or *nach*) in all words in which it occurs: **knyght, droghte.**

l before **f, v, k, m: calf, halve, folk, palmer.**

w in **write, wrecche,** etc.

11. A few additional observations may be made:

ch (*e.g.* in **chivalrie**) always has the sound in *church.*

gg usually represents the hard *g*, but in words where the ModE. word has *dg* (**juggen** "to judge") it is pronounced as in Modern English.

gn in French words (**digne, sovereigne, signes**) is *n.*

h (initially) is silent in words of French origin (**honour, heir**). It is sometimes silent or weakly aspirated in **he, his, him, hem, hit,** and **hadde.**

ng when stressed (**thing, singen**) is like the *ng* in *finger*; but the ending **-ing(e), yng(e)** when unstressed was probably pronounced as it is today, except before a word beginning with a vowel.

12. The ending **-ion, -ioun** is always dissyllabic (**passioun, naciouns**), never like *shun.*

13. In a considerable number of words the accent falls on a different syllable from that which bears it today: **coráge, corál, manére, monéye, persévere, solémpnely, viságe.** Sometimes the principal stress varies: **absénce** or **ábsence, povérte** or **povertée,** and so with **abbéye, natúre, tragédie, walét, welfáre,** and numerous others which may also be accented on the first syllable.

APPENDIX

Open and Close ē, ō in Chaucer

The following rather technical presentation is included for those students who have some knowledge of Old English.

Open and close ō

1. ō is either open (ǫ) or close (ọ) according to its origin.

2. ǭ = (1) OE. ā: **lār** > **lǭre**; **māra** > **mǭre**

   (2) OE. **o** lengthened in an open syllable: **forloren** > **forlǭre**; **to-foran** > **to-fǭre**

   (3) OF. ǫ: **cǫte, restǫre**

3. Chaucer frequently distinguishes between the ǭ from (1) and (2); the second **o** may have been closer, or only half long.

4. ǭ = OE. and ON. ō: **bōn** > ME. **bǭn,** ModE. **boon**

5. Exceptions: Chaucer occasionally rimes ǭ and ǭ in special cases:

dǭm : hǭm (because of the paucity of -om rimes)

gǭ (OE. **gān**) : **dǭ** (OE. **dōn**) when vowel is final

agǫǫn (OE. **agān**) : **dǫǫn** (OE. **dōn**) in TC 2.410

sǫǫth (OE. **sōþ**) : **wrǫǫth** (OE. **wrāþ**)

(These are supposed to be the only cases.)

Open and close ē

1. Distinction maintained, but with more exceptions.

The sources of ę̄:

1. OE. **e** in open syllable, lengthened: **beran** > **bę̄ren; mete** > **mę̄te**
2. OE. **ǣ¹** (WG. **ā** < PG. **ǣ**). This is found only in WS.; Anglian and Kentish have **ę̄.**

WS. **dǣd** (OHG. **tāt**)	non-WS. **dę̄d**
þǣr	**þę̄r**
slǣpan (G. **schlafen**)	**slę̄pen**

Hence ME. **dę̄d** in WS. area, **dę̄d** in non-WS. areas.

3. OE. **ǣ²** (i-umlaut of **ā** < WG. **ai**). This is found everywhere but in Kentish, which has **ę̄.**

Angl. & WS. **dǣlan**	Kentish **dę̄len**
clǣne	**clę̄ne**
ǣnig	**ę̄nig**
sǣ	**sę̄**

Hence ME. **dę̄len** in Angl. and WS. areas, **dę̄len** in Kentish.

4. OE. short **eo** of whatever origin > **ę̄** when lengthened in an open syllable: **meodu** > **mę̄de**
5. OE. **ēa.** This always becomes ME. **ę̄** except that in non-WS. dialects the WS. **ēa** after initial palatals (**c, g, sc**) was **ę̄** and this remains in ME. OE. **dēad** > **dę̄d**, but non-WS. **gę̄r** (WS. **gēar**) > **ȝę̄r**
6. OF. **ę̄**: **prechen, feste**
7. OF. **ai, ei**: **ese, plesen**
8. OF. **e** when lengthened before **r** + consonant: **serchen, percen**

The sources of ME. ē̜

1. OE. **ē** of any origin:
   (a) Gmc. **ē**: **hēr** (adv.) > **hę̄r(e); mēd** > **mę̄ed** (reward)
   (b) i-umlaut of **ō**: **blēdan** (< **blōd**) > **blę̄ed; fēt** (< **fōt**) > **fę̄et**
   (c) In class VII of strong verbs: **hēt** (< **heht** < **hehait**), but this explanation is questioned by Prokosch, *Compar. Gmc. Gram.*, p. 176.
   (d) Latin loanwords: **crēdō, crēda** > **crę̄ed**

2. WS. **ȳ** = Kentish **ē̜** (and Southeast Midl.)
   WS. **gesȳne, gesīene** = Kentish **gesę̄ne** > **y-sę̄ne**
3. OE. **ēo**: **dēop** > **dę̄ep**
4. OF. **ē̜**: **beautee, pitee**
5. OF. **ie** (AN. **ę̄**): **nece, acheven**
6. OF. **ue**: **beef, meve**

INFLECTIONS

By the time of Chaucer the weakening of the inflectional endings of Old English had gone so far as to leave the language in this respect almost like Modern English. The few differences, which generally cause no problem of understanding, are noted in the paragraphs that follow.

Noun

14. The gen. s. and the pl. usually end in **-es**, occasionally **-is**. A few nouns which belonged to declensions in OE. that did not have **-es** and which had not been made to conform to the common pattern occur without **s**, *e.g.*, **fader, herte, hevene, lady, sonne** beside **faderes, hertes,** etc. Some words like **yeer, winter** may remain unchanged in the pl., as do several nouns ending in **s**, such as **hors, vers, caas, paas.** Plurals formed with **-n** or **-en**, like **oxen,** were more common. Examples are **asshen, been, fleen, foon, shoon, toon, peesen,** and **yën** (eyes). For some of these, **s-**plurals also occur. Besides **bretheren** we have occasionally **doghtren** and **sustren.** A petrified dative is preserved in certain set phrases: **on lyve, in (on) honde, to bedde, at a sterte,** and a few others.

Adjective

15. In Old English, as in German today, adjectives were declined in two ways—according to what are called the *strong* and the *weak* (or *definite*) declensions. They were declined according to the weak declension when preceded by a demonstrative, the definite article, a possessive pronoun, and in certain other situations (see §20). Although the endings of the two declensions have weakened and been greatly reduced by Chaucer's time, the distinction is still observed and is apparent in any monosyllabic adjective ending in a consonant. When the adjective in OE. ended in a vowel the formal distinction is lost. The two types may be seen in **blak** and **swete**:

		Strong	*Weak*
Sing.		**blak**	**blake**
Pl.		**blake**	**blake**
Sing.		**swete**	**swete**
Pl.		**swete**	**swete**

16. A few adjectives which ended in a consonant in OE. or OF. regularly or occasionally have a final **-e** by analogy,—*e.g.* **bare** (OE. **bær**), **late** (OE. **læt**), **longe** (OE. **lang**), **tame** (OE. **tam**), **commune** (OF. **comun**). Such an ending not justified by the OE. or OF. form is said to be *inorganic*.

17. Adjectives of more than one syllable like **litel, muchel, blisful,** including comparatives and superlatives in **-er** and **-est,** are uninflected. However, if the accent falls on the last syllable, the word may take **-e** in the def. and pl. forms **(the férfulléste wight).**

18. Predicate adjectives in the plural sometimes have **-e**, sometimes do not **(whan that they were seeke, thise ladyes were not right glad).**

19. Past participles used predicatively **(they were adrad, he was fulfild)** are usually unchanged, but monosyllabic participles occasionally show an inflectional **-e (spradde, fledde).**

20. The weak or definite form is used:

   (1) when the adjective is preceded by

      (a) the definite article: **the olde daunce**

      (b) a demonstrative pronoun: **this goode man**

      (c) a possessive pronoun: **his sweete breeth**

(2) when it is used as a noun: **the faire, for the beste**

(3) when it modifies a following noun in the vocative case: **O leve nece;** but not when it follows the noun: **O cause first**

(4) when it modifies a proper noun: **Of fierse Mars; Of faire, yonge, fresshe Venus free.**

21. The inflectional **-e** in the definite and plural forms of adjectives, while normal, is not invariably found, *e.g.* before a word beginning with a vowel (where it is often elided even when written) or elsewhere in the interest of the rime or meter.

To shewen yow the **goode** Urban the olde	G 177
They were ful **glad** whan I spak to hem faire	D 222

Compare the following pairs of lines:

But, **goode** brother, do now as the oughte	TC 3.264
Now, my **good** em, for Goddes love, I preye	TC 2.309
Ylyche they were bothe gladde and **wrothe**	BD 1294
Ladyes, I prey yow that ye be nat **wrooth** (riming with **gooth**)	E 2350

22. On the other hand the adjective frequently has the final **-e,** when not needed, if it stands at the end of the verse.

And evere a thousand goode ayeyns oon **badde**	A 3155
And made hir bed ful harde and nothyng **softe** (riming with **on-lofte**)	E 228

23. A remnant of the OE. dative survives in certain phrases (**of evene lengthe, of alle cure**), perhaps for the sake of the meter.

The French **-es** or **-s** plural ending occurs sporadically in adjectives of French origin (**places delitables, infernals illusiouns**).

Pronoun

24. The personal pronoun has the following forms:

Singular

First Person	Second Person		Third Person	
N. **I, ich (ik)**	**thou**	**he(e)**	**she**	**hit, hyt**
G. **my, myn**	**thy, thyn**	**his**	**hir(e), her**	**his**
D. **me**	**thee**	**him**	**hir(e), her(e)**	**him**
A. **me**	**thee**	**him**	**hir(e), her(e)**	**hit, hyt**

Plural

N. **we**	**ye**	**they**
G. **oure**	**youre**	**hir(e), her(e)**
D. **us**	**yow, you**	**hem**
A. **us**	**yow, you**	**hem**

25. The form **ik** (Northern) appears only in the speech of the Reeve. As explained under Pronunciation the neuter pronoun **hit, hyt** when unstressed may appear as **it, yt.** The ModE. **its** had not yet developed in Chaucer's time; it first appears at the end of the sixteenth century. The absolute forms of the genitive with **-s** occur in the fem. sg. **hires (heres, hyrs)** and in the pl. forms **oures, youres.**

26. The reflexive pronouns are **myself, myselven, thyself, thyselven,** etc.

27. The demonstrative pronouns are:

Sing.	**this**	that
Pl.	**this(e), these**	tho(o)

— means whole, all, entirely

28. The indefinite pronoun **al** (pl. **alle**) has a gen. pl. **aller,** or **alder** (OE. **ealra**): **hir aller cappe, our alder pris.** Similarly **bother: youre bother love** (the love of you both).

Verb

29. The distinction between strong verbs, which form their past tense and past participle by a change in the vowel of the stem (like ModE. **sing—sang—sung**), and weak verbs, which add **d** or **t** (like **leap—leaped—leaped**) is a feature of the Teutonic languages. It is, of course, characteristic of ME., and there are a few verbs like **helpen—holp—holpen** which are strong verbs in Chaucer, but have since been attracted to the weak conjugation. Some verbs like **slepen** were in the process of changing and have both a strong and a weak preterite (**sleep** and **slepte**). Some show a mixture of strong and weak forms, like **cleven—clefte—cloven.**

30. Infinitive. The infinitive ends in **-en** or **-n** (**speken, gon**), but the **-n** was being lost and forms like **speke, go** are frequent. Verbs are entered in the glossary under the form actually found in the text. The infinitives **doon, seen,** and a few others sometimes (though rarely) appear with an inflectional **-e** (**to done, to sene**) representing the dative case of the OE. gerund or verbal noun.

31. Present participle. The present participle ends in **ynge** or **yng** (**inge, ing**).

32. Past participle. The past participle of strong verbs ends in **-en** or **-e**, of weak verbs in **-ed, -d,** or **-t.** The prefix **y-**(occasionally **i-**), which is fairly common, is the survival in weakened form of the OE. **ge-**, a regular feature of the past participle of verbs without a prefix (**ysonge, ytold**).

33. The inflection of the verb is shown in the following paradigms.

Present Indicative

		Strong	Weak
Sing.	1.	**bere**	**love**
	2.	**berest**	**lovest**
	3.	**bereth**	**loveth**
Pl.		**bere(n)**	**love(n)**

Present Subjunctive

	Strong	Weak
Sing.	**bere**	**love**
Pl.	**bere(n)**	**love(n)**

Preterite Indicative

		Strong	Weak
Sing.	1.	**bar**	**loved(e)**
	2.	**bere, bare**	**lovedest**
	3.	**bar, beer**	**loved(e)**
Pl.		**bere(n), bare(n)**	**lovede(n), loved**

Preterite Subjunctive

Sing.	**bere**	**loved(e)**
Pl.	**bere(n)**	**lovede(n)**

Imperative

Sing.	**ber(e)**	**love**
Pl.	**bereth, ber**	**loveth**

In the above paradigm of **beren** the normal ME. development of the preterite is given first. Where there are alternative forms the second is due to analogical leveling. It will be noticed that the endings of the present tense are the same for both strong and weak verbs.

34. In the present tense the third person singular is sometimes contracted: **bit** beside **biddeth, sit** beside **sitteth**. Other examples are given in the glossary.

35. The imperative singular, except for a few verbs (OE. **jo-**stems), should normally have no ending, but forms with an inorganic **-e** are common.

36. The verbs **chese** and **chose**, **lese** and **lose** are derived from OE. **cēosan** and **lēosan,** which normally developed into **chese** and **lese.** When the diphthong became a rising diphthong (**eó**) it gave rise to the alternative forms **chose** and **lose.** The alternative forms of **meve** and **move, preve** and **prove** (of French origin) are due to the varying position of the accent in the conjugation of the Latin present indicative. A few other verbs of French origin, like **kevere—covere,** show the same alternatives.

37. Preterite-present verbs. A small but important group of verbs shows a mixture of strong and weak features. In these verbs the preterite forms acquired a present meaning and a new (weak) preterite was formed. An example is **witen,** to know.

		Present	Preterite
Sing.	1.	**wot**	**wiste**
	2.	**wost**	**wistest**
	3.	**wot**	**wiste**
Pl.		**wite(n)**	**wiste(n)**
Imper. Sing.		**wite**	*Past part.* **wist**
Pl.	**witteth**		

Others (with full list of forms in the glossary) are:

Present	Preterite
dar	**dorste, durste**
can, pl. **conne(n)**	**coude, couthe**
may, pl. **mowe(n)**	**myghte**
moot	**moste**
owe	**oughte**
shal, pl. **shul(len)**	**sholde**
thar	**thurste** (for **thurfte**)

38. Anomalous verbs. Four verbs depart in various ways from the above patterns: **ben, don, gon,** and **wille.** The regular forms of **ben** are:

		Present Indicative	*Preterite Indicative*
Sing.	1.	**am**	**was**
	2.	**art**	**were**
	3.	**is**	**was**
Pl.		**are, arn, be(n)**	**were(n)**

For the subjunctive and for the forms of **don, gon,** and **wille** see the entries in the glossary.

Adverb

39. Adverbs are commonly formed from adjectives by adding **-e,** unless the adjective itself ends in **-e: bright—brighte, smert—smerte.** Some OE. adverbs ending in a consonant may acquire by analogy an **-e** beside the normal form: **here** beside **her, heer; there** beside **ther;** eke beside **ek, eek.** A number of adverbs end in **-es: hennes, togidres** (beside **togidre**), **unnethes** (beside **unnethe**). Many adverbs end in **-ly** as in ModE., and some in **-liche.** The comparative degree of **fer** and **neigh** shows contraction: **ferre, neer, ner(e).** The adverb **moost, most** when preceded by the definite article commonly takes **-e** as though it were an adjective: **the mooste servysable, the mooste stedefast wyf.**

SYNTAX

40. The syntax of Chaucer's English is essentially like that of today and even the differences present few obstacles to understanding. The construction of sentences is looser, a fact that is partly to be explained by the informal, conversational style. Abrupt change of tense is not infrequent and apparently did not bother the poet. Parataxis—the juxtaposition of sentence elements without connectives or formal syntactical indications —occurs, especially in descriptive passages. Change of construction (anacoluthon) which would now be frowned upon is rather frequent. The agreement of subject and predicate may be disturbed by attraction, and a pronoun may lack an antecedent. Of these irregularities a few examples will be given as a warning to the reader of what may occur. In the following notes on ME. syntax only those usages that are of frequent occurrence or, as experience shows, puzzle the student in the beginning are noted.

41. Change of tense.

But al to deere they **boghte** it er they **ryse.**	B 420
He **kembeth** his lokkes brode, and **made** hym gay.	A 3374
For sternely on me he **gan byholde,**	
So that his loking **dooth** myn herte colde.	*LGW* 239—40

42. Parataxis.

No wonder is, for in hire grete estaat
Hire goost was evere in pleyn humylitee;
No tendre mouth, noon herte delicaat,
No pompe, no semblant of roialtee,

> But ful of pacient benyngnytee,
> Discreet and pridelees, ay honurable,
> And to hire housbonde evere meke and stable.　　　　　E 925–31

43. Change of construction.

> Men wiste nevere womman **han** the care,
> Ne **was** so loth out of a town to fare.　　　　　TC 5.20–1

44. Lack of agreement between subject and predicate.

> His lordes sheep, his neet, his dayerye,
> His swyn, his hors, his stoor, and his pultrye
> **Was** hoolly in this Reves governynge.　　　　　A 597–9

45. Faulty back-reference (pronoun with vague or missing antecedent). The following examples should be examined in context:

> And goon al quit, if he wole **it** reneye　　　　　G 448
> But atte laste . . . **he** han to calle
> Grisilde.　　　　　E 1027–9
> Thanne wol I stynge **hym** with my tonge smerte　　　　　C 413

46. Omission of the subject pronoun.

(a) Anticipatory "it":

> And so **bifel** that　　　　　TC 5.1649
> No wonder **is**　　　　　A 641
> and **seyd is**　　　　　TC 4.1455
> that pite **was** to here　　　　　TC 2.1577
> if so **were** that　　　　　A 1211
> He seyth hym **told is**　　　　　TC 3.796

(b) Other pronouns understood from context:

> 　　　　　There was a king
> That highte Seys, **and had a wif**　　　　　BD 62–3
> This thyng was graunted, and oure othes swore
> With ful glad herte, **and preyden hym also** (we prayed him)　　　　　A 810–1

(c) The relative pronoun:

> With hym ther was a Plowman, **was his brother**　　　　　A 529
> Hastow nat in a book, **lyth in thy cheste**　　　　　LGW 510
> Ye mooten trille a pyn, **stant in his ere**　　　　　F 316
> For he hadde founde a corn, **lay in the yerd**　　　　　B 4365

47. Omission of the sign of the infinitive. Although Chaucer uses **to** and **for to** with infinitives, he also uses the infinitive without either in many places where **to** would be required today.

> And there oure Hoost bigan his hors **areste**　　　　　A 827
> And lothest were of al this world **displese**　　　　　F 1313
> Thanne wolde she ones suffre hym **do** the same　　　　　B 3480
> And she his dreem bigan right thus **expounde**　　　　　B 3940
> the day bigynneth **dawe**　　　　　B 3872
> As gret a craft is **kepe** wel as **wynne**　　　　　TC 3.1634

48. Omission of *of*. In the expression **manner of** the preposition is commonly omitted. The result is a real or apparent apposition.

Now herkeneth, every **maner man**	*HF* 509
And many other **maner pipe**	*HF* 1219
He made alwey a **maner louryng chiere**	D 1266

49. Of is likewise omitted in many partitive constructions.

I hadde levere than a **barel ale**	B 3083
Is ther no **morsel breed** that ye do kepe?	B 3624
Although it be nat worth a **botel hey**	H 14
Than the beste **galon wyn** in Chepe	H 24
And somme woln have a **paire plates** large	A 2121

50. Of is commonly omitted in the construction *one + the +* superlative (singular).

For she was **oon the faireste** under sonne	F 734
The thriftiest and **oon the beste knyght**	*TC* 1.1081
For I have falsed **oon the gentileste**	
That evere was, and **oon the worthieste!**	*TC* 5.1056–7

Even when **of** is not omitted the superlative is still in the singular.

Oon of the beste farynge **man** on lyve	F 932
Oon of the beste entecched **creature**	*TC* 5.832
Oon of the gretteste **auctour** that men rede	B 4174

51. Ellipsis may occur almost anywhere if the omission is easily supplied.

They were [*as*] adrad of hym as of the deeth	A 605
Or be so hardy [*as*] to hire to trespace	B 3093
. . . yet al is seid or schal [*be said*]	*TC* 2.46
Hir hosen weren of fyn scarlet reed,	
Ful streite yteyd, and [*her*] shoes [*weren*] ful moyste and newe	A 456–7
There ys nothyng myssayd nor [*mys*] do.	*BD* 528

Article

52. Both the definite article and the indefinite are omitted in many places where idiom requires them today.

(a) Omission of the definite article:

Descendynge fro the montaigne **into playn**	B 24
From tyme that it first bigynneth to sprynge	A 3018
For ech of hem **made oother** for to wynne	A 427
And but ye come **at day set** into Troye	*TC* 4.1441

(b) Omission of the indefinite article:

Thanne telle I hem ensamples **many oon**	C 435
To stele awey with **swich oon** as he ys	*TC* 5.740
Yong, fressh, strong, and **hardy as lyoun**	*TC* 5.830
That shal be sent **to strange nacioun**	B 268
My lady queene **hath child**	B 734

53. Conversely both the definite and the indefinite article may be used where it would now be omitted.

He moot reherce as ny as evere he kan	
Everich a word, if it be in his charge	A 732–3
He ne hadde for his labour but **a scorn**	A 3388
We have **the deeth** disserved bothe two	A 1716
Thise rokkes sleen myn herte for **the feere**	F 893

54. Occasionally the indefinite article is used where we would use the definite.

Now writ hire thanne, and thow shalt feele sone	
A soth of al (find out the truth about everything)	TC 5.1308–9

Noun

55. Unchanged plural. Nouns expressing number, quantity, length of time, etc. commonly have the singular form with a plural meaning. (Some of these represent unchanged plurals in OE.) Thus we have **an hondred tyme, an hondred sithe, sixty yeer, fourty pound, an hundred mark, in twenty manere.** We even find **fourty dayes and fourty nyght** (D 1885). These and other instances can be identified by reference to the glossary.

56. Group genitive. The group genitive such as *the King of England's nose* takes various forms, usually involving separation of the parts.

this kynges sone of Troie (this son of the king of Troy)	TC 3.1715
The kynges metynge Pharao (Pharaoh the king's dream)	BD 282
the Grekes hors Synoun (Sinon the Greek's horse)	F 209

57. Genitive of description. A noun in the genitive case sometimes has the force of an adjective.

With alle joie and alle **frendes fare** (friendly behavior)	TC 3.605
How sholde a plaunte or **lyves** creature (living)	
Lyve withouten his kynde noriture?	TC 4.767–8
And lat hem in this **hevene** blisse dwelle (heavenly)	TC 3.1322
diluge **of pestilence** (pestilential)	Scogan 14
Ne doute **of reson,** pardee, is ther noon (reasonable)	TC 2.366

For the genitive without –s see §14.

Pronoun

58. Redundant personal pronoun. The personal pronoun is sometimes redundant and when so used imparts an informal or colloquial flavor to the sentence.

but this Miller	
He nolde his wordes for no man forbere	A 3167–8
as doth **he** Ixion in helle	TC 5.212
Ful ofte tyme **he** Pluto and his queene	E 2038
And slow **hym** Olofernus, whil he slepte	E 1368
This marchant, whan that ended was the faire,	
To Seint-Denys **he** gan for to repaire.	B 1515–6

59. *Myself, himself,* **etc. as personal pronouns.** The reflexive and intensive pronouns in **-self, -selven** may be used as personal pronouns.

But though **myself** be gilty in that synne	C 429
Myselven can not telle why	BD 34
. . . but if **hireself** it wolde	TC 4.637
For he hadde power of confessioun,	
As seyde **hymself** . . .	A 218–9
Doth therwithal right as **youreselven** leste.	TC 3.1330

60. Dative of reference. The dative of the personal pronoun, which at times resembles an accusative with reflexive force, may be loosely used as an intensifier. In keeping with Latin grammars some datives of reference are called ethical datives, datives of advantage or disadvantage, etc.

He stal **hym** hoom agayn to his contree.	C 610
er that the cok **hym** croweth	C 362
Thise riotoures thre of whiche I telle . . .	
Were set **hem** in a taverne for to drynke.	C 661–3
That in his bed ther daweth **hym** no day	A 1676

61. *That* **+ personal pronoun.** In addition to the relative pronouns **that, which, whos,** and the combinations **the which, which that,** the group **that** + a personal pronoun may serve as the equivalent.

Ther nas baillif, ne hierde, nor oother hyne,	
That he ne knew **his** sleighte and **his** covyne	
(whose cunning and deceit he did not know)	A 603–4
A Knyght ther was, and that a worthy man,	
That fro the tyme that he first bigan	
To riden out, **he** loved chivalrie.	A 43–5
. . . oon	
That with a spere was thirled **his** brest-boon	A 2709–10

In this construction **which** may replace **that.**

Which alwey for to don wel is **his** wone	
(whose custom is always to do well)	TC 2.318

62. *That* **meaning** *that which, what.*

He kepte **that** he wan in pestilence	A 442
Maistow not heren **that** I do?	HF 1024
That wol mayntene **that** he first bigan	A 1778

63. *This, thise* **with generalizing force.** In colloquial speech today one hears statements like "These bargain sales are not all genuine" or "Beware of your high-pressure salesman," in which *these* and *your* do not identify particular persons or things, but imply that the hearer is familiar with the type referred to. In ME. the generalizing word is usually **thise** or **this.**

As been **thise** wedded men (married men, as you know)	B 1293
And right so as **thise** philosophres write	G 113

As doon **thise** wete brondes in hir brennynge	A 2338
. . . or shrichyng of **thise** owles (screeching of owls, as you know)	TC 5.382
And ay bisyde hym was **this** Pandarus (Pandarus, whom you know about)	TC 5.682

64. The indefinite pronouns *man, men*. Man and the weakened form **men** are used as indefinite pronouns, meaning *one, they*.

She loved as **man** may do hys brother	BD 892
The spices and the wyn **men** forth hem fette	TC 5.852
But **men** (one) myght axe me why soo	BD 30

Verb

65. The impersonal construction. Many verbs which are now used with personal subjects were formerly used impersonally (*it likes me* instead of *I like*). The subject is often not expressed.

So whan **it liked hire** to go to reste	TC 2.911
hir neded no maistresse	C 106
I woot **yow thynketh** straunge (it seems strange to you)	TC 5.120
Hym deyneth not to wreke hym on a flye	LGW 395
anon-right tho **hire mette** (she dreamed)	TC 2.925

66. Reflexive verbs. Many more verbs were used with reflexive pronouns than today. Sometimes it is difficult to say whether the pronoun is used reflexively or as a dative of reference (see §60).

And on hire wey they **spedden hem** to wende	TC 5.501
We shul first **feyne us** cristendom to take	B 351
On bokes for to rede I **me delyte**	LGW 30

67. Infinitive for participle. The infinitive is sometimes used where we use a present participle.

Than found I **sitte** even upryght	BD 451
Ysee who comth here **ride**	TC 2.1253
His lord wel koude he plesen subtilly	
To yeve and lene hym of his owene good.	
(by giving and lending)	A 610–1

68. Past participle for infinitive. The past participle is found, especially after a verb in the perfect tense, where we would expect an infinitive. Possibly the construction arose through the ellipsis of *to have* or *to be*. Although this idiom is not common, its existence is beyond doubt.

And tolde hym al, as ye han herd me **sayd**	F 1547
Thise merchantz han doon **fraught** hir shippes newe	B 171
Hath doon yow **kept**	E 1098
Whan Troilus hadde herd Pandare **assented**	TC 1.1009
Hath mad ful many a lady bright of hewe	
Seyd "weilaway, the day that I was born!"	TC 3.303–4

What is possibly an analogical extension of this construction is

| I was go **walked** fro my tree | BD 387 |

Adverb

69. Position of the adverb. The usual position of the adverb is next to the verb (*he said quietly, he quietly said*). This principle is observed in some cases where today the adverb is put at the end of the clause for emphasis.

Ye, for an heyre clowt to wrappe **in** me	C 736
to quite **with** the Knyghtes tale	A 3119
To saffron **with** my predicacioun	C 345
To store **with** a place that is oures	B 1463

The adverb may be shifted for metrical reasons or for the sake of the rime.

A long surcote of pers **upon** he hade	A 617

70. The negative adverb. The negative adverb is **ne** or **not** (**nat, naught**).

This boke **ne** spak but of such thinges	*BD* 57
It was **not** wele	*BD* 82
Ne falleth **naught** to purpos me to telle	*TC* 1.142

The negative **ne** is frequently combined with the verb.

That in this world **nys** creature lyvynge	A 901
So I **not** what is best to doo	*BD* 29

For other examples (**nyl, nyste**. etc.) see the glossary.

71. The double negative. The double negative is frequent in English down to the eighteenth century. The principle that two negatives make a positive was unknown to Chaucer. A double negative is simply a more emphatic form of negation. Triple negatives are not uncommon.

Ne Deeth, allas, **ne** wol **nat** han my lyf!	C 727
Nowher so bisy a man as he ther **nas**	A 321
Ther **nas no** man **nowher** so vertuous	A 251
He **nevere** yet **no** vileynye **ne** sayde	A 70

72. Intensive or redundant *as*. The adverb *as* is often used with other adverbs and adverbial phrases, a usage which survives in ModE. *as yet*.

And yif I more dorste preye yow **as now**	*TC* 2.1436
That, **as that day,** ther dorste non withstonde	*TC* 2.202
and bad the preest **as faste** (very quickly)	G 1235
Syn ye shul bothe han folk and town **as yerne**	*TC* 4.112
Withouten gilt thou shalt be slayn **as swithe** (immediately)	B 637
Bright was the sonne **as in that someres day**	B 554

73. Hortatory *as* (also), *ther*, *so*. [Exalt someone or thing] An imperative or hortatory subjunctive of wish, imprecation, etc., is commonly introduced by **as, ther,** or **so.**

as beth nat wroth (be not angry)	*TC* 5.145
As lene it me (lend it to me)	A 3777
also God your soule blesse	*HF* 1612
As wolde God (would God that)	*TC* 3.1387
[May] **ther** God his bones corse! [curse]	E 1308
For Goddes love, **as** chees a newe requeste!	D 1060
I bidde God, **so** yeve yow bothe sorwe!	*TC* 3.1470

74. **Exclamatory** *so, so that* **meaning** *how*.

But Lord, **so** she wex sodeynliche red! (how she blushed!)	*TC* 3.956
but Lord! **so that** they lye (how they lie!)	*TC* 3.1380

75. **Interrogative** *wher* (*wheither*). **Wher** or **wheither**, meaning *which of two*, is sometimes used to introduce a direct question, real or rhetorical. Usually alternatives, expressed or implied, are involved, but not always (cf. *HF* 1779 in the examples below).

Wher shal I seye to yow welcom or no? (Shall I)	*TC* 4.831
Wheither seistow this in ernest or in pley?	A 1125
Now **wheither** have I a siker hand or noon?	D 2069
Wher Joves wol me stellyfye?	*HF* 586
What? false theves! **wher** ye wolde	
Be famous good, and nothing nolde	
Deserve why . . .?	*HF* 1779–81

76. The conjunctive adverb *ther*. The conjunctive adverb **ther** (**ther as**) is commonly used in the sense of *where*.

He ferde thus evel **there** he set	*BD* 501
He was an esy man to yeve penaunce	
Ther as he wiste to have a good pitaunce.	A 223–4
and loked on the place	
Ther she was born and **ther** she dwelt hadde ay.	*TC* 5.710–1
Nat fer fro Pedmark, **ther** his dwellyng was	F 801

Preposition

77. Omission of preposition. The preposition is sometimes omitted in adverbial phrases. Cf. ModE. I saw him **this time last year**.

I wil yive hym the alderbeste	
Yifte that ever he abod **hys lyve**.	*BD* 246–7
that evere I saugh **my lyve**	*TC* 2.205
He hath a thousand slayn **this pestilence**	C 679
His owene hand he made laddres thre	A 3624

78. A preposition may follow its noun (especially *bisyde*).

She cleped on hir maistresse **hire bisyde**	F 374
Ye mowe hyt fynde **the see besyde**	*BD* 208
And to his doghter, that stood **hym bisyde**	B 3937

79. The partitive *of*. Like *de* in French, and possibly influenced by French, **of** is occasionally used in the sense of *some*.

Of twenty yeer of age he was, I gesse.	A 82
Of smale houndes hadde she that she fedde	A 146
Cometh up, ye wyves, offreth **of youre wolle**	C 910

80. Idiomatic uses. There is probably nowhere else in English where changes of idiom have been more extensive than in the use of prepositions. This may be seen as well in Shakespeare as in Chaucer. It may be illustrated by Chaucer's use of **of**.

Allas, his wyf ne roghte nat of (*about*) dremes	B 4530
The man hath served yow of (*according to*) his kunnynge	LGW 412
Ther I was fostred of (*as*) a child	E 834
Foond of (*among*) us wommen fooles many oon	E 2278
This millere smyled of (*at*) hir nycetee	A 4046
Therfore no womman of (*by*) no clerk is preysed	D 706
Now wol I stynten of (*concerning*) this Arveragus	F 814
Of (*during*) al that day she saugh hym nat	A 3415
Besoghte mercy of (*for*) hir trespassynge	LGW 155
Hire to delivere of (*from*) wo	B 518
Al myghte a geant passen hym of (*in*) myght	TC 5.838
his herte hadde compassioun/Of (*on*) wommen	A 1770–1
Therfore I passe of (*over*) al this lustiheed	F 288
Withouten wem of (*harm to*) yow	F 121
He was of (*with*) foom al flekked	G 565
worthy of (*with respect to*) his hond/Agayn the Scottes	B 579–80

The varied uses of other prepositions are recorded in the glossary.

81. A few special idioms. Idioms are the lawless parts of language. They are often obscure in origin and sometimes defy logical explanation. They have to be accepted at face value and each one must be learned separately. A few common examples will here suffice.

> **no fors, I do no fors** (no matter, it does not matter to me)
>
> **hit am I, hit weren alle** (it is I, they were all). The verb agrees with the second half of the equation.
>
> **I do no cure** (I do not care)
>
> **which a . . .!** (what a . . .!)
>
> **what me is** (what is the matter with me)
>
> **looke who, looke what,** etc. (whoever, whatever)

Looke who that is most pacient in love	F 771
Looke what day that . . . ye	F 992
And looketh . . . **wher** moost sorwe is	A 3073

> **look how** (just as)

Looke how thou rydest . . .	
To wynne good, thou rekkest nevere how,	
Right so fare I.	D 1452–4

> **wayte what** (whatever)

Wayte what thyng we may nat lightly have,	
Therafter wol we crie al day and crave.	D 517–8

A number of other idiomatic uses have been covered in the preceding paragraphs.

The Versification of Chaucer

THERE IS NO NEED here to explain the elementary principles of prosody. All of Chaucer's verse is iambic in movement ($\smile$ $\diagup$), most of it with either four or five stresses to the line.

> I háve | gret wónd|er, bé | this lýghte.
> Of whích | vertú | engén|dred ís | the floúr.

Like later poets Chaucer felt free to substitute an occasional trochaic foot ($\diagup$ $\smile$):

> Rédy | to wénd|en ón | my píl|grimágë

or to introduce an extra syllable in any foot:

> A Chrís|tophre ón | his brést | of síl|ver sheéne.
> Al spéke | he név|er so rúd|elíche | and lárgë.
> Is lík|ned tíl | a físsh | that is wá|terleés

and sometimes to omit the unstressed syllable at the beginning of the line:

> Whán | that Á|prill wíth | his shoú|res soótë

If it were not for the fact that the word-stress in some words, as explained above, was not the same as it is today and that many words ended in an unstressed **-e, -es, -ed,** etc., which normally constituted a syllable, there would be no problem of scansion for the modern reader of Chaucer. In connection with such syllables a few observations may be useful.

The final **-e** was usually elided before a word beginning with a vowel or the **h** in French words (**honest, honour**). In the examples below a dot under the vowel indicates that it is not pronounced.

> In Gernadę at the seegę eek haddę he be.
> And that ye deignë me so muchę honourë.

It could also be elided before the **h** in a number of common words where this **h** was not strongly aspirated, such as **he, his, him, hem, hadde.**

> At Alisaundrę he was whan it was wonnë.
> He keptę his pacient a ful greet deel.
> And seydę hem thus, as ye shul after herë.
> Ther as this Emelyę haddę hir pleyyngë.

The **e** in inflectional endings (**-ed, -es, -eth,** etc.) and medially before liquids and nasals (**l, r, m, n**) in unstressed syllables is often elided or slurred.

> Al bismoterẹd with his habergeoun
> Grehoundẹs he haddẹ as swift as fowel in flight
> A kynges herte semẹth by hyrs a wrecchë
> Of yonge wommen at his owẹne cost

Certain common words were often pronounced as monosyllables. Such are the possessive pronouns (**hire, oure,** etc.), the verb-forms **have** and **come,** the past tense of auxiliary verbs (**hadde, wolde, koude, were,** etc.) and the plural demonstrative **thise,** to mention only the most important.

> To takẹ ourẹ wey ther as I yow devysë
> And ek the purë wise of hirẹ mevyngë
> I havẹ gret wonder, be this lyghte
> To comẹ to dyner, as he hym bisoughtë
> This ilkë worthy knyght haddẹ been also
> He woldẹ the see werẹ kept for any thyng
> Wel koudẹ she cariẹ a morsel and wel kepë
> But myghtẹ this gold be cariẹd fro this placë
> And as thisẹ clerkës maken mencioun

The above observations should prove helpful because they cover a number of fairly frequent situations, but there is no invariable rule that can be given for the pronunciation or elision of final **-e** or of inflectional endings in which **e** forms a part, except that it is always pronounced at the end of the line and often before the caesura within the line. Otherwise it is pronounced when the meter requires it.

Except in his short lyrics Chaucer did not employ a great variety of verse forms. His earlier poems are in eight-syllable couplets, as can be seen in *The Book of the Duchess* and *The Hous of Fame.* In *The Parlement of Foules* he used for the first time a stanza (*ababbcc*) later known in English poetry as rime royal. It is the stanza which he used again in the *Troilus.* From *The Legend of Good Women* on he wrote chiefly in the ten-syllable couplet, which in its more stylized character as practiced by Dryden and Pope we know as the heroic couplet. This is the verse form of the General Prologue and apparently all the tales written specifically for *The Canterbury Tales.* Other stanza patterns can be seen in the "Monk's Tale stanza" (*ababbcbc*) and the "romance six" of *Sir Thopas* (*aabaab* or *aabccb*), but they call for no comment.

It should be noted that Chaucer occasionally appears to rime a word with itself, but this is actually not the case. Closer examination will show that the two words are used in different senses, or represent different parts of speech. In rare instances they may be merely different grammatical forms of the same word (cf. *telle* at A 408–11). In medieval poetry this is not only permitted but seems to have been looked upon as a special grace, a kind of verbal cleverness. It is known as identical rime (F. *rime riche,* G. *reicher Reim*). Consider the following:

> And I hym folwed, and hyt forth wente
> Doun by a floury grene wente (*path*).   *BD* 397–8

> Whan I first my lady say (*saw*)?
> I was ryght yong, soth to say.   *BD* 1089–90

> And many other maner pipe
> That craftely begunne to pipe.   *HF* 1219–20

By this convention a simple word may rime with a compound containing it (*womman* : *man*), or two words differing only in the prefix (*recorde* : *accorde*), but such rimes can hardly be considered evidence of verbal skill.

BIBLIOGRAPHY

Bibliography

Hammond, E. P. *Chaucer: A Bibliographical Manual*. New York, 1908.

Griffith, D. D. *Bibliography of Chaucer, 1908–1953*. Seattle, 1955.

"Annual Bibliography" [of modern languages and literatures], compiled by Paul A. Brown. Published in *PMLA*.

Annual Bibliography of English Language and Literature, published by the Modern Humanities Research Association.

The Year's Work in Modern Language Studies, published by the Modern Humanities Research Association.

Biography

Life-Records of Chaucer, ed. W. D. Selby, F. J. Furnivall, E. A. Bond, and R. E. G. Kirk. London, 1875–1900. (Chaucer Soc.)

Chute, Marchette. *Geoffrey Chaucer of England*. New York, 1946. (a popular biography)

Hulbert, J. R. *Chaucer's Official Life*. Menasha, 1912.

Kern, A. A. *The Ancestry of Chaucer*. Baltimore, 1906.

Krauss, R. "Chaucerian Problems: Especially the Petherton Forestership and the Question of Thomas Chaucer," in *Three Chaucer Studies*, ed. Carleton Brown. New York, 1932.

Editions

The Complete Works of Geoffrey Chaucer, ed. W. W. Skeat. 7v, Oxford, 1894–7. (Oxford Chaucer) [Skeat]

The Works of Geoffrey Chaucer, ed. A. W. Pollard, M. H. Liddell, H. F. Heath, W. S. McCormick. London, 1898. (Globe Chaucer)

The Works of Geoffrey Chaucer, ed. F. N. Robinson. 2nd ed., Boston, 1957. (New Cambridge Edition) [Robinson]

Manly, J. M., and Edith Rickert. *The Text of the Canterbury Tales*. 8v, Chicago, 1940. [M-R]

Canterbury Tales by Geoffrey Chaucer [selections], ed. J. M. Manly. New York, 1928.

The Book of Troilus and Criseyde by Geoffrey Chaucer, ed. R. K. Root. Princeton, 1926. [Root]

The Parlement of Foulys, ed. D. S. Brewer. London, 1960.

Tatlock, J. S. P., and A. G. Kennedy. *Concordance to the Complete Works of Geoffrey Chaucer and to the Romaunt of the Rose*. Washington, 1927.

Criticism and Interpretation

Baum, P. F. *Chaucer: A Critical Appreciation*. Durham, N. C., 1958.

Bennett, J. A. W. *The Parlement of Foules: An Interpretation*. Oxford, 1957.

Bowden, Muriel. *A Commentary on the General Prologue to the Canterbury Tales*. New York, 1948.

Brewer, D. S. *Chaucer*. London, 1953.

Brusendorff, A. *The Chaucer Tradition*. London, 1925.

Curry, W. C. *Chaucer and the Mediaeval Sciences*. 2nd ed., New York, 1960.

French, R. D. *A Chaucer Handbook*. 2nd ed., New York, 1947.

Hinckley, H. B. *Notes on Chaucer*. Northampton, Mass., 1907.

Kirby, T. A. *Chaucer's Troilus: A Study in Courtly Love*. Baton Rouge, 1940.

Kittredge, G. L. *Chaucer and His Poetry*. Cambridge, Mass., 1915.

Lawrence, W. W. *Chaucer and the Canterbury Tales*. New York, 1950.

Lowes, J. L. "The Prologue to the *Legend of Good Women* as related to the French Marguerite Poems, and the *Filostrato*," *PMLA*, xix (1904). 593–683.

——, "The Prologue to the *Legend of Good Women* Considered in its Chronological Relations," *PMLA*, xx (1905). 749–864.

——, *Geoffrey Chaucer and the Development of His Genius*. Boston, 1934.

Lumiansky, R. M. *Of Sundry Folk: The Dramatic Principle in the Canterbury Tales*. Austin, 1955.

Malone, K. *Chapters on Chaucer*. Baltimore, 1951.

Manly, J. M. *Some New Light on Chaucer*. New York, 1926.

Meech, S. B. *Design in Chaucer's* Troilus. New York, 1959.

Muscatine, C. *Chaucer and the French Tradition: A Study in Style and Meaning*. Berkeley and Los Angeles, 1957.

Patch, H. E. *On Rereading Chaucer*. Cambridge, Mass., 1939.

Pratt, R. A. "The Order of the Canterbury Tales," *PMLA*, lxvi (1951). 1141–67.

Root, R. K. *The Poetry of Chaucer*. 2nd ed., Boston, 1922.

Severs, J. B. *The Literary Relations of Chaucer's* Clerkes Tale. New Haven, 1942.

Shelly, P. V. D. *The Living Chaucer*. Philadelphia, 1940.

Sypherd, W. O. *Studies in Chaucer's Hous of Fame*. London, 1907. (Chaucer Soc.)

Tatlock, J. S. P. *The Development and Chronology of Chaucer's Works*. London, 1907. (Chaucer Soc.)

——, *The Mind and Art of Chaucer*. Syracuse, 1950.

Sources and Influences

Braddy, H. *Chaucer and the French Poet Graunson*. Baton Rouge, 1947.

Bryan, W. F., and Germaine Dempster (edd.). *Sources and Analogues of Chaucer's Canterbury Tales*. Chicago, 1940. [*SA*]

Cummings, H. M. *The Indebtedness of Chaucer's Works to the Italian Works of Boccaccio*. Menasha, 1916.

Fansler, D. S. *Chaucer and the Roman de la Rose*. New York, 1914.

Jefferson, B. L. *Chaucer and the Consolation of Philosophy of Boethius*. Princeton, 1917.

Hamilton, G. L. *The Indebtedness of Chaucer's Troilus and Criseyde to Guido delle Colonne's Historia Trojana*. New York, 1903.

Hazelton, R. "Chaucer and Cato," *Speculum*, xxxv (1960). 357–80.

Pratt, R. A. "Chaucer's Use of the *Teseida*," *PMLA*, lxii (1947). 598–621.

——, "Chaucer's Claudian," *Speculum*, xxii (1947). 419–29.

——, "Jankyn's Book of Wikked Wyves: Medieval Antimatrimonial Propaganda in the Universities," *Annuale Mediaevale*, iii. 5–27.

Shannon, E. F. *Chaucer and the Roman Poets*. Cambridge, Mass., 1929.

Latin, French, and Italian Texts

Le Roman de la Rose, par Guillaume de Lorris et Jean de Meun, ed. E. Langlois. 5v, Paris, 1914–24. (SATF) [*RR*]

Oeuvres de Guillaume de Machaut, ed. E. Hœpffner. 3v, Paris, 1908–21. (SATF)

Oeuvres complètes de Eustache Deschamps, ed. le Marquis de Saint-Hilaire et G. Raynaud. 11v, Paris, 1878–1903. (SATF)

Oeuvres de Froissart: Poésies, ed. A. Scheler. 3v, Bruxelles, 1870–2.

Le Roman de Troie, par Benoit de Sainte-Maure, ed. L. Constans. 6v, Paris, 1904–12. (SATF)

Disticha Catonis, ed. M. Boas and H. J. Botschuyver. Amsterdam, 1952.

Macrobius: Commentary on the Dream of Scipio, trans. with intro. and notes by W. H. Stahl. New York, 1952. (The best Latin text is that of L. von Jan, 2v, Leipzig, 1852).

The Filostrato of Giovanni Boccaccio: A Translation with Parallel Text by N. E. Griffin and A. B. Myrick. Philadelphia, 1929.

Giovanni Boccaccio: Teseida, ed. S. Battaglia. Florence, 1938.

Guido de Columnis: Historia Destructionis Troiae, ed. N. E. Griffin. Cambridge, Mass., 1936.

Alain de Lille: *Anticlaudianus*, ed. Thomas Wright, in *Anglo-Latin Satirical Poets and Epigrammatists* (Rolls Ser.). There is a trans. by W. H. Cornog (Philadelphia, 1935).

——, *De planctu naturae*, ed. Thomas Wright (as above). *The Complaint of Nature*, trans. D. M. Moffat. New York, 1908 (*Yale Stud. in English*, 36).

Boethius: *De consolatione philosophiae*, ed. H. F. Stewart and E. K. Rand. London, 1918 (Loeb Classical Library).

Middle English Literature

Wells, J. E. *A Manual of the Writings in Middle English, 1050–1400*. New Haven, 1916. Nine supplements, 1919–51.

A Literary History of England, ed. A. C. Baugh. New York, 1948 (The Middle English Period, by A. C. Baugh, pp. 107–312).

Language

Baugh, A. C. *A History of the English Language*. 2nd ed., New York, 1957. The standard works on Middle English may be found listed here.

Kökeritz, H. *A Guide to Chaucer's Pronunciation*. New York, 1962.

Mustanoja, T. F. *A Middle English Syntax*. Part I: Parts of Speech. Helsinki, 1960.

Ten Brink, B. *The Language and Metre of Chaucer*, trans. M. B. Smith. London, 1921.

Dictionaries and Reference Books

A New English Dictionary on Historical Principles, ed. J. A. H. Murray and others. 10v, Oxford, 1888–1928. Supplement, 1933. [*NED*]

Middle English Dictionary, ed. H. Kurath and S. M. Kuhn. Ann Arbor, 1952– (in progress). [*MED*]

Carter, H. H. *A Dictionary of Middle English Musical Terms*. Bloomington, 1961.

Godefroy, F. *Dictionnaire de l'ancienne langue française*. 10v, Paris, 1881–1902. [Godefroy]

Magoun, F. P., Jr. *A Chaucer Gazetteer*. Chicago, 1961.

Morawski, J. *Proverbes français antérieurs au XVe siècle*. Paris, 1925. [Morawski]

Singer, S. *Sprichwörter des Mittelalters*. 3v, Bern, 1944–7.

Tobler-Lommatzsch. *Altfranzösisches Wörterbuch*. Berlin and Wiesbaden, 1925– (in progress). [Tobler-Lommatzsch]

Whiting, B. J. *Chaucer's Use of Proverbs*. Cambridge, Mass., 1934.

Political and Social Background

Coulton, G. G. *Chaucer and His England*. 4th ed., London, 1927.

——, *Medieval Panorama*. Cambridge, 1938.

McKisack, M. *The Fourteenth Century, 1307–1399*. Oxford, 1959.

Poole, A. L. (ed.) *Medieval England*. 2v, Oxford, 1958.

Rickert, Edith (compiler). *Chaucer's World*, ed. C. C. Olsen and M. M. Crow. New York, 1948.

Trevelyan, G. M. *England in the Age of Wycliffe*. 4th ed., London, 1909.

ABBREVIATIONS

IN ADDITION to the indications in brackets in the above bibliography, the following abbreviations are used:

Archiv	*Archiv für das Studium der neueren Sprachen.*
EETS	Early English Text Society.
E & S	*Essays and Studies by Members of the English Association.*
ESt	*Englische Studien.*
JEGP	*Journal of English and Germanic Philology.*
MA	*Medium Aevum.*
MLN	*Modern Language Notes.*
MLQ	*Modern Language Quarterly.*
MLR	*Modern Language Review.*
MP	*Modern Philology.*
N & Q	*Notes and Queries.*
PL	*Patrologia Latina (Patrologiae cursus completus: series latina.* 221v, Paris, 1862–4).
PMLA	*Publications of the Modern Language Association of America.*
PQ	*Philological Quarterly.*
RES	*Review of English Studies.*
SATF	Société des anciens textes français.
SP	*Studies in Philology.*

Chaucer's works are referred to by the following abbreviations:

Adam	*Chaucer's Wordes unto Adam.*
BD	*Book of the Duchess.*
Buk	*Lenvoy de Chaucer a Bukton.*
CkT	*Cook's Tale.*
ClT	*Clerk's Tale.*
CT	*Canterbury Tales.*
CYT	*Canon's Yeoman's Tale.*
FranklT	*Franklin's Tale.*
FrT	*Friar's Tale.*
GenProl	*General Prologue* to *The Canterbury Tales.*
Gent	*Gentilesse.*
HF	*Hous of Fame.*
KnT	*Knight's Tale.*
Lak	*Lak of Stedfastnesse.*
LGW	*Legend of Good Women.*
MancT	*Manciple's Tale.*
MerchT	*Merchant's Tale.*
MillT	*Miller's Tale.*
MkT	*Monk's Tale.*
MLT	*Man of Law's Tale.*
NPT	*Nun's Priest's Tale.*

PardT	*Pardoner's Tale*
PF	*Parlement of Foules.*
PhysT	*Physician's Tale.*
PrT	*Prioress's Tale.*
Purse	*Complaynt of Chaucer to his Purse.*
RvT	*Reeve's Tale.*
Rosem	*To Rosemounde.*
Scogan	*Lenvoy de Chaucer a Scogan.*
SNT	*Second Nun's Tale.*
ShipT	*Shipman's Tale.*
SqT	*Squire's Tale.*
SumT	*Summoner's Tale.*
TC	*Troilus and Criseyde.*
Truth	*Truth: Balade de Bon Conseyl.*
WBT	*Wife of Bath's Tale.*

References to *The Canterbury Tales* are by Group and line number (A 10, F 25, etc.).

CHAUCER'S
MAJOR POETRY

The Book of the Duchess

The Book of the Duchess is the earliest of the longer poems of Chaucer which we can date with reasonable certainty. It is preserved in three manuscripts, all of them defective. All are copies at one or more removes of an original which had suffered the loss of a number of lines and contained various mistakes; this archetype was obviously not the poet's copy. At the beginning of the sixteenth century a fourth manuscript was still preserved, and from this Thynne printed the poem in his edition of 1532. This manuscript contained most of the lines missing in the others and had more correct readings in several places, but all the manuscripts agree upon readings in which Chaucer's words have almost certainly been corrupted.

A note in the margin of the Fairfax MS says that the knight who mourns the death of his lady is John of Gaunt, and that Chaucer wrote the poem at his request. The note is in the handwriting of John Stowe, the sixteenth-century antiquary and author of the *Survey of London*, who eagerly sought and copied manuscripts containing the poetry of Chaucer and his contemporaries. At line 948 of the poem the lady is named White, the English translation of *Blanche*, and near the end is a couplet (ll. 1318–19) in which Blanche, Lancaster, John, and Richmond are alluded to in a thinly disguised reference. The poem is then an elegy occasioned by the death of Blanche, Duchess of Lancaster and wife of John of Gaunt, who fell a victim of the plague on September 12, 1369.

The date of her birth is uncertain, but most of the inquisitions post mortem upon her father's death make it likely that she was born in 1340 and was therefore of the same age as her husband. Chaucer was of a like age, possibly a couple of years younger. She was a great heiress since, upon the death of her older sister Maud in 1362, she came into possession of the extensive holdings of her father, Henry, first Duke of Lancaster. What can be learned of her from the chronicles and from contemporary records indicates that she inherited the straightforward character and goodness of her father and that her marriage to John of Gaunt (May 19, 1359) was a very happy one (see Marcia Anderson, *MP*, xlv. 152–159). He erected a handsome effigy and tomb (since destroyed) over her grave in St. Paul's cathedral, ordered costly services each year on the anniversary of her death, and though he twice remarried, directed in his will that his body be buried beside hers. Chaucer's description of her, though it embodies many features which were conventional in medieval descriptions of women and some of them were borrowed from Machaut, seems to be a truthful description and characterization. We may, of course, make allowances for poetic exaggeration.

An elegy too long delayed would lose much of its effect. We may suppose that Chaucer began the poem shortly after Blanche's death. Since John of Gaunt married Constance of Castile in 1372 we may be sure that a poem so laudatory of his first wife and representing him as completely devastated by her death would not have been presented to him after he had married again. We may safely date the poem 1369 or early 1370 at the latest. In the prologue to *The Man of Law's Tale* the Man of Law in enumerating a number of things that Chaucer had written says "In youthe he made of Ceys and Alcione." This has been taken by some to be a separate poem which Chaucer adapted to the purposes of his elegy, in which case this section of the poem would have been written earlier. But it seems better to believe that the Man of Law is speaking of the poem which Chaucer elsewhere refers to as "the Deeth of Blaunche the Duchesse" and "The book of the Duchesse."

It is clear that at the time Chaucer wrote *The Book of the Duchess* his favorite reading had been in Ovid and in certain French poetry then enjoying a great popularity, especially the *Roman de la Rose*, a number of poems of Machaut, and at least one of Froissart. The slower rate at which people read in the Middle Ages and the more or less accurate retention in the memory of what they read, which was one of the consequences of slow reading, together with the fact that all writings were immediately in the public domain and constituted a stock of ideas and images from which anyone was free to borrow—these things must be kept in mind in reading Chaucer's earlier poetry. The opening of his poem is clearly reminiscent of the opening lines of Froissart's *Paradys d'Amours*, and echoes of the *Roman de la Rose* are frequent. But his greatest debt is to two long poems of Machaut, the *Jugement du Roy de Behaigne* (Bohemia) and the *Remède de Fortune*. Occasional lines and passages can be matched more or less closely with lines in some of Machaut's other poems. When all of these parallels are set down *The Book of the Duchess* seems almost a mosaic of borrowed passages. Yet Chaucer's indebtedness does not seem to be that of a man writing with his source books open before him; rather he seems to be writing out of a memory stored with favorite lines and passages.

The elegy is cast in the form of a dream, a conventional device frequently employed in French love poetry of the period. It is sometimes said that Chaucer was the first to employ the convention in an elegy, but this is not true. It had been used by Jean de le Mote in *Li Regret de Guillaume*, an elegy on the death of William of Hainault (1337). Since William of Hainault was Queen Philippa's father and John of Gaunt's grandfather, the *Regret* may well have been known to Chaucer. Otherwise the plan of the poem seems to have been Chaucer's own, and it is not without merit. The story of Ceys and Alcione, by which Chaucer leads up to his own dream, serves the artistic purpose of creating the proper mood for what is to follow, just as Shakespeare (as Coleridge pointed out) strikes the keynote of *Romeo and Juliet* or *Macbeth* in the opening scenes of those plays. The device of the chess game, though not unknown to French love poetry, is here more effectively used, since by making Fortune the knight's opponent Chaucer puts the responsibility for the knight's grief upon fate. By putting the long and laudatory description of Blanche in the mouth of the bereaved husband he escapes the charge of flattery or presumption. Even his pretended stupidity in failing to grasp the meaning of the knight's story, though it taxes our credulity, must be allowed him since it is by this device that he compels the knight to continue his explanation. But what is perhaps the finest manifestation of artistic instinct in the poem is the swiftness with which the poet brings the poem to a close, once the knight has been forced to the plain statement, "She is dead." It would have been easy to allow the situation at this point to become oversentimentalized. Instead, after a brief, shocked exclamation, Chaucer notes that the hunting party with which his adventure began is returning home. The spell is broken and the dream ends. Many a poet of the Middle Ages, or indeed of any time, might well be proud to have written such a first poem.

THE BOOK OF THE DUCHESS

I have gret wonder, be this lyghte,
How that I lyve, for day ne nyghte
I may nat slepe wel nygh noght;
I have so many an ydel thoght,
Purely for defaute of slepe,   5
That, by my trouthe, I take no kepe
Of nothing, how hyt cometh or gooth,
Ne me nys nothyng leef nor looth.
Al is ylyche good to me—
Joye or sorowe, wherso hyt be—   10
For I have felynge in nothyng,
But, as yt were, a mased thyng,
Alway in poynt to falle adoun;
For sorwful ymagynacioun
Ys alway hooly in my mynde.   15
    And wel ye woot, agaynes kynde
Hyt were to lyven in thys wyse;
For nature wolde nat suffyse
To noon erthly creature
Nat longe tyme to endure   20
Withoute slepe and be in sorwe.
And I ne may, ne nyght ne morwe,
Slepe; and thus melancolye
And drede I have for to dye.
Defaute of slepe and hevynesse   25
Hath sleyn my spirit of quyknesse,
That I have lost al lustyhede.

Suche fantasies ben in myn hede,
So I not what is best to doo.
    But men myght axe me why soo   30
I may not sleepe, and what me is.
But natheles, who aske this
Leseth his asking trewely.
Myselven can not telle why
The sothe; but trewly, as I gesse,   35
I holde hit be a sicknesse
That I have suffred this eight yeere,
And yet my boote is never the nere;
For there is phisicien but oon
That may me hele—but that is don.   40
Passe we over untill eft;
That wil not be mot nede be left;
Our first mater is good to kepe.
    So when I saw I might not slepe
Til now late, this other night,   45
Upon my bedde I sat upright
And bad oon reche me a book,
A romaunce, and he it me tok
To rede and drive the night away;
For me thoughte it beter play   50
Then play either at chesse or tables.
And in this boke were written fables
That clerkes had in olde tyme,
And other poets, put in rime

The text is based on the Fairfax MS. The erratic use of the final *e*, often ungrammatical, has been corrected where neces- sary. **3. nat . . . noght.** The double negative is quite correct in Chaucer, as generally in English down to the eighteenth century. **5. defaute,** default, lack. **6. kepe,** heed. **8. Ne,** nor. **nys,** *ne* + *ys*, is not. **9. ylyche,** alike. **12. mased,** dazed, be- wildered. **13. in poynt . . .,** on the point of falling down. **14. ymagynacioun.** Jehan le Bel, a contemporary of Chaucer, in *Li ars d'amour* (Part 2, Bk I, ch. 8 and 10), explains *imagination* as the faculty which retains what is perceived by the senses; here equivalent to memories, thoughts. **16. woot,** know. **agaynes kynde,** against nature. **17. Hyt,** it. **20. Nat,** not. **22. morwe,** morning. **27. lustyhede,** pleasure in life. **29. not,** *ne* + *wot*, know not. **30. men,** one (indef.). **axe,** ask. **31. what me is,** what is the matter with me. **32. natheles,** none the less. **who,** whoever. **aske,** may ask (subjunctive). **33. Leseth,** loses. **35. sothe,** truth. **36–37. a sicknesse That I have suffred this eight yeere.** It has been suggested that Chaucer had paid courtly love to Joan of Kent, wife of the Black Prince (Galway, *MLN*, LX. 431–439) and that she was the "sovereign lady" referred to in the Prologue to the *LGW*. But this protestation of hopeless love is a common conven- tion in French poetry of the time and need not be taken too seriously. **40. that is don,** that is all over. **41. eft,** a later time. **42. That wil not be,** etc. What can't be helped must be endured. **45. Til now late,** until recently. **48. a romaunce.** The word implies a book in French, and since the story of Seys and Alcione (Ceys and Alcione) is from Ovid, the book may have been a French version of the *Metamorphoses* such as the *Ovide Moralisé*. The story is in *Metam.*, XI. 410 ff. It is also told in Machaut's *La Fonteinne Amoureuse*, from which Chaucer derived certain details. **48. tok,** brought. **50. me thoughte,** it seemed to me. **play,** pastime, entertainment. **51. Then,** than. **tables,** backgammon. **53. clerkes,** a general term implying the ability to read and write and a certain amount of learning.

5

To rede, and for to be in minde,
While men loved the lawe of kinde.
This boke ne spak but of such thinges,
Of quenes lives, and of kinges,
And many other thinges smale.   60
Amonge al this I fond a tale
That me thoughte a wonder thing.

    This was the tale: There was a king
That highte Seys, and had a wif,
The beste that mighte bere lyf,
And this quene highte Alcyone.
So it befil thereafter soone,
This king wol wenden over see.
To tellen shortly, whan that he
Was in the see, thus in this wise,   70
Such a tempest gan to rise
That brak her mast and made it falle,
And clefte her ship, and dreinte hem alle,
That never was founde, as it telles,
Bord ne man, ne nothing elles.
Right thus this king Seys loste his lif.   75
    Now for to speken of his wif:
This lady, that was left at hom,
Hath wonder that the king ne com
Hom, for it was a longe terme.
Anon her herte began to erme;   80
And for that her thoughte evermo
It was not wele [he dwelte] so,
She longed so after the king
That, certes, it were a pitous thing
To telle her hertely sorowful lif   85
That she had, this noble wif,
For him she loved alderbest.
Anon she sent bothe eest and west
To seke him, but they founde nought.
"Alas!" quoth shee, "that I was wrought!   90

And wher my lord, my love, be deed?   55
Certes, I nil never ete breed,
I make avowe to my god here,
But I mowe of my lord here!"
Such sorowe this lady to her tok   95
That trewly I, which made this book,
Had such pittee and such rowthe
To rede hir sorwe, that, by my trowthe,
I ferde the worse al the morwe
Aftir, to thenken on hir sorwe.   100
So whan this lady koude here noo word
That no man myghte fynde hir lord,
Ful ofte she swouned and sayed "Alas!"
For sorwe ful nygh wood she was,
Ne she koude no rede but oon;   105
But doun on knees she sat anoon
And wepte, that pittee was to here.
    "A! mercy! swete lady dere!"
Quod she to Juno, hir goddesse,
"Helpe me out of thys distresse,   110
And yeve me grace my lord to se
Soone, or wite wher so he
Or how he fareth; or in what wise;
And I shal make yow sacrifise,
And hooly youres become I shal   115
With good wille, body, herte, and al;
And but thow wilt this, lady swete,
Send me grace to slepe, and mete
In my slepe som certeyn sweven
Wher-thourgh that I may knowe even   120
Whether my lord be quyk or ded."
    With that word she heng doun the hed,
And fel aswowne as cold as ston.
Hyr women kaught hir up anoon,
And broghten hir in bed al naked,   125
And she, forweped and forwaked,

---

56. kinde, nature. **61. wonder**, marvellous. **63. highte**, was named. The verb is active in form, passive in meaning. **and had.** The subject is understood. **65. Alcyone.** The accent is on *-one*. **66. befil**, befell, happened. **67. wol**, will, desires to. **70. gan**, began. **71. That brak**, that (it) broke. **her**, their. **72. dreinte**, drowned. **hem**, them. **73. telles.** The Northern ending is for the rime. **78. ne com**, came not. **80. Anon**, immediately, the usual meaning in Chaucer. **erme**, grieve. **81. her thoughte**, it seemed to her. **84. pitous**, pitiful, sad. **85. hertely**, genuinely. **87. alderbest**, best of all. **91. wher**, whether. The construction is elliptical. **92. Certes**, certainly. **nil**, *ne* + *wil*, will not. **93. avowe**, vow. **94. mowe**, may. **99. ferde**, fared. **104. wood**, mad. **105. rede**, counsel (she knew only one thing to do). **111. yeve**, give. **112. wite**, know. **118. mete**, dream. **119. sweven**, dream. **120. even**, exactly. **122. heng**, hung. **123. aswowne**, in a swoon. **124. anoon**, immediately. **125. broghten hir in bed al naked**, *i.e.* undressed her and put her to bed. People slept without night-clothes in the Middle Ages. **126. forweped and forwaked.** The intensive prefix *for-* implies "worn out from."

Was wery, and thus the dede slepe
Fil on hir, or she tooke kepe,
Throgh Juno, that had herd hir bone,
That made hir to slepe sone. 130
For as she prayede, ryght so was don
In dede; for Juno ryght anon
Called thus hir messager
To doo hir erande, and he com ner.
Whan he was come, she bad hym thus: 135
"Go bet," quod Juno, "to Morpheus,—
Thou knowest hym wel, the god of slepe.
Now understond wel, and tak kepe!
Sey thus that on my halfe, that he
Go faste into the grete se, 140
And byd hym that, on alle thyng,
He take up Seys body the kyng,
That lyeth ful pale and nothyng rody.
Bid hym crepe into the body,
And doo hit goon to Alcione 145
The quene, ther she lyeth allone,
And shewe hir shortly, hit ys no nay,
How hit was dreynt thys other day;
And do the body speke ryght soo,
Ryght as hyt was woned to doo 150
The whiles that hit was alyve.
Goo now faste, and hye the blyve!"

This messager tok leve and wente
Upon hys wey, and never he stente
Til he com to the derke valeye 155
That stant bytwene roches tweye,
Ther never yet grew corn ne gras,
Ne tre, ne noght that ought was,
Beste, ne man, ne noght elles,

Save ther were a fewe welles 160
Came rennynge fro the clyffes adoun,
That made a dedly slepynge soun,
And ronnen doun ryght by a cave
That was under a rokke ygrave
Amydde the valey, wonder depe. 165
There these goddes lay and slepe,
Morpheus and Eclympasteyre,
That was the god of slepes heyre,
That slepe and dide noon other werk.
This cave was also as derk 170
As helle pit overal aboute.
They had good leyser for to route,
To envye who myght slepe beste.
Somme henge her chyn upon hir breste,
And slept upryght, hir hed yhed, 175
And somme lay naked in her bed
And slepe whiles the dayes laste.
This messager com fleynge faste
And cried, "O, ho! awake anoon!"
Hit was for noght; there herde hym non. 180
"Awake!" quod he, "whoo ys lyth there?"
And blew his horn ryght in here eere,
And cried "Awaketh!" wonder hye.
This god of slep with hys oon yë
Cast up, axed, "Who clepeth ther?" 185
"Hyt am I," quod this messager.
"Juno bad thow shuldest goon"—
And tolde hym what he shulde doon,
As I have told yow here-to-fore,—
Hyt ys no nede reherse hyt more— 190
And went hys wey, whan he had sayd.
Anoon this god of slepe abrayd

---

128. Fil, fell. **or,** ere, before. **kepe,** heed, *i.e.* before she knew it. **129. bone,** request. **133. messager,** messenger. **134. he.** Chaucer makes the messenger masculine. In Ovid (and in Machaut) the messenger is Iris. **136. Go bet,** go better, go with full speed. **139. halfe,** behalf. **140. the grete se,** the Mediterranean. **141. on alle thyng,** under any circumstance, without fail. **142. Seys body the kyng,** Ceys the king's body. **143. rody,** ruddy. **145. doo hit,** cause it. **goon,** to go. **146. ther,** where, as frequently in Middle English. **147. hit ys no nay,** it cannot be denied. **148. dreynt,** drowned. **150. woned,** wont. **151. The whiles,** whilst. **152. blyve,** quickly. **154. stente,** stopped. **156. stant,** contraction of *standeth,* stands. **roches tweye,** two rocks. **157. Ther,** where. **corn,** grain. **160. welles,** springs. **161. rennynge,** running. **162. soun,** sound. **163. ronnen,** ran. **164. ygrave,** carved. **166. slepe,** slept. **167. Eclympasteyre.** The name is unknown to classical mythology. However, it occurs near the opening of *Le Paradys d'Amour* (l. 28), where Froissart calls the personage one of the sons of Morpheus. Since Chaucer echoes the opening of the *Paradys,* with its reference to the poet's inability to sleep because of love, he probably got the name from Froissart. **171. helle pit.** That hell was a pit was a medieval commonplace. **overal,** everywhere. **173. To envye,** to vie, contend. **175. upryght,** face upward. **yhed,** hidden. **177. slepe,** slept. **laste,** lasted. **178. com,** came. **fleynge,** flying. **181. whoo ys,** who is it that. **184. with hys oon yë.** This effective detail, which is not in Ovid, is from Machaut (*Font. Amour.,* 632). **185. axed,** asked. **clepeth,** calls. **186. Hyt am I,** it is I, the usual construction in Chaucer. **192. abrayd,** woke up (suddenly), started up.

Out of hys slepe, and gan to goon,
And dyd as he had bede hym doon;
Took up the dreynte body sone   195
And bar hyt forth to Alcione,
Hys wif the quene, ther as she lay
Ryght even a quarter before day,
And stood ryght at hyr beddes fet,
And called hir ryght as she het   200
By name, and sayde, "My swete wyf,
Awake! let be your sorwful lyf!
For in your sorwe there lyth no reed.
For, certes, swete, I am but deed;
Ye shul me never on lyve yse.   205
But, goode swete herte, that ye
Bury my body, suche a tyde
Ye mowe hyt fynde the see besyde;
And farewel, swete, my worldes blysse!
I praye God youre sorwe lysse.   210
To lytel while oure blysse lasteth!"
    With that hir eyen up she casteth
And saw noght. "Allas!" quod she for sorwe,
And deyede within the thridde morwe.
But what she sayede more in that swow   215
I may not telle yow as now;
Hyt were to longe for to dwelle.
My first matere I wil yow telle,
Wherfore I have told this thyng
Of Alcione and Seys the kyng.   220
    For thus moche dar I saye wel,
I had be dolven everydel,
And ded, ryght thurgh defaute of slepe,
Yif I ne had red and take kepe
Of this tale next before.   225
And I wol telle yow wherfore;

For I ne myght, for bote ne bale,
Slepe, or I had red thys tale
Of this dreynte Seys the kyng,
And of the goddes of slepyng.   230
Whan I had red thys tale wel,
And overloked hyt everydel,
Me thoghte wonder yf hit were so;
For I had never herd speke, or tho,
Of no goddes that koude make   235
Men to slepe ne for to wake;
For I ne knew never god but oon.
And in my game I sayde anoon—
And yet me lyst ryght evel to pleye—
"Rather then that y shulde deye   240
Thorgh defaute of slepynge thus,
I wolde yive thilke Morpheus,
Or hys goddesse, dame Juno,
Or som wight elles, I ne roghte who,
To make me slepe and have som reste,—   245
I wil yive hym the alderbeste
Yifte that ever he abod hys lyve.
And here on warde, ryght now, as blyve,
Yif he wol make me slepe a lyte,
Of down of pure dowves white   250
I wil yive hym a fether-bed,
Rayed with gold, and ryght wel cled
In fyn blak satyn doutremer,
And many a pilowe, and every ber
Of clothe of Reynes, to slepe softe;   255
Hym thar not nede to turnen ofte.
And I wol yive hym al that falles
To a chambre; and al hys halles
I wol do peynte with pure gold
And tapite hem ful many-fold   260

---

194. bede, bidden. **195. sone,** soon, quickly. **196. bar,** bore. **197. ther as,** where. **198. a quarter before day,** three hours before dawn. **200. het,** was called. **203. there lyth no reed,** there is no advantage. **205. shul,** shall. **on lyve,** alive. **yse,** see. **206. that ye bury,** understand *look* or *see*. **207. suche a tyde,** at whatever time. All the MSS read *for suche a tyde.* **208. mowe,** may. **210. lysse,** alleviate. **212. eyen,** eyes. **215. swow,** swoon, grievous state. **216. as now,** now. **222–3. dolven everydel, And ded,** dead and buried completely. **224. take kepe,** taken heed. **227. for bote ne bale,** for good nor evil (cf. for better or worse). **228. or,** before. **232. overloked,** looked over. **233. wonder,** wonderful. **234. or tho,** before then. **238. in my game,** in fun. **239. me lyst,** it pleased me: I was in no mood to jest. **242. yive thilke,** give that same. **244. som wight,** somebody. **I ne roghte who,** I didn't care who. **246. alderbeste,** best possible (*lit.,* best of all). **247. abod,** experienced. **hys lyve,** in his life. **248. on warde,** on (my) surety. The MSS read *onward(e).* **249. lyte,** little. **252. Rayed,** striped. **cled,** covered. **253. doutremer,** imported (from beyond the sea). **254. ber,** pillowcase. **255. clothe of Reynes,** a linen fabric from Rennes, often referred to in the fourteenth century. **256. thar not nede.** Tautological, since *thar* means "it is necessary." **257. falles,** belongs. The Northern ending is for the rime. **259. do peynte,** have painted. **260. tapite,** adorn with tapestry. **ful many-fold,** in great variety, but the phrase means little more than "richly."

Of oo sute: this shal he have,
Yf I wiste where were hys cave,
Yf he kan make me slepe sone,
As did the goddesse quene Alcione.
And thus this ylke god, Morpheus,   265
May wynne of me moo fees thus
Than ever he wan; and to Juno,
That ys hys goddesse, I shal soo do,
I trow that she shal holde hir payd.
    I hadde unneth that word ysayd   270
Ryght thus as I have told hyt yow,
That sodeynly, I nyste how,
Such a lust anoon me took
To slepe, that ryght upon my book
Y fil aslepe, and therwith even   275
Me mette so ynly swete a sweven,
So wonderful, that never yit
Y trowe no man had the wyt
To konne wel my sweven rede;
No, not Joseph, withoute drede,   280
Of Egipte, he that redde so
The kynges metynge Pharao,
No more than koude the lest of us;
Ne nat skarsly Macrobeus,
(He that wrot al th'avysyoun   285
That he mette, kyng Scipioun,
The noble man, the Affrikan,—
Suche marvayles fortuned than)
I trowe, arede my dremes even.
Loo, thus hyt was, thys was my sweven.   290
    Me thoghte thus: that hyt was May,
And in the dawenynge I lay
(Me mette thus) in my bed al naked,
And loked forth, for I was waked
With smale foules a gret hepe   295

That had affrayed me out of my slepe,
Thorgh noyse and swetnesse of her song.
And, as me mette, they sate among
Upon my chambre roof wythoute,
Upon the tyles, overal aboute,   300
And songen, everych in hys wyse,
The moste solempne servise
By noote, that ever man, y trowe,
Had herd; for som of hem song lowe,
Som high, and al of oon acorde.   305
To telle shortly, att oo worde,
Was never herd so swete a steven,—
But hyt had be a thyng of heven,—
So mery a soun, so swete entewnes,
That certes, for the toune of Tewnes,   310
I nolde but I had herd hem synge;
For al my chambre gan to rynge
Thurgh syngynge of her armonye.
For instrument nor melodye
Was nowhere herd yet half so swete,   315
Nor of acorde half so mete,
For ther was noon of hem that feyned
To synge, for ech of hem hym peyned
To fynde out mery crafty notes.
They ne spared not her throtes.   320
And, sooth to seyn, my chambre was
Ful wel depeynted, and with glas
Were al the wyndowes wel yglased
Ful clere, and nat an hoole ycrased,
That to beholde hyt was gret joye.   325
For hoolly al the story of Troye
Was in the glasynge ywroght thus,
Of Ector and of kyng Priamus,
Of Achilles and Lamedon,
And eke of Medea and of Jason,   330

261. **Of oo sute,** of one color or pattern, matching. 262. **wiste,** knew. 269. **payd,** satisfied. 270. **unneth,** scarcely. **ysayd,** said. 272. **nyste,** knew not. 273. **lust,** desire. **anoon,** immediately. 276. **Me mette,** I dreamed (impers.). **ynly,** inwardly, supremely. **sweven,** dream. 279. **konne,** know how. **rede,** interpret. 280. **Joseph.** See *Genesis*, 41: 14. **withoute drede,** without doubt. 282. **The kynges metynge Pharao,** the dream of King Pharaoh. The separation of the possessive and its appositive is common in ME. 284. **Macrobeus,** Macrobius, author of a widely known commentary on Cicero's *Somnium Scipionis* (Scipio Africanus). Scipio was not a king, but he is called "roi Scipion" in *RR*, 12. 288. **fortuned,** happened. 289. **arede.** Understand *koude* (l. 283). **dremes.** Chaucer speaks of his dream in the plural apparently to avoid the hiatus of *dremë even*. 295. **foules,** birds. **hepe,** heap, throng. 296. **affrayed,** startled. 297. **noyse,** agreeable sound. 298. **among,** round about. 300. **overal,** everywhere. 301. **everych,** each one. 302. **solempne servise,** *i.e.* their matins. 307. **steven,** voice, sound. 309. **entewnes,** melodies, harmonies. 310. **Tewnes,** Tunis, chosen no doubt for the sake of the rime. 316. **mete,** fitting. 324. **ycrased,** broken. 328. **Ector,** etc. The names of Hector, King Priam, Achilles, Laomedon (father of Priam), Jason and Medea, Paris, Helen, and Lavinia are all associated in one way or another with the story of the Trojan war.

Of Paris, Eleyne, and of Lavyne.
And alle the walles with colours fyne
Were peynted, bothe text and glose,
Of al the Romaunce of the Rose.
My wyndowes were shet echon, 335
And throgh the glas the sonne shon
Upon my bed with bryghte bemes,
With many glade gilde stremes;
And eke the welken was so fair,—
Blew, bryght, clere was the ayr, 340
And ful attempre for sothe hyt was;
For nother to cold nor hoot yt nas,
Ne in al the welken was a clowde.
    And as I lay thus, wonder lowde
Me thoghte I herde an hunte blowe 345
T'assay hys horn, and for to knowe
Whether hyt were clere or hors of soun.
And I herde goynge bothe up and doun
Men, hors, houndes, and other thyng;
And al men speken of huntyng, 350
How they wolde slee the hert with strengthe,
And how the hert had, upon lengthe,
So moche embosed, y not now what.
    Anoon-ryght, whan I herde that,
How that they wolde on-huntynge goon, 355
I was ryght glad, and up anoon
Took my hors, and forth I wente

Out of my chambre; I never stente
Til I com to the feld withoute.
Ther overtok y a gret route 360
Of huntes and eke of foresteres,
With many relayes and lymeres,
And hyed hem to the forest faste
And I with hem. So at the laste
I asked oon, ladde a lymere: 365
"Say, felowe, who shal hunte here?"
Quod I, and he answered ageyn,
"Syr, th'emperour Octovyen,"
Quod he, "and ys here faste by."
"A Goddes halfe, in good tyme!" quod I, 370
"Go we faste!" and gan to ryde.
Whan we came to the forest syde,
Every man dide ryght anoon
As to huntynge fil to doon.
The mayster-hunte anoon, fot-hot, 375
With a gret horn blew thre mot
At the uncouplynge of hys houndes.
Withynne a while the hert [y]founde ys,
Yhalowed, and rechased faste
Longe tyme; and so at the laste 380
This hert rused, and staal away
Fro alle the houndes a privy way.
The houndes had overshote hym alle
And were on a defaute yfalle.

---

333. bothe text and glose, text and commentary. The walls of chambers in palaces and other fine buildings were often painted with historical and legendary scenes. The figures and events were at times identified by scrolls, lozenges, and simple inscriptions, and a fourteenth-century account of the royal palace at Westminster speaks of a "celebrated chamber, on whose walls all the warlike histories of the whole Bible are painted with inexpressible skill, and explained by a regular and complete series of texts, beautifully written in French over each battle." Quoted in, Sypherd, *Studies in Chaucer's Hous of Fame*, p. 84. **334. Romaunce of the Rose.** See intro., above. **Of.** The MSS all read *And*. **335. Shet,** shut. **echon,** each one. **338. gilde stremes.** The small panes of glass in medieval windows were often thick in the center and acted like a convex lens. **339. welken,** sky. **341. attempre,** temperate, mild. **345. hunte,** huntsman. (OE. *hunta*). **346. T'assay,** to try. **349. hors,** plural, as often; cf. *vers,* l. 463. **thyng,** things. **350. speken,** spoke. **351. slee the hert with strengthe.** A hunting expression, used of hunting with hounds, etc. The same meaning attaches to OF. *chassier les cerfs a force.* **352. upòn lengthe,** at length, finally. **353. embosed.** Sometimes explained (following Emerson, *Rom. Rev.*, XIII. 117) as "exhausted." But the verb here is active and seems to represent OF. *en + bois, bos,* with the meaning "to go or hide in the woods," thus corresponding in sense to OF. *embuschier, embuissier.* See *Language,* XXXVII. 539–42. **354. Anoon-ryght,** immediately. **357. Took . . . wente.** The sequence seems to have been influenced by the rime. **358. stente,** stopped. **359. com,** came. **361. huntes,** hunters. **362. relayes,** sets of fresh hunting dogs. **lymeres,** hounds (orig. dogs on a leash). **363. And hyed hem.** The omission of the subject (where we would often use a relative pronoun) is common. Cf. line 369, 473, etc. **365. oon, ladde,** one who led. **368. Octovyen,** the Roman Emperor Octavian of whom a French romance (adapted in Middle English) tells a wholly apocryphal story. In the Middle English versions the name is spelled Octovian. But the reference may be to Augustus Caesar with an implied compliment to Edward III. **370. A Goddes halfe,** on God's behalf, for God's sake. **375. fot-hot,** the usual form in ME. for our *hot foot,* speedily. **376. mot,** notes on the hunting horn. Three long notes were the conventional warning that the hart had been sighted; so Twici (*Rel. Ant.*, i. 152) and cf. *Sir Gawain and the Green Knight,* l. 1141. **379. Yhalowed,** chased with shouts. **rechased,** chased back, headed back. **381. rused.** The hart is said to *ruse* to and fro in order to confuse the tracks and throw the hounds off the scent. See *The Master of Game* (15c.), ed. Baillie-Grohman (1909), p. 31. **staal,** stole. **384. defaute,** loss of the scent.

Therwyth the hunte wonder faste   385
Blew a forloyn at the laste.
  I was go walked fro my tree,
And as I wente, ther cam by mee
A whelp, that fauned me as I stood,
That hadde yfolowed, and koude no good.   390
Hyt com and crepte to me as lowe
Ryght as hyt hadde me yknowe,
Held doun hys hed and joyned hys eres,
And leyde al smothe doun hys heres.
I wolde have kaught hyt, and anoon   395
Hyt fledde, and was fro me goon;
And I hym folwed, and hyt forth wente
Doun by a floury grene wente
Ful thikke of gras, ful softe and swete,
With floures fele, faire under fete,   400
And litel used, hyt semed thus;
For both Flora and Zephirus,
They two that make floures growe,
Had mad her dwellynge ther, I trowe;
For hit was, on to beholde,   405
As thogh the erthe envye wolde
To be gayer than the heven,
To have moo floures, swiche seven,
As in the welken sterres bee.
Hyt had forgete the povertee   410
That wynter, thorgh hys colde morwes,
Had mad hyt suffre, and his sorwes;
All was forgeten, and that was sene.

For al the woode was waxen grene;
Swetnesse of dewe had mad hyt waxe.   415
  Hyt ys no nede eke for to axe
Wher there were many grene greves,
Or thikke of trees, so ful of leves;
And every tree stood by hymselve
Fro other wel ten foot or twelve.   420
So grete trees, so huge of strengthe,
Of fourty or fifty fadme lengthe,
Clene withoute bowgh or stikke,
With croppes brode, and eke as thikke—
They were nat an ynche asonder—   425
That hit was shadewe overal under.
And many an hert and many an hynde
Was both before me and behynde.
Of founes, sowres, bukkes, does
Was ful the woode, and many roes,   430
And many sqwirelles, that sete
Ful high upon the trees and ete,
And in hir maner made festes.
Shortly, hyt was so ful of bestes,
That thogh Argus, the noble countour,   435
Sete to rekene in hys countour,
And rekene[d] with his figures ten—
For by tho figures mowe al ken,
Yf they be crafty, rekene and noumbre,
And telle of every thing the noumbre—   440
Yet shoulde he fayle to rekene even
The wondres me mette in my sweven.

---

386. forloyn. The term seems to be used in more than one sense by Twici (*Rel. Ant.*, I. 152), but here and in the *Book of St. Albans* it implies a signal recalling the hounds when they have got far ahead of the rest of the hunting party or the hart has stolen away. **387. I was go walked,** I had walked. Chaucer uses the construction again in "His felawe (was) go walked into toun" (D 1778). Cf. also C 406, D 354, and F 1580. **my tree,** the tree by which he was posted. A common form of hunting in the Middle Ages consisted of posting the noble participants at advantageous places in the forest or game preserve and driving the hart past their stations to be shot at. **389. whelp,** puppy, small dog. **fauned me.** The construction *faun* + dir. obj. is earlier than *fawn upon*. **390. koude no good,** did not know what to do. **394. heres,** hairs. **398. wente,** path. **400. fele,** many. **402. Flora and Zephirus.** The association of the goddess of flowers and the west wind is a commonplace, but Chaucer could have seen it in *RR*, 8411, which speaks of "Zephirus e Flora sa fame." See *LGW* 171–4. **404. her,** their. **405. on to beholde,** to look upon. **406. envye,** vie. **408. swiche seven,** seven times as many. For the idiom see Klaeber, *MLN*, XVII. 323. **412. his,** its (winter's). **413. sene,** evident. **417. Wher,** whether. **greves,** branches. **418. thikke,** thicket. **422. fadme,** fathom (as a plur.). The word signified either the length of the forearm (= cubit) or, more frequently, that of the outstretched arms, considered to be six feet. This whole passage may be compared with *Romaunt of the Rose*, 1391 ff. **424. croppes,** tops, **426. overal under,** everywhere beneath. **429. founes, sowres, bukkes, does.** From the *Book of St. Albans* (1486) we learn that a buck is called a fawn in its first year, a sore in its fourth, and a buck in its sixth. **434. Shortly,** in short. **435. Argus, the noble countour.** A confusion of the hundred-eyed Argus with Algus (Arabic *al-Khowarazmi*), the Arabic mathematician of the ninth century, whose work on algebra, when translated, made Arabic numerals generally known in Europe. **436. countour,** counting-house. **438. mowe,** may. **ken,** know how, be able. **439–40.** The identical rime involves the verb *noumbre* (to count) and the noun. **441. even,** fully. **442. me mette . . .** I dreamed (*impers.*) in my dream.

But forth they romed ryght wonder faste
Doun the woode; so at the laste
I was war of a man in blak,   445
That sat and had yturned his bak
To an ooke, an huge tree.
"Lord," thoght I, "who may that be?
What ayleth hym to sitten here?"
Anoon-ryght I wente nere;   450
Than found I sitte even upryght
A wonder wel farynge knyght—
By the maner me thoghte so—
Of good mochel, and ryght yong therto,
Of the age of foure and twenty yer,   455
Upon hys berde but lytel her,
And he was clothed al in blak.
I stalked even unto hys bak,
And there I stood as stille as ought,
That, soth to saye, he saw me nought;   460
For-why he heng hys hed adoune,
And with a dedly sorwful soune
He made of ryme ten vers or twelve
Of a compleynte to hymselve,
The moste pitee, the moste rowthe,   465
That ever I herde; for, by my trowthe,
Hit was gret wonder that nature
Myght suffre any creature
To have such sorwe, and be not ded.
Ful pitous pale, and nothyng red,   470
He sayd a lay, a maner song,
Withoute noote, withoute song;
And was thys, for ful wel I kan
Reherse hyt; ryght thus hyt began:

I have of sorwe so gret won   475
That joye gete I never non,
Now that I see my lady bryght,
Which I have loved with al my myght,
Is fro me ded and ys agoon.   479
     Allas, deth, what ayleth the,   481
That thou noldest have taken me,
Whan thou toke my lady swete,
That was so fair, so fresh, so fre,
So good, that men may wel se   485
Of al goodnesse she had no mete!

Whan he had mad thus his complaynte,
Hys sorwful hert gan faste faynte,
And his spirites wexen dede;
The blood was fled for pure drede   490
Doun to hys herte, to make hym warm—
For wel hyt feled the herte had harm—
To wite eke why hyt was adrad
By kynde, and for to make hyt glad;
For hit ys membre principal   495
Of the body; and that made al
Hys hewe chaunge and wexe grene
And pale, for ther noo blood ys sene
In no maner lym of hys.
Anoon therwith whan y sawgh this,   500
He ferde thus evel there he set,
I went and stood ryght at his fet,
And grette hym, but he spak noght,
But argued with his owne thoght,
And in hys wyt disputed faste   505
Why and how hys lyf myght laste,—

445. **war,** aware. **a man in blak,** John of Gaunt, according to the usual interpretation of the poem. See the introduction. 450. **nere,** nearer. 452. **wel farynge,** handsome, attractive. 454. **of good mochel,** of good size, stature. 455. **foure and twenty yer.** John of Gaunt was born in 1340 and was twenty-nine. Chaucer may have understated his age as a compliment, or, as has been suggested, xxviiii was miswritten xxiiii in one of the MSS. Numbers were not always written out. The next line suggests that Chaucer was making him appear young. 458. **stalked,** came up quietly. **even unto,** all the way to. 459. **ought,** anything. 461. **For-why,** because. 470. **pitous,** (used adverbially) piteously. 471-2. **song** in l. 471 refers to the lyric, in l. 472 to the music. 473. **And was.** See note to line 363. 475. **won,** abundance. 480. Thynne inserted a line, most likely spurious: **And thus in sorowe leite me alone.** The line numbering of the Chaucer Soc. is here retained. 482. **noldest,** wouldst not. 486. **mete,** equal. 487. It is sometimes considered a weakness in the poem that the dreamer after hearing the knight's song should not have understood the cause of his grief. French (*JEGP,* LVI. 231–41) suggests that the dreamer considered it a conventional lament of a forlorn lover, exaggerated, and not to be taken seriously. If this is true we must take the lines that follow as also somewhat exaggerated. 489. **wexen,** waxed. 490. **pure,** very, sheer. 493. **wite,** know. **adrad,** afraid. 494. **By kynde,** by (provision of) nature. 496. **that,** the fact that the blood had rushed to his heart. 498. **sene,** visible. 500. From this point Chaucer's poem is often clearly inspired by Machaut's *Le jugement dou Roy de Behainge* (Bohemia). 501. **set,** sat. The normal form is *sat, set* being a back-formation from the pl. *seten.* 503. **grette,** greeted. 505. **wyt,** mind.

Hym thoughte hys sorwes were so smerte
And lay so colde upon hys herte.
So, throgh hys sorwe and hevy thoght,
Made hym that he herde me noght; 510
For he had wel nygh lost hys mynde,
Thogh Pan, that men clepe god of kynde,
Were for hys sorwes never so wroth.

But at the last, to sayn ryght soth,
He was war of me, how y stood 515
Before hym, and did of myn hood,
And had ygret hym as I best koude,
Debonayrly and nothyng lowde.
He sayde, "I prey the, be not wroth.
I herde the not, to seyn the soth, 520
Ne I sawgh the not, syr, trewely."
"A, goode sir, no fors," quod y;
"I am ryght sory yif I have ought
Destroubled yow out of your thought.
Foryive me, yif I have mystake." 525
"Yis, th'amendes is lyght to make,"
Quod he, "for ther lyeth noon therto;
There ys nothyng myssayd nor do."

Loo! how goodly spak thys knyght,
As hit had be another wyght; 530
He made hyt nouther towgh ne queynte.
And I saw that, and gan me aqueynte
With hym, and fond hym so tretable,
Ryght wonder skylful and resonable,
As me thoghte, for al hys bale. 535
Anoon-ryght I gan fynde a tale
To hym, to loke wher I myght ought
Have more knowynge of hys thought.
"Sir," quod I, "this game is doon.

I holde that this hert be goon; 540
These huntes konne hym nowher see."
"Y do no fors therof," quod he;
"My thought ys theron never a del."
"By oure Lord," quod I, "y trow yow wel;
Ryght so me thinketh by youre chere. 545
But, sir, oo thyng wol ye here?
Me thynketh in gret sorowe I yow see.
But certes, sire, yif that yee
Wolde ought discure me youre woo,
I wolde, as wys God helpe me soo, 550
Amende hyt, yif I kan or may.
Ye mowe preve hyt be assay;
For, by my trouthe, to make yow hool,
I wol do al my power hool.
And telleth me of your sorwes smerte; 555
Paraunter hyt may ese youre herte,
That semeth ful seke under your syde."

With that he loked on me asyde,
As who sayth, "Nay, that wol not be."
"Graunt mercy, goode frend," quod he, 560
"I thanke thee that thow woldest soo,
But hyt may never the rather be doo.
No man may my sorwe glade,
That maketh my hewe to falle and fade,
And hath myn understondynge lorn, 565
That me ys wo that I was born!
May noght make my sorwes slyde,
Nought al the remedyes of Ovyde,
Ne Orpheus, god of melodye,
Ne Dedalus with his playes slye; 570
Ne hele me may no phisicien,
Noght Ypocras, ne Galyen.

---

507. **Hym thoughte**, it seemed to him. **smerte**, sharp. 510. **Made.** The subject is understood. 512. **Pan, that men clepe god of kynde.** The conception of Pan as the god of Nature was a commonplace in the Middle Ages, ultimately derived from Servius' commentary on Virgil. 513. **wroth**, grieved, sad. 514. **soth.** The vowel in *soth* (OE. *sōþ*) is close *o*, while that in *wroth* OE. (*wrāþ*) is open. The rime is therefore imperfect (also at 519–20, 1189–90). Such rimes are avoided by Chaucer in his later poetry, though not completely. 516. **did of**, doffed. 517. **ygret**, greeted. 518. **Debonayrly**, politely. 522. **no fors**, no matter. 527. **for ther lyeth noon therto**, for none is needed. 531. **queynte**, strange, with the implication of aloofness. 533. **tretable**, tractable, approachable. 534. **skylful** and **resonable** are synonyms. 536. **a tale**, something to say. 537. **to loke wher**, to see whether. 542. **Y do no fors therof**, it doesn't matter to me. 546. **oo**, one. 548. **yif**, if. 549. **discure**, disclose. 550. **as wys**, assuredly as (assuredly as God may help me). 552. **preve**, prove. 553. **to make yow hool**, to restore you to health. 556. **Paraunter**, peradventure. 559. **As who sayth**, as much as to say. 560. **Graunt mercy**, great thanks. 562. **rather**, sooner. **doo**, done. 563. **glade**, gladden. 564. **falle and fade**, lose color. 565. **lorn**, destroyed. 567. **slyde**, pass away. 568. **the remedyes of Ovyde**, alluding to Ovid's *Remedia Amoris*. 569. **Orpheus**. The music of Orpheus made the tortured in Hades forget their suffering. 570. **Dedalus**, a mythical artist and inventor. He invented artificial wings by which he escaped from his enemies. Here Dedalus with all his crafty devices could not enable the knight to escape from his sorrows. 572. **Ypocras**, Hippocrates, the most famous Greek physician, a contemporary of Socrates. **Galyen**, Galen, another famous Greek physician, born about A.D. 130. See *CT*, A 431.

Me ys wo that I lyve houres twelve.
But whooso wol assay hymselve
Whether his hert kan have pitee   575
Of any sorwe, lat hym see me.
Y wrecche, that deth hath mad al naked
Of al the blysse that ever was maked,
Yworthe worste of alle wyghtes,
That hate my dayes and my nyghtes!   580
My lyf, my lustes, be me loothe,
For al welfare and I be wroothe.
The pure deth ys so ful my foo (foe)
That I wolde deye: hyt wolde not soo;
For whan I folwe hyt, hit wol flee;   585
I wolde have hym: hyt nyl nat me.
This ys my peyne wythoute reed,
Alway deynge and be not deed,
That Cesiphus, that lyeth in helle,
May not of more sorwe telle.   590
And whoso wiste al, by my trouthe,
My sorwe, but he hadde rowthe
And pitee of my sorwes smerte,
That man hath a fendly herte.
For whoso seeth me first on morwe   595
May seyn he hath met with sorwe,
For y am sorwe, and sorwe ys y.
    "Allas! and I wol tel the why;
My song ys turned to pleynynge,   *lamentation*
And al my laughter to wepynge,   600
My glade thoghtes to hevynesse;
In travayle ys myn ydelnesse
And eke my reste; my wele is woo,

My good ys harm, and evermoo
In wrathe ys turned my pleynge,   605
And my delyt into sorwynge.
Myn hele ys turned into seknesse,
In drede ys al my sykernesse;
To derke ys turned al my lyght,
My wyt ys foly, my day ys nyght,   610
My love ys hate, my slepe wakynge,
My myrthe and meles ys fastynge,
My countenaunce ys nycete,
And al abaved, where so I be;
My pees, in pledynge and in werre.   615
Allas! how myghte I fare werre?
My boldnesse ys turned to shame,
For fals Fortune hath pleyed a game
Atte ches with me, allas the while!
The trayteresse fals and ful of gyle,   620
That al behoteth, and nothyng halt;
She goth upryght and yet she halt,
That baggeth foule and loketh faire,
The dispitouse debonaire,
That skorneth many a creature!   625
An ydole of fals portrayture
Ys she, for she wol sone wrien;
She is the monstres hed ywrien,
As fylthe over ystrawed with floures.
Hir moste worshippe and hir flour ys   630
To lyen, for that ys hyr nature;
Withoute feyth, lawe, or mesure
She ys fals; and ever laughynge
With oon eye, and that other wepynge.

---

579. Yworthe, having become; pp. of *worthen.* **581. lustes,** (innocent) pleasures. **582. welfare,** happiness. **wroothe,** *lit.* angry, *i.e.* at enmity. **583. pure,** very. **587. reed,** remedy. **589. Cesiphus,** Sisyphus, whose punishment in Hades was to push a great stone to the top of a hill, after which it always rolled down and had to be pushed up again. But the description "that lyth in helle" fits better Tityus, a giant who lay stretched out in Hades over nine acres. **594. fendly,** fiendish. **599. song.** MSS *sorowe.* This lament of the knight in which all his activities are turned into their opposites was probably suggested by a passage in the *RR (Romaunt of the Rose,* ll. 4706–53) with additional hints from Machaut's *Le jugement dou Roy de Behainge* (ll. 177–87). The ultimate source is perhaps the *De Planctu Naturae* of Alanus de Insulis. **607. hele,** health. **608. drede,** doubt. **sykernesse,** certainty. **613. countenaunce,** composure. **nycete,** shyness. **614. abaved,** abashed. **615. pledynge,** lawsuit. **616. werre,** worse. **617. My boldnesse . . .,** My assurance has become loss of self-esteem. **618. Fortune.** The description of Fortune occurs in several works of Machaut with which Chaucer was acquainted, in long passages of *RR,* and elsewhere. But none offers more than a general similarity of concept or an occasional phrase. The fickleness of Fortune was a commonplace. **618–19. a game Atte ches,** a game at the chess. The experience of several characters is compared to a game of chess in *RR,* 6620 ff., but Chaucer owes scarcely more than an occasional hint or phrase to the account. **621. behoteth,** promises. **halt,** holds, keeps. **622. halt,** halts, limps. **623. baggeth,** squints, **foule,** miserably. **624. dispitouse,** disdainful. **626. of fals portrayture,** *i.e.* falsely represented. **627. wrien,** turn, change her course. **628. ywrien,** covered up, hidden. **629. over ystrawed,** strewn over. **630. worshippe,** renown. **flour,** greatest distinction.

That ys broght up, she set al doun. 635
I lykne hyr to the scorpioun,
That ys a fals, flaterynge beste;
For with his hed he maketh feste,
But al amydde hys flaterynge
With hys tayle he wol stynge 640
And envenyme; and so wol she.
She ys th'envyouse charite
That ys ay fals, and seemeth wele,
So turneth she hyr false whele
Aboute, for hyt ys nothyng stable, 645
Now by the fire, now at table;
For many oon hath she thus yblent.
She ys pley of enchauntement,
That semeth oon and ys not soo.
The false thef! what hath she doo, 650
Trowest thou? By oure Lord I wol the seye.
At the ches with me she gan to pleye;
With hir false draughtes dyvers
She staal on me, and tok my fers, *queen*
And whan I sawgh my fers awaye, 655
Allas! I kouthe no lenger playe,
But seyde, 'Farewel, swete, ywys,
And farewel al that ever ther ys!'
Therwith Fortune seyde 'Chek here!'
And 'Mate!' in myd poynt of the chekkere, 660
With a poune errant, allas!
Ful craftier to pley she was
Than Athalus, that made the game

First of the ches, so was hys name.
But God wolde I had oones or twyes 665
Ykoud and knowe the jeupardyes
That kowde the Grek Pithagores!
I shulde have pleyd the bet at ches,
And kept my fers the bet therby.
And thogh wherto? for trewely, 670
I holde that wyssh nat worth a stree!
Hyt had be never the bet for me.
For Fortune kan so many a wyle,
Ther be but fewe kan hir begile.
And eke she ys the lasse to blame; 675
Myself I wolde have do the same,
Before God, hadde I ben as she;
She oghte the more excused be.
For this I say yet more therto,
Had I be God and myghte have do 680
My wille, whan she my fers kaughte,
I wolde have drawe the same draughte.
For, also wys God yive me reste,
I dar wel swere she took the beste.
But through that draughte I have lorn 685
My blysse; allas! that I was born!
For evermore, y trowe trewly,
For al my wille, my lust holly
Ys turned; but yet, what to doone?
Be oure Lord, hyt ys to deye soone. 690
For nothyng I leve hyt noght,
But lyve and deye ryght in this thoght;

---

635. That, that which. **set,** sets. **636. scorpioun.** In the *Ancrene Riwle* the scorpion is described as "a kind of serpent that has a face somewhat like a woman and is an adder behind, makes a fair showing and flatters with the head and stings with the tail." **638. maketh feste,** shows respect, pays a compliment. **642. envyouse charite.** The phrase is from Machaut's *Remède de Fortune*, l. 1138: C'est l'envieuse charité, in the midst of a series of comparisons similar to but generally not identical with Chaucer's. **644. hyr false whele.** Fortune is commonly represented with a wheel. As it turns it carries mortals to the top and then casts them down. Cf. *TC* 1. 138–41. **646.** This uninspired line, which seems to serve only to complete the couplet, is translated directly from the *Roy de Behaingne*, l. 1074. **647. yblent,** blinded. **649. oon,** one thing. **653. draughtes,** moves. **654. fers,** queen, OF. *fierce, fierge.* Although a *fers* was originally the king's chief counsellor, the piece was commonly called the queen in the Middle Ages (cf. "La roine que nommons fierge," *La Vieille,* l. 1599). It was not so powerful a piece as today, being limited to a move of one diagonal square, but was used defensively as the guardian of the king. The most powerful piece was the rook. The capture of the queen, while not necessarily ending the game, left the king quite vulnerable. The *fers* was the only feminine piece. **656. kouthe,** could. **660. chekkere,** board. **661. poune errant,** a pawn that has been advanced from its original square (*NED*). The capture of the king is taken directly from *RR,* ll. 6652–5: "Eschec e mat li ala dire . . . D'un trait de paonet errant Ou milieu de son eschequier." **663. Athalus,** supposed to be Attalus Philometor, King of Cappadocia, named by Pliny (*Nat. Hist.,* XVIII. 5) The same passage in *RR* (l. 6691) calls Athalus the inventor of chess. **666. Ykoud and knowe,** known and recognized. **jeupardyes,** problems. **667. Pithagores,** Pythagoras, who according to John of Salisbury was interested in games having a numerical basis. **668. bet,** better. **671. stree,** straw. **673. kan,** knows. **675. lasse,** less. **676. have do the same,** *i.e.* taken the queen (had I been in her position). **682. drawe the same draughte,** made the same move. **683. also wys God yive,** as certainly (as) God may give. **688. my lust . . . ys turned,** my joy is reversed. **689. what to doone,** what is to be done? **691. For nothyng . . . noght,** for I believe (trust in) nothing.

For there nys planete in firmament,
Ne in ayr ne in erthe noon element,
That they ne yive me a yifte echone   695
Of wepynge whan I am allone.
For whan that I avise me wel,
And bethenke me every del,
How that ther lyeth in rekenyng,
In my sorwe, for nothyng;   700
And how ther leveth no gladnesse
May glade me of my distresse,
And how I have lost suffisance,
And therto I have no plesance,
Than may I say I have ryght noght.   705
And whan al this falleth in my thoght,
Allas! than am I overcome!
For that ys doon ys not to come.
I have more sorowe than Tantale."
    And whan I herde hym tel thys tale   710
Thus pitously, as I yow telle,
Unnethe myght y lenger dwelle—
Hyt dyde myn herte so moche woo.
"A, goode sir," quod I, "say not soo!
Have som pitee on your nature   715
That formed yow to creature.
Remembre yow of Socrates,
For he ne counted nat thre strees
Of noght that Fortune koude doo."
"No," quod he, "I kan not soo."   720
"Why so? syr, yis parde!" quod y;
"Ne say noght soo, for trewely,
Thogh ye had lost the ferses twelve,

And ye for sorwe mordred yourselve,
Ye sholde be dampned in this cas   725
By as good ryght as Medea was,
That slough hir children for Jason;
And Phyllis also for Demophon
Heng hirself, so weylaway!
For he had broke his terme-day   730
To come to hir. Another rage
Had Dydo, the quene eke of Cartage,
That slough hirself, for Eneas
Was fals; which a fool she was!
And Ecquo died, for Narcisus   735
Nolde nat love hir; and ryght thus
Hath many another foly doon;
And for Dalida died Sampson,
That slough hymself with a pilere.
But ther is no man alyve here   740
Wolde for a fers make this woo!"
"Why so?" quod he, "hyt ys nat soo.
Thou wost ful lytel what thou menest;
I have lost more than thow wenest."
"Loo, [sey] how that may be?" quod y;   745
"Good sir, telle me al hooly
In what wyse, how, why, and wherfore
That ye have thus youre blysse lore."
"Blythely," quod he; "com sytte adoun!
I telle the upon a condicioun   750
That thou shalt hooly, with all thy wyt,
Doo thyn entent to herkene hit."
"Yis, syr." "Swere thy trouthe therto."
"Gladly." "Do thanne holde hereto!"

699–700. The couplet is difficult to construe but appears to mean that there stands in the account nothing that is owing to me in the matter of sorrow. **701. leveth,** remains. **703. suffisance,** contentment. **704. plesance,** pleasure. **708. For that ys doon . . .** Cf. the proverb "What is done cannot be undone." **709. Tantale,** Tantalus, for whom in Hades water and branches of fruit were always just beyond his grasp. **711. pitously,** piteously. **712. Unnethe,** scarcely. **717. Socrates,** described in *RR*, ll. 5846–56, as indifferent to prosperity and adversity. **721. parde,** for *par Dieu*, a mild oath. **723. the ferses twelve.** This makes no sense with respect to chess. It has been suggested that Chaucer has here changed the image to draughts or checkers (S. W. Stevenson, *ELH*, VII. 215–222), but this seems unlikely. F. D. Cooley (*MLN*, LXIII. 35) proposes to omit *the*, making the line mean "even if your loss had been twelve times as great." **726. Medea,** etc. These examples can all be found in various passages of *RR*, but they are so familiar as to require no specific source. Medea, the daughter of the King of Colchis, fell in love with Jason when he came in quest of the Golden Fleece. After helping him to obtain the fleece, she fled with him. Later he deserted her for another love. Medea killed her children by Jason and brought about the death of his new bride. **728. Phyllis,** a Thracian princess married to Demophoon, son of the Athenian Theseus. Once when Demophoon left to go to Athens and did not return at the appointed time Phyllis hanged herself. See *HF* 388–96. **730. terme-day,** appointed day. **731. rage,** madness. For Chaucer's telling of the Dido and Aeneas story see *HF* 140 ff. **734. which a,** what a. **735. Ecquo,** Echo, who was rendered by Juno incapable of speech except in echoing the words of others. Scorned by Narcissus, she nevertheless remained faithful to him until she died. **739. That slough hymself with a pilere.** See *Judges*, 16: 29–30. **743. wost,** knowest. **what thou menest,** what you are saying.

"I shal ryght blythely, so God me save,
Hooly, with al the witte I have,
Here yow, as wel as I kan."
"A Goddes half!" quod he, and began:
"Syr," quod he, "sith first I kouthe
Have any maner wyt fro youthe,   760
Or kyndely understondyng
To comprehende, in any thyng,
What love was, in myn owne wyt,
Dredeles, I have ever yit
Be tributarye and yiven rente   765
To Love, hooly with good entente,
And throgh plesaunce become his thral
With good wille, body, hert, and al.
Al this I putte in his servage,
As to my lord, and dide homage;   770
And ful devoutly I prayed hym to,
He shulde besette myn herte so
That hyt plesance to hym were,
And worship to my lady dere.

   "And this was longe, and many a yere,   775
Or that myn herte was set owhere,
That I dide thus, and nyste why;
I trowe hit cam me kyndely.
Paraunter I was therto most able,
As a whit wal or a table,   780
For hit ys redy to cacche and take
Al that men wil theryn make,
Whethir so men wil portreye or peynte,
Be the werkes never so queynte.

   "And thilke tyme I ferde ryght so,   785
I was able to have lerned tho,
And to have kend as wel or better,
Paraunter, other art or letre;
But for love cam first in my thoght,
Therfore I forgat hyt noght.   790
I ches love to my firste craft;

Therfore hit ys with me laft,
For-why I tok hyt of so yong age
That malyce hadde my corage
Nat that tyme turned to nothyng   795
Thorgh to mochel knowlechyng.
For that tyme Yowthe, my maistresse,
Governed me in ydelnesse;
For hyt was in my firste youthe,
And thoo ful lytel good y couthe,   800
For al my werkes were flyttynge
That tyme, and al my thoght varyinge.
Al were to me ylyche good
That I knew thoo; but thus hit stood.

   "Hit happed that I cam on a day   805
Into a place ther that I say,
Trewly, the fayrest companye
Of ladyes that evere man with yë
Had seen togedres in oo place.
Shal I clepe hyt hap other grace   810
That broght me there? Nay, but Fortune,
That ys to lyen ful comune,
The false trayteresse pervers!
God wolde I koude clepe hir wers!
For now she worcheth me ful woo,   815
And I wol telle sone why soo.

   "Among these ladyes thus echon,
Soth to seyen y sawgh oon
That was lyk noon of the route;
For I dar swere, withoute doute,   820
That as the someres sonne bryght
Ys fairer, clerer, and hath more lyght
Than any other planete in heven,
The moone, or the sterres seven,
For al the world so hadde she   825
Surmounted hem alle of beaute,
Of maner and of comlynesse,
Of stature, and of wel set gladnesse,

---

758. A Goddes half, for God's sake; see above, l. 370. **764. Dredeles,** doubtless. **765. yiven rente,** paid tribute. **767. throgh plesaunce,** with pleasure, willingly. **772. besette,** bestow. **774. worship,** honor. **776. owhere,** anywhere. **777. nyste,** knew not. **779. able,** ready. **783. portreye,** draw. **784. queynte,** ingenious. **785. thilke,** that same. **786. tho,** then. **787. kend,** known. **788. letre,** study, learning. **791. ches,** chose. **792. ys . . . laft,** has remained. **793. For-why,** because. **794. corage,** heart, spirit. **795. turned to nothyng,** destroyed. **801. flyttynge,** changeable. **806. ther that I say,** where I saw. **810. clepe,** call. **other,** or. **812. comune,** accustomed (to). **815. worcheth,** works, causes. **817. echon,** each one. **819. route,** company. **824. the sterres seven.** The allusion here is probably to the Pleiades, a meaning which was already established in Old English. Elsewhere in Chaucer it may mean the planets and sometimes the constellation *Ursa Major*. **826. Surmounted,** surpassed. **828. of,** in. **wel set gladnesse,** fittingly placed cheerfulness.

Of goodlyhede so wel beseye—
Shortly, what shal y more seye?   830
By God, and by his halwes twelve,
Hyt was my swete, ryght as hirselve—
She had so stedfast countenaunce,
So noble port and meyntenaunce.
And Love, that had wel herd my boone,   835
Had espyed me thus soone,
That she ful sone, in my thoght,
As helpe me God, so was ykaught
So sodenly, that I ne tok
No maner counseyl but at hir lok   840
And at myn herte; for-why hir eyen
So gladly, I trow, myn herte seyen,
That purely tho myn owne thoght
Seyde hit were beter serve hir for noght
Than with another to be wel.   845
And hyt was soth, for everydel
I wil anoon-ryght telle thee why.
   "I sawgh hyr daunce so comlily,
Carole and synge so swetely,
Laughe and pleye so womanly,   850
And loke so debonairly,
So goodly speke and so frendly,
That, certes, y trowe that evermore
Nas seyn so blysful a tresore.
For every heer on hir hed,   855
Soth to seyne, hyt was not red,
Ne nouther yelowe, ne broun hyt nas;
Me thoghte most lyk gold hyt was.
And whiche eyen my lady hadde!
Debonaire, goode, glade, and sadde,   860
Symple, of good mochel, noght to wyde.
Therto hir look nas not asyde,
Ne overthwert, but beset so wel
Hyt drew and took up, everydel,

Al that on hir gan beholde.   865
Hir eyen semed anoon she wolde
Have mercy—fooles wenden soo;
But hyt was never the rather doo.
Hyt nas no countrefeted thyng;
Hyt was hir owne pure lokyng   870
That the goddesse, dame Nature,
Had made hem opene by mesure,
And close; for, were she never so glad,
Hyr lokynge was not foly sprad,
Ne wildely, thogh that she pleyde;   875
But ever, me thoght, hir eyen seyde,
'Be God, my wrathe ys al foryive!'
   "Therwith hir lyste so wel to lyve,
That dulnesse was of hir adrad.
She nas to sobre ne to glad;   880
In alle thynges more mesure
Had never, I trowe, creature.
But many oon with hire loke she herte,
And that sat hyr ful lyte at herte,
For she knew nothyng of her thoght;   885
But whether she knew, or knew it nowght,
Algate she ne roughte of hem a stree!
To gete hyr love no ner nas he
That woned at hom, than he in Ynde;
The formest was alway behynde.   890
But goode folk, over al other,
She loved as man may do hys brother;
Of whiche love she was wonder large,
In skilful places that bere charge.
   "But which a visage had she thertoo!   895
Allas! myn herte ys wonder woo
That I ne kan discryven hyt!
Me lakketh both Englyssh and wit
For to undo hyt at the fulle;
And eke my spirites be so dulle   900

---

829. goodlyhede, goodliness. **beseye,** provided. **831. halwes,** saints, apostles. **835. boone,** petition. **839–40. I ne tok No maner counseyl but,** I consulted only. **842. seyen,** regarded. The subj. is *eyen*. **843. purely tho,** verily then. **847. anoon-ryght,** right away. **849. Carole.** To carol was to dance in a ring to the accompaniment of singing. **855.** The description which follows is in accordance with a medieval convention, which was codified by the rhetoricians, especially Matthew de Vendôme and Geoffrey de Vinsauf. The latter offers also an illustration of the method. Chaucer refers elsewhere to Geoffrey de Vinsauf but here he is following mainly *Le jugement dou Roy de Behaingne*. A number of details are paralleled in other French poems which Chaucer is known to have read, but golden hair, beautiful eyes, white and pink complexion, a snowy throat, etc. are commonplaces in the description of feminine beauty. **859. whiche eyen,** what eyes. **860. sadde,** steadfast. **861. of good muchel,** cf. l. 454. **874. foly,** foolishly, wantonly. **885. her,** their. **887. Algate,** at any rate. **stree,** straw. **894. In skilful places that bere charge,** in reasonable situations that justify it (*lit.* bear the weight).

So gret a thyng for to devyse.
I have no wit that kan suffise
To comprehenden hir beaute.
But thus moche dar I sayn, that she
Was whit, rody, fressh, and lyvely hewed,   905
And every day hir beaute newed.
And negh hir face was alderbest;
For certes, Nature had swich lest
To make that fair, that trewly she
Was hir chefe patron of beaute   910
And chefe ensample of al hir werke,
And moustre; for be hyt never so derke,
Me thynketh I se hir ever moo.
And yet moreover, thogh alle thoo
That ever livede were now alyve,   915
[They] ne sholde have founde to discryve
Yn al hir face a wikked sygne;
For hit was sad, symple, and benygne.
   "And which a goodly, softe speche
Had that swete, my lyves leche!   920
So frendly, and so wel ygrounded,
Up al resoun so wel yfounded,
And so tretable to alle goode,
That I dar swere wel by the roode,
Of eloquence was never founde   925
So swete a sownynge facounde,
Ne trewer tonged, ne skorned lasse,
Ne bet koude hele—that, by the masse
I durste swere, thogh the pope hit songe,
That ther was never yet throgh hir tonge   930
Man ne woman gretly harmed;
As for her [ther] was al harm hyd—
Ne lasse flaterynge in hir word,
That purely hir symple record
Was founde as trewe as any bond,   935
Or trouthe of any mannes hond.
Ne chyde she koude never a del;

That knoweth al the world ful wel.
   "But swich a fairnesse of a nekke
Had that swete that boon nor brekke   940
Nas ther non sene that myssat.
Hyt was whit, smothe, streght, and pure flat,
Wythouten hole; or canel-boon,
As be semynge, had she noon.
Hyr throte, as I have now memoyre,   945
Semed a round tour of yvoyre,
Of good gretnesse, and noght to gret.
   "And goode faire White she het;
That was my lady name ryght.
She was bothe fair and bryght;   950
She hadde not hir name wrong.
Ryght faire shuldres and body long
She had, and armes, every lyth
Fattyssh, flesshy, not gret therwith;
Ryght white handes, and nayles rede,   955
Rounde brestes; and of good brede
Hyr hippes were, a streight flat bak.
I knew on hir noon other lak
That al hir lymmes nere pure sewynge
In as fer as I had knowynge.   960
   "Therto she koude so wel pleye,
Whan that hir lyste, that I dar seye
That she was lyk to torche bryght
That every man may take of lyght
Ynogh, and hyt hath never the lesse.   965
Of maner and of comlynesse
Ryght so ferde my lady dere;
For every wight of hir manere
Myght cacche ynogh, yif that he wolde,
Yif he had eyen hir to beholde.   970
For I dar swere wel, yif that she
Had among ten thousand be,
She wolde have be, at the leste,
A chef myrour of al the feste,

---

905. The line is too long. Some edd. omit *whit*, but it is in all the MSS. **907. negh**, almost. **912. moustre**, model. **922. Up**, upon. **923. tretable**, inclinable. **926. So swete a sownynge facounde**, so sweet a sounding eloquence. **933. flaterynge**, leading to false expectation, exaggerating. The construction is awkward and the reading, though supported by the MSS, is probably corrupt. **934. record**, statement. **936. trouthe**, troth, pledge. The normal spelling of *troth* in the fourteenth century was *trouthe* or *trowthe*; it is ultimately the same word as *truth*. **940. brekke**, blemish. **941. sene**, visible. **942. pure**, entirely. **943. canel-boon**, collar bone. **945. memoyre**, remembrance. **948. White**, Blanche. **het**, was called. **949. lady**, lady's. See Language §14. **953. lyth**, limb. **954. Fattyssh**, plump, moderately fat. **956. brede**, breadth. **959. That**, as that. **lymmes**, parts of the body. **nere pure sewynge**, were not perfectly proportioned. **962. hir lyste**, it pleased her. **966. Of**, in.

Thogh they had stonden in a rowe,

To mennes eyen that koude have knowe.

For wher so men had pleyd or waked,

Me thoghte the felawsshyppe as naked

Withouten hir, that sawgh I oones,

As a corowne withoute stones.

Trewly she was, to myn yë,

The soleyn fenix of Arabye;

For ther lyveth never but oon,

Ne swich as she ne knowe I noon.

　"To speke of godnesse, trewly she 985

Had as moche debonairte

As ever had Hester in the Bible,

And more, yif more were possyble.

And, soth to seyne, therwythal

She had a wyt so general, 990

So hool enclyned to alle goode,

That al hir wyt was set, by the rode,

Withoute malyce, upon gladnesse;

And therto I saugh never yet a lesse

Harmful than she was in doynge. 995

I sey nat that she ne had knowynge

What harm was; or elles she

Had koud no good, so thinketh me.

　"And trewly, for to speke of trouthe,

But she had had, hyt hadde be routhe. 1000

Therof she had so moche hyr del—

And I dar seyn and swere hyt wel—

That Trouthe hymself, over al and al

Had chose hys maner principal

In hir, that was his restyng place. 1005

Therto she hadde the moste grace,

To have stedefast perseveraunce,

And esy, atempre governaunce, 975

That ever I knew or wyste yit,

So pure suffraunt was hir wyt. 1010

And reson gladly she understood—

Hyt folowed wel she koude good;

She used gladly to do wel. 980

These were hir maners everydel.

　"Therwith she loved so wel ryght, 1015

She wrong do wolde to no wyght.

No wyght myght do hir noo shame,

She loved so wel hir owne name.

Hyr luste to holde no wyght in honde,

Ne, be thou siker, she wolde not fonde 1020

To holde no wyght in balaunce

By half word ne by countenaunce,

But if men wolde upon hir lye;

Ne sende men into Walakye,

To Pruyse, and into Tartarye, 1025

To Alysaundre, ne into Turkye,

And byd hym faste anoon that he

Goo hoodles to the Drye Se

And come hom by the Carrenare,

And seye 'Sir, be now ryght ware 1030

That I may of yow here seyn

Worshyp, or that ye come ageyn!'

She ne used no suche knakkes smale.

　"But wherfore that y telle my tale?

Ryght on thys same, as I have seyd, 1035

Was hooly al my love leyd;

For certes she was, that swete wif,

My suffisaunce, my lust, my lyf,

Myn hap, myn hele, and al my blesse,

My worldes welfare, and my goddesse, 1040

---

977. wher so, wherever. **men,** one (indef.). **979. That,** as. **982. soleyn,** unique. **fenix of Arabye.** The fabulous bird which, consumed by fire, rises from the ashes, was often mentioned in antiquity and the Middle Ages; it is the subject of an Old English poem, is described in the *Bestiaire* of Philippe de Thaun, etc. Pliny, Bk. x, ch. 2, says: "They say . . . that Arabia has one [bird] that is famous before all others (though perhaps it is fabulous), the phoenix, the only one in the whole world and hardly ever seen." **986. debonairte,** graciousness. **987. Hester,** Esther, queen to King Ahasuerus, who saved her people from being destroyed. **990. a wyt so general,** a mind so comprehending, noble. **998. Had koud,** would have known. **1000. But she had had,** it (understood). **1001. del,** share. **1003. over al and al,** above everything. **1004. maner,** manor, chief residence. **1007. To have,** in having. **1008. atempre,** temperate. **1010. suffraunt,** tolerant. **1012. koude,** knew. **1019. Hyr luste,** it pleased her. **to holde . . . in honde,** to encourage with false hopes. **1020. siker,** sure. **fonde,** strive (OE. *fandian*). **1021. in balaunce,** in suspense. **1023. upon,** concerning. **1024. Walakye,** Wallachia, in Roumania; an allusion to the practice of heroines of romance who set difficult tests for their lovers. **1025. Pruyse,** Prussia. **1026. Alysaundre,** Alexandria. **1027. faste anoon,** without delay. **1028. hoodles to the Drye Se,** without hood to the Gobi Desert. **1029. Carrenare,** Kara-nor or Black Lake on the edge of the Gobi Desert, both on an important trade route to China. For those plausible identifications see Lowes, *MP*, III. 1–46. **1031. here seyn,** hear say. **1032. Worshyp,** honor. **or,** ere. **1033. knakkes,** tricks. **1037. wif,** woman. **1038. suffisaunce,** source of satisfaction. **lust,** joy. **1039. Myn hap . . .,** my good fortune, my well being, my bliss.

And I hooly hires and everydel."
    "By oure Lord," quod I, "y trowe yow wel!
Hardely, your love was wel beset;
I not how ye myghte have do bet."
"Bet? ne no wyght so wel," quod he.   1045
"Y trowe hyt, sir," quod I, "parde!"
"Nay, leve hyt wel!" "Sire, so do I;
I leve yow wel, that trewely
Yow thoghte that she was the beste,
And to beholde the alderfayreste,   1050
Whoso had loked hir with your eyen."
"With myn? nay, alle that hir seyen
Seyde and sworen hyt was soo.
And thogh they ne hadde, I wolde thoo
Have loved best my lady free,   1055
Thogh I had had al the beaute
That ever had Alcipyades,
And al the strengthe of Ercules,
And therto had the worthynesse
Of Alysaunder, and al the rychesse   1060
That ever was in Babyloyne,
In Cartage, or in Macedoyne,
Or in Rome, or in Nynyve;
And therto also hardy be
As was Ector, so have I joye,   1065
That Achilles slough at Troye—
And therfore was he slayn alsoo
In a temple, for bothe twoo
Were slayne, he and Antylegyus,
And so seyth Dares Frygius,   1070
For love of Polixena—
Or ben as wis as Mynerva,

I wolde ever, withoute drede,
Have loved hir, for I moste nede.
'Nede!' nay, trewly, I gabbe now;   1075
Noght 'nede,' and I wol telle how,
For of good wille myn herte hyt wolde,
And eke to love hir I was holde
As for the fairest and the beste.
She was as good, so have I reste,   1080
As ever was Penelopee of Grece,
Or as the noble wif Lucrece,
That was the beste—he telleth thus,
The Romayn, Tytus Lyvyus—
She was as good, and nothyng lyk,   1085
Thogh hir stories be autentyk;
Algate she was as trewe as she.
    "But wherfore that I telle thee
Whan I first my lady say?
I was ryght yong, soth to say,   1090
And ful gret nede I hadde to lerne;
Whan my herte wolde yerne
To love, hyt was a gret empryse.
But as my wyt koude best suffise,
After my yonge childly wyt,   1095
Withoute drede, I besette hyt
To love hir in my beste wyse,
To do hir worship and the servise
That I koude thoo, be my trouthe,
Withoute feynynge outher slouthe;   1100
For wonder feyn I wolde hir se.
So mochel hyt amended me
That, whan I saugh hir first a-morwe,
I was warysshed of al my sorwe

1043. Hardely, assuredly. **1044. not,** know not. **bet,** better. **1046. trowe,** believe. **1047. leve,** believe. **1048-51.** Chaucer is being discreet, offending no other woman by granting that Blanche surpassed all others; but the remark serves also to start the knight off on a further encomium. **1050. to beholde the alderfayreste,** the fairest of all to behold. **1051. loked,** beheld, **eyen,** eyes. **1052. seyen,** saw. **1054. thoo,** still. **1057. Alcipyades,** Alcibiades' fame for beauty is mentioned in *RR*, 8943 and by Boethius (III. 8. 32), but the series of comparisons was a commonplace. **1064. be,** been. **1069. Antylegyus,** a corruption of Archilochus, who with Achilles was lured to the temple of Apollo (Achilles, in the hope of wedding Polyxena) and there attacked by Paris and his followers and slain. **1070. Dares Frygius.** On Dares Phrygius see the introduction to *Troilus and Criseyde*. **1073. withoute drede,** without doubt. **1075. gabbe,** talk idly. **1077. hyt wolde,** wished it. **1078. holde,** bound. **1081. Penelopee,** wife of Ulysses, who during his long absence at the siege of Troy, was compelled to resist many suitors. **1082. Lucrece.** Lucretia, in Roman legend the virtuous wife of Tarquinius Collatinus, who killed herself after being raped by Sextus Tarquinius. The story is in both Ovid and Livy. Chaucer tells it in the *LGW*. Cf. also Shakespeare's *Rape of Lucrece*. **1085. and nothyng lyk.** She was not like Lucretia, but just as good. **1087. Algate,** at any rate. **1089. say,** saw. **1093. empryse,** undertaking. **1094. wyt,** intelligence. **1095. wyt,** understanding. **1096. besette,** employed. **1099. thoo,** then. **1100. outher,** or. **slouthe.** In addition to its ordinary meaning, sloth, as one of the Seven Deadly Sins, had a special sense of laxness in one's obligations to God, *e.g.* failure to do good works, to go to church, etc. In the present passage there is the connotation of laxness in duty to his lady. **1102. mochel,** much. **1103. a-morwe,** in the morning. **1104. warysshed,** cured.

Of al day after, til hyt were eve;   1105
Me thoghte nothyng myghte me greve,
Were my sorwes never so smerte.
And yet she syt so in myn herte,
That, by my trouthe, y nolde noght,
For al thys worlde, out of my thoght   1110
Leve my lady; noo, trewely!"
    "Now, by my trouthe, sir!" quod I,
"Me thynketh ye have such a chaunce
As shryfte wythoute repentaunce."
    "Repentaunce! nay, fy!" quod he,   1115
"Shulde y now repente me
To love? Nay, certes, than were I wel
Wers than was Achitofel,
Or Anthenor, so have I joye,
The traytor that betraysed Troye,   1120
Or the false Genelloun,
He that purchased the tresoun
Of Rowland and of Olyvere.
Nay, while I am alyve here,
I nyl foryete hir never moo."   1125
    "Now, goode syre," quod I thoo,
"Ye han wel told me herebefore,
Hyt ys no nede to reherse it more,
How ye sawe hir first, and where.
But wolde ye tel me the manere   1130
To hire which was your firste speche,
Therof I wolde yow beseche;
And how she knewe first your thoght,
Whether ye loved hir or noght.
And telleth me eke what ye have lore,   1135

I herde yow telle herebefore."
    "Yee!" seyde he, "thow nost what thou
        menest;
I have lost more than thou wenest."
    "What los ys that?" quod I thoo;
"Nyl she not love yow? ys hyt soo?   1140
Or have ye oght doon amys,
That she hath left yow? ys hyt this?
For Goddes love, telle me al."
    "Before God," quod he, "and I shal.
I saye ryght as I have seyd,   1145
On hir was al my love leyd;
And yet she nyste hyt never a del
Noght longe tyme, leve hyt wel!
For be ryght siker, I durste noght,
For al this world, telle hir my thoght,   1150
Ne I wolde have wraththed hir, trewely.
For wostow why? She was lady
Of the body; she had the herte,
And who hath that, may not asterte.
But, for to kepe me fro ydelnesse,   1155
Trewly I did my besynesse
To make songes, as I best koude,
And ofte tyme I song hem loude;
And made songes thus a gret del,
Althogh I koude not make so wel   1160
Songes, ne knewe the art al,
As koude Lamekes sone Tubal,
That found out first the art of songe;
For as hys brothres hamers ronge
Upon hys anvelt up and doun,   1165

1107. **smerte,** bitter. 1108. **syt,** sits. 1113. **such a chaunce . . .** You are in the position of a man who has received absolution without having deserved it. The knight felt highly elated at the sight of his lady before he had any assurance that she would look upon him with favor. 1118. **Achitofel.** On Achitophel, David's trusted counsellor, and his joining the rebellion against David see *2 Samuel*, 17. 1119. **Anthenor.** According to the *Roman de Troie* (ll. 25607 ff) and its derivatives Antenor took away the statue of Pallas Athenae, on which the safety of Troy was supposed to depend, and sent it to Ulysses. Cf. *TC* 4. 204. 1120. **betraysed,** betrayed. 1121. **Genelloun . . .** Roland, Charlemagne's nephew; Oliver, one of the most famous of the Twelve Peers; Ganelon, another of Charlemagne's warriors through whose treachery Roland lost his life at the battle of Roncevalles. See the *Chanson de Roland.* 1122. **purchased,** brought about. **tresoun,** betrayal. 1125. **foryete,** forget. 1126. **thoo,** then. 1135. **lore,** lost. 1136. **I herde yow telle herebefore,** *i.e.* which you mentioned before. 1137. **nost,** knowest not. 1140. **Nyl,** will not. 1147. **nyste,** knew not. 1149. **siker,** sure. 1151. **wraththed hir,** made her angry. 1152-3. **lady Of the body,** as one might say "lord of the manor." She had lordship over his body since, according to a common conception of Courtly Love, the lover's heart was in the possession of his mistress. 1154. **asterte,** escape. 1156. **besynesse,** diligence. 1160. **make,** compose (verses). 1162. **Lamekes sone Tubal.** Tubal and Jubal were frequently confused. Tubalcain was a master artificer. Jubal is called in *Genesis* (4:21) "the father of all such as handle the harp and organ." The legend mentioned in the following lines is found told by Pythagoras in the commentary of Macrobius on the *Somnium Scipionis* (Bk. II, chap. 1) but Chaucer could have derived all his information from the *Aurora* of Peter of Riga, a twelfth-century Latin paraphrase, in verse, of parts of the Bible. See K. Young, *Speculum*, XII. 299-303. 1165. **anvelt,** anvil.

Therof he took the firste soun,—
But Grekes seyn Pictagoras,
That he the firste fynder was
Of the art, Aurora telleth so,—
But therof no fors, of hem two.   1170
Algates songes thus I made
Of my felynge, myn herte to glade;
And, lo! this was the altherferste,—
I not wher hyt were the werste.

Lord, hyt maketh myn herte lyght,   1175
Whan I thenke on that swete wyght
That is so semely on to see;
And wisshe to God hit myght so bee
That she wolde holde me for hir knyght,
My lady, that is so fair and bryght!   1180

"Now have I told thee, soth to say,
My firste song. Upon a day
I bethoghte me what woo
And sorwe that I suffred thoo
For hir, and yet she wyste hyt noght,   1185
Ne telle hir durste I nat my thoght.
'Allas!' thoghte I, 'y kan no reed;
And but I telle hir, I nam but deed;
And yif I telle hyr, to seye ryght soth,
I am adred she wol be wroth.   1190
Allas! what shal I thanne do?'
"In this debat I was so wo,
Me thoghte myn herte braste atweyne!
So at the laste, soth to sayne,
I bethoghte me that Nature   1195
Ne formed never in creature
So moche beaute, trewely,

And bounte, wythoute mercy.
In hope of that, my tale I tolde
With sorwe, as that I never sholde;   1200
For nedes, and mawgree my hed,
I most have told hir or be ded.
I not wel how that I began,
Ful evel rehersen hyt I kan;
And eke, as helpe me God withal,   1205
I trowe hyt was in the dismal,
That was the ten woundes of Egipte;
For many a word I overskipte
In my tale, for pure fere
Lest my wordes mysset were.   1210
With sorweful herte, and woundes dede,
Softe and quakynge for pure drede
And shame, and styntynge in my tale
For ferde, and myn hewe al pale,
Ful ofte I wex bothe pale and red.   1215
Bowynge to hir, I heng the hed;
I durste nat ones loke hir on,
For wit, maner, and al was goon.
I seyde 'mercy!' and no more.
Hyt nas no game, hyt sat me sore.   1220
"So at the laste, soth to seyn,
Whan that myn herte was come ageyn,
To telle shortly al my speche,
With hool herte I gan hir beseche
That she wolde be my lady swete;   1225
And swor, and hertely gan hir hete,
Ever to be stedfast and trewe,
And love hir alwey fresshly newe,
And never other lady have,
And al hir worship for to save   1230
As I best koude; I swor hir this—

1166. **soun**, sound. 1170. **no fors**, no matter. 1171. **Algates**, at any rate. 1172. **glade**, gladden. 1173. **altherferste**, first of all. 1174. **not**, know not. **wher**, whether. 1187. **kan**, know. **reed**, counsel. 1192. **wo**, unhappy. 1193. **braste atweyne**, would burst in two. 1194. **sayne**, say. 1198. **bounte**, goodness. 1200. **With sorwe**. Sometimes taken as an imprecation, but in the light of the explanatory phrase which follows (as though I never should have done so) it is more likely to be understood as "with distress of mind, with some misgivings." 1201. **nedes**, of necessity. **mawgree**, in spite of. 1203. **not**, know not. 1204. **evel**, badly. 1206. **dismal**. The supposed derivation from L. *dies mali*, evil days, can hardly be accepted. See L. Spitzer, *MLN*, LVII. 602–13. Two days in each month were called *dies Ægyptiaci*, according to Vincent of Beauvais. Chaucer apparently took the phrase as meaning *dis mal*, ten evils; hence the allusion to the "ten woundes (L. *plaga*) of Egipte." It was a current superstition. An anonymous tract on the Decalogue in Harl. MS 2398 quotes St. Augustine to the effect that "we scholde nought kepe dayes that beth ycleped egypcians, the whiche, as ich understonde, beth the dayes that men now clepeth dysmale dayes." See *Studies Presented to Sir Hilary Jenkinson* (1957), p. 302. 1210. **mysset**, out of place. 1211. **dede**, deadly. 1212. **Softe**, softly, timidly. **pure drede**, very fear. 1213. **styntynge**, stopping, halting. 1214. **ferde**, fear. 1215. **wex**, waxed. 1218. **maner**, proper behavior. 1220. **Hyt nas no game**. Cf. mod. "it was no joke." **sat me sore**, was painful to me. 1226. **hete**, promise. 1230. **worship**, honor.

'For youres is alle that ever ther ys
For evermore, myn herte swete!
And never to false yow, but I mete,
I nyl, as wys God helpe me soo!'
　"And whan I had my tale ydoo,
God wot, she acounted nat a stree
Of al my tale, so thoghte me.
To telle shortly ryght as hyt ys,
Trewly hir answere hyt was this; 1240
I kan not now wel counterfete
Hyr wordes, but this was the grete
Of hir answere: she sayde 'nay'
Al-outerly. Allas! that day
The sorowe I suffred, and the woo, 1245
That trewly Cassandra, that soo
Bewayled the destruccioun
Of Troye and of Ilyoun,
Had never swich sorwe as I thoo.
I durste no more say thertoo 1250
For pure fere, but stal away;
And thus I lyved ful many a day,
That trewely I hadde no nede
Ferther than my beddes hede
Never a day to seche sorwe; 1255
I fond hyt redy every morwe
For-why I loved hyr in no gere.
　"So hit befel, another yere,
I thoughte ones I wolde fonde
To do hir knowe and understonde 1260
My woo; and she wel understood
That I ne wilned thyng but good,
And worship, and to kepe hir name
Over alle thyng, and drede hir shame,
And was so besy hyr to serve; 1265

And pitee were I shulde sterve,
Syth that I wilned noon harm, ywis.
So whan my lady knew al this,
My lady yaf me al hooly 1270
The noble yifte of hir mercy,
Savynge hir worship by al weyes,—
Dredles, I mene noon other weyes.
And therwith she yaf me a ryng;
I trowe hyt was the firste thyng. 1275
But if myn herte was ywaxe
Glad, that is no nede to axe!
As helpe me God, I was as blyve
Reysed, as fro deth to lyve—
Of al happes the alderbeste,— 1280
The gladdest, and the moste at reste.
For trewely that swete wyght,
Whan I had wrong and she the ryght,
She wolde alway so goodly
Foryeve me so debonairly. 1285
In al my yowthe, in al chaunce,
She took me in hir governaunce.
Therwyth she was alway so trewe,
Our joye was ever ylyche newe;
Oure hertes wern so evene a payre 1290
That never nas that oon contrayre
To that other, for no woo.
For sothe, ylyche they suffred thoo
Oo blysse, and eke oo sorwe bothe;
Ylyche they were bothe gladde and wrothe; 1295
Al was us oon, withoute were.
And thus we lyved ful many a yere
So wel, I kan nat telle how."
　"Sir," quod I, "where is she now?"
"Now?" quod he, and stynte anoon.

1234. but I mete, unless I am dreaming, not responsible. **1235. as wys God helpe,** as certainly (as) God may help. **1237. stree,** straw. **1238. thoghte me,** it seemed to me. **1241. counterfete,** imitate, reproduce. **1242. grete,** gist. **1243.** In the *Roy de Behaingne* the lady, in a similar situation, at first rejects the lover's plea. (cf. ll. 523–48). **1246. Cassandra.** At various points in the *Roman de Troie* Cassandra, daughter of Priam, prophesies the destruction of Troy. For her lamentation in the temple see ll. 26113 ff. **1248. Ilyoun.** Troy and Ilium are, of course, the same, but medieval writers regarded Ilium as the citadel proper. Guido delle Colonne, *Historia Destructionis Troiae*, says that the palace built by Priam was called Ylion (ed. Griffin, p. 49). The distinction between Ilium and Troy is made also in *HF* 151–61, and in the Legend of Dido (*LGW* 936–7) Chaucer says that the "tour of Ylioun . . . of the cite was the chef dongeoun," a direct translation of the *Roman de Troie*, 3041–2. **1249. thoo,** then. **1251. stal,** stole. **1255. seche,** seek. **1257. For-why,** because. **gere,** whim, transient mood. **1259. fonde,** strive. **1260. do,** make. **1262. wilned,** intended. **1265. besy,** eager. **1266. pitee were,** it were a pity that I should die. **1267. ywis,** certainly. **1269. yaf,** gave. **1270. yifte,** gift. **1271. weyes,** means. **1272. Dredles,** of course. **weyes,** way. **1275. ywaxe,** grown. **1276. axe,** ask. **1277. as blyve,** immediately. **1279. Of al happes . . .** the best of all happenings; *al* is redundant. **1284. Foryeve,** forgive. **1285. al chaunce,** every circumstance. **1288. ylyche,** alike. **1294. wrothe,** sad. **1295. were,** doubt. **1299. stynte anoon,** stopped immediately.

etymologically speaking] Lancaster (long + castle

Richmond Rich + Hill or mount

White Fr. (Blanche)

Therwith he wax as ded as stoon,   1300
And seyde, "Allas, that I was bore!
That was the los that here-before
I tolde the that I hadde lorn.
Bethenke how I seyde here-beforn,
'Thow wost ful lytel what thow menest;   1305
I have lost more than thow wenest'—
God wot, allas! ryght that was she!"
    "Allas, sir, how? what may that be?"
    "She ys ded!" "Nay!" "Yis, be my trouthe!"
"Is that youre los? Be God, hyt ys routhe!"
And with that word ryght anoon   1311
They gan to strake forth; al was doon,
For that tyme, the hert-huntyng.
    With that me thoghte that this kyng
Gan homwarde for to ryde   1315
Unto a place, was there besyde,
Which was from us but a lyte:

A long castel with walles white,
Be seynt Johan! on a ryche hil
As me mette; but thus hyt fil.   1320
Ryght thus me mette, as I yow telle,
That in the castell ther was a belle,
As hyt hadde smyten houres twelve.

Therwyth I awook myselve
And fond me lyinge in my bed;   1325
And the book that I hadde red,
Of Alcione and Seys the kyng,
And of the goddes of slepyng,
I fond hyt in myn honde ful even.
Thoghte I, "Thys ys so queynt a sweven   1330
That I wol, be processe of tyme,
Fonde to put this sweven in ryme
As I kan best, and that anoon."
This was my sweven; now hit ys doon.

Explicit the Boke of the Duchesse.

1301. bore, born. **1303. lorn,** lost. **1308. what,** how. **1310. routhe,** pity. **1312. They,** *i.e.* the hunters. **strake forth,** move on, although *strake* here may be the hunting term meaning to blow certain notes on the hunting horn. **1316. was,** (which) was. **1317. lyte,** little. **1318. A long castel,** the English equivalent of *Lancaster.* John of Gaunt was Duke of Lancaster. **walles white, Be seynt Johan,** possibly punning references to Blanche and John of Gaunt, just as in the French love-vision poems the poet sometimes reveals his name in a cryptogram; see the closing lines of the *Panthère d'Amours,* by Nicole de Margivale. **1319. ryche hil,** Richmond (-mount), in Yorkshire, a manor belonging to John of Gaunt at this time. **1320. As me mette,** as I dreamed. **fil,** happened. **1323. As,** since. **houres twelve.** Since the daytime seems called for by the return of the hunting party, the hour must be noon. The bell may refer to a striking clock, the use of which was spreading in Chaucer's day. It is to be noted that the poet only dreams that he hears the bell strike twelve and that this is not necessarily the real time that he awoke. For discussion see B. H. Bronson, *MLN,* LXVIII. 515–521. **1329. ful even,** indeed. **1330. sweven,** dream. **1332. fonde,** strive. **1333. anoon,** immediately.

The Hous of Fame

The Hous of Fame is a triumph of light humor, and is altogether the most delightful of Chaucer's minor poems. It has numerous faults, especially of proportion, but in the invocation to the Third Book Chaucer disclaims any present pretence to "art poetical"; rather, he says "the rym is light and lewed." In spite of its length he seems to have considered it a trifle. He had obviously been reading Dante, and without intending any lack of respect for the *Divine Comedy* borrowed the framework—a marvelous journey, a supernatural guide, the division into three books—and adapted it to his purpose. The mock seriousness and the formal machinery of invocations to the gods and the muses are a part of the design and enhance the humor of the second book.

Only three manuscripts of the poem have come down to us. There are two early printed editions based upon manuscripts now lost. Lydgate does not mention it, at least by title. It is to be inferred that the poem was not widely circulated. All of the versions are incomplete at the end, breaking off in the middle of a sentence just as a "man of greet auctoritee" is about to make an announcement. It is possible that a leaf or more had been lost from the archetype of the existing manuscripts, but it seems more likely that the conclusion was never written. This raises the question why, invites speculation as to what the conclusion would have been, and compels us to consider the reason Chaucer wrote the poem at all.

Early attempts (as by Sandras and Ten Brink) to explain the poem as an allegory of the generous soul chained to vulgar cares and seeking to escape from reality have rightly been discarded. The late Professor Manly suggested that the poem was intended to introduce a series of love stories. Such a view would make it an earlier example of the device of the framed tale seen in *The Legend of Good Women* and *The Canterbury Tales*. But a prologue in three books, each furnished with an Invocation and the whole running to more than 2000 lines, would seem a rather formidable introduction; moreover in the Invocation to Book III Chaucer speaks of "this litel laste book," words which suggest the conclusion of the work rather than a prelude to something else. In 1907 W. O. Sypherd (*Studies in Chaucer's Hous of Fame*) showed that in many ways Chaucer's poem reflects the conventions of a popular type of Old French poetry, the love-vision, of which the *Roman de la Rose* was the progenitor. The study makes clear the literary background against which we should view the poem, but it does not furnish a satisfactory explanation of why Chaucer wrote it. Although Chaucer was following French fashion in making use of the dream convention and although many of his descriptive details can be paralleled in French poetry, nevertheless a considerable gulf separates *The Hous of Fame* from such poems as Nicole de Margival's *Panthère d'Amours* and Froissart's *Paradys d'Amours*.

At the beginning of Book II the poet represents himself as one buried in his books, hermit-like, so that he knows nothing of what is going on in the world or even what is happening to his very neighbors. The tidings of which he is particularly ignorant, in the opinion of Jupiter, are "of Loves folk," and the eagle has been sent by Jupiter because the god has pity on him for having served Venus and Cupid so long without reward. The eagle assures him that when he reaches the Hous of Fame he will hear "Of Loves folke mo tydinges," true and false, than there are grains of sand or "cornes . . . in graunges," and the garrulous bird particularizes such tidings at considerable length. Later, after five companies of petitioners have made requests of the goddess Fame, apparently with no other purpose on Chaucer's part than to show how willful and contrary she is in distributing her rewards and punishments in the form of honorable or shameful reputations, the people in the sixth company acknowledge that they have lived in idleness all their lives, but nevertheless ask that they may have as good fame as those that have done noble deeds and achieved all their desires "As well of love as other thing," whereupon the petitioners ask that the world may judge them to have been people that women loved madly. This comes as a rather sudden particularizing of request after the talk has been in general terms for over two hundred lines. Moreover, the seventh company, which follows immediately, asks "the same bone," and in refusing it the goddess says that they were such as thought that Iseult herself could not have refused them her love although "she that grint at a querne" is too good for them. Finally, when a stranger at the poet's back asks him if he also has come to obtain fame he rejects the idea vigorously and says he is there

> Somme newe tydynges for to lere,
> Somme newe thinges, y not what,
> Tydynges, other this or that,
> *Of love, or suche thinges glad.*

The stranger conducts him to the Hous of Rumour where he will hear what he desires to hear. Consequently, when he enters the Hous of Rumour it is in expectation of hearing tidings "Of love, or swiche thinges glade"; and when, having heard all sorts of other news he has his attention attracted by a great noise in a corner of the hall where "men of love-tydinges tolde," we can hardly doubt that the "man of greet auctoritee" is going to make some statement or announcement, that it will be in the nature of "tydynges," and that it will have to do with love.

This would imply that *The Hous of Fame*, like *The Book of the Duchess*, is an occasional poem. No satisfactory occasion, however, has been proposed. Imelmann (*ESt*, xlv. 397–431) argued that it was intended as a greeting for Anne of Bohemia when she arrived in England for her marriage to King Richard II and that it was a sequel to *The Parlement of Foules*. This reverses the probable order of the poems, and, as has often been observed, an epithalamium would be rather tactless featuring the desertion of Dido by Aeneas and making this story the ground for observing,

> Loo, how a woman doth amis
> To love him that unknowen ys! (269–70).

Brusendorff's attempt to revive the theory (*The Chaucer Tradition*) seems not more convincing. Koch (*ESt*, l. 359–82) would transfer the occasion to the marriage of one of John of Gaunt's daughters, and Riedel (*JEGP*, xxvii. 441–69) sees in the poem a warning to John of Gaunt when he had shocked the court by appearing in public with his mistress. Bronson (*Univ. of Calif. Pub.*, iii, No. 4, pp. 171–92) suggests that the announcement at the end might have been "of dubious credit to the person celebrated: some gossip perhaps of a great man's infidelity in love, some account of a woman's trust betrayed." But this would not be a tiding "Of love, or swiche thinges glad" which the poet is avowedly seeking. A number of features of the poem—the brief telling of a famous classical story, the elementary explanation of how sound travels, the marvelous journey through the air—would have been appropriate if intended for a child, and it might not be fantastic to regard the poem as intended for the young Richard to celebrate his anticipated betrothal to the young French princess Marie, which was being negotiated in 1377—negotiations in which Chaucer may even have had some part—and which, whatever would have been the outcome, was put beyond the realm of possibility by her sudden death. But this is, of course, speculation. If the poem is an occasional poem, the occasion is still to be found.

There are other questions to which it would be unwise to give dogmatic answers. The date 1379 often assigned to *The Hous of Fame* rests on no very firm evidence. The poem shows no indebtedness to Boccaccio, and it could have been written just as well before the poet's second mission to Italy in 1378. An early date is suggested by the use of the eight-syllable couplet, the meter of *The Book of the Duchess*; that the poem is subsequent to his appointment to the customs in 1374 seems a natural inference from lines 652–60. Whether the end is lost or the poem was never finished we shall probably never know. It is possible to see evidences of haste in its composition, but dangerous to press the point. The date December 10, twice mentioned as the date of the poet's dream, has not been convincingly explained, and may be a poetic convention (see the note to l. 63). None of these unsolved problems prevents us from enjoying the humor of Book II and the delicate irony of Book III. The poem has, moreover, an additional appeal because of the numerous auto-biographical allusions and because the poet himself is the principal character. Without being one of Chaucer's greatest poems it is still one of his most delightful compositions.

THE HOUS OF FAME

Book I

Proem

God turne us every dreme to goode !
For hyt is wonder, be the roode,
To my wyt, what causeth swevenes
Eyther on morwes or on evenes;
And why th'effect folweth of somme,   5
And of somme hit shal never come;
Why that is an avisioun,
And this a revelacioun,
Why this a dreme, why that a sweven,
And noght to every man lyche even;   10
Why this a fantome, why these oracles,
I not; but whoso of these myracles
The causes knoweth bet then I,
Devyne he; for I certeynly
Ne kan hem noght, ne never thinke   15

To besily my wyt to swinke,
To knowe of hir signifiaunce
The gendres, neyther the distaunce
Of tymes of hem, ne the causes,
Or why this more then that cause is;   20
As yf folkys complexions
Make hem dreme of reflexions;
Or ellis thus, as other sayn,
For to gret feblenesse of her brayn,
By abstinence, or by sekenesse,   25
Prison, stewe, or gret distresse,
Or ellis by dysordynaunce
Of naturel acustumaunce,
That som man is to curious
In studye, or melancolyous,   30
Or thus, so inly ful of drede,

The text represents basically that of the Fairfax MS. **3. swevenes.** *Dreme* and *sweven* appear to be synonymous in Chaucer, although in l. 9 some distinction is implied. The causes of dreams are considered also in *The Nun's Priest's Tale*, B 4113 ff.; cf. besides *TC* 5.360 ff. and *PF* 99 ff. **7. avisioun . . . revelacioun.** Here *avisioun* seems to be mere fantasy, and *revelacioun* a portent of things to come. **10. lyche even,** exactly alike. **17. signifiaunce The gendres,** the kinds of meaning. **22. reflexions,** illusions, fantasies. See the discussion of dreams in *TC* 5. 358–85. **26. stewe,** brothel. **27. dysordynaunce . . . acustumaunce,** disturbance of normal habit. **29. curious,** eager.

That no man may hym bote bede;
Or ellis that devocion
Of somme, and contemplacion
Causen suche dremes ofte;   35
Or that the cruel lyfe unsofte
Which these ilke lovers leden
That hopen over-muche or dreden,
That purely her impressions
Causen hem avisions;   40
Or yf that spirites have the myght
To make folk to dreme a-nyght;
Or yf the soule, of propre kynde,
Be so parfit, as men fynde,
That yt forwot that ys to come,   45
And that hyt warneth al and some
Of everych of her aventures
Be avisions, or be figures,
But that oure flessh ne hath no myght
To understonde hyt aryght,   50
For hyt is warned to derkly;—
But why the cause is, noght wot I.
Wel worthe, of this thyng, grete clerkys,
That trete of this and other werkes;
For I of noon opinion   55
Nyl as now make mensyon,
But oonly that the holy roode
Turne us every dreme to goode!
For never, sith that I was born,
Ne no man elles me beforn,   60
Mette, I trowe stedfastly,
So wonderful a dreme as I
The tenthe day now of Decembre,
The which, as I kan now remembre,
I wol yow tellen everydel.   65

The Invocation

But at my gynnynge, trusteth wel,
I wol make invocacion,

With special devocion,
Unto the god of slepe anoon,
That duelleth in a cave of stoon   70
Upon a streme that cometh fro Lete,
That is a flood of helle unswete,
Besyde a folk men clepeth Cymerie,—
There slepeth ay this god unmerie
With his slepy thousand sones,   75
That alwey for to slepe hir wone is.
And to this god, that I of rede,
Prey I that he wol me spede
My sweven for to telle aryght,
Yf every dreme stonde in his myght.   80
And he that mover ys of al
That is and was and ever shal,
So yive hem joye that hyt here
Of alle that they dreme to-yere,
And for to stonden alle in grace   85
Of her loves, or in what place
That hem were levest for to stonde,
And shelde hem fro poverte and shonde,
And fro unhap and ech disese,
And sende hem al that may hem plese,   90
That take hit wel and skorne hyt noght,
Ne hyt mysdemen in her thoght
Thorgh malicious entencion.
And whoso thorgh presumpcion,
Or hate, or skorne, or thorgh envye,   95
Dispit, or jape, or vilanye,
Mysdeme hyt, pray I Jesus God
That (dreme he barefot, dreme he shod),
That every harm that any man
Hath had, syth the world began,   100
Befalle hym therof, or he sterve,
And graunte he mote hit ful deserve,
Lo, with such a conclusion
As had of his avision
Cresus, that was kyng of Lyde,   105

---

32. bote bede, offer a remedy. **37. ilke,** same. **43. of propre kynde,** by its own nature. **45. forwot that,** knows in advance what. **47. her,** their. **48. Be,** by. **figures,** phantasms. **51. warned,** foretold. **53. Wel worthe . . .** May great clerks succeed (in understanding). **61. Mette,** dreamed. **I trowe stedfastly,** I firmly believe. **63.** No convincing explanation of this date has been suggested. It may be a poetic convention. Cf. Machaut's *Jugement dou Roy de Navarre* and *Dit dou Lyon*. **70. in a cave of stoon.** The features of the God of Sleep's abode are from Ovid, *Metam.*, XI. 591 ff., as part of the story of Ceyx and Halcione used in the *Book of the Duchess*. **71. Lete,** Lethe. **73. Cymerie.** The Cimmerians, near whom Ovid places the God of Sleep's cave, are thought by some to have been in Scythia, by others near Baiæ in Italy. **76. wone,** custom. **84. to-yere,** this year. **88. shonde,** shame. **89. ech disese,** every discomfort. **92. mysdemen,** have a wrong opinion of. **93. malicious entencion,** ill will. **96. jape,** joke. **99. That.** The conj. is redundant. **101. sterve,** die.

That high upon a gebet dyde!
This prayer shal he have of me;
I am no bet in charyte!
Now herkeneth, as I have yow seyd,
What that I mette, or I abreyd.   110

The Dream

Of Decembre the tenthe day,
Whan hit was nyght, to slepe I lay
Ryght ther as I was wont to done,
And fil on slepe wonder sone,
As he that wery was forgo   115
On pilgrymage myles two
To the corseynt Leonard,
To make lythe of that was hard.
   But as I slepte, me mette I was
Withyn a temple ymad of glas,   120
In which ther were moo ymages
Of gold, stondynge in sondry stages,
And moo ryche tabernacles,
And with perre moo pynacles,
And moo curiouse portreytures,   125
And queynte maner of figures
Of olde werke, then I sawgh ever.
For certeynly, I nyste never
Wher that I was, but wel wyste I,
Hyt was of Venus redely,   130
The temple; for in portreyture,
I sawgh anoon-ryght hir figure
Naked fletynge in a see.

And also on hir hed, pardee,
Hir rose garlond whit and red,   135
And hir comb to kembe hyr hed,
Hir dowves, and daun Cupido,
Hir blynde sone, and Vulcano,
That in his face was ful broun.
   But as I romed up and doun,   140
I fond that on a wall ther was
Thus writen on a table of bras:
"I wol now singen, yif I kan,
The armes, and also the man
That first cam, thorgh his destinee,   145
Fugityf of Troy contree,
In Itayle, with ful moche pyne,
Unto the strondes of Lavyne."
And tho began the story anoon,
As I shal telle yow echon.   150
   First sawgh I the destruction
Of Troye, throgh the Greke Synon,
[That] with his false forswerynge,
And his chere and his lesynge,
Made the hors broght into Troye,   155
Thorgh which Troyens loste al her joye.
And aftir this was grave, allas!
How Ilyon assayled was
And wonne, and kyng Priam yslayn,
And Polytes, his sone, certayn,   160
Dispitously, of daun Pirrus.
And next that sawgh I how Venus,
Whan that she sawgh the castel brende,

---

110. abreyd, woke up. **115. forgo,** exhausted, worn out. This meaning of the past partic. is commonly found in association with *wery;* cf. *he al weri was forgan* (*Cursor Mundi,* l. 3527). Unless this passage is merely an instance of paradoxical humor, the allusion has not been explained. St. Leonard was famous for releasing prisoners, having been granted the privilege by the king of France. In *RR,* 8833 ff. he is mentioned in association with the statement that marriage is an evil bond, but this association of ideas is not in Chaucer's lines. **117. corseynt,** saint (*lit.* holy body). **118. To make lythe of that was hard,** *i.e.* to obtain relief from his pain. **lythe,** easy, soft. **120. a temple.** The closest parallel to Chaucer's description of Venus here and in the *KnT* (A 1949–66) is that pointed out by Lounsbury (*Stud. in. Chaucer,* II. 381–2) in the little treatise of Albricus Philosophus, *Libellus de Deorum Imaginibus.* The *Libellus* is a close adaptation of the prologue to the Latin moralization of Ovid by Bersuire. See also, Wilkins, *Speculum,* XXXII. 511–22. In one detail Chaucer is closer to Bersuire. See J. M. Steadman, *Speculum,* XXXIV. 620–4. Albricus tells how Venus is represented in pictures and Chaucer may be recalling some pictorial representation. No source for the temple itself has been found, but, except that marriage is of glass, it is described only in general terms and the features are found in many descriptions of mythological temples in Old French poetry. **122. stages,** stands or resting places for images. **123. tabernacles,** niches or recesses for images. **124. with perre . . . pynacles,** presumably the pointed terminations over niches, etc., here adorned with precious stones. Cf. l. 1193. **126. queynte maner of figures,** probably the decorative carvings with which architectural features were adorned. **133. fletynge,** floating. **142. table,** tablet. **143. I wol now singen . . .** The translation of the opening lines of Vergil's *Æneid* introduces the paraphrase of the earlier part of the poem which now follows. **155. Made . . . broght,** caused to be brought. **158. Ilyon.** In Chaucer's use this was the citadel proper. See note to *BD* 1248. **160. Polytes,** one of the sons of Priam and Hecuba, who was killed before his parents' eyes by Pyrrhus, the son of Achilles.

Doun fro the hevene gan descende,
And bad hir sone Eneas flee;   165
And how he fledde, and how that he
Escaped was from al the pres,
And took his fader, Anchises,
And bar hym on hys bakke away,
Cryinge, "Allas! and welaway!"   170
The whiche Anchises in hys honde
Bar the goddes of the londe,
Thilke that unbrende were.
    And I saugh next, in al thys fere,
How Creusa, daun Eneas wif,   175
Which that he lovede as hys lyf,
And hir yonge sone Iulo,
And eke Askanius also,
Fledden eke with drery chere,
That hyt was pitee for to here;   180
And in a forest, as they wente,
At a turnynge of a wente,
How Creusa was ylost, allas!
That ded, not I how, she was;
How he hir soughte, and how hir gost   185
Bad hym to flee the Grekes host,
And seyde he moste unto Itayle,
As was hys destynee, sauns faille;
That hyt was pitee for to here,
When hir spirit gan appere,   190
The wordes that she to hym seyde,
And for to kepe hir sone hym preyde.
Ther sawgh I graven eke how he,
Hys fader eke, and his meynee,
With hys shippes gan to saylle   195
Towardes the contree of Itaylle
As streight as that they myghte goo.
Ther saugh I thee, cruel Juno,
That art daun Jupiteres wif,
That hast yhated, al thy lyf,   200
Al the Troianysshe blood,

Renne and crye, as thou were wood,
On Eolus, the god of wyndes,   165
To blowen out, of alle kyndes,
So lowde that he shulde drenche   205
Lord and lady, grome and wenche,
Of al the Troian nacion,
Withoute any savacion.
    Ther saugh I such tempeste aryse,
That every herte myght agryse   210
To see hyt peynted on the wal.
    Ther saugh I graven eke withal,
Venus, how ye, my lady dere,
Wepynge with ful woful chere,
Prayen Jupiter on hye   215
To save and kepe that navye
Of the Troian Eneas,
Syth that he hir sone was.
    Ther saugh I Joves Venus kysse,
And graunted of the tempest lysse.   220
Ther saugh I how the tempest stente,
And how with alle pyne he wente,
And prively tok arryvage
In the contree of Cartage;
And on the morwe, how that he   225
And a knyght, highte Achate,
Mette with Venus that day,
Goynge in a queynt array,
As she had ben an hunteresse,
With wynde blowynge upon hir tresse;   230
How Eneas gan hym to pleyne,
When that he knew hir, of his peyne;
And how his shippes dreynte were,
Or elles lost, he nyste where;
How she gan hym comforte thoo,   235
And bad hym to Cartage goo,
And ther he shulde his folk fynde,
That in the see were left behynde.
    And, shortly of this thyng to pace,

---

174. **fere**, peril. 177. **And eke Askanius.** Iulus was another name or title for Ascanius. Chaucer was not alone in his mis-
understanding of the *Æneid*, IV. 274. See Rand, *Speculum*, I. 222–5. 182. **wente**, path. 200. **That hast yhated . . .** Because
of the judgment of Paris. 215–16. **Prayen Jupiter . . . To save.** Chaucer here departs from Virgil, where Venus does
not appeal to Jupiter until after Æneas has reached land, and Neptune represses Eolus. 219. **Joves.** This form of the name,
which Chaucer uses several times in the poem and in the *Troilus* is the OF. form (nom. case). 220. **lysse**, abatement. 223.
tok arryvage, landed, went ashore. 226. **Achate**, Achates, the close companion of Æneas. 228. **queynt**, strange, curious
(so that Æneas would not recognize her at first).

She made Eneas so in grace 240
Of Dido, quene of that contree,
That, shortly for to tellen, she
Becam hys love, and let hym doo
Al that weddynge longeth too.
What shulde I speke more queynte, 245
Or peyne me my wordes peynte
To speke of love? Hyt wol not be;
I kan not of that faculte.
And eke to telle the manere
How they aqueynteden in-fere, 250
Hyt were a long proces to telle,
And over-long for yow to dwelle.

Ther sawgh I grave how Eneas
Tolde Dido every caas
That hym was tyd upon the see. 255

And after grave was, how shee
Made of hym shortly at oo word
Hyr lyf, hir love, hir lust, hir lord,
And dide hym al the reverence,
And leyde on hym al the dispence, 260
That any woman myghte do,
Wenynge hyt had al be so
As he hir swor; and herby demed
That he was good, for he such semed.
Allas! what harm doth apparence, 265
Whan hit is fals in existence!
For he to hir a traytour was;
Wherfore she slow hirself, allas!
Loo, how a woman doth amys
To love him that unknowen ys! 270
For, be Cryste, lo, thus yt fareth:
"Hyt is not al gold that glareth."
For also browke I wel myn hed,
Ther may be under godlyhed
Kevered many a shrewed vice. 275
Therfore be no wyght so nyce,
To take a love oonly for chere,
Or speche, or for frendly manere,

For this shal every woman fynde,
That som man, of his pure kynde, 280
Wol shewen outward the fayreste,
Tyl he have caught that what him leste;
And thanne wol he causes fynde,
And swere how that she ys unkynde,
Or fals, or privy, or double was. 285
Al this seye I by Eneas
And Dido, and hir nyce lest,
That loved al to sone a gest;
Therfore I wol seye a proverbe,
That "he that fully knoweth th'erbe 290
May saufly leye hyt to his yë";
Withoute drede, this ys no lye.

But let us speke of Eneas,
How he betrayed hir, allas!
And lefte hir ful unkyndely. 295
So when she saw al-utterly,
That he wolde hir of trouthe fayle,
And wende fro hir to Itayle,
She gan to wringe hir hondes two.
"Allas!" quod she, "what me ys woo! 300
Allas! is every man thus trewe,
That every yere wolde have a newe,
Yf hit so longe tyme dure,
Or elles three, peraventure?
As thus: of oon he wolde have fame 305
In magnyfiynge of hys name;
Another for frendshippe, seyth he;
And yet ther shal the thridde be
That shal be take for delyt,
Loo, or for synguler profit." 310
In suche wordes gan to pleyne
Dydo of hir grete peyne,
As me mette redely;
Non other auctour alegge I.
"Allas!" quod she, "my swete herte, 315
Have pitee on my sorwes smerte,
And slee mee not! goo noght awey!

245. **What,** why. **queynte,** subtly. 248. **faculte,** art, science. 250. **aqueynteden in-fere,** became acquainted. 266. **existence,** reality. 272. **glareth,** glitters. 273. **also browke . . .** as I may indeed keep my head. 275. **Kevered,** covered. **shrewed,** wicked. 276. **nyce,** foolish. 277. **chere,** face, looks. 280. **pure kynde,** very nature. 282. **that what him leste,** that which pleases him, what he desires. 285. **privy,** stealthy, furtive, but it may be used for intimacies with the other sex. 287. **nyce lest,** foolish desire. 289. **a proverbe.** The proverb which follows is not common, but it occurs in the *Panthère d'Amours.* See Baugh, *Britannica: Festschrift für Hermann M. Flasdieck* (Heidelberg, 1960), pp. 51–61. 302. **a newe,** a new love. 310. **synguler profit,** special advantage. 313. **me mette,** I dreamed. **redely,** truly.

O woful Dido, welaway!"
Quod she to hirselve thoo.
"O Eneas, what wol ye doo?   320
O that your love, ne your bonde
That ye have sworn with your ryght honde,
Ne my crewel deth," quod she,
"May holde yow stille here with me!
O haveth of my deth pitee!   325
Iwys, my dere herte, ye
Knowen ful wel that never yit,
As ferforth as I hadde wyt,
Agylte [I] yow in thoght ne dede.
O, have ye men such goodlyhede   330
In speche, and never a dele of trouthe?
Allas, that ever hadde routhe
Any woman on any man!
Now see I wel, and telle kan,
We wrechched wymmen konne noon art;   335
For certeyn, for the more part,
Thus we be served everychone.
How sore that ye men konne groone,
Anoon as we have yow receyved,
Certaynly we ben deceyvyd!   340
For, though your love laste a seson,
Wayte upon the conclusyon,
And eke how that ye determynen,
And for the more part diffynen.

    "O, welawey that I was born!   345
For thorgh yow is my name lorn,
And alle myn actes red and songe
Over al thys lond, on every tonge.
O wikke Fame! for ther nys
Nothing so swift, lo, as she is!   350
O, soth ys, every thing ys wyst,
Though hit be kevered with the myst.
Eke, though I myghte duren ever,
That I have don rekever I never,
That I ne shal be seyd, allas,   355

Yshamed be thourgh Eneas,
And that I shal thus juged be,—
'Loo, ryght as she hath don, now she
Wol doo eftsones, hardely;'
Thus seyth the peple prively."   360
But that is don, is not to done;
Al hir compleynt ne al hir moone,
Certeyn, avayleth hir not a stre.
    And when she wiste sothly he
Was forth unto his shippes goon,   365
She into hir chambre wente anoon
And called on hir suster Anne,
And gan hir to compleyne thanne;
And seyde, that she cause was
That she first loved him, allas!   370
And thus counseylled hir thertoo.
But what! when this was seyd and doo,
She rof hirselve to the herte,
And deyde thorgh the wounde smerte.
And al the maner how she deyde,   375
And al the wordes that she seyde,
Whoso to knowe hit hath purpos,
Rede Virgile in Eneydos
Or the Epistle of Ovyde,
What that she wrot or that she dyde;   380
And nere hyt to long to endyte,
Be God, I wolde hyt here write.
    But welaway! the harm, the routhe,
That hath betyd for such untrouthe,
As men may ofte in bokes rede,   385
And al day se hyt yet in dede,
That for to thynken hyt, a tene is.
    Loo, Demophon, duk of Athenys,
How he forswor hym ful falsly,
And traysed Phillis wikkidly,   390
That kynges doghtre was of Trace,
And falsly gan hys terme pace;
And when she wiste that he was fals,

---

329. Agylte, wronged. **335. konne noon art,** are unskilled (in the ways of the world). **338. How,** however. **342. Wayte upon,** wait and see. **343. determynen,** decide. **344. for the more part,** in general. **diffynen,** do at the end. **353. duren,** last, live. **354. That . . . never,** (I might) never make up for what I have done. **355. seyd . . . Yshamed be,** said to be put to shame. **359. eftsones,** again. **361.** What is done is not to be done. **373. rof,** rived, pierced. **378. Eneydos,** gen. case from the fact that titles were often in this form, *e.g. Æneidos liber primus,* etc. **379. the Epistle of Ovyde,** Ovid, *Heroides,* Epist. VII, Dido to Æneas. **381. nere,** were it not. **386. al day,** constantly. **388. Loo, Demophon.** The examples which follow are all represented by epistles in Ovid's *Heroides.* In some cases Chaucer may have remembered details from other versions of the stories encountered in his reading. Demophoon, betrothed to Phyllis, did not appear on his wedding day.

She heng hirself ryght be the hals,
For he had doon hir such untrouthe.   395
Loo! was not this a woo and routhe?
   Eke lo! how fals and reccheles
Was to Breseyda Achilles,
And Paris to Oenone;
And Jason to Isiphile,   400
And eft Jason to Medea;
And Ercules to Dyanira,
For he left hir for Yole,
That made hym cache his deth, parde.
   How fals eke was he Theseus,   405
That, as the story telleth us,
How he betrayed Adriane;
The devel be hys soules bane!
For had he lawghed, had he loured,
He moste have ben al devoured,   410
Yf Adriane ne had ybe.
And, for she had of hym pite,
She made hym fro the dethe escape,
And he made hir a ful fals jape;
For aftir this, withyn a while,   415
He lefte hir slepynge in an ile
Deserte allone, ryght in the se,
And stal away, and let hir be,
And took hir suster Phedra thoo
With him, and gan to shippe goo.   420
And yet he had ysworn to here
On al that ever he myghte swere,

That, so she saved hym hys lyf,
He wolde have take hir to hys wif;
For she desired nothing ellis,   425
In certeyn, as the book us tellis.
   But to excusen Eneas
Fullyche of al his grete trespas,
The book seyth Mercurie, sauns fayle,
Bad hym goo into Itayle,   430
And leve Auffrikes regioun,
And Dido and hir faire toun.
   Thoo sawgh I grave how to Itayle
Daun Eneas is goo to sayle;
And how the tempest al began,   435
And how he loste hys sterisman,
Which that the stere, or he tok kep,
Smot over bord, loo! as he slep.
   And also sawgh I how Sybile
And Eneas, besyde an yle,   440
To helle wente, for to see
His fader, Anchyses the free;
How he ther fond Palinurus,
And Dido, and eke Deiphebus;
And every turment eke in helle   445
Saugh he, which is longe to telle;
Which whoso willeth for to knowe,
He moste rede many a rowe
On Virgile or on Claudian,
Or Daunte, that hit telle kan.   450
   Tho saugh I grave al the aryvayle

394. hals, neck. **398. Breseyda.** In the third epistle of Ovid's *Heroides* (Briseis to Achilles) Briseis, captured by Achilles but given to Agamemnon, chides Achilles for not seeking to get her back, preferring to sulk rather than accept her restoration. **399. Paris to Oenone.** Paris deserted Oenone when he went to fetch Helen. **400. Jason.** Jason deserted Hypsipyle, queen of the island of Lemnos, after she had borne him two children. She died of grief. For Jason's leaving Medea see the note to *BD* 726. **402. Ercules to Dyanira.** The centaur Nessus, attempting to carry off Deinira, was killed by Hercules. Before he died Nessus told Deinira to keep some of his blood and, if it ever became necessary, to use it as a charm to preserve her husband's love. Some time later, jealous of Hercules' attention to the maiden Iole, Deinira dipped one of his robes in the blood. When he wore it he was fatally poisoned. **405. Theseus.** Ariadne, falling in love with Theseus, gave him the sword with which he slew the Minotaur and the thread by which he found his way out of the labyrinth. He promised to marry her, but deserted her on the way home and took her sister Phaedra with him. **409. had he lawghed, had he loured,** *i.e.* under all circumstances. **414. made . . . jape,** played a full false trick on her. **417. Deserte,** desolate. **426. tellis.** The normal form in Chaucer is *telleth* (cf. l. 406); the Northern form is here used for the sake of rime. **429. Mercurie.** In Book IV of the *Æneid* Mercury bears the command of Jove for Æneas to depart. **434. goo,** gone. **435. the tempest,** described in *Æneid,* Book V. **436. hys sterisman,** Palinurus, who was overpowered by Sleep and dashed overboard. **437. the stere,** the tiller, on which Palinurus had a firm grip and which went down with him. **439. Sybile and Eneas.** In Book VI of the *Æneid* Æneas visits the temple of Apollo at Cumae, actually not near the *yle* of Crete, and begs the Sibyl, the priestess of Apollo, to see his father in the underworld. She accompanies him on the journey through Hades. **444. Deiphebus,** son of King Priam. After the death of Paris he married Helen, who treacherously caused his death at the capture of Troy. **448. rowe,** line. **449. Claudian,** Claudius Claudianus, whose *De Raptu Proserpinae* (c. A.D. 400) relates the carrying off by Pluto of Proserpina to become queen of the lower regions, describes the lower world rather by allusion than formally. **450. Daunte,** Dante. **451. aryvayle,** landing.

That Eneas had in Itayle;
And with kyng Latyne hys tretee
And alle the batayles that hee
Was at hymself, and eke hys knyghtis,　　455
Or he had al ywonne hys ryghtis;
And how he Turnus reft his lyf,
And wan Lavina to his wif;
And alle the mervelous signals
Of the goddys celestials;　　460
How, mawgree Juno, Eneas,
For al hir sleight and hir compas,
Acheved al his aventure,
For Jupiter took of hym cure
At the prayer of Venus,—　　465
The whiche I preye alwey save us,
And us ay of oure sorwes lyghte!
　　When I had seen al this syghte
In this noble temple thus,
"A, Lord!" thoughte I, "that madest us,　　470
Yet sawgh I never such noblesse
Of ymages, ne such richesse,
As I saugh graven in this chirche;
But not wot I whoo did hem wirche,
Ne where I am, ne in what contree.　　475
But now wol I goo out and see,
Ryght at the wiket, yf y kan
See owhere any stiryng man,
That may me telle where I am."
　　When I out at the dores cam,　　480

I faste aboute me beheld.
Then sawgh I but a large feld,
As fer as that I myghte see,
Withouten toun, or hous, or tree,
Or bush, or grass, or eryd lond;　　485
For al the feld nas but of sond
As smal as man may se yet lye
In the desert of Lybye;
Ne no maner creature
That ys yformed be Nature　　490
Ne sawgh I, me to rede or wisse.
"O Crist!" thoughte I, "that art in blysse,
Fro fantome and illusion
Me save!" and with devocion
Myn eyen to the hevene I caste.　　495
　　Thoo was I war, lo! at the laste,
That faste be the sonne, as hye
As kenne myghte I with myn yë,
Me thoughte I sawgh an egle sore,
But that hit semed moche more　　500
Then I had any egle seyn.
But this as sooth as deth, certeyn,
Hyt was of gold, and shon so bryght
That never sawe men such a syght,
But yf the heven had ywonne　　505
Al newe of gold another sonne;
So shone the egles fethers bryghte,
And somwhat dounward gan hyt lyghte.

Explicit liber primus.

453. kyng Latyne, the aged king of the country around the mouth of the Tiber, who had been warned in a dream that his daughter Lavinia should marry one from a foreign land. Æneas's destiny seems about to be fulfilled. But Juno's hostility is not yet appeased. She stirs up Turnus, King of the Rutilians, a neighboring tribe, who had hoped to marry Lavinia. In a dream Æneas is advised by Father Tiber to seek the help of the Arcadians a short distance upstream. Aided by them and their friends the Etruscans, he is victorious in the battle which follows. The poem ends as Æneas, in single combat, plunges his sword in Turnus's breast. That he married Lavinia is only inferred. These events, which occupy the last six books of the *Æneid*, are reduced to seventeen lines in Chaucer. **457. he Turnus reft his lyf,** he deprived Turnus of his life. **459. signals,** signs,? manifestations. **462. sleight,** cunning. **compas,** craft. **464. cure,** care. **467. lyghte,** alleviate. **474. did hem wirche,** caused them to be made. **478. owhere,** anywhere. **stiryng,** stirring. **485. eryd,** plowed. **487. smal,** fine. **488. the desert of Lybye.** It has been suggested that the mention of Libya is due to the association with Venus and Jove. See J. M. Steadman, *MLN,* LXXVI. 196–201. **491. rede or wisse,** advise or instruct. **499. an egle.** The description of the eagle seems to be patterned after Dante, *Purgatorio,* IX. 19–21.

Book II

Incipit liber secundus.

Proem

Now herkeneth, every maner man
That Englissh understonde kan,   510
And listeneth of my dreme to lere.
For now at erste shul ye here
So sely an avisyoun,
That Isaye, ne Scipioun,
Ne kyng Nabugodonosor,   515
Pharoo, Turnus, ne Elcanor,
Ne mette such a dreme as this!
Now faire blisfull, O Cipris,
So be my favour at this tyme!
And ye, me to endite and ryme   520
Helpeth, that on Parnaso duelle,
Be Elicon, the clere welle.
O Thought, that wrot al that I mette,
And in the tresorye hyt shette
Of my brayn, now shal men se   525
Yf any vertu in the be,
To telle al my drem aryght.
Now kythe thyn engyn and myght!

The Dream

This egle, of which I have yow told,
That shon with fethres as of gold,   530
Which that so high gan to sore,

I gan beholde more and more,
To se the beaute and the wonder;
But never was ther dynt of thonder,
Ne that thyng that men calle fouder,   535
That smyt somtyme a tour to powder,
And in his swifte comynge brende,
That so swithe gan descende
As this foul, when hyt behelde
That I a-roume was in the felde;   540
And with hys grymme pawes stronge,
Withyn hys sharpe nayles longe,
Me, fleynge, in a swap he hente,
And with hys sours ayen up wente,
Me caryinge in his clawes starke   545
As lyghtly as I were a larke,
How high, I can not telle yow,
For I cam up, y nyste how.
For so astonyed and asweved
Was every vertu in my heved,   550
What with his sours and with my drede,
That al my felynge gan to dede;
For-whi hit was to gret affray.
    Thus I longe in hys clawes lay,
Til at the laste he to me spak   555
In mannes vois, and seyde, "Awak!
And be not agast so, for shame!"

512. at erste, for the first time. **513. sely,** wonderful. **514. Isaye,** see *Isaiah,* 1. **Scipioun,** for the *Somnium Scipionis,* see the note to *PF* 31. **515. Nabugodonsor,** the common form of Nebuchadnezzar in the Middle Ages. For his dream see *Daniel,* 1–4. **516. Pharoo,** Pharaoh; see *Genesis,* 12: 1–7. **Turnus,** probably the Turnus mentioned in l. 457, whom Iris warned (*Æneid,* IX. 1 ff.) of the arrival of Æneas. Elcanor has not been convincingly identified. For the many conjectures see Robinson, p. 782. **517. mette,** dreamed. **518. Cipris,** Venus. **519. favour,** aid, support. **521. Parnaso,** the Italian form, under the influence of Dante, whom this part of the Proem echoes (cf. *Inferno,* II. 7–9; *Paradiso,* I. 16). **522. Elicon,** Helicon, a mountain, but often confused in the Middle Ages with the springs which were upon it. **523. O Thought.** Cf. Dante: "O mente, che scrivesti ciò ch'io vidi" (*Inferno,* II. 8.) **528. engyn,** skill. **529. This egle.** Dante (*Purgatorio,* IX. 28–31) describing the descent of the eagle says, "having wheeled awhile, terrible as lightning, he descended and snatched me up far as the fiery sphere." **535. fouder,** thunderbolt. **536. smyt,** smites. **537. brende.** Chaucer conceives of a thunderbolt as a kind of meteor burning in its swift passage through the air. **538. swithe,** quickly. **539. As this foul.** The meaning is clearer than the syntax. The sense is, "And in its swift coming burned, as this fowl (seemed to), that so quickly began to descend when it perceived. . . ." **540. a-roume,** at large. **543. fleynge,** flying. **swap,** swoop. **hente,** seized. **544. sours,** upward flight. **549. astonyed and asweved,** astonished and bewildered. **550. vertu,** faculty. **heved,** head. **552. dede,** become dead. **553. affray,** fright.

And called me tho by my name,
And, for I shulde the bet abreyde,
Me mette, "Awak," to me he seyde,   560
Ryght in the same vois and stevene
That useth oon I koude nevene;
And with that vois, soth for to seyn,
My mynde cam to me ageyn,
For hyt was goodly seyd to me,   565
So nas hyt never wont to be.
    And herewithal I gan to stere,
And he me in his feet to bere,
Til that he felte that I had hete,
And felte eke tho myn herte bete.   570
And thoo gan he me to disporte,
And with wordes to comforte,
And sayde twyes, "Seynte Marye!
Thou art noyous for to carye,
And nothyng nedeth it, pardee!   575
For, also wis God helpe me,
As thou noon harme shalt have of this;
And this caas that betyd the is,
Is for thy lore and for thy prow.
Let see! darst thou yet loke now?   580
Be ful assured, boldely,
I am thy frend." And therwith I
Gan for to wondren in my mynde.
"O God!" thoughte I, "that madest kynde,
Shal I noon other weyes dye?   585
Wher Joves wol me stellyfye,
Or what thing may this sygnifye?
I neyther am Ennok, ne Elye,
Ne Romulus, ne Ganymede,
That was ybore up, as men rede,   590
To hevene with daun Jupiter

And mad the goddys botiller."
Loo, this was thoo my fantasye!
But he that bar me gan espye
That I so thoughte, and seyde this: 595
"Thow demest of thyself amys;
For Joves ys not theraboute—
I dar wel put the out of doute—
To make of the as yet a sterre.
But er I bere the moche ferre,   600
I wol the telle what I am,
And whider thou shalt, and why I cam
To do thys, so that thou take
Good herte, and not for fere quake."
"Gladly," quod I. "Now wel," quod he,   605
"First, I, that in my fete have the,
Of which thou hast a fere and wonder,
Am dwellynge with the god of thonder,
Which that men callen Jupiter,
That dooth me flee ful ofte fer   610
To do al hys comaundement.
And for this cause he hath me sent
To the; now herke, be thy trouthe!
Certeyn, he hath of the routhe,
That thou so longe trewely   615
Hast served so ententyfly
Hys blynde nevew Cupido,
And faire Venus also,
Withoute guerdon ever yit,
And neverthelesse hast set thy wit—   620
Although that in thy hed ful lyte is—
To make bookes, songes, dytees,
In ryme, or elles in cadence,
As thou best canst, in reverence
Of Love, and of hys servantes eke,   625

559. **abreyde,** come to. 561. **stevene,** voice. 562. **nevene,** name. 573. **Seynte,** presumably the OF. feminine form. 576. **For, also wis . . .,** for so certainly as may God help me, thou shalt have no harm from this. 578. **this caas . . .,** this chance that has happened to thee. 579. **prow,** profit. 586. **Wher,** whether, often used as a mere sign of interrogation; see Language, §75. **stellyfye,** make into a constellation, as were Hercules, Perseus, and others. 588. **Ennok, ne Elye.** Enoch nor Elijah; see *Genesis,* 5: 24, and *2 Kings,* 2: 11. 589. **Romulus,** carried up to heaven by Mars (Ovid, *Metam.,* xiv. 805–28). **Ganymede,** whom Jove in the form of an eagle snatched up to heaven (Ovid, *Metam.,* x. 155–61; Virgil, *Æneid,* i. 28). 592. **the goddys botiller.** Cf. *Ovide Moralisé,* x. 752: *Si le fist bouteillier dou ciel,* and the Latin moralization of Pierre Bersuire: *pincerna deorum effectus.* 597. **ys not theraboute,** does not have in mind. 600. **ferre,** farther. 621. **lyte,** little. 622. **dytees.** In OF. this is a general word for a literary composition of any sort, but also has the meaning *song* (carmen). 623. **cadence.** This is the first instance of the word in English cited by the *NED* and the meaning is uncertain. C. G. Child calls attention to Puttenham, *The Art of English Poesie,* Bk. ii, ch. vii–viii, where it is almost synonymous with *rime,* but probably distinguishes between correspondences such as *subjéction, diréction* and rimes of monosyllables or words accented on the last syllable. For further discussion and references see M. M. Morgan, *MLR,* xlvii. 156–64. The word probably had more than one meaning.

That have hys servyse soght, and seke;
And peynest the to preyse hys art,
Although thou haddest never part;
Wherfore, also God me blesse,
Joves halt hyt gret humblesse, 630
And vertu eke, that thou wolt make
A-nyght ful ofte thyn hed to ake
In thy studye, so thou writest
And evermo of love enditest,
In honour of hym and in preysynges, 635
And in his folkes furtherynges,
And in hir matere al devisest,
And noght hym nor his folk dispisest,
Although thou maist goo in the daunce
Of hem that hym lyst not avaunce. 640
  "Wherfore, as I seyde, ywys,
Jupiter considereth this,
And also, beau sir, other thynges;
That is, that thou hast no tydynges
Of Loves folk yf they be glade, 645
Ne of noght elles that God made;
And noght oonly fro fer contree
That ther no tydynge cometh to thee,
But of thy verray neyghebores,
That duellen almost at thy dores, 650
Thou herist neyther that ne this;
For when thy labour doon al ys,
And hast mad alle thy rekenynges,
In stede of reste and newe thynges,
Thou goost hom to thy hous anoon; 655
And, also domb as any stoon,
Thou sittest at another book
Tyl fully daswed ys thy look,
And lyvest thus as an heremyte,
Although thyn abstynence ys lyte. 660

  "And therfore Joves, thorgh hys grace,
Wol that I bere the to a place
Which that hight the Hous of Fame,
To do the som disport and game,
In som recompensacion 665
Of labour and devocion,
That thou hast had, loo causeles,
To Cupido, the rechcheles!
And thus this god, thorgh his merite,
Wol with som maner thing the quyte, 670
So that thou wolt be of good chere.
For truste wel that thou shalt here,
When we be come there I seye,
Mo wonder thynges, dar I leye,
Of Loves folke moo tydynges, 675
Both sothe sawes and lesynges;
And moo loves newe begonne,
And longe yserved loves wonne,
And moo loves casuelly
That ben betyd, no man wot why, 680
But as a blynd man stert an hare;
And more jolytee and fare,
While that they fynde love of stele,
As thinketh hem, and over-al wele;
Mo discordes, moo jelousies, 685
Mo murmures, and moo novelries,
And moo dissymulacions,
And feyned reparacions;
And moo berdys in two houres
Withoute rasour or sisoures 690
Ymad, then greynes be of sondes;
And eke moo holdynge in hondes,
And also moo renovelaunces
Of olde forleten aqueyntaunces;
Mo love-dayes and acordes 695

---

628. Although thou haddest never part. Lack of skill or success in love is a pretence which Chaucer adopts on several occasions, doubtless for humorous effect and to avoid giving the impression that he writes about love as an expert. **630. halt,** holds. **637. in hir matere,** in matters pertaining to them (thou describest everything). **639. goo in the daunce . . .,** join the circle of those whom it pleases him not to advance. **653. thy rekenynges.** In 1374 Chaucer had been appointed Controller of Wool Customs with the usual stipulation that he keep the books with his own hand. **668. rechcheles,** indifferent. **669. merite,** virtue, righteousness; cf. l. 2019. **671. So that,** provided. **673. there,** where. **674. leye,** wager. **679. casuelly,** by chance, accidentally. **681. stert,** contracted form of *sterteth*, starts, rouses; cf. *stant*, l. 719. **682. fare,** fuss, to-do. **684. over-al wele,** good in every way. **686. novelries,** quarrels, disputes; cf. OF. *novelerie.* **688. reparacions,** amends, reconciliations. **689–91. moo berdys . . . Ymad,** *lit.* more beards trimmed; but *to make a beard* was a common expression meaning "to delude," "get the better of (by trickery)." See A 4096, D 361. **692. holdynge in hondes,** keeping (a lover) hopeful with false hopes. **693. renovelaunces,** renewings. **694. forleten,** abandoned. **695. love-dayes,** reconciliations, agreements. See note to A 258.

Then on instrumentes be cordes;
And eke of loves moo eschaunges
Then ever cornes were in graunges,—
Unnethe maistow trowen this?"
Quod he. "Noo, helpe me God so wys!"   700
Quod I. "Noo? why?" quod he. "For hyt
Were impossible, to my wit,
Though that Fame had alle the pies
In al a realme, and alle the spies,
How that yet she shulde here al this,   705
Or they espie hyt." "O yis, yis!"
Quod he to me, "that kan I preve
Be reson worthy for to leve,
So that thou yeve thyn advertence
To understonde my sentence.   710
    "First shalt thou here where she duelleth,
And so thyn oune bok hyt tellith.
Hir paleys stant, as I shal seye,
Ryght even in myddes of the weye
Betwixen hevene, erthe, and see;   715
That what so ever in al these three
Is spoken, either privy or aperte,
The way therto ys so overte,
And stant eke in so juste a place
That every soune mot to hyt pace,   720
Or what so cometh from any tonge,
Be hyt rouned, red, or songe,
Or spoke in suerte or in drede,
Certeyn, hyt moste thider nede.
    "Now herkene wel, for-why I wille   725
Tellen the a propre skille
And a worthy demonstracioun
In myn ymagynacioun.
    "Geffrey, thou wost ryght wel this,
That every kyndely thyng that is   730
Hath a kyndely stede ther he
May best in hyt conserved be;

Unto which place every thyng,
Thorgh his kyndely enclynyng,
Moveth for to come to,   735
Whan that hyt is awey therfro;
As thus: loo, thou maist alday se
That any thing that hevy be,
As stoon, or led, or thyng of wighte,
And bere hyt never so hye on highte,   740
Lat goo thyn hand, hit falleth doun.
Ryght so seye I be fyre or soun,
Or smoke, or other thynges lyghte;
Alwey they seke upward on highte,
While ech of hem is at his large,   745
Lyght thing upward, and dounward charge.
And for this cause mayst thou see
That every ryver to the see
Enclyned ys to goo by kynde,
And by these skilles, as I fynde,   750
Hath fyssh duellynge in floode and see,
And treës eke in erthe bee.
Thus every thing, by thys reson,
Hath his propre mansyon,
To which hit seketh to repaire,   755
As there hit shulde not apaire.
Loo, this sentence ys knowen kouthe
Of every philosophres mouthe,
As Aristotle and daun Platon,
And other clerkys many oon;   760
And to confirme my resoun,
Thou wost wel this, that spech is soun,
Or elles no man myghte hyt here;
Now herke what y wol the lere.
    "Soun ys noght but eyr ybroken,   765
And every speche that ys spoken,
Lowde or pryvee, foul or fair,
In his substaunce ys but air;
For as flaumbe ys but lyghted smoke,

696. **cordes,** strings (cf. *TC* 5. 443), although often considered a shortened form of *accord*, harmony. The latter is not well attested in ME. and is not supported by OF. Chords were unknown in the instrumental music of Chaucer's time. The bass lute had twenty-four strings, the harp sometimes thirty. See J. B. Colvert, *MLN*, LXIX. 239 ff. **700. wys,** certainly. **703. pies,** magpies, often taught to speak. **709. So that,** provided. **advertence,** attention. **710. sentence,** meaning. **712. thyn oune bok,** your favorite book, Ovid's *Metam.* For the description of the house of Fame see XII. 39–63. **722. rouned,** whispered. **723. in suerte or in drede,** in certainty or in doubt. **726. propre skille,** excellent reason. **727. worthy,** good, excellent. **728. ymagynacioun,** thinking, opinion. **730. every kyndely thyng,** everything in nature. Various sources for parts of the explanation which follows have been suggested, but no satisfactory original has yet been found for the discussion as a whole. **731. stede ther,** place where. **745. at his large,** *i.e.* free to move. **746. charge,** burden, something heavy. **756. apaire,** suffer injury. **757. kouthe,** manifestly.

Ryght soo soune ys air ybroke.   770
But this may be in many wyse,
Of which I wil the twoo devyse,
As soune that cometh of pipe or harpe.
For whan a pipe is blowen sharpe,
The air ys twyst with violence   775
And rent; loo, thys ys my sentence;
Eke, whan men harpe-strynges smyte,
Whether hyt be moche or lyte,
Loo, with the stroke the ayr tobreketh;
And ryght so breketh it when men speketh.   780
Thus wost thou wel what thing is speche.
    "Now hennesforth y wol the teche
How every speche, or noyse, or soun,
Thurgh hys multiplicacioun,
Thogh hyt were piped of a mous,   785
Mot nede come to Fames Hous.
I preve hyt thus—take hede now—
Be experience; for yf that thow
Throwe on water now a stoon,
Wel wost thou, hyt wol make anoon   790
A litel roundell as a sercle,
Paraunter brod as a covercle;
And ryght anoon thow shalt see wel,
That whele wol cause another whel,
And that the thridde, and so forth, brother,   795
Every sercle causynge other
Wydder than hymselve was;
And thus fro roundel to compas,
Ech aboute other goynge
Causeth of othres sterynge   800
And multiplyinge evermoo,
Til that hyt be so fer ygoo,
That hyt at bothe brynkes bee.
Although thou mowe hyt not ysee
Above, hyt gooth yet alway under,   805
Although thou thenke hyt a gret wonder.

And whoso seyth of trouthe I varye,
Bid hym proven the contrarye.
And ryght thus every word, ywys,
That lowde or pryvee spoken ys,   810
Moveth first an ayr aboute,
And of thys movynge, out of doute,
Another ayr anoon ys meved,
As I have of the watir preved,
That every cercle causeth other.   815
Ryght so of ayr, my leve brother;
Everych ayr in other stereth
More and more, and speche up bereth,
Or voys, or noyse, or word, or soun,
Ay through multiplicacioun,   820
Til hyt be atte Hous of Fame,—
Take yt in ernest or in game.
    "Now have I told, yf thou have mynde,
How speche or soun, of pure kynde,
Enclyned ys upward to meve;   825
This, mayst thou fele, wel I preve.
And that [same] place, ywys,
That every thyng enclyned to ys,
Hath his kyndelyche stede:
That sheweth hyt, withouten drede,   830
That kyndely the mansioun
Of every speche, of every soun,
Be hyt eyther foul or fair,
Hath hys kynde place in ayr.
And syn that every thyng that is   835
Out of hys kynde place, ywys,
Moveth thidder for to goo,
Yif hyt aweye be therfroo,
As I have before preved the,
Hyt seweth, every soun, parde,   840
Moveth kyndely to pace
Al up into his kyndely place.
And this place of which I telle,

---

772. devyse, explain, describe. **787. preve**, prove. **788. experience**, experiment. The illustration which follows is found in both Boethius, *De Musica*, Bk. I, ch. 14 (a work which Chaucer refers to in *The Nun's Priest's Tale*, B 4484) and in Vincent of Beauvais, *Speculum Naturale*, Bk. xxv, ch. 58, which cites Boethius, and Bk. v, ch. 18. **791. roundell**, ring. **792. covercle**, pot-lid., **798. fro roundel to compas**, from small ring to large circle. **801. multiplyinge**, increasing in size. **816. leve**, dear. **817. in other . . .**, stirs more and more in another (body of) air. The emendation *another*, proposed by Willert and adopted by Koch and Robinson, is attractive but is without MS authority. **823. yf thou have mynde**, if you remember. **825. meve**, move. **827.** The line is corrupt in all the MSS and, even as amended, does not make very clear sense. The meaning appears to be: Each place (cf. *mansioun*, below) to which every individual thing is inclined to go has its natural location. **840. seweth**, follows.

Ther as Fame lyst to duelle,
Ys set amyddys of these three,   845
Heven, erthe, and eke the see,
As most conservatyf the soun.
Than ys this the conclusyoun,
That every speche of every man,
As y the telle first began,   850
Moveth up on high to pace
Kyndely to Fames place.
    "Telle me this now feythfully,
Have y not preved thus symply,
Withouten any subtilite   855
Of speche, or gret prolixite
Of termes of philosophie,
Of figures of poetrie,
Or colours of rethorike?
Pardee, hit oughte the to lyke!   860
For hard langage and hard matere
Ys encombrous for to here
Attones; wost thou not wel this?"
And y answered and seyde, "Yis."
    "A ha!" quod he, "lo, so I can   865
Lewedly to a lewed man
Speke, and shewe hym swyche skiles
That he may shake hem be the biles,
So palpable they shulden be.
But telle me this, now pray y the,   870
How thinketh the my conclusyon?"
[Quod he]. "A good persuasion,"
Quod I, "hyt is; and lyke to be
Ryght so as thou hast preved me."
"Be God," quod he, "and as I leve,   875
Thou shalt have yet, or hit be eve,
Of every word of thys sentence
A preve by experience,
And with thyn eres heren wel
Top and tayl, and everydel,   880

That every word that spoken ys
Cometh into Fames Hous, ywys,
As I have seyd; what wilt thou more?"
And with this word upper to sore
He gan, and seyde, "Be seynt Jame,   885
Now wil we speken al of game!"
    "How farest thou?" quod he to me.
"Wel," quod I. "Now see," quod he,
"By thy trouthe, yond adoun,
Wher that thou knowest any toun,   890
Or hous, or any other thing.
And whan thou hast of ought knowyng,
Looke that thou warne me,
And y anoon shal telle the
How fer that thou art now therfro."   895
    And y adoun gan loken thoo,
And beheld feldes and playnes,
And now hilles, and now mountaynes,
Now valeyes, now forestes,
And now unnethes grete bestes;   900
Now ryveres, now citees,
Now tounes, and now grete trees,
Now shippes seyllynge in the see.
    But thus sone in a while he
Was flowen fro the ground so hye   905
That al the world, as to myn yë,
No more semed than a prikke;
Or elles was the air so thikke
That y ne myghte not discerne.
With that he spak to me as yerne,   910
And seyde, "Seest thou any token
Or ought that in the world is of spoken?"
I sayde, "Nay." "No wonder nys,"
Quod he, "for half so high as this
Nas Alixandre Macedo,   915
Ne the kyng, Daun Scipio.
That saw in dreme, at poynt-devys,

---

847. conservatyf, preserving. The use of the adjective without *of* is unusual. **858. figures of poetrie,** ornamental or rhetorical devices, especially patterns of thought. **859. colours of rethorike,** figures of speech. This and the preceding expression are not always clearly distinguishable, but cf. the note to *CT,* E 16. See an admirable discussion of the present passage by Florence E. Teager, "Chaucer's Eagle and the Rhetorical Colors," *PMLA,* XLVII. 410–18, and cf. J. W. H. Atkins, *English Literary Criticism: The Medieval Phase,* pp. 108–9. **860. lyke,** please. **866. Lewedly to a lewed man,** in a manner suitable to an unlearned man. **890. Wher,** whether. **900. unnethes,** scarcely, with difficulty. **907. prikke,** point, dot. **910. yerne,** eagerly. **911. token,** characteristic mark. **915. Alixandre Macedo.** In the medieval account of Alexander in the *De Preliis* and in derivatives of it such as the ME. *Wars of Alexander,* Alexander is carried through the air in a car borne by four griffins. **916. Daun Scipio.** See the note to *BD* 284. **917. at poynt-devys,** perfectly.

Helle and erthe and paradys;
Ne eke the wrechche Dedalus,
Ne his child, nyce Ykarus, 920
That fleigh so highe that the hete
Hys wynges malt, and he fel wete
In myd the see, and ther he dreynte,
For whom was maked moch compleynte.
  "Now turn upward," quod he, "thy face, 925
And behold this large space,
This eyr; but loke thou ne be
Adrad of hem that thou shalt se;
For in this region, certeyn,
Duelleth many a citezeyn, 930
Of which that speketh Daun Plato.
These ben the eyryssh bestes, lo!"
And so saw y all that meynee
Boothe goon and also flee.
"Now," quod he thoo, "cast up thyn yë. 935
Se yonder, loo, the Galaxie,
Which men clepeth the Mylky Wey,
For hit ys whit (and somme, parfey,
Kallen hyt Watlynge Strete)
That ones was ybrent with hete, 940
Whan the sonnes sone, the rede,
That highte Pheton, wolde lede
Algate hys fader carte, and gye.
The carte-hors gonne wel espye
That he koude no governaunce, 945
And gonne for to lepe and launce,
And beren hym now up, now doun,
Til that he sey the Scorpioun,

Which that in heven a sygne is yit.
And he, for ferde, loste hys wyt 950
Of that, and let the reynes gon
Of his hors; and they anoon
Gonne up to mounte and doun descende,
Til bothe the eyr and erthe brende;
Til Jupiter, loo, atte laste, 955
Hym slow, and fro the carte caste.
Loo, ys it not a gret myschaunce
To lete a fool han governaunce
Of thing that he can not demeyne?"
And with this word, soth for to seyne, 960
He gan alway upper to sore,
And gladded me ay more and more,
So feythfully to me spak he.
  Tho gan y loken under me
And beheld the ayerissh bestes, 965
Cloudes, mystes, and tempestes,
Snowes, hayles, reynes, wyndes,
And th'engendrynge in hir kyndes,
All the wey thrugh which I cam.
"O God!" quod y, "that made Adam, 970
Moche ys thy myght and thy noblesse!"
And thoo thoughte y upon Boece,
That writ, "A thought may flee so hye,
Wyth fetheres of Philosophye,
To passen everych element; 975
And whan he hath so fer ywent,
Than may be seen, behynde hys bak,
Cloude,"—and al that y of spak.
  Thoo gan y wexen in a were,

---

919. wrechche, wretched. **Dedalus . . . Ykarus.** The story is in Ovid, *Metam.*, VIII. 183 ff. Daedalus to escape from Crete fashioned wings for himself and his son Icarus. In their flight Icarus mounted too near the sun. The heat melted the wax with which the wings were attached; the boy fell into the sea and was drowned. **930. citezeyn,** denizen, inhabitant, possibly suggested by the *vagantes aerios cives* of Alanus de Insulis, *Anticlaudianus*, Bk. IV, ch. 5. **932. eyryssh bestes,** the signs of the Zodiac and constellations such as *Aquila, Pegasus*, etc. W. P. Ker's identification with the *daemones* of the *Anticlaudianus* is open to several objections. Cf. also W. Nelson Francis, *MLN*, LXIV. 339–41. **933. meynee,** company. **934. Boothe goon and also flee,** both walk and also fly. **939. Watlynge Strete,** a name early given to the Roman road which ran from London to Wroxeter (near Shrewsbury). After Chaucer's time it was often applied to other Roman roads. It is one of a number of popular names by which the Milky Way has been known in different countries. **940. That ones was ybrent with hete.** This is perhaps to be inferred but is not stated by Ovid. **942. Pheton,** Phaethon. See Ovid, *Metam.*, II. 31–328. **943. carte,** chariot. **gye,** guide. **948. the Scorpioun,** one of the signs of the Zodiac. **950. for ferde,** for fear. This use of the past part. as a noun almost always occurs in the phrase *for ferde*. See *NED*. **959. demeyne,** manage. **963. feythfully,** reassuringly. **965. ayerissh bestes.** See note to l. 932. **966. Cloudes, mystes,** etc. Probably suggested by the *Anticlaudianus*, Bk. IV, ch. 4. **972. Boece,** Boethius. The passage referred to reads in Chaucer's translation (Bk. IV, Metre i, 1–7: "I [Philosophy] have, forthi, swifte fetheris that surmounten the heighte of the hevene. Whanne the swifte thoght hath clothid itself in tho fetheris, it despiseth the hateful erthes, and surmounteth the rowndnesse of the gret ayr; and it seth the clowdes byhynde his bak. . . ." **975. element,** celestial sphere. **979. were,** state of uncertainty or perplexity.

And seyde, "Y wot wel y am here;   980
But wher in body or in gost
I not, ywys; but God, thou wost!"
For more clere entendement
Nas me never yit ysent.
And than thoughte y on Marcian,   985
And eke on Anteclaudian,
That sooth was her descripsion
Of alle the hevenes region,
As fer as that y sey the preve;
Therfore y kan hem now beleve.   990
    With that this egle gan to crye,
"Lat be," quod he, "thy fantasye!
Wilt thou lere of sterres aught?"
"Nay, certeynly," quod y, "ryght naught."
"And why?" "For y am now to old."   995
"Elles I wolde the have told,"
Quod he, "the sterres names, lo,
And al the hevens sygnes therto,
And which they ben." "No fors," quod y.
"Yis, pardee!" quod he; "wostow why?   1000
For when thou redest poetrie,
How goddes gonne stellifye
Bridd, fissh, best, or him or here,
As the Raven, or eyther Bere,
Or Arionis harpe fyn,   1005
Castor, Pollux, or Delphyn,
Or Athalantes doughtres sevene,
How alle these arn set in hevene;
For though thou have hem ofte on honde,
Yet nostow not wher that they stonde."   1010
"No fors," quod y, "hyt is no nede.
I leve as wel, so God me spede,
Hem that write of this matere,
As though I knew her places here;

And eke they shynen here so bryghte,   1015
Hyt shulde shenden al my syghte
To loke on hem." "That may wel be,"
Quod he. And so forth bar he me
A while, and than he gan to crye,
That never herde I thing so hye,   1020
"Now up the hed, for al ys wel;
Seynt Julyan, loo, bon hostel!
Se here the Hous of Fame, lo!
Maistow not heren that I do?"
"What?" quod I. "The grete soun,"   1025
Quod he, "that rumbleth up and doun
In Fames Hous, full of tydynges,
Bothe of feir speche and chidynges,
And of fals and soth compouned.
Herke wel; hyt is not rouned.   1030
Herestow not the grete swogh?"
"Yis, parde!" quod y, "wel ynogh."
"And what soun is it lyk?" quod hee.
"Peter! lyk betynge of the see,"
Quod y, "ayen the roches holowe,   1035
Whan tempest doth the shippes swalowe;
And lat a man stonde, out of doute,
A myle thens, and here hyt route;
Or elles lyk the last humblynge
After the clappe of a thundringe,   1040
Whan Joves hath the air ybete.
But yt doth me for fere swete!"
"Nay, dred the not therof," quod he.
"Hyt is nothing will byten the;
Thou shalt non harm have trewely."   1045
    And with this word both he and y
As nygh the place arryved were
As men may casten with a spere.
Y nyste how, but in a strete

---

981. wher, whether. **981–2.** See *2 Corinthians*, 12: 2. **983. entendement,** understanding. **985. Marcian,** Martianus Capella (5th c.), author of a work on the Seven Liberal Arts called *De Nuptiis Philologiae et Mercurii*. Book VIII treats of astronomy. **986. Anteclaudian,** the work referred to in the notes to ll. 930, 932. Alanus de Insulis (d. 1202) was the author of another Latin poem, *De Planctu Naturae*, which Chaucer refers to in *PF* 316. **989. sey the preve,** saw the proof. **994. Nay, certeynly.** Chaucer was actually much interested in astronomy, but in his terrifying situation was not in a mood to learn more about it. The reference to his age is not to be taken seriously. **1004. the Raven,** the constellation *Corvus*. **eyther Bere,** Ursa Major or Ursa Minor. **1005. Arionis harpe,** the constellation *Lyra*. **1006. Castor, Pollux, or Delphyn,** the constellations *Gemini* (Castor and Pollux) and *Delphin*, the Dolphin. **1007. Athalantes doughtres sevene,** the *Pleiades* (the seven daughters of Atlas). *Athalante* is the ablative of *Atlas*, a form taken over from Ovid, *Fasti*, v. 83. **1012. leve,** believe. **1016. shenden,** injure. **1020. hye,** loud. **1022. Seynt Julyan,** the patron saint of hospitality. **1024. that,** what. **1029. compouned,** compounded. **1030. rouned,** whispered. **1031. swogh,** sough. **1034. Peter!** A common form of oath; cf. *CT*, D 446, 1332, etc. **1038. route,** roar. **1039. humblynge,** rumbling.

He sette me fayre on my fete,　　　　　　　1050
And seyde, "Walke forth a pas,
And tak thyn aventure or cas,
That thou shalt fynde in Fames place."
　　"Now," quod I, "while we han space
To speke, or that I goo fro the,　　　　　　1055
For the love of God, telle me—
In sooth, that wil I of the lere—
Yf thys noyse that I here
Be, as I have herd the tellen,
Of folk that doun in erthe duellen,　　　　　1060
And cometh here in the same wyse
As I the herde or this devyse;
And that there lives body nys
In al that hous that yonder ys,
That maketh al this loude fare."　　　　　　1065
"Noo," quod he, "by Seynte Clare,
And also wis God rede me!
But o thing y will warne the
Of the whiche thou wolt have wonder.
Loo, to the Hous of Fame yonder,　　　　　1070

Thou wost now how, cometh every speche;
Hyt nedeth noght eft the to teche.
But understond now ryght wel this,
Whan any speche ycomen ys
Up to the paleys, anon-ryght　　　　　　　1075
Hyt wexeth lyk the same wight
Which that the word in erthe spak,
Be hyt clothed red or blak;
And hath so very hys lyknesse
That spak the word, that thou wilt gesse　　1080
That it the same body be,
Man or woman, he or she.
And ys not this a wonder thyng?"
"Yis," quod I tho, "by heven kyng!"
And with this word, "Farewel," quod he,　　1085
"And here I wol abyden the;
And God of heven sende the grace
Some good to lernen in this place."
And I of him tok leve anon,
And gan forth to the paleys gon.　　　　　　1090

Explicit liber secundus.

Book III

Incipit liber tercius.

Invocation
　O God of science and of lyght,
Appollo, thurgh thy grete myght,
This lytel laste bok thou gye!
Nat that I wilne, for maistrye,
Here art poetical be shewed;　　　　　　　1095
But for the ryme ys lyght and lewed,
Yit make hyt sumwhat agreable,
Though som vers fayle in a sillable;
And that I do no diligence

To shewe craft, but o sentence.　　　　　　1100
And yif, devyne vertu, thow
Wilt helpe me to shewe now
That in myn hed ymarked ys—
Loo, that is for to menen this,
The Hous of Fame for to descryve—　　　　1105
Thou shalt se me go as blyve
Unto the nexte laure y see,
And kysse yt, for hyt is thy tree.
Now entre in my brest anoon!

1052. **cas,** chance. 1062. **devyse,** explain. 1063. **lives,** living. 1065. **fare,** "to do." 1066. **Seynte Clare,** St. Clara or Clare (d. 1253), a disciple of St. Francis. The choice of the oath was probably dictated by the rime. 1079. **very,** truly, exactly. 1091. The Invocation was inspired by Dante's opening of the *Paradiso* (ll. 13–27), but Chaucer has given it a playful turn. 1096. **for,** for all that, notwithstanding. 1099. **And that,** continues the force of *for* in l. 1096. 1100. **o,** alone, only. **sentence,** meaning. Chaucer asserts that he is concerned only with what he says, not how he says it. 1103. **ymarked,** fixed, recorded. 1107. **laure,** laurel. 1108. **thy tree.** As the god of music and poetry Apollo is represented as wearing a laurel wreath.

The Dream

Whan I was fro thys egle goon,   1110
I gan beholde upon this place.
And certein, or I ferther pace,
I wol yow al the shap devyse
Of hous and site, and al the wyse
How I gan to thys place aproche,   1115
That stood upon so hygh a roche,
Hier stant ther non in Spayne.
But up I clomb with alle payne,
And though to clymbe it greved me,
Yit I ententyf was to see,   1120
And for to powren wonder lowe,
Yf I koude any weyes knowe
What maner stoon this roche was.
For hyt was lyk alum de glas,
But that hyt shoon ful more clere;   1125
But of what congeled matere
Hyt was, I nyste redely.
But at the laste aspied I,
And found that hit was every del
A roche of yse, and not of stel.   1130
Thoughte I, "By seynt Thomas of Kent!
This were a feble fundament
To bilden on a place hye.
He ought him lytel glorifye
That her-on bilt, God so me save!"   1135
    Tho sawgh I al the half ygrave
With famous folkes names fele,
That had iben in mochel wele,
And her fames wide yblowe.
But wel unnethes koude I knowe   1140
Any lettres for to rede
Hir names by; for, out of drede,

They were almost of-thowed so
That of the lettres oon or two
Was molte away of every name,   1145
So unfamous was woxe hir fame.
But men seyn, "What may ever laste?"
    Thoo gan I in myn herte caste
That they were molte awey with hete,
And not awey with stormes bete.   1150
For on that other syde I say
Of this hille, that northward lay,
How hit was writen ful of names
Of folkes that hadden grete fames
Of olde tyme, and yet they were   1155
As fressh as men had writen hem here
The selfe day, ryght or that houre
That I upon hem gan to poure.
But wel I wiste what yt made;
Hyt was conserved with the shade   1160
Of a castel that stood on high—
Al this writynge that I sigh—
And stood eke on so cold a place
That hete myghte hit not deface.
Thoo gan I up the hille to goon,   1165
And fond upon the cop a woon,
That al the men that ben on lyve
Ne han the kunnynge to descrive
The beaute of that ylke place,
Ne coude casten no compace   1170
Swich another for to make,
That myght of beaute ben hys make,
Ne so wonderlych ywrought;
That hit astonyeth yit my thought,
And maketh al my wyt to swynke,   1175
On this castel to bethynke,

1117. non in Spayne. R. M. Smith suggests that this may refer to the proverbial "castles in Spain," dream castles, mentioned in *RR*, 2442, but the allusion may be merely to the rock of Gibraltar. **1119. greved,** caused bodily discomfort, *i.e.* required quite an effort. **1120. ententyf,** eager. **1121. lowe,** *i.e.* bending or stooping down. **1124. alum de glas,** crystalline alum. The more usual form in ME is *alum glas*, as in the *Canon's Yeoman's Tale* (G 813). The reading is that of the Pepys MS (*alymde glas*) as interpreted by Bradley (*Athenæum*, 1902, I. 563). It appears in corrupted form (*a lymed glas*) in the edd. of Caxton and Thynne. **1130. A roche of yse.** For this admirable notion no direct source has been found. The nearest analogy is the location of the goddess Fortune's house in *La Panthère d'Amours*, by Nicole de Margival, as pointed out by Sypherd. **1131. seynt Thomas of Kent,** St. Thomas à Becket. **1134. him . . . glorifye,** boast, exult. **1136. the half,** one side. **1137. fele,** many. **1148. caste,** conjecture. **1151. say,** saw. **1159. made,** caused it. **1162. sigh,** saw. **1166. cop,** top. **woon,** dwelling. **1170. casten no compace.** The meaning seems to be "to lay out a plan," but the expression has not been recorded elsewhere. In the *Cursor Mundi* (9944–7) occurs "A tour faire of yvory . . . Craftily casten with a compas," where *compas* is app. an instrument. But an earlier meaning of *compas* is "subtlety," "ingenuity," "cunning," so that the phrase in Chaucer could mean "exercise any amount of ingenuity." The accent on *compace* is on the last syllable, as occasionally in Chaucer; cf. 1. 462, 798; A 1889, etc., and Ital. *compasso*. **1175. swynke,** labor.

So that the grete craft, beaute,
The cast, the curiosite
Ne kan I not to yow devyse;
My wit ne may me not suffise. 1180
    But natheles al the substance
I have yit in my remembrance;
For-whi me thoughte, be seynt Gyle!
Al was of ston of beryle,
Bothe the castel and the tour, 1185
And eke the halle and every bour,
Wythouten peces or joynynges.
But many subtil compassinges,
Babewynnes and pynacles,
Ymageries and tabernacles, 1190
I say; and ful eke of wyndowes,
As flakes falle in grete snowes.
And eke in ech of the pynacles
Weren sondry habitacles,
In which stoden, al withoute— 1195
Ful the castel, al aboute—
Of alle maner of mynstralles,
And gestiours, that tellen tales
Both of wepinge and of game,
Of al that longeth unto Fame. 1200
    Ther herde I pleyen on an harpe
That sowned bothe wel and sharpe,
Orpheus ful craftely,
And on his syde, faste by,
Sat the harper Orion, 1205
And Eacides Chiron,

And other harpers many oon,
And the Bret Glascurion;
And smale harpers with her glees
Sate under hem in dyvers sees, 1210
And gunne on hem upward to gape,
And countrefete hem as an ape,
Or as craft countrefeteth kynde.
    Tho saugh I stonden hem behynde,
Afer fro hem, al be hemselve, 1215
Many thousand tymes twelve,
That maden lowde mynstralcyes
In cornemuse and shalemyes,
And many other maner pipe,
That craftely begunne to pipe, 1220
Bothe in doucet and in rede,
That ben at festes with the brede;
And many flowte and liltyng-horne,
And pipes made of grene corne,
As han thise lytel herde-gromes, 1225
That kepen bestis in the bromes.
Ther saugh I than Atiteris,
And of Athenes daun Pseustis,
And Marcia that loste her skyn,
Bothe in face, body, and chyn, 1230
For that she wolde envien, loo!
To pipen bet than Appolloo.
Ther saugh I famous, olde and yonge,
Pipers of the Duche tonge,
To lerne love-daunces, sprynges, 1235
Reyes, and these straunge thynges.

1183. **seynt Gyle,** St. Giles (Aegidius). 1188. **compassinges,** devices, contrivances. 1189. **Babewynnes,** grotesque carvings, gargoyles. 1190. **tabernacles,** niches or recesses for images; cf. l. 123. 1191. **say,** saw. 1194. **habitacles,** niches. 1195. **al withoute,** *i.e.* on the outside of the building. 1197. **Of alle.** The preposition is redundant as in expressions of time (*of al that day* A 3415, *of al a tyde* B 510) though here possibly influenced by the partitive use (*Of smale houndes* A 146). 1198. **gestiours,** reciters of stories, romances, etc. 1200. **longeth unto,** pertains to. It has been pointed out that the whole description shows a striking resemblance to the façade of the Maison des Musiciens at Reims (G. G. Williams, *MLN*, LXXII. 6–9). 1203. **Orpheus.** See the note to *BD* 569. 1205. **Orion,** Arion, a legendary bard of Corinth famous for his skill in playing the cithara or lyre. 1206. **Eacides Chiron,** Chiron, tutor of Achilles, grandson of Aeacus. The genitive *Eacides* is taken over from Ovid's "Æcidae Chiron" (*Ars Amatoria*, I. 17). Chiron, a centaur, had been taught by Apollo and in turn taught Achilles riding, hunting, music, etc. 1208. **the Bret Glascurion,** the Briton Glasgerion, a famous Welsh bard, subject of a well-known ballad (Child, No. 67). 1209. **glees,** musical instruments. 1210. **sees,** seats. 1213. **as craft countrefeteth kynde,** as art imitates nature. 1217. **mynstralcyes,** *i.e.* music. 1218. **cornemuse,** bagpipe. **shalemyes,** shawms, wind instruments of the oboe class. 1221. **doucet,** dulcet, a flute-like instrument. **rede,** a rustic pipe. 1222. **brede,** roast meat. 1223. **liltyng-horne,** trumpet. 1226. **bromes,** broom (a kind of shrub). 1227-8. **Atiteris . . . Pseustis.** Pseustis is a shepherd in the *Ecloga* of Theodulus, who competes with Alithia. The *Ecloga* was a well-known textbook in the Middle Ages (cf. G. L. Hamilton, *MP*, VII. 169–85), to which Chaucer was indebted for other hints in the poem (F. Holthausen, *Anglia*, XVI. 264–6). Holthausen suggested that Atiteris is the shepherd Tityrus of Virgil's first eclogue. 1229. **Marcia,** Marsyas, a satyr who was defeated by Apollo in a trial of musical skill and flayed alive by him (Ovid, *Metam.*, VI. 382–400). Chaucer, perhaps misled by Dante (*Paradiso*, I. 20), has made him a woman. 1231. **envien,** vie (with). 1234. **Pipers . . . tonge.** If this reference has any special significance, it has not been recognized. 1235. **lerne,** teach. **sprynges,** a kind of dance, presumably lively, but not otherwise identified. 1236. **Reyes,** a round dance. The term is Dutch.

Tho saugh I in an other place
Stonden, in a large space,
Of hem that maken blody soun
In trumpe, beme, and claryoun;   1240
For in fyght and blood-shedynge
Ys used gladly clarionynge.
Ther herde I trumpen Messenus,
Of whom that speketh Virgilius.
There herde I trumpe Joab also,   1245
Theodomas, and other mo;
And alle that used clarion
In Cataloigne and Aragon,
That in her tyme famous were
To lerne, saugh I trumpe there.   1250
There saugh I sitte in other sees,
Pleyinge upon sondry glees,
Whiche that I kan not nevene,
Moo than sterres ben in hevene,
Of whiche I nyl as now not ryme,   1255
For ese of yow, and losse of tyme.
For tyme ylost, this knowen ye,
Be no way may recovered be.
Ther saugh I pleye jugelours,
Magiciens, and tregetours,   1260
And phitonesses, charmeresses,
Olde wicches, sorceresses,
That use exorsisacions,
And eke these fumygacions;
And clerkes eke, which konne wel   1265
Al this magik naturel,

That craftely doon her ententes
To make, in certeyn ascendentes,
Ymages, lo, thrugh which magik
To make a man ben hool or syk.   1270
Ther saugh I the quene Medea,
And Circes eke, and Calipsa;
Ther saugh I Hermes Ballenus,
Limote, and eke Symon Magus.
There saugh I, and knew hem by name,   1275
That by such art don men han fame.
Ther saugh I Colle tregetour
Upon a table of sycamour
Pleye an uncouth thyng to telle;
Y saugh him carien a wyndmelle   1280
Under a walsh-note shale.
      What shuld I make lenger tale
Of alle the pepil y ther say,
Fro hennes into domes day?
Whan I had al this folk beholde,   1285
And fond me lous, and nought yholde,
And eft imused longe while
Upon these walles of berile,
That shoone ful lyghter than a glas,
And made wel more than hit was   1290
To semen every thing, ywis,
As kynde thyng of Fames is,
I gan forth romen til I fond
The castel-yate on my ryght hond,
Which that so wel corven was   1295
That never such another nas;

1239. Of hem. See note to l. 1197. Here we may understand *some*, as Skeat suggests, more suitably than in 1197.
1240. beme, trumpet. **1243. Messenus,** Misenus, son of Aeolus, trumpeter to Hector and later to Æneas. The reference is to the *Æneid*, III. 239 or VI. 162–70. **1245. Joab,** mentioned as a trumpeter in *2 Samuel*, 2:28, etc. **1246. Theodomas,** Thiodamas, who succeeded Amphiaraus as augur in the *Thebaid*, VIII. 277 ff. and the *Roman de Thèbes*, ll. 5114–72, is not spoken of as a trumpeter. Chaucer again mentions the two names together in *CT*, E 1719–20. **1253. nevene,** name. **1259. pleye,** perform. **jugelours,** jugglers, but the term also includes various kinds of minstrels. **1260. tregetours,** slight-of-hand performers, magicians. **1261. phitonesses,** witches. The term *pythoness* is often applied to the witch of Endor. See Skeat's note and cf. *1 Chronicles*, 10:13, where "one that had a familiar spirit" (consulted by Saul) is in the Vulgate *pythonissam*. **1264. fumygacions,** fumes raised in incantations. **1266. magik naturel . . . Ymages.** See the note to *CT*, A 417–8. **1271. quene Medea,** Jason's wife, by whose knowledge of herbs and enchantment she restored her father Aeson to youth (Ovid, *Metam.*, VII. 162–293). **1272. Circes,** Circe, who with a magic potion enchanted men and held them captive. The Latin genitive *Circes* frequently occurs in Ovid. **Calipsa,** Calypso, a nymph who fell in love with Odysseus and kept him for seven years. **1273. Hermes Ballenus,** Ballenus (or Belinous) a sage who discovered beneath a statue of Hermes Trismegistus a book containing the secrets of the universe. (Skeat) Hermes is thus an epithet. **1274. Limote.** The Fairfax MS reads *Lymete*, identified by Hales with Elymas the sorcerer of *Acts*, 13:8. **Symon Magus,** see *Acts*, 8:9. **1277. Colle tregetour,** an English magician contemporary with Chaucer whom Royster (*SP*, XXIII. 380–4) found mentioned in a French conversation book of 1396. Cf. l. 1260. **1279. uncouth,** strange. **1280. carien,** convey. **1281. walsh-note shale,** walnut shell. **1282. What,** why. **1292. As kynde thyng . . .,** as is the nature of Fame. **1295. corven,** carved.

And yit it was be aventure
Iwrought, as often as be cure.
Hyt nedeth noght yow more to tellen,
To make yow to longe duellen,   1300
Of this yates florisshinges,
Ne of compasses, ne of kervynges,
Ne how they hatte in masoneries,
As corbetz, ful of ymageries.
But, Lord! so fair yt was to shewe,   1305
For hit was al with gold behewe.
But in I wente, and that anoon.
Ther mette I cryinge many oon,
"A larges, larges, hold up wel!
God save the lady of thys pel,   1310
Our oune gentil lady Fame,
And hem that wilnen to have name
Of us!" Thus herde y crien alle,
And faste comen out of halle
And shoken nobles and sterlynges.   1315
And somme corouned were as kynges,
With corounes wroght ful of losenges;
And many ryban and many frenges
Were on her clothes trewely.
    Thoo atte last aspyed y   1320
That pursevantes and heraudes,
That crien ryche folkes laudes,
Hyt weren alle; and every man
Of hem, as y yow tellen can,
Had on him throwen a vesture   1325
Which that men clepe a cote-armure,
Enbrowded wonderliche ryche,
Although they nere nought ylyche.
But noght nyl I, so mote y thryve,
Ben aboute to dyscryve   1330
Alle these armes that ther weren,

That they thus on her cotes beren,
For hyt to me were impossible;
Men myghte make of hem a bible
Twenty foot thykke, as y trowe.   1335
For certeyn, whoso koude iknowe
Myghte ther alle the armes seen
Of famous folk that han ybeen
In Auffrike, Europe, and Asye,
Syth first began the chevalrie.   1340
    Loo! how shulde I now telle al thys?
Ne of the halle eke what nede is
To tellen yow that every wal
Of hit, and flor, and roof, and al
Was plated half a foote thikke   1345
Of gold, and that nas nothyng wikke,
But, for to prove in alle wyse,
As fyn as ducat in Venyse,
Of which to lite al in my pouche is?
And they were set as thik of nouchis,   1350
Ful of the fynest stones faire
That men rede in the Lapidaire,
As grasses growen in a mede.
But hit were al to longe to rede
The names; and therfore I pace.   1355
    But in this lusty and ryche place,
That Fames halle called was,
Ful moche prees of folk ther nas,
Ne crowdyng for to mochil prees.
But al on hye, above a dees,   1360
Sitte in a see imperiall,
That mad was of a rubee all,
Which that a carbuncle ys ycalled,
Y saugh, perpetually ystalled,
A femynyne creature,   1365
That never formed by Nature

1298. cure, care, intention. **1301. florisshinges,** embellishments. **1302. compasses,** ingenious figures, images. **1304. corbetz,** corbels. **ymageries,** carvings. **1306. with gold behewe,** of carved gold. **1309. hold up wel!** The force of this exclamation is not clear. **1310. pel,** peel, castle. **1313. Of us.** Cf. ll. 1320-3 below. **1315. nobles and sterlynges,** gold coins (6s. 8d.) and silver pennies. **1316. kynges.** Following Skeat this is generally interpreted as kings-at-arms. The title was conferred by the ruler of a kingdom or province by the act of crowning him. See A. R. Wagner, *Heralds and Heraldry in the Middle Ages* (2nd ed., 1956), p. 39. **1317. losenges,** lozenges, diamond-shaped ornaments. **1321. pursevantes.** A pursuivant was a heraldic officer below the rank of herald and often attendant upon a herald. **1326. cote-armure,** a surcoat or outer garment charged with armorial bearings. **1332. beren,** bore. **1334. bible,** book. **1340. chevalrie,** knighthood. **1345. plated,** covered with plates. **1346. wikke,** bad, debased. **1347. for to prove . . .,** to test (it) in every way. **1350. nouchis,** settings for jewels. **1352. Lapidaire,** lapidary, a treatise on precious stones. The *Lapidarium* (11c.) of Marbodus exists also in numerous French (and other) adaptations. **1356. lusty,** pleasant. **1360. above a dees,** upon a dais. **1361. Sitte . . . Y saugh,** I saw sitting. **see,** seat. **1364. ystalled,** installed, seated.

Nas such another thing yseye.
For altherfirst, soth for to seye,
Me thoughte that she was so lyte
That the lengthe of a cubite   1370
Was lengere than she semed be.
But thus sone, in a whyle, she
Hir tho so wonderliche streighte
That with hir fet she erthe reighte,
And with hir hed she touched hevene,   1375
Ther as shynen sterres sevene.
And therto eke, as to my wit,
I saugh a gretter wonder yit,
Upon her eyen to beholde;
But certeyn y hem never tolde.   1380
For as feele eyen hadde she
As fetheres upon foules be,
Or weren on the bestes foure
That Goddis trone gunne honoure,
As John writ in th'Apocalips.   1385
Hir heer, that oundy was and crips,
As burned gold hyt shoon to see;
And, soth to tellen, also she
Had also fele upstondyng eres
And tonges, as on bestes heres;   1390
And on hir fet wexen saugh y
Partriches wynges redely.
   But, Lord! the perry and the richesse
I saugh sittyng on this godesse!
And, Lord! the hevenyssh melodye   1395
Of songes, ful of armonye,
I herde aboute her trone ysonge,
That al the paleys walles ronge!
So song the myghty Muse, she
That cleped ys Caliope,   1400

And hir eighte sustren eke,
That in her face semen meke;
And evermo, eternally,
They songe of Fame, as thoo herd y:
"Heryed be thou and thy name,   1405
Goddesse of Renoun or of Fame!"
   Tho was I war, loo, atte laste,
As I myne eyen gan up caste,
That thys ylke noble quene
On her shuldres gan sustene   1410
Bothe the armes and the name
Of thoo that hadde large fame:
Alexander and Hercules,
That with a sherte hys lyf les!
Thus fond y syttynge this goddesse   1415
In nobley, honour, and rychesse;
Of which I stynte a while now,
Other thing to tellen yow.
   Tho saugh I stonde on eyther syde,
Streight doun to the dores wide,   1420
Fro the dees, many a peler
Of metal that shoon not ful cler;
But though they nere of no rychesse,
Yet they were mad for gret noblesse,
And in hem hy and gret sentence;   1425
And folk of digne reverence,
Of which I wil yow telle fonde,
Upon the piler saugh I stonde.
   Alderfirst, loo, ther I sigh
Upon a piler stonde on high,   1430
That was of led and yren fyn,
Hym of secte saturnyn,
The Ebrayk Josephus, the olde,
That of Jewes gestes tolde;

1367. yseye, seen. **1373. Hir . . . streighte,** stretched herself. **1374. reighte,** reached. **1376. sterres sevene,** the seven planets. **1380. tolde,** counted. **1381. feele,** many. **1383. the bestes foure.** See *Revelation,* 4:6–8. **1385. writ,** writes. **1386. oundy,** wavy. **crips,** curly. **1387. burned,** refined. **1392. Partriches wynges.** Chaucer's description of Fame comes largely from Virgil, *Æneid,* IV. 173–188. Virgil has "swift wings" (*pernicibus alis*) which Chaucer either mistook for *perdicibus* or was following a faulty MS. He translates it correctly in *TC,* 4. 661. **1393. perry,** jewelry or precious stones collectively. **1400. Caliope,** Calliope, the muse of epic poetry. **1401. sustren,** sisters. **1405. Heryed,** praised. **1411. the armes,** the coats of arms. **1414. with a sherte.** The centaur Nessus attempting to carry off Deianira, the wife of Hercules, was killed by the hero. The dying centaur told Deianira to preserve some of his blood, saying that she might use it as a charm to preserve her husband's love. Fearful of his infatuation with Iole, she gave him a garment steeped in the blood. Nessus was revenged when the garment proved poisonous and Hercules died. Cf. *CT,* B 3309 ff. **les,** lost. **1416. nobley,** splendor. **1421. peler,** pillar. **1424. gret noblesse,** *i.e.* persons of great importance. **1427. fonde,** endeavor. **1429. sigh,** saw. **1432. secte saturnyn,** the Jewish religion, which, according to medieval astrology arose in a conjunction of Jupiter and Saturn. See Amanda H. Miller, *MLN,* XLVII. 99–102. **1433. Josephus,** author of a *History of the Jews* (first century). **1434. gestes,** deeds, history.

And he bar on hys shuldres hye 1435
The fame up of the Jewerye.
And by hym stoden other sevene,
Wise and worthy for to nevene,
To helpen hym bere up the charge,
Hyt was so hevy and so large. 1440
And for they writen of batayles,
As wel as other olde mervayles,
Therfor was, loo, thys piler
Of which that I yow telle her,
Of led and yren bothe, ywys, 1445
For yren Martes metal ys,
Which that god is of batayle;
And the led, withouten faille,
Ys, loo, the metal of Saturne,
That hath a ful large whel to turne. 1450

    Thoo stoden forth, on every rowe,
Of hem which that I koude knowe,
Though I hem noght be ordre telle,
To make yow to longe to duelle,
These of whiche I gynne rede. 1455
There saugh I stonden, out of drede,
Upon an yren piler strong
That peynted was, al endelong,
With tigres blode in every place,
The Tholosan that highte Stace, 1460
That bar of Thebes up the fame
Upon his shuldres, and the name
Also of cruel Achilles.

And by him stood, withouten les,
Ful wonder hye on a piler 1465
Of yren, he, the gret Omer;
And with him Dares and Tytus
Before, and eke he Lollius,
And Guydo eke de Columpnis,
And Englyssh Gaufride eke, ywis; 1470
And ech of these, as have I joye,
Was besy for to bere up Troye.
So hevy therof was the fame
That for to bere hyt was no game.
But yet I gan ful wel espie, 1475
Betwex hem was a litil envye.
Oon seyde that Omer made lyes,
Feynynge in hys poetries,
And was to Grekes favorable;
Therfor held he hyt but fable. 1480

    Tho saugh I stonde on a piler,
That was of tynned yren cler,
That Latyn poete, Virgile,
That bore hath up a longe while
The fame of Pius Eneas. 1485

    And next hym on a piler was,
Of coper, Venus clerk, Ovide,
That hath ysowen wonder wide
The grete god of Loves name.
And ther he bar up wel hys fame 1490
Upon his piler, also hye
As I myghte see hyt with myn yë;

1436. Jewerye, Jewish people. 1437. other sevene, presumably Jewish historians. 1438. nevene, name. 1439. charge, load. 1441. writen, wrote. 1450. ful large whel to turne, alluding to the orbit of Saturn, which was the outermost of the planets known in Chaucer's day. 1458. al endelong, from one end to the other. 1459. With tigres blode. As Skeat pointed out, Statius in Book VII of the *Thebaid* describes two tigers, sacred to Bacchus, that broke loose and killed three men. The tigers were wounded and died, whereupon the war was renewed. 1460. Stace, Statius, whose epic the *Thebaid*, written in emulation of the *Æneid*, relates the war between the sons of Oedipus over the rule of Thebes. He is called the *Tholosan* because he was erroneously thought to have been a native of Toulouse. So Dante calls him Tolosano (*Purg.*, XXI. 89). 1464. withouten les, without misrepresentation, truly. 1466. Omer, Homer. 1467. Dares and Tytus, Dares (Phrygius) and Dictys (Cretensis), authors of two prose accounts of the Trojan War. See the introduction to *Troilus and Criseyde*. 1468. Lollius, the supposed author of a work on the Trojan War. See the note to TC 1. 394. 1469. Guydo . . . de Columpnis, Guido delle Colonne (de Columnis), author of the *Historia Destructionis Troiae* (1287). 1470. Englyssh Gaufride, Geoffrey of Monmouth, author of the *Historia Regum Britanniae* (1137), who embodies the tradition that Britain was founded by Brutus, great-grandson of Æneas, hence by a Trojan. 1477. Oon seyde. The preface to Dares, in order to lend credence to the work, attempts to discredit Homer on the ground that he lived long after the time of the Trojan War (Dares claimed to have been in it) and moreover was tried at Athens for representing the gods as fighting with men. Later works often echoed the idea. 1482. tynned yren. It has been cynically suggested that the iron of Homer covered with tin is an admirable description of Virgil (Bell's Chaucer), but this would certainly not have been Chaucer's meaning; rather he would have meant that tin gave an added luster. But it has also been thought that since tin was the metal of Jupiter (cf. CT, G 828) Virgil is represented as Mars controlled by Jupiter. 1487. Ovide. Ovid is called *Venus clerk* because of his poems about love (*Ars Amatoria*, *Remedia Amoris*, etc.) and his image is made of *coper* because this is the metal o` Venus (cf. CT, G 829).

For-why this halle, of which I rede,
Was woxen on highte, length, and brede,
Wel more, be a thousand del,　　　　　1495
Than hyt was erst, that saugh I wel.
　　Thoo saugh I on a piler by,
Of yren wroght ful sternely,
The grete poete, daun Lucan,
And on hys shuldres bar up than,　　　1500
As high as that y myghte see,
The fame of Julius and Pompe.
And by him stoden alle these clerkes
That writen of Romes myghty werkes,
That yf y wolde her names telle,　　　1505
Al to longe most I dwelle.
　　And next him on a piler stood
Of soulfre, lyk as he were wood,
Daun Claudian, the sothe to telle,
That bar up al the fame of helle,　　　1510
Of Pluto, and of Proserpyne,
That quene ys of the derke pyne.
　　What shulde y more telle of this?
The halle was al ful, ywys,
Of hem that writen olde gestes,　　　1515
As ben on treës rokes nestes;
But hit a ful confus matere
Were al the gestes for to here,
That they of write, or how they highte.
　　But while that y beheld thys syghte,　1520
I herde a noyse aprochen blyve,
That ferde as been don in an hive
Ayen her tyme of out-fleynge;
Ryght such a maner murmurynge,
For al the world, hyt semed me.　　　1525
Tho gan I loke aboute and see
That ther come entryng into the halle
A ryght gret companye withalle,
And that of sondry regiouns,
Of alleskynnes condiciouns　　　　　1530
That dwelle in erthe under the mone,

Pore and ryche. And also sone
As they were come in to the halle,
They gonne doun on kneës falle
Before this ilke noble quene,　　　　1535
And seyde, "Graunte us, lady shene,
Ech of us of thy grace a bone!"
And somme of hem she graunted sone,
And somme she werned wel and faire,
And some she graunted the contraire　1540
Of her axyng outterly.
But thus I seye yow, trewely,
What her cause was, y nyste.
For of this folk ful wel y wiste,
They hadde good fame ech deserved　1545
Although they were dyversly served;
Ryght as her suster, dame Fortune,
Ys wont to serven in comune.
　　Now herke how she gan to paye
That gonne her of her grace praye;　　1550
And yit, lo, al this companye
Seyden sooth, and noght a lye.
　　"Madame," seyde they, "we be
Folk that here besechen the
That thou graunte us now good fame,　1555
And let our werkes han that name;
In ful recompensacioun
Of good werkes, yive us good renoun."
　　"I werne yow hit," quod she anon;
"Ye gete of me good fame non,　　　1560
Be God! and therfore goo your wey."
"Allas!" quod they, "and welaway!
Telle us what may your cause be."
"For me lyst hit noght," quod she;
"No wyght shal speke of yow, ywis,　1565
Good ne harm, ne that ne this."
And with that word she gan to calle
Her messanger, that was in halle,
And bad that he shulde faste goon,
Upon peyne to be blynd anon,　　　1570

1493. rede, relate, speak. **1499. daun Lucan.** Lucan's *Pharsalia* deals with the war between Caesar and Pompey.
1508. soulfre, suphur, brimstone, associated with the lower world. **lyk as he were wood,** probably because Claudian
speaks of the poetic *furor* at the beginning of the *De Raptu Proserpinae* and is in his style rhapsodic (see Pratt, *Speculum*, XXII.
425). **1509. Claudian.** See note to l. 449. **1512. pyne,** torment (used for place of torment). **1516. rokes,** rooks', crows'.
1519. write, wrote. **1522. ferde as been don,** went on as bees do. **1523. Ayen,** just before. **1527. come,** came. **1530.
alleskynnes,** of all kinds (of conditions). **1532. also sone,** as soon. **1536. shene,** bright. **1537. bone.** boon. **1539. werned,**
refused. **1548. in comune,** in the same way. **1549. paye,** reward. **1550. That,** those that. **1563. cause,** reason.

For Eolus the god of wynde,—
"In Trace, ther ye shal him fynde,
And bid him bringe his clarioun,
That is ful dyvers of his soun,
And hyt is cleped Clere Laude,   1575
With which he wont is to heraude
Hem that me list ypreised be.
And also bid him how that he
Brynge his other clarioun,
That highte Sklaundre in every toun,   1580
With which he wont is to diffame
Hem that me liste, and do hem shame."
     This messanger gan faste goon,
And found where in a cave of ston,
In a contree that highte Trace,   1585
This Eolus, with harde grace,
Held the wyndes in distresse,
And gan hem under him to presse,
That they gonne as beres rore,
He bond and pressed hem so sore.   1590
     This messanger gan faste crie,
"Rys up," quod he, "and faste hye,
Til thou at my lady be;
And tak thy clariouns eke with the,
And sped the forth." And he anon   1595
Tok to a man, that highte Triton,
Hys clarions to bere thoo,
And let a certeyn wynd to goo,
That blew so hydously and hye
That hyt ne lefte not a skye   1600
In alle the welken longe and brod.
This Eolus nowhere abod
Til he was come to Fames fet,
And eke the man that Triton het;
And ther he stod, as stille as stoon,   1605
And her-withal ther come anoon
Another huge companye
Of goode folk, and gunne crie,
"Lady, graunte us now good fame,

And lat oure werkes han that name   1610
Now in honour of gentilesse,
And also God your soule blesse!
For we han wel deserved hyt,
Therfore is ryght that we ben quyt."
     "As thryve I," quod she, "ye shal faylle!   1615
Good werkes shal yow noght availle
To have of me good fame as now.
But wite ye what? Y graunte yow
That ye shal have a shrewed fame,
And wikkyd loos, and worse name,   1620
Though ye good loos have wel deserved.
Now goo your wey, for ye be served.
And thou, dan Eolus, let see,
Tak forth thy trumpe anon," quod she,
"That is ycleped Sklaundre lyght,   1625
And blow her loos, that every wight
Speke of hem harme and shrewednesse,
In stede of good and worthynesse.
For thou shalt trumpe alle the contrayre
Of that they han don wel or fayre."   1630
     "Allas!" thoughte I, "what aventures
Han these sory creatures!
For they, amonges al the pres,
Shul thus be shamed gilteles.
But what! hyt moste nedes be."   1635
     What dide this Eolus, but he
Tok out hys blake trumpe of bras,
That fouler than the devel was,
And gan this trumpe for to blowe,
As al the world shulde overthrowe,   1640
That throughout every regioun
Wente this foule trumpes soun,
As swifte as pelet out of gonne,
Whan fyr is in the poudre ronne.
And such a smoke gan out-wende   1645
Out of his foule trumpes ende,
Blak, bloo, grenyssh, swartish red,
As doth where that men melte led,

1572. Trace, Thrace. **1587. distresse,** constraint. **1596. Tok to,** delivered to. **Triton.** The Tritons (usually plur.) are often represented with a conch shell as a trumpet. Triton (sing.) in Ovid and Virgil is made to blow his conch. **1598. let,** caused. **1600. skye,** cloud (the orig. meaning). **1604. het,** var. of *hight*, was called. **1611. gentilesse,** true worth or nobility. **1612. also,** as. **1614. quyt,** rewarded. **1617. as now,** at this time. **1619. shrewed,** evil. **1620. wikkyd loos,** bad fame. **1640. As,** as if. **overthrowe,** be overthrown. **1643. pelet,** stone ball, fired from early cannon. **1645. out-wende,** issue. **1647. bloo,** lead-colored. **swartish,** dark.

Loo, al on high fro the tuel.
And therto oo thing saugh I wel,   1650
That the ferther that hit ran,
The gretter wexen hit began,
As dooth the ryver from a welle,
And hyt stank as the pit of helle.
Allas, thus was her shame yronge,   1655
And gilteles, on every tonge!
   Tho come the thridde companye,
And gunne up to the dees to hye,
And doun on knes they fille anon,
And seyde, "We ben everychon   1660
Folk that han ful trewely
Deserved fame ryghtfully,
And praye yow, hit mote be knowe,
Ryght as hit is, and forth yblowe."
"I graunte," quod she, "for me list   1665
That now your goode werkes be wist,
And yet ye shul han better loos,
Right in dispit of alle your foos,
Than worthy is, and that anoon.
Lat now," quod she, "thy trumpe goon,   1670
Thou Eolus, that is so blak;
And out thyn other trumpe tak
That highte Laude, and blow yt soo
That thrugh the world her fame goo
Al esely, and not to faste,   1675
That hyt be knowen atte laste."
"Ful gladly, lady myn," he seyde;
And out hys trumpe of golde he brayde
Anon, and sette hyt to his mouth,
And blew it est, and west, and south,   1680
And north, as lowde as any thunder,
That every wight hath of hit wonder,
So brode hyt ran, or than hit stente.
And, certes, al the breth that wente
Out of his trumpes mouthe smelde   1685
As men a potful bawme helde
Among a basket ful of roses.
This favour dide he til her loses.
   And ryght with this y gan aspye,

Ther come the ferthe companye—   1690
But certeyn they were wonder fewe—
And gunne stonden in a rewe,
And seyden, "Certes, lady bryght,
We han don wel with al our myght,
But we ne kepen have no fame.   1695
Hyde our werkes and our name,
For Goddys love; for certes we
Han certeyn doon hyt for bounte,
And for no maner other thing."
"I graunte yow alle your askyng,"   1700
Quod she; "let your werkes be ded."
   With that aboute y clew myn hed,
And saugh anoon the fifte route
That to this lady gunne loute,
And doun on knes anoon to falle;   1705
And to hir thoo besoughten alle
To hyde her goode werkes ek,
And seyden they yeven noght a lek
For no fame ne for such renoun;
For they for contemplacioun   1710
And Goddes love hadde ywrought,
Ne of fame wolde they nought.
"What?" quod she, "and be ye wood?
And wene ye for to doo good,
And for to have of that no fame?   1715
Have ye dispit to have my name?
Nay, ye shul lyven everychon!
Blow thy trumpes, and that anon,"
Quod she, "thou Eolus, y hote,
And ryng this folkes werk be note,   1720
That al the world may of hyt here."
And he gan blowe her loos so clere
In his golden clarioun
That thrugh the world wente the soun
Also kenely and eke so softe;   1725
But atte last hyt was on-lofte.
   Thoo come the sexte companye,
And gunne faste on Fame crie.
Ryght verraly in this manere
They seyden: "Mercy, lady dere!   1730

1649. tuel, chimney. **1653. welle,** spring. **1655. yronge,** rung, proclaimed. **1663. mote,** may. **1670. Lat . . . goon . . . blak,** *i.e.* lay aside your black trumpet. **1686. potful bawme,** potful of balm. **helde,** poured out (see *NED s.v.* hield). **1688. til her loses,** to their praises. **1695. ne kepen,** care not (to). **1702. clew,** rubbed, scratched (in perplexity). **1710. for contemplacioun . . . love,** out of regard for, and love of, God. **1719. hote,** command. **1720. ryng,** proclaim.

To tellen certeyn as hyt is,
We han don neither that ne this,
But ydel al oure lyf ybe.
But, natheles, yet preye we
That we mowe han as good a fame,   1735
And gret renoun and knowen name,
As they that han doon noble gestes,
And acheved alle her lestes,
As wel of love as other thyng.
Al was us never broche ne ryng,   1740
Ne elles noght, from wymmen sent,
Ne ones in her herte yment
To make us oonly frendly chere,
But myghten temen us upon bere;
Yet lat us to the peple seme   1745
Suche as the world may of us deme
That wommen loven us for wod.
Hyt shal doon us as moche good,
And to oure herte as moche avaylle,
To countrepese ese and travaylle,   1750
As we had wonne hyt with labour;
For that is dere boght honour
At regard of oure grete ese.
And yet thou most us more plese:
Let us be holden eke therto   1755
Worthy, wise, and goode also,
And riche, and happy unto love.
For Goddes love, that sit above,
Thogh we may not the body have
Of wymmen, yet, so God yow save,   1760
Leet men gliwe on us the name!
Sufficeth that we han the fame."
"I graunte," quod she, "be my trouthe!
Now, Eolus, withouten slouthe,
Tak out thy trumpe of gold, let se   1765
And blow as they han axed me,
That every man wene hem at ese,
Though they goon in ful badde lese."

This Eolus gan hit so blowe
That thrugh the world hyt was yknowe.   1770
    Thoo come the seventh route anoon,
And fel on knees everychoon,
And seyde, "Lady, graunte us sone
The same thing, the same bone,
That [ye] this nexte folk han doon."   1775
"Fy on yow," quod she, "everychon!
Ye masty swyn, ye ydel wrechches,
Ful of roten, slowe techches!
What? false theves! wher ye wolde
Be famous good, and nothing nolde   1780
Deserve why, ne never ye roughte?
Men rather yow to hangen oughte!
For ye be lyke the sweynte cat
That wolde have fissh; but wostow what?
He wolde nothing wete his clowes.   1785
Yvel thrift come to your jowes,
And eke to myn, if I hit graunte,
Or do yow favour, yow to avaunte!
Thou Eolus, thou kyng of Trace,
Goo blowe this folk a sory grace,"   1790
Quod she, "anon; and wostow how?
As I shal telle thee ryght now.
Sey: 'These ben they that wolde honour
Have, and do noskynnes labour,
Ne doo no good, and yet han lawde;   1795
And that men wende that bele Isawde
Ne coude hem noght of love werne,
And yet she that grynt at a querne
Ys al to good to ese her herte.' "
This Eolus anon up sterte,   1800
And with his blake clarioun
He gan to blasen out a soun
As lowde as beloweth wynd in helle;
And eke therwith, soth to telle,
This soun was so ful of japes,   1805
As ever mowes were in apes.

1737. gestes, deeds. 1738. lestes, desires. 1740. Al, although. 1742-4. Nor once in their hearts (had they) intended to make us even friendly cheer, but would just as gladly have seen us dead, *lit.* bring us on bier. 1747. for wod, madly. 1750. To countrepese, etc., *i.e.* balancing ease and labor. 1751. As, as if. 1753. At regard of, in comparison with. 1757. unto, in. 1761. gliwe, glue, fasten. 1764. slouthe, tardiness. 1768. lese, pasture. Robinson notes the figure in *TC* 2. 752. 1777. masty, fattened, lazy. 1778. slowe techches, slothful qualities. *Teche* is *lit.* a spot or blemish. 1779. wher, *lit.* whether, but often used to introduce a question where no alternative is implied. 1780. famous, famously. 1783. sweynte, lazy. 1788. avaunte, extol. 1794. noskynnes, of no kind. 1796. Isawde, Iseult. 1797. werne, refuse. 1798. she that grynt at a querne, she that grinds at a hand-mill, *i.e.* a peasant girl. 1806. mowes, grimaces.

And that wente al the world aboute,
That every wight gan on hem shoute,
And for to lawghe as they were wode,
Such game fonde they in her hode.   1810
   Tho come another companye,
That had ydoon the trayterye,
The harm, the grettest wikkednesse
That any herte kouthe gesse;
And prayed her to han good fame,   1815
And that she nolde doon hem no shame,
But yeve hem loos and good renoun,
And do hyt blowe in a clarioun.
"Nay, wis," quod she, "hyt were a vice.
Al be ther in me no justice,   1820
Me lyste not to doo hyt now,
Ne this nyl I not graunte yow."
   Tho come ther lepynge in a route,
And gunne choppen al aboute
Every man upon the crowne,   1825
That al the halle gan to sowne,
And seyden: "Lady, leefe and dere,
We ben suche folk as ye mowe here.
To tellen al the tale aryght,
We ben shrewes, every wyght,   1830
And han delyt in wikkednesse,
As goode folk han in godnesse;
And joye to be knowen shrewes,
And ful of vice and wikked thewes;
Wherfore we praye yow, a-rowe,   1835
That oure fame such be knowe
In alle thing ryght as hit ys."
"Y graunte hyt yow," quod she, "ywis.
But what art thow that seyst this tale,
That werest on thy hose a pale,   1840
And on thy tipet such a belle?"
"Madame," quod he, "soth to telle,
I am that ylke shrewe, ywis,

That brende the temple of Ysidis
In Athenes, loo, that citee."   1845
"And wherfor didest thou so?" quod she.
"By my thrift," quod he, "madame,
I wolde fayn han had a fame,
As other folk hadde in the toun,
Although they were of gret renoun   1850
For her vertu and for her thewes.
Thoughte y, as gret a fame han shrewes,
Though hit be for shrewednesse,
As goode folk han for goodnesse;
And sith y may not have that oon,   1855
That other nyl y noght forgoon.
And for to gette of Fames hire,
The temple sette y al afire.
Now do our loos be blowen swithe,
As wisly be thou ever blythe!"   1860
"Gladly," quod she; "thow Eolus,
Herestow not what they prayen us?"
"Madame, yis, ful wel," quod he,
And I wil trumpen it, parde!"
And tok his blake trumpe faste,   1865
And gan to puffen and to blaste,
Til hyt was at the worldes ende.
   With that y gan aboute wende,
For oon that stood ryght at my bak,
Me thoughte, goodly to me spak,   1870
And seyde, "Frend, what is thy name?
Artow come hider to han fame?"
"Nay, for sothe, frend," quod y;
"I cam noght hyder, graunt mercy,
For no such cause, by my hed!   1875
Sufficeth me, as I were ded,
That no wight have my name in honde.
I wot myself best how y stonde;
For what I drye, or what I thynke,
I wil myselven al hyt drynke,   1880

1810. game, amusement. On the analogy of *TC* 2. 1109–10, *her* should refer to the "seventh route." "To put an ape in one's hood" (cf. *CT*, B 1630) is a different idiom. **1820. Al,** although. **1824. choppen,** strike. **1830. shrewes,** rascals (of either sex). **1834. thewes,** qualities. **1840. pale,** perpendicular stripe, to mark him off from the rest and attract attention. **1844. Ysidis,** Latin genitive form of Isis. One Herostratus, to immortalize his name, set fire to the temple of Diana at Ephesus in 356 B.C. The incident is mentioned by Plutarch, Cicero, and others. When Chaucer made the temple one to Isis and located it in Athens, his memory was doubtless playing him false. **1857. hire,** reward. **1868. wende,** turn. **1877. have . . . in honde,** more commonly *on honde,* to be concerned with. **1879. drye,** suffer. **1880. I wil . . . hyt drynke,** an allusion to the proverb "He who brews bad ale must drink less well."

Certeyn, for the more part,
As ferforth as I kan myn art."
"But what doost thou here than?" quod he.
Quod y, "That wyl y tellen the,
The cause why y stonde here: 1885
Somme newe tydynges for to lere,
Somme newe thinges, y not what,
Tydynges, other this or that,
Of love, or suche thynges glade.
For certeynly, he that me made   1890
To comen hyder, seyde me,
Y shulde bothe here and se,
In this place, wonder thynges;
But these be no suche tydynges
As I mene of." "Noo?" quod he.   1895
And I answered, "Noo, parde!
For wel y wiste ever yit,
Sith that first y hadde wit,
That somme folk han desired fame
Diversly, and loos, and name.   1900
But certeynly, y nyste how
Ne where that Fame duelled, er now,
And eke of her descripcioun,
Ne also her condicioun,
Ne the ordre of her dom,   1905
Unto the tyme y hidder com."
"[Whych] than be, loo, these tydynges,
That thou now [thus] hider brynges,
That thou hast herd?" quod he to me;
"But now no fors, for wel y se   1910
What thou desirest for to here.
Com forth and stond no lenger here,

And y wil thee, withouten drede,
In such another place lede,
Ther thou shalt here many oon."   1915
    Tho gan I forth with hym to goon
Out of the castel, soth to seye.
Tho saugh y stonde in a valeye,
Under the castel, faste by,
An hous, that Domus Dedaly,   1920
That Laboryntus cleped ys,
Nas mad so wonderlych, ywis,
Ne half so queyntelych ywrought.
And evermo, as swyft as thought,
This queynte hous aboute wente,   1925
That never mo hyt stille stente.
And therout com so gret a noyse
That, had hyt stonden upon Oyse,
Men myghte hyt han herd esely
To Rome, y trowe sikerly.   1930
And the noyse which that I herde,
For al the world, ryght so hyt ferde,
As dooth the rowtynge of the ston
That from th'engyn ys leten gon.
And al thys hous of which y rede   1935
Was mad of twigges, falwe, rede,
And grene eke, and somme weren white,
Swiche as men to these cages thwite,
Or maken of these panyers,
Or elles hottes or dossers;   1940
That, for the swough and for the twygges,
This hous was also ful of gygges,
And also ful eke of chirkynges,
And of many other werkynges;

1882. As ferforth as I kan myn art, *i.e.* as far as I am able (know my business). **1895. mene,** speak. **1905. ordre,** usage, customary procedure, hence the character of her judgments. **1908. brynges.** It is customary to explain this word (for *bringest*) as a Northern form. It is unusual in Chaucer. But these three lines present a more serious difficulty. Chaucer has come not to bring, but to hear, tidings. The passage seems to have suffered some corruption in its transmission. Koch's emendation of ll. 1908–9: "That bringe thee hider, and thise thinges / That thou wilt here . . ." is drastic, but offers a more appropriate meaning. **1920. Domus Dedaly.** As Ovid relates (*Metam.*, VIII. 157 ff.), Daedalus constructed a maze of chambers in which the minotaur was confined. Virgil calls it *labyrinthus* (*Æneid*, v. 588). Trevisa in his translation of Higden's *Polychronicon* uses the phrase *laborintus, Dedalus hous*. **1925. wente,** turned. For revolving castles etc. in medieval romance see Sypherd, *Studies in Chaucer's Hous of Fame*, pp. 144 ff. **1928. Oyse,** a river flowing into the Seine a little below Paris. **1933. rowtynge,** roaring. **1934. engyn,** catapult. **1935. rede,** speak. **1936. Was mad of twigges.** Houses made of interwoven branches in the manner of a basket were known in Ireland and other Celtic countries. See Sypherd, *op. cit.*, pp. 141–3. Chaucer may have known of them from observation or hearsay. **1938. thwite,** whittle. **1939. panyers,** baskets. **1940. hottes,** baskets carried on the back or shoulder. The MSS read *hattes*, certainly a mistake. **dossers,** baskets also carried on the back or slung over the backs of beasts of burden. **1942. gygges.** OF. *gigue* is a musical instrument. The *NED*, *gig*, *sb.*[3], suggests "?A squeaking noise"; and cf. Roland Smith, *MLN*, LXV. 529. But in Dante (*Paradiso*, XIV. 118) the sound of the *giga* is *dolce*, and in OF. it is *douce* (See Tobler-Lommatzsch, *s.v. gigue*). **1943. chirkynges,** creakings.

And eke this hous hath of entrees 1945
As fele as of leves ben in trees
In somer, whan they grene been;
And on the roof men may yet seen
A thousand holes, and wel moo,
To leten wel the soun out goo. 1950
And be day, in every tyde,
Been al the dores opened wide,
And by nyght, echon, unshette;
Ne porter ther is noon to lette
No maner tydynges in to pace. 1955
Ne never rest is in that place
That hit nys fild ful of tydynges,
Other loude, or of whisprynges;
And over alle the houses angles
Ys ful of rounynges and of jangles 1960
Of werres, of pes, of mariages,
Of reste, of labour, of viages,
Of abood, of deeth, of lyfe,
Of love, of hate, acord, of stryfe,
Of loos, of lore, and of wynnynges, 1965
Of hele, of seknesse, of bildynges,
Of faire wyndes, and of tempestes,
Of qwalme of folk, and eke of bestes;
Of dyvers transmutacions
Of estats, and eke of regions; 1970
Of trust, of drede, of jelousye,
Of wit, of wynnynge, of folye;
Of plente, and of gret famyne,
Of chepe, of derthe, and of ruyne;
Of good or mys governement, 1975
Of fyr, and of dyvers accident.
  And loo, thys hous, of which I write,
Syker be ye, hit nas not lyte,
For hyt was sixty myle of lengthe.
Al was the tymber of no strengthe, 1980
Yet hit is founded to endure
While that hit lyst to Aventure,
That is the moder of tydynges,
As the see of welles and of sprynges;

And hyt was shapen lyk a cage. 1985
  "Certys," quod y, "in al myn age,
Ne saugh y such an hous as this."
And as y wondred me, ywys,
Upon this hous, tho war was y
How that myn egle, faste by, 1990
Was perched hye upon a stoon;
And I gan streghte to hym gon,
And seyde thus: "Y preye the
That thou a while abide me,
For Goddis love, and lete me seen 1995
What wondres in this place been;
For yit, paraunter, y may lere
Som good thereon, or sumwhat here
That leef me were, or that y wente."
  "Petre! that is myn entente," 2000
Quod he to me; "therfore y duelle.
But certeyn, oon thyng I the telle,
That but I bringe the therinne,
Ne shalt thou never kunne gynne
To come into hyt, out of doute, 2005
So faste hit whirleth, lo, aboute.
But sith that Joves, of his grace,
As I have seyd, wol the solace
Fynally with these thinges,
Unkouthe syghtes and tydynges, 2010
To passe with thyn hevynesse,
Such routhe hath he of thy distresse,
That thou suffrest debonairly—
And wost thyselven outtirly
Disesperat of alle blys, 2015
Syth that Fortune hath mad amys
The fruit of al thyn hertys reste
Languysshe and eke in poynt to breste—
That he, thrugh hys myghty merite,
Wol do the an ese, al be hyt lyte, 2020
And yaf expres commaundement,
To which I am obedient,
To further the with al my myght,
And wisse and teche the aryght

1946. fele, many. **1954. lette,** hinder. **1960. rounynges,** whisperings. **1968. qualme,** plague, death. **1974. chepe,** time of low prices. **1980. Al,** although. **1981. founded,** created. **1982. lyst,** is pleasing. **1984. As the see,** *i.e.* is mother of. **2004. gynne,** begin. **2010. Unkouthe,** unknown, strange. **2011. To passe with . . .,** to pass away thy heaviness with. **2017. The fruit . . .,** the fruition of all that would give thy heart rest. The MSS read *frot, foot.* Caxton and Thynne read *swote.* **2019. That,** continues *sith that* in l. 2007. **2024. wisse,** show.

Where thou maist most tidynges here,   2025
Shaltow here anoon many oon lere."
With this word he ryght anoon
Hente me up bytweene hys toon,
And at a wyndowe yn me broghte,
That in this hous was, as me thoghte—   2030
And therwithalle, me thoughte hit stente,
And nothing hyt aboute wente—
And me sette in the flore adoun.
But which a congregacioun
Of folk, as I saugh rome aboute,   2035
Some wythin and some wythoute,
Nas never seen, ne shal ben eft;
That, certys, in the world nys left
So many formed be Nature,
Ne ded so many a creature;   2040
That wel unnethe in that place
Hadde y a fote-brede of space.
And every wight that I saugh there
Rouned everych in others ere
A newe tydynge prively,   2045
Or elles tolde al openly
Ryght thus, and seyde: "Nost not thou
That ys betyd, lo, late or now?"
"No," quod he, "telle me what."
And than he tolde hym this and that,   2050
And swor therto that hit was soth—
"Thus hath he sayd," and "Thus he doth,"
"Thus shal hit be," "Thus herde y seye,"
"That shal be founde," "That dar I leye"—
That al the folk that ys alyve   2055
Ne han the kunnynge to discryve
The thinges that I herde there,
What aloude, and what in ere.
But al the wondermost was this:
Whan oon had herd a thing, ywis,   2060
He com forth ryght to another wight,
And gan him tellen anon-ryght
The same that to him was told,

Or hyt a forlong way was old,
But gan somwhat for to eche   2065
To this tydynge in this speche
More than hit ever was.
And nat so sone departed nas
Tho fro him, that he ne mette
With the thridde; and or he lette   2070
Any stounde, he told him als;
Were the tydynge soth or fals,
Yit wolde he telle hyt natheles,
And evermo with more encres
Than yt was erst. Thus north and south   2075
Wente every tydyng fro mouth to mouth,
And that encresing evermoo,
As fyr ys wont to quyke and goo
From a sparke spronge amys,
Til al a citee brent up ys.   2080
And whan that was ful yspronge,
And woxen more on every tonge
Than ever hit was, [hit] wente anoon
Up to a wyndowe out to goon;
Or, but hit myghte out there pace,   2085
Hyt gan out crepe at som crevace,
And flygh forth faste for the nones.
And somtyme saugh I thoo at ones
A lesyng and a sad soth sawe,
That gonne of aventure drawe   2090
Out at a wyndowe for to pace;
And, when they metten in that place,
They were achekked bothe two,
And neyther of hem moste out goo
For other, so they gonne crowde,   2095
Til ech of hem gan crien lowde,
"Lat me go first!" "Nay, but let me!
And here I wol ensuren the
Wyth the nones that thou wolt do so,
That I shal never fro the go,   2100
But be thyn owne sworen brother!
We wil medle us ech with other,

2028. **Hente,** snatched. **toon,** toes, claws. 2034. **which,** what. 2038. **left,** left alive. 2044. **Rouned,** whispered. 2048. **That ys betyd . . .** what has happened lately (*lit.* lately ere now). 2054. **leye,** wager. 2064. **a forlong way,** the length of time required to walk a furlong, a very short time. 2065. **eche,** increase, add to. 2070-1. **lette Any stounde,** delayed, let any time pass. Chaucer's description of the activity in the house of rumor amplifies Ovid, *Metam.*, XII. 39 ff. 2071. **als,** also. 1281. **yspronge,** spread. 2089. **a sad soth sawe,** a sober truth. 2094. **moste,** might. 2095. **other,** each other. **so,** thus. 2098. **ensuren,** give assurance. 2099. **Wyth the nones,** on the condition. 2102. **medle,** mix.

That no man, be they never so wrothe,
Shal han that oon [of] two, but bothe
At ones, al besyde his leve,   2105
Come we a-morwe or on eve,
Be we cried or stille yrouned."
Thus saugh I fals and soth compouned
Togeder fle for oo tydynge.

   Thus out at holes gunne wringe   2110
Every tydynge streght to Fame,
And she gan yeven ech hys name,
After hir disposicioun,
And yaf hem eke duracioun,
Somme to wexe and wane sone,   2115
As doth the faire white mone,
And let hem goon. Ther myghte y seen
Wynged wondres faste fleen,
Twenty thousand in a route,
As Eolus hem blew aboute.   2120

   And, Lord, this hous in alle tymes,
Was ful of shipmen and pilgrimes,
With scrippes bret-ful of lesynges,
Entremedled with tydynges,
And eek allone be hemselve.   2125
O, many a thousand tymes twelve
Saugh I eke of these pardoners,
Currours, and eke messangers,
With boystes crammed ful of lyes
As ever vessel was with lyes.   2130

And as I altherfastest wente
About, and dide al myn entente
Me for to pleyen and for to lere,
And eke a tydynge for to here,
That I had herd of som contre   2135
That shal not now be told for me—
For hit no nede is, redely;
Folk kan synge hit bet than I;
For al mot out, other late or rathe,
Alle the sheves in the lathe—   2140
I herde a grete noyse withalle
In a corner of the halle,
Ther men of love-tydynges tolde,
And I gan thiderward beholde;
For I saugh rennynge every wight,   2145
As faste as that they hadden myght;
And everych cried, "What thing is that?"
And somme sayde, "I not never what."
And whan they were alle on an hepe,
Tho behynde begunne up lepe,   2150
And clamben up on other faste,
And up the nose and yën kaste,
And troden fast on others heles,
And stampen, as men doon aftir eles.
Atte laste y saugh a man,   2155
Which that y [nevene] nat ne kan;
But he semed for to be
A man of gret auctorite. . . .

[Unfinished]

2105. **besyde,** without. 2110. **wringe,** squeeze. 2112. **yeven,** give. 2122. **shipmen and pilgrimes,** types of travelers who might bear news. Both had a reputation for exaggerated and false tales. 2123. **scrippes,** bags, wallets. **lesynges,** lies. 2129. **boystes,** boxes. 2130. **lyes,** dregs. 2139. **mot,** must. **rathe,** early. 2140. **lathe,** barn. 2147. **What thing is that?** *i.e.* What's going on? 2152. **And up the nose . . .** I adopt the reading *and yen* of MS Bodl. 638 because *an highen* (F) and *on hyghen* (Th) imply a word in the archetype ending in *en*, therefore not *high*. 2156. **nevene,** name. 2158. **A man of gret auctorite. . . .** It is useless to conjecture concerning the identity of the man who is presumably about to make an announcement. On the incompleteness of the poem see the introduction.

The Parlement of Foules

CHAUCER more than once alludes to the popular notion that on St. Valentine's day the birds choose their mates, and in *The Parlement of Foules* he makes this the ostensible subject of a poem. As in *The Book of the Duchess* and *The Hous of Fame* he employs the conventional device of reporting a dream, the poem opens with a discussion of dreams growing out of the fact that the poet has been reading all day in the *Somnium Scipionis* "of which Macrobye roughte nat a lyte." He dreams that just as Africanus had appeared to the younger Scipio, so he appears to him and conducts him to a garden in which stands a temple of Venus and where eventually he sees a multitude of birds who have assembled to carry out their annual custom, here under the direct supervision of the goddess Nature. The principal birds are three noble eagles who are suing for the affection of a beautiful female eagle that sits on Nature's hand. The lesser birds are irked by the long pleas of the three rivals and the hesitation of the formel eagle, who finally asks for a year (until the next St. Valentine's day) to make up her mind. Not a little of the humor of the poem is in the conflicting opinions expressed by the lesser birds. When they have at last chosen their mates they fly away with such loud chirping that it wakes the poet, who returns to his books in the hope that he may some day come upon something which will enable him "to fare the bet."

As early as Tyrwhitt in the eighteenth century, readers of the poem have felt that it was more than a pleasant bird fable. Since in *The Book of the Duchess* and possibly in *The Hous of Fame* Chaucer found the immediate impulse to composition in some occasion for which a poem would be appropriate, students have tried to find a situation in real life which would fit the poem, especially that part of it which portrays the rivalry of the three noble eagles for the favor of the beautiful formel. The theory that has enjoyed the most favor is that proposed by Koch and modified by Emerson (see bibliography in the notes to the poem). In its modified form the theory sees in the poem a reflection of the projected marriage of Richard II with Anne of Bohemia, which took place January 14, 1382, the rival suitors being considered Friedrich of Meissen and Charles VI of France. Neither of the supposed rivals of Richard has an entirely satisfactory claim to be so considered. Since the parallel between the poem and the facts in the situation is not exact, those who accept the theory are prepared to allow for a certain amount of poetic license. However, other situations have been suggested. Miss Rickert identified the formel eagle with Philippa, eldest daughter of John of Gaunt, whose marriage was under consideration in 1380–81. None of the three persons equated with the male birds in her theory was actually a suitor. Braddy proposed connecting the poem with the peace negotiations of 1377, which according to Froissart included discussion of a marriage between Richard and the young princess Marie of France. In this case there appears to have been only one rival in the field, so that the third eagle is not identified. On the other hand, Manly rejected any historical application and saw in the poem only a conventional valentine poem of the *demande d'amours* type. The weakness of this explanation is that in all other examples of the type the debate is over a much more abstract, or at least general, question. Still other scholars have viewed the poem as a version of the folk-tale *motif* of the contending lovers (Farnham, without rejecting completely an historical application), as an explanation of the nature of love (Langhans), as a discussion of true and false felicity (Lumiansky), etc. From the many attempts to interpret the poem it seems clear that most readers are unwilling to consider it simply a bird fable, and feel that in writing the poem Chaucer meant to represent some situation or topic which would be understood by his courtly audience. Whether that situation has been identified should still be considered an open question.

One is naturally reluctant to suggest a precise date for the composition of the poem. It is generally thought to be later than *The Hous of Fame*, but we cannot be certain when that poem was written (see the introduction to it). If the Richard-Anne theory is accepted, *The Parlement* would presumably fall between the opening of the negotiations in the summer of 1380 and the marriage in January, 1382. The Richard-Marie theory, on the other hand, would carry it back to 1377. If we reject all historical interpretations, we have little on which to base an opinion save the probability (and it is not a certainty) that Chaucer did not know the work of Boccaccio until after his second trip to Italy in 1378.

No direct source of the poem is known, but Chaucer has drawn various features from the *Somnium Scipionis* and Alanus de Insulis's *De Planctu Naturae*, both of which he mentions, and Boccaccio's *Teseida*, which he does not. While retaining the framework of the dream, he has abandoned the eight-syllable couplet of *The Book of the Duchess* and *The Hous of Fame* and now writes in the seven-line stanza which he was to use in the *Troilus*.

THE PARLEMENT OF FOULES

Here begyneth the Parlement of Foules.

The lyf so short, the craft so long to lerne,
Th'assay so hard, so sharp the conquerynge,
The dredful joye, alwey that slit so yerne:
Al this mene I by Love, that my felynge
Astonyeth with his wonderful werkynge   5
So sore iwis, that whan I on hym thynke,
Nat wot I wel wher that I flete or synke.

For al be that I knowe nat Love in dede.
Ne wot how that he quiteth folk here hyre,
Yit happeth me ful ofte in bokes reede   10
Of his myracles and his crewel yre.
There rede I wel he wol be lord and syre;

I dar nat seyn—his strokes been so sore—
But "God save swich a lord!" I can no more.

Of usage—what for lust and what for lore—   15
On bokes rede I ofte, as I yow tolde.
But wherfore that I speke al this? Nat yore
Agon, it happede me for to beholde
Upon a bok, was write with lettres olde,
And therupon, a certeyn thing to lerne,   20
The longe day ful faste I redde and yerne.

For out of olde feldes, as men seyth,
Cometh al this newe corn from yer to yere,

The text is based on Camb. Univ. MS Gg. 4. 27, with the worst of the spelling peculiarities normalized. **1.** The line is a paraphrase of the familiar "Ars longa, vita brevis." **3. dredful.** The meanings "terrifying" and "uncertain," "risky" may both be present. **slit,** slides away. **yerne,** quickly. **5. Astonyeth,** is astonished. **7. Nat wot I . . . wher,** I do not know whether. **flete,** float. **8.** Chaucer's protestations here and elsewhere that he has no personal knowledge of love are not necessarily to be taken seriously. **9. quiteth . . . here hyre,** pays . . . what they have earned. **11. myracles,** wonderful works. **13. nat,** naught. **14. I can no more,** (as we should put it) that's all I can say. **15. lust,** pleasure. **lore,** learning. **17–18. yore Agon,** a long while ago. **21. yerne,** eagerly; cf. the meaning in l. 3. **22. as men seyth,** as one says (*men,* singular number, is the indefinite).

And out of olde bokes, in good feyth,
Cometh al this newe science that men lere.   25
But now to purpos as of this matere;
To rede forth hit gan me so delite
That al that day me thoughte but a lyte.

This bok of which I make mencioun
Entitled was al thus as I shal telle: 30
"Tullyus of the Drem of Scipioun."
Chapitres sevene it hadde, of hevene and helle
And erthe, and soules that therinne dwelle,
Of whiche, as shortly as I can it trete,
Of his sentence I wol yow seyn the greete.   35

Fyrst telleth it, whan Scipion was come
In Affrik, how he meteth Massynisse,
That hym for joie in armes hath inome;
Thanne telleth it here speche and al the blysse
That was betwix hem til the day gan mysse,   40
And how his auncestre, Affrycan so deere,
Gan in his slep that nyght to hym apere.

Thanne telleth it that from a sterry place
How Affrycan hath hym Cartage shewed,
And warnede hym beforn of al his grace,   45
And seyde hym what man, lered other lewed,
That lovede comun profyt, wel ithewed,
He shulde into a blysful place wende,
There as joye is that last withouten ende.

Thanne axede he if folk that here been dede   50
Han lyf and dwellynge in another place.
And Affrican seyde, "Ye, withouten drede,"

And that oure present worldes lyves space
Nis but a maner deth, what wey we trace,
And rightful folk shul gon, after they dye,   55
To hevene; and shewede hym the Galaxye.

Thanne shewede he hym the lytel erthe that
    here is,
At regard of the hevenes quantite;
And after shewede he hym the nyne speres,
And after that the melodye herde he   60
That cometh of thilke speres thryes thre,
That welle is of musik and melodye
In this world here, and cause of armonye.

Than bad he hym, syn erthe was so lyte,
And ful of torment and of harde grace,   65
That he ne shulde hym in the world delyte.
Thanne tolde he hym, in certeyn yeres space
That every sterre shulde come into his place
Ther it was first, and al shulde out of mynde
That in this world is don of al mankynde.   70

Thanne preyede hym Scipion to telle hym al
The wey to come into that hevene blisse.
And he seyde, "Know thyself first immortal,
And loke ay besyly thow werche and wysse
To comun profit, and thow shalt not mysse   75
To comen swiftly to that place deere
That ful of blysse is and of soules cleere.

"But brekers of the lawe, soth to seyne,
And likerous folk, after that they ben dede,

---

25. science, learning, knowledge. **lere,** learn. **28. lyte,** little (time). **31. the Drem of Scipioun.** In 54 B.C. Cicero wrote a treatise on political science (*De Re Publica*), in six books. Long lost, about a third of it has been discovered in modern times. To this treatise the *Somnium Scipionis* formed the epilogue and was preserved separately by Macrobius, a fifth-century antiquarian, who made it the subject of a learned commentary. Chaucer summarizes it in the lines which follow. **35. sentence,** meaning, thought. **greete,** gist. **36. Scipion,** the younger Scipio (185–129 B.C.), who in 146 B.C. destroyed Carthage. In 150 B.C. he went on a mission to Massinissa, King of Numidia. They talked late into the night about Scipio's grandfather, the elder Scipio Africanus, so that when the young man went to bed he dreamed about his distinguished ancestor. See below, ll. 99 ff. **38. inome,** taken. **40. mysse,** fail. **43. sterry,** starry. **45. warnede,** informed; cf. *HF* 893. **of al his grace,** through his kindness. **46. seyde,** told. **what,** whatever. **lered other lewed,** learned or unlearned. **47. ithewed,** endowed with virtues, *i.e.* that lived virtuously. **49. last,** lasts (lasteth). **53. worldes,** worldly. **54. what wey we trace,** whatever course we follow. **56. Galaxye,** the Milky Way (*orbem lacteum* in the *Somnium Scipionis*). **58. At regard of,** in comparison with. **62. welle,** source. **64. lyte,** little. **68. That every sterre shulde come . . .** The *Somnium* says: "But when all the stars have returned to their starting-points and have restored, after long periods, the former configuration of the entire heavens, then that can be truly termed the [cosmic] year. I hardly venture to surmise how many generations of men may be contained within it." The period is about 26,000 years. **69. Ther,** where. **70. of,** by. **72. hevene,** heavenly. **74. wysse,** point the way. **77. cleere,** bright, noble. **79. likerous,** lecherous.

Shul whirle aboute th'erthe alwey in peyne, 80
Tyl many a world be passed, out of drede,
And than, foryeven al hir wikked dede,
Than shul they come into that blysful place,
To which to comen God the sende his grace."

The day gan faylen, and the derke nyght, 85
That reveth bestes from here besynesse,
Berafte me my bok for lak of lyght,
And to my bed I gan me for to dresse,
Fulfyld of thought and busy hevynesse;
For bothe I hadde thyng which that I nolde, 90
And ek I ne hadde that thyng that I wolde.

But fynally, my spirit at the laste,
For-wery of my labour al the day,
Tok reste, that made me to slepe faste,
And in my slep I mette, as that I lay, 95
How Affrican, ryght in the selfe aray
That Scipion hym say byfore that tyde,
Was come and stod right at my beddes syde.

The wery huntere, slepynge in his bed,
To wode ayeyn his mynde goth anon; 100
The juge dremeth how his plees been sped;
The cartere dremeth how his cartes gon;
The riche of gold; the knyght fyght with his
fon;
The syke met he drynketh of the tonne;
The lovere met he hath his lady wonne. 105

Can I nat seyn if that the cause were
For I hadde red of Affrican byforn,
That made me to mete that he stod there;
But thus seyde he: "Thow hast the so wel born
In lokynge of myn olde bok totorn, 110
Of which Macrobye roughte nat a lyte,
That sumdel of thy labour wolde I quyte."

Cytherea, thow blysful lady swete,
That with thy fyrbrond dauntest whom thee
lest,
And madest me this sweven for to mete, 115
Be thow myn helpe in this, for thow mayst best!
As wisly as I sey the north-north-west,
Whan I began my sweven for to write,
So yif me myght to ryme and ek t'endyte!

This forseyde Affrican me hente anon, 120
And forth with hym unto a gate broughte,
Ryght of a park walled with grene ston,
And over the gate, with lettres large iwroughte,
There were vers iwriten, as me thoughte,
On eyther half, of ful gret difference, 125
Of which I shal now seyn the pleyn sentence:

"Thorgh me men gon into that blysful place
Of hertes hele and dedly woundes cure;
Thorgh me men gon unto the welle of grace,129
There grene and lusty May shal evere endure.
This is the wey to al good aventure.

---

80. **whirle aboute th'erthe . . .**, *i.e.* wander about the earth (*terram ipsam volutantur*), not through space. 81. **many a world**, Chaucer's rendering of *multis . . . saeculis, i.e.* until ages have passed. 82. **foryeven**, forgiven. 86. **reveth . . .**, takes away (releases) beasts from their labor. The idea is from Dante, *Inferno*, II. 1–3. 88. **dresse**, direct my course. 89. **busy hevynesse**, disquiet. 90–91. The idea of this couplet is expressed by Boethius (III, pr. 3): ". . . for that the lakkide somwhat that thow woldest nat han lakkid, or elles thou haddest that thow noldest nat han had." 93. **For-wery of**, exhausted from. 95. **mette**, dreamed. 97. **say**, saw. 99–105. This stanza is traced to Claudian by Pratt (*Speculum*, XXII. 422). 103. **fyght**, fights (fighteth). **fon**, foes. 104. **The syke met**, the sick man dreams. **tonne**, wine cask, symbolizing the pleasures of the tavern. 111. **roughte**, cared. 112. **quyte**, repay. 113. **Cytherea**, Venus, 114. **fyrbrond**, the torch with which Venus inflamed the passions; cf. *RR*, 3476, etc. 115. **sweven**, dream. 117. **north-north-west.** The astronomical reference is inexact but sufficiently natural for a layman. Venus would have been in such a position in the years 1374, 1375, 1377, 1379, 1380, 1382, 1383, etc., but would have been visible as an evening star to an observer in England only in 1374, 1377, 1382. One MS reads *north nor west*, which would make Venus a morning star; the reference would fit 1381. Lange suggested that Chaucer may have described the position of Venus with respect to the north of a magnetic needle (cf. ll. 148 ff) rather than the North Star. The phrase is also sometimes taken to mean "in an unpropitious position" or "not at all"; cf. Hamlet's "I am but mad north-north-west." 120. **Affrican**, Scipio Africanus the elder. **hente**, took. 124. **vers**, verses. 126. **pleyn sentence**, full meaning. 127. **Thorgh me men gon . . .** The park is the garden of love, where some find grace and others only sorrow. 128. **hele**, health, well-being. 129. **welle**, spring, source. 130. **There**, where.

Be glad, thow redere, and thy sorwe of-caste;
Al open am I—passe in, and sped thee faste!"

"Thorgh me men gon," than spak that other side,
"Unto the mortal strokes of the spere　　　　135
Of which Disdayn and Daunger is the gyde,
Ther nevere tre shal fruyt ne leves bere.
This strem yow ledeth to the sorweful were
There as the fish in prysoun is al drye;
Th'eschewing is only the remedye!"　　　　140

These vers of gold and blak iwriten were,
Of whiche I gan astonyed to beholde,
For with that oon encresede ay my fere,
And with that other gan myn herte bolde;　　144
That oon me hette, that other dide me colde.
No wit hadde I, for errour, for to chese,
To entre or flen, or me to save or lese.

Right as, betwixen adamauntes two
Of evene myght, a pece of yren set
Ne hath no myght to meve to ne fro—　　　150
For what that oon may hale, that other let—
Ferde I, that nyste whether me was bet
To entre or leve, til Affrycan, my gide,
Me hente and shof in at the gates wide,

And seyde, "It stondeth writen in thy face,　　155
Thyn errour, though thow telle it not to me;
But dred the not to come into this place,
For this writyng nys nothyng ment bi the,
Ne by non but he Loves servaunt be:

For thow of love hast lost thy tast, I gesse,　　160
As sek man hath of swete and bytternesse.

"But natheles, although that thow be dul,
Yit that thow canst not do, yit mayst thow se.
For many a man that may nat stonde a pul,
It liketh hym atte wrastlyng for to be,　　　165
And demeth yit wher he do bet or he.
And if thow haddest connyng for t'endite,
I shal the shewe mater of to wryte."

With that myn hand in his he tok anon,　　　169
Of which I confort caughte, and wente in faste.
But, Lord, so I was glad and wel begoon!
For overal where that I myne eyen caste
Were treës clad with leves that ay shal laste,
Ech in his kynde, of colour fresh and greene
As emeraude, that joye was to seene.　　　175

The byldere ok, and ek the hardy asshe;
The piler elm, the cofre unto carayne;
The boxtre pipere, holm to whippes lashe;
The saylynge fyr; the cipresse, deth to pleyne;
The shetere ew; the asp for shaftes pleyne;　　180
The olyve of pes, and eke the dronke vyne;
The victor palm, the laurer to devyne.

A gardyn saw I ful of blosmy bowes
Upon a ryver, in a grene mede,
There as swetnesse everemore inow is,　　　185
With floures white, blewe, yelwe, and rede,
And colde welle-stremes, nothyng dede,
That swymmen ful of smale fishes lighte,
With fynnes rede and skales sylver bryghte.

---

136. Daunger, an allegorical character in the *Roman de la Rose* who keeps lovers away from the rose. The character symbolizes the quality of shame or modesty in women, which causes them to appear haughty and disposed to repel advances.
137. Ther, where. **138. were,** weir, trap for fish. **140. eschewing,** avoiding. **142. astonyed,** bewildered. **145. hette,**
inflamed. **dide me colde,** chilled. **146. errour,** doubt, uncertainty. Cf. l. 156. **chese,** choose. **147. lese,** lose, be lost.
148. adamauntes, loadstones. **150. meve,** move. **151. hale,** attract. **let,** hinders, repels. **152. Ferde,** fared. **154. shof,**
pushed. **158. nys nothyng ment bi the,** is not meant for thee. **159. by non but,** for any one unless. **163. that,**
what. **165. atte,** at the. **166. wher he do bet or he,** whether this one does better or that one. **171. wel begoon,**
happy. **172. overal,** everywhere. **176. The byldere ok,** etc. The following catalogue of trees is a poetical convention going
back to Ovid (*Metam.*, x. 90–108) and several other Latin poets. It recalls the still more famous catalogue of ships in the
second book of the *Iliad*. **177. piler elm . . .** The elm was planted as a support for the vine, and the wood was commonly
used for coffins. **carayne,** carcases or corpses. Cf. the *De Planctu Naturae*, meter III. **178. boxtre pipere.** Some of the wood-
winds are still made of boxwood. **holm,** holly, used for whip handles. **179. saylynge fyr,** used for masts and spars. **180.
shetere ew . . . asp.** Bows were made of yew, arrows of aspen. **182. laurer,** laurel, sacred to Apollo, used in divination.
187. welle-stremes, springs, or streams flowing therefrom.

On every bow the bryddes herde I synge,   190
With voys of aungel in here armonye;
Some besyede hem here bryddes forth to
     brynge;
The litel conyes to here pley gunne hye;
And ferther al aboute I gan aspye   194
The dredful ro, the buk, the hert and hynde,
Squyreles, and bestes smale of gentil kynde.

Of instrumentes of strenges in acord
Herde I so pleye a ravyshyng swetnesse,
That God, that makere is of al and lord,
Ne herde nevere beter, as I gesse.   200
Therwith a wynd, unnethe it myghte be lesse,
Made in the leves grene a noyse softe
Acordaunt to the foules song alofte.

The air of that place so attempre was   204
That nevere was ther grevaunce of hot ne cold;
There wex ek every holsom spice and gras,
Ne no man may there waxe sek ne old;
Yit was there joye more a thousandfold
Than man can telle; ne nevere wolde it nyghte,
But ay cler day to any manes syghte.   210

Under a tre besyde a welle I say
Cupide, oure lord, his arwes forge and file;
And at his fet his bowe al redy lay;
And Wille, his doughter, temprede al this whyle
The hevedes in the welle, and with hire wile   215
She couchede hem, after as they shulde serve—
Some for to sle and some to wounde and kerve.

Tho was I war of Plesaunce anon-ryght,
And of Aray, and Lust, and Curteysie,   219
And of the Craft that can and hath the myght
To don by force a wight to don folye—
Disfigurat was she, I nyl nat lye;
And by hymself, under an ok, I gesse,
Saw I Delyt, that stod with Gentilesse.

I saw Beute withouten any atyr,   225
And Youthe, ful of game and jolyte;
Foolhardynesse, Flaterye, and Desyr,
Messagerye, and Meede, and other thre—
Here names shul not here be told for me—
And upon pilers greete of jasper longe   230
I saw a temple of bras ifounded stronge.

Aboute that temple daunseden alwey
Women inowe, of whiche some ther weere
Fayre of hemself, and some of hem were
     gay;
In kertels, al dishevele, wente they there: 235
That was here offyce alwey, yer by yeere.
And on the temple, of doves white and fayre
Saw I syttynge many an hundred peyre.

Byfore the temple dore ful soberly
Dame Pees sat, with a curtyn in hire hond,   240
And by hire syde, wonder discretly,
Dame Pacience syttynge there I fond,
With face pale, upon an hil of sond;
And aldernext, withinne and ek withoute,
Byheste and Art, and of here folk a route.   245

---

192. forth to brynge, to bring up. **193. conyes,** rabbits. **195. dredful,** timid, fearful. **201. unnethe,** scarcely.
204. attempre, temperate. **206. wex,** grew. **211. welle,** spring. **say,** saw. **214. Wille.** The name of Cupid's daughter
translates *Volutà* in Boccaccio's *Teseida* (VII, st. 54) and means "sensual pleasure." In the *De Genealogia Deorum* (Bk. IX,
chap. 5) Boccaccio, citing Apuleius, names Psyche as her mother. See K. Malone, *MLR*, XLV (1950). 63. **215. wile,** subtlety.
216. couchede, laid down. **after as,** according as. **217. kerve,** cut. **218. Tho,** then. **war,** aware. **219. Lust,** Pleasure.
220. the Craft. In the *Teseida* (VII, st. 55) this is "l'Arti c' hanno potestate di fare altrui a forza far follia." In Chaucer she
is feminine and singular, but in Boccaccio "nel loro aspetto molto sfigurate da l' imagine nostra." In this series of personi-
fications Chaucer follows Boccaccio almost throughout, if we assume that "il folle Ardire, Lusinghe e Ruffiania [bawd]"
correspond to Chaucer's Fool-hardynesse, Flaterye, and Desyr, but the figures in the next line have nothing to correspond
to in Boccaccio. **226. game,** playfulness. **228. Messagerye,** the allegorical figure represents the carrying of messages.
Meede, Bribery. **229. for,** by. **231.** For a similar description of the temple of Venus see *KnT*, A 1918 ff. **233. inowe,** enough.
235. dishevele, with hair unbound. **240. curtyn.** A tempting suggestion of Prof. Chew (*The Virtues Reconciled*, pp. 121–3)
would make *curtyn* mean "a sword without a point" (see *NED*, s.v. *curtan* and *curtana*), Ital. *cortana*. Since Chaucer is
translating *cortina* (confirmed by the rime) the substitution or mistake must be attributed to Boccaccio or his source. In
Ogier le Danois the hero's sword is named Cortain (ll. 5833, 5960). **243. hil of sond.** The hil of sand is not in Boccaccio.
245. Byheste and Art. In Boccaccio "Promesse e Arte," possibly implying artful promises.

Withinne the temple, of sykes hoote as fyr
I herde a swogh that gan aboute renne,
Whiche sikes were engendered with desyr,
That maden every auter for to brenne
Of newe flaume, and wel espyed I thenne   250
That al the cause of sorwes that they drye
Cam of the bitter goddesse Jelosye.

The god Priapus saw I, as I wente,
Withinne the temple in sovereyn place stonde,
In swich aray as whan the asse hym shente   255
With cri by nyghte, and with his sceptre in
    honde.
Ful besyly men gunne assaye and fonde
Upon his hed to sette, of sondry hewe,
Garlondes ful of freshe floures newe.

And in a prive corner in disport   260
Fond I Venus and hire porter Richesse,
That was ful noble and hautayn of hyre port.
Derk was that place, but afterward lightnesse
I saw a lyte, unnethe it myghte be lesse,
And on a bed of gold she lay to reste   265
Til that the hote sonne gan to weste.

Hyre gilte heres with a golden thred
Ibounden were, untressed as she lay,
And naked from the brest unto the hed

Men myghte hir sen; and, sothly for to say,   270
The remenaunt was wel kevered to my pay,
Ryght with a subtyl coverchef of Valence—
Ther nas no thikkere cloth of no defense.

The place yaf a thousand savours sote,
And Bachus, god of wyn, sat hir besyde,   275
And Ceres next, that doth of hunger boote,
And, as I seyde, amyddes lay Cypride,
To whom on knees two yonge folk ther cryde
To ben here helpe. But thus I let hir lye,
And ferther in the temple I gan espie   280

That, in dispit of Dyane the chaste,
Ful many a bowe ibroke heng on the wal
Of maydenes swiche as gunne here tymes waste
In hyre servyse; and peynted overal
Ful many a story, of which I touche shal   285
A fewe, as of Calyxte and Athalante,
And many a mayde of which the name I wante.

Semyramis, Candace, and Hercules,
Biblis, Dido, Thisbe, and Piramus,
Tristram, Isaude, Paris, and Achilles,   290
Eleyne, Cleopatre, and Troylus,
Silla, and ek the moder of Romulus:
Alle these were peynted on that other syde,
And al here love, and in what plyt they dyde.

246. sykes, sighs. **247. renne,** run. **248. with,** by. **249. auter,** altar. **brenne,** burn. **250. flaume,** flame. **251. drye,** suffer. **253. Priapus.** At night during a festival of Bacchus, Priapus, enamored of the nymph Lotis, was about to embrace her while she slept, when an ass brayed and not only wakened her in time to escape but a host of others to laugh at his discomfiture. Ovid's *Fasti,* I. 415–40. **257. assaye, fonde.** Both words mean "try." **260. in a prive corner.** Boccaccio says, "In più secreta parte del tempio si sta a diletto." **262. hautayn,** haughty. **port,** bearing. **266. weste,** move westward. **268. untressed,** unbraided. **271. pay,** satisfaction. **272. Valence,** presumably the town in France near Lyons. **273. of no defense,** for any protection. **276. boote,** remedy. **277. Cypride,** Venus, from the oblique case of Cyprus (*Cypris*), where she was worshipped. Cf *HF* 518. **279. To ben here helpe,** to help them. **282. bowe ibroke.** Since Diana is regularly represented as a huntress, the broken bows are a symbol of the loss or abandonment of chastity in the encounter with love. **heng,** hung. **284. overal,** all around. **286. A fewe.** The list of lovers which follows is partly from stanzas 61–62 of the *Teseida* (Bk. VII) and partly from the *Inferno,* v. Chaucer adds Candace, Troilus, Scylla, and the mother of Romulus. Most of these names are too well known to need comment. **Calyxte,** Callisto, a nymph beloved by Jove, who changed her into a she-bear to conceal the affair from Juno. **Athalante,** Atalanta, who required her suitors to contend with her in a foot race, and was finally won by Hippomenes, who defeated her, with the help of Venus, by strewing golden apples along the way. **288. Semyramis,** Semiramis, Queen of Assyria, beautiful wife of Ninus; she is the legendary builder of Babylon and its famous hanging gardens. **Candace,** an Indian queen who, according to the Alexander romances, got Alexander into her power. But the name was confused with Canace, who, having borne a child by her brother, killed herself at the command of Aeolus, her father (Ovid, *Heroides,* XI). Cf. *CT,* B 77–80. **Hercules,** whose wife Deianira, in order to keep his love, sent him a shirt dipped in the blood of the centaur killed by him, not knowing that the blood had been poisoned by Hercules' arrow. **289. Biblis,** in love with her brother until finally changed into a fountain. The story is in Ovid (*Metam.,* IX. 454–665). **292. Silla,** Scylla, who for love of Minos cut off her father's hair, upon which his life depended. **moder of Romulus,** Rhea Silvia, who broke her vows as a Vestal Virgin and became the mother of Romulus and Remus. **294. plyt,** plight.

Whan I was come ayen into the place   295
That I of spak, that was so sote and grene,
Forth welk I tho myselven to solace.
Tho was I war wher that ther sat a queene
That, as of lyght the somer sonne shene
Passeth the sterre, right so over mesure   300
She fayrer was than any creature.

And in a launde, upon an hil of floures,
Was set this noble goddesse Nature.
Of braunches were here halles and here boures
Iwrought after here cast and here mesure;   305
Ne there nas foul that cometh of engendrure
That they ne were prest in here presence
To take hire dom and yeve hire audyence.

For this was on seynt Valentynes day,
Whan every foul cometh there to chese his
     make,   310
Of every kynde that men thynke may,
And that so huge a noyse gan they make
That erthe and eyr and tre and every lake
So ful was, that unethe was there space
For me to stonde, so ful was al the place.   315

And right as Aleyn, in the Pleynt of Kynde,
Devyseth Nature of aray and face,
In swich aray men myghte hire there fynde.

This noble emperesse, ful of grace,
Bad every foul to take his owne place,   320
As they were woned alwey fro yer to yeere
Seynt Valentynes day to stonden theere.

That is to seyn, the foules of ravyne
Were hyest set, and thanne the foules smale
That eten as hem Nature wolde enclyne,   325
As worm or thyng of which I telle no tale;
And water-foul sat lowest in the dale;
But foul that lyveth by sed sat on the grene,
And that so fele that wonder was to sene.

There myghte men the royal egle fynde,   330
That with his sharpe lok perseth the sonne,
And othere egles of a lowere kynde,
Of whiche that clerkes wel devyse conne.
Ther was the tiraunt with his fetheres donne
And grey, I mene the goshauk, that doth pyne
To bryddes for his outrageous ravyne.   336

The gentyl faucoun, that with his feet distrayn-
     eth
The kynges hand; the hardy sperhauk eke,
The quayles foo; the merlioun, that payneth
Hymself ful ofte the larke for to seke;   340
There was the douve with hire eyen meke;
The jelous swan, ayens his deth that syngeth;
The oule ek, that of deth the bode bryngeth;

296. **sote**, sweet. 297. **welk**, walked. 299. **shene**, bright. 300. **Passeth**, surpasses. **sterre**, star. **over**, beyond. 302. **launde**, glade, clearing. 303. **Nature**. The source of Chaucer's account, as he indicates in l. 316, is the *De Planctu Naturae* of Alanus de Insulis (*c.* 1128–1203). It is printed in Migne's *Patrologia Latina*, vol. 210. 305. **cast**, plan, design. **mesure**, dimension. 307. **prest**, ready. 308. **dom**, judgment. 309. **seynt Valentynes day**. According to a popular belief in the Middle Ages, the birds chose their mates on this day. In the *Paston Letters* we read, "And, cosyn, uppon Fryday is Seint Valentynes Day, and every brydde chesyth hym a make . . ." (ed. Gairdner, III. 169). A close parallel to the latter part of this stanza has been found in the *Speculum Stultorum*. See R. R. Raymo, *MLN*, LXXI. 159–60. 310. **chese**, choose. **make**, mate. 314. **unethe**, scarcely. 316. **Aleyn**. See note to l. 303. The description of Nature runs to 20 pages. 317. **Devyseth**, describes. 321. **woned**, wont. 323. **foules of ravyne**, birds of prey. The four classes of birds are generally supposed to symbolize four classes of society: birds of prey/nobles, birds that eat worms/bourgeois class, water-fowl/merchant class, seed-fowl/agricultural interests. 327. **lowest**, presumably near the water level, not necessarily lowest in rank. 329. **fele**, many. 330. **royal egle**, *i.e.* the king of birds. 331. **sharpe lok . . .** Skeat noted that Philip de Thaun in his *Bestiaire* says: Egle est rei de oisel. En Latine raisun *cler-veant* le apellum, Ke le solail verat quant il plus cler serat. In the ME. *Bestiary* the eagle flies toward the sun to renew his youth. Cf. Pliny, *Nat. Hist.*, Bk. x, chap. 3. 332. **othere egles**. Skeat notes that six kinds of eagle are enumerated in Pliny (*ibid*), but Chaucer follows more closely suggestions in Alanus de Insulis, where many kinds of birds are represented as pictured on Nature's robe. 333. **wel devyse conne**, know well how to explain. 334. **tiraunt**, tyrant. 335. **pyne**, injury. 336. **ravyne**, rapacity. 337. **faucoun**, falcon. **distrayneth The kinges hand**. In hawking, a sport of the nobility, the hawk was carried perched on the fist. 338. **sperhauk**, sparrowhawk. 339. **merlioun**, merlin, the smallest of the hawks. 342. **ayens his deth that syngeth**. A common notion; cf. Tennyson's *The Dying Swan*. The epithet *jelous* may refer to "the fierceness of the male swan during the breeding season" (Lounsbury). **ayens**, at the approach of. 343. **bode**, omen.

The crane, the geaunt, with his trompes soun;
The thef, the chough; and ek the janglynge
    pye; 345
The skornynge jay; the eles fo, heroun;
The false lapwynge, ful of trecherye;
The stare, that the conseyl can bewrye;
The tame ruddok, and the coward kyte;
The kok, that orloge is of thorpes lyte; 350

The sparwe, Venus sone; the nyghtyngale,
That clepeth forth the grene leves newe;
The swalwe, mortherere of the foules smale
That maken hony of floures freshe of hewe;
The wedded turtil, with hire herte trewe; 355
The pecok, with his aungels fetheres bryghte;
The fesaunt, skornere of the cok by nyghte;

The waker goos; the cukkow ever unkynde;
The popynjay, ful of delicasye;
The drake, stroyere of his owene kynde; 360
The stork, the wrekere of avouterye;
The hote cormeraunt of glotenye;
The raven wys; the crowe with vois of care;
The throstil old; the frosty feldefare.

What shulde I seyn? Of foules every kynde 365
That in this world han fetheres and stature
Men myghten in that place assembled fynde
Byfore the noble goddesse of Nature,
And everich of hem did his besy cure
Benygnely to chese or for to take, 370
By hire acord, his formel or his make.

But to the poynt: Nature held on hire hond
A formel egle, of shap the gentilleste
That evere she among hire werkes fond,
The moste benynge and the goodlieste. 375
In hire was every vertu at his reste,
So ferforth that Nature hireself hadde blysse
To loke on hire, and ofte hire bek to kysse.

Nature, the vicaire of the almyghty Lord, 379
That hot, cold, hevy, lyght, moyst, and dreye
Hath knyt by evene noumbres of acord,
In esy voys began to speke and seye,
"Foules, tak hed of my sentence, I preye,
And for youre ese, in fortheryng of youre
    nede,
As faste as I may speke, I wol me speede. 385

344. **geaunt,** giant (because of its height). **trompes,** trumpet-like. **345. The thef, the chough,** i.e. the chough (that is a) thief. **janglynge,** chattering. **346. skornynge,** because of its querulous screech. **347. trecherye,** deceit. The lapwing pretends to be wounded when its young are in danger. **348. stare,** starling. It has been suggested that the betraying of counsel is a reference to some story like *The Manciple's Tale,* in which a starling rather than a crow speaks. **bewrye,** betray. **349. ruddok,** the (English) robin. **350. orloge,** clock. **thorpes,** villages. **lyte,** little. **351. sparwe, Venus sone.** The sparrow was sacred to Venus, hence popularly considered amorous; cf. *CT,* A 626. **352. clepeth forth . . .,** i.e. calls forth by singing in the Spring. **353. foules smale,** bees, which were sometimes classified as birds. **355. wedded turtil . . .** Alanus says the turtle-dove never takes a second mate. **356. aungels fetheres.** Angels' wings were sometimes represented like peacock feathers; cf. Jameson, *Sacred and Legendary Art,* pp. 111, 136, and for numerous other examples Mary Giffin, *Studies on Chaucer and His Audience* (1956), pp. 49–51. **357. fesaunt.** "Perhaps Chaucer mixed up the description of the pheasant in Alanus with that of the 'gallus silvestris, privatoris galli *deridens* desidiam,' which occurs almost immediately below . . . Or he may allude to the fact, vouched for in Stanley's *Hist. of Birds,* ed. 1880, p. 279, that the Pheasant will breed with the common Hen." (Skeat). It has been suggested also that as the cock crows at dawn, so the pheasant crows at sunset before he goes to roost. **358. waker goos.** The vigilance of the goose was vouched for by the story that in 387 B.C. Manlius repulsed a night attack on the Roman Capitol after being wakened by the sacred geese in the temple of Juno. **unkynde,** unnatural, in that it lays its egg in the nests of other birds and the young cuckoo eventually kills the foster mother; cf. Pliny, *Nat. Hist.,* Bk. x, chap. ii; Baudouin de Condé, *La Messe des Oisiaus,* ll. 381–397. However, the allusion may be to the saying not recorded before *King Lear,* I. iv. 205: The hedge-sparrow fed the cuckoo so long, That it had it head bit off by it young. Cf. below, l. 612. **359. delicasye,** voluptuousness. Pliny says the parrot is "in vino praecipue lasciva" (*Nat. Hist.,* Bk. x, chap. 58). **360. stroyere.** The drake kills young ducks. **361. wrekere,** avenger. **avouterye,** adultery. Skeat cites a story in Alexander Neckam of a stork which had its mate torn to pieces because of her infidelity (*Liber de Naturis Rerum,* Bk. i, chap. 64), and notes other instances illustrative of the supposed characteristic. **362. of glotenye,** gluttonous. **363. raven wys,** because endowed, according to classical legend, with the gift of prophecy. **vois of care,** because the crow is a bird of ill omen. **364. old.** The thrush was supposed to attain a great age. **frosty,** because a winter bird in England. **366. stature,** bodily shape. **369. besy cure,** diligent effort. **371. formel,** normally the female of the eagle or hawk, but here used as mate or companion. **376. at his reste,** at its natural resting place. **377. So ferforth,** to such an extent.

"Ye knowe wel how, seynt Valentynes day,
By my statute and thorgh my governaunce
Ye come for to cheese—and fle youre wey—
Youre makes, as I prike yow with plesaunce;
But natheles, my ryghtful ordenaunce   390
May I nat lete for al this world to wynne,
That he that most is worthi shal begynne.

"The tersel egle, as that ye knowe wel,
The foul royal, above yow in degre,
The wyse and worthi, secre, trewe as stel,   395
Which I have formed, as ye may wel se,
In every part as it best liketh me—
It nedeth not his shap yow to devyse—
He shal first chese and speken in his gyse.

"And after hym by order shul ye chese,   400
After youre kynde, everich as yow lyketh,
And, as youre hap is, shul ye wynne or lese.
But which of yow that love most entriketh,
God sende hym hire that sorest for hym
     syketh!"
And therwithal the tersel gan she calle,   405
And seyde, "My sone, the choys is to the falle.

"But natheles, in this condicioun
Mot be the choys of everich that is heere,
That she agre to his eleccioun,
Whoso he be that shulde be hire feere.   410
This is oure usage alwey, fro yer to yeere,
And whoso may at this tyme have his grace,
In blisful tyme he cam into this place!"

With hed enclyned and with ful humble cheere
This royal tersel spak, and tariede noght.   415
"Unto my sovereyn lady, and not my fere,
I chese, and chese with wil and herte and
     thought,
The formel on youre hond, so wel iwrought,
Whos I am al, and evere wol hire serve,
Do what hire lest, to do me lyve or sterve;   420

"Besekynge hire of merci and of grace,
As she that is my lady sovereyne;
Or let me deye present in this place.
For certes, longe may I nat lyve in payne,
For in myn herte is korven every veyne.   425
Havynge reward only to my trouthe,
My deere herte, have on my wo som routhe.

"And if that I to hyre be founde untrewe,
Disobeysaunt, or wilful necligent,
Avauntour, or in proces love a newe,   430
I preye to yow this be my jugement,
That with these foules I be al torent,
That ilke day that evere she me fynde
To hir untrewe, or in my gilt unkynde.

"And syn that non loveth hire so wel as I,   435
Al be she nevere of love me behette,
Thanne oughte she be myn thourgh hire mercy,
For other bond can I non on hire knette.
Ne nevere for no wo ne shal I lette
To serven hire, how fer so that she wende;   440
Say what yow list, my tale is at an ende."

Ryght as the freshe, rede rose newe
Ayen the somer sonne coloured is,
Ryght so for shame al wexen gan the hewe
Of this formel, whan she herde al this;   445
She neyther answerde wel, ne seyde amys,
So sore abashed was she, tyl that Nature
Seyde, "Doughter, drede yow nought, I yow
     assure."

Another tersel egle spak anon,   449
Of lower kynde, and seyde, "That shal nat be!
I love hire bet than ye don, by seint John,
Or at the leste I love hire as wel as ye,
And lenger have served hire in my degre,
And if she shulde have loved for long
     lovynge,
To me allone hadde be the guerdonynge.   455

389. **plesaunce**, desire. 391. **lete**, abandon. 393. **tersel**, tercel, the male of any variety of hawk. 395. **secre**, discreet. 403. **entriketh**, ensnares. 404. **syketh**, sighs. 407. **in**, on. 408. **Mot**, must. 410. **feere**, companion, mate. 420. **sterve**, die. 425. **is korven**, is cut (and bleeding). 426. **reward**, regard. 427. **routhe**, pity. 429. **Disobeysaunt**, disobedient. **wilful**, willfully. 430. **Avauntour**, boaster. **proces**, the course of time. 432. **torent**, torn to pieces. 433. **ilke**, same. 434. **in my gilt**, by my fault. 435. **syn**, since. 436. **behette**, promised. 438. **knette**, fasten. 439. **lette**, cease. 443. **Ayen**, facing. 444. **wexen**, to increase. 455. **guerdonynge**, reward.

"I dar ek seyn, if she me fynde fals,
Unkynde, janglere, or rebel any wyse,
Or jelous, do me hangen by the hals!
And, but I bere me in hire servyse
As wel as that my wit can me suffyse,   460
From poynt to poynt, hyre honour for to save,
Take she my lif and al the good I have!"

The thridde tercel egle answerde tho,
"Now, sires, ye seen the lytel leyser heere;
For every foul cryeth out to ben ago   465
Forth with his make, or with his lady deere;
And ek Nature hireself ne wol not heere,
For taryinge here, not half that I wolde seye,
And but I speke, I mot for sorwe deye.

"Of long servyse avaunte I me nothing;   470
But as possible is me to deye to-day
For wo as he that hath ben languysshyng
This twenty wynter; and wel happen may,
A man may serven bet and more to pay
In half a yer, although it were no moore,   475
Than som man doth that hath served ful yoore.

"I seye not this by me, for I ne can
Don no servyse that may my lady plese;
But I dar seyn, I am hire treweste man
As to my dom, and faynest wolde hire ese.   480
At shorte wordes, til that deth me sese,
I wol ben heres, whether I wake or wynke,
And trewe in al that herte may bethynke."

Of al my lyf, syn that day I was born,
So gentil ple in love or other thyng   485
Ne herde nevere no man me beforn,
Who that hadde leyser and connyng

For to reherse hire chere and hire spekyng;
And from the morwe gan this speche laste   489
Tyl dounward drow the sonne wonder faste.

The noyse of foules for to ben delyvered
So loude rong, "Have don, and lat us wende!"
That wel wende I the wode hadde al to-
    shyvered.
"Com of!" they criede, "allas, ye wol us shende!
Whan shal youre cursede pletynge have an
    ende?   495
How sholde a juge eyther partie leve
For ye or nay, withouten any preve?"

The goos, the cokkow, and the doke also
So cryede, "Kek kek! kokkow! quek quek!"
    hye,   499
That thourgh myne eres the noyse wente tho.
The goos seyde, "Al this nys not worth a flye!
But I can shape herof a remedie,
And I wol seye my verdit fayre and swythe
For water-foul, whoso be wroth or blythe!" 504

"And I for worm-foul," seyde the fol kokkow,
"For I wol of myn owene autorite,
For comun spede, take on the charge now,
For to delyvere us is gret charite."
"Ye may abyde a while yit, parde!"
Quod the turtil. "If it be youre wille,   510
A wight may speke hym were as fayr be stylle.

"I am a sed-foul, oon the unworthieste,
That wot I wel, and litel of connynge.
But bet is that a wyghtes tonge reste
Than entermeten hym of such doinge,   515
Of which he neyther rede can ne synge;

---

457. janglere, loud talker or one who talks too freely. **458. hals,** neck. **462. good,** property. **463. thridde,** third. **tho,** then. **464. leyser,** leisure, time to spare. **465. ago,** gone. **469. mot,** must. **470. Of long servyse.** The grounds on which the three tercel eagles base their claims should be noticed in connection with the interpretations of the poem discussed in the introduction. **avaunte,** boast. **473. This,** these. **474. bet,** better. **to pay,** satisfactorily. **476. ful yoore,** for a long time. **480. dom,** judgment. **faynest wolde hire ese,** would most gladly please her. **485. ple,** properly a suit or action at law, here applied to a love suit. The legal terminology is continued in what follows. **489. morwe,** morning. **494. Com of!** Come on! **us shende,** ruin us. **495. pletynge,** argument. **496. leve,** believe. **497. preve,** proof. **503. swythe,** quickly. **507. spede,** benefit. **charge,** burden, responsibility. **510–11. If it be youre wille . . . stylle.** This is a difficult passage and probably should be read in the light of the following stanza. On this assumption the turtle's speech may be paraphrased, "Granted that a person may speak, nevertheless it would be as well for him to keep quiet; for in my humble opinion one who meddles in matters which he knows nothing about takes too much upon himself, and officiousness is often annoying." **515. entermeten hym,** meddle.

And whoso it doth, ful foule hymself acloyeth,
For office uncommytted ofte anoyeth."

Nature, which that alwey hadde an ere
To murmur of the lewednesse behynde,   520
With facound voys seyde, "Hold youre tonges
   there!
And I shal sone, I hope, a conseyl fynde
Yow to delyvere, and fro this noyse unbynde:
I juge, of every folk men shul oon calle
To seyn the verdit for yow foules alle."   525

Assented were to this conclusioun
The briddes alle; and foules of ravyne
Han chosen fyrst, by pleyn eleccioun,
The tercelet of the faucoun to diffyne
Al here sentence, and as him lest, termyne;   530
And to Nature hym gonne to presente,
And she accepteth hym with glad entente.

The terslet seyde thanne in this manere:
"Ful hard were it to preve by resoun
Who loveth best this gentil formel heere;   535
For everych hath swich replicacioun
That non by skilles may be brought adoun.
I can not se that argumentes avayle:
Thanne semeth it there moste be batayle."

"Al redy!" quod these egles tercels tho.   540
"Nay, sires," quod he, "if that I durste it seye,
Ye don me wrong, my tale is not ido!
For, sires, ne taketh not agref, I preye,
It may not gon, as ye wolde, in this weye;
Oure is the voys that han the charge in honde,
And to the juges dom ye moten stonde.   546

"And therfore pes! I seye, as to my wit,
Me wolde thynke how that the worthieste
Of knyghthod, and lengest hath used it,

Most of estat, of blod the gentilleste,   550
Were sittyngest for hire, if that hir leste;
And of these thre she wot hireself, I trowe,
Which that he be, for it is light to knowe."

The water-foules han here hedes leid
Togedere, and of a short avysement,   555
Whan everych hadde his large golee seyd,
They seyden sothly, al by oon assent,
How that the goos, with hire facounde gent,
"That so desyreth to pronounce oure nede,
Shal telle oure tale," and preyede "God hir
   spede!"   560

And for these water-foules tho began
The goos to speke, and in hir kakelynge
She seyde, "Pes! now tak kep every man,
And herkeneth which a resoun I shal forth
   brynge!
My wit is sharp, I love no taryinge;   565
I seye I rede hym, though he were my brother,
But she wol love hym, lat hym love another!"

"Lo, here a parfit resoun of a goos!"
Quod the sperhauk; "Nevere mot she thee!
Lo, suche it is to have a tonge loos!   570
Now, parde! fol, yit were it bet for the
Han holde thy pes than shewed thy nycete.
It lyth nat in his wit, ne in his wille,
But soth is seyd, 'a fol can not be stille.'"

The laughter aros of gentil foules alle,   575
And right anon the sed-foul chosen hadde
The turtle trewe, and gonne hire to hem calle,
And preyeden hire to seyn the sothe sadde
Of this matere, and axede what she radde.
And she answerde that pleynly hire entente   580
She wolde shewe, and sothly what she mente.

---

517. acloyeth, overburdens. **520. lewednesse behynde,** ignorance (of those) in the background. **521. facound,** eloquent, authoritative. **524. juge,** decide, rule. **folk,** class of birds. **men . . .,** impers. constr., there shall be one called. **529. diffyne,** state exactly. **530. sentence,** opinion. **termyne,** reach or state a conclusion. **536. replicacioun,** reply rejoinder. **537. skilles,** reasons. **545-6. Oure is the voys . . .** We who have the responsibility for presenting the views of our group may speak, but you must abide by the decision of the judge. **548. Me wolde thynke,** it would seem to me. **551. sittyngest,** fittest. **556. golee,** mouthful. **558. facounde gent,** gentle way of speaking. **563. kep,** heed. **564. which,** what. **566. rede,** advise. **567. But,** unless. **569. thee,** thrive. **572. nycete,** foolishness. **577. turtle,** turtledove. **578. sothe sadde,** sober truth. **579. axede,** asked. **radde,** advised.

"Nay, God forbede a lovere shulde chaunge!"
The turtle seyde, and wex for shame al red,
"Though that his lady everemore be straunge,
Yit lat hym serve hire ever, til he be ded,   585
Forsothe, I preyse nat the goses red,
For, though she deyede, I wolde non other
    make;
I wol ben hirs, til that the deth me take."

"Wel bourded," quod the doke, "by myn hat!
That men shulde loven alwey causeles,   590
Who can a resoun fynde or wit in that?
Daunseth he murye that is myrtheles?
Who shulde recche of that is recheles?
Ye quek!" yit seyde the doke, ful wel and fayre,
"There been mo sterres, God wot, than a
    payre!"   595

"Now fy, cherl!" quod the gentil tercelet,
"Out of the donghil cam that word ful right!
Thow canst nat seen which thyng is wel beset!
Thow farst by love as oules don by lyght: 599
The day hem blent, ful wel they sen by nyght.
Thy kynde is of so low a wrechednesse
That what love is, thow canst nat seen ne gesse."

Tho gan the kokkow putte hym forth in pres
For foul that eteth worm, and seyde blyve:
"So I," quod he, "may have my make in pes,
I reche nat how longe that ye stryve.   606
Lat ech of hem be soleyn al here lyve!
This is my red, syn they may nat acorde;
This shorte lessoun nedeth nat recorde."

"Ye, have the glotoun fild inow his paunche,
Thanne are we wel!" seyde the merlioun;   611

"Thow mortherere of the heysoge on the
    braunche
That broughte the forth, thow [rewthelees]
    glotoun!
Lyve thow soleyn, wormes corrupcioun!
For no fors is of lak of thy nature—   615
Go, lewed be thow whil the world may dure!"

"Now pes," quod Nature, "I comaunde here!
For I have herd al youre opynyoun,
And in effect yit be we nevere the nere.
But fynally, this is my conclusioun,   620
That she hireself shal han the eleccioun
Of whom hire lest; whoso be wroth or blythe,
Hym that she cheseth, he shal hire han as
    swithe.

"For sith it may not here discussed be
Who loveth hire best, as seyde the tercelet,   625
Thanne wol I don hire this favour, that she
Shal han right hym on whom hire herte is set,
And he hire that his herte hath on hire knet:
Thus juge I, Nature, for I may not lye;
To non estat I have non other yë.   630

"But as for conseyl for to chese a make,
If I were Resoun, certes, thanne wolde I
Conseyle yow the royal tercel take,
As seyde the tercelet ful skylfully,
As for the gentilleste and most worthi,   635
Which I have wrought so wel to my plesaunce,
That to yow oughte to been a suffisaunce."

With dredful vois the formel tho answerde,
"My rightful lady, goddesse of Nature,
Soth is that I am evere under youre yerde,   640

584. straunge, distant, unresponsive. 586. red, advice. 589. Wel bourded, that's a joke! 592. murye, merry (merrily). 593. Who shulde recche . . . Who should care about one that does not care? 595. There been mo sterres . . . Proverbial statement, equivalent to "not the only pebble on the beach." 598. wel beset, fitting (properly employed). 599. farst by, dost act in respect to. 600. blent, blinds. 603. putte hym forth in pres, took upon himself (to speak). 604. blyve, soon. 607. soleyn, solitary, single. 609. recorde, supporting argument. 611. we wel, the rest of us satisfied. merlioun, merlin, a small falcon. 612. heysoge, hedge-sparrow. Cf. note to l. 358. 613. broughte the forth, reared thee. rewthelees. The MSS read reufulles, rewfull, rowthfull. The emendation is Skeat's although it had been suggested by Lounsbury earlier. 615. For no fors is . . . The lack of birds of your nature does not matter. 616. lewed, ignorant. dure, last. 619. nevere the nere, no better off (nearer to our purpose). 623. cheseth, chooses. as swithe, at once. 628. knet, fixed. 630. other yë, partiality. 634. skylfully, reasonably. 636. plesaunce, delight. 638. dredful, timid. 640. yerde, rod, correction.

As is everich other creature,
And mot be youres whil my lyf may dure,
And therfore graunteth me my firste bone,
And myn entent I wol yow sey right sone."

"I graunte it yow," quod she; and right anon
This formel egle spak in this degre: 646
"Almyghty queen! unto this yer be gon,
I axe respit for to avise me,
And after that to have my choys al fre:
This al and som that I wol speke and seye.   650
Ye gete no more, although ye do me deye!

"I wol nat serve Venus ne Cupide,
Forsothe as yit, by no manere weye."
"Now, syn it may non otherwise betyde,"
Quod tho Nature, "heere is no more to seye. 655
Thanne wolde I that these foules were aweye,
Ech with his make, for taryinge lengere heere!"
And seyde hem thus, as ye shul after here.

"To yow speke I, ye tercelets," quod Nature,
"Beth of good herte, and serveth alle thre.   660
A yer is nat so longe to endure,
And ech of yow peyne hym in his degre
For to do wel, for, God wot, quyt is she
Fro yow this yer; what after so befalle,
This entremes is dressed for yow alle."   665

And whan this werk al brought was to an ende,
To every foul Nature yaf his make
By evene acord, and on here wey they wende.
And, Lord, the blisse and joye that they make!
For ech of hem gan other in wynges take,   670

And with here nekkes ech gan other wynde,
Thankynge alwey the noble goddesse of kynde.

But fyrst were chosen foules for to synge,
As yer by yer was alwey hir usaunce
To synge a roundel at here departynge,   675
To don to Nature honour and plesaunce.
The note, I trowe, imaked was in Fraunce;
The wordes were swich as ye may here fynde,
The nexte vers, as I now have in mynde.

Now welcome, somer, with thy sonne softe,   680
That hast this wintres wedres overshake,
And driven away the longe nyghtes blake!
Saynt Valentyn, that art ful hy on-lofte,
Thus syngen smale foules for thy sake:
Now welcome, somer, with thy sonne softe,   685
That hast this wintres wedres overshake.

Wel han they cause for to gladen ofte,
Sith ech of hem recovered hath hys make,
Ful blissful mowe they synge when they wake:
Now welcome, somer, with thy sonne softe,   690
That hast this wintres wedres overshake,
And driven away the longe nyghtes blake!

And with the shoutyng, whan the song was do,
That foules maden at here flyght awey,
I wok, and othere bokes tok me to,   695
To reede upon, and yit I rede alwey.
I hope, ywis, to rede so som day
That I shal mete som thyng for to fare
The bet, and thus to rede I nyl nat spare.

Explicit parliamentum Avium in die sancti Valentini tentum, secundum Galfridum Chaucers. Deo gracias.

643. **bone,** petition. 646. **in this degre,** in this wise. 647. **unto,** until. 657. **for taryinge,** to avoid tarrying. 663. **quyt,** freed. 665. **entremes,** a dish served between the courses of a dinner. **dressed,** prepared. 671. **with here nekkes . . . wynde.** Bartholomeus Anglicus says that swans intertwine their necks as a sign of love. For representations in art see E. Mâle, *L' art religieux du XIIe siècle en France* (1922), 355–6. 674. **usaunce,** usage. 675. **roundel,** one of the several types of short poem originating in France. It is generally characterized by the repetition of the opening line or lines as a refrain in the middle and at the end. The example sung by the birds (ABB abAB abbABB) is representative, but there are many variations. See J. Schipper, *Hist. of Eng. Versification,* § 323. 677. **note,** tune, presumably identified by the French line found as a rubric in a few MSS: *Que (i.e. Qui) bien ayme a tarde oublie* (He who loves well is slow to forget). Several poems with this opening line are known. The one which Chaucer is most likely to have been familiar with is by Machaut (*Oeuvres,* ed. Hœpffner, i. 283) but it is not a roundel, and, as Skeat observed, it is difficult to see how Chaucer's poem could be sung to the tune of a poem written in four-stress lines. 681. **overshake,** shaken off. 697–9. Sometimes taken to be a hint for reward, but it may be only a reminder of the opening lines of the poem.

Troilus and Criseyde

FROM THE GREAT BODY of stories that furnished entertainment to medieval audiences few themes have retained their vitality into modern times. None of the Charlemagne romances, not even the famous *Song of Roland*, inspires new creations by modern poets. A few of the Arthurian legends have had the power to stir Swinburne and Tennyson, Richard Wagner, E. A. Robinson, and numerous other poets, to reinterpretations of great beauty. Among classical stories a few drawn from Greek tragedy and pagan mythology continued to find modern interpretations in an age when education was still classical, but the great historical and legendary themes of Alexander, the Trojan war, the siege of Thebes, and the wanderings of Æneas, some of which enjoyed great popularity in medieval retellings, have not had germinating power in modern times. Only the love stories—Anthony and Cleopatra, Troilus and Cressida—as distinct from dramatic episodes of history—inspired Shakespeare and Dryden. And of these the story of Troilus and his consuming love for Cressida was an invention of the Middle Ages.

To western Europe in the Middle Ages Homer was only a name. Benoît de Sainte-Maure calls him a *clers merveillos*—a wonderful clerk. Knowledge of the Trojan war came to the west through Latin versions of two prose works, the *De Excidio Trojae Historia* by Dares Phrygius and the *Ephemeris Belli Trojani* by Dictys Cretensis. The authors pretend to have been eye-witnesses of the war, from the Trojan and Greek sides respectively. The claims are, of course, simple frauds perpetrated to give authority to their narratives; the works were written not earlier than the second century of the Christian era. Dares and Dictys know nothing of the famous love story. Their narratives, however, became the basis of a long French poem, the *Roman de Troie* (30,000 lines), written about 1155–60 by Benoît de Sainte-Maure, mentioned above. With Benoît the narrative comes to life, and both because of its literary merit and the fact that it professed to be the history of an important event of long ago the *Roman de Troie* circulated widely. So highly was it regarded in this latter aspect that in 1287 a Sicilian lawyer, Guido delle Colonne, turned it into Latin prose as the *Historia Trojana*, or *Historia Destructionis Troiae*.

The story of Troilus and Cressida makes it first appearance in literature in the *Roman de Troie*. So far as we can now tell, Benoît invented it, although some scholars (among them Constans and Griffin) believe that he got the suggestion from an expanded version of Dares now lost. It is only an incidental feature of the *Roman de Troie*, introduced to relieve the monotony of the endless encounters and the periods of truce which make up the story of the siege. It begins with the exchange of prisoners (line 13,065), continues at intervals through nine instalments for a total of less than 1500 lines, and ends with the death of Troilus (line 21,512). It says nothing about the courtship or the period during which Troilus enjoyed Briseida's love. (Briseida is the form of the name in the *Roman*.) This part of the story must be inferred from their grief when, as part of the exchange of prisoners, Briseida must leave Troy for the Greek camp.

Such was the material which a youthful Italian poet, Giovanni Boccaccio (1313–1375) saw could be made to serve the purpose of advancing a love affair of his own. Sent by his father to Naples to make his way in business, Boccaccio fell in love with a young woman, Maria d'Aquino, who was not happy in the marriage which had been forced upon her. By her he was commissioned to put into courtly Italian the well-known story of *Floris and Blancheflor*; the result was the *Filocolo*. To her he addressed the long and carefully wrought poem with which we are here concerned, the *Filostrato*. And she inspired all his other romances—the *Teseida*, the *Ameto*, the *Amorosa Visione*, and the *Fiammetta*—some of them written after she had deserted him. Benoît's story of Troilus was of no help in describing the wooing and winning of Criseida (the form of the name used by Boccaccio), and for this part of his poem he drew upon the story of Achilles' love for Polyxena, which runs through much the same part of the *Roman de Troie*, and he also drew suggestions from the romance of *Floris and Blancheflor*, either from his own treatment in the *Filocolo* or from its sources. On the basis of such slender and scattered materials Boccaccio created the famous love story as we know it. Chaucer presumably became acquainted with the *Filostrato* during his second mission to Italy, in 1378, and brought back a manuscript of it to England.

Originality was not one of the primary virtues expected of poets in the Middle Ages. In narrative poetry the authenticity of the story was a better guarantee of audience-appeal. In an age when the conditions of publication had not yet created the concept of property rights in ideas, and the word *plagiarism* did not exist in any language, all literary material was in the public domain and poets took their stories wherever they found them. In deciding to retell Boccaccio's story in English, Chaucer was doing something entirely normal. He might have turned Boccaccio's Italian into English line by line as faithfully as the differences of language would have permitted. This is what many English poets had been doing for a long time and what he himself did in translating the *Roman de la Rose*. But he chose not to do this with the *Filostrato*. Rather he took the plot and the principal personages, followed the sequence of events while making important changes in characterization, and transferred to his own poem lines, stanzas, and longer passages from the Italian where they served his purpose. But he omitted much and added much of his own. Boccaccio's poem contains 5704 lines, Chaucer's poem 8239 lines. But only 2750 lines of the *Filostrato* have their counterpart in the English poem and these are at times condensed, so that more than 5500 lines of *Troilus and Criseyde* are Chaucer's own. But the difference is not one of mere length. Chaucer has introduced significant incidents, such as the dinner at the house of Deiphebus at the end of Book II, and the supper at Pandarus's house, which leads to the lovers' embraces. Chaucer is also responsible for Criseyde's expression of remorse at the end and her realization of the infamy which the world would always attach to her name.

More important are the differences of tone and characterization. Boccaccio in writing his poem had a personal and very practical end in view, that of presenting his own case to Maria d'Aquino and persuading her to return to Naples. Consequently he focuses the attention on Troilus somewhat at the expense of Criseida. Chaucer shows no such favoritism; indeed in his poem Criseyde has become the character of greatest interest to the reader. Most important of all, he has made significant changes in the characterization. Criseyde is at once more complex and more appealing. She is harder to persuade that she should accept Troilus as a lover, and she has more feminine delicacy. In Boccaccio she reaches her decision by a rather straightforward bit of reasoning, appoints the time and place of their rendezvous, and when he arrives at her house conducts him to her bedroom. In the English poem Criseyde's final capitulation is brought about by a ruse, even though she is not unaware of the direction of events and the end to which they will ultimately lead. Chaucer has also made important changes in the character of Pandarus. In Boccaccio he is a young man eager to help a friend. In Chaucer he is older and more worldly wise. He is just as ready to serve Troilus in the cause of love, but perhaps the more so because for a much longer time he has continually "hopped behind" in his own love affairs. In still hoping for better success he appears slightly ridiculous. He knows it and has enough sense of humor to laugh at himself. The whimsical humor of Chaucer's poem springs entirely from the character of Pandarus. There is no humor in the *Filostrato*. But the differences between the *Filostrato* and *Troilus and Criseyde* can only be fully appreciated by reading the two poems. This can be conveniently done in *The Filostrato of Giovanni Boccaccio* (text and translation), by N. E. Griffin and A. B. Myrick (Philadelphia, 1929).

One example, however, may give the reader an idea of the difference. When Pandarus sets out to call on Criseyde and reveal to her the fact of Troilus's love, Boccaccio describes his arrival in a dozen lines:

> La qual veggendo lui a sè venire,
> Levata in piè da lunge il salutava,
> E Pandar lei, che per la man pigliata,
> In una loggia seco l' ha menata.
>
> Quivi con risa e con dolci parole,
> Con lieti motti e con ragionamenti
> Parentevoli assai, sì come suole
> Farsi talvolta tra congiunte genti,
> Si stette alquanto, come quei che vuole
> Al suo proposto con nuovi argomenti
> Venire, se il potrà, e nel bel viso
> Cominciò forte a riguardarla fiso.

[As she saw him come toward her, she stood up and greeted him from afar, and Pandarus her, and he took her by the hand, and led her with him into an apartment.

There he contented himself for a while with laughter and with sweet words, with many jests and with familiar talk, in the fashion usual at such times between relatives, as one who wisheth to come to his point with further arguments, if he may, and began to look into her lovely face very fixedly.]

We have only the factual statement that they exchanged jests and engaged in familiar talk "usual at such times between relatives." In Chaucer's poem the whole scene comes to life:

> Whan he was come unto his neces place,
> "Wher is my lady?" to hire folk quod he;
> And they hym tolde, and he forth in gan pace,
> And fond two othere ladys sete, and she,
> Withinne a paved parlour, and they thre
> Herden a mayden reden hem the geste
> Of the siege of Thebes, while hem leste.
>
> Quod Pandarus, "Madame, God yow see,
> With al youre book, and al the compaignie!"
> "Eye, uncle myn, welcome iwys," quod she;
> And up she roos, and by the hond in hye
> She took hym faste, and seyde, "This nyght thrie,
> To goode mot it turne, of yow I mette."
> And with that word she doun on bench hym sette.
>
> "Ye, nece, yee shal faren wel the bet,
> If God wol, al this yeer," quod Pandarus;
> "But I am sory that I have yow let

To herken of youre book ye preysen thus.
For Goddes love, what seith it? telle it us!
Is it of love? O, som good ye me leere!"
"Uncle," quod she, "youre maistresse is not here."

With that they laughed, and he shows that he knew all along what the story was about. Then he says, "Lay aside your veil and let us dance and celebrate the coming of May."

"I? God forbede!" quod she, "be ye mad?
Is that a widewes lif, so God yow save?
. . . .
Lat maydens gon to daunce, and yonge w yves."

"As evere thryve I," quod this Pandarus,
"Yet koude I telle a thyng to doon yow pleye."
"Now, uncle deere," quod she, "telle it us
For Goddes love; is than th'assege aweye? . . .

"No," says Pandarus, "it is five times better than that." "Ye, holy God," quod she, "what thyng is that? What! bet than swyche fyve?" He must be joking. "But I can't guess what it is, so tell me," "Not I," says Pandarus. "Why not?" she asks. "Because there is no prouder woman in all Troy."

Tho gan she wondren moore than biforn
A thousand fold, and down hire eyghen caste;
For nevere, sith the tyme that she was born,
To knowe thyng desired she so faste . . .

However, she says she won't annoy him by being too persistent. So they talk about other things, and he brings the conversation around to war and the deeds of Hector and Troilus, launching into a long eulogy of the latter. After that, he begins to take his leave. But Criseyde's curiosity has been aroused, and she detains him on the plea that she has some private business to discuss with him. Thereupon the others leave, and in due time he tells her what, of course, he came to tell her. The part of the poem here summarized includes lines 78–280 of Book II. It will be readily apparent that *Troilus and Criseyde* is no simple translation of its Italian source.

In addition to the *Filostrato* Chaucer was acquainted with Benoît de Sainte-Maure's *Roman de Troie* and apparently took a number of small hints from it. Likewise, his knowledge of Guido delle Colonne's *Historia* is beyond doubt, but borrowings in Chaucer's poem are less easy to prove. A number of philosophical reflections, including the extended discussion of predestination and free will, are from Boethius, whose *Consolation of Philosophy* was fresh in his mind because he had translated it only a short time before. There are echoes of Dante, excerpts from the *Teseida* and other works of Boccaccio, indeed phrases and ideas from a memory stored with the reading of a lifetime. The whole poem is a succession of effective *scenes*, as has been shown by F. L. Utley (in *Studies in Medieval Literature*, ed. MacEdward Leach, Philadelphia, 1961, pp. 109–38). The basic inspiration for *Troilus and Criseyde* was the *Filostrato*, but the poem is in the truest sense a work of independent creative art.

While there can be no doubt about the fact that Chaucer used Boccaccio's poem at first hand, the possibility cannot be ignored that he was also acquainted with a French prose translation known as *Le Roman de Troyle et de Criseida*, by Beauvau, Seneschal of Anjou. It has usually been assumed that the French version was written too late to have been used by Chaucer, but Professor Pratt

("Chaucer and *Le Roman de Troyle et de Criseida*," *SP*, LIII. 509–539) has noted the fact that more than one seneschal of Anjou was named Beauvau, that the office seems to have been hereditary in the Beauvau family, and he has suggested that the translation may have been the work of an earlier member of the family than either Pierre or his son Louis, to one or the other of whom it has generally been attributed. He has also shown that in many small matters of wording Chaucer agrees more closely with the French than with the published texts of the *Filostrato*. The problem awaits further investigation.

Chaucer nowhere mentions Boccaccio or the *Filostrato*. In the light of medieval practice this should not cause too much surprise. Boccaccio does not mention his own predecessors, Benoît and Guido, and Guido, though he names Dares and Dictys, does not acknowledge his immediate source, Benoît. It would seem that when medieval poets referred to their predecessors, it was more often to claim authority for their narrative than to record their indebtedness. Chaucer twice credits features of his poem to Lollius—"myn auctour called Lollius," as he says at line 394 of the first book. Elsewhere he is content to cite "myn auctour" or "the storie." Lollius was taken by Chaucer to be the author of a work on the Trojan war, supposedly on the word of Horace at second hand. The notion, in all likelihood, arose through a misreading of the opening lines of Horace's Second Epistle[1] (of Book I). In *The Hous of Fame* Chaucer includes him in a list of genuine authors such as Dares and Dictys who were "besy for to bere up Troye" (l. 1468). In accordance with medieval practice he seeks to give the impression in the *Troilus* that he is following faithfully an ancient authority.

The date of the poem has been subject to two schools of thought. Early opinion held it to be an early work, written before *The Hous of Fame*; later scholars, led by Professor Lowes, stressed its artistic maturity, its abandoning of the eight-syllable couplet, and its relation to Chaucer's journeys to Italy, and placed it in the years 1382–85. An important argument pointing to the later date was the discovery by Professor Root that an astronomical allusion in Book III (624–30) to the conjunction of Jupiter and Saturn in the sign of Cancer, a phenomenon which in Chaucer's day had not occurred for over six hundred years, would have been valid in May, 1385 (R. K. Root and H. N. Russell, "A Planetary Date for Chaucer's *Troilus*," *PMLA*, XXXIX. 48–63). It is made to explain the heavy rain which compels Criseyde to stay overnight at her uncle's house and makes it possible for the lovers to spend the night together. While the allusion is such as might have been added in revision and is to an event that might have been anticipated by an astronomically-minded poet like Chaucer, it is found in all classes of manuscripts of the poem and it seems more natural to think of it as a phenomenon that happened while Chaucer was writing the poem and that suggested to him an excellent reason for Criseyde's not being able to return home. The poem must have occupied Chaucer for a fairly long time, and there is evidence in the surviving manuscripts that it underwent considerable revision, involving both the rewriting of certain lines, occasional deletions, the shifting of stanzas, and the addition of new passages. These revisions are largely concentrated in a few sections of the poem. Elements which were apparently not present in the original draft include such significant additions as Troilus's song in praise of Love (III. 1744–71), his long soliloquy on predestination and free will (IV. 953–1085), and stanzas describing the flight of Troilus's soul to the "holughnesse of the eighte spere" (V. 1807–27). The evidence of the manuscripts suggests that Chaucer was improving his master copy progressively until it reached the stage where revision ceased, and that at various points in the process he permitted copies to be made.

For a proper understanding of some important features of the poem one must bear in mind the conventions of Courtly Love. These had been codified in the twelfth century, especially by Andreas

---

[1] This explanation was first suggested by R. G. Latham in the *Athenaeum*, 1869 (II. 433). The fullest discussion of the problem is the article by G. L. Kittredge, "Chaucer's Lollius," *Harvard Stud. in Class. Phil.*, XXVIII. 47–133. That the misreading actually occurred in a MS of John of Salisbury's *Polycraticus* has been pointed out by R. A. Pratt (*MLN*, LXV. 183–187).

Capellanus in his *De Amore*, and were generally accepted as a guide to polite conduct for lovers and the objects of their desires. Amatory relations outside the publicly accepted moral code have existed in all periods of history, but the conditions governing marriage among the upper classes in the Middle Ages, in which the feelings of the parties most concerned were scarcely considered, were particularly conducive to extramarital intrigue. Courtly Love gave a dubious air of respectability to such intrigues. According to its tenets marriage could not be pleaded as an excuse by a woman for refusing a lover. Indeed love between husband and wife was considered impossible. Marriage was not a goal in the minds of the lovers, even when the woman was unmarried. For this reason a widow was almost as desirable an object of the lover's attention as a married woman. Various rules describe the true lover's conduct and feelings: he can experience true love for only one woman, worships her at first at a distance, fears he may never be accepted, or will not prove worthy, hesitates to declare his love, suffers in secret (though he may have a confidant), conducts his affair with great secrecy to protect his lady's reputation, trembles and turns pale in her presence, suffers sleeplessness, loss of appetite, and the like. On the other hand, the lady was expected to be hard to interest, or should appear so, might be capricious or seemingly heartless, but in the end she should yield her favors willingly. Absolute fidelity was the cardinal virtue of the code. Many of these elements are of course merely the characteristics of romantic love. The basic difference is that Courtly Love envisages possession without benefit of clergy. The springtime of Courtly Love was the twelfth century, its autumn the thirteenth; by Chaucer's day it was merely a literary tradition. But the reader of Chaucer's poem will see how much the attitudes and behavior of the three principal characters reflect the code.

In none of the characters is this more apparent than in Troilus, and as a consequence he appears at a disadvantage in comparison with Diomede, who pursues his course without regard for these conventions. Troilus, although second only to Hector in valor on the battlefield, is timid in love and despairing. He lacks the boldness to present his case directly to Criseyde and accepts a state of helpless yearning until Pandarus assumes the leadership and directs each step of the way. Some of his hesitancy has been attributed to his lack of experience with women. Until he fell in love with Criseyde he had scoffed at love and had taunted those of his friends who had fallen under love's spell. Had he been more experienced with women, it is possible to argue, he might have been less vulnerable and more competent. Under the circumstances he was willing to trust to the judgment of Pandarus, an older man who had had affairs of his own. Moreover, Pandarus might be expected to know his niece better and, besides being free to approach her, might know better what approach would be more likely to succeed with her. All this is doubtless true, and may in part explain Troilus's conduct, but in all his behavior he exemplifies the conventions of the Courtly Love code.

The influence of the code appears in other situations than the wooing. Troilus, for all his intimacy with Criseyde, never loses his attitude of deference toward her. It is not a matter of social position; a king's son need have no fear on that score. But from the beginning she makes it a condition of her surrender that he is not to presume on his royal station, and the knowledge that she could at any time withdraw her favor made him habitually considerate of her wishes. It is this as much as anything that keeps him from taking a firm stand when she is to be exchanged for Antenor and when they must decide on a course of action—this and the fact that at all times he has her reputation to protect.

In the play of Courtly Love he was cast in a role which precluded his appearing as a masterful personality, a man of prompt and forceful decisions. That manifestation was reserved for the final act of his life, an act that at the same time proved the depth of his love and his complete integrity. He was a person of such integrity, was so incapable of going back on his word or changing his affections, that when the lovers were about to be separated and Criseyde assured him that she would be back, he did not question her sincerity. Nor has the reader any reason to question it at this point in the story. Though Troilus did consider the possibility that she might not be able to escape from the Greek camp, her own confidence in being able to manage it overcame his fears; and because she swore to be true, he did not envisage a change of heart on her part, even though he knew from his own experience that she was a person who could be influenced. His love for Criseyde was so unalterable that he counted on an equal permanence in her affection for him. Therein lay his tragedy, and for this neither he nor Courtly Love was to blame.

The behavior of Pandarus in the poem must likewise be judged by the standards of Courtly Love. The rules permitted both the lover and his lady to have a confidant. Pandarus enjoys Troilus's full confidence and to a lesser degree that of Criseyde. However we may condemn his conduct by modern standards, his efforts in behalf of Troilus were sanctioned by the tenets of Courtly Love. The fact that he is at the same time Criseyde's uncle puts him in a more delicate position, one not covered by the rules except in so far as the complete surrender of the woman was tacitly accepted. But beyond his efforts to bring the lover and his lady together he must be judged as a personality in his own right. His ironic humor is Chaucer's contribution and besides being generally delightful in itself serves to relieve the seriousness of the poem. He is a clever strategist and his basic practical wisdom brings success until fate steps in. At the end he is powerless to help. Since his own affections are not involved, he can see the ultimate outcome when Troilus cannot, and he can be mildly cynical about it in asides. He consoles himself with the feeling that he has played his part without thought of advantage to himself and with the sole intention of serving his friend. By medieval standards he deserves a better fame than is suggested by his name today.

Criseyde is one of the great character portrayals of literature. Her hesitation about accepting Troilus's love was in accord with one of Andreas's rules, but it may also have reflected her personal inclination, whether induced by her widowhood or by contentment with her situation. In any case the womanly instinct not to appear too easily won is older than Courtly Love. This may be said, too, of her desire for secrecy. Her only action for which we must invoke the conventions of Courtly Love was her yielding to Troilus's embraces. In this she was excused by the code. Her sin was in not remaining faithful to him.

With such concessions to the medieval conventions under which the love story develops, Criseyde interests us because she is a woman,—complex, baffling, sometimes childishly transparent in the workings of her mind, sometimes inscrutable. Any attempt to indicate her character by a single epithet results in oversimplification. Like everyone else, she was a product of her inheritance and her environment. Her father was an opportunist and a traitor; she shows some of these characteristics. Her father's defection intensified her instinct for self-preservation. Her social and economic position gave her poise and independence, so that in the temple, though "she stood ful lowe and still allone" it was "with ful assured lokyng and manere." She was beautiful, but, while she recognized the fact, it is wrong to call her vain. She was made to be loved and was pleased at the thought of being loved ("But moost hir favour was, for his distresse / Was al for hire."). If at times she was outwardly protesting, inwardly consenting, she was only being human. She was no naive schoolgirl, the easy victim of her uncle's scheming ("It nedeth me ful sleighly for to pleie"). She is not carried away by her feelings; in the quiet of her chamber she goes over in her mind the developing situation. Even when she goes to her uncle's house for dinner, and in spite of Pandarus's assertion that Troilus is out of town, she is not really surprised to find him there; and when Troilus, finally in her bed, says it is useless for her to protest, her reply shows that she had anticipated the possibility ("Ne hadde I er now, my swete herte deere, / Ben yold, ywis, I were now nought heere"). To a large extent Criseyde makes her own decisions.

This is not to say that she could not be influenced by others or would not yield to circumstances. She is a mixture of strength and weakness. Perhaps the circumstance that she was almost alone in the world made her feel the need for someone more than her uncle and her nieces to lean on.

This was possibly a factor in her accepting Troilus's love; it seems to have been even more of a factor in determining her actions, once she found herself in the strange surroundings of the Greek camp. She showed at times surprising resolution, but she was in general not one to struggle against the tide. Though she loved Troilus deeply, it seemed easier to leave him than to defy the decree of the Trojan parliament. Though she wanted to keep her promise and return to her lover, it was easier to remain with her father than to face the risks involved in returning to Troy. And though she never quite succeeded in wiping the memory of Troilus from her mind, it was beyond her power to resist the aggressive wooing of Diomede. Had she possessed the strength to sacrifice all the world for love, the story might have had a different ending. But in Chaucer's phrase, she was "slydynge of corage." This was the tragic flaw in her character. She did not have the strength to do otherwise than she did; she could only feel remorse. Chaucer refrains from condemning her:

> And if I myghte excuse hire any wise,
> For she so sory was for hire untrouthe,
> Iwis, I wolde excuse hire yet for routhe.

Troilus and Criseyde has often been called a psychological novel. While we ordinarily do not think of anything in verse as a novel, still the designation is both justified and illuminating. Like its prose counterpart it tells a story with the emphasis not so much on action and events as on the revelation of character and the workings of the mind, the motives and mental states, the attitudes and emotions which accompany and determine action. *Troilus and Criseyde* is as much a study of character as is Meredith's *Evan Harrington* or Hardy's *Tess of the D'Urbervilles*. In the Middle Ages such character studies are rare, and when they occur, as in Chrétien's *Cliges*, are much more limited in range. Seldom do they reveal people in all the complexity that they might manifest in real life, and therein lies the distinction of Chaucer's portrayal of Criseyde. Though *The Canterbury Tales* is Chaucer's best-known work, and, had he lived to complete it, might have best represented the variety and scope of his genius, *Troilus and Criseyde* stands today as his greatest artistic achievement.

TROILUS AND CRISEYDE

Book I

The double sorwe of Troilus to tellen,	To the clepe I, thow goddesse of torment,
That was the kyng Priamus sone of Troye,	Thow cruwel Furie, sorwynge evere yn peyne,
In lovynge, how his aventures fellen	Help me, that am the sorwful instrument, 10
Fro wo to wele, and after out of joie,	That helpeth loveres, as I kan, to pleyne.
My purpos is, er that I parte fro ye. 5	For wel sit it, the sothe for to seyne,
Thesiphone, thow help me for t'endite	A woful wight to han a drery feere,
Thise woful vers, that wepen as I write.	And to a sorwful tale, a sory chere.

The text is basically that of MS Corpus Christi College, Cambridge, with occasional readings from the Campsall and the St. John's College, Cambridge, MSS. **5. er that I parte fro ye.** Until nearly the end of the Middle Ages literary works of all kinds, but especially in verse, were read aloud by the author or another, instead of being taken in through the eye. Cf. below, ll. 52–4. **ye,** you (unstressed). **6. Thesiphone,** Tisiphone, one of the three Furies, who vented their anger on mortals and punished the wicked. **7. vers,** verses. **wepen.** The subject *that* refers to *vers*, hence the plural form. **8. clepe,** call. **11. pleyne,** complain. **12. sit it,** it is fitting. **seyne,** say. **13. feere,** companion.

(margin, handwritten) ech- each / everyone / every — eek / ek / eke } also

(margin, handwritten) dorste—dare

For I, that God of Loves servantz serve, 15
Ne dar to Love, for myn unliklynesse,
Preyen for speed, al sholde I therfore sterve,
So fer am I from his help in derknesse.
But natheles, if this may don gladnesse
To any lovere, and his cause availle, 20
Have he my thonk, and myn be this travaille!

But ye loveres, that bathen in gladnesse,
If any drope of pyte in yow be,
Remembreth yow on passed hevynesse
That ye han felt, and on the adversite 25
Of othere folk, and thynketh how that ye
Han felt that Love *dare* dorste yow displese,
Or ye han wonne hym with to grete an ese.

And preieth for hem that ben in the cas *plight*
Of Troilus, as ye may after here, 30
That Love hem brynge in hevene to solas.
And ek for me preieth to God so dere
That I have myght to shewe, in som manere,
Swich peyne and wo as Loves folk endure,
In Troilus unsely aventure. 35
(below: un happy)

And biddeth ek for hem that ben despeired *pun*
In love, that nevere nyl recovered be,
And ek for hem that falsly ben apeired *injured*
Thorugh wikked tonges, be it he or she;
Thus biddeth God, for his benignite, *graciousn* 40
So graunte hem soone owt of this world to pace,
That ben despeired out of Loves grace.
(below: in despair of)

And biddeth ek for hem that ben at ese,
That God hem graunte ay good perseveraunce,
And sende hem myght hire ladies so to plese 45
That it to Love be worship and plesaunce.
For so hope I my sowle best avaunce,
To prey for hem that Loves servauntz be,
And write hire wo, and lyve in charite,

And for to have of hem compassioun, 50
(their)
As though I were hire owne brother dere.
Now herkneth with a good entencioun,
For now wil I gon streght to my matere,
In which ye may the double sorwes here
Of Troilus, in lovynge of Criseyde, 55
And how that she forsook hym er she deyde.

Yt is wel wist how that the Grekes, stronge
In armes, with a thousand shippes, wente
To Troiewardes, and the cite longe
Assegeden, neigh ten yer er they stente, 60
And in diverse wise and oon entente,
(carrying)
The ravysshyng to wreken of Eleyne,
By Paris don, they wroughten al hir peyne.

Now fel it so that in the town ther was
Dwellynge a lord of gret auctorite, 65
(soothsayer) *(name)*
A gret devyn, that clepid was Calkas,
That in science so expert was that he
Knew wel that Troie sholde destroied be,
By answere of his god, that highte thus,
Daun Phebus or Appollo Delphicus. 70

So whan this Calkas knew by calkulynge,
And ek by answer of this Appollo,
That Grekes sholden swich a peple brynge,
Thorugh which that Troie moste ben fordo,
He caste anon out of the town to go; 75
For wel wiste he by sort that Troye sholde
Destroyed ben, ye, wolde whoso nolde.

For which for to departen softely
Took purpos ful this forknowynge wise,
And to the Grekes oost ful pryvely 80
(host)
He stal anon; and they, in curteys wise,
Hym diden bothe worship and servyse,
In trust that he hath konnynge hem to rede
In every peril which that is to drede.
(counsel)

15. that God of Loves servantz serve. Cf. the designation of the Pope, "servant of the servants of God." **17. sterve,** die. **21. thonk,** good will. **29. cas,** plight. **35. unsely,** unhappy. **36. biddeth,** pray. **38. apeired,** injured. **42. despeired out of,** in despair of, an unusual idiom used by Chaucer at 5. 713. **51. hire,** their. **52. entencioun,** will. **60. stente,** ceased. **62. wreken,** avenge. **63. hir,** their. **66. devyn,** soothsayer. **clepid,** named. **71. calkulynge,** reckoning. **74. fordo,** destroyed. **75. caste,** determined. **76. sort,** divination. **77. wolde whoso nolde,** equivalent to "willy-nilly" in the preterite. **79. Took purpos . . .,** this foreknowing wise one took full purpose . . . to depart. **80. oost,** host. **81. stal,** stole. **82. worship,** honor. **83. rede,** counsel.

The noise up ros, whan it was first aspied   85
Thorugh al the town, and generaly was spoken,
That Calkas traitour fled was and allied
With hem of Grece, and casten to be wroken
On hym that falsly hadde his feith so broken,
And seyden he and al his kyn at-ones   90
Ben worthi for to brennen, fel and bones.

Now hadde Calkas left in this meschaunce,
Al unwist of this false and wikked dede,
His doughter, which that was in gret penaunce,
For of hire lif she was ful sore in drede,   95
As she that nyste what was best to rede;
For bothe a widewe was she and allone
Of any frend to whom she dorste hir mone.

Criseyde was this lady name al right.
As to my doom, in al Troies cite   100
Nas non so fair, for passynge every wight
So aungelik was hir natif beaute,
That lik a thing inmortal semed she,
As doth an hevenyssh perfit creature,   104
That down were sent in scornynge of nature.

This lady, which that alday herd at ere
Hire fadres shame, his falsnesse and tresoun,
Wel neigh out of hir wit for sorwe and fere,
In widewes habit large of samyt broun,
On knees she fil biforn Ector adown;   110
With pitous vois, and tendrely wepynge,
His mercy bad, hirselven excusynge.

Now was this Ector pitous of nature,
And saugh that she was sorwfully bigon,
And that she was so fair a creature;   115
Of his goodnesse he gladede hire anon,
And seyde, "Lat youre fadres treson gon

Forth with meschaunce, and ye youreself in joie
Dwelleth with us, whil yow good list, in Troie.

"And al th'onour that men may don yow have,
As ferforth as youre fader dwelled here,   121
Ye shul have, and youre body shal men save,
As fer as I may ought enquere or here."

And she hym thonked with ful humble chere,
And ofter wolde, and it hadde ben his wille,   125
And took hire leve, and hom, and held hir stille.

And in hire hous she abood with swich meyne
As til hire honour nede was to holde;
And whil she was dwellynge in that cite,
Kepte hir estat, and both of yonge and olde   130
Ful wel biloved, and wel men of hir tolde.
But wheither that she children hadde or noon,
I rede it naught, therfore I late it goon.

The thynges fellen, as they don of werre,
Bitwixen hem of Troie and Grekes ofte;   135
For som day boughten they of Troie it derre,
And eft the Grekes founden nothing softe
The folk of Troie; and thus Fortune on lofte,
And under eft, gan hem to whielen bothe   139
Aftir hir cours, ay whil that thei were wrothe.

But how this town com to destruccion
Ne falleth naught to purpos me to telle;
For it were here a long digression
Fro my matere, and yow to long to dwelle.
But the Troian gestes, as they felle,   145
In Omer, or in Dares, or in Dite,
Whoso that kan may rede hem as they write.

But though that Grekes hem of Troie shetten,
And hir cite bisegede al aboute,

---

88. casten, the subject *they* is understood. **wroken,** revenged. **91. brennen,** burn. **fel,** skin. **93. unwist,** unaware, ignorant. **98. hir mone,** reveal her sorrow. **99. lady,** lady's. The genitive form represents that of the OE. weak declension. **100. doom,** judgment. **106. alday,** continually. **109. large,** full-cut, flowing. **samyt,** samite, a costly silk. **110. Ector,** Hector. **114. bigon,** overwhelmed. **119. whil yow good list,** as long as you please. **121. As ferforth as,** as long as. **125. and,** for *an*, if. **127. meyne,** household. **133. I rede it naught.** A strange statement since Boccaccio says she had neither son nor daughter. **late,** let. **134. of werre,** in war. **136. som day,** one day. **derre,** more dearly. **137. eft,** again. **139. whielen.** The image is that of Fortune's wheel, carrying them now up, now down. **145. Troian gestes,** Trojan history (deeds). **146. Omer . . .** During most of the Middle Ages Homer was only a name in the West. Chaucer cites him along with Dares (*De Excidio Trojae Historia*) and Dite (Dictys, *Ephemeris de Historia Belli Trojani*) as the authorities known to him, not as his immediate sources. **148. shetten,** shut up.

Hire olde usage nolde they nat letten, 150
As for to honoure hir goddes ful devoute;
But aldirmost in honour, out of doute,
Thei hadde a relik, heet Palladion,
That was hire trist aboven everichon.

And so bifel, whan comen was the tyme 155
Of Aperil, whan clothed is the mede
With newe grene, of lusty Veer the pryme,
And swote smellen floures white and rede,
In sondry wises shewed, as I rede,
The folk of Troie hire observaunces olde, 160
Palladiones feste for to holde.

And to the temple, in al hir beste wise,
In general ther wente many a wight,
To herknen of Palladion the servyse;
And namely, so many a lusty knyght, 165
So many a lady fressh and mayden bright,
Ful wel arayed, bothe meste and leste,
Ye, bothe for the seson and the feste.

Among thise othere folk was Criseyda,
In widewes habit blak; but natheles, 170
Right as oure firste lettre is now an A,
In beaute first so stood she, makeles.
Hire goodly lokyng gladed al the prees.
Nas nevere yet seyn thyng to ben preysed
    derre,
Nor under cloude blak so bright a sterre 175

As was Criseyde, as folk seyde everichone
That hir behelden in hir blake wede.
And yet she stood ful lowe and stille allone,
Byhynden other folk, in litel brede,
And neigh the dore, ay under shames drede, 180

Simple of atire and debonaire of chere,
With ful assured lokyng and manere.

This Troilus, as he was wont to gide
His yonge knyghtes, lad hem up and down
In thilke large temple on every side, 185
Byholding ay the ladyes of the town,
Now here, now there; for no devocioun
Hadde he to non, to reven hym his reste,
But gan to preise and lakken whom hym leste.

And in his walk ful faste he gan to wayten 190
If knyght or squyer of his compaignie
Gan for to syke, or lete his eighen baiten
On any womman that he koude espye,
He wolde smyle and holden it folye,
And seye hym thus, "God woot, she slepeth
    softe 195
For love of the, whan thow turnest ful ofte!

"I have herd told, pardieux, of youre lyvynge,
Ye loveres, and youre lewede observaunces,
And which a labour folk han in wynnynge 199
Of love, and in the kepyng which doutaunces;
And whan youre prey is lost, woo and pen-
    aunces.
O veray fooles, nyce and blynde be ye!
Ther nys nat oon kan war by other be."

And with that word he gan caste up the browe,
Ascaunces, "Loo! is this naught wisely spoken?"
At which the God of Love gan loken rowe 206
Right for despit, and shop for to ben wroken.
He kidde anon his bowe nas naught broken,
For sodeynly he hitte hym atte fulle;
And yet as proud a pekok kan he pulle. 210

150. **letten,** give up, discontinue. 152. **aldirmost,** most of all. 153. **relik, heet Palladion,** *i.e.* an image of Pallas. On the safe custody of the Palladium the preservation of the city depended. It was carried off according to Greek legend by Diomede and Odysseus, but the *Roman de Troie* makes Antenor and Aeneas the traitors (ll. 24301 ff.). See below, 4. 204. **154. trist,** that which they trusted in. **157. of lusty Veer the pryme,** the beginning of spring. **158. swote,** sweet. **162. hir,** their. **169.** The incident in which Troilus is stricken with love for Criseyde in the temple is the invention of Boccaccio. **171. is now an A.** The adverb *now* makes plausible the suggestion of Lowes (*PMLA*, XXIII. 285–306) that Chaucer's comparison is a compliment to Queen Anne after her marriage to Richard II January 14, 1382. **172. makeles,** matchless. **174. derre,** more dearly. **179. brede,** space. **182.** This line, together with the whole stanza, should be noted for the light it throws on Criseyde's personality. **188. reven,** take from. **189. lakken,** disparage. **190. wayten,** watch. **192. syke,** sigh. **baiten,** feast. **198. lewede,** foolish, ignorant. **199. which,** what. **han,** have. **200. which doutaunces,** what uncertainties. **202. nyce,** foolish. **205. Ascaunces,** as if to say. **206. rowe,** angrily. **207. shop,** determined. **wroken,** revenged. **208. kidde,** showed. **210. pulle.** He can pluck as proud a peacock (as Troilus).

O blynde world, O blynde entencioun!
How often falleth al the effect contraire
Of surquidrie and foul presumpcioun;
For kaught is proud, and kaught is debonaire.
This Troilus is clomben on the staire,   215
And litel weneth that he moot descenden;
But alday faileth thing that fooles wenden.

As proude Bayard gynneth for to skippe
Out of the weye, so pryketh hym his corn,
Til he a lasshe have of the longe whippe;   220
Than thynketh he, "Though I praunce al byforn
First in the trays, ful fat and newe shorn,
Yet am I but an hors, and horses lawe
I moot endure, and with my feres drawe";

So ferde it by this fierse and proude knyght:
Though he a worthy kynges sone were,   226
And wende nothing hadde had swich myght
Ayeyns his wille that shuld his herte stere,
Yet with a look his herte wax a-fere,
That he that now was moost in pride above,   230
Wax sodeynly moost subgit unto love.

Forthy ensample taketh of this man,
Ye wise, proude, and worthi folkes alle,
To scornen Love, which that so soone kan
The fredom of youre hertes to hym thralle;   235
For evere it was, and evere it shal byfalle,
That Love is he that alle thing may bynde,
For may no man fordon the lawe of kynde.

That this be soth, hath preved and doth yit.
For this trowe I ye knowen alle or some,   240
Men reden nat that folk han gretter wit
Than they that han be most with love ynome;

And strengest folk ben therwith overcome,
The worthiest and grettest of degree:
This was, and is, and yet men shal it see.   245

And trewelich it sit wel to be so.
For alderwisest han therwith ben plesed;
And they that han ben aldermost in wo,
With love han ben comforted moost and esed;
And ofte it hath the cruel herte apesed,   250
And worthi folk maad worthier of name,
And causeth moost to dreden vice and shame.

Now sith it may nat goodly ben withstonde,
And is a thing so vertuous in kynde,
Refuseth nat to Love for to ben bonde,   255
Syn, as hymselven liste, he may yow bynde.
The yerde is bet that bowen wole and wynde
Than that that brest; and therfore I yow rede
To folowen hym that so wel kan yow lede.

But for to tellen forth in special   260
As of this kynges sone of which I tolde,
And leten other thing collateral,
Of hym thenke I my tale forth to holde,
Bothe of his joie and of his cares colde;
And al his werk, as touching this matere,   265
For I it gan, I wol therto refere.

Withinne the temple he wente hym forth pley-
    inge,
This Troilus, of every wight aboute,
On this lady, and now on that, lokynge,
Wher so she were of town or of withoute;   270
And upon cas bifel that thorugh a route
His eye percede, and so depe it wente,
Til on Criseyde it smot, and ther it stente.

213. **surquidrie,** pride, arrogance. 217. **But alday faileth . . .** Proverbial. Skeat cites a Scottish proverb, "All fails that fools thinks." (*sic*) Cf. also "Moult remaint (*fails*) de ce que fol pense" (Morawski, *Proverbes français*, No 1320), from a thirteenth-century MS. 218. **Bayard,** the name of a horse in *Renaut de Montauban* and in several other chansons de geste. On the origin of the name see P. Rajna, *Le Origini dell' epopea francese,* p. 447. 222. **First in the trays,** as the fore horse in a tandem. 224. **feres,** fellows, companions. 227. **wende,** thought. 228. **stere.** Since the rimes suggest a close *e* the meaning is probably "steer, govern," rather than "stir." Cf. also 3. 910. 229. **a-fere,** afire. The form is Kentish; see Language, § 8. 232. **Forthy,** therefore. **ensample,** example. 238. **fordon . . . kynde,** abolish the law of nature. 239. **preved,** proved (true). 241. **reden,** suppose. 242. **ynome,** taken. 246. **it sit wel,** it is fitting. 247. **alderwisest,** the wisest of all. 256. **Syn,** since. 257. **yerde,** stick. **wynde,** bend. 258. **brest,** breaks. 262. **leten,** let go. **collateral,** incidental. 266. **refere,** return. 270. **Wher so,** whether. 271. **upon cas,** by chance. 273. **stente,** stopped.

And sodeynly he wax therwith astoned,
And gan hir bet biholde in thrifty wise.   275
"O mercy, God," thoughte he, "wher hastow
     woned,
That art so feyr and goodly to devise?"
Therwith his herte gan to sprede and rise,
And softe sighed, lest men myghte hym here,
And caught ayeyn his firste pleyinge chere.   280

She nas nat with the leste of hire stature,
But alle hire lymes so wel answerynge
Weren to wommanhode, that creature
Was nevere lasse mannyssh in semynge.
And ek the pure wise of hire mevynge   285
Shewed wel that men myght in hire gesse
Honour, estat, and wommanly noblesse.

To Troilus right wonder wel with alle
Gan for to like hire mevynge and hire chere,
Which somdel deignous was, for she let falle
Hire look a lite aside in swich manere,   291
Ascaunces, "What! may I nat stonden here?"
And after that hir lokynge gan she lighte,
That nevere thoughte hym seen so good a
     syghte.

And of hire look in him ther gan to quyken   295
So gret desir and such affeccioun,
That in his hertes botme gan to stiken
Of hir his fixe and depe impressioun.
And though he erst hadde poured up and down,
He was tho glad his hornes in to shrinke;   300
Unnethes wiste he how to loke or wynke.

Lo, he that leet hymselven so konnynge,
And scorned hem that Loves peynes dryen,
Was ful unwar that Love hadde his dwellynge

Withinne the subtile stremes of hir yën;   305
That sodeynly hym thoughte he felte dyen,
Right with hire look, the spirit in his herte.
Blissed be Love, that kan thus folk converte!
She, this in blak, likynge to Troilus
Over al thing, he stood for to biholde;   310
Ne his desir, ne wherfore he stood thus,
He neither chere made, ne worde tolde;
But from afer, his manere for to holde,
On other thing his look som tyme he caste,
And eft on hire, while that the servyse laste.   315

And after this, nat fullich al awhaped,
Out of the temple al esilich he wente,
Repentynge hym that he hadde evere ijaped
Of Loves folk, lest fully the descente   319
Of scorn fille on hymself; but what he mente,
Lest it were wist on any manere syde,
His woo he gan dissimulen and hide.

Whan he was fro the temple thus departed,
He streght anon unto his paleys torneth,
Right with hire look thorugh-shoten and
     thorugh-darted,   325
Al feyneth he in lust that he sojorneth;
And al his chere and speche also he borneth,
And ay of Loves servantz every while,
Hymself to wrye, at hem he gan to smyle,

And seyde, "Lord, so ye lyve al in lest,   330
Ye loveres! for the konnyngeste of yow,
That serveth most ententiflich and best,
Hym tit as often harm therof as prow.
Youre hire is quyt ayeyn, ye, God woot how!
Nought wel for wel, but scorn for good servyse.
In feith, youre ordre is ruled in good wise!   336

---

274. astoned, astonished. **275. thrifty,** prudent. **276. woned,** dwelt. **282. alle hire lymes,** all parts of her body. **285. pure wise,** very manner. **289. to like,** to please. **290. deignous,** haughty. **291. lite,** little. **293. lighte,** brighten. **294. thoughte hym seen.** Though the meaning is apparent, the construction is awkward. **298. his,** its (her look). **299. poured,** gazed. **301. wynke,** shut his eyes, not look; *i.e.* he scarcely knew what to do. **302. leet,** considered. **303. dryen,** suffer. **309. She.** The grammar obviously will not bear inspection, but for the combination *she this* with demonstrative force see Mustanoja, p. 137. **312. chere made,** revealed anything by his countenance. **315. eft,** again. **laste,** lasted. **316. awhaped,** disconcerted. **317. esilich,** quietly. **318. ijaped,** made sport. **320. what he mente,** whatever he thought. **326. in lust . . . sojorneth,** remains happy. **327. borneth,** attends to, *lit.* burnishes. **329. wrye,** conceal, cover up. **330. in lest,** in bliss. **333. tit,** contr. of *tideth,* befalls. **prow,** profit. **334. hire,** reward. **quyt,** paid, satisfied.

"In nouncerteyn ben alle youre observaunces,
But it a sely fewe pointes be;
Ne no thing asketh so gret attendaunces
As doth youre lay, and that knowe alle ye;   340
But that is nat the worste, as mote I the!
But, tolde I yow the worste point, I leve,
Al seyde I soth, ye wolden at me greve.

"But take this: that ye loveres ofte eschuwe,
Or elles doon, of good entencioun,   345
Ful ofte thi lady wol it mysconstruwe,
And deme it harm in hire oppynyoun;
And yet if she, for other enchesoun,
Be wroth, than shaltow have a groyn anon.   349
Lord, wel is hym that may ben of yow oon!"

But for al this, whan that he say his tyme,
He held his pees; non other boote hym gayned;
For love bigan his fetheres so to lyme,
That wel unnethe until his folk he fayned
That other besy nedes hym destrayned;   355
For wo was hym, that what to doon he nyste,
But bad his folk to gon wher that hem liste.

And whan that he in chambre was allone,
He doun upon his beddes feet hym sette,
And first he gan to sike, and eft to grone,   360
And thought ay on hire so, withouten lette,
That, as he sat and wook, his spirit mette
That he hire saugh a-temple, and al the wise
Right of hire look, and gan it newe avise.

Thus gan he make a mirour of his mynde,   365
In which he saugh al holly hire figure;
And that he wel koude in his herte fynde,
It was to hym a right good aventure

To love swich oon, and if he dede his cure
To serven hir, yet myghte he falle in grace,   370
Or ellis for oon of hire servantz pace;

Imaginynge that travaille nor grame
Ne myghte for so goodly oon be lorn
As she, ne hym for his desir no shame,
Al were it wist, but in pris and up-born   375
Of alle lovers wel more than biforn.
Thus argumented he in his gynnynge,
Ful unavysed of his woo comynge.

Thus took he purpos loves craft to suwe,
And thoughte he wolde werken pryvely,   380
First to hiden his desir in muwe
From every wight yborn, al-outrely,
But he myghte ought recovered be therby;
Remembryng hym that love to wide yblowe
Yelt bittre fruyt, though swete seed be   385
    sowe.

And over al this, yet muchel more he thoughte
What for to speke, and what to holden inne;
And what to arten hire to love he soughte,
And on a song anon-right to bygynne,
And gan loude on his sorwe for to wynne;   390
For with good hope he gan fully assente
Criseyde for to love, and nought repente.

And of his song naught only the sentence,
As writ myn auctour called Lollius,
But pleinly, save oure tonges difference,   395
I dar wel seyn, in al that Troilus
Seyde in his song, loo! every word right thus
As I shal seyn; and whoso list it here,
Loo, next this vers he may it fynden here.

---

337. **nouncerteyn**, uncertainty. 338. **sely**, insignificant. 340. **lay**, law. 341. **mote I the**, may I prosper. 342. **leve**, believe. 343. **Al**, although. **greve**, feel annoyed. 344. **take**, consider. **that**, that which. **eschuwe . . .**, refrain from doing, or do with good intention. 348. **enchesoun**, reason. 349. **groyn**, grumbling, scolding. 351. **say**, saw. 353. **lyme**, smear with bird lime, whereby he will be caught. 354. **unnethe until**, scarcely unto. 361. **lette**, hindrance. 362. **mette**, dreamed. 363. **a-temple**, in the temple. 364. **it newe avise**, to reflect on it anew. 369. **dede his cure**, devoted his care. 372. **travaille nor grame**, labor nor suffering. 375. **Al . . .**, although it were known. **but in pris.** The construction shifts, with the subj. and pred. implied: but (that he would be) in esteem and respected by all lovers. . . . 378. **unavysed**, unaware. 379. **suwe**, follow. 381. **in muwe**, secretly. A mew was a cage, esp. for hawks when moulting; hence a secret place. 383. **But . . . therby**, unless he might in any way be benefited thereby. 385. **Yelt**, yields. 388. **arten**, induce. 389. **anon-right**, immediately. 390. **to wynne**. For this puzzling word D. C. Fowler (*MLN*, LXIX. 313–315) suggests the meaning "complain" and cites a somewhat similar use in *Piers Plowman*, IV. 53. 393. **sentence**, meaning, thought. 394. **Lollius**. See intro.

Cantus Troili

"If no love is, O God, what fele I so? 400
And if love is, what thing and which is he?
If love be good, from whennes cometh my
   woo?
If it be wikke, a wonder thynketh me,
Whenne every torment and adversite 404
That cometh of hym, may to me savory thinke,
For ay thurst I, the more that ich it drynke.

"And if that at myn owen lust I brenne,
From whennes cometh my waillynge and my
   pleynte?
If harme agree me, wherto pleyne I thenne?
I noot, ne whi unwery that I feynte. 410
O quike deth, O swete harm so queynte,
How may of the in me swich quantite,
But if that I consente that it be?

"And if that I consente, I wrongfully
Compleyne, iwis. Thus possed to and fro, 415
Al sterelees withinne a boot am I
Amydde the see, bitwixen wyndes two,
That in contrarie stonden evere mo.
Allas! what is this wondre maladie?
For hete of cold, for cold of hete, I dye." 420

And to the God of Love thus seyde he
With pitous vois, "O lord, now youres is
My spirit, which that oughte youres be.
Yow thanke I, lord, that han me brought to this.
But wheither goddesse or womman, iwis, 425
She be, I not, which that ye do me serve;
But as hire man I wol ay lyve and sterve.

"Ye stonden in hir eighen myghtily,
As in a place unto youre vertu digne;

Wherfore, lord, if my service or I 430
May liken yow, so beth to me benigne;
For myn estat roial I here resigne
Into hire hond, and with ful humble chere
Bicome hir man, as to my lady dere."

In hym ne deyned spare blood roial 435
The fyr of love—the wherfro God me blesse—
Ne him forbar in no degree for al
His vertu or his excellent prowesse,
But held hym as his thral lowe in destresse,
And brende hym so in soundry wise ay newe,
That sexti tyme a day he loste his hewe. 441

So muche, day by day, his owene thought,
For lust to hire, gan quiken and encresse,
That every other charge he sette at nought.
Forthi ful ofte, his hote fir to cesse, 445
To sen hire goodly lok he gan to presse,
For therby to ben esed wel he wende;
And ay the ner he was, the more he brende.

For ay the ner the fir, the hotter is,—
This, trowe I, knoweth al this compaignye. 450
But were he fer or ner, I dar sey this:
By nyght or day, for wisdom or folye,
His herte, which that is his brestes yë,
Was ay on hire, that fairer was to sene
Than evere was Eleyne or Polixene. 455

Ek of the day ther passed nought an houre
That to hymself a thousand tyme he seyde,
"Good goodly, to whom serve I and laboure,
As I best kan, now wolde God, Criseyde,
Ye wolden on me rewe, er that I deyde! 460
My dere herte, allas! myn hele and hewe
And lif is lost, but ye wol on me rewe."

---

403. wikke, bad. **405. savory thinke,** seem pleasant. **407. lust,** desire. **brenne,** burn. **409. agree me,** please me. **411. queynte,** strange. **415. iwis,** surely. **possed,** pushed, tossed. **416. sterelees,** rudderless. **419. wondre,** strange. **420.** The line may be paraphrased, "I die of cold when I have a fever and of fever when I am cold." **426. not,** know not. **do,** make. **427. sterve,** die. **428. eighen,** eyes. **429. digne,** worthy. **431. liken,** please. **443. lust to,** desire for. **444. charge,** matter of weight, responsibility. **445. cesse,** put an end to. **448. ner,** nearer. **brende,** burned. **450. al this compaignye.** Chaucer pictures himself reading his poem to an audience, as he is shown doing in an illumination in the MS which is the basis of the present text. It is reproduced as the frontispiece to the present volume. **455. Eleyne or Polixene,** Helen, for whom the Trojan War was fought; Polyxena, daughter of Priam, beloved by Achilles. **457. he seyde.** Modern idiom requires a negative. **458. goodly,** pleasing one. **laboure,** *i.e.* to serve.

Alle other dredes weren from him fledde,
Both of th'assege and his savacioun
N'yn him desir noon other fownes bredde,　465
But argumentes to this conclusioun,
That she of him wolde han compassioun,
And he to ben hire man, while he may dure.
Lo, here his lif, and from the deth his cure !

The sharpe shoures felle of armes preve,　470
That Ector or his othere bretheren diden,
Ne made hym only therfore ones meve;
And yet was he, where so men wente or riden,
Founde oon the beste, and lengest tyme abiden
Ther peril was, and dide ek swich travaille　475
In armes, that to thynke it was merveille.

But for non hate he to the Grekes hadde,
Ne also for the rescous of the town,
Ne made hym thus in armes for to madde,
But only, lo, for this conclusioun:　　480
To liken hire the bet for his renoun.
Fro day to day in armes so he spedde,
That the Grekes as the deth him dredde.

And fro this forth tho refte hym love his sleep,
And made his mete his foo; and ek his sorwe
Gan multiplie, that, whoso tok keep,　486
It shewed in his hewe both eve and morwe.
Therfor a title he gan him for to borwe
Of other siknesse, lest men of hym wende
That the hote fir of love hym brende,　490

And seyde he hadde a fevere and ferde amys.
But how it was, certeyn, kan I nat seye,
If that his lady understood nat this,
Or feynede hire she nyste, oon of the tweye;
But wel I rede that, by no manere weye,　495
Ne semed it as that she of hym roughte,
Or of his peyne, or whatsoevere he thoughte.

But thanne felte this Troilus swich wo,
That he was wel neigh wood; for ay his drede
Was this, that she som wight hadde loved so,　500
That nevere of hym she wolde han taken
　　hede,—
For which hym thoughte he felte his herte
　　blede;
Ne of his wo ne dorste he nat bygynne
To tellen hir, for al this world to wynne.

But whan he hadde a space from his care,　505
Thus to hymself ful ofte he gan to pleyne;
He seyde, "O fool, now artow in the snare,
That whilom japedest at loves peyne.
Now artow hent, now gnaw thin owen cheyne !
Thow were ay wont eche lovere reprehende　510
Of thing fro which thou kanst the nat defende.

"What wol now every lovere seyn of the,
If this be wist? but evere in thin absence
Laughen in scorn, and seyn, "Loo, ther goth he
That is the man of so gret sapience,　515
That held us loveres leest in reverence.
Now, thanked be God, he may gon in the
　　daunce
Of hem that Love list febly for to avaunce.

"But, O thow woful Troilus, God wolde,
Sith thow most loven thorugh thi destine,　520
That thow beset were on swich oon that sholde
Know al thi wo, al lakked hir pitee ! —
But also cold in love towardes the
Thi lady is, as frost in wynter moone,
And thow fordon, as snow in fire is soone.　525

"God wold I were aryved in the port
Of deth, to which my sorwe wol me lede !
A, Lord, to me it were a gret comfort;
Than were I quyt of languisshyng in drede.

---

464. **savacioun**, preservation, safety. 465. **fownes**, fawns, *i.e.* smaller desires. 470. **shoures felle**, combats cruel. **preve**, proof. 472. **Ne . . . meve**, did not make him move once on that account. 473. **wente or riden**, walked or rode. 474. **oon the beste**, one of the best. **lengest tyme**, and (one of those who) remained the longest time where there was danger. 478. **rescous**, rescue. 479. **madde**, rage. 480. **conclusioun**, end, purpose. 481. **liken**, please. **bet**, better. 483. **deth**, pestilence. 484. **tho**, then. 488. **title**, name. 491. **ferde amys**, was not well. 496. **roughte**, cared. 499. **wood**, mad. 505. **a space from his care**, a period of freedom from responsibility. 508. **japedest at**, joked about. 509. **hent**, caught. 519. **God wolde**, would God. 522. **al lakked . . .**, although pity were lacking in her. 525. **fordon**, done for. 529. **drede**, doubt.

For, by myn hidde sorwe iblowe on brede,   530
I shal byjaped ben a thousand tyme
More than that fool of whos folie men ryme.

"But now help, God, and ye, swete, for whom
I pleyne, ikaught, ye, nevere wight so faste!
O mercy, dere herte, and help me from   535
The deth, for I, while that my lyf may laste,
More than myself wol love yow to my laste.
And with som frendly look gladeth me, swete,
Though nevere more thing ye me byhete."

Thise wordes, and ful many an other to,   540
He spak, and called evere in his compleynte
Hire name, for to tellen hire his wo,
Til neigh that he in salte teres dreynte.
Al was for nought: she herde nat his pleynte;
And whan that he bythought on that folie,   545
A thousand fold his wo gan multiplie.

Bywayling in his chambre thus allone,
A frend of his, that called was Pandare,
Com oones in unwar, and herde hym groone,
And say his frend in swich destresse and care.
"Allas," quod he, "who causeth al this fare?   551
O mercy, God! what unhap may this meene?
Han now thus soone Grekes maad yow leene?

"Or hastow som remors of conscience,
And art now falle in som devocioun,   555
And wailest for thi synne and thin offence,
And hast for ferde caught attricioun?
God save hem that biseged han oure town,
That so kan leye oure jolite on presse,
And bringe oure lusty folk to holynesse!"   560

Thise wordes seyde he for the nones alle,
That with swich thing he myght hym angry
   maken,

And with an angre don his wo to falle,
As for the tyme, and his corage awaken.
But wel he wist, as fer as tonges spaken,   565
Ther nas a man of gretter hardinesse
Thanne he, ne more desired worthinesse.

"What cas," quod Troilus, "or what aventure
Hath gided the to sen me langwisshinge,
That am refus of every creature?   570
But for the love of God, at my preyinge,
Go hennes awey, for certes my deyinge
Wol the disese, and I mot nedes deye;
Therfore go wey, ther is na more to seye.

"But if thow wene I be thus sik for drede,   575
It is naught so, and therfore scorne nought.
Ther is another thing I take of hede
Wel more than aught the Grekes han yet
   wrought,
Which cause is of my deth, for sorowe and
   thought.
But though that I now telle it the ne leste,   580
Be thow naught wroth; I hide it for the beste."

This Pandare, that neigh malt for wo and routhe,
Ful ofte seyde, "Allas! what may this be?
Now frend," quod he, "if evere love or trouthe
Hath ben, or is, bitwixen the and me,   585
Ne do thow nevere swich a crueltee
To hiden fro thi frend so gret a care!
Wostow naught wel that it am I, Pandare?

"I wol parten with the al thi peyne,
If it be so I do the no comfort,   590
As it is frendes right, soth for to seyne,
To entreparten wo as glad desport.
I have, and shal, for trewe or fals report,
In wrong and right iloved the al my lyve:
Hid nat thi wo fro me, but telle it blyve."   595

---

530. **iblowe on brede,** blown abroad. 532. The allusion would fit a number of fabliaux. 539. **byhete,** promised. 543. **dreynte,** drowned. 545. **bythought,** reflected. 549. **unwar,** unawares. 550. **say,** saw. 551. **fare,** going on, to do. 557. **ferde,** fear. **attricioun,** a mild form of contrition. 559. **leye . . . on presse,** put away. 561. **for the nones,** for the occasion. 563. **angre,** a feeling or fit of anger. 564. **As for the tyme,** for the time being. 568. **cas . . . aventure,** accident . . . chance. 570. **refus of,** rejected by. 573. **mot,** must. 580. **now . . . leste,** do not please to tell it to thee now. 582. **malt,** melted. 589. **parten,** share. 592. **entreparten,** share. 595. **blyve,** quickly.

Than gan this sorwful Troylus to syke,
And seide hym thus: "God leve it be my beste
To telle it the; for sith it may the like,
Yet wol I telle it, though myn herte breste.
And wel woot I thow mayst do me no reste; 600
But lest thow deme I truste nat to the,
Now herke, frend, for thus it stant with me.

"Love, ayeins the which whoso defendeth
Hymselven most, hym alderlest avaylleth,
With disespeyr so sorwfulli me offendeth, 605
That streight unto the deth myn herte sailleth.
Therto desir so brennyngly me assailleth,
That to ben slayn it were a gretter joie
To me than kyng of Grece ben and Troye.

"Suffiseth this, my fulle frend Pandare, 610
That I have seyd, for now wostow my wo;
And for the love of God, my colde care
So hide it wel—I tolde it nevere to mo.
For harmes myghten folwen mo than two,
If it were wist; but be thow in gladnesse, 615
And lat me sterve, unknowe, of my destresse."

"How hastow thus unkyndely and longe
Hid this fro me, thow fol?" quod Pandarus.
"Paraunter thow myghte after swich oon longe,
That myn avys anoon may helpen us." 620
"This were a wonder thing," quod Troilus.
"Thow koudest nevere in love thiselven wisse:
How devel maistow brynge me to blisse?"

"Ye, Troilus, now herke," quod Pandare;
"Though I be nyce, it happeth often so, 625
That oon that excesse doth ful yvele fare
By good counseil kan kepe his frend therfro.
I have myself ek seyn a blynd man goo
Ther as he fel that couthe loken wide;
A fool may ek a wis man ofte gide. 630

"A wheston is no kervyng instrument,
But yet it maketh sharpe kervyng tolis.
And there thow woost that I have aught mys-
went,
Eschuwe thow that, for swich thing to the
scole is;
Thus often wise men ben war by foolys. 635
If thow do so, thi wit is wel bewared;
By his contrarie is every thyng declared.

"For how myghte evere swetnesse han ben
knowe
To him that nevere tasted bitternesse?
Ne no man may ben inly glad, I trowe, 640
That nevere was in sorwe or som destresse.
Eke whit by blak, by shame ek worthinesse,
Ech set by other, more for other semeth,
As men may se, and so the wyse it demeth.

"Sith thus of two contraries is o lore, 645
I, that have in love so ofte assayed
Grevances, oughte konne, and wel the more,
Counseillen the of that thow art amayed.
Ek the ne aughte nat ben yvel appayed,
Though I desyre with the for to bere 650
Thyn hevy charge; it shal the lasse dere.

"I woot wel that it fareth thus be me
As to thi brother, Paris, an herdesse,
Which that icleped was Oënone,
Wrot in a compleynte of hir hevynesse. 655
Yee say the lettre that she wrot, I gesse."
"Nay nevere yet, ywys," quod Troilus.
"Now," quod Pandare, "herkne, it was thus:

596. syke, sigh. 597. God leve, God grant. 604. hym alderlest avaylleth, it avails him least of all. 617. unkyndely, unnaturally. 619. after swich oon longe, long for such a one. 622. wisse, manage. 623. How devel, how the devil. 625. nyce, foolish. 626. excesse doth . . . fare, emotional intemperance causes to fare badly. 631. wheston, whetstone. 632. tolis, tools. 633. there, where. 634. to the scole is, is a lesson to thee. 636. bewared, expended. 643. Ech set . . .. Each thing set beside its opposite seems more distinct because of the other. 645. o lore, one thing that may be learned. 646. assayed, experienced. 648. amayed, dismayed. 649. yvel appayed, dissatisfied. 651. charge, burden. dere, harm. 653–4. Paris . . . Oënone. The nymph Oënone, deserted by Paris when he went to fetch Helen, pleaded with him by letter to be faithful to her. The letter constitutes Ovid's *Heroides*, v. 656. say, saw.

" 'Phebus, that first fond art of medicyne,'
Quod she, 'and couthe in every wightes care 660
Remedye and reed, by herbes he knew fyne,
Yet to hymself his konnyng was ful bare;
For love hadde hym so bounden in a snare,
Al for the doughter of the kyng Amete,
That al his craft ne koude his sorwes bete.' 665

"Right so fare I, unhappily for me,
I love oon best, and that me smerteth sore;
And yet, peraunter, kan I reden the,
And nat myself; repreve me na more.
I have no cause, I woot wel, for to sore 670
As doth an hauk that listeth for to pleye;
But to thin help yet somwhat kan I seye.

"And of o thyng right siker maistow be,
That certein, for to dyen in the peyne,
That I shal nevere mo discoveren the; 675
Ne, by my trouthe, I kepe nat restreyne
The fro thi love, theigh that it were Eleyne
That is thi brother wif, if ich it wiste:
Be what she be, and love hire as the liste!

"Therfore, as frend, fullich in me assure, 680
And telle me plat now what is th'enchesoun
And final cause of wo that ye endure;
For douteth nothyng, myn entencioun
Nis nat to yow of reprehencioun,
To speke as now, for no wight may byreve 685
A man to love, tyl that hym list to leve.

"And witteth wel that bothe two ben vices,
Mistrusten alle, or elles alle leve.
But wel I woot, the mene of it no vice is,
For for to trusten som wight is a preve 690

Of trouth, and forthi wolde I fayn remeve
Thi wronge conseyte, and do the som wyght
     triste
Thi wo to telle; and tel me, if the liste.

"The wise seith, 'Wo hym that is allone,
For, and he falle, he hath non helpe to ryse'; 695
And sith thow hast a felawe, tel thi mone;
For this nys naught, certein, the nexte wyse
To wynnen love, as techen us the wyse,
To walwe and wepe as Nyobe the queene,
Whos teres yet in marble ben yseene. 700

"Lat be thy wepyng and thi drerynesse,
And lat us lissen wo with oother speche;
So may thy woful tyme seme lesse.
Delyte nat in wo thi wo to seche,
As don thise foles that hire sorwes eche 705
With sorwe, whan thei han mysaventure,
And listen naught to seche hem other cure.

"Men seyn, 'to wrecche is consolacioun
To have another felawe in hys peyne.'
That owghte wel ben oure opynyoun, 710
For, bothe thow and I, of love we pleyne.
So ful of sorwe am I, soth for to seyne,
That certeinly namore harde grace
May sitte on me, for-why ther is no space.

"If God wol, thow art nat agast of me, 715
Lest I wolde of thi lady the bygyle!
Thow woost thyself whom that I love, parde,
As I best kan, gon sithen longe while.
And sith thow woost I do it for no wyle,
And seyst I am he that thow trustest moost, 720
Telle me somwhat, syn al my wo thow woost."

659. **Phebus**, Apollo. The story of Apollo's love for the daughter of Admetus is probably from a gloss to ll. 151–2 of the epistle mentioned in the previous note. In one such gloss the daughter's name is given as Perimele. See Meech, *PMLA*, XLV. 113. Admetus was a king in Thessaly, whose flocks for a time were tended by Apollo. 665. **bete,** amend. 674. **for to dyen in the peyne,** to the extent of dying under torture. Cf. *CT*, A 1133, B 1327. 676. **kepe,** care. 677. **theigh,** though. 678. **brother,** brother's (OE. *r*-declension, unchanged in gen.). 681. **plat,** flatly. **enchesoun,** reason. 685. **byreve,** *lit.* deprive. The meaning "prevent" and the constr. with *to* are unusual. 686. **to leve,** to leave off. 688. **Mistrusten . . . leve,** to mistrust everything or else believe everything. 690. **preve,** proof. 691. **remeve,** remove. 692. **do,** cause. **triste,** trust. 694. **The wise,** the wise man, *i.e.* Solomon; cf. *Eccles.*, 4:10. 697. **the nexte wyse,** the nearest way. 699. **Nyobe,** Niobe, Queen of Thebes, whose pride was punished by the death of her children. As she wept, she was turned to stone, even to her tears. Cf. Ovid, *Metam.*, VI. 312: lacrimas etiam nunc marmora manant. 700. **yseene,** visible. 702. **lissen,** alleviate. 704. **seche,** here perhaps in the sense of "examine, scrutinize," hence "dwell upon." 705. **eche,** increase.

Yet Troilus for al this no word seyde,
But longe he ley as stylle as he ded were;
And after this with sikynge he abreyde,
And to Pandarus vois he lente his ere,   725
And up his eighen caste he, that in feere
Was Pandarus, lest that in frenesie
He sholde falle, or elles soone dye;

And cryde "Awake!" ful wonderlich and
     sharpe;
"What! slombrestow as in a litargie?   730
Or artow lik an asse to the harpe,
That hereth sown whan men the strynges plye,
But in his mynde of that no melodie
May sinken hym to gladen, for that he
So dul ys of his bestialite?"   735

And with that, Pandare of his wordes stente;
And Troilus yet hym nothyng answerde,
For-why to tellen nas nat his entente
To nevere no man, for whom that he so ferde.
For it is seyd, "man maketh ofte a yerde   740
With which the maker is hymself ybeten
In sondry manere," as thise wyse treten;

And namelich in his counseil tellynge
That toucheth love that oughte ben secree;
For of himself it wol ynough out sprynge,   745
But if that it the bet governed be.
Ek som tyme it is a craft to seme fle
Fro thyng whych in effect men hunte faste:
Al this gan Troilus in his herte caste.

But natheles, whan he hadde herd hym crye
"Awake!" he gan to syken wonder soore,   751
And seyde, "Frend, though that I stylle lye,
I am nat deef. Now pees, and crye namore,
For I have herd thi wordes and thi lore;
But suffre me my meschief to bywaille,   755
For thi proverbes may me naught availle.

"Nor other cure kanstow non for me.
Ek I nyl nat ben cured; I wol deye.
What knowe I of the queene Nyobe?
Lat be thyne olde ensaumples, I the preye."   760
"No," quod tho Pandarus, "therfore I seye,
Swych is delit of foles to bywepe
Hire wo, but seken bote they ne kepe.

"Now knowe I that ther reson in the failleth.
But telle me if I wiste what she were   765
For whom that the al this mysaunter ailleth.
Dorste thow that I tolde hir in hire ere
Thi wo, sith thow darst naught thiself for feere,
And hire bysoughte on the to han som routhe?"
"Why, nay," quod he, "by God and by my
     trouthe!"   770

"What? nat as bisyly," quod Pandarus,
"As though myn owene lyf lay on this nede?"
"No, certes, brother," quod this Troilus.
"And whi?"—"For that thow scholdest nevere
     spede."
"Wostow that wel?"—"Ye, that is out of
     drede,"   775
Quod Troilus; "for al that evere ye konne,
She nyl to noon swich wrecche as I ben
     wonne."

Quod Pandarus, "Allas! what may this be,
That thow dispeired art thus causeles?
What! lyveth nat thi lady, bendiste?   780
How wostow so that thow art graceles?
Swich yvel is nat alwey booteles.
Why, put nat impossible thus thi cure,
Syn thyng to come is oft in aventure.

"I graunte wel that thow endurest wo   785
As sharp as doth he Ticius in helle,
Whos stomak foughles tiren evere moo
That hightyn volturis, as bokes telle.

---

724. **sikynge**, sighing. **abreyde**, started up. 731. **lik an asse**. See Boethius, I, pr. iv. 3. 735. **bestialite**, animal nature. 739. **ferde**, fared. 742. **treten**, tell. 744. **that**, that which. 745. **himself**, itself. 747. **craft**, wise policy. 754. **lore**, teaching, advice. 755. **meschief**, misfortune. 766. **mysaunter**, misadventure. 771. **bisyly**, zealously. 775. **drede**, doubt. 780. **bendiste**, benedicite. 784. **in aventure**, uncertain. 786. **Ticius**, a giant who attempted violence on Diana and was cast into Hades, where he lay stretched out while two vultures devoured his liver. 787. **tiren**, tear.

But I may nat endure that thow dwelle
In so unskilful an oppynyoun   790
That of thi wo is no curacioun.

"But oones nyltow, for thy coward herte,
And for thyn ire and folissh wilfulnesse,
For wantrust, tellen of thy sorwes smerte,
Ne to thyn owen help don bysynesse   795
As muche as speke a resoun moore or lesse,
But lyest as he that lest of nothyng recche.
What womman koude loven swich a wrecche?

"What may she demen oother of thy deeth,
If thow thus deye, and she not why it is,   800
But that for feere is yolden up thy breth,
For Grekes han biseged us, iwys?
Lord, which a thonk than shaltow han of this!
Thus wol she seyn, and al the town attones,   804
'The wrecche is ded, the devel have his bones!'

"Thow mayst allone here wepe and crye and knele,
But love a womman that she woot it nought,
And she wol quyte it that thow shalt nat fele.
Unknowe, unkist, and lost, that is unsought!
What! many a man hath love ful deere ybought
Twenty wynter that his lady wiste,   811
That nevere yet his lady mouth he kiste.

"What? sholde he therfore fallen in dispayr,
Or be recreant for his owne tene,
Or slen hymself, al be his lady fair?   815
Nay, nay, but evere in oon be fressh and grene
To serve and love his deere hertes queene,
And thynk it is a guerdon, hire to serve,
A thousand fold moore than he kan deserve."

And of that word took hede Troilus,   820
And thoughte anon what folie he was inne,
And how that soth hym seyde Pandarus,

That for to slen hymself myght he nat wynne,
But bothe don unmanhod and a synne,
And of his deth his lady naught to wite;   825
For of his wo, God woot, she knew ful lite.

And with that thought he gan ful sore syke,
And seyde, "Allas! what is me best to do?"
To whom Pandare answerde, "If the like,
The beste is that thow telle me al thi wo;   830
And have my trouthe, but thow it fynde so
I be thi boote, or that it be ful longe,
To pieces do me drawe, and sithen honge!"

"Ye, so thow seyst," quod Troilus tho, "allas!
But, God woot, it is naught the rather so.   835
Ful hard were it to helpen in this cas,
For wel fynde I that Fortune is my fo;
Ne al the men that riden konne or go
May of hire cruel whiel the harm withstonde;
For, as hire list, she pleyeth with free and bonde."   840

Quod Pandarus, "Than blamestow Fortune
For thow art wroth, ye, now at erst I see.
Woost thow nat wel that Fortune is comune
To everi manere wight in som degree?
And yet thow hast this comfort, lo, parde,   845
That, as hire joies moten overgon,
So mote hire sorwes passen everechon.

"For if hire whiel stynte any-thyng to torne,
Than cessed she Fortune anon to be.
Now, sith hire whiel by no way may sojourne,
What woostow if hire mutabilite   851
Right as thyselven list, wol don by the,
Or that she be naught fer fro thyn helpynge?
Paraunter thow hast cause for to synge.

"And therfore wostow what I the biseche?   855
Lat be thy wo and tornyng to the grounde;

790. **unskilful**, unreasonable. 794. **wantrust**, mistrust. 797. **lest**, pleases, wishes. **recche**, care. 799. **oother**, either, otherwise. 800. **not**, know not. 803. **which**, what. 804. **attones**, at once. 807. **that she woot**, who knows. 808. **quyte it that**, requite it so that. 812. **lady**. On the form see note to l. 99 above. 814. **recreant**, vanquished, faint-hearted. **tene**, vexation. 816. **evere in oon**, constantly. 818. **guerdon**, reward. 823. **for to slen**, by slaying. **wynne**, gain anything. 825. **wite**, know. 826. **lite**, little. 832. **or**, before. 833. **do me drawe**, cause me to be drawn. 835. **rather**, sooner. 838. **go**, walk. 842. **at erst**, for the first time, at last. 846. **moten overgon**, must pass away. 848. **any-thyng**, at all.

For whoso list have helyng of his leche,
To hym byhoveth first unwrye his wownde.
To Cerberus yn helle ay be I bounde,
Were it for my suster, al thy sorwe, 860
By my wil she sholde al be thyn to-morwe.

"Look up, I seye, and telle me what she is
Anon, that I may gon aboute thy nede.
Knowe ich hire aught? For my love, telle me
    this.
Thanne wolde I hopen rather for to spede." 865
Tho gan the veyne of Troilus to blede,
For he was hit, and wax al reed for shame.
"A ha!" quod Pandare, "here bygynneth
    game."

And with that word he gan hym for to shake,
And seyde, "Thef, thow shalt hyre name telle."
But tho gan sely Troilus for to quake 871
As though men sholde han led hym into helle,
And seyde, "Allas! of al my wo the welle,
Thanne is my swete fo called Criseyde!" 874
And wel neigh with the word for feere he deide.

And whan that Pandare herde hire name nevene,
Lord, he was glad, and seyde, "Frend so deere,
Now fare aright, for Joves name in hevene.
Love hath byset the wel; be of good cheere!
For of good name and wisdom and manere 880
She hath ynough, and ek of gentilesse.
If she be fayr, thow woost thyself, I gesse.

"Ne I nevere saugh a more bountevous
Of hire estat, n'a gladder, ne of speche
A frendlyer, n'a more gracious 885
For to do wel, ne lasse hadde nede to seche

What for to don; and al this bet to eche,
In honour, to as fer as she may strecche,
A kynges herte semeth by hyrs a wrecche.

"And forthy loke of good comfort thou be; 890
For certainly, the firste poynt is this:
Of noble corage and wel ordayné,
A man to have pees with himself, ywis.
So oughtest thou, for nought but good it is
To loven wel, and in a worthy place; 895
The oughte nat to clepe it hap, but grace.

"And also thynk, and therwith glade the,
That sith thy lady vertuous is al,
So foloweth it that there is som pitee
Amonges alle thise other in general; 900
And forthi se that thow, in special,
Requere naught that is ayeyns hyre name;
For vertu streccheth naught hymself to shame.

"But wel is me that evere that I was born,
That thow biset art in so good a place; 905
For by my trouthe, in love I dorste have sworn
The sholde nevere han tid thus fayr a grace.
And wostow why? For thow were wont to
    chace
At Love in scorn, and for despit him calle
'Seynt Idyot, lord of thise foles alle.' 910

"How often hastow maad thi nyce japes,
And seyd that Loves servantz everichone
Of nycete ben verray Goddes apes;
And some wolde mucche hire mete allone, 914
Liggyng abedde, and make hem for to grone;
And som, thow seydest, hadde a blaunche fevere,
And preydest God he sholde nevere kevere.

---

858. **unwrye,** uncover. The MSS vary between *unwre* and *unwrye, unwrie.* The former is historically better, but the latter are the usual spellings in Chaucer's day. Cf. also 2. 380. **859. Cerberus,** the three-headed dog guarding the entrance to Hades. **868. here bygynneth game.** Now the fun begins! **871. sely Troilus,** poor Troilus. **873. welle,** spring, source. **876. nevene,** name (heard tell her name). **883. bountevous,** full of goodness, kind. **887. eche,** increase, add to. **890. forthy,** therefore. **890–96.** This stanza is found only in α MSS, representing the earliest form of the poem. Chaucer may have removed it in revision either (as Root suggests) because it shifts the argument from the character of Criseyde, or because he was dissatisfied with the complicated syntax. **892. ordayné,** OF. *ordené,* regulated. **900. thise other,** these other virtues. **903.** For a virtue (such as pity) must not be stretched so far as to result in shame. **905. biset,** bestowed. **907. The . . . tid,** should never have happened to thee. **908-9. to chace at,** to rail at. **911. nyce japes,** foolish jokes. **913. Of nycete,** through foolishness. **verray,** true. **Goddes apes,** natural born fools; see *NED,* ape, 4. **914. mucche,** munch. **915. Liggyng,** lying. **916. som,** one. **blaunche fevere,** love-sickness. **917. kevere,** recover.

"And som of hem tooke on hem, for the cold,
More than ynough, so seydestow ful ofte.
And som han feyned ofte tyme, and told   920
How that they waken, whan thei slepen softe;
And thus they wolde han brought hemself
    alofte,
And natheles were under at the laste.
Thus seydestow, and japedest ful faste.

"Yet seydestow, that for the moore part,   925
Thise loveres wolden speke in general,
And thoughten that it was a siker art,
For faylyng, for t'assayen overal.
Now may I jape of the, if that I shal;
But natheles, though that I sholde deye,   930
That thow art non of tho, I dorste saye.

"Now bet thi brest, and sey to God of Love,
'Thy grace, lord, for now I me repente,
If I mysspak, for now myself I love.'
Thus sey with al thyn herte in good entente."
Quod Troilus, "A, lord! I me consente,   936
And preye to the my japes thow foryive,
And I shal nevere more whyle I live."

"Thow seist wel," quod Pandare, "and now I
    hope
That thow the goddes wrathe hast al apesed;
And sithen thow hast wopen many a drope,   941
And seyd swych thyng wherwith thi god is
    plesed,
Now wolde nevere god but thow were esed!
And thynk wel, she of whom rist al thi wo
Hereafter may thy comfort be also.   945

"For thilke grownd that bereth the wedes wikke
Bereth ek thise holsom herbes, as ful ofte
Next the foule netle, rough and thikke,

The rose waxeth swoote and smothe and
    softe;
And next the valeye is the hil o-lofte;   950
And next the derke nyght the glade morwe;
And also joie is next the fyn of sorwe.

"Now loke that atempre be thi bridel,
And for the beste ay suffre to the tyde,
Or elles al oure labour is on ydel: 955
He hasteth wel that wisely kan abyde.
Be diligent and trewe, and ay wel hide;
Be lusty, fre; persevere in thy servyse,
And al is wel, if thow werke in this wyse.

"But he that parted is in everi place   960
Is nowher hol, as writen clerkes wyse.
What wonder is, though swich oon have no
    grace?
Ek wostow how it fareth of som servise,
As plaunte a tree or herbe, in sondry wyse,
And on the morwe pulle it up as blyve!   965
No wonder is, though it may nevere thryve.

"And sith that God of Love hath the bistowed
In place digne unto thi worthinesse,
Stond faste, for to good port hastow rowed;
And of thiself, for any hevynesse,   970
Hope alwey wel; for, but if drerinesse
Or over-haste oure bothe labour shende,
I hope of this to maken a good ende.

"And wostow why I am the lasse afered
Of this matere with my nece trete?   975
For this have I herd seyd of wyse lered,
Was nevere man or womman yet bigete
That was unapt to suffren loves hete,
Celestial, or elles love of kynde;
Forthy som grace I hope in hire to fynde.   980

918. **tooke on.** The expression is ambiguous, but seems to mean "made much ado about." 922. **brought hemself alofte** . . . They thought to have succeeded but in the end failed. 926. **in general,** generally. 927. **a siker art** . . . a sure method against failing was to try everywhere. 941. **wopen,** wept. 944. **rist,** arises. 946. **wikke,** evil. 952. **fyn,** end. 953. **atempre,** restrained. 954. **suffre to the tyde,** submit to the time, *i.e.* be patient. 955. **on ydel,** in vain. 956. **He hasteth wel** . . . A form of the proverb quoted in 4. 1568. It occurs again in the *Melibeus,* 2243. 957. **hide.** The reference is probably to the courtly love requirement of secrecy; cf. ll. 991–3 below. 965. **as blyve,** immediately. 970. **for,** notwithstanding. 971. **drerinesse,** gloominess. The corresponding expression in the *Filostrato* is *pianto,* complaint. 979. **Celestial** . . . **kynde,** *i.e.* heavenly or earthly love.

"And for to speke of hire in specyal,
Hire beaute to bithynken and hire youthe,
It sit hire naught to ben celestial
As yet, though that hire liste bothe and kowthe;
But trewely, it sate hire wel right nowthe　　985
A worthi knyght to loven and cherice,
And but she do, I holde it for a vice.

"Wherfore I am, and wol ben, ay redy
To peyne me to do yow this servyse;
For bothe yow to plese thus hope I　　990
Herafterward; for ye ben bothe wyse,
And konne it counseil kepe in swych a wyse
That no man schal the wiser of it be;
And so we may ben gladed alle thre.

"And, by my trouthe, I have right now of the
A good conceyte in my wit, as I gesse,　　996
And what it is, I wol now that thow se.
I thenke, sith that Love, of his goodnesse,
Hath the converted out of wikkednesse,
That thow shalt ben the beste post, I leve,　　1000
Of al his lay, and moost his foos to greve.

"Ensample why, se now thise wise clerkes,
That erren aldermost ayeyn a lawe,
And ben converted from hire wikked werkes
Thorugh grace of God that list hem to hym
　　drawe,　　1005
Thanne arn they folk that han moost God in awe,
And strengest feythed ben, I undirstonde,
And konne an errowr alderbest withstonde."

Whan Troilus hadde herd Pandare assented
To ben his help in lovyng of Cryseyde,　　1010
Weex of his wo, as who seith, untormented,
But hotter weex his love, and thus he seyde,

With sobre chere, although his herte pleyde:
"Now blisful Venus helpe, er that I sterve,
Of the, Pandare, I mowe som thank deserve.

"But, deere frend, how shal my wo be lesse　1016
Til this be doon? And good, ek telle me this:
How wiltow seyn of me and my destresse,
Lest she be wroth—this drede I moost, ywys—
Or nyl nat here or trowen how it is?　　1020
Al this drede I, and eke for the manere
Of the, hire em, she nyl no swich thyng here."

Quod Pandarus, "Thow hast a ful gret care
Lest that the cherl may falle out of the moone!
Whi, Lord! I hate of the thi nyce fare!　　1025
Whi, entremete of that thow hast to doone!
For Goddes love, I bidde the a boone:
So lat m'alone, and it shal be thi beste."

"Whi, frend," quod he, "now do right as the
　　leste.

"But herke, Pandare, o word, for I nolde　1030
That thow in me wendest so gret folie,
That to my lady I desiren sholde
That toucheth harm or any vilenye;
For dredeles me were levere dye
Than she of me aught elles understode　　1035
But that that myghte sownen into goode."

Tho lough this Pandare, and anon answerde,
"And I thi borugh? fy! no wight doth but so.
I roughte naught though that she stood and
　　herde
How that thow seist! but farewel, I wol go.
Adieu! be glad! God spede us bothe two!　1041
Yef me this labour and this bisynesse,
And of my spede be thyn al that swetnesse."

---

982. bithynken, consider. **984. though . . . kowthe,** though she would and could (Tatlock). **985. sate,** would befit.
nowthe, now. **990. bothe yow,** you both. **992. counseil,** a secret. **998. sith,** since. **1000. post . . . lay,** supporter
of his law. **1003. erren,** transgress. **1008. errowr,** false belief, heresy. **1009. assented,** elliptical for *to have assented.* See
Language, § 51. **1011. Weex,** he became. **as who seith,** as one might say. **1015. Of the . . .,** that I may do something
(in return), Pandare, to deserve thanks. **1017. good,** good friend. **1021. for the manere . . .,** considering the circumstance that you are her uncle. **1022. em,** uncle. Although the word (OE. *ēam*) is used by Chaucer only in this poem, it is
used fairly often and the student should become familiar with it. **1024. cherl . . .,** that the man in the moon may fall out.
1025. fare, behavior. **1026. entremete . . .,** mind your own affairs. **1028. thi beste,** best for you. **1033. That,** that
which. **1034. dredeles,** without doubt. **1036. sownen into,** be conducive to. **1037. lough,** laughed. **1038. And I thi
borugh?** And am I your surety? **no wight . . .,** every lover says the same thing. **1039. I roughte naught,** I would not care.

Tho Troilus gan doun on knees to falle,
And Pandare in his armes hente faste,   1045
And seyde, "Now, fy on the Grekes alle!
Yet, parde, God shal helpe us atte laste.
And dredelees, if that my lyf may laste,
And God toforn, lo, som of hem shal smerte;
And yet m'athinketh that this avant m'asterte!

"Now, Pandare, I kan na more seye,   1051
But, thow wis, thow woost, thow maist, thow
     art al!
My lif, my deth, hol in thyn honde I leye.
Help now!" Quod he, "Yis, by my trowthe, I
     shal."
"God yelde the, frend, and this in special,"   1055
Quod Troilus, "that thow me recomande
To hire that to the deth me may comande."

This Pandarus, tho desirous to serve
His fulle frend, than seyde in this manere: 1059
"Farwell, and thenk I wol thi thank deserve!
Have here my trowthe, and that thow shalt wel
     here,"—
And went his wey, thenkyng on this matere,
And how he best myghte hire biseche of grace,
And fynde a tyme therto, and a place.

For everi wight that hath an hous to founde   1065
Ne renneth naught the werk for to bygynne

With rakel hond, but he wol bide a stounde,
And sende his hertes line out fro withinne
Aldirfirst his purpos for to wynne.
Al this Pandare in his herte thoughte,   1070
And caste his werk ful wisely or he wroughte.

But Troilus lay tho no lenger down,
But up anon upon his stede bay,
And in the feld he pleyde the leoun;
Wo was that Grek that with hym mette a-day!
And in the town his manere tho forth ay   1076
Soo goodly was, and gat hym so in grace,
That ecch hym loved that loked on his face.

For he bicom the frendlieste wight,
The gentilest, and ek the mooste fre,   1080
The thriftiest and oon the beste knyght,
That in his tyme was or myghte be.
Dede were his japes and his cruelte,
His heighe port and his manere estraunge,
And ecch of tho gan for a vertu chaunge.   1085

Now lat us stynte of Troilus a stounde,
That fareth lik a man that hurt is soore,
And is somdeel of akyngge of his wownde
Ylissed wel, but heeled no deel moore,
And, as an esy pacyent, the loore   1090
Abit of hym that gooth aboute his cure;
And thus he dryeth forth his aventure.

Explicit liber primus.

1050. **m'athinketh . . .,** I am sorry that this boast escaped from me. 1052. **thou wis,** thou, being wise. 1055. **God yelde the,** God grant thee, although the expression may have its commoner meaning, "God reward thee." 1065. **founde,** build (set the foundation for). 1067. **rakel,** rash. 1068. **hertes line,** imaginary line. The sense is that by considering the matter the builder will arrive at the best way to proceed. The passage is based, as Robinson notes, on the *Nova Poetria*, ll. 43–5, of Geoffrey de Vinsauf. 1075. **a-day,** by day. 1086. **stynte,** cease. **a stounde,** a while. 1089. **Ylissed,** relieved. Although relieved somewhat of pain, he is no nearer being cured. 1090. **the loore Abit,** awaits the advice. 1092. **dryeth forth,** continues to endure.

Book II

Incipit prohemium secundi libri.

Owt of thise blake wawes for to saylle,
O wynd, o wynd, the weder gynneth clere;
For in this see the boot hath swych travaylle,
Of my connyng, that unneth I it steere.
This see clepe I the tempestous matere   5
Of disespeir that Troilus was inne;
But now of hope the kalendes bygynne.

O lady myn, that called art Cleo,
Thow be my speed fro this forth, and my Muse,
To ryme wel this book til I have do;   10
Me nedeth here noon other art to use.
Forwhi to every lovere I me excuse,
That of no sentement I this endite,
But out of Latyn in my tonge it write.

Wherfore I nyl have neither thank ne blame
Of al this werk, but prey yow mekely,   16
Disblameth me, if any word be lame,
For as myn auctour seyde, so sey I.
Ek though I speke of love unfelyngly,
No wondre is, for it nothyng of newe is;   20
A blynd man kan nat juggen wel in hewis.

Ye knowe ek that in forme of speche is chaunge
Withinne a thousand yeer, and wordes tho
That hadden pris, now wonder nyce and
straunge

Us thinketh hem, and yet thei spake hem so,
And spedde as wel in love as men now do;   26
Ek for to wynnen love in sondry ages,
In sondry londes, sondry ben usages.

And forthi if it happe in any wyse,
That here be any lovere in this place   30
That herkneth, as the storie wol devise,
How Troilus com to his lady grace,
And thenketh, "so nold I nat love purchace,"
Or wondreth on his speche or his doynge,
I noot; but it is me no wonderynge.   35

For every wight which that to Rome went
Halt nat o path, or alwey o manere;
Ek in som lond were al the game shent,
If that they ferde in love as men don here,
As thus, in opyn doyng or in chere,   40
In visityng, in forme, or seyde hire sawes;
Forthi men seyn, ecch contree hath his lawes.

Ek scarsly ben ther in this place thre
That have in love seid lik, and don, in al;
For to thi purpos this may liken the,   45
And the right nought, yet al is seid or schal;
Ek som men grave in tree, some in ston wal,
As it bitit; but syn I have bigonne,
Myn auctour shal I folwen, if I konne.

Explicit prohemium secundi libri.

1. wawes, waves. **4. Of my connyng.** If, as seems most likely, these opening lines follow Dante (the beginning of the *Purgatorio*), this phrase is to be construed with *boot*. Dante has "la navicella del mio ingegno." **7. kalendes,** the first day of the month, therefore the beginning of a new period of time or of anything. **8. Cleo,** Clio, the Muse of history. **13. sentement,** personal experience or knowledge. **14. Latyn.** Chaucer continues to claim a Latin source. Cf. 1. 394. **16. Of,** for. **17. Disblameth,** excuse. **30-1.** Chaucer envisages an audience of listeners. **36. went,** for *wendeth*, goes. **37. Halt,** holds. **38. shent,** spoiled. **40. in opyn doyng . . .,** in overt act or in countenance. **41. in forme,** in behavior according to the rules of etiquette. **seyde hire sawes,** expressed themselves. **42. his,** its. **43. in this place.** Cf. note to 30-1. **44. lik,** alike. **46. is seid or schal,** is said sooner or later. **47. grave,** carve. **48. bitit,** for *bitideth*, happens.

Incipit liber secundus.

In May, that moder is of monthes glade, 50
That fresshe floures, blew and white and rede,
Ben quike agayn, that wynter dede made,
And ful of bawme is fletyng every mede;
Whan Phebus doth his bryghte bemes sprede,
Right in the white Bole, it so bitidde, 55
As I shal synge, on Mayes day the thrydde,

That Pandarus, for al his wise speche,
Felt ek his part of loves shotes keene,
That, koude he nevere so wel of lovyng preche,
It made his hewe a-day ful ofte greene. 60
So shop it that hym fil that day a teene
In love, for which in wo to bedde he wente,
And made, er it was day, ful many a wente.

The swalowe Proigne, with a sorowful lay,
Whan morwen com, gan make hire wayment-
  ynge, 65
Whi she forshapen was; and ever lay
Pandare abedde, half in a slomberynge,
Til she so neigh hym made hire cheterynge
How Tereus gan forth hire suster take,
That with the noyse of hire he gan awake, 70

And gan to calle, and dresse hym up to ryse,
Remembryng hym his erand was to doone
From Troilus, and ek his grete emprise;
And caste and knew in good plit was the moone
To doon viage, and took his weye ful soone 75
Unto his neces palays ther biside.
Now Janus, god of entree, thow hym gyde!

Whan he was come unto his neces place,
"Wher is my lady?" to hire folk quod he;
And they hym tolde, and he forth in gan pace,
And fond two othere ladys sete, and she, 81
Withinne a paved parlour, and they thre
Herden a mayden reden hem the geste
Of the siege of Thebes, while hem leste.

Quod Pandarus, "Madame, God yow see, 85
With al youre book, and al the compaignie!"
"Ey, uncle myn, welcome iwys," quod she;
And up she roos, and by the hond in hye
She took hym faste, and seyde, "This nyght
  thrie,
To goode mot it turne, of yow I mette." 90
And with that word she doun on bench hym
  sette.

"Ye, nece, yee shal faren wel the bet,
If God wol, al this yeer," quod Pandarus;
"But I am sory that I have yow let
To herken of youre book ye preysen thus. 95
For Goddes love, what seith it? telle it us!
Is it of love? O, som good ye me leere!"
"Uncle," quod she, "youre maistresse is nat
  here."

With that thei gonnen laughe, and tho she
  seyde,
"This romaunce is of Thebes that we rede; 100
And we han herd how that kyng Layus deyde
Thorugh Edippus his sone, and al that dede;

53. is fletyng, abounds in, "is swimming in." 55. Bole, Taurus. The epithet *white* is not clear, but was attributed by Skeat to reminiscence of Ovid, *Metam.*, II. 852. it so bitidde, it so happened. 56. The reason for the date is not certainly known. It is likewise the date on which Palemon escapes from prison and witnesses Arcite doing "his observaunce to May" (*KnT*, A 1462 ff.) as well as that on which Chauntecleer is carried off by the fox (*NPT*, B 4380). J. P. McCall (*MLN*, LXXVI. 201–5) makes the plausible suggestion that the date represents the culmination of the Floralia, a particularly licentious Roman festival, and therefore associated with love. 61. So shop it, it so happened. teene, grief. 63. wente, twisting and turning. 64. The swalowe Proigne. The story is told by Ovid, *Metam.*, VI. Progne was wedded to Tereus, King of Thrace. Tereus, enamored of her sister Philomela, violated her. After taking a terrible vengeance on Tereus by feeding him the flesh of his own son, Progne was metamorphosed (*forshapen*) into a swallow and Philomela into a nightingale. 74. caste, calculated astrologically. in good plit, in a favorable position. 76. ther biside, nearby. 77. Janus, guardian deity of gates, represented with two faces looking in opposite directions. 81. sete, were sitting. 84. siege of Thebes, the subject of the *Thebaid* of Statius and well-known in the Middle Ages through the *Roman de Thèbes*. 88. in hye, quickly, soon. 90. mette, dreamed. 94. let, hindered. 95. preysen, value, esteem. 97. leere, teach. 99. tho, then.

And here we stynten at thise lettres rede,
How the bisshop, as the book kan telle,   104
Amphiorax, fil thorugh the ground to helle."

Quod Pandarus, "Al this knowe I myselve,
And al th'assege of Thebes and the care;
For herof ben ther maked bookes twelve.
But lat be this, and telle me how ye fare.
Do wey youre barbe, and shewe youre face
     bare;   110
Do wey youre book, rys up, and lat us daunce,
And lat us don to May som observaunce."

"I? God forbede!" quod she, "be ye mad?
Is that a widewes lif, so God yow save?
By God, ye maken me ryght soore adrad!   115
Ye ben so wylde, it semeth as ye rave.
It sate me wel bet ay in a cave
To bidde and rede on holy seyntes lyves;
Lat maydens gon to daunce, and yonge wyves."

"As evere thryve I," quod this Pandarus,   120
"Yet koude I telle a thyng to doon yow pleye."
"Now, uncle deere," quod she, "telle it us
For Goddes love; is than th'assege aweye?
I am of Grekes so fered that I deye."
"Nay, nay," quod he, "as evere mote I thryve,
It is a thing wel bet than swyche fyve."   126

"Ye, holy God," quod she, "what thyng is that?
What! bet than swyche fyve? I! nay, ywys!
For al this world ne kan I reden what
It sholde ben; som jape, I trowe, is this;   130
And but youreselven telle us what it is,
My wit is for t'arede it al to leene.
As help me God, I not nat what ye meene."

"And I youre borugh, ne nevere shal, for me,   134
This thyng be told to yow, as mote I thryve!"
"And whi so, uncle myn? whi so?" quod she.
"By God," quod he, "that wol I telle as blyve!
For prouder womman is ther noon on lyve,
And ye it wist, in al the town of Troye.
I jape nought, as evere have I joye!"   140

Tho gan she wondren moore than biforn
A thousand fold, and down hire eyghen caste;
For nevere, sith the tyme that she was born,
To knowe thyng desired she so faste;
And with a syk she seyde hym atte laste,   145
"Now, uncle myn, I nyl yow nought displese,
Nor axen more that may do yow disese."

So after this, with many wordes glade,
And frendly tales, and with merie chiere,
Of this and that they pleide, and gonnen wade
In many an unkouth glad and dep matere,   151
As frendes doon whan thei ben mette yfere,
Tyl she gan axen hym how Ector ferde,
That was the townes wal and Grekes yerde.

"Ful wel, I thonk it God," quod Pandarus,   155
"Save in his arm he hath a litel wownde;
And ek his fresshe brother Troilus,
The wise, worthi Ector the secounde,
In whom that alle vertu list habounde,
As alle trouth and alle gentilesse,   160
Wisdom, honour, fredom, and worthinesse."

"In good feith, em," quod she, "that liketh me;
Thei faren wel, God save hem bothe two!
For trewelich I holde it gret deynte,
A kynges sone in armes wel to do,   165

---

103. lettres rede, rubric, evidently summarizing the next section. **104–5. the bisshop . . . Amphiorax.** Amphiorax, a famous Greek soothsayer, was consulted by Adrastus, king of Argos, before setting out on the expedition against Thebes. Lydgate always speaks of him as *bishop*, a common anachronism in the Middle Ages. He foretold the evils that would result from the war and predicted that he himself would perish. In the midst of the fighting he was swallowed up by the earth. See the closing lines of Book VII of the *Thebaid*. **108. bookes twelve,** the number of books in the *Thebaid*. **110. barbe,** "a piece of white plaited linen, passed over or under the chin, and reaching midway to the waist." (*NED*) It was worn by widows as well as nuns. **117. sate,** would befit. **118. bidde,** pray. **121. doon yow pleye,** make you be merry. **123. assege,** besieging force. **129. reden,** think, guess. **130. jape,** joke. **133. not nat,** know not. **134. youre borugh,** *i.e.* I give you my word. **137. as blyve,** immediately. **144. faste,** eagerly. **149. frendly,** pleasant. **152. yfere,** together. **154. yerde,** rod, cudgel. **164. gret deynte,** a very estimable thing.

And ben of goode condiciouns therto;
For gret power and moral vertu here
Is selde yseyn in o persone yfere."

"In good faith, that is soth," quod Pandarus.
"But, by my trouthe, the kyng hath sones
    tweye,—   170
That is to mene, Ector and Troilus,—
That certeynly, though that I sholde deye,
Thei ben as voide of vices, dar I seye,
As any men that lyven under the sonne.
Hire myght is wyde yknowe, and what they
    konne.   175

"Of Ector nedeth it namore for to telle:
In al this world ther nys a bettre knyght
Than he, that is of worthynesse welle;
And he wel moore vertu hath than myght.
This knoweth many a wis and worthi wight.
The same pris of Troilus I seye;   181
God help me so, I knowe nat swiche tweye."

"By God," quod she, "of Ector that is sooth.
Of Troilus the same thyng trowe I;
For, dredeles, men tellen that he doth   185
In armes day by day so worthily,
And bereth hym here at hom so gentily
To every wight, that alle pris hath he
Of hem that me were levest preysed be."

"Ye sey right sooth, ywys," quod Pandarus; 190
"For yesterday, whoso hadde with hym ben,
He myghte han wondred upon Troilus;
For nevere yet so thikke a swarm of been
Ne fleigh, as Grekes fro hym gonne fleen,
And thorugh the feld, in everi wightes eere,
There nas no cry but 'Troilus is there!'   196

"Now here, now ther, he hunted hem so faste,
Ther nas but Grekes blood,—and Troilus.

Now hym he hurte, and hym al down he
    caste;
Ay wher he wente, it was arayed thus: 200
He was hir deth, and sheld and lif for us;
That, as that day, ther dorste non withstonde,
Whil that he held his blody swerd in honde.

"Therto he is the friendlieste man
Of gret estat, that evere I saugh my lyve,   205
And wher hym lest, best felawshipe kan
To swich as hym thynketh able for to thryve."
And with that word tho Pandarus, as blyve,
He took his leve, and seyde, "I wol gon henne."
"Nay, blame have I, myn uncle," quod she
    thenne.   210

"What aileth yow to be thus wery soone,
And namelich of wommen? wol ye so?
Nay, sitteth down; by God, I have to doone
With yow, to speke of wisdom er ye go."
And everi wight that was aboute hem tho,   215
That herde that, gan fer awey to stonde,
Whil they two hadde al that hem liste in
    honde.

Whan that hire tale al brought was to an ende,
Of hire estat and of hire governaunce,
Quod Pandarus, "Now is it tyme I wende.   220
But yet, I say, ariseth, lat us daunce,
And cast youre widewes habit to mischaunce!
What list yow thus youreself to disfigure,
Sith yow is tid thus fair an aventure?"   224

"A! wel bithought! for love of God," quod she,
"Shal I nat witen what ye meene of this?"
"No, this thing axeth leyser," tho quod he,
"And eke me wolde muche greve, iwys,
If I it tolde, and ye it toke amys.
Yet were it bet my tonge for to stille   230
Than seye a soth that were ayeyns youre wille.

181. **pris,** praise. 188-9. . . . he hath all the praise of them by whom I should like best to be praised. 193. **been,** bees.
194. **fleigh,** flew. **fleen,** flee. 200. **arayed,** destined. 202. **as that day,** that day. 206. **kan,** can (show). 207. **thryve.** The
connotation is not clear; possibly "to grow (or continue) in virtue." 209. **henne,** hence. 214. **wisdom,** a wise thing to do.
217. **al . . . in honde,** all the business they wished to transact. 218. **tale,** talk. 222. **to mischaunce,** to the devil. 223.
disfigure, destroy your attractiveness (by wearing widow's weeds).

"For, nece, by the goddesse Mynerve,
And Jupiter, that maketh the thondre rynge,
And by the blisful Venus that I serve,
Ye ben the womman in this world
    lyvynge,   235
Withouten paramours, to my wyttynge,
That I best love, and lothest am to greve,
And that ye weten wel yourself, I leve."

"Iwis, myn uncle," quod she, "grant mercy.
Youre frendshipe have I founden evere yit;   240
I am to no man holden, trewely,
So muche as yow, and have so litel quyt;
And with the grace of God, emforth my wit,
As in my gylt I shal yow nevere offende;
And if I have er this, I wol amende.   245

"But, for the love of God, I yow biseche,
As ye ben he that I love moost and triste,
Lat be to me youre fremde manere speche,
And sey to me, youre nece, what yow liste."
And with that word hire uncle anoon hire kiste,
And seyde, "Gladly, leve nece dere!   251
Tak it for good, that I shal sey yow here."

With that she gan hire eighen down to caste,
And Pandarus to coghe gan a lite,
And seyde, "Nece, alwey, lo! to the laste,   255
How so it be that som men hem delite
With subtyl art hire tales for to endite,
Yet for al that, in hire entencioun,
Hire tale is al for som conclusioun.

"And sithen th'ende is every tales strengthe,
And this matere is so bihovely,   261
What sholde I peynte or drawen it on lengthe
To yow, that ben my frend so feythfully?"
And with that word he gan right inwardly
Byholden hire and loken on hire face,   265
And seyde, "On swiche a mirour goode grace!"

Than thought he thus: "If I my tale endite
Aught harde, or make a proces any whyle,
She shal no savour have therin but lite,
And trowe I wolde hire in my wil bigyle;   270
For tendre wittes wenen al be wyle
Theras thei kan nought pleynly understonde;
Forthi hire wit to serven wol I fonde"—

And loked on hire in a bysi wyse,
And she was war that he byheld hire so,   275
And seyde, "Lord! so faste ye m'avise!
Sey ye me nevere er now—What sey ye, no?"
"Yis, yis," quod he, "and bet wole er I go!
But, be my trouthe, I thoughte, now if ye
Be fortunat, for now men shal it se,   280

"For to every wight som goodly aventure
Som tyme is shape, if he it kan receyven;
And if that he wol take of it no cure,
Whan that it commeth, but wilfully it weyven,
Lo, neyther cas ne fortune hym deceyven,   285
But ryght his verray slouthe and wrecched-
    nesse;
And swich a wight is for to blame, I gesse.

"Good aventure, o beele nece, have ye
Ful lightly founden, and ye konne it take;
And, for the love of God, and ek of me,   290
Cache it anon, lest aventure slake!
What sholde I lenger proces of it make?
Yif me youre hond, for in this world is noon,
If that yow list, a wight so wel bygon.

"And sith I speke of good entencioun,   295
As I to yow have told wel here-byforn,
And love as wel youre honour and renoun
As creature in al this world yborn,
By alle the othes that I have yow sworn,
And ye be wrooth therfore, or wene I lye,   300
Ne shal I nevere sen yow eft with yë.

236. **Withouten paramours,** except my lady loves. 241. **holden,** indebted. 243. **emforth,** to the extent of. 244. **As in my gylt,** through my fault. 248. **fremde,** strange. 251. **leve,** dear. 255. **to the laste,** in the end, after all. 261. **bihovely,** profitable. 262. **What,** why. 264. **inwardly,** intently. 266. Blessing on such a mirror! 268. **make a proces any whyle,** make a long story (of it). 270. **trowe,** (she will) believe. 273. Therefore I will try to adapt myself to her intelligence. 274. **in a bysi wyse,** attentively. 276. **faste,** steadily. **avise,** stare at. 277. **Sey,** saw. 283. **cure,** heed (care). 284. **weyven,** cast aside. 291. **aventure slake,** good fortune wane. 294. **wel bygon,** fortunate. 300. **And,** if.

"Beth naught agast, ne quaketh naught!
  Wherto?
Ne chaungeth naught for fere so youre hewe!
For hardely the werst of this is do,   304
And though my tale as now be to yow newe,
Yet trist alwey ye shal me fynde trewe;
And were it thyng that me thoughte unsittynge,
To yow wolde I no swiche tales brynge."

"Now, my good em, for Goddes love, I preye,"
Quod she, "come of, and telle me what it is!
For both I am agast what ye wol seye,   311
And ek me longeth it to wite, ywys;
For whethir it be wel or be amys,
Say on, lat me nat in this feere dwelle."
"So wol I doon; now herkeneth! I shal telle:

"Now, nece myn, the kynges deere sone,   316
The goode, wise, worthi, fresshe, and free,
Which alwey for to don wel is his wone,
The noble Troilus, so loveth the,
That, but ye helpe, it wol his bane be.   320
Lo, here is al! What sholde I moore seye?
Do what yow lest, to make hym lyve or deye.

"But if ye late hym deye, I wol sterve—
Have here my trouthe, nece, I nyl nat lyen—
Al sholde I with this knyf my throte kerve."
With that the teris breste out of his yën,   326
And seide, "If that ye don us bothe dyen,
Thus gilteles, than have ye fisshed fayre!
What mende ye, though that we booth appaire?

"Allas! he which that is my lord so deere,   330
That trewe man, that noble gentil knyght,
That naught desireth but youre frendly cheere,
I se hym deyen, ther he goth upryght,
And hasteth hym with al his fulle myght
For to ben slayn, if his fortune assente.   335
Allas, that God yow swich a beaute sente!

"If it be so that ye so cruel be,
That of his deth yow liste nought to recche,
That is so trewe and worthi, as ye se,
Namoore than of a japer or a wrecche,—   340
If ye be swich, youre beaute may nat strecche
To make amendes of so cruel a dede.
Avysement is good byfore the nede.

"Wo worth the faire gemme vertulees!
Wo worth that herbe also that dooth no
  boote!
Wo worth that beaute that is routheles!   346
Wo worth that wight that tret ech undir foote!
And ye, that ben of beaute crop and roote,
If therwithal in yow ther be no routhe,
Than is it harm ye lyven, by my trouthe!   350

"And also think wel that this is no gaude;
For me were levere thow and I and he
Were hanged, than I sholde ben his baude,
As heigh as men myghte on us alle ysee!
I am thyn em; the shame were to me,   355
As wel as the, if that I sholde assente,
Thorough myn abet, that he thyn honour shente.

"Now understonde, for I yow nought requere
To bynde yow to hym thorugh no byheste,
But only that ye make hym bettre chiere   360
Than ye han doon er this, and moore feste,
So that his lif be saved atte leeste:
This al and som, and pleynly oure entente.
God help me so, I nevere other mente!

"Lo, this requeste is naught but skylle, ywys,
Ne doute of reson, pardee, is ther noon.   366
I sette the worste, that ye dreden this:
Men wolde wondren sen hym come or goon.
Ther-ayeins answere I thus anoon,
That every wight, but he be fool of kynde,   370
Wol deme it love of frendshipe in his mynde.

---

310. come of, come on. **329. What mende ye?** what do you gain? **appaire,** suffer harm. **333. deyen, ther he goth upryght,** *i.e.* dying on his feet. **340. japer,** trickster. **344.** An allusion to the belief that precious stones had magical and other useful properties. **347. tret,** treads. **348. crop,** top (of a tree). *Crop and roote* is a common phrase signifying the whole of anything. **351. gaude,** trickery. **357. shente,** injured. **359. byheste,** promise. **361. feste,** encouragement. **363. al and som,** the sum total. **pleynly,** entirely. **365. skylle,** reason. **366. doute of reson,** reasonable fear. **367.** I assume the worst. **370. fool of kynde,** a natural fool.

"What? who wol demen, though he se a man
To temple go, that he th'ymages eteth?
Thenk ek how wel and wisely that he kan   374
Governe hymself, that he no thyng foryeteth,
That where he cometh, he pris and thank hym
    geteth;
And ek therto, he shal come here so selde,
What fors were it though al the town byhelde?

"Swych love of frendes regneth al this town;
And wry yow in that mantel evere moo;   380
And, God so wys be my savacioun,
As I have seyd, youre beste is to do soo.
But alwey, goode nece, to stynte his woo,
So lat youre daunger sucred ben a lite,
That of his deth ye be naught for to wite."   385

Criseyde, which that herde hym in this wise,
Thoughte, "I shal felen what he meneth, ywis."
"Now em," quod she, "what wolde ye devise?
What is youre reed I sholde don of this?"

"That is wel seyd," quod he, "certein, best is
That ye hym love ayeyn for his lovynge,   391
As love for love is skilful guerdonynge.

"Thenk ek how elde wasteth every houre
In eche of yow a partie of beautee;
And therfore, er that age the devoure,   395
Go love; for olde, ther wol no wight of the.
Lat this proverbe a loore unto yow be:
'To late ywar, quod beaute, whan it paste';
And elde daunteth daunger at the laste.

"The kynges fool is wont to crien loude,   400
Whan that hym thinketh a womman berth hire
    hye,
'So longe mote ye lyve, and alle proude,
Til crowes feet be growen under youre yë,
And sende yow than a myrour in to prye,

In which that ye may se youre face a-morwe!'
Nece, I bidde wisshe yow namore sorwe."   406

With this he stynte, and caste adown the heed,
And she began to breste a-wepe anoon,
And seyde, "Allas, for wo! Why nere I deed?
For of this world the feyth is al agoon.   410
Allas! what sholden straunge to me doon,
When he, that for my beste frend I wende,
Ret me to love, and sholde it me defende?

"Allas! I wolde han trusted, douteles,
That if that I, thorugh my disaventure,   415
Hadde loved outher hym or Achilles,
Ector, or any mannes creature,
Ye nolde han had no mercy ne mesure
On me, but alwey had me in repreve.
This false world, allas! who may it leve?   420

"What! is this al the joye and al the feste?
Is this youre reed? Is this my blisful cas?
Is this the verray mede of youre byheeste?
Is al this paynted proces seyd, allas!
Right for this fyn? O lady myn, Pallas!   425
Thow in this dredful cas for me purveye,
For so astoned am I that I deye."

Wyth that she gan ful sorwfully to syke.
"A! may it be no bet?" quod Pandarus;   429
"By God, I shal namore come here this wyke,
And God toforn, that am mystrusted thus!
I se ful wel that ye sette lite of us,
Or of oure deth! allas, I, woful wrecche!
Might he yet lyve, of me is nought to recche.

"O cruel god, O dispitouse Marte,   435
O Furies thre of helle, on yow I crye!
So lat me nevere out of this hous departe,
If that I mente harm or vilenye!"

---

378. **What fors were it,** what would it matter. 380. **wry,** wrap. 384. **daunger,** distant manner, haughtiness. **sucred,** sugared. 385. **wite,** blame. 387. **felen,** find out. 388. **devise,** suggest, recommend. 392. **skilful guerdonynge,** reasonable reward. 398. **ywar,** watchful, on guard. Bohn's *Hand-book of Proverbs* gives "Too late to grieve when the chance is past." 406. **I bidde wisshe yow . . . ,** do not intend to wish you more sorrow. Cf. G. V. Smithers, *English and Germanic Studies,* I (1947–8). 101–13. 409. **nere,** were not. 411. **straunge,** strangers. 413. **Ret,** for *redeth,* advises. **defende,** forbid. 417. **mannes,** of mankind, human. 423. **mede,** fulfillment. 424. **paynted proces,** highly-coloured account. 426. **purveye,** provide. 428. **syke,** sigh. 438. **vilenye,** anything improper.

But sith I se my lord mot nedes dye,
And I with hym, here I me shryve, and seye
That wikkedly ye don us bothe deye.   441

"But sith it liketh yow that I be ded,
By Neptunus, that god is of the see,
Fro this forth shal I nevere eten bred
Til I myn owen herte blood may see;   445
For certeyn I wol deye as soone as he."—
And up he sterte, and on his wey he raughte,
Til she agayn hym by the lappe kaughte.

Criseyde, which that wel neigh starf for feere,
So as she was the ferfulleste wight   450
That myghte be, and herde ek with hire ere
And saugh the sorwful ernest of the knyght,
And in his preier ek saugh noon unryght,
And for the harm that myghte ek fallen moore,
She gan to rewe, and dredde hire wonder
     soore,   455

And thoughte thus: "Unhappes fallen thikke
Alday for love, and in swych manere cas
As men ben cruel in hemself and wikke;
And if this man sle here hymself, allas!
In my presence, it wol be no solas.   460
What men wolde of hit deme I kan nat seye:
It nedeth me ful sleighly for to pleie."

And with a sorowful sik she sayde thrie,
"A! Lord! what me is tid a sory chaunce!
For myn estat lith now in jupartie,   465
And ek myn emes lif is in balaunce;
But natheles, with Goddes governaunce,
I shal so doon, myn honour shal I kepe,
And ek his lif,"—and stynte for to wepe.

"Of harmes two, the lesse is for to chese;   470
Yet have I levere maken hym good chere
In honour, than myn emes lyf to lese.
Ye seyn, ye nothyng elles me requere?"

"No, wis," quod he, "myn owen nece dere."
"Now wel," quod she, "and I wol doon my
     peyne;   475
I shal myn herte ayeins my lust constreyne.

"But that I nyl nat holden hym in honde;
Ne love a man ne kan I naught, ne may,
Ayeins my wyl; but elles wol I fonde,
Myn honour sauf, plese hym fro day to day.
Therto nolde I nat ones han seyd nay,   481
But that I dredde, as in my fantasye;
But cesse cause, ay cesseth maladie.

"And here I make a protestacioun,
That in this proces if ye depper go,   485
That certeynly, for no salvacioun
Of yow, though that ye sterven bothe two,
Though al the world on o day be my fo,
Ne shal I nevere of hym han other routhe."
"I graunte wel," quod Pandare, "by my
     trowthe.   490

"But may I truste wel therto," quod he,
"That of this thyng that ye han hight me here,
Ye wole it holden trewely unto me?"
"Ye, doutelees," quod she, "myn uncle deere."
"Ne that I shal han cause in this matere,"   495
Quod he, "to pleyne, or ofter yow to preche?"
"Why, no, parde; what nedeth moore speche?"

Tho fillen they in other tales glade,
Tyl at the laste, "O good em," quod she tho,
"For his love, which that us bothe made,   500
Tel me how first ye wisten of his wo.
Woot noon of it but ye?"—He seyde, "No."—
"Kan he wel speke of love?" quod she; "I preye
Tel me, for I the bet me shal purveye."

Tho Pandarus a litel gan to smyle,   505
And seyde, "By my trouthe, I shal yow telle.
This other day, naught gon ful longe while,

447. raughte, started, proceeded. 448. lappe, a flap or fold of a garment. 449. starf, perished. 457. Alday, continually. 460. solas, consolation, perhaps "laughing matter." 462. sleighly, cautiously. 463. thrie, three times. 474. wis, certainly. 475. doon my peyne, do what is necessary. 480. honour, reputation, good name. 482. dredde, was afraid. 485. proces, matter. 492. hight, promised. 504. That I may be the better prepared.

In-with the paleis gardyn, by a welle,
Gan he and I wel half a day to dwelle,
Right for to speken of an ordinaunce,   510
How we the Grekes myghten disavaunce.

"Soon after that bigonne we to lepe,
And casten with oure dartes to and fro,
Tyl at the laste he seyde he wolde slepe,
And on the gres adoun he leyde hym tho;   515
And I afer gan romen to and fro,
Til that I herde, as that I welk alone,
How he bigan ful wofully to grone.

"Tho gan I stalke hym softely byhynde,
And sikirly, the soothe for to seyne,   520
As I kan clepe ayein now to my mynde,
Right thus to Love he gan hym for to pleyne:
He seyde, 'Lord, have routhe upon my peyne,
Al have I ben rebell in myn entente;
Now, *mea culpa*, lord, I me repente!   525

" 'O god, that at thi disposicioun
Ledest the fyn, by juste purveiaunce,
Of every wight, my lowe confessioun
Accepte in gree, and sende me swich penaunce
As liketh the, but from disesperaunce,   530
That may my goost departe awey fro the,
Thow be my sheld, for thi benignite.

" 'For certes, lord, so soore hath she me
     wounded,
That stood in blak, with lokyng of hire eyen,
That to myn hertes botme it is ysounded,   535
Thorugh which I woot that I moot nedes deyen.
This is the werste, I dar me nat bywreyen;
And wel the hotter ben the gledes rede,
That men hem wrien with asshen pale and dede.'

'Wyth that he smot his hed adown anon,   540
And gan to motre, I noot what, trewely.
And I with that gan stille awey to goon,

And leet therof as nothing wist had I,
And com ayein anon, and stood hym by,
And seyde, 'awake, ye slepen al to longe!   545
It semeth nat that love doth yow longe,

" 'That slepen so that no man may yow wake.
Who sey evere or this so dul a man?'
'Ye, frend,' quod he, 'do ye youre hedes ake
For love, and lat me lyven as I kan.'   550
But though that he for wo was pale and wan,
Yet made he tho as fressh a countenaunce
As though he sholde have led the newe
     daunce.

"This passed forth til now, this other day,
It fel that I com romyng al allone   555
Into his chaumbre, and fond how that he lay
Upon his bed; but man so soore grone
Ne herde I nevere, and what that was his mone
Ne wist I nought; for, as I was comynge,
Al sodeynly he lefte his complaynynge.   560

"Of which I took somwat suspecioun,
And ner I com, and fond he wepte soore;
And God so wys be my savacioun,
As nevere of thyng hadde I no routhe moore.
For neither with engyn, ne with no loore,   565
Unnethes myghte I fro the deth hym kepe,
That yet fele I myn herte for hym wepe.

"And God woot, nevere, sith that I was born,
Was I so besy no man for to preche,
Ne nevere was to wight so depe isworn,   570
Or he me told who myghte ben his leche.
But now to yow rehercen al his speche,
Or alle his woful wordes for to sowne,
Ne bid me naught, but ye wol se me swowne.

"But for to save his lif, and elles nought,   575
And to noon harm of yow, thus am I dryven;
And for the love of God, that us hath wrought,

510. **ordinaunce**, plan. 511. **disavaunce**, injure, repel. 513. **dartes**, javelins. 517. **welk**, walked. 519. **stalke**, approach quietly. 521. **clepe**, call. 525. ***mea culpa***, I acknowledge my fault. 527. **Ledest the fyn**, guidest the end. **purveiaunce**, providence. 529. **in gree**, graciously. 530. **disesperaunce**, despair. 539. **wrien**, cover. 543. **leet**, pretended. 546. **longe**, pertain to, *i.e.* you are not in love or you wouldn't sleep so well. 548. **sey**, saw. 549. **do ye youre hedes ake**, do you (lovers) make your heads ache. 562. **ner**, nearer. 565. **engyn**, subtlety. **loore**, counsel. 571. **Or**, ere.

Swich cheer hym dooth, that he and I may
    lyven!
Now have I plat to yow myn herte shryven;
And sith ye woot that myn entent is cleene,
Take heede therof, for I non yvel meene.   581

"And right good thrift, I prey to God, have ye,
That han swich oon ykaught withouten net!
And, be ye wis as ye be fair to see,
Wel in the ryng than is the ruby set.   585
Ther were nevere two so wel ymet,
Whan ye ben his al hool, as he is youre:
Ther myghty God yet graunte us see that
    houre!"

"Nay, therof spak I nought, ha, ha!" quod she;
"As helpe me God, ye shenden every deel!"   590
"O, mercy, dere nece," anon quod he,
"What so I spak, I mente naught but wel,
By Mars, the god that helmed is of steel!
Now beth naught wroth, my blood, my nece
    dere."   594
"Now wel," quod she, "foryeven be it here!"

With this he took his leve, and home he wente;
And, Lord, so he was glad and wel bygon!
Criseyde aros, no lenger she ne stente,
But streght into hire closet wente anon,
And set hire doun as stylle as any ston,   600
And every word gan up and down to wynde
That he had seyd, as it com hire to mynde;

And was somdel astoned in hire thought,
Right for the newe cas; but whan that she
Was ful avysed, tho fond she right nought   605
Of peril, why she ought afered be.
For man may love, of possibilite,
A womman so, his herte may tobreste, breaking to
And she naught love ayein, but if hire leste.

But as she sat allone and thoughte thus,   610
Ascry aros at scarmuch al withoute,
And men cride in the strete, "Se, Troilus
Hath right now put to flighte the Grekes route!"
With that gan al hire meyne for to shoute,
"A, go we se! cast up the yates wyde!   615
For thorwgh this strete he moot to paleys ride;

"For other wey is fro the yate noon
Of Dardanus, there opyn is the cheyne."
With that com he and al his folk anoon
An esy pas rydyng, in routes tweyne,   620
Right as his happy day was, sooth to seyne,
For which, men seyn, may nought destourbed
    be   happen by
That shal bityden of necessitee.

This Troilus sat on his baye steede,
Al armed, save his hed, ful richely;   625
And wownded was his hors, and gan to blede,
On which he rood a pas ful softely.
But swich a knyghtly sighte, trewely,
As was on hym, was nought, withouten faille,
To loke on Mars, that god is of bataille.   630

So lik a man of armes and a knyght
He was to seen, fulfilled of heigh prowesse;
For bothe he hadde a body and a myght
To don that thing, as wel as hardynesse;
And ek to seen hym in his gere hym dresse,
So fressh, so yong, so weldy semed he,   636
It was an heven upon hym for to see.

His helm tohewen was in twenty places,
That by a tyssew heng his bak byhynde;
His sheeld todasshed was with swerdes and
    maces,   640
In which men myght many an arwe fynde
That thirled hadde horn and nerf and rynde;

579. shryven, disclosed. 588. Ther, an exclamatory intensive introducing a wish or imprecation. See Language, § 73. 590. ye shenden every deel, you spoil everything. 601. wynde, turn over. 611. Ascry, outcry, shout. 614. meyne, household. 615. yates, gates. One MS reads latis (lattice), which makes better sense. 618. Dardanus, according to Guido, the strongest of the six gates of Troy. 621. his happy day, his lucky day. That which is destined to happen can not be prevented. 628-30. To look on Mars . . . was in no way such a knightly sight as to look on him. 635. hym dresse, hold himself erect. 636. weldy, vigorous. 642. thirled, pierced. horn . . . rynde, the materials with which shields were covered or bound,—horn, sinew, and hide(?).

And ay the peple cryde, "Here cometh oure
   joye,
And, next his brother, holder up of Troye!"

For which he wex a litel reed for shame,   645
Whan he the peple upon hym herde cryen,
That to byholde it was a noble game,
How sobrelich he caste down his yën.
Criseÿda gan al his chere aspien,
And leet it so softe in hire herte synke,   650
That to hireself she seyde, "Who yaf me
   drynke?"

For of hire owen thought she wex al reed,
Remembryng hire right thus, "Lo, this is he
Which that myn uncle swerith he moot be deed,
But I on hym have mercy and pitee."   655
And with that thought, for pure ashamed, she
Gan in hire hed to pulle, and that as faste,
Whil he and alle the peple forby paste;

And gan to caste and rollen up and down
Withinne hire thought his excellent prowesse,
And his estat, and also his renown,   661
His wit, his shap, and ek his gentilesse;
But moost hir favour was, for his distresse
Was al for hire, and thoughte it was a routhe
To sleen swich oon, if that he mente trouthe.

Now myghte som envious jangle thus: 666
"This was a sodeyn love; how myght it be
That she so lightly loved Troilus,
Right for the firste syghte, ye, parde?"
Now whoso seith so, mote he nevere ythe!   670
For every thyng, a gynnyng hath it nede
Er al be wrought, withowten any drede.

For I sey nought that she so sodeynly
Yaf hym hire love, but that she gan enclyne
To like hym first, and I have told yow whi;   675
And after that, his manhod and his pyne
Made love withinne hire herte for to myne,
For which, by proces and by good servyse,
He gat hire love, and in no sodeyn wyse.

And also blisful Venus, wel arrayed,   680
Sat in hire seventhe hous of hevene tho,
Disposed wel, and with aspectes payed,
To helpe sely Troilus of his woo.
And, soth to seyne, she nae not al a foo
To Troilus in his nativitee;   685
God woot that wel the sonner spedde he.

Now lat us stynte of Troilus a throwe,
That rideth forth, and lat us torne faste
Unto Criseyde, that heng hire hed ful lowe,
Ther as she sat allone, and gan to caste   690
Where on she wolde apoynte hire atte laste,
If it so were hire em ne wolde cesse
For Troilus upon hire for to presse.

And, Lord! so she gan in hire thought argue
In this matere of which I have yow told,   695
And what to doone best were, and what eschue,
That plited she ful ofte in many fold.
Now was hire herte warm, now was it cold;
And what she thoughte, somwhat shal I write,
As to myn auctour listeth for t'endite   700

She thoughte wel that Troilus persone
She knew by syghte, and ek his gentilesse,
And thus she seyde, "Al were it nat to doone
To graunte hym love, yet for his worthynesse

---

651. drynke. Commentators following Skeat interpret the word as "love potion," for which there seems to be no authority. It seems better to interpret it in one of its common meanings, "intoxicating beverage," something which goes to her head or makes her head swim. **657. as faste,** very fast. **663. favour,** favorable feeling. **670. ythe,** thrive. **677. myne,** penetrate. **678. by proces,** at length. **681. hous.** The usual meaning is a sign of the zodiac in which a given planet exerts its greatest influence, but here it seems to refer to one of the twelve equal sections of the heavens, six above and six below the horizon, marked by imaginary circles passing through the north and south points of the horizon. The houses are counted from the east, the first six being below the earth. The seventh house is the first above the horizon in the west, a propitious position for Venus, the planet concerned with matters of love. As the poet says in ll. 684–5 Venus was also not unfavorably situated at Troilus's birth. **682. payed,** made propitious by the aspects of other planets. **691. Where on she wolde apoynte hire,** what she would decide upon. **697. plited,** folded, turned back and forth. **703. Al,** although.

It were honour, with pley and with gladnesse,
In honestee with swich a lord to deele, 706
For myn estat, and also for his heele.

"Ek wel woot I my kynges sone is he;
And sith he hath to se me swich delit,
If I wolde outreliche his sighte flee, 710
Peraunter he myghte have me in dispit,
Thorugh whicch I myghte stonde in worse plit.
Now were I wis, me hate to purchace,
Withouten nede, ther I may stonde in grace?

"In every thyng, I woot, there lith mesure. 715
For though a man forbede dronkenesse,
He naught forbet that every creature
Be drynkeles for alwey, as I gesse.
Ek sith I woot for me is his destresse,
I ne aughte nat for that thing hym despise, 720
Sith it is so, he meneth in good wyse.

"And eke I knowe, of longe tyme agon,
His thewes goode, and that he is nat nyce.
N'avantour, seith men, certein, he is noon;
To wis is he to doon so gret a vice; 725
Ne als I nyl hym nevere so cherice
That he may make avaunt, by juste cause,
He shal me nevere bynde in swich a clause.

"Now sette a caas: the hardest is, ywys,
Men myghten demen that he loveth me. 730
What dishonour were it unto me, this?
May ich hym lette of that? Why, nay, parde!
I knowe also, and alday heere and se,
Men loven wommen al biside hire leve; 734
And whan hem leste namore, lat hem byleve!

"I thenke ek how he able is for to have
Of al this noble town the thriftieste,
To ben his love, so she hire honour save.

For out and out he is the worthieste,
Save only Ector, which that is the beste; 740
And yet his lif al lith now in my cure.
But swich is love, and ek myn aventure.

"Ne me to love, a wonder is it nought;
For wel woot I myself, so God me spede,
Al wolde I that noon wiste of this thought, 745
I am oon the faireste, out of drede,
And goodlieste, whoso taketh hede,
And so men seyn, in al the town of Troie.
What wonder is though he of me have joye?

"I am myn owene womman, wel at ese, 750
I thank it God, as after myn estat,
Right yong, and stonde unteyd in lusty leese,
Withouten jalousie or swich debat.
Shal noon housbonde seyn to me "chek mat!"
For either they ben ful of jalousie, 755
Or maisterfull, or loven novelrie.

"What shal I doon? To what fyn lyve I thus?
Shal I nat love, in cas if that me leste?
What, par dieux! I am naught religious.
And though that I myn herte sette at reste 760
Upon this knyght, that is the worthieste,
And kepe alwey myn honour and my name,
By alle right, it may do me no shame."

But right as when the sonne shyneth brighte
In March, that chaungeth ofte tyme his face, 765
And that a cloude is put with wynd to flighte,
Which oversprat the sonne as for a space,
A cloudy thought gan thorugh hire soule pace,
That overspradde hire brighte thoughtes alle,
So that for feere almost she gan to falle. 770

That thought was this: "Allas! syn I am free,
Sholde I now love, and put in jupartie

---

707. estat, condition, position. **heele,** welfare. **711. have me in dispit,** feel resentful toward me, bear a grudge against me. **717. forbet,** forbids. We should expect "bids." One is tempted to interpret the prefix as an intensive, as in many other words, but it is not recorded of *forbid.* **723. thewes,** qualities. **nyce,** foolish. **724. avantour,** one who boasts of his love affairs; cf. 3. 288 ff. **726. so cherice,** treat with so much affection. **728. clause,** stipulation (a legal metaphor). **732. lette,** prevent. **734. biside,** without. **735. lat hem byleve,** let them remain behind. **737. thriftieste,** worthiest. **746. drede,** doubt. **750. myn owene womman,** my own mistress. **751. as after,** with respect to. **estat,** condition, position. **752. lusty leese,** pleasant pasture. **759. religious,** a nun (so to speak). **767. oversprat,** overspreads.

My sikernesse, and thrallen libertee?
Allas! how dorst I thenken that folie?
May I naught wel in other folk aspie   775
Hire dredfull joye, hire constreinte, and hire
    peyne?
Ther loveth noon, that she nath why to pleyne.

"For love is yet the mooste stormy lyf,
Right to hymself, that evere was bigonne;
For evere som mystrust or nice strif   780
Ther is in love, som cloude is over that sonne.
Therto we wrecched wommen nothing konne,
Whan us is wo, but wepe and sitte and thinke;
Oure wrecche is this, oure owen wo to drynke.

"Also thise wikked tonges ben so prest   785
To speke us harm, ek men ben so untrewe,
That, right anon as cessed is hire lest,
So cesseth love, and forth to love a newe.
But harm ydoon is doon, whoso it rewe;
For though thise men for love hem first torende,
Ful sharp bygynnyng breketh ofte at ende.   791

"How ofte tyme hath it yknowen be,
The tresoun that to wommen hath ben do!
To what fyn is swich love I kan nat see,
Or wher bycometh it, whan it is ago.   795
Ther is no wight that woot, I trowe so,
Where it bycometh; lo, no wight on it sporneth:
That erst was nothing, into nought it torneth.

"How bisy, if I love, ek most I be   799
To plesen hem that jangle of love, and dremen,
And coye hem, that they seye noon harm of me!
For though ther be no cause, yet hem semen
Al be for harm that folk hire frendes quemen;

And who may stoppen every wikked tonge,   804
Or sown of belles whil that thei ben ronge?"

And after that, hire thought gan for to clere,
And seide, "He which that nothing under-
    taketh,
Nothyng n'acheveth, be hym looth or deere."
And with an other thought hire herte quaketh;
Than slepeth hope, and after drede awaketh;   810
Now hoot, now cold; but thus, bitwixen
    tweye,
She rist hire up, and went here for to pleye.

Adown the steyre anon-right tho she wente
Into the garden, with hire neces thre,
And up and down ther made many a wente,
Flexippe, she, Tharbe, and Antigone,   816
To pleyen, that it joye was to see;
And other of hire wommen, a gret route,
Hire folowede in the garden al abowte.   819

This yerd was large, and rayled alle th' aleyes,
And shadewed wel with blosmy bowes grene,
And benched newe, and sonded alle the weyes,
In which she walketh arm in arm bitwene,
Til at the laste Antigone the shene
Gan on a Troian song to singen cleere,   825
That it an heven was hire vois to here.

She seyd: "O Love, to whom I have and shal
Ben humble subgit, trewe in myn entente,
As I best kan, to yow, lord, yeve ich al,
For everemo, myn hertes lust to rente.   830
For nevere yet thi grace no wight sente
So blisful cause as me, my lif to lede
In alle joie and seurte, out of drede.

---

773. **thrallen,** enthrall. 777. Although the MS evidence is overwhelmingly in favor of *wey*, I adopt the minority reading *why* on the score of sense (as do Skeat, the Globe editors, and Robinson). 784. **wrecche,** misfortune. 785. **prest,** ready. 787. **lest,** desire. 790. **torende,** tear to pieces. 791. Apparently a proverb; a gloss in one MS reads "Acriores in principi[o] franguntur in fine." 797. **sporneth,** kicks it (accidentally), trips over it. 801. **coye,** quiet, pacify. 802-3. To them, all things that people do to please their friends seem for harm. 812. **rist . . . went,** rises . . . goes. 813. **Adown the steyre.** The living quarters of a medieval house were almost never on the ground floor. 815. **wente,** turn. 816. Where Chaucer found the names of Criseyde's nieces is not known. Like the nieces themselves, the names seem to be Chaucer's invention. 820. **rayled,** enclosed (possibly with hedges or the like). 822. **benched,** provided with benches. In medieval gardens these were sometimes mounds covered with turf. Cf. *MchT*, E 2235. **sonded,** sanded. **weyes,** paths. 830. **to rente,** in payment due.

"Ye, blisful god, han me so wel byset
In love, iwys, that al that bereth lif   835
Ymagynen ne koude how to be bet;
For, lord, withouten jalousie or strif,
I love oon which that is moost ententif
To serven wel, unweri or unfeyned,   839
That evere was, and leest with harm desteyned.

"As he that is the welle of worthynesse,
Of trouthe grownd, mirour of goodlihed,
Of wit Apollo, stoon of sikernesse,
Of vertu roote, of lust fynder and hed,
Thorough which is alle sorwe fro me ded,   845
Iwis, I love hym best, so doth he me;
Now good thrift have he, wherso that he be!

"Whom shulde I thanken but yow, god of
    Love,
Of al this blisse, in which to bathe I gynne?
And thanked be ye, lord, for that I love!   850
This is the righte lif that I am inne,
To flemen alle manere vice and synne:
This dooth me so to vertu for t'entende,
That day by day I in my wille amende.

"And whoso seith that for to love is vice,   855
Or thraldom, though he feele in it destresse,
He outher is envyous, or right hyce,   *very foolish*
Or is unmyghty, for his shrewednesse,
To loven; for swich manere folk, I gesse,
Defamen Love, as nothing of him knowe: 860
Thei speken, but thei benten nevere his bowe!

Nature
"What is the sonne wers, of kynde right,
Though that a man, for feeblesse of his yën,
May nought endure on it to see for bright?
Or love the wers, though wrecches on it crien?
No wele is worth that may no sorwe dryen.   866

And forthi, who that hath an hed of verre,
Fro caste of stones war hym in the werre!

"But I with al myn herte and al my myght,
As I have seyd, wol love unto my laste,   870
My deere herte, and al myn owen knyght,
In which myn herte growen is so faste,
And his in me, that it shal evere laste.
Al dredde I first to love hym to bigynne,
Now woot I wel, ther is no peril inne."   875

And of hir song right with that word she stente,
And therwithal, "Now nece" quod Cryseyde,
"Who made this song now with so good entente?"
Antygone answerde anoon and seyde,
"Madame, iwys, the goodlieste mayde   880
Of gret estat in al the town of Troye,
And let hire lif in moste honour and joye."

"Forsothe, so it semeth by hire song,"
Quod tho Criseyde, and gan therwith to sike,
And seyde, "Lord, is ther swych blisse among
Thise loveres, as they konne faire endite?"   886
"Ye, wis," quod fresshe Antigone the white,
"For alle the folk that han or ben on lyve
Ne konne wel the blisse of love discryve.

"But wene ye that every wrecche woot   890
The parfite blisse of love? Why, nay, iwys!
They wenen all be love, if oon be hoot.
Do wey, do wey, they woot no thyng of this!
Men mosten axe at seyntes if it is
Aught fair in hevene (why? for they kan telle),
And axen fendes is it foul in helle."   896

Criseyde unto that purpos naught answerde,
But seyde, "Ywys, it wol be nyght as faste."
But every word which that she of hire herde,

She gan to prenten in hire herte faste,   900
And ay gan love hire lasse for t'agaste
Than it dide erst, and synken in hire herte,
That she wex somwhat able to converte.

The dayes honour, and the hevenes yë,   904
The nyghtes foo—al this clepe I the sonne—
Gan westren faste, and downward for to wrye,
As he that hadde his dayes cours yronne;
And white thynges wexen dymme and donne
For lakke of lyght, and sterres for t'apere,
That she and alle hire folk in went yfeere.   910

So whan it liked hire to go to reste,
And voided weren thei that voiden oughte,
She seyde that to slepen wel hire leste.
Hire wommen soone til hire bed hire broughte.
Whan al was hust, than lay she stille and
     thoughte   915
Of al this thing; the manere and the wise
Reherce it nedeth nought, for ye ben wise.

A nyghtyngale, upon a cedir grene,
Under the chambre wal ther as she ley,
Ful loude song ayein the moone shene,   920
Peraunter, in his briddes wise, a lay
Of love, that made hire herte fressh and gay.
That herkned she so longe in good entente,
Til at the laste the dede slep hire hente.

And as she slep, anon-right tho hire mette   925
How that an egle, fethered whit as bon,
Under hire brest his longe clawes sette,
And out hire herte he rente, and that anon,
And dide his herte into hire brest to gon,
Of which she nought agroos, ne nothyng
     smerte;   930
And forth he fleigh, with herte left for herte.

Now lat hire slepe, and we oure tales holde
Of Troilus, that is to paleis riden
Fro the scarmuch of the which I tolde,
And in his chaumbre sit, and hath abiden,   935
Til two or thre of his messages yeden
For Pandarus, and soughten hym ful faste,
Til they hym founde and broughte hym at the
     laste.

This Pandarus com lepyng in atones,
And seyde thus, "Who hath ben wel ibete   940
To-day with swerdes and with slynge-stones,
But Troilus, that hath caught hym an hete?"
And gan to jape, and seyde, "Lord, so ye swete!
But ris, and lat us soupe and go to reste."
And he answerde hym, "Do we as the leste."   945

With al the haste goodly that they myghte,
They spedde hem fro the soper unto bedde;
And every wight out at the dore hym dyghte,
And where hym liste upon his wey him spedde.
But Troilus, that thoughte his herte bledde   950
For wo, til that he herde som tydynge,
He seyde, "Frend, shal I now wepe or synge?"

Quod Pandarus, "Ly stylle, and lat me slepe,
And don thyn hood; thy nedes spedde be!
And chese if thow wolt synge or daunce or lepe!
At shorte wordes, thow shalt trowen me: 956
Sire, my nece wol do wel by the,
And love the best, by God and by my trouthe,
But lakke of pursuyt make it in thi slouthe.

"For thus ferforth I have thi werk bigonne,
Fro day to day, til this day by the morwe   961
Hire love of frendshipe have I to the wonne,
And also hath she leyd hire feyth to borwe.
Algate a foot is hameled of thi sorwe!"

901. lasse, less. **t'agaste,** to frighten. **903. converte,** change her mind. **906. wrye,** turn. **920. ayein the moone shene,** in the moonlight. Cf. *CT,* A 1509. **930. agroos,** was frightened. **936. messages,** messengers. **yeden,** went. **942. hete,** temperature, fever. **943. jape,** joke. **948. hym dyghte,** betook himself. **954. don thyn hood,** be at ease (said to a person who has doffed his hat out of courtesy). For another interpretation see F. G. Cassidy, *JEGP,* LVII. 739–42. **959. But lakke of pursuyt,** unless lack of suit (entreaty) make it a matter of negligence on your part. **960. thus ferforth,** thus far. **961. til this day by the morwe,** until this morning. **962. of frendshipe,** out of friendship. **963. to borwe,** in pledge. **964. Algate,** at any rate. **hameled,** cut off. The three toes of the forefeet were required by the forest laws to be cut off ("hambled," "lawed") of all dogs within or adjacent to a royal forest.

What sholde I lenger sermon of it holde?   965
As ye han herd byfore, al he hym tolde.

But right as floures, thorugh the cold of nyght
Iclosed, stoupen on hire stalkes lowe,
Redressen hem ayein the sonne bright,
And spreden on hire kynde cours by rowe,   970
Right so gan tho his eighen up to throwe
This Troilus, and seyde, "O Venus deere,
Thi myght, thi grace, yheried be it here!"

And to Pandare he held up bothe his hondes,
And seyde, "Lord, al thyn be that I have!   975
For I am hool, al brosten ben my bondes.
A thousand Troyes whoso that me yave,
Ech after other, God so wys me save,
Ne myghte me so gladen; lo, myn herte,
It spredeth so for joie, it wol tosterte!   980

"But, Lord, how shal I doon? How shal I lyven?
Whan shal I next my deere herte see?
How shal this longe tyme awey be dryven,
Til that thow be ayein at hire fro me?
Thow maist answer, 'abid, abid,' but he   985
That hangeth by the nekke, soth to seyne
In grete disese abideth for the peyne."

"Al esily, now, for the love of Marte,"
Quod Pandarus, "for every thing hath tyme.
So longe abid, til that the nyght departe;   990
For al so siker as thow list here by me,
And God toforn, I wyl be ther at pryme;
And forthi, werk somwhat as I shal seye,
Or on som other wight this charge leye.

"For, pardee, God woot I have evere yit   995
Ben redy the to serve, and to this nyght
Have I naught fayned, but emforth my wit

Don al thi lust, and shal with al my myght.
Do now as I shal seyn, and fare aright;
And if thow nylt, wite al thiself thi care!   1000
On me is nought along thyn yvel fare.

"I woot wel that thow wiser art than I
A thousand fold, but if I were as thow,
God help me so, as I wolde outrely,
Of myn owen hond, write hire right now   1005
A lettre, in which I wolde hire tellen how
I ferde amys, and hire biseche of routhe.
Now help thiself, and leve it nought for slouthe!

"And I myself wol therwith to hire gon;
And whan thow woost that I am with hire
        there,   1010
Worth thow upon a courser right anon,
Ye, hardily, right in thi beste gere,
And ryd forth by the place, as nought ne were,
And thow shalt fynde us, if I may, sittynge
At som wyndow, into the strete lokynge.   1015

"And if the list, than maistow us salue;
And upon me make thow thi countenaunce;
But, by thi lif, be war and faste eschue
To tarien ought,—God shilde us fro mes-
        chaunce!
Rid forth thi wey, and hold thi governaunce;
And we shal speek of the somwhat, I trowe,   1021
Whan thow art gon, to don thyn eris glowe!

"Towchyng thi lettre, thou art wys ynough.
I woot thow nylt it dygneliche endite,
As make it with thise argumentes tough;   1025
Ne scryvenyssh or craftily thow it write;
Biblotte it with thi teris ek a lite;
And if thow write a goodly word al softe,
Though it be good, reherce it nought to ofte.

---

965. sermon, discourse. **970. on hire kynde cours by rowe,** in the natural course of events. **973. yheried,** praised. **980. tosterte,** burst. **987. disese,** discomfort. **992. pryme,** nine o'clock. **996. to this nyght,** tonight. **997. emforth my wit,** to the extent of my ability. **1000. wite al thiself,** blame your trouble only on yourself. **1001. On me . . . along,** dependant upon me, through my fault. **fare,** condition, state. **1004. outrely,** absolutely. **1011. Worth thow upon,** get on. **1013. as nought ne were,** as though nothing had happened or been arranged. **1017. upon . . . countenaunce,** direct your look towards me. **1020. hold thi governaunce,** behave properly. **1024. dygneliche,** haughtily. **1025. tough.** In spite of the fact that in other contexts the phrase *to make it tough* has special meanings the word here probably has its commoner meaning "difficult." **1026. scryvenyssh,** like a scrivener, in a formal or stilted style.

"For though the beste harpour upon lyve   1030
Wolde on the beste sowned joly harpe
That evere was, with alle his fyngres fyve,
Touche ay o streng, or ay o werbul harpe,
Were his nayles poynted nevere so sharpe,
It sholde maken every wight to dulle,   1035
To here his glee, and of his strokes fulle.

"Ne jompre ek no discordant thyng yfeere,
As thus, to usen termes of phisik
In loves termes; hold of thi matere
The forme alwey, and do that it be lik;   1040
For if a peyntour wolde peynte a pyk
With asses feet, and hedde it as an ape,
It cordeth naught, so nere it but a jape."

This counseil liked wel to Troilus,
But, as a dredful lovere, he seyde this: 1045
"Allas, my deere brother Pandarus,
I am ashamed for to write, ywys,
Lest of myn innocence I seyde amys,
Or that she nolde it for despit receyve;   1049
Than were I ded, ther myght it nothyng weyve."

To that Pandare answerid, "If the lest,
Do that I seye, and lat me therwith gon;
For by that Lord that formede est and west,
I hope of it to brynge answere anon
Right of hire hond; and if that thow nylt noon,
Lat be, and sory mote he ben his lyve,   1056
Ayeins thi lust that helpeth the to thryve."

Quod Troilus, "Depardieux, ich assente!
Sith that the list, I wil arise and write;
And blisful God prey ich with good entente,
The viage, and the lettre I shal endite,   1061
So spede it; and thow, Minerva, the white,
Yif thow me wit my lettre to devyse."
And sette hym down, and wrot right in this
    wyse.

First he gan hire his righte lady calle,   1065
His hertes lif, his lust, his sorwes leche,
His blisse, and ek thise other termes alle
That in swich cas thise loveres alle seche;
And in ful humble wise, as in his speche,
He gan hym recomaunde unto hire grace;   1070
To telle al how, it axeth muchel space.

And after this, ful lowely he hire preyde
To be nought wroth, thogh he, of his folie,
So hardy was to hire to write, and seyde
That love it made, or elles most he die;   1075
And pitously gan mercy for to crye;
And after that he seyde, and leigh ful loude,
Hymself was litel worth, and lasse he koude;

And that she sholde han his konnyng excused,
That litel was, and ek he dredde hire soo;   1080
And his unworthynesse he ay acused;
And after that than gan he telle his woo;
But that was endeles, withouten hoo;
And seyde he wolde in trouth alwey hym
    holde,—
And radde it over, and gan the lettre folde.

And with his salte teris gan he bathe   1086
The ruby in his signet, and it sette
Upon the wex deliverliche and rathe.
Therwith a thousand tymes, er he lette,
He kiste tho the lettre that he shette,   1090
And seyde, "Lettre, a blisful destine
The shapyn is: my lady shal the see!"

This Pandare tok the lettre, and that bytyme
A-morwe, and to his neces paleis sterte,   1094
And faste he swor that it was passed prime,
And gan to jape, and seyde, "Ywys, myn herte,
So fressh it is, although it sore smerte,
I may naught slepe nevere a Mayes morwe;
I have a joly wo, a lusty sorwe."

1033. **werbul**, tune. 1035. **to dulle**, to become bored. 1036. **glee**, music. **fulle**, surfeited. 1037. **jompre**, jumble. 1038. **termes of phisik In loves termes**, *i.e.* don't mix together terms of medicine and love. 1040. **lik**, shortened form of *ylike*, suitable. 1041. **pyk**, pike (fish). 1043. **cordeth**, accords. **so nere it but a jape**, unless it were only a joke. 1050. **weyve**, remove. 1057. **lust**, desire, wish. 1062. **Minerva**, goddess of wisdom, here accented Mínervá. 1063. **Yif**, give. 1077. **leigh**, lied. **ful loude**, openly, palpably. 1078. **koude**, knew. 1081. **acused**, blamed. 1083. **hoo**, ceasing. 1088. **deliverliche and rathe**, deftly and soon. 1089. **lette**, left off. 1093. **bytyme**, betimes, early. 1095. **prime**, nine o'clock.

Criseyde, whan that she hire uncle herde,   1100
With dredful herte, and desirous to here
The cause of his comynge, thus answerde:
"Now, by youre fey, myn uncle," quod she,
    "dere,
What manere wyndes gydeth yow now here?
Tel us youre joly wo and youre penaunce.   1105
How ferforth be ye put in loves daunce?"

"By God," quod he, "I hoppe alwey byhynde!"
And she to-laugh, it thoughte hire herte brest.
Quod Pandarus, "Loke alwey that ye fynde
Game in myn hood; but herkneth, if yow lest!
Ther is right now come into town a gest,   1111
A Greek espie, and telleth newe thinges,
For which I come to telle yow tydynges.

"Into the gardyn go we, and ye shal here,
Al pryvely, of this a long sermoun."   1115
With that they wenten arm in arm yfeere
Into the gardyn from the chaumbre down;
And whan that he so fer was that the sown
Of that he spak, no man heren myghte,   1119
He seyde hire thus, and out the lettre plighte:

"Lo, he that is al holy youres free
Hym recomaundeth lowely to youre grace,
And sent yow this lettre here by me.
Avyseth yow on it, whan ye han space,   1124
And of som goodly answere yow purchace;
Or, helpe me God, so pleynly for to seyne,
He may nat longe lyven for his peyne."

Ful dredfully tho gan she stonden stylle,   1128
And took it naught, but al hire humble chere
Gan for to chaunge, and seyde, "Scrit ne bille,

For love of God, that toucheth swich matere,
Ne brynge me noon; and also, uncle deere,
To myn estat have more rewarde, I preye,
Than to his lust! What sholde I more seye?

"And loketh now if this be resonable,   1135
And letteth nought, for favour ne for slouthe,
To seyn a sooth; now were it covenable
To myn estat, by God and by youre trouthe,
To taken it, or to han of hym routhe,
In harmyng of myself, or in repreve?   1140
Ber it ayein, for hym that ye on leve!"

This Pandarus gan on hire for to stare,
And seyde, "Now is this the grettest wondre
That evere I seigh! Lat be this nyce fare!
To dethe mot I smyten be with thondre,   1145
If for the citee which that stondeth yondre,
Wold I a lettre unto yow brynge or take
To harm of yow! What list yow thus it make?

"But thus ye faren, wel neigh alle and some,
That he that most desireth yow to serve,   1150
Of hym ye recche leest wher he bycome,
And whethir that he lyve or elles sterve.
But for al that that ever I may deserve,
Refuse it naught," quod he, and hente hire faste,
And in hire bosom the lettre down he thraste,

And seyde hire, "Now cast it awey anon,   1156
That folk may seen and gauren on us tweye."
Quod she, "I kan abyde til they be gon";
And gan to smyle, and seyde hym, "Em, I
    preye,
Swich answere as yow list youreself purveye,
For trewely I nyl no lettre write."   1161
"No? than wol I," quod he, "so ye endite."

1106. **How ferforth be ye put,** how far have you got. **loves daunce.** The fifteenth-century *Dance aux Aveugles,* by Pierre Michault, describes "la Dance du Dieu Damours." 1108. **to-laugh,** laughed heartily (although the form should be *to-lough*). 1109. **fynde Game in myn hood,** make a joke at my expense. 1111. **gest,** stranger. 1117. **down.** See note to 2. 813, above. 1120. **plighte,** plucked. 1123. **sent,** sendeth. 1125. **yow purchace,** provide for yourself. 1130. **Scrit ne bille,** writing nor letter. A *bille* may be any statement in writing. 1134. **lust,** desire. 1136. **letteth nought,** do not be prevented. 1141. **Ber it,** take it away. 1144. **nyce fare,** foolish behavior. 1146. **citee.** The word may at times mean a fortified enclosure, a citadel, and the reference here could be to the palace of King Priam, but it is more likely that Pandarus is indicating, as by a wave of the hand, the houses which stretch out (*stondeth yondre*) from Criseyde's dwelling. 1149. **alle and some,** entirely, in all respects. 1151. **wher he bycome,** *lit.* where he goes, *i.e.* what becomes of him. 1157. **gauren,** gape (at). 1160. **purveye,** provide. 1162. **endite,** compose, dictate.

Therwith she lough, and seyde, "Go we dyne."
And he gan at hymself to jape faste,
And seyde, "Nece, I have so gret a pyne   1165
For love, that everich other day I faste—"
And gan his beste japes forth to caste,
And made hire so to laughe at his folye,
That she for laughter wende for to dye.

And whan that she was comen into halle,   1170
"Now, em," quod she, "we wol go dyne anon."
And gan some of hire wommen to hire calle,
And streght into hire chambre gan she gon;
But of hire besynesses this was on,
Amonges othere thynges, out of drede,   1175
Ful pryvely this lettre for to rede.

Avysed word by word in every lyne,
And fond no lakke, she thoughte he koude good;
And up it putte, and wente hire in to dyne.
But Pandarus, that in a studye stood,   1180
Er he was war, she took hym by the hood,
And seyde, "Ye were caught er that ye wiste."
"I vouchesauf," quod he, "do what you liste."

Tho wesshen they, and sette hem down, and ete;
And after noon ful sleighly Pandarus   1185
Gan drawe hym to the wyndowe next the strete,
And seyde, "Nece, who hath araied thus
The yonder hous, that stant aforyeyn us?"
"Which hous?" quod she, and gan for to by-
        holde,   1189
And knew it wel, and whos it was hym tolde;

And fillen forth in speche of thynges smale,
And seten in the windowe bothe tweye.
Whan Pandarus saugh tyme unto his tale.
And saugh wel that hire folk were alle aweye,
"Now, nece myn, tel on," quod he. "I seye,
How liketh yow the lettre that ye woot?   1196
Kan he theron? For, by my trouthe, I noot."

Therwith al rosy hewed tho wex she,
And gan to homme, and seyde, "So I trowe."
"Aquite hym wel, for Goddes love," quod he;
"Myself to medes wol the lettre sowe."   1201
And held his hondes up, and sat on knowe;
"Now, goode nece, be it nevere so lite,
Yif me the labour it to sowe and plite."

"Ye, for I kan so writen," quod she tho;   1205
"And ek I noot what I sholde to hym seye."
"Nay, nece," quod Pandare, "sey nat so.
Yet at the leeste thonketh hym, I preye,
Of his good wille, and doth hym nat to
        deye.
Now, for the love of me, my nece deere,   1210
Refuseth nat at this tyme my prayere!"

"Depardieux," quod she, "God leve al be wel!
God help me so, this is the firste lettre
That evere I wroot, ye, al or any del."
And into a closet, for t'avise hire bettre,   1215
She wente allone, and gan hire herte unfettre
Out of desdaynes prison but a lite,
And sette hire down, and gan a lettre write,

Of which to telle in short is myn entente
Th'effect, as fer as I kan understonde.   1220
She thanked hym of al that he wel mente
Towardes hire, but holden hym in honde
She nolde nought, ne make hireselven bonde
In love; but as his suster, hym to plese,   1224
She wolde ay fayn, to doon his herte an ese.

She shette it, and in to Pandare gan goon,
Ther as he sat and loked into the strete,
And down she sette hire by hym on a stoon
Of jaspre, upon a quysshyn gold-ybete,
And seyde, "As wisly help me God the grete,
I nevere dide thing with more peyne   1231
Than writen this, to which ye me constreyne";

1163. **Go we dyne,** let us go to dinner. Dinner was at ten o'clock or shortly thereafter; cf. 2. 1557. **1178. koude good,** knew what was proper, *i.e.* wrote politely. **1180. in a studye,** in thought, meditation. **1184. wesshen,** washed. **1199. homme,** hum. **1201. to medes,** in return; *lit.* as a reward. **sowe,** *lit.* sew, but one suspects confusion with the noun *seal* (OF. *sceau*). Troilus's letter was sealed (cf. ll. 1086–8) and in the *Filostrato* Criseida seals hers. **1202. sat on knowe,** knelt down **1204. plite,** fold. **1212. leve,** grant. **1215. closet,** small room. **1222. holden hym in honde,** lead him on with false hopes. **1229. gold-ybete,** embroidered or interwoven with gold threads. **1230. wisly,** certainly.

And took it hym. He thonked hire and seyde,
"God woot, of thyng ful often looth bygonne
Comth ende good; and nece myn, Criseyde,
That ye to hym of hard now ben ywonne   1236
Oughte he be glad, by God and yonder sonne;
For-whi men seith, 'impressiounes lighte
Ful lightly ben ay redy to the flighte.'   1239

"But ye han played the tirant neigh to longe,
And hard was it youre herte for to grave.
Now stynt, that ye no lenger on it honge,
Al wolde ye the forme of daunger save,
But hasteth yow to doon hym joye have;
For trusteth wel, to longe ydoon hardnesse   1245
Causeth despit ful often for destresse."

And right as they declamed this matere,
Lo, Troilus, right at the stretes ende,
Com rydyng with his tenthe som yfere,
Al softely, and thiderward gan bende   1250
Ther as they sete, as was his way to wende
To paleis-ward; and Pandarus hym aspide,
And seyde, "Nece, ysee who comth here ride!

"O fle naught in (he seeth us, I suppose),   1254
Lest he may thynken that ye hym eschuwe."
"Nay, nay," quod she, and wex as red as rose.
With that he gan hire humbly to saluwe,
With dredful chere, and oft his hewes muwe;
And up his look debonairly he caste,
And bekked on Pandare, and forth he paste.

God woot if he sat on his hors aright,   1261
Or goodly was biseyn, that ilke day!
God woot wher he was lik a manly knyght!
What sholde I drecche, or telle of his aray?
Criseyde, which that alle thise thynges say,   1265
To telle in short, hire liked al in-fere,
His person, his aray, his look, his chere,

His goodly manere, and his gentilesse,
So wel that nevere, sith that she was born,
Ne hadde she swych routh of his destresse;   1270
And how so she hath hard ben here-byforn,
To God hope I, she hath now kaught a thorn,
She shal nat pulle it out this nexte wyke.
God sende mo swich thornes on to pike!

Pandare, which that stood hire faste by,   1275
Felte iren hoot, and he bygan to smyte,
And seyde, "Nece, I pray yow hertely,
Telle me that I shal axen yow a lite.
A womman, that were of his deth to wite,   1279
Withouten his gilt, but for hire lakked routhe,
Were it wel doon?" Quod she, "Nay, by my
    trouthe!"

"God help me so," quod he, "ye sey me soth.
Ye felen wel youreself that I nought lye.
Lo, yond he rit!" "Ye," quod she, "so he doth!"
"Wel," quod Pandare, "as I have told yow
    thrie,   1285
Lat be youre nyce shame and youre folie,
And spek with hym in esyng of his herte;
Lat nycete nat do yow bothe smerte."

But theron was to heven and to doone.
Considered al thing it may nat be;   1290
And whi, for shame; and it were ek to soone
To graunten hym so grete a libertee.
For pleynly hire entente, as seyde she,
Was for to love hym unwist, if she myghte,
And guerdon hym with nothing but with
    sighte.   1295

But Pandarus thought, "It shal nought be so,
Yif that I may; this nyce opynyoun
Shal nought be holden fully yeres two."
What sholde I make of this a long sermoun?

1236. **of hard,** with difficulty. 1241. **grave,** make an impression on. 1242. **stynt,** cease. **honge,** remain undecided. 1243. **Al wolde ye . . .,** even though you would preserve the appearance of haughtiness. 1249. **his tenthe som,** with ten others. 1250. **bende,** turn. 1258. **muwe,** change. 1260. **bekked on,** nodded to. 1264. **drecche,** torment, become tiresome. 1265. **say,** saw. 1266. **in-fere,** together. 1268. **gentilesse,** nobility. 1279. **wite,** blame. 1289. **But . . . doone,** but on this matter there was much that called for exertion and had to be done. 1290. This line reflects Criseyde's thoughts. 1294. **unwist,** without his knowing it.

He moste assente on that conclusioun,   1300
As for the tyme; and whan that it was eve,
And al was wel, he roos and tok his leve.

And on his wey ful faste homward he spedde,
And right for joye he felte his herte daunce;
And Troilus he fond allone abedde,   1305
That lay, as do thise lovers, in a traunce
Bitwixen hope and derk disesperaunce.
But Pandarus, right at his in-comynge,
He song, as who seyth, "Somwhat I brynge,"

And seyde, "Who is in his bed so soone   1310
Iburied thus?" "It am I, frend," quod he.
"Who, Troilus? Nay, help me so the moone,"
Quod Pandarus, "thow shalt arise and see
A charme that was sent right now to the,
The which kan helen the of thyn accesse,   1315
If thow do forthwith al thi bisynesse."

"Ye, thorugh the myght of God," quod Troilus.
And Pandarus gan hym the lettre take,
And seyde, "Parde, God hath holpen us!
Have here a light, and loke on al this blake."
But ofte gan the herte glade and quake   1321
Of Troilus, whil that he gan it rede,
So as the wordes yave hym hope or drede.

But finaly, he took al for the beste   1324
That she hym wroot, for somwhat he byheld,
On which hym thoughte he myghte his herte
    reste,
Al covered she the wordes under sheld.
Thus to the more worthi part he held,
That, what for hope and Pandarus byheste,
His grete wo foryede he at the leste.   1330

But as we may alday oureselven see,
Thorugh more wode or col, the more fir,
Right so encrees of hope, of what it be,
Therwith ful ofte encresseth ek desir;
Or as an ook comth of a litel spir,   1335
So thorugh this lettre, which that she hym sente,
Encressen gan desir, of which he brente.

Wherfore I seye alwey, that day and nyght
This Troilus gan to desiren moore
Thanne he did erst, thorugh hope, and did his
    myght   1340
To preessen on, as by Pandarus loore,
And writen to hire of his sorwes soore.
Fro day to day he leet it nought refreyde,
That by Pandare he wroot somwhat or seyde;

And dide also his other observaunces   1345
That til a lovere longeth in this cas;
And after that thise dees torned on chaunces,
So was he outher glad or seyde "allas!"
And held after his gestes ay his pas;
And after swiche answeres as he hadde,   1350
So were his dayes sory outher gladde.

But to Pandare alwey was his recours,
And pitously gan ay to hym to pleyne,
And hym bisoughte of reed and som socours;
And Pandarus, that sey his woode peyne,   1355
Wex wel neigh ded for routhe, sooth to seyne,
And bisily with al his herte caste
Som of his wo to slen, and that as faste;

And seyde, "Lord, and frend, and brother dere,
God woot that thi disese doth me wo.   1360
But wiltow stynten al this woful cheere,

1306. traunce, state of suspense. **1312. help me so the moone.** Although much influence was attributed to the moon by medieval astrology, there seems to be no special significance in the present appeal, which was doubtless for the sake of rime. **1315. accesse,** an attack of illness, esp. a fever. **1330. foryede,** abandoned. **1335. spir,** shoot. **1343. refreyde,** grow cold. **1347. after that,** according as. **dees,** dice. **1349. after his gestes.** The phrase is of uncertain meaning. Root adopts the form *gistes,* connects it with OF. *gist.* L. *jactus,* and notes that one meaning of *jactus* is a throw of the dice. But the *s* in *gist* would have to be analogical, and the Latin meaning is not recorded in OF. or in English. On the other hand, *gist* (*gest*), OF. *giste,* "a stopping place," "lodging," which Robinson adopts in the sense "stations or stages of a journey" is not recorded in English in the latter sense until the sixteenth century. Accordingly it seems best to understand the word in Chaucer as "deeds," "accomplishments" and interpret the line, "And regulated his pace according to his achievements." **1355. woode,** mad. **1358. as faste,** very quickly.

And, by my trouthe, er it be dayes two,
And God toforn, yet shal I shape it so,
That thow shalt come into a certeyn place,
There as thow mayst thiself hire preye of grace.

"And certeynly, I noot if thow it woost,   1366
But tho that ben expert in love it seye,
It is oon of the thynges forthereth most,
A man to han a layser for to preye,
And siker place his wo for to bywreye;   1370
For in good herte it mot som routhe impresse,
To here and see the giltlees in distresse.

"Peraunter thynkestow: though it be so,
That Kynde wolde don hire to bygynne
To have a manere routhe upon my woo,   1375
Seyth Daunger, 'Nay, thow shalt me nevere
   wynne!'
So reulith hire hir hertes gost withinne,
That though she bende, yeet she stant on roote;
What in effect is this unto my boote?   1379

"Thenk here-ayeins: whan that the stordy ook,
On which men hakketh ofte, for the nones,
Receyved hath the happy fallyng strook,
The greete sweigh doth it come al at ones,
As don thise rokkes or thise milnestones;   1384
For swifter cours comth thyng that is of
   wighte,
Whan it descendeth, than don thynges lighte.

"And reed that boweth down for every blast,
Ful lightly, cesse wynd, it wol aryse;
But so nyl nought an ook, whan it is cast;
It nedeth me nought the longe to forbise.   1390
Men shal rejoissen of a gret empryse
Acheved wel, and stant withouten doute,
Al han men ben the lenger theraboute.

"But, Troilus, yet telle me, if the lest,
A thing which that I shal now axen the: 1395
Which is thi brother that thow lovest best,
As in thi verray hertes privetee?"
"Iwis, my brother Deiphebus," quod he.
"Now," quod Pandare, "er houres twyes
   twelve,
He shal the ese, unwist of it hymselve.   1400

"Now lat m'alone, and werken as I may,"
Quod he; and to Deiphebus wente he tho,
Which hadde his lord and grete frend ben ay;
Save Troilus, no man he loved so.
To telle in short, withouten wordes mo,   1405
Quod Pandarus, "I pray yow that ye be
Frend to a cause which that toucheth me."

"Yis, parde," quod Deiphebus, "wel thow
   woost,
In al that evere I may, and God tofore,
Al nere it but for man I love moost,   1410
My brother Troilus; but sey wherfore
It is; for sith that day that I was bore,
I nas, ne nevere mo to ben I thynke,
Ayeins a thing, that myghte the forthynke."

Pandare gan hym thank, and to hym seyde,
"Lo, sire, I have a lady in this town,   1416
That is my nece, and called is Criseyde,
Which some men wolden don oppressioun,
And wrongfully han hire possessioun;
Wherfore I of youre lordship yow biseche   1420
To ben oure frend, withouten more speche."

Deiphebus hym answerde, "O, is nat this,
That thow spekest of to me thus straungely,
Criseyda, my frend?" He seyde, "Yis."
"Than nedeth," quod Deiphebus, "hardyly,

1369. **layser,** opportunity. 1370. **bywreye,** reveal. 1371. **impresse,** urge, enforce. 1378. **on roote,** well rooted. 1383. **sweigh,** falling motion. 1390. **longe to forbise,** show by multiplying examples. The form should be *forbisne.* 1392. **stant,** it stands. 1393. **Al,** to be construed with *the lenger.* 1401. The episode at the house of Deiphebus is Chaucer's invention. Boccaccio in the seventh book of the *Filostrato* has Deiphebus discover the cause of Troilus's despondency, when Criseida fails to return, and speaks of him as one for whom Troilus had much affection. 1410. **Al nere it but,** unless it were; *i.e.* he would do as much for Pandarus as for anyone with the possible exception of Troilus. 1414. **that myghte the forthynke,** if it (my opposition) would diplease you.

Namore to speke, for trusteth wel that I   1426
Wol be hire champioun with spore and yerde;
I roughte nought though alle hire foos it herde.

"But telle me, thow that woost al this matere,
How I myght best avaylen."—"Now lat se,"
Quod Pandarus; "if ye, my lord so dere,   1431
Wolden as now do this honour to me,
To preyen hire to-morwe, lo, that she
Come unto yow, hire pleyntes to devise,
Hire adversaries wolde of it agrise   1435

"And yif I more dorste preye yow as now,
And chargen yow to han so grete travaille,
To han som of youre bretheren here with yow,
That myghten to hire cause bet availle,
Than wot I wel she myghte nevere faille   1440
For to ben holpen, what at youre instaunce,
What with hire other frendes governaunce."

Deiphebus, which that comen was of kynde
To alle honour and bounte to consente,
Answerd, "It shal be don; and I kan fynde   1445
Yet grettere help to this, in myn entente.
What wiltow seyn, if I for Eleyne sente
To speke of this? I trowe it be the beste,
For she may leden Paris as hire leste.   1449

"Of Ector, which that is my lord, my brother,
It nedeth naught to preye hym frend to be;
For I have herd hym, o tyme and ek oother,
Speke of Cryseyde swich honour, that he
May seyn no bet, swich hap to hym hath she.
It nedeth naught his helpes for to crave;   1455
He shal be swich, right as we wol hym have.

"Spek thow thiself also to Troilus
On my byhalve, and prey hym with us dyne."
"Syre, al this shal be don," quod Pandarus,
And took his leve, and nevere gan to fyne,   1460

But to his neces hous, as streyght as lyne,
He com; and fond hire fro the mete arise,
And sette hym down, and spak right in this
     wise.

He seide, "O verray God, so have I ronne!
Lo, nece myn, se ye nought how I swete?   1465
I not wheither ye the more thank me konne.
Be ye naught war how false Poliphete
Is now aboute eftsones for to plete,
And brynge on yow advocacies newe?"   1469
"I? no," quod she, and chaunged al hire hewe.

"What is he more aboute, me to drecche
And don me wrong? What shal I doon, allas?
Yet of hymself nothing ne wolde I recche,
Nere it for Antenor and Eneas,
That ben his frendes in swich manere cas.   1475
But, for the love of God, myn uncle deere,
No fors of that, lat hym han al yfeere.

"Withouten that I have ynough for us."
"Nay," quod Pandare, "it shal nothing be so.
For I have ben right now at Deiphebus,   1480
At Ector, and myn oother lordes moo,
And shortly maked eche of hem his foo,
That, by my thrift, he shal it nevere wynne,
For aught he kan, whan that so he bygynne."

And as thei casten what was best to doone,   1485
Deiphebus, of his owen curtesie,
Com hire to preye, in his propre persone,
To holde hym on the morwe compaignie
At dyner; which she nolde nought denye,
But goodly gan to his preier obeye.   1490
He thonked hire, and went upon his weye.

Whan this was don, this Pandare up anon,
To telle in short, and forth gan for to wende
To Troilus, as stille as any ston;

1427. with spore and yerde, speedily, eagerly. **1428. roughte,** would care. **1434. devise,** relate. **1435. agrise,** tremble. **1441. instaunce,** urging. **1442. governaunce,** management. **1443. of kynde,** by nature. **1454. hap,** favor. **1460. fyne,** finish, end. **1467. Poliphete.** Chaucer probably took the name of a Trojan priest in the *Æneid* (VI. 484). It is not in Boccaccio. **1468. plete,** bring suit. **1469. advocacies,** charges. **1471. me to drecche,** to cause me trouble. **1483. by my thrift,** by my profitable management, but here merely a mild oath.

And al this thyng he tolde hym, word and
    ende,   1495
And how that he Deiphebus gan to blende,
And seyde hym, "Now is tyme, if that thow
    konne,
To bere the wel tomorwe, and al is wonne.

"Now spek, now prey, now pitously com-
    pleyne;
Lat nought for nyce shame, or drede, or _foolish_
    slouthe!
Somtyme a man mot telle his owen peyne. 1501
Bileve it, and she shal han on the routhe;
Thow shalt be saved by thi feyth, in trouthe.
But wel woot I that thow art now in drede,
And what it is, I leye, I kan arede.   1505

"Thow thynkest now, ' How sholde I don al
    this?
For by my cheres mosten folk aspie
That for hire love is that I fare amys;
Yet hadde I levere unwist for sorwe dye.'
Now thynk nat so, for thow dost gret folie;
For I right now have founden o manere   1511
Of sleyghte, for to coveren al thi cheere.

"Thow shalt gon over nyght, and that bylyve,
Unto Deiphebus hous, as the to pleye,
Thi maladie awey the bet to dryve,—   1515
For-whi thow semest sik, soth for to seye.
Soone after that, down in thi bed the leye,
And sey, thow mayst no lenger up endure,
And lye right there, and bide thyn aventure.

"Sey that thi fevre is wont the for to take,   1520
The same tyme, and lasten til a-morwe;
And lat se now how wel thow kanst it make,
For, parde, sik is he that is in sorwe.

Go now, farwel! and Venus here to borwe,
I hope, and thow this purpos holde ferme,   1525
Thi grace she shal fully ther conferme."

Quod Troilus, "Iwis, thow nedeles
Conseilest me that siklich I me feyne,
For I am sik in ernest, douteles,
So that wel neigh I sterve for the peyne."   1530
Quod Pandarus, "Thow shalt the bettre
    pleyne,
And hast the lasse nede to countrefete,
For hym men demen hoot that men seen
    swete.

"Lo, hold the at thi triste cloos, and I
Shal wel the deer unto thi bowe dryve."   1535
Therwith he took his leve al softely,
And Troilus to paleis wente blyve.
So glad ne was he nevere in al his lyve,
And to Pandarus reed gan al assente,
And to Deiphebus hous at nyght he wente.   1540

What nedeth yow to tellen al the cheere
That Deiphebus unto his brother made,
Or his accesse, or his sikliche manere,
How men gan hym with clothes for to lade,
Whan he was leyd, and how men wolde hym
    glade?   1545
But al for nought; he held forth ay the wyse
That ye han herd Pandare er this devyse.

But certayn is, er Troilus hym leyde,
Deiphebus had hym preied over-nyght
To ben a frend and helpyng to Criseyde.   1550
God woot that he it graunted anon-right,
To ben hire fulle frend with al his myght;
But swich a nede was to preye hym thenne,
As for to bidde a wood man for to renne.
    bid a madman run

1495. word and ende, earlier *ord and ende*, beginning and end. **1496. blende,** hoodwink. **1500. Lat nought,** leave nothing undone. **1505. I leye,** I wager. **arede,** conjecture. **1507. cheres,** looks. **1512. sleyghte,** trick. **1513. bylyve,** quickly, soon. **1514. as,** as if. **1522. it make,** perform your part. **1524. Venus here to borwe,** *i.e.* with Venus's help (as your surety). **1533. swete,** sweat. **1534. triste,** appointed place or station (a hunting term). In medieval hunting the hunters stationed themselves at suitable spots while the huntsmen and dogs drove the deer in their direction. **1537. blyve,** soon. **1543. accesse.** See note to l. 1315. **1544. clothes,** bed-clothes. **lade,** load. **1554. bidde a wood man for to renne,** bid a madman run.

The morwen com, and neighen gan the tyme
Of meeltide, that the faire queene Eleyne   1556
Shoop hire to ben, an houre after the prime,
With Deiphebus, to whom she nolde feyne;
But as his suster, homly, soth to seyne,
She com to dyner in hire pleyne entente.   1560
But God and Pandare wist al what this mente.

Com ek Criseyde, al innocent of this,
Antigone, hire suster Tarbe also.
But fle we now prolixitee best is,
For love of God, and lat us faste go   1565
Right to th'effect, withouten tales mo,
Whi al this folk assembled in this place;
And lat us of hire saluynges pace.

Gret honour did hem Deiphebus, certeyn,   1569
And fedde hem wel with al that myghte like;
But evere mo "Allas!" was his refreyn,
"My goode brother Troilus, the syke,
Lith yet"—and therwithal he gan to sike;
And after that, he peyned hym to glade
Hem as he myghte, and cheere good he made.

Compleyned ek Eleyne of his siknesse   1576
So feythfully, that pite was to here,
And every wight gan waxen for accesse
A leche anon, and seyde, "In this manere
Men curen folk."—"This charme I wol yow
 leere."   1580
But ther sat oon, al list hire nought to teche,
That thoughte, "Best koude I yet ben his
 leche."

After compleynte, hym gonnen they to preyse,
As folk don yet, whan som wight hath
 bygonne
To preise a man, and up with pris hym reise   1585

A thousand fold yet heigher than the sonne:
"He is, he kan, that fewe lordes konne."
And Pandarus, of that they wolde afferme,
He naught forgat hire preisynge to conferme.

Herde al this thyng Criseyde wel inough,   1590
And every word gan for to notifie;
For which with sobre cheere hire herte lough.
For who is that ne wolde hire glorifie,
To mowen swich a knyght don lyve or dye?
But al passe I, lest ye to longe dwelle;   1595
For for o fyn is al that evere I telle.

The tyme com fro dyner for to ryse,
And as hem aughte, arisen everichon.
And gonne a while of this and that devise.
But Pandarus brak al this speche anon,   1600
And seide to Deiphebus, "Wol ye gon,
If it youre wille be, as I yow preyde,
To speke here of the nedes of Criseyde?"

Eleyne, which that by the hond hire held,
Took first the tale, and seyde, "Go we blyve";
And goodly on Criseyde she biheld,   1606
And seyde, "Joves lat hym nevere thryve,
That doth yow harm, and brynge hym soone of
 lyve,
And yeve me sorwe, but he shal it rewe,
If that I may, and alle folk be trewe!"   1610

"Telle thow thi neces cas," quod Deiphebus
To Pandarus, "for thow kanst best it telle."
"My lordes and my ladys, it stant thus:
What sholde I lenger," quod he, "do yow
 dwelle?"
He rong hem out a proces lik a belle   1615
Upon hire foo, that highte Poliphete,
So heynous, that men myghte on it spete.

Answerde of this ech werse of hem than other,
And Poliphete they gonnen thus to warien:
"Anhonged be swich oon, were he my brother!
And so he shal, for it ne may nought varien!"
What shold I lenger in this tale tarien?   1622
Pleynliche, alle at ones, they hire highten
To ben hire helpe in al that evere they myghten.

Spak than Eleyne, and seyde, "Pandarus,   1625
Woot ought my lord, my brother, this matere,
I meene Ector? or woot it Troilus?"
He seyde, "Ye, but wole ye now me here?
Me thynketh this, sith that Troilus is here,
It were good, if that ye wolde assente,   1630
She tolde hireself hym al this, er she wente.

"For he wol have the more hir grief at herte,
By cause, lo, that she a lady is;
And, by youre leve, I wol but in right sterte
And do yow wyte, and that anon, iwys,   1635
If that he slepe, or wol ought here of this."
And in he lepte, and seyde hym in his ere,
"God have thi soule, ibrought have I thi
    beere!"

To smylen of this gan tho Troilus,
And Pandarus, withouten rekenynge,   1640
Out wente anon to Eleyne and Deiphebus,
And seyde hem, "So ther be no taryinge,
Ne moore prees, he wol wel that ye brynge
Criseÿda, my lady, that is here;
And as he may enduren, he wol here.   1645

"But wel ye woot, the chaumbre is but lite,
And fewe folk may lightly make it warm;
Now loketh ye (for I wol have no wite,
To brynge in prees that myghte don hym
    harm,
Or hym disesen, for my bettre arm)   1650

Wher it be bet she bide til eftsonys;
Now loketh ye, that knowen what to doon is.

"I sey for me, best is, as I kan knowe,
That no wight in ne wente but ye tweye,
But it were I, for I kan in a throwe   1655
Reherce hire cas unlik that she kan seye;
And after this, she may hym ones preye
To ben good lord, in short, and take hire leve.
This may nought muchel of his ese hym reve.

"And ek, for she is straunge, he wol forbere 1660
His ese, which that hym thar nought for yow;
Ek oother thing, that toucheth nought to here,
He wol yow telle—I woot it wel right now—
That secret is, and for the townes prow."   1664
And they, that nothyng knewe of his entente,
Withouten more, to Troilus in they wente.

Eleyne, in al hire goodly softe wyse,
Gan hym salue, and wommanly to pleye,
And seyde, "Iwys, ye moste alweies arise!
Now, faire brother, beth al hool, I preye!" 1670
And gan hire arm right over his shulder leye,
And hym with al hire wit to reconforte;
As she best koude, she gan hym to disporte.

So after this quod she, "We yow biseke,
My deere brother, Deiphebus, and I,   1675
For love of God—and so doth Pandare eke—
To ben good lord and frend, right hertely,
Unto Criseyde, which that certeynly
Receyveth wrong, as woot weel here Pandare,
That kan hire cas wel bet than I declare."   1680

This Pandarus gan newe his tong affile,
And al hire cas reherce, and that anon.
Whan it was seyd, soone after in a while,
Quod Troilus, "As sone as I may gon,   1684

1619. warien, curse. **1621. varien,** be otherwise. **1623. highten,** promised. **1634. I wol . . . sterte,** I will just pop in. **1638. thi beere.** Pandarus jests about his feigned fever. **1640. rekenynge,** rendering an account, *i.e.* giving him further details. **1648. have . . . wite,** incur blame. **1651. eftsonys,** later. **1655. throwe,** brief time, moment. **1656. unlik that,** in a manner different from what. **1660. straunge,** not one of the family. **forbere,** forgo. **1661. hym thar nought,** he does not need. **1662. here,** her. **1684. gon,** walk.

I wol right fayn with al my myght ben oon,
Have God my trouthe, hire cause to sustene."
"Good thrift have ye!" quod Eleyne the
    queene.

Quod Pandarus, "And it youre wille be,
That she may take hire leve, er that she go?"
"O, elles God forbede it," tho quod he,   1690
"If that she vouchesauf for to do so."
And with that word quod Troilus, "Ye two,
Deiphebus and my suster lief and deere,
To yow have I to speke of o matere,   1694

To ben avysed by youre reed the bettre—"
And fond, as hap was, at his beddes hed,
The copie of a tretys and a lettre,
That Ector hadde hym sent to axen red
If swych a man was worthi to ben ded,
Woot I nought who; but in a grisly wise   1700
He preyede hem anon on it avyse.

Deiphebus gan this lettre for t'onfolde
In ernest greet; so did Eleyne the queene;
And romyng outward, faste it gonne byholde,
Downward a steire, into an herber greene.   1705
This ilke thing they redden hem bitwene,
And largely the mountance of an houre
Thei gonne on it to reden and to poure.

Now lat hem rede, and torne we anon
To Pandarus, that gan ful faste prye   1710
That al was wel, and out he gan to gon
Into the grete chaumbre, and that in hye,
And seyde, "God save al this compaynye!
Come, nece myn; my lady queene Eleyne
Abideth yow, and ek my lordes tweyne.   1715

"Rys, take with yow youre nece Antigone,
Or whom yow list; or no fors; hardyly
The lesse prees, the bet; com forth with me,
And loke that ye thonken humblely
Hem alle thre, and whan ye may goodly   1720
Youre tyme se, taketh of hem youre leeve,
Lest we to longe his restes hym byreeve."

Al innocent of Pandarus entente,
Quod tho Criseyde, "Go we, uncle deere";
And arm in arm inward with hym she wente,
Avysed wel hire wordes and hire cheere;   1726
And Pandarus, in ernestful manere,
Seyde, "Alle folk, for Godes love, I preye,
Stynteth right here, and softely yow pleye.

"Aviseth yow what folk ben hire withinne,   1730
And in what plite oon is, God hym amende!"
And inward thus, "Ful softely bygynne,
Nece, I conjure and heighly yow defende,
On his half which that soule us alle sende,
And in the vertu of corones tweyne,   1735
Sle naught this man, that hath for yow this
    peyne!

"Fy on the devel! thynk which oon he is,
And in what plite he lith; com of anon!
Thynk al swich taried tyde but lost it nys.
That wol ye bothe seyn, whan ye ben oon.   1740
Secoundely, ther yet devyneth noon
Upon yow two; come of now, if ye konne!
While folk is blent, lo, al the tyme is wonne.

"In titeryng, and pursuyte, and delayes,
The folk devyne at waggyng of a stree;   1745
And though ye wolde han after mirye dayes,

1689. take hire leve, say good-by. **1700. grisly,** terrifying, serious. **1703. in ernest greet,** in great earnest. **1704. romyng outward,** going outdoors. The stairs mentioned in the next line were, as generally in the Middle Ages, on the outside of the house. **1707. largely,** fully; **mountance,** extent, duration. **1710. prye,** look closely. **1712. in hye,** hastily. **1725. inward,** in. **1732. inward,** on the way in. **1733. defende,** forbid. **1734. sende,** sent. **1735. corones tweyne.** Chaucer refers to *corones tweye, corones two,* in *The Second Nun's Tale* (270, 279), garlands of roses and lilies, but such an allusion does not seem adequate for the present passage. Other suggestions such as that they are nuptial crowns, or symbols of Pity and Bountee, Justice and Mercy, etc. are no more convincing. Pandarus's earnestness seems to require something more solemn. The line remains obscure. **1738. com of,** come on! **1741. yet devyneth noon,** no one suspects anything. **1744. In titeryng . . .,** In vacillation, and entreaty, and procrastination. **1745. waggyng of a stree,** waving or fluttering of a straw, a mere trifle. **1746. han after,** have afterwards.

Than dar ye naught; and whi? for she, and she
Spak swych a word; thus loked he, and he!
Allas tyme iloste! I dar nought with yow dele.
Com of, therfore, and bryngeth hym to hele!"

But now to yow, ye loveres that ben here,   1751
Was Troilus nought in a kankedort,

That lay, and myghte whisprynge of hem here,
And thoughte, "O Lord, right now renneth my
    sort
Fully to deye, or han anon comfort!"   1755
And was the firste tyme he shulde hire preye
Of love; O myghty God, what shal he seye?

Explicit liber secundus.

Book III

Incipit prohemium tercii libri.

O blisful light, of which the bemes clere
Adorneth al the thridde heven faire,
O sonnes lief, O Joves doughter deere,
Plesance of love, O goodly debonaire,
In gentil hertes ay redy to repaire!   5
O veray cause of heele and of gladnesse,
Iheryed be thy myght and thi goodnesse!

In hevene and helle, in erthe and salte see
Is felt thi myght, if that I wel descerne;
As man, brid, best, fissh, herbe, and grene tree
Thee fele in tymes with vapour eterne.   11
God loveth, and to love wol nought werne;
And in this world no lyves creature
Withouten love is worth, or may endure.

Ye Joves first to thilk effectes glade,   15
Thorough which that thynges lyven alle and be,
Comeveden, and amorous him made
On mortal thyng, and as yow list, ay ye

Yeve hym in love ese or adversitee;
And in a thousand formes down hym sente   20
For love in erthe, and whom yow liste, he hente.

Ye fierse Mars apaisen of his ire,
And as yow list, ye maken hertes digne;
Algates hem that ye wol sette a-fyre,
They dreden shame, and vices they resygne;   25
Ye do hem corteys be, fresshe and benigne;
And heighe or lowe, after a wight entendeth,
The joies that he hath, youre myght him sendeth.

Ye holden regne and hous in unitee;
Ye sothfast cause of frendshipe ben also;   30
Ye knowe al thilke covered qualitee
Of thynges, which that folk on wondren so,
Whan they kan nought construe how it may jo
She loveth hym, or whi he loveth here,
As whi this fissh, and naught that, comth to
    were.   35

1749. **dele,** contend, argue. **1752. kankedort,** predicament, pickle. The origin of the word is unknown and the meaning must be inferred from the context. For suggested etymologies see *MLN*, LXIV. 264 (Spargo) and 503 (Spitzer). **1754. sort,** lot, destiny. **1.** The invocation to Venus, which constitutes the principal feature of the Proem, is from the *Filostrato*, III, st. 74–9. **2. thridde heven,** the third sphere, in which the planet Venus was supposed to be; therefore the *blisful light* is Venus. **3. O sonnes lief,** darling of the sun. **4. debonaire,** here used as a noun, *i.e.* a gracious person. **5. repaire,** reside. **7. Iheryed,** praised. **11. Thee fele . . .,** feel thee at (certain) seasons with eternal emanation (influence). **12. to love . . . werne,** will deny nothing to love. **13. lyves,** gen. s. of *lyf,* used as an adj.: no living creature; see Language, § 57. **14. worth,** of value, worthy. **15. Ye Joves . . . comeveden.** The construction is clear in the order *Ye comeveden Joves,* ye instigated Jove. The same word order appears in ll. 22, 36, and 44. **26. fresshe,** active, vigorous. **27. after a wight entendeth,** as a person wishes. **29. regne,** kingdom. The sense of the line is that Venus holds all the world together, which is what Boccaccio says (*Filostrato,* III, st. 78). **33. jo.** The word is otherwise unknown. Skeat connects it with OF. *joer,* to play. The sense here seems to be *happen.* **35. to were,** in the weir, an enclosure of stakes for trapping fish.

Ye folk a lawe han set in universe,
And this knowe I by hem that lovers be,
That whoso stryveth with yow hath the
    werse.
Now, lady bryght, for thi benignite,
At reverence of hem that serven the,   40
Whos clerc I am, so techeth me devyse
Som joye of that is felt in thi servyse.

Ye in my naked herte sentement
Inhielde, and do me shewe of thy swetnesse.
Caliope, thi vois be now present,   45
For now is nede; sestow nought my destresse,
How I mot telle anon-right the gladnesse
Of Troilus, to Venus heryinge?
To which gladnesse, who nede hath, God hym
    brynge!

Explicit prohemium tercii libri.

Incipit liber tercius.

Lay al this mene while Troilus,   50
Recordyng his lesson in this manere:
"Mafay," thoughte he, "thus wol I sey, and
    thus;
Thus wol I pleyne unto my lady dere;
That word is good, and this shal be my cheere;
This nyl I nought foryeten in no wise."   55
God leve hym werken as he kan devyse!

And, Lord, so that his herte gan to quappe,
Heryng hire come, and shorte for to sike!
And Pandarus, that ledde hire by the lappe,
Com ner, and gan in at the curtyn pike,   60
And seyde, "God do boot on alle syke!
Se who is here yow comen to visite;
Lo, here is she that is youre deth to wite."

Therwith it semed as he wepte almost.
"A-ha," quod Troilus so reufully,   65
"Wher me be wo, O myghty God, thow
    woost!
Who is al ther? I se nought trewely."
"Sire," quod Criseyde, "it is Pandare and I."

"Ye, swete herte? allas, I may nought rise,
To knele and do yow honour in som wyse."   70
And dressed hym upward, and she right tho
Gan bothe hire hondes softe upon hym leye.
"O, for the love of God, do ye nought so
To me," quod she, "I! what is this to seye?
Sire, comen am I to yow for causes tweye: 75
First, yow to thonke, and of youre lordshipe eke
Continuance I wolde yow biseke."

This Troilus, that herde his lady preye
Of lordshipe hym, wax neither quyk ne ded,
Ne myghte o word for shame to it seye,   80
Although men sholde smyten of his hed.
But, Lord, so he wex sodeynliche red,
And sire, his lessoun, that he wende konne
To preyen hire, is thorugh his wit ironne.

Criseyde al this aspied wel ynough,   85
For she was wis, and loved hym nevere the lasse,
Al nere he malapert, or made it tough,
Or was to bold, to synge a fool a masse.

---

36. folk, for folk. **40. At reverence of,** out of respect for. **41. devyse,** describe, relate. **43. naked,** unfurnished, ill-equipped. **44. Inhielde,** pour in. **do me shewe,** give me a manifestation. **45. Caliope,** Calliope, the Muse of epic poetry. **48. to
Venus heryinge,** to Venus's praise. **51. Recordyng,** rehearsing. **52. Mafay,** upon my faith! **57. so that,** how, introducing an exclamatory clause; cf. l. 82. **quappe,** flutter. **59. lappe,** flap or folded part of a garment. **61. syke,** sick people. **63.
youre deth to wite,** to blame for your death. **66. Wher me be wo,** whether I am unhappy. **71. dressed hym,** raised himself. **74. what is this to seye,** what means this. **76. lordshipe,** protection, patronage. **80. shame,** modesty, embarrassment.
87-8. Al nere he . . . masse. These two lines present four difficulties: (1) the usual meaning of *Al nere he* is "although
he were not," whereas we should expect "because he was not"; (2) the meaning of *made it tough* varies in different contexts;
(3) the force of *to synge a fool a masse*, although the phrase is apparently proverbial, is unknown; and (4) the relation of this
phrase to the rest of the sentence is ambiguous. Without dogmatism I paraphrase the two lines: "all the more because he
did not behave insolently, or haughtily, or overboldly to accomplish no useful purpose." For a different interpretation see
Professor Robinson's note to the passage.

But whan his shame gan somwhat to passe,
His resons, as I may my rymes holde, 90
I wol yow telle, as techen bokes olde.
In chaunged vois, right for his verray drede,
Which vois ek quook, and therto his manere
Goodly abaist, and now his hewes rede,
Now pale, unto Criseyde, his lady dere, 95
With look down cast and humble iyolden chere,
Lo, the alderfirste word that hym asterte
Was, twyes, "Mercy, mercy, swete herte!"

And stynte a while, and whan he myghte out-
brynge,
The nexte word was, "God woot, for I have, 100
As ferforthly as I have had konnynge,
Ben youres al, God so my soule save,
And shal, til that I, woful wight, be grave!
And though I ne dar, ne kan, unto yow pleyne,
Iwis, I suffre nought the lasse peyne. 105

"Thus muche as now, O wommanliche wif,
I may out-brynge, and if this yow displese,
That shal I wreke upon myn owen lif
Right soone, I trowe, and do youre herte an ese,
If with my deth youre wreththe I may apese. 110
But syn that ye han herd me somwhat seye,
Now recche I nevere how soone that I deye."

Therwith his manly sorwe to biholde,
It myghte han mad an herte of stoon to rewe;
And Pandare wep as he to water wolde, 115
And poked evere his nece new and newe,
And seyde, "Wo bygon ben hertes trewe!
For love of God, make of this thing an ende,
Or sle us both at ones, er ye wende."

"I! what?" quod she, "by God and by my
trouthe, 120
I not nat what ye wilne that I seye."

"I! what?" quod he, "that ye han on hym
routhe,
For Goddes love, and doth hym nought to
deye."
"Now thanne thus," quod she, "I wolde hym
preye
To telle me the fyn of his entente. 125
Yet wist I nevere wel what that he mente."

"What that I mene, O swete herte deere?"
Quod Troilus, "O goodly, fresshe free,
That with the stremes of youre eyen cleere
Ye wolde somtyme frendly on me see, 130
And thanne agreen that I may ben he,
Withouten braunche of vice on any wise,
In trouthe alwey to don yow my servise,

"As to my lady right and chief resort,
With al my wit and al my diligence; 135
And I to han, right as yow list, comfort,
Under yowre yerde, egal to myn offence,
As deth, if that I breke youre defence;
And that ye deigne me so muche honoure,
Me to comanden aught in any houre; 140

"And I to ben youre verray humble trewe,
Secret, and in my paynes pacient,
And evere mo desiren fresshly newe
To serve, and ben ay ylike diligent,
And with good herte al holly youre talent 145
Receyven wel, how sore that me smerte,—
Lo, this mene I, myn owen swete herte."

Quod Pandarus, "Lo, here an hard requeste,
And resonable, a lady for to werne!
Now, nece myn, by natal Joves feste, 150
Were I a god, ye sholden sterve as yerne,
That heren wel this man wol nothing yerne
But youre honour, and sen hym almost sterve,
And ben so loth to suffren hym yow serve."

94. Goodly abaist, becomingly abashed. **96. iyolden,** submissive. **97. asterte,** escaped. **101. ferforthly,** far. **106. as now,** now. **wommanliche wif,** pattern of womanhood. **125. fyn,** end. **128. free,** gracious (lady). **132. braunche,** species. **134. resort,** source of aid. **137. yerde,** correction. **138. defence,** prohibition. **141. trewe,** true servant. **145. talent,** inclination, desire. **149. werne,** deny. **150. by natal Joves feste,** probably, as Skeat suggested, by the feast of Jupiter as the god who presided over nativities. If Chaucer had meant Jupiter's natal feast (Root), he could have written *Joves natal feste* with no violence to the meter. **151-2. yerne . . . yerne.** A nice example of identical rime, the first *yerne* meaning "quickly," the second "desire."

With that she gan hire eyen on hym caste　　155
Ful esily and ful debonairly, *graciously*
Avysyng hire, and hied nought to faste
With nevere a word, but seyde hym softely, *still*
"Myn honour sauf, I wol wel trewely,　　✳
And in swich forme as he gan now devyse,　　160
Receyven hym fully to my servyse,

"Bysechyng hym, for Goddes love, that he
Wolde, in honour of trouthe and gentilesse,
As I wel mene, eke mene wel to me,
And myn honour with wit and bisynesse　　165
Ay kepe; and if I may don hym gladnesse, *will not*
From hennesforth, iwys, I nyl nought feyne.
Now beth al hool; no lenger ye ne pleyne.

"But natheles, this warne I yow," quod she,
"A kynges sone although ye be, ywys,　　170
Ye shal namore han sovereignete
Of me in love, than right in that cas is;
N'y nyl forbere, if that ye don amys,
To wratthe yow; and whil that ye me serve,
Chericen yow right after ye disserve.　　175

"And shortly, deere herte and al my knyght,
Beth glad, and draweth yow to lustinesse,
And I shal trewely, with al my myght,
Youre bittre tornen al into swetenesse;
If I be she that may yow do gladnesse,　　180
For every wo ye shal recovere a blisse."
And hym in armes took, and gan hym kisse.

✳ Fil Pandarus on knees, and up his eyen
To heven threw, and held his hondes highe,
"Immortal god," quod he, "that mayst nought
　　deyen,　　185
Cupide I mene, of this mayst glorifie;
And Venus, thow mayst maken melodie!

Withouten hond, me semeth that in towne,
For this merveille, ich here ech belle sowne.

"But ho! namore as now of this matere;　　190
For-whi this folk wol comen up anon,
That han the lettre red; lo, I hem here.
But I conjure the, Criseyde, and oon,
And two, thow Troilus, whan thow mayst
　　goon,
That at myn hous ye ben at my warnynge,　　195
For I ful well shal shape youre comynge;

"And eseth there youre hertes right ynough;
And lat se which of yow shal bere the belle,
To speke of love aright!"—therwith he
　　lough—
"For ther have ye a leiser for to telle."　　200
Quod Troilus, "How longe shal I dwelle,
Er this be don?" Quod he, "Whan thow mayst
　　ryse,
This thyng shal be right as I yow devyse."

With that Eleyne and also Deiphebus　　204
Tho comen upward, right at the steires ende;
And Lord, so thanne gan gronen Troilus,
His brother and his suster for to blende.
Quod Pandarus, "It tyme is that we wende.
Tak, nece myn, youre leve at alle thre,
And lat hem speke, and cometh forth with
　　me."　　210

She took hire leve at hem ful thriftily,
As she wel koude, and they hire reverence
Unto the fulle diden, hardyly,
And wonder wel speken, in hire absence,
Of hire, in preysing of hire excellence,　　215
Hire governaunce, hire wit; and hire manere
Comendeden, it joie was to here.

---

156. **esily,** softly. 160. **devyse,** set forth. 165. **with wit and bisynesse,** mindfully and diligently. 167. **feyne,** hold back, dissemble. 174. **wratthe yow,** be angry with you. 177. **lustinesse,** vigor, enjoyment of life. 186. **of this mayst glorifie,** in this mayest thou exult. 188. **Withouten hond.** There are numerous instances, as in the ballads, of bells ringing spontaneously. 192. **lo, I hem here,** *i.e.* they will be looking for him. 193. **and oon, And two,** both one and the other. 194. **whan thow mayst goon,** when you are able to walk. 195. **warnynge,** command (invitation). 196. **shape,** arrange. 198. **bere the belle,** (like the bellwether) be the first, take the prize. 203. **devyse,** shall explain. 211. **thriftily,** in a becoming manner. 212-3. **reverence . . . diden,** paid their respects. 214. **speken,** spoke. 216. **governaunce,** demeanour. **wit,** intelligence, good sense.

Now lat hire wende unto hire owen place,
And torne we to Troilus ayein,
That gan ful lightly of the lettre pace   220
That Deiphebus hadde in the gardyn seyn;
And of Eleyne and hym he wolde feyn
Delivered ben, and seyde that hym leste
To slepe, and after tales have reste.

Eleyne hym kiste, and took hire leve blyve, 225
Deiphebus ek, and hom wente every wight;
And Pandarus, as faste as he may dryve,
To Troilus tho com, as lyne right,
And on a paillet al that glade nyght
By Troilus he lay, with mery chere,   230
To tale; and wel was hem they were yfeere.

Whan every wight was voided but they two,
And alle the dores weren faste yshette,
To telle in short, withouten wordes mo,
This Pandarus, withouten any lette,   235
Up roos, and on his beddes syde hym sette,
And gan to speken in a sobre wyse
To Troilus, as I shal yow devyse:

"Myn alderlevest lord, and brother deere,
God woot, and thow, that it sat me so soore,
When I the saugh so langwisshyng to-yere 241
For love, of which thi wo wax alwey moore,
That I, with al my myght and al my loore,
Have evere sithen don my bisynesse
To brynge the to joye out of distresse,   245

"And have it brought to swich plit as thow
    woost,
So that thorugh me thow stondest now in weye
To faren wel; I sey it for no bost,
And wostow whi? for shame it is to seye:
For the have I bigonne a gamen pleye,   250
Which that I nevere do shal eft for other,
Although he were a thousand fold my brother.

"That is to seye, for the am I bicomen,
Bitwixen game and ernest, swich a meene
As maken wommen unto men to comen;   355
Al sey I nought, thow wost wel what I meene.
For the have I my nece, of vices cleene,
So fully maad thi gentilesse triste,
That al shal ben right as thiselven liste.

"But God, that al woot, take I to witnesse, 260
That nevere I this for coveitise wroughte,
But oonly for t'abregge that distresse
For which wel neigh thow deidest, as me
    thoughte.
But, goode brother, do now as the oughte,
For Goddes love, and kep hire out of blame, 265
Syn thow art wys, and save alwey hire name.

"For wel thow woost, the name as yet of here
Among the peeple, as who seyth, halwed is;
For that man is unbore, I dar wel swere,
That evere wiste that she dide amys.   270
But wo is me, that I, that cause al this,
May thynken that she is my nece deere,
And I hire em, and traitour eke yfeere!

"And were it wist that I, thorugh myn engyn,
Hadde in my nece yput this fantasie,   275
To doon thi lust and holly to ben thyn,
Whi, al the world upon it wolde crie,
And seyn that I the werste trecherie
Dide in this cas that evere was bigonne,
And she forlost, and thow right nought ywonne.

"Wherfore, er I wol ferther gon a pas,   281
Yet eft I the biseche and fully seye,
That privete go with us in this cas,
That is to seyn, that thow us nevere wreye;
And be nought wroth, though I the ofte preye
To holden secree swich an heigh matere, 286
For skilfull is, thow woost wel, my praiere.

---

220. of the lettre pace, glance over the letter, (or perhaps) treat it lightly. **224. tales,** talks. **227. dryve,** hasten. **228. as lyne right,** directly. **231. To tale,** to talk things over. **wel was hem . . .,** they were happy to be together. **235. lette,** delay. **241. to-yere,** this year. **243. loore,** knowledge, "science." **246. plit,** state of affairs. **249. for shame it is to seye,** I am ashamed to say it. **254. meene,** go-between. **262. l'abregge,** to abridge, shorten. **268. halwed,** reverenced. **274. engyn,** contrivance, devices. **275. fantasie,** idea. **276. lust.** pleasure.

"And thynk what wo ther hath bitid er this,
For makyng of avantes, as men rede;
And what meschaunce in this world yet ther is,
Fro day to day, right for that wikked dede;   291
For which thise wise clerkes that ben dede
Han evere thus proverbed to us yonge,
That 'firste vertu is to kepe tonge.'

"And nere it that I wilne as now t'abregge   295
Diffusioun of speche, I koude almoost
A thousand olde stories the allegge
Of wommen lost through fals and foles bost.
Proverbes kanst thiself ynowe and woost,
Ayeins that vice, for to ben a labbe,   300
Al seyde men soth as often as thei gabbe.

"O tonge, allas! so often here-byforn
Hath mad ful many a lady bright of hewe
Seyd 'weilaway, the day that I was born!'
And many a maydes sorwe for to newe;   305
And for the more part, al is untrewe
That men of yelpe, and it were brought to preve.
Of kynde non avauntour is to leve.

"Avauntour and a lyere, al is on;
As thus: I pose, a womman graunte me   310
Hire love, and seith that other wol she non,
And I am sworn to holden it secree,
And after I go telle it two or thre;
Iwis, I am avauntour at the leeste,
And lyere, for I breke my biheste.   315

"Now loke thanne, if they be nought to blame,
Swich manere folk—what shal I clepe hem?
     what?—
That hem avaunte of wommen, and by name,
That nevere yet bihyghte hem this ne that,
Ne knewe hem more than myn olde hat!   320

No wonder is, so God me sende hele,
Though wommen dreden with us men to dele.

"I sey nought this for no mistrust of yow,
Ne for no wise men, but for foles nyce,
And for the harm that in the werld is now,   325
As wel for folie ofte as for malice;
For wel woot I, in wise folk that vice
No womman drat, if she be wel avised;
For wyse ben by foles harm chastised.

"But now to purpos; leve brother deere,   330
Have al this thyng that I have seyd in mynde,
And kep the clos, and be now of good cheere,
For at thi day thow shalt me trewe fynde.
I shal thi proces set in swych a kynde,
And God toforn, that it shal the suffise,   335
For it shal be right as thow wolt devyse.

"For wel I woot, thow menest wel, parde;
Therfore I dar this fully undertake.
Thow woost ek what thi lady graunted the,
And day is set, the chartres up to make.   340
Have now good nyght, I may no lenger wake;
And bid for me, syn thow art now in blysse,
That God me sende deth or soone lisse."

Who myghte tellen half the joie or feste
Whiche that the soule of Troilus tho felte,   345
Heryng th'effect of Pandarus byheste?
His olde wo, that made his herte swelte,
Gan tho for joie wasten and tomelte,
And al the richesse of his sikes sore
At ones fledde; he felte of hem namore.   350

But right so as thise holtes and thise hayis,
That han in wynter dede ben and dreye,
Revesten hem in grene, when that May is,

---

296. Diffusioun, prolixity. **298. foles**, gen. as adj., foolish. **301. gabbe**, lie, boast. **302. O tonge**, *i.e.* a single tongue. **304. Seyd**, elliptical for *to have seyd*. For similar ellipsis see *TC* 1. 1009 and Language, § 68. **308. Of kynde . . .**, by nature no boaster is to be believed. **310. pose**, put a case. **315. biheste**, promise. **329. For wyse . . .**, for wise men learn their lesson (*lit.* are punished) from the harm done by fools. **333. at thi day**, *i.e.* at the proper time. **338. dar . . . undertake**, venture to assert, **340. And day is set . . .**, a legal metaphor: a time is appointed for making matters definite. **342. bid**, pray. **343. lisse**, joy. **346. byheste.** The word here connotes both promise and command. **347. swelte**, perish. **349. the richesse of his sikes**, his abundant sighs. **351. holtes and . . . hayis**, woods and hedges.

Whan every lusty liketh best to pleye;
Right in that selve wise, soth to seye,   355
Wax sodeynliche his herte ful of joie,
That gladder was ther nevere man in Troie.

"And gan his look on Pandarus up caste
Ful sobrely, and frendly for to se,
And seyde, "Frend, in Aperil the laste,—   360
As wel thow woost, if it remembre the,—
How neigh the deth for wo thow fowndest me,
And how thow dedest al thi bisynesse
To knowe of me the cause of my destresse.

"Thow woost how longe ich it forbar to seye
To the, that art the man that I best triste;   366
And peril non was it to the bywreye,
That wist I wel, but telle me, if the liste,
Sith I so loth was that thiself it wiste,
How dorst I mo tellen of this matere,   370
That quake now, and no wight may us here?

"But natheles, by that God I the swere,
That, as hym list, may al this world governe,—
And, if I lye, Achilles with his spere
Myn herte cleve, al were my lif eterne,   375
As I am mortal, if I late or yerne
Wolde it bewreye, or dorst, or sholde konne,
For al the good that God made under sonne—

"That rather deye I wolde, and determyne,
As thynketh me, now stokked in prisoun,   380
In wrecchidnesse, in filthe, and in vermyne,
Caytif to cruel kyng Agamenoun;
And this in all the temples of this town
Upon the goddes alle, I wol the swere
To-morwe day, if that it liketh the here.   385

"And that thow hast so muche ido for me
That I ne may it nevere more diserve,
This know I wel, al myghte I now for the

A thousand tymes on a morwe sterve.
I kan namore, but that I wol the serve   390
Right as thi sclave, whider so thow wende,
For evere more, unto my lyves ende.

"But here, with al myn herte, I the biseche
That nevere in me thow deme swich folie
As I shal seyn; me thoughte by thi speche   395
That this which thow me dost for compaignie,
I sholde wene it were a bauderye.
I am nought wood, al-if I lewed be!
It is nought so, that woot I wel, parde!

"But he that gooth, for gold or for ricchesse,
On swich message, calle hym what the list;   401
And this that thow doost, calle it gentilesse,
Compassioun, and felawship, and trist.
Departe it so, for wyde-wher is wist
How that ther is diversite requered   405
Bytwixen thynges like, as I have lered.

"And, that thow knowe I thynke nought, ne
    wene,
That this servise a shame be or jape,
I have my faire suster Polixene,
Cassandre, Eleyne, or any of the frape,   410
Be she nevere so faire or wel yshape,
Tel me which thow wilt of everychone,
To han for thyn, and lat me thanne allone.

"But sith thow hast idon me this servyse,
My lif to save, and for non hope of mede,   415
So, for the love of God, this grete emprise
Perfourme it out, for now is moste nede;
For heigh and lough, withouten any drede,
I wol alwey thyn hestes alle kepe.
Have now good nyght, and lat us bothe slepe."

Thus held hym ech of other wel apayed,   421
That al the world ne myghte it bet amende;

---

354. lusty, one who is full of the joy of life. **376. yerne,** soon. **379. determyne,** come to an end. **380. stokked,** set in the stocks. **382. Agamenoun,** Agamemnon, king of Mycenae and leader of the Greek expedition against Troy. **385. To-morwe day,** tomorrow morning (daybreak). **here,** *i.e.* to hear me take this oath. **396. compaignie,** companionship, friendship. **397. bauderye,** the act of a bawd. **398. I am nought wood . . .,** I am not mad even if I am ignorant. **404. Departe it so,** make such a distinction. **wyde-wher,** far and wide, everywhere. **408. jape,** trick. **410. frape,** pack. **413. lat me thanne allone,** leave the rest to me.

And on the morwe, whan they were arayed,
Ech to his owen nedes gan entende.
But Troilus, though as the fir he brende   425
For sharp desir of hope and of plesaunce,
He nought forgat his gode governaunce.

But in hymself with manhod gan restreyne
Ech racle dede and ech unbridled chere,
That alle tho that lyven, soth to seyne,   430
Ne sholde han wist, by word or by manere,
What that he mente, as touchyng this matere.
From every wight as fer as is the cloude
He was, so wel dissimulen he koude.

And al the while which that I yow devyse,   435
This was his lif: with all his fulle myght,
By day, he was in Martes heigh servyse,
This is to seyn, in armes as a knyght;
And for the more part, the longe nyght   439
He lay and thoughte how that he myghte serve
His lady best, hire thonk for to deserve.

Nil I naught swere, although he lay ful softe,
That in his thought he nas somwhat disesed,
Ne that he torned on his pilwes ofte,   444
And wold of that hym missed han ben sesed.
But in swich cas man is nought alwey plesed,
For aught I woot, namore than was he;
That kan I deme of possibilitee.

But certeyn is, to purpos for to go,
That in this while, as writen is in geeste,   450
He say his lady somtyme, and also
She with hym spak, whan that she dorst and
     leste;
And by hire bothe avys, as was the beste,
Apoynteden full warly in this nede,
So as they durste, how they wolde procede.   455

But it was spoken in so short a wise,
In swich await alwey, and in swich feere,

Lest any wight devynen or devyse
Wolde of hem two, or to it laye an ere,
That al this world so leef to hem ne were   460
As that Cupide wolde hem grace sende
To maken of hire speche aright an ende.

But thilke litel that they spake or wroughte,
His wise goost took ay of al swych heede,
It semed hire he wiste what she thoughte   465
Withouten word, so that it was no nede
To bidde hym ought to doon, or ought for-
     beede;
For which she thought that love, al come it
     late,
Of alle joie hadde opned hire the yate.

And shortly of this proces for to pace,   470
So wel his werk and wordes he bisette,
That he so ful stood in his lady grace,
That twenty thousand tymes, er she lette,
She thonked God that evere she with hym
     mette.
So koude he hym governe in swich
     servyse,   475
That al the world ne myght it bet devyse.

For whi she fond hym so discret in al,
So secret, and of swich obëisaunce,
That wel she felte he was to hire a wal
Of stiel, and sheld from every displesaunce;   480
That to ben in his goode governaunce,
So wis he was, she was namore afered,—
I mene, as fer as oughte ben requered.

And Pandarus, to quike alwey the fir,
Was evere ylike prest and diligent;   485
To ese his frend was set al his desir.
He shof ay on, he to and fro was sent;
He lettres bar whan Troilus was absent;
That nevere man, as in his frendes nede,
Ne bar hym bet than he, withouten drede.   490

---

429. **racle**, rash. 443. **disesed**, troubled. 445. **of that hym missed han ben sesed**, have been in possession of what he lacked. 451. **say**, saw. 452. **leste**, pleased. 453. **hire bothe avys**, the judgment of them both. 457. **swich await**, such watchfulness. 458. **devyse**, conjecture. 462. **aright**, quickly. 473. **lette**, left off, ceased. 482. **namore afered**, no longer afraid. 485. **evere ylike**, uniformly. **prest**, ready. 489. **as in**, in.

But now, paraunter, som man wayten wolde
That every word, or soonde, or look, or cheere
Of Troilus that I rehercen sholde,
In al this while unto his lady deere.
I trowe it were a long thyng for to here;   495
Or of what wight that stant in swich disjoynte,
His wordes alle, or every look, to poynte.

For sothe, I have naught herd it don er this
In story non, ne no man here, I wene;
And though I wolde, I koude nought, ywys;
For ther was som epistel hem bitwene,   501
That wolde, as seyth myn autour, wel contene
Neigh half this book, of which hym liste nought
    write.
How sholde I thanne a lyne of it endite?

But to the grete effect. Than sey I thus,   505
That stondyng in concord and in quiete,
Thise ilke two, Criseyde and Troilus,
As I have told, and in this tyme swete,—
Save only often myghte they nought mete,
Ne leiser have hire speches to fulfelle,—   510
That it bifel right as I shal yow telle:

That Pandarus, that evere dide his myght
Right for the fyn that I shal speke of here,
As for to bryngen to his hows som nyght
His faire nece and Troilus yfere,   515
Wher as at leiser al this heighe matere,
Touchyng here love, were at the fulle up-
    bounde,
Hadde out of doute a tyme to it founde.

For he with gret deliberacioun
Hadde every thyng that herto myght availle 520
Forncast and put in execucioun,
And neither left for cost ne for travaile.

Come if hem list, hem sholde no thyng faille;
And for to ben in ought aspied there,
That, wiste he wel, an impossible were.   525

Dredeles, it clere was in the wynd
From every pie and every lette-game;
Now al is wel, for al the world is blynd
In this matere, bothe fremed and tame.
This tymbur is al redy up to frame;   530
Us lakketh nought but that we witen wolde
A certeyn houre, in which she comen sholde.

And Troilus, that al this purveiaunce
Knew at the fulle, and waited on it ay,
Hadde hereupon ek made gret ordinaunce, 535
And found his cause, and therto his aray,
If that he were missed, nyght or day,
Ther-while he was aboute this servyse,—
That he was gon to don his sacrifise,

And moste at swich a temple allone wake, 540
Answered of Apollo for to be;
And first to sen the holy laurer quake,
Er that Apollo spake out of the tree,
To telle hym next whan Grekes sholde flee,—
And forthy lette hym no man, God forbede, 545
But prey Apollo helpen in this nede.

Now is ther litel more for to doone,
But Pandare up, and shortly for to seyne,
Right sone upon the chaungynge of the moone,
Whan lightles is the world a nyght or tweyne,
And that the wolken shop hym for to reyne, 551
He streght o morwe unto his nece wente;
Ye han wel herd the fyn of his entente.

Whan he was come, he gan anon to pleye
As he was wont, and of hymself to jape; 555
And finaly he swor and gan hire seye,

---

491. wayten, expect. **496. disjoynte,** difficult situation. **499. ne no man here, I wene.** Chaucer envisages an audience. **502. contene,** occupy, fill. **505. grete effect,** main point. **510. fulfelle,** a Kentish form adopted by Thynne (1532) and required by the rime, but all MSS have *fulfille.* **517. were . . . up-bounde,** might be bound up (completed). **523. Come if hem list,** if it pleased them to come. **525. an impossible,** an impossibility. **526. it clere was in the wynd From . . .,** i.e. the wind was blowing directly away from every magpie (a tell-tale bird) and spoil-sport. **529. fremed and tame,** wild and tame, i.e. everybody. **530. This tymbur . . .,** the figure is from putting up the framework of a house. **frame,** cut and set in place. **531. we.** This seems to be the "editorial we." **witen wolde,** should know. **533. purveiaunce,** preparation, prearrangement. **534. waited on,** observed. **536. aray,** arrangement. **542. holy laurer.** The laurel was sacred to Apollo. **545. lette,** hinder. **551. wolken,** sky. **shop hym,** prepared itself. **553. the fyn of his entente,** his object.

By this and that, she sholde hym nought escape,
Ne lenger don hym after hire to gape;
But certeynly she moste, by hire leve,
Come soupen in his hous with hym at eve.　　560

At which she lough, and gan hire faste excuse,
And seyde, "It reyneth; lo, how sholde I gon?"
"Lat be," quod he, "ne stond nought thus to muse.
This moot be don! Ye shal be ther anon."
So at the laste herof they fille aton,　　565
Or elles, softe he swor hire in hire ere,
He nolde nevere comen ther she were.

Soone after this, she to hym gan to rowne,
And axed hym if Troilus were there.
He swor hire nay, for he was out of towne,　　570
And seyde, "Nece, I pose that he were;
Yow thurste nevere han the more fere;
For rather than men myghte hym ther aspie,
Me were levere a thousand fold to dye."

Nought list myn auctour fully to declare　　575
What that she thoughte whan he seyde so,
That Troilus was out of towne yfare,
As if he seyde therof soth or no;
But that, withowten await, with hym to go,
She graunted hym, sith he hire that bisoughte,
And, as his nece, obeyed as hire oughte.　　581

But natheles, yet gan she hym biseche,
Although with hym to gon it was no fere,
For to ben war of goosish poeples speche,　　584
That dremen thynges whiche that nevere were,

And wel avyse hym whom he broughte there;
And seyde hym, "Em, syn I moste on yow triste,
Loke al be wel, and do now as yow liste."

He swor hire yis, by stokkes and by stones,
And by the goddes that in hevene dwelle,　　590
Or elles were hym levere, fel and bones,
With Pluto kyng as depe ben in helle
As Tantalus!—what sholde I more telle?
Whan al was wel, he roos and took his leve,
And she to soper com, whan it was eve,　　595

With a certein of hire owen men,
And with hire faire nece Antigone,
And other of hire wommen nyne or ten.
But who was glad now, who, as trowe ye,
But Troilus, that stood and myght it se　　600
Thoroughout a litel wyndow in a stuwe,
Ther he bishet syn mydnyght was in mewe,

A little peephole in Closet.

Unwist of every wight but of Pandare?
But to the point; now whan that she was come,
With alle joie and alle frendes fare,　　605
Hire em anon in armes hath hire nome,
And after to the soper, alle and some,
Whan tyme was, ful softe they hem sette.
God woot, ther was no deynte for to fette!

And after soper gonnen they to rise,　　610
At ese wel, with hertes fresshe and glade,
And wel was hym that koude best devyse
To liken hire, or that hire laughen made.
He song; she pleyde; he tolde tale of Wade.

---

558. to gape (after), wish for, long for. **563. stond . . . to muse,** hesitate to make up one's mind, wonder what to do. **568. rowne,** whisper. **571. I pose that he were,** suppose he was. **572. Yow thurste,** *lit.* it would be needful to you, you would need. The form *thurste* (clearly supported by the MSS) is irregular. We should expect *thurfte.* The *s* is due to the early confusion of the forms of *tharf* and *dare* (see *NED*). **579. await,** delay, though the suggestion of "watchfulness," "caution," usual in the word at this time, may be present. **583. it was no fere,** she was not afraid. **584. goosish,** silly. **587. moste.** The MS variants (*must, mot*) suggest that *moste* was felt to be an auxiliary verb. Both Root and Robinson, however, consider it the adverb "most," and this interpretation is supported by 2. 247. At 3. 916 the construction is again open to either interpretation. **589. stokkes and . . . stones,** *i.e.* sacred images or idols, often used contemptuously of such objects because made of wood and stone. **591. fel,** skin. **592. Pluto,** god of the lower world. **593. Tantalus.** See note to *BD* 709. **601. stuwe,** a small heated room, generally for bathing (OF. *estuve*). **602. mewe,** coop, *i.e.* confined in a small space. **605. frendes fare,** friendly behavior. **609. for to fette,** lacking, to be fetched. **613. liken,** please. **614. Wade.** A hero of romance, several times mentioned in Middle English. No romance of Wade has survived. He is mentioned in *Beves of Hampton* (ll. 2599–2608) along with Lancelot and Guy of Warwick as having fought a dragon. Chaucer mentions his boat in *The Merchant's Tale* (E 1424) and Walter Map relates an episode in the *De Nugis Curialium.* It is possible that the phrase *tale of Wade* here means simply a tall story.

weather condition.

But at the laste, as every thyng hath ende, 615
She took hire leve, and nedes wolde wende.

But O Fortune, executrice of wyrdes!
O influences of thise hevenes hye!
Soth is, that under God ye ben oure hierdes,
Though to us bestes ben the causes wrie. 620
This mene I now, for she gan homward hye,
But execut was al bisyde hire leve
The goddes wil; for which she moste bleve.

The bente moone with hire hornes pale,
Saturne, and Jove, in Cancro joyned were, 625
That swych a reyn from heven gan avale,
That every maner womman that was there
Hadde of that smoky reyn a verray feere;
At which Pandare tho lough, and seyde
  thenne,
"Now were it tyme a lady to gon henne! 630

"But goode nece, if I myghte evere plese
Yow any thyng, than prey ich yow," quod he,
"To don myn herte as now so grete an ese
As for to dwelle here al this nyght with me,
For-whi this is youre owen hous, parde. 635
For, by my trouthe, I sey it nought a-game,
To wende as now, it were to me a shame."

Criseyde, which that koude as muche good
As half a world, took hede of his preyere;
And syn it ron, and al was on a flod, 640
She thoughte, "As good chepe may I dwellen
  here,
And graunte it gladly with a frendes chere,

And have a thonk, as grucche and thanne abide;
For hom to gon, it may nought wel bitide."

"I wol," quod she, "myn uncle lief and deere;
Syn that yow list, it skile is to be so. 646
I am right glad with yow to dwellen here;
I seyde but a-game, I wolde go."
"Iwys, graunt mercy, nece," quod he tho,
"Were it a-game or no, soth for to telle, 650
Now am I glad, syn that yow list to dwelle."

Thus al is wel; but tho bigan aright
The newe joie and al the feste agayn.
But Pandarus, if goodly hadde he myght,
He wolde han hyed hire to bedde fayn, 655
And seyde, "Lord, this is an huge rayn!
This were a weder for to slepen inne;
And that I rede us soone to bygynne.

"And, nece, woot ye wher I wol yow leye,
For that we shul nat liggen far asonder, 660
And for ye neither shullen, dar I seye,
Heren noyse of reynes nor of thonder?
By God, right in my litel closet yonder.
And I wol in that outer hous allone
Be wardein of youre wommen everichone. 665

"And in this myddel chaumbre that ye se
Shul youre wommen slepen, wel and softe;
And there I seyde shal youreselven be;
And if ye liggen wel to-nyght, com ofte,
And careth nought what weder is alofte. 670
The wyn anon, and whan so that yow leste,
So go we slepe; I trowe it be the beste."

616. wende, *i.e.* go home. **617. wyrdes,** fates. **619. hierdes,** guardians, referring to *wyrdes* or *influences*. **620. bestes,** creatures. **wrie,** hidden. **622. But execut . . .,** all was carried out at the will of the gods, without her leave. **623. bleve,** remain. **624.** The astronomical conjunction here referred to (Jupiter and Saturn in the sign Cancer) is a rare one, occurring only once in roughly six hundred years. The conditions described were fulfilled in May, 1385. For its bearing on the date of the poem see the introduction. **626. avale,** descend. **636. a-game,** in jest. **638. koude . . . world,** was no fool. **640. ron,** rained (OE. *rān*, strong pret. of *rīnan*). **641. As good chepe,** as cheaply, hence easily. **642. frendes,** friendly; cf. l. 605, above. **643. grucche,** complain, grumble. **644. bitide,** happen, take place. **654. myght,** ability; if he had been able fittingly. **659. leye,** cause to lie. **663. closet,** a small room (adjoining the main hall). The supper was in the hall. Afterwards, in preparation for the night, we must suppose that a curtain (*travers*) was drawn across the hall dividing it into what Pandarus calls the *myddel chaumbre*, where Criseyde's women will sleep, and the *outer hous*, which he will occupy. For an excellent discussion of the interior arrangement of Pandarus's house, so far as it can be inferred, see H. M. Smyser, *Speculum*, XXXI. 297–315. **668. there I seyde,** where I mentioned, *i.e.* the "litel closet" of l. 663. **671. The wyn.** Wine was drunk before retiring in the Middle Ages, accompanied by spices and often cakes, dates, figs, raisins, etc. The little repast was called the *voidee* (cf. l. 674).

Ther nys no more, but hereafter soone,
The voidë dronke, and travers drawe anon,
Gan every wight that hadde nought to done 675
More in the place out of the chaumbre gon.
And evere mo so sterneliche it ron,
And blew therwith so wondirliche loude,
That wel neigh no man heren other koude.

Tho Pandarus, hire em, right as hym oughte, 680
With wommen swiche as were hire most aboute,
Ful glad unto hire beddes syde hire broughte,
And took his leve, and gan ful lowe loute,
And seyde, "Here at this closet dore withoute,
Right overthwart, youre wommen liggen alle,
That, whom yow list of hem, ye may here
    calle."   686

So whan that she was in the closet leyd,
And alle hire wommen forth by ordinaunce
Abedde weren, ther as I have seyd,
There was nomore to skippen nor to traunce,
But boden go to bedde, with meschaunce,   691
If any wight was steryng anywhere,
And lat hem slepen that abedde were.

But Pandarus, that wel koude eche a deel
The olde daunce, and every point therinne,   695
Whan that he sey that alle thyng was wel,
He thought he wolde upon his werk bigynne,
And gan the stuwe doore al softe unpynne,
And stille as stoon, withouten lenger lette,
By Troilus adown right he hym sette.   700

And, shortly to the point right for to gon,
Of al this werk he tolde hym word and ende,
And seyde, "Make the redy right anon,
For thow shalt into hevene blisse wende."
"Now, blisful Venus, thow me grace sende!"
Quod Troilus, "For nevere yet no nede   706
Hadde ich er now, ne halvendel the drede."

Quod Pandarus, "Ne drede the nevere a deel,
For it shal be right as thow wolt desire;
So thryve I, this nyght shal I make it weel,   710
Or casten al the gruwel in the fire."
"Yet, blisful Venus, this nyght thow me en-
    spire,"
Quod Troilus, "As wys as I the serve,
And evere bet and bet shal, til I sterve.

"And if ich hadde, O Venus ful of myrthe,   715
Aspectes badde of Mars or of Saturne,
Or thow combust or let were in my birthe,
Thy fader prey al thilke harm disturne
Of grace, and that I glad ayein may turne,
For love of hym thow lovedest in the shawe,   720
I meene Adoun, that with the boor was slawe.

"O Jove ek, for the love of faire Europe,
The which in forme of bole awey thow fette,
Now help! O Mars, thow with thi blody cope,
For love of Cipris, thow me nought ne lette! 725
O Phebus, thynk whan Dane hireselven shette
Under the bark, and laurer wax for drede,
Yet for hire love, O help now at this nede!

---

674. voidë, wine, with cakes, etc.; see note to l. 671. **travers,** curtain forming a screen. **677. so sterneliche it ron,** it rained so hard. **683. loute,** bow. **684. withoute,** *i.e.* outside the door. **685. overthwart,** opposite. **688. by ordinaunce,** as had been arranged. **690.** There was to be no more skipping and tramping around (by the servants), but they were bidden to go to bed, with a malediction upon any who stirred. **694. eche a deel The olde daunce,** all the tricks of the game (of love); cf. *CT*, A 476. **696. sey,** saw. **702. word and ende,** from beginning to end. See note to 2. 1495, above. **704. hevene,** gen. as adj., heavenly. **711. casten al the gruwel in the fire,** *i.e.* give it up as a bad job; apparently a proverbial expression not noted elsewhere. The expression "the fat is in the fire" has a different meaning. **713. wys,** certainly. **716. Aspectes badde.** Mars and Saturn in certain relative positions were baleful planets. **717. combust,** *lit.* burnt up, the position of a planet within 8.5° of the sun. The influence of Venus for good was destroyed under these circumstances. Her influence could also be hindered (*let*) by other astronomical conditions. **718. Thy fader,** Jupiter. **disturne,** turn aside. **719. Of grace,** through grace, graciously. **720. shawe,** wood. **721. Adoun,** Adonis. Ovid tells the story, *Metam.,* x. 708 ff. Venus loved Adonis so greatly that after he had been killed hunting a wild boar she persuaded Pluto, with the help of Jove, to let him return to earth for the spring and summer of each year. **722. Europe,** Europa. Jupiter, to obtain the maiden Europa, assumed the form of a bull and carried her off on his back. Cf. Ovid, *Metam.,* x. 833 ff. **724. blody cope.** The description is appropriate to the god of war. **725. Cipris,** Venus. **726. Dane,** Daphne. With the help of her father, the river-god, Daphne became a laurel to escape from the pursuit of Apollo. See Ovid, *Metam.,* I. 452 ff.

"Mercurie, for the love of Hierse eke,
For which Pallas was with Aglawros wroth, 730
Now help! and ek Diane, I the biseke,
That this viage be nought to the looth.
O fatal sustren, which, er any cloth
Me shapen was, my destine me sponne,
So helpeth to this werk that is bygonne!" 735

Quod Pandarus, "Thow wrecched mouses
    herte,
Artow agast so that she wol the bite?
Why, don this furred cloke upon thy sherte,
And folwe me, for I wol have the wite.
But bide, and lat me gon biforn a lite." 740
And with that word he gan undon a trappe,
And Troilus he brought in by the lappe.

The sterne wynd so loude gan to route
That no wight oother noise myghte heere;
And they that layen at the dore withoute, 745
Ful sikerly they slepten alle yfere;
And Pandarus, with a ful sobre cheere,
Goth to the dore anon, withouten lette,
There as they laye, and softely it shette.

And as he com ayeynward pryvely, 750
His nece awook, and axed, "Who goth there?"
"My dere nece," quod he, "it am I.
Ne wondreth nought, ne have of it no fere."
And ner he com, and seyde hire in hire ere,
"No word, for love of God, I yow biseche! 755
Lat no wight risen and heren of oure speche."

"What! which wey be ye comen, benedicite?"
Quod she, "and how thus unwist of hem alle?"

"Here at this secre trappe-dore," quod he. 759
Quod tho Criseyde, "Lat me som wight calle!"
"I! God forbede that it sholde falle,"
Quod Pandarus, "that ye swich folye wroughte!
They myghte demen thyng they nevere er
    thoughte.

"It is nought good a slepyng hound to wake,
Ne yeve a wight a cause to devyne. 765
Youre wommen slepen alle, I undertake,
So that, for hem, the hous men myghte myne,
And slepen wollen til the sonne shyne.
And whan my tale brought is to an ende,
Unwist, right as I com, so wol I wende. 770

"Now, nece myn, ye shul wel understonde,"
Quod he, "so as ye wommen demen alle,
That for to holde in love a man in honde,
And hym hire lief and deere herte calle,
And maken hym an howve above a calle, 775
I meene, as love another in this while,
She doth hireself a shame, and hym a gyle.

"Now, wherby that I telle yow al this:
Ye woot yourself, as wel as any wight,
How that youre love al fully graunted is 780
To Troilus, the worthieste knyght
Oon of this world, and therto trouthe yplight,
That, but it were on hym along, ye nolde
Hym nevere falsen while ye lyven sholde.

"Now stant it thus, that sith I fro yow wente,
This Troilus, right platly for to seyn, 786
Is thorough a goter, by a pryve wente,

729. Mercurie . . . Hierse. Pallas (Minerva), displeased by Aglauros, made her envious of her sister Herse. When Aglauros tried to thwart Mercury in his love for Herse, she was turned into stone by Mercury. See Ovid, Metam., II. 708 ff. 731. Diane. Troilus beseeches Diana, the chaste goddess, that his undertaking may not be displeasing to her. 732. viage, undertaking. 733. fatal sustren, the Fates, who spun the web of his destiny before any cloth was woven for him. 737. so that, that. 739. wite, blame. 740. bide, wait. 741. trappe, trapdoor. The stuwe where Troilus had been concealed was presumably above (or below) the room in which Criseyde was sleeping. Stairs (possibly in the wall) would have connected the two rooms. That Pandarus brought Troilus in "by the lappe" need be thought of as referring only to the moment of entrance. 765. devyne, conjecture. 773. holde in love a man in honde, lead a man on with false hopes. 775. maken hym an howve above a calle, engage in double dealing, such as loving another at the same time (l. 776). A calle (caul) is a close-fitting cap; a howve is a hood. 782. Oon, a variation in word order of oon the worthieste knyght. On the idiom see Language, §50. therto trouthe yplight, and your troth is plighted to him. 783. but it were on hym along, unless it were chargeable to him. 787. goter, gutter. In the legend of Hypermnestra (LGW 2703–10), which is not included in the present volume, Lino is offered escape from an upper room by means of a gutter. wente, passage.

Into my chaumbre come in al this reyn,
Unwist of every manere wight, certeyn,
Save of myself, as wisly have I joye,		790
And by that feith I shal Priam of Troie.

"And he is come in swich peyne and distresse
That, but he be al fully wood by this,
He sodeynly mot falle into wodnesse,
But if God helpe; and cause whi this is,		795
He seith hym told is of a frend of his,
How that ye sholden love oon hatte Horaste;
For sorwe of which this nyght shal ben his
    laste."

Criseyde, which that al this wonder herde,
Gan sodeynly aboute hire herte colde,		800
And with a sik she sorwfully answerde,
"Allas! I wende, whoso tales tolde,
My deere herte wolde me nought holde
So lightly fals! Allas! conceytes wronge,
What harm they don, for now lyve I to
    longe!

"Horaste! allas, and falsen Troilus?		806
I knowe hym nought, God helpe me so," quod
    she.
"Allas, what wikked spirit tolde hym thus?
Now certes, em, tomorwe, and I hym se,
I shal therof as ful excusen me,		810
As evere dide womman, if hym like."
And with that word she gan ful soore sike.

"O God!" quod she, "so worldly selynesse,
Which clerkes callen fals felicitee,
Imedled is with many a bitternesse!		815
Ful angwissous than is, God woot," quod she,
"Condicioun of veyn prosperitee;
For either joies comen nought yfeere,
Or elles no wight hath hem alwey here.

"O brotel wele of mannes joie unstable!		820
With what wight so thow be, or how thow
    pleye,
Either he woot that thow, joie, art muable,
Or woot it nought; it mot ben oon of tweye.
Now if he woot it nought, how may he seye
That he hath verray joie and selynesse,		825
That is of ignoraunce ay in derknesse?

"Now if he woot that joie is transitorie,
As every joie of worldly thyng mot flee,
Than every tyme he that hath in memorie,
The drede of lesyng maketh hym that he		830
May in no perfit selynesse be;
And if to lese his joie he sette a myte,
Than semeth it that joie is worth ful lite.

"Wherfore I wol diffyne in this matere,
That trewely, for aught I kan espie,		835
Ther is no verray weele in this world heere.
But O thow wikked serpent, jalousie,
Thow mysbyleved and envyous folie,
Why hastow Troilus mad to me untriste,
That nevere yet agylt hym, that I wiste?"		840

Quod Pandarus, "Thus fallen is this cas—"
"Why, uncle myn," quod she, "who tolde hym
    this?
Why doth my deere herte thus, allas?"
"Ye woot, ye, nece myn," quod he, "what is.
I hope al shal be wel that is amys;		845
For ye may quenche al this, if that yow leste.
And doth right so, for I holde it the beste."

"So shal I do to-morwe, ywys," quod she,
And God toforn, so that it shal suffise."
"To-morwe? allas, that were a fair!" quod he.
"Nay, nay, it may nat stonden in this wise.		851
For, nece myn, thus writen clerkes wise,

---

791. shal, owe to; cf. *NED, s.v.*, I. 1b. **793. wood**, mad. **797. sholden love**, are said to love. **Horaste**, Orestes. Chaucer adopts a well-known name for Pandarus' invented story. **800. colde**, grow cold. **813**. Criseyde's philosophical speculation is based on Boethius, II, pr. 4. **selynesse**, happiness. **820. brotel**, brittle. **822. muable**, changeable. **834. diffyne**, conclude, state. **838. mysbyleved**, misbelieving. **839. untriste**, distrustful (toward). **840. agylt**, wronged. **841. Thus fallen in this cas**, that is how matters stand. **850. that were a fair**, that would be a fine thing to do.

That peril is with drecchyng in ydrawe;
Nay, swiche abodes ben nought worth an hawe.

"Nece, alle thyng hath tyme, I dar avowe,   855
For whan a chaumbre afire is, or an halle,
Wel more nede is, it sodeynly rescowe
Than to dispute and axe amonges alle
How is this candele in the straw i-falle.
A, *benedicite!* for al among that fare   860
The harm is don, and farewel feldefare!

"And nece myn—ne take it naught agrief—
If that ye suffre hym al nyght in this wo,
God help me so, ye hadde hym nevere lief,
That dar I seyn, now ther is but we two.   865
But wel I woot that ye wol nat do so;
Ye ben to wys to doon so gret folie,
To putte his lif al nyght in jupertie."

"Hadde I hym nevere lief? by God, I weene
Ye hadde nevere thyng so lief!" quod she.   870
"Now by my thrift," quod he, "that shal be
   seene!
For syn ye make this ensaumple of me,
If ich al nyght wolde hym in sorwe se,
For al the tresour in the town of Troie,
I bidde God I nevere mote have joie.   875

"Now loke thanne, if ye that ben his love
Shul putte his lif al night in jupertie
For thyng of nought, now, by that God above,
Naught oonly this delay comth of folie,
But of malice, if that I shal naught lie.   880
What! platly, and ye suffre hym in destresse,
Ye neyther bounte don ne gentilesse."

Quod tho Criseyde, "Wol ye don o thyng,
And ye therwith shal stynte al his disese?

Have heere, and bereth hym this blewe
   ryng,   885
For ther is nothyng myghte hym bettre plese,
Save I myself, ne more hys herte apese;
And sey my deere herte, that his sorwe
Is causeles, that shal be sene to-morwe."

"A ryng?" quod he, "ye, haselwodes shaken!
Ye, nece myn, that ryng moste han a stoon   891
That myhte dede men alyve maken;
And swich a ryng trowe I that ye have non.
Discrecioun out of youre hed is gon;
That fele I now," quod he, "and that is routhe.
O tyme ilost, wel maistow corsen slouthe!   896

"Woot ye not wel that noble and heigh corage
Ne sorweth nought, ne stynteth ek, for lite?
But if a fool were in a jalous rage,
I nolde setten at his sorwe a myte,   900
But feffe hym with a fewe wordes white
Anothir day, whan that I myghte hym fynde;
But this thyng stant al in another kynde.

"This is so gentil and so tendre of herte,
That with his deth he wol his sorwes wreke;   905
For trusteth wel, how sore that hym smerte,
He wol to yow no jalous wordes speke.
And forthi, nece, er that his herte breke,
So speke youreself to hym of this matere;
For with o word ye may his herte stere.   910

"Now have I told what peril he is inne,
And his comynge unwist is to every wight;
Ne, parde, harm may ther be non, ne synne;
I wol myself be with yow al this nyght.
Ye knowe ek how it is youre owen knyght,   915
And that bi right ye moste upon hym triste,
And I al prest to fecche hym whan yow liste."

853. peril . . . in ydrawe, danger is introduced by delay. 854. abodes, waiting, delays. 860. among that fare, in the course of, during the time of that procedure. 861. farewel feldefare, a proverbial expression signifying "the bird has flown," "it's too late." 862. agrief, amiss. 871. by my thrift. See note to 2. 1483. 872. ensaumple, example for comparison. 890. haselwodes shaken, a form of asseveration, found only here. At 5. 505 Pandarus uses haselwode alone as an ejaculation. 891. a stoon. Various stones were supposed to have magical properties and were described in medieval lapidaries. See P. Studer and Joan Evans, Anglo-Norman Lapidaries (Paris, 1924). 894. Discrecioun, good sense. 896. corsen, curse. 897-8. that noble . . . lite, that a noble heart neither sorrows nor ceases to sorrow because of little things. 901. feffe, grant, bestow upon. wordes white, fair or specious words. 904. This, this man. 910. stere, steer, govern. See note to 1. 228.

This accident so pitous was to here,
And ek so like a sooth, at prime face, *on first appearance*
And Troilus hire knyght to hir so deere, 920
His prive comyng, and the siker place,
That, though that she did hym as thanne a
  grace,
Considered alle thynges as they stoode,
No wonder is, syn she did al for goode.

Criseyde answerde, "As wisly God at reste 925
My soule brynge, as me is for hym wo! *I am sorry for him*
And, em, iwis, fayn wolde I don the beste, *uncle truly glady*
If that ich hadde grace to do so.
But whether that ye dwelle or for hym go,
I am, til God me bettre mynde sende, 930
At dulcarnoun, right at my wittes ende."
Completely perplexed

Quod Pandarus, "Yee, nece, wol ye here?
Dulcarnoun called is 'flemyng of wrecches. *banishment of the miserable*
It semeth hard, for wrecches wol nought lere,
For verray slouthe or other wilfull tecches: *faults* 935
This seyd by hem that ben nought worth two *this is*
  fecches. *beans*
But ye ben wis, and that we han on honde
Nis neither hard, ne skilful to withstonde."

"Than, em," quod she, "doth herof as yow list. *undo*
But er he come, I wil up first arise, 940
And, for the love of God, syn al my trist
Is on yow two, and ye ben bothe wise,
So werketh now in so discret a wise
That I honour may have, and he plesaunce;
For I am here al in youre governaunce." 945

"That is wel seyd," quod he, "my nece deere. *there be*
Ther good thrift on that wise gentil herte!
But liggeth stille, and taketh hym right here;
lie still

It nedeth nought no ferther for hym sterte. *go/move*
And ech of yow ese otheres sorwes smerte, 950
For love of God; and Venus, I the herye;
For soone, hope I, we shul ben alle merye."

This Troilus ful soone on knees hym sette *Troilus appears kneels by the bed.*
Ful sobrely, right be hyre beddes hed,
And in his beste wyse his lady grette. 955
But, Lord, so she wex sodeynliche red! *she blushes*
Ne though men sholde smyten of hire hed,
She kouthe nought a word aright out-brynge
So sodeynly, for his sodeyn comynge.

But Pandarus, that so wel koude feele 960
In every thyng, to pleye anon bigan,
And seyde, "Nece, se how this lord kan knele!
Now, for youre trouthe, se this gentil man!"
And with that word he for a quysshen ran, 964 *Brings him a cushion to make him comfortable.*
And seyde, "Kneleth now, while that yow
  leste,
There God youre hertes brynge soone at reste!"

Kan I naught seyn, for she bad hym nought rise,
If sorwe it putte out of hire remembraunce,
Or elles that she took it in the wise
Of dewete, as for his observaunce; 970
But wel fynde I she dede hym this pleasaunce,
That she hym kiste, although she siked sore,
And bad hym sitte adown withouten more.
she tells him to sit down.

Quod Pandarus, "Now wol ye wel bigynne.
Now doth hym sitte, goode nece deere, 975 *on the bed*
Upon youre beddes syde al ther withinne, *inside the curtains*
That ech of yow the bet may other heere."
And with that word he drow hym to the feere, *fire; fireplace*
And took a light, and fond his contenaunce *assumed an appearance*
As for to looke upon an old romaunce. 980
Pandarus gets a book + goes to

---

919. at prime face, *prima facie*, on first appearance. **926. as me is for hym wo!** I am sorry for him! **931. At dulcar-noun,** completely perplexed. As Skeat pointed out the expression comes from an Arabic epithet meaning two-horned, applied to Alexander the Great because of his supposed descent from Jupiter Ammon, represented as having horns. It was also the name of the 47th proposition of Euclid. **933. flemyng of wrecches,** a translation of *fuga miserorum*, corresponding to *Eleufuga*, a name for Euclid's 5th proposition (also a difficult one). The phrase means "banishment of the miserable." **935. tecches,** faults. **936. This,** this is. **fecches,** vetches, beans. **947. Ther.** See note to 2. 588 and Language, § 73. **949. sterte,** go, move. **954. sobrely,** humbly. **960. feele,** understand. **970. observaunce,** attention, respect decreed by custom. **976. withinne,** inside the curtains. **978. feere,** (Kentish form), fire, fireplace; see Language, § 8. **979. fond his countenaunce,** assumed an appearance.

Criseyde, that was Troilus lady right,
And cler stood on a ground of sikernesse,
Al thoughte she hire servant and hire knyght
Ne sholde of right non untrouthe in hire gesse,
Yet natheles, considered his distresse,   985
And that love is in cause of swich folie,
Thus to hym spak she of his jalousie:

"Lo, herte myn, as wolde the excellence
Of love, ayeins the which that no man may
Ne oughte ek goodly make resistence;   990
And ek bycause I felte wel and say
Youre grete trouthe and servise every day,
And that youre herte al myn was, soth to
     seyne,—
This drof me for to rewe upon youre peyne.

"And youre goodnesse have I founde alwey yit,
Of which, my deere herte and al my knyght, 996
I thonke it yow, as fer as I have wit,
Al kan I nought as muche as it were right;
And I, emforth my connyng and my might,
Have and ay shal, how sore that me smerte, 1000
Ben to yow trewe and hool with al myn herte;

"And dredeles, that shal be founde at preve.
But, herte myn, what al this is to seyne
Shal wel be told, so that ye nought yow greve,
Though I to yow right on youreself compleyne.
For therwith mene I fynaly the peyne   1006
That halt youre herte and myn in hevynesse
Fully to slen, and every wrong redresse.

"My goode myn, noot I for-why ne how
That jalousie, allas! that wikked wyvere,   1010
Thus causeles is cropen into yow,
The harm of which I wolde fayn delyvere.
Allas, that he, al hool, or of hym slyvere,

Shuld han his refut in so digne a place,
Ther Jove hym soone out of youre herte arace!

"But O, thow Jove, O auctour of nature,   1016
Is this an honour to thi deyte,
That folk ungiltif suffren hire injure,
And who that giltif is, al quyt goth he?
O, were it leful for to pleyn on the,   1020
That undeserved suffrest jalousie,
Of that I wolde upon the pleyne and crie!

"Ek al my wo is this, that folk now usen
To seyn right thus, 'Ye, jalousie is love!'
And wolde a busshel venym al excusen,   1025
For that o greyn of love is on it shove.
But that woot heighe God that sit above,
If it be likkere love, or hate, or grame;
And after that, it oughte bere his name.

"But certeyn is, som manere jalousie   1030
Is excusable more than som, iwys;
As whan cause is, and som swich fantasie
With piete so wel repressed is
That it unnethe doth or seyth amys,
But goodly drynketh up al his distresse;   1035
And that excuse I, for the gentilesse.

"And som so ful of furie is and despit
That it sourmounteth his repressioun.
But, herte myn, ye be nat in that plit,
That thonke I God; for which youre passioun
I wol nought calle it but illusioun,   1041
Of habundaunce of love and besy cure,
That doth youre herte this disese endure.

"Of which I am right sory, but nought wroth;
But, for my devoir and youre hertes reste,   1045
Wherso yow list, by ordal or by oth,

983. Al, although. **986. in cause of,** responsible for, to blame for. **988. wolde,** would suggest. **991. say,** saw. **999. emforth,** to the extent of. **1007. halt,** holds. **1009. My goode myn,** my very own; cf. *O goodly myn,* 3. 1473, below. **noot I,** I do not know. **1010. wyvere,** viper, snake. **1011. cropen,** crept. **1013. slyvere,** portion (sliver). **1014. refut,** refuge. **1015. arace,** root out. **1017. deyte,** deity. **1018. injure,** injury. **1020. leful,** lawful, permissible. **1026. o,** one. **1028. likkere,** more like. **grame,** sorrow, anger. **1032-5. and som swich . . .,** and some imagining of this kind is so well repressed through a sense of duty that it scarcely does or says anything amiss, but patiently drinks up its (cup of) distress. **1039. herte,** sweetheart. **1040. passioun,** suffering. **1041. nought . . . but,** only. **1042. besy cure,** diligence, zeal.

By sort, or in what wise so yow leste,
For love of God, lat preve it for the beste;
And if that I be giltif, do me deye!
Allas, what myght I more don or seye?" 1050

With that a fewe brighte teris newe
Owt of hire eighen fille, and thus she seyde,
"Now God, thow woost, in thought ne dede untrewe
To Troilus was nevere yet Criseyde." 1054
With that here heed down in the bed she leyde,
And with the sheete it wreigh, and sighte soore,
And held hire pees; nought o word spak she more.

But now help God to quenchen al this sorwe!
So hope I that he shal, for he best may.
For I have seyn, of a ful misty morwe 1060
Folowen ful ofte a myrie someris day;
And after wynter foloweth grene May.
Men sen alday, and reden ek in stories,
That after sharpe shoures ben victories.

This Troilus, whan he hire wordes herde, 1065
Have ye no care, hym liste nought to slepe;
For it thought hym no strokes of a yerde
To heere or seen Criseyde, his lady, wepe;
But wel he felt about his herte crepe,
For everi tere which that Criseyde asterte, 1070
The crampe of deth, to streyne hym by the herte.

And in his mynde he gan the tyme acorse
That he com there, and that he was born;
For now is wikke torned into worse,
And al that labour he hath don byforn, 1075
He wende it lost; he thoughte he nas but lorn.
"O Pandarus," thoughte he, "allas, thi wile
Serveth of nought, so weylaway, the while!"

And therwithal he heng adown the heed,
And fil on knees, and sorwfully he sighte. 1080
What myghte he seyn? He felte he nas but deed,
For wroth was she that sholde his sorwes lighte.
But natheles, whan that he speken myghte,
Than seyde he thus, "God woot that of this game, 1084
Whan al is wist, than am I nought to blame."

Therwith the sorwe so his herte shette,
That from his eyen fil ther nought a tere,
And every spirit his vigour in-knette,
So they astoned or oppressed were.
The felyng of his sorwe, or of his fere, 1090
Or of aught elles, fled was out of towne;
And down he fel al sodeynly aswowne.

This was no litel sorwe for to se;
But al was hust, and Pandare up as faste,—
"O nece, pes, or we be lost!" quod he, 1095
"Beth naught agast!" but certeyn, at the laste,
For this or that, he into bed hym caste,
And seyde, "O thef, is this a mannes herte?"
And of he rente al to his bare sherte;

And seyde, "Nece, but ye helpe us now, 1100
Allas, youre owen Troilus is lorn!"
"Iwis, so wolde I, and I wiste how,
Ful fayn," quod she; "Allas, that I was born!"
"Yee, nece, wol ye pullen out the thorn
That stiketh in his herte," quod Pandare, 1105
"Sey 'al foryeve,' and stynt is al this fare!"

"Ye, that to me," quod she, "ful levere were
Than al the good the sonne aboute gooth."
And therwithal she swor hym in his ere,
"Iwys, my deere herte, I am nought wroth, 1110
Have here my trouthe!" and many an other oth;

1047. **sort**, divination. 1048. **lat preve it,** let it be proved. 1056. **wreigh,** covered. 1064. **shoures,** battles. 1070. **asterte,** escaped from. 1088. **every spirit,** *i.e.* the vital spirit (in the heart), the natural spirit (in the liver), and the animal spirit (in the brain). These controlled life. **his vigour in-knette,** contracted its vigor. 1094. **hust,** silent. 1099. **of . . . rente,** tore away. 1106. **stynt is al this fare,** all this business will have stopped. 1108. **al the good,** *i.e.* the whole world (all the property that the sun goes around).

"Now speke to me, for it am I, Criseyde!"
But al for nought; yit myght he nought
   abreyde.

Therwith his pous and paumes of his hondes
They gan to frote, and wete his temples
   tweyne;   1115
And to deliveren hym fro bittre bondes,
She ofte hym kiste; and shortly for to seyne,
Hym to revoken she did al hire peyne.
And at the laste, he gan his breth to drawe,
And of his swough sone after that adawe,   1120

And gan bet mynde and reson to hym take,
But wonder soore he was abayst, iwis.
And with a sik, whan he gan bet awake,
He seyde, "O mercy, God, what thyng is
   this?"
"Why do ye with youreselven thus amys?" 1125
Quod tho Criseyde; "Is this a mannes game?
What, Troilus, wol ye do thus for shame?"

And therwithal hire arm over hym she leyde,
And al foryaf, and ofte tyme hym keste.
He thonked hire, and to hire spak, and seyde
As fil to purpos for his hertes reste;   1131
And she to that answerde hym as hire leste,
And with hire goodly wordes hym disporte
She gan, and ofte his sorwes to comforte.

Quod Pandarus, "For aught I kan aspien,   1135
This light, nor I, ne serven here of nought.
Light is nought good for sike folkes yën!
But, for the love of God, syn ye ben brought
In thus good plit, lat now no hevy thought
Ben hangyng in the hertes of yow tweye"—
And bar the candele to the chymeneye.   1141

Soone after this, though it no nede were,
Whan she swiche othes as hire leste devyse

Hadde of hym take, hire thoughte tho no
   fere,
Ne cause ek non to bidde hym thennes rise. 1145
Yet lasse thyng than othes may suffise
In many a cas; for every wyght, I gesse,
That loveth wel, meneth but gentilesse.

But in effect she wolde wite anon
Of what man, and ek wheer, and also why 1150
He jalous was, syn ther was cause non;
And ek the sygne that he took it by,
She badde hym that to telle hire bisily;
Or elles, certeyn, she bar hym on honde
That this was don of malice, hire to fonde. 1155

Withouten more, shortly for to seyne,
He most obeye unto his lady heste;
And for the lasse harm, he moste feyne.
He seyde hire, whan she was at swiche a feste,
She myght on hym han loked at the leste,— 1160
Noot I nought what, al deere ynough a rysshe,
As he that nedes most a cause fisshe.

And she answerde, "Swete, al were it so,
What harm was that, syn I non yvel mene?
For, by that God that bought us bothe two, 1165
In alle thyng is myn entente cleene.
Swiche argumentes ne ben naught worth a
   beene.
Wol ye the childissh jalous contrefete?
Now were it worthi that ye were ybete."

Tho Troilus gan sorwfully to sike;   1170
Lest she be wroth, hym thoughte his herte
   deyde;
And seyde, "Allas, upon my sorwes sike
Have mercy, swete herte myn, Criseyde!
And if that in tho wordes that I seyde
Be any wrong, I wol no more trespace.   1175
Doth what yow list, I am al in youre grace."

1113. abreyde, come to. **1114. pous,** pulse. **1118. revoken,** restore to consciousness. **1120. adawe,** awaken. **1141. chymeneye,** fireplace. **1154. bar hym on honde,** asserted, accused him. **1155. fonde,** test. **1161. al deere ynough a rysshe,** although worthless (worth no more than a rush). **1163. al,** even if. **1170. sike,** sigh.

And she answerde, "Of gilt misericorde!
That is to seyn, that I foryeve al this.
And evere more on this nyght yow recorde,
And beth wel war ye do namore amys," 1180
"Nay, dere herte myn," quod he, "iwys!"
"And now," quod she, "that I have don yow smerte,
Foryeve it me, myn owene swete herte."

This Troilus, with blisse of that supprised,
Putte al in Goddes hand, as he that mente 1185
Nothyng but wel; and sodeynly avysed,
He hire in armes faste to hym hente.
And Pandarus, with a ful good entente,
Leyde hym to slepe, and seyde, "If ye be wise,
Swouneth nought now, lest more folk arise!"

What myghte or may the sely larke seye, 1191
Whan that the sperhauk hath it in his foot?
I kan namore, but of thise ilke tweye,—
To whom this tale sucre be or soot,—
Though that I tarie a yer, somtyme I moot, 1195
After myn auctour, tellen hire gladnesse,
As wel as I have told hire hevynesse.

Criseyde, which that felte hire thus itake,
As writen clerkes in hire bokes olde,
Right as an aspes leef she gan to quake, 1200
Whan she hym felte hire in his armes folde.
But Troilus, al hool of cares colde,
Gan thanken tho the blisful goddes sevene.
Thus sondry peynes bryngen folk to hevene.

This Troilus in armes gan hire streyne, 1205
And seyde, "O swete, as evere mot I gon,
Now be ye kaught, now is ther but we tweyne!
Now yeldeth yow, for other bote is non!"
To that Criseyde answerde thus anon, 1209

"Ne hadde I er now, my swete herte deere,
Ben yold, ywis, I were now nought heere!"
O, sooth is seyd, that heled for to be
As of a fevre, or other gret siknesse,
Men moste drynke, as men may ofte se,
Ful bittre drynke; and for to han gladnesse, 1215
Men drynken ofte peyne and gret distresse;
I mene it here, as for this aventure,
That thorugh a peyne hath founden al his cure.

And now swetnesse semeth more swete,
That bitternesse assaied was byforn; 1220
For out of wo in blisse now they flete;
Non swich they felten syn that they were born.
Now is this bet than bothe two be lorn.
For love of God, take every womman heede
To werken thus, if it comth to the neede. 1225

Criseyde, al quyt from every drede and tene,
As she that juste cause hadde hym to triste,
Made hym swich feste, it joye was to seene,
Whan she his trouthe and clene entente wiste;
And as aboute a tree, with many a twiste, 1230
Bytrent and writh the swote wodebynde,
Gan eche of hem in armes other wynde.

And as the newe abaysed nyghtyngale,
That stynteth first whan she bygynneth to synge,
Whan that she hereth any herde tale, 1235
Or in the hegges any wyght stirynge,
And after siker doth hire vois out rynge,
Right so Criseyde, whan hire drede stente,
Opned hire herte, and tolde hym hire entente.

And right as he that seth his deth yshapen, 1240
And dyen mot, in ought that he may gesse,
And sodeynly rescous doth hym escapen,

1179. evere more on this nyght yow recorde, always remember this night. 1184. supprised, seized, overtaken. 1186. sodeynly avysed, by a sudden resolution. 1187. hente, caught. 1189. Leyde hym to slepe, i.e. went to bed. 1194. sucre . . . or soot, sugar or soot (in the Middle Ages often referred to as bitter). 1195. moot, must. 1200. aspes leef, leaf of the aspen, aspen leaf. 1203. goddes sevene, the planets. 1204. sondry peynes . . ., an aphorism, as we say "every cloud has a silver lining." 1210. Ne hadde I er now . . . Ben yold . . . The importance of Criseyde's statement should be noted. 1218. his, its. 1224. take every womman heede, let every woman take heed. 1231. Bytrent and writh, encircles and twines around. 1233. abaysed, startled. 1235. any herde tale, any shepherd speak. 1241. in ought that he may gesse, so far as he can tell. 1242. rescous, OF. rescous, help, rescue. doth, causes, enables.

[handwritten top margin: wel–well / wol, wole > will / wolde – 146 / ne ded / Pleyne – complain / lament / pleye(n) play / be merry / wood – mad / rouThe – pity / wo, woo – war, sorrow / un happy]

And from his deth is brought in sykernesse,
For al this world, in swych present gladnesse
Was Troilus, and hath his lady swete.   1245
With worse hap God lat us nevere mete!

[handwritten: Enjoys her body]

Hire armes smale, hire streghte bak and softe,
Hire sydes longe, flesshly, smothe, and white
He gan to stroke, and good thrift bad ful ofte
Hire snowisshe throte, hire brestes rounde and
      lite.   1250
Thus in this hevene he gan hym to delite,
And therwithal a thousand tyme hire kiste,
That what to don, for joie unnethe he wiste.

[handwritten: Scarcely Knew]

Than seyde he thus, "O Love, O Charite!
Thi moder ek, Citherea the swete,   1255
After thiself next heried be she,
Venus mene I, the wel-willy planete!
And next that, Imeneus, I the grete;
For nevere man was to yow goddes holde
As I, which ye han brought fro cares colde.   1260

"Benigne Love, thow holy bond of thynges,
Whoso wol grace, and list the nought honouren,
Lo, his desir wol fle withouten wynges.
For noldestow of bownte hem socouren
That serven best and most alwey labouren,   1265
Yet were al lost, that dar I wel seyn certes,
But if thi grace passed oure desertes.

"And for thow me, that leest koude disserve
Of hem that noumbred ben unto thi grace,
Hast holpen, ther I likly was to sterve,   1270
And me bistowed in so heigh a place
That thilke boundes may no blisse pace,
I kan namore; but laude and reverence
Be to thy bounte and thyn excellence!"

And therwithal Criseyde anon he kiste,   1275
Of which certein she felte no disese.

And thus seyde he, "Now wolde God I wiste,
Myn herte swete, how I yow myght plese!
What man," quod he, "was evere thus at ese
As I, on which the faireste and the beste   1280
That evere I say, deyneth hire herte reste?

"Here may men seen that mercy passeth right;
Th'experience of that is felt in me,
That am unworthi to so swete a wight.
But herte myn, of youre benignite,   1285
So thynketh, though that I unworthi be,
Yet mot I nede amenden in som wyse,
Right thorugh the vertu of youre heigh
      servyse.

"And for the love of God, my lady deere,
Syn God hath wrought me for I shall yow
      serve,—   1290
As thus I mene, he wol ye be my steere,
To do me lyve, if that yow liste, or sterve,—
So techeth me how that I may disserve
Youre thonk, so that I thorugh myn ignoraunce,
Ne do no thing that yow be displesaunce.   1295

"For certes, fresshe wommanliche wif,
This dar I seye, that trouth and diligence,
That shal ye fynden in me al my lif;
N'y wol nat, certein, breken youre defence;
And if I do, present or in absence,   1300
For love of God, lat sle me with the dede,
If that it like unto youre wommanhede."

"Iwys," quod she, "myn owen hertes list,
My ground of ese, and al myn herte deere,
Gramercy, for on that is al my trist!   1305
But lat us falle awey fro this matere,
For it suffiseth, this that seyd is heere,
And at o word, withouten repentaunce,
Welcome, my knyght, my pees, my suffi-
      saunce!"

1249. **thrift,** fortune. He invoked many a blessing on her snowy throat, etc. 1255. **Citherea,** Venus. 1257. **wel-willy,** beneficent. 1258. **Imeneus,** Hymen, god of marriage. 1262. **wol,** wishes. 1263. **fle,** fly. 1283. **experience,** proof. 1287. **mot,** must. 1291. **steere,** pilot. 1296. **wif,** woman; cf. 3. 106, above. 1299. **breken youre defence,** do what you forbid. 1301. **dede,** death, pestilence; may I die of the plague. 1303. **list,** pleasure. 1308. **repentaunce,** regret, sorrow for what is past.

[handwritten notes in margins: A carnal heaven on earth: not trivial; To a certain extent they are particular; it is universal love; the holy bond of things. Chance views this whole as a fuller one, wherein Bk 4, 5; Prayer to Charity; nothing to do w/ Bidily Love; To Venus (Redemption of mankind); mercy passeth right; returns him to have it sig.; Star / Pilot; fresh / vigorous — pattern of womanhood; wife; do what you forbid; slay; Indeed; ground of ese / foundation; please; ease; trust; Mother making / source of satisfaction; peace; Let's cut it short. Pandarus same; She is more del. note]

Of hire delit, or joies oon the leeste,　　1310
Were impossible to my wit to seye;
But juggeth ye that han ben at the feste
Of swich gladnesse, if that hem liste pleye!
I kan namore, but thus thise ilke tweye,
That nyght, bitwixen drede and sikernesse,　　1315
Felten in love the grete worthynesse.

O blisful nyght, of hem so longe isought,
How blithe unto hem bothe two thow
　　weere!
Why nad I swich oon with my soule ybought,
Ye, or the leeste joie that was theere?　　1320
Awey, thow foule daunger and thow feere,
And lat hem in this hevene blisse dwelle,
That is so heigh that al ne kan I telle!

But soth is, though I kan nat tellen al,
As kan myn auctour, of his excellence,　　1325
Yet have I seyd, and God toforn, and shal
In every thyng the grete of his sentence;
And if that ich, at Loves reverence,
Have any word in eched for the beste,
Doth therwithal right as youreselven leste.　　1330

For myne wordes, heere and every part,
I speke hem alle under correccioun
Of yow that felyng han in loves art,
And putte it al in youre discrecioun
T' encresse or maken dymynucioun　　1335
Of my langage, and that I yow biseche.
But now to purpos of my rather speche.

Thise ilke two, that ben in armes laft,
So loth to hem asonder gon it were,
That ech from other wenden ben biraft,　　1340
Or elles, lo, this was hir mooste feere,
That al this thyng but nyce dremes were;

For which ful ofte ech of hem seyde, "O swete,
Clippe ich yow thus, or elles I it meete?"

And Lord! so he gan goodly on hire se,　　1345
That nevere his look ne bleynte from hire face,
And seyde, "O deere herte, may it be
That it be soth, that ye ben in this place?"
"Yee, herte myn, God thank I of his grace,"
Quod tho Criseyde, and therwithal hym kiste,
That where his spirit was, for joie he nyste.　　1351

This Troilus ful ofte hire eyen two
Gan for to kisse, and seyde, "O eyen clere,
It weren ye that wroughte me swich wo,
Ye humble nettes of my lady deere!　　1355
Though ther be mercy writen in youre cheere,
God woot, the text ful hard is, soth, to fynde!
How koude ye withouten bond me bynde?"

Therwith he gan hire faste in armes take,
And wel an hondred tymes gan he syke,　　1360
Naught swiche sorwfull sikes as men make
For wo, or elles when that folk ben sike,
But esy sykes, swiche as ben to like,
That shewed his affeccioun withinne;
Of swiche sikes koude he nought bilynne.　　1365

Soone after this they spake of sondry thynges,
As fel to purpos of this aventure,
And pleyinge entrechaungeden hire rynges,
Of whiche I kan nought tellen no scripture;
But wel I woot, a broche, gold and asure,　　1370
In which a ruby set was lik an herte,
Criseyde hym yaf, and stak it on his sherte.

Lord, trowe ye a coveytous or a wrecche,
That blameth love, and halt of it despit,
That of tho pens that he kan mokre and crecche

1310. joies oon the leeste, the least of their joys. **1315. drede and sikernesse,** doubt and security. **1321. thow foule daunger.** In the *Roman de la Rose* Daunger represents the power to hinder the lover. **1329. in eched,** added. **1334. discrecioun,** judgment. **1337. rather,** earlier. **1344. Clippe,** embrace. **I it meete?** do I dream it? **1346. bleynte,** turned away. **1355. humble,** modest. **nettes,** *i.e.* in which the lover is caught. **1363. to like,** to be liked. **1365. bilynne,** cease. **1369. scripture,** posy, inscription on a ring. The inscriptions were engraved on the outside of the shanks of rings. There are fourteenth-century specimens in the South Kensington Museum. See Wm. Jones, *Finger-Ring Lore*, p. 397, and especially Joan Evans, *English Posies and Posy Rings* (London, 1931). **1370. asure,** usually taken to be lapis lazuli, but here possibly blue enamel. **1375. mokre,** hoard. **crecche,** snatch, grab (see *NED cratch*). The reading is found in only two MSS, and these belong to the α (unrevised) group. Variant readings include *theche*, *tecche*, and *kecche*, which involve other difficulties.

Was evere yit yyeven hym swich delit 1376
As is in love, in o poynt, in som plit?
Nay, douteles, for also God me save,
So perfit joie may no nygard have.

They wol seyn "yis," but Lord! so that they lye,
Tho besy wrecches, ful of wo and drede! 1381
Thei callen love a woodnesse or folie,
But it shall falle hem as I shal yow rede;
They shal forgon the white and ek the rede,
And lyve in wo, ther God yeve hem meschaunce,
And every lovere in his trouthe avaunce! 1386

As wolde God tho wrecches that dispise
Servise of love hadde erys also longe
As hadde Mida, ful of coveytise,
And therto dronken hadde as hoot and stronge
As Crassus dide for his affectis wronge, 1391
To techen hem that coveytise is vice,
And love is vertu, though men holde it nyce.

Thise ilke two, of whom that I yow seye,
Whan that hire hertes wel assured were, 1395
Tho gonne they to speken and to pleye,
And ek rehercen how, and whan, and where
Thei knewe hem first, and every wo and feere
That passed was; but al swich hevynesse,
I thank it God, was torned to gladnesse. 1400

And evere mo, when that hem fel to speke
Of any wo of swich a tyme agoon,
With kissyng al that tale sholde breke,
And fallen in a newe joye anoon;
And diden al hire myght, syn they were oon,
For to recoveren blisse and ben at eise, 1406
And passed wo with joie contrepeise.

Resoun wol nought that I speke of slep,
For it acordeth nought to my matere.
God woot, they took of that ful litel kep! 1410
But lest this nyght, that was to hem so deere,
Ne sholde in veyn escape in no manere,
It was byset in joie and bisynesse
Of al that souneth into gentilesse.

But whan the cok, comune astrologer, 1415
Gan on his brest to bete and after crowe,
And Lucyfer, the dayes messager,
Gan for to rise, and out hire bemes throwe,
And estward roos, to hym that koude it knowe,
Fortuna Major, that anoon Criseyde, 1420
With herte soor, to Troilus thus seyde:

"Myn hertes lif, my trist, and my plesaunce,
That I was born, allas, what me is wo,
That day of us moot make disseveraunce!
For tyme it is to ryse and hennes go, 1425
Or ellis I am lost for evere mo!
O nyght, allas! why nyltow over us hove,
As longe as whan Almena lay by Jove?

"O blake nyght, as folk in bokes rede,
That shapen art by God this world to hide 1430
At certeyn tymes wyth thi derke wede,
That under that men myghte in reste abide,
Wel oughten bestes pleyne, and folk the chide,
That there as day wyth labour wolde us breste,
That thow thus fleest, and deynest us nought
    reste. 1435

"Thow doost, allas, to shortly thyn office,
Thow rakle nyght, ther God, maker of kynde,
The, for thyn haste and thyn unkynde vice,

1377. **plit**, situation. 1380. **so that**, how! 1381. **besy**, anxious, worried. 1384. **white . . . rede**, silver . . . gold. 1389. **Mida**, Midas. 1391. **Crassus**, slain in battle by the king of Parthia, who had molten gold poured into his mouth because in life he had been so greedy for wealth. **affectis**, desires. 1407. **passed**, past. **contrepeise**, counterbalance. 1413. **byset**, employed. 1414. **souneth into**, conduces to. 1417. **Lucyfer**, the morning star (the planet Venus). 1420. *Fortuna Major*. A designation for Jupiter, but the allusion is supposed to be to a group of six stars in the constellations Aquarius and Pegasus. The group would be rising in the east in England at the date of the poem. Curry (*MLN*, xxxviii. 94–96) interprets it as the Sun, but this would leave the phrase "to him that coude it knowe" almost meaningless. **that.** Chaucer has either lost his way in this long sentence or the construction is violently elliptical: it was then that. **1421-8.** The stanza expresses the idea of the *albe* (Prov. *alba*) or dawn song, in which lovers lament the coming of day when they must part. 1427. **hove**, hover. 1428. **Almena**, Alcmena, the mother of Hercules by Jove, lengthened the night in which Jove lay with her. 1431. **wede**, cloak, garment. 1434. **breste**, crush, overwhelm. 1436. **office**, duty, task. 1437. **rakle**, hasty. **ther**, introducing a curse; see Language, § 73.

So faste ay to oure hemysperie bynde,
That nevere more under the ground thow
   wynde!   1440
For now, for thow so hiest out of Troie,
Have I forgon thus hastili my joie!"

This Troilus, that with tho wordes felte,
As thoughte hym tho, for pietous distresse,
The blody teris from his herte melte,   1445
As he that nevere yet swich hevynesse
Assayed hadde, out of so gret gladnesse,
Gan therwithal Criseyde, his lady deere,
In armes streyne, and seyde in this manere:

"O cruel day, accusour of the joie   1450
That nyght and love han stole and faste
   iwryen,
Acorsed be thi comyng into Troye,
For every bore hath oon of thi bryghte yën!
Envyous day, what list the so to spien?
What hastow lost, why sekestow this place?   1455
Ther God thi light so quenche, for his grace!

"Allas! what have thise loveris the agylt,
Dispitous day? Thyn be the peyne of helle!
For many a lovere hastow slayn, and wilt;
Thy pourynge in wol nowher lat hem dwelle.
What profrestow thi light here for to selle?   1461
Go selle it hem that smale selys grave;
We wol the nought, us nedeth no day have."

And ek the sonne, Titan, gan he chide,
And seyde, "O fool, wel may men the dispise,
That hast the Dawyng al nyght by thi syde,   1466
And suffrest hire so soone up fro the rise,
For to disese loveris in this wyse.
What! holde youre bed ther, thow, and ek thi
   Morwe!
I bidde God, so yeve yow bothe sorwe!"   1470

Therwith ful soore he syghte, and thus he seyde:
"My lady right, and of my wele or wo
The welle and roote, O goodly myn, Criseyde,
And shal I rise, allas, and shal I so?
Now fele I that myn herte moot a-two.   1475
For how sholde I my lif an houre save,
Syn that with yow is al the lyf ich have?

"What shal I don? For, certes, I not how,
Ne whan, allas! I shal the tyme see
That in this plit I may ben eft with yow.   1480
And of my lif, God woot how that shal be,
Syn that desir right now so biteth me,
That I am ded anon, but I retourne.
How sholde I longe, allas, fro yow sojourne?

"But natheles, myn owen lady bright,   1485
Yit were it so that I wiste outrely
That I, youre humble servant and youre knyght,
Were in youre herte iset as fermely
As ye in myn, the which thyng, trewely,
Me levere were than thise worldes tweyne,   1490
Yet sholde I bet enduren al my peyne."

To that Criseyde answerde right anon,
And with a sik she seyde, "O herte deere,
The game, ywys, so ferforth now is gon,
That first shal Phebus fallen fro his spere,   1495
And everich egle ben the dowves feere,
And everi roche out of his place sterte,
Er Troilus out of Criseydes herte.

"Ye ben so depe in-with myn herte grave,
That, though I wolde it torne out of my thought,
As wisly verray God my soule save,   1501
To dyen in the peyne, I koude nought.
And, for the love of God that us hath wrought,
Lat in youre brayn non other fantasie
So crepe, that it cause me to dye!   1505

1440. wynde, revolve. **1442. forgon**, lost. **1443. felte.** The object is the infinitive phrase in l. 1445. **1450. accusour**, betrayer. **1451. iwryen**, covered, hidden. **1453. bore**, hole, chink. **1457. what**, how; so also in l. 1461. **1462. that smale selys grave**, who engrave small seals, and therefore need a good light. **1464. Titan**, the sun, confused with Tithonus, the husband of Aurora. **1466. Dawyng**, Aurora. **1469. Morwe**, same as Dawyng. **1470. I bidde God**, I pray God. *So* is intensive; see Language, § 74. **1480. plit**, situation. **1483. but**, unless. **1490. thise worldes tweyne**, two worlds such as this. **1495. spere**, sphere. **1496. feere**, companion. **1502. To dyen in the peyne**, even if I were tortured to death.

Trowe – Beleve   Plit situation   erst-before Er

"And that ye me wolde han as faste in mynde
As I have yow, that wolde I yow biseche;
And if I wiste sothly that to fynde, _point_
God myghte nought a poynt my joies eche.
But herte myn, withouten more speche,   1510
Beth to me trewe, or ellis were it routhe;
For I am thyn, by God and by my trouthe!

"Beth glad, forthy, and lyve in sikernesse!
Thus seyde I nevere er this, ne shal to mo;
And if to yow it were a gret gladnesse   1515
To torne ayeyn soone after that ye go, _return again_
As fayn wolde I as ye that it were so, _gladly_
As wisly God myn herte brynge at reste!"
And hym in armes tok, and ofte keste.

Agayns his wil, sith it mot nedes be,   1520
This Troilus up ros, and faste hym cledde,
And in his armes took his lady free
An hondred tyme, and on his wey hym spedde;
And with swiche voys as though his herte
   bledde,
He seyde, "Farewel, dere herte swete,   1525
Ther God us graunte sownde and soone to
   mete!" _he eth_

To which no word for sorwe she answerde,
So soore gan his partyng hire distreyne;
And Troilus unto his paleys ferde,
As wo-bygon as she was, soth to seyne.   1530
So harde hym wrong of sharp desir the peyne,
For to ben eft there he was in plesaunce,
That it may nevere out of his remembraunce.

Retorned to his real paleys soone, _royal_
He softe into his bed gan for to slynke,   1535
To slepe longe, as he was wont to doone. _the wink_
But al for nought; he may wel ligge and wynke,
But slep ne may ther in his herte synke,

Thynkyng how she, for whom desir hym
   brende,   1539
A thousand fold was worth more than he wende.

And in his thought gan up and down to wynde
Hire wordes alle, and every countenaunce,
And fermely impressen in his mynde
The leeste point that to him was plesaunce;
And verraylich, of thilke remembraunce,   1545
Desir al newe hym brende, and lust to brede
Gan more than erst, and yet took he non hede. _before_

Criseyde also, right in the same wyse,
Of Troilus gan in hire herte shette
His worthynesse, his lust, his dedes wise,   1550
His gentilesse, and how she with hym mette,
Thonkynge Love he so wel hire bisette;
Desiryng eft to han hire herte deere
In swich a plit, she dorste make hym cheere. _situation_

who in the morning had
Pandare, o-morwe which that comen was   1555
Unto his nece and gan hire faire grete,
Seyde, "Al this nyght so reyned it, allas,
That al my drede is that ye, nece swete,
✷ Han litel laiser had to slepe and mete. _dream_
Al nyght," quod he, "hath reyn so do me wake,
That som of us, I trowe, hire hedes ake."   1561

stands goes it
And ner he com, and seyde, "How stant it now
This mury morwe? Nece, how kan ye fare?" _merry morning_
Criseyde answerde, "Nevere the bet for yow,
Fox that ye ben! God yeve youre herte kare!
God help me so, ye caused al this fare, _behaving_ 1566
Trowe I," quod she, "for al youre wordes white. _believe_
O, whoso seeth yow, knoweth yow ful lite."

cover
With that she gan hire face for to wrye
With the shete, and wax for shame al reed;   1570
And Pandarus gan under for to prie,

1514. **Thus seyde I nevere er this.** In substance Criseyde says she had never fallen in love before romantically. Her marriage had doubtless been arranged by her parents. **1516. torne,** return. **1526. sownde,** health. **1528. distreyne,** distress. **1534. real,** royal. **1537. wynke,** close his eyes. **1546. lust,** desire. **brede,** grow. **1552. bisette,** laid siege to, occupied (in the military sense). **1554. In swich a plit . . .,** in a situation where she could make him happy. **1555. o-morwe which . . .,** who in the morning had come. **1566. al this fare,** all this business. **1569. wrye,** cover.

And seyde, "Nece, if that I shal be ded,
Have here a swerd and smyteth of myn hed!"
With that his arm al sodeynly he thriste   1574
Under hire nekke, and at the laste hire kyste.

I passe al that which chargeth nought to seye.
What! God foryaf his deth, and she al so
Foryaf, and with here uncle gan to pleye,
For other cause was ther noon than so.
But of this thing right to the effect to go,   1580
Whan tyme was, hom to here hous she wente,
And Pandarus hath fully his entente.

Now torne we ayeyn to Troilus,
That resteles ful longe abedde lay,
And pryvely sente after Pandarus,   1585
To hym to com in al the haste he may.
He com anon, nought ones seyde he nay;
And Troilus ful sobrely he grette,
And down upon his beddes syde hym sette.

This Troilus, with al th'affeccioun   1590
Of frendes love that herte may devyse,
To Pandarus on knowes fil adown,
And er that he wolde of the place arise,
He gan hym thonken in his beste wise
An hondred sythe, and gan the tyme blesse   1595
That he was born, to brynge hym fro destresse.

He seyde, "O frend of frendes the alderbeste
That evere was, the sothe for to telle,
Thow hast in hevene ybrought my soule at reste
Fro Flegetoun, the fery flood of helle;   1600
That, though I myght a thousand tymes selle,
Upon a day, my lif in thi servise,
It myghte naught a moote in that suffise.

"The sonne, which that al the world may se,
Saugh nevere yet my lif, that dar I leye,   1605
So inly fair and goodly as is she,
Whos I am al, and shal, tyl that I deye.

And that I thus am hires, dar I seye,
That thanked be the heighe worthynesse
Of Love, and ek thi kynde bysynesse.   1610

"Thus hastow me no litel thing yyive,
For which to the obliged be for ay
My lif, and whi? For thorugh thyn help I lyve,
Or elles ded hadde I ben many a day."
And with that word down in his bed he lay,
And Pandarus ful sobrely hym herde   1616
Til al was seyd, and than he thus answerde:

"My deere frend, if I have don for the
In any cas, God wot, it is me lief;
And am as glad as man may of it be,   1620
God help me so; but tak it nat a-grief
That I shal seyn, be war of this meschief,
That, there as thow now brought art in thy
     blisse,
That thow thiself ne cause it nat to misse.

"For of fortunes sharpe adversitee   1625
The worste kynde of infortune is this,
A man to han ben in prosperitee,
And it remembren, whan it passed is.
Th'art wis ynough, forthi do nat amys:
Be naught to rakel, theigh thow sitte warme;
For if thow be, certeyn, it wol the harme.   1631

"Thow art at ese, and hold the wel therinne;
For also seur as reed is every fir,
As gret a craft is kepe wel as wynne.
Bridle alwey wel thi speche and thi desir,   1635
For worldly joie halt nought but by a wir.
That preveth wel it brest alday so ofte;
Forthi nede is to werken with it softe."

Quod Troilus, "I hope, and God toforn,
My deere frend, that I shal so me beere,   1640
That in my gylt ther shal nothyng be lorn,
N'y nyl nought rakle as for to greven heere.

1576. chargeth nought, is not important. **1577. his deth,** those responsible for the crucifixion. **1582. hath fully his entente,** has accomplished all he intended to. **1591. devyse,** conceive. **1592. knowes,** knees. **1600. Flegetoun,** Phlege-thon, the fiery river of Hades (cf. Virgil, *Æneid,* vi. 550–1). **1603. moote,** particle. **1605. my lif,** in my life. **1622. mes-chief,** unfortunate condition. **1623. there as,** whereas. **1641. in my gylt,** through my fault. **1642. rakle,** act rashly.

It nedeth naught this matere ofte stere;
For wystestow myn herte wel, Pandare,
God woot, of this thow woldest litel care." 1645

Tho gan he telle hym of his glade nyght,
And wherof first his herte dred, and how,
And seyde, "Frend, as I am trewe knyght,
And by that feyth I shal to God and yow,
I hadde it nevere half so hote as now; 1650
And ay the more that desir me biteth
To love hire best, the more it me deliteth.

"I not myself naught wisly truly what it is;
But now I feele a newe qualitee,
Yee, al another than I dide er this." 1655
Pandare answerd, and seyde thus, that he
That ones may in hevene blisse be,—
"He feleth other weyes, dar I leye,
Than thilke tyme he first herde of it seye."

This is o word for al; this Troilus 1660
Was nevere ful to speke of this matere,
And for to preisen unto Pandarus
The bounte of his righte lady deere,
And Pandarus to thanke and maken cheere.
This tale was ay span-newe to bygynne, 1665
Til that the nyght departed hem atwynne.

Soon after this, for that Fortune it wolde,
Icomen was the blisful tyme swete
That Troilus was warned that he sholde,
There he was erst, Criseyde his lady mete; 1670
For which he felte his herte in joie flete,
And feithfully gan alle the goddes herie; Praise
And lat se now if that he kan be merie!

And holden was the forme and al the wise
Of hire commyng, and ek of his also, 1675
As it was erst, which nedeth nought devyse.
But pleynly to th'effect right for to go,

In joie and suerte Pandarus hem two
Abedde brought, whan that hem bothe leste,
And thus they ben in quyete and in reste. 1680

Nought nedeth it to yow, syn they ben met,
To axe at me if that they blithe were;
For if it erst was wel, tho was it bet
A thousand fold; this nedeth nought enquere.
Agon was every sorwe and every feere; 1685
And bothe, ywys, they hadde, and so they
    wende,
As muche joie as herte may comprende. contain

This is no litel thyng of for to seye;
This passeth every wit for to devyse;
For eche of hem gan otheres lust obeye. wish, desire 1690
Felicite, which that thise clerkes wise
Comenden so, ne may nought here suffise;
This joie may nought writen be with inke;
This passeth al that herte may bythynke.

But cruel day, so wailaway the stounde! 1695
Gan for t'aproche, as they by sygnes knewe;
For which hem thoughte feelen dethis wownde.
So wo was hem that changen gan hire hewe,
And day they gonnen to despise al newe,
Callyng it traitour, envyous, and worse, 1700
And bitterly the dayes light thei corse.

Quod Troilus, "Allas, now am I war
That Pirous and tho swifte steedes thre,
Which that drawen forth the sonnes char,
Han gon som bi-path in dispit of me; 1705
That maketh it so soone day to be;
And, for the sonne hym hasteth thus to rise,
Ne shal I nevere don him sacrifise."

But nedes day departe hem moste soone, 1709
And whan hire speche don was and hire cheere,
They twynne anon, as they were wont to doone,

1643. stere, urge. **1649. shal,** owe; cf. 3. 791, above. **1650. I hadde it nevere half so hote,** I never felt half so intensely. **1653. wisly,** certainly, truly. **1660. This is o word for al,** *i.e.* to put it in a nutshell. **1661. ful,** satiated. **1664. maken cheere,** be pleasant or agreeable. **1665. span-newe,** brand-new, *lit.* chip new. **1672. herie,** praise. **1687. comprende,** contain. **1690. lust,** wish, desire. **1703. Pirous,** Pyroïs, one of the four horses of the sun. Their names are given by Ovid, *Metam.,* II. 153–4. **1705. Han gon som bi-path . . .,** *i.e.* have taken a shortcut to spite me.

And setten tyme of metyng eft yfeere.
And many a nyght they wroughte in this
   manere,
And thus Fortune a tyme ledde in joie
Criseyde, and ek this kynges sone of Troie.   1715

In suffisaunce, in blisse, and in singynges,
This Troilus gan al his lif to lede.
He spendeth, jousteth, maketh festeynges;
He yeveth frely ofte, and chaungeth wede,
And held aboute hym alwey, out of drede,   1720
A world of folk, as com hym wel of kynde,
The fresshest and the beste he koude fynde;

That swich a vois was of hym and a stevene
Thoroughout the world, of honour and largesse,
That it up rong unto the yate of hevene.   1725
And, as in love, he was in swich gladnesse,
That in his herte he demed, as I gesse,
That ther nys lovere in this world at ese
So wel as he; and thus gan love hym plese.

The goodlihede or beaute which that kynde
In any other lady hadde yset   1731
Kan nought the montance of a knotte unbynde,
Aboute his herte, of al Criseydes net.
He was so narwe ymasked and yknet,
That it undon on any manere syde,—   1735
That nyl naught ben, for aught that may bitide.

And by the hond ful ofte he wolde take
This Pandarus, and into gardyn lede,
And swich a feste and swich a proces make
Hym of Criseyde, and of hire womanhede,   1740
And of hire beaute, that, withouten drede,

It was an hevene his wordes for to here;
And thanne he wolde synge in this manere:—

"Love, that of erthe and se hath governaunce,
Love, that his hestes hath in hevenes hye,   1745
Love, that with an holsom alliaunce
Halt peples joyned, as hym lest hem gye,
Love, that knetteth lawe of compaignie,
And couples doth in vertu for to dwelle,
Bynd this acord, that I have told and telle.   1750

"That that the world with feith, which that is
   stable,
Diverseth so his stowndes concordynge,
That elementz that ben so discordable
Holden a bond perpetuely durynge,   1754
That Phebus mote his rosy day forth brynge,
And that the mone hath lordshipe over the
   nyghtes,—
Al this doth Love, ay heried be his myghtes!

"That that the se, that gredy is to flowen,
Constreyneth to a certeyn ende so
His flodes that so fiersly they ne growen   1760
To drenchen erthe and al for evere mo;
And if that Love aught lete his bridel go,
Al that now loveth asondre sholde lepe,
And lost were al that Love halt now to-hepe.

"So wolde God, that auctour is of kynde,   1765
That with his bond Love of his vertu liste
To cerclen hertes alle, and faste bynde,
That from his bond no wight the wey out
   wiste;
And hertes colde, hem wolde I that he twiste

1712. **yfeere,** together. 1716. **suffisaunce,** contentment. 1718. **festeynges,** festivities. 1721. **as com hym wel of kynde,** as was quite natural for him. 1732. **montance,** extent (of a single knot). 1734. **narwe ymasked,** closely enmeshed. **yknet,** knit together. 1735. **it undon on any manere syde,** to undo it in any way. 1739. **a feste . . . make.** The phrase may mean either "to make merry" or "to pay a compliment." **swich a proces make,** talk so much; but the whole line of course, means merely that Troilus was bubbling over with good spirits and enthusiasm for Criseyde and her virtues. 1745. **hestes,** commands. 1748. **compaignie,** companionship. The stanza and the next three are based on Boethius, II, met. 8, in which Chaucer's translation of the equivalent line reads, "Love endyteth lawes to trewe felawes." From the circumstance that this song of Troilus is absent from some MSS it is thought to have been added in the revision. The song of Troilus in the *Filostrato* had already been used by Chaucer in the Proem to this book (ll. 1–38). 1751. **That that.** The repetition of *that* here and at the beginning of the next stanza has not been explained. The corresponding statement in the Boethius is "That the world with stable feith varieth acordable changinges" and "that the see, greedy to flowen, constreyneth with a certein ende hise flodes . . ." It seems to be equivalent to "the fact that." 1752. **Diverseth . . . concordynge,** so varies its harmonious seasons (*i.e.* its seasons harmoniously). 1761. **drenchen,** drown.

To make hem love, and that hem liste ay
  rewe   1770
On hertes sore, and kepe hem that ben
  trewe!"—

In alle nedes, for the townes werre,
He was, and ay, the first in armes dyght,
And certeynly, but if that bokes erre,
Save Ector most ydred of any wight;   1775
And this encres of hardynesse and myght
Com hym of love, his ladies thank to wynne,
That altered his spirit so withinne.

In tyme of trewe, on haukyng wolde he ride,
Or elles honte boor, beer, or lyoun;   1780
The smale bestes leet he gon biside.
And whan that he com ridyng into town,
Ful ofte his lady from hire wyndow down,
As fressh as faukoun comen out of muwe,
Ful redy was hym goodly to saluwe.   1785

And moost of love and vertu was his speche,
And in despit hadde alle wrecchednesse;
And douteles, no nede was hym biseche
To honouren hem that hadde worthynesse,
And esen hem that weren in destresse.   1790
And glad was he if any wyght wel ferde,
That lovere was, whan he it wiste or herde.

For, soth to seyne, he lost held every wyght,
But if he were in Loves heigh servise,—

I mene folk that oughte it ben of right.   1795
And over al this, so wel koude he devyse
Of sentement, and in so unkouth wise,
Al his array, that every lovere thoughte
That al was wel, what so he seyde or wroughte.

And though that he be come of blood roial, 1800
Hym liste of pride at no wight for to chace;
Benigne he was to ech in general,
For which he gat hym thank in every place.
Thus wolde Love, yheried be his grace,
That pride, envye, and ire, and avarice   1805
He gan to fle, and everich other vice.

Thow lady bryght, the doughter to Dyone,
Thy blynde and wynged sone ek, daun Cupide,
Yee sustren nyne ek, that by Elicone
In hil Pernaso listen for t'abide,   1810
That ye thus fer han deyned me to gyde,
I kan namore, but syn that ye wol wende,
Ye heried ben for ay withouten ende!

Thorugh yow have I seyd fully in my song
Th'effect and joie of Troilus servise,   1815
Al be that ther was som disese among,
As to myn auctour listeth to devise.
My thridde bok now ende ich in this wyse,
And Troilus in luste and in quiete
Is with Criseyde, his owen herte swete.   1820

Explicit liber tercius.

1773. the first in armes dyght, the first one armed. **1779. trewe,** truce. **1781. leet he gon biside,** he disregarded. **1787. wrecchednesse,** meanness. **1797. unkouth,** unusual, marvellous. **1801. to chace.** An unusual use of the verb, though it sometimes has the meaning "to harass or persecute." Contextually the meaning here seems "act in a proud or haughty manner." **1805. pride,** etc. Four of the seven deadly sins; the others are sloth, gluttony, and lechery. **1807. Thow lady bryght,** Venus. Boccaccio (*De Genealogia Deorum,* xi, chap. iii) in saying that Venus was the daughter of Jove and Dione, refers to Homer and Cicero as his authorities. It was, however, a commonplace. **1809. Elicone.** See note to *HF* 522. Chaucer was not alone in thinking Helicon was near mount Parnassus. **1812. I kan namore, but,** *i.e.* I can only say. **1816. among,** all the while. **1819. luste,** pleasure, happiness.

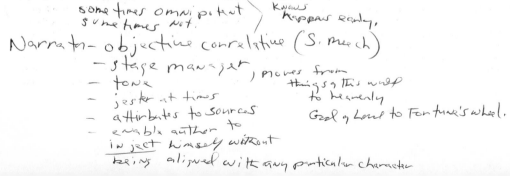

Book IV

Incipit prohemium quarti libri.

But al to litel, weylaway the whyle,
Lasteth swich joie, ythonked be Fortune,
That semeth trewest whan she wol bygyle,
And kan to fooles so hire song entune, 4
That she hem hent and blent, traitour comune!
And whan a wight is from hire whiel ythrowe,
Than laugheth she, and maketh hym the mowe.

From Troilus she gan hire brighte face
Awey to writhe, and tok of hym non heede,
But caste hym clene out of his lady grace, 10
And on hire whiel she sette up Diomede;
For which right now myn herte gynneth blede,
And now my penne, allas! with which I write,
Quaketh for drede of that I moste endite.

For how Criseyde Troilus forsook, 15
Or at the leeste, how that she was unkynde,
Moot hennesforth ben matere of my book,
As writen folk thorugh which it is in mynde.
Allas! that they sholde evere cause fynde
To speke hire harm, and if they on hire lye, 20
Iwis, hemself sholde han the vilanye.

O ye Herynes, Nyghtes doughtren thre,
That endeles compleignen evere in pyne,
Megera, Alete, and ek Thesiphone;
Thow cruel Mars ek, fader to Quyryne, 25
This ilke ferthe book me helpeth fyne,
So that the losse of lyf and love yfeere
Of Troilus be fully shewed heere.

Explicit prohemium quarti libri.

Incipit liber quartus.

Liggyng in oost, as I have seyd er this,
The Grekys stronge aboute Troie town, 30
Byfel that, whan that Phebus shynyng is
Upon the brest of Hercules lyoun,
That Ector, with ful many a bold baroun,
Caste on a day with Grekes for to fighte,
As he was wont, to greve hem what he
    myghte.

Not I how longe or short it was bitwene 36
This purpos and that day they fighten mente;
But on a day wel armed, brighte and shene,
Ector and many a worthi wight out wente,

With spere in honde and bigge bowes bente; 40
And in the berd, withouten lenger lette,
Hire fomen in the feld anon hem mette.

The longe day, with speres sharpe igrounde,
With arwes, dartes, swerdes, maces felle,
They fighte and bringen hors and man to
    grounde,
And with hire axes out the braynes quelle. 45
But in the laste shour, soth for to telle,
The folk of Troie hemselven so mysledden
That with the wors at nyght homward they
    fledden.

---

5. hent and blent, catches and blinds (contracted forms). **7. maketh hym the mowe,** makes a face at him. **21. vilanye,** reproach. **22. Herynes,** Erinyes, Furies. **25. Quyryne,** another name for Romulus. Romulus and Remus were sons of Mars (Ovid, *Fasti*, II. 419, 476). **26. fyne,** finish. **29. Liggyng in oost,** lying in a host, as an army. **32. Hercules lyoun.** Since one of the labors of Hercules was the killing of the Nemaean lion, the lion was a symbol of the hero. The sun was in the sign Leo in late July and early August. The purpose is to indicate the time of the year. **34. Caste,** decided, resolved. **41. in the berd,** resolutely, face to face. **lette,** delay. **46. quelle,** dash, knock (out). **47. shour,** assault, encounter. **48. hemselven so mysledden,** conducted themselves so badly.

At whiche day was taken Antenore,   50
Maugre Polydamas or Monesteo,
Santippe, Sarpedon, Polynestore,
Polite, or ek the Trojan daun Rupheo,
And other lasse folk as Phebuseo;
So that, for harm, that day the folk of Troie   55
Dredden to lese a gret part of hire joie.

Of Priamus was yeve, at Grekes requeste,
A tyme of trewe, and tho they gonnen trete,
Hire prisoners to chaungen, meste and leste,
And for the surplus yeven sommes grete.   60
This thing anon was couth in every strete,
Bothe in th'assege, in town and everywhere,
And with the firste it com to Calkas ere.

Whan Calkas knew this tretis sholde holde,
In consistorie, among the Grekes soone   65
He gan in thringe forth with lordes olde,
And sette hym there as he was wont to doone;
And with a chaunged face hem bad a boone,
For love of God, to don that reverence,
To stynte noyse, and yeve hym audience.   70

Than seyde he thus, "Lo, lordes myn, ich was
Troian, as it is knowen out of drede;
And, if that yow remembre, I am Calkas,
That alderfirst yaf comfort to youre nede,
And tolde wel how that ye shulden spede.   75
For dredeles, thorugh yow shal in a stownde
Ben Troie ybrend, and beten down to grownde.

"And in what forme, or in what manere wise,
This town to shende, and al youre lust t'acheve,
Ye han er this wel herd me yow devyse.   80
This knowe ye, my lordes, as I leve.

And, for the Grekis weren me so leeve,
I com myself, in my propre persone,
To teche in this how yow was best to doone,

"Havyng unto my tresor ne my rente   85
Right no resport, to respect of youre ese.
Thus al my good I lefte and to yow wente,
Wenyng in this yow, lordes, for to plese.
But al that los ne doth me no disese.
I vouchesauf, as wisly have I joie,   90
For yow to lese al that I have in Troie,

"Save of a doughter that I lefte, allas!
Slepyng at hom, whanne out of Troie I sterte.
O sterne, O cruel fader that I was!
How myghte I have in that so harde an herte?
Allas, I ne hadde ibrought hire in hire sherte!   96
For sorwe of which I wol nought lyve to-
    morwe,
But if ye lordes rewe upon my sorwe.

"For, by that cause I say no tyme er now
Hire to delivere, ich holden have my pees;   100
But now or nevere, if that it like yow,
I may hire have right soone, douteles.
O help and grace! amonges al this prees,
Rewe on this olde caytyf in destresse,
Syn I thorough yow have al this hevynesse.   105

"Ye have now kaught and fetered in prisoun
Troians ynowe; and if youre willes be,
My child with oon may han redempcioun,
Now, for the love of God and of bounte,
Oon of so fele, allas, so yive hym me!   110
What nede were it this preiere for to werne,
Syn ye shul bothe han folk and town as yerne?

---

51. Maugre Polydamas . . ., in spite of Polydamas, Menestheus, Xantippus (King of Frisia, an ally), Sarpedon, Polymnestor (also an ally), Polites (one of the sons of Priam), Riphaeus. In these names Chaucer follows the form in Boccaccio. Chaucer has apparently added the name Phebuseo from his own invention. In the light of subsequent events the importance of this reverse for the Trojans lies in the capture of Antenor. **62. in th' assege,** in the besieging force. **64. tretis,** treaty. **65. consistorie,** council. **66. thringe,** press. Perhaps we should read *inthringe*, a verb recorded in the next century. **68. with a chaunged face.** The phrase usually connotes a change of color. **76. stownde,** a space of time. **83. com,** came. **86. resport,** regard. **to respect of,** with respect to, in comparison with. **87. good,** property. **90. I vouchesauf,** I am willing. **96. Allas . . . ibrought,** alas that I did not bring. **99. by that cause,** because. **say,** saw. **110. hym,** one of the prisoners for exchange. **111. werne,** refuse. **112. as yerne,** very soon.

"On peril of my lif, I shal nat lye,
Appollo hath me told it feithfully;
I have ek founde it be astronomye,   115
By sort, and by augurye ek, trewely,
And dar wel say, the tyme is faste by
That fire and flaumbe on al the town shal
  sprede,
And thus shal Troie torne to asshen dede.

"For certein, Phebus and Neptunus bothe,   120
That makeden the walles of the town,
Ben with the folk of Troie alwey so wrothe,
That they wol brynge it to confusioun,
Right in despit of kyng Lameadoun.
Bycause he nolde payen hem here hire,   125
The town of Troie shal ben set on-fire."

Tellyng his tale alwey, this olde greye,
Humble in his speche, and in his lokyng eke,
The salte teris from his eyen tweye
Ful faste ronnen down by either cheke.   130
So longe he gan of socour hem biseke
That, for to hele hym of his sorwes soore,
They yave hym Antenor, withouten moore.

But who was glad ynough but Calkas tho?
And of this thyng ful soone his nedes leyde   135
On hem that sholden for the tretis go,
And hem for Antenor ful ofte preyde
To bryngen hom kyng Toas and Criseyde.
And whan Priam his save-garde sente,
Th'embassadours to Troie streight they wente.

The cause itold of hire comyng, the olde   141
Priam, the kyng, ful soone in general
Let her-upon his parlement to holde,
Of which th'effect rehercen yow I shal.
Th'embassadours ben answerd for fynal,   145

Th'eschaunge of prisoners and al this nede
Hem liketh wel, and forth in they procede.

This Troilus was present in the place,
Whan axed was for Antenor Criseyde;
For which ful soone chaungen gan his face,   150
As he that with tho wordes wel neigh deyde.
But natheles he no word to it seyde,
Lest men sholde his affeccioun espye;
With mannes herte he gan his sorwes drye,

And ful of angwissh and of grisly drede   155
Abod what lordes wolde unto it seye;
And if they wolde graunte, as God forbede,
Th'eschaunge of hire, than thoughte he thynges
  tweye,
First, how to save hire honour, and what weye
He myghte best th'eschaunge of hire with-
  stonde;   160
Ful faste he caste how al this myghte stonde.

Love hym made al prest to don hire byde,
And rather dyen than she sholde go;
But resoun seyde hym, on that other syde,
"Withouten assent of hire ne do nat so,   165
Lest for thi werk she wolde be thy fo,
And seyn that thorugh thy medlynge is iblowe
Youre bother love, ther it was erst unknowe."

For which he gan deliberen, for the beste,
That though the lordes wolde that she wente,
He wolde lat hem graunte what hem leste,   171
And telle his lady first what that they mente;
And whan that she hadde seyd hym hire en-
  tente,
Therafter wolde he werken also blyve,
Theigh al the world ayeyn it wolde stryve.   175

---

120. **Phebus and Neptunus.** According to Benoît de Sainte-Maure (*Roman de Troye*, 25, 921 ff.) Neptune built the walls and Apollo dedicated them, but he merely says they were badly deceived. Ovid and others relate that when Neptune and Apollo were for a time condemned to serve Laomedon the latter refused them their wages. 133. **moore,** more ado. 138. **Toas,** Thoas, king of Calydon, who with Criseyde was to be exchanged for Antenor. 139. **save-garde,** safe conduct. 143. **parlement.** Properly the council, but Chaucer apparently has in mind the English meaning. 145. **for fynal,** finally. 146. **al this nede,** everything necessary. 154. **drye,** endure. 162. **to don hire byde,** to have her remain. 167. **iblowe,** spread abroad. 168. **Youre bother love,** the love of you both. 174. **also blyve,** very quickly.

Ector, which that wel the Grekis herde,
For Antenor how they wolde han Criseyde,
Gan it withstonde, and sobrely answerde:
"Syres, she nys no prisonere," he seyde;
"I not on yow who that this charge leyde,   180
But, on my part, ye may eftsone hem telle,
We usen here no wommen for to selle."

The noyse of peple up stirte thanne at ones,
As breme as blase of straw iset on-fire;
For infortune it wolde, for the nones,   185
They sholden hire confusioun desire.
"Ector," quod they, "what goost may yow en-
     spyre,
This womman thus to shilde, and don us leese
Daun Antenor—a wrong wey now ye chese—

"That is so wys and ek so bold baroun?   190
And we han nede of folk, as men may se.
He is ek oon the grettest of this town.
O Ector, lat tho fantasies be!
O kyng Priam," quod they, "thus sygge we,
That al oure vois is to forgon Criseyde."   195
And to deliveren Antenor they preyde.

O Juvenal, lord! trewe is thy sentence,
That litel wyten folk what is to yerne
That they ne fynde in hire desire offence;
For cloude of errour lat hem nat discerne   200
What best is. And lo, here ensample as yerne:
This folk desiren now deliveraunce
Of Antenor, that brought hem to meschaunce.

For he was after traitour to the town
Of Troye; allas, they quytte hym out to rathe!
O nyce world, lo, thy discrecioun!   206

Criseyde, which that nevere dide hem scathe,
Shal now no lenger in hire blisse bathe;
But Antenor, he shal com hom to towne,
And she shal out; thus seyden here and howne.

For which delibered was by parlement,   211
For Antenor to yelden out Criseyde,
And it pronounced by the president,
Altheigh that Ector "nay" ful ofte preyde.
And fynaly, what wight that it withseyde,   215
It was for nought; it moste ben and sholde,
For substaunce of the parlement it wolde.

Departed out of parlement echone,
This Troilus, withouten wordes mo,
Unto his chambre spedde hym faste allone,   220
But if it were a man of his or two,
The which he bad out faste for to go,
Bycause he wolde slepen, as he seyde,
And hastily upon his bed hym leyde.

And as in wynter leves ben biraft,   225
Ech after other, til the tree be bare,
So that ther nys but bark and braunche ilaft,
Lith Troilus, byraft of ech welfare,
Ibounden in the blake bark of care,
Disposed wood out of his wit to breyde,   230
So sore hym sat the chaungynge of Criseyde.

He rist hym up, and every dore he shette
And wyndow ek, and tho this sorwful man
Upon his beddes syde adown hym sette,
Ful lik a ded ymage, pale and wan;   235
And in his brest the heped wo bygan
Out breste, and he to werken in this wise
In his woodnesse, as I shal yow devyse.

181. **eftsone,** immediately. 183. **The noyse of peple.** . . . C. Brown (*MLN*, XXVI. 208–211) sees in this passage an allusion to the Peasants' Revolt of 1381, with *straw* as a possible punning reference to Jack Straw. 184. **breme,** fierce. 185. **infortune,** ill fortune. 186. **confusioun,** destruction, ruin. 197. **Juvenal.** See the Satires, x. 2–4: "Few are able to distinguish true good from what is very different, separated by a cloud of error." 198. **what is to yerne,** what is to be desired. 200. **lat,** lets. 201. **as yerne,** very soon. 205. **quytte . . . to rathe,** they released him too soon. 210. **here and howne,** an alliterative phrase apparently meaning "all and sundry,' but it has not been explained. The speculations of Skeat and Root (both unconvincing) are summarized by Robinson. The *NED s.v. howne* says "Meaning unknown." 215. **it withseyde,** spoke against it. 216. **sholde,** would have to be done. 217. **substaunce,** majority. 225. **biraft,** taken away. 230. **breyde,** go suddenly. 232. **rist,** rises. In ME. the verb *rise* is sometimes used with a reflexive pronoun or a dative of reference.

[handwritten top margin: Wrecche – wretch | (righte) right | algate – At any rate
Wreche – Vengeaunce | nverye exactly | ay – ever always
Wrecche – Afliction: misfortune | directe]

Right as the wylde bole bygynneth sprynge,
Now her, now ther, idarted to the herte, 240
And of his deth roreth in compleynynge,
Right so gan he aboute the chaumbre sterte,
Smytyng his brest ay with his fistes smerte;
His hed to the wal, his body to the grounde
Ful ofte he swapte, hymselven to confounde.

His eyen two, for piete of herte, 246
Out stremeden as swifte welles tweye;
The heighe sobbes of his sorwes smerte
His speche hym refte; unnethes myghte he
  seye,
"O deth, allas! why nyltow do me deye? 250
Acorsed be that day which that Nature
Shop me to ben a lyves creature!"

But after, whan the furie and al the rage
Which that his herte twiste and faste threste,
By lengthe of tyme somwhat gan aswage, 255
Upon his bed he leyde hym down to reste.
But tho bygonne his teeris more out breste,
That wonder is the body may suffise
To half this wo, which that I yow devyse.

Than seyde he thus, "Fortune, allas the while!
What have I don? What have I thus agylt? 261
How myghtestow for rowthe me bygile?
Is ther no grace, and shal I thus be spilt?
Shal thus Criseyde awey, for that thow wilt?
Allas! how maistow in thyn herte fynde 265
To ben to me thus cruwel and unkynde?

"Have I the nought honoured al my lyve,
As thow wel woost, above the goddes alle?
Whi wiltow me fro joie thus deprive?
O Troilus, what may men now the calle 270
But wrecche of wrecches, out of honour falle
Into miserie, in which I wol bewaille
Criseyde, allas! til that the breth me faille?

"Allas, Fortune! if that my lif in joie
Displesed hadde unto thi foule envye, 275
Why ne haddestow my fader, kyng of Troye,
Byraft the lif, or don my bretheren dye,
Or slayn myself, that thus compleyne and crye,
I, combre-world, that may of nothyng serve,
But evere dye and nevere fulli sterve? 280

"If that Criseyde allone were me laft,
Nought roughte I whider thow woldest me
  steere;
And hire, allas! than hastow me biraft.
But everemore, lo, this is thi manere,
To reve a wight that most is to hym deere, 285
To preve in that thi gerful violence.
Thus am I lost, ther helpeth no diffence.

"O verrey lord, O Love! O god, allas!
That knowest best myn herte and al my thought,
What shal my sorwful lif don in this cas, 290
If I forgo that I so deere have bought?
Syn ye Criseyde and me han fully brought
Into youre grace, and bothe oure hertes seled,
How may ye suffre, allas! it be repeled?

"What shal I don? I shal, while I may dure 295
On lyve in torment and in cruwel peyne,
This infortune of this disaventure,
Allone as I was born, iwys, compleyne;
Ne nevere wol I seen it shyne or reyne,
But ende I wol, as Edippe, in derknesse 300
My sorwful lif, and dyen in distresse.

"O wery goost, that errest to and fro,
Why nyltow fleen out of the wofulleste
Body that evere myghte on grounde go?
O soule, lyrkynge in this wo, unneste, 305
Fle forth out of myn herte, and lat it breste,
And folowe alwey Criseyde, thi lady dere.
Thi righte place is now no lenger here.

---

240. idarted, pierced with a dart. **245. swapte,** struck. **246. piete,** pity, compassion. **252. lyves,** living. **254. twiste and . . . threste,** wrung and pierced. **258. suffise to,** be adequate for, capable of bearing. **275. envye,** malice. **279. combreworld,** an encumbrance to the world (by living too long). **285. that,** that which. **286. gerful,** changeable, wayward. **300. Edippe,** Oedipus, who put out his eyes when he learned that, after killing his father Laius, he had married his own mother. **305. unneste,** go out of thy nest.

"O woful eyen two, syn youre disport
Was al to sen Criseydes eyen brighte,   310
What shal ye don but, for my discomfort,
Stonden for naught, and wepen out youre
    sighte,
Syn she is queynt, that wont was yow to lighte?
In vayn fro this forth have ich eyen tweye
Ifourmed, syn youre vertu is aweye.   315

"O my Criseyde, O lady sovereigne
Of thilke woful soule that thus crieth,
Who shal now yeven comfort to the peyne?
Allas! no wight; but whan myn herte dieth,
My spirit, which that so unto yow hieth,   320
Receyve in gree, for that shal ay yow serve;
Forthi no fors is, though the body sterve.

"O ye loveris, that heigh upon the whiel
Ben set of Fortune, in good aventure,
God leve that ye fynde ay love of stiel,   325
And longe mote youre lif in joie endure!
But whan ye comen by my sepulture,
Remembreth that youre felawe resteth there;
For I loved ek, though ich unworthi were.

"O oold, unholsom, and myslyved man,   330
Calkas I mene, allas! what eileth the,
To ben a Grek, syn thow art born Troian?
O Calkas, which that wolt my bane be,
In corsed tyme was thow born for me!
As wolde blisful Jove, for his joie,   335
That I the hadde wher I wolde, in Troie!"

A thousand sikes, hotter than the gleede,
Out of his brest ech after other wente,
Medled with pleyntes new, his wo to feede,
For which his woful teris nevere stente;   340
And shortly, so his peynes hym torente,
And wex so mat, that joie nor penaunce
He feleth non, but lith forth in a traunce.

Pandare, which that in the parlement
Hadde herd what every lord and burgeys seyde,
And how ful graunted was by oon assent   346
For Antenor to yelden so Criseyde,
Gan wel neigh wood out of his wit to breyde,
So that, for wo, he nyste what he mente,
But in a rees to Troilus he wente.   350

A certeyn knyght, that for the tyme kepte
The chambre door, undide it hym anon;
And Pandare, that ful tendreliche wepte,
Into the derke chambre, as stille as ston,
Toward the bed gan softely to gon,   355
So confus that he nyste what to seye;
For verray wo his wit was neigh aweye.

And with his chiere and lokyng al totorn,
For sorwe of this, and with his armes folden,
He stood this woful Troilus byforn,   360
And on his pitous face he gan byholden.
But, Lord, so ofte gan his herte colden,
Seyng his frend in wo, whos hevynesse
His herte slough, as thoughte hym, for des-
    tresse.

This woful wight, this Troilus, that felte   365
His frend Pandare ycomen hym to se,
Gan as the snow ayeyn the sonne melte;
For which this sorwful Pandare, of pitee,
Gan for to wepe as tendreliche as he;
And specheles thus ben thise ilke tweye,   370
That neither myghte o word for sorwe seye.

But at the laste this woful Troilus,
Neigh ded for smert, gan bresten out to rore,
And with a sorwful noise he seyde thus,
Among hise sobbes and his sikes sore: 375
"Lo, Pandare, I am ded, withouten more.
Hastow nat herd at parlement," he seyde,
"For Antenor how lost is my Criseyde?"

---

312. Stonden for naught. Perhaps a punning allusion to the fact that in the Middle Ages the eyes were represented as zeroes, with the nose and eyebrows as M forming the word *omo*. It is referred to by Dante, *Purgatorio*, XXIII. 31–33. See A. F. Kornbluth, *N & Q*, CCIV. 243. **313. queynt**, quenched, extinguished. **318. the peyne**, distress. **325. leve**, grant. **330. unholsom**, corrupt. **myslyved**, of evil life. **335. As**, see Language, § 73. **342. mat**, worn out, dejected. **penaunce**, sorrow. **343. forth**, continually. **349. mente**, intended. **350. rees**, rush (OE. *rǽs*, rush, act of running). **358. totorn**, distraught, *lit.* torn to pieces. **364. slough**, slew.

This Pandarus, ful dede and pale of hewe,
Ful pitously answerde and seyde, "Yis !   380
As wisly were it fals as it is trewe,
That I have herd, and woot al how it is.
O mercy, God, who wolde have trowed this?
Who wolde have wend that in so litel a
    throwe
Fortune oure joie wold han overthrowe?   385

"For in this world ther is no creature,
As to my dom, that ever saw ruyne
Straunger than this, thorugh cas or aventure.
But who may al eschue, or al devyne.
Swich is this world! forthi I thus diffyne: 390
Ne trust no wight to fynden in Fortune
Ay propretee; hire yiftes ben comune.

"But telle me this, whi thow art now so mad
To sorwen thus? Whi listow in this wise,
Syn thi desire al holly hastow had,   395
So that, by right, it oughte ynough suffise?
But I, that nevere felte in my servyse
A frendly cheere, or lokyng of an eye,
Lat me thus wepe and wailen til I deye.

"And over al this, as thow wel woost thiselve,
This town is ful of ladys al aboute;   401
And, to my doom, fairer than swiche twelve
As evere she was, shal I fynde in som route,
Yee, on or two, withouten any doute.
Forthi be glad, myn owen deere brother!   405
If she be lost, we shal recovere an other.

"What! God forbede alwey that ech plesaunce
In o thyng were, and in non other wight!
If oon kan synge, an other kan wel daunce;
If this be goodly, she is glad and light;   410

And this is fair, and that kan good aright.
Ech for his vertu holden is for deere,
Both heroner and faucoun for ryvere.

"And ek, as writ Zanzis, that was ful wys,
'The newe love out chaceth ofte the olde;'   415
And upon newe cas lith newe avys.
Thenk ek, thi lif to saven artow holde.
Swich fir, by proces, shal of kynde colde;
For syn it is but casuel plesaunce,
Som cas shal putte it out of remembraunce.   420

"For also seur as day comth after nyght,
The newe love, labour, or oother wo,
Or elles selde seynge of a wight,
Don olde affecciouns alle overgo.
And, for thi part, thow shalt have oon of tho
T'abregge with thi bittre peynes smerte;   426
Absence of hire shal dryve hire out of herte."

Thise wordes seyde he for the nones alle,
To help his frend, lest he for sorwe deyde;
For douteles, to don his wo to falle,   430
He roughte nought what unthrift that he
    seyde.
But Troilus, that neigh for sorwe deyde,
Took litel heede of al that evere he mente;
Oon ere it herde, at the other out it wente.

But at the laste he answerde, and seyde,
"Frend,   435
This lechecraft, or heeled thus to be,
Were wel sittyng, if that I were a fend,
To trayson hir that trewe is unto me!
I pray God lat this conseil nevere ythe;
But do me rather sterve anon-right here,   440
Er I thus do as thow me woldest leere!

381. **were it,** would that it were. 384. **throwe,** space of time. 390. **diffyne,** conclude, state. 392. **propretee,** fitness. **comune,** common to all. 402. **fairer . . . twelve,** twelve times as fair. 413. **heroner,** falcon trained to catch herons. **for ryvere,** beside the river. 414. **Zanzis** (some MSS read *Zauzis*), Zeuxis. The assignment of the saying is Chaucer's; Boccaccio and Ovid cite no authority. In the *PhysT* (C 16) Chaucer refers to Zanzis (Zeuxis the painter), but Robinson suggests that the reference here may be to a sage of that name in the Alexander story. 416. **And upon newe cas . . .,** a new situation requires new consideration. 419. **casuel,** the result of chance. 425. **oon of tho,** one of those experiences, although the reference could be to the other women mentioned at 401. 428. **for the nones,** for the time being. 431. **unthrift,** impropriety. 433. **mente,** said.

"She that I serve, iwis, what so thow seye,
To whom myn herte enhabit is by right,
Shal han me holly hires til that I deye.
For, Pandarus, syn I have trouthe hire hight,
I wol nat ben untrewe for no wight;   446
But as hire man I wol ay lyve and sterve,
And nevere other creature serve.

"And ther thow seist thow shalt as faire fynde
As she, lat be, make no comparisoun   450
To creature yformed here by kynde!
O leve Pandare, in conclusioun,
I wol nat ben of thyn opynyoun,
Touchyng al this; for which I the biseche,
So hold thi pees; thow sleest me with thi
     speche!   455

"Thow biddest me I shulde love another
Al fresshly newe, and lat Criseyde go!
It lith nat in my power, leeve brother;
And though I myght, I wolde nat do so.
But kanstow playen raket, to and fro,   460
Nettle in, dok out, now this, now that, Pan-
     dare?
Now foule falle hire for thi wo that care!

"Thow farest ek by me, thow Pandarus,
As he that, whan a wight is wo bygon,   464
He cometh to hym a paas, and seith right thus,
'Thynk nat on smert, and thow shalt fele non.'
Thow moost me first transmewen in a ston,
And reve me my passiones alle,
Er thow so lightly do my wo to falle.

"The deth may wel out of my brest departe   470
The lif, so longe may this sorwe myne;
But fro my soule shal Criseydes darte
Out nevere mo; but down with Proserpyne,
Whan I am ded, I wol go wone in pyne,

And ther I wol eternaly compleyne   475
My wo, and how that twynned be we tweyne.

"Thow hast here made an argument, for fyn,
How that it sholde a lasse peyne be
Criseyde to forgon, for she was myn,
And lyved in ese and in felicite.   480
Whi gabbestow, that seydest thus to me
That 'hym is wors that is fro wele ythrowe,
Than he hadde erst noon of that wele yknowe?'

"But tel me now, syn that the thynketh so lyght
To changen so in love ay to and fro,   485
Whi hastow nat don bysyly thi myght
To chaungen hire that doth the al thi wo?
Why nyltow lete hire fro thyn herte go?
Whi nyltow love an other lady swete,
That may thyn herte setten in quiete?   490

"If thou hast had in love ay yet myschaunce,
And kanst it not out of thyn herte dryve,
I, that levede in lust and in plesaunce
With hire, as muche as creature on lyve,
How sholde I that foryete, and that so blyve?
O, where hastow ben hid so longe in muwe, 496
That kanst so wel and formaly arguwe?

"Nay, God wot, nought worth is al thi red,
For which, for what that evere may byfalle,
Withouten wordes mo, I wol be ded.   500
O deth, that endere art of sorwes alle,
Com now, syn I so ofte after the calle;
For sely is that deth, soth for to seyne,
That, ofte ycleped, cometh and endeth peyne.

"Wel wot I, whil my lyf was in quyete,   505
Er thow me slowe, I wolde have yeven hire;
But now thi comynge is to me so swete
That in this world I nothing so desire.

443. enhabit, devoted. 445. hight, promised. 460. raket, the game of rackets, a kind of tennis played off a wall; court tennis. 461. Nettle in, dok out, the first words of a charm for removing the sting of a nettle. 462. Now foule falle hire . . ., i.e. bad luck to any lady that may care about your love-sickness. 465. a paas, apace. 470. departe, remove. 471. myne. Elsewhere in Chaucer this verb is used in the sense "to penetrate, undermine." The present passage seems to require "go on," for which there is no authority in ME., unless it represents OE. mynian, to direct one's course, go. 473. Proserpyne, queen of Hades. 477. for fyn, finally. 481. gabbestow, dost thou talk nonsense. seydest thus to me. See 3. 1625–28. 503. sely, blissful. 506. hire, ransom; I would have ransomed myself from Death.

O deth, syn with this sorwe I am a-fyre,
Thow other do me anoon in teris drenche,	510
Or with thi colde strok myn hete quenche.

"Syn that thou sleest so fele in sondry wyse
Ayens hire wil, unpreyed, day and nyght,
Do me at my requeste this servise:
Delyvere now the world, so dostow right,	515
Of me, that am the wofulleste wyght
That evere was; for tyme is that I sterve,
Syn in this world of right nought may I serve."

This Troylus in teris gan distille,
As licour out of a lambic ful faste;	520
And Pandarus gan holde his tunge stille,
And to the ground his eyen doun he caste.
But natheles, thus thought he at the laste:
"What! parde, rather than my felawe deye,
Yet shal I somwhat more unto hym seye."	525

And seyde: "Frend, syn thow hast swych dis-
	tresse,
And syn thee list myn arguments to blame,
Why nylt thiselven helpen don redresse,
And with thy manhod letten al this grame?
Go ravisshe hire ne kanstow not? for shame!	530
And other lat hire out of towne fare,
Or hold hire stille, and leve thi nyce fare.

"Artow in Troie, and hast non hardyment
To take a womman which that loveth the,
And wolde hireselven ben of thyn assent?	535
Now is nat this a nyce vanitee?
Ris up anon, and lat this wepyng be,
And kith thow art a man; for in this houre
I wol ben ded, or she shal bleven oure."

To this answerde hym Troilus ful softe,	540
And seyde, "Parde, leve brother deere,

Al this have I myself yet thought ful ofte,
And more thyng than thow devysest here.
But whi this thyng is laft, thow shalt wel
	here;
And whan thow me hast yeve an audience,	545
Therafter maystow telle al thi sentence.

"First, syn thow woost this town hath al this
	werre
For ravysshyng of wommen so by myght,
It sholde nought be suffred me to erre,
As it stant now, ne don so gret unright.	550
I sholde han also blame of every wight.
My fadres graunt if that I so withstoode,
Syn she is chaunged for the townes goode.

"I have ek thought, so it were hire assent,
To axe hire at my fader, of his grace;	555
Than thynke I, this were hire accusement,
Syn wel I woot I may hire nought purchace.
For syn my fader, in so heigh a place
As parlement, hath hire eschaunge enseled,
He nyl for me his lettre be repeled.	560

"Yet drede I moost hire herte to perturbe
With violence, if I do swich a game;
For if I wolde it openly desturbe,
It mooste be disclaundre to hire name.
And me were levere ded than hire diffame,	565
As nolde God but if I sholde have
Hire honour levere than my lif to save!

"Thus am I lost, for aught that I kan see.
For certeyn is, syn that I am hire knyght,
I moste hire honour levere han than me	570
In every cas, as lovere ought of right.
Thus am I with desir and reson twight:
Desir for to destourben hire me redeth,
And reson nyl nat, so myn herte dredeth."

520. **lambic,** alembic, a retort used in distilling. 529. **letten . . . grame,** stop all this grief. 530. **ravisshe,** carry off by force. 531. **other,** either. 532. **nyce fare,** foolish behavior. 538. **kith,** show. 539. **bleven,** remain. 547. **hath al this werre . . .,** has all this war because of the carrying off of women. Hesione, Priam's sister, was carried off by Telamon, and when the Greeks refused to give her up Paris in retaliation took Helen. 554. **so it were . . .,** provided she agreed. 555. **at,** of. 556. **hire accusement,** disclosure or betrayal of her. 557. **Syn,** since. **purchace,** obtain. 560. **lettre,** decree. 563. **it . . . desturbe,** interfere with the arrangement. 564. **disclaundre,** a reproach. 566. **As nolde God but if . . .,** God forbid that I should not hold her honor dearer than saving my life. 572. **twight,** pulled, pinched. 574. **dredeth,** is very apprehensive.

Thus wepyng that he koude nevere cesse,   575
He seyde, "Allas! how shal I, wrecche, fare?
For wel fele I alwey my love encresse,
And hope is lasse and lasse alway, Pandare.
Encressen ek the causes of my care.
So weilaway, whi nyl myn herte breste?   580
For, as in love, ther is but litel reste."

Pandare answerde, "Frend, thow maist, for me,
Don as the list; but hadde ich it so hoote,
And thyn estat, she sholde go with me,
Though al this town cride on this thyng by note.
I nolde sette at al that noys a grote!   586
For whan men han wel cryd, than wol they
     rowne;
Ek wonder last but nyne nyght nevere in towne.

"Devyne not in resoun ay so depe
Ne corteisly, but help thiselve anon.   590
Bet is that othere than thiselven wepe,
And namely syn ye two ben al on.
Ris up, for by myn hed, she shal not goon!
And rather be in blame a lite ifounde
Than sterve here as a gnat, withouten wounde.

"It is no shame unto yow ne no vice,   596
Hire to withholden that ye love moost.
Peraunter, she myghte holde the for nyce,
To late hire go thus to the Grekis oost.
Thenk ek Fortune, as wel thiselven woost,   600
Helpeth hardy man to his enprise,
And weyveth wrecches for hire cowardise.

"And though thy lady wolde a lite hire greve,
Thow shalt thiself thi pees hereafter make,
But as for me, certeyn, I kan nat leve   605
That she wolde it as now for yvel take.
Whi sholde thanne of ferd thyn herte quake?

Thenk ek how Paris hath, that is thi brother,
A love; and whi shaltow nat have another?

"And Troilus, o thyng I dar the swere,   610
That if Criseyde, which that is thi lief,
Now loveth the as wel as thow dost here,
God help me so, she nyl nat take a-grief,
Theigh thow do boote anon in this meschief.
And if she wilneth fro the for to passe,   615
Thanne is she fals; so love hire wel the lasse.

"Forthi tak herte, and thynk right as a knyght,
Thorugh love is broken alday every lawe.
Kith now somwhat thi corage and thi myght;
Have mercy on thiself, for any awe.   620
Lat nat this wrecched wo thyn herte gnawe,
But manly sette the world on six and sevene;
And if thow deye a martyr, go to hevene!

"I wol myself ben with the at this dede,
Theigh ich and al my kyn, upon a stownde,   625
Shulle in a strete as dogges liggen dede,
Thorugh-girt with many a wide and blody
     wownde,
In every cas I wol a frend be founde.
And if the list here sterven as a wrecche,
Adieu, the devel spede hym that it recche!"   630

This Troilus gan with tho wordes quyken,
And seyde, "Frend, graunt mercy, ich assente.
But certeynly thow maist nat so me priken,
Ne peyne non ne may me so tormente,
That, for no cas, it is nat myn entente,   635
At shorte wordes, though I deyen sholde,
To ravysshe hire, but if hireself it wolde."

"Whi, so mene I," quod Pandarus, "al this day.
But telle me thanne, hastow hire wil assayed,

---

575. that, as if. **581. as in,** in. **585. by note,** in unison. **587. rowne,** quiet down, *lit.* whisper. The line looks like a proverb; that in the next line is, of course, common. **589. Devyne.** The basic meaning of the word is "to foretell as a soothsayer," but contextually it suggests here the action of looking closely or examining. **590. corteisly,** with respect for others. One MS (Cx) reads *curyously*. **597. withholden,** retain. **602. weyveth,** abandons, forsakes. **614. do boote,** adopt a remedy. **618. alday,** continually. **620. for any awe,** regardless of fear. **622. sette the world on six and sevene,** stake the world on the throw of the dice. The present meaning of "at sixes and sevens" seems to be a later development and hardly fits the present passage. **625. upon a stownde,** in one hour (Skeat). **627. Thorugh-girt,** pierced through. **630. recche,** may care about. **633. priken,** goad on. **637. ravysshe,** carry off.

That sorwest thus?" And he answerde hym,
  "Nay."   640
"Wherof artow," quod Pandare, "thanne
  amayed,
That nost nat that she wol ben yvele appayed,
To ravysshe hire, syn thow hast nought ben
  there,
But if that Jove told it in thyn ere?

"Forthi ris up, as nought ne were, anon,   645
And wassh thi face, and to the kyng thow wende,
Or he may wondren whider thow art goon.
Thow most with wisdom hym and othere
  blende,
Or, upon cas, he may after the sende,
Er thow be war; and shortly, brother deere,   650
Be glad, and lat me werke in this matere.

"For I shal shape it so, that sikerly
Thow shalt this nyght som tyme, in som
  manere,
Come speken with thi lady pryvely
And by hire wordes ek, and by hire cheere,   655
Thow shalt ful sone aperceyve and wel here
Al hire entente, and of this cas the beste.
And fare now wel, for in this point I reste."

The swifte Fame, which that false thynges
Egal reporteth lik the thynges trewe,   660
Was thoroughout Troie yfled with preste wynges
Fro man to man, and made this tale al newe,
How Calkas doughter, with hire brighte hewe,
At parlement, withouten wordes more,
Ygraunted was in chaunge of Antenore.   665

The whiche tale anon-right as Criseyde
Hadde herd, she, which that of hire fader
  roughte,
As in this cas, right nought, ne whan he deyde,
Ful bisily to Jupiter bisoughte

Yeve hem meschaunce that this tretis broughte.
But shortly, lest thise tales sothe were,   671
She dorst at no wight asken it, for fere.

As she that hadde hire herte and al hire mynde
On Troilus iset so wonder faste,
That al this world ne myghte hire love un-
  bynde,   675
Ne Troilus out of hire herte caste,
She wol ben his, while that hire lif may laste.
And thus she brenneth both in love and drede,
So that she nyste what was best to reede.

But as men seen in towne, and al aboute,   680
That wommen usen frendes to visite,
So to Criseyde of wommen com a route,
For pitous joie, and wenden hire delite;
And with hire tales, deere ynough a myte,   684
Thise wommen, which that in the cite dwelle,
They sette hem down, and seyde as I shall telle.

Quod first that oon, "I am glad, trewely,
Bycause of yow, that shal youre fader see."
Another seyde, "Ywis, so nam nat I;
For al to litel hath she with us be."   690
Quod tho the thridde, "I hope, ywis, that she
Shal bryngen us the pees on every syde,
That, whan she goth, almyghty God hire gide !"

Tho wordes and tho wommanysshe thynges,
She herde hem right as though she thennes
  were;   695
For, God it woot, hire herte on othir thyng is.
Although the body sat among hem there,
Hire advertence is alwey elleswhere;
For Troilus ful faste hire soule soughte;   699
Withouten word, on hym alwey she thoughte.

Thise wommen, that thus wenden hire to plese,
Aboute naught gonne alle hire tales spende.

---

641. amayed, dismayed. **642. yvele appayed,** ill pleased. **643. To ravysshe hire.** The constr. is elliptical, but in a different word order would be clear: that knowest not that, to carry her off (*i.e.* by your carrying her off) she will be displeased. **648. with wisdom,** wisely. **blende,** blind. **649. upon cas,** perchance. **661. preste,** swift. **667. roughte,** cared. **683. wenden hire delite,** thought to please her. **684. deere ynough a myte,** dear enough at a mite. **689. so nam nat I,** so am not I. **695. thennes were,** were somewhere else. **702. Aboute naught,** for nothing.

WENden

Swich vanyte ne kan don hire non ese,
As she that al this mene while brende
Of other passioun than that they wende,   705
So that she felte almost hire herte dye
For wo and wery of that compaignie.

For which no lenger myghte she restreyne
Hir teeris, so they gonnen up to welle,
That yaven signes of the bittre peyne   710
In which hir spirit was, and moste dwelle;
Remembryng hir, fro heven into which helle
She fallen was, syn she forgoth the syghte
Of Troilus, and sorwfully she sighte.

And thilke fooles sittynge hire aboute   715
Wenden that she wepte and siked sore
Bycause that she sholde out of that route
Departe, and nevere pleye with hem more.
And they that hadde yknowen hire of yore
Seigh hire so wepe, and thoughte it kynde-
nesse,   720
And ech of hem wepte eke for hire destresse.

And bisyly they gonnen hire comforten
Of thyng, God woot, on which she litel
thoughte;
And with hire tales wenden hire disporten,
And to be glad they often hire bysoughte.   725
But swich an ese therwith they hire wroughte,
Right as a man is esed for to feele,
For ache of hed, to clawen hym on his heele!

But after al this nyce vanyte   *foolish + idle talk*
They toke hire leve, and hom they wenten
alle.
Criseyde, ful of sorweful pite,   731
Into hire chambre up went out of the halle,
And on hire bed she gan for ded to falle,
In purpos nevere thennes for to rise;   734
And thus she wroughte, as I shal yow devyse.

Hire ownded heer, that sonnyssh was of hewe,
She rente, and ek hire fyngeres longe and smale
She wrong ful ofte, and bad God on hire rewe,
And with the deth to doon boote on hire bale.
Hire hewe, whilom bright, that tho was pale,
Bar witnesse of hire wo and hire constreynte;
And thus she spak, sobbyng in hire com-   742
pleynte:

"Allas!" quod she, "out of this regioun
I, woful wrecche and infortuned wight,
And born in *cursed* corsed constellacioun,   745
myst Moot goon, and thus departen fro my knyght.
Wo worth, allas! that ilke dayes light
On which I saugh hym first with eyen tweyne,
That causeth me, and ich hym, al this peyne!"

Therwith the teris from hire eyen two   750
Down fille, as shour in Aperill ful swithe;
Hire white brest she bet, and for the wo
After the deth she cryed a thousand sithe,
Syn he that wont hire wo was for to lithe,
She moot forgon; for which disaventure   755
She held hireself a forlost creature.

She seyde, "How shal he don, and ich also?
How sholde I lyve, if that I from hym twynne?
O deere herte eke, that I love so,
Who shal that sorwe slen that ye ben inne?   760
O Calkas, fader, thyn be al this synne!
O moder myn, that cleped were Argyve,
Wo worth that day that thow me bere on lyve!
didst bear

"To what fyn sholde I lyve and sorwen thus?
How sholde a fissh withouten water dure?   765
What is Criseyde worth, from Troilus?
How sholde a plaunte or lyves creature
Lyve withouten his kynde noriture?
For which ful ofte a by-word here I seye,
That 'rooteles moot grene soone deye.'   770

707. **wery,** being weary. 729. **nyce vanyte,** foolish futility, foolish and idle talk. 731. **sorweful pite,** *i.e.* pitiful sorrow. 736. **ownded,** wavy, curly. 741. **constreynte,** distress. 745. **corsed constellacioun,** unfavorable position of the planets. 754. **lithe,** alleviate. 757. **How,** what. 762. **Argyve.** The name of Criseyde's mother is added by Chaucer. No source has been found. 763. **bere,** didst bear. 767. **lyves,** living; cf. l. 252 above. 769. **by-word,** proverb.

"I shal doon thus, syn neither swerd ne darte
Dar I noon handle, for the crueltee,
That ilke day that I from yow departe,
If sorwe of that nyl nat my bane be,
Thanne shal no mete or drynke come in me 775
Til I my soule out of my breste unshethe;
And thus myselven wol I don to dethe.

"And, Troilus, my clothes everychon
Shul blake ben in tokenyng, herte swete,
That I am as out of this world agon, 780
That wont was yow to setten in quiete;
And of myn ordre, ay til deth me mete,
The observance evere, in youre absence,
Shal sorwe ben, compleynt, and abstinence.

"Myn herte and ek the woful goost therinne
Byquethe I, with youre spirit to compleyne 786
Eternaly, for they shal nevere twynne.
For though in erthe ytwynned be we tweyne,
Yet in the feld of pite, out of peyne,
That highte Elisos, shal we ben yfeere, 790
As Orpheus with Erudice, his fere.

"Thus, herte myn, for Antenor, allas!
I soone shal be chaunged, as I wene.
But how shul ye don in this sorwful cas;
How shal youre tendre herte this sustene? 795
But, herte myn, foryete this sorwe and tene,
And me also; for, sothly for to seye,
So ye wel fare, I recche naught to deye."

How myghte it evere yred ben or ysonge,
The pleynte that she made in hire destresse?
I not; but as for me, my litel tonge, 801
If I discryven wolde hire hevynesse,
It sholde make hire sorwe seme lesse
Than that it was, and childisshly deface 804
Hire heigh compleynte, and therfore ich it pace.

Pandare, which that sent from Troilus
Was to Criseyde—as ye han herd devyse
That for the beste it was acorded thus,
And he ful glad to doon hym that servyse—
Unto Criseyde, in a ful secree wise, 810
Ther as she lay in torment and in rage,
Com hire to telle al hoolly his message,

And fond that she hireselven gan to trete
Ful pitously; for with hire salte teris
Hire brest, hire face, ybathed was ful wete. 815
The myghty tresses of hire sonnysshe heeris,
Unbroiden, hangen al aboute hire eeris;
Which yaf hym verray signal of martire
Of deth, which that hire herte gan desire. 819

Whan she hym saugh, she gan for sorwe anon
Hire tery face atwixe hire armes hide;
For which this Pandare is so wo-bygon
That in the hous he myghte unnethe abyde,
As he that pite felt on every syde. 824
For if Criseyde hadde erst compleyned soore,
Tho gan she pleyne a thousand tymes more.

And in hire aspre pleynte thus she seyde:
"Pandare first of joies mo than two
Was cause causyng unto me, Criseyde,
That now transmewed ben in cruel wo. 830
Wher shal I seye to yow welcom or no,
That alderfirst me broughte unto servyse
Of love, allas! that endeth in swich wise?

"Endeth thanne love in wo? Ye, or men lieth!
And alle worldly blisse, as thynketh me. 835
The ende of blisse ay sorwe it occupieth;
And whoso troweth nat that it so be,
Lat hym upon me, woful wrecche, ysee,
That myself hate, and ay my burthe acorse,
Felyng alwey, fro wikke I go to worse. 840

782. **ordre**, order, as in "a religious order." **789–90. feld of pite . . . Elisos**, Elysian field. **790. yfeere**, together. **791. fere**, companion. **796. herte**, sweetheart. **798. I recche naught to deye**, I care not if I die. **813. hireselven to trete**, to behave. **817. Unbroiden**, unbraided, dishevelled. **818. signal**, sign. **818-9. martire Of deth**, a martyr by death. **827. aspre**, bitter. **831. Wher**, whether, but used as an introductory intensive; see Language, § 75. **836. The ende . . . occupieth**, sorrow always takes possession of the end of bliss. **839. acorse**, curse.

Nas — was not
Ngt — not
Not but — nothing but

1.930-V-lie

168   TROILUS AND CRISEYDE   [*Book IV, 841–910*]

"Whoso me seeth, he seeth sorwe al atonys,
Peyne, torment, pleynte, wo, distresse!
Absent From Out of my woful body harm ther noon is,
As angwissh, langour, cruel bitternesse,
Anoy, smert, drede, fury, and ek siknesse.   845
I trowe, ywys, from hevene teeris reyne
For pite of myn aspre and cruel peyne."

"And thow, my suster, ful of discomfort,"
Quod Pandarus, "what thynkestow to do?
Whi ne hastow to thyselven som resport? *regard*   850
Whi wiltow thus thiself, allas, fordo?
Leef al this werk, and tak now heede to
That I shal seyn; and herkne of good entente
This, which by me thi Troilus the sente."

Tearing hirto pieces   (composing)
Tornede hire tho Criseyde, a wo makynge   855
So gret that it a deth was for to see.
"Allas!" quod she, "what wordes may ye brynge?
What wol my deere herte seyn to me,
Which that I drede *fear* nevere mo to see?
Wol he han pleynte or teris, er I wende?   860
I have ynough, if he therafter sende!"
if he sends for any.

She was right swich to seen in hire visage
As is that wight that men on beere bynde;
Hire face, lik of Paradys the ymage,
Was al ychaunged in another kynde.   865
The pleye, the laughter, men *one* was wont to fynde
In hire, and ek hire joies everichone,
Ben fled, and thus lith now Criseyde allone.

Goes Around Aboute hire eyen two a purpre ryng
Bytrent, in sothfast tokenyng of hire peyne,   870
That to biholde it was a dedly thyng;
For which Pandare myghte nat restreyne
The teeris from his eighen for to reyne.
But natheles, as he best myghte, he seyde
From Troilus thise wordes to Criseyde: 875

"Lo, nece, I trowe wel ye han herd al how
The kyng with othere lordes, for the beste,
Hath mad eschaunge of Antenor and yow,
That cause is of this sorwe and this unreste.
But how this cas dooth Troilus moleste,   880
That may non erthely mannes tonge seye;
For verray wo his wit is al aweye.

"For which we han so sorwed, he and I,
almost That into litel bothe it hadde us slawe;
But thorugh my conseyl this day, finaly,   885
He somwhat is fro wepynge now withdrawe,
And semeth me that he desireth fawe *willingly*
With yow to ben al nyght, for to devyse
Remedie in this, if ther were any wyse.

"This, short and pleyn, th'effect of my message,
As ferforth as my wit kan comprehende;   891
For ye, that ben of torment in swich rage,
May to no long prologe as now entende.
And hereupon ye may answere hym sende;
And, for the love of God, my nece deere,   895
So lef this wo er Troilus be here!"

"Gret is my wo," quod she, and sighte soore,
As she that feleth dedly sharp distresse;
"But yit to me his sorwe is muchel more,
That love hym bet than he hymself, I gesse.   900
Allas! for me hath he swich hevynesse? *Sorrow*
Kan he for me so pitously compleyne?
Iwis, this sorwe doubleth al my peyne.

"Grevous to me, God woot, is for to twynne,"
Quod she, "but yet it harder is to me   905
To sen that sorwe which that he is inne;
For wel woot I it wol my bane be,
And deye I wol in certeyn," tho quod she;
"But bid hym come, *Before* er deth, that thus me threteth,
Dryve out that goost which in myn herte beteth."   910

---

843. **Out of,** absent from. 850. **resport,** regard. 859. **drede,** fear. 861. **if he therafter sende,** if he sends for any. 866. **men,** one (indefinite, weakened form). 870. **Bytrent,** goes around; cf. 3. 1231. 884. **into litel,** almost. 887. **fawe,** willingly. 893. **entende,** attend, give attention. 896. **lef,** leave. 897. **sighte,** sighed. 909. **threteth,** threatens.

Thise wordes seyd, she on hire armes two
Fil gruf, and gan to wepen pitously.
Quod Pandarus, "Allas! whi do ye so,
Syn wel ye woot the tyme is faste by,
That he shal come? Aris up hastily,   915
That he yow nat bywopen thus ne fynde,
But ye wole have hym wood out of his
    mynde.

"For wiste he that ye ferde in this manere,
He wolde hymselven sle; and if I wende
To han this fare, he sholde nat come here   920
For al the good that Priam may dispende.
For to what fyn he wolde anon pretende,
That knowe ich wel; and forthi yet I seye,
So lef this sorwe, or platly he wol deye.

"And shapeth yow his sorwe for t'abregge,   925
And nought encresse, leeve nece swete!
Beth rather to hym cause of flat than egge,
And with som wisdom ye his sorwe bete.
What helpeth it to wepen ful a strete,
Or though ye bothe in salte teeris dreynte?   930
Bet is a tyme of cure ay than of pleynte.

"I mene thus: whan ich hym hider brynge,
Syn ye be wise, and bothe of oon assent,
So shapeth how destourbe youre goynge,
Or come ayeyn, soon after ye be went.   935
Women ben wise in short avysement;
And lat sen how youre wit shal now availle,
And what that I may helpe, it shal nat faille."

"Go," quod Criseyde, "and uncle, trewely,
I shal don al my myght me to restreyne   940
From wepyng in his sighte, and bisily,

Hym for to glade I shal don al my peyne,
And in myn herte seken every veyne.
If to this sore ther may be fonden salve,
It shal nat lakke, certeyn, on my halve."   945

Goth Pandarus, and Troilus he soughte,
Til in a temple he fond hym al allone,
As he that of his lif no lenger roughte;
But to the pitouse goddes everichone   949
Ful tendrely he preyed, and made his mone,
To doon hym sone out of this world to pace;
For wel he thoughte ther was non other grace.

And shortly, al the sothe for to seye,
He was so fallen in despeir that day,
That outrely he shop hym for to deye.   955
For right thus was his argument alway:
He seyde, he nas but lorn, so weylawey!
"For al that comth, comth by necessitee:
Thus to ben lorn, it is my destinee.

"For certeynly, this wot I wel," he seyde,   960
"That forsight of divine purveyaunce
Hath seyn alwey me to forgon Criseyde,
Syn God seeth every thyng, out of doutaunce,
And hem disponyth, thorugh his ordinaunce,
In hire merites sothly for to be,   965
As they shul comen by predestyne.

"But natheles, allas! whom shal I leeve?
For ther ben grete clerkes many oon,
That destyne thorugh argumentes preve;
And som men seyn that nedely ther is noon,   970
But that fre chois is yeven us everychon.   971
O, welaway! so sleighe arn clerkes olde,
That I not whos opynyoun I may holde.

912. **gruf,** face down. 916. **bywopen,** disfigured from crying. 917. **But,** unless. 920. **fare,** behavior. 921. **good,** wealth. 922. **pretende,** tend toward (a course of action). 927. **cause of flat than egge.** In the conferring of knighthood the candidate was touched with the flat of a sword; hence the beneficial effect caused by the flat as opposed to the edge of a blade. 928. **bete,** assuage (OE. *bētan,* to make better). 929. **ful a strete,** a streetful. 931. **tyme of cure . . .,** time spent on a remedy rather than in complaining. 934. **shapeth how desturbe . . .,** plan how to frustrate your going or how you may come back. 943. **seken every veyne,** search out every vein to find the cause of an illness and prescribe a remedy. 957 **ff.** Troilus's reasoning about predestination and free will is not in Boccaccio. The reflection is based on Boethius, v, pr. 2 and especially 3. Since the whole passage is absent from one group of MSS, it is probable that it is an addition made in revision. 961. **purveyaunce,** providence. 962. **forgon,** lose. 970. **nedely ther is noon,** there cannot be any such thing.

Handwritten top margin: Nede – need; necessity / Nedelyf of necessity / Nedly / Nedfully – of necessity

"For som men seyn, if God seth al biforn,
Ne God may nat deceyved ben, parde,
Than moot it fallen, theigh men hadde it sworn,   975
That purveiance hath seyn before to be.
Wherfore I sey, that from eterne if he
Hath wist byforn oure thought ek as oure dede,
We han no fre chois, as thise clerkes rede.   980

"For other thought, nor other dede also,
Myghte nevere ben, but swich as purveyaunce,
Which may nat ben deceyved nevere mo,
Hath feled byforn, withouten ignoraunce.
For yf ther myghte ben a variaunce   985
To writhen out fro Goddis purveyinge,
Ther nere no prescience of thyng comynge,

"But it were rather an opynyoun
Uncerteyn, and no stedfast forseynge.
And certes, that were an abusioun,   990
That God sholde han no parfit cler wytynge,
More than we men that han doutous wenynge.
But swich an errour upon God to gesse
Were fals and foul, and wikked corsednesse.

"Ek this is an opynyoun of some   995
That han hire top ful heighe and smothe yshore:
They seyn right thus, that thyng is nat to come
For that the prescience hath seyn byfore

That it shal come; but they seyn that therfore
That it shal come, therfore the purveyaunce   1000
Woot it byforn, withouten ignoraunce;

"And in this manere this necessite
Retorneth in his part contrarie agayn.
For nedfully byhoveth it nat to bee
That thilke thynges fallen in certayn   1005
That ben purveyed; but nedly, as they sayn,
Byhoveth it that thynges whiche that falle,
That they in certayn ben purveyed alle.

"I mene as though I laboured me in this,
To enqueren which thyng cause of which thyng
     be: 1010
As wheither that the prescience of God is
The certeyn cause of the necessite
Of thynges that to comen ben, parde;
Or if necessite of thyng comynge
Be cause certeyn of the purveyinge.   1015

"But now n'enforce I me nat in shewynge
How the ordre of causes stant; but wel woot I
That it byhoveth that the byfallynge
Of thynges wiste byforen certeynly
Be necessarie, al seme it nat therby   1020
That prescience put fallynge necessaire
To thyng to come, al falle it foule or faire.

974. For som men seyn. . . . The passage in Boethius (Chaucer's translation) reads: "For yif so be that god loketh alle thinges biforn, and god ne may nat ben desseived in no manere, than mot it nedes been, that alle thinges bityden the which that the purviaunce of god hath seyn biforn to comen. For which, yif that god knoweth biforn nat only the werkes of men, but also hir conseiles and hir willes, thanne ne shal ther be no libertee of arbitre" (prose 3). **977. That,** that which. **981. For other thought, nor other dede.** . . . Boethius: "ne, certes, ther ne may be noon other dede, ne no wil, but thilke which that the divyne purviaunce, that may nat ben desseived, hath feled biforn." **982. purveyaunce,** providence. **985. variaunce,** uncertainty, varying alternatives. Boethius: "But yif that god wot . . . that thinges mowen ben doon or elles nat y-doon—what is thilke prescience that ne comprehendeth no certein thing ne stable?" (prose 3). **986. writhen,** squirm. **purveyinge,** providence. **987. prescience,** fore-knowledge. **988. But it were rather an opynyoun** . . . Boethius: "For if that they mighten wrythen awey in othre manere than they ben purveyed, than sholde ther be no stedefast prescience of thing to comen, but rather an uncertein opinioun; the whiche thing to trowen of god, I deme it felonye and unleveful." **990. abusioun,** absurdity. **993. gesse,** imagine. **996. yshore,** shorn. **997. They seyn right thus** . . . Boethius: "For, certes, they seyn that thing nis nat to comen for that the purviaunce of god hath seyn it biforn that is to comen, but rather the contrarye, and that is this: that, for that the thing is to comen, therefore ne may it nat ben hid fro the purviaunce of god." **998. For that,** because. **1002-22. And in this manere** . . . The corresponding sentence in Boethius reads, "and in this manere this necessitee slydeth ayein into the contrarye partye: ne it ne bihoveth nat, nedes, that thinges bityden that ben purvyed, but it bihoveth, nedes, that thinges that ben to comen ben y-porveyed: but as it were y-travailed . . . to enqueren, the whiche thing is cause of the whiche thing:—as, whether the prescience is cause of the necessitee of thinges to comen, or elles that the necessitee of thinges to comen is cause of the purviaunce. But I ne enforce me nat now to shewen it, that the bitydinge of thinges ywist biforn is necessarie, how so or in what manere that the ordre of causes hath itself; although that it ne seme nat that the prescience bringe in necessitee of bitydinge to thinges to comen. **1006. purveyed,** foreseen.

Handwritten bottom margin: Shaved heads indicative of some degree of clergy in middle Ages. / tonsure – shaved head.

"For if ther sitte a man yond on a see,
Than by necessite bihoveth it
That, certes, thyn opynyoun sooth be,　　1025
That wenest or conjectest that he sit.
And further over now ayeynward yit,
Lo, right so is it of the part contrarie,
As thus,—nowe herkne, for I wol nat tarie:

"I sey, that if the opynyoun of the　　1030
Be soth, for that he sitte, than sey I this,
That he mot siten by necessite;
And thus necessite in eyther is.
For in hym nede of sittynge is, ywys,
And in the nede of soth; and thus, forsothe,
There mot necessite ben in yow bothe.　　1036

"But thow mayst seyn, the man sit nat therfore,
That thyn opynyoun of his sittynge soth is;
But rather, for the man sit ther byfore,
Therfore is thyn opynyoun soth, ywis.　　1040
And I seye, though the cause of soth of this
Comth of his sittyng, yet necessite
Is entrechaunged both in hym and the.

"Thus in this same wise, out of doutaunce,
I may wel maken, as it semeth me,　　1045
My resonyng of Goddes purveyaunce
And of the thynges that to comen be;
By which resoun men may wel yse
That thilke thynges that in erthe falle,
That by necessite they comen alle.　　1050

"For although that, for thyng shal come, ywys,
Therfore is it purveyed, certeynly,
Nat that it comth for it purveyed is;
Yet natheles, bihoveth it nedfully,
That thing to come be purveyd, trewely;　　1055
Or elles, thynges that purveyed be,
That they bitiden by necessite.

"And this suffiseth right ynough, certeyn,
For to destruye oure fre chois every del.
But now is this abusioun, to seyn　　1060
That fallyng of the thynges temporel
Is cause of Goddes prescience eternel.
Now trewely, that is a fals sentence,
That thyng to come sholde cause his prescience.

"What myght I wene, and I hadde swich a
thought,　　1065
But that God purveyeth thyng that is to come
For that it is to come, and ellis nought?
So myghte I wene that thynges alle and some,
That whilom ben byfalle and overcome,
Ben cause of thilke sovereyne purveyaunce　　1070
That forwoot al withouten ignoraunce.

"And over al this, yet sey I more herto,
That right as whan I wot ther is a thyng,
Iwys, that thyng moot nedfully be so;
Ek right so, whan I woot a thyng comyng,　　1075
So mot it come; and thus the bifallyng

1023. For if ther sitte . . . The example comes from the same passage in Boethius: "For certes, if that any wight sitteth it behoveth by necessitee that the opinioun be sooth of him that conjecteth that he sitteth; and ayeinward also is it of the contrarye: yif the opinoun be sooth of any wight for that he sitteth, it bihoveth by necessitee that he sitte. Thanne is heer necessitee in that oon and in that other: for in that oon is necessitee of sittinge, and, certes, in that other is necessitee of sooth." **see,** seat. **1027. ayeynward,** on the other hand. **1037. But thow mayst seyn** . . . Boethuis: "But therfore ne sitteth nat a wight, for that the opinioun of the sittinge is sooth; but the opinioun is rather sooth, for that a wight sitteth biforn. And thus, although that the cause of the sooth cometh of that other syde . . ., algates yit is ther comune necessitee in that oon and in that other." **1043. entrechaunged,** reciprocal. **1044. Thus in this same wise** . . . Boethius: "Thus sheweth it, that I may make semblable skiles [reasons] of the purviaunce of god and of thinges to comen." **1051. For although** . . . Boethuis: "For althogh that, for that thinges ben to comen, therfore ben they purveyed, nat, certes, for that they ben purveyed, therfore ne bityde they nat. Yit natheles, bihoveth it by necessitee, that either the thinges to comen ben y-purveyed of god, or elles that the thinges that ben purveyed of god bityden." **1058. And this suffiseth** . . . Boethius: "And this thing only suffiseth ynough to destroyen the freedom of oure arbitre, that is to seyn, of oure free wil. But now, certes, sheweth it wel, how fer fro the sothe and how up-so-doun is this thing that we seyn, that the bitydinge of temporel thinges is cause of the eterne prescience." **1065. What myght I wene** . . . Boethius: "But for to wenen that god purvyeth the thinges to comen for they ben to comen, what other thing is it but for to wene that thilke thinges that bitidden whylom ben causes of thilke sovereyn purvyaunce that is in god?" **1066. purveyeth,** foresees. **1072. And over al this** . . . Boethius: "And herto I adde yit this thing: that, right as whan that I wot that a thing is, it bihoveth by necessitee that thilke selve thing be; and eek, whan I have knowe that any thing shal bityden, so byhoveth it by necessitee that thilke thing bityde:—so folweth it thanne, that the bitydinge of the thing y-wist biforn ne may nat ben eschued."

Of thynges that ben wist bifore the tyde,
They mowe nat ben eschued on no syde."

Thanne seyde he thus: "Almyghty Jove in
 trone,
That woost of al this thyng the sothfastnesse,
Rewe on my sorwe, and do me deyen sone, 1081
Or bryng Criseyde and me fro this destresse!"
And whil he was in al this hevynesse,
Disputyng with hymself in this matere,   1084
Com Pandare in, and seyde as ye may here.

"O myghty God," quod Pandarus, "in trone,
I! who say evere a wis man faren so?
Whi, Troilus, what thinkestow to doone?
Hastow swich lust to ben thyn owen fo?
What, parde, yet is nat Criseyde ago!   1090
Whi list the so thiself fordoon for drede,
That in thyn hed thyne eyen semen dede?

"Hastow nat lyved many a yer byforn
Withouten hire, and ferd ful wel at ese?
Artow for hire and for noon other born? 1095
Hath Kynde the wrought al only hire to plese?
Lat be, and thynk right thus in thi disese:
That, in the dees right as ther fallen chaunces,
Right so in love ther come and gon plesaunces.

"And yet this is my wonder most of alle, 1100
Whi thow thus sorwest, syn thow nost nat yit,
Touchyng hire goyng, how that it shal falle,
Ne yif she kan hireself destourben it.
Thow hast nat yet assayed al hire wit.
A man may al bytyme his nekke beede   1105
Whan it shal of, and sorwen at the nede.

"Forthi tak hede of that I shal the seye:
I have with hire yspoke, and longe ybe,
So as acorded was bitwixe us tweye;
And evere mo me thynketh thus, that she 1110
Hath somwhat in hire hertes privete,

Wherwith she kan, if I shal right arede,
Destourbe al this of which thow art in drede.

"For which my counseil is, whan it is nyght,
Thow to hire go, and make of this an ende; 1115
And blisful Juno, thorugh hire grete myght,
Shal, as I hope, hire grace unto us sende.
Myn herte seyth, 'Certeyn, she shal nat wende.'
And forthi put thyn herte a while in reste,
And hold thi purpos, for it is the beste."   1120

This Troilus answerd, and sighte soore:
"Thow seist right wel, and I wol don right so."
And what hym liste, he seyde unto it more.
And whan that it was tyme for to go,
Ful pryvely hymself, withouten mo,   1125
Unto hire com, as he was wont to doone;
And how they wroughte, I shal yow tellen
 soone.

Soth is, that whan they gonnen first to mete,
So gan the peyne hire hertes for to twiste,
That neyther of hem other myghte grete, 1130
But hem in armes toke, and after kiste.
The lasse woful of hem bothe nyste
Wher that he was, ne myghte o word out
 brynge,
As I seyde erst, for wo and for sobbynge.

Tho woful teeris that they leten falle   1135
As bittre weren, out of teris kynde,
For peyne, as is ligne aloes or galle.
So bittre teeris weep nought, as I fynde,
The woful Mirra thorough the bark and rynde;
That in this world ther nys so hard an herte, 1140
That nolde han rewed on hire peynes smerte.

But whan hire wofulle weri goostes tweyne
Retourned ben ther as hem oughte to dwelle,
And that somwhat to wayken gan the peyne
By lengthe of pleynte, and ebben gan the welle

1090. **ago,** gone. 1091. **fordoon,** destroy. 1098. **dees,** dice. 1105. **al bytyme his nekke beede,** in good time offer his neck. 1136. **out of teris kynde,** beyond the nature of tears. 1137. **ligne aloes,** lign-aloes, an aromatic wood. 1139. **Mirra,** Myrrha, changed into a myrrh tree for deceiving her father into an incestuous relation, wept tears of myrrh. See Ovid, *Metam.*, x. 298–518. 1142. **hire,** their. 1144. **wayken,** diminish.

Of hire teeris, and the herte unswelle,　　1146
With broken vois, al hoors forshright, Criseyde
To Troilus thise ilke wordes seyde:

"O Jove, I deye, and mercy I beseche!
Help, Troilus!" and therwithal hire face　　1150
Upon his brest she leyde, and loste speche;
Hire woful spirit from his propre place,
Right with the word, alwey o poynt to pace.
And thus she lith with hewes pale and grene,
That whilom fressh and fairest was to sene.　　1155

This Troilus, that on hire gan biholde,
Clepyng hire name,—and she lay as for ded,
Withoute answere, and felte hir lymes colde,
Hire eyen throwen upward to hire hed,—
This sorwful man kan now noon other red,　　1160
But ofte tyme hire colde mowth he kiste.
Wher hym was wo, God and hymself it wiste!

He rist hym up, and long streght he hire leyde;
For signe of lif, for aught he kan or may,
Kan he non fynde in nothyng on Criseyde,　　1165
For which his song ful ofte is "weylaway!"
But whan he saugh that specheles she lay,
With sorweful vois, and herte of blisse al bare,
He seyde how she was fro this world
　　　yfare.　　1169

So after that he longe hadde hire compleyned,
His hondes wrong, and seyd that was to seye,
And with his teeris salt hire brest byreyned,
He gan tho teeris wypen of ful dreye,
And pitously gan for the soule preye,　　1174
And seyde, "O Lord, that set art in thi trone,
Rewe ek on me, for I shal folwe hire sone!"

She cold was, and withouten sentement,
For aught he woot, for breth ne felte he non;
And this was hym a pregnant argument

That she was forth out of this world agon.　　1180
And whan he say ther was non other woon
He gan hire lymes dresse in swich manere
As men don hem that shal ben layd on beere.

And after this, with sterne and cruel herte,　　1184
His swerd anon out of his shethe he twighte,
Hymself to slen, how sore that hym smerte,
So that his soule hire soule folwen myghte
Ther as the doom of Mynos wolde it dighte;
Syn Love and cruel Fortune it ne wolde,
That in this world he lenger lyven sholde.　　1190

Than seyde he thus, fulfild of heigh desdayn:
"O cruel Jove, and thow, Fortune adverse,
This al and som, that falsly have ye slayn
Criseyde, and syn ye may do me no werse,
Fy on youre myght and werkes so dyverse!　　1195
Thus cowardly ye shul me nevere wynne;
Ther shal no deth me fro my lady twynne.

"For I this world, syn ye have slayn hire thus,
Wol lete, and folwe hire spirit low or hye.
Shal nevere lovere seyn that Troilus　　1200
Dar nat, for fere, with his lady dye;
For, certeyn, I wol beere hire compaignie.
But syn ye wol nat suffre us lyven here,
Yet suffreth that oure soules ben yfere.

"And thow, cite, which that I leve in wo,　　1205
And thow, Priam, and bretheren al yfeere,
And thow, my moder, farwel! for I go;
And Atropos, make redy thow my beere.
And thow, Criseyde, o swete herte deere,
Receyve now my spirit!" wolde he seye,　　1210
With swerd at herte, al redy for to deye.

But, as God wolde, of swough therwith
　　sh'abreyde,
And gan to sike, and "Troilus" she cride;

1147. **al hoors forshright,** shrieked completely hoarse. 1152. **his,** its. 1153. **o poynt to pace,** on the point of passing. 1163. **long streght,** stretched out. 1177. **sentement,** sensation, feeling. 1179. **pregnant,** convincing. 1181. **say,** saw. **woon,** course, alternative. 1186. **how,** however. 1188. **Mynos,** the king of Crete who after his death became one of the judges of the shades in the lower world. **dighte,** ordain. 1193. **This al and som,** this is the sum and substance of the matter. 1208. **Atropos,** that one of the three Fates that cut the thread of life.

Primes & Thisbe — *Romeo + Juliet*

henne—hennce forth

Desides to live.

And he answerde, "Lady myn, Criseyde,
Lyve ye yet?" and leet his swerd down glide.
"Ye, herte myn, that thonked be Cipride!" 1216
Quod she, and therwithal she soore syghte,
And he bigan to glade hire as he myghte;

Took hire in armes two, and kiste hire ofte,
And hire to glade he did al his entente; 1220
For which hire goost, that flikered ay on lofte,
Into hire woful herte ayeyn it wente.
But at the laste, as that hire eye glente
Asyde, anon she gan his swerd espie,
As it lay bare, and gan for fere crye, 1225

And asked hym, whi he it hadde out drawe.
And Troilus anon the cause hire tolde,
And how hymself therwith he wolde han slawe;
For which Criseyde upon hym gan biholde,
And gan hym in hire armes faste folde, 1230
And seyde, "O mercy, God, lo, which a dede!
Allas, how neigh we weren bothe dede!

Criseyde is impressed

"Than if I nadde spoken, as grace was,
Ye wolde han slayn yourself anon?" quod she.
Yes, undoubtedly "Yee, douteles"; and she answerde, "Allas! 1235
I would not have For, by that ilke Lord that made me,
I nolde a forlong wey on lyve have be,
After youre deth, to han ben crowned queene
Of al the lond the sonne on shyneth sheene.

Would she have killed herself??

"But with this selve swerd, which that here is,
Myselve I wolde han slayn," quod she tho. 1241
"But hoo, for we han right ynough of this,
And lat us rise, and streght to bedde go,
And there lat us speken of oure wo.
They go to bed. For, by the morter which that I se brenne, 1245
candle *burning*
Knowe I ful wel that day is nat far henne."
hence

Whan they were in hire bed, in armes folde,
Naught was it lik tho nyghtes here-byforn.
For pitously ech other gan byholde,

As they that hadden al hire blisse ylorn, 1250
Bywaylinge ay the day that they were born;
Til at the laste this sorwful wight, Criseyde,
To Troilus thise ilke wordes seyde:

"Lo, herte myn, wel woot ye this," quod she,
"That if a wight alwey his wo compleyne, 1255
And seketh nought how holpen for to be,
It nys but folie and encrees of peyne;
And syn that here assembled be we tweyne
To fynde boote of wo that we ben inne,
It were al tyme soone to bygynne. 1260

"I am a womman, as ful wel ye woot,
And as I am avysed sodeynly,
So wol I telle yow, whil it is hoot.
Me thynketh thus, that nouther ye nor I
Ought half this wo to maken, skilfully; 1265
For ther is art ynough for to redresse
That yet is mys, and slen this hevynesse.

"Soth is, the wo, the which that we ben inne,
For aught I woot, for nothyng ellis is
But for the cause that we sholden twynne. 1270
Considered al, ther nys namore amys.
But what is thanne a remede unto this,
But that we shape us soone for to meete?
This al and som, my deere herte sweete.

"Now, that I shal wel bryngen it aboute, 1275
To come ayeyn, soone after that I go,
Therof am I no manere thyng in doute.
For, dredeles, withinne a wowke or two, *week*
I shal ben here; and that it may be so
By alle right, and in a wordes fewe, 1280
I shal yow wel an heep of weyes shewe.

"For which I wol nat make long sermoun,
For tyme ylost may nought recovered be;
But I wol gon to my conclusioun,
And to the beste, in aught that I kan see. 1285

1216. Cipride, Venus. **1223. glente,** glanced. **1245. morter,** mortar, a night light consisting either of a wax candle or a bowl of wax or oil with a wick. It was made to last a certain number of hours. **1262. am avysed,** have come to a conclusion. **1266. art,** plan, means. **1269–70. for nothyng . . . twynne,** is only because we must separate. **1278. wowke,** week (OE. *wucu,* var. of *wice*). **1285. to the beste,** for the best.

And, for the love of God, foryeve it me,
If I speke aught ayeyns youre hertes reste,
For trewely, I speke it for the beste;

"Makyng alwey a protestacioun,
That now thise wordes, which that I shal seye,
Nis but to shewen yow my mocioun   1291
To fynde unto oure help the beste weye;
And taketh it non other wise, I preye.
For in effect, what so ye me comaunde,
That wol I don, for that is no demaunde.   1295

"Now herkneth this: ye han wel understonde,
My goyng graunted is by parlement
So ferforth that it may nat be withstonde
For al this world, as by my jugement.
And syn ther helpeth non avisement   1300
To letten it, lat it passe out of mynde,
And lat us shape a bettre wey to fynde.

"The soth is this: the twynnyng of us tweyne
Wol us disese and cruelich anoye;
But hym byhoveth somtyme han a peyne,   1305
That serveth Love, if that he wol have joye.
And syn I shal no ferther out of Troie
Than I may ride ayeyn on half a morwe,   ✳
It oughte lesse causen us to sorwe;

"So as I shal not so ben hid in mewe,   ✳   1310
That day by day, myn owne herte deere,
Syn wel ye woot that it is now a trewe,
Ye shal ful wel al myn estat yheere.
And er that trewe is doon, I shal ben heere;
And thanne have ye both Antenore ywonne
And me also. Beth glad now, if ye konne,   1316

"And thenk right thus, 'Criseyde is now agon.
But what! she shal come hastiliche ayeyn!'
And whanne, allas? By God, lo, right anon,
Er dayes ten, this dar I saufly seyn.   1320
And than at erste shal we be so feyn,

So as we shal togideres evere dwelle,
That al this world ne myghte oure blisse teile.

"I se that ofte tyme, there as we ben now,
That for the beste, oure counseyl for to hide,
Ye speke nat with me, nor I with yow   1326
In fourtenyght, ne se yow go ne ride.
May ye naught ten dayes thanne abide,
For myn honour, in swich an aventure?
Iwys, ye mowen ellis lite endure!   1330

"Ye knowe ek how that al my kyn is heere,
But if that onliche it my fader be;
And ek myn othere thynges alle yfeere,
And nameliche, my deere herte, ye,
Whom that I nolde leven for to se   1335
For al this world, as wyd as it hath space;
Or ellis se ich nevere Joves face!

"Whi trowe ye my fader in this wise
Coveyteth so to se me, but for drede
Lest in this town that folkes me despise   1340
Because of hym, for his unhappy dede?
What woot my fader what lif that I lede?
For if he wiste in Troie how wel I fare,
Us neded for my wendyng nought to care.

"Ye sen that every day ek, more and more,   1345
Men trete of pees; and it supposid is
That men the queene Eleyne shal restore,
And Grekis us restoren that is mys.
So, though ther nere comfort non but this,
That men purposen pees on every syde,   1350
Ye may the bettre at ese of herte abyde.

"For if that it be pees, myn herte deere,
The nature of the pees moot nedes dryve
That men moost entrecomunen yfeere,
And to and fro ek ride and gon as blyve   1355
Alday as thikke as been fleen from an hyve,
And every wight han liberte to bleve
Where as hym liste the bet, withouten leve.

1291. mocioun, proposal. 1295. for that is no demaunde, of that there is no question. 1301. letten, prevent. 1312. trewe, truce. 1321. than at erste, then indeed, at last. 1324. there as we ben now, in our present situation. 1335. nolde leven for to se, would not cease to see. 1351. at ese . . . abyde, rest at ease. 1353. dryve, compel. 1356. Alday, continually. as been fleen, as bees fly. 1357. bleve, remain.

"And though so be that pees ther may be non,
Yet hider, though ther nevere pees ne were,
I moste come; for whider sholde I gon,   1361
Or how, meschaunce, sholde I dwelle there
Among tho men of armes evere in feere?
For which, as wisly God my soule rede,
I kan nat sen wherof ye sholden drede.   1365

"Have here another wey, if it so be
That al this thyng ne may yow nat suffise.
My fader, as ye knowen wel, parde,
Is old, and elde is ful of coveytise;
And I right now have founden al the gise,   1370
Withouten net, wherwith I shal hym hente.
And herkeneth now, if that ye wol assente.

"Lo, Troilus, men seyn that hard it is
The wolf ful, and the wether hool to have;
This is to seyn, that men ful ofte, iwys,   1375
Mote spenden part the remenant for to save.
For ay with gold men may the herte grave
Of hym that set is upon coveytise;
And how I mene, I shal it yow devyse.

"The moeble which that I have in this town
Unto my fader shal I take, and seye,   1381
That right for trust and for savacioun
It sent is from a frend of his or tweye,
The whiche frendes ferventliche hym preye
To senden after more, and that in hie,   1385
Whil that this town stant thus in jupartie.

"And that shal ben an huge quantite,—
Thus shal I seyn,—but lest it folk espide,
This may be sent by no wight but by me.

I shal ek shewen hym, yf pees bitide,   1390
What frendes that ich have on every side
Toward the court, to don the wrathe pace
Of Priamus, and don hym stonde in grace.

"So, what for o thyng and for oother, swete,
I shal hym so enchaunten with my sawes,   1395
That right in hevene his sowle is, shal he meete.
For al Appollo, or his clerkes lawes,
Or calkulyng, availeth nought thre hawes;
Desir of gold shal so his soule blende,
That, as me list, I shal wel make an ende.   1400

"And yf he wolde aught by his sort it preve,
If that I lye, in certayn I shal fonde
Distourben hym, and plukke hym by the sleve,
Makynge his sort, and beren hym on honde
He hath not wel the goddes understonde;   1405
For goddes speken in amphibologies,
And for oo sooth they tellen twenty lyes.

"Eke drede fond first goddes, I suppose,—
Thus shal I seyn,—and that his coward herte
Made hym amys the goddes text to glose,   1410
Whan he for fered out of Delphos sterte.
And but I make hym soone to converte,
And don my red withinne a day or tweye,
I wol to yow oblige me to deye."

And treweliche, as writen wel I fynde,   1415
That al this thyng was seyd of good entente;
And that hire herte trewe was and kynde
Towardes hym, and spak right as she mente,
And that she starf for wo neigh, whan she
          wente,

1362. **meschaunce,** confound it! 1370. **gise,** method. 1374. **ful,** *i.e.* whose hunger has been satisfied. **wether,** sheep. 1377. **grave,** make an impression on. 1380. **moeble,** personal possessions. 1382. **for trust,** because they trust him. **savacioun,** salvation, safe keeping. 1385. **in hie,** speedily. 1392. **Toward,** in the direction of. **to don . . . pace,** to cause the wrath of Priam to pass. 1396. **meete,** dream. 1397. **or.** We would say *and.* 1398. **calkulyng,** reckoning, divination. 1399. **blende,** blind. 1401. **sort,** lot, divination; **preve,** put to the test. 1402. **fonde . . .,** try to disturb him . . . while he is making his divination. 1404. **beren hym on honde,** make him believe. 1406. **amphibologies,** ambiguities. 1408. **drede fond first goddes,** fear first found gods. The idea goes back to classical times and was a commonplace in the Middle Ages. Robinson cites many examples. 1410. **glose,** interpret. The word is usually associated with explaining or commenting upon a (Biblical) *text,* and this accounts for Criseyde's phrase. We should say "utterance." 1411. **fered,** fear. **Delphos,** Delphi. **sterte,** started (away). 1412. **converte,** change his mind. 1413. **don my red,** to follow my advice. 1414. **oblige me,** pledge myself. 1415. **And treweliche . . .** The construction is loose. The *that* clauses depending upon *finde* have taken over the thought. 1419. **starf for wo neigh,** nearly died for woe. In this and the following line Chaucer anticipates the future action.

And was in purpos evere to be trewe: 1420
Thus writen they that of hire werkes knewe.

This Troilus, with herte and erys spradde,
Herde al this thyng devysen to and fro;
And verrayliche hym semed that he hadde
The selve wit; but yet to late hire go   1425
His herte mysforyaf hym evere mo.
But fynaly, he gan his herte wreste
To trusten hire, and took it for the beste.

For which the grete furie of his penaunce
Was queynt with hope, and therwith hem bi-
   twene   1430
Bigan for joie th'amorouse daunce.
And as the briddes, whanne the sonne is shene,
Deliten in hire song in leves grene,
Right so the wordes that they spake yfeere
Delited hem, and made hire hertes clere.   1435

But natheles, the wendyng of Criseyde,
For al this world, may nat out of his mynde;
For which ful ofte he pitously hire preyde
That of hire heste he myghte hire trewe fynde,
And seyde hire, "Certes, if ye be unkynde,   1440
And but ye come at day set into Troye,
Ne shal I nevere have hele, honour, ne joye.

"For also soth as sonne uprist o-morwe—
And God, so wisly thow me, woful wrecche,
To reste brynge out of this cruel sorwe—   1445
I wol myselven sle if that ye drecche!
But of my deeth though litel be to recche,

Yet, er that ye me causen so to smerte,
Dwelle rather here, myn owen swete herte.

"For trewely, myn owne lady deere,   1450
Tho sleghtes yet that I have herd yow stere
Ful shaply ben to faylen alle yfeere.
For thus men seyth, 'that on thenketh the
   beere,
But al another thenketh his ledere.'
Youre syre is wys; and seyd is, out of drede   1455
'Men may the wise atrenne, and naught atrede.'

"It is ful hard to halten unespied
Byfore a crepel, for he kan the craft;
Youre fader is in sleght as Argus eyed;
For al be that his moeble is hym biraft,   1460
His olde sleighte is yet so with hym laft,
Ye shal nat blende hym for youre womman-
   hede,
Ne feyne aright; and that is al my drede.

"I not if pees shal evere mo bitide;
But pees or no, for ernest ne for game,   1465
I woot, syn Calkas on the Grekis syde
Hath ones ben, and lost so foule his name,
He dar nomore come here ayeyn for shame;
For which that wey, for aught I kan espie,
To trusten on, nys but a fantasie.   1470

"Ye shal ek sen, youre fader shal yow glose
To ben a wif, and as he kan wel preche,
He shal som Greke so preyse and wel alose,
That ravysshen he shal yow with his speche,

1422. spradde, open wide, receptive. **1423. Herde . . . devysen.** Cf. the modern construction *heard tell.* **1425. The selve wit,** the same mind. **1426. mysforyaf,** had misgivings. **1427. wreste,** dispose. **1429. For which,** as a result of which. **penaunce,** suffering, woe. **1430. queynt,** quenched, extinguished. **1432. shene,** bright. **1435. clere,** unclouded, cheerful. **1436. wendyng,** departure. **1439. heste,** promise. **1444. wisly,** surely. **1446.** (just so surely) will I slay myself if you linger. **1447. recche,** care, matter. **1451. Tho sleghtes,** those tricks or stratagems. **stere,** propose. **1452. shaply,** likely. **1453. that on thenketh the beere . . .** The bear thinks one thing, his leader another. Chaucer indicates that the saying is proverbial. In OF the saying is fairly common as applied to the ass. It occurs in Arabic in reference to the camel (Singer, *Sprichwörter des Mittelalters,* I. 88). **1455. and seyd is,** and it is said. **1456. Men may the wise . . .** Another proverb, which occurs in a variant form in the *KnT,* 2449: Men may the old outrun and still not outwit, in which form it occurs in the *Proverbs of Alfred.* **1457. halten,** limp; still another proverb. **1458. kan the craft,** knows the trade, trick. **1459. sleght,** cunning, trickery. **as Argus eyed,** provided with as many eyes as Argus, *i.e.* a hundred. **1462. for youre wommanhede,** notwithstanding your woman's wiles. **1463. aright,** properly, *i.e.* successfully. **1464. not,** do not know. **1465. for ernest ne for game,** under any circumstances. **1471. glose,** persuade by smooth talking. **1473. alose,** praise, commend. **1474. ravysshen . . . yow,** carry you away.

Or do yow don by force as he shal teche;   1475
And Troilus, of whom ye nyl han routhe,
Shal causeles so sterven in his trouthe!

"And over al this, youre fader shal despise
Us alle, and seyn this cite nys but lorn,
And that th'assege nevere shal aryse,   1480
For-whi the Grekis han it alle sworn,
Til we be slayn, and down oure walles torn.
And thus he shal yow with his wordes fere,
That ay drede I, that ye wol bleven there.

"Ye shal ek seen so many a lusty knyght   1485
Among the Grekis, ful of worthynesse,
And ech of hem with herte, wit, and myght
To plesen yow don al his bisynesse,
That ye shul dullen of the rudenesse
Of us sely Troians, but if routhe   1490
Remorde yow, or vertu of youre trouthe.

"And this to me so grevous is to thynke,
That fro my brest it wol my soule rende;
Ne dredeles, in me ther may nat synke
A good opynyoun, if that ye wende;   1495
For whi youre fadres sleghte wol us shende.
And if ye gon, as I have told yow yore,
So thenk I n'am but ded, withoute more.

"For which, with humble, trewe, and pitous
  herte,
A thousand tymes mercy I yow preye;   1500
So rueth on myn aspre peynes smerte,
And doth somwhat as that I shal yow seye,
And lat us stele awey bitwixe us tweye;

And thynk that folie is, whan man may chese,
For accident his substaunce ay to lese.   1505

"I mene thus: that syn we mowe er day
Wel stele awey, and ben togidere so,
What wit were it to putten in assay,
In cas ye sholden to youre fader go,
If that ye myghten come ayeyn or no?   1510
Thus mene I, that it were a gret folie
To putte that sikernesse in jupertie.

"And vulgarly to speken of substaunce
Of tresour, may we bothe with us lede
Inough to lyve in honour and plesaunce,   1515
Til into tyme that we shal ben dede;
And thus we may eschuen al this drede.
For everich other wey ye kan recorde,
Myn herte, ywys, may therwith naught acorde.

"And hardily, ne dredeth no poverte,   1520
For I have kyn and frendes elleswhere
That, though we comen in oure bare sherte,
Us sholde neyther lakken gold ne gere,
But ben honured while we dwelten there.
And go we anon; for, as in myn entente,   1525
This is the beste, if that ye wole assente."

Criseyde, with a sik, right in this wise,
Answerde, "Ywys, my deere herte trewe,
We may wel stele awey, as ye devyse,
And fynden swich unthrifty weyes newe;   1530
But afterward, ful soore it wol us rewe.
And helpe me God so at my mooste nede,
As causeles ye suffren al this drede!

1475. **do yow don,** cause you to do. **1480. aryse,** be lifted. **1483. fere,** frighten. **1484. bleven,** remain. **1489. dullen,** grow weary. **1490. sely,** simple, unsophisticated. **but if,** unless. **1491. Remorde,** cause remorse. **vertu of youre trouthe,** quality of loyalty. **1494–5. in me . . . opynyoun.** While the general import of the statement is clear, the exact value to be attached to *synke* and *opynyoun* is not certain. In the sixteenth century *opynyoun* has as one of its senses "expectation of what will happen," a meaning that fits well enough the present passage. The use of *synke* may have been dictated by the needs of rime. We may venture the interpretation, "A favorable expectation cannot enter into my thought." **wende,** go away. **1496. shende,** ruin. **1499. pitous,** sorrowful. **1501. aspre,** sharp, bitter. **1505. accident . . . substaunce.** The substance is *that which truly is,* accident the variable quality (or sum of qualities) that accompanies it, *e.g.* stone as opposed to the hardness, whiteness, etc. of a particular stone; hence the distinction is between what is real, and therefore certain, and what permits of variation, and is therefore uncertain. See *PardT,* C 539. **1506. syn,** since. **1508. putten in assay,** try the experiment (to see . . .). **1513. vulgarly,** in the ordinary sense. Troilus is here contrasting his use of the word *substaunce* with the philosophical sense in which he has just used it. **1514. lede,** carry, take. **1516. Til into,** until. **1517. eschuen,** avoid. **drede,** uncertainty. **1518. recorde,** relate, call to mind (OF. *recorder*). **1523. gere,** goods (clothing, household utensils, etc.). **1525. go we,** let us go. **entente,** opinion. **1527. sik,** sigh. **1530. unthrifty,** unprofitable, resulting in no good.

"For thilke day that I for cherisynge
Or drede of fader, or for other wight,   1535
Or for estat, delit, or for weddynge,
Be fals to yow, my Troilus, my knyght,
Saturnes doughter, Juno, thorugh hire myght,
As wood as Athamante do me dwelle
Eternalich in Stix, the put of helle!   1540

"And this on every god celestial
I swere it yow, and ek on ech goddesse,
On every nymphe and deite infernal,
On satiry and fawny more and lesse,
That halve goddes ben of wildernesse;   1545
And Attropos my thred of lif tobreste,
If I be fals! now trowe me if yow leste!

"And thow, Symois, that as an arwe clere
Thorugh Troie rennest ay downward to the se,
Ber witnesse of this word that seyd is here,   1550
That thilke day that ich untrewe be
To Troilus, myn owene herte fre,
That thow retourne bakward to thi welle,
And I with body and soule synke in helle!

"But that ye speke, awey thus for to go   1555
And leten alle youre frendes, God forbede,
For any womman, that ye sholden so!
And namely syn Troie hath now swich nede
Of help. And ek of o thyng taketh hede:
If this were wist, my lif lay in balaunce,   1560
And youre honour; God shilde us fro mes-
    chaunce!

"And if so be that pees heerafter take,
As alday happeth after anger game,
Whi, Lord, the sorwe and wo ye wolden make,
That ye ne dorste come ayeyn for shame!   1565
And er that ye juparten so youre name,
Beth naught to hastif in this hoote fare;
For hastif man ne wanteth nevere care.

"What trowe ye the peple ek al aboute
Wolde of it seye? It is ful light t'arede.   1570
They wolden seye, and swere it, out of doute,
That love ne drof yow naught to don this dede,
But lust voluptuous and coward drede.
Thus were al lost, ywys, myn herte deere,
Youre honour, which that now shyneth so clere.

"And also thynketh on myn honeste,   1576
That floureth yet, how foule I sholde it shende,
And with what filthe it spotted sholde be,
If in this forme I sholde with yow wende.
Ne though I lyved unto the werldes ende,   1580
My name sholde I nevere ayeynward wynne.
Thus were I lost, and that were routhe and
    synne.

"And forthi sle with resoun al this hete!
Men seyn, 'the suffrant overcomith,' parde;
Ek 'whoso wol han lief, he lief moot lete.'   1585
Thus maketh vertu of necessite
By pacience, and thynk that lord is he
Of Fortune ay, that naught wole of hire recche;
And she ne daunteth no wight but a wrecche.

1536. estat, economic or social condition. **1539. wood,** mad. **Athamante,** from the oblique cases of *Athamas* (prob. through Dante). Athamas was driven mad by Juno, who pursued him to the lower world. **1540. Stix, the put of helle.** The river Styx was commonly equated with hell-pit in the Middle Ages. **1544. satiry and fawny,** satyrs and fauns. **1545. halve goddes,** demigods. **of wildernesse.** Satyrs and fauns haunted the woods and glades. **1546. Attropos,** Atropos, that one of the three Fates who cut the thread of life. **tobreste,** break in two. **1548. Symois,** a river in Troy. **1553. welle,** source. **1556. leten,** forsake. **1560. lay,** would lie. **1562. take,** take place. **1563. alday,** continually. **game,** mirth. **1566. juparten,** put in jeopardy. **1567. hoote fare,** rash conduct. **1568. care,** sorrow. A proverb, the basic idea of which appears in Haste makes waste, Better safe than sorry, etc. **1570. arede,** explain, foretell. **1576. honeste,** good repute. **1579. forme,** manner, way. **1581. name,** good name. **ayeynward wynne,** get back. **1584. the suffrant overcomith,** a translation of the Latin proverb, He who suffers conquers (*Vincit qui patitur*), frequently found in glosses to one of the precepts in the *Distichs of Cato* (I. 38). *Piers Plowman* has *Pacientes vincunt* (B XIII. 134). **1585. whoso wol han lief . . .,** he who will fain have something, must give up something he would fain have. A widely known proverb in the Middle Ages: *Qui ne done ke il aime, ne prent que desire (Proverbia Rusticorum)*. I have cited numerous other examples in *MLN*, LXXVI. 1–4. **1586. maketh,** imperative. The proverb occurs in *KnT*, 3042, and elsewhere in Chaucer. **1588. recche,** reck, care. The virtue of defying fortune is, of course, a commonplace.

"And trusteth this, that certes, herte swete,   1590
Er Phebus suster, Lucina the sheene,
The Leoun passe out of this Ariete,
I wol ben here, withouten any wene.
I mene, as helpe me Juno, hevenes quene,
The tenthe day, but if that deth m'assaile,   1595
I wol yow sen, withouten any faille."

"And now, so this be soth," quod Troilus,
"I shal wel suffre unto the tenthe day,
Syn that I se that nede it mot be thus.
But, for the love of God, if it be may,   1600
So late us stelen prively away;
For evere in oon, as for to lyve in reste,
Myn herte seyth that it wol be the beste."

"O mercy, God, what lif is this?" quod she.
"Allas, ye sle me thus for verray tene!   1605
I se wel now that ye mystrusten me,
For by youre wordes it is wel yseene.
Now, for the love of Cinthia the sheene,
Mistrust me nought thus causeles, for routhe,
Syn to be trewe I have yow plight my trouthe.

"And thynketh wel, that somtyme it is wit   1611
To spende a tyme, a tyme for to wynne.
Ne, parde, lorn am I naught fro yow yit,
Though that we ben a day or two atwynne.
Drif out the fantasies yow withinne,   1615
And trusteth me, and leveth ek youre sorwe,
Or here my trouthe, I wol naught lyve tyl
     morwe.

"For if ye wiste how soore it doth me smerte,
Ye wolde cesse of this; for, God, thow wost,
The pure spirit wepeth in myn herte   1620
To se yow wepen that I love most,
And that I mot gon to the Grekis oost.

Ye, nere it that I wiste remedie
To come ayeyn, right here I wolde dye!

"But certes, I am naught so nyce a wight   1625
That I ne kan ymaginen a wey
To come ayeyn that day that I have hight.
For who may holde a thing that wol awey?
My fader naught, for al his queynte pley!
And by my thrift, my wendyng out of Troie
Another day shal torne us alle to joie.   1631

"Forthi with al myn herte I yow biseke,
If that yow list don ought for my preyere,
And for that love which that I love yow eke,
That er that I departe fro yow here,   1635
That of so good a confort and a cheere
I may yow sen, that ye may brynge at reste
Myn herte, which that is o poynt to breste.

"And over al this I prey yow," quod she tho,
"Myn owene hertes sothfast suffisaunce,   1640
Syn I am thyn al hol, withouten mo,
That whil that I am absent, no plesaunce
Of oother do me fro youre remembraunce.
For I am evere agast, forwhy men rede
That love is thyng ay ful of bisy drede.   1645

"For in this world ther lyveth lady non,
If that ye were untrewe (as God defende!),
That so bitraised were or wo-bigon
As I, that alle trouthe in yow entende.
And douteles, if that ich other wende,   1650
I ner but ded, and er ye cause fynde,
For Goddes love, so beth me naught unkynde!"

To this answerde Troilus and seyde,
"Now God, to whom ther nys no cause ywrye,
Me glade, as wys I nevere unto Criseyde,   1655

1591. **Lucina the sheene,** Lucina the bright, *i.e.* the moon. 1592. **The Leoun . . .,** *i.e.* before the moon, having left the sign Aries, passes Leo (and Taurus, Gemini, and Cancer in between). This, as Skeat calculated, would take a little more than nine days. 1593. **wene,** doubt. 1602. **evere in oon,** ever alike, invariably. 1605. **tene,** sorrow. 1608. **Cinthia,** the moon. 1614. **atwynne,** separated. 1620. **pure spirit,** (my) very soul. 1623. **wiste remedie,** knew an effective means. 1625. **nyce,** stupid, resourceless. 1626. **ymaginen,** devise. 1627. **hight,** promised. 1629. **queynte pley,** cunning devices. 1630. **by my thrift,** a mild oath, as in 2. 1483, etc. 1633. **for,** at, in response to. 1644. **forwhy men rede,** wherefore men say. 1645. **bisy drede,** anxiety. 1647. **defende,** forbid. 1648. **so bitraised were,** would be so betrayed. 1649. **entende,** am aware of, apprehend. 1650. **other wende,** thought otherwise. 1654. **ywrye,** hidden. 1655. **as wys I,** as surely as I.

Syn thilke day I saugh hire first with yë,
Was fals, ne nevere shal til that I dye.
At shorte wordes, wel ye may me leve:
I kan no more, it shal be founde at preve."

"Grant mercy, goode myn, iwys!" quod she,
"And blisful Venus lat me nevere sterve   1661
Er I may stonde of plesaunce in degree
To quyte hym wel, that so wel kan deserve.
And while that God my wit wol me conserve,
I shal so don, so trewe I have yow founde,   1665
That ay honour to me-ward shal rebounde.

"For trusteth wel, that youre estat roial,
Ne veyn delit, nor only worthinesse
Of yow in werre or torney marcial,
Ne pompe, array, nobleye, or ek richesse   1670
Ne made me to rewe on youre destresse;
But moral vertu, grounded upon trouthe,
That was the cause I first hadde on yow routhe!

"Eke gentil herte and manhod that ye hadde,
And that ye hadde, as me thoughte, in despit
Every thyng that souned into badde,   1676
As rudenesse and poeplissh appetit,
And that youre resoun bridlede youre delit;
This made, aboven every creature,   1679
That I was youre, and shal while I may dure.

"And this may lengthe of yeres naught fordo,
Ne remuable Fortune deface.
But Juppiter, that of his myght may do
The sorwful to be glad, so yeve us grace,
Or nyghtes ten, to meten in this place,   1685
So that it may youre herte and myn suffise!
And fareth now wel, for tyme is that ye rise."

And after that they longe ypleyned hadde,
And ofte ykist, and streite in armes folde,
The day gan rise, and Troilus hym cladde,   1690
And rewfullich his lady gan byholde,
As he that felte dethes cares colde,
And to hire grace he gan hym recomaunde.
Wher him was wo, this holde I no demaunde.

For mannes hed ymagynen ne kan,   1695
N'entendement considere, ne tonge telle
The cruele peynes of this sorwful man,
That passen every torment down in helle.
For whan he saugh that she ne myghte
        dwelle,
Which that his soule out of his herte rente,   1700
Withouten more, out of the chaumbre he
        wente.

Explicit liber quartus.

1658. leve, believe. **1660. goode myn,** my "treasure." **1662. of plesaunce . . .,** in the condition of happiness to requite him. **1664. God . . . conserve,** God will preserve for me my mind. **1668. only,** unique. **1675. despit,** disdain. **1676. souned into badde,** tended toward evil. **1677. poeplissh,** vulgar. **1678. delit,** gratification of desire. **1681. fordo,** destroy. **1682. remuable,** changeable. **1683. do,** cause. **1689. streite,** tightly. **folde,** folded, clasped (each other). **1694. Wher,** whether. **demaunde,** question. **1696. entendement,** understanding.

Book V

Incipit liber quintus.

Aprochen gan the fatal destyne
That Joves hath in disposicioun,
And to yow, angry Parcas, sustren thre,
Committeth, to don execucioun;
For which Criseyde moste out of the town,   5
And Troilus shal dwellen forth in pyne
Til Lachesis his thred no lenger twyne.

The golde-tressed Phebus heighe on-lofte
Thries hadde alle with his bemes clene
The snowes molte, and Zepherus as ofte   10
Ibrought ayeyn the tendre leves grene,
Syn that the sone of Ecuba the queene
Bigan to love hire first for whom his sorwe
Was al, that she departe sholde a-morwe.

Ful redy was at prime Diomede,   15
Criseyde unto the Grekis oost to lede,
For sorwe of which she felt hire herte blede,
As she that nyste what was best to rede.
And trewely, as men in bokes rede,
Men wiste nevere womman han the care,   20
Ne was so loth out of a town to fare.

This Troilus, withouten reed or loore,
As man that hath his joies ek forlore,
Was waytyng on his lady evere more

As she that was the sothfast crop and more   25
Of al his lust or joies here-bifore.
But Troilus, now far-wel al thi joie,
For shaltow nevere sen hire eft in Troie!

Soth is that while he bood in this manere,
He gan his woful manly for to hide,   30
That wel unnethe it sene was in his chere;
But at the yate ther she sholde out ride,
With certeyn folk he hoved hire t'abide,
So wo-bigon, al wolde he naught hym pleyne,
That on his hors unnethe he sat for peyne.   35

For ire he quook, so gan his herte gnawe,
Whan Diomede on horse gan hym dresse,
And seyde to hymself this ilke sawe:
"Allas!" quod he, "thus foul a wrecchednesse,
Whi suffre ich it? Whi nyl ich it redresse?   40
Were it nat bet atones for to dye
Than evere more in langour thus to drye?

"Whi nyl I make atones riche and pore
To have inough to doone, er that she go?
Why nyl I brynge al Troie upon a roore?   45
Whi nyl I slen this Diomede also?
Why nyl I rather with a man or two
Stele hire away? Whi wol I this endure?
Whi nyl I helpen to myn owen cure?"

1. Jove is represented as controlling the Parcas (accusative form) or Fates, to whom he commits the carrying out (*to don execucioun*) of destiny. The three Fates are the sisters, Clotho (who spins the thread of life), Lachesis (who determines its length), and Atropos (who cuts it off). Atropos is mentioned at 4. 1546. **7. twyne,** twist, spin. The distinct functions of the three Fates were not always carefully observed. **10. molte,** melted. The melting of winter's snow and the return of spring, symbolized by Zephyrus, the West Wind, three times give us the duration of the action. Troilus first observed Criseyde at the Palladion, in April; cf. 1. 156. **12. sone of Ecuba.** Troilus was the son of Hecuba. **15. prime,** sunrise, the first hour. **Diomede,** the Greek warrior next in bravery to Achilles. Observe in this stanza the rimes *Diomede: blede* (with close *e*), *lede: rede* (with open *e*). The same careful distinction is made in the next stanza between the open ō in *loore, evere more* (from OE. *ā*) and the open ō in *forlore, more* (root), *here-bifore* (representing OE. ō lengthened in an open syllable). We do not know the precise difference between these two sounds, but Chaucer is generally careful to keep them apart and it is clear that they had not yet fallen together in his pronunciation. **18-19. rede . . . rede.** *Rime riche* or identical rime: the first *rede* means to "counsel or decide," the second "read." **20. care,** sorrow. **22. reed or loore,** counsel or advice. **24. waytyng on,** waiting for. **25. crop,** top (as of a tree), **more,** root; we would say "the beginning and end." **26. lust,** pleasure. **29. bood,** abode. **33. hoved,** remained. **34. al,** although. **36. gnawe,** used intransitively where we should expect a reflexive pronoun. **37. on horse . . . dresse,** to mount his horse. **41. atones,** at once, once and for all. **42. drye,** suffer, endure, go on living. **45. roore,** uproar.

But why he nolde don so fel a dede,   50
That shal I seyn, and whi hym liste it spare:
He hadde in herte alweyes a manere drede
Lest that Criseyde, in rumour of this fare,
Sholde han ben slayn; lo, this was al his care.
And ellis, certeyn, as I seyde yore,   55
He hadde it don, withouten wordes more.

Criseyde, whan she redy was to ride,
Ful sorwfully she sighte, and seyde "allas!"
But forth she moot, for aught that may bitide,
And forth she rit ful sorwfully a pas.   60
Ther is non other remedie in this cas.
What wonder is, though that hire sore smerte,
Whan she forgoth hire owen swete herte?

This Troilus, in wise of curteysie,   64
With hauke on honde, and with an huge route
Of knyghtes, rood and did hire companye,
Passyng al the valeye fer withoute;
And ferther wolde han riden, out of doute,
Ful fayn, and wo was hym to gon so sone;
But torne he moste, and it was ek to done.   70

And right with that was Antenor ycome
Out of the Grekis oost, and every wight
Was of it glad, and seyde he was welcome.
And Troilus, al nere his herte light,
He peyned hym with al his fulle myght   75
Hym to withholde of wepyng atte leeste,
And Antenor he kiste, and made feste.

And therwithal he moste his leve take,
And caste his eye upon hire pitously,
And neer he rood, his cause for to make,   80
To take hire by the honde al sobrely.

And Lord! so she gan wepen tendrely!
And he ful softe and sleighly gan hire seye,
"Now holde youre day, and do me nat to
     deye."

With that his courser torned he aboute   85
With face pale, and unto Diomede
No word he spak, ne non of al his route;
Of which the sone of Tideus took hede,
As he that koude more than the crede
In swich a craft, and by the reyne hire hente;   90
And Troilus to Troie homward he wente.

This Diomede, that ledde hire by the bridel,
Whan that he saugh the folke of Troie aweye,
Thoughte, "Al my labour shal nat ben on ydel,
If that I may, for somwhat shal I seye.   95
For at the werste it may yet shorte oure weye.
I have herd seyd ek tymes twyes twelve,
'He is a fool that wole foryete hymselve.' "

But natheles, this thoughte he wel ynough,
That "certeynlich I am aboute nought,   100
If that I speke of love, or make it tough;
For douteles, if she have in hire thought
Hym that I gesse, he may nat ben ybrought
So soon awey; but I shal fynde a meene,   104
That she naught wite as yet shal what I mene."

This Diomede, as he that koude his good,
Whan this was don, gan fallen forth in speche
Of this and that, and axed whi she stood
In swich disese, and gan hire ek biseche,
That if that he encresse myghte or eche   110
With any thyng hire ese, that she sholde
Comaunde it hym, and seyde he don it wolde.

50. fel, wicked. **51. spare,** refrain from. **53. in rumour of this fare,** upon the report of this conduct. **59. for aught that may bitide,** whatever may happen. **62. hire sore smerte,** it pained her sorely. **64. in wise of curteysie,** in courteous wise. **65. With hauke on honde.** The nobility, out riding, are often so pictured in the Middle Ages. It is not known whether falconry was practiced in the eastern Mediterranean at this time, but it was known even earlier in China. **70. it was ek to done,** it had to be done. **74. al nere . . .,** although his heart was not light. **77. made feste,** showed him honor, made much of him. **80. neer,** nearer. **his cause for to make,** to plead his case; cf. l. 84. **81. sobrely,** gravely, sadly. **88. sone of Tideus,** Diomede. **89. koude . . . craft,** *i.e.* had more than elementary knowledge of such a business. **94. on ydel,** in vain. **100. I am aboute nought,** I am acting to no purpose, accomplishing nothing. **101. make it tough,** am too forward. The phrase has different meanings in different contexts. See notes to 2. 1025, 3. 87. **106. koude his good,** knew what was best for him, knew what he was about (Skeat). **107. Whan this was don.** The reference may be either to Diomede's taking Criseyde's bridle and setting out or to the decision as to his course of conduct. The β manuscripts read *Whan tyme was,* *i.e.* in due time, when it seemed opportune. **109. disese,** distress. **110. eche,** increase.

For treweliche he swor hire, as a knyght,
That ther nas thyng with which he myghte hire
   plese,
That he nolde don his peyne and al his myght
To don it, for to done hire herte an ese;   116
And preyede hire, she wolde hire sorwe apese,
And seyde, "Iwis, we Grekis kan have joie
To honouren yow, as wel as folk of Troie."

He seyde ek thus, "I woot yow thynketh
   straunge,—   120
Ne wonder is, for it is to yow newe,—
Th'aquayntaunce of thise Troians to chaunge
For folk of Grece, that ye nevere knewe.
But wolde nevere God but if as trewe
A Grek ye sholde among us alle fynde   125
As any Troian is, and ek as kynde.

"And by the cause I swor yow right, lo, now,
To ben youre frend, and helply, to my myght,
And for that more aquayntaunce ek of yow
Have ich had than another straunger wight,   130
So fro this forth, I pray yow, day and nyght,
Comaundeth me, how soore that me smerte,
To don al that may like unto youre herte;

"And that ye me wolde as youre brother trete;
And taketh naught my frendshipe in despit;   135
And though youre sorwes be for thynges grete,
Not I nat whi, but out of more respit,
Myn herte hath for t'amende it gret delit.
And if I may youre harmes nat redresse,
I am right sory for youre hevynesse.   140

"For though ye Troians with us Grekes wrothe
Han many a day ben alwey yet, par le,
O god of Love in soth we serven bothe.
And, for the love of God, my lady fre,   144
Whomso ye hate, as beth nat wroth with me;

For trewely, ther kan no wyght yow serve,
That half so loth youre wratthe wold disserve.

"And nere it that we ben so neigh the tente
Of Calcas, which that sen us bothe may,
I wolde of this yow telle al myn entente;   150
But this enseled til anothir day.
Yeve me youre hond; I am, and shal ben ay,
God helpe me so, while that my lyf may dure,
Youre owene aboven every creature.

"Thus seyde I nevere er now to womman born;
For, God myn herte as wisly glade so,   156
I loved never womman here-biforn
As paramours, ne nevere shal no mo.
And, for the love of God, beth nat my fo,
Al kan I naught to yow, my lady deere,   160
Compleyne aright, for I am yet to leere.

"And wondreth nought, myn owen lady bright,
Though that I speke of love to yow thus blyve;
For I have herd er this of many a wight,
Hath loved thyng he nevere saigh his lyve.   165
Ek I am nat of power for to stryve
Ayeyns the god of Love, but hym obeye
I wole alwey; and mercy I yow preye.

"Ther ben so worthi knyghtes in this place,
And ye so fayr, that everich of hem alle   170
Wol peynen hym to stonden in youre grace.
But myghte me so faire a grace falle,
That ye me for youre servant wolde calle,
So lowely ne so trewely yow serve
Nil non of hem, as I shal, til I sterve."   175

Criseyde unto that purpos lite answerde,
As she that was with sorwe oppressed so
That, in effect, she naught his tales herde
But her and ther, now here a word or two.

---

117. apese, quiet. **120. yow thynketh straunge,** it seems to you strange. **124. But wolde nevere God . . .,** but God forbid . . . that you should not find . . . **127. by the cause,** because. **128. helply, to my myght,** helpful to the best of my ability. **132. how,** however. **me smerte,** it causes me pain. **133. like,** be pleasing. **137. out of more respit,** without further delay. **138. it,** *i.e.* Criseyede's state of mind implied in *sorwes*. **143. O,** one. **147. loth,** reluctantly. **151. this,** contraction of *this is;* **enseled,** sealed up. **156. For, God . . .,** as certainly as may God gladden my heart. **158. As paramours,** in the manner of a lover. **161. I am yet to leere,** I have yet to learn. **163. blyve,** quickly, soon. **176. purpos,** proposal, subject.

Hire thoughte hire sorwful herte brast a-two;
For whan she gan hire fader fer espie,   181
Wel neigh down of hire hors she gan to sye.

But natheles she thonked Diomede
Of al his travaile and his goode cheere,
And that hym list his frendshipe hire to bede;
And she accepteth it in good manere,   186
And wol do fayn that is hym lief and dere,
And trusten hym she wolde, and wel she
          myghte,
As seyde she; and from hire hors sh'alighte.

Hire fader hath hire in his armes nome,   190
And twenty tyme he kiste his doughter sweete,
And seyde, "O deere doughter myn, wel-
          come!"
She seyde ek, she was fayn with hym to mete,
And stood forth muwet, milde, and mansuete.
But here I leve hire with hire fader dwelle,   195
And forth I wol of Troilus yow telle.

To Troie is come this woful Troilus,
In sorwe aboven alle sorwes smerte,
With feloun look and face dispitous.
Tho sodeynly doun from his hors he sterte,   200
And thorugh his paleis, with a swollen herte,
To chaumbre he wente; of nothyng took he
          hede,
Ne non to hym dar speke a word for drede.

And ther his sorwes that he spared hadde
He yaf an issue large, and "deth!" he criede;
And in his throwes frenetik and madde   206
He corseth Jove, Appollo, and ek Cupide,
He corseth Ceres, Bacus, and Cipride,
His burthe, hymself, his fate, and ek nature,
And, save his lady, every creature.   210

To bedde he goth, and walweth ther and torn-
          eth
In furie, as doth he Ixion in helle;
And in this wise he neigh til day sojorneth.
But tho bigan his herte a lite unswelle
Thorugh teris, which that gonnen up to welle;
And pitously he cryde upon Criseyde,   216
And to hymself right thus he spak, and seyde:

"Wher is myn owene lady, lief and deere?
Wher is hire white brest? wher is it, where?
Wher ben hire armes and hire eyen cleere,   220
That yesternyght this tyme with me were?
Now may I wepe allone many a teere,
And graspe aboute I may, but in this place,
Save a pilowe, I fynde naught t'enbrace.

"How shal I do? whan shal she come ayeyn?   225
I not, allas! whi lete ich hire to go.
As wolde God ich hadde as tho ben sleyn!
O herte myn, Criseyde, O swete fo!
O lady myn, that I love and na mo!
To whom for evermo myn herte I dowe,   230
Se how I dey, ye nyl me nat rescowe!

"Who seth yow now, my righte lode-sterre?
Who sit right now or stant in youre presence?
Who kan conforten now youre hertes werre?
Now I am gon, whom yeve ye audience?   235
Who speketh for me right now in myn ab-
          sence?
Allas, no wight; and that is al my care!
For wel woot I, as yvele as I ye fare.

"How sholde I thus ten dayes ful endure,
Whan I the firste nyght have al this tene?   240
How shal she don ek, sorwful creature?
For tendernesse, how shal she ek sustene

---

180. Hire thoughte, it seemed to her. **brast,** would burst (subjunctive). **181. fer,** afar. **182. sye,** sink down, fall. **184. Of al his travaile,** for all his trouble (labor). **185. bede,** offer. **187. wol do fayn,** will fain do. **190. nome,** taken. **194. mansuete,** gentle, meek. **196. forth,** further. **199. feloun,** angry, sullen. **dispitous,** cruel, contemptuous. **204. spared,** refrained from. **205. yaf an issue large,** gave free vent to. **206. frenetik,** frantic. **208. Cipride,** Venus. **212. Ixion.** Because Ixion tried to make love to Juno, Jupiter had him chained hand and foot to a revolving wheel. **213. sojorneth,** remains. **214. tho,** then. **223. graspe,** grope. **227. As.** Introducing an exclamation: Would God . . .! **as tho,** then. **230. dowe,** give, bequeath. **233. sit, stant,** contracted forms of *sitteth, standeth.* **234. werre,** war, struggle. **242. For tendernesse,** because of her gentle nature.

Swich wo for me? O pitous, pale, and grene
Shal ben youre fresshe, wommanliche face
For langour, er ye torne unto this place."   245

And whan he fil in any slomberynges,
Anon bygynne he sholde for to grone,
And dremen of the dredefulleste thynges
That myghte ben; as, mete he were allone
In place horrible, makyng ay his mone,   250
Or meten that he was amonges alle
His enemys, and in hire hondes falle.

And therwithal his body sholde sterte,
And with the sterte al sodeynliche awake,
And swich a tremour fele aboute his herte,   255
That of the fere his body sholde quake;
And therwithal he sholde a noyse make,
And seme as though he sholde falle depe
From heighe o-lofte; and thanne he wolde wepe,

And rewen on hymself so pitously,   260
That wonder was to here his fantasie.
Another tyme he sholde myghtyly
Conforte hymself, and sein it was folie,
So causeles swich drede for to drye,
And eft bygynne his aspre sorwes newe,   265
That every man myght on his sorwes rewe.

Who koude telle aright or ful discryve
His wo, his pleynt, his langour, and his pyne?
Naught alle the men that han or ben on lyve.
Thow, redere, maist thiself ful wel devyne   270
That swich a wo my wit kan nat diffyne.
On ydel for to write it sholde I swynke,
Whan that my wit is wery it to thynke.

On hevene yet the sterres weren seene,
Although ful pale ywoxen was the moone;   275

And whiten gan the orisonte shene
Al estward, as it wont is for to doone;
And Phebus with his rosy carte soone
Gan after that to dresse hym up to fare
Whan Troilus hath sent after Pandare.   280

This Pandare, that of al the day biforn
Ne myghte han comen Troilus to se,
Although he on his hed it hadde sworn,
For with the kyng Priam alday was he,
So that it lay nought in his libertee   285
Nowher to gon,—but on the morwe he wente
To Troilus, whan that he for hym sente.

For in his herte he koude wel devyne
That Troilus al nyght for sorwe wook;
And that he wolde telle hym of his pyne,   290
This knew he wel ynough, withoute book.
For which to chaumbre streght the wey he
     took,
And Troilus tho sobrelich he grette,
And on the bed ful sone he gan hym sette.

"My Pandarus," quod Troilus, "the sorwe   295
Which that I drye, I may nat longe endure.
I trowe I shal nat lyven til to-morwe.
For which I wolde alweys, on aventure,
To the devysen of my sepulture
The forme; and of my moeble thow dispone,   300
Right as the semeth best is for to done.   301

"But of the fir and flaumbe funeral
In which my body brennen shal to glede,
And of the feste and pleyes palestral
At my vigile, I prey the, tak good hede   305
That that be wel; and offre Mars my steede,
My swerd, myn helm, and, leve brother deere,
My sheld to Pallas yef, that shyneth cleere.

243. grene, often coupled in ME. with wan and having much the same meaning. 245. torne, return. 249. mete, dream; so meten, l. 251. 252. hire, their. 254. awake, awaken. 260. rewen on, pity. 261. fantasie, delusion. 264. drye, suffer. 269. han, have (been). 272. swynke, labor. 276. And whiten . . ., and the bright horizon began to grow white in all the east. 278. carte, chariot. 279. dresse hym, prepare. 282. Ne myghte han comen, was not able to come. 284. alday, continually. 298. on aventure, on the chance. 299. devysen, describe, suggest. 300. moeble, goods. dispone, dispose. 303. brennen shal to glede, shall burn to ashes (ember). 304. pleyes palestral, athletic contests. An account of the funeral games in honor of Patroclus occupies Book XXIII of the Iliad. 305. vigile, wake. 306. offre, offer up to, as a sacrifice. 307. leve, dear. 308. yef, give.

"The poudre in which myn herte ybrend shal
   torne,
That preye I the thow take and it conserve   310
In a vessell that men clepeth an urne,
Of gold, and to my lady that I serve,
For love of whom thus pitouslich I sterve,
So yeve it hire, and do me this plesaunce,
To preyen hire kepe it for a remembraunce.

"For wele I fele, by my maladie,   316
And by my dremes now and yore ago,
Al certeynly that I mot nedes dye.
The owle ek, which that hette Escaphilo,
Hath after me shright al thise nyghtes two.   320
And, god Mercurye! of me now, woful
   wrecche,
The soule gyde, and, whan the liste, it fecche!"

Pandare answerde and seyde, "Troilus,
My deere frend, as I have told the yore,
That it is folye for to sorwen thus,   325
And causeles, for which I kan namore.
But whoso wil nought trowen reed ne loore,
I kan nat sen in hym no remedie,
But lat hym worthen with his fantasie.

"But, Troilus, I prey the, tel me now   330
If that thow trowe, er this, that any wight
Hath loved paramours as wel as thow?
Ye, God woot! and fro many a worthi knyght
Hath his lady gon a fourtenyght,
And he nat yet made halvendel the fare.   335
What nede is the to maken al this care?

"Syn day by day thow maist thiselven se
That from his love, or ellis from his wif,
A man mot twynnen of necessite,
Ye, though he love hire as his owene lif;   340
Yet nyl he with hymself thus maken strif.

For wel thou woost, my leve brother deere,
That alwey frendes may nat ben yfeere.

"How don this folk that seen hire loves wedded
By frendes myght, as it bitit ful ofte,   345
And sen hem in hire spouses bed ybedded?
God woot, they take it wisly, faire, and softe,
Forwhi good hope halt up hire herte o-lofte.
And, for they kan a tyme of sorwe endure,
As tyme hem hurt, a tyme doth hem cure.   350

"So sholdestow endure, and laten slide
The tyme, and fonde to ben glad and light.
Ten dayes nys so longe nought t'abide.
And syn she the to comen hath bihyght,
She nyl hire heste breken for no wight.   355
For dred the nat that she nyl fynden weye
To come ayein; my lif that dorste I leye.

"Thy swevenes ek and al swich fantasie
Drif out, and lat hem faren to meschaunce;
For they procede of thi malencolie,   360
That doth the fele in slep al this penaunce.
A straw for alle swevenes signifiaunce!
God helpe me so, I counte hem nought a bene!
Ther woot no man aright what dremes mene.

"For prestes of the temple tellen this,   365
That dremes ben the revelaciouns
Of goddes, and as wel they telle, ywis,
That they ben infernals illusiouns;
And leches seyn that of complexiouns
Proceden they, or fast, or glotonye.   370
Who woot in soth thus what thei signifie?

"Ek oother seyn that thorugh impressiouns,
As if a wight hath faste a thyng in mynde,
That therof cometh swiche avysiouns;
And other seyn, as they in bokes fynde,   375

---

314. plesaunce, favor. **319. owle.** The screeching of the owl has been considered a foreboding of death since classical times. **Escaphilo,** Ascalaphus, who, because he tattled on Proserpina, was changed into an owl. **327. trowen reed ne loore,** believe advice or teaching. **329. worthen,** dwell. **332. paramours,** as a lover, passionately. **335. halvendel the fare,** half the fuss. **339. twynnen,** separate, be parted. **344. yfeere,** together. **345. this folk,** these people. **By frendes myght,** *i.e.* the influence of relatives. **bitit,** happens. **347. faire,** quietly. **350. hurt,** hurts. **351. slide,** pass. **352. fonde,** strive. **359. faren to meschaunce,** go to the devil; cf. 2. 222. **361. doth,** makes. **penaunce,** suffering. **368. infernals,** an example of the romance plural, infrequent in Chaucer's verse. **369. leches,** physicians. **374. cometh,** properly *comen.*

That after tymes of the yer, by kynde,
Men dreme, and that th'effect goth by the
   moone.
But leve no drem, for it is nought to doone.

"Wel worthe of dremes ay thise olde wives,
And treweliche ek augurye of thise fowles,   380
For fere of which men wenen lese here lyves,
As revenes qualm, or shrichyng of thise owles.
To trowen on it bothe fals and foul is.
Allas, allas, so noble a creature
As is a man shal dreden swich ordure!   385

"For which with al myn herte I the biseche,
Unto thiself that al this thow foryyve;
And ris now up withowten more speche,
And lat us caste how forth may best be dryve
This tyme, and ek how fresshly we may lyve 390
Whan that she comth, the which shal be right
   soone.
God helpe me so, the beste is thus to doone.

"Ris, lat us speke of lusty lif in Troie
That we han led, and forth the tyme dryve;
And ek of tyme comyng us rejoie,   395
That bryngen shal oure blisse now so blyve;
And langour of thise twyes dayes fyve
We shal therwith so foryete or oppresse,
That wel unneth it don shal us duresse.

"This town is ful of lordes al aboute,
And trewes lasten al this mene while.   400
Go we pleye us in som lusty route
To Sarpedoun, nat hennes but a myle;
And thus thow shalt the tyme wel bygile,
And dryve it forth unto that blisful morwe, 405
That thow hire se, that cause is of thi sorwe.

"Now ris, my deere brother Troilus,
For certes, it non honour is to the
To wepe, and in thi bedde to jouken thus.
For trewelich, of o thyng trust to me,   410
If thow thus ligge a day, or two, or thre,
The folk wol wene that thow, for cowardise,
The feynest sik, and that thow darst nat rise!"

This Troilus answerde, "O brother deere,
This knowen folk that han ysuffred peyne, 415
That though he wepe and make sorwful cheere,
That feleth harm and smert in every veyne,
No wonder is; and though ich evere pleyne,
Or alwey wepe, I am no thyng to blame,
Syn I have lost the cause of al my game.   420

"But syn of fyne force I mot arise,
I shal arise as soone as evere I may;
And God, to whom myn herte I sacrifice,
So sende us hastely the tenthe day!
For was ther nevere fowel so fayn of May   425
As I shal ben, whan that she comth in Troie,
That cause is of my torment and my joie.

"But whider is thi reed," quod Troilus,
"That we may pleye us best in al this town?"
"By God, my conseil is," quod Pandarus,   430
"To ride and pleye us with kyng Sarpedoun."
So longe of this they speken up and down,
Til Troilus gan at the laste assente
To rise, and forth to Sarpedoun they wente.

This Sarpedoun, as he that honourable   435
Was evere his lyve, and ful of heigh largesse,
With al that myghte yserved ben on table,
That deynte was, al coste it gret richesse,
He fedde hem day by day, that swich noblesse,

376. **after tymes,** according to the seasons. 378. **leve,** believe. **nought to doone,** not to be done. 379. **Wel worthe . . .,** well be it ever to these old women as for dreams, *i.e.* let them believe in dreams. 380. **of thise fowles,** from these birds. 381. **wenen lese** (infin.), think they will lose. 382. **As,** such as. **qualm,** croaking. 384. **Allas . . .,** alas (that). 385. **ordure,** nonsense (*lit.* filth). 387. **Unto thiself . . . foryyve,** have mercy on thyself (translating the Italian *a te stesso perdona*). 389. **dryve,** driven away, made to pass. 390. **fresshly,** eagerly. 396. **blyve,** soon. 398. **oppresse,** suppress. 399. **duresse,** hardship. 401. **trewes,** truces, or days of truce (Skeat). 402. **pleye us,** amuse ourselves. **route,** band, company. 403. **Sarpedoun.** See note to 4. 52. There is no mention of Sarpedon's return to Troy after being captured by the Greeks. 409. **jouken,** lie at rest; *lit.* to roost (OF. *jouqier*). 411. **ligge,** lie. 418. **evere,** forever. 421. **of fyne force,** of sheer necessity (OF. *par fine force, a fine force*). 428. **whider is thi reed,** whither (in what way) is it your opinion. 432. **up and down.** We should say "backwards and forwards." 438. **al . . .,** although it cost a fortune. 439. **noblesse,** splendor.

As seyden bothe the mooste and ek the leeste,
Was nevere er that day wist at any feste. 441

Nor in this world ther is non instrument
Delicious, thorough wynd or touche of corde,
As fer as any wight hath evere ywent,
That tonge telle or herte may recorde, 445
That at that feste it nas wel herd acorde;
Ne of ladys ek so fair a compaignie
On daunce, er tho, was nevere iseye with ië.

But what availeth this to Troilus,
That for his sorwe nothyng of it roughte? 450
For evere in oon his herte pietous
Ful bisyly Criseyde, his lady, soughte.
On hire was evere al that his herte thoughte,
Now this, now that, so faste ymagenynge,
That glade, iwis, kan hym no festeyinge. 455

Thise ladies ek that at this feste ben,
Syn that he saugh his lady was aweye,
It was his sorwe upon hem for to sen,
Or for to here on instruments so pleye.
For she, that of his herte berth the keye, 460
Was absent, lo, this was his fantasie,
That no wight sholde maken melodie.

Nor ther nas houre in al the day or nyght,
Whan he was there as no wight myghte hym
     heere,
That he ne seyde, "O lufsom lady bryght, 465
How have ye faren syn that ye were here?
Welcome, ywis, myn owne lady deere!"
But weylaway, al this nas but a maze.
Fortune his howve entended bet to glaze!

The lettres ek that she of olde tyme 470
Hadde hym ysent, he wolde allone rede

An hondred sithe atwixen noon and prime,
Refiguryng hire shap, hire wommanhede,
Withinne his herte, and every word or dede
That passed was; and thus he drof t'an ende 475
The ferthe day, and seyde he wolde wende.

And seyde, "Leve brother Pandarus,
Intendestow that we shal here bleve
Til Sarpedoun wol forth congeyen us?
Yet were it fairer that we toke oure leve. 480
For Goddes love, lat us now soone at eve
Oure leve take, and homward lat us torne;
For treweliche, I nyl nat thus sojourne."

Pandare answerde, "Be we comen hider
To fecchen fir, and rennen hom ayein? 485
God help me so, I kan nat tellen whider
We myghte gon, if I shal sothly seyn,
Ther any wight is of us more feyn
Than Sarpedoun; and if we hennes hye
Thus sodeynly, I holde it vilanye, 490

"Syn that we seyden that we wolde bleve
With hym a wowke; and now, thus sodeynly,
The ferthe day to take of hym owre leve,
He wolde wondren on it, trewely!
Lat us holde forth oure purpos fermely. 495
And syn that ye bihighten hym to bide,
Holde forward now, and after lat us ride."

Thus Pandarus, with alle peyne and wo,
Made hym to dwelle; and at the wikes ende,
Of Sarpedoun they toke hire leve tho, 500
And on hire wey they spedden hem to wende.
Quod Troilus, "Now Lord me grace sende,
That I may fynden, at myn hom-comynge
Criseyde comen!" and therwith gan he synge.

---

445. recorde, remember. **448. On daunce,** in the dance. **451. evere in oon,** continually, without variation. **455. glade,** make glad. **festeyinge,** festivity, entertainment. **456. Thise ladies.** *Thise* is generalizing, as often. **458. sen,** look upon. **460. For,** because. **461. fantasie,** notion, idea. **464. there as,** where. **466. faren,** fared. **468. maze,** delusion. **469. his howve . . . to glaze.** *Howve,* hood; to glaze one's hood is to mock or delude a person. See 2. 867–8, where to have a glass head is to be vulnerable. **472. sithe,** (in plural sense) times. **prime,** sunrise. **476. wende,** go, leave. **479. congeyen,** bid us goodbye, *i.e.* invite us to go. **481. soone,** promptly, without delay. **485. and rennen . . .,** *i.e.* before the live coals die out. **488. Ther,** where. **490. vilanye,** bad manners (the conduct of a villein). **492. wowke,** week; see note to 4.1278. **496. bihighten,** promised.

"Ye, haselwode!" thoughte this Pandare,   505
And to hymself ful softeliche he seyde,
"God woot, refreyden may this hote fare,
Er Calkas sende Troilus Criseyde!"
But natheles, he japed thus, and pleyde,   509
And swor, ywys, his herte hym wel bihighte,
She wolde come as soone as evere she myghte.

Whan they unto the paleys were ycomen
Of Troilus, they doun of hors alighte,
And to the chambre hire wey than han they
    nomen.
And into tyme that it gan to nyghte,   515
They spaken of Criseÿde the brighte;
And after this, whan that hem bothe leste,
They spedde hem fro the soper unto reste.

On morwe, as soone as day bygan to clere,
This Troilus gan of his slep t'abrayde,   520
And to Pandare, his owen brother deere,
"For love of God," ful pitously he sayde,
"As go we sen the palais of Criseyde;
For syn we yet may have namore feste,
So lat us sen hire paleys atte leeste."   525

And therwithal, his meyne for to blende,
A cause he fond in towne for to go,
And to Criseydes hous they gonnen wende.
But Lord! this sely Troilus was wo!   529
Hym thoughte his sorwful herte braste a-two.
For, whan he saugh hire dores spered alle,
Wel neigh for sorwe adoun he gan to falle.

Therwith, whan he was war and gan biholde
How shet was every wyndow of the place,   534
As frost, hym thoughte, his herte gan to colde;
For which with chaunged dedlich pale face,
Withouten word, he forthby gan to pace,

And, as God wolde, he gan so faste ride,
That no wight of his contenance espide.

Than seide he thus: "O paleys desolat,   540
O hous of houses whilom best ihight,
O paleys empty and disconsolat,
O thow lanterne of which queynt is the light,
O paleys, whilom day, that now art nyght,
Wel oughtestow to falle, and I to dye,   545
Syn she is went that wont was us to gye!

"O paleis, whilom crowne of houses alle,
Enlumyned with sonne of alle blisse!
O ryng, fro which the ruby is out falle,
O cause of wo, that cause hast ben of lisse!   550
Yet, syn I may no bet, fayn wolde I kisse
Thy colde dores, dorste I for this route;
And farwel shryne, of which the seynt is oute!"

Therwith he caste on Pandarus his yë,   554
With chaunged face, and pitous to biholde;
And whan he myghte his tyme aright aspie,
Ay as he rood, to Pandarus he tolde
His newe sorwe, and ek his joies olde,
So pitously and with so ded an hewe,
That every wight myghte on his sorwe rewe.

Fro thennesforth he rideth up and down,   561
And every thyng com hym to remembraunce
As he rood forby places of the town
In which he whilom hadde al his plesaunce.
"Lo, yonder saugh ich last my lady daunce;   565
And in that temple, with hire eyen cleere,
Me kaughte first my righte lady dere.

"And yonder have I herd ful lustyly
Me dere herte laugh; and yonder pleye
Saugh ich hire ones ek ful blisfully.   570

---

505. **haselwode.** Cf. note to 3. 890. 507. **refreyden,** cool off. **this hote fare,** eager anticipation, impatience. 509. **japed,** dissembled (joked). 510. **his herte . . . bihighte,** his heart told him (*lit.* promised). 515. **into tyme,** until the time. **to nyghte,** to grow dark. 519. **to clere,** to grow light, to dawn. 520. **abrayde,** start, wake up. 523. **As,** hortatory *as:* let us go. 526. **his meyne,** the members of his household. **blende,** blind. 530. **braste,** would burst (pt. subj.). 531. **spered,** barred. 537. **forthby . . . to pace,** to go away. 539. **espide,** caught sight (of). 541. **ihight,** called. 543. **queynt,** quenched, extinguished. 545. **oughtestow,** oughtest thou. 546. **gye,** guide. 550. **lisse,** peace, joy. 551. **may no bet,** may do no better. 552. **for this route,** because of this crowd, although it can also mean "before this crowd." 559. **ded,** deadly, wan.

And yonder ones to me gan she seye,
'Now goode swete, love me wel, I preye;'
And yond so goodly gan she me biholde,
That to the deth myn herte is to hire holde.

"And at that corner, in the yonder hous,   575
Herde I myn alderlevest lady deere
So wommanly, with vois melodious,
Syngen so wel, so goodly, and so clere,
That in my soule yet me thynketh ich here
The blisful sown; and in that yonder place   580
My lady first me took unto hire grace."

Thanne thoughte he thus, "O blisful lord Cu-
    pide,
Whan I the proces have in my memorie,
How thow me hast wereyed on every syde,
Men myght a book make of it, lik a storie.   585
What nede is the to seke on me victorie,
Syn I am thyn, and holly at thi wille?
What joie hastow thyn owen folk to spille?

"Wel hastow, lord, ywroke on me thyn ire,
Thow myghty god, and dredefull for to greve!
Now mercy, lord! thow woost wel I desire   591
Thi grace moost of alle lustes leeve,
And lyve and dye I wol in thy byleve;
For which I n'axe in guerdoun but o bone,
That thow Criseyde ayein me sende sone.   595

"Distreyne hire herte as faste to retorne,
As thow doost myn to longen hire to see,
Than woot I wel that she nyl naught sojorne.
Now blisful lord, so cruel thow ne be
Unto the blood of Troie, I preye the,   600
As Juno was unto the blood Thebane,
For which the folk of Thebes caughte hire
    bane."

And after this he to the yates wente
Ther as Criseyde out rood a ful good paas,   604
And up and down ther made he many a wente,
And to hymself ful ofte he seyde, "Allas!
Fro hennes rood my blisse and my solas!
As wolde blisful God now, for his joie,
I myghte hire sen ayein come into Troie!

"And to the yonder hille I gan hire gyde,   610
Allas, and ther I took of hire my leve!
And yond I saugh hire to hire fader ride,
For sorwe of which myn herte shal tocleve.
And hider hom I com whan it was eve,
And here I dwelle out cast from alle joie,   615
And shal, til I may sen hire eft in Troie."

And of hymself ymagened he ofte
To ben defet, and pale, and waxen lesse
Than he was wont, and that men seyden softe,
"What may it be? Who kan the sothe gesse
Whi Troilus hath al this hevynesse?"   621
And al this nas but his malencolie,
That he hadde of hymself swich fantasie.

Another tyme ymaginen he wolde
That every wight that wente by the weye   625
Hadde of hym routhe, and that they seyen
    sholde,
"I am right sory Troilus wol deye."
And thus he drof a day yet forth or tweye,
As ye have herd; swich lif right gan he lede,
As he that stood bitwixen hope and drede.   630

For which hym likede in his songes shewe
Th'enchesoun of his wo, as he best myghte,
And made a song of wordes but a fewe,
Somwhat his woful herte for to lighte.

---

574. holde, bound. **576. alderlevest,** dearest of all. **580. sown,** sound. **584. wereyed,** made war. **585. storie,** history (the usual meaning) or, since he thinks of himself as a martyr to love, saint's legend (the ecclesiastical sense). **590. dredefull,** terrible. **592. lustes leeve,** dear delights. **593. byleve,** belief, creed. **594. o bone,** one boon. **596. Distreyne,** constrain. **faste,** firmly. **598. Than,** then. **sojorne,** delay, tarry. **601. As Juno was.** Juno's hostility towards Thebes is often referred to; cf. the *Teseida,* III. 1, etc. It was due to her resentment of Jove's infidelities with Theban women, including Semele (by whom he had Bacchus) and Alcmene (by whom he had Hercules). **604. Ther as,** where. **paas,** distance. **605. wente,** turn. **608. As wolde . . . God,** would God! **613. tocleve,** split in two. **618. defet,** wasted away, disfigured. **628. drof . . . forth,** caused to pass. **632. enchesoun,** cause, reason.

And whan he was from every mannes syghte,
With softe vois he of his lady deere,   636
That absent was, gan synge as ye may heere.

Canticus Troili

"O sterre, of which I lost have al the light,
With herte soor wel oughte I to biwaille,   639
That evere derk in torment, nyght by nyght,
Toward my deth with wynd in steere I saille;
For which the tenthe nyght, if that I faille
The gydyng of thi bemes bright an houre,
My ship and me Caribdis wol devoure."

This song whan he thus songen hadde, soone
He fil ayeyn into his sikes olde;   646
And every nyght, as was his wone to doone,
He stood the brighte moone to byholde,
And al his sorwe he to the moone tolde,
And seyde, "Ywis, whan thow art horned
     newe,
I shal be glad, if al the world be trewe!   651

"I saugh thyn hornes olde ek by the morwe,
Whan hennes rood my righte lady dere,
That cause is of my torment and my sorwe;
For which, O brighte Latona the clere,   655
For love of God, ren faste aboute thy spere!
For whan thyne hornes newe gynnen sprynge,
Than shal she come that may my blisse brynge."

The dayes moore, and lenger every nyght,   659
Than they ben wont to be, hym thoughte tho,
And that the sonne went his cours unright
By lenger weye than it was wont to do;
And seyde, "Ywis, me dredeth evere mo,
The sonnes sone, Pheton, be on lyve,
And that his fader carte amys he dryve."   665

Upon the walles faste ek wolde he walke,
And on the Grekis oost he wolde se,
And to hymself right thus he wolde talke:
"Lo, yonder is myn owene lady free,
Or ellis yonder, ther the tentes be.   670
And thennes comth this eyr, that is so soote,
That in my soule I fele it doth me boote.

"And hardily this wynd, that more and moore
Thus stoundemele encresseth in my face,
Is of my ladys depe sikes soore.   675
I preve it thus, for in noon othere place
Of al this town, save onliche in this space,
Fele I no wynd that sowneth so lik peyne:
It seyth, 'Allas! whi twynned be we tweyne?' "

This longe tyme he dryveth forth right thus,
Til fully passed was the nynthe nyght;   681
And ay bisyde hym was this Pandarus,
That bisily did al his fulle myght
Hym to conforte, and make his herte light,   684
Yevyng hym hope alwey, the tenthe morwe
That she shal come, and stynten al his sorwe.

Upon that other syde ek was Criseyde,
With wommen fewe, among the Grekis
     stronge;
For which ful ofte a day "Allas!" she seyde,   689
"That I was born! Wel may myn herte longe
After my deth; for now lyve I to longe.
Allas! and I ne may it nat amende!
For now is wors than evere yet I wende.

"My fader nyl for nothyng do me grace
To gon ayeyn, for naught I kan hym queme;   696
And if so be that I my terme pace,
My Troilus shal in his herte deme

---

641. in steere, astern. **642. faille,** fail to have, am without. **644. Caribdis.** Scylla and Charybdis were two rocks between Sicily and Italy. On the latter dwelt a monster of the name who swallowed the waters of the channel and spewed them out again. In other accounts Charybdis is simply a whirlpool that sucked in ships, which would suit the present reference. **646. sikes,** sighes. **647. wone,** custom; he watched every night for the new moon. **652. thyn hornes olde,** *i.e.* the moon was in the last quarter. **655. Latona,** prob. a mistake for *Lucina*, the moon. **656. spere,** sphere (the first of the seven in which the planets were thought to revolve). **664. Pheton,** Phaethon. For Chaucer's telling of the story see *HF* 940 ff. **on lyve,** alive. **667. se,** look. **671. soote,** sweet. **673. hardily,** assuredly. **674. stoundemele,** hour by hour, gradually. **678. no,** *i.e.* any. **sowneth,** soundeth. **686. stynten,** stop, put an end to. **689. ful ofte a day,** many times a day. **691. After,** for. **695. for . . . queme,** for anything I can do to please him.

That I am fals, and so it may wel seme;
Thus shal ich have unthank on every side.
That I was born, so weilaway the tide!　　700

"And if that I me putte in jupartie,
To stele awey by nyght, and it bifalle
That I be kaught, I shal be holde a spie;
Or elles—lo, this drede I moost of alle—
If in the hondes of som wrecche I falle,　　705
I nam but lost, al be myn herte trewe.
Now, myghty God, thow on my sorwe rewe!"

Ful pale ywaxen was hire brighte face,
Hire lymes lene, as she that al the day　　709
Stood, whan she dorste, and loked on the place
Ther she was born and ther she dwelt hadde ay;
And al the nyght wepyng, allas, she lay.
And thus despeired out of alle cure
She ladde hire lif, this woful creature.

Ful ofte a day she sighte ek for destresse,　　715
And in hirself she wente ay purtrayinge
Of Troilus the grete worthynesse,
And al his goodly wordes recordynge
Syn first that day hire love bigan to springe.
And thus she sette hire woful herte afire　　720
Thorugh remembraunce of that she gan desire.

In al this world ther nys so cruel herte
That hire hadde herd compleynen in hire sorwe,
That nolde han wepen for hire peynes smerte,
So tendrely she wepte, bothe eve and morwe.
Hire nedede no teris for to borwe!　　726
And this was yet the werste of al hire peyne,
Ther was no wight to whom she dorste hire
　pleyne.

Ful rewfully she loked upon Troie,
Biheld the toures heigh and ek the halles.　　730
"Allas!" quod she, "the plesance and the joie,
The which that now al torned into galle is,
Have ich had ofte withinne tho yonder walles!
O Troilus, what dostow now?" she seyde.
"Lord! wheyther thow yet thenke upon Cri-
　seyde?　　735

"Allas, I ne hadde trowed on youre loore,
And went with yow, as ye me redde er this!
Than hadde I now nat siked half so soore.
Who myghte have seyd that I hadde don amys
To stele awey with swich oon as he ys?　　740
But al to late comth the letuarie,
Whan men the cors unto the grave carie.

"To late is now to speke of that matere.
Prudence, allas, oon of thyne eyen thre
Me lakked alwey, er that I come here!　　745
On tyme ypassed wel remembred me,
And present tyme ek koud ich wel ise,
But future tyme, er I was in the snare,
Koude I nat sen; that causeth now my care.

"But natheles, bityde what bityde,　　750
I shal to-morwe at nyght, by est or west,
Out of this oost stele on som manere syde,
And gon with Troilus where as hym lest.
This purpos wol ich holde, and this is best.
No fors of wikked tonges janglerie,　　755
For evere on love han wrecches had envye.

"For whoso wol of every word take hede,
Or reulen hym by every wightes wit,
Ne shal he nevere thryven, out of drede;

699. **unthank,** blame. 703. **holde,** considered. 713. **despeired out of,** in despair of. See note to 1.42. 715. **sighte,** sighed. 716. **in hireself . . . purtrayinge,** picturing to herself. 718. **recordynge,** recalling. 723. **hadde,** subj. (if he had). 724. **wepen,** wept. 735. **wheyther,** introducing a rhetorical question: Do you . . .? See Language, § 75. 736. **I ne hadde . . . loore,** that I did not follow your advice. 737. **redde,** advised. 741. **letuarie,** electuary, medicine in the form of a syrup. 744. **thyne eyen thre.** Prudence, who looks to the past, the present, and the future, is one of the four Cardinal Virtues. Dante refers to them (collectively) in *Purgatorio,* XXIX. 130–2, where the one who leads the others "avea tre occhi in testa." She is identified by a fourteenth-century commentator as Prudence. In medieval art, Prudence is usually represented with the normal two eyes, and holds a mirror in her hand, but a Dante MS in the Pierpont Morgan Library (MS 676, fol. 83 verso) has an illumination showing clearly the three eyes, and she is so represented in the frescoes of Ambrogio Lorenzetti in the Palazzo Pubblico of Siena (cf. Symonds, *Intro. to the Study of Dante,* p. 122). 750. **bityde what bityde,** come what may. 752. **on som manere syde,** on one side or the other. 755. **No fors of . . . janglerie,** the prating of wicked tongues doesn't matter. 758. **wit,** opinion.

For that that som men blamen evere yit,
Lo, other manere folk comenden it.
And as for me, for al swich variaunce,
Felicite clepe I my suffisaunce.

"For which, withouten any wordes mo,
To Troie I wole, as for conclusioun." 765
But God it wot, er fully monthes two,
She was ful fer fro that entencioun!
For bothe Troilus and Troie town
Shal knotteles thoroughout hire herte slide;
For she wol take a purpos for t'abyde. 770

This Diomede, of whom yow telle I gan,
Goth now withinne hymself ay arguynge
With al the sleghte, and al that evere he kan,
How he may best, with shortest taryinge,
Into his net Criseydes herte brynge. 775
To this entent he koude nevere fyne,
To fisshen hire, he leyde out hook and lyne.

But natheles, wel in his herte he thoughte,
That she nas nat withoute a love in Troie;
For nevere, sythen he hire thennes broughte,
Ne koude he sen hire laughe or maken joie.
He nyst how best hire herte for t'acoye.
"But for t'asay," he seyde, "it naught ne
greveth;
For he that naught n'asaieth, naught n'acheveth."

Yet seide he to hymself upon a nyght, 785
"Now am I nat a fool, that woot wel how
Hire wo for love is of another wight,
And hereupon to gon assaye hire now?
I may wel wite, it nyl nat ben my prow.
For wise folk in bookes it expresse, 790
'Men shal nat wowe a wight in hevynesse.'

But whoso myghte wynnen swich a flour 760
From hym for whom she morneth nyght and
day,
He myghte seyn he were a conquerour."
And right anon, as he that bold was ay, 795
Thoughte in his herte, "Happe how happe may,
Al sholde I dye, I wol hire herte seche!
I shal namore lesen but my speche."

This Diomede, as bokes us declare,
Was in his nedes prest and corageous, 800
With sterne vois and myghty lymes square,
Hardy, testif, strong, and chivalrous
Of dedes, lik his fader Tideus.
And som men seyn he was of tonge large; 805
And heir he was of Calydoigne and Arge.

Criseyde mene was of hire stature,
Therto of shap, of face, and ek of cheere,
Ther myghte ben no fairer creature.
And ofte tyme this was hire manere,
To gon ytressed with hire heres clere 810
Doun by hire coler at hire bak byhynde, 779
Which with a thred of gold she wolde bynde.

And, save hire browes joyneden yfere,
Ther nas no lak, in aught I kan espien.
But for to speken of hire eyen cleere, 815
Lo, trewely, they writen that hire syen,
That Paradis stood formed in hire yën.
And with hire riche beaute evere more
Strof love in hire ay, which of hem was more.

She sobre was, ek symple, and wys withal,
The best ynorisshed ek that myghte be, 821
And goodly of hire speche in general,
Charitable, estatlich, lusty, and fre;

763. **Felicite . . . suffisaunce,** happiness is enough for me. 765. **as for conclusioun,** in conclusion. 773. **sleghte,** cunning, skill. **al that evere he kan,** everything that he can do. 776. **fyne,** cease. 782. **t' acoye,** to quiet, tame. 783. **But . . . greveth,** but it does no harm to try. 789. **prow,** profit. 796. **Happe how happe may.** The meaning is the same as that of *bityde what bityde,* l. 750 above. 797. **seche,** seek. 800. **prest,** ready, resourceful. 802. **testif,** impetuous. **chivalrous,** doughty. 804. **of tonge large,** free with his tongue, fluent (?), perhaps rendering *parlante quant' altro Greco mai* (Filostrato, VI. 33). 805. **Calydoigne.** Tydeus, Diomede's father (l. 803), was king of Calydon. **Arge,** Argos. 806. **mene,** average. 810. **ytressed,** braided. 813. **browes joyneden.** Chaucer considers knit eyebrows a blemish, but it is often a feature of medieval descriptions of women and in ancient Greece was a mark of beauty. Cf. N. E. Griffin, *JEGP,* xx. 39–46. 816. **they . . . syen,** they write who saw her. 821. **ynorisshed,** brought up. 823. **estatlich,** dignified. **lusty,** cheerful, lively. **fre,** generous, noble.

Ne nevere mo ne lakked hire pite;
Tendre-herted, slydynge of corage;   825
But trewely, I kan nat telle hire age.

And Troilus wel woxen was in highte,
And complet formed by proporcioun
So wel that kynde it nought amenden myghte;
Yong, fressh, strong, and hardy as lyoun;   830
Trewe as steel in ech condicioun;
Oon of the beste entecched creature
That is, or shal, whil that the world may dure.

And certeynly in storye it is yfounde,
That Troilus was nevere unto no wight,   835
As in his tyme, in no degree secounde
In durryng don that longeth to a knyght.
Al myghte a geant passen hym of myght,
His herte ay with the first and with the beste
Stood paregal, to durre don that hym leste.   840

But for to tellen forth of Diomede:
It fel that after, on the tenthe day
Syn that Criseyde out of the citee yede,
This Diomede, as fressh as braunche in May,
Com to the tente, ther as Calkas lay,   845
And feyned hym with Calkas han to doone;
But what he mente, I shal yow tellen soone.

Criseyde, at shorte wordes for to telle,
Welcomed hym, and down hym by hire sette;
And he was ethe ynough to maken dwelle!
And after this, withouten longe lette,   851
The spices and the wyn men forth hem fette;
And forth they speke of this and that yfeere,
As frendes don, of which som shal ye heere.

He gan first fallen of the werre in speche   855
Bitwixe hem and the folk of Troie town;
And of th'assege he gan hire ek biseche
To telle hym what was hire opynyoun.
Fro that demaunde he so descendeth down
To axen hire, if that hire straunge thoughte   860
The Grekis gise, and werkes that they wroughte;

And whi hire fader tarieth so longe
To wedden hire unto som worthy wight.
Criseyde, that was in hire peynes stronge
For love of Troilus, hire owen knyght,   865
As ferforth as she konnyng hadde or myght,
Answerde hym tho; but, as of his entente,
It semed nat she wiste what he mente.

But natheles, this ilke Diomede
Gan in hymself assure, and thus he seyde: 870
"If ich aright have taken of yow hede,
Me thynketh thus, O lady myn, Criseyde,
That syn I first hond on youre bridel leyde,
Whan ye out come of Troie by the morwe,
Ne koude I nevere sen yow but in sorwe.   875

"Kan I nat seyn what may the cause be,
But if for love of som Troian it were,
The which right sore wolde athynken me;
That ye for any wight that dwelleth there
Sholden spille a quarter of a tere,   880
Or pitously youreselven so bigile,
For dredeles, it is nought worth the while.

"The folk of Troie, as who seyth, alle and some
In prisoun ben, as ye youreselven se;
Nor thennes shal nat oon on-lyve come   885
For al the gold atwixen sonne and se.
Trusteth wel, and understondeth me,
Ther shal nat oon to mercy gon on-lyve,
Al were he lord of worldes twiës fyve!

---

825. slydynge of corage, unstable of heart. **828. complet,** adj. used as an adv. **831. ech,** *i.e.* every. **832. entecched.** The normal meaning is "infected, stained," but with a qualifying adverb it has the neutral sense "imbued with." **beste entecched,** best endowed. **837. durryng don . . . knyght,** daring to do what belongs to a knight. *Durryng* is a verbal noun from OE. *durran,* to dare; cf. l. 840. **840. paregal,** fully equal. **842. fel,** fell, happened. **845. lay,** lodged. **850. ethe,** easy. **851. lette,** delay. **859. demaunde,** question. **861. gise,** ways,—if the Greek ways seemed strange to her. **864. in hire peynes stronge,** grieving greatly. **866. konnyng,** ability. **875. Ne koude I nevere sen,** I have never been able to see. **878. wolde athynken me,** would repent me, cause regret. **881. bigile,** delude. **883. as who seyth,** as one may say. **alle and some,** each and every one. **888. to mercy gon on-lyve,** *i.e.* escape the Greek wrath alive.

"Swiche wreche on hem, for fecchynge of
    Eleyne,   890
Ther shal ben take, er that we hennes wende,
That Manes, which that goddes ben of peyne,
Shal ben agast that Grekes wol hem shende.
And men shul drede, unto the worldes ende,
From hennesforth to ravysshen any queene,   895
So cruel shal oure wreche on hem be seene.

"And but if Calkas lede us with ambages,
That is to seyn, with double wordes slye,
Swiche as men clepen a word with two
    visages,
Ye shal wel knowen that I naught ne lye,   900
And al this thyng right sen it with youre yë,
And that anon, ye nyl nat trowe how sone.
Now taketh hede, for it is for to doone.

"What! wene ye youre wise fader wolde
Han yeven Antenor for yow anon,   905
If he ne wiste that the cite sholde
Destroied ben? Whi, nay, so mote I gon!
He knew ful wel ther shal nat scapen oon
That Troian is; and for the grete feere,
He dorste nat ye dwelte lenger there.   910

"What wol ye more, lufsom lady deere?
Lat Troie and Troian fro youre herte pace!
Drif out that bittre hope, and make good
    cheere,
And clepe ayeyn the beaute of youre face,
That ye with salte teris so deface.   915
For Troie is brought in swich a jupartie,
That it to save is now no remedie.

"And thenketh wel, ye shal in Grekis fynde
A moore parfit love, er it be nyght,

Than any Troian is, and more kynde,   920
And bet to serven yow wol don his myght.
And if ye vouchesauf, my lady bright,
I wol ben he to serven yow myselve,
Yee, levere than be lord of Greces twelve!"

And with that word he gan to waxen red,   925
And in his speche a litel wight he quok,
And caste asyde a litle wight his hed,
And stynte a while; and afterward he wok,
And sobreliche on hire he threw his lok,
And seyde, "I am, al be it yow no joie,   930
As gentil man as any wight in Troie.

For if my fader Tideus," he seyde,
"Ilyved hadde, ich hadde ben, er this,
Of Calydoyne and Arge a kyng, Criseyde!
And so hope I that I shal yet, iwis.   935
But he was slayn, allas! the more harm is,
Unhappily at Thebes al to rathe,
Polymytes and many a man to scathe.

"But herte myn, syn that I am youre man,—
And ben the first of whom I seche grace,—   940
To serve yow as hertely as I kan,
And evere shal, whil I to lyve have space,
So, er that I departe out of this place,
Ye wol me graunte that I may to-morwe,
At bettre leyser, tellen yow my sorwe."   945

What sholde I telle his wordes that he seyde?
He spak inough, for o day at the meeste.
It preveth wel, he spak so that Criseyde
Graunted, on the morwe, at his requeste,
For to speken with hym at the leeste,   950
So that he nolde speke of swich matere.
And thus to hym she seyde, as ye may here,

---

890. **wreche,** vengeance. 892. **Manes,** the shades of the dead, sometimes spoken of as gods; that they were gods of pain seems to be without foundation in classical times. 893. **shende,** put to shame. 897. **ambages,** *lit.* circumlocutions; hence, ambiguities. In English this is the first instance of the word, which Chaucer has taken over from his Italian source; therefore he explains it in the next line. 901. **sen,** infin. with *shal.* 903. **it is for to doone,** it is well (or necessary) to do so. 914. **clepe ayeyn,** recall. 917. **is,** there is. 926. **a litel wight,** a little bit. 928. **wok,** aroused himself. 930. **al be it yow,** although it be to you. 938. **Polymytes,** Polynices. In the war between the brothers Eteocles and Polynices for the rule of Thebes, Tydeus fought on the side of Polynices. Therefore his death was a misfortune to Polynices and his supporters. **scathe,** harm, injury. 940. **ben.** The construction is loose, as is that of the clause which follows, but the subject of *ben* is *ye* understood, implied by *youre.* 946. **What,** why.

As she that hadde hire herte on Troilus
So faste, that ther may it non arace;
And strangely she spak, and seyde thus: 955
"O Diomede, I love that ilke place
Ther I was born; and Joves, for his grace,
Delyvere it soone of al that doth it care!
God, for thy myght, so leve it wel to fare!

"That Grekis wolde hire wrath on Troie
   wreke,
If that they myght, I knowe it wel, iwis.   961
But it shal naught byfallen as ye speke,
And God toforn! and forther over this,
I woot my fader wys and redy is;
And that he me hath bought, as ye me tolde,
So deere, I am the more unto hym holde.   966

"That Grekis ben of heigh condicioun,
I woot ek wel; but certeyn, men shal fynde
As worthi folk withinne Troie town,
As konnyng, and as parfit, and as kynde,   970
As ben bitwixen Orkades and Inde.
And that ye koude wel yowre lady serve,
I trowe ek wel, hire thank for to deserve.

"But as to speke of love, ywis," she seyde,
"I hadde a lord, to whom I wedded was,   975
The whos myn herte al was, til that he deyde;
And other love, as help me now Pallas,
Ther in myn herte nys, ne nevere was.
And that ye ben of noble and heigh kynrede,
I have wel herd it tellen, out of drede.   980

"And that doth me to han so gret a wonder,
That ye wol scornen any womman so.
Ek, God woot, love and I ben fer ysonder!
I am disposed bet, so mot I go,
Unto my deth, to pleyne and maken wo.   985

What I shal after don, I kan nat seye;
But trewelich, as yet me list nat pleye.

"Myn herte is now in tribulacioun,
And ye in armes bisy day by day.
Herafter, whan ye wonnen han the town,   990
Peraunter, thanne so it happen may,
That whan I se that nevere yit I say,
Than wol I werke that I nevere wroughte!
This word to yow ynough suffisen oughte.   994

"To-morwe ek wol I speken with yow fayn,
So that ye touchen naught of this matere.
And whan yow list, ye may come here ayayn;
And er ye gon, thus muche I sey yow here:
As help me Pallas with hire heres clere,
If that I sholde of any Grek han routhe,   1000
It sholde be yourselven, by my trouthe!

"I say nat therfore that I wol yow love,
N'y say nat nay; but in conclusioun,
I mene wel, by God that sit above!"
And therwithal she caste hire eyen down,   1005
And gan to sike, and seyde, "O Troie town,
Yet bidde I God, in quiete and in reste
I may yow sen, or do myn herte breste."

But in effect, and shortly for to seye,
This Diomede al fresshly newe ayeyn   1010
Gan pressen on, and faste hire mercy preye;
And after this, the sothe for to seyn,
Hire glove he took, of which he was ful feyn.
And finaly, whan it was woxen eve,
And al was wel, he roos and tok his leve.   1015

The brighte Venus folwede and ay taughte
The wey ther brode Phebus down alighte;
And Cynthea hire char-hors overraughte

954. **arace,** root out. 955. **strangely,** coldly, distantly. 958. **doth it care,** causes it to feel anxiety, although *care* could be construed as a noun. 963. **forther over this,** furthermore. 966. **holde,** beholden, under obligation. 971. **Orkades,** the Orkney Islands, on the western edge of the known world. For the notion that India marked the eastern limit of the world see F. L. Utley in *Names*, v. 212. 974. **as to speke of,** speaking of. 977. **Pallas,** Pallas Athene, upon the preservation of whose image the safety of Troy depended. 978. **Ther . . . was,** Criseyde is, of course, lying. 982. **scornen,** mock. 986. **after,** in the future. 992. **That . . . say,** what I never saw before. 993. **werke . . . wroughte,** do what I never did. 999. **heres clere,** bright hair, 1008. **do,** make. 1016. **Venus,** here the evening star. 1017. **brode,** plainly. **Phebus,** the sun. 1018. **Cynthea,** the moon. In 4. 1591 Criseyde had promised that she would return before the moon passed out of the sign of Leo. **char-hors,** chariot horses. **overraughte,** reached over (in the act of urging the horses on).

To whirle out of the Leoun, if she myghte;
And Signifer his candels sheweth brighte,   1020
Whan that Criseyde unto hire bedde wente
Inwith hire fadres faire brighte tente,

Retornyng in hire soule ay up and down
The wordes of this sodeyn Diomede,
His grete estat, and perel of the town,   1025
And that she was allone and hadde nede
Of frendes help; and thus bygan to brede
The cause whi, the sothe for to telle,
That she took fully purpos for to dwelle.

The morwen com, and gostly for to speke,   1030
This Diomede is come unto Criseyde;
And shortly, lest that ye my tale breke,
So wel he for hymselven spak and seyde,
That alle hire sikes soore adown he leyde.
And finaly, the sothe for to seyne,   1035
He refte hire of the grete of al hire peyne.

And after this the storie telleth us
That she hym yaf the faire baye stede,
The which he ones wan of Troilus;   1039
And ek a broche—and that was litel nede—
That Troilus was, she yaf this Diomede.
And ek, the bet from sorwe hym to releve,
She made hym were a pencel of hire sleve.

I fynde ek in the stories elleswhere,   1044
Whan thorugh the body hurt was Diomede
Of Troilus, tho wepte she many a teere,
Whan that she saugh his wyde wowndes blede;
And that she took, to kepen hym, good hede;
And for to helen hym of his sorwes smerte,
Men seyn—I not—that she yaf hym hire
    herte.   1050

But trewely, the storie telleth us,
Ther made nevere woman moore wo
Than she, whan that she falsed Troilus.
She seyde, "Allas! for now is clene ago
My name of trouthe in love, for everemo!   1055
For I have falsed oon the gentileste
That evere was, and oon the worthieste!

"Allas! of me, unto the worldes ende,
Shal neyther ben ywriten nor ysonge
No good word, for thise bokes wol me shende.
O, rolled shal I ben on many a tonge!   1061
Thorughout the world my belle shal be
    ronge!
And wommen moost wol haten me of alle.
Allas, that swich a cas me sholde falle!

"Thei wol seyn, in as muche as in me is,   1065
I have hem don dishonour, weylaway!
Al be I nat the first that dide amys,
What helpeth that to don my blame awey?
But syn I se ther is no bettre way,
And that to late is now for me to rewe,   1070
To Diomede algate I wol be trewe.

"But, Troilus, syn I no bettre may,
And syn that thus departen ye and I,
Yet prey I God, so yeve yow right good day,
As for the gentileste, trewely,   1075
That evere I say, to serven feythfully,
And best kan ay his lady honour kepe";—
And with that word she brast anon to wepe.

"And certes, yow ne haten shal I nevere;
And frendes love, that shal ye han of me,   1080
And my good word, al sholde I lyven evere.
And, trewely, I wolde sory be

1020. Signifer, the sign-bearer, the zodiac. **1023. Retornyng,** turning over. **1024. sodeyn,** impetuous. **1029. took . . . purpos,** made up her mind. **1030. gostly,** solemnly, *i.e.* to tell the truth. **1032. breke,** cut short, *i.e.* lest I weary you with too long a story. **1034. adown . . . leyde,** allayed. **1036. grete,** chief part. **1039. wan,** won. Diomede won the horse in battle and according to other accounts (*e.g. Roman de Troie,* ll. 14286–14300) sent it to Criseyde. Cf. Shakespeare's *Troilus and Cressida,* V, v. 1–5. She here gives it back to him. **1041. That Troilus was,** that was Troilus's. **1043. pencel,** a token, often in the form of a small banner or streamer. **1048. took, to kepen hym, good hede,** took good care to look after him. **1061. rolled,** *i.e.* turned over and over. **1062. my belle shal be ronge,** app. a slang or proverbial expression, here implying "my reputation will be noised abroad." **1070. rewe,** repent. **1071. algate,** in any case. **1073. departen,** separate. **1076. say,** saw. **1078. to wepe,** into weeping.

For to seen yow in adversitee; *believe*
And gilteles, I woot wel, I yow leve. 1084
But al shal passe; and thus take I my leve."

But trewely, how longe it was bytwene
That she forsok hym for this Diomede,
Ther is non auctour telleth it, I wene.
Take every man now to his bokes heede;
He shal no terme fynden, out of drede. 1090
For though that he bigan to wowe hire soone,
Er he hire wan, yet was ther more to doone.

Ne me ne list this sely womman chyde
Forther than the storye wol devyse.
Hire name, allas! is punysshed so wide, 1095
That for hire gilt it oughte ynough suffise.
And if I myghte excuse hire any wise,
For she so sory was for hire untrouthe,
Iwis, I wolde excuse hire yet for routhe. *pity*

This Troilus, as I byfore have told, 1100
Thus driveth forth, as wel as he hath myght.
But often was his herte hoot and cold,
And namely that ilke nynthe nyght,
Which on the morwe she hadde hym bihight
To com ayeyn: God woot, ful litel reste 1105
Hadde he that nyght; nothyng to slepe hym
  leste.

The laurer-crowned Phebus, with his heete,
Gan, in his course ay upward as he wente,
To warmen of the est see the wawes weete,
And Nysus doughter song with fressh entente, *vigor*
Whan Troilus his Pandare after sente; 1111
And on the walles of the town they pleyde,
To loke if they kan sen aught of Criseyde.

Tyl it was noon, they stoden for to se
Who that ther come; and every maner wight
That com fro fer, they seyden it was she, 1116
Til that thei koude knowen hym aright.
Now was his herte dul, now was it light.
And thus byjaped stonden for to stare *fooled*
Aboute naught this Troilus and Pandare. 1120

To Pandarus this Troilus tho seyde,
"For aught I woot, byfor noon, sikirly,
Into this town ne comth nat here Criseyde.
She hath ynough to doone, hardyly,
To wynnen from hire fader, so trowe I. 1125
Hire olde fader wol yet make hire dyne
Er that she go; God yeve hys herte pyne!"

Pandare answerde, "It may wel be, certeyn.
And forthi lat us dyne, I the byseche, 1129
And after noon than maystow come ayeyn."
And hom they go, withoute more speche,
And comen ayeyn; but longe may they seche
Er that they fynde that they after gape.
Fortune hem bothe thenketh for to jape!

Quod Troilus, "I se wel now that she 1135
Is taried with hire olde fader so,
That er she come, it wol neigh even be.
Com forth, I wole unto the yate go.
Thise porters ben unkonnyng evere mo,
And I wol don hem holden up the yate 1140
As naught ne were, although she come late." *As though there were no special reason*

The day goth faste, and after that com eve,
And yet com nought to Troilus Criseyde.
He loketh forth by hegge, by tre, by greve, *thicket*
And fer his hed over the wal he leyde, 1145
  further *laid*

1084. leve, believe. 1095. punysshed, made to suffer. 1109. est see, not certainly identified, but Chaucer could have derived the idea of a sea lying to the east of Troy from Guido della Colonna. See Pratt, *MLN*, LXI. 541–3. F. P. Magoun suggests the Indian Ocean (*Medieval Stud.*, XV. 117). The allusion could even be to the continuous waters supposed to surround the habitable earth on all sides (cf. Pliny, Book II. chap. 66). 1110. Nysus doughter, Scylla, who, for the love of Minos, caused her father's death. To save her from the vengeance about to overtake her she was changed into a bird. entente, vigor, endeavor. 1119. byjaped, fooled. 1122. noon, with the modern sense. Troilus and Pandarus have not yet eaten (cf. l. 1129, below), although the usual hour for dinner was ten o'clock. 1125. To wynnen from, to get away from. 1134. jape, trick, mock. 1138. yate, gate (in the city wall). 1140. yate, portcullis. 1141. As naught ne were, as though there were no special reason. although, even though. 1144. greve, thicket.

And at the laste he torned hym and seyde,
"By God, I woot hire menyng now, Pandare!
Almoost, ywys, al newe was my care.

"Now douteles, this lady kan hire good;
I woot, she meneth riden pryvely.   1150
I comende hire wisdom, by myn hood!
She wol nat maken peple nycely
Gaure on hire whan she comth; but softely
By nyghte into the town she thenketh ride.
And, deere brother, thynk not longe t'abide.

"We han naught elles for to don, ywis.   1156
And Pandarus, now woltow trowen me?
Have here my trouthe, I se hire! yond she is!
Heve up thyn eyen, man! maistow nat se?"
Pandare answerede, "Nay, so mote I the!   1160
Al wrong, by God! What saistow, man, where
     arte?
That I se yond nys but a fare-carte."

"Allas! thow seyst right soth," quod Troilus.
"But, hardily, it is naught al for nought
That in myn herte I now rejoysse thus.   1165
It is ayeyns som good I have a thought.
Not I nat how, but syn that I was wrought,
Ne felte I swich a comfort, dar I seye;
She comth to-nyght, my lif that dorste I
     leye!"   1169

Pandare answerde, "It may be, wel ynough,"
And held with hym of al that evere he seyde.
But in his herte he thoughte, and softe lough,
And to hymself ful sobreliche he seyde,
"From haselwode, there joly Robyn pleyde,
Shal come al that that thow abidest heere.   1175
Ye, fare wel al the snow of ferne yere!"

The warden of the yates gan to calle
The folk which that withoute the yates were,
And bad hem dryven in hire bestes alle,
Or al the nyght they moste bleven there.   1180
And fer withinne the nyght, with many a teere,
This Troilus gan homward for to ride;
For wel he seth it helpeth naught t'abide.

But natheles, he gladed hym in this:
He thought he misacounted hadde his day,   1185
And seyde, "I understonde have al amys.
For thilke nyght I last Criseyde say,
She seyde, 'I shal ben here, if that I may,
Er that the moone, O deere herte swete,
The Leoun passe, out of this Ariete.'   1190

"For which she may yet holde al hire byheste."
And on the morwe unto the yate he wente,
And up and down, by west and ek by este,
Upon the walles made he many a wente;   1194
But al for nought; his hope alwey hym blente.
For which at nyght, in sorwe and sikes sore
He wente hym hom, withouten any more.

His hope al clene out of his herte fledde;
He nath wheron now lenger for to honge;
But for the peyne hym thoughte his herte
     bledde,   1200
So were his throwes sharpe and wonder stronge.
For whan he saugh that she abood so longe,
He nyste what he juggen of it myghte,
Syn she hath broken that she hym bihighte.

The thridde, ferthe, fifte, sexte day   1205
After tho dayes ten of which I tolde,
Bitwixen hope and drede his herte lay,
Yet somwhat trustyng on hire hestes olde.

1149. kan hire good, knows what is good for her. **1152. nycely,** stupidly. **1153. Gaure on,** stare at. **1155. thynk . . . abide,** *i.e.* don't expect to have to wait very long. **1162. fare-carte,** cart for produce (?). The word is not found elsewhere. **1166. It . . . thought,** *i.e.* I believe it forebodes some good, or I would not feel such a comfort. **1171. held with hym of,** agreed with him in. **1174. From haselwode . . . Shal come,** *i.e.* will not come at all. But the expression and its exact meaning are unknown. Robin is a common name for a young shepherd in the medieval pastourelle. In Chaucer *haselwode* always has some connotation besides the literal meaning "a thicket of hazel bushes"; cf. the note to 3. 890. **1176. ferne yere,** last year. **1180. bleven,** remain. **1187. say,** saw. **1190. Leoun.** See 4. 1592 and note. **1197. withouten any more,** without more ado.

But whan he saugh she nolde hire terme holde,
He kan now sen non other remedie   1210
But for to shape hym soone for to dye.
    Prepare

Therwith the wikked spirit, God us blesse,
Which that men clepeth the woode jalousie, *mad*
Gan in hym crepe, in al this hevynesse;
For which, by cause he wolde soone dye,   1215
He ne et ne drank, for his malencolye,
And ek from every compaignye he fledde:
This was the lif that al the tyme he ledde.

He so defet was, that no manere man
Unneth hym myghte knowen ther he wente;
So was he lene, and therto pale and wan,   1221
And feble, that he walketh by potente;
And with his ire he thus hymselve shente. *rage destroyed*
And whoso axed hym wherof hym smerte,
He seyde, his harm was al aboute his herte.   1225

Priam ful ofte, and ek his moder deere,
His bretheren and his sustren gonne hym freyne
Whi he so sorwful was in al his cheere,
And what thyng was the cause of al his peyne;
But ai for naught. He nolde his cause pleyne,
But seyde he felte a grevous maladie   1231
Aboute his herte, and fayn he wolde dye.

So on a day he leyde hym doun to slepe,
And so byfel that in his slep hym thoughte
That in a forest faste he welk to wepe   1235
For love of here that hym these peynes
    wroughte;
And up and doun as he the forest soughte,
He mette he saugh a bor with tuskes grete,
That slepte ayeyn the bryghte sonnes hete.

And by this bor, faste in his armes folde,   1240
Lay, kissyng ay his lady bryght, Criseyde.
For sorwe of which, whan he it gan byholde,
    Because of indignation
And for despit, out of his slep he breyde, *started*
And loude he cride on Pandarus and seyde:
"O Pandarus, now know I crop and roote *root & branch*   1245
I n'am but ded; ther nys non other bote.

"My lady bryght, Criseyde, hath me bytrayed,
In whom I trusted most of any wight.
She elliswhere hath now here herte apayed.
The blysful goddes, thorugh here grete myght,
Han in my drem yshewed it ful right.   1251
Thus in my drem Criseyde have I byholde"—
And al this thing to Pandarus he tolde.

"O my Criseyde, allas! what subtilte,   1254
What newe lust, what beaute, what science,
What wratthe of juste cause have ye to me?
What gilt of me, what fel experience,
Hath fro me raft, allas! thyn advertence?
O trust, O feyth, O depe aseuraunce,   1259
Who hath me reft Criseyde, al my plesaunce?

"Allas! whi leet I you from hennes go,
For which wel neigh out of my wit I breyde?
Who shal now trowe on any othes mo?
God wot, I wende, O lady bright, Criseyde,
That every word was gospel that ye seyde!   1265
But who may bet bigile, yf hym lyste,
Than he on whom men weneth best to triste?

"What shal I don, my Pandarus, allas?
I fele now so sharp a newe peyne,
Syn that ther is no remedye in this cas,   1270
That bet were it I with myn honde tweyne

1211. **shape hym,** prepare. 1213. **woode,** mad. 1219. **defet,** wasted away. 1222. **by potente,** with a crutch. 1223. **ire,** rage. **shente,** injured, destroyed. 1224. **wherof hym smerte,** of what he suffered. 1227. **freyne,** ask. 1230. **his cause pleyne,** explain his case. 1235. **welk,** walked, roamed. 1237. **soughte,** explored. 1238. **mette,** dreamed. 1239. **slepte ayeyn,** slept exposed to. 1243. **for despit,** because of indignation. **breyde,** started. 1245. **crop and roote,** root and branch. 1249. **apayed,** satisfied. 1254. **subtilte.** It is not possible to say with certainty what connotation the word carries here. Its range of meanings includes acuteness of mind, cunning, guile, trick, stratagem, and even abstruse knowledge. It is part of the sequence of possible causes (new desire or pleasure, beauty, knowledge, just anger, fault of mine, dreadful experience) that have diverted Criseyde's mind from Troilus. He seems to be including every possiblity that he can think of. 1258. **advertence,** consideration. 1262. **breyde,** am going (suddenly).

Myselven slow than thus alwey to pleyne.
For thorugh my deth my wo shold han an ende,
Ther every day with lyf myself I shende.''

Pandare answerde and seyde, ''Allas the while
That I was born! Have I nat seyd er this,   1276
That dremes many a maner man bigile?
And whi? For folk expounden hem amys.
How darstow seyn that fals thy lady ys,   1279
For any drem, right for thyn owene drede?
Lat be this thought; thow kanst no dremes rede.

''Peraunter, ther thow dremest of this boor,
It may so be that it may signifie
Hire fader, which that old is and ek hoor,
Ayeyn the sonne lith, o poynt to dye,   1285
And she for sorwe gynneth wepe and crie,
And kisseth hym, ther he lith on the grounde:
Thus sholdestow thi drem aright expounde!''

''How myghte I than don,'' quod Troilus,   1289
''To knowe of this, yee, were it nevere so lite?''
''Now seystow wisly,'' quod this Pandarus.
''My rede is this, syn thow kanst wel endite,
That hastily a lettre thow hire write,
Thorough which thow shalt wel bryngyn it
   aboute,
To know a soth of that thow art in doute.   1295

''And se now whi; for this I dar wel seyn,
That if so is that she untrewe be,
I kan nat trowen that she wol write ayeyn.
And if she write, thow shalt ful sone yse
As wheither she hath any liberte   1300
To come ayeyn; or ellis in som clause,
If she be let, she wol assigne a cause.

''Thow hast nat writen hire syn that she wente,
Nor she to the; and this I dorste laye,

Ther may swich cause ben in hire entente,
That hardily thow wolt thiselven saye   1306
That hire abod the best is for yow twaye.
Now writ hire thanne, and thow shalt feele sone
A soth of al; ther is namore to done.''

Acorded ben to this conclusioun,   1310
And that anon, thise ilke lordes two;
And hastily sit Troilus adown,
And rolleth in his herte to and fro,
How he may best discryven hire his wo.
And to Criseyde, his owen lady deere,   1315
He wrot right thus, and seyde as ye may here:

Litera Troili
''Right fresshe flour, whos I ben have and shal,
Withouten part of elleswhere servyse,
With herte, body, lif, lust, thought, and al,
I, woful wyght, in everich humble wise   1320
That tonge telle or herte may devyse,
As ofte as matere occupieth place,
Me recomaunde unto youre noble grace.

''Liketh yow to witen, swete herte,
As ye wel knowe, how longe tyme agon   1325
That ye me lefte in aspre peynes smerte,
Whan that ye wente, of which yit boote non
Have I non had, but evere wors bigon
Fro day to day am I, and so mot dwelle,   1329
While it yow list, of wele and wo my welle.

''For which to yow, with dredful herte trewe,
I write, as he that sorwe drifth to write,
My wo, that everich houre encresseth newe,
Compleynyng, as I dar or kan endite.
And that defaced is, that may ye wite   1335
The teris which that fro myn eyen reyne,
That wolden speke, if that they koude, and
   pleyne.

1272. slow, slew. **1274.** shende, reproach. **1280. For . . . drede,** *i.e.* fear causes him to see in his dream an ill omen. **1281. rede,** intrepret. **1291. Now seystow wisly,** now you are talking sense. **1295. a soth,** in truth. **1302. let,** prevented. **1304. laye,** wager. **1305. entente,** mind. **1307. abod,** delay. **1308. feele . . . al,** find out the truth about everything. **1313. rolleth,** revolves. **1318. Withouten . . . servyse,** with no part of my service bestowed elsewhere. **1324. Liketh . . . witen,** may it please you to recall. **1327. boote,** remedy, relief. **1328. wors bigon,** worse beset. **1329. mot dwelle,** must remain. **1335. wite,** blame.

"Yow first biseche I that youre eyen clere
To loke on this, defouled ye nat holde;
And over al this, that ye, my lady deere,   1340
Wol vouchesauf this lettre to byholde.
And by the cause ek of my cares colde,
That sleth my wit, if aught amys m'asterte,
Foryeve it me, myn owen swete herte!

"If any servant dorste or oughte of right   1345
Upon his lady pitously compleyne,
Thanne wene I that ich oughte be that wight,
Considered this, that ye thise monthes tweyne
Han taried, ther ye seyden, soth to seyne,
But dayes ten ye nolde in oost sojourne,—   1350
But in two monthes yet ye nat retourne.

"But for as muche as me moot nedes like
Al that yow liste, I dar nat pleyne moore,
But humblely, with sorwful sikes sike,
Yow write ich myn unresty sorwes soore,   1355
Fro day to day desiryng evere moore
To knowen fully, if youre wille it weere,
How ye han ferd and don whil ye be theere;

"The whos welfare and hele ek God encresse
In honour swich, that upward in degree   1360
It growe alwey, so that it nevere cesse.
Right as youre herte ay kan, my lady free,
Devyse, I prey to God so moot it be,
And graunte it that ye soone upon me rewe,
As wisly as in al I am yow trewe.   1365

"And if yow liketh knowen of the fare
Of me, whos wo ther may no wit discryve,
I kan namore but, chiste of every care,
At wrytyng of this lettre I was on-lyve,
Al redy out my woful gost to dryve;   1370
Which I delaye, and holde hym yet in honde,
Upon the sighte of matere of youre sonde.

"Myn eyen two, in veyn with which I se,
Of sorwful teris salte arn waxen welles;
My song, in pleynte of myn adversitee;   1375
My good, in harm; myn ese ek woxen helle is;
My joie, in wo; I kan sey yow naught ellis,
But torned is, for which my lif I warie,
Everich joie or ese in his contrarie.   1379

"Which with youre comyng hom ayeyn to
    Troie
Ye may redresse, and more a thousand sithe
Than evere ich hadde, encressen in me joie.
For was ther nevere herte yet so blithe
To han his lif as I shal ben as swithe
As I yow se; and though no manere routhe   1385
Commeve yow, yet thynketh on youre trouthe.

"And if so be my gilt hath deth deserved,
Or if yow list namore upon me se,
In guerdoun yet of that I have yow served,
Byseche I yow, myn owen lady free,   1390
That hereupon ye wolden write me,
For love of God, my righte lode-sterre,
That deth may make an ende of al my werre.

"If other cause aught doth yow for to dwelle,
That with youre lettre ye me recomforte;   1395
For though to me youre absence is an helle,
With pacience I wol my wo comporte,
And with youre lettre of hope I wol desporte.
Now writeth, swete, and lat me thus nat pleyne;
With hope, or deth, delivereth me fro peyne.

"Iwis, myne owene deere herte trewe,   1401
I woot that, whan ye next upon me se,
So lost have I myn hele and ek myn hewe,
Criseyde shal nought konne knowen me.
Iwys, myn hertes day, my lady free,   1405
So thursteth ay myn herte to byholde
Youre beute, that my lif unnethe I holde.

1338. **that youre eyen . . . holde,** that you do not consider your eyes defiled by looking on this. **1342. by the cause,** because. **1343. m' asterte,** escapes from me. **1348. Considered this,** this being considered. **1349. ther,** whereas. **1350. in oost,** *i.e.* in the Greek host. **1354. with . . . sike,** sick from. **1355. unresty,** unquiet. **1365. wisly,** certainly. **1366. fare,** condition, state. **1368. chiste,** chest, container. **1372. sonde,** message. **1378. warie,** curse. **1395. That,** depending upon *Byseche I yow* (l. 1390). **1398. desporte,** take consolation or cheer. **1404. konne,** be able.

"I say namore, al have I for to seye
To yow wel more than I telle may,
But wheither that ye do me lyve or deye,   1410
Yet praye I God, so yeve yow right good day!
And fareth wel, goodly, faire, fresshe may,
As ye that lif or deth may me comande!
And to youre trouthe ay I me recomande,

"With hele swich that, but ye yeven me   1415
The same hele, I shal non hele have.
In yow lith, whan yow liste that it so be,
The day in which me clothen shal my grave;
In yow my lif, in yow myght for to save
Me fro disese of alle peynes smerte;   1420
And far now wel, myn owen swete herte!
                le vostre T."

This lettre forth was sent unto Criseyde,
Of which hire answere in effect was this:
Ful pitously she wroot ayeyn, and seyde,
That also sone as that she myghte, ywys,   1425
She wolde come, and mende al that was mys.
And fynaly she wroot and seyde hym thenne,
She wolde come, ye, but she nyste whenne.

But in hire lettre made she swich festes
That wonder was, and swerth she loveth hym
      best;   1430
Of which he fond but botmeles bihestes.
But Troilus, thow maist now, est or west,
Pipe in an ivy lef, if that the lest!
Thus goth the world. God shilde us fro mes-
      chaunce,
And every wight that meneth trouthe avaunce!

Encressen gan the wo fro day to nyght   1436
Of Troilus, for tarying of Criseyde;
And lessen gan his hope and ek his myght,
For which al down he in his bed hym leyde.

He ne eet, ne dronk, ne slep, ne no word seyde,
Ymagynyng ay that she was unkynde,   1441
For which wel neigh he wex out of his mynde.

This drem, of which I told have ek byforn,
May nevere come out of his remembraunce.
He thought ay wel he hadde his lady lorn,   1445
And that Joves, of his purveyaunce,
Hym shewed hadde in slep the signifiaunce
Of hire untrouthe and his disaventure,
And that the boor was shewed hym in figure.

For which he for Sibille his suster sente,   1450
That called was Cassandre ek al aboute,
And al his drem he tolde hire er he stente,
And hire bisoughte assoilen hym the doute
Of the stronge boor with tuskes stoute;
And fynaly, withinne a litel stounde,   1455
Cassandre hym gan right thus his drem ex-
      pounde.

She gan first smyle, and seyde, "O brother
      deere,
If thow a soth of this desirest knowe,
Thow most a fewe of olde stories heere,
To purpos, how that Fortune overthrowe   1460
Hath lordes olde; thorugh which, withinne a
      throwe,
Thow wel this boor shalt knowe, and of what
      kynde
He comen is, as men in bokes fynde.

"Diane, which that wroth was and in ire
For Grekis nolde don hire sacrifise,   1465
Ne encens upon hire auter sette afire,
She, for that Grekis gonne hire so despise,
Wrak hire in a wonder cruel wise;
For with a boor as gret as ox in stalle
She made up frete hire corn and vynes alle.   1470

1415. With, together with. **1419. in yow.** Understand *lith* from l. 1417. **1421. le vostre T,** your T. **1426. mys,** wrong. **1429. festes,** what pleases, *i.e.* she was so pleasant. **1431. botmeles bihestes,** empty promises. **1433. Pipe in an ivy lef,** go whistle. Chaucer uses the expression also in *KnT*, 1838. **1438. myght,** strength. **1441. unkynde,** cruel, untrue. **1446. purveyaunce,** providence, foreknowledge. **1447. signifiaunce,** sign. **1449. in figure,** symbolically. **1450. Sibille,** (properly) prophetess, but Chaucer uses it as another name for Cassandra. **1453. assoilen,** release from. **doute,** fear, uncertainty. **1460. To purpos,** pertinent to the subject. **1461. throwe,** short space of time. **1468. Wrak,** avenged. **1470. up frete hire corn,** eat up their grain.

"To sle this boor was al the contre raysed,
Amonges which ther com, this boor to se,
A mayde, oon of this world the beste ypreysed;
And Meleagre, lord of that contree,
He loved so this fresshe mayden free,   1475
That with his manhod, er he wolde stente,
This boor he slough, and hire the hed he sente;

"Of which, as olde bokes tellen us,
Ther ros a contek and a gret envye;
And of this lord descended Tideus   1480
By ligne, or ellis olde bookes lye.
But how this Meleagre gan to dye
Thorough his moder, wol I yow naught telle,
For al to longe it were for to dwelle."

She tolde ek how Tideus, er she stente,   1485
Unto the stronge citee of Thebes,
To cleymen kyngdom of the citee, wente,
For his felawe, daun Polymytes,
Of which the brother, daun Ethiocles,
Ful wrongfully of Thebes held the strengthe;
This tolde she by proces, al by lengthe.   1491

She tolde ek how Hemonydes asterte,
Whan Tideus slough fifty knyghtes stoute.

She tolde ek alle the prophecyes by herte,
And how that seven kynges with hire route
Bysegeden the citee al aboute;   1496
And of the holy serpent, and the welle,
And of the furies, al she gan hym telle;

Of Archymoris burying and the pleyes,
And how Amphiorax fil thorugh the grounde,
How Tideus was sleyn, lord of Argeyes,   1501
And how Ypomedoun in litel stounde
Was dreynt, and ded Parthonope of wownde;
And also how Capaneus the proude   1504
With thonder-dynt was slayn, that cride loude.

She gan ek telle hym how that eyther brother,
Ethiocles and Polymyte also,
At a scarmuche ech of hem slough other,
And of Argyves wepynge and hire wo;   1509
And how the town was brent, she tolde ek tho.
And so descendeth down from gestes olde
To Diomede, and thus she spak and tolde.

"This ilke boor bitokneth Diomede,
Tideus sone, that down descended is
Fro Meleagre, that made the boor to blede.   1515
And thy lady, wherso she be, ywis,

1474. Meleagre, Meleager son of the Calydonian king and leader of the band that slew the monster (a boar) which was devastating the country. The story is told by Ovid, *Metam.,* VIII. 271–444. The maiden is Atalanta. **1479. contek and . . . envye,** strife and enmity. **1480. Tideus,** properly the half-brother, not the descendant of Meleager. **1482. But how this Meleagre gan to dye.** His mother's brothers protested his giving the head to Atalanta, whereupon he slew them. When he was an infant the Fates had declared that he would die when a certain piece of wood on the hearth was consumed. His mother, Althaea, had extinguished it and concealed it. Now in her rage she threw it into the fire. **1485.** This and the following three stanzas summarize the *Thebaid* of Statius. Eteocles and Polynices (whom Chaucer calls Polymites), sons of Oedipus, agreed to rule Thebes in alternative years. When at the end of a year Eteocles refused to let Polynices take his turn, the latter enlisted the help of his father-in-law Adrastus, king of Argos. The other daughter of Adrastus was married to Tydeus. **1491. by proces,** in due course. **1492. Hemonydes,** Maeon, son of Haemon. **asterte,** escaped. **1493. fifty knyghtes,** really the other forty-nine. The fifty had been sent by Eteocles against Tydeus. **1494. alle the prophecyes.** Amphiaraus, a great prophet at Argos, had foretold the fatal outcome of the war. **1495. seven kynges,** the seven heroes (including Polynices) who besieged Thebes—the Seven against Thebes. **1497. holy serpent.** A serpent sent by Jove stung to death the child Archemorus when its nurse left it to guide the host of the Seven at one point in their march. **the welle,** the stream to which the nurse was guiding them. **1498. the furies.** In Statius (Book V) Hypsipyle recalls how the women of Lemnos, acting like furies, killed all their husbands (for having left them and taken concubines from Thrace). **1499. Archymoris,** Archimorus; see note to l. 1497. **the pleyes,** the Nemean games, instituted by the Seven on their way to Thebes. **1500. Amphiorax,** Amphiaraus; see note to l. 1494 and 2. 104–5. In addition to being a prophet he was a famous warrior. One of the few still living at the end of the war, he was swallowed up by the earth when he was about to be taken prisoner. **1501. Argeyes,** Argives, citizens of Argos. **1502. Ypomedoun,** Hippomedon, one of the Seven, as were Parthenopeus and Capaneus. Capaneus boasted that even the fire of Zeus would not prevent him from scaling the walls, whereupon Zeus struck him with a thunderbolt. **1503. ded,** (was) dead. **1508. scarmuche,** skirmish. **1509. Argyves wepynge.** Although the form of the name is peculiar, the reference is usually explained as to Argia, Polynices' wife, whose grief is described in the *Thebaid,* XII. 111–16. But it may more plausibly be taken as a reference to the grief of the women of Argos for their husbands and relatives, among whom Argia is only the first of those mentioned by name, as they proceed, partly guided by the gods, to the scene of the disaster (see *Thebaid,* XII, 205–40).

This Diomede hire herte hath, and she his,
Wep if thow wolt, or lef! For, out of doute,
This Diomede is inne, and thow art oute."

"Thow seyst nat soth," quod he, "thow sor-
     ceresse,   1520
With al thy false goost of prophecye!
Thow wenest ben a gret devyneresse!
Now sestow nat this fool of fantasie
Peyneth hire on ladys for to lye?   1524
Awey!" quod he, "ther Joves yeve the sorwe!
Thow shalt be fals, peraunter, yet tomorwe!

"As wel thow myghtest lien on Alceste,
That was of creatures, but men lye,
That evere weren, kyndest and the beste!
For whan hire housbonde was in jupertye   1530
To dye hymself, but if she wolde dye,
She ches for hym to dye and gon to helle,
And starf anon, as us the bokes telle."

Cassandre goth, and he with cruel herte
Foryat his wo, for angre of hire speche;   1535
And from his bed al sodeynly he sterte,
As though al hool hym hadde ymad a leche.
And day by day he gan enquere and seche
A sooth of this with al his fulle cure;   1539
And thus he drieth forth his aventure.   1540

Fortune, which that permutacioun
Of thynges hath, as it is hire comitted
Thorugh purveyaunce and disposicioun
Of heighe Jove, as regnes shal be flitted   1544
Fro folk in folk, or when they shal be smytted,
Gan pulle awey the fetheres brighte of Troie
Fro day to day, til they ben bare of joie.

Among al this, the fyn of the parodie
Of Ector gan aprochen wonder blyve.
The fate wolde his soule sholde unbodye,   1550
And shapen hadde a mene it out to dryve,
Ayeyns which fate hym helpeth nat to stryve;
But on a day to fighten gan he wende,
At which, allas! he caught his lyves ende.

For which me thynketh every manere wight
That haunteth armes oughte to biwaille   1556
The deth of hym that was so noble a knyght;
For as he drough a kyng by th'aventaille,
Unwar of this, Achilles thorugh the maille   1559
And thorugh the body gan hym for to ryve;
And thus this worthi knyght was brought of
     lyve.

For whom, as olde bokes tellen us,
Was mad swich wo, that tonge it may nat telle;
And namely, the sorwe of Troilus,
That next hym was of worthynesse welle.   1565
And in this wo gan Troilus to dwelle,
That, what for sorwe, and love, and for unreste,
Ful ofte a day he bad his herte breste.

But natheles, though he gan hym dispaire,
And dradde ay that his lady was untrewe,   1570
Yet ay on hire his herte gan repaire.
And as thise loveres don, he soughte ay newe
To gete ayeyn Criseyde, brighte of hewe;
And in his herte he wente hire excusynge,
That Calkas caused al hire tariynge.   1575

And ofte tyme he was in purpos grete
Hymselven lik a pilgrym to desgise,
To seen hire; but he may nat contrefete

1518. lef, leave (it) undone. 1523. sestow, a rhetorical question not directed to Cassandra. fantasie, fantasy, delusion. 1527. Alceste, Alcestis, whose husband Admetus had been promised by the Fates deliverance from death if his father, mother, or wife would die for him. She is the principal character in the Prol. to the *LGW*. 1539. cure, care. 1540. drieth forth, goes through with. 1544. regnes . . . flitted, kingdoms shall be transferred. 1545. smytted, smutted, sullied. 1547. they, *i.e.* the Trojans. 1548. parodie, period, duration. The end (*fin*) of Hector's life-period was rapidly approaching. 1550. unbodye, leave the body. 1558. drough, drew. aventaille, a wide band of chain-mail protecting the lower part of the face, the neck, and the upper chest. 1559. Unwar of this, without knowing it. 1564. namely, especially. 1566. dwelle, remain, continue. 1567. unreste, disturbed state of mind. 1572. newe, anew. 1574. wente, went on. 1577. pilgrym. An anachronism here, but the device is not uncommon in medieval romance and in real life. Cf. B. J. Whiting, *MLN*, LX. 47–49.

To ben unknowen of folk that weren wise,
Ne fynde excuse aright that may suffise,   1580
If he among the Grekis knowen were;
For which he wep ful ofte and many a tere.

To hire he wroot yet ofte tyme al newe
Ful pitously,—he lefte it nought for slouthe,
Bisechyng hire, syn that he was trewe,   1585
That she wol come ayeyn and holde hire trouthe.
For which Criseyde upon a day, for routhe,—
I take it so,—touchyng al this matere,
Wrot hym ayeyn, and seyde as ye may here:

Litera Criseydis

"Cupides sone, ensample of goodlyheede,   1590
O swerd of knyghthod, sours of gentilesse,
How myght a wight in torment and in drede
And heleles, yow sende as yet gladnesse?
I herteles, I sik, I in destresse!
Syn ye with me, nor I with yow, may dele,   1595
Yow neyther sende ich herte may nor hele.

"Youre lettres ful, the papir al ypleynted,
Conceyved hath myn hertes pietee.
I have ek seyn with teris al depeynted   1599
Youre lettre, and how that ye requeren me
To come ayeyn, which yet ne may nat be.
But whi, lest that this lettre founden were,
No mencioun ne make I now, for feere.

"Grevous to me, God woot, is youre unreste,
Youre haste, and that the goddes ordinaunce
It semeth nat ye take it for the beste.   1606
Nor other thyng nys in youre remembraunce,
As thynketh me, but only youre plesaunce.
But beth nat wroth, and that I yow biseche;
For that I tarie is al for wikked speche.   1610

"For I have herd wel moore than I wende,
Touchyng us two, how thynges han ystonde;
Which I shal with dissymulyng amende
And beth nat wroth, I have ek understonde
How ye ne do but holden me in honde.   1615
But now no force, I kan nat in yow gesse
But alle trouthe and alle gentilesse.

"Come I wole; but yet in swich disjoynte
I stonde as now, that what yer or what day
That this shal be, that kan I naught apoynte.
But in effect I pray yow, as I may,   1621
Of youre good word and of youre frendship ay.
For trewely, while that my lif may dure,
As for a frend ye may in me assure.

"Yet preye ich yow, on yvel ye ne take   1625
That it is short which that I to yow write;
I dar nat, ther I am, wel lettres make,
Ne nevere yet ne koude I wel endite.
Ek gret effect men write in place lite;
Th'entente is al, and nat the lettres space.   1630
And fareth now wel, God have yow in his grace!
                          La vostre C."

This Troilus this lettre thoughte al straunge,
Whan he it saugh, and sorwfullich he sighte.
Hym thoughte it lik a kalendes of chaunge
But fynaly, he ful ne trowen myghte   1635
That she ne wolde hym holden that she hyghte;
For with ful yvel wille list hym to leve,
That loveth wel, in swich cas, though hym
    greve.

But natheles, men seyen that at the laste,
For any thyng, men shal the soothe se.   1640
And swich a cas bitidde, and that as faste,

1584. slouthe, failure to do what is necessary. **1593. heleles,** devoid of health or well-being. **1594. herteles,** without heart (spirit). **sik,** sick. **1596. Yow . . . hele,** I can send you neither courage nor health. **1598. Conceyved . . . pietee,** has aroused (engendered) my heart's pity. **1605. haste,** impatience. **1615. holden . . . in honde,** lead on with false expectation. **1616. gesse,** suppose. **1618. disjoynte,** difficult situation. **1620. apoynte,** set a time, say definitely. **1624. assure,** feel secure. **1629. Ek gret effect,** also people write matters of great consequence in little space. **1630. the lettres space,** the extent of the letter. **1634. kalendes,** beginning, lit. the first day of the month. **1637. leve,** believe. Although the e in leve (believe) is variable, it is normally close, and in the four other occurrences in the poem of the rime leve: greve the meaning of leve (believe) is unequivocal. The meaning of the present couplet appears to be: He who loves well is unwilling to believe (the evidence), in such a case, although he is troubled. **1641. as faste,** very soon.

That Troilus wel understod that she
Nas nought so kynde as that hire oughte be.
And fynaly, he woot now, out of doute,
That al is lost that he hath ben aboute. 1645

Stood on a day in his malencolie
This Troilus, and in suspecioun
Of hire for whom he wende for to dye.
And so bifel that thoroughout Troye town,
As was the gise, iborn was up and down 1650
A manere cote-armure, as seith the storie,
Byforn Deiphebe, in signe of his victorie;

The whiche cote, as telleth Lollius,
Deiphebe it hadde rent fro Diomede
The same day. And whan this Troilus 1655
It saugh, he gan to taken of it hede,
Avysyng of the lengthe and of the brede,
And al the werk; but as he gan byholde,
Ful sodeynly his herte gan to colde,

As he that on the coler fond withinne 1660
A broche, that he Criseyde yaf that morwe
That she from Troie moste nedes twynne,
In remembraunce of hym and of his sorwe.
And she hym leyde ayeyn hire feith to borwe
To kepe it ay! But now ful wel he wiste, 1665
His lady nas no lenger on to triste.

He goth hym hom, and gan ful soone sende
For Pandarus, and al this newe chaunce,
And of this broche, he tolde hym word and ende,
Compleynyng of hire hertes variaunce, 1670
His longe love, his trouthe, and his penaunce.
And after deth, withouten wordes moore,
Ful faste he cride, his reste hym to restore.

Than spak he thus, "O lady myn, Criseyde, 1674
Where is youre feith, and where is youre biheste?

Where is youre love? where is youre trouthe?"
 he seyde.
"Of Diomede have ye now al this feeste!
Allas! I wolde han trowed atte leeste
That, syn ye nolde in trouthe to me stonde,
That ye thus nolde han holden me in honde!

"Who shal now trowe on any othes mo? 1681
Allas! I nevere wolde han wend, er this,
That ye, Criseyde, koude han chaunged so;
Ne, but I hadde agilt and don amys,
So cruel wende I nought youre herte, ywis, 1685
To sle me thus! Allas, youre name of trouthe
Is now fordon, and that is al my routhe.

"Was ther non other broche yow liste lete
To feffe with youre newe love," quod he,
"But thilke broch that I, with teris wete, 1690
Yow yaf, as for a remembraunce of me?
Non other cause, allas, ne hadde ye
But for despit, and ek for that ye mente
Al outrely to shewen youre entente.

"Thorugh which I se that clene out of youre
 mynde 1695
Ye han me cast; and I ne kan nor may,
For al this world, withinne myn herte fynde
To unloven yow a quarter of a day!
In corsed tyme I born was, weilaway,
That yow, that doon me al this wo endure, 1700
Yet love I best of any creature!

"Now God," quod he, "me sende yet the grace
That I may meten with this Diomede!
And trewely, if I have myght and space,
Yet shal I make, I hope, his sydes blede. 1705
O God," quod he, "that oughtest taken heede
To fortheren trouthe, and wronges to punyce,
Whi nyltow don a vengeaunce of this vice?

1650. gise, custom. 1651. cote-armure, coat-armor, a tunic with heraldic devices worn over armor, naturally an anachronism here. 1653. Lollius. See intro. 1654. Deiphebe, Deiphebus, brother of Troilus; cf. 2. 1398. 1662. twynne, depart. 1664. to borwe, in pledge. 1666. on to triste, to put trust in. 1668. chaunce, unexpected occurrence. 1669. word and ende, properly *ord and ende*, beginning and end. 1671. penaunce, suffering. 1672. after deth . . . cride, called upon death. 1677. feeste, enjoyment, cf. OF. *aveir feste. This* is used in a generalizing sense. 1680. holden me in honde. See note to l. 1615, above. 1682. wend, weened. 1687. fordon, destroyed. 1688. lete, give up. 1689. To feffe, enfeoff. 1708. vice, wrong, evil.

"O Pandarus, that in dremes for to triste
Me blamed hast, and wont art oft upbreyde,
Now maistow se thiself, if that the liste, 1711
How trewe is now thi nece, bright Criseyde!
In sondry formes, God it woot," he seyde,
"The goddes shewen bothe joie and tene
In slep, and by my drem it is now sene. 1715

"And certeynly, withouten moore speche,
From hennesforth, as ferforth as I may,
Myn owen deth in armes wol I seche.
I recche nat how soone be the day!
But trewely, Criseyde, swete may, 1720
Whom I have ay with al my myght yserved,
That ye thus doon, I have it nat deserved."

This Pandarus, that al thise thynges herde,
And wiste wel he seyde a soth of this,
He nought a word ayeyn to hym answerde;
For sory of his frendes sorwe he is, 1726
And shamed for his nece hath don amys,
And stant, astoned of thise causes tweye,
As stille as ston; a word ne kowde he seye.

But at the laste thus he spak, and seyde: 1730
"My brother deer, I may do the namore.
What sholde I seyen? I hate, ywys, Cryseyde;
And, God woot, I wol hate hire evermore!
And that thow me bisoughtest don of yoore,
Havyng unto myn honour ne my reste 1735
Right no reward, I dide al that the leste.

"If I dide aught that myghte liken the,
It is me lief; and of this tresoun now,
God woot that it a sorwe is unto me!
And dredeles, for hertes ese of yow, 1740
Right fayn I wolde amende it, wiste I how.
And fro this world, almyghty God I preye
Delivere hire soon! I kan namore seye."

Gret was the sorwe and pleynte of Troilus;
But forth hire cours Fortune ay gan to holde.
Criseyde loveth the sone of Tideus, 1746
And Troilus moot wepe in cares colde.
Swich is this world, whoso it kan byholde:
In ech estat is litel hertes reste.
God leve us for to take it for the beste! 1750

In many cruel bataille, out of drede,
Of Troilus, this ilke noble knyght,
As men may in thise olde bokes rede,
Was seen his knyghthod and his grete myght.
And dredeles, his ire, day and nyght, 1755
Ful cruwely the Grekis ay aboughte;
And alwey moost this Diomede he soughte.

And ofte tyme, I fynde that they mette
With blody strokes and with wordes grete,
Assayinge how hire speres weren whette; 1760
And, God it woot, with many a cruel hete
Gan Troilus upon his helm to bete!
But natheles, Fortune it naught ne wolde,
Of oothers hond that eyther deyen sholde.

And if I hadde ytaken for to write 1765
The armes of this ilke worthi man,
Than wolde ich of his batailles endite;
But for that I to writen first bigan
Of his love, I have seyd as I kan,—
His worthi dedes, whoso list hem heere, 1770
Rede Dares, he kan telle hem alle ifeere—

Bysechyng every lady bright of hewe,
And every gentil womman, what she be,
That al be that Criseyde was untrewe,
That for that gilt she be nat wroth with me.
Ye may hire giltes in other bokes se; 1776
And gladlier I wol write, if yow leste,
Penelopeës trouthe and good Alceste.

1728. astoned, dumfounded. **1736. reward,** regard. **1737. liken,** please. **1738. It is me lief,** I am glad. **1764. Of oothers,** of the other's. **1766. armes,** deeds of arms; cf. the opening words of the *Æneid*. **1771. Dares.** See note to 1. 146. It is not certain that Chaucer used Dares. The allusion is an example of the practice of medieval authors of referring to an ancient authority, rather than to a more immediate source. **1778. Penelopeës trouthe and good Alceste,** an indication that Chaucer already had in mind *The Legend of Good Women*.

N'y sey nat this aloonly for thise men,
But moost for wommen that bitraised be 1780
Thorough false folk; God yeve hem sorwe, amen!
That with hire grete wit and subtilte
Bytraise yow! And this commeveth me
To speke, and in effect yow alle I preye,
Beth war of men, and herkneth what I seye!—

Go, litel book, go, litel myn tragedye, 1786
Ther God thi makere yet, er that he dye,
So sende myght to make in som comedye!
But litel book, no makyng thow n'envie,
But subgit be to alle poesye; 1790
And kis the steppes, where as thow seest pace
Virgile, Ovide, Omer, Lucan, and Stace.

And for ther is so gret diversite
In Englissh and in writyng of oure tonge,
So prey I God that non myswrite the, 1795
Ne the mysmetre for defaute of tonge.
And red wherso thow be, or elles songe,
That thow be understonde, God I biseche!
But yet to purpos of my rather speche.—

The wrath, as I bigan yow for to seye, 1800
Of Troilus the Grekis boughten deere.
For thousandes his hondes maden deye,
As he that was withouten any peere,
Save Ector, in his tyme, as I kan heere.
But weilawey, save only Goddes wille! 1805
Despitously hym slough the fierse Achille.

And whan that he was slayn in this manere,
His lighte goost ful blisfully is went
Up to the holughnesse of the eighte spere,
In convers letyng everich element; 1810
And ther he saugh, with ful avysement,
The erratik sterres, herkenyng armonye
With sownes ful of hevenyssh melodie.

And down from thennes faste he gan avyse
This litel spot of erthe, that with the se 1815
Embraced is, and fully gan despise
This wrecched world; and held al vanite
To respect of the pleyn felicite
That is in hevene above; and at the laste, 1819
Ther he was slayn, his lokyng down he caste.

And in hymself he lough right at the wo
Of hem that wepten for his deth so faste;
And dampned al oure werk that foloweth so
The blynde lust, the which that may nat laste,
And sholden al oure herte on heven caste. 1825
And forth he wente, shortly for to telle,
Ther as Mercurye sorted hym to dwelle.

Swich fyn hath, lo, this Troilus for love!
Swich fyn hath al his grete worthynesse!
Swich fyn hath his estat real above, 1830
Swich fyn his lust, swich fyn hath his noblesse!
Swych fyn hath false worldes brotelnesse!
And thus bigan his lovyng of Criseyde,
As I have told, and in this wise he deyde.

1779. aloonly, solely. **1787. he,** *i.e.* the author, implied in the preceding line. **1788. to make in,** compose. It was formerly thought that the lines were intended to announce another poem which Chaucer had in mind, but they may express no more than the hope that he will live to write something with a happier ending. **1789. no makyng thow n' envie,** do not vie with other poetry. **1790. But subgit be . . .,** *i.e.* be one of poetry's simple subjects. **1799. rather,** earlier. **1805. weilawey, save only Goddes wille,** alas, except that it was God's will. **1809. eighte spere.** The reading *eighte* is found in only three MSS, including Caxton (the others reading *seventhe*), but is the number in Chaucer's source for this passage (Boccaccio's *Teseida*). It is uncertain whether Chaucer numbered the spheres outward from the earth or inward from that of the fixed stars. The former is suggested by the phrase *up to the holughnesse of,* in which case the sphere referred to would be that of the fixed stars, next to the outermost or *primum mobile.* See also M. W. Bloomfield, *MLR,* LIII. 408–10. **1810. In convers,** a mistranslation or intentional alteration of Boccaccio's *convessi* (convexities). Chaucer's phrase means 'on the other side, behind.' As the spirit of Troilus rose through the spheres it left behind fire, air, earth, and water (*everich element*). **1811. avysement,** contemplation. **1812. The erratik sterres,** the seven planets. **herkenyng armonye,** *i.e.* while listening to the music of the spheres. **1814. avyse,** contemplate. **1818. To respect of,** in comparison with. **pleyn,** full, perfect. **1820. lokyng,** look, gaze. **1823. dampned . . . werk,** condemned all our activity. **1825. And sholden,** *i.e.* when we should. **1827. Ther as Mercurye,** *i.e.* to the place which Mercury allotted to him. One of Mercury's functions was to conduct the shades to the other world. **1828. fyn,** end. **1830. real,** royal. **1832. brotelnesse,** fragility, insecurity.

O yonge, fresshe folkes, he or she,			1835
In which that love up groweth with youre age,
Repeyreth hom fro worldly vanyte,
And of youre herte up casteth the visage
To thilke God that after his ymage
Yow made, and thynketh al nys but a faire		1840
This world, that passeth soone as floures faire.

And loveth hym, the which that right for love
Upon a crois, oure soules for to beye,
First starf, and roos, and sit in hevene above;
For he nyl falsen no wight, dar I seye,			1845
That wol his herte al holly on hym leye.
And syn he best to love is, and most meke,
What nedeth feynede loves for to seke?
Lo here, of payens corsed olde rites!
Lo here, what alle hire goddes may availle!		1850
Lo here, thise wrecched worldes appetites!
Lo here, the fyn and guerdoun for travaille

Of Jove, Appollo, of Mars, of swich rascaille!
Lo here, the forme of olde clerkis speche
In poetrie, if ye hire bokes seche!			1855

O moral Gower, this book I directe
To the and to the, philosophical Strode,
To vouchen sauf, ther nede is, to correcte,
Of youre benignites and zeles goode.			1859
And to that sothefast Crist, that starf on rode,
With al myn herte of mercy evere I preye,
And to the Lord right thus I speke and seye:

Thow oon, and two, and thre, eterne on lyve,
That regnest ay in thre, and two, and oon,
Uncircumscript, and al maist circumscrive,		1865
Us from visible and invisible foon
Defende, and to thy mercy, everichon,
So make us, Jesus, for thi mercy digne,
For love of mayde and moder thyn benigne.
	Amen.

Explicit liber Troili et Criseydis.

1840. **faire,** fair. The phrase *cherry fair*, a fair held in a cherry orchard and a scene of much gaiety, was a symbol of the fleeting pleasures of life. For examples see *NED, s.v. cherry-fair*. 1844. **starf . . . sit,** died . . . sits. 1848. **feynede,** false, deceptive, *i.e.* only heavenly love is real, all earthly love an illusion. 1853. **rascaille,** worthless folk. 1854. **forme,** shape, beauty. 1856. **Gower,** John Gower, poet and friend of Chaucer (see the Life of Chaucer above, p. xiv). The adjective *moral* is not derogatory. 1857. **philosophical Strode,** probably Ralph Strode, a contemporary philosopher and theologian, a fellow of Merton College, Oxford. He may be the same as the Ralph Strode who is found later practising law in London and who died in 1387. 1863. **Thow oon, and two, and thre,** Father, Son, and Holy Ghost. 1866. **foon,** foes.

The Legend of Good Women

The Legend of Good Women is named by Chaucer in the Introduction to *The Man of Law's Tale* "the Seintes Legende of Cupide." In his playful way he thus suggested comparison with Christian legendaries or collections of saints' lives. The plan involved the telling of a number of stories, most likely twenty, of women who had suffered martyrdom for love and consequently qualified for canonization under the religion of the god of Love. The collection is set in a framework by a prologue which explains how the stories came to be written. In its humble way it anticipates *The Canterbury Tales*.

Hardly any other work of Chaucer has been the object of so much scholarly controversy. An early controversial issue arose from the fact that the Prologue, the most interesting part of the poem, exists in two forms: one commonly known in the past as the B version but often referred to now as the F version, from the Fairfax manuscript, one of the twelve manuscripts in which it is preserved; the other commonly called the A version, because when it was first discovered it was believed to be an early draft of the Prologue, of which B represented the finished state. The A version is now often called the G version from the single manuscript in the Cambridge University library (Gg. 4.27) in which it is found. Since the letters A and B inevitably carry some implication of a chronological sequence and since there is grave doubt about the priority of the A version, it seems better to refer to them simply by the symbols for manuscripts in which they are found, and the two forms of the Prologue will here be designated F and G. Only the former is included in the present volume.

The priority of G was perhaps too hastily assumed and, once assumed, was buttressed by arguments which seemed to support it. Since the F version is preserved in most of the manuscripts it seemed to be the version which Chaucer released for circulation, and in many individual lines and passages it is patently superior to G. In the belief that any changes which Chaucer made would be for the better it was easy to persuade oneself that F was the revision of G. However, in 1892 ten Brink undertook to reverse the current opinion. While his views were challenged by those who upheld the older order, he gained a few converts. The most important evidence in support of the reversal was brought forward by Lowes in an article (*PMLA*, xix. 593–683) which, though claiming too much for certain supposed resemblances, threw new light on the poem. He showed that the Prologue must be viewed against the background of a clearly recognizable French tradition, observable in a number of the longer and shorter poems in praise of the *marguerite* (daisy). Two of the long poems in this tradition are Deschamps' *Lai de Franchise* and Froissart's *Paradys d'Amours*, and there are a number of short *Dits*. With the *Paradys* Chaucer had been familiar even when he wrote *The Book of the Duchess*; his acquaintance with the *Lai de Franchise* is open to doubt. In those passages which contain recollections of the French *marguerite* poems the differences between the two prologues can best be accounted for on the assumption that version G is a revision of version F. But the most telling argument for the later date of G is the omission by G of a couplet referring to Queen Anne. In version F Alceste, in directing the poet to write the lives of women true in love, tells him to present the finished work to the queen at "Eltham or at Shene." Queen Anne died June 7, 1394. These were the favorite royal manors of Richard II and Queen Anne. So great was the king's grief when the queen died that he ordered the palace at Sheen to be torn down. The most natural explanation, pointed out by ten Brink and emphasized by Lowes (*PMLA*, xx. 749–864), is that Chaucer removed the couplet in the revision to avoid reviving in the king a painful memory.

While it may be said that the question of priority between the two versions of the Prologue has been settled and it is agreed by all scholars that the version printed in the present volume presents the poem in its original form, it is not so easy to account for some of the changes made in the revision or indeed to suggest a reason for the poet's undertaking the revision at all. By 1394 Chaucer had been engaged for seven or eight years on a much more challenging work, *The Canterbury Tales*, and had completed nearly a quarter of it according to his original plan. He had presumably discarded the collection of legends for what must have seemed to him, as it does to us, a better idea. Of the twenty legends which he had implied in the Prologue he wrote only nine, and the ninth is incomplete. One usually does not embark on an extensive revision of an abandoned work unless he has decided to complete it. We do not know what external circumstance or inner urge[1] would have induced him to interrupt his labors on *The Canterbury Tales* to continue his collection of tragic love stories. But there is also another circumstance connected with the revised prologue which is even more puzzling. This is the fact that readers, even the uninitiated, almost invariably prefer the earlier version and can point to many beautiful lines which have been spoiled in revision. We cannot attribute the deterioration to the failing powers of the poet. If the revision is thought of as undertaken soon after the death of the queen (it could, of course, have been considerably later), this is approximately the time we believe Chaucer was composing the Marriage Group in *The Canterbury Tales*, and he was certainly then in the full possession of his powers. The only respect in which Version G of the Prologue has been thought superior to the earlier version is in certain small matters of structure, the more logical grouping of associated ideas, obtained by condensation and the shifting of a number of passages. In the latter half of the Prologue the changes are slight except for omissions. All the differences between the two versions could be accounted for on the theory that version G was the work of some one other than Chaucer, possibly attempting to restore from memory an imperfect copy, were it not for a rather long passage in which the god of Love reminds the poet of books in his library in which he might have found an abundance of stories about good women. Some of them are books which Chaucer was especially interested in when he was composing the tales that make up the Marriage Group. The passage, while not up to his best, is not un-Chaucerian.

Another controversial question which has been argued is whether the character of Alceste, and consequently of the god of Love, are meant to suggest real persons. Many scholars at the end of the last century, and well into the present, were quite sure that in Alceste the poet was paying a delicate compliment to Queen Anne. Such a view, however, is difficult to reconcile with Alceste's command:

> And whan this book ys maad, yive it the quene,
> On my behalf, at Eltham or at Sheene.

There are scholars who deny any historical references in the poem. Yet the tradition of the French *marguerite* poems, in which the poet himself often furnishes the clue to the identity of the

---

[1] The suggestion has been made that Chaucer may have undertaken to revise the Prologue for presentation to Isabel, the seven-year-old French princess whom Richard married in 1396. It would give point to one detail, the fact that the garland of rose leaves worn by the god of Love was "Stiked al with lylye floures newe." But in general the changes do not seem to adapt the poem in any significant way to the new occasion.

person symbolized by the daisy, and Chaucer's own practice in other occasional poems make it seem likely to others that Alceste is intended to represent some real person, someone whose identity would have been clear to the court circle for which Chaucer wrote. Accordingly other identifications have from time to time been proposed, often with so little to recommend them that it would not be profitable to discuss them here.

One interpretation that has been advanced, however, is rather arresting, put forward by Miss Margaret Galway ("Chaucer's Sovereign Lady," *MLR*, XXXIII. 145–99, followed by other articles which make minor modifications and have not generally strengthened her case). Noting that in the poem the god of Love is a king as well as a god and wears a halo instead of a crown, she seeks a king who has died and whose widow has remained faithful to his memory. No actual king of England meets the requirement at the time the Prologue was written, but Edward III had invested his three sons with coronets during his lifetime. Of these the eldest, Edward the Black Prince, had died in 1376 and his wife Joan, known as the Fair Maid of Kent, had not married again. Various details are noted which are reported in the notes to the text below. One historical circumstance seems to offer an occasion for the writing of the poem. In June, 1385, shortly before Richard set out for a campaign in Scotland, he arranged for his mother to stay at Wallingford (south of Oxford) and designated Sir Lewis Clifford and a dozen other men to attend her there. Chaucer is not named in the document but the group included a number of his friends and he may well have been of the party. The little arbor, in which he goes to sleep and dreams, would in this case have been at Wallingford. The fact that while there Joan died (August 7) can be seen as a reason for Chaucer's leaving the work unfinished. A theory of this kind cannot be proved; though it has more to recommend it than some of the other interpretations that have been suggested, there are scholars who will have none of it.

In its original form the Prologue can be dated with fair approximation. That it is a relatively late work can be inferred from the list of Chaucer's poems which Alceste, in coming to his defense, says he had previously written. One of the offenses which the god of Love charges against him is the writing of *Troilus and Criseyde*. Since it is likely that the *Troilus* was not finished before May, 1385, we can hardly assign the Prologue of the *Legend* to an earlier date. It was formerly argued that Chaucer showed in the Prologue an acquaintance with Deschamps' *Lai de Franchise*, which was written for May Day, 1385, and could hardly have reached Chaucer before 1386. But, as we have said above, his acquaintance with the *Lai de Franchise* must be regarded as not proved. On the other hand, it seems most likely that by April, 1387, Chaucer had begun *The Canterbury Tales*, another collection of stories in a framework. The more likely period, therefore, for the composition of the Prologue in its original form would seem to be 1385–86. Those who are persuaded that the sovereign lady for whom Chaucer expresses his devotion was Joan of Kent will assign it to the summer of 1385, but in any case such a date can hardly be far wrong. The later version must be dated sometime after the death of Queen Anne in June, 1394.

Some of the legends may have been written before the Prologue, but the reasons advanced in individual cases are not conclusive. Nor can we say why, as it has come down to us, the collection is incomplete. The existence of twelve manuscripts with the probability that at one time there were as many more, even though several of those we have are fragmentary, suggests that the work enjoyed considerable circulation, all the more surprising if it was never completed. Comparison with *The Canterbury Tales* in this respect is hardly proper. And yet, it must be admitted that probability is in favor of its never having been completed. That Chaucer tired of his task is not impossible; some of the legends seem to be related in a rather perfunctory way. That the death of Joan of Kent came as a shock to the court, even though she had been in poor health, is not to be doubted. The circumstance could have interrupted his work, whether or not he had begun it for her entertainment. These are matters of conjecture. But there is one certainty. He was on the point of beginning another collection of stories of much more varied character, in a framework with much more dramatic possibilities. That the plan was taking shape in his mind before the April in which the Canterbury pilgrims set out on their journey no one can doubt. And no one will regret his devoting the energies of his remaining years to this incomparably greater project.

The text is basically that of the Fairfax MS.

THE LEGEND OF GOOD WOMEN

THE PROLOGUE

(Text F)

A thousand tymes have I herd men telle
That ther ys joy in hevene and peyne in helle,
And I acorde wel that it ys so;
But, natheles, yet wot I wel also
That ther nis noon dwellyng in this contree, 5
That eyther hath in hevene or helle ybe,
Ne may of hit noon other weyes witen,
But as he hath herd seyd, or founde it writen;
For by assay ther may no man it preve.
But God forbede but men shulde leve 10
Wel more thing then men han seen with yë!
Men shal not wenen every thing a lye
But yf himself yt seeth, or elles dooth;
For, God wot, thing is never the lasse sooth,
Thogh every wight ne may it nat ysee. 15
Bernard the monk ne saugh nat all, pardee!

  Than mote we to bokes that we fynde,
Thurgh whiche that olde thinges ben in mynde,
And to the doctrine of these olde wyse,
Yeve credence, in every skylful wise, 20
That tellen of these olde appreved stories
Of holynesse, of regnes, of victories,
Of love, of hate, of other sondry thynges,

Of whiche I may not maken rehersynges.
And yf that olde bokes were awey, 25
Yloren were of remembraunce the key.
Wel ought us thanne honouren and beleve
These bokes, there we han noon other preve.

  And as for me, though that I konne but lyte,
On bokes for to rede I me delyte, 30
And to hem yive I feyth and ful credence,
And in myn herte have hem in reverence
So hertely, that ther is game noon
That fro my bokes maketh me to goon,
But yt be seldom on the holyday, 35
Save, certeynly, whan that the month of May
Is comen, and that I here the foules synge,
And that the floures gynnen for to sprynge.
Farewel my bok and my devocioun!

  Now have I thanne eek this condicioun, 40
That, of al the floures in the mede,
Thanne love I most thise floures white and rede,
Swiche as men callen daysyes in our toun.
To hem have I so gret affeccioun,
As I seyde erst, whanne comen is the May, 45
That in my bed ther daweth me no day

3. **acorde,** agree. 10. **leve,** believe. 11. **thing,** things. 13. **himself,** sing. because *men* (l. 12), the indefinite pronoun, is construed as a singular. 16. **Bernard the monk.** Several identifications have been suggested, but the statement seems to have been proverbial and associated with Bernard of Clairvaux (1091–1153), who was the head of the band of monks which established the Cistercian abbey with which his name is associated. 17. **mote,** may, must. 20. **skylful wise,** reasonable manner. 21. **appreved,** tried and true. 26. **Yloren,** lost. 27. **ought us,** impers. construction, as usual. 40. **condicioun,** personal characteristic. 42. **Thanne love I most . . .** These lines reflect a cult of the daisy (Fr. *marguerite*), which several contemporary French poems imply, such as Machaut's *Dit de la Marguerite,* Deschamps' *Lai de Franchise,* and Froissart's *Paradys d'Amours* (ll. 1620–1653), a poem with which Chaucer was already acquainted when he wrote *The Book of the Duchess.* **white and rede.** The red color refers to the tips of the petals. 46. **daweth,** dawns.

That I nam up and walkyng in the mede
To seen this flour ayein the sonne sprede,
Whan it upryseth erly by the morwe.
That blisful sight softneth al my sorwe, 50
So glad am I, whan that I have presence
Of it, to doon it alle reverence,
As she that is of alle floures flour,
Fulfilled of al vertu and honour,
And evere ilyke faire and fressh of hewe; 55
And I love it, and ever ylike newe,
And evere shal, til that myn herte dye.
Al swere I nat, of this I wol nat lye;
Ther loved no wight hotter in his lyve.
And whan that hit ys eve, I renne blyve, 60
As sone as evere the sonne gynneth weste,
To seen this flour, how it wol go to reste,
For fere of nyght, so hateth she derknesse.
Hire chere is pleynly sprad in the brightnesse
Of the sonne, for ther yt wol unclose. 65
Allas, that I ne had Englyssh, ryme or prose,
Suffisant this flour to preyse aryght!
But helpeth, ye that han konnyng and myght,
Ye lovers that kan make of sentement;
In this cas oghte ye be diligent 70
To forthren me somwhat in my labour,
Whethir ye ben with the leef or with the flour.
For wel I wot that ye han her-biforn
Of makyng ropen, and lad awey the corn,
And I come after, glenyng here and there, 75
And am ful glad yf I may fynde an ere
Of any goodly word that ye han left.
And thogh it happen me rehercen eft
That ye han in your fresshe songes sayd,

Forbereth me, and beth nat evele apayd, 80
Syn that ye see I do yt in the honour
Of love, and eke in service of the flour
Whom that I serve as I have wit or myght.
She is the clerenesse and the verray lyght 84
That in this derke world me wynt and ledeth.
The hert in-with my sorwfull brest yow dredeth
And loveth so sore that ye ben verrayly
The maistresse of my wit, and nothing I.
My word, my werk ys knyt so in youre bond
That, as an harpe obeieth to the hond 90
And maketh it soune after his fyngerynge,
Ryght so mowe ye oute of myn herte bringe
Swich vois, ryght as yow lyst, to laughe or
   pleyne.
Be ye my gide and lady sovereyne!
As to myn erthely god to yow I calle, 95
Bothe in this werk and in my sorwes alle.
   But wherfore that I spak, to yive credence
To olde stories and doon hem reverence,
And that men mosten more thyng beleve 99
Then men may seen at eighe, or elles preve,—
That shal I seyn, whanne that I see my tyme;
I may not al attones speke in ryme.
My besy gost, that thursteth alwey newe
To seen this flour so yong, so fressh of hewe,
Constreyned me with so gledy desire 105
That in myn herte I feele yet the fire
That made me to ryse, er yt were day—
And this was now the firste morwe of May—
With dredful hert and glad devocioun,
For to ben at the resureccioun 110
Of this flour, whan that yt shulde unclose

51-2. have presence Of it, have its presence. The constr. is unusual, although Chaucer uses it again in the legend of Ariadne: "and for to han presence Of yow" (l. 2048). **53. she.** The pronoun is here feminine because the flower symbolizes Alceste. **55. ilyke,** equally. **60. blyve,** quickly. **61. weste,** travel toward the west. **69. make,** write poetry. **72. with the leef or with the flour.** In France and perhaps in England a courtly rivalry existed between those who professed to favor the flower and those who maintained the superiority of the leaf, not always consistently. Deschamps composed two ballades in support of the flower and one praising the leaf. Chaucer asserts his neutrality. The fullest discussion of the poetic references is G. L. Marsh, "The Flower and the Leaf," *MP*, iv. 121–67, 281–327, primarily concerned with a fifteenth-century English poem bearing the same title and formerly attributed to Chaucer. **73. For wel I wot . . .** Chaucer here acknowledges in a delicate compliment his indebtedness to the French courtly poets from whom he borrowed. **74. makyng,** the composing of poetry. **ropen,** reaped. **80. Forbereth me,** bear with me. **evele apayd,** displeased. **84. She is the clerenesse . . .** Chaucer now addresses himself to the lady symbolized by the daisy, Alceste. **85. wynt,** directs (*lit.* turns). **89. knyt so in youre bond,** bound so in your fetters. **91. And maketh it soune,** and (the hand) makes it sound. **100. at eighe,** before one's eye, hence plainly. **103. besy gost,** eager spirit. **newe,** anew. **105. Constreyned,** compelled. **gledy,** glowing, burning. **109. dredful,** fearful, timorous. **110. For to ben.** The infin. depends upon *constreyned me.*

Agayn the sonne, that roos as red as rose,
That in the brest was of the beste that day
That Agenores doghtre ladde away.
And doun on knes anoon-ryght I me sette, 115
And, as I koude, this fresshe flour I grette,
Knelyng alwey, til it unclosed was,
Upon the smale, softe, swote gras,
That was with floures swote enbrouded al,
Of swich swetnesse and swich odour overal, 120
That, for to speke of gomme, or herbe, or tree,
Comparisoun may noon ymaked bee;
For yt surmounteth pleynly alle odoures,
And of riche beaute alle floures.
Forgeten had the erthe his pore estat 125
Of wynter, that hym naked made and mat,
And with his swerd of cold so sore greved;
Now hath th'atempre sonne all that releved,
That naked was, and clad him new agayn.
The smale foules, of the sesoun fayn, 130
That from the panter and the net ben scaped,
Upon the foweler, that hem made awhaped
In wynter, and distroyed hadde hire brood,
In his dispit hem thoghte yt did hem good
To synge of hym, and in hir song despise 135
The foule cherl that for his coveytise
Had hem betrayed with his sophistrye.
This was hire song, "The foweler we deffye,
And al his craft." And somme songen clere
Layes of love, that joye it was to here, 140
In worshipynge and preysinge of hir make;
And for the newe blisful somers sake,
Upon the braunches ful of blosmes softe,
In hire delyt they turned hem ful ofte,
And songen, "Blessed be Seynt Valentyne, 145

For on his day I chees yow to be myne,
Withouten repentyng, myn herte swete!"
And therwithalle hire bekes gonnen meete,
Yeldyng honour and humble obeysaunces
To love, and diden hire other observaunces 150
That longeth onto love and to nature;
Construeth that as yow lyst, I do no cure.
And thoo that hadde doon unkyndenesse—
As dooth the tydif, for newfangelnesse—
Besoghte mercy of hir trespassynge, 155
And humblely songen hire repentynge,
And sworen on the blosmes to be trewe,
So that hire makes wolde upon hem rewe,
And at the laste maden hire acord.
Al founde they Daunger for a tyme a lord, 160
Yet Pitee, thurgh his stronge gentil myght,
Forgaf, and made Mercy passen Ryght,
Thurgh innocence and ruled curtesye.
But I ne clepe nat innocence folye,
Ne fals pitee, for vertu is the mene, 165
As Etik seith; in swich maner I mene.
And thus thise foweles, voide of al malice,
Acordeden to love, and laften vice
Of hate, and songen alle of oon acord,
"Welcome, somer, oure governour and lord!"
    And Zepherus and Flora gentilly 171
Yaf to the floures, softe and tenderly,
Hire swoote breth, and made hem for to sprede,
As god and goddesse of the floury mede;
In which me thoghte I myghte, day by day,
Dwellen alwey, the joly month of May, 176
Withouten slep, withouten mete or drynke.
Adoun ful softely I gan to synke,
And lenynge on myn elbowe and my syde,

112. **Agayn,** towards. 113. **the beste.** Jupiter in the form of a bull carried Europa (*Agenores doghtre*) away on his back. Chaucer is saying that on that day the sun was in the part of the sign Taurus corresponding to the breast of the bull. 116. **grette,** greeted. 120. **overal,** everywhere. The attribution of fragrance to the daisy is a poetic fiction taken over from French marguerite poems. 126. **mat,** vanquished. 131. **panter,** snare, net. 132. **Upon,** with respect to. **awhaped,** frightened, bewildered. 137. **sophistrye,** cunning, trickery. 146. **chees,** chose. For St. Valentine's day as the day on which birds were said to choose their mates see note to *PF* 309. 151. **longeth onto,** pertain to. 152. **I do no cure,** I do not care. 153. **thoo,** those. 154. **tydif.** It is not certain what bird is meant. In the *SqT* (F 648) Chaucer mentions it among other "false fowles,"—"tercelettes, owles." **newfangelnesse,** love of novelty. 158. **So that,** provided. 160. **Al,** although. **Daunger,** Haughtiness, or the quality of being difficult to approach. 162. **Ryght,** righteousness. 163. **ruled,** marked by self-control. 164. **But I ne clepe nat . . .** I do not call folly or false pity innocence. 165. **mene.** We would say the "golden mean." 166. **Etik.** Probably a reference at second-hand to the *Nicomachean Ethics* of Aristotle. There were at least four translations, in whole or in part, of the *Ethics* by Chaucer's time, but the idea had become a commonplace in the Middle Ages. 168. **laften,** left. 171. **Zepherus and Flora.** See note to *BD* 402.

The longe day I shoop me for t'abide   180
For nothing elles, and I shal nat lye,
But for to loke upon the dayesie,
That wel by reson men it calle may
The "dayesye," or elles the "ye of day,"
The emperice and flour of floures alle.   185
I pray to God that faire mote she falle,
And alle that loven floures, for hire sake!
But natheles, ne wene nat that I make
In preysing of the flour agayn the leef,
No more than of the corn agayn the sheef;   190
For, as to me, nys lever noon ne lother.
I nam withholden yit with never nother;
Ne I not who serveth leef, ne who the flour.
Wel browken they her service or labour;
For this thing is al of another tonne,   195
Of olde storye, er swich stryf was begonne.
    Whan that the sonne out of the south gan
      weste,
And that this flour gan close and goon to reste
For derknesse of the nyght, the which she
      dredde,
Hom to myn hous ful swiftly I me spedde   200
To goon to reste, and erly for to ryse,
To seen this flour to sprede, as I devyse.
And in a litel herber that I have,
That benched was, on turves fressh ygrave,
I bad men sholde me my couche make;   205
For deyntee of the newe someres sake,
I bad hem strawen floures on my bed.

Whan I was leyd, and had myn eyen hed,
I fel on slepe in-with an houre or twoo.
Me mette how I lay in the medewe thoo,   210
To seen this flour that I so love and drede;
And from afer com walkyng in the mede
The god of Love, and in his hand a quene,
And she was clad in real habit grene.
A fret of gold she hadde next her heer,   215
And upon that a whit corowne she beer
With flourouns smale, and I shal nat lye;
For al the world, ryght as a dayesye
Ycorouned ys with white leves lyte,
So were the flowrouns of hire coroune white.
For of o perle fyne, oriental,   221
Hire white coroune was ymaked al;
For which the white coroune above the grene
Made hire lyke a daysie for to sene,
Considered eke hir fret of gold above.   225
    Yclothed was this myghty god of Love
In silk, enbrouded ful of grene greves,
In-with a fret of rede rose-leves,
The fresshest syn the world was first bygonne.
His gilte heer was corowned with a sonne,   230
Instede of gold, for hevynesse and wyghte.
Therwith me thoghte his face shoon so bryghte
That wel unnethes myghte I him beholde;
And in his hand me thoghte I saugh him holde
Twoo firy dartes, as the gledes rede,   235
And aungelyke hys wynges saugh I sprede.
And al be that men seyn that blynd ys he,

---

180. shoop me, prepared myself. **184. ye of day.** This is the correct meaning of the word (OE. *dæges-eage*). **186. faire mote she falle,** good fortune befall her. **188. ne wene nat . . .** See note to l. 72. **make,** compose (my poem). **191. lother,** more displeasing. **192. witholden . . . with,** committed to the service of. **never nother,** neither one nor the other. **193. not,** do not know (*ne wot*). **194. browken they,** may they enjoy. **195. of another tonne,** *lit.* out of another cask; *i.e.* about a different matter. **197. weste,** travel westward. **199. dredde,** dreaded. **203. herber,** arbor. For the bearing of the word on the date of the poem see the introduction. It should be noted that Chaucer's description, confirmed by other evidence, indicates that the word meant in Chaucer's day a grass yard with benches sometimes made of turf. There is a somewhat fuller description of such an *herber* in *The Flower and the Leaf*, ll. 49 ff. **204. benched,** provided with benches. **206. deyntee,** pleasure. If *sake* is not to be considered tautological, *deyntee of the newe someres* must be construed as a group genitive. **208. hed,** hidden. **212. com,** came. **214. real,** royal. **215. fret,** a cap-like net for the head, a caul. **217. flourouns,** properly, little flowers, but the word is found in ME. only in Chaucer (here and at ll. 220 and 529). However, Froissart uses it twice in the *Dittié de la Flour de la Margherite* (166, 187) in the sense of petals, and since this is where Chaucer probably found the word, he may be using it in the same sense. **221. o perle,** a single pearl. **oriental,** eastern, but implying superior quality. **224. sene,** appear. **227. enbrouded,** embroidered, the only form of the word found in Chaucer. **greves,** sprigs, branches. **228. fret.** The exact meaning here is uncertain. It may mean network, but the later version substitutes "A garlond on his hed of rose-leves, Sticked al with lylye flowres newe," so that the present passage may mean that the green sprigs were surrounded by a garland of rose-leaves. If the description has heraldic significance, the fret would consist of interlaced bands, but the word is not recorded so early in this sense. **rose-leves,** rose petals. **230. corowned with a sonne.** The halo is important to Miss Galway's theory that the god of Love represents Edward the Black Prince, who had died about ten years before (1376). See Introduction. **231. for,** on account of. **wyghte,** weight.

Algate me thoghte that he myghte se;
For sternely on me he gan byholde,
So that his loking dooth myn herte colde.   240
And by the hand he held this noble quene,
Corowned with white, and clothed al in grene,
So womanly, so benigne, and so meke,
That in this world, thogh that men wolde seke,
Half hire beaute shulde men nat fynde   245
In creature that formed ys by kynde.
And therfore may I seyn, as thynketh me,
This song in preysyng of this lady fre.

Balade

Hyd, Absolon, thy gilte tresses clere;
Ester, ley thou thy mekenesse al adown;   250
Hyd, Jonathas, al thy frendly manere;
Penalopee and Marcia Catoun,
Make of youre wifhod no comparysoun;
Hyde ye youre beautes, Ysoude and Eleyne:
My lady cometh, that al this may disteyne.   255

Thy faire body, lat yt nat appere,
Lavyne; and thou, Lucresse of Rome toun,
And Polixene, that boghten love so dere,

And Cleopatre, with al thy passyoun,
Hyde ye your trouthe of love and your re-
noun;   260
And thou, Tisbe, that hast for love swich peyne:
My lady cometh, that al this may disteyne.

Herro, Dido, Laudomia, alle yfere,
And Phillis, hangyng for thy Demophoun,
And Canace, espied by thy chere,   265
Ysiphile, betrayed with Jasoun,
Maketh of your trouthe neythir boost ne soun;
Nor Ypermystre or Adriane, ye tweyne:
My lady cometh, that al this may dysteyne.

This balade may ful wel ysongen be,   270
As I have seyd erst, by my lady free;
For certeynly al thise mowe nat suffise
To apperen wyth my lady in no wyse.
For as the sonne wole the fyr disteyne,
So passeth al my lady sovereyne,   275
That ys so good, so faire, so debonayre,
I prey to God that ever falle hire faire!
For, nadde comfort ben of hire presence,
I hadde ben ded, withouten any defence,

---

240. dooth. We should expect the past tense. **249. Absolon,** Absalom, son of David, famous for his beauty and especially the luxuriance of his hair; cf. *2 Sam.*, 14–15. That his hair was blond or golden Chaucer probably learned from *RR*, 13870, though it seems to have been a medieval commonplace. **250. Ester,** Esther, chosen queen by king Ahasuerus; see note to *BD* 986. **251. Jonathas,** Jonathan, whose friendship for David saved the latter's life; see *1 Samuel*. 19: 1–7. **252. Penalopee,** wife of Ulysses; see note to *BD* 1081. **Marcia Catoun.** Opinion has fluctuated between Marcia, the wife of Cato of Utica, and Marcia, the daughter of Cato, as the person referred to. Since no likely source has been suggested in which Chaucer might have found the story of Cato's wife, whereas the refusal of Cato's daughter to marry again is mentioned by St. Jerome *Against Jovinian* (referred to in the later version of the Prologue, l. 281) and is told at length by Deschamps in the *Miroir de Mariage* (ll. 5435–5527), it seems that the balance of probability lies with the latter. **254. Ysoude and Eleyne,** Iseult and Helen. **255. disteyne,** outshine, make pale. **257. Lavyne,** Lavinia, wife of Aeneas. **Lucresse,** Lucretia, having been violated by Sextus Tarquinius, slew herself. The story is told by Chaucer in the fifth of the legends. **258. Polixene,** Polyxena, daughter of King Priam, beloved by Achilles and sacrificed at the bidding of Achilles' ghost. **259. Cleopatre.** See the legend of Cleopatra below. **261. Tisbe,** Thisbe, whose story is told in the second of the legends. **263. Herro,** Hero, beloved by Leander. When he was drowned she threw herself into the sea. **Dido.** Chaucer had told her story in *HF* (*q.v.*) but told it again in the third legend. **Laudomia,** Laodamia, wife of Protesilaus. After his death he was brought back to earth in order that his wife might talk to him, and when he died a second time she also died. **264. Phillis,** Phyllis, whose story forms the eighth legend. The daughter of a Thracian king, she killed herself when Demophoon did not return at the appointed time to marry her. **265. Canace.** The story of the unnatural love of brother and sister is told by Ovid in the *Heroides*, XI. Although Chaucer mentions Canace here among women surpassed by the god of Love's queen, he could hardly have intended to tell a story of which he expresses strong disapproval in the introduction to *The Man of Law's Tale* (B 78 ff.). **espied by thy chere.** Canace's condition was first discovered by her nurse from her countenance. **266. Ysiphile,** Hypsipyle, queen of the island of Lemnos. Deserted by Jason after she had borne him two children, she remained faithful to him and died of grief. Her story is told in the fourth legend. **268. Ypermystre,** Hypermnestra, who spared her husband's life though sworn to kill him. The story is begun in the ninth legend but is unfinished. **Adriane,** Ariadne, whose legend is the sixth of those that Chaucer wrote. She fell in love with Theseus, and gave him the sword with which he slew the Minotaur and the thread by which he found his way out of the labyrinth. Promising to marry her, he deserted her on the way home. **271. by,** concerning. **273. apperen,** be the peer of. **277. falle hire faire,** good fortune befall her. **278. nadde,** *ne hadde,* had not. **279. withouten any defence,** inevitably.

For drede of Loves wordes and his chere, 280
As, when tyme ys, herafter ye shal here.
    Behynde this god of Love, upon the grene,
I saugh comyng of ladyes nyntene,
In real habit, a ful esy paas, 284
And after hem coome of wymen swich a traas
That, syn that God Adam hadde mad of erthe,
The thridde part of mankynde, or the ferthe,
Ne wende I not by possibilitee
Had ever in this wide world ybee; 289
And trewe of love thise women were echon.
    Now wheither was that a wonder thing or
    non,
That ryght anoon as that they gonne espye
Thys flour, which that I clepe the dayesie,
Ful sodeynly they stynten al attones,
And kneled doun, as it were for the nones, 295
And songen with o vois, "Heel and honour
To trouthe of womanhede, and to this flour
That bereth our alder pris in figurynge!
Hire white corowne bereth the witnessynge."
And with that word, a-compas enviroun, 300
They setten hem ful softely adoun.
First sat the god of Love, and syth his quene
With the white corowne, clad in grene,
And sithen al the remenaunt by and by,
As they were of estaat, ful curteysly; 305
Ne nat a word was spoken in the place
The mountaunce of a furlong wey of space.
    I, knelyng by this flour, in good entente,
Abood to knowen what this peple mente,
As stille as any ston; til at the laste 310
This god of Love on me hys eyen caste,

And seyde, "Who kneleth there?" and I an-
    swerde
Unto his askynge, whan that I it herde,
And seyde, "Sir, it am I," and com him nere,
And salwed him. Quod he, "What dostow here
So nygh myn oune floure, so boldely? 316
Yt were better worthy, trewely,
A worm to neghen ner my flour than thow."
"And why, sire," quod I, "and yt lyke yow?"
"For thow," quod he, "art therto nothing able.
Yt is my relyke, digne and delytable, 321
And thow my foo, and al my folk werreyest,
And of myn olde servauntes thow mysseyest,
And hynderest hem with thy translacioun,
And lettest folk from hire devocioun 325
To serve me, and holdest it folye
To serve Love. Thou maist yt nat denye,
For in pleyn text, withouten nede of glose,
Thou hast translated the Romaunce of the
    Rose,
That is an heresye ayeins my lawe, 330
And makest wise folk fro me withdrawe;
And of Creseyde thou hast seyd as the lyste,
That maketh men to wommen lasse triste,
That ben as trewe as ever was any steel.
Of thyn answere avise the ryght weel; 335
For thogh thou reneyed hast my lay,
As other wrecches han doon many a day,
By Seynt Venus, that my moder ys,
If that thou lyve, thou shalt repenten this
So cruelly that it shal wel be sene!" 340
Thoo spak this lady, clothed al in grene,
And seyde, "God, ryght of youre curtesye,

---

281. when tyme ys, when there is time. **285. traas,** train (of persons). **287. The thridde part . . .** The phrase *of mankynde* causes trouble, but the meaning seems to be "I did not think a third or a quarter as many people had been in the world since the time of Adam." **290. echon,** each one. **292. That.** The conjunction is redundant. **298. our alder pris in figurynge,** the prize of us all symbolically. **300. a-compas enviroun,** in a circle round about. **304. by and by,** one after the other. **307. mountaunce of a furlong wey,** the amount of time required to walk a furlong. Skeat estimates 2½ minutes. **314. it am I,** (the normal ME. idiom) it is I. **com,** came. **nere,** nearer. **315. salwed,** saluted. **dostow,** dost thou. **317. better worthy,** more fitting. **318. neghen,** approach. **319. and yt lyke yow,** if it may please you. **320. able,** fit. **321. relyke,** treasure. Miss Galway, who interprets Alceste as Joan of Kent, widow of Edward the Black Prince (the god of Love according to her theory), would see in the words *my relyke* an "allegorical equivalent of 'my relict'." *Relicte,* widow, was in use in French at this time, but *relict* is not recorded in English until the sixteenth century. **322. werreyest,** makest war upon. **323. servauntes,** *i.e.* lovers. **325. lettest,** hinderest. **328. glose,** explanation. **329. Romaunce of the Rose.** Of the ME. translation of the *Roman de la Rose* which has come down to us (representing about a fourth of the original) only the first 1705 lines are believed to be by Chaucer. The part of the poem that is cynical about love is not in the ME. version so far as we have it. **333. lasse triste,** trust less. **336. reneyed,** renounced. **lay,** law.

Ye moten herken yf he can replye
Agayns al this that ye have to him meved.
A god ne sholde nat be thus agreved, 345
But of hys deitee he shal be stable,
And therto gracious and merciable.
And yf ye nere a god, that knowen al,
Thanne myght yt be as I yow tellen shal:
This man to yow may falsly ben accused, 350
That as by right him oughte ben excused.
For in youre court ys many a losengeour,
And many a queynte totelere accusour,
That tabouren in youre eres many a soun,
Ryght after hire ymagynacioun, 355
To have youre daliance, and for envie.
Thise ben the causes, and I shal not lye.
Envie ys lavendere of the court alway,
For she ne parteth, neither nyght ne day,
Out of the hous of Cesar; thus seith Dante; 360
Whoso that gooth, algate she wol nat wante.
And eke, peraunter, for this man ys nyce,
He myghte doon yt, gessyng no malice,
But for he useth thynges for to make;
Hym rekketh noght of what matere he take.
Or him was boden maken thilke tweye 366
Of som persone, and durste yt nat withseye;
Or him repenteth outrely of this.
He ne hath nat doon so grevously amys,
To translaten that olde clerkes writen, 370
As thogh that he of malice wolde enditen
Despite of love, and had himself yt wroght.

This shoolde a ryghtwis lord have in his thoght,
And nat be lyk tirauntez of Lumbardye,
That han no reward but at tyrannye, 375
For he that kynge or lord ys naturel,
Hym oghte nat be tiraunt ne crewel,
As is a fermour, to doon the harm he kan.
He moste thinke yt is his lige man,
And is his tresour, and his gold in cofre. 380
This is the sentence of the philosophre:
A kyng to kepe his liges in justice;
Withouten doute, that is his office.
Al wol he kepe his lordes hire degree,
As it ys ryght and skilful that they bee 385
Enhaunced and honoured, and most dere—
For they ben half-goddes in this world here—
Yit mot he doon bothe ryght, to poore and
ryche,
Al be that hire estaat be nat yliche,
And han of poore folk compassyoun. 390
For loo, the gentil kynde of the lyoun!
For whan a flye offendeth him or biteth,
He with his tayle awey the flye smyteth
Al esely; for, of hys genterye,
Hym deyneth not to wreke hym on a flye, 395
As dooth a curre, or elles another best.
In noble corage oughte ben arest,
And weyen every thing by equytee,
And ever have reward to his degree.
For, syr, yt is no maistrye for a lord 400
To dampne a man without answere of word,

343. moten, must. 344. meved, moved, urged. 348. nere, were not. that knowen al, that knows everything. 352. losengeour, deceiver. 353. queynte, cunning. totelere, tattling (though the word is properly a noun). accusour, one who blames or accuses. 354. tabouren, beat, drum. 356. To have youre daliance, to enjoy your conversation or company. 358. lavendere, washerwoman. 359. parteth, departs. 360. the hous of Cesar, a symbol of high places. thus seith Dante. The passage is in the *Inferno* (XIII. 64–67), where Envy is called a harlot (*meretrice*). Chaucer's suggestion of one who washes dirty linen is a nicer touch. 361. Whoso . . . wante, no matter who goes away, she (Envy) will never be wanting. 362. for, because. nyce, foolish. 363. gessyng, supposing, intending. 364. useth thynges for to make, is accustomed to compose things (poetry). 365. Hym rekketh noght, he does not care. 366. boden, commanded. 367. Of, by. withseye, refuse (*lit.* contradict). 370. that, what. clerkes, writers. 371. As thogh that, as if. 372. Despite, disdain. 375. reward, regard. 376. lord . . . naturel, a lord by right of his rank or position as contrasted with one who purchases his office (*fermour*), and might at times abuse his privilege (*to doon the harm he kan*). 379. yt, *i.e.* that he. 381. the philosophre, probably Aristotle. Skeat notes that Chaucer's friend Gower reports at length Aristotle's advice to Alexander on the policy of kings in the *Confessio Amantis*, Book VII. The discussion of justice begins at l. 2695. Gower refers to Aristotle both by name and as "the Philosophre." 388. to poore and ryche. Gower makes the same point ("to the povere and to the riche," l. 2743), follows his discussion of justice with a treatment of pity as an attribute of kings ("It sit a king to be pitious," l. 3125) and describes the nobility of the lion (ll. 3387–3416) though not with respect to a fly. 394. genterye, nobility. 395. wreke, avenge. 397. corage, heart. arest, restraint. 398. weyen. The infinitive depends upon *oughte*, so that *arest* must be taken as the subject. 399. reward, regard 400. yt is no maistrye, it is no great achievement. 401. dampne, condemn.

And, for a lord, that is ful foul to use.
And if so be he may hym nat excuse,
But asketh mercy with a sorweful herte,
And profereth him, ryght in his bare sherte,
To ben ryght at your owen jugement,   406
Than oght a god, by short avysement,
Consydre his owne honour and hys trespas.
For, syth no cause of deth lyeth in this caas,
Yow oghte to ben the lyghter merciable;   410
Leteth youre ire, and beth sumwhat tretable.
The man hath served yow of his kunnyng,
And furthred wel youre lawe in his makyng.
Al be hit that he kan nat wel endite,
Yet hath he maked lewed folk delyte   415
To serve yow, in preysing of your name.
He made the book that hight the Hous of Fame,
And eke the Deeth of Blaunche the Duchesse,
And the Parlement of Foules, as I gesse,
And al the love of Palamon and Arcite   420
Of Thebes, thogh the storye ys knowen lyte;
And many an ympne for your halydayes,
That highten balades, roundels, virelayes;
And, for to speke of other holynesse,
He hath in prose translated Boece,   425
And maad the lyf also of Seynt Cecile.
He made also, goon ys a gret while,
Origenes upon the Maudeleyne.
Hym oughte now to have the lesse peyne;
He hath maad many a lay and many a thing.

Now as ye be a god, and eke a kyng,   431
I, your Alceste, whilom quene of Trace,
Y aske yow this man, ryght of your grace,
That ye him never hurte in al his lyve;
And he shal swere to yow, and that as blyve,   435
He shal no more agilten in this wyse,
But he shal maken, as ye wol devyse,
Of wommen trewe in lovyng al hire lyf,
Wher so ye wol, of mayden or of wyf,
And forthren yow, as muche as he mysseyde   440
Or in the Rose or elles in Creseyde."
    The god of Love answerde hire thus anoon:
"Madame," quod he, "it is so long agoon
That I yow knew so charitable and trewe,
That never yit, syn that the world was newe,   445
To me ne found y better noon than yee.
If that I wol save my degree,
I may, ne wol, nat werne your requeste.
Al lyeth in yow; dooth wyth hym what yow
    leste.
I al foryeve, withouten lenger space;   450
For whoso yeveth a yift, or dooth a grace,
Do it bytyme, his thank ys wel the more.
And demeth ye what he shal doo therfore.
Goo thanke now my lady here," quod he.
    I roos, and doun I sette me on my knee,   455
And seyde thus, "Madame, the God above
Foryelde yow, that ye the god of Love
Han maked me his wrathe to foryive,

408. his . . . hys, *i.e.* the Lord's . . . the subject's. **411. Leteth,** give up. **tretable,** open to appeal. **412. of his kun-nyng,** according to his ability. **417. He made the book . . .** Chaucer uses a similar device for listing his works in the introduction to the *MLT.* **420. Palamon and Arcite,** later incorporated into *The Canterbury Tales* as the *KnT,* pro-bably because it had not been widely circulated. **422. ympne . . . halydayes.** The words *hymn* and *holy days* carry out the image of the god of Love. **423. balades, roundels, virelayes,** Fixed French forms of which only a few by Chaucer have survived. The balade consists in Chaucer of three stanzas (and sometimes an *envoy*), each ending in an identical line. An example will be found in ll. 249–269 above, and in several of the Shorter Poems. **425. Boece.** Chaucer's translation of the *Consolation of Philosophy* by Boethius is not included in the present volume. **426. the lyf . . . of Seynt Cecile.** This poem is now *The Second Nun's Tale.* **428. Origenes upon the Maudeleyne,** now lost but presumed to be a translation of a sermon formerly attributed to Origen (*c.* 185–*c.* 253). **429. Hym oughte . . . to have.** The construction is not incorrect, though a little forced. The dative *hym* with the impersonal verb *oughte* is made to serve as the subject of the infinitive. **430. lay,** a difficult word to define since it was used for both lyric and narrative poems. **432. quene of Trace.** Professor Magoun points out (*Medieval Stud,* xv. 132) that Chaucer has substituted Thrace for Thessaly. **433. this man,** points forward to *him* as the object of *hurte.* **435. as blyve,** immediately. **436. agilten,** sin, offend. **441. Or . . . or,** either . . . or. **443. it is so long agoon.** The theory that the god of Love, who is represented as both a king and a god (l. 431, etc.), stands for the Black Prince, sees a special fitness in this statement, since Edward, crowned during his father's lifetime, died ten years before the poem is believed to have been written. The statement may, however, mean no more than that the god of Love has known his queen to be true for so long a time that he has never known of anyone better since the world began. **447. If . . . degree,** if I wish to preserve my standing as a king. **448. werne,** refuse. **452. bytyme,** early, promptly. **453. demeth,** judge, decide. **457. Foryelde,** requite. **458. me his wrathe to foryive,** to give up his wrath toward me.

And yeve me grace so long for to lyve,
That I may knowe soothly what ye bee, 460
That han me holpe and put in this degree.
But trewely I wende, as in this cas,
Naught have agilt, ne doon to love trespas.
For-why a trewe man, withouten drede,
Hath nat to parten with a theves dede; 465
Ne a trewe lover oght me not to blame,
Thogh that I speke a fals lovere som shame.
They oghte rather with me for to holde,
For that I of Creseyde wroot or tolde,
Or of the Rose; what so myn auctour mente,
Algate, God woot, yt was myn entente 471
To forthren trouthe in love and yt cheryce,
And to ben war fro falsnesse and fro vice
By swich ensample; this was my menynge."
And she answerde, "Lat be thyn arguynge, 475
For Love ne wol nat countrepleted be
In ryght ne wrong; and lerne that of me!
Thow hast thy grace, and hold the ryght therto.
Now wol I seyn what penance thou shalt do
For thy trespas, and understonde yt here: 480
Thow shalt, while that thou lyvest, yer by yere,
The moste partye of thy tyme spende
In makyng of a glorious legende
Of goode wymmen, maydenes and wyves,
That weren trewe in lovyng al hire lyves; 485
And telle of false men that hem bytraien,
That al hir lyf ne do nat but assayen
How many women they may doon a shame;
For in youre world that is now holde a game.
And thogh the lyke nat a lovere bee, 490
Speke wel of love; this penance yive I thee.

And to the god of Love I shal so preye
That he shal charge his servantz, by any weye,
To forthren thee, and wel thy labour quyte.
Goo now thy wey, this penaunce ys but
lyte. 495
And whan this book ys maad, yive it the quene,
On my byhalf, at Eltham or at Sheene."
The god of Love gan smyle, and than he
sayde:
"Wostow," quod he, "wher this be wyf or
mayde,
Or queene, or countesse, or of what degre, 500
That hath so lytel penance yiven thee,
That hast deserved sorer for to smerte?
But pite renneth soone in gentil herte;
That maistow seen, she kytheth what she ys."
And I answered, "Nay, sire, so have I blys, 505
No moore but that I see wel she is good."
"That is a trewe tale, by myn hood!"
Quod Love, "and that thou knowest wel, par-
dee,
If yt be so that thou avise the.
Hastow nat in a book, lyth in thy cheste, 510
The grete goodnesse of the quene Alceste,
That turned was into a dayesye;
She that for hire housbonde chees to dye,
And eke to goon to helle, rather than he,
And Ercules rescowed hire, parde, 515
And broght hir out of helle agayn to blys?"
And I answerd ageyn, and sayde, "Yis,
Now knowe I hire. And is this good Alceste,
The dayesie, and myn owene hertes reste?
Now fele I weel the goodnesse of this wyf, 520

---

460. Here and at l. 499 Chaucer seems to forget that Alceste has mentioned her name at l. 432. **461. holpe,** helped. **degree,** condition. **462. wende,** thought, supposed. **464. trewe,** honest. **465. parten with,** participate in, *i.e.* share the consequences of. **467. speke . . . shame,** reproach. **473. to ben war,** *i.e.* to warn others. **476. countrepleted,** argued against. **478. hold the ryght therto,** preserve the right to it. **483. legende,** collection of saints' lives. **489. holde,** held. **490. the lyke,** it pleases thee. **496. yive it the quene . . .** Queen Anne. This command makes it impossible to identify Alceste with Queen Anne, as has sometimes been done. **497. Eltham or at Sheene,** the two favorite palaces of Richard and Anne, a few miles up the river from London. **499. Wostow . . .** The god of Love is saying, "Do you have any idea who this is?" According to Miss Galway's identification of Alceste with the widow of the Black Prince the mention of the title *countesse* has special significance, since Joan in her own right was Countess of Kent. **503. But pite renneth . . .** Chaucer's favorite line. It occurs four times in his poetry. **504. kytheth,** makes known, shows plainly. **510. cheste,** *i.e.* bookcase. Books were commonly kept in chests in the Middle Ages. **511. Alceste.** The story of Alcestis, the wife of Admetus, king of Pherae in Thessaly, was well known and was told by Gower, *Conf. Aman.*, VII. 1917–49. When her husband lay ill and was believed beyond recovery, Alcestis prayed Minerva. Minerva promised to restore him to health if Alcestis would die instead. She did so and Admetus recovered. Later she was brought back to the earth by Hercules. In none of the versions of the story now known is Alcestis turned into a daisy.

That both aftir hir deth and in hir lyf
Hir grete bounte doubleth hire renoun.
Wel hath she quyt me myn affeccioun,
That I have to hire flour, the dayesye.
No wonder ys thogh Jove hire stellyfye,   525
As telleth Agaton, for hire goodnesse!
Hire white corowne berith of hyt witnesse;
For also many vertues hadde shee
As smale florouns in hire corowne bee.
In remembraunce of hire and in honour   530
Cibella maade the daysye and the flour
Ycrowned al with white, as men may see;
And Mars yaf to hire corowne reed, pardee,
In stede of rubyes, sette among the white."
    Therwith this queene wex reed for shame a
      lyte,   535
Whan she was preysed so in hire presence.
Thanne seyde Love, "A ful gret necligence
Was yt to the, that ylke tyme thou made
'Hyd, Absolon, thy tresses,' in balade,
That thou forgate hire in thi song to sette,   540
Syn that thou art so gretly in hire dette,
And wost so wel that kalender ys shee
To any woman that wol lover bee.
For she taught al the craft of fyn lovynge,
And namely of wyfhod the lyvynge,   545
And al the boundes that she oghte kepe.
Thy litel wit was thilke tyme aslepe.
But now I charge the, upon thy lyf,
That in thy legende thou make of thys wyf,

Whan thou hast other smale ymaad before;   550
And fare now wel, I charge the namore.
But er I goo, thus muche I wol the telle:
Ne shal no trewe lover come in helle.
Thise other ladies sittynge here a–rowe
Ben in thy balade, yf thou kanst hem knowe,   555
And in thy bookes alle thou shalt hem fynde.
Have hem now in thy legende al in mynde;
I mene of hem that ben in thy knowynge.
For here ben twenty thousand moo sittynge
Than thou knowest, goode wommen alle,   560
And trewe of love, for oght that may byfalle.
Make the metres of hem as the leste—
I mot goon hom (the sonne draweth weste)
To paradys, with al this companye—
And serve alwey the fresshe dayesye.   565
At Cleopatre I wol that thou begynne,
And so forth, and my love so shalt thou wynne.
For lat see now what man that lover be,
Wol doon so strong a peyne for love as she.
I wot wel that thou maist nat al yt ryme,   570
That swiche lovers diden in hire tyme;
It were to long to reden and to here.
Suffiseth me thou make in this manere,
That thou reherce of al hir lyf the grete,
After thise olde auctours lysten to trete.   575
For whoso shal so many a storye telle,
Sey shortly, or he shal to longe dwelle."
And with that word my bokes gan I take,
And ryght thus on my Legende gan I make.

Explicit prohemium.

---

522. bounte, goodness. **525. stellyfye,** should make into a star. **526. Agaton.** Agathon was a Greek tragic poet, a friend of Euripides. In Plato's *Symposium* the banquet which furnishes the occasion for the discussion was given at Agathon's house, but the work Chaucer cites is unknown. **529. florouns.** See note to l. 217. **531. Cibella,** Cybele, goddess of fertility, and therefore said to have made the daisy. **533. reed.** See note to l. 42. **535. shame,** modesty. **539. Hyd, Absolon.** See ll. 249–269. **542. kalender,** guide. The proper meaning is "almanac." **545. namely,** especially. **550. other smale,** other less important legends. The implication of the line is that the story of Alceste was to be the final legend of the collection. **562. as the leste,** as it pleases thee. **572. and to here.** Note that Chaucer refers here to a listening audience. **574. grete,** gist, substance.

I

THE LEGEND OF CLEOPATRA

Incipit legenda Cleopatrie, Martiris, Egipti regine.

After the deth of Tholome the kyng, 580
That al Egipt hadde in his governyng,
Regned hys queene Cleopataras;
Til on a tyme befel ther swich a cas,
That out of Rome was sent a senatour,
For to conqueren regnes and honour 585
Unto the toun of Rome, as was usaunce,
To have the world at hir obeysaunce,
And sooth to seye, Antonius was his name.
So fil it, as Fortune hym oughte a shame,
Whan he was fallen in prosperitee, 590
Rebel unto the toun of Rome is hee.
And over al this, the suster of Cesar,
He lafte hir falsly, er that she was war,
And wolde algates han another wyf;
For which he took with Rome and Cesar strif.
Natheles, forsooth, this ilke senatour 596
Was a ful worthy gentil werreyour,
And of his deth it was ful gret damage.
But love had broght this man in swich a rage,
And him so narwe bounden in his laas, 600
Al for the love of Cleopataras,
That al the world he sette at no value.
Him thoghte ther nas nothyng to him so due
As Cleopatras for to love and serve;
Him roghte nat in armes for to sterve 605
In the defence of hir and of hir ryght.

This noble queene ek lovede so this knyght,
Thurgh his desert, and for his chivalrye;
As certeynly, but if that bokes lye,
He was, of persone and of gentillesse, 610
And of discrecioun and hardynesse,
Worthy to any wyght that lyven may;
And she was fair as is the rose in May.
And, for to maken shortly is the beste,
She wax his wif, and hadde him as hir leste.
     The weddyng and the feste to devyse, 616
To me, that have ytake swich empryse
Of so many a story for to make,
It were to longe, lest that I sholde slake
Of thing that bereth more effect and charge;
For men may overlade a ship or barge. 621
And forthy to th'effect thanne wol I skyppe,
And al the remenaunt, I wol lete it slyppe.
     Octovyan, that wood was of this dede,
Shop hym an ost on Antony to lede 625
Al outerly for his destruccioun.
With stoute Romayns, crewel as lyoun,
To ship they wente, and thus I lat hem sayle.
Antonius was war, and wol nat fayle
To meten with thise Romayns, if he may; 630
Took eke his rede and bothe, upon a day,
His wyf and he, and al his ost, forth wente
To shippe anon, no lengere they ne stente;

Incipit legenda, etc. Here begins the legend of Cleopatra the martyr, Queen of Egypt. **580. Tholome,** Ptolemy. Ptolemy was the name of Cleopatra's father, who died 51 B.C., and also the name of his two sons. Cleopatra, then seventeen, was appointed Queen of Egypt, to reign in conjunction with the elder of the brothers. She was driven out by her brother but reinstated by Julius Caesar. In the Alexandrine war which resulted Ptolemy was killed, and since the other child was a mere boy Cleopatra became, at least in fact, sole ruler. The words *hys queene* make it likely that it is the elder brother who is referred to by Chaucer. **583. befel . . . cas,** it happened. **585. regnes,** kingdoms. **589. oughte,** owed, *i.e.* had in store for him. **590. in,** upon. **592. the suster of Cesar,** Octavia, sister of Octavianus (Caesar Augustus). **594. algates,** under any circumstances. **599. rage,** passion. **600. laas,** net, snare. **603. him so due,** so incumbent upon him. **615. as hir leste,** as she pleased. **616. devyse,** describe. **617. empryse,** undertaking. **619. slake (of),** slight. **620. bereth more effect and charge,** carries more weight. **622. effect,** result. **633. stente,** stopped.

And in the see it happed hem to mete.   634
Up goth the trompe, and for to shoute and
     shete,
And peynen hem to sette on with the sonne.
With grisly soun out goth the grete gonne,
And heterly they hurtelen al atones,
And fro the top doun cometh the grete stones.
In goth the grapenel, so ful of crokes;   640
Among the ropes renne the sheryng-hokes.
In with the polax preseth he and he;
Byhynde the mast begyneth he to fle,
And out agayn, and dryveth hym overbord;
He styngeth hym upon hys speres ord;   645
He rent the sayl with hokes lyke a sithe;
He bryngeth the cuppe, and biddeth hem be
     blithe;
He poureth pesen upon the hacches slidre;
With pottes ful of lyme they goon togidre;
And thus the longe day in fight they spende,
Til at the laste, as every thing hath ende,   651
Antony is shent, and put hym to the flyghte,
And al hys folk to-go, that best go myghte.
     Fleeth ek the queen, with al hir purpre sayl,
For strokes, which that wente as thik as hayl; 655
No wonder was she myghte it nat endure.
And whan that Antony saugh that aventure,
"Allas," quod he, "the day that I was born!
My worship in this day thus have I lorn."
And for dispeyr out of his wit he sterte,   660
And rof hymself anon thurghout the herte,
Er that he ferther wente out of the place.
Hys wyf, that koude of Cesar have no grace,
To Egipt is fled for drede and for destresse.

But herkeneth, ye that speken of kyndenesse,
Ye men that falsly sweren many an ooth   666
That ye wol dye, if that youre love be wrooth,
Here may ye seen of women which a trouthe!
This woful Cleopatre hath mad swich routhe
That ther nys tonge noon that may it telle.   670
But on the morwe she wol no lenger dwelle,
But made hir subtil werkmen make a shryne
Of al the rubies and the stones fyne
In al Egipte, that she koude espye,
And putte ful the shryne of spicerye,   675
And let the cors enbaume, and forth she fette
This dede cors, and in the shryne yt shette.
And next the shryne a pit than doth she grave,
And al the serpents that she myghte have,
She putte hem in that grave, and thus she
     sayde: 680
"Now, love, to whom my sorweful hert
     obeyde
So ferforthly that fro that blisful houre
That I yow swor to ben al frely youre—
I mene yow, Antonius, my knyght—
That never wakyng, in the day or nyght,   685
Ye nere out of myn hertes remembraunce,
For wele or wo, for carole or for daunce;
And in myself this covenaunt made I thoo,
That ryght swich as ye felten, wel or woo,
As ferforth as it in my power lay,   690
Unreprovable unto my wifhod ay,
The same wolde I felen, life or deeth,—
And thilke covenant, whil me lasteth breeth,
I wol fulfille; and that shal wel be sene,
Was never unto hir love a trewer quene."   695

---

635. **trompe,** trumpet. 636. **to sette on with the sonne,** to attack with the sun at their backs. 637. **out goth the grete gonne,** the great gun goes off, an anachronism. 638. **heterly,** violently. **hurtelen,** clash. 640. **grapenel,** an instrument with iron claws, hurled by a rope, or chain, to lash ships together. **crokes,** hooks. 641. **renne the sheryng-hokes,** shear-hooks "a sickle-shaped hook intended to destroy the enemy's rigging" (*NED*). 643. **he,** this one. 644. **hym,** that one; and so in the following lines. 645. **styngeth,** pierces. **ord,** point. 646. **rent,** rends. 648. **poureth pesen,** pour peas (to make the enemy slip). The practice is recorded by George Gascoigne in 1572. See W. T. Furniss, *MLN*, LXVIII. 117. **hacches,** movable planks forming a deck. **slidre,** slippery. 649. **lyme,** quicklime, to be thrown into the eyes. The description of the battle follows the practice of Chaucer's day. Many of the details are found in the accounts of naval engagements, *e.g.* in Froissart's description of the battle beside Sluys (*Chron.*, trans. Johnes, I. 72–73). 652. **put hym,** puts himself. 653. **to-go,** dispersed. 657. **aventure,** misfortune. 659. **worship,** honor. 661. **rof,** pierced. 662. **Er that he ferther wente . . .** Actually Anthony stabbed himself a year later at Alexandria. 668. **which a,** what a. 672. **subtil,** skilful. **shryne,** casket. 676. **let,** caused. **fette,** fetched. 677. **shette,** shut, enclosed. 678. **doth she grave,** she causes (them) to dig. 682. **So ferforthly,** to such an extent. 687. **for carole or for daunce,** *i.e.* for anything. 688. **thoo,** then. 691. **Unreprovable,** without reproach. 694. **sene,** evident.

And with that word, naked, with ful good
  herte,
Among the serpents in the pit she sterte,
And ther she chees to have hir buryinge.
Anon the neddres gonne hir for to stynge,
And she hir deeth receyveth with good chere,
For love of Antony that was hir so dere.   701
And this is storial sooth, it is no fable.
Now, er I fynde a man thus trewe and stable,
And wol for love his deeth so frely take,
I prey God let oure hedes nevere ake!   705

Explicit Legenda Cleopatre, martiris.

697. **sterte,** leaped. Where Chaucer got this idea is unknown. 698. **chees,** chose. 699. **neddres,** adders. 702. **storial sooth,** historical truth. **Explicit . . .** Here ends the legend of Cleopatra the martyr.

The Canterbury Tales

The Canterbury Tales is a collection of stories bound together in a framework. We have become accustomed to volumes of stories, sometimes by a single author but just as often not, which we read because each story is interesting in itself. But we also have collections like *The Adventures of Sherlock Holmes* or the various books of *Uncle Remus* stories. Such integrated collections belong to a literary type that has been traced back as far as ancient Egypt (see H. B. Hinckley, "The Framing-Tale," *MLN*, xlviii. 69–80), and was highly developed in India. One of the largest and best-known examples is *The Arabian Nights' Entertainments*, or *A Thousand and One Nights*, but though its beginnings go back as far as the tenth century, it did not assume its present form until after Chaucer's death and was not known to him. Two medieval collections of the twelfth century which Chaucer must have known about were *The Seven Sages* (in French, later turned into English) and the *Disciplina Clericalis* of Petrus Alfonsus (in Latin). In the latter a series of moral apothegms and longer narratives is strung on a slender thread of dialogue. In the former a prince is forbidden to speak for seven days. Each night his hostile stepmother tells a story to persuade the king to order his execution, and each morning one of the prince's masters tells a story urging delay. When the prince is finally able to speak he reveals the stepmother's iniquity and she is put to death.

Two other more nearly contemporary collections of framed tales were in existence before Chaucer began *The Canterbury Tales* and are of much greater interest. *The Decameron* consists of a hundred stories in prose and was written by Giovanni Boccaccio, whose *Teseida*, *Filostrato*, and other works were drawn upon heavily by Chaucer, albeit he never mentions Boccaccio by name. Ten men and women of gentle birth have withdrawn to a suburb of Florence to avoid the plague then raging in the city. To pass the time each tells a story a day, which the others invariably approve. While the stories are of many kinds, some of them are quite indecorous and are inappropriate both to the teller and to the rest of the group. Boccaccio's framework is much less flexible than Chaucer's. *The Decameron* and *The Canterbury Tales* have five stories in common, and it is natural to ask whether Chaucer was indebted to Boccaccio for the idea of his collection and for any of his tales. Early editors took the matter for granted, but later opinion has been divided. It is sufficient to note here that except for *The Clerk's Tale* of patient Griselda, in which Chaucer follows more closely Petrarch's Latin version, the resemblances between tales are limited to the basic plot; the divergences are great, and in some cases closer analogues have been found elsewhere. Apart from the fact that *The Decameron* seems to have had more limited circulation in Italy than Boccaccio's poetry and is not known to have reached England until after Chaucer's death, it is hard to believe that Chaucer would not have made use of such a wealth of stories if he had known the work. The most that can be said is that he might have heard of it on one of his trips to Italy.

The other collection of framed tales alluded to above, the *Novelle* of Giovanni Sercambi, is of special interest because the framework, like Chaucer's, is a pilgrimage. During the outbreak of the plague in Lucca in 1374 a number of men and women of different walks of life and a few members of the clergy decide to leave Lucca and go on a trip to various places in Italy. One of their number suggests that they choose a leader, and he is himself promptly chosen. The pilgrims travel down one coast and up the other, and tales are related on the road and during the stopovers. There are here certain resemblances to Chaucer's plan. There are also certain differences. For example, all the tales are told by the author rather than by the members of the company. The survival of Sercambi's work in a single manuscript suggests that it did not have wide circulation. As in the case of *The Decameron*, there is no evidence that Chaucer derived any of his stories from it, and it remains doubtful whether he knew of its existence. For the present, at least, it would seem that while the literary device of combining stories in some kind of framework was familiar to him— indeed he had already used it in *The Legend of Good Women*—he conceived the idea of a pilgrimage from what was after all a common occurrence.

Route of Canterbury Pilgrims

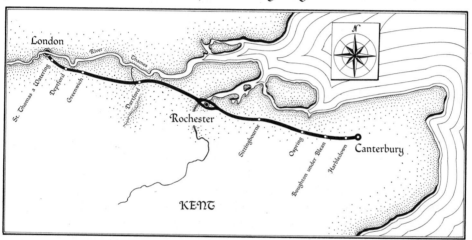

The framework of a pilgrimage had one great advantage. A religious pilgrimage was the one occasion in the Middle Ages when class barriers could to a certain degree be overlooked, and when the association of such diverse classes as a knight, a prioress, a London cook, and a vulgar miller was conceivable. Consequently Chaucer was able to include a wide variety of persons and, unlike Boccaccio, fit many of his stories to them with obvious appropriateness. Moreover, while the seven gentlewomen and three well-born men who tell the stories in *The Decameron* are hardly distinguishable, with the possible exception of the humorous Dioneo, Chaucer could endow most of his pilgrims with vivid personalities, besides making them representative of a class. This he has done partly in the wonderful series of character-sketches which makes up most of the General Prologue but also in the remarks and the behavior of the pilgrims as they react to one another and as they reveal themselves in the preliminaries to their own narratives. Occasionally the pilgrims show such individual characteristics, not at all necessary to the description of a type, as to suggest that some of the portraits may have been drawn from life. Such a procedure would have been entirely natural, and the late Professor Manly (*Some New Light on Chaucer*) called attention to a number of persons in real life who (with proper precautions on Chaucer's part) could have been the originals of some of the pilgrims.

The plan which is set out in the General Prologue calls for four stories from each pilgrim, two on the way to Canterbury and two on the journey back. Since thirty pilgrims (nine and twenty plus himself) are envisaged by Chaucer, the collection of tales would have totaled 120, a "long hundred" and therefore a round number to a medieval mind. Since the poet began work on *The Canterbury Tales* rather late in life, such a program was clearly overambitious, and occasional remarks in the course of the journey (especially I 25 and 47) envision only one story per pilgrim each way, or possibly one story each all-told. Even this limited number seems to have proved beyond the poet's strength, and the poem remains unfinished.

Twenty-four tales (two of them fragmentary) constitute the work as we have it today. They divide rather evenly between serious and humorous. Some of them, such as *The Knight's Tale* and the story of St. Cecilia told by the Second Nun, had been written earlier; others of which this is probably true are mentioned in the introductory notes to the separate tales. Some, it must be admitted, can hardly qualify as entertainment even by medieval standards. Two are excluded from the present volume because they are not in verse. *The Knight's Tale* by reason of its length is hardly suited to the occasion, but we must not inquire too closely into such matters or ask whether any of the stories could have been heard by thirty people on horseback as they rode along a rather bad road. We gladly invoke Coleridge's dictum of "the willing suspension of disbelief."

In addition to reducing the number of tales that would be told along the way, Chaucer seems to have changed his mind about other things as he worked on his project. It is apparent, for example, that the tale which the Man of Law tells does not carry out the promise of his preliminary remarks that he will "speke in prose," and it has been accepted practically without question that originally Chaucer had intended him to tell the *Melibee*. But why did he make the change?

It is reasonable to assume that when Chaucer began *The Canterbury Tales* he had a certain amount of material on hand that could be used in the new project. It would be natural if he fitted this material into his plan early. Such a procedure would give him a good start. If he had other tales in mind but not yet written—also a reasonable assumption—he could make a mental note of how he might use them. As the collection took shape and as he worked on it from week to week and month to month, he must have had second thoughts, as every author has. *The Man of Law's Tale* clearly represents such a second thought. The Custance story was one which a learned man like the Sergeant of the Law might well have read, and so Chaucer gave it to him, confident that he could place the Melibeus elsewhere—if indeed he had not already reached the point where he saw how effectively he could use it to satisfy the Host, who had so bluntly cut short his narrative of *Sir Thopas*.

But a hundred and twenty tales is a large number, and Chaucer must have been constantly on the lookout for stories that would serve his purpose. In so doing he would not reject a possibility merely because the pilgrim for which a newly found story would be most appropriate was already provided for. The story of the knight and the loathly lady is a case in point. It exemplifies perfectly the Wife of Bath's philosophy that a husband should be ruled by his wife in everything. But the Wife of Bath had already been provided with a tale. Only a few students have doubted that *The Shipman's Tale* was written for a woman, and the only woman on the pilgrimage who could have told an immoral story was the Wife of Bath. Chaucer made the substitution and gave the story of the lover's gift returned to the Shipman. Fortunately, at the time, he did not take the trouble to revise the opening lines and remove the tell-tale evidence of his earlier intention. At times, after giving a pilgrim a particular tale, he must have come upon a story that would point up the clash of personalities or contribute effectively to the drama of the journey. It is for some such reason, it seems, that the story told by the Merchant, which I believe was originally intended for the Friar, was taken from the Friar, in order to free him to tell a story that carries out the quarrel between the Friar and the Summoner.

We shall, of course, never know how many changes of this sort Chaucer made without leaving any tell-tale clues to arouse our suspicion. If he had lived to finish his great work, the little contradictions and inconsistencies that we notice would doubtless have been removed. In his eagerness to push on with the writing he did not always stop to make the necessary changes. Details of this sort could be taken care of at leisure, or at such time as the work was nearing completion. This time never came. And so, in a few cases, we can see beyond the existing manuscripts and, as it were, look over the poet's shoulder as he worked.

The unfinished state of *The Canterbury Tales* presents us with another problem, about which a word must be said. To the general reader it might seem that the order of the tales as he reads them in a modern edition was that of the author, such being what he would expect in reading a later poet. But if he were to examine editions of Chaucer from Thynne (1532) down he would find considerable differences in the arrangement. And the same thing would be true if he consulted the many manuscripts in which *The Canterbury Tales* has come down to us.

At the time of his death Chaucer had probably not decided on the final arrangement to be adopted or, indeed, the exact position of some of the parts that he had completed. If he had been a very methodical person, he might have drawn up an outline which he could follow in writing his poem. But clearly no such outline was among his papers, and those who put together the earliest manuscripts were compelled to arrange what they found in what seemed to them the best order. In this they were helped somewhat by the fact that certain tales are linked together by remarks of the Host or of the pilgrims and thus constitute Groups or Fragments which could be treated as units. But later scribes interpreted some of the links differently, or altered them, or even composed spurious links to give an appearance of continuity to their text and to justify their arrangement. There are also occasional places along the road and the time of day, which could be taken into account but which were sometimes ignored. In any case, the arrangement in the manuscripts is that of what we would call "literary executors" and of later scribes, and it is the opinion of present-day scholars that (in the words of Manly) "none of the extant manuscripts exhibits an arrangement which with any probability can be ascribed to Chaucer" (*The Text of the Canterbury Tales*, II. 489).

It would seem then that we are thrown back on internal evidence—allusions which seem to refer to something that has been said before, references to the time of day and to places along the way, as said above, and other inferences from particular passages. It is not likely that Chaucer would have written "Loo, Rouchestre stant heer faste by!" (B 3116) if he had intended *The Monk's Tale* to come after the Wife of Bath's *Prologue*, at the end of which the Summoner promises to tell two or three tales about friars "er I come to Sidyngborne" (D 847). Rochester would have been several miles behind them as the pilgrims approached Sittingbourne. Even though his listeners might not all have picked up the detail, Chaucer was too familiar with the road to Canterbury to have made so obvious a mistake. When Furnivall in 1868 wrote his *Temporary Preface* to the six-text edition of *The Canterbury Tales*, published by the Chaucer Society, and discussed at some length the probable sequence of the stories, he arrived (with the help of Henry Bradshaw) at an arrangement of the unified Groups based upon internal evidence and the inferences he drew from that evidence. He designated the successive Groups in his arrangement A, B, C, etc. Those later editors who have adopted the arrangement of the tales in the Ellesmere MS (not only a handsome manuscript but textually and linguistically one of the best) have designated the Groups as Fragments and numbered them I, II, III, etc. Furnivall's arrangement of the Groups, adopted by the Chaucer Society, gives a highly satisfactory sequence in all respects except as to the position which he assigned to the Physician-Pardoner pair (Group C), which he placed, on very slender grounds, after *The Nun's Priest's Tale*.

Modern editors have adopted one of the two sequences just indicated. Skeat in the seven-volume Oxford edition (1894–7) followed the arrangement of the Chaucer Society, though with a protest against the position of Group C. The text of this edition was reproduced in one volume which he brought out (1897), and the Chaucer Society sequence was followed in the Globe edition (1898), edited by Pollard and a group of collaborators. These were the most conveniently available and widely used editions until 1933, when Professor F. N. Robinson edited the *Complete Works* for the Cambridge Poets series (revised, 1957) and adopted the order of the Ellesmere MS, as had Manly in his selections of 1928 (see Bibliography p. xliii).

The latter procedure can be justified on the ground that we cannot now tell what would have been Chaucer's arrangement of the tales, and that it represents at least an arrangement found in a carefully written manuscript produced within about ten years after his death. But as we have said above, the arrangement in none of the extant manuscripts can be attributed to Chaucer, and the Ellesmere sequence involves a dislocation of places along the way which Chaucer would not have intended.

The most difficult group to place is Group C (Physician-Pardoner) because it is without any reference to time or place except the not very helpful remark of the Pardoner that before he tells his tale he must stop for a draught of ale and a bite of cake. We are thus left with nothing else to go on than its position in the manuscripts. One cannot but be impressed by the quality and number of the manuscripts in which this group immediately precedes the group that begins with *The Shipman's Tale* (Group B_2), and over a dozen manuscripts of what is called the *d* type contain a spurious link connecting the two groups. If CB_2 could be considered a unit, it could be argued that it should be placed as a unit, and some scholars (Koch, Moore, and at one time Manly) have suggested a position immediately after *The Man of Law's Tale* (B_1). But this involves difficulties. Also, in manuscripts regarded as the best (including Ellesmere) CB_2 consistently follows *The Franklin's Tale*. This arrangement results in the dislocation of the reference in B_2 to Rochester. It would seem best to regard the close association of C and B_2 as due to an early scribe, and to try to place each of these fragments separately. Since there is reason for placing B_2 before the Wife of Bath's Prologue, and since C causes no difficulty if left to occupy the position after *The Franklin's Tale*, where it is found in excellent manuscripts, that is where it is placed in the present edition. Professor Pratt, by a process of elimination, has argued for this location in his article "The Order of the Canterbury Tales," *PMLA*, LXVI. 1141–67, to which the student is referred for an excellent study of the problem.

Except for Group A (and then only because of the length of *The Knight's Tale*) B_2 is the largest and most completely integrated group of tales in the whole of *The Canterbury Tales*. It consists of six tales all closely and dramatically tied together by links, the effectiveness of which is not surpassed anywhere else in *The Canterbury Tales*. Compared with these two groups all other groups are noticeably fragmentary. In only one are there more than two tales—Group D, which links the opposing tales of the Friar and Summoner with the quarrel between them that is brewing early in the Wife's Prologue. The rest of the collection consists of single tales or simple pairs of tales; they seem like pieces later to be fitted into the picture, though an occasional allusion to time or place suggests that Chaucer may have thought of some of them as material for the latter part of the journey. It is natural in writing a book to begin at the beginning and complete as much as possible as one goes along, even though one may have to leave small gaps to be completed later. From this point of view it would seem more reasonable to think that so extensive and complete a section as Group B_2 was largely completed early in the course of the project and that Chaucer had proceeded fairly continuously through Groups A, B_1, and B_2 while his energy and enthusiasm were still high. The fact that much that went into Group B_2 was material that he already had on hand—*The Prioress's Tale*, the *Sir Thopas*, the *Melibeus*, and *The Monk's Tale*—would have made such a procedure all the easier, and such reasoning does not preclude the possibility that *The Nun's Priest's Tale*, which comes at the end, might have been added later, perhaps when he had become interested in the collection of pieces which formed the contents of Jankyn's book and when the Wife's Prologue was taking shape in his mind.

Because of the nature and limitations of the evidence we have to go on no sequence of the groups is entirely free from objections. The arrangement here adopted is that which does least violence to the allusions to places along the way, and although any intentions of the poet would have been subject to later change, these allusions were due to Chaucer himself and had not been changed at the time of his death.

A number of small questions connected with *The Canterbury Tales* have engaged the attention of scholars. They do not affect our enjoyment of the poem, but to the true Chaucerian everything that has to do with the poet and his work is of interest. How many pilgrims actually were there? How many days did they spend on the road? Did Chaucer intend certain tales to form a Marriage Group? Some of these questions are referred to in the notes to particular passages and in the introductions to individual tales, but a brief statement concerning them is not out of place here. That Chaucer had in mind thirty pilgrims, counting himself, who were to tell stories, and Harry Bailly, the genial Host of the Tabard Inn who offers to go along as their guide, is not questioned. But the mention of three priests in the company of the Prioress (A 164) results in too many pilgrims. The reading of the manuscripts is probably not due to Chaucer (see the note to the line), and it seems certain that there was only one priest in the Prioress's company, the one who tells the tale of the cock and the fox. Then there is the fact that although Chaucer says that the group of pilgrims that he joined at the Tabard Inn consisted of "wel nyne and twenty," he actually mentions only twenty-eight when he comes to enumerate and describe them in the course of the General Prologue. The deficiency is made up when, well along the way to Canterbury, they are joined by a Canon and his Yeoman, neither of whom has been mentioned before. The Yeoman talks so freely about his master that the Canon rides off in shame, but the Yeoman remains and tells a story of the frauds which the Canon practices as an alchemist. It is one of the most realistic and dramatic of the episodes that occur on the trip. Some have gone so far as to suggest that Chaucer planned the incident from the beginning and purposely left his description of the company one pilgrim short in order to allow for it. But it is more likely that the omission in the General Prologue was an oversight, and that when he discovered it, rather than revise the Prologue, he achieved the desired number in the manner indicated. He retrieved himself brilliantly.

How many days the pilgrims were on the road and at what places they stopped for the night Chaucer does not tell us. They certainly did not make the fifty-five mile journey in one day. We know of a dozen persons in real life who made the trip, and they took from one to four days, depending on the need for haste. One of those who did it in a single day was Joan of Kent, the mother of Richard II (see the introduction to *The Legend of Good Women*), who, menaced by Wat Tyler and his rebels in the Peasants' Revolt of 1381, made the trip from Canterbury to London without stopping. Most travelers took four days, with stops at Dartford, Rochester, and Ospring, or three days, with stops at Dartford and either Rochester or Ospring. It is not necessary to be dogmatic. To the present editor the probability seems to favor three overnight stops (the intervals are then about fifteen miles each), with ten miles to go on the fourth day, but the possibility of a three-day journey is not to be denied.

The situation at the end is not entirely clear. No one, I believe, doubts that Chaucer intended to have *The Parson's Tale* conclude the story telling. Now, *The Parson's Tale* and *The Manciple's Tale*, which immediately precedes it (Groups H and I) are linked together and really constitute a single Group. Yet their linking presents a difficulty. When the Manciple begins his tale it is still morning and presumably fairly early. The tale which he tells is one of the shortest in the collection, a little over 250 lines. Yet when he finishes, it is four o'clock in the afternoon, as we are told. This has led to speculation. Manly suggested (*SP*, xxviii. 613–7) that *The Parson's Tale* was intended to be told not on the way to Canterbury but rather to end the tales of the homeward journey; Root, perhaps following a suggestion of Ten Brink, proposed (*MLN*, xliv. 493) that *The Manciple's Tale* be considered the opening tale of the return trip. But these speculations seem to the present writer to raise more problems than the one they are intended to solve. It is better to recognize the limitations of our knowledge and believe that the discrepancy is one of those flaws in the surviving work that would have been removed in the final revision.

The Man of Law's Tale evidently begins a new day, presumably the second day of the pilgrimage, and the mention of the date ("it was the eightetethe day of Aprill") by the Host in calling upon the Man of Law for a story offers a possible clue to the year as well. Accepting the probability that *The Canterbury Tales* was begun after, rather than before, *The Legend of Good Women*—that is, not earlier than 1386—Skeat showed that certain years could be eliminated as possibilities: in 1389, for example, April 18 was Easter; in 1386 it fell within Holy Week when the Prioress, the Parson, and other pilgrims had responsibilities; in 1388 it was a Saturday. For the discussion the student may consult the *Oxford Chaucer* (III. 408–9). It is sufficient to note here that in 1387 Easter was early, April 18 was a Thursday, and the pilgrims could have reached their destination comfortably on Saturday. They would then have been able to attend services in the cathedral on Sunday. Such a date agrees with what we otherwise know about Chaucer's activity at this period of his life, and we may assume with considerable probability that 1387 was the year in which he began the General Prologue and proceeded to carry out the project outlined in it.

It is hardly likely that a work of such magnitude and one begun so late in life could have been carried forward at a constant rate. We must allow for illness and temporary loss of energy. The poet's appointment in 1389 as Clerk of the King's Works involved considerable travel and on-the-job supervision. It must have interrupted or slowed down his progress on *The Canterbury Tales*. On the other hand, it would appear that there were times when he was able to return to the work with renewed enthusiasm. There is at least one sequence of stories within the collection as a whole that seems to represent "a fresh impulse to Chaucer's imagination," to use Miss Hammond's admirable phrase. *The Wife of Bath's Prologue* and *Tale* and the six tales which follow (Group D, E, F) form a sequence that is observed with fair consistency in the manuscripts, although the tales making up Groups E and F are not always in the correct order. A number of stories in these three groups present various aspects of marriage, and as long ago as 1908 Miss Hammond observed, "Yet a third class of narratives in the Canterbury Tales is what I may term the Marriage Group, the mass of material suggested or enriched by Jerome adversus Jovinianum, and developed in the Wife of Bath's Prologue, The Merchant's Tale, and the inserted passage in the Franklin's romance, lines 639 ff." (*Chaucer: A Bibliographical Manual*, p. 256). But the observation passed almost unnoticed, and it is doubtful if Miss Hammond herself perceived much more than the existence of a common source for some of the material in the tales she mentions. In 1913, in a notable essay, Kittredge developed the idea that Groups D, E, and F offered an extended treatment of marriage (interrupted by the quarrel of the Friar and the Summoner, and possibly by the fragmentary *Squire's Tale*), full of dramatic contrasts and the interplay of personality, and culminating in the enlightened views of the Franklin ("Chaucer's Discussion of Marriage," *MP*, IX. 435–67). The Wife of Bath frankly maintains that wives should dominate their husbands, as she has dominated the five that she has had thus far, and the story she tells is meant to enforce her doctrine. In due time the Clerk, outraged by the Wife of Bath's sensualism and by her philosophy of marriage, answers her with the story of patient Griselda, in which a wife's patience and submission are ultimately rewarded. *The Merchant's Tale* of January and May presents one of the problems that may arise where there is great discrepancy in age between the married pair, and the Franklin both exemplifies in his story and specifically advocates mutual tolerance and forbearance on both sides.

A Marriage Group, as such, has been denied by some, by others has been accepted completely, and by still others has been extended to include additional tales, both earlier and later. Other tales, such as the *Melibeus* and *The Nun's Priest's Tale*, have been suggested as additions to the Group, while these and the tales of the Miller, the Shipman, and the Manciple have been cited as evidence that there are discussions of marriage elsewhere and that the concept of a Marriage Group has been overemphasized. Whether Chaucer consciously planned a Marriage Group within the larger framework of *The Canterbury Tales* may be open to question, but he could hardly have been unaware of the dramatic possibilities in the juxtaposition of certain tales and their sequence in the three fragments in question. What seems fairly clear is that at a certain stage in the composition of *The Canterbury Tales* he became interested in the *Miroir de Mariage* of Eustache Deschamps and in a collection of antifeminist tracts of which St. Jerome's letter *Adversus Jovinianum* formed the most important part. Borrowings from these works in portions of the Marriage Group (and from the *Miroir* in the later version of the Prologue to *The Legend of Good Women*) suggest a date for the Marriage Group *c.* 1393–96.

Many types of medieval literature are represented in *The Canterbury Tales*. Varieties of the romance are illustrated by *The Knight's Tale*, the unfinished *Squire's Tale*, and the Arthurian story told by the Wife of Bath. Even the kind of Middle English romance that Chaucer was clearly contemptuous of is present in the humorous parody, *Sir Thopas*. The shorter romance known as the Breton lai is the tale told by the Franklin, while the romance's poor relation, the fabliau, featuring a humorous and generally indecent or unconventional incident, is fully exemplified, especially in the tales told by representatives of the lower classes such as the Miller, the Reeve, the Shipman, the Summoner, and others. One of the best examples of the Renart the Fox fables, popular on the Continent, is the tale of the cock and the fox told by the Nun's Priest. It is the more notable because the beast epic is not well represented in Middle English. Other narrative types are the classical legend (Man of Law, Physician), the saint's life (Second Nun), the *exemplum* or story useful to preachers (Pardoner), the Miracle of the Virgin (Prioress), and the moral apologue (Manciple, Chaucer). Tragedy, which in the Middle Ages was the story of one who had fallen from high places, often a collection of such chastening stories, is abundantly represented by *The Monk's Tale*—too abundantly in the judgment of the Knight and Harry Bailly. We even have a sermon, delivered by the Parson, and in *The Canon's Yeoman's Tale* an example of what came to be known in Elizabethan times as the cony-catching pamphlet. Any one who reads the whole of *The Canterbury Tales* will have a fair idea of the literary types that make up the great body of Middle English literature.

But *The Canterbury Tales* is much more than a collection of stories. It is an unfolding drama of human personalities who are brought into temporary association with one another. Some are gentle, some aristocratic, and some are coarse and vulgar. Some are not easy to get along with when sober, and they are not all sober. They are on a holiday, even though it is also a religious pilgrimage. The Reeve is a "sclendre colerick man," quick to suspect an affront and to take offence. Some in the company make themselves ridiculous by their remarks or their actions. The Cook is so drunk that he falls off his horse and can be put back on his mount only with much straining and pulling by the other pilgrims. Quarrels break out; one of the group glowers at another and promises to get back at him. The Knight and Host at times have to intercede and restore peace. Above all, it is Harry Bailly, the capable and forthright proprietor of the Tabard Inn, who keeps everything moving, who regulates the journey, calls on the pilgrims for their tales, comments freely on both tale and teller, and holds the whole series of stories together. This unfolding drama is sometimes achieved, or at least accented, by the juxtaposition of stories, as when the Clerk replies to the Wife of Bath with the tale of patient Griselda or when the Friar and the Summoner tell stories uncomplimentary to each other, but it is developed mostly in the introductions to and links between the tales. These interludes of dialogue and action are Chaucer's great contribution to the technique of the literary device of the framed tale. By means of them he has produced what has fittingly been called an English *comédie humaine*.

The text that follows is basically that of the Ellesmere MS.

THE CANTERBURY TALES

Group A (Fragment I)

GENERAL PROLOGUE

Here bygynneth the Book of the Tales of Caunterbury.

Whan that Aprill with his shoures soote
The droghte of March hath perced to the roote,
And bathed every veyne in swich licour
Of which vertu engendred is the flour;
Whan Zephirus eek with his sweete breeth   5
Inspired hath in every holt and heeth
The tendre croppes, and the yonge sonne
Hath in the Ram his halve cours yronne,
And smale foweles maken melodye,
That slepen al the nyght with open yë   10
(So priketh hem nature in hir corages),—
Thanne longen folk to goon on pilgrimages,
And palmeres for to seken straunge strondes,
To ferne halwes, kowthe in sondry londes;
And specially from every shires ende   15
Of Engelond to Caunterbury they wende,
The hooly blisful martir for to seke,
That hem hath holpen whan that they were
      seeke.
Bifil that in that seson on a day,
In Southwerk at the Tabard as I lay   20
Redy to wenden on my pilgrymage,
To Caunterbury with ful devout corage,
At nyght was come into that hostelrye
Wel nyne and twenty in a compaignye,
Of sondry folk, by aventure yfalle   25
In felaweshipe, and pilgrimes were they alle,
That toward Caunterbury wolden ryde.
The chambres and the stables weren wyde,
And wel we weren esed atte beste.

1. Aprill, accented on the first syllable. **his,** its. **shoures soote,** showers sweet. The earlier form of *soote* is *swote* (OE. *swōt,* influenced by the adv. *swōte*). The usual form of the word in Chaucer is *swete,* as in l. 5 below, representing OE. *swēte.* The opening, though conventional, tells us the time of year when the pilgrimage of the poem took place. **3. swich licour,** such moisture. **5. Zephirus,** the west wind, associated with spring. **6. Inspired,** breathed upon. **holt,** woodland. **7. croppes,** shoots. **yonge sonne.** The sun was supposed to begin its journey with the vernal equinox. Hence it was just starting out. **8. Ram,** the sign of the Zodiac, Aries. **halve cours.** During the month of April the sun passed through the last half of Aries and the first half of Taurus. **9. foweles,** birds. **10. with open yë.** Only a slight exaggeration. My friend Dr. R. C. Murphy, Curator Emeritus of Oceanic Birds at the American Museum of Natural History, writes me, "Chaucer was a keenly observant naturalist . . . I am confident that his reference to the open eye refers to the fact that most birds are light sleepers and that they take their slumber in snatches rather than in the human manner." **11. corages,** hearts. **13. palmeres,** professional pilgrims. **14. ferne halwes,** distant shrines (*lit..* saints). **kowthe,** known. **17. blisful martir,** Thomas à Becket, who through his martyrdom entered into eternal bliss; but *blisful* may simply mean "blessed." **18. holpen,** helped. **seeke,** sick, ill. **19. Bifil,** it befell. **20. Tabard,** an inn in Southwark, a district of London south of the Thames. The inn was identified by a pictorial sign showing a *tabard,* a short coat worn over armor and embroidered with the arms of the knight or noble In a broader sense the word designated any smock-shaped surcoat, without embroidery. The plowman on the pilgrimage was wearing a tabard (see l. 541 below). **lay,** lodged, was stopping overnight. **24. Wel nyne and twenty.** The meaning is "fully" or, "as many as" twenty-nine. Chaucer's intention was plainly to have thirty story-telling pilgrims, of which he would make the thirtieth. Assuming only one priest (see note to l. 164) there are only twenty-eight besides Chaucer. When at the end of the Prologue the Host (who at A 4358 is named Herry Bailly) offers to accompany the group and act as guide, it is clear that he is not to be one of the story tellers (cf. l. 814). Chaucer apparently discovered the error later and corrected it by the device of having the company joined at Boughton-under-Blee by a canon and his yeoman, the latter of whom continues with the pilgrims and tells a story. **25. aventure,** chance. **28. chambres,** bedrooms. **wyde,** spacious. **29. atte,** at the.

And shortly, whan the sonne was to reste, 30
So hadde I spoken with hem everichon
That I was of hir felaweshipe anon,
And made forward erly for to ryse,
To take oure wey ther as I yow devyse.

But nathelees, whil I have tyme and space, 35
Er that I ferther in this tale pace,
Me thynketh it acordaunt to resoun
To telle yow al the condicioun
Of ech of hem, so as it semed me,
And whiche they weren, and of what degree, 40
And eek in what array that they were inne;
And at a knyght than wol I first bigynne.

A **Knyght** ther was, and that a worthy man,
That fro the tyme that he first bigan
To riden out, he loved chivalrie, 45
Trouthe and honour, fredom and curteisie.
Ful worthy was he in his lordes werre,
And therto hadde he riden, no man ferre,

As wel in cristendom as in hethenesse,
And evere honoured for his worthynesse. 50
At Alisaundre he was whan it was wonne.
Ful ofte tyme he hadde the bord bigonne
Aboven alle nacions in Pruce;
In Lettow hadde he reysed and in Ruce,
No Cristen man so ofte of his degree. 55
In Gernade at the seege eek hadde he be
Of Algezir, and riden in Belmarye.
At Lyeys was he and at Satalye,
Whan they were wonne; and in the Grete See
At many a noble armee hadde he be. 60
At mortal batailles hadde he been fiftene,
And foughten for oure feith at Tramyssene
In lystes thries, and ay slayn his foo.
This ilke worthy knyght hadde been also
Somtyme with the lord of Palatye 65
Agayn another hethen in Turkye.
And everemoore he hadde a sovereyn prys;

---

30. shortly, briefly. **31. everichon,** every one (*lit.* ever each one). **32. anon,** at once. **33. forward,** agreement. The subject of *made* is "we" understood. **34. devyse,** will describe, relate. The pres. tense has been a normal form for expressing the future, usually indicated by an adverb, from Old English times. **35. nathelees,** nevertheless. **38. condicioun,** status (social, economic, etc.). **40. whiche,** what. **degree,** rank. **42. wol,** will. **43. worthy,** distinguished, honorable. **45. riden out,** take to the field, go on military expeditions. **chivalrie,** knighthood. **46. fredom,** nobility, liberality. **curteisie.** In addition to all the connotation of *courtesy* today, the word in the Middle Ages implies the manners supposed to belong to the court. **47. his lordes,** of his overlord. **werre,** warfare. **48. ferre,** farther. **49. hethenesse,** non-Christian territory. **50. honoured,** (had been) honored. **51. Alisaundre,** Alexandria, captured in 1365. In enumerating the important battles and sieges in which the Knight had participated Chaucer was of course intending to indicate his extensive and distinguished military career. All the campaigns mentioned were against the infidel,—Saracens, Turks, and pagans in northeastern Europe (Russia and Lithuania). Many knights volunteered for service of this kind, either as free-lances or under their overlords. Whether Chaucer's Knight fought under his overlord depends on the interpretation of *therto* in l. 48, which may mean "in connection therewith" or "in addition to that." The fact that all the sieges which we can date in Chaucer's enumeration occurred between 1342 and 1367 suggests a long military career and indicates that in 1387 the Knight was in his fifties; yet he had just returned from another "viage," as a result of which his gypon still bore stains from his coat of mail. Attempts have been made to find an actual original for him in real life, Cook favoring Henry, Earl of Lancaster, who, however, died before some of the sieges mentioned, Manly suggesting a composite of various members of the Scrope family. For information on the battles see Manly in *Trans. Amer. Philol. Assn*, XXXVIII. 89–107, and Cook, *Trans. Conn. Acad.*, XX. 161–240. **52. he hadde the bord bigonne,** he had sat at the head of the table or in the place of honor, perhaps at banquets of the Teutonic Order, in Prussia. **53. Pruce,** Prussia. **54. Lettow,** Lithuania. **reysed,** made a military expedition. **Ruce,** Russia. **56. Gernade,** Grenada. **57. Algezir,** Algeciras, captured from the Moorish king of Grenada in 1344. **riden,** see note to l. 45. **Belmarye,** now Benmarin, and like Tramyssene (modern Tlemcen), in l. 62, a Moorish kingdom in northwest Africa, opposite Spain. The dates of these campaigns are not known, but Manly cites the *Chron. de Sir Bertrand du Guesclin* as authority for an invasion of Belmarye planned in 1365. **58. Lyeys,** Ayas, near Antioch, won temporarily from the Turks in 1367. **Satalye,** Adalia, captured in 1361. Adalia and Alexandria were both taken under the leadership of Pierre de Lusignan, King of Cyprus. **59. Grete See,** Mediterranean. **60. armee,** an armed expedition. **63. In lystes thries.** Battles settled by single combat between champions representing the respective sides are common in the romances. The practice is here implied in actual warfare. **ilke,** same. **65. Somtyme with the lord of Palatye . . .** This and the following line have all the appearance of being a reference to a particular person. Palatia is the ancient Miletus at the mouth of the Meander. The principality of Menteshē was formed around the middle of the fourteenth century and its sultan was known as *dominus de Palatia*. In 1355 the then Sultan Yakoub was at war with Saroukhan, Sultan of Magnesia (See Mas Latrie, *Trésor de Chronologie,* col. 1801). If, as seems likely, this is the incident referred to, Chaucer could hardly have known of it except by oral report, and if he is painting his portrait of the Knight from life, these lines may contain the clue to the identity of his model. **Somtyme,** for a time. **67. a sovereyn prys,** the highest reputation.

And though that he were worthy, he was wys,
And of his port as meeke as is a mayde.
He nevere yet no vileynye ne sayde 70
In al his lyf unto no maner wight.
He was a verray parfit, gentil knyght.
But, for to tellen yow of his array,
His hors were goode, but he was nat gay.
Of fustian he wered a gypoun 75
Al bismotered with his habergeoun,
For he was late ycome from his viage,
And wente for to doon his pilgrymage.
With hym ther was his sone, a yong **Squier,**
A lovyere and a lusty bacheler, 80
With lokkes crulle as they were leyd in presse.
Of twenty yeer of age he was, I gesse.
Of his stature he was of evene lengthe,
And wonderly delyvere, and of greet strengthe.
And he hadde been somtyme in chyvachie 85
In Flaundres, in Artoys, and Pycardie,
And born hym weel, as of so litel space,
In hope to stonden in his lady grace.
Embrouded was he, as it were a meede
Al ful of fresshe floures, whyte and reede. 90

Syngynge he was, or floytynge, al the day;
He was as fressh as is the monthe of May.
Short was his gowne, with sleves longe and
wyde.
Wel koude he sitte on hors and faire ryde.
He koude songes make and wel endite, 95
Juste and eek daunce, and weel purtreye and
write.
So hoote he lovede that by nyghtertale
He slepte namoore than dooth a nyghtyngale.
Curteis he was, lowely, and servysable,
And carf biforn his fader at the table. 100
A **Yeman** hadde he and servantz namo
At that tyme, for hym liste ride so,
And he was clad in cote and hood of grene.
A sheef of pecok arwes, bright and kene,
Under his belt he bar ful thriftily 105
Wel koude he dresse his takel yemanly:
His arwes drouped noght with fetheres lowe—
And in his hand he baar a myghty bowe.
A not-heed hadde he, with a broun visage,
Of wodecraft wel koude he al the usage. 110
Upon his arm he baar a gay bracer,

---

68. worthy, full of worth, eminent. **wys,** prudent. **69. port,** bearing. **70. vileynye,** what is characteristic of a villain, rudeness, evil. **71. no maner wight,** person of any kind. **72. verray,** true. **gentil,** courteous, polite. **74. hors,** horses. Knights regularly traveled with extra horses, and he was fresh from an expedition. Note the contrast between the goodness of his horses and his own casual appearance. **gay,** dressed up. **75. fustian,** a coarse cloth made of cotton and flax. **gypoun,** tunic. **76. bismotered with,** soiled (stained) by. **habergeoun,** coat of mail. **77. viage,** a journey of any kind, but since he has been wearing a coat of mail, presumably here a military expedition. **79. Squier,** an attendant on a knight. **80. lovyere,** lover. **lusty,** vigorous, lively. **bacheler,** aspirant to knighthood. **81. crulle,** curly. **as they were,** as if they had been. **82. Of twenty yeer.** The noun is an older form of the plural; the partitive use of *of* is due to French influence. Cf. *de quinze mètres de longueur.* **I gesse.** This use of *guess,* now obsolete in England, is preserved in American English. **83. evene lengthe,** average or proper height. **84. delyvere,** active, agile. **85. chyvachie,** expedition. The English campaign of 1383 fits the next line. **87. as of so litel space,** considering the shortness of the time. **88. lady,** lady's. For the possessive without *s* see Language, § 14. **89. Embrouded,** embroidered. The doublet among the well-to-do was commonly embroidered, but here and in l. 93 Chaucer seems to suggest a somewhat excessive observance of current fashion. A statute of 1363 forbade esquires and gentlemen below the status of knight to wear any sort of embroidered garment unless they had an income of £200 a year, but we cannot be sure it was enforced. **91. floytynge,** playing the flute or (possibly) whistling. But whistling in public may not have been polite, as in some parts of Europe today. **94. faire,** adv. **95. He koude songes make . . .** This and the succeeding lines express the fashionable accomplishments of a young squire: compose the music (*songs make*) and the words (*endite*) . . . draw or paint (*purtreye*) and write, the last a much less widespread ability than today. **96. Juste,** joust. **97. hoote,** hotly, fervently. **nyghtertale,** nighttime. **98.** During the mating season the nightingale sings all night, or nearly so. **99. lowely,** modest in demeanor. **100. carf,** carved; one of the functions of a squire. **101. Yeman.** The Yeoman, in rank above a groom, is in the service of the Knight, and from the description was probably one of his foresters, a kind of game warden. Therefore *he* refers back to the Knight. **servantz namo.** Chaucer is careful to indicate that the Yeoman was not the only servant that the Knight had, but the only one who accompanied him on the pilgrimage. **102. hym liste,** it pleased him, he chose. **104. pecok arwes.** Ascham in his *Toxophilus* is rather critical of peacock feathers for the arrow, the feathers of the goose being the best. But other evidence makes it clear that this was not the opinion in Chaucer's day. **105. Under,** below. **thriftily,** appropriately. **106. takel,** bow and arrow, although the word sometimes means "arrow" or "arrows" (collectively). **yemanly,** as a good yeoman should. **109. not-heed,** close-cropped head. **110. koude,** knew. **111. bracer,** leather shield for the arm to prevent friction of the bowstring. **gay,** here and in l. 113 suggest something ornamented or fancy.

And by his syde a swerd and a bokeler,
And on that oother syde a gay daggere
Harneised wel and sharp as point of spere;
A Cristophre on his brest of silver sheene. 115
An horn he bar, the bawdryk was of grene;
A forster was he, soothly, as I gesse.
 Ther was also a Nonne, a **Prioresse**
That of hir smylyng was ful symple and coy;
Hire gretteste ooth was but by Seinte Loy; 120
And she was cleped madame Eglentyne.
Ful weel she soong the service dyvyne,
Entuned in hir nose ful semely,
And Frenssh she spak ful faire and fetisly,
After the scole of Stratford atte Bowe, 125
For Frenssh of Parys was to hire unknowe.
At mete wel ytaught was she with-alle:
She leet no morsel from hir lippes falle,
Ne wette hir fyngres in hir sauce depe;
Wel koude she carie a morsel and wel kepe 130
That no drope ne fille upon hire brest.

In curteisie was set ful muchel hir lest.
Hir over-lippe wyped she so clene
That in hir coppe ther was no ferthyng sene
Of grece, whan she dronken hadde hir draughte.
Ful semely after hir mete she raughte. 136
And sikerly she was of greet desport,
And ful plesaunt, and amyable of port,
And peyned hire to countrefete cheere
Of court, and to been estatlich of manere, 140
And to ben holden digne of reverence.
But, for to speken of hire conscience,
She was so charitable and so pitous
She wolde wepe, if that she saugh a mous
Kaught in a trappe, if it were deed or bledde. 145
Of smale houndes hadde she that she fedde
With rosted flessh, or milk and wastel-breed.
But soore wepte she if oon of hem were deed,
Or if men smoot it with a yerde smerte;
And al was conscience and tendre herte. 150
Ful semyly hir wympul pynched was,

---

114. Harneised, mounted. **115. Christophre,** an image of St. Christopher, according to Manly the patron saint of foresters, worn as a charm. **sheene,** bright. **116. bawdryk,** baldrick, a band or cord hanging from the shoulder to below the other arm. **119. coy,** quiet. **120. Seinte Loy,** St. Eligius (Fr. *Eloi*). Several unconvincing explanations of the choice of the saint have been proposed,—that he refused on one occasion to swear, was a courtly person like the fastidious Prioress, was a patron of travelers, etc. Identification has also been suggested with St. Eulalia, with a change of sex, as has happened in the name of a Burgundian village (J. J. Lynch, *MLN*, LXXII. 242–9). But the name may have been dictated by rime. **121. cleped,** named. **madame Eglentyne.** At the priory of St. Leonard's at Stratford atte Bowe (see l. 125) there was a nun in 1375 and perhaps earlier) named madam Argentyn, as Manly showed (*Some New Light on Chaucer*). Argentyn is a variant of the family name Eglentyne. When Chaucer was a page in the household of the Countess of Ulster the Countess visited the priory, and Chaucer may have been in the retinue. Manly believed that the portrait of the Prioress was drawn from this sister. Later, finding that madam Argentyn was never prioress, he withdrew the suggestion. But too much literalness is not to be expected in a work of fiction, and certain features of the portrait (a large woman, an unusually broad forehead) suggest that Chaucer may have been recalling an actual nun. **123. Entuned in hir nose.** Whether Chaucer is making gentle fun of a fashionable affectation is not known. **124. Frenssh . . .** That the Prioress's French was dialectal is clear. The French spoken in England was often ridiculed at this time by those who spoke the standard French of Paris. By 1387 there was no need for any one in England to speak French, but it was doubtless cultivated at St. Leonard's because of its former association with the English upper class. **fetisly,** elegantly. **125. Stratford atte Bowe,** about two miles outside of London (to the east of Aldgate, where Chaucer had lived for some twelve years). The priory of St. Leonard's while less exclusive than Barking, which was also on the outskirts of London, had some claim to social distinction. Many of the Prioress's efforts "to countrefete cheere of court" are readily understood if we assume a desire on her part to have her house, though on a smaller scale, not inferior to Barking. The nine nuns and their prioress could boast among their number Elizebeth of Hainault, the sister of Queen Philippa. **127. At mete.** The description of the Prioress's table manners is largely borrowed from the *Roman de la Rose*, but this does not lessen Chaucer's intention of showing that in matters of etiquette the Prioress showed care in following the rules of the socially proper. **129. sauce,** sauce, gravy. **130. kepe,** take care. **131. fille,** fell. **132. curteisie,** etiquette. **lest,** delight. **134. coppe,** cup. **ferthyng,** small spot, like the tiny English coin. **sene,** visible. A fifteenth-century curtesy book for the young says "Wype thi mouthe when thou wyll drinke, Lest it foule thi copys brinke." (*Babees Book*, p. 23). **136. mete,** food. **raughte,** reached. **137. sikerly,** certainly. **desport,** agreeableness, charm. **139. countrefete,** copy, imitate, **cheere,** behavior, bearing. **140. estatlich,** stately, dignified. **141. digne,** worthy. **143. pitous,** tenderhearted. **146. Of smale houndes,** some little dogs. To keep pets of this sort would have required a dispensation, and this in turn implies that the Prioress or her house had influence. **147. wastel-breed,** a fine white bread (Fr. *gâteau*, cake). Four grades of bread were recognized: payndemayn, wastel, and two cheaper kinds. Wastel bread was the best of the grades in ordinary use. Since the Prioress fed it to her little dogs, it is implied that St. Leonard's ate only the best. **148. soore,** sorely. **149. men,** one. **yerde,** stick, rod. **smerte,** smartly. **150. conscience,** tenderness, sensibility (in the eighteenth-century sense). **151. wympul.** The wimple was a linen covering for the head, the sides of the face, and the neck. **pynched,** pleated.

Hir nose tretys, hir eyen greye as glas,
Hir mouth ful smal, and therto softe and reed.
But sikerly she hadde a fair forheed,—
It was almoost a spanne brood, I trowe,— 155
For, hardily, she was nat undergrowe.
Ful fetys was hir cloke, as I was war.
Of smal coral aboute hire arm she bar
A peire of bedes, gauded al with grene, 159
And theron heng a brooch of gold ful sheene,
On which ther was first write a crowned A,
And after *Amor vincit omnia.*

Another **Nonne** with hire hadde she,
That was hir chapeleyne, and preestes thre.

A **Monk** ther was, a fair for the maistrie, 165
An outridere, that lovede venerie,
A manly man, to been an abbot able.
Ful many a deyntee hors hadde he in stable,
And whan he rood, men myghte his brydel heere
Gynglen in a whistlynge wynd als cleere 170
And eek as loude as dooth the chapel belle
Ther as this lord was kepere of the celle.

The reule of seint Maure or of seint Beneit,
By cause that it was old and somdel streit
This ilke Monk leet olde thynges pace, 175
And heeld after the newe world the space.
He yaf nat of that text a pulled hen
That seith that hunters been nat hooly men,
Ne that a monk, whan he is recchelees,
Is likned til a fissh that is waterlees,— 180
This is to seyn, a monk out of his cloystre.
But thilke text heeld he nat worth an oystre;
And I seyde his opinioun was good.
What sholde he studie and make hymselven wood,
Upon a book in cloystre alwey to poure, 185
Or swynken with his handes, and laboure,
As Austyn bit? How shal the world be served?
Lat Austyn have his swynk to hym reserved!
Therfore he was a prikasour aright;
Grehoundes he hadde as swift as fowel in flight.
Of prikyng and of huntyng for the hare 191
Was al his lust; for no cost wolde he spare.
I seigh his sleves ypurfiled at the hond

---

152. tretys, slender, well-proportioned. In medieval descriptions a lady's nose is always *tretys.* **greye,** hazel. Although a bluish tint is not excluded, the interpretation "blue" is not justified. See A. K. Moore, *PQ,* XXVI. 307–12. **155. trowe,** believe. **156. hardily,** assuredly. **157. fetys,** neat, elegant. **158. smal coral.** Since coral is a substance, the adjective implies that Chaucer is using the word for stones or pieces of coral. **159. A peire of bedes,** a string of beads, a rosary. **gauded,** divided into groups by "gauds," beads of distinct size, material, color, or ornamentation, the purpose of which in Chaucer's day is still not certain. The modern use of reciting a *Paternoster* between decades or tens of *Aves* (Hail Mary's) is not known before the fifteenth century. See Beverly Boyd, *MLQ,* XI. 404–16. **160. heng,** hung. **brooch,** ornament. **162. Amor vincit omnia,** Love (divine) conquers all. **163. Another Nonne.** The Prioress naturally traveled with a companion. The chaplain was a kind of adminstrative assistant to the Prioress. **164. preestes thre.** It is almost certain that there was only one priest on the pilgrimage. Only one is ever referred to elsewhere and he tells a story. It is likely that Chaucer left the end of the line to be completed later and that the present reading is due to a scribe. Miss Rickert's suggestion that the original reading was "and the priest is three" is ingenious but not convincing. **165. for the maistrie,** pre-eminently; hence the meaning is "a fine example of a monk." **166. outridere,** an officer in a monastery whose duty it was to look after the manors belonging to it. **venerie,** hunting. A monk of Chaucer's time notorious for his addiction to hunting was William Clown, abbot of a house of Austin canons at Leicester. See Ramona Bressie, *MLN,* LIV. 476–90, and, for comment, Dom David Knowles. *The Religious Orders in England* (2v, Cambridge, 1950–57), II. 365–6. **168. deyntee,** valuable. **170. Gynglen,** jingle. It was fashionable to hang small bells on the bridle and other parts of the harness. **172. Ther as,** where. **celle,** a priory or dependent house. **173. seint Maure . . . seint Beneit.** St. Maurus was credited with introducing the Benedictine rule into France. **176. somdel streit,** somewhat strict. **176. the space,** meanwhile (Manly), the course or custom (Skeat; *NED*). **177. that text.** O. F. Emerson (*MP,* I. 105–15) believed that the text referred to was the *Decretum* of Gratian, C. XI, which cites St. Jerome's commentary on Psalm 90. But that it is a reference to Nimrod (*Genesis,* 10:9) is not impossible. **pulled hen,** a plucked hen. **179. recchelees,** negligent of his duty. **180. a fissh that is waterlees.** The idea in *Piers Plowman* (A 201–7, etc.) is credited to the *Moralia* of Pope Gregory. The comparison of the cloisterless monk to a fish out of water goes back to the *Vitae Patrum* (the *Vita Antonii* by Athanasuis); cf. *PL,* LXXIII. 858. It is found also in Wyclif. See Constance Rosenthal, *The Vitae Patrum in Old and Middle English Literature* (Philadelphia, 1936), p. 128. **184. What,** why. **wood,** mad. **186. swynken,** work. **187. Austyn bit,** St. Augustine bids. Although St. Augustine's teachings on labor are to be found in his *De Opere Monachorum* (*PL,* XL. 547 ff.), it is probable that Chaucer was here remembering the *RR* (cf. ed. Langlois, III. 316). **189. prikasour,** hard rider (but cf. note on l. 191). **aright,** truly. **191. prikyng,** following the tracks (of a hare). **192. lust,** pleasure. **193. seigh,** saw. **ypurfiled,** edged.

With grys, and that the fyneste of a lond;
And, for to festne his hood under his chyn,   195
He hadde of gold ywroght a ful curious pyn;
A love-knotte in the gretter ende ther was.
His heed was balled, that shoon as any glas,
And eek his face, as he hadde been enoynt.
He was a lord ful fat and in good poynt;   200
His eyen stepe, and rollynge in his heed,
That stemed as a forneys of a leed;
His bootes souple, his hors in greet estaat.
Now certeinly he was a fair prelaat;
He was nat pale as a forpyned goost.   205
A fat swan loved he best of any roost.
His palfrey was as broun as is a berye.

    A **Frere** ther was, a wantowne and a merye,
A lymytour, a ful solempne man.
In alle the ordres foure is noon that kan   210
So muchel of daliaunce and fair langage.
He hadde maad ful many a mariage
Of yonge wommen at his owene cost.
Unto his ordre he was a noble post.
Ful wel biloved and famulier was he   215
With frankeleyns over al in his contree,

And eek with worthy wommen of the toun;
For he hadde power of confessioun,
As seyde hymself, moore than a curat,
For of his ordre he was licenciat.   220
Ful swetely herde he confessioun,
And plesaunt was his absolucioun:
He was an esy man to yeve penaunce
Ther as he wiste to have a good pitaunce.
For unto a povre ordre for to yive   225
Is signe that a man is wel yshryve;
For if he yaf, he dorste make avaunt,
He wiste that a man was repentaunt;
For many a man so hard is of his herte,
He may nat wepe, althogh hym soore
    smerte.   230
Therfore in stede of wepynge and preyeres
Men moote yeve silver to the povre freres.
His typet was ay farsed ful of knyves
And pynnes, for to yeven faire wyves.
And certeinly he hadde a murye note;   235
Wel koude he synge and pleyen on a rote;
Of yeddynges he baar outrely the pris.
His nekke whit was as the flour-de-lys;

194. **grys,** an expensive gray fur, probably squirrel (cf. F. *petit-gris*). 196. **curious,** carefully or beautifully made. 198. **balled,** bald. 199. **as,** as if. **enoynt,** anointed. 200. **in good poynt,** in good condition; but cf. F. *embonpoint*, stoutness. 201. **stepe,** It is impossible to tell whether the word here means "prominent" or "bright." The word was used in both senses to describe the eyes. 202. **stemed,** glowed. **forneys of a leed,** furnace under a cauldron. 205. **forpyned,** wasted away. 208. **Frere.** The friar was a member of one of the four mendicant orders (see note to l. 210), but of which one we do not know. The shortcomings of the class were widely criticized in Chaucer's day. **a wantowne,** a person given to pleasure, but, as the description which follows shows, he was a wanton in the modern sense. 209. **A lymytour,** a friar having the exclusive right to beg within an assigned district or limit. **solempne,** important. 210. **ordres foure.** The four orders of friars were the Franciscan, founded by St. Francis of Assisi in 1209, also known as Gray Friars or friars minor; the Dominican, founded by St. Dominic in 1206, also known as Black Friars or friars-preachers; the Carmelite or White Friars; and the Augustinian or Austin Friars, organized about the middle of the thirteenth century (their habit was also black). **kan,** knows. 211. **daliaunce.** The word covers anything from conversation to amorous play. 212. **maad,** arranged. 213. **at his owene cost,** *i.e.* possibly because they had been his mistresses. 214. **post,** *i.e.* he was "a pillar of (his) society." 216. **frankeleyns,** country gentlemen. See the description of the Frankeleyn, below (ll. 331 ff.). **over al,** everywhere. **contree,** region, although the word is frequently used where we would say "county." 217. **worthy,** respectable, but here probably also implying well-to-do. **wommen of the toun,** townswomen. 218. **power of confessioun.** One of the great causes of friction between the friars and the parish priests was the license which the friars had to hear confession, with accompanying loss of income for the parish priest. 219. **moore than a curat.** The friar could give absolution for certain more serious offenses which ordinarily were referred to the bishop. **curat,** parish priest, parson. 220. **licenciat.** By a papal bull of 1300 (*Super Cathedram*) the mendicant orders were required to designate those members who should be licensed to hear confession. 224. **Ther as he wiste to have,** where he knew he would have. **pitaunce,** a pious donation, often probably a good dinner. 226. **yshryve,** shriven. 227. **yaf,** gave. **avaunt,** boast. 230. **hym. . . smerte,** it may pain him. 232. **Men moote,** people may. 233. **typet,** a streamer of cloth attached to the hood or sleeve, but it seems here to be furnished with a pocket. **farsed,** stuffed. **knyves And pynnes.** Wiclif inveighs against the friars for becoming pedlars of knives, pins, purses, etc. and also for giving them to women "to gete love of hem." See Skeat's note for this and other contemporary references to the practice. 235. **a murye note,** a pleasant singing voice; cf. a bird's note. 236. **rote,** a musical instrument resembling a lyre. It generally had five to eight strings and was plucked. See illustrations in F. W. Galpin, *Old English Instruments of Music* (London, 1911). 237. **yeddynges,** songs, generally narrative, "*idem quod geest* (or rowmawnce . . .)" according to the *Promptorium Parvulorum.* **outrely the pris,** absolutely the prize. 238. **nekke whit,** regarded in the Middle Ages as a mark of sensuality.

Therto he strong was as a champioun.

He knew the tavernes wel in every toun   240

And everich hostiler and tappestere

Bet than a lazar or a beggestere;

For unto swich a worthy man as he

Acorded nat, as by his facultee,

To have with sike lazars aqueyntaunce.   245

It is nat honeste, it may nat avaunce,

For to deelen with no swich poraille,

But al with riche and selleres of vitaille.

And over al ther as profit sholde arise

Curteis he was and lowely of servyse.   250

Ther nas no man nowher so vertuous.

He was the beste beggere in his hous;

[And yaf a certeyn ferme for the graunt;   252a

Noon of his bretheren cam ther in his

     haunt;]   252b

For thogh a wydwe hadde noght a sho,

So plesaunt was his *"In principio,"*

Yet wolde he have a ferthyng, er he wente.   255

His purchas was wel bettre than his rente.

And rage he koude, as it were right a whelpe.

In love-dayes ther koude he muchel helpe,

For ther he was nat lyk a cloysterer

With a thredbare cope, as is a povre scoler,   260

But he was lyk a maister or a pope.

Of double worstede was his semycope,

That rounded as a belle out of the presse.

Somwhat he lipsed, for his wantownesse,

To make his Englissh sweete upon his

     tonge;   265

And in his harpyng, whan that he hadde

     songe,

His eyen twynkled in his heed aryght,

As doon the sterres in the frosty nyght.

This worthy lymytour was cleped Huberd.

   A **Marchant** was ther with a forked berd,   270

In mottelee, and hye on horse he sat;

Upon his heed a Flaundryssh bevere hat,

His bootes clasped faire and fetisly.

His resons he spak ful solempnely,

Sownynge alwey th'encrees of his wynnyng.

He wolde the see were kept for any

     thyng   276

239. champioun, champion wrestler or athlete. **241. hostiler,** innkeeper. **tappestere,** barmaid. The ending *-ster* originally signified a female (cf. *spinster*), but the significance was being largely lost. **242. Bet,** better. **lazar,** leper (from *Lazarus*), but here probably (as often) any poor or diseased person. **beggestere,** beggar. **244. as by,** in view of. **facultee,** profession, occupation. **246. honeste,** respectable, becoming. **avaunce,** profit one. **247. poraille,** poor people, the rabble. **248. riche,** rich people. **selleres of vitaille.** The merchants of the victualing trade, at least in London, were an influential class. **249. over al ther as,** everywhere where. **250. Curteis . . . servyse.** See l. 99 and note. **251. vertuous,** capable. Note the emphasis conveyed by the triple negative. **252a. And yaf a certeyn ferme . . .** This couplet is entirely Chaucerian but is found in only a few manuscripts. **ferme,** a lump sum which the Friar paid for his monopoly. **254.** *In principio,* the opening words of the gospel of St. John, the first fourteen verses of which were the favorite devotion of friars upon entering a house. See R. A. Law, *PMLA,* xxxvii. 208–15, and M. W. Bloomfield, *MLN,* lxx. 559–65. **256. purchas,** profit (from begging). The word sometimes has the suggestion of ill-gotten gains. **rente,** generally interpreted as "regular income" and in this sense the statement "He made more by purchase than by his rent" is found elsewhere, but since it is difficult to see what could be meant by the Friar's regular income other than the proceeds of his activities as described, the interpretation of *rente* as his payment for the privileges which he enjoyed cannot be entirely ruled out. A pun may even be intended on the two meanings of the word. **257. rage,** carry on, behave wantonly or foolishly. **whelpe,** puppy. **258. love-dayes,** attempts to settle disputes by arbitration out of court. See Josephine W. Bennett, "The Mediaeyal Loveday," *Speculum,* xxxiii. 351–70, and R. H. Bowers, "A Middle-English Poem on Lovedays," *MLR,* xlvii. 374–5. **261. maister,** presumably used in the learned sense of *magister,* whose knowledge or opinion is considered authoritative. **262. double worstede,** a stout worsted cloth 45 inches wide. See *Language,* xxxvii. 542–3. **semycope,** a short cloak, but this is the only occurrence of the word quoted in the *NED.* **263. presse,** mould. **264. lipsed.** Lisping was an affectation associated with wantonness, but *for his wantownesse* is taken by Skeat as meaning "by way of mannerism." This would be in keeping with the next line. **270. forked berd.** In Chaucer's time this was one of a number of fashionable shapes of beard. **271. mottelee,** cloth with a woven figure in the same or different color. **hye on horse,** *i.e.* he used a high saddle, which made him more imposing. **272. Flaundryssh,** of Flemish style, probably imported from Flanders. **bevere** fur of the beaver or an imitation of it. **273. fetisly,** neatly. **274. resons,** opinions. **solempnely,** importantly. **275. Sownynge,** conducing to. Although usually followed by a preposition (*to, into,* etc.) it may be followed by a direct object. **276. wolde,** wished. **kept,** guarded, protected. **for any thyng,** under all circumstances. Pirates were a constant danger, and whenever France and England were at war privateers on both sides attacked the other nation's ships.

Bitwixe Middelburgh and Orewelle.
Wel koude he in eschaunge sheeldes selle.
This worthy man ful wel his wit bisette:
Ther wiste no wight that he was in dette,   280
So estatly was he of his governaunce
With his bargaynes and with his chevyssaunce.
For sothe he was a worthy man with-alle,
But, sooth to seyn, I noot how men hym calle.

A **Clerk** ther was of Oxenford also,   285
That unto logyk hadde longe ygo.
As leene was his hors as is a rake,
And he nas nat right fat, I undertake,
But looked holwe, and therto sobrely.
Ful thredbare was his overeste courtepy;   290
For he hadde geten hym yet no benefice,
Ne was so worldly for to have office.
For hym was levere have at his beddes heed
Twenty bookes, clad in blak or reed,
Of Aristotle and his philosophie,   295
Than robes riche, or fithele, or gay sautrie.
But al be that he was a philosophre,

Yet hadde he but litel gold in cofre;
But al that he myghte of his freendes hente,
On bookes and on lernynge he it spente,   300
And bisily gan for the soules preye
Of hem that yaf hym wherwith to scoleye.
Of studie took he moost cure and moost
    heede,
Noght o word spak he moore than was neede,
And that was seyd in forme and reverence,   305
And short and quyk and ful of hy sentence.
Sownynge in moral vertu was his speche,
And gladly wolde he lerne and gladly teche.

A **Sergeant of the Lawe,** war and wys,
That often hadde been at the Parvys,   310
Ther was also, ful riche of excellence.
Discreet he was and of greet reverence—
He semed swich, his wordes weren so wise.
Justice he was ful often in assise,
By patente and by pleyn commissioun.   315
For his science and for his heigh renoun,
Of fees and robes hadde he many oon.

---

277. Middelburgh, a port on an island off the coast of the Netherlands. **Orewelle,** a river in Suffolk, on which was Ipswich, one of the English wool staples. Wool and certain other major items of English export could be sent from only a small number of English ports and received at a still smaller number abroad. These ports were known as staples and there the customs were checked and paid. As J. W. Hales pointed out (*Folia Litteraria,* pp. 99–102) Middleburgh was a staple for only four years, 1384–1388, and it would be most natural for Chaucer to write the line during this period. The objections of Knott and of Manly are of little force. The Merchant's concern would lose most of its point unless Middleburgh were a normal staple. A further inference is that he was a merchant of the staple, since only such were allowed to export the commodities subject to the restriction. **278. eschaunge sheeldes selle.** This activity, which we would call foreign exchange, was illegal. Sheeldes were gold coins known as florins d'escu, worth (according to Tyrwhitt) about three shillings four pence. **279. bisette,** employed. **281. So estatly . . .,** so dignified was he in the conduct of his business. **282. bargaynes . . . chevyssaunce.** The two words are several times associated in fourteenth-century quotations and involve money lending. Chevyssaunce means "usury." A sells a cargo of goods to B, who cannot pay for it until he has resold it; in return for the credit which A extends, B enters into a bond to pay A a sum considerably greater than the original sale price. See A. H. Thomas, *Trans. Royal Hist. Soc.,* 4th Ser., IV. 90. **284. noot,** know not. **285. Clerk,** student preparing for the priesthood. **Oxenford,** Oxford. **286. ygo,** betaken himself. **290. overeste courtepy,** outermost short cloak. **291. geten,** obtained. **292. office,** secular employment. Persons of his education were often employed in government offices. **293. hym was levere,** he preferred. **294. Twenty bookes,** a very large collection at this time. **296. fithele,** fiddle. **sautrie,** psaltery, a flat musical instrument generally in the shape of a triangle or trapezoid, with eight to twenty strings. It was held upright or on the lap. **297. philosophre,** a play on the word, which was also applied to alchemists. **299. hente,** get. **301. gan,** did. **302. scoleye,** study, attend school. **303. studie,** reflection. **cure,** care. **304. o word,** one word. **305. forme and reverence,** propriety and respect. **306. hy sentence,** weighty significance. **307. Sownynge in,** conducing to, reflecting. **309. Sergeant of the Lawe,** not an everyday lawyer, but one of a very small number who attained to this rank. Appointment was by the king and induction involved a seven-day ceremony with an expensive dinner and costly gifts to the important guests. Manly believed that Chaucer drew his portrait from a Sergeant named Thomas Pynchbek. See *Some New Light on Chaucer,* chap. v. **310. Parvys,** the porch of St. Paul's cathedral, a favorite place for lawyers to congregate in the sixteenth-century and presumably in the fourteenth. In the reign of Queen Elizabeth sergeants at law at the time of their induction were assigned a location on the parvis. **312. reverence,** respect. **314. Justice,** judge. **assise,** the county court, held periodically, to which justices were sent on temporary appointment by the king. **315. patente,** the letter patent by which he was appointed. **pleyn commissioun,** full commission to hear all cases. **316. science,** learning. **317. fees and robes,** representing payment by his clients. Payment in kind for professional services was quite common.

So greet a purchasour was nowher noon:
Al was fee symple to hym in effect;
His purchasyng myghte nat been infect. 320
Nowher so bisy a man as he ther nas,
And yet he semed bisier than he was.
In termes hadde he caas and doomes alle
That from the tyme of kyng William were falle.
Therto he koude endite, and make a thyng, 325
Ther koude no wight pynche at his writyng;
And every statut koude he pleyn by rote.
He rood but hoomly in a medlee cote,
Girt with a ceint of silk, with barres smale;
Of his array telle I no lenger tale. 330
A **Frankeleyn** was in his compaignye.
Whit was his berd as is the dayesye;
Of his complexioun he was sangwyn.
Wel loved he by the morwe a sop in wyn;
To lyven in delit was evere his wone, 335
For he was Epicurus owene sone,
That heeld opinioun that pleyn delit

Was verray felicitee parfit.
An housholdere, and that a greet, was he;
Seint Julian he was in his contree. 340
His breed, his ale, was alweys after oon;
A bettre envyned man was nowher noon.
Withoute bake mete was nevere his hous,
Of fissh and flessh, and that so plentevous,
It snewed in his hous of mete and drynke, 345
Of alle deyntees that men koude thynke.
After the sondry sesons of the yeer,
So chaunged he his mete and his soper.
Ful many a fat partrich hadde he in muwe,
And many a breem and many a luce in stuwe.
Wo was his cook but if his sauce were 351
Poynaunt and sharp, and redy al his geere.
His table dormant in his halle alway
Stood redy covered al the longe day.
At sessiouns ther was he lord and sire; 355
Ful ofte tyme he was knyght of the shire.
An anlaas and a gipser al of silk

---

318. purchasour, usually explained as "conveyancer," but no example of the word used in this sense is known. There are, however, many references, generally expressing disapproval, to those who bought up land and property, as Wiclif says speaking of lawyers, "to be peers with knights and barons." See *EETS*, 74, p. 183. **319. fee symple.** Property held in fee simple is owned without conditions, or limitations, and descends to women in default of male heirs. **320. infect,** invalidated. **321. nas,** *i.e.* ne was; note the double negative. **323. termes,** probably the Year Books, which were compiled from notes taken at trials and were valuable to lawyers and students as a record of precedents. See W. C. Bolland, *The Year Books* (Cambridge, 1927), esp. p. 6, and the introductions to the various volumes in the series published by the Selden Soc. They covered the cases of a single law term and are headed *Placita de Termino Sancti Hillarii . . .*, etc. **caas and doomes,** cases and judgments. Chaucer is indulging in poetic exaggeration in saying that the Sergeant had Year Books reaching back to William the Conqueror. The earliest now known date from the reign of Edward I. **325. endite, and make a thyng,** compose and draw up legal papers. **326. pynche,** find fault. If Manly's identification is correct (see note to l. 309), this may be a punning reference to Pynchbek. **327. koude . . . rote,** he knew completely by heart. **328. hoomly,** unpretentiously, dressed informally. **medlee,** cloth made of wool dyed before weaving. It could be of one color, or variegated, or in stripes. **329. ceint,** girdle. **barres,** *i.e.* to keep the silk spread. The word is taken by some to mean "stripes," but in the *Romaunt of the Rose* Rychesse wears a girdle of satin and "the barres were of gold ful fyne" (l. 1103), each of the weight of a bezant. The girdle was often worn at the level of the hips rather than at the waist. **331. Frankeleyn.** It is significant that the Sergeant of the Law was travelling with a well-to-do country gentleman. **333. complexioun.** There were four complections or temperaments: sanguine, choleric, phlegmatic, and melancholic, which were determined by the fluids or humors of the body. A *sangwyn* complection resulted from a dominance of blood. **334. by the morwe,** in the morning. **sop in wyn,** pieces of toasted bread or cake in wine. **335. wone,** custom. **336. Epicurus,** Greek philosopher who held that the highest good was pleasure. **337. pleyn,** full. **338. verray,** true. **340. Seint Julian,** patron saint of hospitality. **contree,** region, county. **341. after oon,** of uniform quality. **342. envyned,** stocked with wine. **343. bake mete,** a pie in which meat or fish is baked with fruit, spices, etc. A number of recipes are given in *Two Fifteenth-Century Cookery-Books* (EETS, 91), p. 47, some of them quite elaborate. **344. plentevous,** plentiful. **346. deyntees,** delicacies. **347. After,** according to. **348. mete,** dinner. The author of the fifteenth-century courtesy book printed in *EETS*, 148, after describing in full the serving of dinner, says "as all these sayd servantes and offecers have don at mete so to do at souper" (p. 14). **349. muwe,** coop. **350. breem . . . luce,** bream or carp . . . pike. **stuwe,** fishpond. In the Middle Ages private fishponds were common. **351. but if,** unless. **352. Poynaunt,** piquant. **geere,** equipment (knives, etc.). **353. table dormant,** an article of furniture often mentioned in wills and inventories and occasionally in romances, but unfortunately not described. Its distinctive feature would seem to be that it remained standing, whereas the tables on which people dined consisted of boards on trestles and were removed after the meal. It was occasionally quite large. There are instances in which people were seated. **halle,** the main room of the house, also used for meals. **355. sessiouns,** meetings of the Justices of the Peace, at which he presided. At these sessions (four a year) indicted persons were tried. **356. knyght of the shire,** member of Parliament for his county. **357. anlaas,** a broad two-edged dagger. **gipser,** purse, pouch.

Heeng at his girdel, whit as morne milk.
A shirreve hadde he been, and a contour.
Was nowher swich a worthy vavasour. 360

An **Haberdasshere** and a **Carpenter**,
A **Webbe**, a **Dyere**, and a **Tapycer**,—
And they were clothed alle in o lyveree
Of a solempne and a greet fraternitee.
Ful fressh and newe hir geere apiked was: 365
Hir knyves were chaped noght with bras
But al with silver; wroght ful clene and weel
Hire girdles and hir pouches everydeel.
Wel semed ech of hem a fair burgeys
To sitten in a yeldehalle on a deys. 370
Everich, for the wisdom that he kan,
Was shaply for to been an alderman.
For catel hadde they ynogh and rente,
And eek hir wyves wolde it wel assente;

And elles certeyn were they to blame. 375
It is ful fair to been ycleped "madame,"
And goon to vigilies al bifore,
And have a mantel roialliche ybore.

A **Cook** they hadde with hem for the nones
To boille the chiknes with the marybones, 380
And poudre-marchant tart and galyngale.
Wel koude he knowe a draughte of Londoun
ale.
He koude rooste, and sethe, and broille, and
frye,
Maken mortreux, and wel bake a pye.
But greet harm was it, as it thoughte me, 385
That on his shyne a mormal hadde he.
For blankmanger, that made he with the beste.

A **Shipman** was ther, wonynge fer by
weste;

---

358. Heeng, hung. **morne.** morning. **359. shirreve,** sheriff. **contour.** One of the important duties of the sheriff was to collect the revenue of his county and bring it twice a year to the Exchequer at Westminster. He made final settlement for the year at Michaelmas and cleared his account. It is difficult not to see in Chaucer's *contour* a reference to this function, although the word has also other meanings. **360. vavasour.** In the French chansons de geste it indicates a baron or a member of the lesser nobility. In the feudal hierarchy it represented a grade below the baron and in England sometimes a rather small free-man. In the fourteenth century it was archaic, and Chaucer's use of the term for the Franklin is probably mildly humorous. **361. Haberdasshere,** a dealer in hats or in what we call in the United States "notions" (small wares). **362. Webbe,** weaver. **Tapycer,** primarily a maker of tapestry and carpets. **363. in o lyveree . . .** The fact that they were all wearing one livery shows that they were not dressed in the livery of their respective craft gilds. The *solempne and . . . greet fraternitee* must therefore refer to a parish gild, a religious and fraternal organization of which there were many. The most plausible identification of the gild here meant is that of Thomas J. Garbaty, *JEGP,* LIX. 691–709, who presents good evidence for the gild of St. Fabian and St. Sebastian, attached to St. Botolph's in Aldersgate. All the crafts represented by the five gildsmen belonged to the nonvictualing group, which was supported by John of Gaunt in its struggle with the victualers for the con-trol of the city. They were, however, not among the more belligerent crafts in the group. **365. geere,** apparel. **apiked,** cleaned, adorned. **366. chaped.** A *chape* was a small plate or tip, usually on the end of a scabbard, and the word was some-times used for the scabbard itself. It is difficult to tell whether Chaucer is here referring to the scabbards or the mountings of the knives. **370. yeldehalle,** gildhall. **deys,** dais or platform where the mayor and aldermen sat. **372. shaply,** fit. **alder-man,** the head of the gild and hence a member of the Common Council of the town. **373. catel,** property, possessions. **rente,** income. To maintain the dignity of his office an alderman required money, and the expense was even greater if he were later chosen as mayor. **374. assente.** The verb was sometimes used without a preposition. **376. ycleped "madame."** The wives of aldermen assumed the title "lady." See S. L. Thrupp, *The Merchant Class of Medieval London* (Chicago, 1948), p. 18. **377. vigilies,** vigils, religious services or devotional exercises on the eve of a holy day. Liddell notes that the reference here is probably to vigils on the eve of a gild festival. **al bifore,** at the head of the procession. **379. for the nones,** *lit.* for the occasion, but the phrase came to have little or no meaning and seems often used merely as a convenient device for filling out the line or supplying an easy rime. For an attempt to distinguish shades of meaning see R. M. Lumiansky, *Neophilologus,* XXXV. 29–36. **380. marybones,** an old spelling for "marrowbones." A glance through a medieval cookbook shows a much commoner use of marrow in the recipes than nowadays. **381. poudre-marchant.** Except that it was a kind of spice and was, as Chaucer says, tart, we do not know what it was. The word occurs several times outside of Chaucer, e.g. in *Two Fifteenth-Century Cookery-Books* (EETS, 91), p. 25, where it is added to a kind of pork stew. **galyngale,** a spice made from an aromatic East Indian root, often mentioned in medieval cookery. **383. sethe,** boil. **384. mortreux,** generally explained as a thick soup, and this seems to be one meaning (cf. "mortrewes and potages," *Piers Plowman,* C XVI. 47, but a few lines farther on "mortrews and poddynges," l. 66). The numerous recipes in the fifteenth-century cookbooks referred to in the note to l. 381 above, even those under "potage dyvers" indicate a kind of hash (ground pork or fish, bread crumbs, yolk of egg, spices, etc.). **pye,** meat (or fish) pie. **385. thoughte,** seemed. **386. shyne,** shin. **mormal,** an open sore. For the causes as described by medieval authorities on medicine the reader may consult W. C. Curry, *MLN,* XXXVI. 274–6, incorporated in *Chaucer and the Mediaeval Sciences* (1926). **387. blankmanger,** not the blanc-mange of today, but a dish made (according to one fifteenth-century recipe) by boiling rice and ground almonds in milk, then adding capon in small pieces, sugar, and salt (EETS, 91, p. 85). **388. Shipman,** a ship owner.

Darmouth

For aught I woot, he was of Dertemouthe.
He rood upon a <u>rouncy</u>, as he kouthe, 390
In a gowne of faldyng to the knee.
A daggere hangynge on a laas hadde he
Aboute his nekke, under his arm adoun.
The hoote somer hadde maad his hewe al broun.
rascal
And certeinly he was a good felawe; 395
Ful many a draughte of wyn had he ydrawe
Fro Burdeux-ward, whil that the chapman
    sleep. (steal wine while they sleep)
foolish
Of nyce conscience took he no keep.
If that he faught, and hadde the hyer hond,
By water he sente hem hoom to every lond. 400
But of his craft to rekene wel his tydes,
His stremes, and his daungers hym bisides,
His herberwe, and his moone, his lodemenage,
Ther nas noon swich from Hulle to Cartage.
Hardy he was and wys to undertake; 405
With many a tempest hadde his berd been shake.
He knew alle the havenes, as they were,
Fro Gootlond to the cape of Fynystere,

And every cryke in Britaigne and in Spayne.
His barge ycleped was the **Maudelayne**. 410 Anti-climax
    With us ther was a **Doctour of Phisik;**
In al this world ne was ther noon hym lik,
To speke of phisik and of surgerye,
For he was grounded in astronomye.
He kepte his pacient a ful greet deel 415
In houres by his magyk natureel.
Wel koude he fortunen the ascendent
Of his ymages for his pacient.
He knew the cause of everich maladye, 419
Were it of hoot, or coold, or moyste, or drye,
originated
And where engendred, and of what humour.
He was a verray, parfit praktisour:
The cause yknowe, and of his harm the roote,
Anon he yaf the sike man his boote. remedy
Ful redy hadde he his apothecaries 425
To sende hym drogges and his letuaries,
For ech of hem made oother for to wynne—
Hir frendshipe nas nat newe to bigynne.
Wel knew he the olde Esculapius,

---

389. Dertemouthe. Chaucer's suggestion that the Shipman might have been from Dartmouth was a natural one at the time, since Dartmouth was not only a major port in the Middle Ages but for several years around the time of the Prologue was notorious for the piratical activities of its shipmen. Manly (*New Light*) suggested that Chaucer may have had in mind one Peter Risshenden, who was engaged in such activities and was master of a ship (in 1391) named the *Maudeleyne*. The port records, however, refer to a number of ships with this name. The most famous ship owner and pirate at the time was John Hawley, but he was mayor of Dartmouth and a more important person than Chaucer's Shipman seems to have been. **390. rouncy,** a horse of small size, originally a pack horse, often used for riding (cf. *Romania*, XLVIII. 115–7). **as he kouthe,** as (well as) he could. **391. faldyng,** a soft woolen cloth, of a solid color, often of Irish manufacture. **392. laas,** cord. **394. hoote,** hot. **395. a good felawe.** The expression was sometimes used ironically in the sense of "rascal," and that seems to be the intention here. **396. draughte,** a drink or a quantity drawn off. **397. chapman,** merchant, who was traveling with his cargo. **sleep,** slept. **398. nyce,** foolish. **conscience,** conscience, but the word also means "compassion," "feeling," and this interpretation, suggested by Liddell, has been followed by some commentators. Cf. l. 150. **keep,** heed. **402. stremes,** currents. **daungers hym bisides,** dangers even near at hand, *i.e.* hazards of all kinds. Later *daungers* has a nautical sense of submerged rocks, which would fit the passage well, but the use is not recorded at so early a date. **403. herberwe,** harbor. This is the accepted interpretation. But the word has an astronomical use: "The 'house,' or mansion, position of the sun or a planet in the zodiac." (*NED*) Chaucer uses it in this sense in *The Franklin's Tale* (F 1035), and coupled, as it is in the present line, with *his moone*, it may indicate an element in the Shipman's *lodemenage*, which Bullokar defined in 1616 as "skill of navigation." The usual meaning of lodemenage is "piloting," but a *lodesman* is one who steers a ship at sea as well as in harbors. (see Gower, *Conf. Amant.*, III. 996). **404. Cartage,** Carthage, frequently mentioned by Chaucer, although, as suggested by Manly and earlier by Heidrich, the reference here may be to Cartagena in Spain. **405. wys to undertake,** showed good judgment in his undertakings or risks. **408. Gootlond,** Gotland, an island in the Baltic belonging to Sweden. **cape of Fynystere,** on the northwestern coast of Spain. **409. cryke,** harbor, port (mod. *creek*). **Britaigne,** Brittany. **410. barge,** a sailing vessel of medium size. **411. Phisik,** medicine. **413. To speke of,** in the matter of. **414. astronomye.** The influence of the heavens was considered important in the practice of medieval medicine. See Lynn Thorndike, *A History of Magic and Experimental Science* (8v, 1923–58). **415. kepte,** watched over. **416. magyk natureel,** *i.e.* astrology. **417-8. fortunen the ascendent Of his ymages,** determine the favorable time for making his images. On the making of astrological images, which may be moulded or inscribed, see Curry, chap. I. In astrology the ascendant is "The point of the ecliptic, or degree of the zodiac, which at any moment (esp. *e.g.* at the birth of a child) is just rising above the eastern horizon." (*NED*) **420. of hoot, or coold,** etc. The four humors, the proper balance of which in the body was necessary to health. **421. engendred,** originated. **423. yknowe,** known. **424. boote,** remedy. **426. letuaries,** electuaries, medicines mixed with syrup. **427. wynne,** profit. **429. Esculapius,** etc. The men here mentioned were the authors of the chief medical books of the Middle Ages. Esculapius was the reputed author of a treatise, *De Morborum . . . Causis, Descriptionibus, et Cura,* probably of the seventh century.

And Deyscorides, and eek Rufus,   430
Olde Ypocras, Haly, and Galyen,
Serapion, Razis, and Avycen,
Averrois, Damascien, and Constantyn,
Bernard, and Gatesden, and Gilbertyn.
Of his diete mesurable was he,   435
For it was of no superfluitee,
But of greet norissyng and digestible.
His studie was but litel on the Bible.
In sangwyn and in pers he clad was al,
Lyned with taffata and with sendal;   440
And yet he was but esy of dispence.
He kepte that he wan in pestilence,
For gold in phisik is a cordial;
Therefore he lovede gold in special.

    A good **Wif** was ther of biside **Bathe**,   445
But she was somdel deef, and that was scathe.
Of clooth-makyng she hadde swich an haunt,
She passed hem of Ypres and of Gaunt.
In al the parisshe wif ne was ther noon

That to the offrynge bifore hire sholde goon;   450
And if ther dide, certeyn so wrooth was she,
That she was out of alle charitee.
Hir coverchiefs ful fyne weren of ground;
I dorste swere they weyeden ten pound
That on a Sonday weren upon hir heed.   455
Hir hosen weren of fyn scarlet reed,
Ful streite yteyd, and shoes ful moyste and
   newe.
Boold was hir face, and fair, and reed of hewe.
She was a worthy womman al hir lyve:
Housbondes at chirche dore she hadde fyve,   460
Withouten oother compaignye in youthe,—
But therof nedeth nat to speke as nowthe.
And thries hadde she been at Jerusalem;
She hadde passed many a straunge strem;
At Rome she hadde been, and at Boloigne,   465
In Galice at Seint-Jame, and at Coloigne.
She koude muchel of wandrynge by the weye.
Gat-tothed was she, soothly for to seye.

430. Deyscorides, Dioscorides Pedanius, a Greek botanist and army doctor of the first century A.D. **Rufus,** Rufus of Ephesus, c. A.D. 100, a number of whose medical writings have been preserved. **431. Ypocras,** Hippocrates, the most famous of the Greek physicians, a contemporary of Socrates. **Haly,** Ali Ben el-Abbas, Arabic physician of the tenth century. **Galyen,** Galen, court physician in Rome under Marcus Aurelius (second century A.D.). **432. Serapion, Razis, and Avycen,** Syriac and Arabic authorities. The most famous, although primarily a compiler, was Avicenna (early eleventh century). **433. Averrois,** Averroës, author of a compendium of medicine in Arabic (twelfth century). **Damascien,** probably the younger Serapion (c. 1100). **Constantyn,** Constantinus Africanus (eleventh century), who became a monk at Monte Cassino. See M. Bassan, *Mediaeval Studies,* XXIV. 127–40, and cf. E 1810. **434. Bernard,** etc. These three were all famous physicians a generation or so before Chaucer. Bernard de Gordon taught medicine at Montpellier. John Gaddesden taught at Merton College, Oxford. **Gilbertyn,** Gilbertus Anglicus, was also an English physician. **439. sangwyn,** blood-red. Strutt (*Dress and Habits,* II. 164) interpets the word as "purple," which agrees with the illumination in the Ellesmere MS. **pers,** blue or bluish gray. In the Ellesmere illumination he wears a blue hood trimmed with white fur. Both words are used for cloth of the indicated color. **440. taffata . . . sendal.** Both words refer to kinds of thin and expensive silk. **441. esy of dispence,** careful about spending. **442. in pestilence,** during periods of the plague. **443. cordial,** a medicine good for the heart. In medieval medicine gold was administered in the form of *aurum potabile,* and sometimes a few grains of the metal were mixed with other drugs. **445. good Wif.** As the accentuation shows this was in effect a compound like "gentleman." **446. scathe,** matter for regret (*lit.* harm). **447. haunt,** skill. **448. Ypres . . . Gaunt.** Ypres, Ghent, and other towns in the Low Countries were noted for their fine cloth. **450. to the offrynge bifore hire.** In the *Parson's Tale* (I. 408) the desire of a person to "goon to offryng biforn his neighebor" is one of the sins of pride. **453. coverchiefs,** kerchiefs, scarfs for covering the head. **ground,** texture. **454. ten pound.** Although the *coverchiefs* were often large, draped over wire frames, hung down far in back, and were sometimes ornamented, Chaucer was (Manly notwithstanding) clearly exaggerating here. According to D. E. Wretlind (*MLN,* LXIII. 381–2), the fashion of wearing large headdresses was introduced by Queen Anne. **457. streite yteyd,** tightly fastened. **moyste,** soft, not dried out. The meaning "unworn" suggested by the *NED* is unsupported by any other quotation. **459. worthy.** The word has, of course, numerous overtones, but I take it to imply here that she enjoyed a comfortable economic and social position. **460. at chirche dore.** In the Middle Ages the marriage was performed by the priest on the church porch or in the vestibule, after which the married couple and their friends went inside for the mass. **461. Withouten.** The word may mean "without" or "not to speak of," "besides." While La Vielle in *RR,* 12781, lamenting her lost youth, speaks of "autre compaignie" and Chaucer took the phrase along with other hints from the passage, the ambiguity here is doubtless intended. **462. as nowthe,** at present. **465-6. at Boloigne . . . at Coloigne.** The Wife of Bath had been on pilgrimages to all the famous shrines,—the Holy Sepulchre at Jerusalem, the many churches at Rome, the well-known image of the Virgin at Boulogne, the shrine of St. James of Compostella in Galicia (northwest Spain), the relics of the Three Kings at Cologne. **467. koude,** knew. **468. Gat-tothed,** gap-toothed. Curry (*PMLA,* XXXVII. 30–51) quotes early works on physiognomy where this feature is supposed to indicate a nature vain, bold, lascivious, etc.

Upon an amblere esily she sat,
Ywympled wel, and on hir heed an hat   470
As brood as is a bokeler or a targe;
A foot-mantel aboute hir hipes large,
And on hir feet a paire of spores sharpe.
In felaweshipe wel koude she laughe and carpe.
Of remedies of love she knew per chaunce,   475
For she koude of that art the olde daunce.

  A good man was ther of religioun,
And was a povre **Persoun** of a toun,
But riche he was of hooly thoght and werk.
He was also a lerned man, a clerk,   480
That Cristes gospel trewely wolde preche;
His parisshens devoutly wolde he teche.
Benygne he was, and wonder diligent,
And in adversitee ful pacient,
And swich he was ypreved ofte sithes.   485
Ful looth were hym to cursen for his tithes,
But rather wolde he yeven, out of doute,
Unto his povre parisshens aboute
Of his offryng and eek of his substaunce.
He koude in litel thyng have suffisaunce.   490
Wyd was his parisshe, and houses fer asonder,
But he ne lefte nat, for reyn ne thonder,
In siknesse nor in meschief to visite
The ferreste in his parisshe, muche and lite,
Upon his feet, and in his hand a staf.   495

This noble ensample to his sheep he yaf,
That first he wroghte, and afterward he taughte.
Out of the gospel he tho wordes caughte,
And this figure he added eek therto,
That if gold ruste, what shal iren do?   500
For if a preest be foul, on whom we truste,
No wonder is a lewed man to ruste;
And shame it is, if a preest take keep,
A shiten shepherde and a clene sheep.
Wel oghte a preest ensample for to yive,   505
By his clennesse, how that his sheep sholde lyve.
He sette nat his benefice to hyre
And leet his sheep encombred in the myre
And ran to Londoun unto Seinte Poules
To seken hym a chaunterie for soules,   510
Or with a bretherhed to been withholde;
But dwelte at hoom, and kepte wel his folde,
So that the wolf ne made it nat myscarie;
He was a shepherde and noght a mercenarie.
And though he hooly were and vertuous,   515
He was to synful men nat despitous,
Ne of his speche daungerous ne digne,
But in his techyng discreet and benygne.
To drawen folk to hevene by fairnesse,
By good ensample, this was his bisynesse.   520
But it were any persone obstinat,
What so he were, of heigh or lough estat,

469. **amblere,** a saddle horse. The Ellesmere MS pictures her riding astride, but this was not uncommon. The statement of some editors that Queen Anne introduced the custom of riding side-saddle is open to question. See Thomas Wright, *Homes of Other Days*, pp. 84, 129, etc. The seal of Joan de Stuteville, about 1229, shows her riding side-saddle. See J. H. Round, *Quar. Rev.*, ccv. 541. **470. Ywympled.** See note to l. 151. **471. targe,** shield. The picture of the Wife of Bath in the Camb. Univ. Library MS (Gg. 4. 27) bears out this description. See the appendix to the Chaucer Soc. text of the Ellesmere MS for reproduction. **472. foot-mantel.** In the Ellesmere MS this is a blue apron-like skirt. **474. carpe,** joke. **475. remedies of love.** The phrase was associated with Ovid's *Remedia Amoris*. **476. the olde daunce,** all the tricks of the game. **478. Persoun,** parson or parish priest. **482. parisshens,** parishioners. **485. ypreved,** proved. **ofte sithes,** oftentimes. **486. cursen,** excommunicate. Wyclif says that "wordly clerkis cursen for dymes (tithes) and offryngis, though men ben ful pore" (*English Works*, ed. Matthew, p. 214). The full form of the curse is printed in John Myrk's *Instructions for Parish Priests* (*EETS*, 31), pp. 66–7. **487. yeven,** give. **489. offryng.** In addition to the tithes, fixed by law, the people made voluntary offerings. **substaunce,** fixed income, derived from his benefice (*i.e.* the land, house, barn, etc., including the right to graze his stock on the common pasture) and from tithes, the right, or obligation to collect two shillings in the pound from each member of the parish (paid generally in kind). For an excellent account of the parson's income see J. R. H. Moorman, *Church Life in England in the Thirteenth Century* (Cambridge, 1946). **492. lefte,** left, omitted. **493. meschief,** trouble. **494. ferreste,** farthest. **muche and lite,** the great and small. **496. ensample,** example. **498. tho,** those. **502. lewed,** ignorant. **503. keep,** heed. **504. shiten,** befouled. **507. He sette nat . . .** The practice here alluded to is the subject of much criticism. A priest could engage a curate, generally for much less than the income from his benefice, and become a chantry priest in London. Chantries were established by the well-to-do, the endowment of which paid the stipend of a priest to say masses for the souls of the benefactor and his relatives. The duties of a chantry priest were light. Skeat notes that there were thirty-five of these chantries at St. Paul's, served by fifty-four priests. **508. leet,** left. **511. bretherhed,** gild or fraternity. **withholde,** supported. **516. despitous,** contemptuous. **517. daungerous,** haughty. **digne,** dignified, superior. **520. bisynesse,** constant endeavor. **521. But it were . . .** Elliptical: But if it happened that any person was obstinate.

Hym wolde he snybben sharply for the nonys.
A bettre preest I trowe that nowher noon ys.
He waited after no pompe and reverence,   525
Ne maked hym a spiced conscience,
But Cristes loore and his apostles twelve
He taughte, but first he folwed it hymselve.
  With hym ther was a **Plowman,** was his
      brother,
That hadde ylad of dong ful many a fother;   530
A trewe swynkere and a good was he,
Lyvynge in pees and parfit charitee.
God loved he best with al his hoole herte
At alle tymes, thogh him gamed or smerte,
And thanne his neighebore right as hymselve.
He wolde thresshe, and therto dyke and delve,
For Cristes sake, for every povre wight,   537
Withouten hire, if it lay in his myght.
His tithes payde he ful faire and wel,
Bothe of his propre swynk and his catel.   540
In a tabard he rood upon a mere.
  Ther was also a **Reve,** and a **Millere,**
A **Somnour,** and a **Pardoner** also,
A **Maunciple,** and myself—ther were namo.

The **Millere** was a stout carl for the nones;
Ful byg he was of brawn, and eek of bones.   546
That proved wel, for over al ther he cam,
At wrastlynge he wolde have alwey the ram.
He was short-sholdred, brood, a thikke knarre;
Ther was no dore that he nolde heve of harre,
Or breke it at a rennyng with his heed.   551
His berd as any sowe or fox was reed,
And therto brood, as though it were a spade.
Upon the cop right of his nose he hade
A werte, and theron stood a toft of herys,   555
Reed as the brustles of a sowes erys;
His nosethirles blake were and wyde.
A swerd and bokeler bar he by his syde.
His mouth as greet was as a greet forneys.
He was a janglere and a goliardeys,   560
And that was moost of synne and harlotries.
Wel koude he stelen corn and tollen thries;
And yet he hadde a thombe of gold, pardee.
A whit cote and a blew hood wered he.   564
A baggepipe wel koude he blowe and sowne,
And therwithal he broghte us out of towne.
  A gentil **Maunciple** was ther of a temple,

---

523. snybben, rebuke. **for the nonys,** on the occasion. **525. waited after,** looked for. **526. spiced conscience,** over-scrupulous nature. **527. loore,** teaching. **529. Plowman.** From the description (especially ll. 536–8) it would seem that the Plowman was a freeman rather than a serf. Cf. A. L. Poole, *Obligations of Society in the XII and XIII Centuries* (Oxford, 1946), chap. II. **was his brother.** For the omission of the relative pronoun see Language, §46. **530. ylad,** led, carried. **fother,** cart load. **534. gamed or smerte,** was pleasant or unpleasant. **536. dyke and delve,** make ditches and dig. **540. his propre swynk and his catel,** his own labor and his goods. **541. tabard,** a kind of smock, often confined at the waist by a belt. **mere,** mare, only ridden by the poor. **545. carl,** fellow. **547. That proved wel,** proved . . . to be true (understood). **over al ther,** everywhere where. **548. the ram,** the traditional prize at wrestling matches. Cf. Masefield's *The Widow in the Bye Street.* **549. short-sholdred,** stocky(?). This is the only recorded instance of the word. The *NED* conjectures "thick-set," but this would seem to duplicate the following *thikke.* **knarre,** knotty fellow (LG. *knorre,* a knot in wood). **550. of harre,** off its hinge(s). Several modern instances are on record and Whiting has called attention to one in Trevisa (*MLN,* LXIX. 309–11). **554. cop,** top. **555. werte,** wart. **557. nosethirles,** nostrils. **559. forneys,** cauldron. **560. janglere,** loud talker. **goliardeys,** ribald speaker or story teller. The *scholares vagantes* or wandering scholars of the twelfth century were known as Goliards, from Golias, their supposed leader. Their songs and poems, in Latin, were clever, satirical, scurrilous, and often indecent. **561. harlotries,** vulgarities, ribaldries. **562. tollen,** take his toll or percentage of the grain which he ground. The amount varied with the grain and the custom of the manor, but it was generally between a twentieth or twenty-fourth (by statute) and a sixteenth (in practice), sometimes as much as a thirteenth for a serf. Since the miller generally farmed the mill for a fixed yearly rent, the temptation to increase his profit was great. See H. S. Bennett, *Life on the English Manor* (Cambridge, 1938), chap. VI. **563. thombe of gold.** A miller's thumb is said to become enlarged from constantly feeling the flour and might be regarded as the source of his wealth. On the other hand, the proverb "An honest miller has a thumb of gold" meant that there were no honest millers. **567. Maunciple.** A manciple was a minor employee of an institution, such as a college or one of the Inns of Court, whose principal function was to purchase provisions. **a temple,** one of the Inns of Court: Lincoln's Inn, Gray's Inn, the Inner Temple, and the Middle Temple, all in London. The last two owed their names to the fact that they occupied buildings which had earlier belonged to the Knights Templars. Each had about 200 students or apprentices. Most of these were of noble or gentle birth. Many had no intention of becoming lawyers but wanted to be able to look after their property. They studied the common law and also pursued certain liberal studies. The masters were below the rank of sergeant. The teaching was by lectures and argument. The governing body consisted of the Benchers, equivalent to the Fellows of Oxford and Cambridge. With considerable change of function the Inns of Court still exist. See W. S. Holdsworth, *A History of English Law,* II. 414–31.

Of which achatours myghte take exemple
For to be wise in byynge of vitaille;
For wheither that he payde or took by taille,
Algate he wayted so in his achaat 571
That he was ay biforn and in good staat.
Now is nat that of God a ful fair grace
That swich a lewed mannes wit shal pace
The wisdom of an heep of lerned men? 575
Of maistres hadde he mo than thries ten,
That weren of lawe expert and curious,
Of which ther were a duszeyne in that hous
Worthy to been stywardes of rente and lond
Of any lord that is in Engelond, 580
To make hym lyve by his propre good
In honour dettelees (but if he were wood),
Or lyve as scarsly as hym list desire;
And able for to helpen al a shire
In any caas that myghte falle or happe; 585
And yet this Manciple sette hir aller cappe.

The **Reve** was a sclendre colerik man.
His berd was shave as ny as ever he kan;
His heer was by his erys ful round yshorn;
His top was dokked lyk a preest biforn. 590
Ful longe were his legges and ful lene,
Ylyk a staf; ther was no calf ysene.

Wel koude he kepe a gerner and a bynne;
Ther was noon auditour koude on him wynne.
Wel wiste he by the droghte and by the reyn 595
The yeldynge of his seed and of his greyn.
His lordes sheep, his neet, his dayerye,
His swyn, his hors, his stoor, and his pultrye
Was hoolly in this Reves governynge,
And by his covenant yaf the rekenynge, 600
Syn that his lord was twenty yeer of age.
Ther koude no man brynge hym in arrerage.
Ther nas baillif, ne hierde, nor oother hyne,
That he ne knew his sleighte and his covyne;
They were adrad of hym as of the deeth. 605
His wonyng was ful faire upon an heeth;
With grene treës shadwed was his place.
He koude bettre than his lord purchace.
Ful riche he was astored pryvely:
His lord wel koude he plesen subtilly, 610
To yeve and lene hym of his owene good,
And have a thank, and yet a cote and hood.
In youthe he hadde lerned a good myster;
He was a wel good wrighte, a carpenter.
This Reve sat upon a ful good stot, 615
That was al pomely grey and highte Scot.
A long surcote of pers upon he hade,

568. **achatours,** purchasers, what we call "purchasing agents." 570. **by taille,** by tally, on account. The tally was a piece of wood on which the amounts were indicated by notches. It was then spilt and the buyer and seller each retained half. 571. **Algate,** always. **wayted,** watched. **achaat,** purchase. 572. **ay biforn,** always ahead. 574. **lewed,** unlearned. 577. **curious,** skilful. 579. **stywardes.** A steward was the chief officer or supervisor of the manors of a lord, and presided at the manor court in the absence of the lord. **rente,** income. 581. **by his propre good,** on his income. 582. **wood,** mad. 583. **scarsly,** economically. 584. **al a shire,** a whole county. 586. **sette hir aller cappe,** made a fool of them all. This slang or colloquial expression is not known outside of Chaucer. Cf. A 3143. 587. **Reve.** Unlike the steward, the reeve was attached to the manor, was responsible for whatever was produced, saw that the work was done, and kept a full account. He was chosen from among the serfs, and, having lived among them all his life, knew all their tricks (cf. l. 604). His appointment was for one year, but many reeves were reappointed (as they accounts show) year after year, sometimes over a period of twenty years and more (cf. l. 601). Most were illiterate; they depended for their records upon an excellent memory and notches in the gate post, until a professional scribe drew up the account for audit by the steward and other representatives of the owner. The reeve received a stipend (generally five shillings a year) and other perquisites,—free grazing, exemption from customary works, etc. There were also many opportunities for taking a little here and a little there (cf. l. 609). See N. J. Hone, *The Manor and Manorial Records* (1925) and an excellent discussion in H. S. Bennett, *Life on the English Manor,* chap. VII. 590. **dokked,** cut short (across the forehead). 592. **ysene,** visible. 593. **gerner,** garner, storehouse for grain. 594. **on him wynne,** get the better of him. 597. **neet,** cattle. **dayerye,** milch cows. 598. **stoor,** live stock. 600. **covenant,** terms of his appointment. **yaf,** gave. 603. **hierde,** herdsman. **hyne,** hind, farm laborer. 604. **sleighte,** cunning. **covyne,** fraud, deceit. 605. **the deeth,** the plague. 606. **wonyng,** habitation. **heeth,** a piece of uncultivated land. 608. **purchace,** increase his possessions. 609. **astored,** supplied, stocked. **pryvely,** privately (in view of the two following lines), rather than secretly. 610. **His lord,** etc. He could please his lord by lending him what he had stolen from him. 613. **myster,** craft, trade. 615. **stot,** probably a "farm horse." The *Catholicon Anglicum* (EETS, 75) in the note on p. 366 cites many occurrences of the word, mostly in association with other farm animals. 616. **pomely,** dappled. **highte,** was named. **Scot,** still said to be a common name for a horse in Norfolk. 617. **surcote,** an outer coat, more often characteristic of the upper classes; also worn by knights over armor and embroidered with a heraldic device. **pers,** blue, bluish gray.

And by his syde he baar a rusty blade.
Of Northfolk was this Reve of which I telle,
Biside a toun men clepen Baldeswelle. 620
Tukked he was as is a frere aboute,
And evere he rood the hyndreste of oure route.
 A **Somonour** was ther with us in that place,
That hadde a fyr-reed cherubynnes face,
For saucefleem he was, with eyen narwe. 625
As hoot he was and lecherous as a sparwe,
With scalled browes blake and piled berd.
Of his visage children were aferd.
Ther nas quyksilver, lytarge, ne brymstoon,
Boras, ceruce, ne oille of tartre noon, 630
Ne oynement that wolde clense and byte,
That hym myghte helpen of his whelkes white,
Nor of the knobbes sittynge on his chekes.
Wel loved he garleek, oynons, and eek lekes,
And for to drynken strong wyn, reed as
 blood; 635
Thanne wolde he speke and crie as he were
 wood.
And whan that he wel dronken hadde the wyn,

Thanne wolde he speke no word but Latyn.
A fewe termes hadde he, two or thre,
That he had lerned out of som decree; 640
No wonder is—he herde it al the day;
And eek ye knowen wel how that a jay
Kan clepen "Watte" as wel as kan the pope.
But whoso koude in oother thyng hym grope,
Thanne hadde he spent al his philosophie; 645
Ay "*Questio quid iuris*" wolde he crie.
He was a gentil harlot and a kynde;
A bettre felawe sholde men noght fynde.
He wolde suffre for a quart of wyn
A good felawe to have his concubyn 650
A twelf-monthe, and excuse hym atte fulle;
Ful prively a fynch eek koude he pulle.
And if he foond owher a good felawe,
He wolde techen hym to have noon awe
In swich caas of the ercedekenes curs, 655
But if a mannes soule were in his purs;
For in his purs he sholde ypunysshed be.
"Purs is the ercedekenes helle," seyde he.
But wel I woot he lyed right in dede;

620. Baldeswelle, Bawdswell, in northern Norfolk. For a conjecture on the identity of the Reeve, see Manly, *Some New Light on Chaucer.* **622. route,** company. **623. Somonour.** A summoner was a petty officer who cited persons to appear in court; but in the fourteenth century the term generally refers to such an officer of the archdeacon. The archdeacon (cf. l. 658) was the principal administrative assistant to the bishop, looking after the church revenues and the repair of property, supervising and disciplining the clergy, and even making visitations. Until largely stripped of power by the Council of Trent (1553) the archdeacon exercised extensive authority. From the point of view of Chaucer's Summoner one of his main functions was to preside over the archdeacon's court, which had jurisdiction in matrimonial cases and in moral offenses such as adultery and fornication, both clerical and lay. Bribery was not unknown and from other contemporary references besides Chaucer's (see also *The Friar's Tale*) the corruption which he attributes to the Summoner was widespread. There is a study of the English summoner by L. A. Haselmayer in *Speculum*, XII. 43–57. **624. fyr-reed cherubynnes face.** The red face with which cherubs were painted in the Middle Ages was proverbial. The description which follows of the Summoner's repulsive appearance indicates, as Curry has shown, *alopicia*, considered by medieval medical authorities as a form of leprosy. It must be remembered, however, that many diseases were not well defined in the Middle Ages, and that even the terms *leper* and *leprous* could refer to other things than leprosy. **625. saucefleem,** afflicted with red pimples and inflammation of the skin. **eyen narwe.** The slit-like eyes, produced by the swelling of the face and eyelids, were characteristic of alopicia. **626. lecherous as a sparwe.** That the sparrow was lecherous is a common medieval notion. In *PF* 351 Chaucer calls the bird Venus's son. **627. scalled,** scabby. **piled berd.** The falling of the hair is compared by medieval writers to the shedding of the fox in summer. **629. lytarge,** litharge, protoxide of lead, also white lead. In this enumeration Chaucer is also following the prescription of medical authorities of the time. **630. Boras,** borax. **ceruce,** ceruse, another name for white lead. **oille of tartre,** cream of tartar. **632. whelkes,** pimples filled with pus. **634. garleek . . . lekes.** An echo of *Num.* 11:5, sometimes coupled in the Middle Ages with moral depravity (see R. E. Kaske, *MLN*, LXXIV. 481–4). **640. decree,** ordinance. **642. jay,** a noisy bird, with some of the characteristics of the magpie and parrot. **643. Kan clepen "Watte",** can say Walter. **644. grope,** probe, test. **646. *Questio quid iuris*.** The question is, "what point of the law (applies)?" J. W. Spargo, *MLN*, LXII. 119–22, takes it as a reference to the writ of *Quid iuris clamat*, but the explanation is open to doubt. **647. harlot,** fellow. **650. good felawe,** used ironically with (contextual) implications of rascality. Cf. l. 395, above. **650. to have his concubyn.** Sometimes taken to refer to priests who lived with women, but there is nothing in the text to indicate this. **651. atte fulle,** completely. **652. a fynch eek koude he pulle.** The expression to *pull a finch* (i.e. to pluck a bird) normally means "to cheat a person," but Kittredge showed (*MP*, VII. 475–7) that it also had an obscene sense and that the Summoner had immoral relations with women. **653. foond owher,** found anywhere. **655. ercedekenes curs,** archdeacon's excommunication. **656. But if,** provided.

Of cursyng oghte ech gilty man him drede, 660
For curs wol slee right as assoillyng savith,
And also war hym of a *Significavit.*
In daunger hadde he at his owene gise
The yonge girles of the diocise,
And knew hir conseil, and was al hir reed. 665
A gerland hadde he set upon his heed
As greet as it were for an alestake.
A bokeleer hadde he maad hym of a cake.
    With hym ther rood a gentil **Pardoner**
Of Rouncivale, his freend and his compeer, 670
That streight was comen fro the court of Rome.
Ful loude he soong "Com hider, love, to me!"
This Somonour bar to hym a stif burdoun;
Was nevere trompe of half so greet a soun.
This Pardoner hadde heer as yelow as wex, 675
But smothe it heeng as dooth a strike of flex;
By ounces henge his lokkes that he hadde,
And therwith he his shuldres overspradde;
But thynne it lay, by colpons oon and oon.
But hood, for jolitee, wered he noon, 680

For it was trussed up in his walet.
Hym thoughte he rood al of the newe jet;
Dischevelee, save his cappe, he rood al bare.
Swiche glarynge eyen hadde he as an hare.
A vernycle hadde he sowed upon his cappe. 685
His walet lay biforn hym in his lappe,
Bretful of pardoun, comen from Rome al hoot.
A voys he hadde as smal as hath a goot.
No berd hadde he, ne nevere sholde have;
As smothe it was as it were late shave. 690
I trowe he were a geldyng or a mare.
But of his craft, fro Berwyk into Ware,
Ne was ther swich another pardoner;
For in his male he hadde a pilwe-beer,
Which that he seyde was Oure Lady veyl: 695
He seyde he hadde a gobet of the seyl
That Seint Peter hadde, whan that he wente
Upon the see, til Jhesu Crist hym hente.
He hadde a croys of latoun ful of stones,
And in a glas he hadde pigges bones. 700
But with thise relikes, whan that he fond

661. slee, slay. **assoillyng,** absolution. **662. war hym,** beware. ***Significavit,*** the opening word in the writ issued by the civil authorites at the request of the bishop to seize the convicted party. **663. In daunger,** in his power. **at his owene gise.** The phrase occurs also at A 1789, where the meaning is "at will," "as he pleases," which fits the present line as well. The phrase thus corresponds to OF. *a sa guise;* see Tobler-Lommatzsch, *s.v.* With *gise* in the commoner sense of "way, manner" Chaucer generally uses *in.* **664. girles.** The word means "young people of either sex," but at A 3769 Chaucer uses it for a young woman and it may well have its modern meaning here. Cf. M. W. Bloomfield, *PQ,* xxviii. 503–7. **665. counseil,** confidence, secrets. **reed,** counsel, but here seems to be used in the sense of "adviser." **666. gerland,** garland, wreath. **667. alestake.** A horizontal pole, usually above the door, extending out from an alehouse, with a garland on the end. The garland was not always in the shape of a wreath. **669. Pardoner.** A pardoner was generally a minor ecclesiastic, but some pardoners were laymen. They purchased small strips of parchment with papal seals attached—Manly estimates the cost as not more than a penny apiece—and then sold them to the public. The little "pardons" were bulls of indulgence and could be purchased in lieu of other forms of penance. Some were forgeries. The proceeds went supposedly to a religious house, but there were many dishonest pardoners. In addition to selling indulgences, pardoners exhibited false relics. The class was often satirized and condemned, even by the most devout members of the Church. **670. Rouncivale,** at Charing Cross, then on the edge of London. It was a cell (consisting of a hospital and a chapel) of the convent of Our Lady of Roncevalles in Navarre. **compeer,** comrade. **672. "Com hider, love, to me!"** a line, probably the refrain, of a popular song. **673. a stif burdoun,** a strong bass. In part singing the *burden* in England was the lowest voice (on the Continent the highest). See Gustave Reese, *Music in the Middle Ages,* p. 339. As Miss Dieckmann notes (*MP,* xxvi. 279–82), it was probably droned. **674. trompe,** trumpet. **676. heeng,** hung. **strike,** hank. **flex,** flax. **677. ounces,** small strands. **679. colpons,** shreds. **oon and oon,** one by one. **680. jolitee,** fun, levity. **681. trussed,** packed. **walet,** bag, knapsack. Note the accent here on the final syllable but cf. l. 686. **682. of the newe jet,** in the latest style. **683. Dischevelee,** loose, unconfined. **bare,** bareheaded. **684. glarynge,** staring. **685. vernycle,** a copy of the handkerchief, preserved at Rome, given by St. Veronica to Christ when carrying the cross. It received an imprint of His face. **687. Bretful,** brimfull. **pardoun,** indulgence. **691. geldyng,** eunuch. **692. craft,** occupation, trade. **fro Berwyk into Ware.** Berwick-on-Tweed is on the Scottish border. Ware, in Hertfordshire, is about twenty miles north of London. The phrase means from one end of England to the other. The choice of Ware was doubtless dictated by the rime. **694. male,** bag; cf. *mail*-bag. **pilwe-beer,** pillowcase. **695. Lady,** Lady's. **696. gobet,** gobbet, piece. Nowadays the word is likely to suggest grossness, a large piece or chunk, and this meaning is as old as Chaucer. See *NED, s.v. gobbet,* 3. **seyl,** sail (of St. Peter's boat). **698. hente,** caught hold of. The reference is to Christ's extending a helping hand to Peter when he walked on the water and became afraid. See *Matthew,* 14: 29–31. **699. croys,** cross. **latoun,** a metal made of copper and zinc; brass. **stones,** precious stones (or imitations). **700. glas,** glass container.

A povre person dwellynge upon lond,
Upon a day he gat hym moore moneye
Than that the person gat in monthes tweye;
And thus, with feyned flaterye and japes, 705
He made the person and the peple his apes.
But trewely to tellen atte laste,
He was in chirche a noble ecclesiaste.
Wel koude he rede a lessoun or a storie,
But alderbest he song an offertorie; 710
For wel he wiste, whan that song was songe,
He moste preche and wel affile his tonge
To wynne silver, as he ful wel koude;
Therefore he song the murierly and loude.
Now have I toold you shortly, in a clause, 715
Th'estaat, th'array, the nombre, and eek the
cause
Why that assembled was this compaignye
In Southwerk at this gentil hostelrye
That highte the Tabard, faste by the Belle.
But now is tyme to yow for to telle 720
How that we baren us that ilke nyght,
Whan we were in that hostelrie alyght;
And after wol I telle of oure viage
And al the remenaunt of oure pilgrimage.
But first I pray yow, of youre curteisye, 725
That ye n'arette it nat my vileynye,
Thogh that I pleynly speke in this mateere,
To telle yow hir wordes and hir cheere,
Ne thogh I speke hir wordes proprely.
For this ye knowen al so wel as I, 730
Whoso shal telle a tale after a man,

He moot reherce as ny as evere he kan
Everich a word, if it be in his charge,
Al speke he never so rudeliche and large,
Or ellis he moot telle his tale untrewe, 735
Or feyne thyng, or fynde wordes newe.
He may nat spare, althogh he were his brother;
He moot as wel seye o word as another.
Crist spak hymself ful brode in hooly writ,
And wel ye woot no vileynye is it. 740
Eek Plato seith, whoso kan hym rede,
The wordes moote be cosyn to the dede.
Also I prey yow to foryeve it me,
Al have I nat set folk in hir degree
Heere in this tale, as that they sholde stonde, 745
My wit is short, ye may wel understonde.
Greet chiere made oure Hoost us everichon,
And to the soper sette he us anon.
He served us with vitaille at the beste; 749
Strong was the wyn, and wel to drynke us leste.
A semely man **Oure Hooste** was withalle
For to been a marchal in an halle.
A large man he was with eyen stepe—
A fairer burgeys was ther noon in Chepe—
Boold of his speche, and wys, and wel ytaught,
And of manhod hym lakkede right naught. 756
Eek therto he was right a myrie man,
And after soper pleyen he bigan,
And spak of myrthe amonges othere thynges,
Whan that we hadde maad our rekenynges, 760
And seyde thus: "Now, lordynges, trewely,
Ye been to me right welcome, hertely;

---

702. **person,** parson. **upon lond,** in the country. 703. **gat,** got. 705. **japes,** deceits. 706. **He made. . . apes,** i.e. he made monkeys of them. 707. **atte laste,** finally, after all. 709. **lessoun,** a "lectio," one of the passages from the Bible or patristic literature read at matins, evensong, or any of the canonical hours. **storie,** a "historia" or series of "lectiones," such as the life of a saint or other appropriate narrative. On this liturgical term see K. Young, *MLN,* xxx. 97–9. 710. **offertorie,** the chant (verses of a psalm and an antiphon) preparatory to the ceremonial offering of the Bread and Wine, at which time the people made their offerings. 712. **He moste preche.** Since the offering that accompanied the offertory went to the church, the Pardoner's sermon was presumably to prepare the people to buy his pardons and pay to see or touch his relics. See the Prologue to *The Pardoner's Tale.* **affile,** make smooth. 715. **in a clause,** in a few words. 719. **the Belle.** See the note to l. 20. **the Belle,** presumably another inn, but it cannot be identified. See Baum, *MLN,* xxxiv. 307–9. 721. **ilke,** same. 723. **viage,** trip, journey. 726. **n'arette,** do not attribute. **my vileynye,** to my ill-breeding. 728. **cheere,** behavior. 729. **proprely,** exactly. 732. **moot,** must. 733. **charge,** power. 734. **Al,** although. **large,** broadly. 736. **feyne,** invent. 738. **moot,** may. **o word,** one word. 741. **Plato.** Chaucer knew Plato only at second hand. He found this statement in Boethius (III, pr. 12) or in *RR,* 7104 ff. 744. **Al,** although. 747. **chiere,** welcome. 750. **us leste,** it pleased us. 752. **marchal in an halle.** The marshall was the person in authority at the serving of meals, supervised the servants, and quelled disturbances if necessary. He also assigned guests to their rooms and saw that they were properly provided for. His duties are described in detail in a fifteenth-century courtesy book published in *EETS,* 148. 753. **stepe.** See note to l. 201 above. 754. **burgeys,** a substantial citizen. **Chepe,** Cheapside, the main business street of London in Chaucer's day. 758. **pleyen,** joke, be sociable. 760. **maad our rekenynges,** i.e. paid our bills. 761. **lordynges,** used for "ladies and gentlemen."

For by my trouthe, if that I shal nat lye,
I saugh nat this yeer so myrie a compaignye
Atones in this herberwe as is now.   765
Fayn wolde I doon yow myrthe, wiste I how.
And of a myrthe I am right now bythoght,
To doon yow ese, and it shal coste noght.

    Ye goon to Caunterbury—God yow speede!
The blisful martir quite yow youre meede!   770
And wel I woot, as ye goon by the weye,
Ye shapen yow to talen and to pleye;
For trewely, confort ne myrthe is noon
To ride by the weye doumb as a stoon;
And therfore wol I maken yow disport,   775
As I seyde erst, and doon yow som confort.
And if yow liketh alle by oon assent
For to stonden at my juggement,
And for to werken as I shal yow seye,
To-morwe, whan ye riden by the weye,   780
Now, by my fader soule that is deed,
But ye be myrie, I wol yeve yow myn heed!
Hoold up youre hondes, withouten moore
    speche.”

    Oure conseil was nat longe for to seche.   784
Us thoughte it was noght worth to make it wys,
And graunted hym withouten moore avys,
And bad him seye his voirdit as hym leste.
“Lordynges,” quod he, “now herkneth for the
    beste;
But taak it nought, I prey yow, in desdeyn.
This is the poynt, to speken short and pleyn,   790
That ech of yow, to shorte with oure weye,
In this viage shal telle tales tweye
To Caunterbury-ward, I mene it so,

And homward he shal tellen othere two,
Of aventures that whilom han bifalle.   795
And which of yow that bereth hym best of alle,
That is to seyn, that telleth in this caas
Tales of best sentence and moost solaas,
Shal have a soper at oure aller cost
Heere in this place, sittynge by this post,   800
Whan that we come agayn fro Caunterbury.
And for to make yow the moore mury,
I wol myselven goodly with yow ryde,
Right at myn owene cost, and be youre gyde;
And whoso wole my juggement withseye   805
Shal paye al that we spenden by the weye.
And if ye vouchesauf that it be so,
Tel me anon withouten wordes mo,
And I wol erly shape me therfore.”

    This thyng was graunted, and oure othes
    swore   810
With ful glad herte, and preyden hym also
That he wolde vouchesauf for to do so,
And that he wolde been oure governour,
And of our tales juge and reportour,
And sette a soper at a certeyn pris,   815
And we wol reuled been at his devys
In heigh and lough; and thus by oon assent
We been acorded to his juggement.
And therupon the wyn was fet anon;
We dronken, and to reste wente echon,   820
Withouten any lenger taryynge.

    A-morwe, whan that day bigan to sprynge,
Up roos oure Hoost, and was oure aller cok,
And gadrede us togidre alle in a flok,
And forth we riden a litel moore than paas   825

---

765. Atones, at one time. **herberwe,** inn. **768. To doon yow ese,** to please or entertain you. **769. goon,** are going. **770 quite,** repay, give in return. **meede,** reward. **772. shapen . . . pleye,** intend to talk or tell anecdotes and have a good time. **773. ne,** nor. **775. disport,** pleasure, amusement. **776. erst,** before. **782. yeve,** give. **784. conseil,** counsel, deliberation. **785. Us thoughte,** it seemed to us. **worth to make it wys,** worth while deliberating. Although this is the only instance of the phrase known to the *NED*, the use of the phrase *to make it* with other adjectives is fairly common. Cf. *to make it tough, quaint,* etc. (*BD* 531, *TC* 3. 87, etc.). **787. voirdit,** verdict, decision. **791. to shorte . . . weye,** to shorten our way with. **794. othere two.** This plan which calls for four tales from each pilgrim was never completed, By the time Chaucer got to the Parson's Prologue he had come to think in terms of one story each. See the introduction. **795. whilom,** once upon a time. **798. sentence,** wisdom, moral truth. **799. oure aller cost,** the cost of us all. **802. mury,** merry. **803. goodly,** gladly. **805. withseye,** oppose, *lit.* contradict. **809. shape me,** prepare myself. **811. preyden.** The subject is understood. **814. reportour.** As Manly observes, this must mean that he was to report on their merits. **816. devys,** will, desire. **817. In heigh and lough,** in all respects. The phrase is patterned after the Latin *in alto et basso;* see any Law Dictionary. **819. the wyn was fet.** It was the custom to drink a little wine before going to bed. **fet,** fetched. **820. echon,** each one. **822. A-morwe,** in the morning. **823. oure aller cok,** the rooster who wakened us all. **825. riden,** rode. **paas,** a foot-pace or walk.

Unto the wateryng of Seint Thomas;
And there oure Hoost bigan his hors areste
And seyde, "Lordynges, herkneth, if yow leste.
Ye woot youre foreward, and I it yow recorde.
If even-song and morwe-song accorde, 830
Lat se now who shal telle the firste tale.
As evere mote I drynke wyn or ale,
Whoso be rebel to my juggement
Shal paye for al that by the wey is spent. 834
Now draweth cut, er that we ferrer twynne;
He which that hath the shorteste shal bigynne.
Sire Knyght," quod he, "my mayster and my
    lord,
Now draweth cut, for that is myn accord.
Cometh neer," quod he, "my lady Prioresse.
And ye, sire Clerk, lat be youre shamefastnesse,
Ne studieth noght; ley hond to, every man!"

Anon to drawen every wight bigan, 842
And shortly for to tellen as it was,
Were it by aventure, or sort, or cas,
The sothe is this, the cut fil to the Knyght, 845
Of which ful blithe and glad was every wyght,
And telle he moste his tale, as was resoun,
By foreward and by composicioun,
As ye han herd; what nedeth wordes mo?
And whan this goode man saugh that it was so,
As he that wys was and obedient 851
To kepe his foreward by his free assent,
He seyde, "Syn I shal bigynne the game,
What, welcome be the cut, a Goddes name!
Now lat us ryde, and herkneth what I seye." 855
And with that word we ryden forth oure weye,
And he bigan with right a myrie cheere
His tale anon, and seyde as ye may heere.

The Knight's Tale

Heere bigynneth the Knyghtes Tale.

Whilom, as olde stories tellen us,
Ther was a duc that highte Theseus; 860
Of Atthenes he was lord and governour,
And in his tyme swich a conquerour,
That gretter was ther noon under the sonne.
Ful many a riche contree hadde he wonne;
What with his wysdom and his chivalrie, 865
He conquered al the regne of Femenye,
That whilom was ycleped Scithia,

And weddede the queene Ypolita,
And broghte hire hoom with hym in his contree
With muchel glorie and greet solempnytee, 870
And eek hir yonge suster Emelye.
And thus with victorie and with melodye
Lete I this noble duc to Atthenes ryde,
And al his hoost in armes hym bisyde.
    And certes, if it nere to long to heere, 875
I wolde have toold yow fully the manere

826. the wateryng of Seint Thomas, St. Thomas a Watering, a brook at the second milestone on the London-Canterbury road. 828. leste, may please. 829. foreward, agreement. recorde, recall. 832. mote, may. 835. draweth cut, draw lots. The form draweth is the imper. plur., used in polite address. The material used was pieces of straw of different lengths. 838. accord, decision, but the use of the word seems to be somewhat forced. 840. shamefastnesse, shyness, bashfulness. 844. by aventure, or sort, or cas. All three words mean "by chance." 848. composicioun, agreement. 854. a Goddes name, in God's name.

The Knight's Tale. In the Prologue to The Legend of Good Women, (see ll. 414 ff.) Alceste, in coming to the defense of the poet when he has been upbraided by the God of Love, mentions among the poems which he has written "in preysing of your name" one which she describes as "al the love of Palamon and Arcite of Thebes, thogh the storye ys knowen lyte."

859. Whilom, once upon a time. 865. chivalrie, knightly exploits. 866. regne, kingdom. Femenye, the country of the Amazons (L. femina, "woman"), also called Amazonia. Bartholomew Anglicus in the thirteenth century located it "partly in Asia, partly in Europe." 868. Ypolita, Hippolyta. 870. muchel . . . solempnytee, much pomp and ceremony. 871. suster, sister. 872. with victorie, victoriously. 875. nere, were not.

How wonnen was the regne of Femenye
By Theseus and by his chivalrye;
And of the grete bataille for the nones
Bitwixen Atthenes and Amazones;   880
And how asseged was Ypolita,
The faire, hardy queene of Scithia;
And of the feste that was at hir weddynge,
And of the tempest at hir hoom-comynge;
But al that thyng I moot as now forbere.   885
I have, God woot, a large feeld to ere,
And wayke been the oxen in my plough.
The remenant of the tale is long ynough.
I wol nat letten eek noon of this route;
Lat every felawe telle his tale aboute,   890
And lat se now who shal the soper wynne;
And ther I lefte, I wol ayeyn bigynne.

This duc, of whom I make mencioun,
Whan he was come almoost unto the toun,
In al his wele and in his mooste pride,   895
He was war, as he caste his eye aside,
Where that ther kneled in the heighe weye

A compaignye of ladyes, tweye and tweye,
Ech after oother, clad in clothes blake;
But swich a cry and swich a wo they make   900
That in this world nys creature lyvynge
That herde swich another waymentynge;
And of this cry they nolde nevere stenten
Til they the reynes of his brydel henten.
"What folk been ye, that at myn hom-
comynge   905
Perturben so my feste with criynge?"
Quod Theseus. "Have ye so greet envye
Of myn honour, that thus compleyne and crye?
Or who hath yow mysboden or offended?
And telleth me if it may been amended,   910
And why that ye been clothed thus in blak."

The eldeste lady of hem alle spak,
Whan she hadde swowned with a deedly cheere,
That it was routhe for to seen and heere.
She seyde: "Lord, to whom Fortune hath yiven
Victorie, and as a conqueror to lyven,   916
Nat greveth us youre glorie and youre honour,

This is, of course, the subject of *The Knight's Tale* and indicates that what now constitutes the first of the stories told on the road to Canterbury had been written earlier as a separate poem. Like *Troilus and Criseyde* this poem is based on an Italian original, the *Teseida of Boccaccio, a poem of nearly 10,000 lines*. Chaucer's narrative is less than a quarter its length, and he has taken from Boccaccio little more than the outline of the story. Only a few hundred lines scattered through *The Knight's Tale* can properly be described as "translated."

While the story grows out of the love of Palamon and Arcite for the same lady, it is a tale of chivalry and sentiment rather than a love story. There is in it little or none of the psychological complexity which enriches the *Troilus* with so many overtones. Emily, the heroine, by her very position in the story, can do nothing; she can appear only as a young woman of grace and beauty for whom Palamon and Arcite strive. We are thus deprived of any equivalent of the struggle that goes on in the mind of Criseyde, and to that extent it lacks the subtlety and the modern appeal of *Troilus and Criseyde*. In its own way, however, it is a carefully wrought narrative.

Earlier scholars such as Ten Brink, Koch, and Skeat believed that the poem was originally written in seven-line stanzas. They also considered its date of composition to have been in the early 1370's. The stanzaic theory was questioned by Pollard (Globe *Chaucer*) and by Mather (Furnivall *Miscellany*) and disposed of by Tatlock in his *Development and Chronology of Chaucer's Works*. Moreover, so early a date has likewise been generally abandoned. Instead, it would seem that a date around 1381–2 would best fit the facts, especially if we accept the interpretation of lines 884 and 2459 as allusions to the arrival of Anne of Bohemia in England (Dec. 18, 1381) and the Peasants' Revolt (May-June, 1381). It is not impossible that Chaucer touched the poem up in places when fitting it into *The Canterbury Tales;* thus he may have added or rewritten some lines in the account of the tournament at a date subsequent to the tournament at Smithfield in 1390, for which he supervised the erection of the scaffolds (see J. Parr, *PMLA*, LX. 315–324, and cf. R. A. Pratt, *ibid.*, LXIII. 726–39). Basically, however, it is a good example of Chaucer's transference of earlier work to the larger project of *The Canterbury Tales* when he had individual pieces on hand and could fit them into his plan.

878. chivalrye, body of knights. **879. for the nones,** one of the cases where the phrase may be intensive, "especially." Lumiansky, *Neophilologus*, XXXV. 31, however, suggests that here it means "for that purpose." **881. asseged,** besieged. **884. the tempest at hir hoom-comynge.** Since there is no mention of a tempest at their home-coming in the *Teseida*, Lowes suggested that this is an allusion to the violent storm (*maris commotio*) which occurred after the landing of Anne of Bohemia in England. See *MLN*, XIX. 240–3. W. C. Curry, however, argues (*MLN*, XXXVI. 272–4) that Chaucer is merely referring to the noise and tumult of the crowd. **886. ere,** plow. **889. I wol nat letten,** I don't wish to hinder. This and the three following lines must have been part of the revision mentioned in the introductory note. **890. aboute,** in his turn. **892. ther,** where. **898. tweye and tweye,** two by two. **902. waymentynge,** lamentation. **903. stenten,** stop. **904. henten,** seized. **908. compleyne,** (ye) complain. **909. mysboden,** insulted.

But we biseken mercy and socour.
Have mercy on oure wo and oure distresse!
Som drope of pitee, thurgh thy gentillesse, 920
Upon us wrecched wommen lat thou falle.
For, certes, lord, ther is noon of us alle,
That she ne hath been a duchesse or a queene.
Now be we caytyves, as it is wel seene,
Thanked be Fortune and hire false wheel, 925
That noon estaat assureth to be weel.
And certes, lord, to abyden youre presence,
Heere in this temple of the goddesse Clemence
We han ben waitynge al this fourtenyght.
Now help us, lord, sith it is in thy myght. 930
    I, wrecche, which that wepe and wayle thus,
Was whilom wyf to kyng Cappaneus,
That starf at Thebes—cursed be that day!
And alle we that been in this array
And maken al this lamentacioun, 935
We losten alle oure housbondes at that toun,
Whil that the seege theraboute lay.
And yet now the olde Creon, weylaway!
That lord is now of Thebes the citee,
Fulfild of ire and of iniquitee, 940
He, for despit and for his tirannye,
To do the dede bodyes vileynye
Of alle oure lordes whiche that been yslawe,
Hath alle the bodyes on an heep ydrawe,
And wol nat suffren hem, by noon assent, 945
Neither to been yburyed nor ybrent,
But maketh houndes ete hem in despit."
    And with that word, withouten moore
        respit,
They fillen gruf and criden pitously, 949
"Have on us wrecched wommen som mercy,
And lat oure sorwe synken in thyn herte."
    This gentil duc doun from his courser sterte

With herte pitous, whan he herde hem speke.
Hym thoughte that his herte wolde breke,
Whan he saugh hem so pitous and so maat, 955
That whilom weren of so greet estaat;
And in his armes he hem alle up hente,
And hem conforteth in ful good entente,
And swoor his ooth, as he was trewe knyght,
He wolde doon so ferforthly his myght 960
Upon the tiraunt Creon hem to wreke,
That al the peple of Grece sholde speke
How Creon was of Theseus yserved
As he that hadde his deeth ful wel deserved.
    And right anoon, withouten moore abood,
His baner he desplayeth, and forth rood 966
To Thebes-ward, and al his hoost biside.
No neer Atthenes wolde he go ne ride,
Ne take his ese fully half a day,
But onward on his wey that nyght he lay, 970
And sente anon Ypolita the queene,
And Emelye, hir yonge suster sheene,
Unto the toun of Atthenes to dwelle,
And forth he rit; ther is namoore to telle.
    The rede statue of Mars, with spere and
        targe, 975
So shyneth in his white baner large,
That alle the feeldes glyteren up and doun;
And by his baner born is his penoun
Of gold ful riche, in which ther was ybete 979
The Mynotaur, which that he slough in Crete.
Thus rit this duc, thus rit this conquerour,
And in his hoost of chivalrie the flour,
Til that he cam to Thebes and alighte
Faire in a feeld, ther as he thoughte to fighte.
    But shortly for to speken of this thyng, 985
With Creon, which that was of Thebes kyng,
He faught, and slough hym manly as a knyght

918. **biseken**, beseech. 924. **caytyves**, wretched creatures. 926. **assureth**. The subject is Fortune. 927. **abyden**, await. 928. **Clemence**, Mercy. 932. **Cappaneus**, Capaneus, one of the leaders supporting Polynices (the Seven against Thebes). He was killed in the seige of Thebes. 933. **starf**, died. 934. **array**, condition. 938. **Creon**. After the death of Eteocles and Polynices, sons of Oedipus, Creon became king of Thebes. 940. **Fulfild**, filled with. 942. **vileynye**, disgrace. 943. **yslawe**, slain. 946. **ybrent**, burned. 948. **respit**, delay. 949. **fillen gruf**, fell face down; cf. Mod. E. *groveling*. 952. **sterte**, started, leaped. 953. **pitous**, pitying; cf l. 955 where the sense is "pitiful." 955. **maat**, downcast, cf. *checkmate*. 957. **hente**, took. 960. **so ferforthly**, to a great extent, to the extent of his power. **doon . . . his myght**, exert his strength. 961. **wreke**, avenge. 966. **His baner he desplayeth**. A sign that he was setting out on his campaign against Creon. 967. **biside**, with him. 968. **neer**, nearer. **go**, walk. 970. **lay**, lodged. 972. **sheene**, bright, fair. 974. **rit**, rides. 975. **rede statue**, red image. **targe**, shield. 978. **penoun**, a narrow streamer. 979. **Of gold . . . ybete**, woven or embroidered with gold thread. 983. **alighte**, alighted. 984. **ther as**, where. 987. **manly**, in a manly manner.

In pleyn bataille, and putte the folk to flyght;
And by assaut he wan the citee after,
And rente adoun bothe wall and sparre and
  rafter;   990
And to the ladyes he restored agayn
The bones of hir housbondes that were slayn,
To doon obsequies, as was tho the gyse.
But it were al to longe for to devyse
The grete clamour and the waymentynge 995
That the ladyes made at the brennynge
Of the bodies, and the grete honour
That Theseus, the noble conquerour,
Dooth to the ladyes, whan they from hym
  wente;
But shortly for to telle is myn entente. 1000
Whan that this worthy duc, this Theseus,
Hath Creon slayn, and wonne Thebes thus,
Stille in that feeld he took al nyght his reste,
And dide with al the contree as hym leste.
To ransake in the taas of bodyes dede, 1005
Hem for to strepe of harneys and of wede,
The pilours diden bisynesse and cure
After the bataille and disconfiture.
And so bifel that in the taas they founde,
Thurgh-girt with many a grevous blody
  wounde, 1010
Two yonge knyghtes liggynge by and by,
Bothe in oon armes, wroght ful richely,
Of whiche two Arcita highte that oon,
And that oother knyght highte Palamon.
Nat fully quyke, ne fully dede they were, 1015
But by hir cote-armures and by hir gere
The heraudes knewe hem best in special
As they that weren of the blood roial
Of Thebes, and of sustren two yborn.

Out of the taas the pilours han hem torn, 1020
And han hem caried softe unto the tente
Of Theseus; and he ful soone hem sente
To Atthenes, to dwellen in prisoun
Perpetuelly,—he nolde no raunsoun. 1024
And whan this worthy duc hath thus ydon,
He took his hoost, and hoom he rit anon
With laurer crowned as a conquerour;
And ther he lyveth in joye and in honour
Terme of his lyf; what nedeth wordes mo?
And in a tour, in angwissh and in wo, 1030
This Palamon and his felawe Arcite
For everemoore; ther may no gold hem quite.
This passeth yeer by yeer and day by day,
Til it fil ones, in a morwe of May,
That Emelye, that fairer was to sene 1035
Than is the lylie upon his stalke grene,
And fressher than the May with floures newe—
For with the rose colour stroof hire hewe,
I noot which was the fyner of hem two—
Er it were day, as was hir wone to do, 1040
She was arisen and al redy dight;
For May wole have no slogardie a-nyght.
The sesoun priketh every gentil herte,
And maketh hym out of his slep to sterte,
And seith "Arys, and do thyn observaunce."
This maked Emelye have remembraunce 1046
To doon honour to May, and for to ryse.
Yclothed was she fressh, for to devyse:
Hir yelow heer was broyded in a tresse
Bihynde hir bak, a yerde long, I gesse. 1050
And in the gardyn, at the sonne upriste,
She walketh up and doun, and as hire liste
She gadereth floures, party white and rede,
To make a subtil gerland for hire hede;

988. **In pleyn bataille,** in open battle. 990. **sparre,** beam. 996. **brennynge,** burning. 1005. **taas,** heap. 1006. **strepe,** strip. **harneys,** armor. 1007. **pilours,** pillagers. **cure,** care. 1010. **Thurgh-girt,** pierced through. 1011. **liggynge,** lying. **by and by,** side by side. 1012. **in oon armes,** in the same coat-of-arms. Since they belonged to the same family they had the same heraldic device painted on their shields or embroidered on their surcoats (the *cote-armures* of l. 1016). Chaucer is here attributing a medieval practice to antiquity. 1015. **quyke,** alive. 1016. **gere,** trappings. 1017. **heraudes,** heralds (another medieval touch). 1021. **softe,** softly, gently. 1024. **nolde,** did not wish, *i.e.* would not accept. 1027. **laurer,** laurel. 1029. **Terme,** duration. 1030. **tour,** tower, dungeon. 1032. **For everemoore,** understand *lyven,* carried over from *lyveth* in l. 1028. **quite,** ransom. 1034. **it fil,** it happened. 1038. **stroof,** strove. 1039. **noot,** know not. 1040. **day,** *i.e.* daylight. **wone,** wont. 1041. **dight,** dressed, *lit.* prepared. 1042. **slogardie,** laziness. **a-nyght,** at night. The observance of May was widespread in the Middle Ages and the Renaissance. 1048. **for to devyse,** *i.e.* as I may describe. 1049. **Hir yelow heer was broyded in a tresse,** her blond hair was braided in a plait. 1051. **sonne upriste,** sun's uprising; *sonne* represents the OE. genitive *sunnan.* 1052. **as hire liste,** as it pleased her. 1053. **party,** particolored. 1054. **subtil,** skilfully woven, ingenious.

And as an aungel hevenysshly she soong.   1055
  The grete tour, that was so thikke and stroong,
Which of the castle was the chief dongeoun,
(Ther as the knyghtes weren in prisoun
Of whiche I tolde yow and tellen shal)
Was evene joynant to the gardyn wal   1060
Ther as this Emelye hadde hir pleyynge.
Bright was the sonne and cleer that morwen-
    ynge,
And Palamoun, this woful prisoner,
As was his wone, by leve of his gayler,
Was risen and romed in a chambre an heigh,
In which he al the noble citee seigh,   1066
And eek the gardyn, ful of braunches grene,
Ther as this fresshe Emelye the shene
Was in hir walk, and romed up and doun.
This sorweful prisoner, this Palamoun,   1070
Goth in the chambre romynge to and fro,
And to hymself compleynynge of his wo.
That he was born, ful ofte he seyde, "allas!"
  And so bifel, by aventure or cas,   1074
That thurgh a wyndow, thikke of many a barre
Of iren greet and square as any sparre,
He cast his eye upon Emelya,
And therwithal he bleynte and cride, "A!"
As though he stongen were unto the herte.
And with that cry Arcite anon up sterte,   1080
And seyde, "Cosyn myn, what eyleth thee,
That art so pale and deedly on to see?
Why cridestow? Who hath thee doon offense?
For Goddes love, taak al in pacience
Oure prisoun, for it may noon oother be.   1085
Fortune hath yeven us this adversitee.
Som wikke aspect or disposicioun
Of Saturne, by sum constellacioun,   1088
Hath yeven us this, although we hadde it sworn:
So stood the hevene whan that we were born.

We moste endure it; this is the short and playn."
  This Palamon answerde and seyde agayn:
"Cosyn, for sothe of this opinioun
Thow hast a veyn ymaginacioun.
This prison caused me nat for to crye,   1095
But I was hurt right now thurghout myn yë
Into myn herte, that wol my bane be.
The fairnesse of that lady that I see
Yond in the gardyn romen to and fro
Is cause of al my criyng and my wo.   1100
I noot wher she be womman or goddesse,
But Venus is it soothly, as I gesse."
And therwithal on knees doun he fil,
And seyde: "Venus, if it be thy wil
Yow in this gardyn thus to transfigure   1105
Bifore me, sorweful, wrecched creature,
Out of this prisoun help that we may scapen.
And if so be my destynee be shapen
By eterne word to dyen in prisoun,
Of oure lynage have som compassioun,   1110
That is so lowe ybroght by tirannye."
  And with that word Arcite gan espye
Wher as this lady romed to and fro,
And with that sighte hir beautee hurte hym so,
That, if that Palamon was wounded soore,   1115
Arcite is hurt as muche as he, or moore.
And with a sigh he seyde pitously:
"The fresshe beautee sleeth me sodeynly
Of hire that rometh in the yonder place,
And but I have hir mercy and hir grace,   1120
That I may seen hire atte leeste weye,
I nam but deed; ther nis namoore to seye."
  This Palamon, whan he tho wordes herde,
Dispitously he looked and answerde,   1124
"Wheither seistow this in ernest or in pley?"
  "Nay," quod Arcite, "in ernest, by my fey!
God helpe me so, me list ful yvele pleye."

1060. **evene**, directly, quite. **joynant**, adjoining. 1061. **pleyynge**, recreation. 1062. **morwenynge**, early morning. 1078. **bleynte**, turned pale. 1083. **offense**, injury. 1085. **noon oother**, not otherwise. 1087. **wikke**, evil. **aspect**, relative position of heavenly bodies. Saturn in astrology was a malignant planet. **disposicioun**, the situation of a planet as it affects one's horoscope. 1088. **constellacioun**, the position of the planets, supposed to affect human affairs. 1089. **although we hadde it sworn**, regardless of anything we might have done. 1094. **a veyn ymaginacioun**, *i.e.* you have the wrong idea; see note to BD 14. 1109. **eterne**, eternal, irrevocable. 1121. **atte leeste weye**, leastwise. 1123. **tho**, those. 1125. **Wheither**. *Wheither* means "which of two" and is sometimes used to introduce a direct question involving alternatives, expressed or implied; see Language, § 75. **seistow**, sayest thou. **pley**, jest. 1127. **me list ful yvele pleye**, it pleases me full ill to jest.

This Palamon gan knytte his browes tweye.
"It nere," quod he, "to thee no greet honour
For to be fals, ne for to be traitour 1130
To me, that am thy cosyn and thy brother
Ysworn ful depe, and ech of us til oother,
That nevere, for to dyen in the peyne,
Til that the deeth departe shal us tweyne,
Neither of us in love to hyndre oother, 1135
Ne in noon oother cas, my leeve brother;
But that thou sholdest trewely forthren me
In every cas, as I shal forthren thee,—
This was thyn ooth, and myn also, certeyn;
I woot right wel, thou darst it nat withseyn.
Thus artow of my conseil, out of doute, 1141
And now thow woldest falsly been aboute
To love my lady, whom I love and serve,
And evere shal til that myn herte sterve.
Nay, certes, false Arcite, thow shalt nat so.
I loved hire first, and tolde thee my wo 1146
As to my conseil and my brother sworn
To forthre me, as I have toold biforn.
For which thou art ybounden as a knyght
To helpen me, if it lay in thy myght, 1150
Or elles artow fals, I dar wel seyn."
    This Arcite ful proudly spak ageyn:
"Thow shalt," quod he, "be rather fals than I;
And thou art fals, I telle thee outrely,
For paramour I loved hire first er thow. 1155
What wiltow seyen? Thou woost nat yet now
Wheither she be a womman or goddesse!
Thyn is affeccioun of hoolynesse,
And myn is love, as to a creature;
For which I tolde thee myn aventure 1160

As to my cosyn and my brother sworn.
I pose that thow lovedest hire biforn;
Wostow nat wel the olde clerkes sawe,
That 'who shal yeve a lovere any lawe?'
Love is a gretter lawe, by my pan, 1165
Than may be yeve to any erthely man;
And therfore positif lawe and swich decree
Is broken alday for love in ech degree.
A man moot nedes love, maugree his heed.
He may nat flee it, thogh he sholde be deed,
Al be she mayde or wydwe, or elles wyf. 1171
And eek it is nat likly al thy lif
To stonden in hir grace; namoore shal I;
For wel thou woost thyselven, verraily,
That thou and I be dampned to prisoun 1175
Perpetuelly; us gayneth no raunsoun.
We stryve as dide the houndes for the boon;
They foughte al day, and yet hir part was noon.
Ther cam a kyte, whil that they were so wrothe,
And baar awey the boon bitwixe hem bothe.
And therfore, at the kynges court, my brother,
Ech man for hymself, ther is noon oother. 1182
Love, if thee list, for I love and ay shal;
And soothly, leeve brother, this is al.
Heere in this prisoun moote we endure, 1185
And everich of us take his aventure."
    Greet was the strif and long bitwix hem
        tweye,
If that I hadde leyser for to seye,
But to th'effect. It happed on a day,
To telle it yow as shortly as I may, 1190
A worthy duc that highte Perotheus,
That felawe was unto duc Theseus

1132. Ysworn ful depe. This is an allusion to the medieval custom of swearing blood brotherhood, not uncommon in the romances. The ceremony sometimes involved the mingling of blood from slight incisions and swearing an oath, at other times merely an oath. It is a feature of the romance of *Athelston*, and there is a good example of the swearing of such an oath in the *Pardoner's Tale* (C 697–704). **1133. for to dyen in the peyne,** to the extent of dying by torture. **1140. withseyn,** contradict, deny. **1141. of my conseil,** in my confidence, *i.e.* you know about my love for the lady in the garden. **1142. been aboute,** undertake. **1144. sterve,** die. **1147. conseil,** counsellor. Although this meaning of the word is not elsewhere recorded in Middle English, it is found in Old French. **1150. lay,** should lie (subjunctive). **1154. outrely,** plainly. **1155. paramour,** as a lover. **1158. affeccioun of hoolynesse,** religious feeling. **1160. aventure,** experience. **1162. I pose,** I put the hypothetical case. **biforn,** first. **1163. the olde clerkes sawe.** The reference is to Boethius, *Cons. Phil.*, III, met. 12. **1165. pan,** skull. **1167. positif lawe,** law established by enactment or decree, hence man-made, as opposed to laws of nature, morality, etc. **1168. alday,** constantly. **in ech degree,** in every class or rank of society. **1169. moot nedes,** must needs. **maugree,** in spite of. **1171. Al be she,** even if she be. **1172. al thy lyf,** no matter how long you live. **1176. us gayneth,** impers. constr., we shall win. **1178. hir,** their. **1181-2. at the kynges court . . . Ech man for hymself.** A proverb. **ther is noon oother,** there is no other way. **1185. moote we endure,** must we remain.

Syn thilke day that they were children lite,
Was come to Atthenes his felawe to visite,
And for to pleye as he was wont to do;   1195
For in this world he loved no man so,
And he loved hym als tendrely agayn.
So wel they lovede, as olde bookes sayn,
That whan that oon was deed, soothly to telle,
His felawe wente and soughte hym doun in
    helle,—   1200
But of that storie list me nat to write.
Duc Perotheus loved wel Arcite,
And hadde hym knowe at Thebes yeer by yere,
And finally at requeste and preyere
Of Perotheus, withouten any raunsoun,   1205
Duc Theseus hym leet out of prisoun
Frely to goon wher that hym liste over-al,
In swich a gyse as I you tellen shal.
   This was the forward, pleynly for t'endite,
Bitwixen Theseus and hym Arcite   1210
That if so were that Arcite were yfounde
Evere in his lif, by day or nyght, oo stounde
In any contree of this Theseus,
And he were caught, it was acorded thus,
That with a swerd he sholde lese his heed.   1215
Ther nas noon oother remedie ne reed;
But taketh his leve, and homward he him
    spedde.
Lat hym be war! His nekke lith to wedde.
   How greet a sorwe suffreth now Arcite!
The deeth he feeleth thurgh his herte smyte;
He wepeth, wayleth, crieth pitously;   1221
To sleen hymself he waiteth prively.—
He seyde, "Allas that day that I was born!
Now is my prisoun worse than biforn;
Now is me shape eternally to dwelle   1225

Nat in purgatorie, but in helle.
Allas, that evere knew I Perotheus!
For elles hadde I dwelled with Theseus,
Yfetered in his prisoun everemo.   1229
Thanne hadde I been in blisse, and nat in wo.
Oonly the sighte of hire whom that I serve,
Though that I nevere hir grace may deserve,
Wolde han suffised right ynough for me.
O deere cosyn Palamon," quod he,
"Thyn is the victorie of this aventure.   1235
Ful blisfully in prison maistow dure,—
In prison? certes nay, but in paradys!
Wel hath Fortune yturned thee the dys,
That hast the sighte of hire, and I th'absence.
For possible is, syn thou hast hire presence,   1240
And art a knyght, a worthy and an able,
That by som cas, syn Fortune is chaungeable,
Thow maist to thy desir somtyme atteyne.
But I, that am exiled and bareyne
Of alle grace, and in so greet dispeir,   1245
That ther nys erthe, water, fir, ne eir,
Ne creature that of hem maked is,
That may me helpe or doon confort in this,
Wel oughte I sterve in wanhope and distresse.
Farwel my lif, my lust, and my gladnesse!   1250
   Allas, why pleynen folk so in commune
On purveiaunce of God, or of Fortune,
That yeveth hem ful ofte in many a gyse
Wel bettre than they kan hemself devyse?
Som man desireth for to han richesse,   1255
That cause is of his moerdre or greet siknesse;
And som man wolde out of his prisoun fayn,
That in his hous is of his meynee slayn.
Infinite harmes been in this mateere.
We witen nat what thing we preyen heere: 1260

1193. lite, little. 1197. he, i.e. Theseus. 1200. doun in helle. This mistake comes probably from RR, 8153. Theseus had accompanied Pirithous to the underworld in his attempt to carry off Proserpina. 1201. to write. Chaucer either forgets that the Knight is speaking or this is evidence that the story was not originally written for the CT. 1203. knowe, known. yeer by yere, year after year. 1207. over-al, everywhere. 1209. forward, agreement. 1212. oo stounde, one moment. 1216. reed, help. 1217. taketh, he takes. The ellipsis is not uncommon, but is here awkward because the subject must be inferred from the terms of the agreement. 1218. to wedde, in pawn. 1222. waiteth, watches for an opportunity. prively, unobserved. 1225. Now is me shape, now it is determined for me, I am destined. 1236. dure, continue. 1240. syn, since. 1242. cas, chance. 1244. bareyne, barren. 1246. erthe, water, etc. Since these were the four elements of which everything was composed, the statement implies "there is nothing in the world or any creature that can help me." 1249. sterve in wanhope, die in despair. 1250. lust . . . gladnesse, pleasure . . . happiness. 1251. pleynen, complain. in commune, commonly. 1252. On purveiaunce, about the providence. 1253. in many a gyse, in many ways. 1256. moerdre, murder. 1257. wolde . . . fayn, would gladly be. 1258. meynee, household.

We faren as he that dronke is as a mous.
A dronke man woot wel he hath an hous,
But he noot which the righte wey is thider,
And to a dronke man the wey is slider.
And certes, in this world so faren we;　　1265
We seken faste after felicitee,
But we goon wrong ful often, trewely.
Thus may we seyen alle, and namely I,
That wende and hadde a greet opinioun
That if I myghte escapen from prisoun,　　1270
Thanne hadde I been in joye and perfit heele,
Ther now I am exiled fro my wele.
Syn that I may nat seen you, Emelye,
I nam but deed; ther nys no remedye."

　　Upon that oother syde Palamon,　　1275
Whan that he wiste Arcite was agon,
Swich sorwe he maketh that the grete tour
Resouneth of his youlyng and clamour.
The pure fettres on his shynes grete
Weren of his bittre, salte teeres wete.　　1280
"Allas," quod he, "Arcita, cosyn myn,
Of al oure strif, God woot, the fruyt is thyn.
Thow walkest now in Thebes at thy large,
And of my wo thow yevest litel charge.
Thou mayst, syn thou hast wisdom and man-
　　hede,　　1285
Assemblen alle the folk of oure kynrede,
And make a werre so sharp on this citee,
That by som aventure or som tretee
Thow mayst have hire to lady and to wyf
For whom that I moste nedes lese my lyf.　　1290
For, as by wey of possibilitee,
Sith thou art at thy large, of prisoun free,
And art a lord, greet is thyn avauntage
Moore than is myn, that sterve here in a cage.
For I moot wepe and wayle, whil I lyve,　　1295

With al the wo that prison may me yive,
And eek with peyne that love me yeveth also,
That doubleth al my torment and my wo."
Therwith the fyr of jalousie up sterte　　1299
Withinne his brest, and hente him by the herte
So woodly that he lyk was to biholde
The boxtree or the asshen dede and colde.

　　Thanne seyde he, "O crueel goddes that
　　governe
This world with byndyng of youre word eterne,
And writen in the table of atthamaunt　　1305
Youre parlement and youre eterne graunt,
What is mankynde moore unto you holde
Than is the sheep that rouketh in the folde?
For slayn is man right as another beest,
And dwelleth eek in prison and arreest,　　1310
And hath siknesse and greet adversitee,
And ofte tymes giltelees, pardee.
What governance is in this prescience,
That giltelees tormenteth innocence?
And yet encresseth this al my penaunce,　　1315
That man is bounden to his observaunce,
For Goddes sake, to letten of his wille,
Ther as a beest may al his lust fulfille.
And whan a beest is deed he hath no peyne;
But man after his deeth moot wepe and pleyne,
Though in this world he have care and wo.　1321
Withouten doute it may stonden so.
The answere of this lete I to dyvynys,
But wel I woot that in this world greet pyne ys.
Allas, I se a serpent or a theef,　　1325
That many a trewe man hath doon mescheef,
Goon at his large, and where hym list may turne.
But I moot been in prisoun thurgh Saturne,
And eek thurgh Juno, jalous and eek wood,
That hath destroyed wel ny al the blood　1330

1261. **dronke is as a mous,** a proverbial expression which in later English was replaced by "drunk as a rat." See Skeat *Early Eng. Proverbs;* cf. D 246. **1262.** The illustration is from Boethius, *Cons. Phil.,* III, pr. 1. **1263. noot,** doesn't know **1264. slider,** slippery. **1268. namely,** particularly. **1269. wende,** thought. **1271. heele,** well-being. **1272. Ther,** whereas **wele,** happiness, good fortune. **1275. Upon that oother syde,** on the other hand. **1276. agon,** gone away. **1279. pure,** very. **1283. at thy large,** at large. **1284. charge,** weight. **1285. manhede,** courage. **1301. woodly,** madly. **1305. table of atthamaunt,** tablet of adamant. **1306. parlement,** decision (resulting from deliberation). **1307. holde,** considered. **1308. rouketh,** cowers. **1313. What governance,** what kind of management. **prescience,** foreknowledge. **1315. penaunce,** suffering. **1316. is bounden to his observaunce,** is under obligation. **1317. letten of,** desist from. **1318. Ther as,** whereas. **lust,** desire. **1320. pleyne,** lament. **1322. it may stonden so,** such is the case. **1323. dyvynys,** those learned in divinity. **1324. pyne,** suffering. **1325. serpent,** a treacherous person. **1329. And eek thurgh Juno.** See note to *TC* 5. 601

Of Thebes with his waste walles wyde;
And Venus sleeth me on that oother syde
For jalousie and fere of hym Arcite."
    Now wol I stynte of Palamon a lite,
And lete hym in his prisoun stille dwelle,   1335
And of Arcita forth I wol yow telle.
    The somer passeth, and the nyghtes longe
Encressen double wise the peynes stronge
Bothe of the lovere and the prisoner.
I noot which hath the wofuller mester.   1340
For, shortly for to seyn, this Palamoun
Perpetuelly is dampned to prisoun,

In cheynes and in fettres to been deed;
And Arcite is exiled upon his heed
For evere mo, as out of that contree,   1345
Ne nevere mo he shal his lady see.
    Yow loveres axe I now this questioun:
Who hath the worse, Arcite or Palamoun?
That oon may seen his lady day by day,
But in prison he moot dwelle alway;   1350
That oother wher hym list may ride or go,
But seen his lady shal he nevere mo.
Now demeth as yow liste, ye that kan,
For I wol telle forth as I bigan.

Explicit prima pars.

Sequitur pars secunda.

   Whan that Arcite to Thebes comen was,   1355
Ful ofte a day he swelte and seyde "Allas!"
For seen his lady shal he nevere mo.
And shortly to concluden al his wo,
So muche sorwe hadde nevere creature   1359
That is, or shal, whil that the world may dure.
His slep, his mete, his drynke, is hym biraft,
That lene he wex and drye as is a shaft;
His eyen holwe, and grisly to biholde,
His hewe falow and pale as asshen colde,
And solitarie he was and evere allone,   1365
And waillynge al the nyght, makynge his mone;
And if he herde song or instrument,
Thanne wolde he wepe, he myghte nat be stent.
So feble eek were his spiritz, and so lowe,   1369
And chaunged so, that no man koude knowe
His speche nor his voys, though men it herde.
And in his geere for al the world he ferde,

Nat oonly lik the loveris maladye
Of Hereos, but rather lyk manye,
Engendred of humour malencolik,   1375
<u>Biforen, in his celle fantastik.</u>
And shortly, turned was al up so doun
Bothe habit and eek disposicioun
Of hym, this woful lovere daun Arcite.
    What sholde I al day of his wo endite?   1380
Whan he endured hadde a yeer or two
This crueel torment and this peyne and wo,
At Thebes, in his contree, as I seyde,
Upon a nyght in sleep as he hym leyde,
Hym thoughte how that the wynged god Mer-
    curie   1385
Before Biforn hym stood and bad hym to be murie.
His slepy yerde in hond he bar uprighte;
An hat he werede upon his heris brighte.
Arrayed was this god, as he took keep,

1333. For jalousie. The jealousy, of course, is felt by Palamon. **1340. mester,** occupation. **1344. upon his heed,** on pain of losing his head. **1345. as out of,** out of. **1347. questioun.** The question which follows is typical of those discussed in the courts of love. **1351. go,** walk. **1356. swelte,** languished. **1358. concluden,** sum up. **1364. falow,** pale brown. **1368. stent,** stopped. **1372. geere,** fits of passion, changeable mood. **ferde,** fared. **1373–4. the loveris maladye Of Hereos.** First explained by Lowes (*MP*, XI. 491–546). *Hereos* or *amor hereos* was an illness recognized by medical authorities of the Middle Ages, the symptoms of which were loss of appetite, sleeplessness, hysterical outbursts, etc. **1374. manye,** mania. **1376. Biforen, in his celle fantastik.** The brain was believed to have three cells, front, middle, and back. The front cell is called the fantastic cell because mania was supposed to be located there. See Lowes, as above, and Professor Robinson's note, p. 673. **1377. up so doun.** The older form of "upside down." **1378. habit,** character. **1387. slepy yerde,** the wand or caduceus of Mercury, called by Ovid (*Metam.*, I. 671–2) *virgam somniferam.* After he had lulled the hundred-eyed Argus to sleep Mercury waved his wand over him to insure his staying asleep until he had cut off his head. **1389. keep,** heed.

As he was whan that Argus took his sleep; 1390
And seyde hym thus: "To Atthenes shaltou
  wende,
Ther is thee shapen of thy wo an ende."
And with that word Arcite wook and sterte.
"Now trewely, hou soore that me smerte," 1394
Quod he, "to Atthenes right now wol I fare,
Ne for the drede of deeth shal I nat spare
To se my lady, that I love and serve.
In hire presence I recche nat to sterve."
  And with that word he caughte a greet
  mirour,
And saugh that chaunged was al his colour, 1400
And saugh his visage al in another kynde.
And right anon it ran hym in his mynde,
That, sith his face was so disfigured
Of maladye the which he hadde endured,
Hy myghte wel, if that he bar hym lowe, 1405
Lyve in Atthenes everemoore unknowe
And seen his lady wel ny day by day.
  And right anon he chaunged his array,
And cladde hym as a povre laborer,
And al allone, save oonly a squier 1410
That knew his privetee and al his cas,
Which was disgised povrely as he was,
To Atthenes is he goon the nexte way.
And to the court he wente upon a day,
And at the gate he profreth his servyse 1415
To drugge and drawe, what so men wol devyse.
And shortly of this matere for to seyn,
He fil in office with a chamberleyn
The which that dwellynge was with Emelye;
For he was wys and koude soone espye 1420
Of every servaunt which that serveth here.
Wel koude he hewen wode, and water bere,
For he was yong and myghty for the nones,
And therto he was long and big of bones

To doon that any wight kan hym devyse. 1425
  A yeer or two he was in this servyse,
Page of the chambre of Emelye the brighte;
And Philostrate he seyde that he highte.
But half so wel biloved a man as he
Ne was ther nevere in court of his degree; 1430
He was so gentil of condicioun
That thurghout al the court was his renoun.
They seyden that it were a charitee
That Theseus wolde enhauncen his degree,
And putten hym in worshipful servyse, 1435
Ther as he myghte his vertu exercise.
And thus withinne a while his name is spronge,
Bothe of his dedes and his goode tonge,
That Theseus hath taken hym so neer,
That of his chambre he made hym a squier, 1440
And gaf hym gold to mayntene his degree.
And eek men broghte hym out of his contree,
From yeer to yeer, ful pryvely his rente;
But honestly and slyly he it spente, 1444
That no man wondred how that he it hadde.
And thre yeer in this wise his lif he ladde,
And bar hym so, in pees and eek in werre,
Ther was no man that Theseus hath derre.
And in this blisse lete I now Arcite,
And speke I wole of Palamon a lite. 1450
  In derknesse and horrible and strong prisoun
Thise seven yeer hath seten Palamoun
Forpyned, what for wo and for distresse.
Who feeleth double soor and hevynesse
But Palamon, that love destreyneth so 1455
That wood out of his wit he goth for wo?
And eek therto he is a prisoner
Perpetuelly, noght oonly for a yer.
Who koude ryme in Englyssh proprely
His martirdom? for sothe it am nat I; 1460
Therfore I passe as lightly as I may.

1393. **sterte,** gave a start. 1394. **smerte,** it may hurt me. 1396. **spare,** refrain. 1398. **I recche nat to sterve,** *i.e.* I care not if I die. 1401. **al in another kynde,** completely changed. 1403. **disfigured,** altered. 1404. **Of maladye,** by illness. 1411. **privetee,** private affairs. 1413. **nexte,** nearest, shortest. 1416. **drugge,** drudge. **devyse,** tell, suggest. 1418. **fil in office,** fell into service. 1421. **here,** her. 1428. **that he highte,** that his name was. 1430. **degree,** social position. 1431. **condicioun,** manner, disposition. 1433. **it were a charitee,** it would be an act of justice. 1434. **enhauncen his degree,** improve his status. 1435. **worshipful,** honorable. 1436. **vertu,** natural ability. 1437. **spronge,** spread abroad. 1443. **rente,** income. 1444. **honestly,** fittingly, modestly. **slyly,** cautiously. 1448. **derre,** more dearly. 1453. **Forpyned,** tormented. 1454. **soor,** sorrow, the reading (*sorowe*) of many manuscripts. 1455. **destreyneth,** oppresses. 456. **wood,** madly. 1460. **it am nat I.** This is the usual idiom in ME.

It fel that in the seventhe yer, of May
The thridde nyght, (as olde bookes seyn,
That al this storie tellen moore pleyn)
Were it by aventure or destynee— 1465
As, whan a thyng is shapen, it shal be—
That soone after the mydnyght Palamoun,
By helpyng of a freend, brak his prisoun
And fleeth the citee faste as he may go.
For he hadde yeve his gayler drynke so 1470
Of a clarree maad of a certeyn wyn,
With nercotikes and opie of Thebes fyn,
That al that nyght, thogh that men wolde him
shake,
The gayler sleep—he myghte nat awake;
And thus he fleeth as faste as evere he may. 1475
The nyght was short and faste by the day,
That nedes cost he moot hymselven hyde;
And til a grove faste ther bisyde
With dredeful foot thanne stalketh Palamoun.
For, shortly, this was his opinioun, 1480
That in that grove he wolde hym hyde al day,
And in the nyght thanne wolde he take his way
To Thebes-ward, his freendes for to preye
On Theseus to helpe hym to werreye;
And shortly, outher he wolde lese his lif, 1485
Or wynnen Emelye unto his wyf.
This is th'effect and his entente pleyn.
    Now wol I turne to Arcite ageyn,

That litel wiste how ny that was his care, 1489
Til that Fortune had broght him in the snare.
    The bisy larke, messager of day,
Salueth in hir song the morwe gray,
And firy Phebus riseth up so brighte
That al the orient laugheth of the lighte,
And with his stremes dryeth in the greves 1495
The silver dropes hangynge on the leves.
And Arcita, that in the court roial
With Theseus is squier principal,
Is risen and looketh on the myrie day.
And for to doon his observaunce to May, 1500
Remembrynge on the poynt of his desir,
He on a courser, startlynge as the fir,
Is riden into the feeldes hym to pleye,
Out of the court, were it a myle or tweye.
And to the grove of which that I yow tolde
By aventure his wey he gan to holde 1506
To maken hym a gerland of the greves
Were it of wodebynde or hawethorn leves,
And loude he song ayeyn the sonne shene:
"May, with alle thy floures and thy grene, 1510
Welcome be thou, faire, fresshe May,
In hope that I som grene gete may."
And from his courser, with a lusty herte,
Into the grove ful hastily he sterte,
And in a path he rometh up and doun, 1515
Theras by aventure this Palamoun

1463. **The thridde nyght.** Although Manly believed this to refer to the night before May 3, Skeat observed that the third night was followed by the fourth day, and this seems the more natural interpretation. If, as Skeat assumed, Chaucer was writing with the calendar of the year in which he was writing in his mind, the reference may give a clue to the date of composition. When Palamon and Arcite met the next morning it was on a Friday (see l. 1534), and the next day when they fought (see l. 1610) was Saturday, May 5. After interrupting the fight, Theseus orders them to settle their differences at a tournament "this day fifty wykes, fer ne ner" (l. 1850). Boccaccio says "un anno intero," and it is assumed that this is Chaucer's meaning, the loose expression being dictated by the necessity of the rime and the meter. When the knights assemble on May 5 the following year, it is on a Sunday (l. 2188). May 5 fell on a Sunday in 1381 and 1387. The latter year is too late. The Prologue to the *LGW*, which mentions the story of Palamon and Arcite among Chaucer's works, was almost certainly written before 1387. If this calculation based on the mention of days and dates in the poem is significant, it suggests that Chaucer was writing it in 1381. It is, however, a long poem and its composition may well have extended into 1382. The arrival of the future Queen Anne in England, which is probably alluded to (see note to l. 884), did not take place until December 18, 1381. It is possible that Chaucer chose May 3 because according to medieval superstition this was one of a number of unlucky days in the year. For this point of view see Manly's note (*Canterbury Tales*, pp. 549–51). For another suggestion see the note to *TC* 2. 56, above. 1464. **pleyn,** fully. 1466. **shapen,** determined. 1471. **clarree,** wine to which honey and spices were added. 1472. **opie of Thebes fyn.** The reference is to the Egyptian Thebes on the Nile, which was famous for its opium. Palamon may have had the drug in his possession because it was a recognized remedy for love melancholy. See O. F. Emerson, *MP*, XVII. 289–91. 1473. **men,** one. 1474. **sleep,** slept. 1476. **faste by,** near. 1477. **nedes cost,** necessarily. 1478. **til,** to. 1479. **stalketh,** walks stealthily. 1484. **werreye,** wage war. 1487. **effect,** purport. **entente pleyn,** full intention. 1492. **Salueth,** salutes. 1495. **greves,** bushes. 1502. **startlynge,** prancing. 1507. **greves,** branches. 1509. **ayeyn the sonne shene,** in the sunshine; cf. *TC* 2. 920. 1512. **grene,** something green, green leaves or branches.

Was in a bussh, that no man myghte hym se,
For soore afered of his deeth was he.
Nothyng ne knew he that it was Arcite;
God woot he wolde have trowed it ful lite.   1520
But sooth is seyd, gon sithen many yeres, *(many years ago)*
That "feeld hath eyen and the wode hath eres."
(It is desireble)
It is ful fair a man to bere hym evene,
For alday meeteth men at unset stevene.
Ful litel woot Arcite of his felawe, *(rascal)*   1525
That was so ny to herknen al his sawe,
For in the bussh he sitteth now ful stille.

Whan that Arcite hadde romed al his fille,
And songen al the roundel lustily,
Into a studie he fil sodeynly,   1530
As doon thise loveres in hir queynte geres, *(strange behaviors)*
Now in the crope, now doun in the breres,
Now up, now doun, as boket in a welle.
Right as the Friday, soothly for to telle, *(friday it is clear another it rains)*
Now it shyneth, now it reyneth faste,   1535
Right so kan geery Venus overcaste *(changeable)*
The hertes of hir folk; right as hir day
Is gereful, right so chaungeth she array.
Selde is the Friday al the wowke ylike.   1539 *(like all the rest of the week)*

Whan that Arcite had songe, he gan to sike,
And sette hym doun withouten any moore.
"Allas," quod he, "that day that I was bore!
How longe, Juno, thurgh thy crueltee,
Woltow werreyen Thebes the citee?
Allas, ybroght is to confusioun   1545
The blood roial of Cadme and Amphioun,—
Of Cadmus, which that was the firste man
That Thebes bulte, or first the toun bigan,

And of the citee first was crouned kyng.
Of his lynage am I and his ofspryng   1550
By verray ligne, as of the stok roial,
And now I am so caytyf and so thral,
That he that is my mortal enemy,
I serve hym as his squier povrely.
And yet dooth Juno me wel moore shame,   1555
For I dar noght biknowe myn owene name; *(acknowledged)*
But ther as I was wont to highte Arcite,
Now highte I Philostrate, noght worth a myte.
Allas, thou felle Mars! allas, Juno!
Thus hath youre ire oure lynage al fordo,   1560
Save oonly me and wrecched Palamoun,
That Theseus martireth in prisoun.
And over al this, to sleen me outrely,
Love hath his firy dart so brennyngly
Ystiked thurgh my trewe, careful herte, *(sorrowful)*   1565
That shapen was my deeth erst than my sherte. *(determined)*
Ye sleen me with youre eyen, Emelye!
Ye been the cause wherfore that I dye.
Of al the remenant of myn oother care
Ne sette I nat the montance of a tare,   1570 *(Provided)*
So that I koude doon aught to youre plesaunce."
And with that word he fil doun in a traunce
A longe tyme, and after he up sterte.

This Palamoun, that thoughte that thurgh his herte
He felte a coold swerd sodeynliche glyde,   1575
For ire he quook, no lenger wolde he byde.
And whan that he had herd Arcites tale,
As he were wood, with face deed and pale, *(mad) (deathly)*
He stirte hym up out of the buskes thikke, *(bushes)*

1519. Nothyng, not at all. **1521. gon sithen many yeres,** since many years ago; cf. F 536: *goon sithen many a day. Gon* is the past.participle. **1522. feeld hath eyen . . .** A proverb found in English and other languages. "Champ ont yeulx et bois ont oreillez" occurs in *Renard Contrefait*. For this and many other examples see S. Singer, *Sprichwörter des Mittelalters*, I.72. **1523. It is ful fair,** it is desirable. **to bere hym evene,** restrain himself. **1524. alday,** continually. **at unset stevene,** at an unappointed time, unexpectedly. This was a common proverb of which Zupitza notes a number of instances in his edition of "The Proverbis of Wysdom," *Archiv.* xc. 251. **1526. al his sawe,** all that he said. **1529. roundel,** rondel (Mod. *rondeau*), a short lyric, originally accompanying a dance, using only two rimes, with the opening line or couplet repeated in the middle and at the end. **1531. queynte geres,** strange behaviors, moods. **1532. crope . . . breres,** top . . . briars, *i.e.* now in high spirits, now in low. **1534. Right as the Friday.** Alexander Neckam says that Friday's weather is the opposite of that in the preceding days of the week. It therefore varies. Friday is Venus's day. **1535. Now . . . now,** *i.e.* one Friday it is clear, another it rains. **1536. geery,** changeable; so also *gereful.* **overcaste,** overcloud, darken. **1539. al the wowke ylike,** like all the (rest of the) week. **1546. Cadme,** Cadmus, legendary founder of Thebes. **Amphioun,** Amphion, who built the fortifications. **1551. verray ligne,** true descent. **1552. thral,** enslaved. **1554. povrely,** in a lowly manner. **1556. biknowe,** acknowledge. **1559. felle,** cruel. **1560. fordo,** destroyed. **1565. careful,** sorrowful. **1566. shapen,** determined. **erst than,** before. The superlative is sometimes used in the simple sense of "earlier," "before." Cf. E 336. **1571. So that,** provided. **1578. deed,** deathly. **1579. buskes,** bushes.

And seide: "Arcite, false traytour wikke,   1580
Now artow hent, that lovest my lady so,
For whom that I have al this peyne and wo,
And art my blood, and to my conseil sworn,
As I ful ofte have told thee heerbiforn,
And hast byjaped heere duc Theseus,   1585
And falsly chaunged hast thy name thus!
I wol be deed, or elles thou shalt dye.
Thou shalt nat love my lady Emelye,
But I wol love hire oonly and namo;
For I am Palamon, thy mortal foo.   1590
And though that I no wepene have in this place,
But out of prison am astert by grace,
I drede noght that outher thow shalt dye,
Or thow ne shalt nat loven Emelye.
Chees which thou wolt, for thou shalt nat
   asterte!"   1595
   This Arcite, with ful despitous herte,
Whan he hym knew, and hadde his tale herd,
As fiers as leon pulled out his swerd,
And seyde thus: "By God that sit above,
Nere it that thou art sik and wood for love,   1600
And eek that thow no wepne hast in this place,
Thou sholdest nevere out of this grove pace,
That thou ne sholdest dyen of myn hond.
For I defye the seurete and the bond   1604
Which that thou seist that I have maad to thee.
What, verray fool, thynk wel that love is free,
And I wol love hire maugree al thy myght!
But for as muche thou art a worthy knyght,
And wilnest to darreyne hire by bataille,
Have heer my trouthe, tomorwe I wol nat faille,
Withoute wityng of any oother wight,   1611
That heere I wol be founden as a knyght,
And bryngen harneys right ynough for thee;
And ches the beste, and leve the worste for me.
And mete and drynke this nyght wol I brynge

Ynough for thee, and clothes for thy beddynge.
And if so be that thou my lady wynne,   1617
And sle me in this wode ther I am inne,
Thow mayst wel have thy lady as for me."
   This Palamon answerde, "I graunte it thee."
And thus they been departed til a-morwe,   1621
Whan ech of hem had leyd his feith to borwe.
   O Cupide, out of alle charitee!
O regne, that wolt no felawe have with thee!
Ful sooth is seyd that love ne lordshipe   1625
Wol noght, his thankes, have no felaweshipe.
Wel fynden that Arcite and Palamoun.
Arcite is riden anon unto the toun,
And on the morwe, er it were dayes light,
Ful prively two harneys hath he dight,   1630
Bothe suffisaunt and mete to darreyne
The bataille in the feeld bitwix hem tweyne;
And on his hors, allone as he was born,
He carieth al the harneys hym biforn.
And in the grove, at tyme and place yset,   1635
This Arcite and this Palamon ben met.
Tho chaungen gan the colour in hir face,
Right as the hunters in the regne of Trace,
That stondeth at the gappe with a spere,
Whan hunted is the leon or the bere,   1640
And hereth hym come russhyng in the greves,
And breketh bothe bowes and the leves,
And thynketh, "Heere cometh my mortal en-
   emy!
Withoute faile, he moot be deed, or I;
For outher I moot sleen hym at the gappe,   1645
Or he moot sleen me, if that me myshappe,"—
So ferden they in chaungyng of hir hewe,
As fer as everich of hem oother knewe.
   Ther nas no good day, ne no saluyng,
But streight, withouten word or rehersyng,   1650
Everich of hem heelp for to armen oother

1580. wikke, wicked. **1581. hent,** caught. **1585. byjaped,** tricked. **1592. astert,** escaped. **1596. despitous,** scornful. **1599. sit,** sits, contraction of *sitteth*. **1600. Nere it,** were it not. **1604. seurete,** pledge. **1609. darreyne,** decide (a claim to). **1611. wityng,** knowledge. **1613. harneys,** equipment. **1619. as for me,** as far as I am concerned. **1621. departed,** separated. **a-morwe,** the next day. **1622. to borwe,** in pledge. **1624. regne,** rule, dominion. **felawe,** associate. **1626. his thankes,** willingly. **1630. harneys,** sets of equipment. **dight,** prepared. **1631. darreyne The bataille,** vindicate his claim (by single combat). **1638. regne,** kingdom. Statius in the *Thebadi*, IV. 494 ff, imitated in the *Teseida*, VII, st. 106, describes the hunter as very bold until the lion appears, whereupon he loses his courage. **1641. greves,** bushes. **1646. me myshappe,** *lit.* it mishaps me (I am unfortunate). **1648. As fer as . . .,** to the extent that each recognized the character of his opponent. **1649. saluyng,** saluting, greeting. **1651. heelp,** helped.

As freendly as he were his owene brother;
And after that, with sharpe speres stronge
They foynen ech at oother wonder longe.
Thou myghtest wene that this Palamoun　1655
In his fightyng were a wood leoun,
And as a crueel tigre was Arcite;
As wilde bores gonne they to smyte,
That frothen whit as foom for ire wood.
Up to the ancle foghte they in hir blood.　1660
And in this wise I lete hem fightyng dwelle,
And forth I wole of Theseus yow telle.

　The destinee, ministre general,
That executeth in the world over-al　1664
The purveiaunce that God hath seyn biforn,
So strong it is that, though the world had sworn
The contrarie of a thyng by ye or nay,
Yet somtyme it shal fallen on a day
That falleth nat eft withinne a thousand yeer.
For certeinly, oure appetites heer,　1670
Be it of werre, or pees, or hate, or love,
Al is this reuled by the sighte above.

　This mene I now by myghty Theseus,
That for to hunten is so desirus,
And namely at the grete hert in May,　1675
That in his bed ther daweth hym no day
That he nys clad, and redy for to ryde
With hunte and horn and houndes hym bisyde.
For in his huntyng hath he swich delit
That it is al his joye and appetit　1680
To been hymself the grete hertes bane,
For after Mars he serveth now Dyane.

　Cleer was the day, as I have toold er this,
And Theseus with alle joye and blis,
With his Ypolita, the faire queene,　1685
And Emelye, clothed al in grene,
On huntyng be they riden roially.
And to the grove that stood ful faste by,
In which ther was an hert, as men hym tolde,

Duc Theseus the streighte wey hath holde.　1690
And to the launde he rideth hym ful right,
For thider was the hert wont have his flight,
And over a brook, and so forth on his weye.
This duc wol han a cours at hym or tweye
With houndes swiche as that hym list com-
　aunde.　1695
　And whan this duc was come unto the launde,
Under the sonne he looketh, and anon
He was war of Arcite and Palamon,
That foughten breme, as it were bores two.
The brighte swerdes wenten to and fro　1700
So hidously that with the leeste strook
It semed as it wolde felle an ook.
But what they were, nothyng he ne woot.
This duc his courser with his spores smoot,
And at a stert he was bitwix hem two,　1705
And pulled out a swerd, and cride, "Hoo!
Namoore, up peyne of lesynge of youre heed!
By myghty Mars, he shal anon be deed
That smyteth any strook that I may seen.
But telleth me what myster men ye been,　1710
That been so hardy for to fighten heere
Withouten juge or oother officere,
As it were in a lystes roially."
　This Palamon answerde hastily,
And seyde, "Sire, what nedeth wordes mo?　1715
We have the deeth disserved bothe two.
Two woful wrecches been we, two caytyves,
That been encombred of oure owene lyves;
And as thou art a rightful lord and juge,
Ne yeve us neither mercy ne refuge,　1720
But sle me first, for seinte charitee!
But sle my felawe eek as wel as me;
Or sle hym first, for though thow knowest it
　lite,
This is thy mortal foo, this is Arcite,
That fro thy lond is banysshed on his heed,　1725

1654. foynen, thrust. **1659. ire wood,** mad anger. **1661. dwelle,** continue. **1664. over-al,** everywhere. **1665. pur-**
veiaunce, providence. **seyn biforn,** foreseen. **1670. appetites,** desires. **1676. daweth hym,** dawns for him. **1678.**
hunte, huntsman. **1682. Dyane,** Diana, the huntress. **1691. launde,** an open space in the woods, a glade. **1694. cours,**
charge, here the action of pursuing game. **1697. Under the sonne he looketh,** looks around (perhaps shading his eyes).
The expression is discussed in several articles in *MLN*, xxxvii, xxxviii, xliv, li. **1699. breme,** fiercely. **1703. what,** who.
nothyng, not at all. **1705. at a stert,** in a moment. **1707. up,** upon. **1710. myster,** trade, *i.e.* what kind of men you are.
1713. lystes. lists, properly plur. but sometimes treated as sing. **1714. hastily,** quickly, promptly. **1718. encombred of,**
weary of. **1720. refuge,** protection. **1725. on his heed,** under penalty of losing his head.

For which he hath deserved to be deed.
For this is he that cam unto thy gate
And seyde that he highte Philostrate.
Thus hath he japed thee ful many a yer,
And thou hast maked hym thy chief squier; 1730
And this is he that loveth Emelye.
For sith the day is come that I shal dye,
I make pleynly my confessioun
That I am thilke woful Palamoun
That hath thy prisoun broken wikkedly. 1735
I am thy mortal foo, and it am I
That loveth so hoote Emelye the brighte
That I wol dye present in hir sighte.
Wherfore I axe deeth and my juwise;
But sle my felawe in the same wise, 1740
For bothe han we deserved to be slayn."
  This worthy duc answerde anon agayn,
And seyde, "This is a short conclusioun.
Youre owene mouth, by youre confessioun,
Hath dampned yow, and I wol it recorde; 1745
It nedeth noght to pyne yow with the corde.
Ye shal be deed, by myghty Mars the rede!"
  The queene anon, for verray wommanhede,
Gan for to wepe, and so dide Emelye,
And alle the ladyes in the compaignye. 1750
Greet pitee was it, as it thoughte hem alle,
That evere swich a chaunce sholde falle;
For gentil men they were of greet estaat,
And no thyng but for love was this debaat;
And saugh hir blody woundes wyde and soore,
And alle crieden, bothe lasse and moore, 1756
"Have mercy, Lord, upon us wommen alle!"
And on hir bare knees adoun they falle,
And wolde have kist his feet ther as he stood;
Til at the laste aslaked was his mood, 1760
For pitee renneth soone in gentil herte.
And though he first for ire quook and sterte,
He hath considered shortly, in a clause,
The trespas of hem bothe, and eek the cause,

And although that his ire hir gilt accused, 1765
Yet in his resoun he hem bothe excused,
As thus: he thoghte wel that every man
Wol helpe hymself in love, if that he kan,
And eek delivere hymself out of prisoun.
And eek his herte hadde compassioun 1770
Of wommen, for they wepen evere in oon;
And in his gentil herte he thoughte anon,
And softe unto hymself he seyde, "Fy
Upon a lord that wol have no mercy,
But been a leon, bothe in word and dede, 1775
To hem that been in repentaunce and drede,
As well as to a proud despitous man
That wol mayntene that he first bigan.
That lord hath litel of discrecioun,
That in swich cas kan no divisioun, 1780
But weyeth pride and humblesse after oon."
And shortly, whan his ire is thus agoon,
He gan to looken up with eyen lighte,
And spak thise same wordes al on highte:
  { "The god of love, a, *benedicite!* 1785
  { How myghty and how greet a lord is he!
  (Ayeyns his myght ther gayneth none obstacles.
He may be cleped a god for his myracles;
For he kan maken, at his owene gyse,
Of everich herte as that hym list divyse. 1790
Lo heere this Arcite and this Palamoun,
That quitly weren out of my prisoun,
And myghte han lyved in Thebes roially,
And witen I am hir mortal enemy,
And that hir deth lith in my myght also; 1795
And yet hath love, maugree hir eyen two,
Broght hem hyder bothe for to dye.
Now looketh, is nat that an heigh folye?
Who may been a fool, but if he love?
Bihoold, for Goddes sake that sit above, 1800
Se how they blede! be they noght wel arrayed?
Thus hath hir lord, the god of love, ypayed
Hir wages and hir fees for hir servyse!

1737. hoote, fervently. 1739. juwise, sentence. 1745. recorde, declare as a verdict. 1746. pyne, torture. 1760. aslaked, allayed. 1761. For pittee renneth soone in gentil herte. Chaucer's favorite line; cf. E 1986, F 479, LGW 503. 1763. in a clause, in a few words. 1765. hir gilt accused, condemned their offense. 1771. evere in oon, always in the same way. 1777. despitous, scornful. 1779. discrecioun, discernment. 1780. kan no divisioun, makes no distinction. 1781. after oon, alike, by one standard. 1782. agoon, past. 1784. al on highte, out loud. 1787. gayneth, avails. 1789. at his owene gyse, at will 1792. quitly, freely. 1798. heigh, great. 1799. but if, provided. For the use of *but if* see A 656.

And yet they wenen for to been ful wyse
That serven love, for aught that may bifalle.
But this is yet the beste game of alle, 1806
That she for whom they han this jolitee
Kan hem therfore as muche thank as me.
She woot namoore of al this hoote fare,
By God, than woot a cokkow or an hare! 1810
But all moot ben assayed, hoot and coold;
A man moot ben a fool, or yong or oold,—
I woot it by myself ful yore agon,
For in my tyme a servant was I oon.
And therfore, syn I knowe of loves peyne, 1815
And woot hou soore it kan a man distreyne,
As he that hath ben caught ofte in his laas,
I yow foryeve al hoolly this trespaas,
At requeste of the queene, that kneleth heere,
And eek of Emelye, my suster deere. 1820
And ye shul bothe anon unto me swere
That nevere mo ye shal my contree dere,
Ne make werre upon me nyght ne day,
But been my freendes in al that ye may.
I yow foryeve this trespas every deel." 1825
And they hym sworen his axyng faire and
    weel,
And hym of lordshipe and of mercy preyde,
And he hem graunteth grace, and thus he
    seyde:
    "To speke of roial lynage and richesse,
Though that she were a queene or a princesse,
Ech of your bothe is worthy, doutelees, 1831
To wedden whan tyme is, but nathelees
I speke as for my suster Emelye,
For whom ye have this strif and jalousye.
Ye woot yourself she may nat wedden two 1835
Atones, though ye fighten everemo.
That oon of you, al be hym looth or lief,
He moot go pipen in an yvy leef;

This is to seyn, she may nat now han bothe,
Al be ye never so jalouse ne so wrothe. 1840
And forthy I yow putte in this degree,
That ech of yow shal have his destynee
As hym is shape, and herkneth in what wyse;
Lo heere youre ende of that I shal devyse.
    My wyl is this, for plat conclusioun, 1845
Withouten any repplicacioun,—
If that you liketh, take it for the beste:
That everich of you shal goon where hym leste
Frely, withouten raunson or daunger;
And this day fifty wykes fer ne ner, 1850
Everich of you shal brynge an hundred
    knyghtes
Armed for lystes up at alle rightes,
Al redy to darreyne hire by bataille.
And this bihote I yow withouten faille,
Upon my trouthe, and as I am a knyght, 1855
That wheither of yow bothe that hath
    myght,—
This is to seyn, that wheither he or thow
May with his hundred, as I spak of now,
Sleen his contrarie, or out of lystes dryve,
Thanne shal I yeve Emelya to wyve 1860
To whom that Fortune yeveth so fair a grace.
The lystes shal I maken in this place,
And God so wisly on my soule rewe,
As I shal evene juge been and trewe.
Ye shul noon oother ende with me maken 1865
That oon of yow ne shal be deed or taken.
And if yow thynketh this is weel ysayd,
Seyeth youre avys, and holdeth you apayd.
This is youre ende and youre conclusioun."
    Who looketh lightly now but Palamoun?
Who spryngeth up for joye but Arcite? 1871
Who kouthe telle, or who kouthe it endite,
The joye that is maked in the place

1806. game, joke. 1807. jolitee, passion, desire. 1808. Kan hem . . . thank, is under obligation to them. 1809. hoote
fare, fervent behavior, "carrying on." 1813. yore agon. The expression is redundant but in common use; cf. l. 1941
below and *PF* 17. 1814. servant, servant of love. 1816. distreyne, oppress. 1817. laas, noose. 1822. dere, injure. 1827.
lordshipe, the protection of an overlord. 1838. go pipen in an yvy leef, go whistle. The expression occurs also in *TC* 5.
1433. 1841. degree, condition. 1843. shape, determined. 1844. ende, destiny. 1845. plat, plain, flat. 1846. repplicacioun,
rejoinder, protest. 1850. fer ne ner, more or less. See note to l. 1463. 1852. up, here an intensive adverb (as in "dressed
up"). at alle rightes, at all points. 1853. to darreyne hire, to establish (your) claim to her. 1854. bihote, promise. 1856.
wheither, whichever. 1859. contrarie, adversary. 1860. to wyve, for wife. 1863. And God . . . rewe, and may God
so surely have pity on my soul. 1864. evene, impartial. 1865. ende, agreement. 1868. avys, opinion. apayd, satisfied. 1869.
This . . . conclusioun, this ends the matter.

Whan Theseus hath doon so fair a grace?   1874
But doun on knees wente every maner wight,
And thonked hym with al hir herte and myght,
And namely the Thebans often sithe.

And thus with good hope and with herte blithe
They taken hir leve, and homward gonne they ride
To Thebes, with his olde walles wyde.   1880

Explicit secunda pars.

Sequitur pars tercia.

I trowe men wolde deme it necligence
If I foryete to tellen the dispence
Of Theseus, that gooth so bisily
To maken up the lystes roially,
That swich a noble theatre as it was,   1885
I dar wel seyn in this world ther nas.
The circuit a myle was aboute,
Walled of stoon, and dyched al withoute.
Round was the shape, in manere of compas,
Ful of degrees, the heighte of sixty pas,   1890
That whan a man was set on o degree,
He letted nat his felawe for to see.
    Estward ther stood a gate of marbul whit,
Westward right swich another in the opposit.
And shortly to concluden, swich a place   1895
Was noon in erthe, as in so litel space;
For in the lond ther was no crafty man
That geometrie or ars-metrik kan,
Ne portreyour, ne kervere of ymages,
That Theseus ne yaf him mete and wages,   1900
The theatre for to maken and devyse.
And for to doon his ryte and sacrifise,
He estward hath, upon the gate above,
In worshipe of Venus, goddesse of love,
Doon make an auter and an oratorie;   1905
And on the gate westward, in memorie
Of Mars, he maked hath right swich another,
That coste largely of gold a fother.
And northward, in a touret on the wal,
Of alabastre whit and reed coral,   1910

An oratorie, riche for to see,
In worshipe of Dyane of chastitee,
Hath Theseus doon wroght in noble wyse.
    But yet hadde I foryeten to devyse
The noble kervyng and the portreitures,   1915
The shape, the contenaunce, and the figures,
That weren in thise oratories thre.
    First in the temple of Venus maystow se
Wroght on the wal, ful pitous to biholde,
The broken slepes, and the sikes colde,   1920
The sacred teeris, and the waymentynge,
The firy strokes of the desirynge
That loves servantz in this lyf enduren;
The othes that hir covenantz assuren;
Plesaunce and Hope, Desir, Foolhardynesse,   1925
Beautee and Youthe, Bauderie, Richesse,
Charmes and Force, Lesynges, Flaterye,
Despense, Bisynesse, and Jalousye,
That wered of yelewe gooldes a gerland,
And a cokkow sittynge on hir hand;   1930
Festes, instrumentz, caroles, daunces,
Lust and array, and alle the circumstaunces
Of love, whiche that I rekned and rekne shal,
By ordre weren peynted on the wal,
And mo than I kan make of mencioun.   1935
For soothly al the mount of Citheroun,
Ther Venus hath hir principal dwellynge,
Was shewed on the wal in portreyynge,
With al the gardyn and the lustynesse.
Nat was foryeten the porter, Ydelnesse,   1940

1877. **often sithe**, repeatedly. 1882. **dispence**, expenditure. 1885. **theatre**, amphitheater. 1890. **degrees**, steps. **pas**, paces (yards). 1892. **letted**, hindered. 1896. **as in so litel space**, of its size. 1897. **crafty**, skilled. 1898. **ars-metrik**, arithmetic. 1899. **portreyour**, painter. 1905. **Doon make**, caused to be made. 1908. **fother**, cartload. 1910. Such luxury is characteristic of medieval romances. 1914. **hadde I foryeten**, I would have forgotten, came near forgetting. **devyse**, describe. 1915. **portreitures**, representations. 1920. **sikes**, sighs. 1926. **Bauderie**, Mirth or Gaiety. 1927. **Lesynges**, Lies. 1928. **Despense**, Expense. 1929. **gooldes**, marigolds. 1936. **mount of Citheroun**, a confusion with the island of Cythera, beside which Venus rose from the sea. Chaucer got the idea that Venus had her "principal dwellynge" there from *RR*, 15669. 1939. **lustynesse**, pleasure. 1940. **the porter, Ydelnesse**. Ydleness is the porter who guards the gate of the garden in *RR*.

Ne Narcisus the faire of yore agon,
Ne yet the folye of kyng Salamon,
Ne yet the grete strengthe of Ercules—
Th'enchauntementz of Medea and Circes—
Ne of Turnus, with the hardy fiers corage, 1945
The riche Cresus, kaytyf in servage.
Thus may ye seen that wysdom ne richesse,
Beautee ne sleighte, strengthe ne hardynesse,
Ne may with Venus holde champartie,
For as hir list the world than may she gye. 1950
Lo, alle thise folk so caught were in hir las,
Til they for wo ful ofte seyde "allas!"
Suffiseth heere ensamples oon or two,
And though I koude rekene a thousand mo.

    The statue of Venus, glorious for to se, 1955
Was naked, fletynge in the large see,
And fro the navele doun al covered was
With wawes grene, and brighte as any glas.
A citole in hir right hand hadde she,
And on hir heed, ful semely for to se, 1960
A rose gerland, fressh and wel smellynge;
Above hir heed hir dowves flikerynge.
Biforn hire stood hir sone Cupido;
Upon his shuldres wynges hadde he two,
And blynd he was, as it is often seene; 1965
A bowe he bar and arwes brighte and kene.

    Why sholde I noght as wel eek telle yow al
The portreiture that was upon the wal
Withinne the temple of myghty Mars the rede?
Al peynted was the wal, in lengthe and brede,
Lyk to the estres of the grisly place 1971
That highte the grete temple of Mars in Trace,
In thilke colde, frosty regioun

Ther as Mars hath his sovereyn mansioun.
    First on the wal was peynted a forest, 1975
In which ther dwelleth neither man ne best,
With knotty, knarry, bareyne trees olde,
Of stubbes sharpe and hidouse to biholde,
In which ther ran a rumbel in a swough, 1979
As though a storm sholde bresten every bough.
And dounward from an hille, under a bente,
Ther stood the temple of Mars armypotente,
Wroght al of burned steel, of which the entree
Was long and streit, and gastly for to see.
And therout cam a rage and swich a veze 1985
That it made al the gate for to rese.
The northren lyght in at the dores shoon,
For wyndowe on the wal ne was ther noon,
Thurgh which men myghten any light discerne.
The dore was al of adamant eterne, 1990
Yclenched overthwart and endelong
With iren tough; and for to make it strong,
Every pyler, the temple to sustene,
Was tonne-greet, of iren bright and shene.
    Ther saugh I first the derke ymaginyng 1995
Of Felonye, and al the compassyng;
The crueel Ire, reed as any gleede;
The pykepurs, and eek the pale Drede;
The smylere with the knyfe under the cloke;
The shepne brennynge with the blake
    smoke; 2000
The tresoun of the mordrynge in the bedde;
The open werre, with woundes al bibledde;
Contek, with blody knyf and sharp manace.
Al ful of chirkyng was that sory place.
The sleere of hymself yet saugh I ther,— 2005

1941. Narcisus. Narcissus pined away for love of his own image in a fountain. **1945. Turnus,** represented in the *Æneid* as a brave warrior, killed by Æneas (the battle occupies the twelfth book). **fiers corage,** proud heart. **1946. The riche Cresus.** The wealth of Croesus, king of Lydia (560–546 B.C.), is proverbial, but the phrase *kaytyf in servage* (wretched in servitude) refers to his capture by Cyrus. Chaucer tells part of the story at the end of the *Monk's Tale*. **1948. sleighte,** cunning. **1949. champartie,** equal power. **1950. gye,** direct. **1951. las,** noose, net. **1956. fletynge,** floating. **large,** broad. For Chaucer's source for this description see the note to *HF* 120. **1959. citole,** a pear-shaped stringed instrument, though Chaucer's probable source describes her with a conch in her right hand. **1971. estres,** the (upper) parts or rooms of a building. **grisly,** horrible. **1977. knarry,** gnarled. **1978. stubbes,** the remains of broken branches. **1979. in,** in the form of. **1981. under a bente,** below a grassy slope. **1982. armypotente,** powerful in arms. **1983. burned,** burnished. **entree,** entrance. **1984. streit,** narrow. **1985. rage, veze,** violent wind. rush of air. **1986. rese,** shake. **1987. northren lyght,** here simply "the light from the north," not the Aurora Borealis. **1991. Yclenched,** bound. **overthwart and endelong,** crosswise and lengthwise. **1994. tonne-greet,** large as a tun. **1996. compassyng,** contriving, scheming. **2000. shepne,** stable, shed. **2001. mordrynge in the bedde,** possibly alluding to the story of Hypermnestra, which Chaucer left unfinished in the *LGW*. **2003. Contek,** strife. **2004. chirkyng,** harsh noise. **2005. sleere of hymself,** suicide.

His herte-blood hath bathed al his heer;
The nayl ydryven in the shode a-nyght;
The colde deeth, with mouth gapyng upright.
Amyddes of the temple sat Meschaunce,
With disconfort and sory contenaunce.   2010
Yet saugh I Woodnesse, laughynge in his rage,
Armed Compleint, Outhees, and fiers Outrage;
The careyne in the busk, with throte ycorve;
A thousand slayn, and nat of qualm ystorve;
The tiraunt, with the pray by force yraft;   2015
The toun destroyed, ther was nothyng laft.
Yet saugh I brent the shippes hoppesteres;
The hunte strangled with the wilde beres;
The sowe freten the child right in the cradel;
The cook yscalded, for al his longe ladel.   2020
Noght was foryeten by the infortune of Marte
The cartere overryden with his carte:
Under the wheel ful lowe he lay adoun.
Ther were also, of Martes divisioun,   2024
The barbour, and the bocher, and the smyth,
That forgeth sharpe swerdes on his styth.
And al above, depeynted in a tour,
Saugh I Conquest, sittynge in greet honour,
With the sharpe swerd over his heed
Hangynge by a soutil twynes threed.   2030
Depeynted was the slaughtre of Julius,
Of grete Nero, and of Antonius;
Al be that thilke tyme they were unborn,
Yet was hir deth depeynted ther-biforn
By manasynge of Mars, right by figure.   2035

So was it shewed in that portreiture,
As is depeynted in the sterres above
Who shal be slayn or elles deed for love.
Suffiseth oon ensample in stories olde;
I may nat rekene hem alle though I wolde.   2040
The statue of Mars upon a carte stood
Armed, and looked grym as he were wood;
And over his heed ther shynen two figures
Of sterres, that been cleped in scriptures,
That oon Puella, that oother Rubeus—   2045
This god of armes was arrayed thus.
A wolf ther stood biforn hym at his feet
With eyen rede, and of a man he eet;
With soutil pencel was depeynt this storie
In redoutynge of Mars and of his glorie.   2050
Now to the temple of Dyane the chaste,
As shortly as I kan, I wol me haste,
To telle yow al the descripsioun.
Depeynted been the walles up and doun
Of huntyng and of shamefast chastitee.   2055
Ther saugh I how woful Calistopee,
Whan that Diane agreved was with here,
Was turned from a womman til a bere,
And after was she maad the loode-sterre;   2059
Thus was it peynted, I kan sey yow no ferre.
Hir sone is eek a sterre, as men may see.
Ther saugh I Dane, yturned til a tree,—
I mene nat the goddesse Diane,
But Penneus doghter, which that highte Dane.
Ther saugh I Attheon an hert ymaked,   2065

2007. shode, top of the head. **2010. disconfort,** discouragement, grief. **2011. Woodnesse,** Madness. **2012. Outhees,** outcry, clamor. **2013. careyne,** dead body. **busk,** bush. **ycorve,** cut. **2014. qualm,** pestilence. **ystorve,** having died. **2015. pray,** booty. **yraft,** taken away. **2016. ther,** where. **2017. hoppesteres.** The word properly means "dancers," but the phrase *the shippes hoppesteres* represents *le navi bellatrici* (the fighting ships) of the *Teseida* (VII, st. 37). Chaucer may have misread the word or his manuscript may have read *ballatrici, i.e.* dancing ships. **2018. hunte,** hunter. **with** by. **2019. freten,** having eaten. **2021. by,** with respect to. **infortune of Marte,** malevolent influence of Mars. Chaucer is here thinking of the planet identified with the god. **2022. overryden,** run over. **2024. divisioun.** Liddell notes that the crafts were under the protection of Mars. **2026. styth,** anvil. **2030. soutil,** slender. **2035. manasynge,** threatening, *i.e.* the foreseen malignancy of Mars. The prepositional phrase modifies. *deth* **by figure.** The phrase is of uncertain meaning, but probably has reference to the astrological interpretation of the stars. **2043. two figures. . . .** This passage was first explained by Skeat in the *Academy*, March 2, 1889. Figures were arrangements of dots, of which sixteen types were recognized in the "science" of geomancy. Puella and Rubeus were the names of two of them, ⠒ Puella, ⠆ Rubeus. Skeat's explanation can conveniently be read in his note on the passage in the *Oxford Chaucer*, **2046. arrayed thus,** so provided. **2048. eet,** ate. **2050. redoutynge,** reverence. **2055. shamefast,** modest. **2056. Calistopee,** Callisto. Diana was angry with her because she had been embraced by Jove and was no longer a virgin. Juno changed her into a bear and Jove placed her in the heavens as Ursa Major and her son as Ursa Minor. The *loode-sterre* or polestar is actually in Ursa Minor. Chaucer in calling her a star identifies her with the constellation, and refers in the same way to her son in l. 2061. **2060. ferre,** farther. **2062. Dane,** Daphne, pursued by Apollo, escaped by being changed into a laurel. **2064. Penneus,** Peneus, the river-god in Thessaly. **2065. Attheon,** Actaeon, a huntsman, changed into a stag because he came upon Diana and her nymphs bathing.

For vengeaunce that he saugh Diane al naked;
I saugh how that his houndes have hym caught
And freeten hym, for that they knewe hym naught.
Yet peynted was a litel forther moor
How Atthalante hunted the wilde boor, 2070
And Meleagre, and many another mo,
For which Dyane wroghte hym care and wo.
Ther saugh I many another wonder storie,
The whiche me list nat drawen to memorie.

This goddesse on an hert ful hye seet, 2075
With smale houndes al aboute hir feet;
And undernethe hir feet she hadde a moone,—
Wexynge it was and sholde wanye soone.
In gaude grene hir statue clothed was,
With bowe in honde, and arwes in a cas. 2080
Hir eyen caste she ful lowe adoun,
Ther Pluto hath his derke regioun.
A womman travaillynge was hire biforn;
But for hir child so longe was unborn,
Ful pitously Lucyna gan she calle, 2085
And seyde, "Help, for thou mayst best of alle!"
Wel koude he peynten lifly that it wroghte;
With many a floryn he the hewes boghte.

Now been thise lystes maad, and Theseus,
That at his grete cost arrayed thus 2090
The temples and the theatre every deel,
Whan it was doon, hym lyked wonder weel.
But stynte I wole of Theseus a lite,
And speke of Palamon and of Arcite.

The day approcheth of hir retournynge, 2095
That everich sholde an hundred knyghtes brynge
The bataille to darreyne, as I yow tolde.
And til Atthenes, hir covenant for to holde,

Hath everich of hem broght an hundred knyghtes,
Wel armed for the werre at alle rightes. 2100
And sikerly ther trowed many a man
That nevere sithen that the world bigan,
As for to speke of knyghthod of hir hond,
As fer as God hath maked see or lond,
Nas of so fewe so noble a compaignye. 2105
For every wight that lovede chivalrye,
And wolde, his thankes, han a passant name,
Hath preyed that he myghte been of that game;
And wel was hym that therto chosen was.
For if ther fille tomorwe swich a cas, 2110
Ye knowen wel that every lusty knyght
That loveth paramours and hath his myght,
Were it in Engelond or elleswhere,
They wolde, hir thankes, wilnen to be there,—
To fighte for a lady, *benedicitee!* 2115
It were a lusty sighte for to see.

And right so ferden they with Palamon.
With hym ther wenten knyghtes many on;
Som wol ben armed in an haubergeoun,
And in a brestplate and a light gypoun; 2120
And somme woln have a paire plates large;
And somme woln have a Pruce sheeld or a targe;
Somme woln ben armed on hir legges weel,
And have an ax, and somme a mace of steel—
Ther is no newe gyse that it nas old. 2125
Armed were they, as I have yow told,
Everych after his opinioun.

Ther maistow seen comynge with Palamoun
Lygurge hymself, the grete kyng of Trace.
Blak was his berd and manly was his face; 2130

The cercles of his eyen in his heed,
They gloweden bitwixen yelow and reed,
And lik a grifphon looked he aboute,
With kempe heeris on his browes stoute;   2134
His lymes grete, his brawnes harde and stronge,
His shuldres brode, his armes rounde and longe;
And as the gyse was in his contree,
Ful hye upon a chaar of gold stood he,
With foure white boles in the trays.
In stede of cote-armure over his harnays,   2140
With nayles yelewe and brighte as any gold,
He hadde a beres skyn, col-blak for old.
His longe heer was kembd bihynde his bak;
As any ravenes fethere it shoon for blak;   2144
A wrethe of gold, arm-greet, of huge wighte,
Upon his heed, set ful of stones brighte,
Of fyne rubyes and of dyamauntz.
Aboute his chaar ther wenten white alauntz,
Twenty and mo, as grete as any steer,
To hunten at the leoun or the deer,   2150
And folwed hym with mosel faste ybounde,
Colered of gold, and tourettes fyled rounde.
An hundred lordes hadde he in his route,
Armed ful wel, with hertes stierne and stoute.
   With Arcita, in stories as men fynde,   2155
The grete Emetreus, the kyng of Inde,
Upon a steede bay trapped in steel,
Covered in clooth of gold, dyapred weel,
Cam ridynge lyk the god of armes, Mars.
His cote-armure was of clooth of Tars   2160

Couched with perles white and rounde and
   grete;
His sadel was of brend gold newe ybete;
A mantelet upon his shulder hangynge,
Bret-ful of rubyes rede as fyr sparklynge;
His crispe heer lyk rynges was yronne,   2165
And that was yelow, and glytered as the sonne.
His nose was heigh, his eyen bright citryn,
His lippes rounde, his colour was sangwyn;
A fewe frakenes in his face yspreynd,
Bitwixen yelow and somdel blak ymeynd;   2170
And as a leoun he his lookyng caste.
Of fyve and twenty yeer his age I caste.
His berd was wel bigonne for to sprynge;
His voys was as a trompe thonderynge.
Upon his heed he wered of laurer grene   2175
A gerland, fressh and lusty for to sene.
Upon his hand he bar for his deduyt
An egle tame, as any lilye whyt.
An hundred lordes hadde he with hym there,
Al armed, save hir heddes, in al hir gere,   2180
Ful richely in alle maner thynges.
For trusteth wel that dukes, erles, kynges
Were gadered in this noble compaignye,
For love and for encrees of chivalrye.
Aboute this kyng ther ran on every part   2185
Ful many a tame leoun and leopart.
And in this wise thise lordes, alle and some,
Been on the Sonday to the citee come
Aboute pryme, and in the toun alight.   2189

2131. cercles, spheres (*i.e.* his eyeballs). **2133. grifphon,** griffin. **2134. kempe,** shaggy. **2135. brawnes,** muscles. **2138. chaar,** chariot. **2139. boles,** bulls. **trays,** traces. **2140. cote-armure,** coat armor, a vest embroidered with a heraldic device. **harnays,** armor. **2142. for old,** for age. It is not always easy to tell when in Chaucer (and ME generally) *for* is to be taken as a preposition and when as an intensive prefix. Each instance must be considered in context, and in some contexts either interpretation is possible. **2143. kembd,** combed. **2144. for blak,** for blackness. **2145. wighte,** weight. **2148. alauntz,** wolf-hounds. **2151. mosel,** muzzle. **2152. Colered,** furnished with collars. **and tourettes,** and (with) little rings for attaching a leash. **fyled,** filed, finished with a file. **2154. stierne,** stern. **2156. Emetreus.** The character has not been identified. Some have seen resemblances to Richard II and to Henry, Earl of Derby. Curry has proposed an astrological explanation for Lycurgus and Emetreus (*Chaucer and the Medieval Sciences*). **2157. trapped in steel,** with steel trappings. **2158. clooth of gold,** cloth with narrow strips of gold, or gold threads, in the wool. **dyapred weel,** well covered with figures or a pattern. **2160. clooth of Tars,** a rich cloth frequently mentioned in inventories of church vestments. The origin of the name is not certain but the designation seems to be derived from Tarsia in Chinese Turkestan. It was almost always purple. Many quotations are gathered together in Francisque-Michel, *Recherches sur le commerce, la fabrication et l' usage des étoffes de soie, etc.* (2v, Paris, 1852–4), II. 164–6. **2161. Couched,** overlaid, decorated. **2162. brend,** refined. **2164. Bret-ful,** brimful. **2165. crispe,** curly. **yronne,** *lit.* run, but the use seems rather forced. **2167. citryn,** lemon-colored. **2168. sangwyn,** ruddy. **2169. frakenes,** freckles. **yspreynd,** sprinkled. **2170. ymeynd,** mingled. **2172. caste,** estimate. **2175. laurer,** laurel. **2177. deduyt,** delight. **2180. gere,** armor. **2184. chivalrye,** knightly distinction. **2185. part,** side. **2187. alle and some,** one and all. **2189. pryme,** 9 A.M.

This Theseus, this duc, this worthy knyght,
Whan he had broght hem into his citee,
And inned hem, everich at his degree,
He festeth hem, and dooth so greet labour
To esen hem and doon hem al honour,
That yet men wenen that no mannes wit   2195
Of noon estaat ne koude amenden it.

    The mynstralcye, the service at the feeste,
The grete yiftes to the meeste and leeste,
The riche array of Theseus paleys,
Ne who sat first ne last upon the deys,   2200
What ladyes fairest been or best daunsynge,
Or which of hem kan dauncen best and synge,
Ne who moost felyngly speketh of love;
What haukes sitten on the perche above,
What houndes liggen on the floor adoun,—
Of al this make I now no mencioun,   2206
But al th'effect, that thynketh me the beste.
Now cometh the point, and herkneth if yow
    leste.
    The Sonday nyght, er day bigan to sprynge,
Whan Palamon the larke herde synge,   2210
Although it nere nat day by houres two,
Yet song the larke; and Palamon right tho,
With hooly herte and with an heigh corage,
He roos to wenden on his pilgrymage
Unto the blisful Citherea benigne,—   2215
I mene Venus, honurable and digne.
And in hir houre he walketh forth a pas
Unto the lystes ther hire temple was,
And doun he kneleth, and with humble cheere
And herte soor, he seyde as ye shal heere: 2220
    "Faireste of faire, O lady myn, Venus,
Doughter to Jove, and spouse of Vulcanus,
Thow gladere of the mount of Citheron,
For thilke love thow haddest to Adoon,
Have pitee of my bittre teeris smerte,   2225
And taak myn humble preyere at thyn herte.
Allas! I ne have no langage to telle

Th'effectes ne the tormentz of myn helle;
Myn herte may myne harmes nat biwreye;
I am so confus that I kan noght seye   2230
But, 'Mercy, lady bright, that knowest weele
My thought, and seest what harmes that I feele!'
Considere al this and rewe upon my soore,
As wisly as I shal for everemoore,
Emforth my myght, thy trewe servant be,   2235
And holden werre alwey with chastitee.
That make I myn avow, so ye me helpe!
I kepe noght of armes for to yelpe,
Ne I ne axe nat tomorwe to have victorie,
Ne renoun in this cas, ne veyne glorie   2240
Of pris of armes blowen up and doun;
But I wolde have fully possessioun
Of Emelye, and dye in thy servyse.
Fynd thow the manere hou, and in what wyse.
I recche nat, but it may bettre be,   2245
To have victorie of hem, or they of me,
So that I have my lady in myne armes.
For though so be that Mars is god of armes,
Youre vertu is so greet in hevene above
That if yow list, I shal wel have my love.   2250
Thy temple wol I worshipe everemo,
And on thyn auter, where I ride or go,
I wol doon sacrifice and fires beete.
And if ye wol nat so, my lady sweete,
Thanne preye I thee, tomorwe with a spere   2255
That Arcita me thurgh the herte bere.
Thanne rekke I noght, whan I have lost my lyf,
Though that Arcita wynne hire to his wyf.
This is th'effect and ende of my preyere:
Yif me my love, thow blisful lady deere."   2260
    Whan the orison was doon of Palamon,
His sacrifice he dide, and that anon,
Ful pitously, with alle circumstaunces,
Al telle I noght as now his observaunces;
But atte laste the statue of Venus shook,   2265
And made a signe, wherby that he took

2192. inned, lodged. at his degree, according to his rank. 2198. meeste, most important. 2207. al th' effect, the general effect. 2211. houres two. Two hours before sunrise on Monday, the twenty-third hour of Sunday began, an hour assigned to the planet Venus (cf. l. 2217). Chaucer explains the distribution of hours in his Astrolabe, II, par. 12. 2212. and, At this point the construction changes. 2213. corage, spirit. 2216. digne, worthy. 2220. soor, sore (with love). 2224. Adoon, Adonis. 2229. biwreye, reveal. 2230. confus, bewildered. 2235. Emforth, to the extent of. 2238. kepe, care. yelpe, boast. 2247. So that, provided. 2252. where . . . go, whether I ride or walk. 2253. beete, kindle. 2264. Al, although.

That his preyere accepted was that day.
For thogh the signe shewed a delay,
Yet wiste he wel that graunted was his boone;
And with glad herte he wente hym hoom ful soone. 2270
   The thridde houre inequal that Palamon
Bigan to Venus temple for to gon,
Up roos the sonne, and up roos Emelye,
And to the temple of Dyane gan hye.
Hir maydens, that she thider with hire ladde,
Ful redily with hem the fyr they hadde, 2276
Th'encens, the clothes, and the remenant al
That to the sacrifice longen shal;
The hornes fulle of meeth, as was the gyse,
Ther lakked noght to doon hir sacrifise. 2280
Smokynge the temple, ful of clothes faire,
This Emelye, with herte debonaire,
Hir body wessh with water of a welle.
But hou she dide hir ryte I dar nat telle,
But it be any thing in general; 2285
And yet it were a game to heeren al.
To hym that meneth wel it were no charge;
But it is good a man been at his large.
Hir brighte heer was kembd, untressed al;
A coroune of a grene ook cerial 2290
Upon hir heed was set ful fair and meete.
Two fyres on the auter gan she beete,
And dide hir thynges, as men may biholde
In Stace of Thebes and thise bookes olde.
Whan kyndled was the fyr, with pitous cheere
Unto Dyane she spak as ye may heere: 2296
   "O chaste goddesse of the wodes grene,
To whom bothe hevene and erthe and see is sene,
Queene of the regne of Pluto derk and lowe,

Goddesse of maydens, that myn herte hast knowe 2300
Ful many a yeer, and woost what I desire,
As keep me fro thy vengeaunce and thyn ire,
That Attheon aboughte cruelly.
Chaste goddesse, wel wostow that I
Desire to ben a mayden al my lyf, 2305
Ne nevere wol I be no love ne wyf.
I am, thow woost, yet of thy compaignye,
A mayde, and love huntynge and venerye,
And for to walken in the wodes wilde,
And noght to ben a wyf and be with childe, 2310
Noght wol I knowe the compaignye of man.
Now help me, lady, sith ye may and kan,
For tho thre formes that thou hast in thee.
And Palamon, that hath swich love to me,
And eek Arcite, that loveth me so soore,— 2315
This grace I preye thee withoute moore:
As sende love and pees bitwixe hem two,
And fro me turne awey hir hertes so
That al hire hoote love and hir desir,
And al hir bisy torment, and hir fir 2320
Be queynt, or turned in another place.
And if so be thou wolt nat do me grace,
Or if my destynee be shapen so
That I shal nedes have oon of hem two,
As sende me hym that moost desireth me. 2325
Bihoold, goddesse of clene chastitee,
The bittre teeris that on my chekes falle.
Syn thou art mayde and kepere of us alle,
My maydenhede thou kepe and wel conserve,
And whil I lyve, a mayde I wol thee serve." 2330
   The fires brenne upon the auter cleere,
Whil Emelye was thus in hir preyere.
But sodeynly she saugh a sighte queynte,

2271. **houre inequal.** The equal hours are each a twenty-fourth of the solar day, but the "inequal" hours are a twelfth of the time between sunrise and sunset. Thus the length of the hours in the daytime and at night varied with the season. The hours assigned to the different planets were the inequal hours. **that,** after. The first hour of Monday was assigned to the moon, hence Diana. 2277. **clothes,** cloths, hangings. 2278. **longen,** belong. 2279. **meeth,** mead. 2281. **Smokynge.** The line in the *Teseida* (VII, st. 72) reads *Fu mondo il templo . . .*, the temple was clean. Chaucer's translation implies *Fumando*, which might have been the reading of his MS. 2283. **wessh,** washed. **welle,** spring. 2286. **a game,** a pleasure. 2287. **it were no charge,** it wouldn't matter. 2288. **at his large,** at liberty (not to speak). 2289. **untressed,** loose. 2290. **ook cerial,** a species of oak (*Quercus cerris*). 2291. **meete,** fitting. 2294. **Stace,** Statius, author of the *Thebaid*. 2298. **sene,** visible, manifest. 2299. **regne,** kingdom. 2302. **As,** introducing an imperative; cf. Language, § 73. See note to l. 2065 above. 2303. **Attheon,** Actaeon. **aboughte,** atoned for. 2308. **venerye,** the chase. 2313. **tho thre formes.** She is called Luna in heaven, Diana on earth, Proserpina in hell. 2321. **queynt,** quenched. 2328. **Syn,** since. 2331. **brenne,** burn. 2333. **queynte,** strange.

For right anon oon of the fyres queynte, *was quenched*
And quyked agayn, and after that anon 2335
That oother fyr was queynt and al agon;
And as it queynte it made a whistelynge,
As doon thise *those* wete brondes in hir brennynge,
And at the brondes ende out ran anon
As it were blody dropes many oon; 2340
For which so soore agast was Emelye
That she was wel ny mad, and gan to crye,
For she ne wiste what it signyfied;
But oonly for the feere thus hath she cried,
And weep that it was pitee for to heere. 2345
And therwithal Dyane gan appeere,
With bowe in honde, right as an hunteresse,
And seyde, "Doghter, stynt thyn hevynesse.
Among the goddes hye it is affermed, 2349
And by eterne word writen and confermed,
Thou shalt ben wedded unto oon of tho
That han for thee so muchel care and wo;
But unto which of hem I may nat telle.
Farwel, for I ne may no lenger dwelle.
The fires whiche that on myn auter brenne 2355
Shulle thee declaren, er that thou go henne,
Thyn aventure of love, as in this cas."
And with that word, the arwes in the caas
Of the goddesse clateren faste and rynge,
And forth she wente, and made a vanysshynge;
For which this Emelye astoned was, 2361
And seyde, "What amounteth this, allas?
I putte me in thy proteccioun,
Dyane, and in thy disposicioun."
And hoom she goth anon the nexte weye. 2365
This is th'effect; ther is namoore to seye.

The nexte houre of Mars folwynge this,
Arcite unto the temple walked is
Of fierse Mars, to doon his sacrifise,
With alle the rytes of his payen wyse. 2370
With pitous herte and heigh devocioun,
Right thus to Mars he seyde his orisoun: *prayer*

"O stronge god, that in the regnes colde
Of Trace honoured art and lord yholde,
And hast in every regne and every lond 2375
Of armes al the brydel in thyn hond,
And hem fortunest as thee lyst devyse, *givest (good or bad) fortune*
Accepte of me my pitous sacrifise.
If so be that my youthe may deserve,
And that my myght be worthy for to
      serve 2380
Thy godhede, that I may been oon of thyne,
Thanne preye I thee to rewe upon my pyne.
For thilke peyne, and thilke hoote fir
In which thow whilom brendest for desir,
Whan that thow usedest the beautee 2385
Of faire, yonge, fresshe Venus free,
And haddest hire in armes at thy wille—
Although thee ones on a tyme mysfille, *it went wrong with thee*
Whan Vulcanus hadde caught thee in his las, *net*
And foond thee liggynge by his wyf, allas!—
For thilke sorwe that was in thyn herte, 2391
Have routhe as wel upon my peynes smerte. *pity*
I am yong and unkonnynge, as thow woost,
And, as I trowe, with love offended moost
That evere was any lyves creature; 2395
For she that dooth me al this wo endure
Ne reccheth nevere wher I synke or fleete.
And wel I woot, er she me mercy heete, *promise*
I moot with strengthe wynne hire in the place; *battle-fields: lists*
And wel I woot, withouten help or grace 2400
Of thee, ne may my strengthe noght availle.
Thanne help me, lord, tomorwe in my
      bataille,
For thilke fyr that whilom brente thee,
As wel as thilke fyr now brenneth me, *burned*
And do that I tomorwe have victorie. 2405 *bring it about*
Myn be the travaille, and thyn be the glorie!
Thy sovereyn temple wol I moost honouren
Of any place, and alwey moost labouren
In thy plesaunce and in thy craftes stronge,

2334. **queynte,** was quenched. 2338. **thise,** these (in a generalizing sense, where we say *those*). 2361. **astoned,** stunned. 2367. **The nexte houre of Mars.** This would be the fourth hour of Monday. 2370. **payen,** pagan. 2372. **orisoun,** prayer. 2373. **regnes,** kingdoms. 2377. **fortunest,** givest (good or bad) fortune. 2388. **thee . . . mysfille,** it went wrong with thee. The story is told by Ovid in the *Metam.,* IV. 171–89, and in the *Ars Amat.,* II. 561–600. 2389. **las,** net. 2390. **liggynge,** lying. 2395. **lyves,** living. 2397. **fleete,** float. 2398. **heete,** may promise. 2399. **place,** battle-field, *i.e.* the lists. 2403. **brente,** burned. 2405. **do,** bring it about.

And in thy temple I wol my baner honge 2410
And alle the armes of my compaignye;
And everemo, unto that day I dye,
Eterne fir I wol biforn thee fynde.
And eek to this avow I wol me bynde:
My beerd, myn heer, that hongeth long adoun,
That nevere yet ne felte offensioun 2416
Of rasour nor of shere, I wol thee yive,
And ben thy trewe servant whil I lyve.
Now, lord, have routhe upon my sorwes soore;
Yif me the victorie, I aske thee namoore." 2420
     The preyere stynt of Arcita the stronge,
The rynges on the temple dore that honge,
And eek the dores, clatereden ful faste,
Of which Arcita somwhat hym agaste.
The fyres brenden upon the auter brighte, 2425
That it gan al the temple for to lighte;
A sweete smel the ground anon up yaf,
And Arcita anon his hand up haf,
And moore encens into the fyr he caste,
With othere rytes mo; and atte laste 2430
The statue of Mars bigan his hauberk rynge;
And with that soun he herde a murmurynge
Ful lowe and dym, and seyde thus, "Victorie!"
For which he yaf to Mars honour and glorie
And thus with joye and hope wel to fare 2435
Arcite anon unto his in is fare,
As fayn as fowel is of the brighte sonne.
     And right anon swich strif ther is bigonne,
For thilke grauntyng, in the hevene above,
Bitwixe Venus, the goddesse of love, 2440
And Mars, the stierne god armypotente,
That Juppiter was bisy it to stente;
Til that the pale Saturnus the colde,

That knew so manye of aventures olde,
Foond in his olde experience an art 2445
That he ful soone hath plesed every part.
As sooth is seyd, elde hath greet avantage;
In elde is bothe wysdom and usage;
Men may the olde atrenne, and noght atrede.
Saturne anon, to stynten strif and drede, 2450
Al be it that it is agayn his kynde,
Of al this strif he gan remedie fynde.
"My deere doghter Venus," quod Saturne,
"My cours, that hath so wyde for to turne,
Hath moore power than woot any man. 2455
Myn is the drenchyng in the see so wan;
Myn is the prison in the derke cote;
Myn is the stranglyng and hangyng by the
     throte,
The murmure and the cherles rebellyng,
The groynynge, and the pryvee empoysonyng;
I do vengeance and pleyn correccioun, 2461
Whil I dwelle in the signe of the leoun.
Myn is the ruyne of the hye halles,
The fallynge of the toures and of the walles
Upon the mynour or the carpenter. 2465
I slow Sampsoun, shakynge the piler;
And myne be the maladyes colde,
The derke tresons, and the castes olde;
My lookyng is the fader of pestilence.
Now weep namoore, I shal doon diligence 2470
That Palamon, that is thyn owene knyght,
Shal have his lady, as thou hast him hight.
Though Mars shal helpe his knyght, yet nathe-
     lees
Bitwixe yow ther moot be som tyme pees,
Al be ye noght of o compleccioun, 2475

2413. **fynde,** provide for. 2416. **offensioun,** damage. Robinson notes that the dedication of hair and beard was an actual custom and cites Fraser, *The Golden Bough.* 2424. **hym agaste,** was frightened. 2428. **haf,** lifted. 2430. **atte,** at the. 2441. **armypotente,** powerful in arms. 2442. **was bisy it to stente,** had much to do to put an end to it. 2446. **every part,** all sides. 2448. **usage,** experience. 2449. **Men . . . atrede.** One may outrun the old but not outwit; cf. *TC* 4. 1456. 2451. **agayn his kynde,** against his nature, which was to cause strife. 2453. **doghter,** perhaps loosely used for granddaughter. 2454. **turne,** *i.e.* with his sphere. 2456. **drenchyng,** drowning. 2457. **cote.** Skeat renders the word "dungeon," which fits the context, but I do not know of any other example of this meaning in OE. or ME. 2459. **the cherles rebellyng,** supposed to be an allusion to the Peasants' Revolt in 1381, but some would attribute the action to the influence of Saturn (see J. Parr, *MLN,* LXIX. 393–4). There is no reason why both considerations should not have been in Chaucer's mind, and the word *cherles* seems quite pointed. 2460. **groynynge,** discontent. 2461. **correccioun,** punishment. 2462. **in the signe of the leoun,** The influence of the planet Saturn was particularly malign while in the sign Leo. 2467. **maladyes colde,** illnesses due to an excess of cold; cf. A 420. 2468. **castes,** plots, deceits. 2469. **lookyng,** aspect. 2475. **compleccioun,** disposition.

That causeth al day swich divisioun.
I am thyn aiel, redy at thy wille;
Weep now namoore, I wol thy lust fulfille."
   Now wol I stynten of the goddes above,

Of Mars, and of Venus, goddesse of love, 2480
And telle yow as pleynly as I kan
The grete effect, for which that I bygan.

Explicit tercia pars.

Sequitur pars quarta.

Greet was the feeste in Atthenes that day,
And eek the lusty seson of that May 2484
Made every wight to been in swich plesaunce
That al that Monday justen they and daunce,
And spenden it in Venus heigh servyse.
But by the cause that they sholde ryse
Eerly, for to seen the grete fight,
Unto hir reste wenten they at nyght. 2490
And on the morwe, whan that day gan sprynge,
Of hors and harneys noyse and claterynge
Ther was in hostelryes al aboute;
And to the paleys rood ther many a route
Of lordes upon steedes and palfreys. 2495
Ther maystow seen devisynge of harneys
So unkouth and so riche, and wroght so weel
Of goldsmythrye, of browdynge, and of steel;
The sheeldes brighte, testeres, and trappures,
Gold-hewen helmes, hauberkes, cote-armures;
Lordes in paramentz on hir courseres, 2501
Knyghtes of retenue, and eek squieres
Nailynge the speres, and helmes bokelynge;
Giggynge of sheeldes, with layneres lacynge—
There as nede is they weren no thyng ydel;
The fomy steedes on the golden brydel 2506
Gnawynge, and faste the armurers also
With fyle and hamer prikynge to and fro;
Yemen on foote, and communes many oon

With shorte staves, thikke as they may goon;
Pypes, trompes, nakers, clariounes, 2511
That in the bataille blowen blody sounes;
The paleys ful of peple up and doun,
Heere thre, ther ten, holdynge hir questioun,
Dyvynynge of thise Thebane knyghtes two. 2515
Somme seyden thus, somme seyde "it shal be
   so";
Somme helden with hym with the blake berd,
Somme with the balled, somme with the thikke
   herd;
Somme seyde he looked grymme, and he wolde
   fighte;
"He hath a sparth of twenty pound of wighte."
Thus was the halle ful of divynynge, 2521
Longe after that the sonne gan to sprynge.
   The grete Theseus, that of his sleep awaked
With mynstralcie and noyse that was maked,
Heeld yet the chambre of his paleys riche,
Til that the Thebane knyghtes, bothe yliche
Honured, were into the paleys fet. 2527
Duc Theseus was at a wyndow set,
Arrayed right as he were a god in trone.
The peple preesseth thiderward ful soone 2530
Hym for to seen, and doon heigh reverence,
And eek to herkne his heste and his sentence.
An heraud on a scaffold made an "Oo!"

2477. **aiel,** grandfather, forefather. 2478. **lust,** desire. 2491. **on the morwe.** Tuesday, Mars' day was traditionally a day for battles. See K. Garvin, *MLN,* XLVI. 453–4. 2496. **devisynge,** preparation. 2497. **unkouth,** unusual, marvelous. 2498. **browdynge,** embroidery. 2499. **testeres,** head-pieces. **trappures,** coverings for horses, either protective or decorative. 2500. **Gold-hewen,** made of gold. 2501. **paramentz,** decorated robes. 2503. **Nailynge the speres,** nailing the head of a lance to the shaft. 2504. **Giggynge,** fitting with straps. **layneres,** thongs. 2508. **prikynge,** spurring their horses. 2509. **Yemen,** yeomen. **communes,** common people. 2511. **nakers,** generally interpreted as "kettle-drums," but it is here in a list of wind instruments and in OF. (see Godefroy, *s.v. nacaire*) as in Middle English it is associated in some quotations with tabors and in others with trumpets. It may designate a wind instrument in the present passage. The word is Arabic and Robinson notes that there are two rather similar words in Arabic, one meaning "drum," the other "trumpet." 2512. **blody sounes.** Chaucer uses the expression in *HF* 1239, where he goes on to explain it. The meaning, however, is sufficiently obvious. 2513. **up and doun,** everywhere. 2514. **holdynge hir questioun,** carrying on discussion. 2515. **Dyvynynge of,** guessing about. 2518. **balled,** bald. **thikke herd,** thick-haired. 2519. **he . . . he,** this one . . . that one. 2520. **sparth,** battle-axe. 2521. **divynynge,** conjecture. 2526. **yliche,** equally. 2527. **fet,** fetched. 2529. **in trone,** on a throne. 2532. **heste,** bidding. 2533. **Oo,** Ho!

Til al the noyse of peple was ydo,   2534
And whan he saugh the peple of noyse al stille,
Tho shewed he the myghty dukes wille.
    "The lord hath of his heigh discrecioun
Considered that it were destruccioun
To gentil blood to fighten in the gyse
Of mortal bataille now in this emprise.   2540
Wherfore, to shapen that they shal nat dye,
He wol his firste purpos modifye.
No man therfore, up peyne of los of lyf,
No maner shot, ne polax, ne short knyf
Into the lystes sende, or thider brynge;   2545
Ne short swerd, for to stoke with poynt
    bitynge,
No man ne drawe, ne bere it by his syde.
Ne no man shal unto his felawe ryde
But o cours, with a sharpe ygrounde spere;
Foyne, if hym list, on foote, hymself to were.
And he that is at meschief shal be take   2551
And noght slayn, but be broght unto the stake
That shal ben ordeyned on either syde;
But thider he shal by force, and there abyde.
And if so falle the chieftayn be take   2555
On outher syde, or elles sleen his make,
No lenger shal the turneiynge laste.
God spede you! gooth forth, and ley on faste!
With long swerd and with maces fighteth youre
    fille.
Gooth now youre wey, this is the lordes wille."
    The voys of peple touchede the hevene,   2561
So loude cride they with murie stevene,
"God save swich a lord, that is so good!
He wilneth no destruccion of blood."
Up goon the trompes and the melodye,   2565
And to the lystes rit the compaignye,
By ordinance, thurghout the citee large,

Hanged with clooth of gold, and nat with sarge.
    Ful lik a lord this noble duc gan ryde,
Thise two Thebans upon either syde;   2570
And after rood the queene, and Emelye,
And after that another compaignye
Of oon and oother, after hir degree.
And thus they passen thurghout the citee,
And to the lystes come they by tyme.   2575
It nas nat of the day yet fully pryme
Whan set was Theseus ful riche and hye,
Ypolita the queene, and Emelye,
And othere ladys in degrees aboute.
Unto the seetes preesseth al the route.   2580
And westward, thurgh the gates under Marte,
Arcite and eek the hondred of his parte,
With baner reed is entred right anon;
And in that selve moment Palamon
Is under Venus, estward in the place,   2585
With baner whyt, and hardy chiere and face.
In al the world, to seken up and doun,
So evene, withouten variacioun,
Ther nere swiche compaignyes tweye;
For ther was noon so wys that koude seye   2590
That any hadde of oother avauntage
Of worthynesse, ne of estaat, ne age,
So evene were they chosen, for to gesse.
And in two renges faire they hem dresse.
Whan that hir names rad were everichon,   2595
That in hir nombre gyle were ther noon,
Tho were the gates shet, and cried was loude:
"Do now youre devoir, yonge knyghtes
    proude!"
    The heraudes lefte hir prikyng up and doun;
Now ryngen trompes loude and clarioun.   2600
Ther is namoore to seyn, but west and est
In goon the speres ful sadly in arrest;

2534. ydo, done, ended. 2537. discrecioun, sagacity, wisdom. 2543. up peyne of, upon pain of. 2544. shot, arrow. 2546. stoke, stab. 2549. cours, charge. 2550. Foyne, let him thrust. were, defend. 2551. at meschief, in misfortune. 2552. stake. In the account of a tourney quoted by Skeat from Strutt's *Sports and Pastimes* there was on each side a stake at which there were "two kyngs of arms, with penne, and inke, and paper, to write the names of all them that were yolden." 2554. by force, perforce, of necessity. 2555. if so falle, if it so happen. 2556. outher, either. sleen, (shall) slay. 2562. murie stevene, merry voice or sound. 2566. rit, rides. 2568. sarge, serge. 2576. pryme. *Prime* sometimes includes the first three hours after sunrise, here it probably means that it was not yet nine o'clock. 2581. Marte, Mars. 2583. baner reed. A red banner is appropriate for one who fights under the protection of Mars, often described as red (cf. l. 1969 above). 2584. selve, same. 2594. renges, ranks, rows. 2595. rad, read. 2596. were ther, there should be. 2598. devoir, duty. 2602. sadly in arrest, firmly in their rests; firmly couched. A *rest* or *arest* was a concave device attached to the breastplate and extending under the right arm. It is illustrated in A. Demmin, *Weapons of War* (1870), pp. 199, 226.

In gooth the sharpe spore into the syde.
Ther seen men who kan juste and who kan
  ryde;   2604
Ther shyveren shaftes upon sheeldes thikke;
He feeleth thurgh the herte-spoon the prikke.
Up spryngen speres twenty foot on highte;
Out goon the swerdes as the silver brighte;
The helmes they tohewen and toshrede;   2609
Out brest the blood with stierne stremes rede;
With myghty maces the bones they tobreste.
He thurgh the thikkeste of the throng gan
  threste;
Ther stomblen steedes stronge, and doun gooth
  al;
He rolleth under foot as dooth a bal;
He foyneth on his feet with his tronchoun, 2615
And he hym hurtleth with his hors adoun;
He thurgh the body is hurt and sithen ytake,
Maugree his heed, and broght unto the stake:
As forward was, right ther he moste abyde.
Another lad is on that oother syde.   2620
And som tyme dooth hem Theseus to reste,
Hem to refresshe and drynken, if hem leste.
Ful ofte a day han thise Thebanes two
Togydre ymet, and wroght his felawe wo;
Unhorsed hath ech oother of hem tweye.   2625
Ther nas no tygre in the vale of Galgopheye,
Whan that hir whelp is stole whan it is lite,
So crueel on the hunte as is Arcite
For jelous herte upon this Palamoun.
Ne in Belmarye ther nys so fel leoun,   2630
That hunted is, or for his hunger wood,
Ne of his praye desireth so the blood,
As Palamon to sleen his foo Arcite.
The jelous strokes on hir helmes byte;
Out renneth blood on bothe hir sydes rede. 2635
  Som tyme an ende ther is of every dede.

For er the sonne unto the reste wente,
The stronge kyng Emetreus gan hente
This Palamon, as he faught with Arcite,
And made his swerd depe in his flessh to byte;
And by the force of twenty is he take   2641
Unyolden, and ydrawe unto the stake.
And in the rescus of this Palamoun
The stronge kyng Lygurge is born adoun,
And kyng Emetreus, for al his strengthe,   2645
Is born out of his sadel a swerdes lengthe,
So hitte him Palamoun er he were take;
But al for noght—he was broght to the stake.
His hardy herte myghte hym helpe naught:
He most abyde, whan that he was caught,   2650
By force and eek by composicioun.
  Who sorweth now but woful Palamoun,
That moot namoore goon agayn to fighte?
And whan that Theseus hadde seyn this sighte,
Unto the folk that foghten thus echon   2655
He cryde, "Hoo! namoore, for it is doon!
I wol be trewe juge, and no partie.
Arcite of Thebes shal have Emelie,
That by his fortune hath hire faire ywonne."
Anon ther is a noyse of peple bigonne   2660
For joye of this, so loude and heighe withalle,
It semed that the lystes sholde falle.
  What kan now faire Venus doon above?
What seith she now? What dooth this queene
  of love,
But wepeth so, for wantynge of hir wille,   2665
Til that hir teeres in the lystes fille?
She seyde, "I am ashamed, doutelees."
  Saturnus seyde, "Doghter, hoold thy pees!
Mars hath his wille, his knyght hath al his
  boone,   2669
And, by myn heed, thow shalt been esed soone."
  The trompours, with the loude mynstralcie,

2603. spore, spur. 2606. herte-spoon, the depression below the breastbone. 2607. on highte, on high, in the air. 2609. tohewen, hew to pieces. toshrede, reduce to shreds. 2610. brest, bursts. stierne, terrible, gruesome. 2611. tobreste, break in pieces. 2612. He, this one. Cf. l. 2519. threste, thrust, push. 2615. tronchoun, broken shaft of spear. 2616. hurtleth . . . adoun, strikes down. 2619. forward, agreement. 2623. a day, during the day. 2626. Galgopheye. Skeat's suggestion is the most plausible—the vale of Gargaphie, where Actaeon was torn to pieces by his dogs (Ovid, *Metam.*, III. 155 ff.). 2627. lite, little. 2628. on the hunte, toward the hunter. 2629. upon, toward. 2630. Belmarye, in northwest Spain. See note to l. 57 above. 2634. jelous, eager. 2638. hente, catch. 2642. Unyolden, not having given up. 2643. rescus, rescue. 2651. By force, of necessity. composicioun, *i.e.* what he had agreed to. 2661. heighe, vociferously. 2666. fille, fell. 2667. ashamed, put to shame.

The heraudes, that ful loude yelle and crie,
Been in hire wele for joye of daun Arcite.
But herkneth me, and stynteth noyse a lite,
Which a myracle ther bifel anon.   2675
  This fierse Arcite hath of his helm ydon,
And on a courser, for to shewe his face,
He priketh endelong the large place,
Lokynge upward upon this Emelye;
And she agayn hym caste a freendlich yë   2680
(For wommen, as to speken in comune,
Thei folwen alle the favour of Fortune)
And was al his, in chiere, as in his herte.
  Out of the ground a furie infernal sterte,
From Pluto sent at requeste of Saturne,   2685
For which his hors for fere gan to turne,
And leep aside, and foundred as he leep;
And er that Arcite may taken keep,
He pighte hym on the pomel of his heed,
That in the place he lay as he were deed,   2690
His brest tobrosten with his sadel-bowe.
As blak he lay as any cole or crowe,
So was the blood yronnen in his face.
Anon he was yborn out of the place,
With herte soor, to Theseus paleys.   2695
Tho was he korven out of his harneys,
And in a bed ybrought ful faire and blyve;
For he was yet in memorie and alyve,
And alwey criynge after Emelye.
  Duc Theseus, with al his compaignye,   2700
Is comen hoom to Atthenes his citee,
With alle blisse and greet solempnitee.
Al be it that this aventure was falle,
He nolde noght disconforten hem alle.
Men seyde eek that Arcite shal nat dye;   2705
He shal been heeled of his maladye.
And of another thyng they weren as fayn,
That of hem alle was ther noon yslayn,

Al were they soore yhurt, and namely oon
That with a spere was thirled his brest-boon.
To othere woundes and to broken armes   2711
Somme hadden salves, and somme hadden
   charmes;
Fermacies of herbes, and eek save
They dronken, for they wolde hir lymes have.
For which this noble duc, as he wel kan,   2715
Conforteth and honoureth every man,
And made revel al the longe nyght
Unto the straunge lordes, as was right.
Ne ther was holden no disconfitynge
But as a justes, or a tourneiynge;   2720
For soothly ther was no disconfiture.
For fallyng nys nat but an aventure,
Ne to be lad by force unto the stake
Unyolden, and with twenty knyghtes take,
O persone allone, withouten mo,   2725
And haryed forth by arme, foot, and too,
And eke his steede dryven forth with staves
With footmen, bothe yemen and eek knaves,—
It nas arretted hym no vileynye;
Ther may no man clepen it cowardye.   2730
For which anon duc Theseus leet crye,
To stynten alle rancour and envye,
The gree as wel of o syde as of oother,
And eyther syde ylik as ootheres brother;
And yaf hem yiftes after hir degree,   2735
And fully heeld a feeste dayes three,
And conveyed the kynges worthily
Out of his toun a journee largely.
And hoom wente every man the righte way.
Ther was namoore but "Fare wel, have good
   day!"   2740
Of this bataille I wol namoore endite,
But speke of Palamon and of Arcite.
  Swelleth the brest of Arcite, and the soore

2676. **fierse**, proud, noble. **of** . . . **ydon**, removed. 2680. **agayn**, toward. 2681. **in comune**, in general. 2683. **in chiere**, in her countenance. 2689. **pighte**, pitched. **pomel**, top (round part). 2691. **tobrosten**, broken to pieces, shattered. **with**, by. 2696. **korven**, cut, *i.e.* the laces. 2698. **in memorie**, conscious. 2703. **aventure**, accident. 2704. **disconforten**, dishearten. 2709. **Al**, although. 2710. **That . . . his**, whose. **thirled**, pierced. 2712. **charmes**, commonly used by physicians in Chaucer's day. 2713. **Fermacies**, medicines. **save**, the herb sage, or an infusion of many herbs. 2714. **lymes**, limbs, which originally designated any of the organs of the body. 2718. **straunge**, foreign. 2719. **disconfitynge**, defeat in battle. 2720. **justes**, jousting-match; actually a plural here used in the sing. 2725. **O**, one. 2726. **haryed**, dragged. 2729. **arretted**, imputed. **vileynye**, disgrace. 2731. **leet crye**, caused to be proclaimed. 2732. **To stynten**, in order to stop. **envye**, illwill. 2733. **gree**, good-will. 2734. **ylik**, equal. 2738. **journee**, the distance traveled in a day. **largely**, fully. 2743. **soore**, pain, injury.

Encreesseth at his herte moore and moore.
The clothered blood, for any lechecraft,   2745
Corrupteth, and is in his bouk ylaft,
That neither veyne-blood, ne ventusynge,
*Ne drynke of herbes may ben his helpynge.
The vertu expulsif, or animal,
Fro thilke vertu cleped natural   2750
Ne may the venym voyden ne expelle.
The pipes of his longes gonne to swelle,
And every lacerte in his brest adoun
Is shent with venym and corrupcioun.
Hym gayneth neither, for to gete his lif,   2755
Vomyt upward, ne dounward laxatif.
Al is tobrosten thilke regioun;
Nature hath now no dominacioun.
And certeinly, ther Nature wol nat wirche,
Fare wel phisik! go ber the man to chirche!   2760
This al and som, that Arcita moot dye;
For which he sendeth after Emelye,
And Palamon, that was his cosyn deere.
Thanne seyde he thus, as ye shal after heere:
"Naught may the woful spirit in myn herte   2765
Declare o point of alle my sorwes smerte
To yow, my lady, that I love moost;
But I biquethe the servyce of my goost
To yow aboven every creature,
Syn that my lyf may no lenger dure.   2770
Allas, the wo! allas, the peynes stronge,
That I for yow have suffred, and so longe!
Allas, the deeth! allas, myn Emelye!
Allas, departynge of oure compaignye!
Allas, myn hertes queene! allas, my wyf!   2775
Myn hertes lady, endere of my lyf!

What is this world? what asketh men to have?
Now with his love, now in his colde grave
Allone, withouten any compaignye.
Fare wel, my swete foo, myn Emelye!   2780
And softe taak me in youre armes tweye,
For love of God, and herkneth what I seye.
    I have heer with my cosyn Palamon
Had strif and rancour many a day agon
For love of yow, and for my jalousye.   2785
And Juppiter so wys my soule gye,
To speken of a servaunt proprely,
With alle circumstances trewely—
That is to seyn, trouthe, honour, knyghthede,
Wysdom, humblesse, estaat, and heigh kynrede,
Fredom, and al that longeth to that art—   2791
So Juppiter have of my soule part,
As in this world right now ne knowe I non
So worthy to ben loved as Palamon,
That serveth yow, and wol doon al his lyf.   2795
And if that evere ye shul ben a wyf,
Foryet nat Palamon, the gentil man."
And with that word his speche faille gan,
For from his feet up to his brest was come
The coold of deeth, that hadde hym overcome,
And yet mooreover, for in his armes two   2801
The vital strengthe is lost and al ago.
Oonly the intellect, withouten moore,
That dwelled in his herte syk and soore,
Gan faillen whan the herte felte deeth.   2805
Dusked his eyen two, and failled breeth,
But on his lady yet caste he his yë;
His laste word was, "Mercy, Emelye!"
His spirit chaunged hous and wente ther,

2745. clothered, clotted. **for,** in spite of. **2746. bouk,** trunk of the body. **2747. veyne-blood,** letting blood from a vein, although this use of the word is unusual. **ventusynge,** bloodletting. **2749. vertu expulsif, or animal.** According to medieval medicine there were three *virtues* controlling the body: natural (in the liver), vital (in the heart), and animal (working through the brain). Chaucer identifies the expulsive virtue with the animal virtue, rather than the natural, but this was a matter of controversy among medical authorities. See Curry, *Chaucer and the Medieval Sciences*, pp. 140 ff. What Chaucer seems to be saying is that the injured brain is not able to actuate the muscles producing a cough and thus expel what is injurious to the natural virtue. **2753. lacerte,** muscle. **2754. shent,** corrupted. **corrupcioun,** decomposed matter. **2755. Hym gayneth,** there profits him. **2759. wirche,** work. **2761. This al and som,** this (is) the whole of the matter. **2766. o point,** one particle. **2768. goost,** spirit, soul, *i.e.* after death. **2775. wyf.** In the *Teseida* Arcita marries Emelia on his deathbed, but here Arcite may be thinking of her as having been awarded to him as his wife. **2776. endere of my lyf,** cause of my death. **2777. men,** one. **2786. wys,** certainly. **2787. of a servaunt,** as a servant. **2792. part,** possession. **2803. Oonly . . .** The intellect only began to fail when . . . The unusual word-order is influenced by the *Teseida*, "sol nello intelletto," with a different construction. The heart as the seat of the intellect survives in our expression "to learn by heart." **2806. Dusked,** grew dim.

As I cam nevere, I kan nat tellen wher.   2810
Therfore I stynte, I nam no divinistre;
Of soules fynde I nat in this registre,
Ne me ne list thilke opinions to telle
Of hem, though that they writen wher they
    dwelle.
Arcite is coold, ther Mars his soule gye!   2815
Now wol I speken forth of Emelye.
    Shrighte Emelye, and howleth Palamon,
And Theseus his suster took anon
Swownynge, and baar hire fro the corps away.
What helpeth it to tarien forth the day   2820
To tellen how she weep bothe eve and morwe?
For in swich cas wommen have swich sorwe,
Whan that hir housbondes ben from hem ago,
That for the moore part they sorwen so,
Or ellis fallen in swich maladye,   2825
That at the laste certeinly they dye.
    Infinite been the sorwes and the teeres
Of olde folk, and folk of tendre yeeres,
In al the toun for deeth of this Theban.
For hym ther wepeth bothe child and man;   2830
So greet wepyng was ther noon, certayn,
Whan Ector was ybroght, al fressh yslayn,
To Troye. Allas, the pitee that was ther,
Cracchynge of chekes, rentynge eek of heer.
"Why woldestow be deed," thise wommen
    crye,   2835
"And haddest gold ynough, and Emelye?"
    No man myghte gladen Theseus,
Savynge his olde fader Egeus,
That knew this worldes transmutacioun,
As he hadde seyn it chaunge bothe up and doun,
Joye after wo, and wo after gladnesse,   2841
And shewed hem ensamples and liknesse.
    "Right as ther dyed nevere man," quod he,
"That he ne lyvede in erthe in som degree,
Right so ther lyvede never man," he seyde,   2845

"In al this world, that som tyme he ne deyde.
This world nys but a thurghfare ful of wo,
And we been pilgrymes, passynge to and fro.
Deeth is an ende of every worldly soore."
And over al this yet seyde he muchel moore   2850
To this effect, ful wisely to enhorte
The peple that they sholde hem reconforte.
    Duc Theseus, with al his bisy cure,
Caste now wher that the sepulture
Of goode Arcite may best ymaked be,   2855
And eek moost honurable in his degree.
And at the laste he took conclusioun
That ther as first Arcite and Palamoun
Hadden for love the bataille hem bitwene,
That in that selve grove, swoote and grene,   2860
Ther as he hadde his amorouse desires,
His compleynte, and for love his hoote fires,
He wolde make a fyr in which the office
Funeral he myghte al accomplice;
And leet comande anon to hakke and hewe   2865
The okes olde, and leye hem on a rewe
In colpons wel arrayed for to brenne.
His officers with swifte feet they renne
And ryde anon at his comandement.
And after this, Theseus hath ysent   2870
After a beere, and it al overspradde
With clooth of gold, the richeste that he hadde.
And of the same suyte he cladde Arcite.
Upon his hondes hadde he gloves white,
Eek on his heed a coroune of laurer grene,   2875
And in his hond a swerd ful bright and kene.
He leyde hym, bare the visage, on the beere;
Therwith he weep that pitee was to heere.
And for the peple sholde seen hym alle,
Whan it was day, he broghte hym to the halle,
That roreth of the criyng and the soun.   2881
    Tho came this woful Theban Palamoun,
With flotery berd and ruggy, asshy heeres,

2810. **As,** where. 2811. **Therfore I stynte.** The passage in the *Teseida* describing the flight of Arcite's soul to heaven Chaucer had used, or was to make use of, in *TC* 5. 1807–1827. **divinistre,** diviner. 2812. **registre.** The word, which can hardly mean "narrative" as Skeat suggests, is evidently used humorously and, like the rest of the passage, serves to break the mood of tragedy. 2815. **ther,** the expletive use introducing a wish. **gye** guide. 2817. **Shrighte,** shrieked. **howleth.** The verb *howl*, "to utter a mournful cry," is not intended to be ludicrous. 2820. **to tarien forth the day,** to spend the whole day. 2834. **Cracchynge,** scratching. **rentynge,** tearing. 2851. **enhorte,** urge. 2853. **bisy cure,** diligent attention. 2854. **Caste,** considered. 2860. **swoote,** sweet. The funeral pyre is apparently in the neighborhood of the amphitheater. Cf. l. 1862. 2867. **colpons,** (cut) pieces. **arrayed,** arranged. 2868. **renne,** run. 2873. **suyte,** color, pattern. 2874. **gloves white,** used as mourning at the funeral of an unmarried person. 2883. **flotery,** fluttering, possibly "wavy." **ruggy,** shaggy. **asshy,** covered with ashes.

In clothes blake, ydropped al with teeres;
And, passynge othere of wepynge, Emelye,
The rewefulleste of al the compaignye.　　2886
In as muche as the servyce sholde be
The moore noble and riche in his degree,
Duc Theseus leet forth thre steedes brynge,
That trapped were in steel al gliterynge,　　2890
And covered with the armes of daun Arcite.
Upon thise steedes, that weren grete and
　white,
Ther seten folk, of whiche oon baar his sheeld,
Another his spere up on his hondes heeld,
The thridde baar with hym his bowe Turkeys
(Of brend gold was the caas and eek the
　harneys);　　2896
And riden forth a paas with sorweful cheere
Toward the grove, as ye shul after heere.
The nobleste of the Grekes that ther were
Upon his shuldres caryeden the beere,　　2900
With slakke paas, and eyen rede and wete,
Thurghout the citee by the maister strete,
That sprad was al with blak, and wonder hye
Right of the same is the strete ywrye.
Upon the right hond wente olde Egeus,　　2905
And on that oother syde duc Theseus,
With vessels in hir hand of gold ful fyn,
Al ful of hony, milk, and blood, and wyn;
Eek Palamon, with ful greet compaignye;
And after that cam woful Emelye,　　2910
With fyr in honde, as was that tyme the gyse,
To do the office of funeral servyse.
　Heigh labour and ful greet apparaillynge
Was at the service and the fyr-makynge,　　2914
That with his grene top the hevene raughte;
And twenty fadme of brede the armes
　straughte—
This is to seyn, the bowes weren so brode.

Of stree first ther was leyd ful many a lode.
But how the fyr was maked upon highte,
Ne eek the names that the trees highte,　　2920
As ook, firre, birch, asp, alder, holm, popler,
Wylugh, elm, plane, assh, box, chasteyn, lynde,
　laurer,
Mapul, thorn, bech, hasel, ew, whippeltree,—
How they weren feld, shal nat be toold for me;
Ne hou the goddes ronnen up and doun,　　2925
Disherited of hire habitacioun,
In which they woneden in reste and pees,
Nymphes, fawnes and amadrides;
Ne hou the beestes and the briddes alle
Fledden for fere, whan the wode was falle;　2930
Ne how the ground agast was of the light,
That was nat wont to seen the sonne bright;
Ne how the fyr was couched first with stree,
And thanne with drye stikkes cloven a thre,
And thanne with grene wode and spicerye,　2935
And thanne with clooth of gold and with
　perrye,
And gerlandes, hangynge with ful many a
　flour;
The mirre, th'encens, with al so greet odour;
Ne how Arcite lay among al this,
Ne what richesse aboute his body is;　　2940
Ne how that Emelye, as was the gyse,
Putte in the fyr of funeral servyse;
Ne how she swowned whan men made the fyr,
Ne what she spak, ne what was hir desir;
Ne what jeweles men in the fyre caste,　　2945
Whan that the fyr was greet and brente faste;
Ne how somme caste hir sheeld, and somme hir
　spere,
And of hire vestimentz, whiche that they were,
And coppes fulle of wyn, and milk, and blood,
Into the fyr, that brente as it were wood;　2950

2884. **ydropped,** sprinkled. 2885. **passynge othere of wepynge,** weeping more than the others. 2888. **in his degree,** in conformance with his rank. 2889. **leet . . . brynge,** caused to be brought. 2893. **Ther seten folk.** At the funeral of a knight it was customary to have his shield, sword, etc. carried by a herald or a relative. See Rock, *Church of Our Fathers,* cited by Skeat. 2895. **Turkeys,** Turkish. 2896. **harneys,** fittings. 2897. **a paas,** at a walk 2901. **slakke paas,** slow pace. 2904. **ywrye,** covered, draped. 2911. **With fyr in honde,** *i.e.* to light the funeral pyre. 2913. **Heigh,** great. **apparail-lynge,** preparation. 2915. **his,** its, referring to the pile of wood and branches implied in *fyr-makynge.* **raughte,** reached. 2917. **bowes,** boughs. 2918. **stree,** straw. 2919. **upon highte,** on high. 2921. **holm,** holly. 2922. **Wylugh,** willow. **chasteyn,** chestnut. 2923. **whippeltree,** dogwood. 2925. **ronnen,** ran. 2926. **Disherited,** deprived, disinherited. 2927. **woneden,** dwelt. 2928. **amadrides,** hamadryads, dryads. 2933. **couched,** laid. 2934. **a thre,** in three. 2935. **spicerye,** spices. 2936. **perrye,** precious stones, jewelry. 2938. **mirre,** myrrh.

Ne how the Grekes, with an huge route,
Thries riden al the fyr aboute
Upon the left hand, with a loud shoutynge,
And thries with hir speres claterynge;
And thries how the ladyes gonne crye;   2955
Ne how that lad was homward Emelye;
Ne how Arcite is brent to asshen colde;
Ne how that lyche-wake was yholde
Al thilke nyght; ne how the Grekes pleye
The wake-pleyes, ne kepe I nat to seye;   2960
Who wrastleth best naked with oille enoynt,
Ne who that baar hym best, in no disjoynt.
I wol nat tellen eek how that they goon
Hoom til Atthenes, whan the pley is doon;
But shortly to the point thanne wol I wende,
And maken of my longe tale an ende.   2966
  By processe and by lengthe of certeyn yeres,
Al stynted is the moornynge and the teres
Of Grekes, by oon general assent.
Thanne semed me ther was a parlement   2970
At Atthenes, upon certein pointz and caas;
Among the whiche pointz yspoken was,
To have with certein contrees alliaunce,
And have fully of Thebans obeisaunce.
For which this noble Theseus anon   2975
Leet senden after gentil Palamon,
Unwist of hym what was the cause and why;
But in his blake clothes sorwefully
He cam at his comandement in hye.
Tho sente Theseus for Emelye.   2980
Whan they were set, and hust was al the place,
And Theseus abiden hadde a space
Er any word cam fram his wise brest,
His eyen sette he ther as was his lest,
And with a sad visage he siked stille,   2985

And after that right thus he seyde his wille:
  "The Firste Moevere of the cause above,
Whan he first made the faire cheyne of love,
Greet was th'effect, and heigh was his entente.
Wel wiste he why, and what therof he mente;
For with that faire cheyne of love he bond   2991
The fyr, the eyr, the water, and the lond
In certeyn boundes, that they may nat flee.
That same Prince and that Moevere," quod he,
"Hath stablissed in this wrecched world adoun
Certeyn dayes and duracioun   2996
To al that is engendred in this place,
Over the whiche day they may nat pace,
Al mowe they yet tho dayes wel abregge.
Ther nedeth noon auctoritee t'allegge,   3000
For it is preeved by experience,
But that me list declaren my sentence.
Thanne may men by this ordre wel discerne
That thilke Moevere stable is and eterne.
Wel may men knowe, but it be a fool,   3005
That every part dirryveth from his hool;
For nature hath nat taken his bigynnyng
Of no partie or cantel of a thyng,
But of a thyng that parfit is and stable,
Descendynge so til it be corrumpable.   3010
And therfore, of his wise purveiaunce,
He hath so wel biset his ordinaunce,
That speces of thynges and progressiouns
Shullen enduren by sucessiouns,
And nat eterne, withouten any lye.   3015
This maystow understonde and seen at yë.
  Loo the ook, that hath so long a norisshynge
From tyme that it first bigynneth to sprynge,
And hath so long a lif, as we may see,
Yet at the laste wasted is the tree.   3020

2958. **lyche-wake,** wake. Chaucer uses a medieval term and applies it to the watch over the funeral pyre. 2960. **wake-pleyes,** the funeral games or athletic contests with which the death of a hero was celebrated. **kepe,** care, am concerned. 2962. **in no disjoynt,** in any difficult situation. The negative continues the two previous negatives. 2967. **By processe,** in the course of events. 2970. **parlement,** discussion. 2973. **with certein contrees alliaunce.** Some have seen in this phrase an allusion to the alliance of England with Bohemia (and the marriage of Richard and Anne), but this is hardly necessary. Theseus as lord of Athens had destroyed Creon, tyrant of Thebes, and devastated the city. In sanctioning the marriage of the Theban Palamon to Emelye it would be natural for Theseus to come to some sort of agreement with the people of Thebes. 2976. **Leet,** caused. 2979. **in hye,** quickly. 2981. **hust,** hushed. 2985. **siked stille,** sighed quietly. 2988. **cheyne of love.** The idea that all things are bound together by love could have come from Boethius (*Cons. Phil.*, II, met. 8) or *RR*, 16786, but it is as old as Plato. The speech as a whole follows Boethius. 2999. **Al mowe they,** although they may. **abregge,** abridge. 3003. **ordre,** disposition of things. 3008. **cantel,** portion. 3010. **corrumpable,** corruptible. 3016. **at yë,** evidently.

Considereth eek how that the harde stoon
Under oure feet, on which we trede and goon,
Yet wasteth it as it lyth by the weye.
The brode ryver somtyme wexeth dreye;
The grete tounes se we wane and wende. 3025
Thanne may ye se that al this thyng hath ende.
　　Of man and womman seen we wel also
That nedes, in oon of thise termes two,
This is to seyn, in youthe or elles age,
He moot be deed, the kyng as shal a page; 3030
Som in his bed, som in the depe see,
Som in the large feeld, as men may see;
Ther helpeth noght, al goth that ilke weye.
Thanne may I seyn that al this thyng moot
　　deye. *All powerful and*
　　What maketh this but Juppiter, the kyng, 3035
That is prince and cause of alle thyng,
Convertynge al unto his propre welle
From which it is dirryved, sooth to telle?
And heer-agayns no creature on lyve,
Of no degree, availleth for to stryve. 3040
　　Thanne is it wysdom, as it thynketh me,
To maken vertu of necessittee,
And take it weel that we may nat eschue,
And namely that to us alle is due.
And whoso gruccheth ought, he dooth folye,
And rebel is to hym that al may gye. 3046
And certeinly a man hath moost honour
To dyen in his excellence and flour,
Whan he is siker of his goode name;
Thanne hath he doon his freend, ne hym, no
　　shame. 3050
And gladder oghte his freend been of his deeth,
Whan with honour up yolden is his breeth,
Than whan his name apalled is for age,
For al forgeten is his vassellage.
Thanne is it best, as for a worthy fame, 3055
To dyen whan that he is best of name.
　　The contrarie of al this is wilfulnesse.
Why grucchen we, why have we hevynesse,

That goode Arcite, of chivalrie flour,
Departed is with duetee and honour 3060
Out of this foule prisoun of this lyf?
Why grucchen heere his cosyn and his wyf
Of his welfare, that loved hem so weel?
Kan he hem thank? Nay, God woot, never a
　　deel,
That bothe his soule and eek hemself offende,
And yet they mowe hir lustes nat amende. 3066
　　What may I conclude of this longe serye?
But after wo I rede us to be merye,
And thanken Juppiter of al his grace.
And er that we departen from this place 3070
I rede that we make of sorwes two
O parfit joye, lastynge everemo.
And looketh now wher moost sorwe is herinne,
Ther wol we first amenden and bigynne.
　　"Suster," quod he, "this is my fulle assent,
With al th'avys heere of my parlement, 3076
That gentil Palamon, youre owene knyght,
That serveth yow with wille, herte, and myght,
And ever hath doon syn ye first hym knewe,
That ye shul of youre grace upon hym rewe,
And taken hym for housbonde and for lord. 3081
Lene me youre hond, for this is oure accord.
Lat se now of youre wommanly pitee.
He is a kynges brother sone, pardee;
And though he were a povre bacheler, 3085
Syn he hath served yow so many a yeer,
And had for yow so greet adversitee,
It moste been considered, leeveth me;
For gentil mercy oghte to passen right." 3089
　　Thanne seyde he thus to Palamon the knight:
"I trowe ther nedeth litel sermonyng
To make yow assente to this thyng.
　　Com neer, and taak youre lady by the hond."
Bitwixen hem was maad anon the bond
That highte matrimoigne or mariage, 3095
By al the conseil and the baronage.
And thus with alle blisse and melodye

3026. **al this thyng,** everything. 3037. **welle,** will. 3043. **that,** that which. 3050. **hym,** himself. 3052. **yolden,** yielded. 3053. **apalled,** enfeebled. 3054. **vassellage,** prowess. 3060. **duetee,** respect. 3062. **his wyf.** Cf. note to l. 2775. 3066. **hir lustes,** their happiness. 3067. **serye,** succession of points in an argument. 3072. **O,** one. 3073. **looketh now wher,** wherever. 3082. **Lene,** lend. 3084. **brother.** The possessive case was sometimes the same as the nominative. Cf. Language, § 14.

Hath Palamon ywedded Emelye.
And God, that al this wyde world hath
wroght,
Sende hym his love that hath it deere aboght;
For now is Palamon in alle wele, 3101
Lyvynge in blisse, in richesse, and in heele,

And Emelye hym loveth so tendrely,
And he hire serveth also gentilly,
That nevere was ther no word hem bitwene
Of jalousie or any oother teene. 3106
Thus endeth Palamon and Emelye;
And God save al this faire compaignye! Amen.

Heere is ended the Knyghtes Tale. *Reminds us of other pilgrims*

The Miller's Tale

THE MILLER'S PROLOGUE

Heere folwen the wordes bitwene the Hoost and the Millere.

Whan that the Knyght had thus his tale
ytoold,
In al the route nas ther yong ne oold 3110
That he ne seyde it was a noble storie
And worthy for to drawen to memorie,
And namely the gentils everichon.
Oure Hooste lough and swoor, "So moot I gon,
This gooth aright; unbokeled is the male. 3115
Lat se now who shal telle another tale;
For trewely the game is wel bigonne.
Now telleth ye, sire Monk, if that ye konne
Somwhat to quite with the Knyghtes tale."
The Millere, that fordronken was al pale, 3120
So that unnethe upon his hors he sat,
He nolde avalen neither hood ne hat,
Ne abyde no man for his curteisie,
But in Pilates voys he gan to crie,
And swoor, "By armes, and by blood and
bones, 3125

I kan a noble tale for the nones,
With which I wol now quite the Knyghtes
tale."
Oure Hooste saugh that he was dronke of ale,
And seyde, "Abyd, Robyn, my leeve brother;
Som bettre man shal telle us first another. 3130
Abyd, and lat us werken thriftily."
"By Goddes soule," quod he, "that wol nat I;
For I wol speke, or elles go my wey."
Oure Hoost answerde, "Tel on, a devel wey!
Thou art a fool; thy wit is overcome." 3135
"Now herkneth," quod the Millere, "alle and
some!
But first I make a protestacioun
That I am dronke, I knowe it by my soun;
And therfore if that I mysspeke or seye,
Wyte it the ale of Southwerk, I you preye. 3140
For I wol telle a legende and a lyf
Bothe of a carpenter and of his wyf,

3110. **route**, company. 3112. **drawen to memorie**, call to mind. 3113. **namely**, particularly. 3115. **unbokeled is the male**, the bag is opened, *i.e.* we have made a good beginning. 3119. **to quite with**, to match. 3120. **fordronken**, very drunk. 3121. **unnethe**, scarcely. 3122. **avalen**, lower (the visor of the helmet), *i.e.* take off. 3124. **in Pilates voys**. In the medieval mystery plays Pilate usually rants. 3125. **By armes.** . . . The arms, bones, etc. of Christ, the nails of the crucifixion, and other sacred objects were often sworn by in medieval profanity. 3126. **kan**, know. **for the nones**, for the occasion, but possibly here also a phrase that has become a meaningless cliché. 3129. **leeve**, dear. 3131. **thriftily**, properly. 3134. **a devel wey**, another common oath, *lit.* on the way to the devil, go to the devil, what the devil. 3136. **alle and some**, one and all. 3138. **my soun**, *i.e.* the sound of my voice. 3139. **seye**, missay. 3140. **Wyte it**, attribute it to.

How that a clerk hath set the wrightes cappe."

   The Reve answerde and seyde, "Stynt thy clappe!

Lat be thy lewed dronken harlotrye.   3145

It is a synne and eek a greet folye

To apeyren any man, or hym defame,

And eek to bryngen wyves in swich fame.

Thou mayst ynogh of othere thynges seyn."

   This dronke Millere spak ful soone ageyn

And seyde, "Leve brother Osewold,   3151

Who hath no wyf, he is no cokewold.

But I sey nat therfore that thou art oon;

Ther been ful goode wyves many oon,   3154

And evere a thousand goode ayeyns oon badde.

That knowestow wel thyself, but if thou madde.

Why artow angry with my tale now?

I have a wyf, pardee, as wel as thow;

Yet nolde I, for the oxen in my plogh,

Take upon me moore than ynogh,   3160

As demen of myself that I were oon;

I wol bileve wel that I am noon.

An housbonde shal nat been inquisityf

Of Goddes pryvetee, nor of his wyf.

So he may fynde Goddes foyson there,   3165

Of the remenant nedeth nat enquere."

   What sholde I moore seyn, but this Millere

He nolde his wordes for no man forbere,

But tolde his cherles tale in his manere.

M'athynketh that I shal reherce it heere.   3170

And therfore every gentil wight I preye,

For Goddes love, demeth nat that I seye

Of yvel entente, but for I moot reherce

Hir tales alle, be they bettre or werse,

Or elles falsen som of my mateere.   3175

And therfore, whoso list it nat yheere,

Turne over the leef and chese another tale;

For he shal fynde ynowe, grete and smale,

Of storial thyng that toucheth gentillesse,

And eek moralitee and hoolynesse.   3180

Blameth nat me if that ye chese amys.

The Millere is a cherl, ye knowe wel this;

So was the Reve eek and othere mo,

And harlotrie they tolden bothe two.

Avyseth yow, and put me out of blame;   3185

And eek men shal nat maken ernest of game.

3143. **set the wrightes cappe,** made a fool of the carpenter. 3144. **Stynt thy clappe,** hold your tongue, stop your idle talking. The Reeve was by trade a carpenter; cf. above, A 614. 3145. **harlotrye,** ribaldry. 3147. **apeyren,** injure. 3152. **Who . . . cokewold,** a proverbial saying. A man whose wife was guilty of infidelity was known as a cuckold, and was supposed to develop horns. 3156. **but if thou madde,** unless you are out of your mind. 3165. **foyson,** plenty, *i.e.* as long as he finds God's plenty in his wife. 3166. **nedeth nat,** it is unnecessary (to). 3170. **M'athynketh,** it causes me regret. This is an obvious way for Chaucer to excuse himself for telling a vulgar story. 3174. **Hir,** their. 3176. **yheere,** hear, the infin. (OE. *gehieran*). 3179. **storial,** historical, authentic. 3186. **ernest,** a serious matter, *i.e.* take a joke seriously.

THE MILLER'S TALE

Heere bigynneth the Millere his tale.

Whilom ther was dwellynge at Oxenford
A riche gnof, that gestes heeld to bord,
And of his craft he was a carpenter.   3189
With hym ther was dwellynge a povre scoler,
Hadde lerned art, but al his fantasye
Was turned for to lerne astrologye,
And koude a certeyn of conclusiouns,
To demen by interrogaciouns,
If that men asked hym in certein houres   3195
Whan that men sholde have droghte or elles
    shoures,
Or if men asked hym what sholde bifalle
Of every thyng; I may nat rekene hem alle.
    This clerk was cleped hende Nicholas.
Of deerne love he koude and of solas;   3200
And therto he was sleigh and ful privee,
And lyk a mayden meke for to see.
A chambre hadde he in that hostelrye
Allone, withouten any compaignye,
Ful fetisly ydight with herbes swoote;   3205
And he hymself as sweete as is the roote
Of lycorys, or any cetewale.

His Almageste, and bookes grete and smale,
His astrelabie, longynge for his art,
His augrym stones layen faire apart,   3210
On shelves couched at his beddes heed;
His presse ycovered with a faldyng reed;
And al above ther lay a gay sautrie,
On which he made a-nyghtes melodie
So swetely that al the chambre rong;   3215
And *Angelus ad virginem* he song;
And after that he song the kynges noote.
Ful often blessed was his myrie throte.
And thus this sweete clerk his tyme spente
After his freendes fyndyng and his rente.   3220
    This carpenter hadde wedded newe a wyf,
Which that he lovede moore than his lyf;
Of eighteteene yeer she was of age.
Jalous he was, and heeld hire narwe in cage,
For she was wylde and yong, and he was old,
And demed hymself been lik a cokewold.   3226
He knew nat Catoun, for his wit was rude,
That bad man sholde wedde his simylitude.
Men sholde wedden after hire estaat,

The Miller's Tale is a fabliau, *i.e.* a humorous story almost always indecent in subject and often in treatment. While many such stories were given literary treatment and were written down, many more doubtless circulated orally and were recited by minstrels. Chaucer's source has not been found, but there are numerous analogues.

3188. gnof, churl. **gestes,** guests. **3191. Hadde,** (who) had. **art,** the trivium (grammar, rhetoric, logic). **fantasye,** fancy, inclination. **3193. koude a certeyn,** knew a certain number. **conclusiouns,** propositions, astrological procedures. **3194. To demen by interrogaciouns,** to express an opinion with respect to questions, according to the hour at which the question was asked. The hour determined the position of the heavenly bodies on which the prognostication was based. **3199. cleped,** called. **hende,** gracious, gentle. **3200. deerne,** secret. **koude,** knew (much). **3201. privee,** secretive. **3203. hostelrye,** lodging house. **3205. fetisly ydight,** agreeably furnished or supplied. **swoote,** sweet. **3207. cetewale,** an herb (setwall or zedoary). **3208. Almageste,** a book on astrology, or possibly that by Ptolemy, the most famous. **3209. astrelabie,** astrolabe, an instrument consisting of circular plates and two revolving pointers, used for determining certain positions of heavenly bodies. It is now replaced by the sextant. Chaucer wrote a treatise on the use of the instrument for his little son, Lewis. **3209. longynge for,** appropriate to. **3210. augrym stones,** small stones used for doing problems in arithmetic. *Augrym* is a normal development from OF. *algorisme,* which in turn represents the name of an Arab mathematician. **3211. couched,** placed, arranged. **3212. presse,** cupboard or (more likely) a chest, for his clothes and other possessions. **faldyng,** a coarse cloth. **3213. sautrie,** psaltery; see note to A 296. **3216. *Angelus ad virginem,*** a hymn of the Annunciation, printed in Dreves and Blume, *Ein Jahrtausend Lateinischer Hymnendichtung,* II. 242. **3217. the kynges noote.** All attempts to identify this song or tune are unconvincing. **3220. After,** in accordance with. **fyndyng,** money provided. **rente,** income. **3221. newe,** lately. **3223. Of eighteteene yeer,** eighteen years. Cf. A 82. **3226. been lik,** likely to be. **3227. Catoun.** The reference is to the *Disticha Catonis,* a collection of aphorisms often used as a schoolbook. The advice which Chaucer attributes to Cato is not in the *Disticha,* but is found in another medieval courtesy book, the *Liber Faceti* or *Facetus* (the polite man), which was also widely known. **3228. That bad man,** that bade that one. **his simylitude,** his like.

For youthe and elde is often at debaat. 3230
But sith that he was fallen in the snare,
He moste endure, as oother folk, his care.

    Fair was this yonge wyf, and therwithal
As any wezele hir body gent and smal.
A ceynt she werede, barred al of silk, 3235
A barmclooth eek as whit as morne milk
Upon hir lendes, ful of many a goore.
Whit was hir smok, and broyden al bifoore
And eek bihynde, on hir coler aboute,
Of col-blak silk, withinne and eek withoute.
The tapes of hir white voluper 3241
Were of the same suyte of hir coler;
Hir filet brood of silk, and set ful hye.
And sikerly she hadde a likerous yë;
Ful smale ypulled were hire browes two, 3245
And tho were bent and blake as any sloo.
She was ful moore blisful on to see
Than is the newe pere-jonette tree,
And softer than the wolle is of a wether.
And by hir girdel heeng a purs of lether, 3250
Tasseled with silk, and perled with latoun.
In al this world, to seken up and doun,
There nys no man so wys that koude thenche
So gay a popelote or swich a wenche.
Ful brighter was the shynyng of hir hewe 3255
Than in the Tour the noble yforged newe.
But of hir song, it was as loude and yerne
As any swalwe sittynge on a berne.
Therto she koude skippe and make game,
As any kyde or calf folwynge his dame. 3260
Hir mouth was sweete as bragot or the meeth,

Or hoord of apples leyd in hey or heeth.
Wynsynge she was as is a joly colt,
Long as a mast, and upright as a bolt.
A brooch she baar upon hir lowe coler, 3265
As brood as is the boos of a bokeler.
Hir shoes were laced on hir legges hye.
She was a prymerole, a piggesnye,
For any lord to leggen in his bedde,
Or yet for any good yeman to wedde. 3270

    Now, sire, and eft, sire, so bifel the cas,
That on a day this hende Nicholas
Fil with this yonge wyf to rage and pleye,
Whil that hir housbonde was at Oseneye,
As clerkes ben ful subtile and ful queynte; 3275
And prively he caughte hire by the queynte,
And seyde, "Ywis, but if ich have my wille,
For deerne love of thee, lemman, I spille."
And heeld hire harde by the haunche-bones,
And seyde, "Lemman, love me al atones, 3280
Or I wol dyen, also God me save!"
And she sproong as a colt dooth in the trave,
And with hir heed she wryed faste awey,
And seyde, "I wol nat kisse thee, by my fey!
Why, lat be," quod she, "lat be, Nicholas,
Or I wol crie, 'out, harrow' and 'allas'! 3286
Do wey youre handes, for youre curteisye!"

    This Nicholas gan mercy for to crye,
And spak so faire, and profred him so faste,
That she hir love hym graunted atte laste, 3290
And swoor hir ooth, by seint Thomas of Kent,
That she wol been at his comandement,
Whan that she may hir leyser wel espie.

3230. **is.** We should expect **ben.** 3234. **gent,** graceful. 3235. **ceynt,** girdle. **barred,** striped, possibly crosswise. 3236. **barmclooth,** apron. 3237. **lendes,** loins. 3238. **smok,** undergarment, chemise. **broyden,** embroidered. 3241. **voluper,** cap, bonnet. 3242. **suyte,** color, material. **of hir coler,** as her collar. 3243. **filet,** a band for the hair. 3244. **likerous,** wanton. 3245. **Ful smale ypulled.** The plucking of the eyebrows was familiar to the Middle Ages. 3246. **sloo,** sloe, the purple-black fruit of the blackthorn. 3248. **pere-jonette,** a type of early pear. Chaucer alludes to the beauty of the tree when in blossom. 3251. **perled with latoun,** ornamented with beads or drops of brass. 3253. **thenche,** imagine. 3254. **popelote,** lovable young woman. **wenche,** prob. here has the meaning "wanton woman," common in Chaucer's day but not the only meaning. 3256. **Tour,** Tower of London, where the London mint was located. **noble,** a gold coin about the size of a half-crown or American half-dollar, though much thinner, worth 6s. 8d. 3257. **yerne,** eager, lively. 3261. **bragot,** a drink made of ale and honey fermented together. **meeth,** mead. 3262. **heeth,** heather. 3263. **Wynsynge,** skittish. 3264. **bolt,** crossbow-bolt. Cf. "bolt-upright." 3265. **baar,** wore. 3266. **boos of a bokeler,** the boss in the center of a shield. 3268. **prymerole, piggesnye,** names of flowers applied to women as we say "peach," "daisy." *Prymerole* is a primrose. *piggesnye* (pig's eye) is a dialect word in Essex for cuckoo flower. See Manly's note. 3269. **leggen,** lay. 3274. **Oseneye,** Osney, an island in the river Thames, one-half mile west of Oxford. It contained an Augustinian abbey, referred to at l. 3666, below. 3275. **queynte,** cunning. 3276. **queynte,** pudendum. 3277. **ich,** I. 3278. **deerne,** secret. **spille,** am ruined. 3280. **al atones,** immediately. 3282. **trave,** an enclosure of rails in which an unruly horse is put to be shod. 3283. **wryed,** turned. 3293. **leyser,** opportunity.

"Myn housbonde is so ful of jalousie
That but ye wayte wel and been privee,   3295
I woot right wel I nam but deed," quod she.
"Ye moste been ful deerne, as in this cas."
    "Nay, therof care thee noght," quod
        Nicholas.
"A clerk hadde litherly biset his whyle,
But if he koude a carpenter bigyle."   3300
And thus they been accorded and ysworn
To wayte a tyme, as I have told biforn.
    Whan Nicholas had doon thus everideel,
And thakked hire aboute the lendes weel,
He kist hire sweete and taketh his sawtrie,   3305
And pleyeth faste, and maketh melodie.
    Thanne fil it thus, that to the paryssh chirche,
Cristes owene werkes for to wirche,
This goode wyf wente on an haliday.
Hir forheed shoon as bright as any day,   3310
So was it wasshen whan she leet hir werk.
Now was ther of that chirche a parissh clerk,
The which that was ycleped Absolon.
Crul was his heer, and as the gold it shoon,
And strouted as a fanne large and brode;   3315
Ful streight and evene lay his joly shode.
His rode was reed, his eyen greye as goos.
With Poules wyndow corven on his shoos,
In hoses rede he wente fetisly.
Yclad he was ful smal and proprely   3320
Al in a kirtel of a lyght waget;
Ful faire and thikke been the poyntes set.
And therupon he hadde a gay surplys

As whit as is the blosme upon the rys.
A myrie child he was, so God me save.   3325
Wel koude he laten blood and clippe and
    shave,
And maken a chartre of lond or acquitaunce.
In twenty manere koude he trippe and daunce
After the scole of Oxenforde tho,
And with his legges casten to and fro,   3330
And pleyen songes on a smal rubible;
Therto he song som tyme a loud quynyble;
And as wel koude he pleye on a giterne.
In al the toun nas brewhous ne taverne
That he ne visited with his solas,   3335
Ther any gaylard tappestere was.
But sooth to seyn, he was somdeel squaymous
Of fartyng, and of speche daungerous.
    This Absolon, that jolif was and gay,
Gooth with a sencer on the haliday,   3340
Sensynge the wyves of the parisshe faste;
And many a lovely look on hem he caste,
And namely on this carpenteris wyf.
To looke on hire hym thoughte a myrie lyf,
She was so propre and sweete and likerous.   3345
I dar wel seyn, if she hadde been a mous,
And he a cat, he wolde hire hente anon.
This parissh clerk, this joly Absolon,
Hath in his herte swich a love-longynge
That of no wyf took he noon offrynge;   3350
For curteisie, he seyde, he wolde noon.
    The moone, whan it was nyght, ful brighte
        shoon,

3295. **wayte**, watch. 3299. **litherly biset his whyle**, badly employed his time. 3304. **thakked**, slapped, patted. **lendes**, buttocks. 3305. **kist**, kisses. The form is a contraction of *kiseth*. **sweete**, sweetly. 3307. **fil**, befell. 3308. **wirche**, work, per-form. 3313. **ycleped**, called. 3314. **Crul**, curly. 3315. **strouted**, stuck out. 3316. **shode**, the part in the hair. 3317. **rode**, complexion. 3318. **Poules wyndow.** It was fashionable to have the upper leather of shoes cut in a variety of open work, some of which resembled the stone tracery in church windows. Absolon's red hose showed through. The reference here is to St. Paul's cathedral in London. 3319. **fetishly**, neatly. 3320. **smal**, quietly. **proprely**, finely. 3321. **waget**, blue. 3322. **thikke**, close together. **poyntes**, laces. 3324. **rys**, branch. 3325. **child**, young man. 3326. **laten blood**, let blood. **clippe**, cut hair. 3327. **chartre**, charter. 3329. **scole**, fashion. **tho**, then. 3331. **rubible**, rebeck, an early type of violin. See numerous illustrations in F. W. Galpin, *Old English Instruments of Music*. 3332. **quynyble**, high treble. 3333. **giterne**, a form of guitar. 3335. **solas**, entertainment. 3336. **Ther**, where. **gaylard tappestere**, lively barmaid. 3337. **squaymous**, delicate, modest. 3338. **daungerous**, fastidious, dainty. 3340. **Gooth with a sencer.** There are differ-ences of opinion as to whether the censing was in the church or in the houses of the people. Cutts (*Scenes and Characters of the Middle Ages.*, p. 219) favors the latter, since it was one of the parish clerk's duties to asperse with holy water the people in their homes. Skeat expresses the opposite view, "for there is an allusion to the ladies coming forward with the usual offering (l. 3350)." But lines 3350–51 say that Absolon would not accept any offering (*he wolde noon*) from the women, whereas in the church he would have had no such discretionary power. His censing was probably in a perambulation of the parish, as Cutts thought. 3343. **namely**, especially. 3345. **propre**, good-looking. **likerous**, tempting. 3347. **hente**, seize.

And Absolon his gyterne hath ytake,
For paramours he thoghte for to wake.
And forth he gooth, jolif and amorous, 3355
Til he cam to the carpenteres hous
A litel after cokkes hadde ycrowe,
And dressed hym up by a shot-wyndowe
That was upon the carpenteris wal.
He syngeth in his voys gentil and smal, 3360
"Now, deere lady, if thy wille be,
I praye yow that ye wole rewe on me,"
Ful wel acordaunt to his gyternynge.
This carpenter awook, and herde him synge,
And spak unto his wyf, and seyde anon, 3365
"What! Alison! herestow nat Absolon,
That chaunteth thus under oure boures wal?"
And she answerde hir housbonde therwithal,
"Yis, God woot, John, I heere it every deel."
　This passeth forth; what wol ye bet than
　　weel? 3370
Fro day to day this joly Absolon
So woweth hire that hym is wo bigon.
He waketh al the nyght and al the day;
He kembeth his lokkes brode, and made hym
　gay;
He woweth hire by meenes and brocage, 3375
And swoor he wolde been hir owene page;
He syngeth, brokkynge as a nyghtyngale;
He sente hire pyment, meeth, and spiced ale,
And wafres, pipyng hoot out of the gleede;
And, for she was of towne, he profred meede.
For som folk wol ben wonnen for richesse, 3381
And somme for strokes, and somme for gen-
　tillesse.
　Somtyme, to shewe his lightnesse and
　　maistrye,
He pleyeth Herodes upon a scaffold hye.

But what availleth hym as in this cas? 3385
She loveth so this hende Nicholas
That Absolon may blowe the bukkes horn;
He ne hadde for his labour but a scorn.
And thus she maketh Absolon hire ape,
And al his ernest turneth til a jape. 3390
Ful sooth is this proverbe, it is no lye,
Men seyn right thus, "Alwey the nye slye
Maketh the ferre leeve to be looth."
For though that Absolon be wood or wrooth,
By cause that he fer was from hire sighte, 3395
This nye Nicholas stood in his lighte.
　Now bere thee wel, thou hende Nicholas,
For Absolon may waille and synge "allas."
And so bifel it on a Saterday,
This carpenter was goon til Osenay; 3400
And hende Nicholas and Alisoun
Acorded been to this conclusioun,
That Nicholas shal shapen hym a wyle
This sely jalous housbonde to bigyle;
And if so be the game wente aright, 3405
She sholde slepen in his arm al nyght,
For this was his desir and hire also.
And right anon, withouten wordes mo,
This Nicholas no lenger wolde tarie,
But dooth ful softe unto his chambre carie 3410
Bothe mete and drynke for a day or tweye,
And to hire housbonde bad hire for to seye,
If that he axed after Nicholas,
She sholde seye she nyste where he was,
Of al that day she saugh hym nat with yë; 3415
She trowed that he was in maladye,
For for no cry hir mayde koude hym calle,
He nolde answere for thyng that myghte falle.
This passeth forth al thilke Saterday,
That Nicholas stille in his chambre lay, 3420

3354. **For paramours**, for love's sake (Skeat). 3355. **jolif**, gay. 3358. **dressed hym up**, stationed himself. **shot-wyn-dowe**, a casement window. 3359. **upon**, in. 3370. **This . . . weel.** We should say, "This goes on; what more do you expect?" 3372. **woweth**, woos. 3375. **by meenes and brocage**, by go-betweens and the use of agents, but *brocage* often implies bribery. 3377. **brokkynge**, trilling, quavering. 3378. **pyment**, wine to which honey and spices have been added. **meeth**, mead. 3379. **wafres.** These were baked in an iron form resembling the modern waffle-iron. 3380. **of towne**, *i.e.* in contrast to a country girl. **meede**, reward (money). 3381. **for**, by. 3384. **Herodes**, Herod, *i.e.* he played the part of Herod in a mystery play. **scaffold hye.** The temporary outdoor stage, about on the level of a man's head, was commonly called a scaffold. 3387. **blowe the bukkes horn.** Cf. the modern "go whistle," and "go pipen in an yvy leef" at A 1838. 3389. **hire ape.** Cf. A 706. 3390. **til**, to. 3392. **nye slye**, the nearby clever one. 3393. **ferre leeve**, distant dear one. The proverb is similar to "out of sight, out of mind." 3394. **wood**, mad. 3404. **sely**, poor. 3407. **hire**, hers. 3419. **This passeth forth**, this goes on, continues. Cf. A 3370.

And eet and sleep, or dide what hym leste,
Til Sonday, that the sonne gooth to reste.
This sely carpenter hath greet merveyle
Of Nicholas, or what thyng myghte hym eyle,
And seyde, "I am adrad, by Seint Thomas, 3425
It stondeth nat aright with Nicholas.
God shilde that he deyde sodeynly!
This world is now ful tikel, sikerly.
I saugh to-day a cors yborn to chirche
That now, on Monday last, I saugh hym
      wirche. 3430

  "Go up," quod he unto his knave anoon,
"Clepe at his dore, or knokke with a stoon.
Looke how it is, and tel me boldely."

  This knave gooth hym up ful sturdily, 3434
And at the chambre dore whil that he stood,
He cride and knokked as that he were wood,
"What! how! what do ye, maister Nicholay?
How may ye slepen al the longe day?"

  But al for noght, he herde nat a word.
An hole he foond, ful lowe upon a bord, 3440
Ther as the cat was wont in for to crepe,
And at that hole he looked in ful depe,
And at the laste he hadde of hym a sighte.
This Nicholas sat evere capyng uprighte,
As he had kiked on the newe moone. 3445
Adoun he gooth, and tolde his maister soone
In what array he saugh this ilke man.

  This carpenter to blessen hym bigan,
And seyde, "Help us, seinte Frydeswyde!
A man woot litel what hym shal bityde. 3450
This man is falle, with his astromye,
In som woodnesse or in som agonye.

I thoghte ay wel how that it sholde be!
Men sholde nat knowe of Goddes pryvetee.
Ye, blessed be alwey a lewed man 3455
That noght but oonly his bileve kan!
So ferde another clerk with astromye;
He walked in the feeldes, for to prye
Upon the sterres, what ther sholde bifalle,
Til he was in a marle-pit yfalle; 3460
He saugh nat that. But yet, by seint Thomas,
Me reweth soore of hende Nicholas.
He shal be rated of his studiyng,
If that I may, by Jhesus, hevene kyng!
Get me a staf, that I may underspore, 3465
Whil that thou, Robyn, hevest up the dore.
He shal out of his studiyng, as I gesse"—
And to the chambre dore he gan hym dresse.
His knave was a strong carl for the nones,
And by the haspe he haaf it of atones; 3470
Into the floor the dore fil anon.
This Nicholas sat ay as stille as stoon,
And evere caped upward into the eir.
This carpenter wende he were in despeir,
And hente hym by the sholdres myghtily, 3475
And shook hym harde, and cride spitously,
"What! Nicholay! what, how! what, looke
  adoun!
Awake, and thenk on Cristes passioun!
I crouche thee from elves and fro wightes."
Therwith the nyght-spel seyde he anon-rightes
On foure halves of the hous aboute, 3481
And on the thresshfold of the dore withoute:
"Jhesu Crist and seïnt Benedight,
Blesse this hous from every wikked wight,

3422. **that**, the time when. 3427. **shilde**, forbid. 3428. **tikel**, uncertain. 3429. **cors**, body, corpse. 3430. **wirche**, work. 3431. **knave**, servant. 3432. **Clepe**, call. 3444. **capyng**, gaping, staring. 3445. **As he had kiked**, as if he were gazing. 3448. **blessen hym**, cross himself. 3449. **seinte Frydeswyde.** St. Frideswide was a natural saint for the carpenter to swear by, since she was the patroness of the city and university of Oxford. Fragments of the priory of St. Frideswide are preserved in parts of Christ Church, the cathedral and the college. She also was noted for her power to heal the sick. 3451. **astromye**, the carpenter's mispronunciation of *astronomye*. 3452. **woodnesse**, madness. **agonye**, fit. 3453. **I thoghte.** . . . I always thought this would happen. 3455. **lewed**, ignorant. 3456. **his bileve kan**, knows his Creed. 3458. **prye**, gaze. 3460. **marle-pit**, pit from which marl (clay containing lime) is dug. The anectode is as old as Plato. 3463. **rated of**, scolded for. 3465. **underspore**, pry up. 3468. **dresse**, direct his course. 3470. **haaf it of**, heaved it off. 3474. **wende**, weened. 3476. **spitously**, vigorously. 3479. **crouche**, protect by the sign of the cross. 3480. **nyght-spel**, charm against evil spirits, said at night. **anon-rightes**, immediately. 3481. **halves**, sides. 3482. **thresshfold**, threshold. 3483. **Benedight**, Benedict. The charm is partly nonsense, as with many charms. The White Paternoster is an actual bedtime prayer, of which several versions are printed in *Folklore Rec.*, I. 145–54, II. 127–34; but St. Peter's sister (apparently a mistake for his daughter, St. Petronilla) remains unexplained. Skeat has a long note on the charm. E. T. Donaldson (*MLN*, LXIX. 310–3) would emend *verye* to *nerye* "save."

For nyghtes verye, the white *pater-noster!*   3485
Where wentestow, seïnt Petres soster?"
    And atte laste this hende Nicholas
Gan for to sike soore, and seyde, "Allas!
Shal al the world be lost eftsoones now?"   3489
    This carpenter answerde, "What seystow?
What! thynk on God, as we doon, men that
        swynke."
    This Nicholas answerde, "Fecche me drynke,
And after wol I speke in pryvetee
Of certeyn thyng that toucheth me and thee.
I wol telle it noon oother man, certeyn."   3495
    This carpenter goth doun, and comth ageyn,
And broghte of myghty ale a large quart;
And whan that ech of hem had dronke his part,
This Nicholas his dore faste shette,
And doun the carpenter by hym he sette.   3500
    He seyde "John, myn hooste, lief and deere,
Thou shalt upon thy trouthe swere me heere
That to no wight thou shalt this conseil wreye;
For it is Cristes conseil that I seye,
And if thou telle it man, thou art forlore;   3505
For this vengeaunce thou shalt han therfore,
That if thou wreye me, thou shalt be wood."
"Nay, Crist forbede it, for his hooly blood!"
Quod tho this sely man, "I nam no labbe;
Ne, though I seye, I nam nat lief to gabbe.   3510
Sey what thou wolt, I shal it nevere telle
To child ne wyf, by hym that harwed helle!"
    "Now John," quod Nicholas, "I wol nat lye;
I have yfounde in myn astrologye,
As I have looked in the moone bright,   3515
That now a Monday next, at quarter nyght,
Shal falle a reyn, and that so wilde and wood,
That half so greet was nevere Noes flood.
This world," he seyde, "in lasse than an hour
Shal al be dreynt, so hidous is the shour.   3520

Thus shal mankynde drenche, and lese hir lyf."
    This carpenter answerde, "Allas, my wyf!
And shal she drenche? allas, myn Alisoun!"
For sorwe of this he fil almoost adoun,   3524
And seyde, "Is ther no remedie in this cas?"
    "Why, yis, for Gode," quod hende Nicholas,
"If thou wolt werken after loore and reed.
Thou mayst nat werken after thyn owene heed;
For thus seith Salomon, that was ful trewe,
'Werk al by conseil, and thou shalt nat rewe.'
And if thou werken wolt by good conseil,   3531
I undertake, withouten mast and seyl,
Yet shal I saven hire and thee and me.
Hastow nat herd hou saved was Noe,
Whan that oure Lord hadde warned hym
        biforn   3535
That al the world with water sholde be lorn?"
    "Yis," quod this Carpenter, "ful yoore ago."
    "Hastou nat herd," quod Nicholas, "also
The sorwe of Noe with his felaweshipe,
Er that he myghte gete his wyf to shipe?   3540
Hym hadde be levere, I dar wel undertake
At thilke tyme, than alle his wetheres blake
That she hadde had a ship hirself allone.
And therfore, woostou what is best to doone?
This asketh haste, and of an hastif thyng   3545
Men may nat preche or maken tariyng.
    Anon go gete us faste into this in
A knedyng trogh, or ellis a kymelyn,
For ech of us, but looke that they be large,
In which we mowe swymme as in a barge,   3550
And han therinne vitaille suffisant
But for a day,—fy on the remenant!
The water shal aslake and goon away
Aboute pryme upon the nexte day.   3554
But Robyn may nat wite of this, thy knave,
Ne eek thy mayde Gille I may nat save;

3489. eftsoones, soon. 3491. swynke, work. 3493. in pryvetee, confidentially. 3499. shette, shut. 3503. wreye, betray. 3505. man, to any one. forlore, lost. 3509. labbe, blab. 3512. hym that harwed helle, Christ, who between the Cruci-fixion and the Resurrection released from hell the souls of those whose condemnation was only because they had lived before the Incarnation. The subject was included in many of the mystery cycles in England and on the Continent. 3516. at quarter nyght, about a quarter of the way through the night. 3519. lasse, less. 3520. dreynt, drowned. 3521. drenche, drown. 3526. for, before. 3529. thus seith Salomon. *Ecclesiasticus*, 32:19, where it is said by Jesus, son of Sirach. 3530. rewe, be sorry. 3539. The sorwe of Noe. In the English mystery plays Noah's wife is represented as a scold who refuses to enter the ark unless she can bring her "gossips" along, is beaten by Noah, etc. felaweshipe, those who accom-panied him in the ark. 3542. wetheres, wethers, sheep. 3545. hastif thyng, urgent matter. 3548. kymelyn, tub for brewing, salting meat, etc. 3550. swymme, float. 3553. aslake, grow less. 3554. pryme, nine o'clock. 3555. wite, know.

Axe nat why, for though thou aske me,
I wol nat tellen Goddes pryvetee.
Suffiseth thee, but if thy wittes madde,
To han as greet a grace as Noe hadde.   3560
Thy wyf shal I wel saven, out of doute.
Go now thy wey, and speed thee heer-aboute.
    But whan thou hast, for hire and thee and
      me,
Ygeten us thise knedyng tubbes thre,   3564
Thanne shaltow hange hem in the roof ful hye,
That no man of oure purveiaunce spye.
And whan thou thus hast doon, as I have seyd,
And hast oure vitaille faire in hem yleyd,
And eek an ax, to smyte the corde atwo,   3569
Whan that the water comth, that we may go,
And breke an hole an heigh, upon the gable,
Unto the gardyn-ward, over the stable,
That we may frely passen forth oure way,
Whan that the grete shour is goon away,
Thanne shaltou swymme as myrie, I undertake,
As dooth the white doke after hire drake.   3576
Thanne wol I clepe, 'How, Alison! how, John!
Be myrie, for the flood wol passe anon.'
And thou wolt seyn, 'Hayl, maister Nicholay!
Good morwe, I se thee wel, for it is day.'   3580
And thanne shul we be lordes al oure lyf
Of al the world, as Noe and his wyf.
    But of o thyng I warne thee ful right:
Be wel avysed on that ilke nyght
That we ben entred into shippes bord,   3585
That noon of us ne speke nat a word,
Ne clepe, ne crie, but been in his preyere;
For it is Goddes owene heeste deere.
    Thy wyf and thou moote hange fer atwynne;
For that bitwixe yow shal be no synne,   3590
Namoore in lookyng than ther shal in deede.
This ordinance is seyd. Go, God thee speede!

Tomorwe at nyght, whan men ben alle aslepe,
Into oure knedyng-tubbes wol we crepe,
And sitten there, abidyng Goddes grace.   3595
Go now thy wey, I have no lenger space
To make of this no lenger sermonyng.
Men seyn thus, 'sende the wise, and sey no
    thyng:'
Thou art so wys, it needeth thee nat teche.
Go, save oure lyf, and that I the biseche."   3600
    This sely carpenter goth forth his wey.
Ful ofte he seide "allas" and "weylawey,"
And to his wyf he tolde his pryvetee,
And she was war, and knew it bet than he,
What al this queynte cast was for to seye.   3605
But nathelees she ferde as she wolde deye,
And seyde, "Allas! go forth thy wey anon,
Help us to scape, or we been dede echon!
I am thy trewe, verray wedded wyf;   3609
Go, deere spouse, and help to save oure lyf."
    Lo, which a greet thyng is affeccioun!
Men may dyen of ymaginacioun,
So depe may impressioun be take.
This sely carpenter bigynneth quake;
Hym thynketh verraily that he may see   3615
Noes flood come walwynge as the see
To drenchen Alisoun, his hony deere.
He wepeth, weyleth, maketh sory cheere;
He siketh with ful many a sory swogh;
He gooth and geteth hym a knedyng trogh,   3620
And after that a tubbe and a kymelyn,
And pryvely he sente hem to his in,
And heng hem in the roof in pryvetee.
His owene hand he made laddres thre,
To clymben by the ronges and the stalkes   3625
Unto the tubbes hangynge in the balkes,
And hem vitailled, bothe trogh and tubbe,
With breed and chese, and good ale in a jubbe,

3559. madde, go mad. 3565. in the roof. The hall was usually open to the roof, and was provided with cross beams. The stable adjoins the hall on the side toward the garden. 3566. purveiaunce, provision. 3588. heeste, commandment. 3589. moote, must. fer atwynne, far apart. 3598. sende the wise. . . . Ray, Handbook of Proverbs (Bohn ed., p. 143) has "Send a wise man of an errand, and say nothing to him." 3605. queynte cast . . . seye, ingenious plan was about. 3606. ferde, behaved. as, as if. 3611. which a, what a. affeccioun, emotion, state of mind. 3616. walwynge, surging. 3619. siketh, sighs. swogh, audible sigh. 3621. kymelyn, tub, vat. 3622. in, lodging. 3623. heng, hung. 3624. His owene hand, with his own hand. See Language, § 77. 3625. stalkes, shafts (grasped with the hands while climbing). 3626. balkes, beams (stretching from wall to wall). 3628. jubbe, jug. In a fourteenth-century account (see NED) one such vessel held four gallons, but there may have been other sizes.

Suffisynge right ynogh as for a day.
But er that he hadde maad al this array,   3630
He sente his knave, and eek his wenche also,
Upon his nede to London for to go.
And on the Monday, whan it drow to nyght,
He shette his dore withoute candel-lyght,
And dressed alle thyng as it sholde be.   3635
And shortly, up they clomben alle thre;
They seten stille wel a furlong way.
   "Now, *Pater-noster*, clom!" seyde Nicolay,
And "clom," quod John, and "clom," seyde
   Alisoun.
This carpenter seyde his devocioun,   3640
And stille he sit, and biddeth his preyere,
Awaitynge on the reyn, if he it heere.
   The dede sleep, for wery bisynesse,
Fil on this carpenter right, as I gesse,
Aboute corfew-tyme, or litel moore;   3645
For travaille of his goost he groneth soore,
And eft he routeth, for his heed myslay.
Doun of the laddre stalketh Nicholay,
And Alisoun ful softe adoun she spedde;
Withouten wordes mo they goon to bedde,
Ther as the carpenter is wont to lye.   3651
Ther was the revel and the melodye;
And thus lith Alison and Nicholas,
In bisynesse of myrthe and of solas,
Til that the belle of laudes gan to rynge,   3655
And freres in the chauncel gonne synge.
   This parissh clerk, this amorous Absolon,
That is for love alwey so wo bigon,
Upon the Monday was at Oseneye   3659
With compaignye, hym to disporte and pleye,
And axed upon cas a cloisterer
Ful prively after John the carpenter;
And he drough hym apart out of the chirche,

And seyde, "I noot, I saugh hym heere nat
   wirche
Syn Saterday; I trowe that he be went   3665
For tymber, ther oure abbot hath hym sent;
For he is wont for tymber for to go,
And dwellen at the grange a day or two;
Or elles he is at his hous, certeyn.
Where that he be, I kan nat soothly seyn."   3670
   This Absolon ful joly was and light,
And thoghte, "Now is tyme to wake al nyght;
For sikirly I saugh hym nat stirynge
Aboute his dore, syn day bigan to sprynge.
So moot I thryve, I shal, at cokkes crowe,
Ful pryvely knokken at his wyndowe   3676
That stant ful lowe upon his boures wal.
To Alison now wol I tellen al
My love-longynge, for yet I shal nat mysse
That at the leeste wey I shal hire kisse.   3680
Som maner confort shal I have, parfay.
My mouth hath icched al this longe day;
That is a signe of kissyng atte leeste.
Al nyght me mette eek I was at a feeste.   3684
Therfore I wol go slepe an houre or tweye,
And al the nyght thanne wol I wake and
   pleye."
   Whan that the firste cok hath crowe, anon
Up rist this joly lovere Absolon,
And hym arraieth gay, at poynt-devys.
But first he cheweth greyn and lycorys,   3690
To smellen sweete, er he hadde kembd his
   heer.
Under his tonge a trewe-love he beer,
For therby wende he to ben gracious.
He rometh to the carpenteres hous,   3694
And stille he stant under the shot-wyndowe—
Unto his brest it raughte, it was so lowe—

3630. **array,** preparation. 3635. **dressed,** arranged. 3637. **a furlong way,** the length of time it takes to walk a furlong, about 2½ minutes. 3638. **clom,** mum, *i.e.* say a paternoster and then keep quiet. 3641. **sit,** sits. 3645. **corfew-tyme,** curfew time, usually 8 P.M., announced by a bell, when, according to a regulation, fires were to be covered for the night. 3646. **travaille of his goost,** laboring of his spirit. 3647. **routeth,** snores. 3648. **stalketh,** goes quietly. 3652. **revel . . . melodye,** apparently a variation of the stock phrase *mirth and melody*. 3655. **laudes.** Lauds followed Matins and came about four-thirty in the morning. 3661. **upon cas,** by chance. 3664. **noot,** don't know. **saugh . . . . wirche,** I have not seen him working here. 3665. **Syn,** since. 3666. **ther,** where. 3668. **grange,** an outlying farm-house and associated buildings belonging to the religious house of the cloisterer. 3677. **stant,** stands. 3684. **me mette,** I dreamed. 3687. **the firste cok hath crowe,** traditionally shortly after midnight. 3688. **rist,** riseth, rises. 3689. **at poynt-devys,** to a point of perfection, fastidiously. 3690. **greyn,** presumably the aromatic spice known as grain of Paradise. 3692. **a trewe-love,** identified in Gerard's *Herbal* with herb-paris (*Paris quadrifolia*). **beer,** bore. 3695. **shot-wyndowe,** casement window.

Phraseology
from
Song
of Songs

And softe he cougheth with a semy soun:
"What do ye, hony-comb, sweete Alisoun,
My faire bryd, my sweete cynamome?   3699
Awaketh, lemman myn, and speketh to me!
Wel litel thynken ye upon my wo,
That for youre love I swete ther I go.
No wonder is thogh that I swelte and swete;
I moorne as dooth a lamb after the tete.   3704
Ywis, lemman, I have swich love-longynge,
That lik a turtel trewe is my moornynge.
I may nat ete na moore than a mayde."
    "Go fro the wyndow, Jakke fool," she sayde;
"As help me God, it wol nat be 'com pa me.'
I love another—and elles I were to blame—
Wel bet than thee, by Jhesu, Absolon.   3711
Go forth thy wey, or I wol caste a ston,
And lat me slepe, a twenty devel wey!"
    "Allas," quod Absolon, "and weylawey,
That trewe love was evere so yvel biset!   3715
Thanne kysse me, syn it may be no bet,
For Jhesus love, and for the love of me."
    "Wiltow thanne go thy wey therwith?"
        quod she.
    "Ye, certes, lemman," quod this Absolon.
    "Thanne make thee redy," quod she, "I come
        anon."   3720
And unto Nicholas she seyde stille,
"Now hust, and thou shalt laughen al thy fille."
    This Absolon doun sette hym on his knees
And seyde, "I am a lord at alle degrees;
For after this I hope ther cometh moore.   3725
Lemman, thy grace, and sweete bryd, thyn
        oore!"
    The wyndow she undoth, and that in haste.
"Have do," quod she, "com of, and speed the
        faste,

Lest that oure neighebores thee espie."   3729
    This Absolon gan wype his mouth ful drie.
Derk was the nyght as pich, or as the cole,
And at the wyndow out she putte hir hole,
And Absolon, hym fil no bet ne wers,
But with his mouth he kiste hir naked ers
Ful savourly, er he were war of this.   3735
Abak he stirte, and thoughte it was amys,
For wel he wiste a womman hath no berd.
He felte a thyng al rough and long yherd,
And seyde, "Fy! allas! what have I do?"
    "Tehee!" quod she, and clapte the wyndow
        to,   3740
And Absolon gooth forth a sory pas.
    "A berd! a berd!" quod hende Nicholas,
"By Goddes corpus, this goth faire and weel."
    This sely Absolon herde every deel,
And on his lippe he gan for anger byte,   3745
And to hymself he seyde, "I shal thee quyte."
    Who rubbeth now, who froteth now his
        lippes
With dust, with sond, with straw, with clooth,
        with chippes,
But Absolon, that seith ful ofte, "Allas!"
"My soule bitake I unto Sathanas,   3750
But me were levere than al this toun," quod he,
"Of this despit awroken for to be.
Allas," quod he, "allas, I ne hadde ybleynt!"
His hoote love was coold and al yqueynt;
For fro that tyme that he hadde kist hir ers,   3755
Of paramours he sette nat a kers;
For he was heeled of his maladie.
Ful ofte paramours he gan deffie,
And weep as dooth a child that is ybete.
A softe paas he wente over the strete   3760
Until a smyth men cleped daun Gerveys,

3697. semy, thin, small, 3699. bryd, bird. cynamome, cinnamon. 3700. lemman, sweetheart. 3702. swete ther, sweat wherever. 3703. swelte, grow faint (from heat), swelter. *Swelte and swete* is a common alliterative phrase. 3704. moorne, feel longing. tete, teat. 3706. turtel, turtle-dove. moornynge, yearning. 3708. Jakke fool. Cf. mod. "Tom fool." 3709. com pa me, come kiss me. Chaucer has ba (kiss) at D 433. 3715. yvel biset, ill bestowed. 3722. hust, hush. 3724. at alle degrees, in all respects. 3726. oore, favor. In an anecdote reported by Giraldus Cambrensis (ed. Rolls Ser., II. 120) "Swete lamman, dhin are" is the refrain of a love-song. 3728. Have do . . . com of. Have done . . . come on. 3738. yherd, haired. 3741. a sory pas, sorrowfully. 3742. A berd! a joke, a trick! (with double meaning). 3743. corpus, body. 3746. quyte, repay. 3747. froteth, rubs. 3750. bitake, commit. Sathanas, Satan. 3752. awroken, avenged. 3753. I ne hadde ybleynt, *i.e.* that I had not abstained. 3754. yqueynt, quenched. 3756. kers, cress (a trifling thing). 3757. heeled, cured. 3758. deffie, denounce. 3759. weep, wept. 3760. A softe paas, quietly, slowly.

That in his forge smythed plough harneys;
He sharpeth shaar and kultour bisily.
This Absolon knokketh al esily, 3764
And seyde, "Undo, Gerveys, and that anon."
    "What, who artow?" "It am I, Absolon."
"What, Absolon! for Cristes sweete tree,
Why rise ye so rathe? ey, *benedicitee!*
What eyleth yow? Som gay gerl, God it woot,
Hath broght yow thus upon the viritoot. 3770
By seinte Note, ye woot wel what I mene."
    This Absolon ne roghte nat a bene
Of al his pley; no word agayn he yaf;
He hadde moore tow on his distaf
Than Gerveys knew, and seyde, "Freend so
        deere, 3775
That hoote kultour in the chymenee heere,
As lene it me, I have therwith to doone,
And I wol brynge it thee agayn ful soone."
    Gerveys answerde, "Certes, were it gold,
Or in a poke nobles alle untold, 3780
Thou sholdest have, as I am trewe smyth.
Ey, Cristes foo! what wol ye do therwith?"
    "Therof," quod Absolon, "be as be may.
I shal wel telle it thee to-morwe day"—
And caughte the kultour by the colde stele.
Ful softe out at the dore he gan to stele, 3786
And wente unto the carpenteris wal.
He cogheth first, and knokketh therwithal
Upon the wyndowe, right as he dide er.
    This Alison answerde, "Who is ther 3790
That knokketh so? I warante it a theef."
    "Why, nay," quod he, "God woot, my
        sweete leef,

I am thyn Absolon, my deerelyng.
Of gold," quod he, "I have thee broght a ryng.
My mooder yaf it me, so God me save; 3795
Ful fyn it is, and therto wel ygrave.
This wol I yeve thee, if thou me kisse."
    This Nicholas was risen for to pisse,
And thoughte he wolde amenden al the jape;
He sholde kisse his ers er that he scape. 3800
And up the wyndowe dide he hastily,
And out his ers he putteth pryvely
Over the buttok, to the haunche-bon;
And therwith spak this clerk, this Absolon,
"Spek, sweete bryd, I noot nat where thou
        art." 3805
    This Nicholas anon leet fle a fart,
As greet as it had been a thonder-dent,
That with the strook he was almoost yblent;
And he was redy with his iren hoot,
And Nicholas amydde the ers he smoot. 3810
    Of gooth the skyn an hande-brede aboute,
The hoote kultour brende so his toute,
And for the smert he wende for to dye.
As he were wood, for wo he gan to crye, 3814
"Help! water! water! help, for Goddes herte!"
    This carpenter out of his slomber sterte,
And herde oon crien "water" as he were wood,
And thoughte, "Allas, now comth Nowelis
        flood!"
He sit hym up withouten wordes mo,
And with his ax he smoot the corde atwo, 3820
And doun gooth al; he foond neither to selle
Ne breed ne ale, til he cam to the celle
Upon the floor, and ther aswowne he lay.

3762. **harneys,** parts, fittings. 3763. **shaar,** plowshare. **kultour,** vertical blade in front of the plowshare. 3764. **esily,** quietly. 3767. **tree,** rood tree, cross. 3768. **rathe,** early. 3769. **gerl,** girl, although the word may mean a young person of either sex. 3770. **viritoot.** No satisfactory explanation of this word has been found. Spitzer's suggestion(*Lang.*,XXVI. 389–93) involves a phonological difficulty, since Chaucer's word has [ọ] riming with *woot*. 3771. **seinte Note,** St. Neot, a ninth-century monk of Glastonbury. Tradition credited King Alfred with the founding of Oxford University on the advice of St. Neot. 3774. **moore tow on his distaf,** a proverbial expression meaning "to have more business in hand." **tow,** flax. 3776. **chymenee,** fireplace. 3777. **As lene,** lend. 3780. **poke,** bag, sack. **nobles,** see note to A 3256. **untold,** uncounted. 3782. **foo,** generally supposed to be an intentional substitution for *foot*, but *Christes foo* may quite possibly mean "the devil." 3785. **stele,** handle, shank. 3793. **deerelyng,** darling. 3799. **amenden,** improve. **jape,** joke. 3801. **up . . . dide,** opened. 3806. **fle,** fly. 3811. **hande-brede,** handbreadth. 3812. **toute,** rump. 3818. **Nowelis,** another of the carpenter's malapropisms. 3821–2. **he foond neither to selle Ne breed ne ale.** The statement, which means that he didn't stop, is paralleled by two instances in OF. fabliaux, pointed out by Tyrwhitt and Wright. **celle,** floor board. Since the word represents OE. *syll*, *celle* must be a Kentish form adopted for the sake of the rime. 3823. **floor,** the ground underneath the floor. **aswowne,** unconscious.

Up stirte hire Alison and Nicholay,   3824
And criden "out" and "harrow" in the strete.
The neighebores, bothe smale and grete,
In ronnen for to gauren on this man,
That yet aswowne lay, bothe pale and wan,
For with the fal he brosten hadde his arm.
But stonde he moste unto his owene harm;   3830
For whan he spak, he was anon bore doun
With hende Nicholas and Alisoun.
They tolden every man that he was wood,
He was agast so of Nowelis flood
Thurgh fantasie, that of his vanytee   3835
He hadde yboght hym knedyng tubbes thre,
And hadde hem hanged in the roof above;
And that he preyed hem, for Goddes love,
To sitten in the roof, *par compaignye.*

The folk gan laughen at his fantasye;   3840
Into the roof they kiken and they cape,
And turned al his harm unto a jape.
For what so that this carpenter answerde,
It was for noght, no man his reson herde.
With othes grete he was so sworn adoun   3845
That he was holde wood in al the toun;
For every clerk anonright heeld with other.
They seyde, "The man is wood, my leeve
    brother";
And every wight gan laughen at this stryf.
Thus swyved was this carpenteris wyf,   3850
For al his kepyng and his jalousye;
And Absolon hath kist hir nether yë;
And Nicholas is scalded in the towte.
This tale is doon, and God save al the rowte!

Heere endeth the Millere his tale.

The Reeve's Tale

THE REEVE'S PROLOGUE

The prologe of the Reves Tale.

Whan folk hadde laughen at this nyce cas
Of Absolon and hende Nicholas,   3856
Diverse folk diversely they seyde,
But for the moore part they loughe and pleyde.
Ne at this tale I saugh no man hym greve,
But it were oonly Osewold the Reve.   3860
By cause he was of carpenteris craft,
A litel ire is in his herte ylaft;
He gan to grucche, and blamed it a lite.

"So theek," quod he, "ful wel koude I thee
    quite
With bleryng of a proud milleres yë,   3865
If that me liste speke of ribaudye.
But ik am oold, me list not pley for age;
Gras tyme is doon, my fodder is now forage;
This white top writeth myne olde yeris;
Myn herte is also mowled as myne heris,   3870
But if I fare as dooth an open-ers:

3827. **ronnen**, ran. **gauren**, stare. 3829. **brosten**, broken. 3830. **stonde . . . harm**, he must accept the responsibility for his misfortune. 3832. **With**, by. 3835. **vanytee**, foolishness. 3840. **fantasye**, delusion, silly notion. 3841. **kiken**, gaze. **cape**, gape. 3850. **swyved**, embraced sexually. 3858. **loughe**, laughed. **pleyde**, made merry. 3863. **grucche**, grumble. 3864. **So theek**, a contraction of *so thee ik*, so may I thrive. The form *ik* (< OE *ic*) is often spoken of as Northern, but it is found wherever Scandinavian influence was strong. This explains its occurence in the Reeve's Norfolk dialect, which is properly speaking not Northern. 3865. **bleryng . . . yë**, getting the better of. 3866. **ribaudye**, ribaldry. 3868. **forage**, dry winter food. 3870. **mowled**, grown mouldy. 3871. **open-ers**, medlar (tree), the fruit of which cannot be eaten until it has become mushy.

That ilke fruyt is ever lenger the wers,
Til it be roten in mullok or in stree.
We olde men, I drede, so fare we:
Til we be roten, kan we nat be rype; 3875
We hoppen ay whil that the world wol pype.
For in oure wyl ther stiketh evere a nayl,
To have an hoor heed and a grene tayl,
As hath a leek; for thogh oure myght be goon,
Oure wyl desireth folie evere in oon. 3880
For whan we may nat doon, than wol we speke;
Yet in oure asshen olde is fyr yreke.
    Foure gleedes han we, whiche I shal devyse,—
Avauntyng, liyng, anger, coveitise;
Thise foure sparkles longen unto eelde. 3885
Oure olde lemes mowe wel been unweelde,
But wyl ne shal nat faillen, that is sooth.
And yet ik have alwey a coltes tooth,
As many a yeer as it is passed henne
Syn that my tappe of lif bigan to renne. 3890
For sikerly, whan I was bore, anon
Deeth drough the tappe of lyf and leet it gon;
And ever sithe hath so the tappe yronne
Til that almoost al empty is the tonne. 3894
The streem of lyf now droppeth on the chymbe.
The sely tonge may wel rynge and chymbe

Of wrecchednesse that passed is ful yoore;
With olde folk, save dotage, is namoore!"
    Whan that oure Hoost hadde herd this ser-
        monyng,
He gan to speke as lordly as a kyng. 3900
He seide, "What amounteth al this wit?
What shul we speke alday of hooly writ?
The devel made a reve for to preche,
Or of a soutere a shipman or a leche.
Sey forth thy tale, and tarie nat the tyme. 3905
Lo Depeford! and it is half-wey pryme.
Lo Grenewych, ther many a shrewe is inne!
It were al tyme thy tale to bigynne."
    "Now, sires," quod this Osewold the Reve,
"I pray yow alle that ye nat yow greve, 3910
Thogh I answere, and somdeel sette his howve;
For leveful is with force force of-showve.
    This dronke Millere hath ytoold us heer
How that bigyled was a carpenteer,
Peraventure in scorn, for I am oon. 3915
And, by youre leve, I shal hym quite anoon;
Right in his cherles termes wol I speke.
I pray to God his nekke mote tobreke;
He kan wel in myn eye seen a stalke,
But in his owene he kan nat seen a balke." 3920

3873. **mullok,** refuse. **stree,** straw. 3876. **hoppen,** dance. 3877. **ther stiketh evere a nayl,** *i.e.* there is always something that holds us, or compels us. 3878. **tayl,** stalk. 3880. **evere in oon,** always in the same way. 3882. **yreke,** raked up. 3883. **gleedes,** burning coals, embers. 3886. **lemes,** limbs. **mowe,** may. **unweelde,** weak. 3888. **a coltes tooth,** *i.e.* having the desires of youth. The Wife of Bath uses the expression in an almost identical line (D 602) when describing herself. 3889. **henne,** hence. 3892. **drough the tappe,** drew the tap. The tap was originally a tapered peg which fitted into a hole; hence the expression here. But it came to be used for the opening itself. 3894. **tonne,** tun, cask. 3895. **chymbe,** rim of the barrel. 3896. **chymbe,** chime. 3902. **What shul,** why must. **alday,** continually. 3904. **soutere,** shoemaker. **leche,** physician. 3905. **tarie,** prolong, delay. 3906. **Lo Depeford,** Deptford, a little less than four miles from Southwark. **half-wey pryme,** about seven-thirty, or, according to a different interpretation, about six-thirty. See E. A. Block, *Speculum,* XXXII. 826–33. 3907. **Grenewych.** Greenwich, one-half mile beyond Deptford. Both towns lie to the left of the road. The reference to *many a shrewe* (rascal) may be a sly dig by the Host at Chaucer, who was probably living in Greenwich at this time. 3911. **sette his howve,** make him look foolish. *Howve* means "hood." 3912. **with force force of-showve,** to repel force with force. 3919–20. **stalke . . . balke.** The words correspond exactly with the Latin of the Vulgate (*Matthew,* 7:3): *festucam* (stalk) and *trabs* (beam). The so-called Wiclif Bible has *festu* and *beme.*

THE REEVE'S TALE

Heere bigynneth the Reves Tale.

At Trumpyngtoun, nat fer fro Cantebrigge,
Ther gooth a brook, and over that a brigge,
Upon the whiche brook ther stant a melle;
And this is verray sooth that I yow telle.
A millere was ther dwellynge many a day;   3925
As any pecok he was proud and gay.
Pipen he koude and fisshe, and nettes beete,
And turne coppes, and wel wrastle and sheete.
Ay by his belt he baar a long panade,
And of a swerd ful trenchant was the blade.
A joly poppere baar he in his pouche;   3931
Ther was no man, for peril, dorste hym touche.
A Sheffeld thwitel baar he in his hose.
Round was his face, and camuse was his nose;
As piled as an ape was his skulle.   3935
He was a market-betere atte fulle:
Ther dorste no wight hand upon hym legge,
That he ne swoor he sholde anon abegge.
A theef he was forsothe of corn and mele,
And that a sly, and usaunt for to stele.   3940
His name was hoote deynous Symkyn.
A wyf he hadde, ycomen of noble kyn;
The person of the toun hir fader was.

With hire he yaf ful many a panne of bras,
For that Symkyn sholde in his blood allye.   3945
She was yfostred in a nonnerye;
For Symkyn wolde no wyf, as he sayde,
But she were wel ynorissed and a mayde,
To saven his estaat of yomanrye.
And she was proud, and peert as is a pye.   3950
A ful fair sighte was it upon hem two;
On halydayes biforn hire wolde he go
With his typet bounde aboute his heed,
And she cam after in a gyte of reed;
And Symkyn hadde hosen of the same.   3955
Ther dorste no wight clepen hire but "dame";
Was noon so hardy that wente by the weye
That with hire dorste rage or ones pleye,
But if he wolde be slayn of Symkyn
With panade, or with knyf, or boidekyn.   3960
For jalous folk ben perilous everemo;
Algate they wolde hire wyves wenden so.
And eek, for she was somdel smoterlich,
She was as digne as water in a dich,
And ful of hoker and of bisemare.   3965
Hir thoughte that a lady sholde hire spare,

The Reeve's Tale, like the Miller's is a fabliau. While the exact source of Chaucer's story does not exist, two versions of a French fabliau offer a close analogue. See *Sources and Analogues*, pp. 124–47, where both texts are printed.
3921. Trumpyngtoun, Trumpington, about three miles south of Cambridge. **3923. melle,** mill. **3927. Pipen.** That the miller of the tale could play the bagpipe is one of a number of details by which the Reeve suggests to the pilgrims the possible identification of the character with the Miller. **beete,** mend. **3928. turne coppes,** usually explained as "to turn wooden cups on a lathe," which carries on the activities mentioned in the preceding line, but Pratt suggests (*JEGP*, LIX. 208–11) "drink," "carouse" on the basis of a folk custom of Sussex reported in 1862, in which the accompanying chant ends "the cup is turn'd over." **sheete,** shoot. **3929. panade,** large knife, cutlass. **3930. trenchant,** sharp. **3931. poppere,** dagger. **3933. thwitel,** knife. Sheffield is still famous for its fine steel. **3934. camuse,** flat, "pug." **3935. piled,** deprived of hair, bald. **3936. market-betere,** swaggerer. **atte fulle,** completely. **3937. legge,** lay. **3938. abegge,** pay for it. **3940. usaunt,** accustomed. **3941. hoote,** called. **deynous,** scornful. **3943. person,** parson. **3944. panne of bras.** Her father was willing to give her a good dowry because she was presumably illegitimate. **3945. in his blood allye,** *i.e.* enter into alliance with the priest's offspring. **3949. saven,** preserve. He was evidently a freeman, and by preserving his status he would not have to perform the customary services of the manor to which his village belonged and would furthermore enjoy the protection of his rights and property in the king's court. **3950. pye,** magpie. **3952. biforn hire.** Note that he walks before her, a symbol of masculine superiority not unknown among the peasantry in parts of Europe today. **3953. typet,** a scarf or streamer normally hanging from the hood. **3954. gyte,** long cloak (OF. *guite*). The *g* is hard. **3958. rage,** behave wantonly. **3959. But if,** unless. **wolde,** wished. **3960. boidekyn,** dagger. **3962. wenden,** should think. **3963. somdel smoterlich,** somewhat besmirched (by her illegitimacy). **3964. digne as water in a dich,** "stinking with pride" (*NED*). **3965. hoker,** scorn. **bisemare,** contemptuous behavior. **3966. hire spare,** be reserved.

What for hire kynrede and hir nortelrie
That she hadde lerned in the nonnerie.
  A doghter hadde they bitwixe hem two
Of twenty yeer, withouten any mo,   3970
Savynge a child that was of half yeer age;
In cradel it lay and was a propre page.
This wenche thikke and wel ygrowen was,
With kamuse nose, and eyen greye as glas,
With buttokes brode, and brestes rounde and
     hye;   3975
But right fair was hire heer, I wol nat lye.
  This person of the toun, for she was feir,
In purpos was to maken hire his heir,
Bothe of his catel and his mesuage,
And straunge he made it of hir mariage.   3980
His purpos was for to bistowe hire hye
Into som worthy blood of auncetrye;
For hooly chirches good moot been despended
On hooly chirches blood, that is descended.
Therfore he wolde his hooly blood hon-
     oure,   3985
Though that he hooly chirche sholde devoure.
  Greet sokene hath this millere, out of doute,
With whete and malt of al the land aboute;
And nameliche ther was a greet collegge   3989
Men clepen the Soler Halle at Cantebregge;
Ther was hir whete and eek hir malt ygrounde.
And on a day it happed, in a stounde,
Sik lay the maunciple on a maladye;
Men wenden wisly that he sholde dye.   3994
For which this millere stal bothe mele and corn
An hundred tyme moore than biforn;

For therbiforn he stal but curteisly,
But now he was a theef outrageously,
For which the wardeyn chidde and made fare.
But therof sette the millere nat a tare;   4000
He craketh boost, and swoor it was nat so.
  Thanne were ther yonge povre scolers two,
That dwelten in this halle, of which I seye.
Testif they were, and lusty for to pleye,
And, oonly for hire myrthe and revelrye,   4005
Upon the wardeyn bisily they crye
To yeve hem leve, but a litel stounde,
To goon to mille and seen hir corn ygrounde;
And hardily they dorste leye hir nekke   4009
The millere sholde nat stele hem half a pekke
Of corn by sleighte, ne by force hem reve;
And at the laste the wardeyn yaf hem leve.
John highte that oon, and Aleyn highte that
     oother;
Of o toun were they born, that highte Strother,
Fer in the north, I kan nat telle where.   4015
  This Aleyn maketh redy al his gere,
And on an hors the sak he caste anon.
Forth goth Aleyn the clerk, and also John,
With good swerd and with bokeler by hir syde.
John knew the wey,—hem nedede no gyde,—   4020
And at the mille the sak adoun he layth.
Aleyn spak first, "Al hayl, Symond, y-fayth!
Hou fares thy faire doghter and thy wyf?"
  "Aleyn, welcome," quod Symkyn, "by my
     lyf!
And John also, how now, what do ye
     heer?"   4025

3967. What for, in view of. **nortelrie,** education. **3972. propre page,** good-looking boy. **3974. kamuse,** Cf. l. 3934 above. According to a medieval treatise on physiognomy, a pug nose suggests a sensual person. See W. A. Turner, *N & Q*, cxcix. 232. **3977. for,** because. **she,** *i.e.* the miller's daughter. **3979. catel,** chattels, wealth. **his mesuage,** his house and its purtenances. **3980. straunge he made it of,** he raised difficulties about. The meaning is assured by the quotations in the *NED*. **3983. good,** goods. **moot,** must. **3987. sokene.** The soken was the monopoly by which all the tenants on a manor were required to have their grain ground at the lord's mill. It was generally farmed to the miller for a fixed annual rent. The business of the mill would be increased if there were an institution like the Cambridge college, about to be mentioned, which did not have its own mill. **3990. Solar Halle,** King's Hall, now a part of Trinity College. It got its name probably from the size or importance of its *solarium*, frequently mentioned in the early records of the college. The *solarium* was a room or rooms, a kind of sun-parlor, forming the upper story. **Cantebregge,** Cambridge. **3992. in a stounde,** at one time. **3993. maunciple.** On the duties of a manciple see the note to A 567. **on,** of. **3994. wisly,** surely. **3995. stal,** stole. **3997. curteisly,** like a gentleman. **3999. made fare,** made a to-do. **4001. craketh boost,** blusters, talks loudly. **4002. povre,** poor. **4004. Testif,** headstrong. **4007. yeve,** give. **stounde,** while. **4009. leye,** wager. **4011. reve,** take away. **4013. highte,** was named. **4014. Strother.** No town of this name has been found, but there was a Strother castle in Northumberland, which was *Fer in the north*. **4020. hem nedede,** lit. was neede to them. **4023. fares.** The students speak in the Northern dialect, in which the 3 pl. of verbs ended in -*s*.

"Symond," quod John, "by God, nede has na
　　peer.
Hym boes serve hymself that has na swayn,
Or elles he is a fool, as clerkes sayn.
Oure manciple, I hope he wil be deed,
Swa werkes ay the wanges in his heed;　　4030
And forthy is I come, and eek Alayn,
To grynde oure corn and carie it ham agayn;
I pray yow spede us heythen that ye may."
　　"It shal be doon," quod Symkyn, "by my
　　fay!　　　　　　　　　　　　　　　　4034
What wol ye doon whil that it is in hande?"
　　"By God, right by the hopur wil I stande,"
Quod John, "and se how that the corn gas in.
Yet saugh I nevere, by my fader kyn,
How that the hopur wagges til and fra."
　　Aleyn answerde, "John, and wiltow swa?
Thanne wil I be bynethe, by my croun,　　4041
And se how that the mele falles doun
Into the trough; that sal be my disport.
For John, y-faith, I may been of youre sort;
I is as ille a millere as ar ye."　　　　　4045
　　This millere smyled of hir nycetee,
And thoghte, "Al this nys doon but for a wyle.
They wene that no man may hem bigyle,
But by my thrift, yet shal I blere hir yë,
For al the sleighte in hir philosophye.　　4050
The moore queynte crekes that they make,
The moore wol I stele whan I take.
In stide of flour yet wol I yeve hem bren.
'The gretteste clerkes been noght wisest men,'
As whilom to the wolf thus spak the mare.

Of al hir art ne counte I noght a tare."　　4056
　　Out at the dore he gooth ful pryvely,
Whan that he saugh his tyme, softely.
He looketh up and doun til he hath founde
The clerkes hors, ther as it stood ybounde　　4060
Bihynde the mille, under a levesel;
And to the hors he goth hym faire and wel;
He strepeth of the brydel right anon.
And whan the hors was laus, he gynneth gon
Toward the fen, ther wilde mares renne,　　4065
And forth with "wehee," thurgh thikke and
　　thurgh thenne.
　　This millere gooth agayn, no word he seyde,
But dooth his note, and with the clerkes
　　pleyde,
Til that hir corn was faire and weel ygrounde.
And whan the mele is sakked and ybounde,　4070
This John goth out and fynt his hors away,
And gan to crie "Harrow!" and "Weylaway!
Oure hors is lorn, Alayn, for Goddes banes,
Step on thy feet! Com of, man, al atanes!
Allas, oure wardeyn has his palfrey lorn."　　4075
This Aleyn al forgat, bothe mele and corn;
Al was out of his mynde his housbondrie.
"What, whilk way is he geen?" he gan to crie.
　　The wyf cam lepynge inward with a ren.
She seyde, "Allas! youre hors goth to the fen
With wilde mares, as faste as he may go.　　4081
Unthank come on his hand that boond hym so,
And he that bettre sholde han knyt the reyne!"
　　"Allas," quod John, "Aleyn, for Cristes
　　peyne,

4026. **nede has na peer,** necessity has no equal. The more usual form of the proverb is "Necessity knows no law."
The verb *has,* which seems quite natural to us, is another Northern form, the London dialect having *hath.* Likewise *na* for
no is Northern. In general it may be said that Chaucer has done an excellent job of suggesting the Northern speech of the
students. His few inconsistencies may even represent Midland forms that have crept into their speech from their residence
in Cambridge. 4027. **boes,** behooves, a distinctly Northern contraction. 4029. **hope,** expect. 4030. **werkes,** more correctly
warkes, ache. **wanges,** cheek-teeth, molars. 4031. **forthy,** therefore. **is I,** Northern. 4032. **ham,** home. OE *ā,* which had
become *ō* in the other dialects, remained *a* in the north. 4033. **heythen,** hence. In Chaucer's own dialect the word was *hennes.*
4037. **gas,** goes. 4039. **til and fra,** to and fro. 4040. **swa,** so. 4043. **sal,** Northern for *shal.* 4045. **ar.** This now familiar
form is due to Scandinavian influence and is chiefly Northern at this time. Chaucer normally uses *been.* 4046. **nycetee,**
foolishness. 4047. **wyle,** wile, trick. 4049. **blere hir yë,** blear their eye, get the better of them. 4050. **sleighte,** craftiness.
4051. **queynte crekes,** clever tricks. 4055. **thus spak the mare.** The story is quite common and occurs in some of the
Renard the Fox collections. The fox persuades the wolf (who is hungry) to buy a mare's foal. The mare says the price is
written on her hind foot. When the wolf examines her foot she kicks him. The fox observes that the best clerks are not the
wisest men. See Baum, *MLN,* XXXVII. 350–3. 4060. **ther as,** where. 4061. **levesel,** leafy arbor. 4063. **strepeth,** strips.
4064. **laus,** loose. 4068. **note,** work. 4071. **fynt,** finds. 4073. **lorn,** lost. **banes,** bones. 4074. **Com of,** come on. **al atanes,**
right away. 4077. **housbondrie,** careful management. 4078. **whilk,** which. **geen,** gone. 4079. **ren,** run. 4082. **Unthank,**
the opposite of thanks (bad luck, a curse).

Lay doun thy swerd, and I wil myn alswa.

I is ful wight, God waat, as is a raa;   4086

By Goddes herte, he sal nat scape us bathe!

Why nadstow pit the capul in the lathe?

Il-hayl! by God, Alayn, thou is a fonne!"

   This sely clerkes han ful faste yronne   4090

Toward the fen, bothe Aleyn and eek John.

   And whan the millere saugh that they were
     gon,

He half a busshel of hir flour hath take,

And bad his wyf go knede it in a cake.

He seyde, "I trowe the clerkes were aferd,   4095

Yet kan a millere make a clerkes berd,

For al his art; now lat hem goon hir weye!

Lo, wher he gooth! ye, lat the children pleye.

They gete hym nat so lightly, by my croun."

   Thise sely clerkes rennen up and doun   4100

With "Keep! keep! stand! stand! jossa, war-
     derere,

Ga whistle thou, and I shal kepe hym heere!"

But shortly, til that it was verray nyght,

They koude nat, though they dide al hir myght,

Hir capul cacche, he ran alwey so faste,   4105

Til in a dych they caughte hym atte laste.

   Wery and weet, as beest is in the reyn,

Comth sely John, and with him comth Aleyn.

"Allas," quod John, "the day that I was born!

Now are we dryve til hethyng and til scorn.

Oure corn is stoln, men wil us fooles calle,   4111

Bathe the wardeyn and oure felawes alle,

And namely the millere, weylaway!"

   Thus pleyneth John as he gooth by the way

Toward the mille, and Bayard in his hond.

The millere sittynge by the fyr he fond,   4116

For it was nyght, and forther myghte they
     noght;

But for the love of God they hym bisoght

Of herberwe and of ese, as for hir peny.   4119

   The millere seyde agayn, "If ther be eny,

Swich as it is, yet shal ye have youre part.

Myn hous is streit, but ye han lerned art;

Ye konne by argumentes make a place

A myle brood of twenty foot of space.

Lat se now if this place may suffise,   4125

Or make it rowm with speche, as is youre gise."

   "Now, Symond," seyde John, "by seint Cut-
     berd,

Ay is thou myrie, and this is faire answerd.

I have herd seyd, 'man sal taa of twa thynges

Slyk as he fyndes, or taa slyk as he brynges.'

But specially I pray thee, hooste deere,   4131

Get us som mete and drynke, and make us
     cheere,

And we wil payen trewely atte fulle.

With empty hand men may na haukes tulle;

Loo, heere oure silver, redy for to spende."

   This millere into toun his doghter sende   4136

For ale and breed, and rosted hem a goos,

And boond hire hors, it sholde namoore go
     loos;

And in his owene chambre hem made a bed,

With sheetes and with chalons faire yspred   4140

Noght from his owene bed ten foot or twelve.

His doghter hadde a bed, al by hirselve,

Right in the same chambre by and by.

It myghte be no bet, and cause why?   4144

Ther was no roumer herberwe in the place.

They soupen and they speke, hem to solace,

And drynken evere strong ale atte beste.

Aboute mydnyght wente they to reste.

   Wel hath this millere vernysshed his heed;

Ful pale he was fordronken, and nat reed.   4150

He yexeth, and he speketh thurgh the nose

As he were on the quakke, or on the pose.

4085. alswa, also. **4086. wight,** fleet, swift. **raa,** roe. **4087. bathe,** both. **4088. pit,** put. **capul,** horse. **lathe,** barn. **4089. Il-hayl,** bad luck to you. **thou is a fonne,** thou art a fool. **4096. make a . . . berd,** fool, get the better of. **4101. jossa,** down here. **warderere,** look behind. **4102. Ga,** go. **4110. til hethyng,** into derision, contempt. **4113. namely,** particularly. **4122. streit,** narrow, small. **4126. rowm,** roomy. **4127. Cutberd,** Cuthbert, a Northumberland saint. **4129. sal taa,** shall take. One must take what he finds or what he brings. **4134. tulle,** lure. **4136. sende,** sent. **4140. chalons,** bedspreads. **4143. by and by,** one after the other, in order. **4145. roumer,** roomier. **herberwe,** lodging. **4146. soupen,** sup. **4149. vernysshed his heed,** made himself drunk. Cf. F. *être verni,* to be drunk, and the modern "shel-lacked." **4150. fordronken,** very drunk. Cf. A 3120. **4151. yexeth,** hiccups. **4152. on the quakke,** hoarse. **on the pose,** suffering from a cold in the head.

To bedde he goth, and with hym goth his wyf.
As any jay she light was and jolyf,
So was hir joly whistle wel ywet.   4155
The cradel at hir beddes feet is set,
To rokken, and to yeve the child to sowke.
And whan that dronken al was in the crowke,
To bedde wente the doghter right anon;
To bedde gooth Aleyn and also John;   4160
Ther nas na moore,—hem nedede no dwale.
This millere hath so wisly bibbed ale
That as an hors he fnorteth in his sleep,
Ne of his tayl bihynde he took no keep.
His wyf bar hym a burdon, a ful strong;   4165
Men myghte hir rowtyng heere two furlong;
The wenche rowteth eek, *par compaignye.*

    Aleyn the clerk, that herde this melodye,
He poked John, and seyde, "Slepestow?
Herdestow evere slyk a sang er now?   4170
Lo, swilk a complyn is ymel hem alle,
A wilde fyr upon thair bodyes falle!
Wha herkned evere slyk a ferly thyng?
Ye, they sal have the flour of il endyng.
This lange nyght ther tydes me na reste;   4175
But yet, na fors, al sal be for the beste.
For, John," seyde he, "als evere moot I thryve,
If that I may, yon wenche wil I swyve.
Som esement has lawe yshapen us;
For, John, ther is a lawe that says thus,   4180
That gif a man in a point be agreved,
That in another he sal be releved.
Oure corn is stoln, sothly, it is na nay,
And we han had an il fit al this day;
And syn I sal have neen amendement   4185
Agayn my los, I will have esement.
By Goddes saule, it sal neen other bee!"

This John answerde, "Alayn, avyse thee!
The millere is a perilous man," he seyde,
"And gif that he out of his sleep abreyde,   4190
He myghte doon us bathe a vileynye."
Aleyn answerde, "I counte hym nat a flye."
And up he rist, and by the wenche he crepte.
This wenche lay uprighte, and faste slepte,
Til he so ny was, er she myghte espie,   4195
That it had been to late for to crie,
And shortly for to seyn, they were aton.
Now pley, Aleyn, for I wol speke of John.

    This John lith stille a furlong wey or two,
And to hymself he maketh routhe and wo.   4200
"Allas!" quod he, "this is a wikked jape;
Now may I seyn that I is but an ape.
Yet has my felawe somwhat for his harm;
He has the milleris doghter in his arm.
He auntred hym, and has his nedes sped,   4205
And I lye as a draf-sak in my bed;
And when this jape is tald another day,
I sal been halde a daf, a cokenay!
I wil arise and auntre it, by my fayth!
'Unhardy is unseely,' thus men sayth."   4210
And up he roos, and softely he wente
Unto the cradel, and in his hand it hente,
And baar it softe unto his beddes feet.
    Soone after this the wyf hir rowtyng leet,
And gan awake, and wente hire out to
    pisse,   4215
And cam agayn, and gan hir cradel mysse,
And groped heer and ther, but she foond noon.
"Allas!" quod she, "I hadde almoost mysgoon;
I hadde almoost goon to the clerkes bed.
Ey, benedicite! thanne hadde I foule ysped."
And forth she gooth til she the cradel fond.   4221

4157. **sowke,** suck. 4158. **crowke,** jug, pitcher. 4161. **dwale,** sleeping potion. 4162. **wisly,** certainly. 4163. **fnorteth,** snores. The reading is doubtful and the meaning still more so. A number of manuscripts have *snorteth* and Ln reads *frontith* (kicks). But cf. B 790. 4165. **burdon,** a bass accompaniment. See note to A 673. 4166. **rowtyng,** snoring. 4170. **slyk a sang,** such a song. 4171. **complyn,** compline, the last canonical hour, the service sung before retiring. **ymel,** among. 4172. **wilde fyr,** erysipelas. 4173. **ferly,** strange. 4174. **flour of il endyng,** the choicest of an evil end. 4175. **tydes,** comes to. 4178. **swyve,** have intercourse with. 4179. **esement,** redress. 4181. **gif,** if. 4184. **il fit,** unfortunate experience. 4187. **saule,** soul. **neen other bee,** not be otherwise. 4191. **doon us bathe a vileynye,** do us both harm. 4194. **uprighte,** upon her back. 4195. **espie,** become aware. 4199. **a furlong wey or two,** the time it takes to walk a furlong or two. 4205. **auntred hym,** took a chance. 4206. **draf-sak,** a sack of refuse. 4208. **daf,** fool. **cokeney,** cockney, which originally meant a poor or worthless thing. 4209. **auntre,** venture. 4210. **Unhardy is unseely.** The timid man is unlucky. Cf. the modern proverb "Nothing ventured, nothing gained." 4212. **hente,** took. 4214. **hir rowtyng leet,** stopped snoring.

She gropeth alwey forther with hir hond,
And foond the bed, and thoghte noght but
    good,
By cause that the cradel by it stood,
And nyste wher she was, for it was derk;   4225
But faire and wel she creep in to the clerk,
And lith ful stille, and wolde han caught a
    sleep.
Withinne a while this John the clerk up leep,
And on this goode wyf he leith on soore.
So myrie a fit ne hadde she nat ful yoore;   4230
He priketh harde and depe as he were mad.
This joly lyf han thise two clerkes lad
Til that the thridde cok bigan to synge.

    Aleyn wax wery in the dawenynge,
For he had swonken al the longe nyght,   4235
And seyde, "Fare weel, Malyne, sweete wight!
The day is come, I may no lenger byde;
But everemo, wher so I go or ryde,
I is thyn awen clerk, swa have I seel!"
    "Now, deere lemman," quod she, "go, fare-
        weel!   4240
But er thow go, o thyng I wol thee telle:
Whan that thou wendest homward by the
    melle,
Right at the entree of the dore bihynde
Thou shalt a cake of half a busshel fynde
That was ymaked of thyn owene mele,   4245
Which that I heelp my sire for to stele.
And, goode lemman, God thee save and kepe!"
And with that word almoost she gan to wepe.
    Aleyn up rist, and thoughte, "Er that it dawe,
I wol go crepen in by my felawe";   4250
And fond the cradel with his hand anon.
"By God," thoughte he, "al wrang I have
    mysgon.
Myn heed is toty of my swynk tonyght,

That maketh me that I go nat aright.
I woot wel by the cradel I have mysgo;   4255
Heere lith the millere and his wyf also."
And forth he goth, a twenty devel way,
Unto the bed ther as the millere lay.
He wende have cropen by his felawe John,
And by the millere in he creep anon,   4260
And caughte hym by the nekke, and softe he
    spak.
He seyde, "Thou John, thou swynes-heed,
    awak,
For Cristes saule, and heer a noble game.
For by that lord that called is seint Jame,
As I have thries in this shorte nyght   4265
Swyved the milleres doghter bolt upright,
Whil thow hast, as a coward, been agast."
    "Ye, false harlot," quod the millere, "hast?
A, false traitour! false clerk!" quod he,
"Thow shalt be deed, by Goddes dignitee!   4270
Who dorste be so boold to disparage
My doghter, that is come of swich lynage?"
And by the throte-bolle he caughte Alayn,
And he hente hym despitously agayn,   4274
And on the nose he smoot hym with his fest.
Doun ran the blody streem upon his brest;
And in the floor, with nose and mouth tobroke,
They walwe as doon two pigges in a poke;
And up they goon, and doun agayn anon,
Til that the millere sporned at a stoon,   4280
And doun he fil bakward upon his wyf,
That wiste no thyng of this nyce stryf;
For she was falle aslepe a lite wight
With John the clerk, that waked hadde al
    nyght,
And with the fal out of hir sleep she
    breyde.   4285
"Help! hooly croys of Bromeholm," she seyde,

4226. creep, crept. 4228. leep, leaped. 4233. the thridde cok. In popular tradition the cock crows at midnight, about three o'clock in the morning, and an hour before dawn. 4235. swonken, *lit*. labored. 4236. Malyne, a familiar variant of Matilda. 4239. awen, own. seel, prosperity, *i.e.* so may I prosper. 4242. melle, mill. 4246. heelp, helped. 4249. rist, rises. dawe, dawns. 4252. wrang, wrong. 4253. toty, dizzy, befuddled. 4259. cropen, crept. 4263. a noble game, a good joke. 4267. agast, afraid. 4268. harlot, rascal. 4271. disparage, dishonor. 4273. throte-bolle, Adam's apple. 4274. hente, seized. despitously. angrily. agayn, in return. 4277. in, on. 4278. walwe, wallow, wrestle. 4280. sporned at, tripped over. 4283. wight, while. 4285. breyde, started. 4286. hooly croys of Bromeholm. Bromholm, in Norfolk, is some seventy-five miles from Trumpington. In 1223, according to Roger of Wendover, a piece of the true cross was brought from Constantinople to the priory there, and miracles began to be reported. See Pratt, *MLN*, LXX. 324-5.

In manus tuas! Lord, to thee I calle!

Awak, Symond! the feend is on me falle.

Myn herte is broken; help! I nam but deed!

Ther lyth oon upon my wombe and on myn
    heed.   4290

Help, Symkyn, for the false clerkes fighte!"

    This John stirte up as faste as ever he
    myghte,

And graspeth by the walles to and fro,

To fynde a staf; and she stirte up also,

And knew the estres bet than dide this John,

And by the wal a staf she foond anon,   4296

And saugh a litel shymeryng of a light,

For at an hole in shoon the moone bright;

And by that light she saugh hem bothe two,

But sikerly she nyste who was who,   4300

But as she saugh a whit thyng in hir yë.

And whan she gan this white thyng espye,

She wende the clerk hadde wered a volupeer,

And with the staf she drow ay neer and neer,

And wende han hit this Aleyn at the fulle,   4305

And smoot the millere on the pyled skulle,

That doun he gooth, and cride, "Harrow! I
    dye!"

Thise clerkes beete hym weel and lete hym lye;

And greythen hem, and tooke hir hors anon,

And eek hire mele, and on hir wey they gon.

And at the mille yet they tooke hir cake   4311

Of half a busshel flour, ful wel ybake.

    Thus is the proude millere wel ybete,

And hath ylost the gryndynge of the whete,

And payed for the soper everideel   4315

Of Aleyn and of John, that bette hym weel.

His wyf is swyved, and his doghter als.

Lo, swich it is a millere to be fals!

And therfore this proverbe is seyd ful sooth,

"Hym thar nat wene wel that yvele dooth";

A gylour shal hymself bigyled be.   4321

And God, that sitteth heighe in magestee,

Save al this compaignye, grete and smale!

Thus have I quyt the Millere in my tale.   4324

Heere is ended the Reves tale.

The Cook's Tale

THE COOK'S PROLOGUE

The prologe of the Cokes Tale.

    The Cook of Londoun, whil the Reve spak,

For joye him thoughte he clawed him on the
    bak.

"Ha! ha!" quod he, "for Cristes passioun,

This millere hadde a sharp conclusioun

Upon his argument of herbergage!

Wel seyde Salomon in his langage,   4330

'Ne brynge nat every man into thyn hous';

For herberwynge by nyghte is perilous.

Wel oghte a man avysed for to be

Whom that he broghte into his pryvetee.

I pray to God, so yeve me sorwe and care   4335

4287. *In manus tuas!* Into thy hands! Cf. *Luke*, 23:46. **4293. graspeth,** gropes. **4295. estres,** the inside of the building, rooms. **4301. But as,** except that. **in her yë,** with her eye. **4303. wered a volupeer,** worn a nightcap. **4304. neer and neer,** nearer and nearer. **4305. wende han.** thought to have. **4306. the pyled skulle,** his bald head. **4309. greythen,** prepare. **4317. als,** also. **4320. Hym thar . . .** He that does evil need not expect well. **4321. gylour,** one who practices deceit. **4326. him thoughte,** (as) it seemed to him, *i.e.* the joy which he felt. **clawed him on the bak,** complimented him. **4329. herbergage,** lodging. **4330. Salomon.** Cf. *Ecclesiasticus*, 11:29. **4334. pryvetee,** privacy.

If evere, sitthe I highte Hogge of Ware,
Herde I a millere bettre yset a-werk.
He hadde a jape of malice in the derk.
But God forbede that we stynte heere;
And therfore, if ye vouchesauf to heere   4340
A tale of me, that am a povre man,
I wol yow telle, as wel as evere I kan,
A litel jape that fil in oure citee."
    Oure Hoost answerde and seide, "I graunte
        it thee.
Now telle on, Roger, looke that it be good;
For many a pastee hastow laten blood,   4346
And many a Jakke of Dovere hastow soold
That hath been twies hoot and twies coold.
Of many a pilgrym hastow Cristes curs,
For of thy percely yet they fare the wors,   4350

That they han eten with thy stubbel goos;
For in thy shoppe is many a flye loos.
Now telle on, gentil Roger by thy name.
But yet I pray thee, be nat wroth for game;
A man may seye ful sooth in game and pley."
    "Thou seist ful sooth," quod Roger, "by my
        fey!   4356
But 'sooth pley, quaad pley,' as the Flemyng
    seith.
And therfore, Herry Bailly, by thy feith,
Be thou nat wrooth, er we departen heer,
Though that my tale be of an hostileer.   4360
But nathelees I wol nat telle it yit;
But er we parte, ywis, thou shalt be quit."
And therwithal he lough and made cheere,
And seyde his tale, as ye shul after heere.

THE COOK'S TALE

Heere bigynneth the Cookes Tale.

    A prentys whilom dwelled in oure citee,   4365
And of a craft of vitailliers was hee.
Gaillard he was as goldfynch in the shawe,
Broun as a berye, a propre short felawe,
With lokkes blake, ykembd ful fetisly.
Dauncen he koude so wel and jolily   4370
That he was cleped Perkyn Revelour.
He was as ful of love and paramour
As is the hyve ful of hony sweete:
Wel was the wenche with hym myghte meete.
At every bridale wolde he synge and
    hoppe;   4375

He loved bet the taverne than the shoppe.
For whan ther any ridyng was in Chepe,
Out of the shoppe thider wolde he lepe—
Til that he hadde al the sighte yseyn,
And daunced wel, he wolde nat come ayeyn—
And gadered hym a meynee of his sort   4381
To hoppe and synge and maken swich disport;
And ther they setten stevene for to meete,
To pleyen at the dys in swich a streete.
For in the toune nas ther no prentys   4385
That fairer koude caste a paire of dys
Than Perkyn koude, and therto he was free

4336. highte, was called. **Hogge,** Hodge (Roger). **Ware,** in eastern Hertfordshire, about 30 miles from London. **4337. yset a-werk,** imposed upon, duped. Cf. D 215 and glossary. **4338. a jape of malice,** a mean trick. **4339. stynte,** stop. **4346. pastee,** meat-pie. **laten blood,** let blood, *i.e.* drawn off the gravy, done to unsold pies to keep them from getting soggy. **4347. Jakke of Dovere,** probably a stale or warmed-over pie, though the meaning is not certain. **4350. percely,** parsley. **4351. stubbel goos,** goose fed on stubble. **4352. many a flye,** *i.e.* which got mixed with the parsley stuffing. **4357. sooth pley, quaad pley,** *i.e.* a true jest is a bad jest (Flemish *quaad,* bad). **4358. Herry Bailly.** We here learn the name of the Host, which is actually found as the name of an innkeeper in Southwark in a Subsidy Roll for 1380–81. See Manly, *New Light,* pp. 79–82. **4361. I wol nat telle it yit.** The Cook means to tell it later, since according to the original plan each pilgrim was to tell four tales. **4367. Gaillard,** lively, merry. **shawe,** grove, thicket. **4368. propre,** well proportioned. **4369. fetisly,** neatly. **4375. hoppe,** dance. **4377. ridyng,** procession. **Chepe,** Cheapside, the principal business street, and part of the main thorofare, in Chaucer's London. **4383. setten stevene,** made an appointment. **4387-8. was free Of his dispense,** spent freely.

Of his dispense, in place of pryvetee.
That fond his maister wel in his chaffare;
For often tyme he foond his box ful bare.   4390
For sikerly a prentys revelour
That haunteth dys, riot, or paramour,
His maister shal it in his shoppe abye,
Al have he no part of the mynstralcye.
For thefte and riot, they been convertible,   4395
Al konne he pleye on gyterne or ribible.
Revel and trouthe, as in a lowe degree,
They been ful wrothe al day, as men may see.
  This joly prentys with his maister bood,
Til he were ny out of his prentishood,   4400
Al were he snybbed bothe erly and late,
And somtyme lad with revel to Newegate.
But atte laste his maister hym bithoghte,
Upon a day, whan he his papir soghte,
Of a proverbe that seith this same word,   4405

"Wel bet is roten appul out of hoord
Than that it rotie al the remenaunt."
So fareth it by a riotous servaunt;
It is ful lasse harm to lete hym pace,   4409
Than he shende alle the servantz in the place.
Therfore his maister yaf hym acquitance,
And bad hym go, with sorwe and with mes-
  chance!
And thus this joly prentys hadde his leve.
Now lat hym riote al the nyght or leve.   4414
And for ther is no theef withoute a lowke,
That helpeth hym to wasten and to sowke
Of that he brybe kan or borwe may,
Anon he sente his bed and his array
Unto a compeer of his owene sort,
That lovede dys, and revel, and disport,   4420
And hadde a wyf that heeld for contenance
A shoppe, and swyved for hir sustenance

4389. chaffare, business. **4393. abye,** pay for. **4394. Al,** although. **mynstralcye,** entertainment. **4395. convertible,** interchangeable terms. **4396. Al konne he pleye . . .** Regardless of the interpretation of these lines, the two *al* (although) clauses stylistically leave something to be desired. Skeat took *he* of l. 4396 to refer to the apprentice, but this spoils the word-play on *mynstralcye*. I take *he* to refer to the master, who has no part in the minstrelsy even though he may know how to play a guitar or rebeck (see note to A 3331). **4397. Revel and truthe . . .,** riotous living and honesty, in one of low station, are always (*al day*) at enmity. **4399. bood,** lived. **4401. snybbed,** reproved. **4402. lad with revel to Newegate.** Newgate was a prison in London. Those arrested were by law conducted from Newgate to the pillory or other place of punishment accompanied by minstrelsy, no doubt to attract a crowd and increase their public disgrace. See Riley, *Liber Albus,* pp. 394–6. Chaucer implies that they were also conducted in this way to prison. **4404. whan he his papir soghte.** The most plausible interpretation is that of R. Blenner-Hassett (*MLN*, LVII. 34–5). The paper is the indenture of apprenticeship, which Perkyn asks to be released from. His master gave him acquittance for the reason explained in the text. **4407. rotie,** corrupt. **4410. shende** harm. **4414. or leve,** desist, *i.e.* not riot. **4415. lowke,** accomplice. **4416. to sowke Of,** to extract. **4417. that,** what. **brybe,** purloin. **4421. for contenance,** for the sake of appearances. **4422. swyved,** was a courtesan. The tale is unfinished. At this point Chaucer probably decided that three vulgar stories in a row would be too many. The Cook reappears in the Manciple's Prologue.

The Man of Law's Tale

Group B₁ (Fragment II)

INTRODUCTION TO THE MAN OF LAW'S TALE

The wordes of the Hoost to the compaignye.

Oure Hooste saugh wel that the brighte sonne
The ark of his artificial day hath ronne
The ferthe part, and half an houre and moore,
And though he were nat depe ystert in loore,
He wiste it was the eightetethe day   5
Of Aprill, that is messager to May;
And saugh wel that the shadwe of every tree
Was as in lengthe the same quantitee
That was the body erect that caused it.
And therfore by the shadwe he took his wit 10
That Phebus, which that shoon so clere and
    brighte,
Degrees was fyve and fourty clombe on highte;
And for that day, as in that latitude,
It was ten of the clokke, he gan conclude,
And sodeynly he plighte his hors aboute. 15
  "Lordynges," quod he, "I warne yow, al this
    route,

The fourthe party of this day is gon.
Now, for the love of God and of Seint John,
Leseth no tyme, as ferforth as ye may.
Lordynges, the tyme wasteth nyght and day, 20
And steleth from us, what pryvely slepynge,
And what thurgh necligence in oure wakynge,
As dooth the streem that turneth nevere agayn,
Descendynge fro the montaigne into playn.
Wel kan Senec and many a philosophre   25
Biwaillen tyme moore than gold in cofre;
For 'los of catel may recovered be,
But los of tyme shendeth us,' quod he.
It wol nat come agayn, withouten drede,
Namoore than wole Malkynes maydenhede, 30
Whan she hath lost it in hir wantownesse.
Lat us nat mowlen thus in ydelnesse.
  "Sire Man of Lawe," quod he, "so have ye
    blis,

The Man of Law's Tale. There is nothing at the end of the Cook's unfinished narrative to indicate what was to follow, and no reference in the *Prologue to the Man of Law's Tale* to a preceding narrator. But since it follows *The Cook's Tale* or the spurious *Tale of Gamelin* (which some manuscripts insert after *The Cook's Tale*) in all branches of the manuscript tradition, it is clear that those who put Chaucer's papers together after his death, or gathered together parts of the collection already perhaps in the hands of friends, found *The Man of Law's Tale* standing after *The Cook's Tale* in Chaucer's papers or decided that it belonged there. The arrangement has been followed in all subsequent editions. The introduction tells us the day of the month and advertises Chaucer's other works,—both features usually associated with the beginning of a literary work—facts which led Carleton Brown to the belief that in Chaucer's original intention the *Man of Law's Prologue* was to follow immediately after the *General Prologue* (SP, xxxiv. 8-35), and Manly to the conclusion that it belongs to later in the morning of the first day of the journey (Manly-Rickert, ii. 491). Brown's view has been reaffirmed (with additional arguments) by C. A. Owen, Jr., *Mediaeval Stud.*, xxi. 202-10. But in the existing text it is necessary to regard *The Man of Law's Introduction and Tale* as beginning a new day.
2. artificial day, the time between sunrise and sunset. Chaucer so defines it in the *Astrolabe.* **4. ystert.** In ME. the verb *sterte* implies a quick or sudden motion. The use here seems strange, and a number of manuscripts have *expert.* **10. wit,** judgment. **15. plighte,** pulled. **19. ferforth,** far. **26. tyme,** *i.e.* time lost. **27. catel,** wealth. The closest approximation to this aphorism in Seneca is in the first of his epistles. **30. Malkynes maydenhede.** Malkin was the proverbial name for a wanton woman. **32. mowlen,** grow mouldy.

Telle us as tale anon, as forward is.   34
Ye been submytted, thurgh youre free assent,
To stonden in this cas at my juggement.
Acquiteth yow now of youre biheeste;
Thanne have ye do youre devoir atte leeste."
    "Hooste," quod he, "*depardieux*, ich assente;
To breke forward is nat myn entente.   40
Biheste is dette, and I wole holde fayn
Al my biheste, I kan no bettre sayn.
For swich lawe as a man yeveth another
    wight,
He sholde hymselven usen it, by right;
Thus wole oure text. But nathelees, certeyn,   45
I kan right now no thrifty tale seyn
That Chaucer, thogh he kan but lewedly
On metres and on rymyng craftily,
Hath seyd hem in swich Englissh as he kan
Of olde tyme, as knoweth many a man;   50
And if he have noght seyd hem, leve brother,
In o book, he hath seyd hem in another.
For he hath toold of loveris up and doun
Mo than Ovide made of mencioun
In his Episteles, that been ful olde.   55
What sholde I tellen hem, syn they ben tolde?
    In youthe he made of Ceys and Alcione,
And sitthen hath he spoken of everichone,
Thise noble wyves and thise loveris eke.
Whoso that wole his large volume seke,   60
Cleped the Seintes Legende of Cupide,
Ther may be seen the large woundes wyde

Of Lucresse, and of Babilan Tesbee;
The swerd of Dido for the false Enee;
The tree of Phillis for hire Demophon;   65
The pleinte of Dianire and of Hermyon,
Of Adriane, and of Isiphilee;
The bareyne yle stondynge in the see;
The dreynte Leandre for his Erro;
The teeris of Eleyne, and eek the wo   70
Of Brixseyde, and of the, Ladomya;
The crueltee of the, queen Medea,
Thy litel children hangynge by the hals,
For thy Jason, that was of love so fals!
O Ypermystra, Penelopee, Alceste,   75
Youre wifhode he comendeth with the
    beste!
    But certeinly no word ne writeth he
Of thilke wikke ensample of Canacee,
That loved hir owene brother synfully;
(Of swiche cursed stories I sey fy!)   80
Or ellis of Tyro Appollonius,
How that the cursed kyng Antiochus
Birafte his doghter of hir maydenhede,
That is so horrible a tale for to rede,
Whan he hir threw upon the pavement.   85
And therfore he, of ful avysement,
Nolde nevere write in none of his sermons
Of swiche unkynde abhomynacions,
Ne I wol noon reherce, if that I may.
    But of my tale how shal I doon this day?   90
Me were looth be likned, doutelees,

34. forward, agreement. **37. biheeste,** promise. **38. devoir,** duty. **45. wole oure text,** our text requires. The word text seems to be used here in the general sense of "code" or "standard of conduct," but Professor Robinson notes that the principle is actually stated in the *Digests* of Justinian. **46. thrifty,** profitable. **47. lewedly,** simply, unskilfully. **50. Of olde tyme,** for a long time. **57. Ceys and Alcione.** See *The Book of the Duchess.* **61. the Seintes Legende of Cupide,** the *Legend of Good Women.* As we have it, the poem is unfinished and includes only nine legends: Cleopatra, Thisbe, Dido, Hypsipyle and Medea, Lucrétia, Ariadne, Philomela, Phyllis, Hypermnestra (incomplete). In the present passage the Man of Law fails to mention two, Cleopatra and Philomela. The others will be easily recognized in their medieval forms. But the list includes eight additional names, for which Chaucer apparently still intended at this time to write legends. But the list does not correspond with another enumeration in the Prologue to *LGW* (see ll. 249–69). Chaucer had probably not reached a final decision as to the nineteen legends (plus that of Alceste) which would have made up the finished poem. It should be added that this is not a device of Chaucer's for calling attention to his other works, or at least his only purpose. He omits some of the most important. The emphasis is on stories of virtuous or wronged women. Tatlock suggested (*Dev. and Chron.,* p. 174) that it may be a further answer to the criticism which led to the writing of *LGW.* **68. The bareyne yle . . .,** in the story of Ariadne **70. Eleyne,** Helen of Troy. **71. Brixseyde,** Briseis, beloved by Achilles. **Ladomya,** Laodamia, wife of Protesilaus, killed in the landing of the Greeks at Troy. **73. hals,** neck. **75. Alceste.** See the Prologue to *LGW.* **78–81. Canacee . . . Tyro Appollonius** (Apollonius of Tyre). These stories are told by Gower in *Conf. Aman.,* though Gower does not include in the latter the detail of the pavement. The present passage is supposed by some to have caused an estrangement between the two poets. **88. unkynde,** unnatural.

To Muses that men clepe Pierides—
Methamorphosios woot what I mene;
But nathelees, I recche noght a bene
Though I come after hym with hawebake.   95

I speke in prose, and lat him rymes make."
And with that word he, with a sobre cheere,
Bigan his tale, as ye shal after heere.

The prologe of the Mannes Tale of Lawe.

O hateful harm, condicion of poverte!
With thurst, with coold, with hunger so con-
    foundid!   100
To asken help thee shameth in thyn herte;
If thou noon aske, with nede artow so woundid
That verray nede unwrappeth al thy wounde
    hid!
Maugree thyn heed, thou most for indigence
Or stele, or begge, or borwe thy despence!   105

Thow blamest Crist, and seist ful bitterly,
He mysdeparteth richesse temporal;
Thy neighebore thou wytest synfully,
And seist thou hast to lite, and he hath al.
"Parfay," seistow, "somtyme he rekene shal,   110
Whan that his tayl shal brennen in the gleede,
For he noght helpeth needfulle in hir neede."

Herkne what is the sentence of the wise:
"Bet is to dyen than have indigence";
"Thy selve neighebor wol thee despise."   115

If thou be povre, farwel thy reverence!
Yet of the wise man take this sentence:
"Alle the dayes of povre men been wikke."
Be war, therfore, er thou come to that prikke!

If thou be povre, thy brother hateth thee,   120
And alle thy freendes fleen from thee, allas!
O riche marchauntz, ful of wele been yee,
O noble, o prudent folk, as in this cas!
Youre bagges been nat fild with *ambes as,*
But with *sys cynk,* that renneth for youre
    chaunce;   125
At Cristemasse myrie may ye daunce!

Ye seken lond and see for yowre wynnynges;
As wise folk ye knowen al th'estaat
Of regnes; ye been fadres of tidynges
And tales, bothe of pees and of debaat.   130
I were right now of tales desolaat,
Nere that a marchant, goon is many a yeere,
Me taughte a tale, which that ye shal heere.

---

92. Pierides, the nine daughters of Pierus, who challenged unsuccessfully the Muses to a contest of song. The story is told at length in *Metam.,* v. 294–678. **93. Methamorphosios,** the *Book of the Metamorphoses.* Titles were often cited in the genitive case, here sing. instead of plur. **95. hawebake,** baked haw, "something that could just be eaten by a very hungry person." (Skeat). **96. I speke in prose.** Since the tale which follows is in verse, it is clear that the Prologue was written with another tale in mind. **99. poverte.** The next three stanzas are a paraphrase of a passage in Pope Innocent's *De Contemptu Mundi,* a work which Chaucer tells us (*LGW,* revised version of the Prol., l. 414) he translated. **104. Maugree thyn heed,** in spite of thy head. **105. Or . . . or,** either . . . or. **107. mysdeparteth,** distributes unjustly. **108. wytest,** reproachest. **109. lite,** little. **111. brennen in the gleede,** burn in the hot coals. **112. needfulle,** the needy. **113. sentence,** opinion. **the wise,** *Ecclesiasticus,* 40:28. **115. selve,** very. Cf. *Proverbs,* 14:20. **117. the wise man.** Cf. *Proverbs,* 15:15. **118. wikke,** evil. **119. prikke,** point. **124. ambes as,** double (both) aces. In dice an ace counted only one. To throw two aces was to lose the throw and your turn. **125. sys cynk,** six and five. **125. youre chaunce.** The player called a number, often seven. If he threw two aces or a two and an ace or two sixes, he lost. If he threw seven or eleven, he won. If he threw another number (called the caster's *chance*) he went on playing until he cast a winning or losing throw. **126. myrie,** merrily. **127. see for,** look out for. **129. regnes,** kingdoms. **130. debaat,** strife. **132. Nere,** were it not.

THE MAN OF LAW'S TALE

Heere begynneth the Man of Lawe his tale.

In Surrye whilom dwelte a compaignye
Of chapmen riche, and therto sadde and trewe,
That wyde-where senten hir spicerye,   136
Clothes of gold, and satyns riche of hewe.
Hir chaffare was so thrifty and so newe
That every wight hath deyntee to chaffare
With hem, and eek to sellen hem hire ware.

Now fil it that the maistres of that sort   141
Han shapen hem to Rome for to wende;
Were it for chapmanhode or for disport,
Noon oother message wolde they thider sende,
But comen hemself to Rome, this is the ende;
And in swich place as thoughte hem avantage
For hire entente, they take hir herbergage.   147

Sojourned han thise marchantz in that toun
A certein tyme, as fil to hire plesance.
And so bifel that th'excellent renoun   150
Of the Emperoures doghter, dame Custance,
Reported was, with every circumstance,
Unto thise Surryen marchantz in swich wyse,
Fro day to day, as I shal yow devyse.   154

This was the commune voys of every man:
"Oure Emperour of Rome—God hym see!—

A doghter hath that, syn the world bigan,
To rekene as wel hir goodnesse as beautee,
Nas nevere swich another as is shee.
I prey to God in honour hire susteene,   160
And wolde she were of al Europe the queene.

"In hire is heigh beautee, withoute pride,
Yowthe, withoute grenehede or folye;
To alle hire werkes vertu is hir gyde;
Humblesse hath slayn in hire al tirannye.   165
She is mirour of alle curteisye;
Hir herte is verray chambre of hoolynesse,
Hir hand, ministre of fredam for almesse."

And al this voys was sooth, as God is trewe.
But now to purpos lat us turne agayn.   170
Thise marchantz han doon fraught hir shippes
     newe,
And whan they han this blisful mayden sayn,
Hoom to Surrye been they went ful fayn,
And doon hir nedes as they han doon yoore,
And lyven in wele; I kan sey yow namoore.   175

Now fil it that thise marchantz stode in grace
Of hym that was the Sowdan of Surrye;
For whan they cam from any strange place,

The Man of Law's Tale. The story of Constance which the Man of Law claims to have heard from a merchant many years before belongs to a type of widespread story in which the heroine is persecuted by her mother-in-law or some other vicious person, suffers exile and other hardships, but is finally cleared of all accusations and happily reunited with her husband (and her children), while the wicked causes of her troubles are duly punished. On the type see Margaret Schlauch, *Chaucer's Constance and Accused Queens* (1927). Chaucer's source, notwithstanding the Man of Law's statement, is an Anglo-Norman prose *Chronicle* by Nicholas Trivet. The pertinent part of Trivet's *Chronicle* is printed in *SA*. The story is also told by Gower in the *Confessio Amantis*, who drew upon the same source. While the remarks in the *Introduction* to *The Man of Law's Tale* suggest that Chaucer was familiar with the *Confessio Amantis*, Chaucer's indebtedness to Gower's version, which scholars have both claimed and denied, is difficult to prove, and the question must remain open. Early scholarly opinion consistently regarded *The Man of Law's Tale* as an early work revised for *The Canterbury Tales*, but since Tatlock's vigorous attack on this view it has been customary to date it about 1390, possibly not much before 1394.
    134. Surrye, Syria. **135. sadde,** trustworthy. **136. wyde-where,** widely, everywhere. **spicerye,** spices. **138. chaffare,** merchandise. **thrifty,** suitable, profitable. **139. hath deyntee to chaffare,** is pleased to do business. **141. sort,** group, company. **142. Han shapen hem,** made plans, decided. **143. chapmanhode or . . . disport,** business or pleasure. **144. message,** messenger. **156. see,** protect. **163. grenehede,** *i.e.* youth without its unripeness. **165. tirannye,** cruelty, imperious behaviour. **167. verray,** true. **168. almesse,** alms. **171. doon fraught,** caused to be loaded. **newe,** anew. **172. sayn,** seen. **176. fil it,** it happened.

He wolde, of his benigne curteisye,
Make hem good chiere, and bisily espye   180
Tidynges of sondry regnes, for to leere
The wondres that they myghte seen or heere.

Amonges othere thynges, specially,
Thise marchantz han hym toold of dame Cus-
    tance
So greet noblesse in ernest, ceriously,   185
That this Sowdan hath caught so greet
    plesance
To han hir figure in his remembrance,
That al his lust and al his bisy cure
Was for to love hire whil his lyf may dure.

Paraventure in thilke large book   190
Which that men clepe the hevene ywriten was
With sterres, whan that he his birthe took,
That he for love sholde han his deeth, allas !
For in the sterres, clerer than is glas,
Is writen, God woot, whoso koude it rede,   195
The deeth of every man, withouten drede.

In sterres, many a wynter therbiforn,
Was writen the deeth of Ector, Achilles,
Of Pompei, Julius, er they were born;
The strif of Thebes; and of Ercules,   200
Of Sampson, Turnus, and of Socrates
The deeth; but mennes wittes ben so dulle
That no wight kan wel rede it atte fulle.

This Sowdan for his privee conseil sente,
And, shortly of this matiere for to pace,   205
He hath to hem declared his entente,
And seyde hem, certein, but he myghte have
    grace
To han Custance withinne a litel space,
He nas but deed; and charged hem in hye
To shapen for his lyf som remedye.   210

Diverse men diverse thynges seyden;
They argumenten, casten up and doun;
Many a subtil resoun forth they leyden;
They speken of magyk and abusioun.
But finally, as in conclusioun,   215
They kan nat seen in that noon avantage,
Ne in noon oother wey, save mariage.

Thanne sawe they therinne swich difficultee
By wey of reson, for to speke al playn,
By cause that ther was swich diversitee   220
Bitwene hir bothe lawes, that they sayn
They trowe, "that no Cristen prince wolde fayn
Wedden his child under oure lawes sweete
That us were taught by Mahoun, oure
    prophete."

    And he answerde, "Rather than I lese   225
Custance, I wol be cristned, douteles.
I moot been hires, I may noon oother chese.
I prey yow hoold youre argumentz in pees;
Saveth my lyf, and beth noght recchelees
To geten hire that hath my lyf in cure;   230
For in this wo I may nat longe endure."

    What nedeth gretter dilatacioun?
I seye, by tretys and embassadrie,
And by the popes mediacioun,
And al the chirche, and al the chivalrie,   235
That in destruccioun of maumettrie,
And in encrees of Cristes lawe deere,
They been acorded, so as ye shal heere:

How that the Sowdan and his baronage
And alle his liges sholde ycristned be,   240
And he shal han Custance in mariage,
And certein gold, I noot what quantitee;
And heer-to founden sufficient suretee.
This same accord was sworn on eyther syde;
Now, faire Custance, almyghty God thee gyde!

180. espye, seek to learn. **181. regnes,** kingdoms. **185. ceriously,** in detail. **187. figure,** person. **188. lust,** desire. **bisy
cure,** diligent effort. **191. the hevene,** heaven. **205. to pace,** to pass over. **209. in hye,** speedily. **214. abusioun,** deception. **219. By wey of reson,** as a practical matter. **221. lawes,** religions. **222. fayn,** willingly. **224. Mahoun,** Mahomet.
225. lese, should lose. **229. recchelees To geten,** careless about getting. **230. in cure,** in custody. **232. gretter dilatacioun,** greater amplification. **233. tretys,** negotiation. **embassadrie,** the work of ambassadors. **235. chivalrie,** knightly
class. **236. maumettrie,** idolatry from *maumet,* an idol, which in turn comes from the name Mahomet). **242. noot,**
know not.

Now wolde som men waiten, as I gesse,   246
That I sholde tellen al the purveiance
That th'Emperour, of his grete noblesse,
Hath shapen for his doghter, dame Custance.
Wel may men knowen that so greet ordinance
May no man tellen in a litel clause   251
As was arrayed for so heigh a cause.

Bisshopes been shapen with hire for to wende,
Lordes, ladies, knyghtes of renoun,
And oother folk ynowe, this is th'ende;   255
And notified is thurghout the toun
That every wight, with greet devocioun,
Sholde preyen Crist that he this mariage
Receyve in gree, and spede this viage.

The day is comen of hir departynge;   260
I seye, the woful day fatal is come,
That ther may be no lenger tariynge,
But forthward they hem dressen, alle and some.
Custance, that was with sorwe al overcome,
Ful pale arist, and dresseth hire to wende;   265
For wel she seeth ther is noon oother ende.

Allas! what wonder is it thogh she wepte,
That shal be sent to strange nacioun
Fro freendes that so tendrely hire kepte,
And to be bounden under subjeccioun   270
Of oon, she knoweth nat his condicioun?
Housbondes been alle goode, and han ben
      yoore;
That knowen wyves; I dar sey yow na moore.

"Fader," she seyde, "thy wrecched child
      Custance,
Thy yonge doghter fostred up so softe,   275
And ye, my mooder, my soverayn plesance
Over alle thyng, out-taken Crist on-lofte,
Custance youre child hire recomandeth ofte
Unto youre grace, for I shal to Surrye,
Ne shal I nevere seen yow moore with yë.   280

"Allas! unto the Barbre nacioun
I moste anon, syn that it is youre wille;
But Crist, that starf for our redempcioun
So yeve me grace his heestes to fulfille!
I, wrecche womman, no fors though I spille! 285
Wommen are born to thraldom and penance,
And to been under mannes governance."

I trowe at Troye, whan Pirrus brak the wal,
Or Ilion brende, [at] Thebes the citee,
N'at Rome, for the harm thurgh Hanybal   290
That Romayns hath venquysshed tymes thre,
Nas herd swich tendre wepyng for pitee
As in the chambre was for hire departynge;
But forth she moot, wher so she wepe or synge.

O firste moevyng, crueel firmament,   295
With thy diurnal sweigh that crowdest ay
And hurlest al from est til occident
That naturelly wolde holde another way,
Thy crowdyng set the hevene in swich array
At the bigynnyng of this fiers viage,   300
That crueel Mars hath slayn this mariage.

---

246. **waiten,** expect. 247. **purveiance,** provision. 250. **ordinance,** preparation, arrangement. 252. **arrayed,** made ready. 253. **shapen,** appointed. 259. **in gree,** favorably. **viage,** journey. 263. **forthward,** forward. **hem dressen,** proceed. **alle and some,** one and all. 265. **arist,** arises. **dresseth hire to wende,** prepares to go. 277. **out-taken,** excepted. 281. **Barbre,** Barbary, heathen. The word is often not capitalized, and perhaps should not be here, but the capital is retained because it is so written in the Ellesmere MS. 283. **starf,** died. 284. **heestes,** commandments. 285. **wrecche,** wretched. **no fors though I spille,** it doesn't matter though I perish. 288. **Pirrus,** Pyrrhus, son of Achilles. 289. **Ilion,** the citadel proper; see note to *BD* 1248. **brende,** burned. 294. **wher so,** whether. 295. **firste moevyng,** the *primum mobile* or outermost sphere, whose motion from east to west, as Chaucer says, carried everything with it, contrary to what would seem the natural motion as judged by the advance of the sun along the ecliptic and through the successive signs of the zodiac. 296. **diurnal sweigh,** daily motion (*lit.* sway). **crowdest,** pressest on; hence *crowdyng* (299), driving force. 300. **fiers viage,** merciless journey. 301. **crueel Mars.** The influence of Mars is made responsible for the misfortunes to come. The astronomical allusions in the next stanza have been differently interpreted. The *ascendent tortuous* is the movement of a planet in one of the "tortuous signs," which as Chaucer tells us in the *Astrolabe* (II. 28) are those between Capricorn and Gemini. One of these is Aries, of which Mars is lord. Mars is said to have fallen out of *his angle into the derkeste hous.* The zodiacal circle was divided into twelve "houses"; the four beginning at the cardinal points, north, south, east, and west, were called "angles." Mars had a second "house," Scorpio, into which he had fallen. In this position his influence was particularly baleful. Manly attaches a different meaning to *hous.*

Infortunat ascendent tortuous,
Of which the lord is helplees falle, allas,
Out of his angle into the derkeste hous!
O Mars, o atazir, as in this cas! 305
O fieble moone, unhappy been thy paas!
Thou knyttest thee ther thou art nat receyved;
Ther thou were weel, fro thennes artow weyved.

Inprudent Emperour of Rome, allas!
Was ther no philosophre in al thy toun? 310
Is no tyme bet than oother in swich cas?
Of viage is ther noon eleccioun,
Namely to folk of heigh condicioun?
Noght whan a roote is of a burthe yknowe?
Allas, we been to lewed or to slowe! 315

To ship is brought this woful faire mayde
Solempnely, with every circumstance.
"Now Jhesu Crist be with yow alle!" she sayde;
Ther nys namoore, but "Farewel, faire Cus-
  tance!"
She peyneth hire to make good contenance;
And forth I lete hire saille in this manere, 321
And turne I wole agayn to my matere.

The mooder of the Sowdan, welle of vices,
Espied hath hir sones pleyn entente,
How he wol lete his olde sacrifices; 325
And right anon she for hir conseil sente,
And they been come to knowe what she mente.
And whan assembled was this folk in-feere,
She sette hire doun, and seyde as ye shal heere.

"Lordes," quod she, "ye knowen everichon,
How that my sone in point is for to lete 331

The hooly lawes of oure Alkaron,
Yeven by Goddes message Makomete.
But oon avow to grete God I heete,
The lyf shall rather out of my body sterte 335
Or Makometes lawe out of myn herte!

"What sholde us tyden of this newe lawe
But thraldom to oure bodies and penance,
And afterward in helle to be drawe,
For we reneyed Mahoun oure creance? 340
But, lordes, wol ye maken assurance,
As I shal seyn, assentynge to my loore,
And I shal make us sauf for everemoore?"

They sworen and assenten, every man,
To lyve with hire and dye, and by hire stonde,
And everich, in the beste wise he kan, 346
To strengthen hire shal alle his frendes fonde;
And she hath this emprise ytake on honde,
Which ye shal heren that I shal devyse,
And to hem alle she spak right in this wyse: 350

"We shul first feyne us cristendom to take,—
Coold water shal nat greve us but a lite!
And I shal swich a feeste and revel make
That, as I trowe, I shal the Sowdan quite.
For thogh his wyf be cristned never so white, 355
She shal have nede to wasshe awey the rede,
Thogh she a font-ful water with hire lede."

O Sowdanesse, roote of iniquitee!
Virago, thou Semyrame the secounde!
O serpent under femynynytee, 360
Lik to the serpent depe in helle ybounde!
O feyned womman, al that may confounde

305. atazir, an Arabic word meaning "influence," used by astrologers in certain complicated calculations (in which the position of the moon played a part) for prognosticating the fortunes of individuals. **306. O fieble moone.** See preceding note. The moon is presumably in conjunction with Mars in Scorpio, and has passed from a more favorable position. **307. knyttest thee,** joinest thyself, thou art in conjunction. **receyved,** received, supported by a lucky planet. (Skeat). **308. weyved,** banished. **310. Was ther no philosophre . . .** It should have been known that the stars were unfavorable for setting out on a journey. **312. eleccioun,** favorable time (a technical term in the language of astrology). **314. a roote . . . of a burthe,** the exact moment of nativity, from which the favorable or unfavorable aspect of the heavens could be determined. **315. lewed,** ignorant. **324. pleyn entente,** full intention. **325. lete,** abandon. **328. in-feere,** together. **332. Alkaron,** the Koran. **333. message,** messenger. **Makomete,** Mahomet. **334. heete,** promise. **335. rather,** sooner. **336. Or,** before. **337. tyden,** happen. **of,** as a result of. **340. For we reneyed . . .,** because we renounced our faith in Mahomet (dat.). **342. loore,** teaching, advice. **343. sauf,** safe. **347. fonde,** try (to persuade). **348. emprise,** undertaking. **352. lite,** little. **354. quite,** satisfy. **357. lede,** carry, bring. **359. Semyrame,** Semiramis, Assyrian queen who had her husband murdered. **361. serpent depe in helle.** The serpent that tempted Eve was often described and pictured as having the face of a woman.

Vertu and innocence, thurgh thy malice,
Is bred in thee, as nest of every vice!

O Sathan, envious syn thilke day   365
That thou were chaced from oure heritage,
Wel knowestow to wommen the olde way!
Thou madest Eva brynge us in servage;
Thou wolt fordoon this Cristen mariage.
Thyn instrument so, weylawey the while!   370
Makestow of wommen, whan thou wolt bigile.

   This Sowdanesse, whom I thus blame and
     warye,
Leet prively hire conseil goon hire way.

What sholde I in this tale lenger tarye?
She rydeth to the Sowdan on a day   375
And seyde hym that she wolde reneye hir lay,
And cristendom of preestes handes fonge,
Repentynge hire she hethen was so longe;

Bisechynge hym to doon hire that honour,
That she moste han the Cristen folk to feeste,—
"To plesen hem I wol do my labour."   381
The Sowdan seith, "I wol doon at youre heeste";
And knelynge thanketh hire of that requeste.
So glad he was, he nyste what to seye.
She kiste hir sone, and hoom she gooth hir
     weye.   385

Explicit prima pars.

Sequitur pars secunda.

   Arryved been this Cristen folk to londe
In Surrye, with a greet solempne route,
And hastifliche this Sowdan sente his sonde,
First to his mooder, and al the regne aboute,
And seyde his wyf was comen, out of doute, 390
And preyde hire for to ryde agayn the queene,
The honour of his regne to susteene.

Greet was the prees, and riche was th'array
Of Surryens and Romayns met yfeere;
The mooder of the Sowdan, riche and gay,   395
Receyveth hire with also glad a cheere
As any mooder myghte hir doghter deere,
And to the nexte citee ther bisyde
A softe paas solempnely they ryde.

   Noght trowe I the triumphe of Julius,   400
Of which that Lucan maketh swich a boost,
Was roialler ne moore curius
Than was th'assemblee of this blisful hoost.

But this scorpioun, this wikked goost,
The Sowdanesse, for al hire flaterynge,   405
Caste under this ful mortally to stynge.

   The Sowdan comth hymself soone after this
So roially, that wonder is to telle,
And welcometh hire with alle joye and blis.
And thus in murthe and joye I lete hem dwelle;
The fruyt of this matiere is that I telle.   411
Whan tyme cam, men thoughte it for the
    beste
That revel stynte, and men goon to hir reste.

   The tyme cam, this olde Sowdanesse
Ordeyned hath this feeste of which I tolde,   415
And to the feeste Cristen folk hem dresse
In general, ye, bothe yonge and olde.
Heere may men feeste and roialtee biholde,
And deyntees mo than I kan yow devyse;
But al to deere they boghte it er they ryse.   420

369. **wolt fordoon**, wishest to destroy. 372. **warye**, curse. 374. **What**, why. 376. **lay**, law, religion. 377. **fonge**, receive. 380. **moste**, might. 387. **solempne route**, distinguished company. 388. **sonde**, messenger. 391. **agayn**, toward. 394. **yfeere**, together. 396. **also**, as. 399. **solempnely**, ceremoniously. 401. **Lucan maketh swich a boost**. It has often been noted that Chaucer is here mistaken. In his account of the struggle between Caesar and Pompey in the *Pharsalia* Lucan explains that Caesar did not celebrate his victory with a triumph. 402. **curius**, elaborate. 404. **wikked goost**, evil spirit. 405. **flaterynge**, false friendliness. 406. **Caste**, schemed, intended. 413. **stynte**, stop. 418. **feeste**, festivity. 419. **devyse**, describe.

O sodeyn wo, that evere art successour
To worldly blisse, spreynd with bitternesse!
The ende of the joye of oure worldly labour!
Wo occupieth the fyn of oure gladnesse.
Herke this conseil for thy sikernesse: 425
Upon thy glade day have in thy mynde
The unwar wo or harm that comth bihynde.

For shortly for to tellen, at o word,
The Sowdan and the Cristen everichone
Been al tohewe and stiked at the bord,   430
But it were oonly dame Custance allone.
This olde Sowdanesse, cursed krone,
Hath with hir freendes doon this cursed dede,
For she hirself wolde al the contree lede.

Ne ther was Surryen noon that was converted,
That of the conseil of the Sowdan woot,   436
That he nas al tohewe er he asterted.
And Custance han they take anon, foot-hoot,
And in a ship al steerelees, God woot,
They han hir set, and bidde hire lerne saille   440
Out of Surrye agaynward to Ytaille.

A certein tresor that she thider ladde,
And, sooth to seyn, vitaille greet plentee
They han hire yeven, and clothes eek she
   hadde,
And forth she sailleth in the salte see.   445
O my Custance, ful of benignytee,
O Emperoures yonge doghter deere,
He that is lord of Fortune be thy steere!

She blesseth hire, and with ful pitous voys
Unto the croys of Crist thus seyde she: 450
"O cleere, o welful auter, hooly croys,
Reed of the Lambes blood ful of pitee,
That wessh the world fro the olde iniquitee,
Me fro the feend and fro his clawes kepe,
That day that I shal drenchen in the depe.   455

Victorious tree, proteccioun of trewe,
That oonly worthy were for to bere
The Kyng of Hevene with his woundes newe,
The white Lamb, that hurt was with a spere,
Flemere of feendes out of hym and here   460
On which thy lymes feithfully extenden,
Me kepe, and yif me myght my lyf
   t'amenden."

Yeres and dayes fleet this creature
Thurghout the See of Grece unto the Strayte
Of Marrok, as it was hire aventure.   465
On many a sory meel now may she bayte;
After hir deeth ful often may she wayte,
Er that the wilde wawes wol hire dryve
Unto the place ther she shal arryve.   469

Men myghten asken why she was nat slayn
Eek at the feeste? who myghte hir body save?
And I answere to that demande agayn,
Who saved Danyel in the horrible cave
Ther every wight save he, maister and knave,
Was with the leon frete er he asterte?   475
No wight but God, that he bar in his herte.

---

421. O sodeyn wo . . . A common sentiment, partly inspired by *Proverbs*, 14:13. Cf. B 4395. **422. spreynd,** sprinkled.
424. fyn, end. **427. unwar,** unforeseen. **430. tohewe,** cut to pieces. **stiked,** stabbed. **431. But it were,** except. **434. lede,**
govern. **436. woot,** knows. **437. asterted,** escaped. **438. foot-hoot,** hastily. **441. agaynward,** back again. **442. ladde,**
brought. **444. yeven,** given. **448. steere,** helmsman. **449. pitous,** pitiful. **450. croys,** cross. This twelve-line prayer to the
cross reads like a paraphrase of a Latin hymn to the cross, of which there are many. A close parallel to the opening lines is
in stanza 15 of *Salva Christi crux praeclara* (Dreves-Blume, *Ein Jahrtausend Lat. Hymnendichtung,* II. 83–4): Salve, clara crucis
ara, Rubens agni sanguine Quam sacravit, qui nos lavit Ab antiquo crimine . . . Lines 456–7 are a commonplace, occurring in the office for the feast of the Invention of the Cross and elsewhere (see *Breviarium ad usum* . . . *Sarum,* ed. Procter
and Wordsworth, II. 507, III. 274, etc.). **451. welful auter,** blessed altar. **452. Reed of,** red from. **453. wessh,** washed.
455. drenchen, drown. **456. trewe,** true people, the faithful. **460. Flemere,** one who drives out or expels. **hym and
here,** him and her, *i.e.* man and woman. **461. lymes,** limbs, *i.e.* the arms of the cross. **463. fleet,** floats. **464. See of
Grece.** Pliny (IV. 51) says that the Romans call that part of the Aegean Sea that washes the coast of Greece the Grecian
Sea, but in the Middle Ages the name was commonly used for the eastern Mediterranean. **Strayte of Marrok,** Strait
of Gibraltar. **466. bayte,** feed. **467. After hir deeth** . . ., many times may she expect to die. **468. wawes,** waves. **469.
ther,** where. **474. knave,** servant. **475. frete,** devoured. **asterte,** escaped.

God liste to shewe his wonderful myracle
In hire, for we sholde seen his myghty werkis;
Crist, which that is to every harm triacle,
By certeine meenes ofte, as knowen clerkis,   480
Dooth thyng for certein ende that ful derk is
To mannes wit, that for oure ignorance
Ne konne noght knowe his prudent
    purveiance.

Now sith she was nat at the feeste yslawe,
Who kepte hire fro the drenchyng in the see?
Who kepte Jonas in the fisshes mawe   486
Til he was spouted up at Nynyvee?
Wel may men knowe it was no wight but he
That kepte peple Ebrayk from hir drenchynge,
With drye feet thurghout the see passynge.   490

Who bad the foure spirites of tempest
That power han t'anoyen lond and see,
Bothe north and south, and also west and est,
"Anoyeth, neither see, ne land, ne tree"?
Soothly, the comandour of that was he   495
That fro the tempest ay this womman kepte
As wel whan she wook as whan she slepte.

Where myghte this womman mete and
    drynke have
Thre yeer and moore? how lasteth hire vitaille?
Who fedde the Egipcien Marie in the cave,   500
Or in desert? No wight but Crist, sanz faille.
Fyve thousand folk it was as greet mervaille
With loves fyve and fisshes two to feede.
God sente his foyson at hir grete neede.

She dryveth forth into oure occian   505
Thurghout oure wilde see, til atte laste
Under an hoold that nempnen I ne kan,
Fer in Northhumberlond the wawe hire caste,
And in the sond hir ship stiked so faste
That thennes wolde it noght of al a tyde;   510
The wyl of Crist was that she sholde abyde.

The constable of the castel doun is fare
To seen this wrak, and al the ship he soghte,
And foond this wery womman ful of care;
He foond also the tresor that she broghte.   515
In hir langage mercy she bisoghte,
The lyf out of hire body for to twynne,
Hire to delivere of wo that she was inne.

A maner Latyn corrupt was hir speche,
But algates therby was she understonde.   520
The constable, whan hym lyst no lenger seche,
This woful womman broghte he to the londe.
She kneleth doun and thanketh Goddes sonde;
But what she was she wolde no man seye,
For foul ne fair, thogh that she sholde deye.   525

She seyde she was so mazed in the see   526
That she forgat hir mynde, by hir trouthe.
The constable hath of hire so greet pitee,
And eek his wyf, that they wepen for routhe.
She was so diligent, withouten slouthe,   530
To serve and plesen everich in that place,
That alle hir loven that looken in hir face.

This constable and dame Hermengyld, his wyf,
Were payens, and that contree everywhere;

---

477. **God liste,** it pleased God. **myracle,** miraculous power. 478. **for,** in order that. 479. **triacle,** ointment, remedy. 483. **purveiance,** provision. 487. **spouted,** spewed. *Jonah,* 2:10. 490. **the see passynge.** *Exodus,* 14:22. 491. **the foure spirites of tempest.** *Revelation,* 7:1–3. 500. **the Egipcien Marie.** St. Mary of Egypt, in repentance for her early life as a prostitute, lived for forty-seven years on three loaves of bread in the desert beyond the Jordan. 504. **foyson,** plenty. 507. **hoold,** stronghold, castle. 508. **Northhumberlond,** originally the district north of the Humber River, which included the present Yorkshire. The coast of Yorkshire is probably where Custance's boat was cast ashore, since in both Trivet and Gower the castle is said to be near the Humber. 509. **sond,** sand. 510. **of al a tyde.** The meaning is uncertain. ME. *tyde* may mean "time" or "tide." It is also used specifically to designate an hour, and to indicate a more general period of time, as a season, a while. The phrase *al a* means "a whole" *(al a day, al a year, al a country);* see *MED, s.v.* al, 2a. The prep. *of* may have the sense "during." Skeat took the expression in Chaucer to mean "for the whole of an hour." The more general sense "for quite a while" is also possible. However, *of* is often used by Chaucer in phrases indicating the agent, so that the meaning "by a whole tide" (including the ebb and flow) or "by a full (high) tide" can hardly be ruled out. There is no equivalent of this line in Trivet. 513. **soghte,** searched. 517. **twynne,** sever, separate. 520. **algates,** nevertheless. 523. **sonde,** dispensation. 525. **deye,** die. 527. **forgat hir mynde,** lost her memory. 531. **everich,** every one. 534. **payens,** pagans.

But Hermengyld loved hire right as hir lyf, 535
And Custance hath so longe sojourned there,
In orisons, with many a bitter teere,
Til Jhesu hath converted thurgh his grace
Dame Hermengyld, constablesse of that place.

In al that lond no Cristen dorste route; 540
Alle Cristen folk been fled fro that contree
Thurgh payens, that conquereden al aboute
The plages of the north, by land and see.
To Walys fledde the Cristyanytee
Of olde Britons dwellynge in this ile; 545
Ther was hir refut for the meene while.

But yet nere Cristene Britons so exiled
That ther nere somme that in hir privetee
Honoured Crist and hethen folk bigiled,
And ny the castel swiche ther dwelten three. 550
That oon of hem was blynd and myghte nat see,
But it were with thilke eyen of his mynde
With whiche men seen, after that they ben
   blynde.

Bright was the sonne as in that someres day,
For which the constable and his wyf also 555
And Custance han ytake the righte way
Toward the see a furlong wey or two,
To pleyen and to romen to and fro;
And in hir walk this blynde man they mette,
Croked and oold, with eyen faste yshette. 560

"In name of Crist," cride this blinde Britoun,
"Dame Hermengyld, yif me my sighte agayn!"
This lady weex affrayed of the soun,
Lest that hir housbonde, shortly for to sayn,
Wolde hire for Jhesu Cristes love han slayn, 565

Til Custance made hire boold, and bad hire
   wirche
The wyl of Crist, as doghter of his chirche.

The constable weex abasshed of that sight,
And seyde, "What amounteth al this fare?"
Custance answerde, "Sire, it is Cristes myght,
That helpeth folk out of the feendes snare." 571
And so ferforth she gan oure lay declare
That she the constable, er that it was eve
Converted, and on Crist made hym bileve.

This constable was nothyng lord of this place
Of which I speke, ther he Custance fond, 576
But kepte it strongly many wyntres space
Under Alla, kyng of al Northhumbrelond,
That was ful wys, and worthy of his hond
Agayn the Scottes, as men may wel heere; 580
But turne I wole agayn to my mateere.

Sathan, that evere us waiteth to bigile,
Saugh of Custance al hire perfeccioun,
And caste anon how he myghte quite hir while,
And made a yong knyght that dwelte in that
   toun 585
Love hire so hoote, of foul affeccioun,
That verraily hym thoughte he sholde spille,
But he of hire myghte ones have his wille.

He woweth hire, but it availleth noght;
She wolde do no synne, by no weye. 590
And for despit he compassed in his thoght
To maken hire on shameful deeth to deye.
He wayteth whan the constable was aweye,
And pryvely upon a nyght he crepte
In Hermengyldes chambre, whil she slepte. 595

539. constablesse, constable's wife. **540. route,** assemble. **542. Thurgh,** on account of. **543. plages,** regions. **544. Cristyanytee,** body of Christians. **546. refut,** refuge. **547. nere,** were not. **548. in hir privetee,** privately. **557. a furlong wey or two.** A furlong is an eighth of a mile. The phrase here, as elsewhere in Chaucer, is a measure of time, two and half minutes, the time required to walk a furlong. It is often simply a way of indicating a short time. **563. weex,** waxed **.566. wirche,** work, perform. **567.** J. Burke Severs (*MLN*, LXXIV, 193–8) has plausibly suggested that at this point a stanza has been lost, describing the actual miracle and corresponding to the account in his source, where Hermengyld makes the sign of the cross over the blind man's eyes and bids him see. **569. amounteth,** means. **fare.** going-on, business. **572. so ferforth,** to such an extent. **lay,** law, doctrine. **575. nothyng,** in no wise. **578. Alla,** Ælla (latter half of the sixth cent.), who was the king of the slave boys in the story of Gregory and his vow to convert the English to Christianity, as told by Bede. **579. worthy of his hond,** worthy with respect to his hand, strong. **582. waiteth,** lies in wait. **584. quite hir while,** repay her for her trouble. **586. of foul affeccioun,** with sinful love. **587. spille,** die. **589. woweth,** woos. **591. compassed,** planned. **592. on,** one, a, but possibly a preposition. **593. wayteth,** watches.

Wery forwaked in hire orisouns,
Slepeth Custance, and Hermengyld also.
This knyght, thurgh Sathanas temptaciouns,
Al softely is to the bed ygo,
And kitte the throte of Hermengyld atwo,   600
And leyde the blody knyf by dame Custance,
And wente his wey, ther God yeve hym mes-
    chance!

Soone after cometh this constable hoom
    agayn,
And eek Alla, that kyng was of that lond,
And saugh his wyf despitously yslayn,   605
For which ful ofte he weep and wroong his hond,
And in the bed the blody knyf he fond
By Dame Custance. Allas! what myghte she
    seye?
For verray wo hir wit was al aweye.   609

To kyng Alla was toold al this meschance,
And eek the tyme, and where, and in what wise
That in a ship was founden this Custance,
As heerbiforn that ye han herd devyse.
The kynges herte of pitee gan agryse,
Whan he saugh so benigne a creature   615
Falle in disese and in mysaventure.

For as the lomb toward his deeth is broght,
So stant this innocent bifore the kyng.
This false knyght, that hath this tresoun wroght,
Berth hire on hond that she hath doon thys
    thyng.   620
But nathelees, ther was greet moornyng
Among the peple, and seyn they kan nat gesse
That she had doon so greet a wikkednesse;

For they han seyn hire evere so vertuous,
And lovynge Hermengyld right as hir lyf.   625
Of this baar witnesse everich in that hous,
Save he that Hermengyld slow with his knyf.
This gentil kyng hath caught a greet motyf
Of this witnesse, and thoghte he wolde enquere
Depper in this, a trouthe for to lere.   630

Allas! Custance, thou hast no champioun,
Ne fighte kanstow noght, so weylaway!
But he that starf for oure redempcioun,
And boond Sathan (and yet lith ther he lay),
So be thy stronge champion this day!   635
For, but if Crist open myracle kithe,
Withouten gilt thou shalt be slayn as swithe.

She sette hire doun on knees, and thus she sayde:
"Immortal God, that savedest Susanne
Fro false blame, and thou, merciful mayde,   640
Marie I meene, doghter of Seint Anne,
Bifore whos child angeles synge Osanne,
If I be giltlees of this felonye,
My socour be, for ellis shal I dye!"

Have ye nat seyn somtyme a pale face,   645
Among a prees, of hym that hath be lad
Toward his deeth, wher as hym gat no grace,
And swich a colour in his face hath had,
Men myghte knowe his face that was bistad,
Amonges alle the faces in that route?   650
So stant Custance, and looketh hire aboute.

O queenes, lyvynge in prosperitee,
Duchesses, and ye ladyes everichone,
Haveth som routhe on hire adversitee!

---

596. forwaked, worn out through staying awake. **600. kitte,** cut. **atwo,** in two. **602. ther,** intensive. See Language, § 73. **605. despitously,** cruelly. **606. weep,** wept. **610. meschance,** calamity. **613. herd devyse,** heard tell. **614. agryse,** shudder. **615. benigne,** gracious, kindly. **616. disese,** misery. **mysaventure,** misfortune. **618. stant,** stands. **620. Berth hire on hond,** bears her in hand, *i.e.* accuses her falsely. The expression sometimes means "to deceive" "to lead on with false hopes," etc. See Glossary. **622. gesse,** suppose. imagine. **627. he,** for *him*. **628. hath caught a greet motyf,** was strongly moved. **629. Of,** by. **witnesse,** public testimony. **630. Depper,** more deeply. **lere,** learn. **633. starf,** died. **634. and yet lith . . .,** and (he) still lies where he (then) lay. **636. but if,** unless. **open myracle kithe,** manifests a public miracle. **637. as swithe,** quickly. **639. Susanne.** In the Old Testament apocryphal *History of Susanna*, Susanna re- fuses to lie with the two elders, who thereupon bring a false accusation against her and condemn her to death. Her prayers, however, are answered when David, examining the elders separately, causes them to convict themselves by giving contradictory testimony. **646. prees,** crowd. **lad,** led. **649. his face that was bistad,** the face of him who was beset by enemies, in trouble. **651. stant,** stands.

An Emperoures doghter stant allone;   655
She hath no wight to whom to make hir mone.
O blood roial, that stondest in this drede,
Fer been thy freendes at thy grete nede!

    This Alla kyng hath swich compassioun,
As gentil herte is fulfild of pitee,   660
That from his eyen ran the water doun.
"Now hastily do fecche a book," quod he,
"And if this knyght wol sweren how that she
This womman slow, yet wol we us avyse
Whom that we wole that shal been oure jus-
    tise."   665

A Britoun book, written with Evangiles,
Was fet, and on this book he swoor anoon
She gilty was, and in the meene whiles
An hand hym smoot upon the nekke-boon,
That doun he fil atones as a stoon,   670
And bothe his eyen broste out of his face
In sighte of every body in that place.

    A voys was herd in general audience,
And seyde, "Thou hast desclaundred, giltelees,
The doghter of hooly chirche in heigh presence;
Thus hastou doon, and yet holde I my pees!" 676
Of this mervaille agast was al the prees;
As mazed folk they stoden everichone,
For drede of wreche, save Custance allone.

    Greet was the drede and eek the repentance
Of hem that hadden wrong suspecioun   681
Upon this sely innocent, Custance;
And for this miracle, in conclusioun,
And by Custances mediacioun,
The kyng, and many another in that place,   685
Converted was, thanked be Cristes grace!

    This false knyght was slayn for his untrouthe
By juggement of Alla hastifly;
And yet Custance hadde of his deeth greet
    routhe.
And after this Jhesus, of his mercy,   690
Made Alla wedden ful solempnely
This hooly mayden, that is so bright and sheene;
And thus hath Crist ymaad Custance a queene.

But who was woful, if I shal nat lye,
Of this weddyng but Donegild, and namo,   695
The kynges mooder, ful of tirannye?
Hir thoughte hir cursed herte brast atwo.
She wolde noght hir sone had do so;
Hir thoughte a despit that he sholde take
So strange a creature unto his make.   700

    Me list nat of the chaf, ne of the stree,
Maken so long a tale as of the corn.
What sholde I tellen of the roialtee
At mariage, or which cours goth biforn;
Who bloweth in a trumpe or in an horn?   705
The fruyt of every tale is for to seye:
They ete, and drynke, and daunce, and synge,
    and pleye.

They goon to bedde, as it was skile and right;
For thogh that wyves be ful hooly thynges,
They moste take in pacience at nyght   710
Swiche manere necessaries as been plesynges
To folk that han ywedded hem with rynges,
And leye a lite hir hoolynesse aside,
As for the tyme,—it may no bet bitide.

On hire he gat a knave child anon,   715
And to a bisshop, and his constable eke,
He took his wyf to kepe, whan he is gon

---

666. **A Britoun book . . . Evangiles,** a book containing the Gospels in Celtic. According to Trivet the accuser was a Christian. 667. **fet,** fetched. 669. **nekke-boon,** a vertebra at the nape of the neck, or the nape of the neck itself. 670. **atones,** at once. 671. **broste,** burst. 673. **audience,** hearing. 678. **mazed,** bewildered. 679. **wreche,** vengeance. 688. **hastifly,** quickly. 695. **namo,** no more. 697. **Hir thoughte hir cursed herte brast atwo,** it seemed to her that her cursed heart would burst in two. 699. **despit,** outrage. 700. **make,** mate. 701. **stree,** straw. 702. **corn,** grain, wheat. 703. **What,** why. 704. **cours,** procedure at the wedding. 706. **fruyt,** *i.e.* the valuable or enjoyable part. **for to seye,** to be told. 708. **skile,** reason. 711. **plesynges.** The form is probably one of the French plurals which Chaucer sometimes uses, but it may be a noun (pleasures). In any case it was probably dictated by the rime. 714. **bet,** better. 717. **kepe,** preserve, look after.

To Scotlond-ward, his foomen for to seke.
Now faire Custance, that is so humble and
  meke,
So longe is goon with childe, til that stille   720
She halt hire chambre, abidyng Cristes wille.

The tyme is come a knave child she beer;
Mauricius at the font-stoon they hym calle.
This constable dooth forth come a messageer,
And wroot unto his kyng, that cleped was Alle,
How that this blisful tidyng is bifalle,   726
And othere tidynges spedeful for to seye.
He taketh the lettre, and forth he gooth his
  weye.

This messager, to doon his avantage,
Unto the kynges mooder rideth swithe,   730
And salueth hire ful faire in his langage:
"Madame," quod he, "ye may be glad and
  blithe,
And thanketh God an hundred thousand sithe!
My lady queene hath child, withouten doute,
To joye and blisse to al this regne aboute.   735

Lo, heere the lettres seled of this thyng,
That I moot bere with al the haste I may.
If ye wol aught unto youre sone the kyng,
I am youre servant, bothe nyght and day."
Donegild answerde, "As now at this tyme, nay;
But heere al nyght I wol thou take thy reste,   741
To-morwe wol I seye thee what me leste."

This messager drank sadly ale and wyn,
And stolen were his lettres pryvely
Out of his box, whil he sleep as a swyn;   745
And countrefeted was ful subtilly

Another lettre, wroght ful synfully,
Unto the kyng direct of this mateere
Fro his constable, as ye shal after heere.

The lettre spak the queene delivered was   750
Of so horrible a feendly creature
That in the castel noon so hardy was
That any while dorste ther endure.
The mooder was an elf, by aventure
Ycomen, by charmes or by sorcerie,   755
And everich wight hateth hir compaignye.

Wo was this kyng whan he this lettre had
  sayn,
But to no wight he tolde his sorwes soore,
But of his owene hand he wroot agayn,
"Welcome the sonde of Crist for everemoore
To me that am now lerned in his loore!   761
Lord, welcome be thy lust and thy plesaunce;
My lust I putte al in thyn ordinaunce.

Kepeth this child, al be it foul or feir,
And eek my wyf, unto myn hoom-comynge.
Crist, whan hym list, may sende me an heir   766
Moore agreable than this to my likynge."
This lettre he seleth, pryvely wepynge,
Which to the messager was take soone,
And forth he gooth; ther is na moore to doone.

O messager, fulfild of dronkenesse,   771
Strong is thy breeth, thy lymes faltren ay,
And thou biwreyest alle secreenesse.
Thy mynde is lorn, thou janglest as a jay,
Thy face is turned in a newe array.   775
Ther dronkenesse regneth in any route,
Ther is no conseil hyd, withouten doute.

---

720. **stille,** constantly. 721. **halt,** holds (stays in). 722. **The tyme is come,** understand *when*. 724. **dooth,** causes, has. 725. **cleped was,** was named. 727. **spedeful,** advantageous, to the purpose. 729. **to doon his avantage,** for his own advantage. The messenger hoped to be rewarded for carrying the news to the king's mother. 730. **swithe,** rapidly. 731. **salueth,** salutes, greets. 733. **sithe,** (plur.) times. 736. **lettres,** plur. used like the Latin *literae* in a sing. sense. 737. **moot,** must. 741. **wol,** wish. 743. **sadly,** deeply. 745. **sleep,** slept. 748. **direct,** directed. **of,** concerning. 750. **spak,** said. 752. **was.** The rime, as Skeat noted, would be improved by reading *nas* (was not), but *nas* is found in only one MS. 753. **endure,** remain. 754. **elf,** evil spirit, though elves are not necessarily evil. 757. **sayn,** seen. 760. **sonde,** dispensation. 762. **lust,** desire, pleasure. 764. **Kepeth,** take care of. 769. **take,** given. 771. **fulfild of,** filled with. 773. **secreenesse,** secrecy. 774. **lorn,** lost. **janglest,** chatterest (talkest volubly). 775. **is turned in a newe array,** is changed in appearance. 776. **Ther,** where. **route,** company.

O Donegild, I ne have noon Englissh digne
Unto thy malice and thy tirannye!
And therfore to the feend I thee resigne; 780
Lat hym enditen of thy traitorie!
Fy, mannysh, fy!—o nay, by God, I lye—
Fy, feendlych spirit, for I dar wel telle,
Thogh thou heere walke, thy spirit is in helle!

This messager comth fro the kyng agayn, 785
And at the kynges moodres court he lighte,
And she was of this messager ful fayn,
And plesed hym in al that ever she myghte.
He drank, and wel his girdel underpighte;
He slepeth, and he fnorteth in his gyse 790
Al nyght, til the sonne gan aryse.

Eft were his lettres stolen everychon,
And countrefeted lettres in this wyse:
"The king comandeth his constable anon,
Up peyne of hangyng, and on heigh juyse, 795
That he ne sholde suffren in no wyse
Custance in-with his reawme for t'abyde
Thre dayes and o quarter of a tyde;

"But in the same ship as he hire fond,
Hire, and hir yonge sone, and al hir geere, 800
He sholde putte, and croude hire fro the lond,
And charge hire that she never eft coome
  theere."
O my Custance, wel may thy goost have feere,
And, slepynge, in thy dreem been in penance,
Whan Donegild cast al this ordinance. 805

This messager on morwe, whan he wook,
Unto the castel halt the nexte way,
And to the constable he the lettre took;
And whan that he this pitous lettre say,

Ful ofte he seyde, "Allas! and weylaway!" 810
"Lord Crist," quod he, "how may this world
  endure,
So ful of synne is many a creature?

"O myghty God, if that it be thy wille,
Sith thou art rightful juge, how may it be
That thou wolt suffren innocentz to spille, 815
And wikked folk regne in prosperitee?
O goode Custance, allas! so wo is me
That I moot be thy tormentour, or deye
On shames deeth; ther is noon oother weye."

Wepen bothe yonge and olde in al that place
Whan that the kyng this cursed lettre sente, 821
And Custance, with a deedly pale face,
The ferthe day toward hir ship she wente.
But nathelees she taketh in good entente 824
The wyl of Crist, and knelynge on the stronde,
She seyde, "Lord, ay welcome be thy sonde!

"He that me kepte fro the false blame
While I was on the lond amonges yow,
He kan me kepe from harm and eek fro shame
In salte see, althogh I se noght how. 830
As strong as evere he was, he is yet now.
In hym triste I, and in his mooder deere,
That is to me my seyl and eek my steere."

Hir litel child lay wepyng in hir arm,
And knelynge, pitously to hym she seyde, 835
"Pees, litel sone, I wol do thee noon harm."
With that hir coverchief of hir heed she
  breyde,
And over his litel eyen she it leyde,
And in hir arm she lulleth it ful faste,
And into hevene hire eyen up she caste. 840

---

778. **digne Unto**, worthy of (describing). 782. **mannysh**, characteristic of a man rather than a woman. 786. **lighte**, alights. 789. **underpighte**, propped up. 790. **fnorteth**, snores, but see note to A 4163. **in his gyse**, in his accustomed manner. 795. **juyse**, justice (OF. *juise*). 797. **in-with**, within. 798. **tyde**. The meaning "hour" rather than "tide" seems more appropriate here. The force of the line would then be "three days and only the shortest possible time more." The phrase *o quarter of a tyde* may have been added for the sake of the rime. 799. **as he hire fond**, as he found her in. 800. **geere**, equipment, belongings. 801. **croude**, push. 803. **goost**, spirit. 804. **penance**, distress. 805. **cast al this ordinance**, contrived all this plan. 807. **halt the nexte way**, takes the shortest route. 809. **say**, saw. 815. **spille**, be destroyed. 826. **sonde**, dispensation. 833. **steere**, rudder. 834. **Hir litel child** . . . This and the following five stanzas are almost entirely Chaucer's addition.

"Mooder," quod she, "and mayde bright, Marie,
Sooth is that thurgh wommanes eggement
Mankynde was lorn, and dampned ay to dye,
For which thy child was on a croys yrent.
Thy blisful eyen sawe al his torment;   845
Thanne is ther no comparison bitwene
Thy wo and any wo man may sustene.

"Thow sawe thy child yslayn bifore thyne yën,
And yet now lyveth my litel child, parfay!   849
Now, lady bright, to whom alle woful cryen,
Thow glorie of wommanhede, thow faire may,
Thow haven of refut, brighte sterre of day,
Rewe on my child, that of thy gentillesse,
Rewest on every reweful in distresse.

"O litel child, allas! what is thy gilt,   855
That nevere wroghtest synne as yet, pardee?
Why wil thyn harde fader han thee spilt?

O mercy, deere constable," quod she,
"As lat my litel child dwelle heer with thee;
And if thou darst nat saven hym, for blame,   860
So kys hym ones in his fadres name!"

Therwith she looked bakward to the londe,
And seyde, "Farewel, housbonde routhelees!"
And up she rist, and walketh doun the stronde
Toward the ship,—hir folweth al the prees,—
And evere she preyeth hire child to holde his pees;   866
And taketh hir leve, and with an hooly entente
She blisseth hire, and into ship she wente.

Vitailled was the ship, it is no drede,
Habundantly for hire ful longe space,   870
And othere necessaries that sholde nede
She hadde ynogh, heryed be Goddes grace!
For wynd and weder almyghty God purchace,
And brynge hire hoom! I kan no bettre seye,
But in the see she dryveth forth hir weye.   875

Explicit secunda pars.

Sequitur pars tercia.

Alla the kyng comth hoom soone after this
Unto his castle, of the which I tolde,
And asketh where his wyf and his child is.
The constable gan aboute his herte colde,
And pleynly al the manere he hym tolde   880
As ye han herd—I kan telle it no bettre—
And sheweth the kyng his seel and eek his lettre,

And seyde, "Lord, as ye comanded me
Up peyne of deeth, so have I doon, certein."
This messager tormented was til he   885
Moste biknowe and tellen, plat and pleyn,
Fro nyght to nyght, in what place he had leyn;
And thus, by wit and sotil enquerynge,
Ymagined was by whom this harm gan sprynge.

The hand was knowe that the lettre wroot,
And al the venym of this cursed dede,   891
But in what wise, certeinly, I noot.
Th'effect is this, that Alla, out of drede,
His mooder slow—that may men pleynly rede—
For that she traitoure was to hire ligeance.   895
Thus endeth olde Donegild, with meschance!

The sorwe that this Alla nyght and day
Maketh for his wyf, and for his child also,
Ther is no tonge that it telle may.
But now wol I unto Custance go,   900
That fleteth in the see, in peyne and wo,
Fyve yeer and moore, as liked Cristes sonde,
Er that hir ship approched unto londe.

842. eggement, instigation. **844. yrent,** torn. **852. refut,** refuge. **854. reweful,** pitiful creature. **857. han thee spilt,** have thee destroyed. **859. As,** hortatory *as*, introducing a petition, prayer, etc. **864. rist,** riseth. **871. nede,** be necessary. **872. heryed,** praised. **873. purchace,** provide. **879. colde,** grow cold. **885. tormented,** tortured. **886. Moste biknowe,** had to confess. **plat and pleyn,** plainly and openly. **890. knowe,** recognized. **892. noot,** know not. **893. out of drede,** without doubt. **894. slow,** slew. **896. with meschance,** a curse upon her! **901. fleteth,** floats.

Under an hethen castel, atte laste,   904
Of which the name in my text noght I fynde,
Custance, and eek hir child, the see up caste.
Almyghty God, that saveth al mankynde,
Have on Custance and on hir child som mynde,
That fallen is in hethen hand eftsoone,
In point to spille, as I shal telle yow soone.   910

Doun fro the castle comth ther many a wight
To gauren on this ship and on Custance.
But shortly, from the castle, on a nyght,
The lordes styward—God yeve hym mes-
    chance!—
A theef that hadde reneyed oure creance,   915
Cam into ship allone, and seyde he sholde
Hir lemman be, wher so she wolde or nolde.

Wo was this wrecched womman tho bigon;
Hir child cride, and she cride pitously.
But blisful Marie heelp hire right anon;   920
For with hir struglyng wel and myghtily
The theef fil over bord al sodeynly,
And in the see he dreynte for vengeance;
And thus hath Crist unwemmed kept Custance.

O foule lust of luxurie, lo, thyn ende !   925
Nat oonly that thou feyntest mannes mynde,
But verraily thou wolt his body shende.
Th'ende of thy werk, or of thy lustes blynde,
Is compleynyng. Hou many oon may men
    fynde
That noght for werk somtyme, but for th'en-
    tente   930
To doon this synne, been outher slayn or shente !

How may this wayke womman han this
    strengthe
Hire to defende agayn this renegat?
O Golias, unmesurable of lengthe,
Hou myghte David make thee so maat,   935
So yong and of armure so desolaat?
Hou dorste he looke upon thy dredful face?
Wel may men seen, it nas but Goddes grace.

Who yaf Judith corage or hardynesse
To sleen hym Olofernus in his tente,   940
And to deliveren out of wrecchednesse
The peple of God? I seye, for this entente,
That right as God spirit of vigour sente
To hem, and saved hem out of meschance,
So sente he myght and vigour to Custance.   945

Forth gooth hir ship thurghout the narwe
    mouth
Of Jubaltare and Septe, dryvynge ay
Somtyme west, and somtyme north and south,
And somtyme est, ful many a wery day,
Til Cristes mooder—blessed be she ay !—   950
Hath shapen, thurgh hir endelees goodnesse,
To make an ende of al hir hevynesse.

Now lat us stynte of Custance but a throwe,
And speke we of the Romayn Emperour,
That out of Surrye hath by lettres knowe   955
The slaughtre of cristen folk, and dishonour
Doon to his doghter by a fals traytour,
I mene the cursed wikked Sowdanesse
That at the feeste leet sleen bothe moore and
    lesse.

---

905. Of which the name . . . Trivet merely calls it *un chastel de un admiral de paens.* **909. eftsoone,** again. **912. gauren,** stare. **915. reneyed oure creance,** renounced our faith. **917. lemman,** lover. **wher so,** whether. **918. Wo . . . bigon,** woe begone, wretched. **tho,** then. **920. heelp,** helped. **923. for vengeance,** as he deserved; *lit.* by retribution. **924. unwemmed,** unblemished. **925. luxurie,** lechery. **926. feyntest,** enfeeblest. **927. shende,** ruin. **929. compleynyng,** grief. In the Latin of Pope Innocent's *De Contemptu Mundi,* from which this stanza is derived, the corresponding words are *dolor et penitentia.* **930.** *for werk,* for the act. **931. shente,** brought to shame, ruined. **932. wayke,** weak. **934. Golias,** Goliath. Cf. *1 Samuel,* 17:4–51. **935. maat,** overcome, vanquished. **936. desolaat,** completely without. David was without armor. **939. Judith.** The story of Judith and Holofernes is the subject of the book of *Judith,* among the apocryphal books of the Old Testament. Chaucer relates it briefly in the *Monk's Tale* (B 3741–64), **942. for this entente,** in this matter (consideration) **946–7. the narwe mouth Of Jubaltare and Septe,** the Strait of Gibraltar. Septe is Ceuta on the opposite coast of Africa. The identification may be confirmed by two references in Chevalier, *Répertoire des sources hist., s.v.* Ceuta. **953. stynte,** leave off. **throwe,** while. **955. Surrye,** Syria. **959. leet sleen,** caused to be slain.

For which this Emperour hath sent anon   960
His senatour, with roial ordinance,
And othere lordes, God woot, many oon,
On Surryens to taken heigh vengeance.
They brennen, sleen, and brynge hem to mes-
   chance
Ful many a day; but shortly, this is th'ende,   965
Homward to Rome they shapen hem to wende.

This senatour repaireth with victorie
To Rome-ward, saillynge ful roially,
And mette the ship dryvynge, as seith the storie,
In which Custance sit ful pitously.   970
Nothyng ne knew he what she was, ne why
She was in swich array, ne she nyl seye
Of hire estaat, althogh she sholde deye.

He bryngeth hire to Rome, and to his wyf
He yaf hire, and hir yonge sone also;   975
And with the senatour she ladde hir lyf.
Thus kan Oure Lady bryngen out of wo
Woful Custance, and many another mo.
And longe tyme dwelled she in that place,
In hooly werkes evere, as was hir grace.   980

The senatoures wyf hir aunte was,
But for al that she knew hire never the moore.
I wol no lenger tarien in this cas,
But to kyng Alla, which I spak of yoore,
That for his wyf wepeth and siketh soore,   985
I wol retourne, and lete I wol Custance
Under the senatoures governance.

Kyng Alla, which that hadde his mooder
   slayn,
Upon a day fil in swich repentance
That, if I shortly tellen shal and playn,   990

To Rome he comth to receyven his penance;
And putte hym in the Popes ordinance
In heigh and logh, and Jhesu Crist bisoghte
Foryeve his wikked werkes that he wroghte.

The fame anon thurgh Rome toun is born,
How Alla kyng shal comen in pilgrymage,   996
By herbergeours that wenten hym biforn;
For which the senatour, as was usage,
Rood hym agayns, and many of his lynage,
As wel to shewen his heighe magnificence   1000
As to doon any kyng a reverence.

Greet cheere dooth this noble senatour
To kyng Alla, and he to hym also;
Everich of hem dooth oother greet honour.
And so bifel that in a day or two   1005
This senatour is to kyng Alla go
To feste, and shortly, if I shal nat lye,
Custances sone wente in his compaignye.

Som men wolde seyn at requeste of Cus-
   tance
This senatour hath lad this child to feeste;   1010
I may nat tellen every circumstance,—
Be as be may, ther was he at the leeste.
But sooth is this, that at his moodres heeste
Biforn Alla, durynge the metes space,   1014
The child stood, lookyng in the kynges face.

This Alla kyng hath of this child greet wonder,
And to the senatour he seyde anon,
"Whos is that faire child that stondeth yonder?"
"I noot," quod he, "by God, and by seint John!
A mooder he hath, but fader hath he noon   1020
That I of woot"—and shortly, in a stounde,
He tolde Alla how that this child was founde.

---

961. ordinance, orders, directive. **964. meschance,** ruin. **965. shortly,** in brief. Chaucer here condenses Trivet. **967. This senatour.** His name is given in Trivet as Arsemius, and his wife's name (cf. l. 974) as Helen. **972. array,** condition. **981. aunte,** actually her cousin. Helen was the daughter of the Emperor's brother. **983. in this cas,** over this matter. **985. siketh,** sighs. **986. lete,** leave. **996. shal comen.** The tense is a little awkward after the three preceding lines: *bisoghte* is the past tense, and therefore *putte* is probably the past tense. **997. herbergeours,** attendants sent ahead to provide lodging. **999. hym agayns,** to meet him. **1000-1. As wel . . . as,** both . . . and. **reverence,** respect. **1009. Som men wolde seyn . . .** Generally taken to be an allusion to Trivet or Gower, but neither mentions any such suggestion by Custance. The statement may mean simply "Some people would suppose that . . ." But cf. l. 1086. **1010. this child.** According to Trivet he was beginning his eighteenth year. **1013. heeste,** behest. **1014. durynge the metes space,** in the course of the dinner. **1021. in a stounde,** in a (short) space of time.

"But God woot," quod this senatour also,
"So vertuous a lyvere in my lyf
Ne saugh I nevere as she, ne herde of mo,   1025
Of worldly wommen, mayde, ne of wyf.
I dar wel seyn hir hadde levere a knyf
Thurghout hir brest, than ben a womman
      wikke;
There is no man koude brynge hire to that
      prikke."

    Now was this child as lyk unto Custance   1030
As possible is a creature to be.
This Alla hath the face in remembrance
Of dame Custance, and ther on mused he
If that the childes mooder were aught she
That is his wyf, and pryvely he sighte,   1035
And spedde hym fro the table that he myghte.

"Parfay," thoghte he, "fantome is in myn heed!
I oghte deme, of skilful juggement,
That in the salte see my wyf is deed."
And afterward he made his argument: 1040
"What woot I if that Crist have hyder ysent
My wyf by see, as wel as he hire sente
To my contree fro thennes that she wente?"

And after noon, hoom with the senatour
Goth Alla, for to seen this wonder chaunce.   1045
This senatour dooth Alla greet honour,
And hastifly he sente after Custaunce.
But trusteth weel, hire liste nat to daunce,
Whan that she wiste wherfore was that sonde;
Unnethe upon hir feet she myghte stonde.   1050

    Whan Alla saugh his wyf, faire he hire grette,
And weep, that it was routhe for to see;
For at the firste look he on hire sette,

He knew wel verraily that it was she.
And she, for sorwe, as doumb stant as a tree,
So was hir herte shet in hir distresse,   1056
Whan she remembred his unkyndenesse.

Twyes she swowned in his owene sighte;
He weep, and hym excuseth pitously.
"Now God," quod he, "and alle his halwes
      brighte   1060
So wisly on my soule as have mercy,
That of youre harm as giltelees am I
As is Maurice my sone, so lyk youre face;
Elles the feend me fecche out of this place!"

    Long was the sobbyng and the bitter peyne,
Er that hir woful hertes myghte cesse;   1066
Greet was the pitee for to heere hem pleyne,
Thurgh whiche pleintes gan hir wo encresse.
I pray yow alle my labour to relesse;
I may nat telle hir wo until to-morwe,   1070
I am so wery for to speke of sorwe.

But finally, whan that the sothe is wist
That Alla giltelees was of hir wo,
I trowe an hundred tymes been they kist,
And swich a blisse is ther bitwix hem two   1075
That, save the joye that lasteth everemo,
Ther is noon lyk that any creature
Hath seyn or shal, whil that the world may dure.

Tho preyde she hir housbonde mekely,
In relief of hir longe, pitous pyne,   1080
That he wolde preye hir fader specially
That of his magestee he wolde enclyne
To vouchesauf som day with hym to dyne.
She preyde hym eek he sholde by no weye
Unto hir fader no word of hire seye.   1085

1024. lyvere, living person. 1028. wikke, wicked. 1029. prikke, point, condition. 1034. aught, in any wise. 1035. sighte, sighed. 1036. spedde . . . that he myghte, went away as quickly as possible. 1037. fantome, delusion. I am having a "brain storm." 1038. skilful, rational. 1041. What woot I if, how do I know whether. 1045. to seen this wonder chaunce, to look into this miraculous possibility. 1048. hire liste nat to daunce, she was in no mood to dance. It must be remembered that so far as Custance knows she was put to sea on the orders of her husband. 1049. sonde, message. 1052. weep, wept. 1056. shet, shut. 1060. halwes, saints. 1061. wisly, surely. as have, have. See Language, § 73. 1064. Elles the feend me fecche, otherwise may the devil carry me off. 1066. hir, their. 1071. wery for to speke, weary of speaking. 1080. In relief of . . ., to relieve her long suffering.

Som men wolde seyn how that the child
    Maurice
Dooth this message unto this Emperour;
But, as I guesse, Alla was nat so nyce
To hym that was of so sovereyn honour
As he that is of Cristen folk the flour,   1090
Sente any child, but it is bet to deeme
He wente hymself, and so it may wel seeme.

    This Emperour hath graunted gentilly
To come to dyner, as he hym bisoughte;
And wel rede I he looked bisily   1095
Upon this child, and on his doghter thoghte.
Alla goth to his in, and as hym oghte,
Arrayed for this feste in every wise
As ferforth as his konnyng may suffise.   1099

    The morwe cam, and Alla gan hym dresse,
And eek his wyf, this Emperour to meete;
And forth they ryde in joye and in gladnesse.
And whan she saugh hir fader in the strete,
She lighte doun, and falleth hym to feete.
"Fader," quod she, "youre yonge child Cus-
    tance   1105
Is now ful clene out of youre remembrance.

I am youre doghter Custance," quod she,
"That whilom ye han sent unto Surrye.
It am I, fader, that in the salte see
Was put allone and dampned for to dye.   1110
Now, goode fader, mercy I yow crye!
Sende me namoore unto noon hethenesse,
But thonketh my lord heere of his kyndenesse."

    Who kan the pitous joye tellen al
Bitwixe hem thre, syn they been thus ymette?
But of my tale make an ende I shal;   1116

The day goth faste, I wol no lenger lette.
This glade folk to dyner they hem sette;
In joye and blisse at mete I lete hem dwelle
A thousand foold wel moore than I kan telle.

    This child Maurice was sithen Emperour   1121
Maad by the Pope, and lyved cristenly;
To Cristes chirche he dide greet honour.
But I lete al his storie passen by;
Of Custance is my tale specially.   1125
In the olde Romayn geestes may men fynde
Maurices lyf; I bere it noght in mynde.

    This kyng Alla, whan he his tyme say,
With his Custance, his hooly wyf so sweete,
To Engelond been they come the righte way,
Wher as they lyve in joye and in quiete.   1131
But litel while it lasteth, I yow heete,
Joye of this world, for tyme wol nat abyde;
Fro day to nyght it changeth as the tyde.

    Who lyved euere in swich delit o day   1135
That hym ne moeved outher conscience,
Or ire, or talent, or somkynnes affray,
Envye, or pride, or passion, or offence?
I ne seye but for this ende this sentence,
That litel while in joye or in plesance   1140
Lasteth the blisse of Alla with Custance.

    For deeth, that taketh of heigh and logh his
    rente,
Whan passed was a yeer, evene as I gesse,
Out of this world this kyng Alla he hente,
For whom Custance hath ful greet hevynesse.
Now lat us prayen God his soule blesse!   1146
And dame Custance, finally to seye,
Toward the toun of Rome goth hir weye.

1086. Som men wolde seyn . . . Here the statement (cf. l. 1009) seems to be a reference to the way others tell the story, since in both Trivet and Gower Maurice is sent to convey the invitation to the emperor. Although Chaucer has Alla go in person, it is evident that Maurice accompanied him (cf. l. 1095). **1088. nyce,** foolish. **1091. Sente,** that he would send. **1094. bisoughte,** beseeched. **1097. in,** inn, lodging. **1098. Arrayed,** prepared. **1099. As ferforth as,** as far as. **1100. dresse,** prepare. **1110. dampned,** condemned. **1117. lette,** delay, prolong matters. **1126. geestes,** histories. The allusion here is not to the *Gesta Romanorum*. **1128. say,** saw. **1131. Wher as,** where. **1132. heete,** assure. This and the observations immediately following are inspired by Pope Innocent's *De Contemptu Mundi*. **1135. o day,** a single day. **1136. conscience,** sense of guilt. **1137. talent,** desire, appetite. **somkynnes affray,** alarm of some kind. **1139. sentence,** opinion. **1142. rente,** cf. ModE. "toll". **1144. he hente,** he (death) seized.

To Rome is come this hooly creature,
And fyndeth hire freendes hoole and sounde;
Now is she scaped al hire aventure.   1151
And whan that she hir fader hath yfounde,
Doun on hir knees falleth she to grounde;
Wepynge for tendrenesse in herte blithe,
She heryeth God an hundred thousand sithe.

In vertu and in hooly almus-dede   1156
They lyven alle, and nevere asonder wende;
Til deeth departed hem, this lyf they lede.
And fareth now weel! my tale is at an ende.
Now Jhesu Crist, that of his myght may sende
Joye after wo, governe us in his grace,   1161
And kepe us alle that been in this place! Amen

Heere endeth the tale of the Man of Lawe.

MAN OF LAW'S ENDLINK

Here endith the Man of Lawe his tale. And next folwith the Shipman his prolog.

Owre Hoost upon his stiropes stood anon,
And seyde, "Goode men, herkeneth everych on!
This was a thrifty tale for the nones!   1165
Sir Parisshe Prest," quod he, "for Goddes bones,
Telle us a tale, as was thi forward yore.
I se wel that ye lerned men in lore
Can moche good, by Goddes dignite!"
   The Parson him answerde, "*Benedicite!*   1170
What eyleth the man, so synfully to swere?"
Oure Host answerde, "O Jankin, be ye there?
I smelle a Lollere in the wynd," quod he.
"Now! goode men," quod oure Host, "herken-
   eth me;
Abydeth, for Goddes digne passioun,   1175

For we schal han a predicacioun;
This Lollere heer wil prechen us somwhat."
   "Nay, by my fader soule, that schal he nat!"
Seyde the Shipman; "heer schal he nat preche;
He schal no gospel *glosen* here ne teche.   1180
We leven alle in the grete God," quod he;
"He wolde sowen som difficulte,
Or springen cokkel in our clene corn.
And therfore, Hoost, I warne thee biforn,
My joly body schal a tale telle,   1185
And I schal clynken you so mery a belle,
That I schal waken al this compaignie.
But it schal not ben of philosophie,
Ne phislyas, ne termes queinte of lawe.
Ther is but litel Latyn in my mawe!"   1190

Here endith the Shipman his prolog. And next folwyng he bigynneth his tale &c.

1154. tendrenesse, womanishness. 1155. heryeth, praises, worships. sithe, times.
   Man of Law's Endlink. The link which is here designated the Man of Law's Endlink is sometimes called the Epilogue of *The Man of Law's Tale*, though it is not so called in any of the manuscripts. It is found in more than thirty of the manuscripts and in the great majority of them serves to introduce *The Squire's Tale*; consequently l. 1179 reads "Seyde the Squire." Some manuscripts, however, read "Somnour" and four read "Shipman." In one of these, the Selden MS (generally a poor manuscript), it is followed by *The Shipman's Tale*.
   It is apparent that at this point Chaucer changed his mind, possibly when he transferred the story which the Shipman tells from the Wife of Bath to the Shipman (see the Introductory Note to *The Shipman's Tale*). In any case, the link always follows *The Man of Law's Tale*, and since the order of the tales here adopted is mainly that of the Chaucer Society, the link here serves as the Shipman's Prologue. Since the endlink is omitted from the Ellesmere MS (and a score of others), the text here printed follows in the main the Corpus MS. The rubrics are from the Selden MS. **1165. a thrifty tale**, echoing the Man of Law's words in line B 46. **for the nones**, for the occasion. **1167. as . . . yore**, as you agreed formerly. **1169. Can,** know. **1172. Jankin,** a diminutive of John. Priests were commonly called Sir John, and the form Jankin is used derisively. **1173. Lollere,** Lollard, a name applied to the followers of Wiclif. **1178. fader,** the possessive case; see Language, § 14. **1180. glosen,** explain. **1181. leven,** believe. **1183. springen cokkel,** scatter cockle (corn cockle, a weed). **corn,** grain, wheat. **1189. phislyas.** The meaning and origin of the word are unknown. Some MSS read *phisik*.

Group B₂ (Fragment VII)

The Shipman's Tale

Heere bigynneth the Shipmannes Tale.

A marchant whilom dwelled at Seint-Denys,
That riche was, for which men helde hym wys.
A wyf he hadde of excellent beautee;
And compaignable and revelous was she,
Which is a thyng that causeth more dispence
Than worth is al the chiere and reverence 1196
That men hem doon at festes and at daunces.
Swiche salutaciouns and contenaunces
Passen as dooth a shadwe upon the wal;
But wo is hym that payen moot for al! 1200
The sely housbonde, algate he moot paye,
He moot us clothe, and he moot us arraye,
Al for his owene worship richely,
In which array we daunce jolily.
And if that he noght may, par aventure, 1205
Or ellis list no swich dispence endure,
But thynketh it is wasted and ylost,
Thanne moot another payen for oure cost,
Or lene us gold, and that is perilous.
This noble marchaunt heeld a worthy hous,

For which he hadde alday so greet repair 1211
For his largesse, and for his wyf was fair,
That wonder is; but herkneth to my tale.
Amonges alle his gestes, grete and smale,
Ther was a monk, a fair man and a boold— 1215
I trowe a thritty wynter he was oold—
That evere in oon was drawynge to that place.
This yonge monk, that was so fair of face,
Aqueynted was so with the goode man,
Sith that hir firste knoweliche bigan, 1220
That in his hous as famulier was he
As it is possible any freend to be.
     And for as muchel as this goode man,
And eek this monk, of which that I bigan,
Were bothe two yborn in o village, 1225
The monk hym claymeth as for cosynage;
And he agayn, he seith nat ones nay,
But was as glad therof as fowel of day;
For to his herte it was a greet plesaunce.
Thus been they knyt with eterne alliaunce, 1230

The Shipman's Tale. Since *The Shipman's Tale* was apparently intended to be told by a woman (see ll. 1201–9) and is of such a character that neither the Prioress nor the Second Nun could have told it, it is generally believed to have been earlier assigned to the Wife of Bath. She would have been quite capable of telling it. It is a fabliau and concerns an immoral intrigue between a monk and the wife of a merchant, as a concomitant of which the husband is cheated out of a considerable sum of money.
     The fabliau which the Shipman tells belongs to a well-known type of folk-tale, known as the lover's gift regained, which has been studied by John W. Spargo in *Chaucer's Shipman's Tale: The Lover's Gift Regained* (Helsinki, 1930; *FF Communications*, No. 91). There is a briefer discussion by the same author in *Sources and Analogues*. Chaucer's source was probably an Old French fabliau which has not come down to us. A similar story is told by Boccaccio in the *Decameron* (the first story of the eighth day) and by Sercambi in his *Novelle* (No. 19), but it is unlikely that Chaucer knew either of these collections.
     Like the fabliaux told by the Miller and the Reeve, it probably was written for *The Canterbury Tales*, rather near the beginning of the period of composition of the *Tales*, but nothing very definite can be said about the date except that it was almost certainly written before the Prologue to *The Wife of Bath's Tale* was fully conceived. For a discussion of a number of points on which scholarly opinion has differed see W. W. Lawrence, "Chaucer's *Shipman's Tale*," *Speculum*, XXXIII. 56–68.
     1191. whilom, once upon a time. **Seint-Denys,** Saint-Denis, about four miles north of Paris. It was the site of a famous monastery where many of the early kings of France were buried. **1194. revelous,** pleasure loving. **1195. dispence,** spending. **1196. chiere,** pleasure, attention. **1198. contenaunces,** behavior of one person toward another. **1200. moot,** must. **1201. sely,** simple. **algate,** always, in any case. **1202. us.** See introductory note. **1206. list,** wishes. **1209. lene,** lend. **1211. alday,** constantly. **repair,** frequenting (of his house). **1217. evere in oon,** continually. **1220. knoweliche,** acquaintance. **1226. for cosynage,** for kinship, as a relation.

And ech of hem gan oother for t'assure
Of bretherhede, whil that hir lyf may dure.
  Free was daun John, and namely of dispence,
As in that hous, and ful of diligence
To doon plesaunce, and also greet costage. 1235
He noght forgat to yeve the leeste page
In al that hous; but after hir degree,
He yaf the lord, and sitthe al his meynee,
Whan that he cam, som manere honest thyng;
For which they were as glad of his comyng 1240
As fowel is fayn whan that the sonne up riseth.
Na moore of this as now, for it suffiseth.
  But so bifel, this marchant on a day
Shoop hym to make redy his array
Toward the toun of Brugges for to fare, 1245
To byen there a porcioun of ware;
For which he hath to Parys sent anon
A messager, and preyed hath daun John
That he sholde come to Seint-Denys to pleye
With hym and with his wyf a day or tweye, 1250
Er he to Brugges wente, in alle wise.
  This noble monk, of which I yow devyse,
Hath of his abbot, as hym list, licence,
By cause he was a man of heigh prudence,
And eek an officer, out for to ryde, 1255
To seen hir graunges and hire bernes wyde,
And unto Seint-Denys he comth anon.
Who was so welcome as my lord daun John,
Oure deere cosyn, ful of curteisye?
With hym broghte he a jubbe of malvesye, 1260
And eek another, ful of fyn vernage,
And volatyl, as ay was his usage.
And thus I lete hem ete and drynke and pleye,

This marchant and this monk, a day or tweye.
  The thridde day, this marchant up ariseth,
And on his nedes sadly hym avyseth, 1266
And up into his countour-hous gooth he
To rekene with hymself, as wel may be,
Of thilke yeer how that it with hym stood,
And how that he despended hadde his good,
And if that he encressed were or noon. 1271
His bookes and his bagges many oon
He leith biforn hym on his countyng-bord.
Ful riche was his tresor and his hord, 1274
For which ful faste his countour-dore he shette;
And eek he nolde that no man sholde hym lette
Of his acountes, for the meene tyme;
And thus he sit til it was passed pryme.
  Daun John was rysen in the morwe also,
And in the gardyn walketh to and fro, 1280
And hath his thynges seyd ful curteisly.
  This goode wyf cam walkynge pryvely
Into the gardyn, there he walketh softe,
And hym saleweth, as she hath doon ofte.
A mayde child cam in hire compaignye, 1285
Which as hir list she may governe and gye,
For yet under the yerde was the mayde.
"O deere cosyn myn, daun John," she sayde,
"What eyleth yow so rathe for to ryse?"
  "Nece," quod he, "it oghte ynough suffise
Fyve houres for to slepe upon a nyght, 1291
But it were for an old appalled wight,
As been thise wedded men, that lye and dare
As in a fourme sit a wery hare,
Were al forstraught with houndes grete and
  smale. 1295

1232. bretherhede. See note to D 1405. dure, last. 1233. daun, don (L. *dominus*). namely, especially. 1234. As in, in. 1235. costage, expense. 1238. sitthe, afterwards. meynee, household. 1244. Shoop hym, prepared. array, clothing and other necessities. 1249. to pleye, to have a good time. 1251. in alle wise, by all means, *lit.* in all respects. 1252. devyse, tell, relate. 1255. out for to ryde. His office was that of an outrider. See note to A 166. 1256. graunges; granges, outlying farmhouses and associated buildings belonging to his monastery. bernes, barns. 1259. cosyn, kinsman. 1260. jubbe, a large jug. See note to A 3628. malvesye, a sweet wine, originally from Greece. 1261. vernage, a sweet Italian wine, sometimes red but generally white; the Italian *vernaccia* is a white wine. 1262. volatyl, wild fowl. 1266. sadly, seriously. hym avyseth, reflects. 1267. countour-hous, counting-house, office. 1270. despended, spent. good, property, wealth. 1275. shette, shut. 1276. nolde, did not wish. lette, interrupt, keep from. 1278. sit, sits. pryme, 9 A.M. 1281. his thynges, *i.e.* the divine office in his Breviary. curteisly, graciously, *i.e.* as he should. 1284. saleweth, greets. 1286. gye, guide. 1287. yerde, rod, *i.e.* subject to discipline, quite young. 1289. rathe, early. 1290. Nece. Niece, like cousin, was often used without regard for the degree of relationship. 1292. But it were, except. appalled wight, enfeebled person. 1293. dare, lie motionless, not the same word as *dare*, to have courage, etc. 1294. fourme, rabbit burrow. sit, sits. 1295. Were, if it were. forstraught, distraught. The word is apparently a coinage of Chaucer's. No other instance is recorded in the *MED*.

But deere nece, why be ye so pale?
I trowe, certes, that oure goode man
Hath yow laboured sith the nyght bigan,
That yow were nede to resten hastily."
And with that word he lough ful murily,   1300
And of his owene thought he wax al reed.

    This faire wyf gan for to shake hir heed
And seyde thus, "Ye, God woot al," quod she.
"Nay, cosyn myn, it stant nat so with me;
For, by that God that yaf me soule and lyf,   1305
In al the reawme of France is ther no wyf
That lasse lust hath to that sory pley.
For I may synge 'allas and weylawey
That I was born,' but to no wight," quod she,
"Dar I nat telle how that it stant with me.   1310
Wherfore I thynke out of this land to wende,
Or elles of myself to make an ende,
So ful am I of drede and eek of care."

    This monk bigan upon this wyf to stare,
And seyde, "Allas, my nece, God forbede   1315
That ye, for any sorwe or any drede,
Fordo youreself; but telleth me youre grief.
Paraventure I may, in youre meschief,
Conseille or helpe; and therfore telleth me
Al youre anoy, for it shal been secree.   1320
For on my porthors here I make an ooth
That nevere in my lyf, for lief ne looth,
Ne shal I of no conseil yow biwreye."

    "The same agayn to yow," quod she, "I seye.
By God and by this porthors I yow swere,   1325
Though men me wolde al into pieces tere,
Ne shal I nevere, for to goon to helle,
Biwreye a word of thyng that ye me telle,
Nat for no cosynage ne alliance,
But verraily, for love and affiance."   1330
Thus been they sworn, and heerupon they kiste,
And ech of hem tolde oother what hem liste.

    "Cosyn," quod she, "if that I hadde a space,

As I have noon, and namely in this place,
Thanne wolde I telle a legende of my lyf,   1335
What I have suffred sith I was a wyf
With myn housbonde, al be he youre cosyn."
    "Nay," quod this monk, "by God and seint
      Martyn,
He is na moore cosyn unto me
Than is this leef that hangeth on the tree!   1340
I clepe hym so, by Seint Denys of Fraunce,
To have the moore cause of aqueyntaunce
Of yow, which I have loved specially
Aboven alle wommen, sikerly.
This swere I yow on my professioun.   1345
Telleth youre grief, lest that he come adoun;
And hasteth yow, and gooth youre wey anon."
    "My deere love," quod she, "O my daun
      John,
Ful lief were me this conseil for to hyde.
But out it moot; I may namoore abyde.   1350
Myn housbonde is to me the worste man
That evere was sith that the world bigan.
But sith I am a wyf, it sit nat me
To tellen no wight of oure privetee,
Neither abedde, ne in noon oother place;   1355
God shilde I sholde it tellen, for his grace!
A wyf ne shal nat seyn of hir housbonde
But al honour, as I kan understonde;
Save unto yow thus muche I tellen shal:
As helpe me God, he is noght worth at al   1360
In no degree the value of a flye.
But yet me greveth moost his nygardye.
And wel ye woot that wommen naturelly
Desiren thynges sixe as wel as I:
They wolde that hir housbondes sholde be   1365
Hardy, and wise, and riche, and therto free,
And buxom unto his wyf, and fressh abedde.
But by that ilke Lord that for us bledde,
For his honour, myself for to arraye,

1300. lough, laughed. **1304. stant,** stands. **1307. lasse,** less. **1317. Fordo,** should destroy. **1318. meschief,** trouble, difficulty. **1320. secree,** secret. **1321. porthors,** Breviary. **1323. conseil,** confidence. **biwreye,** betray. **1327. for to goon,** to the extent of going. Cf. *TC* 1. 674 and A 1133. **1329. cosynage,** relationship. **1330. affiance,** good faith. **1333. space,** *i.e.* of time. **1335. legende,** a tale of martyrdom or suffering. **1338. seint Martyn,** St. Martin of Tours (d. 399). **1341, clepe,** call. **of Fraunce,** because there were other saints of this name (Dionysius). St. Denis was the first bishop of Paris (third cent.). **1344. sikerly,** certainly. **1345. professioun,** monastic vow. **1352. sith,** since. **1353. sit,** becomes. **1356. shilde,** forbid. **1359. Save,** except that. **1362. nygardye,** stinginess. **1367. buxom,** obedient.

A Sonday next I moste nedes paye 1370
An hundred frankes, or ellis I am lorn.
Yet were me levere that I were unborn
Than me were doon a sclaundre or vileynye;
And if myn housbonde eek it myghte espye,
I nere but lost; and therfore I yow preye, 1375
Lene me this somme, or ellis moot I deye.
Daun John, I seye, lene me thise hundred
    frankes.
Pardee, I wol nat faille yow my thankes,
If that yow list to doon that I yow praye.
For at a certeyn day I wol yow paye, 1380
And doon to yow what plesance and service
That I may doon, right as yow list devise.
And but I do, God take on me vengeance
As foul as evere hadde Genylon of France."
    This gentil monk answerde in this manere:
"Now trewely, myn owene lady deere, 1386
I have," quod he, "on yow so greet a routhe
That I yow swere, and plighte yow my trouthe,
That whan youre housbonde is to Flaundres
    fare,
I wol delyvere yow out of this care; 1390
For I wol brynge yow an hundred frankes."
And with that word he caughte hire by the
    flankes,
And hire embraceth harde, and kiste hire ofte.
"Gooth now youre wey," quod he, "al stille and
    softe,
And lat us dyne as soone as that ye may; 1395
For by my chilyndre it is pryme of day.

Gooth now, and beeth as trewe as I shal be."
    "Now elles God forbede, sire," quod she;
And forth she gooth as jolif as a pye,
And bad the cookes that they sholde hem hye,
So that men myghte dyne, and that anon. 1401
Up to hir housbonde is this wyf ygon,
And knokketh at his countour boldely.
    "*Qui la?*" quod he. "Peter! it am I," 1404
Quod she; "what, sire, how longe wol ye faste?
How longe tyme wol ye rekene and caste
Youre sommes, and youre bookes, and youre
    thynges?
The devel have part on alle swiche rekenynges!
Ye have ynough, pardee, of Goddes sonde;
Com doun to-day, and lat youre bagges stonde.
Ne be ye nat ashamed that daun John 1411
Shal fasting al this day alenge goon?
What! lat us heere a messe, and go we dyne."
    "Wyf," quod this man, "litel kanstow devyne
The curious bisynesse that we have. 1415
For of us chapmen, also God me save,
And by that lord that clepid is Seint Yve,
Scarsly amonges twelve tweye shul thryve
Continuelly, lastynge unto oure age.
We may wel make chiere and good visage, 1420
And dryve forth the world as it may be,
And kepen oure estaat in pryvetee,
Til we be deed, or elles that we pleye
A pilgrymage, or goon out of the weye.
And therfore have I greet necessitee 1425
Upon this queynte world t'avyse me;

1370. A, on. **1371. lorn,** lost. **1375. nere but,** would not be otherwise than. **1376. Lene,** lend. **deye,** die. **1384. Genylon,** Ganelon in the *Chanson de Roland*, whose enmity toward Roland caused the latter's death at Roncesvalles. He was torn to pieces by wild horses. **1389. fare,** gone. **1396. chilyndre,** a cylindrical instrument which worked on the principle of the sun-dial. **pryme of day,** 9 A.M. Dinner was usually at ten o'clock or before. **1399. jolif as a pye,** jolly as a magpie. **1400. hye,** hurry. **1401. men,** used as an indefinite pronoun, one. **1404. *Qui la,*** who is there? **Peter,** *i.e.* St. Peter. **1408. The devel have part,** equivalent to the modern "The devil take . . . !" or "A curse on . . . !" That *part* does not imply "a portion of" the merchant's profits or wealth is to be inferred from the use of the imprecation in the OF. *Farce du Pasté et de la Tarte* (*Ancien théâtre français*, II. 71): *Que le dyable y puist avoir part,* where the context makes such an interpretation of *part* impossible. This is likewise true of two other instances (*Le diable y ait part*) in *La Farce du Pauvre Jouhan,* ed. E. Droz and M. Roques (Geneva, 1959), ll. 61 and 83. **1409. sonde,** dispensation, gift. **1412. alenge,** long and weary. **1413. messe,** mass. **1415. curious,** troublesome, involving much care. **1417. Seint Yve,** St. Ives, but which of several saints of the name it is impossible to say. The name furnishes a convenient rime for *thryve*. **1421. dryve forth,** endure, pass through. **1422. kepen oure estaat in pryvetee,** keep our affairs (financial condition) to ourselves, or look after them quietly. **1423. pleye,** perform. The word is sometimes taken to imply that pleasure or relaxation was one of the objects of a pilgrimage (Skeat), as indeed it was, but the word does not always carry such an implication. **1424. goon out of the weye,** *i.e.* go off somewhere. In these five lines the merchant seems to say that they have two alternatives,—either to maintain a cheerful countenance, accept what life brings, and keep their affairs to themselves (or, quietly look after their financial condition) until they die, or else to make a pilgrimage or go off somewhere (to avoid their creditors).

For everemoore we moote stonde in drede
Of hap and fortune in oure chapmanhede.
   To Flaunders wol I go to-morwe at day,
And come agayn, as soone as evere I may.   1430
For which, my deere wyf, I thee biseke,
As be to every wight buxom and meke,
And for to kepe oure good be curious,
And honestly governe wel oure hous.
Thou hast ynough, in every maner wise,   1435
That to a thrifty houshold may suffise.
Thee lakketh noon array ne no vitaille;
Of silver in thy purs shaltow nat faille."
And with that word his countour-dore he shette,
And doun he gooth, no lenger wolde he lette.
But hastily a messe was ther seyd,   1441
And spedily the tables were yleyd,
And to the dyner faste they hem spedde,
And richely this monk the chapman fedde.
   At after-dyner daun John sobrely   1445
This chapman took apart, and prively
He seyde hym thus: "Cosyn, it standeth so,
That wel I se to Brugges wol ye go.
God and seint Austyn spede yow and gyde!
I prey yow, cosyn, wisely that ye ryde.   1450
Governeth yow also of youre diete
Atemprely, and namely in this hete.
Bitwix us two nedeth no strange fare;
Farewel, cosyn; God shilde yow fro care!
And if that any thyng by day or nyght,   1455
If it lye in my power and my myght,
That ye me wol comande in any wyse,
It shal be doon, right as ye wol devyse.
   O thyng, er that ye goon, if it may be,
I wolde prey yow: for to lene me   1460

An hundred frankes, for a wyke or tweye,
For certein beestes that I moste beye,
To stoore with a place that is oures.
God helpe me so, I wolde it were youres!
I shal nat faille surely of my day,   1465
Nat for a thousand frankes, a mile way.
But lat this thyng be secree, I yow preye,
For yet to-nyght thise beestes moot I beye.
And fare now wel, myn owene cosyn deere;
Graunt mercy of youre cost and of youre
   cheere."   1470
   This noble marchant gentilly anon
Answerde and seyde, "O cosyn myn, daun John,
Now sikerly this is a smal requeste.
My gold is youres, whan that it yow leste,
And nat oonly my gold, but my chaffare.   1475
Take what yow list, God shilde that ye spare.
   But o thyng is, ye knowe it wel ynogh,
Of chapmen, that hir moneie is hir plogh.
We may creaunce whil we have a name;
But goldlees for to be, it is no game.   1480
Paye it agayn whan it lith in youre ese;
After my myght ful fayn wolde I yow plese."
   Thise hundred frankes he fette forth anon,
And prively he took hem to daun John.
No wight in al this world wiste of this lone, 1485
Savynge this marchant and daun John allone.
They drynke, and speke, and rome a while and
   pleye,
Til that daun John rideth to his abbeye.
   The morwe cam, and forth this marchant
   rideth
To Flaundres-ward; his prentys wel hym
   gydeth,   1490

1428. oure chapmanhede, the conduct of our business. **1432. buxom,** gracious. **1433. curious,** careful. **1434. honestly,** honorably. **1439. shette,** shut. **1440. lette,** linger, delay. **1445. At after-dyner.** It is possible to consider *at after* as a comp. prep. (= after), but since the noun *after-mete* (cf. E 1921) is found in ME. preceded by *an, the, this* (see *MED*) it is fair to assume that *after-dyner* (cf. also F 918) and *after-soper* (F 302, 1219) are already valid compounds in Chaucer, although not otherwise recorded until the sixteenth cent. The time indicated here is the late forenoon. **sobrely,** gravely. **1449. seint Austyn,** St Augustine. **1452. Atemprely,** temperately. **namely,** especially. **1453. strange fare,** the behavior of strangers, formality. **1460. lene,** lend. **1461. wyke,** week. **1462. beye,** buy. **1463. To stoore with a place,** to stock a piece of land with. **1466. a mile way,** *i.e.* by as much time as it takes to walk a mile. **1467. secree,** confidential. **1468. moot I beye,** must I buy. **1470. Graunt mercy,** many thanks. **cost,** *i.e.* of his entertainment. **1471. gentilly,** courteously. **1473 sikerly,** surely. **1474. whan that it yow leste,** when you please. **1475. chaffare,** wares, goods. **1476. God shilde . . .,** God fobid that you should refrain. **1477. But o thyng is . . . Of chapmen,** but there is one thing about business men. **1478. plogh,** plow, what they work with. **1479. creaunce,** receive on credit. **1483. fette,** fetched. **1484. took,** delivered, handed. **1485. lone,** loan.

Til he cam into Brugges murily.
Now gooth this marchant faste and bisily
Aboute his nede, and byeth and creaunceth.
He neither pleyeth at the dees ne daunceth,
But as a marchaunt, shortly for to telle, 1495
He let his lyf, and there I lete hym dwelle.

The Sonday next the marchant was agon,
To Seint-Denys ycomen is daun John,
With crowne and berd al fressh and newe
  yshave.
In al the hous ther nas so litel a knave, 1500
Ne no wight elles, that he nas ful fayn
For that my lord daun John was come agayn.
And shortly to the point right for to gon,
This faire wyf acorded with daun John
That for thise hundred frankes he sholde al nyght
Have hire in his armes bolt upright; 1506
And this acord parfourned was in dede.
In myrthe al nyght a bisy lyf they lede
Til it was day, that daun John wente his way,
And bad the meynee "farewel, have good day!"
For noon of hem, ne no wight in the toun, 1511
Hath of daun John right no suspecioun.
And forth he rydeth hoom to his abbeye,
Or where hym list; namoore of hym I seye.

This marchant, whan that ended was the faire,
To Seint-Denys he gan for to repaire, 1516
And with his wyf he maketh feeste and cheere,
And telleth hire that chaffare is so deere
That nedes moste he make a chevyssaunce;
For he was bounden in a reconyssaunce 1520
To paye twenty thousand sheeld anon.
For which this marchant is to Parys gon
To borwe of certeine freendes that he hadde
A certeyn frankes; and somme with him he
  ladde.

And whan that he was come into the toun, 1525
For greet chiertee and greet affeccioun,
Unto daun John he gooth hym first, to pleye;
Nat for to axe or borwe of hym moneye,
But for to wite and seen of his welfare,
And for to tellen hym of his chaffare, 1530
As freendes doon whan they been met yfeere.
Daun John hym maketh feeste and murye
  cheere,
And he hym tolde agayn, ful specially,
How he hadde wel yboght and graciously,
Thanked be God, al hool his marchandise; 1535
Save that he moste, in alle maner wise,
Maken a chevyssaunce, as for his beste,
And thanne he sholde been in joye and reste.
Daun John answerde, "Certes, I am fayn
That ye in heele ar comen hom agayn. 1540
And if that I were riche, as have I blisse,
Of twenty thousand sheeld sholde ye nat
  mysse,
For ye so kyndely this oother day
Lente me gold; and as I kan and may,
I thanke yow, by God and by seint Jame! 1545
But nathelees, I took unto oure dame,
Youre wyf, at hom, the same gold ageyn
Upon youre bench; she woot it wel, certeyn,
By certeyn tokenes that I kan yow telle.
Now, by youre leve, I may no lenger dwelle;
Oure abbot wole out of this toun anon, 1551
And in his compaignye moot I goon.
Grete wel oure dame, myn owene nece sweete,
And fare wel, deere cosyn, til we meete!"

This marchant, which that was ful war and
  wys, 1555
Creanced hath, and payd eek in Parys
To certeyn Lumbardes, redy in hir hond,

1491. **murily,** pleasantly, without mishap. 1493. **creaunceth,** obtains credit. 1494. **dees,** dice. 1496. **He let his lyf,** he lives. *Let* is the contracted form of *ledeth,* the reading of some manuscripts. 1500. **knave,** boy. 1504. **acorded,** agreed. 1506. **upright,** face up; *bolt* implies "as straight as an arrow," therefore she was stretched out. 1510. **meynee,** household. The line is not to be understood literally; he departed before any of the household were up. 1515. **faire,** fair, market. 1518. **chaffare,** merchandise. 1519. **make a chevyssaunce,** arrange a loan. 1520. **reconyssaunce,** recognizance, a kind of promissory note. 1521. **sheeld,** gold coins. See note to A 278. 1524. **A certeyn frankes,** a certain number of frances. **he ladde,** he took along. These he paid for the loan, but he still had to pay the loan in full. This seems to have been a way of circumventing the ecclesiastical condemnation of interest. 1526. **chiertee,** fondness. 1530. **chaffare,** dealings. 1531. **yfeere,** together. 1532. **maketh feeste,** welcomes, makes much of. 1536. **in alle maner wise,** under any circumstances. 1537. **as for his beste,** in the best way he could. 1540. **heele,** health. 1549. **tokenes,** evidence, proof. 1556. **Creanced hath,** obtained credit. 1557. **Lumbardes,** famous as bankers and money-lenders.

The somme of gold, and gat of hem his bond;
And hoom he gooth, murie as a papejay,
For wel he knew he stood in swich array   1560
That nedes moste he wynne in that viage
A thousand frankes aboven al his costage.
  His wyf ful redy mette hym atte gate,
As she was wont of oold usage algate,
And al that nyght in myrthe they bisette;   1565
For he was riche and cleerly out of dette.
Whan it was day, this marchant gan embrace
His wyf al newe, and kiste hire on hir face,
And up he gooth and maketh it ful tough.
  "Namoore," quod she, "by God, ye have
        ynough!"   1570
And wantownely agayn with hym she pleyde,
Til atte laste thus this marchant seyde:
"By God," quod he, "I am a litel wrooth
With yow, my wyf, although it be me looth.
And woot ye why? by God, as that I gesse   1575
That ye han maad a manere straungenesse
Bitwixen me and my cosyn daun John.
Ye sholde han warned me, er I had gon,
That he yow hadde an hundred frankes payed
By redy tokene; and heeld hym yvele apayed,
For that I to hym spak of chevyssaunce;   1581
Me semed so, as by his contenaunce.
But nathelees, by God, oure hevene kyng,
I thoughte nat to axen hym no thyng.
I prey thee, wyf, ne do namoore so;   1585
Telle me alwey, er that I fro thee go,
If any dettour hath in myn absence
Ypayed thee, lest thurgh thy necligence
I myghte hym axe a thing that he hath payed."
  This wyf was nat afered nor affrayed,   1590

But boldely she seyde, and that anon;
"Marie, I deffie the false monk, daun John!
I kepe nat of his tokenes never a deel;
He took me certeyn gold, that woot I weel,—
What! yvel thedam on his monkes snowte!   1595
For, God it woot, I wende, withouten doute,
That he hadde yeve it me bycause of yow,
To doon therwith myn honour and my prow,
For cosynage, and eek for beele cheere
That he hath had ful ofte tymes heere.   1600
But sith I se I stonde in this disjoynt,
I wol answere yow shortly to the poynt.
Ye han mo slakkere dettours than am I!
For I wol paye yow wel and redily
Fro day to day, and if so be I faille,   1605
I am youre wyf; score it upon my taille,
And I shal paye as soone as ever I may.
For by my trouthe, I have on myn array,
And nat on wast, bistowed every deel;
And for I have bistowed it so weel   1610
For youre honour, for Goddes sake, I seye,
As be nat wrooth, but lat us laughe and pleye.
Ye shal my joly body have to wedde;
By God, I wol nat paye yow but a-bedde!
Forgyve it me, myn owene spouse deere;   1615
Turne hiderward, and maketh bettre cheere."
  This marchant saugh ther was no remedie,
And for to chide it nere but folie,
Sith that the thyng may nat amended be.
"Now wyf," he seyde, "and I foryeve it thee;
But, by thy lyf, ne be namoore so large.   1621
Keep bet my good, this yeve I thee in charge."
Thus endeth now my tale, and God us sende
Taillynge ynough unto oure lyves ende. Amen

Heere endeth the Shipmannes Tale.

1558. **and gat of hem his bond.** The merchant in Bruges from whom he obtained a loan has apparently (we would say) discounted his note with Lombard money-lenders in Paris. 1559. **murie as a papejay,** merry as a popinjay (parrot). Cf. our "happy as a lark." 1560. **stood in swich array,** was in such a position. 1561. **in that viage,** on that trip. 1562. **costage,** expenses. 1563. **atte,** at the. 1564. **algate,** always. 1565. **bisette,** occupied. 1569. **maketh it ful tough,** shows great vigor. 1580. **By redy tokene,** by clear evidence. **heeld hym yvele apayed,** (he) took it amiss, was displeased. 1590. **affrayed,** frightened, afraid. 1592. **Marie,** by the Virgin Mary. **deffie,** defy, repudiate. 1593. **I kepe nat,** I care not. 1594. **took,** handed. 1595. **yvel thedam,** misfortune; *lit.* ill thriving. 1596. **I wende,** I thought. 1598. **prow,** profit, advantage. 1599. **beele cheere,** hospitality. 1601. **disjoynt,** awkward situation. 1606. **taille,** tally, *i.e.* charge it to my account; but it is clear that an obscene pun is involved. 1609. **wast,** wastefulness. 1612. **As be,** be. 1613. **to wedde,** as a pledge. 1618. **nere,** were not (it would be nothing). 1621. **large,** liberal, free in spending. 1622. **bet,** better. **this yeve I thee in charge,** I charge thee. 1624. **Taillynge.** See comment on line 1606. It may be observed that the note on which the tale ends is repeated in the closing lines of *The Wife of Bath's Tale.*

Bihoold the murie wordes of the Hoost to the Shipman and to the lady Prioresse.

"Wel seyd, by *corpus dominus*," quod oure
  Hoost,   1625
"Now longe moote thou saille by the cost,
Sire gentil maister, gentil maryneer!
God yeve the monk a thousand last quade yeer!
A ha! felawes! beth war of swich a jape!
The monk putte in the mannes hood an ape,
And in his wyves eek, by Seint Austyn!   1631
Draweth no monkes moore unto youre in.
  But now passe over, and lat us seke aboute,

Who shal now telle first of al this route
Another tale;" and with that word he sayde,
As curteisly as it had been a mayde,   1636
"My lady Prioresse, by youre leve,
So that I wiste I sholde yow nat greve,
I wolde demen that ye tellen sholde
A tale next, if so were that ye wolde.   1640
Now wol ye vouchesauf, my lady deere?"
  "Gladly," quod she, and seyde as ye shal
  heere.

The Prioress's Tale

PROLOGUE OF THE PRIORESS'S TALE

The Prologe of the Prioresses Tale.

Domine dominus noster

"O Lord, oure Lord, thy name how merveil-
  lous
Is in this large world ysprad," quod she;
"For noght oonly thy laude precious   1645
Parfourned is by men of dignitee,
But by the mouth of children thy bountee
Parfourned is, for on the brest soukynge
Somtyme shewen they thyn heriynge.

Wherfore in laude, as I best kan or may,   1650
Of thee and of the white lylye flour

Which that the bar, and is a mayde alway,
To telle a storie I wol do my labour;
Nat that I may encreessen hir honour,
For she hirself is honour and the roote   1655
Of bountee, next hir Sone, and soules boote.

O mooder Mayde! o mayde Mooder free!
O bussh unbrent, brennynge in Moyses sighte,
That ravysedest doun fro the Deitee,
Thurgh thyn humblesse, the Goost that in
  th'alighte,   1660

1625. corpus dominus, properly *domini*, the Lord's body, but allowance must be made for the Host's Latin. **1626. moote,** mayest. **1628. last,** load (sing. for plur. as in *ten foot, two ton*, etc.). **quade,** bad. The phrase means "a thousand loads of bad years." **1630. putte in the mannes hood an ape.** Although the expression has not been found elsewhere in Middle English, it clearly means to make a fool of someone. **1631. And in his wyves eek,** and also in his wife's. **1632. in,** lodging, dwelling-place. **1634. route,** company. **1638. So that,** provided. **1639. demen,** judge, decide. **1643. *Domine dominus noster*** . . . The phrase, translated in this and the following lines, is the opening of Psalm 8, which is recited at the beginning of the first nocturn of Matins in the *Little Office of the Blessed Virgin.* **1646. Parfourned,** carried out, brought to pass. **1649. heriynge,** praise. **1651. white lylye flour,** a common symbol of the Virgin. **1652. Which that the bar,** which bore thee. **1658. O bussh unbrent . . .** The burning bush which remained uninjured (cf. *Exodus*, 3:2–4) was a frequent symbol of the Virgin's purity in spite of motherhood. The idea is elaborated in Chaucer's *ABC*, a hymn to the Virgin. **1659. ravysedest,** *lit.* snatched (drew). The antecedent of *That* is *mooder.*

Of whos vertu, whan he thyn herte lighte,
Conceyved was the Fadres sapience,
Help me to telle it in thy reverence!

Lady, thy bountee, thy magnificence,
Thy vertu, and thy grete humylitee,   1665
Ther may no tonge expresse in no science;
For somtyme, Lady, er men praye to thee,
Thou goost biforn of thy benyngnytee,
And getest us the lyght, of thy preyere,
To gyden us unto thy Sone so deere.   1670

My konnyng is so wayk, o blisful Queene,
For to declare thy grete worthynesse
That I ne may the weighte nat susteene;
But as a child of twelf monthe oold, or lesse,
That kan unnethe any word expresse,   1675
Right so fare I, and therfore I yow preye,
Gydeth my song that I shal of yow seye."

Explicit.

THE PRIORESS'S TALE

Heere bigynneth the Prioresses Tale.

Ther was in Asye, in a greet citee,
Amonges Cristene folk, a Jewerye,
Sustened by a lord of that contree   1680
For foul usure and lucre of vileynye,
Hateful to Crist and to his compaignye;
And thurgh the strete men myghte ride or
  wende,
For it was free and open at eyther ende.

A litel scole of Cristen folk ther stood   1685
Doun at the ferther ende, in which ther were
Children an heep, ycomen of Cristen blood,
That lerned in that scole yeer by yere
Swich manere doctrine as men used there,
This is to seyn, to syngen and to rede,   1690
As smale children doon in hire childhede.

1661. **lighte.** The sense may be either "cheered" or "illuminated," as Skeat shows. 1662. **sapience,** wisdom (Christ). 1666. **science,** art, manifestation of skill. 1669. **of,** by, through. 1671. **wayk,** weak. 1675. **unnethe,** scarcely. 1677. **song,** poem, narrative. The word was at times used where musical accompaniment is unlikely, as in *Genesis and Exodus* (l. 13) or *On God Ureisun of Ure Lefdi* (l. 170), although the possibility of some form of chant can seldom be ruled out.
 The Prioress's Tale. The story told by the Prioress belongs to the medieval literary type known as a Miracle of the Virgin. Nearly 2000 examples of such stories have been found (see the index by *incipits* in *Analecta Bollandiana*, Vol. XXI). A good account of the type will be found in Eileen Power's introduction to Johannes Herolt's *Miracles of the Blessed Virgin Mary* in the *Broadway Medieval Library*. Most Miracles of the Virgin are in Latin, but medieval versions of a number are to be found in all the vernacular languages of western Europe. Each narrative records an instance in which the Virgin intercedes in behalf of some one in need of help, some one who has earned the Virgin's favor by his devotion to her. A well-known modern example is John Davidson's *Ballad of a Nun*. The many versions of the story told by the Prioress are discussed in Carleton Brown's *A Study of the Miracle of Our Lady Told by Chaucer's Prioress* (1910; *Chaucer Soc.*, 2nd Ser., 45), which should be supplemented by Margaret H. Statler's "The Analogues of Chaucer's Prioress' Tale: the Relation of Group C to Group A," *PMLA*, lxv. 896–910. Brown's own later views are found in his discussion in *Sources and Analogues*. The tale is generally believed to belong to the period of *The Canterbury Tales* and to have been written for the Prioress, but it is in the seven-line stanza associated with the period of the *Troilus* and may have been written before work on *The Canterbury Tales* had begun.
 1678. **Asye,** possibly here meaning Asia Minor, as Tyrwhitt suggested. 1679. **Jewerye,** a Jews' quarter. 1680. **Sustened,** maintained. 1681. **usure,** usury, which included all lending of money for interest, a practice forbidden by the Church. **lucre of vileynye,** wicked gain, the English equivalent of *turpe lucrum* in medieval canon law. It sometimes included usury, sometimes was coupled with it (as in the present line). It then meant excessive profit, speculative gain, profit through deception, etc. See J. A. Yunck, *N & Q*, ccv. 165–7, and J. Baldwin, *Medieval Theories of the Just Price* (Philadelphia, 1959). 1689. **doctrine,** teaching, things taught.

Among thise children was a wydwes sone,
A litel clergeoun, seven yeer of age,
That day by day to scole was his wone,
And eek also, where as he saugh th'ymage   1695
Of Cristes mooder, hadde he in usage,
As hym was taught, to knele adoun and seye
His *Ave Marie*, as he goth by the weye.

Thus hath this wydwe hir litel sone ytaught
Oure blisful Lady, Cristes mooder deere,   1700
To worshipe ay, and he forgat it naught,
For sely child wol alday soone leere.
But ay, whan I remembre on this mateere,
Seint Nicholas stant evere in my presence,
For he so yong to Crist dide reverence.   1705

This litel child, his litel book lernynge,
As he sat in the scole at his prymer,
He *Alma redemptoris* herde synge,
As children lerned hire antiphoner;
And as he dorste, he drough hym ner and
     ner,   1710
And herkned ay the wordes and the noote,
Til he the firste vers koude al by rote.

Noght wiste he what this Latyn was to seye,
For he so yong and tendre was of age.
But on a day his felawe gan he preye   1715
T'expounden hym this song in his langage,
Or telle hym why this song was in usage;

This preyde he hym to construe and declare
Ful often tyme upon his knowes bare.

His felawe, which that elder was than he,   1720
Answerde hym thus: "This song, I have herd
     seye,
Was maked of oure blisful Lady free,
Hire to salue, and eek hire for to preye
To been oure help and socour whan we deye.
I kan namoore expounde in this mateere;   1725
I lerne song, I kan but smal grammeere."

"And is this song maked in reverence
Of Cristes mooder?" seyde this innocent.
"Now, certes, I wol do my diligence
To konne it al er Cristemasse be went.   1730
Though that I for my prymer shal be shent,
And shal be beten thries in an houre,
I wol it konne Oure Lady for to honoure!"

His felawe taughte hym homward prively,
Fro day to day, til he koude it by rote,   1735
And thanne he song it wel and boldely.
Fro word to word, acordynge with the note.
Twies a day it passed thurgh his throte,
To scoleward and homward whan he wente;
On Cristes mooder set was his entente.   1740

As I have seyd, thurghout the Juerie,
This litel child, as he cam to and fro,

1693. clergeoun, pupil. For an illuminating discussion of the little schoolboy, the type of school implied, the character of his instruction, and the schoolbook which he studied see Carleton Brown, "Chaucer's 'Litel Clergeon,'" *MP*, III. 467–91. These matters will be touched on in later notes. **1694. was his wone,** *i.e.* was accustomed to go. **That . . . his,** whose. See language, § 61 for additional examples. **1695. where as,** where. **1698. Ave Marie,** Hail, Mary,—the beginning of a prayer constructed from the words of the Annunciation; cf. *Luke,* 1:28 and 42. **1702. For sely child wol alday soone leere,** a common proverb: the good child will always learn quickly. **1703. But ay . . .** Whenever I think about this I always see before me St. Nicholas because . . . In the *Legenda Aurea* we are told that as an infant he took the breast only once on Wednesdays and Fridays. Here the association of ideas is all the more natural since St. Nicholas was the patron saint of schoolboys. **1707. prymer,** a prayer-book for the laity containing psalms and other devotional exercises; it was sometimes called a Book of Hours (*Horae Beatae Mariae Virginis*). It was commonly used as an elementary schoolbook, in which case it often contained at the beginning the alphabet, the Lord's Prayer, the Apostle's Creed, the Ten Commandments, etc. It was originally in Latin (as was probably the little clergeon's) and the child learned the contents by rote, later construing the sentences in the process of learning his grammar. See the article by Carleton Brown, mentioned in the note to l. 1693, and C. Wordsworth and H. Littlehales, *The Old Service-Books of the English Church* (London, 1904), chap. IX. **1708. Alma redemptoris,** an antiphon, used especially in the offices from Advent to Candlemas: *Alma redemptoris mater, quae pervia coeli porta manes,* etc. (Beloved mother of the Redeemer, who remainest heaven's open gate . . .). **1709. antiphoner,** a service book containing antiphons (and other chants) for the Canonical Hours. **1710. ner and ner,** nearer and nearer. **1711. noote,** music. **1712. koude,** knew. **1713. was to seye,** meant. **1719. knowes,** knees. **1723. salue,** salute, greet. **1726. kan,** know. **1731. shent,** shamed, scolded (for not knowing his primer).

Ful murily than wolde he synge and crie
O *Alma redemptoris* everemo.
The swetnesse hath his herte perced so   1745
Of Cristes mooder that, to hire to preye,
He kan nat stynte of syngyng by the weye.

Oure firste foo, the serpent Sathanas,
That hath in Jues herte his waspes nest,
Up swal, and seide, "O Hebrayk peple,
    allas!   1750
Is this to yow a thyng that is honest,
That swich a boy shal walken as hym lest
In youre despit, and synge of swich sentence,
Which is agayn youre lawes reverence?"

Fro thennes forth the Jues han conspired   1755
This innocent out of this world to chace.
An homycide therto han they hyred,
That in an aleye hadde a privee place;
And as the child gan forby for to pace,
This cursed Jew hym hente, and heeld hym
    faste,   1760
And kitte his throte, and in a pit hym caste.

I seye that in a wardrobe they hym threwe
Where as thise Jewes purgen hire entraille.
O cursed folk of Herodes al newe,
What may youre yvel entente yow availle? 1765
Mordre wol out, certeyn, it wol nat faille,
And namely ther th'onour of God shal sprede;
The blood out crieth on youre cursed dede.

O martir, sowded to virginitee,
Now maystow syngen, folwynge evere in
    oon   1770

The white Lamb celestial—quod she—
Of which the grete evaungelist, Seint John,
In Pathmos wroot, which seith that they that
    goon
Biforn this Lamb, and synge a song al newe,
That nevere, flesshly, wommen they ne
    knewe.   1775

This povre wydwe awaiteth al that nyght
After hir litel child, but he cam noght;
For which, as soone as it was dayes lyght,
With face pale of drede and bisy thoght,
She hath at scole and elleswhere hym soght, 1780
Til finally she gan so fer espie
That he last seyn was in the Juerie.

With moodres pitee in hir brest enclosed,
She gooth, as she were half out of hir mynde,
To every place where she hath supposed   1785
By liklihede hir litel child to fynde;
And evere on Cristes mooder meeke and kynde
She cride, and atte laste thus she wroghte:
Among the cursed Jues she hym soghte.

She frayneth and she preyeth pitously   1790
To every Jew that dwelte in thilke place,
To telle hire if hir child wente oght forby.
They seyde "nay"; but Jhesu, of his grace,
Yaf in hir thoght, inwith a litel space,
That in that place after hir sone she cryde,   1795
Where he was casten in a pit bisyde.

O grete God, that parfournest thy laude
By mouth of innocentz, lo, heere thy myght!
This gemme of chastite, this emeraude,

1743. murily, merrily. 1747. stynte of, stop, cease from. 1750. Up swal, swelled up. 1751. honest, honorable. 1752. as hym lest, as he pleases. 1753. sentence, meaning, subject. 1759. forby, by. pace, pass. 1760. hente, seized. 1761. kitte, cut. 1762. wardrobe, privy. 1764. Herodes . . . newe, new Herods. 1766. Mordre wol out, murder will out. 1769. sowded to, made fast in. 1770. evere in oon, always, continually. 1771. quod she. Chaucer momentarily forgets that the Prioress herself is speaking. 1773. Pathmos, Patmos, a small island in the Aegean, in which St. John was exiled and where it is commonly believed he wrote the Apocalypse. For the vision of the 144,000 virgins, referred to in the next two lines see *Revelation*, 14:1–4. Children dying in their early years (innocents) were regarded as properly associated with the group. See *Pearl*, ed. E. V. Gordon, (Oxford, 1953), pp. xxv–xxvi, to which my attention was directed by Prof. Robinson's note. 1775. flesshly, carnally. 1779. bisy thoght, anxiety. 1781. espie, find out. 1783. pitee, tenderness. 1788. wroghte, acted, did. 1790. frayneth, inquires. 1792. oght, at all. 1794. Yaf in hir thoght, gave her an idea. inwith, within. space, space of time. 1795. That, so that. 1796. bisyde, nearby. 1797. parfournest, bringest to pass. 1798. lo, heere thy myght! behold here thy might! 1799. emeraude. The emerald and the ruby were associated with chastity and martyrdom repectively. See J. J. Lynch, *MLN*, LVII. 440–1.

And eek of martirdom the ruby bright, 1800
Ther he with throte ykorven lay upright,
He *Alma redemptoris* gan to synge
So loude that al the place gan to rynge.

The Cristene folk that thurgh the strete wente
In coomen for to wondre upon this thyng, 1805
And hastily they for the provost sente;
He cam anon withouten tariyng,
And herieth Crist that is of hevene kyng,
And eek his mooder, honour of mankynde,
And after that the Jewes leet he bynde. 1810

This child with pitous lamentacioun
Up taken was, syngynge his song alway,
And with honour of greet processioun
They carien hym unto the nexte abbay.
His mooder swownynge by his beere lay; 1815
Unnethe myghte the peple that was theere
This newe Rachel brynge fro his beere.

With torment and with shameful deeth echon
This provost dooth thise Jewes for to sterve
That of this mordre wiste, and that anon. 1820
He nolde no swich cursednesse observe.
"Yvele shal have that yvele wol deserve";
Therfore with wilde hors he dide hem drawe,
And after that he heng hem by the lawe.

Upon this beere ay lith this innocent 1825
Biforn the chief auter, whil the masse laste;
And after that, the abbot with his covent
Han sped hem for to burien hym ful faste;
And whan they hooly water on hym caste,
Yet spak this child, whan spreynd was hooly
  water, 1830
And song *O Alma redemptoris mater!*

This abbot, which that was an hooly man,
As monkes been—or elles oghte be—
This yonge child to conjure he bigan,
And seyde, "O deere child, I halse thee, 1835
In vertu of the hooly Trinitee,
Tel me what is thy cause for to synge,
Sith that thy throte is kut to my semynge?"

"My throte is kut unto my nekke-boon,"
Seyde this child, "and, as by wey of kynde, 1840
I sholde have dyed, ye, longe tyme agon.
But Jesu Crist, as ye in bookes fynde,
Wil that his glorie laste and be in mynde,
And for the worship of his Mooder deere
Yet may I synge *O Alma* loude and cleere. 1845

"This welle of mercy, Cristes mooder sweete,
I loved alwey, as after my konnynge;
And whan that I my lyf sholde forlete,
To me she cam, and bad me for to synge
This anthem verraily in my deyynge, 1850
As ye han herd, and whan that I hadde songe,
Me thoughte she leyde a greyn upon my tonge.

"Wherfore I synge, and synge moot certeyn,
In honour of that blisful Mayden free,
Til fro my tonge of taken is the greyn; 1855
And after that thus seyde she to me:
'My litel child, now wol I fecche thee,
Whan that the greyn is fro thy tonge ytake.
Be nat agast, I wol thee nat forsake.'"

This hooly monk, this abbot, hym meene
  I, 1860
His tonge out caughte, and took awey the
  greyn,
And he yaf up the goost ful softely.
And whan this abbot hadde this wonder seyn,

1801. **Ther,** where. **ykorven,** cut. **upright,** face up. 1805. **coomen,** came. **wondre,** show amazement. 1806. **provost,** chief magistrate. 1808. **herieth,** praises. 1810. **leet he bynde,** he caused to be bound. 1814. **nexte,** nearest. 1816. **Unnethe,** scarcely. 1817. **Rachel,** Rachel symbolized the grieving mothers of Israel at the slaughter of the innocents. 1818. **torment,** torture. 1819. **dooth,** causes. **sterve,** die. 1821. **observe,** tolerate. 1823. **hors,** horses. 1824. **heng,** hanged. 1826. **auter,** altar. 1827. **covent,** convent, the body of monks. 1830. **spreynd,** sprinkled. 1835. **halse,** conjure, beseech. 1840. **by wey of kynde,** in the course of nature. 1843. **Wil,** wills. 1848. **forlete,** give up. 1852. **greyn,** seed, probably the grain of paradise (*cardamom*), as suggested by Father Beichner, *Speculum,* XXXVI. 302–7. 1855. **of,** off, away.

His salte teeris trikled doun as reyn,
And gruf he fil al plat upon the grounde,　　1865
And stille he lay as he had ben ybounde.

The covent eek lay on the pavement
Wepynge, and herying Cristes mooder deere,
And after that they ryse, and forth been went,
And tooken awey this martir from his
　　beere;　　　　　　　　　　　　　　　　1870
And in a tombe of marbul stones cleere

Enclosen they his litel body sweete.
Ther he is now, God leve us for to meete!

　　O yonge Hugh of Lyncoln, slayn also
With cursed Jewes, as it is notable,　　1875
For it is but a litel while ago,
Preye eek for us, we synful folk unstable,
That, of his mercy, God so merciable
On us his grete mercy multiplie,
For reverence of his mooder Marie. Amen　1880

Heere is ended the Prioresses Tale.

Sir Thopas

PROLOGUE TO SIR THOPAS

Bihoold the murye wordes of the Hoost to Chaucer.

Whan seyd was al this miracle, every man
As sobre was that wonder was to se,
Til that oure Hooste japen tho bigan,
And thanne at erst he looked upon me,　　1884
And seyde thus: "What man artow?" quod he;
"Thou lookest as thou woldest fynde an hare,
For evere upon the ground I se thee stare.

"Approche neer, and looke up murily.
Now war yow, sires, and lat this man have place!
He in the waast is shape as wel as I;　　1890
This were a popet in an arm t'enbrace
For any womman, smal and fair of face.

He semeth elvyssh by his contenaunce,
For unto no wight dooth he daliaunce.　　1894

"Sey now somwhat, syn oother folk han sayd;
Telle us a tale of myrthe, and that anon."
"Hooste," quod I, "ne beth nat yvele apayd,
For oother tale certes kan I noon,
But of a rym I lerned longe agoon."
"Ye, that is good," quod he; "now shul we
　　heere　　　　　　　　　　　　　　　1900
Som deyntee thyng, me thynketh by his
　　cheere."

Explicit.

1865. **gruf,** grovelling (adv.). **plat,** flat. 1868. **herying,** praising. 1869. **ryse.** Some MSS read *roos.* 1873. **Ther . . . meete!** God grant that we may meet where he is now! 1874. **Hugh of Lyncoln,** a boy supposed to have been murdered by Jews in 1255. The incident is reported by the St. Albans chronicler, Matthew Paris. 1877. **unstable,** subject to the vicissitudes of fortune. 1882. **As . . . to se,** so sober that it was amazing. 1883. **japen,** joke. 1884. **at erst.** The phrase seems often to be a mere intensive: "then finally," "then indeed." 1886. **Thou lookest . . .** Chaucer's whimsical description of himself need not be taken literally down to the last detail, but in its main lines it agrees with the description in *Lenvoy a Scogan,* at least with respect to his portliness. He was, however, quite willing to make fun of himself, and the reference to his shyness, if he had the opposite reputation among his friends may have been intended to get a laugh. 1891. **popet,** poppet, a small or dainty person. 1893. **elvyssh,** abstracted, peevish. 1894. **dooth he daliaunce,** engages in conversation, is sociable. 1897. **yvele apayd,** dissatisfied, displeased. 1901. **deyntee,** worthwhile. The word (L. *dignitatem*) is from the same root as *digne,* worthy (L. *dignus*).

SIR THOPAS

Heere bigynneth Chaucers Tale of Thopas.

The First Fit

Listeth, lordes, in good entent,
And I wol telle verrayment
  Of myrthe and of solas;
Al of a knyght was fair and gent   1905
In bataille and in tourneyment,
  His name was sire Thopas.

Yborn he was in fer contree,
In Flaundres, al biyonde the see,
  At Poperyng, in the place.   1910
His fader was a man ful free,
And lord he was of that contree,
  As it was Goddes grace.

Sire Thopas wax a doghty swayn;
Whit was his face as payndemayn,   1915
  His lippes rede as rose;
His rode is lyk scarlet in grayn,
And I yow telle in good certayn,
  He hadde a semely nose.

His heer, his berd was lyk saffroun,   1920
That to his girdel raughte adoun;
  His shoon of cordewane.
Of Brugges were his hosen broun,
His robe was of syklatoun,
  That coste many a jane.   1925

Sir Thopas, *Sir Thopas* is a parody of one type of English metrical romance. The metrical romance originally had had aristocratic appeal, but by the end of the fourteenth century it had fallen somewhat in the social scale and was to end its career in the seventeenth century as material for penny chapbooks. It is clear that Chaucer, whose taste had been formed on the *Roman de la Rose* and other French allegorical love poetry, was mildly contemptuous of such minstrel entertainment, but he could not have failed to hear some of these stories recited many times during his life. In their plot, characters, jog-trot rhythm, and verbal clichés they lent themselves readily to burlesque. The basic verse form is that known as "romance sixes," six-line stanzas riming *aabaab* or *aabccb*, often combined in pairs to form stanzas of twelve lines.

It is altogether likely that at some time Chaucer had amused himself by undertaking a parody of the type. The skit is not something that he would have been likely to carry through to the end. But he was also not one to waste material which he had on hand when an opportunity to make use of it presented itself, and *The Canterbury Tales* must have offered a number of such opportunites. But how use the *Sir Thopas?* Any one of the pilgrims who recited it would invite ridicule. Chaucer solved the problem by assigning it to himself. But how use something that was incomplete? Chaucer solved this problem with dramatic effectiveness by having Harry Baily interrupt him and refuse to let him go on.

If the suggestion here made is valid, it does not preclude the possibility that Chaucer combined with his satire of a literary type satirical thrusts at the Flemings. That satire of the Flemings was intended was argued by Miss Winstanley and, with differences, by the late Professor Manly (see the former's edition of *The Prioress's Tale* and *Sir Thopas* (Cambridge, 1922), and the latter's paper in *E & S*, vol. XIII), but their views were convincingly challenged by W. W. Lawrence (*PMLA*, L. 81–91). So questionable a theory can hardly be made the basis for dating the little extravaganza, and its date of composition must remain open.

Parallels to situations, ideas, particular phrases, and clichés in Chaucer's parody have been found in many Middle English romances, for they are ubiquitous. They are especially numerous in *Guy of Warwick*. A generous representation will be found in the discussion of the tale by Laura Hibbard Loomis in *Sources and Analogues*. That Chaucer had some extensive collection of romances, such as that in the famous Auchinleck MS, is suggested by Mrs. Loomis in the volume just mentioned and in her paper in *Essays and Studies in Honor of Carleton Brown* (New York, 1940). But whether his acquaintance with them was through the eye or the ear, or both, the best preparation for the enjoyment of Chaucer's satire would be the reading of one or more of those which he mentions.

1902. Listeth, lordes . . ., A very common formula for the opening of romances and other types of narrative recited by minstrels. *Lordes* is a complimentary term with little more force than our "Ladies and gentlemen." In the notes that follow, similar clichés will be pointed out only in exceptional cases. **1903. verrayment,** truly. **1905. gent,** well-bred. **1907. Thopas.** The word is the same as *topaz* and as Skeat remarked "an excellent title for such a gem of a knight." No other symbolism need be supposed. **1908. fer,** far. **1910. Poperyng,** Poperinge, a small Flemish town, which makes ridiculous the phrase *in fer contree* (another romance commonplace). **in the place,** probably a mere rimetag, but it may mean "market-place," the center of town, or "manor-house," as Skeat suggests. **1915. payndemayn,** *panis dominicus* (bread of our Lord), white bread of the finest quality. **1917. rode,** complexion. **grayn,** Scarlet Grain, an insect, the female of the cochineal, used to produce the dye of that name. **1921. raughte,** reached. **1922. cordewane,** Cordovan leather. **1924. syklatoun,** a light-weight, costly material, generally red. The word *scarlet* is etymologically related. **1925. jane,** a small silver coin of Genoa.

He koude hunte at wilde deer,
And ride an haukyng for river
  With grey goshauk on honde; *(a lower grade of hawk)*
Therto he was a good archeer;
Of wrastlyng was ther noon his peer,   1930
  Ther any ram shal stonde. *he wrestles. The Miller does, Thus, Not Knight.*

Ful many a mayde, bright in bour,
They moorne for hym paramour,
  Whan hem were bet to slepe;
But he was chaast and no lechour,   1935
And sweete as is the brembul flour
  That bereth the rede hepe.

And so bifel upon a day,
For sothe, as I yow telle may,
  Sire Thopas wolde out ride.   1940
He worth upon his steede gray,
And in his hand a launcegay,
  A long swerd by his side.

PUN → He prikesth thurgh a fair forest,
Therinne is many a wilde best,   1945
  Ye, bothe bukke and hare;
And as he priketh north and est,
I telle it yow, hym hadde almost
  Bitid a sory care.

Ther spryngen herbes grete and smale,   1950
The lycorys and the cetewale,
  And many a clowe-gylofre;
And notemuge to putte in ale,
Wheither it be moyste or stale,
  Or for to leye in cofre.   1955

The briddes synge, it is no nay,
The sparhauk and the papejay,
  That joye it was to heere;
The thrustelcok made eek his lay,
The wodedowve upon the spray   1960
  She sang ful loude and cleere.

Sire Thopas fil in love-longynge,
Al whan he herde the thrustel synge,
  And pryked as he were wood.
His faire steede in his prikynge   1965
So swatte that men myghte him wrynge;
  His sydes were al blood.

Sire Thopas eek so wery was
For prikyng on the softe gras,
  So fiers was his corage,   1970
That doun he leyde him in that plas
To make his steede som solas, *entertaining.*
  And yaf hym good forage.

"O seinte Marie, *benedicite!*
What eyleth this love at me   1975
  To bynde me so soore?
Me dremed al this nyght, pardee,
An elf-queene shal my lemman be
  And slepe under my goore.

"An elf-queene wol I love, ywis,   1980
For in this world no womman is
  Worthy to be my make
      In towne;
  Alle othere wommen I forsake,
And to an elf-queene I me take   1985
  By dale and eek by downe!"

1926. wilde deer, wild animals. **1927. for river,** beside the river, a favorite place for hawking. As the rimes show, *river* is accented on the last syllable and is possibly an adaptation of OF. *riviere,* also spelled *rivere* (see quotations in Godefroy). The prep. *for* is not easy to explain; possibly to be taken, as Skeat suggests, with *ride,* in the sense of "toward." **1928. goshauk,** inferior type of hawk used by yeomen. **1931. Ther,** where. For a ram as the usual prize in wrestling cf. A 548. **stonde,** *i.e.* be put up for competition. **1933. moorne,** long. **paramour,** ardently. **1937. hepe,** hip, fruit of the wild rose. **1941. worth upon,** got on (*lit.* became on). **1942. launcegay,** a kind of lance, apparently short. **1944. priketh,** spurs his horse. **1948. hym hadde . . . Bitid,** there happened to him. **1951. cetewale.** The modern form is *setwall.* These "herbes" would naturally not be found growing in Flanders. **1952. clowe-gylofre,** clove. **1953. notemuge,** nutmeg. **1954. moyste or stale,** new or old (as applied to ale). *Stale* is applied to ale that has stood long enough to become clear, hence old and strong. **1955. cofre,** box or chest. **1957. sparhauk,** sparrow-hawk. **papejay,** popinjay, parrot. **1959. thrustelcok,** thrush. **1960. wodedowve,** wood-pidgeon. **1962. fil,** fell. **1964. wood,** mad. **1966. swatte,** sweat. **1967. al blood,** covered with blood. **1970. corage,** heart, zeal. **1973. forage,** food, grazing. **1974. benedicite,** pronounced *bén-cité.* **1979. goore,** a section of a garment, here used (as often) for the whole garment. **1982. make,** mate. **1985. take,** betake.

Into his sadel he clamb anon,
And priketh over stile and stoon
  An elf-queene for t'espye,
Til he so longe hath riden and goon   1990
That he foond, in a pryve woon,
  The contree of Fairye
              So wilde;
For in that contree was ther noon
That to him durste ride or goon,   1995
  Neither wyf ne childe;

Til that ther cam a greet geaunt,
His name was sire Olifaunt,
  A perilous man of dede.
He seyde, "Child, by Termagaunt!   2000
But if thou prike out of myn haunt,
  Anon I sle thy steede
              With mace.
Heere is the queene of Fairye,
With harpe and pipe and symphonye,   2005
  Dwellynge in this place."

The child seyde, "Also moote I thee,
Tomorwe wol I meete with thee,
  Whan I have myn armoure;
And yet I hope, par ma fay,   2010
That thou shalt with this launcegay
  Abyen it ful sowre.
              Thy mawe
Shal I percen, if I may,
Er it be fully pryme of day,   2015
  For heere thow shalt be slawe."

Sire Thopas drow abak ful faste;
This geant at hym stones caste

Out of a fel staf-slynge;
But faire escapeth child Thopas,   2020
And al it was thurgh Goddes gras,
  And thurgh his fair berynge.

Yet listeth, lordes, to my tale
Murier than the nightyngale,
  For now I wol yow rowne   2025
How sir Thopas, with sydes smale,
  Prikyng over hill and dale,
  Is comen agayn to towne.

His myrie men comanded he
To make hym bothe game and glee,   2030
  For nedes moste he fighte
With a geaunt with hevedes three,
For paramour and jolitee
  Of oon that shoon ful brighte.

"Do come," he seyde, "my mynstrales,   2035
And geestours for to tellen tales,
  Anon in myn armynge,
Of romances that been roiales,
Of popes and of cardinales,
  And eek of love-likynge."   2040

They fette hym first the sweete wyn,
And mede eek in a mazelyn,
  And roial spicerye
Of gyngebreed that was ful fyn,
And lycorys, and eek comyn,   2045
  With sugre that is trye.

He dide next his white leere,
Of clooth of lake fyn and cleere,

1987. clamb, climbed. Of course, he should have leaped into his saddle **1991. woon,** place, region. **1998. sire Olifaunt,** Sir Elephant, an appropriate name for a giant. **2000. Termagaunt,** according to Christians a Mohammedan god. **2002. sle,** will slay. **2005. symphonye,** drum. **2007. Also moote I thee,** as may I thrive or prosper. **2012. Abyen,** pay for. **sowre,** bitterly. **2013. mawe,** stomach, belly. **2015. fully pryme,** 9 A.M. **2016. slawe,** slain. **2019. fel staf-slynge,** a terrible slingshot. **2020. faire,** fairly, safely. **child,** often used in the ballads for a young knight. **2023. Yet listeth . . .** This and the next two lines closely resemble the opening of *Beves of Hampton*. **2025. rowne,** whisper, tell. **2026. with sydes smale.** In Middle English the phrase is generally found in descriptions of women. Cf. "Hir myddel smal", E 1602. **2028. Is comen agayn to towne,** has returned again. **2030. glee,** music, entertainment. **2032. hevedes,** heads. **2033. paramour,** love. **jolitee,** amusement. **2035. Do come . . . my mynstrales,** have my minstrels come, *i.e.* summon them. **2036. geestours,** another name for minstrels, in their capacity of story-tellers; cf. *chanson de geste*. **2041. fette,** fetched. **2042. mazelyn,** mazer, a wooden bowl, especially of maplewood. **2043. spicerye.** The word covered not only spices but things containing spices. **2044. Of,** consisting of, including. **gyngebreed,** preserved ginger. **2045. comyn,** now spelled *cumin*. **2046. trye,** choice, excellent. **2047. dide,** put on. **leere,** flesh. **2048. clooth of lake,** linen.

A breech and eek a sherte;
And next his sherte an aketoun, 2050
And over that an haubergeoun
  For percynge of his herte;

And over that a fyn hawberk,
Was al ywroght of Jewes werk,
  Ful strong it was of plate; 2055
And over that his cote-armour
As whit as is a lilye flour,
  In which he wol debate.

His sheeld was al of gold so reed,
And therinne was a bores heed, 2060
  A charbocle bisyde;
And there he swoor on ale and breed
How that the geaunt shal be deed,
  Bityde what bityde!

His jambeux were of quyrboilly, 2065
His swerdes shethe of yvory,
  His helm of latoun bright;
His sadel was of rewel-boon,
His brydel as the sonne shoon,
  Or as the moone light. 2070

His spere was of fyn ciprees,
That bodeth werre, and nothyng pees,

The heed ful sharpe ygrounde;
His steede was al dappull gray,
It gooth an ambil in the way 2075
  Ful softely and rounde
        In londe.
Loo, lordes myne, heere is a fit!
If ye wol any moore of it,
  To telle it wol I fonde. 2080

The Second Fit

Now holde youre mouth, *par chritee*,
Bothe knyght and lady free,
  And herkneth to my spelle;
Of bataille and of chivalry,
And of ladyes love-drury 2085
  Anon I wol yow telle.

Men speken of romances of prys,
Of Horn child and of Ypotys,
  Of Beves and sir Gy,
Of sir Lybeux and Pleyndamour,— 2090
But sir Thopas, he bereth the flour
  Of roial chivalry!

His goode steede al he bistrood,
And forth upon his wey he glood
  As sparcle out of the bronde; 2095

2050. **aketoun**, a short vest-like garment, padded or guilted, worn under the hauberk. 2051. **haubergeoun**, coat of mail. 2052. **For**, as a protection against. 2053. **hawberk**, the hauberk, worn outside the habergeon, was made of plates, as here. 2054. **Jewes werk**. The Jews were known as craftsmen and metal workers. See H. S. Ficke, *PQ*, VII. 82–5. 2056. **cote-armour**, the surcoat worn over the knight's armor. It should have had Sir Thopas' coat of arms embroidered on it. 2058. **debate**, *i.e.* fight, dispute the ground with his opponent. 2059. **reed**, red. 2061. **A charbocle bisyde**, together with a carbuncle. The boar's head and the carbuncle were painted on the shield. 2062. **he swoor on ale and breed**. Knights usually swore on more aristocratic objects such as a peacock or heron. 2064. **Bityde what bityde**, come what may. 2065. **jambeux**, protections for the shins. **quyrboilly**, leather soaked in hot water and dried (after being shaped). 2067. **latoun**, brass. 2068. **rewel-boon**, whalebone, ivory. 2071. **ciprees**, cypress. Although the lance was usually made of ash, as the OE. *æsc* "spear" indicates, the wood of the cypress is close-grained and extremely durable. Among the ancients the cypress was a symbol of the dead, and its ill-boding nature may be the reason for the statement in the next line. 2072. **werre**, war. 2074. **dappull gray**, dappled gray. 2075. **ambil**, amble, hardly associated with the gait of a war-horse. 2077. **In londe**, a tag of little meaning, common in romances in stanzas. 2080. **fonde**, strive. 2081. **holde youre mouth**. Although the openings of many romances and other poems intended for recitation request the audience to pay attention by "Listeth," "Herkneth," "Holdeth your peace," etc., none to my knowledge says "Shut your mouth." The rudeness here is part of the exaggeration. 2083. **spelle**, discourse (frequent in the romances). 2085. **love-drury, etc.** Such lists of romances and themes are common both in the romances themselves and in didactic works which compare such entertainment (unfavorably) with the work about to be presented. Of the titles here mentioned all but one are easily identified. *Horn child* is the romance known as *King Horn*, possibly in the version in the Auchinleck MS where it has the title *Horn Childe; Beves* and *sir Gy* are *Beves of Hampton* and *Guy of Warwick; sir Lybeux* is *Libeus Desconus* (The Fair Unknown). *Ypotys* is not a romance but an exposition of Christian doctrine in the form of a dialogue between Ypotis and the emperor of Rome. *Pleyndamour* cannot be identified, although the name Sir Playne de Amours occurs in Malory's *Morte Darthur.* 2087. **of prys**, of worth, renoun. 2094. **glood**, glided. 2095. **sparcle**, spark.

Upon his creest he bar a tour,
And therinne stiked a lilie flour,—
  God shilde his cors fro shonde!

And for he was a knyght auntrous,
He nolde slepen in noon hous, 2100
  But liggen in his hoode;

His brighte helm was his wonger,
And by hym baiteth his dextrer
  Of herbes fyne and goode.

Hymself drank water of the well, 2105
As dide the knyght sire Percyvell
  So worthy under wede,
Til on a day—

The Link between Sir Thopas and The Tale of Melibee

Heere the Hoost stynteth Chaucer of his tale of Thopas.

"Namoore of this, for Goddes dignitee,"
Quod oure Hooste, "for thou makest me 2110
So wery of thy verray lewednesse
That, also wisly God my soule blesse,
Myne eres aken of thy drasty speche.
Now swich a rym the devel I biteche!
This may wel be rym dogerel," quod he. 2115
  "Why so?" quod I, "why wiltow lette me
Moore of my tale than another man,
Syn that it is the beste rym I kan?"
  "By God," quod he, "for pleynly, at a word,
Thy drasty rymyng is nat worth a toord! 2120
Thou doost noght elles but despendest tyme.
Sire, at o word, thou shalt no lenger ryme.
Lat se wher thou kanst tellen aught in geeste,
Or telle in prose somwhat, at the leeste,
In which ther be som murthe or som doc-
    tryne." 2125

"Gladly," quod I, "by Goddes sweete pyne!
I wol yow telle a litel thyng in prose
That oghte liken yow, as I suppose,
Or elles, certes, ye been to daungerous.
It is a moral tale vertuous, 2130
Al be it told somtyme in sondry wyse
Of sondry folk, as I shal yow devyse.
  As thus: ye woot that every Evaungelist,
That telleth us the peyne of Jhesu Crist,
Ne seith nat alle thyng as his felawe dooth; 2135
But nathelees hir sentence is al sooth,
And alle acorden as in hire sentence,
Al be ther in hir tellyng difference.
For somme of hem seyn moore, and somme
    seyn lesse,
Whan they his pitous passioun expresse— 2140
I meene of Mark, Mathew, Luc, and John—
But doutelees hir sentence is al oon.

2096. **creest,** top of the helmet. 2098. **cors,** body. **shonde,** harm. 2099. **auntrous,** adventurous. 2102. **wonger,** pillow. The word was apparently old-fashioned in Chaucer's day. 2103. **baiteth,** feeds. **dextrer,** steed (destrier). 2104. **herbes,** herbage. 2105. **well,** spring. 2106. **sire Percyvell,** in the romance of *Sir Perceval de Galles.* 2107. **worthy under wede** (clothing), a common alliterate phrase.
  Rubric. stynteth, stops. 2111. **lewednesse,** the qualities of the *lewd* or ignorant. 2112. **also wisly . . .,** as certainly as may God bless my soul. 2113. **drasty,** wretched (*lit.* filthy). 2114. **biteche,** consign to. 2116. **lette,** hinder, prevent. 2121. **despendest,** wastest. 2123. **aught in geeste,** *i.e.* anything worth listening to, such as a story of famous deeds or historical fact. The phrase *in geeste* may be meant to suggest the meter of the chansons de geste, eight or ten syllable lines riming in couplets or grouped by assonance into larger units called *laisses.* 2125. **doctryne,** teaching. 2126. **pyne,** suffering. 2128. **liken,** be pleasing to. 2129. **daungerous,** difficult, hard to please. 2132. **devyse,** tell, explain. 2136. **sentence,** meaning. **sooth,** true. 2137. **acorden,** agree.

Therfore, lordynges alle, I yow biseche,

If that yow thynke I varie as in my speche,

As thus, though that I telle somwhat moore

Of proverbes than ye han herd bifoore   2146

Comprehended in this litel tretys heere,

To enforce with th' effect of my mateere,

And though I nat the same wordes seye

As ye han herd, yet to yow alle I preye   2150

Blameth me nat; for, as in my sentence,

Shul ye nowher fynden difference

Fro the sentence of this tretys lyte

After the which this murye tale I write,

And therfore herkneth what that I shal seye,

And lat me tellen al my tale, I preye."   2156

Explicit.

THE TALE OF MELIBEE

The "tale" which is introduced by the above lines is indeed no tale, but a prose treatise on good counsel, and since the present volume is limited to Chaucer's poetry it is here omitted.

In his absence from home Melibeus has been attacked by his enemies, who have entered his house, beaten his wife Prudence, and seriously wounded his daughter Sophie. Upon returning he is at first grief-stricken and eager for revenge. He calls together a large number of people for advice. Some counsel patience, some war, and he decides on war. But his wife urges him to reconsider his decision, and presents at great length the wisdom of many sages on the subject of revealing one's private affairs to others, choosing one's counselors, weighing their advice, changing one's decision when it seems wise to do so, and similar topics. The presentation is in the form of conversation in which Dame Prudence does most of the talking; she is the mouthpiece through which the author expresses his ideas.

The source of the treatise is a French work entitled *Le Livre de Mellibee et Prudence*, by a Dominican friar, Renaud de Louens, which Chaucer translates very closely. Renaud's work in turn goes back to a thirteenth-century Latin treatise of Albertano of Brescia, the *Liber Consolationis et Consilii*, which he freely condenses and adapts.

The *Melibeus* is not without interest today to one who can feel at home in the moral and intellectual atmosphere of the Middle Ages. But with full recognition of the medieval taste for discussions of this sort, it is hard to believe that Chaucer would have deliberately written a treatise of this kind for the diversion of pilgrims on the road. It is likely that he made the translation independently of *The Canterbury Tales*, possibly before he had begun work on the latter collection. We can admire the great skill with which he contrived the situation whereby he could place the responsibility for this didactic discourse on the Host and satisfy the latter's request for a narrative in which there would be "som doctryne."

2153. lyte, little. **2154. I write.** Chaucer forgets that he is speaking to the pilgrims.

The Monk's Tale
THE PROLOGUE TO THE MONK'S TALE

The murye wordes of the Hoost to the Monk.

Whan ended was my tale of Melibee,
And of Prudence and hire benignytee,   3080
Oure Hooste seyde, "As I am feithful man,
And by that precious corpus Madrian,
I hadde levere than a barel ale
That Goodelief, my wyf, hadde herd this tale!
For she nys no thyng of swich pacience   3085
As was this Melibeus wyf Prudence.
By Goddes bones! whan I bete my knaves,
She bryngeth me forth the grete clobbed
      staves,
And crieth, 'Slee the dogges everichoon,
And brek hem, bothe bak and every
      boon!'   3090
  And if that any neighebore of myne
Wol nat in chirche to my wyf enclyne,
Or be so hardy to hire to trespace,
Whan she comth hoom she rampeth in my
      face,
And crieth, 'False coward, wrek thy wyf!   3095
By corpus bones, I wol have thy knyf,
And thou shalt have my distaf and go spynne!'
Fro day to nyght right thus she wol bigynne.
'Allas!' she seith, 'that evere I was shape
To wedden a milksop, or a coward ape,   3100

That wol been overlad with every wight!
Thou darst nat stonden by thy wyves right!'
  This is my lif, but if that I wol fighte;
And out at dore anon I moot me dighte,
Or elles I am but lost, but if that I   3105
Be lik a wilde leoun, fool-hardy.
I woot wel she wol do me slee som day
Som neighebore, and thanne go my way;
For I am perilous with knyf in honde,
Al be it that I dar nat hire withstonde,   3110
For she is byg in armes, by my feith:
That shal he fynde that hire mysdooth or
      seith,—
But lat us passe awey fro this mateere.
  My lord, the Monk," quod he, "be myrie of
      cheere,
For ye shul telle a tale trewely.   3115
Loo, Rouchestre stant heer faste by!
Ryde forth, myn owene lord, brek nat oure
      game.
But, by my trouthe, I knowe nat youre name.
Wher shal I calle yow my lord daun John,
Or daun Thomas, or elles daun Albon?   3120
Of what hous be ye, by youre fader kyn?
I vowe to God, thou hast a ful fair skyn;

3081. **feithful man,** a man true to my (Christian) faith. 3082. **corpus Madrian,** the body of St. Madrian, but no saint of that name is known and no plausible explanation of the name has been offered. It probably represents one of the flaws in Harry Baily's learning, about which it is idle to speculate. 3083. **barel ale,** a barrel of ale. The omission of the partitive is not unusual. See Language, § 49. 3084. **Goodelief.** It has been shown that the name is found as that of women in Kentish records. 3088. **clobbed,** club-shaped, thick at one end. 3092. **enclyne,** bow. 3093. **to hire to trespace,** as to commit an offence against her. The verb was more commonly used with *to* (*unto, til*) than with *against.* 3094. **rampeth,** storms. Cf. the mod. "ramp and rage." 3095. **wrek,** avenge. 3096. **By corpus bones,** another of the Host's singular oaths. **corpus,** body. 3099. **shape,** destined. 3101. **overlad with every wight,** domineered over by every one. 3103. **but if,** unless. 3104. **me dighte,** betake myself. 3107. **do me slee,** cause me to slay. 3108. **go my way,** die (be hanged). 3116. **Loo, Rouchestre.** Rochester, 30 miles from London, is a little more than halfway to Canterbury. **stant,** stands. 3117. **forth,** forward. 3119. **Wher,** whether, used to introduce a direct question involving alternatives. 3120. As we learn from l. 3982 the Monk's name was Piers (Peter). 3121. **hous,** religious establishment. **fader,** father's.

It is a gentil pasture ther thow goost.
Thou art nat lyk a penant or a goost:
Upon my feith, thou art som officer, 3125
Som worthy sexteyn, or som celerer,
For by my fader soule, as to my doom,
Thou art a maister whan thou art at hoom;
No povre cloysterer, ne no novys,
But a governour, wily and wys, 3130
And therwithal of brawnes and of bones,
A wel farynge persone for the nones.
I pray to God, yeve hym confisioun,
That first thee broghte unto religioun!
Thou woldest han been a tredefowel aright.
Haddestow as greet a leeve, as thou thast
    myght, 3136
To parfourne al thy lust in engendrure,
Thou haddest bigeten many a creature.
Allas, why werestow so wyd a cope?
God yeve me sorwe, but, and I were a
    pope, 3140
Nat oonly thou, but every myghty man,
Though he were shorn ful hye upon his pan,
Sholde have a wyf; for al the world is lorn!
Religioun hath take up al the corn 3144
Of tredyng, and we borel men been shrympes.
Of fieble trees ther comen wrecched ympes.
This maketh that oure heires been so sklendre
And feble that they may nat wel engendre.
This maketh that oure wyves wole assaye
Religious folk, for ye mowe bettre paye 3150
Of Venus paiementz than mowe we;
God woot, no lussheburghes payen ye!
But be nat wrooth, my lord, though that I pleye.
Ful ofte in game a sooth I have herd seye!"
    This worthy Monk took al in pacience, 3155
And seyde, "I wol doon al my diligence,
As fer as sowneth into honestee,
To telle yow a tale, or two, or three.
And if yow list to herkne hyderward,
I wol yow seyn the lyf of Seint Edward; 3160
Or ellis, first, tragedies wol I telle,
Of whiche I have an hundred in my celle.
Tragedie is to seyn a certeyn storie,
As olde bookes maken us memorie,
Of hym that stood in greet prosperitee, 3165
And is yfallen out of heigh degree
Into myserie, and endeth wrecchedly.
And they ben versified communely
Of six feet, which men clepen exametron.
In prose eek been endited many oon, 3170
And eek in meetre, in many a sondry wyse.
Lo, this declaryng oghte ynogh suffise.
    Now herkneth, if yow liketh for to heere.
But first I yow biseeke in this mateere,
Though I by ordre telle nat thise thynges, 3175
Be it of popes, emperours, or kynges,
After hir ages, as men writen fynde,
But tellen hem som before and som bihynde,
As it now comth unto my remembraunce,
Have me excused of myn ignoraunce." 3180

Explicit.

3123. It is a gentil pasture . . ., i.e. you eat well. ther, where. 3124. penant, penitent, one doing penance. 3126. sexteyn, sacristan. celerer, cellarer. Both were obedientiaries or administrative officers, and their offices were supported by separate endowments. At Ely the sacristan often entertained parties of his fellow monks and townsmen at one of his granges or farmhouses. He was in charge of the church fabric, with special attention to the altar, lights, vestments, etc. The cellarer was responsible for all the food and drink, including the proper dispensing of them, and had charge of the servants. 3127. as to my doom, in my judgment. 3132. wel farynge, handsome. for the nones, for the nonce, but here apparently little more than a rime-tag. 3134. unto religioun, into a monastic life. 3140. and, properly an, if. 3143. lorn, lost, i.e. the loser. 3145. borel men, ordinary men. Borel or burel is coarse woollen cloth. shrympes, puny persons,— apparently the earliest occurence of the word in this sense. 3146. ympes, shoots. The saying is proverbial. 3147. sklendre, weak, not robust. 3152. lussheburges, coins of inferior metal from Luxembourg. 3157. sowneth into honestee, is conducive to or consonant with virtue. 3160. Seint Edward, either Edward, king and martyr, whose murder in 978 earned him the title of martyr, or Edward the Confessor, who was canonized in 1161. 3161. tragedies, used not in the modern sense but as explained in the lines which follow. The accent is on the second syllable. 3169. clepen, call. exametron, the Latin hexameter. 3174. biseeke, beseech. 3177. After hir ages, in chronological order.

THE MONK'S TALE

Heere bigynneth the Monkes Tale De Casibus Virorum Illustrium.

I wol biwaille, in manere of tragedie,
The harm of hem that stoode in heigh degree,
And fillen so that ther nas no remedie
To brynge hem out of hire adversitee.
For certein, whan that Fortune list to flee,   3185
Ther may no man the cours of hire withholde.
Lat no man truste on blynd prosperitee;
Be war by thise ensamples trewe and olde.

Lucifer

At Lucifer, though he an angel were,
And nat a man, at hym wol I bigynne.   3190
For though Fortune may noon angel dere,
From heigh degree yet fel he for his synne
Doun into helle, where as he yet is inne.
O Lucifer, brightest of angels alle,   3194
Now artow Sathanas, that mayst nat twynne
Out of miserie, in which that thou art falle.

Adam

Loo Adam, in the feeld of Damyssene,
With Goddes owene fynger wroght was he,
And nat bigeten of mannes sperme unclene,
And welte al paradys savynge o tree.   3200
Hadde nevere worldly man so heigh degree
As Adam, til he for mysgovernaunce
Was dryven out of hys hye prosperitee
To labour, and to helle, and to meschaunce.

Sampson

Loo Sampsoun, which that was annunciat
By th' angel, longe er his nativitee,   3206
And was to God Almyghty consecrat,
And stood in noblesse whil he myghte see.
Was nevere swich another as was hee,
To speke of strengthe, and therwith hardy-
nesse;   3210

The Monk's Tale. Collections of stories illustrating the fall of well-known persons from prosperity to adversity were a favorite product of literary activity in the Middle Ages, reminding man of the instability of this life and urging him, sometimes explicitly, to set his mind on the life to come. The most extensive collection of this kind in English is Lydgate's *Fall of Princes*, and it is a commentary on the taste of the age that his poem not only runs to over 36,000 lines but was written (as he tells us) at the request of Humphrey, Duke of Gloucester. Before Chaucer Boccaccio had written in Latin the *De Casibus Virorum Illustrium*, which fills a folio volume of nearly 300 pages. For evidence that the interest in such stories did not die with the Middle Ages we have only to recall the *Mirror for Magistrates*.

Under the circumstances it is not surprising that Chaucer should have begun such a collection. Each tragedy is a separate vignette, sometimes confined to a single stanza, sometimes extending to a dozen or more. It could well have been worked on at odd times. But it is generally held to be early work (perhaps in the 1370's), with the "modern instances" added or retouched later. Like other collections it is made to exemplify the perversity of Fortune, and in this respect may be said to derive from the *Roman de la Rose*, where Reason castigates the goddess and illustrates her frowardness in the fates of a number of historical persons, both classical and contemporary. But Chaucer's sources for the individual stories are various, sometimes difficult to pin down, and need not detain us. More important is it to recognize that in addition to the general moral which could be drawn from such a collection, the reader or listener could pick up a variety of facts and anecdotes, topics for conversation and discussion, and go away feeling that he had derived profit as well as entertainment from his experience.

In the manuscripts the position of the modern instances varies. In the greater number they are inserted after the story of Zenobia, as here, but in the group which is generally regarded as the best (and which includes the Ellesmere MS) they are placed at the end. Whether the latter arrangement is due to Chaucer or to the orderly impluse of a scribe it is impossible to say. The question involves the link which follows and which exists in a longer and shorter form (see note to line 3957). The order followed in the present edition, which ties the link (in its longer form) more closely with the last stanza of the story of Croessus, seems on the whole the better one to adopt for the modern reader.

3183. fillen, fell. **3188. Be war,** take warning. **3189. Lucifer.** The name means light-bringer, therefore the morning-star. From its use in *Isaiah,* 14:12 it was applied to Satan. **3191. dere,** harm. **3195. twynne,** depart. **3197. feeld of Damyssene.** The field in which Adam was created was identified in the Middle Ages with the site on which Damascus was later built. It is mentioned in Peter Comestor's *Historia Scholastica* (PL, CXCVIII. 1067) and elsewhere. **3200. welte,** wielded, ruled over. **3205. Sampsoun.** The mother of Samson, who was barren, was told by an angel that she would bear a son (*Judges,* 13:3). **annunciat,** announced, foretold. **3208. whil he myghte see,** until his eyes were put out by the Philistines.

But to his wyves toolde he his secree,
Thurgh which he slow hymself for wrecched-
    nesse.

Sampsoun, this noble almyghty champioun,
Withouten wepen, save his handes tweye,
He slow and al torente the leoun,   3215
Toward his weddyng walkynge by the weye.
His false wyf koude hym so plese and preye
Til she his conseil knew; and she, untrewe,
Unto his foos his conseil gan biwreye,   3219
And hym forsook, and took another newe.

Thre hundred foxes took Sampson for ire,
And alle hir tayles he togydre bond,
And sette the foxes tayles alle on fire,
For he on every tayl had knyt a brond;   3224
And they brende alle the cornes in that lond,
And alle hire olyveres, and vynes eke.
A thousand men he slow eek with his hond,
And hadde no wepen but an asses cheke.

Whan they were slayn, so thursted hym that he
Was wel ny lorn, for which he gan to preye
That God wolde on his peyne han som
    pitee,   3231
And sende hym drynke, or elles most he deye;
And of this asses cheke, that was dreye,
Out of a wang-tooth sprang anon a welle,
Of which he drank ynogh, shortly to seye;
Thus heelp hym God, as *Judicum* can telle.   3236

By verray force at Gazan, on a nyght,
Maugree Philistiens of that citee,
The gates of the toun he hath up plyght,
And on his bak ycaryed hem hath hee   3240
Hye on an hill whereas men myghte hem see.

O noble, almyghty Sampsoun, lief and deere,
Had thou nat toold to wommen thy secree,
In al this world ne hadde been thy peere!

This Sampson nevere ciser drank ne wyn,   3245
Ne on his heed cam rasour noon ne sheere,
By precept of the messager divyn,
For alle his strengthes in his heeres weere.
And fully twenty wynter, yeer by yeere,
He hadde of Israel the governaunce.   3250
But soone shal he wepe many a teere,
For wommen shal hym bryngen to meschaunce!

Unto his lemman Dalida he tolde
That in his heeris al his strengthe lay,
And falsely to his foomen she hym solde.   3255
And slepynge in hir barm, upon a day,
She made to clippe or shere his heres away,
And made his foomen al this craft espyen;
And whan that they hym foond in this array,
They bounde hym faste and putten out his
    yën.   3260

But er his heer were clipped or yshave,
Ther was no boond with which men myghte
    him bynde;
But now is he in prison in a cave,
Where as they made hym at the queerne
    grynde.   3264
O noble Sampsoun, strongest of mankynde,
O whilom juge, in glorie and in richesse!
Now maystow wepen with thyne eyen blynde,
Sith thou fro wele art falle in wrecchednesse.

The ende of this caytyf was as I shal seye.
His foomen made a feeste upon a day,   3270
And made hym as hire fool biforn hem pleye;

3211. his secree. The first "secret" was the riddle by which he lost his wager with certain Philistines, and the second was the source of his strength. **3215. torente,** tore to pieces. **3216. Toward his weddyng,** on the way to his wedding. The best commentary on what follows is *Judges,* ch. 14–16. **3224. knyt,** tied. **3225. cornes,** crops. **3226. olyveres,** olive trees. **3227. slow,** slew. **3228. cheke,** cheekbone. **3234. wang-tooth,** cheektooth, molar. **welle,** pool. **3236. heelp,** helped. *Judicum, Liber Judicum,* Book of Judges. **3237. Gazan,** Gaza. **3238. Maugree,** in spite of. **3239. plyght,** plucked. **3244. ne hadde been,** would not have been. **3245. ciser,** strong drink (*siceram* in the Vulgate). **3253. lemman,** sweetheart. **Dalida,** Dalila. **3255. solde.** The Philistines bribed Dalila with a large sum of money. **3256. barm,** lap. **3257. made,** caused. **3260. yën,** eyes. **3264. queerne,** handmill. **3269. caytyf,** captive, wretched person.

And this was in a temple of greet array.
But atte laste he made a foul affray;   3273
For he two pilers shook and made hem falle,
And doun fil temple and al, and ther it lay,—
And slow hymself, and eek his foomen alle.

This is to seyn, the prynces everichoon,
And eek thre thousand bodyes, were ther slayn
With fallynge of the grete temple of stoon.
Of Sampson now wol I namoore sayn.   3280
Beth war by this ensample oold and playn
That no men telle hir conseil til hir wyves
Of swich thyng as they wolde han secree fayn,
If that it touche hir lymes or hir lyves.

Hercules

Of Hercules, the sovereyn conquerour,   3285
Syngen his werkes laude and heigh renoun;

For in his tyme of strengthe he was the flour.
He slow, and rafte the skyn of the leoun;
He of Centauros leyde the boost adoun;
He Arpies slow, the crueel bryddes felle;   3290
He golden apples rafte of the dragoun;
He drow out Cerberus, the hound of helle;

He slow the crueel tyrant Busirus,
And made his hors to frete hym, flessh and boon;
He slow the firy serpent venymus;   3295
Of Acheloys two hornes he brak oon;
And he slow Cacus in a cave of stoon;
He slow the geant Antheus the stronge;
He slow the grisly boor, and that anon;
And bar the hevene on his nekke longe.   3300

Was nevere wight, sith that this world bigan,
That slow so manye monstres as dide he.

3272. **of greet array,** richly adorned, splendid. 3273. **foul affray,** miserable commotion. 3282. **til,** to. 3286. **werkes,** deeds, labors. 3288. **rafte,** took away. **the leoun.** Hercules as the offspring of Jupiter and Alcmene was hated by Juno, who naturally resented her husband's affairs with other women. Most of the dangerous exploits of Hercules were ordained by Juno. Chaucer alludes to some of the more famous of his Twelve Labors and to some of his other exploits. The labors were imposed upon him by his cousin Eurystheus, to whom he was made subject after he had slain his children during a period of madness. His first labor was to rid the valley of Nemea of a lion and bring back the skin. This he accomplished by strangling the lion. 3289. **Centauros,** Centaurs. In performing his fourth labor of bringing back alive the Erymanthian boar, he got into a quarrel with some of the centaurs over a cask of wine and killed them. **leyde the boost adoun,** humbled, overcame. 3290. **Arpies.** The harpies were the Stymphalian birds, so-called from the town of Stymphalus. They had brass beaks and claws and fed on human flesh. Hercules flushed them with the noise of a brass rattle given him by Minerva and as they attempted to fly away he shot them with his arrows. 3291. **golden apples.** This was the eleventh labor of Hercules. The apples were a wedding-present to Juno and were guarded by the Hesperides, daughters of Atlas, and by the dragon Ladon. Hercules persuaded Atlas to fetch the apples, meanwhile supporting the heavens on his own shoulders. When Atlas returned and refused to take back his burden, Hercules outwitted him by asking him to bear the load long enough for him to get a pad for his shoulders and then making off with the apples. 3292. **drow,** drew. **Cerberus.** The twelfth labor was to bring from the lower world Cerberus the three-headed dog that guarded the entrance to Hades. He persuaded Pluto to let him carry Cerberus into the upper world provided he could do it without using any weapon. He overpowered the monster, carried it to Eurystheus (mentioned in the note to l. 3288) for him to see, and then returned it to the lower world. 3293. **Busirus,** Busiris, an Egyptian tyrant who put to death all foreigners until Hercules killed him. But Chaucer (or his source) has confused this feat with the eighth labor, which concerns a Thracian king, Diomedes, who fed his horses human flesh. Hercules killed Diomedes and threw his body to the same horses. 3294. **frete,** devour. 3295. **serpent,** the Lernean hydra, a serpent with nine heads, the middle one immortal. Each time Hercules struck off one of the heads two others appeared in its place. He finally accomplished his task by having a companion promptly sear the point of decapitation and by burying the immortal head under a rock. This is regarded as the second labor of Hercules. **firy.** This is a strange adjective to apply to the hydra. My colleague in the Classics department, Prof. Wm. C. McDermott, suggests that it represents a misconstruing of *Æneid,* VI. 287–8: *belua Lernae horrendum stridens flammisque armata Chimaera* (the beast of Lerna hissing (hisses) to be shuddered at, and the Chimaera armed with flames). In an unpunctuated text the enclitic in *flammisque* could easily be misconstrued. **venymus,** presumably referring to the fact that Hercules dipped his arrows in the monster's bile, and consequently a wound inflicted by them was incurable. 3296. **Acheloys.** Achelous, the river god, fought with Hercules over Deianire, whom both loved. Beaten in wrestling, Achelous took the form of a bull and had one of his horns broken off by Hercules. 3297. **Cacus,** a giant, the son of Vulcan, who lived in a cave on Mt. Aventine, in Italy. He stole some of the oxen that Hercules had taken in Spain and dragged them into this cave by their tails so that they would leave no footprints. Their lowing when the other oxen passed the entrance to the cave revealed their whereabouts, and Hercules slew Cacus. This and the following exploit are not numbered among the Twelve Labors. 3298. **Antheus,** a giant wrestler whose strength was overpowering as long as he was in contact with the earth. Hercules lifted him up and strangled him in the air. 3299. **grisly boor,** the Erymanthian boar alluded to in the note to l. 3289. Hercules chased it through deep snow until it was exhausted and then captured it with a net. 3300. **bar the hevene,** bore the heavens. See note to l. 3291. **longe,** a long while.

Thurghout this wyde world his name ran,
What for his strengthe and for his heigh
    bountee,
And every reawme wente he for to see.   3305
He was so stroong that no man myghte hym
    lette.
At bothe the worldes endes, seith Trophee,
In stide of boundes he a pileer sette.

A lemman hadde this noble champioun,
That highte Dianira, fressh as May;   3310
And as thise clerkes maken mencioun,
She hath hym sent a sherte, fressh and gay.
Allas! this sherte, allas and weylaway!
Envenymed was so subtilly withalle,
That er that he had wered it half a day,   3315
It made his flessh al from his bones falle.

But nathelees somme clerkes hire excusen
By oon that highte Nessus, that it maked.
Be as be may, I wol hire noght accusen;
But on his bak this sherte he wered al
    naked,   3320
Til that his flessh was for the venym blaked.
And whan he saugh noon oother remedye,
In hoote coles he hath hymselven raked,
For with no venym deigned hym to dye.

Thus starf this worthy, myghty Hercules.   3325
Lo, who may truste on Fortune any throwe?
For hym that folweth al this world of prees,
Er he be war, is ofte yleyd ful lowe.
Ful wys is he that kan hymselven knowe!   3329
Beth war, for whan that Fortune list to glose,
Thanne wayteth she her man to overthrowe
By swich a wey as he wolde leest suppose.

Nabugodonosor

The myghty trone, the precious tresor,
The glorious ceptre, and roial magestee
That hadde the kyng Nabugodonosor   3335
With tonge unnethe may discryved bee.
He twyes wan Jerusalem the citee;
The vessel of the temple he with hym ladde.
At Babiloigne was his sovereyn see,
In which his glorie and his delit he hadde.   3340

The faireste children of the blood roial
Of Israel he leet do gelde anoon,
And maked ech of hem to been his thral.
Amonges othere Daniel was oon,
That was the wiseste child of everychon;   3345
For he the dremes of the kyng expowned,
Where as in Chaldeye clerk ne was ther noon
That wiste to what fyn his dremes sowned.

3304. **bountee**, worth, excellence. 3306. **lette**, hinder, "stop." 3307. **At bothe the worldes endes.** Hercules was supposed to have set up pillars at both the eastern and western limits of the world. The pillars of Hercules in Spain and Africa (at the Strait of Gibraltar) were well known. Those at the eastern end of the world were shown by Kittredge (*Putnam Anniv. Volume*, 545–66) to have been mentioned quite frequently, particularly in the various treatments of Alexander the Great. More recently Pratt has called attention to a commentary on Walter Map's *Epistola Valerii ad Rufinum* in which both are mentioned. See *Studies in Honor of* [B. L.] *Ullman* (St. Louis, 1960), pp. 118–25. **Trophee.** The reference has long been a puzzle. The Ellesmere and Hengwrt manuscripts contain a marginal gloss *Ille vates Chaldeorum Tropheus*, brilliantly explained by Tupper (*MLN*, xxxi. 13–14) as a conflation of two glosses which in an earlier manuscript were juxtaposed in the inner margins of an opening, one to *Trophee* and the other to *Daniel* (l. 3344) but this does not account for the name. Kittredge (in the article cited in the previous note) suggested that some one (not necessarily Chaucer) took the word *trophaea* (sign, monument) in the *Epistola Alexandri Macedonis ad Aristotelem* as a proper name. 3310. **Dianira.** See note to l. 3296. 3311. **thise clerkes**, learned writers. 3312. **a sherte.** The story alluded to in this and the following stanza runs as follows: On one occasion when the centaur Nessus attempted to carry off Deianira, Hercules killed him with an arrow. Before dying, Nessus told Deianira to keep some of his blood, saying that it could be used as a charm to preserve her husband's love. A few years later Deianira, jealous of Hercules' attention to the maiden Iole, dipped one of his robes in the blood. When he wore it he was fatally poisoned by the blood. Hercules, realizing that he would die, built a funeral pyre, lay down upon it, and had his friend Philoctetes apply the torch. 3318. **By**, on account of. **highte**, was named. 3325. **starf**, died. 3326. **throwe**, a (short) space of time. 3327. **world of prees**, busy world. 3330. **glose**, flatter, beguile. 3331. **wayteth**, watches for an opportunity. 3333. **trone**, throne. 3335. **Nabugodonosor**, a common form of the name Nebuchadnezzar in the Middle Ages. 3336. **unnethe**, scarcely. 3337. **wan**, won, captured. 3338. **vessel**, (collective) vessels. **ladde**, carried off. 3339. **Babiloigne**, Babylon. **see**, seat (of government). 3342. **leet do gelde**, had castrated. 3344. **othere**, others. 3345. **of everychon**, of all. 3346. **expowned**, interpreted. 3348. **fyn**, end. **sowned**, tended.

This proude kyng leet maken a statue of gold,
Sixty cubites long and sevene in brede;   3350
To which ymage bothe yong and oold
Comanded he to loute, and have in drede,
Or in a fourneys, ful of flambes rede,
He shal be brent that wolde noght obeye.
But nevere wolde assente to that dede   3355
Daniel, ne his yonge felawes tweye.

This kyng of kynges proud was and elaat;
He wende that God, that sit in magestee,
Ne myghte hym nat bireve of his estaat.
But sodeynly he loste his dignytee,   3360
And lyk a beest hym semed for to bee,
And eet hey as an oxe, and lay theroute
In reyn; with wilde beestes walked hee,
Til certein tyme was ycome aboute.

And lik an egles fetheres wax his heres;   3365
His nayles lyk a briddes clawes weere;
Til God relessed hym a certeyn yeres,
And yaf hym wit, and thanne with many a
    teere
He thanked God, and evere his lyf in feere
Was he to doon amys or moore trespace;   3370
And til that tyme he leyd was on his beere,
He knew that God was ful of myght and grace.

Balthasar

His sone, which that highte Balthasar,
That heeld the regne after his fader day,
He by his fader koude noght be war,   3375
For proud he was of herte and of array;
And eek an ydolastre was he ay.
His hye estaat assured hym in pryde;
But Fortune caste hym doun, and ther he lay,
And sodeynly his regne gan divide.   3380

A feeste he made unto his lordes alle,
Upon a tyme, and bad hem blithe bee;
And thanne his officeres gan he calle:
"Gooth, bryngeth forth the vesseles," quod he,
"Whiche that my fader in his prosperitee   3385
Out of the temple of Jerusalem birafte;
And to oure hye goddes thanke we
Of honour that oure eldres with us lafte."

Hys wyf, his lordes, and his concubynes
Ay dronken, whil hire appetites laste,   3390
Out of thise noble vessels sondry wynes.
And on a wal this kyng his eyen caste,
And saugh an hand, armlees, that wroot ful
    faste,
For feere of which he quook and siked soore.
This hand, that Balthasar so soore agaste,   3395
Wroot *Mane*, *techel*, *phares*, and namoore.

In al that land magicien was noon
That koude expoune what this lettre mente;
But Daniel expowned it anoon,
And seyde, "Kyng, God to thy fader lente
Glorie and honour, regne, tresour, rente;   3401
And he was proud, and nothyng God ne
    dradde,
And therfore God greet wreche upon hym
    sente,
And hym birafte the regne that he hadde.

He was out cast of mannes compaignye;   3405
With asses was his habitacioun,
And eet hey as a beest in weet and drye,
Til that he knew, by grace and by resoun,
That God of hevene hath domynacioun
Over every regne and every creature;   3410
And thanne hadde God of hym compassioun,
And hym restored his regne and his figure.

3352. **loute,** bow down. 3353. **flambes,** flames. 3354. **brent,** burnt. 3356. **felawes tweye,** two companions, a mistake for three (Shadrach, Meshach, and Abednego). 3357. **elaat,** lofty, arrogant. 3358. **sit,** sits. 3359. **bireve,** deprive. 3360. **dignytee,** high estate. 3362. **eet,** ate. 3367. **a certeyn yeres,** a certain number of years. 3373. **Balthasar,** Belshazzar. 3374. **regne,** kingdom. **fader,** father's. 3375. **be war,** take warning. 3376. **array,** attire. 3377. **ydolastre,** idolater. 3378. **assured,** confirmed. 3386. **birafte,** carried off. 3388. **Of,** for. 3390. **laste,** lasted. 3394. **quook and siked,** quaked and sighed. 3395. **soore agaste,** sorely terrified. 3401. **rente,** revenue. 3402. **nothyng God ne dradde,** feared God not at all. 3403. **wreche,** vengeance. 3412. **figure,** (human) shape.

Eek thou, that art his sone, art proud also,
And knowest alle thise thynges verraily,
And art rebel to God, and art his foo. 3415
Thou drank eek of his vessels boldely;
Thy wyf eek, and thy wenches, synfully
Dronke of the same vessels sondry wynys;
And heryest false goddes cursedly;
Therfore to thee yshapen ful greet pyne ys. 3420

This hand was sent from God that on the wal
Wroot *Mane, techel, phares,* truste me;
Thy regne is doon, thou weyest noght at al.
Dyvyded is thy regne, and it shal be
To Medes and to Perses yeven," quod he. 3425
And thilke same nyght this kyng was slawe,
And Darius occupieth his degree,
Thogh he therto hadde neither right ne lawe.

Lordynges, ensample heerby may ye take
How that in lordshipe is no sikernesse; 3430
For whan Fortune wole a man forsake,
She bereth awey his regne and his richesse,
And eek his freendes, bothe moore and lesse.
For what man that hath freendes thurgh Fortune,
Mishap wol maken hem enemys, I gesse; 3435
This proverbe is ful sooth and ful commune.

Cenobia

Cenobia, of Palymerie queene,
As writen Persiens of hir noblesse,
So worthy was in armes and so keene,
That no wight passed hire in hardynesse, 3440
Ne in lynage, ne in oother gentillesse.
Of kynges blood of Perce is she descended.
I seye nat that she hadde moost fairnesse,
But of hir shape she myghte nat been amended.

From hire childhede I fynde that she fledde 3445
Office of wommen, and to wode she wente,
And many a wilde hertes blood she shedde
With arwes brode that she to hem sente.
She was so swift that she anon hem hente;
And whan that she was elder, she wolde kille 3450
Leouns, leopardes, and beres al torente,
And in hir armes weelde hem at hir wille.

She dorste wilde beestes dennes seke,
And rennen in the montaignes al the nyght,
And slepen under a bussh, and she koude eke 3455
Wrastlen, by verray force and verray myght,
With any yong man, were he never so wight.
Ther myghte no thyng in hir armes stonde.
She kepte hir maydenhod from every wight;
To no man deigned hire for to be bonde. 3460

But atte laste hir freendes han hire maried
To Odenake, a prynce of that contree,
Al were it so that she hem longe taried.
And ye shul understonde how that he
Hadde swiche fantasies as hadde she. 3465
But natheless, whan they were knyt in-feere,
They lyved in joye and in felicitee;
For ech of hem hadde oother lief and deere.

Save o thyng, that she wolde nevere assente,
By no wey, that he sholde by hire lye 3470
But ones, for it was hir pleyn entente
To have a child, the world to multiplye;
And also soone as that she myghte espye
That she was nat with childe with that dede,

3419. heryest, (thou) worshipest. **3420. pyne,** punishment. **3423. weyest noght at al,** hast no importance. **3426. slawe,** slain. **3427. degree,** rank. **3435. Mishap,** misfortune. **3437. Cenobia,** Zenobia. **Palymerie,** Palmyra, a city on an oasis in the desert east of Syria. Zenobia, who ruled it, was defeated by the Emperor Aurelian in A.D. 272. The city was destroyed in 273. **3442. Perce,** Persia, apparently a mistake. She was descended from the Ptolemies of Egypt. **3446. Office,** function, employment. Chaucer was apparently translating *officiis* in Boccaccio. **3451. torente,** tear to pieces. **3454. rennen,** run. **3457. wight,** strong. **3458. in hir armes stonde,** *i.e.* in wrestling. **3460. deigned hire,** she deigned. **3462. Odenake,** Odenathus. **3463. hem . . . taried,** kept them waiting. **3464. how that,** that. **3465. fantasies,** inclinations, desires. **3466. in-feere,** together. **3468. hadde oother,** held the other. **3471. pleyn,** full. **3473. also,** as.

Thanne wolde she suffre hym doon his fantasye   3475
Eftsoone, and nat but oones, out of drede.

And if she were with childe at thilke cast,
Namoore sholde he pleyen thilke game
Til fully fourty wikes weren past;
Thanne wolde she ones suffre hym do the
   same.   3480
Al were this Odenake wilde or tame,
He gat namoore of hire, for thus she seyde,
It was to wyves lecherie and shame,
In oother caas, if that men with hem pleyde.

Two sones by this Odenake hadde she,   3485
The whiche she kepte in vertu and lettrure;
But now unto oure tale turne we.
I seye, so worshipful a creature,
And wys therwith, and large with mesure,
So penyble in the werre, and curteis eke,   3490
Ne moore labour myghte in werre endure,
Was noon, though al this world men sholde
   seke.

Hir riche array ne myghte nat be told,
As wel in vessel as in hire clothyng.
She was al clad in perree and in gold,   3495
And eek she lafte noght, for noon huntyng,
To have of sondry tonges ful knowyng,
Whan that she leyser hadde; and for to entende
To lerne bookes was al hire likyng,
How she in vertu myghte hir lyf dispende. 3500

And shortly of this storie for to trete,
So doghty was hir housbonde and eek she,
That they conquered manye regnes grete
In the orient, with many a fair citee

Apertenaunt unto the magestee   3505
Of Rome, and with strong hond held hem ful
   faste,
Ne nevere myghte hir foomen doon hem flee,
Ay whil that Odenakes dayes laste.

Hir batailles, whoso list hem for to rede,
Agayn Sapor the kyng and othere mo,   3510
And how that al this proces fil in dede,
Why she conquered, and what title had therto,
And after, of hir meschief and hire wo,
How that she was biseged and ytake,—
Lat hym unto my maister Petrak go,   3515
That writ ynough of this, I undertake.

Whan Odenake was deed, she myghtily
The regnes heeld, and with hire propre hond
Agayn hir foos she faught so cruelly
That ther nas kyng ne prynce in al that lond
That he nas glad, if he that grace fond,   3521
That she ne wolde upon his lond werreye.
With hire they maden alliance by bond
To been in pees, and lete hire ride and pleye.

The Emperour of Rome, Claudius   3525
Ne hym bifore, the Romayn Galien,
Ne dorste nevere been so corageus,
Ne noon Ermyn, ne noon Egipcien,
Ne Surrien, ne noon Arabyen,
Withinne the feeld that dorste with hire
   fighte,   3530
Lest that she wolde hem with hir handes slen,
Or with hir meignee putten hem to flighte.

In kynges habit wente hir sones two,
As heires of hir fadres regnes alle,
And Hermanno and Thymalao   3535

3476. Eftsoone, again. **nat but,** only. **drede,** doubt. **3477. cast,** occasion. **3479. wikes,** weeks. **3481. wilde or tame,** amorous or not. **3486. lettrure,** learning. **3488. worshipful,** honorable. **3489. mesure,** moderation. **3490. penyble,** indefatigable. **werre,** war. **3493. array,** accouterment, equipment. **3494. vessel,** (collective) vessels. **3495. perree,** precious stones. **3497. tonges,** languages. **3498. entende,** endeavor. **3503. regnes,** kingdoms. **3505. Apertenaunt,** belonging. **3507. doon hem flee,** put them to rout. **3510. Sapor,** Sapor (or Shapur) I, King of Persia (c. 240–c.272). **3511. proces,** course of events. **fil,** happened (fell). **3515. Petrak,** Petrarch, apparently a mistake for Boccaccio. **3519. Agayn,** against. **3522. werreye,** wage war. **3525. Claudius,** Claudius II, Emperor of Rome (268–270). **3526. Galien,** Galienus (253–268). **3528. Ermyn,** Armenian. **3529. Surrien,** Syrian. **3532. meignee,** company, followers. **3535. Hermanno and Thymalao,** Herennianus and Timoleon.

Hir names were, as Persiens hem calle.
But ay Fortune hath in hire hony galle;
This myghty queene may no while endure.
Fortune out of hir regne made hire falle
To wrecchednesse and to mysaventure.   3540

Aurelian, whan that the governaunce
Of Rome cam into his handes tweye,
He shoop upon this queene to doon vengeaunce.
And with his legions he took his weye
Toward Cenobie, and, shortly for to seye,   3545
He made hire flee, and atte laste hire hente,
And fettred hire, and eek hire children tweye,
And wan the land, and hoom to Rome he
    wente.

Amonges othere thynges that he wan,
Hir chaar, that was with gold wroght and
    perree,   3550
This grete Romayn, this Aurelian,
Hath with hym lad, for that men sholde it see.
Biforen his triumphe walketh shee,
With gilte cheynes on hire nekke hangynge.
Coroned was she, as after hir degree,   3555
And ful of perree charged hire clothynge.

Allas, Fortune! she that whilom was
Dredeful to kynges and to emperoures,
Now gaureth al the peple on hire, allas!
And she that helmed was in starke stoures,   3560
And wan by force townes stronge and toures,
Shal on hir heed now were a vitremyte;
And she that bar the ceptre ful of floures
Shal bere a distaf, hire cost for to quyte.

De Petro Rege Ispannie

O noble, O worthy Petro, glorie of Spayne,
Whom Fortune heeld so hye in magestee,   3566
Wel oghten men thy pitous deeth complayne!
Out of thy land thy brother made thee flee,
And after, at a seege, by subtiltee,
Thou were bitraysed and lad unto his tente,   3570
Where as he with his owene hand slow thee,
Succedynge in thy regne and in thy rente.

The feeld of snow, with th'egle of blak therinne,
Caught with the lymerod coloured as the
    gleede,
He brew this cursednesse and al this synne.   3575
The wikked nest was werkere of this nede.
Noght Charles Olyver, that took ay heede

3541. **Aurelian,** Aurelianus (270–275). 3543. **shoop,** planned. 3546. **hente,** seized, captured. 3548. **wan,** won. 3550. **chaar,** chariot. 3552. **for that,** in order that. 3556. **charged,** loaded. 3558. **Dredeful,** terrifying. 3559. **gaureth,** gape, stare. 3560. **starke stoures,** hard battles. 3562. **were,** wear. **vitremyte.** Skeat calls this word perhaps the greatest crux in Chaucer. It is found nowhere else. Of the various guesses that have been hazarded as to the origin of the word Skeat's seems still the best: L. *vitream mitram,* a glass cap or headdress. Since the phrase *his howve to glaze* (to glaze his hood) is used by Chaucer in the *Troilus* (v. 469) in the sense of "to make a fool of him," the meaning of *vitremyte* might be something like a "fool's cap." For further discussion see K. Young, *SP,* XL (1943). 494–501. 3563. **ful of floures.** I can only suppose that Zenobia's sceptre was ornamented with gold flowers. 3564. **hire cost for to quyte,** *i.e.* by which to earn her keep. 3565. **Petro, glorie of Spayne.** Petro the Cruel, King of Castile (1350–1369). Chaucer's interest in this modern instance was probably in part the result of the fact that, as we now know, he was in Spain in February, 1366 (see biographical sketch, p. xiii). The throne was wrested from Pedro by one of his nine illegitimate half-brothers, Enrique of Trastamare, aided by the king of Castile and Charles V of France. Edward, the Black Prince, by a campaign in 1367 restored Pedro to the throne temporarily. Pedro's daughter Constance became the wife of John of Gaunt in 1371. The best account of the background for Chaucer's two stanzas is P. E. Russell, *The English Intervention in Spain and Portugal in the Time of Edward III and Richard II* (Oxford, 1955). 3570. **bitraysed,** betrayed. Contemporary accounts of the betrayal differ as to details and the name of the agent. Pedro was besieged in the castle of Montiel, with almost no provisions. According to the Spanish chronicler Ayala he offered money and gifts to one of the principal besiegers, Bertrand du Guesclin, to help him escape. Du Guesclin informed Enrique, who persuaded him to lure Pedro to his tent with a promise of safety. There an encounter between Pedro and Enrique took place in which Pedro was stabbed by Enrique. 3572. **rente,** revenue. 3573. **The feeld of snow . . .** These two lines identify du Guesclin by his arms, which, in Furnivall's words, were "a black double-headed eagle displayed on a silver shield, with a red band across the whole, from left to right—'the lymrod coloured as the gleede,' " or in heraldic language: argent an eagle sable, over all a bend dexter gules. 3574. **lymerod,** a rod smeared with birdlime. 3575. **brew,** brewed. 3576. **The wikked nest.** Skeat first pointed out that the phrase translates OF. *mau ni (mal nid),* and thus reveals Sir Oliver de Mauny as the second traitor. Mauny's part in the affair is unknown, but Chaucer's line implies that he planned or carried out the treachery which brought Pedro to such straits. **nede,** violence. 3577. **Noght Charles Olyver . . .,** Not Charlemagne's Oliver, who was always heedful of truth and honor, but the "Ganelon" Oliver of Brittany (Armorica), corrupted by bribery . . . Sir Oliver de Mauny was from Brittany. In the *Chanson de Roland* Oliver is a stalwart member of Charlemagne's company. Ganelon is the traitor responsible for Roland's death.

Of trouthe and honour, but of Armorike
Genylon Olyver, corrupt for meede,
Broghte this worthy kyng in swich a brike. 3580

De Petro Rege de Cipro

O worthy Petro, kyng of Cipre, also,
That Alisandre wan by heigh maistrie,
Ful many an hethen wroghtestow ful wo,
Of which thyne owene liges hadde envie,
And for no thyng but for thy chivalrie 3585
They in thy bed han slayn thee by the morwe.
Thus kan Fortune hir wheel governe and gye,
And out of joye brynge men to sorwe.

De Barnabo de Lumbardia

Off Melan grete Barnabo Viscounte,
God of delit, and scourge of Lumbardye, 3590
Why sholde I nat thyn infortune acounte,
Sith in estaat thow cloumbe were so hye?
Thy brother sone, that was thy double allye,
For he thy nevew was, and sone-in-lawe,
Withinne his prisoun made thee to dye,— 3595
But why, ne how, noot I that thou were slawe.

De Hugelino Comite de Pize

Off the Erl Hugelyn of Pyze the langour
Ther may no tonge telle for pitee.
But litel out of Pize stant a tour,
In which tour in prisoun put was he, 3600

And with hym been his litel children thre;
The eldeste scarsly fyf yeer was of age.
Allas, Fortune! it was greet crueltee
Swiche briddes for to putte in swich a cage!

Dampned was he to dyen in that prisoun, 3605
For Roger, which that bisshop was of Pize,
Hadde on hym maad a fals suggestioun,
Thurgh which the peple gan upon hym rise,
And putten hym to prisoun, in swich wise
As ye han herd, and mete and drynke he
   hadde 3610
So smal, that wel unnethe it may suffise,
And therwithal it was ful povre and badde.

And on a day bifil that in that hour
Whan that his mete wont was to be broght,
The gayler shette the dores of the tour. 3615
He herde it wel, but he spak right noght,
And in his herte anon ther fil a thoght
That they for hunger wolde doon hym dyen.
"Allas!" quod he, "allas, that I was wroght!"
Therwith the teeris fillen from his yën. 3620

His yonge sone, that thre yeer was of age,
Unto hym seyde, "Fader, why do ye wepe?
Whanne wol the gayler bryngen oure potage?
Is ther no morsel breed that ye do kepe?
I am so hungry that I may nat slepe. 3625
Now wolde God that I myghte slepen evere!

3580. **brike**, trap. 3581. **Petro, kyng of Cipre,** Pierre de Lusignan, King of Cyprus. He captured Alexandria in 1365 (see note to A 51, in the General Prologue). He had twice visited England. Chaucer's account is at variance with the known facts of his death and seems to have been derived from Machaut's *Prise d' Alexandrie*. See Haldeen Braddy, *MLN*, LXII. 173–5. 3585. **for thy chivalrie.** The assassination of Pierre in 1369 was occasioned by his own headstrong conduct and cruelty. Chaucer's favorable opinion of him has been traced to Machaut's *Prise d' Alexandrie* by Braddy (*PMLA*, L. 78–80). 3587. **gye**, guide. 3589. **Melan**, Milan. **Barnabo Viscounte.** Chaucer's interest in Barnabò Visconti may have been stimulated by the fact that Barnabò's niece Violanta was married to Lionel, Duke of Clarence, and a daughter Donnina was the wife of the celebrated adventurer Sir John Hawkwood, leader of a mercenary band known as the White Company. Lionel was Chaucer's first patron (see biographical sketch) and it is practically certain that some of Chaucer's business on his mission to Italy in 1378 was with Barnabò and Hawkwood (see R. A. Pratt, *ELH*, XVI, 188–93). Barnabò was Lord of Milan (with his nephew and son-in-law Gian Galeazzo Visconti) until the latter had him imprisoned and put to death in 1385. The circumstances of his death are unknown, but he was probably poisoned. The present stanza was presumably written soon after the news of his death reached England. 3593. **brother**, brother's. 3597. **Hugelyn of Pyze,** Ugolino, one of the leaders of the Guelfs in Pisa in their struggle with the Ghibellines, headed by Ruggiero (the Roger of l. 3606), Archbishop of Pisa. Seizing a favorable opportunity, the archbishop had him thrown into prison, together with four of his sons and grandsons, where he died (1289) of starvation. Chaucer's knowledge of Ugolino comes mainly from Dante (*Inf.*, XXXIII. 1–90), but he has changed some details and added others. **langour**, woeful plight. 3599. **stant**, stands. 3601. **thre.** Dante mentions four children, but after one has died he refers to the three remaining in a somewhat ambiguous way. 3604. **briddes**, birds. 3607. **suggestioun**, accusation. 3611. **unnethe**, scarcely. 3612. **povre**, poor. 3615. **shette**, shut. 3618. **doon**, make. 3620. **fillen from his yën**, fell from his eyes. 3624. **morsel breed**, morsel of bread.

Thanne sholde nat hunger in my wombe crepe;
Ther is no thyng, but breed, that me were
     levere."

Thus day by day this child bigan to crye,
Til in his fadres barm adoun it lay,   3630
And seyde, "Farewel, fader, I moot dye!"
And kiste his fader, and dyde the same day.
And whan the woful fader deed it say,
For wo his armes two he gan to byte.
And seyde, "Allas, Fortune, and weylaway!
Thy false wheel my wo al may I wyte."   3636

His children wende that it for hunger was
That he his armes gnow, and nat for wo,
And seyde, "Fader, do nat so, allas!
But rather ete the flessh upon us two.   3640
Oure flessh thou yaf us, take oure flessh us fro,
And ete ynogh,"—right thus they to hym seyde,
And after that, withinne a day or two,
They leyde hem in his lappe adoun and deyde.

Hymself, despeired, eek for hunger starf;   3645
Thus ended is this myghty Erl of Pize.
From heigh estaat Fortune awey hym carf.
Of this tragedie it oghte ynough suffise;
Whoso wol here it in a lenger wise,
Redeth the grete poete of Ytaille   3650
That highte Dant, for he kan al devyse
Fro point to point, nat o word wol he faille.

Nero

Although that Nero were as vicius
As any feend that lith ful lowe adoun,

Yet he, as telleth us Swetonius,   3555
This wyde world hadde in subjeccioun,
Bothe est and west, south, and septemtrioun.
Of rubies, saphires, and of peerles white
Were alle his clothes brouded up and doun;
For he in gemmes greetly gan delite.   3660

Moore delicaat, moore pompous of array,
Moore proud was nevere emperour than he;
That ilke clooth that he hadde wered o day,
After that tyme he nolde it nevere see.   3664
Nettes of gold threed hadde he greet plentee
To fisshe in Tybre, whan hym liste pleye.
His lustes were al lawe in his decree,
For Fortune as his freend hym wolde obeye.

He Rome brende for his delicasie;
The senatours he slow upon a day   3670
To heere how that men wolde wepe and crie;
And slow his brother, and by his suster lay.
His mooder made he in pitous array,
For he hire wombe slitte to biholde
Where he conceyved was; so weilaway!   3675
That he so litel of his mooder tolde.

No teere out of his eyen for that sighte
Ne cam, but seyde, "A fair womman was she!"
Greet wonder is how that he koude or myghte
Be domesman of hire dede beautee.   3680
The wyn to bryngen hym comanded he,
And drank anon,—noon oother wo he made.
Whan myght is joyned unto crueltee,
Allas, to depe wol the venym wade!

3627. **wombe,** stomach. 3630. **barm,** lap. 3631. **moot,** must. 3633. **say,** saw. 3636. **may I wyte,** may I lay the blame upon. 3637. **wende,** weened, thought. 3638. **gnow,** gnawed. 3645. **starf,** died. 3647. **carf,** *lit.* carved. 3653. **Nero,** emperor from 54 to 68. 3654. **lith ful lowe adoun,** *i.e.* in Hell. 3655. **Swetonius,** Suetonius (*c.* 69–*c.* 140), whose *Lives of the Twelve Caesars* includes an account of Nero. Chaucer, like many medieval authors, was fond of referring to ancient authorities, including some he had not read. The reference here may be an instance, since most of the material in the story of Nero could have been found in the *Roman de la Rose* and Boethius. Certain details in this and in other tragedies related by the Monk have been traced to the great thirteenth-century encyclopedia by Vincent of Beauvais, the *Speculum Historiale* (see Pauline Aiken, *Speculum,* XVII. 56–68); but since the *Speculum* is completely derivative, is an enormous compilation (the 1494 edition fills nearly 1000 large folio pages), and the brief passages which Chaucer might have used are widely scattered, his acquaintance with the work can only be considered a possibility. 3657. **septemtrioun,** north. 3659. **brouded,** adorned (*lit.* embroidered). 3661. **delicaat,** fastidious. 3663. **That ilke clooth,** that same robe. **o day,** one day. 3667. **lustes,** desires. **decree,** code. 3669. **delicasie,** delight. 3670. **slow,** slew. 3673. **array,** condition. 3676. **tolde,** accounted. 3678. **but seyde,** but he said. 3680. **domesman,** judge. 3684. **wade,** go.

In yowthe a maister hadde this emperour   3685
To teche hym letterure and curteisye,
For of moralitee he was the flour,
As in his tyme, but if bookes lye;
And whil this maister hadde of hym maistrye,
He maked hym so konnyng and so sowple   3690
That longe tyme it was er tirannye
Or any vice dorste on hym uncowple.

This Seneca, of which that I devyse,
By cause Nero hadde of hym swich drede,
For he fro vices wolde hym ay chastise   3695
Discreetly, as by word and nat by dede,—
"Sire," wolde he seyn, "an emperour moot nede
Be vertuous and hate tirannye—"
For which he in a bath made hym to blede
On bothe his armes, til he moste dye.   3700

This Nero hadde eek of acustumaunce
In youthe agayns his maister for to ryse,
Which afterward hym thoughte a greet grev-
   aunce;
Therfore he made hym dyen in this wise.
But natheless this Seneca the wise   3705
Chees in a bath to dye in this manere
Rather than han another tormentise;
And thus hath Nero slayn his maister deere.

Now fil it so that Fortune liste no lenger
The hye pryde of Nero to cherice,   3710
For though that he were strong, yet was she
   strenger.
She thoughte thus, "By God! I am to nyce
To sette a man that is fulfild of vice

In heigh degree, and emperour hym calle.
By God! out of his sete I wol hym trice;   3715
Whan he leest weneth, sonnest shal he falle."

The peple roos upon hym on a nyght
For his defaute, and whan he it espied,
Out of his dores anon he hath hym dight
Allone, and ther he wende han been allied,   3720
He knokked faste, and ay the moore he cried,
The fastere shette they the dores alle.
Tho wiste he wel, he hadde himself mysgyed,
And wente his wey; no lenger dorste he calle.

The peple cride and rombled up and doun,   3725
That with his erys herde he how they seyde,
"Where is this false tiraunt, this Neroun?"
For fere almoost out of his wit he breyde,
And to his goddes pitously he preyde
For socour, but it myghte nat bityde.   3730
For drede of this, hym thoughte that he deyde,
And ran into a gardyn hym to hyde.

And in this gardyn foond he cherles tweye
That seten by a fyr ful greet and reed.
And to thise cherles two he gan to preye   3735
To sleen hym, and to girden of his heed,
That to his body, whan that he were deed,
Were no despit ydoon for his defame.
Hymself he slow, he koude no bettre reed,   3739
Of which Fortune lough, and hadde a game.

De Oloferno

Was nevere capitayn under a kyng
That regnes mo putte in subjeccioun,
Ne strenger was in feeld of alle thyng,
As in his tyme, ne gretter of renoun,   3744

3686. letterure, book learning. **3692. uncowple,** let loose. **3693. Seneca,** Lucius Annaeus Seneca (*c.* 5 B.C.–A.D. 65), states-man and moralist, the author of numerous prose works and nine verse tragedies. **3693. devyse,** relate, explain. **3695. For he fro vices . . .** The actual cause of Seneca's death was not that given by Chaucer. He was accused of participation in the Pisonian conspiracy to assassinate Nero. **3701. This Nero . . .** Chaucer describes the death of Seneca twice, presum-ably because he was following two sources. In addition to *RR* and Boethius the story is told in the *Legenda Aurea* (life of St. Peter). **hadde . . . of acustumaunce,** was accustomed. **3702. agayns,** in the presence of. **3706. Chees,** chose. Seneca was allowed to choose the way in which he should die. **3707. tormentise,** torture. **3712. nyce,** foolish. **3715. trice,** pluck. **3720. allied,** possessed of allies. **3722. shette,** shut. **3723. Tho,** then. **mysgyed,** misguided. **3725. rombled,** made a tumult. **3728. breyde,** started. **3731. deyde,** would have died. **3736. girden of,** strike off. **3739. reed,** counsel. **3740. lough,** laughed. **game,** sport, amusement. **3742. regnes mo,** more kingdoms. **3743. of alle thyng,** in every respect.

Ne moore pompous in heigh presumpcioun
Than Oloferne, which Fortune ay kiste
So likerously, and ladde hym up and doun,
Til that his heed was of, er that he wiste.

Nat oonly that this world hadde hym in awe
For lesynge of richesse or libertee,   3750
But he made every man reneyen his lawe.
"Nabugodonosor was god," seyde hee;
"Noon oother god sholde adoured bee."
Agayns his heeste no wight dorste trespace,
Save in Bethulia, a strong citee,   3755
Where Eliachim a preest was of that place.

But taak kepe of the deeth of Oloferne:
Amydde his hoost he dronke lay a-nyght,
Withinne his tente, large as is a berne,
And yet, for al his pompe and al his myght, 3760
Judith, a womman, as he lay upright
Slepynge, his heed of smoot, and from his tente
Ful pryvely she stal from every wight,
And with his heed unto hir toun she wente.

De Rege Anthiocho illustri

What nedeth it of kyng Anthiochus   3765
To telle his hye roial magestee,
His hye pride, his werkes venymus?
For swich another was ther noon as he.
Rede which that he was in Machabee,
And rede the proude wordes that he seyde, 3770
And why he fil fro heigh prosperitee,
And in an hill how wrecchedly he deyde.

Fortune hym hadde enhaunced so in pride
That verraily he wende he myghte attayne
Unto the sterres upon every syde,   3775

And in balance weyen ech montayne,
And alle the floodes of the see restrayne.
And Goddes peple hadde he moost in hate;
Hem wolde he sleen in torment and in payne,
Wenynge that God ne myghte his pride abate.

And for that Nichanore and Thymothee   3781
Of Jewes weren venquysshed myghtily,
Unto the Jewes swich an hate hadde he
That he bad greithen his chaar ful hastily,
And swoor, and seyde ful despitously   3785
Unto Jerusalem he wolde eftsoone,
To wreken his ire on it ful cruelly;
But of his purpos he was let ful soone.

God for his manace hym so soore smoot
With invisible wounde, ay incurable,   3790
That in his guttes carf it so and boot
That his peynes weren importable.
And certeinly the wreche was resonable,
For many a mannes guttes dide he peyne.   3794
But from his purpos cursed and dampnable,
For al his smert, he wolde hym nat restreyne,

But bad anon apparaillen his hoost;
And sodeynly, er he was of it war,
God daunted al his pride and al his boost.
For he so soore fil out of his char   3800
That it his limes and his skyn totar,
So that he neyther myghte go ne ryde,
But in a chayer men aboute hym bar,
Al forbrused, bothe bak and syde.

The wreche of God hym smoot so cruelly   3805
That thurgh his body wikked wormes crepte,
And therwithal he stank so horribly

3745. **pompous**, arrogant. 3746. **Oloferne**, Holofernes; cf. the book of *Judith* in the Old Testament Apocrypha. 3747. **likerously**, sweetly, wantonly. 3750. **lesynge**, (fear of) losing. 3751. **reneyen**, abjure. 3754. **heeste**, behest, command. 3756. **Eliachim**, the name of the high priest in the Vulgate; in the Authorized Version it is Joakim. 3759. **berne**, barn. 3761. **upright**, face up. 3763. **stal**, stole. 3765. **Anthiochus**, Antiochus, King of Syria (*c.* 173–162 B.C.). 3769. **which that**, what. **Machabee**. Cf. *2 Maccabees*, 9:1–28, in the Old Testament Apocrypha. 3772. **in**, on. Cf. l. 3817. 3776. **balance**, scales. 3780. **abate**, bring down, destroy. 3781. **Nichanore and Thymothee**. "And while he was at Ecbatana, news was brought him what had happened unto Nicanor and the forces of Timotheus." 2 *Maccabees*, 9:3. 3784. **greithen**, prepared. **chaar**, chariot. 3786. **wolde**, wished to go. 3788. **let**, prevented. 3789. **manace**, threat. 3791. **carf**, cut. **boot**, bit. 3793. **wreche**, retribution, vengeance. 3794. **peyne**, inflict pain upon. 3797. **apparaillen**, prepare. **hoost**, army. 3800. **soore**, violently. **char**, chariot. 3801. **totar**, tore to pieces. 3802. **go**, walk. 3803. **chayer**, chair, litter. **bar**, bore. 3804. **forbrused**, severely bruised.

That noon of al his meynee that hym kepte,
Wheither so he wook, or ellis slepte,
Ne myghte noght the stynk of hym endure. 3810
In this meschief he wayled and eek wepte,
And knew God lord of every creature.

To al his hoost and to hymself also
Ful wlatsom was the stynk of his careyne;
No man ne myghte hym bere to ne fro.   3815
And in this stynk and this horrible peyne,
He starf ful wrecchedly in a monteyne.
Thus hath this robbour and this homycide,
That many a man made to wepe and pleyne,
Swich gerdoun as bilongeth unto pryde.   3820

De Alexandro

The storie of Alisaundre is so commune
That every wight that hath discrecioun
Hath herd somwhat or al of his fortune.
This wyde world, as in conclusioun,   3824
He wan by strengthe, or for his hye renoun
They weren glad for pees unto hym sende.
The pride of man and beest he leyde adoun,
Wher so he cam, unto the worldes ende.

Comparisoun myghte nevere yet been maked
Bitwixe hym and another conquerour;   3830
For al this world for drede of hym hath quaked.
He was of knyghthod and of fredom flour;
Fortune hym made the heir of hire honour.
Save wyn and wommen, no thing myghte
      aswage
His hye entente in armes and labour,   3835
So was he ful of leonyn corage.

What pris were it to hym, though I yow tolde
Of Darius, and an hundred thousand mo

Of kynges, princes, dukes, erles bolde
Whiche he conquered, and broghte hem into
      wo?   3840
I seye, as fer as man may ryde or go,
The world was his,—what sholde I moore de-
      vyse?
For though I write or tolde yow everemo
Of his knyghthode, it myghte nat suffise.

Twelf yeer he regned, as seith Machabee. 3845
Philippes sone of Macidoyne he was,
That first was kyng in Grece the contree.
O worthy, gentil Alisandre, allas,
That evere sholde fallen swich a cas!
Empoysoned of thyn owene folk thou weere;
Thy *sys* Fortune hath turned into *aas*, 3851
And yet for thee ne weep she never a teere.

Who shal me yeven teeris to compleyne
The deeth of gentillesse and of franchise,
That al the world weelded in his demeyne,
And yet hym thoughte it myghte nat suf-
      fise?   3856
So ful was his corage of heigh emprise.
Allas! who shal me helpe to endite
False Fortune, and poyson to despise,
The whiche two of al this wo I wyte?   3860

De Julio Cesare

By wisedom, manhede, and by greet labour,
From humble bed to roial magestee
Up roos he Julius, the conquerour,
That wan al th'occident by land and see,
By strengthe of hand, or elles by tretee, 3865
And unto Rome made hem tributarie;
And sitthe of Rome the emperour was he,
Til that Fortune weex his adversarie.

3808. meynee, household, following. **kepte,** took care of. **3812. knew,** acknowledged. **3814. wlatsom,** nauseating, loathsome. **careyne,** carcass. **3817. starf,** died. **in,** on. The Vulgate reads *in montibus*. **3820. gerdoun,** reward. **3821. so commune.** The story of Alexander the Great, with many legendary additions, circulated in a number of Latin versions and in romances in all the vernacular languages of Europe. **3822. hath discrecioun,** is grown up. **3824. as in conclusioun,** in short. **3834. aswage,** lessen. **3837. pris,** esteem, fame: How would it enhance his fame, though I told you . . . **3841. ryde or go.** Cf. l. 3802. **3843. write,** wrote. **3845. Machabee,** 1 *Maccabees,* 1:1–7. **3849. cas,** event, situation. **3851. *sys*,** six (in dice). **aas,** ace, one. See note to B 125. **3852. weep,** wept. **3853. yeven,** give. **3854. franchise,** courtesy,—the death of one characterized by nobility and courtesy. **3855. demeyne,** dominion, territory owned or controlled by him. **3857. corage,** heart. **emprise,** endeavor. **3858. endite,** indict. **3860. wyte,** blame. **3868. weex,** grew, became.

O myghty Cesar, that in Thessalie
Agayn Pompeus, fader thyn in lawe,   3870
That of the orient hadde al the chivalrie
As fer as that the day bigynneth dawe,
Thou thurgh thy knyghthod hast hem take and
    slawe,
Save fewe folk that with Pompeus fledde,
Thurgh which thou puttest al th'orient in awe.
Thanke Fortune, that so wel thee spedde!   3876

But now a litel while I wol biwaille
This Pompeus, this noble governour
Of Rome, which that fleigh at this bataille.
I seye, oon of his men, a fals traitour,   3880
His heed of smoot, to wynnen hym favour
Of Julius, and hym the heed he broghte.
Allas, Pompeye, of th'orient conquerour,
That Fortune unto swich a fyn thee broghte!

To Rome agayn repaireth Julius   3885
With his triumphe, lauriat ful hye;
But on a tyme Brutus Cassius,
That evere hadde of his hye estaat envye,
Ful prively hath maad conspiracye
Agayns this Julius in subtil wise,   3890
And caste the place in which he sholde dye
With boydekyns, as I shal yow devyse.

This Julius to the Capitolie wente
Upon a day, as he was wont to goon,

And in the Capitolie anon hym hente   3895
This false Brutus and his othere foon,
And stiked hym with boydekyns anoon
With many a wounde, and thus they lete hym
    lye;
But nevere gronte he at no strook but oon,
Or elles at two, but if his storie lye.   3900

So manly was this Julius of herte,
And so wel lovede estaatly honestee,
That though his deedly woundes soore smerte,
His mantel over his hypes caste he,
For no man sholde seen his privetee;   3905
And as he lay of diyng in a traunce,
And wiste verraily that deed was hee,
Of honestee yet hadde he remembraunce.

Lucan, to thee this storie I recomende,
And to Swetoun, and to Valerius also,   3910
That of this storie writen word and ende,
How that to thise grete conqueroures two
Fortune was first freend, and sitthe foo.
No man ne truste upon hire favour longe,
But have hire in awayt for everemoo;   3915
Witnesse on alle thise conqueroures stronge.

Cresus

This riche Cresus, whilom kyng of Lyde,
Of which Cresus Cirus soore hym dradde,
Yet was he caught amyddes al his pryde,

3870. Pompeus, Pompey, who was really his son-in-law. Writers before Chaucer seem to have confused Pompeius Rufus (who was Caesar's father-in-law) with Gnaeus Pompeius (Pompey the Great), who won his greatest fame by his campaigns in the East, and who was married to Caesar's daughter Julia. Caesar defeated him in 48 B.C. at Pharsalus in Thessaly. Pompey escaped but was stabbed to death as he landed in Egypt. **3871. chivalrie,** men-at-arms collectively. **3872. dawe,** dawn, *i.e.* as far as where the sun rises. **3873. hem,** referring to *chivalrie.* **take and slawe,** taken and slain. **3876. spedde,** favored, advanced. **3879. fleigh,** fled. **3881. His heed of smoot,** smote off his head. **hym,** himself. **3884. fyn,** end. **3886. lauriat,** crowned with laurel. **3887. Brutus Cassius.** Chaucer was not the first to make one person out of Brutus and Cassius. **3891. caste,** planned. **3892. boydekyns,** bodkins, daggers. **3893. Capitolie,** Capitol. **3895. hente,** seized. **3896. foon,** foes. **3899. gronte,** groaned. **3902. estaatly honestee,** majestic decorum. **3903. soore smerte,** sorely smarted. **3909–10. Lucan.** Lucan (39–65), author of a long poem called *Pharsalia,* relating the struggle between Caesar and Pompey. **Swetoun,** Suetonius (*c.* 69–*c.* 140), author of prose *Lives of the (Twelve) Caesars.* **Valerius,** Valerius Maximus (*fl.* A.D. 30), author of *Factorum ac Dictorum Memorabilium Libri IX.* **recomende,** commit, refer for authority. These two lines are not to be taken as evidence that Chaucer drew his material from these sources, although some have argued that he did. **3911. word and ende,** a common Middle English corruption of *ord and ende* (beginning and end). **3913. sitthe,** afterwards. **3914. No man ne truste,** let no man trust. **3915. But have hire in awayt,** keep a watchful eye on her. **3916. Witnesse on,** an idiom used several times by Chaucer with the meaning "take or consider as a witness . . ." Cf. *Witnesse on Myda* . . . (D 951), *Witnesse on Job* (D 1491), etc. **3917. Cresus,** Croesus, the last king of Lydia (*c.* 560–546 B.C.), overthrown by the Persian king Cyrus. His death early became the subject of legend. **whilom,** at one time. **3919. amyddes,** amidst.

And to be brent men to the fyr hym ladde. 3920
But swich a reyn doun fro the welkne shadde
That slow the fyr, and made hym to escape;
But to be war no grace yet he hadde,
Til Fortune on the galwes made hym gape.

Whanne he escaped was, he kan nat stente
For to bigynne a newe werre agayn.   3926
He wende wel, for that Fortune hym sente
Swich hap that he escaped thurgh the rayn,
That of his foos he myghte nat be slayn;
And eek a swevene upon a nyght he mette, 3930
Of which he was so proud and eek so fayn
That in vengeance he al his herte sette.

Upon a tree he was, as that hym thoughte,
Ther Juppiter hym wessh, bothe bak and syde,
And Phebus eek a fair towaille hym
    broughte   3935
To dryen hym with; and therfore wax his
    pryde,
And to his doghter, that stood hym bisyde,
Which that he knew in heigh sentence ha-
    bounde,

He bad hire telle hym what it signyfyde,   3939
And she his dreem bigan right thus expounde:

"The tree," quod she, "the galwes is to meene,
And Juppiter bitokneth snow and reyn,
And Phebus, with his towaille so clene,
Tho been the sonne stremes for to seyn.
Thou shalt anhanged be, fader, certeyn;   3945
Reyn shal thee wasshe, and sonne shal thee
    drye."
Thus warned hym ful plat and eek ful pleyn
His doghter, which that called was Phanye.

Anhanged was Cresus, the proude kyng;
His roial trone myghte hym nat availle.   3950
Tragedies noon oother maner thyng
Ne kan in syngyng crie ne biwaille
But that Fortune alwey wole assaille
With unwar strook the regnes that been proude;
For whan men trusteth hire, thanne wol she
    faille,   3955
And covere hire brighte face with a clowde.

Explicit Tragedia.

Heere stynteth the Knyght the Monk of his tale.

3921. welkne, clouds, sky. **shadde,** fell, poured. **3922. slow,** slew, quenched. **3923. war,** cautious, *i.e.* he did not yet have the good fortune to be cautious. **3925. stente,** desist. **3927. wende,** supposed. **3928. hap,** (good) fortune. **3930. a swevene . . . he mette,** he dreamed a dream. **3932. in,** upon. **3933. hym thoughte,** it seemed to him. **3934. Ther,** where. **wessh,** washed. **3938. heigh sentence,** deep insight. **habounde,** to abound. **3941. meene,** signify. **3947. plat,** flatly, plainly. **pleyn,** plainly. **3951. Tragedies.** The observation comes from Boethius, ii, pr. 2: "what other thyng by-waylen the cryinges of tragedyes but oonly the dedes of Fortune, that with unwar strook overturneth the realmes of greet nobleye." **3954. unwar,** unexpected. **regnes,** kingdoms.

The Nun's Priest's Tale

THE PROLOGUE OF THE NUN'S PRIEST'S TALE

The Prologe of the Nonnes Preestes Tale.

"Hoo!" quod the Knyght, "good sire, na-
 moore of this!
That ye han seyd is right ynough, ywis,
And muchel moore; for litel hevynesse
Is right ynough to muche folk, I gesse.   3960
I seye for me, it is a greet disese,
Whereas men han been in greet welthe and ese,
To heeren of hire sodeyn fal, allas!
And the contrarie is joye and greet solas,
As whan a man hath been in povre estaat,   3965
And clymbeth up and wexeth fortunat,
And there abideth in prosperitee.
Swich thyng is gladsom, as it thynketh me,
And of swich thyng were goodly for to telle."
"Ye," quod oure Hooste, "by seint Poules belle!
Ye seye right sooth; this Monk he clappeth
 lowde.   3971
He spak how Fortune covered with a clowde
I noot nevere what; and also of a tragedie
Right now ye herde, and, pardee, no remedie
It is for to biwaille ne compleyne   3975
That that is doon, and als it is a peyne,
As ye han seyd, to heere of hevynesse.
 Sire Monk, namoore of this, so God yow blesse!
Youre tale anoyeth al this compaignye.
Swich talkyng is nat worth a boterflye,   3980
For therinne is ther no desport ne game.
Wherfore, sire Monk, or daun Piers by youre
 name,
I pray yow hertely telle us somwhat elles;

For sikerly, nere clynkyng of youre belles,
That on youre bridel hange on every syde,
By hevene kyng, that for us alle dyde,   3986
I sholde er this han fallen doun for sleep,
Althogh the slough had never been so deep;
Thanne hadde youre tale al be toold in veyn.
For certeinly, as that thise clerkes seyn,   3990
Whereas a man may have noon audience,
Noght helpeth it to tellen his sentence.
 And wel I woot the substance is in me,
If any thyng shal wel reported be.
Sire, sey somwhat of huntyng, I yow preye."
 "Nay," quod this Monk, "I have no lust to
 pleye.   3996
Now lat another telle, as I have toold."
Thanne spak oure Hoost with rude speche and
 boold,
And seyde unto the Nonnes Preest anon,
"Com neer, thou preest, com hyder, thou sir
 John!   4000
Telle us swich thyng as may oure hertes glade.
Be blithe, though thou ryde upon a jade.
What thogh thyn hors be bothe foul and lene?
If he wol serve thee, rekke nat a bene.
Looke that thyn herte be murie everemo."   4005
 "Yis, sire," quod he, "yis, Hoost, so moot I go,
But I be myrie, ywis I wol be blamed."
And right anon his tale he hath attamed,
And thus he seyde unto us everichon,   4009
This sweete preest, this goodly man sir John.

Explicit.

3957. The Prologue exists in two forms, a shorter and a longer. In the shorter, and almost certainly the earlier, version the Host, rather than the Knight, interrupts the Monk (as in a number of manuscripts). In the longer form lines 3961–80 were added and the Knight was substituted for the Host in line 3957. 3958. That, what. 3961. disese, discomfort. 3970. seint Poules, St. Paul's church in London. 3971. clappeth, talks, carrying out the figure of the bell. 3973. noot, know not. 3976. als, also. peyne, painful experience. 3977. As ye han seyd, referring to the Knight's words. 3984. nere, were (there) not. 3986. hevene, heaven's. dyde, died. 3988. slough, mire. 3993. substance, basis, foundation (NED). Presumably the sense is "I have the capacity to understand." 3996. lust, desire. 4000. sir John, a common and rather contemptuous designation for a priest. 4008. attamed, begun.

THE NUN'S PRIEST'S TALE

Heere bigynneth the Nonnes Preestes Tale of the Cok and Hen, Chauntecleer and Pertelote.

A povre wydwe, somdeel stape in age
Was whilom dwellyng in a narwe cotage,
Biside a grove, stondynge in a dale.
This wydwe, of which I telle yow my tale,
Syn thilke day that she was last a wyf, 4015
In pacience ladde a ful symple lyf,
For litel was hir catel and hir rente.
By housbondrie of swich as God hire sente
She foond hirself and eek hir doghtren two.
Thre large sowes hadde she, and namo, 4020
Three keen, and eek a sheep that highte Malle.
Ful sooty was hir bour and eek hir halle,
In which she eet ful many a sklendre meel.
Of poynaunt sauce hir neded never a deel.
No deyntee morsel passed thurgh hir throte;
Hir diete was accordant to hir cote. 4026
Repleccioun ne made hire nevere sik;
Attempree diete was al hir phisik,
And excercise, and hertes suffisaunce.
The goute lette hire nothyng for to
daunce, 4030
N'apoplexie shente nat hir heed.
No wyn ne drank she, neither whit ne reed;
Hir bord was served moost with whit and
blak,—
Milk and broun breed, in which she foond no
lak, 4034
Seynd bacoun, and somtyme an ey or tweye;
For she was, as it were, a maner deye.
A yeerd she hadde, enclosed al aboute
With stikkes, and a drye dych withoute,
In which she hadde a cok, hight Chauntecleer.
In al the land, of crowyng nas his peer. 4040
His voys was murier than the murie orgon
On messe-dayes that in the chirche gon.
Wel sikerer was his crowyng in his logge

The Nun's Priest's Tale. The Nun's Priest's story of the cock and the fox belongs to the general class of narratives known as the beast fable. Of this class the most popular collection in the Middle Ages was the French beast epic, the *Roman de Renart*, with derivatives in the Middle High German *Reinhard Fuchs*, the Flemish *Roman van den Vos Reinaerde*, and others. In England there is no parallel collection until Caxton printed in 1481 *The History of Reynard the Fox*, the translation of a Flemish prose version. Indeed there are only scanty evidences of an interest in these stories, such as *The Fox and the Wolf* and Chaucer's tale. The immediate source of *The Nun's Priest's Tale* is unknown, although stories of the craftiness of the fox at the expense of a fowl go back as far as Aesop's fable of the fox and the crow in Greek. In some respects Chaucer's story is closer to the Flemish than to the French *Roman*, but it would be going too far to conclude that he derived his material directly from Flemish. The story of the cock and the fox was one of the most popular episodes incorporated in the *Roman de Renart*, and separate versions of it, oral as well as written, were in circulation. The basic plot forms a relatively small part of the tale, elaborated as it is with features of character, exchanges of opinion, moral observations, and descriptive details. Much of this material may be the poet's additions. Apart from the allusion to the Peasant's Revolt of 1381 (see note to l. 4584) there is nothing by which we can determine the date of the composition. It is in the meter of the General Prologue and was probably written during the period of *The Canterbury Tales*. Elements which Chaucer could have derived from "Jankyn's book" suggest that its date may not be far from that of the Wife's *Prologue*. It is appropriate to the teller and may well have been written with him in mind.

4011. wydwe, widow. **stape,** advanced (ME. *stapen*, to step, advance). Cf. E 1514: *stapen is in age*. **4016. ladde,** led. **4017. catel,** possessions. **rente,** income. **4018. housbondrie,** careful management. **4019. foond hirself,** provided for herself. **4021. keen,** cows (kine). **highte Malle,** was named Malle. The sheep was evidently something of a pet. **4022. hir bour and eek hir halle.** It is not certain whether the widow's house had a separate chamber for sleeping (bower) or whether the bower was a portion of the hall separated by a curtain at night. **4024. hir neded,** (impersonal constr.) she needed. **4026. cote,** cottage. **4027. Repleccioun,** repletion, surfeit. **4028. Attempree,** temperate. **4029. excercise,** physical activity. **suffisaunce,** content. **4030. lette,** hindered. **4031. shente,** injured. **4033. whit and blak,** elaborated in the next line. **4035. Seynd,** broiled (*lit.* singed). **ey or tweye,** an egg or two. **4036. a maner deye,** a kind of dairywoman, whose duties included looking after the livestock. **4039. hight,** called. **4041. murier,** merrier, pleasanter. **orgon,** organ, properly sing. at this date, although the verb *gon* is plur. **4042. messe-dayes,** feast days (*lit.* mass days). **4043. sikerer,** more certain. **logge,** lodge. While the word was often loosely used, it may here have humorous overtones.

Than is a clokke or an abbey orlogge.
By nature he knew ech ascencioun   4045
Of the equynoxial in thilke toun;
For whan degrees fiftene weren ascended,
Thanne crew he, that it myghte nat been
     amended.
✗His coomb was redder than the fyn coral,
And batailled as it were a castel wal;   4050
His byle was blak, and as the jeet it shoon;
Lyk asure were his legges and his toon;
His nayles whitter than the lylye flour,
And lyk the burned gold was his colour.
This gentil cok hadde in his governaunce   4055
Sevene hennes for to doon al his plesaunce,
Whiche were his sustres and his paramours,
And wonder lyk to hym, as of colours;
⁕ Of whiche the faireste hewed on hir throte
Was cleped faire damoysele Pertelote.   4060
Curteys she was, discreet, and debonaire,
And compaignable, and bar hyrself so faire,
Syn thilke day that she was seven nyght oold,
That trewely she hath the herte in hoold
Of Chauntecleer, loken in every lith;   4065
He loved hire so that wel was hym therwith.
But swich a joye was it to here hem synge,
Whan that the brighte sonne gan to sprynge,
In sweete accord, "My lief is faren in londe!"
For thilke tyme, as I have understonde,   4070
Beestes and briddes koude speke and synge.
     And so bifel that in a dawenynge,
As Chauntecleer among his wyves alle
Sat on his perche, that was in the halle,
And next hym sat this faire Pertelote,   4075
This Chauntecleer gan gronen in his throte,

As man that in his dreem is drecched soore.
And whan that Pertelote thus herde hym roore,
She was agast, and seyde, "Herte deere,
What eyleth yow, to grone in this manere?   4080
Ye been a verray sleper; fy, for shame!"
     And he answerde, and seyde thus: "Madame,
I pray yow that ye take it nat agrief.
By God, me mette I was in swich meschief
Right now, that yet myn herte is soore
     afright.   4085
Now God," quod he, "my swevene recche
     aright,
And kepe my body out of foul prisoun!
Me mette how that I romed up and doun
Withinne our yeerd, wheer as I saugh a beest
Was lyk an hound, and wolde han maad
     areest   4090
Upon my body, and wolde han had me deed.
His colour was bitwixe yelow and reed,
And tipped was his tayl and bothe his eeris
With blak, unlyk the remenant of his heeris;
His snowte smal, with glowynge eyen tweye.
Yet of his look for feere almoost I deye;   4096
This caused me my gronyng, doutelees."
     "Avoy!" quod she, "fy on yow, hertelees!
Allas!" quod she, "for, by that God above,
Now han ye lost myn herte and al my love.
I kan nat love a coward, by my feith!   4101
For certes, what so any womman seith,
We alle desiren, if it myghte bee,
To han housbondes hardy, wise, and free,
And secree, and no nygard, ne no fool,   4105
Ne hym that is agast of every tool,
Ne noon avauntour, by that God above!

4044. orlogge, clock. **4045. ascencioun Of the equynoxial.** The equinoctial, the celestial equator, was an imaginary circle which made one revolution every twenty-four hours. An hour therefore represents 15° on the equinoctial, and if twenty-four imaginary points are marked on it, one will rise above the horizon each hour. Chauntecleer knew each such point of time. Since the time varied with the position of the observer, Chaucer adds *in thilke toun.* **4048. crew,** crowed. **4050. batailled,** crenelated. **4052. asure,** lapis lazuli. **toon,** toes. **4054. burned,** burnished. **4058. as of,** in respect to. **4063. Syn,** since. **4064. in hoold,** in her keeping. **4065. loken in every lith,** locked in every limb or joint. **4069. My lief is faren in londe,** my sweetheart has gone away (into the country). It was probably the beginning (or the refrain) of a popular song. Skeat published (*Athenaeum,* Oct. 24, 1896) a seven-line stanza (*c.* 1500) with this as the opening line, containing also the line "She hath my hert in hold." It may be older than the manuscript in which it survives. **4072. dawenynge,** dawn. **4077. drecched,** troubled in his sleep. **4081. Ye been a verray sleper,** you're a fine sleeper! **4083. agrief,** amiss. **4084. me mette,** I dreamed. **4086. recche aright,** interpret favorably, make my dream turn out well. **4090–1. maad areest Upon,** taken prisoner. **4094. remenant,** rest. **4095. eyen,** eyes. **4098. hertelees,** timid. **4104. free,** generous. **4105. secree,** able to keep a secret, especially not betraying love affairs. **4106. tool,** sword, weapon. **4107. avauntour,** boaster.

How dorste ye seyn, for shame, unto youre love
That any thyng myghte make yow aferd?
Have ye no mannes herte, and han a berd?   4110
Allas! and konne ye been agast of swevenys?
Nothyng, God woot, but vanitee in swevene is.
Swevenes engendren of replecciouns,
And ofte of fume and of complecciouns,   4114
Whan humours been to habundant in a wight.
Certes this dreem, which ye han met to-nyght,
Cometh of the greete superfluytee
Of youre rede colera, pardee,
Which causeth folk to dreden in hir dremes
Of arwes, and of fyr with rede lemes,   4120
Of rede beestes, that they wol hem byte,
Of contek, and of whelpes, grete and lyte;
Right as the humour of malencolie
Causeth ful many a man in sleep to crie
For feere of blake beres, or boles blake,   4125
Or elles blake develes wole hem take.
Of othere humours koude I telle also
That werken many a man in sleep ful wo;
But I wol passe as lightly as I kan.   4129
      Lo Catoun, which that was so wys a man,
Seyde he nat thus, 'Ne do no fors of dremes?'
      Now sire," quod she, "whan we flee fro the
            bemes,
For Goddes love, as taak som laxatyf.
Up peril of my soule and of my lyf,
I conseille yow the beste, I wol nat lye,   4135
That bothe of colere and of malencolye
Ye purge yow; and for ye shal nat tarie,
Though in this toun is noon apothecarie,

I shal myself to herbes techen yow
That shul been for youre heele and for youre
      prow;   4140
And in oure yeerd tho herbes shal I fynde
The whiche han of hire propretee by kynde
To purge yow bynethe and eek above.
Foryet nat this, for Goddes owene love!
Ye been ful coleryk of compleccioun;   4145
Ware the sonne in his ascencioun
Ne fynde yow nat repleet of humours hoote.
And if it do, I dar wel leye a grote,
That ye shul have a fevere terciane,
Or an agu, that may be youre bane.   4150
A day or two ye shul have digestyves
Of wormes, er ye take youre laxatyves
Of lawriol, centaure, and fumetere,
Or elles of ellebor, that groweth there,
Of katapuce, or of gaitrys beryis,   4155
Of herbe yve, growyng in oure yeerd, ther
      mery is;
Pekke hem up right as they growe and ete hem
      yn.
Be myrie, housbonde, for youre fader kyn!
Dredeth no dreem, I kan sey yow namoore."
      "Madame," quod he, "graunt mercy of youre
            loore.   4160
But nathelees, as touchyng daun Catoun,
That hath of wysdom swich a greet renoun,
Though that he bad no dremes for to drede,
By God, men may in olde bookes rede
Of many a man moore of auctorite   4165
Than evere Caton was, so moot I thee,

4113. **engendren of,** spring from. Chaucer several times refers to the causes of dreams; see in particular the beginning of *The Hous of Fame*. **replecciouns,** cf. l. 4027. 4114. **fume,** vapor rising to the head, especially from drinking. **complecciouns,** see note to A 333. 4116. **met,** dreamed. **to-nyght,** last night. 4118. **rede colera,** red choler or bile. 4119. **dreden . . . of,** dread. 4120. **lemes,** flames. 4122. **contek,** strife. **lyte,** little. 4123. **malencolie,** black bile. 4125. **beres, or boles,** bears, or bulls. 4128. **That . . . wo,** that produce for many a man full troublesome sleep. 4130. **Catoun,** Cato. The references is to the *Disticha Catonis*, II. 31: *Somnia ne cures* (trust not dreams). 4131. **Ne do no fors of dremes,** pay no attention to dreams. 4132. **flee,** fly. **bemes,** beams. 4133. **as take,** take. 4134. **Up,** upon. 4139. **techen,** guide. 4140. **prow,** benefit. 4141. **tho,** those. 4145. **coleryk,** bilious. 4146. **Ware,** beware (that). **in his ascencioun,** as it increases in altitude. 4148. **grote.** The groat, a small silver coin, was worth four pence in Chaucer's day. 4149. **fevere terciane,** an intermittent fever increasing every third day, counting both ends of the series,—therefore, every other day. 4151. **digestyves.** For Pertelote's remedies see Curry, *Chaucer and the Medieval Sciences* (New York, 1926), p. 225, who shows that Pertelote was well informed on medieval medicine. *Digestyves* are "medicines for absorbing or dissipating melancholy and choler." They must be taken for some time before administering the laxatives mentioned: *lawriol* (laurus nobilis), *centaure* (centauria), *fumetere* (fumaria or fumus terre), *ellebor* (elleborus), *katapuce* (euphorbium), *gaitrys beryis* (rhamus), and *herbe yve* (coronopus). 4156. **ther mery is,** where it is pleasant. 4160. **graunt mercy,** great thanks. **loore,** instruction, advice. 4166. **so moot I thee,** so may I prosper.

That al the revers seyn of this sentence,
And han wel founden by experience
That dremes been significaciouns
As wel of joye as of tribulaciouns   4170
That folk enduren in this lif present.
Ther nedeth make of this noon argument;
The verray preeve sheweth it in dede.

    Oon of the gretteste auctour that men rede
Seith thus: that whilom two felawes wente   4175
On pilgrimage, in a ful good entente;
And happed so, they coomen in a toun
Wher as ther was swich congregacioun
Of peple, and eek so streit of herbergage,
That they ne founde as muche as o cotage   4180
In which they bothe myghte ylogged bee.
Wherfore they mosten of necessitee,
As for that nyght, departen compaignye;
And ech of hem gooth to his hostelrye,
And took his loggyng as it wolde falle.   4185
That oon of hem was logged in a stalle,
Fer in a yeerd, with oxen of the plough;
That oother man was logged wel ynough,
As was his aventure or his fortune,
That us governeth alle as in commune.   4190

    And so bifel that, longe er it were day,
This man mette in his bed, ther as he lay,
How that his felawe gan upon hym calle,
And seyde, 'Allas! for in an oxes stalle
This nyght I shal be mordred ther I lye.   4195
Now help me, deere brother, or I dye.
In alle haste com to me!' he sayde.
This man out of his sleep for feere abrayde;
But whan that he was wakened of his sleep,
He turned hym, and took of this no keep.   4200
Hym thoughte his dreem nas but a vanitee.
Thus twies in his slepyng dremed hee;

And atte thridde tyme yet his felawe
Cam, as hym thoughte, and seide, 'I am now
    slawe.
Bihoold my bloody woundes depe and wyde!
Arys up erly in the morwe tyde,   4206
And at the west gate of the toun,' quod he,
'A carte ful of donge ther shaltow se,
In which my body is hid ful prively;
Do thilke carte arresten boldely.   4210
My gold caused my mordre, sooth to sayn.'
And tolde hym every point how he was slayn,
With a ful pitous face, pale of hewe.
And truste wel, his dreem he foond ful trewe,
For on the morwe, as soone as it was day,   4215
To his felawes in he took the way;
And whan that he cam to this oxes stalle,
After his felawe he bigan to calle.

    The hostiler answerede hym anon,
And seyde, 'Sire, youre felawe is agon.   4220
As soone as day he wente out of the toun.'

    This man gan fallen in suspecioun,
Remembrynge on his dremes that he mette,
And forth he gooth—no lenger wolde he
    lette—
Unto the west gate of the toun, and fond   4225
A dong-carte, wente as it were to donge lond,
That was arrayed in that same wise
As ye han herd the dede man devyse.
And with an hardy herte he gan to crye
Vengeance and justice of this felonye.   4230
'My felawe mordred is this same nyght,
And in this carte he lith gapyng upright.
I crye out on the ministres,' quod he,
'That sholden kepe and reulen this citee.
Harrow! allas! heere lith my felawe slayn!' 4235
What sholde I moore unto this tale sayn?

4167. revers, reverse. **4173. verray preeve**, experience itself. **4174. Oon of the gretteste auctour.** On the construction see Language, § 50. The author is either Cicero or Valerius Maximus, both of whom tell the stories, but Chaucer probably had them at second hand. Cf. *Sources and Analogues*, pp. 662–3, and Skeat, Oxford Chaucer, v. 253. **4177. happed**, it happened. **4179. so streit of herbergage**, so scanty of accommodations. **4180. o cotage**, a single cottage. **4183. departen compaignye**, part company. **4187. Fer in a yeerd**, *i.e.* in a remote part of a yard. **4190. as in commune**, generally. **4192. mette**, dreamed. **ther as** and **ther** (l. 4195), where; they are equivalent expressions. **4198. abrayde**, started. **4200. took of this no keep**, took no heed of this. **4204. slawe**, slain. **4206. morwe**, morning. **4210. Do thilke carte arresten**, have that cart stopped. **4216. in**, lodging. **4219. hostiler**, innkeeper. **4222. gan fallen in suspecioun**, began to be suspicious. **4224. lette**, delay. **4226. wente**, (which) went. **4227. arrayed**, prepared (loaded). **4228. devyse**, describe. **4230. of**, for. **4232. lith gapyng upright**, lies on his back with his mouth open. **4233. ministres**, magistrates, law officers.

The peple out sterte and caste the cart to
    grounde,
And in the myddel of the dong they founde
The dede man, that mordred was al newe.
O blisful God, that art so just and trewe,   4240
Lo, how that thou biwreyest mordre alway!
Mordre wol out, that se we day by day.
Mordre is so wlatsom and abhomynable
To God, that is so just and resonable,
That he ne wol nat suffre it heled be,   4245
Though it abyde a yeer, or two, or thre.
Mordre wol out, this my conclusioun.
And right anon, ministres of that toun
Han hent the cartere and so soore hym pyned,
And eek the hostiler so soore engyned,   4250
That they biknewe hire wikkednesse anon,
And were anhanged by the nekke-bon.
    Heere may men seen that dremes been to
        drede.
And certes in the same book I rede,
Right in the nexte chapitre after this—   4255
I gabbe nat, so have I joye or blis—
Two men that wolde han passed over see,
For certeyn cause, into a fer contree,
If that the wynd ne hadde been contrarie,
That made hem in a citee for to tarie   4260
That stood ful myrie upon an haven-syde;
But on a day, agayn the even-tyde,
The wynd gan chaunge, and blew right as hem
    leste.
Jolif and glad they wente unto hir reste,
And casten hem ful erly for to saille.   4265
But to that o man fil a greet mervaille:
That oon of hem, in slepyng as he lay,
Hym mette a wonder dreem agayn the day.

Hym thoughte a man stood by his beddes syde,
And hym comanded that he sholde abyde,   4270
And seyde hym thus: 'If thou tomorwe wende,
Thow shalt be dreynt; my tale is at an ende.'
He wook, and tolde his felawe what he mette,
And preyde hym his viage for to lette;
As for that day, he preyde hym to byde.   4275
His felawe, that lay by his beddes syde,
Gan for to laughe, and scorned him ful faste.
'No dreem,' quod he, 'may so myn herte agaste
That I wol lette for to do my thynges.
I sette nat a straw by thy dremynges,   4280
For swevenes been but vanytees and japes.
Men dreme alday of owles and of apes,
And eek of many a maze therwithal;
Men dreme of thyng that nevere was ne shal.
But sith I see that thou wolt heere abyde,   4285
And thus forslewthen wilfully thy tyde,
God woot, it reweth me; and have good day!'
And thus he took his leve, and wente his way.
But er that he hadde half his cours yseyled,
Noot I nat why, ne what myschaunce it
    eyled,   4290
But casuelly the shippes botme rente,
And ship and man under the water wente
In sighte of othere shippes it bisyde,
That with hem seyled at the same tyde.
And therfore, faire Pertelote so deere,   4295
By swiche ensamples olde maistow leere
That no man sholde been to recchelees
Of dremes; for I seye thee, doutelees,
That many a dreem ful soore is for to drede.
    Lo, in the lyf of Seint Kenelm I rede,   4300
That was Kenulphus sone, the noble kyng
Of Mercenrike, how Kenelm mette a thyng.

4237. sterte, started. **4239. al newe,** very recently. **4241. biwreyest,** betrayest, revealest. **4243. wlatsom,** loathsome. **4245. heled,** concealed. **4247. this,** this (is). **4249. hent,** seized. **pyned,** tortured. **4250. engyned,** racked. **4251. biknewe,** acknowledged. **4253. to drede,** to be feared. **4255. in the nexte chapitre.** Since this is not true of either Cicero or Valerius Maximus, it is probable that Chaucer took the stories from a source not yet identified. **4256. gabbe,** talk idly, lie. **4257. Two men.** Chaucer gets involved in parenthetical ideas, and *two men* remains without a principal verb. **4262. agayn the even-tyde,** toward evening. **4263. leste,** it pleased. **4264. Jolif,** cheerful. **4265. casten,** planned, arranged. **4268. agayn the day,** toward morning. **4272. dreynt,** drowned. **4274. viage,** voyage. **lette,** put off. **4278. agaste,** frighten. **4281. japes,** tricks, deceits. **4282. alday,** continually. **4283. maze,** delusion. fantasy. **4284. ne shal,** nor shall be. **4286. forslewthen,** waste in sloth, idle away. **4290. Noot I nat why,** I know not why (double negative). **4291. casuelly,** by chance. **4293. it bisyde,** present, near at hand. Cf. A 402. **4296. leere,** learn. **4297. recchelees,** disregardful. **4300. Seint Kenelm,** the seven-year-old son of King Kenulph (Cenwulf) of Mercia, who after his father's death was murdered at the instigation of his aunt (819). **4302. Mercenrike,** kingdom of Mercia.

A lite er he was mordred, on a day,
His mordre in his avysioun he say.
His norice hym expowned every deel   4305
His swevene, and bad hym for to kepe hym
   weel
For traisoun; but he nas but seven yeer oold,
And therfore litel tale hath he toold
Of any dreem, so hooly was his herte.
By God! I hadde levere than my sherte   4310
That ye hadde rad his legende, as have I.
   Dame Pertelote, I sey yow trewely,
Macrobeus, that writ the avisioun
In Affrike of the worthy Cipioun,   4314
Affermeth dremes, and seith that they been
Warnynge of thynges that men after seen.
And forthermoore, I pray yow, looketh wel
In the olde testament, of Daniel,
If he heeld dremes any vanitee.
Reed eek of Joseph, and ther shul ye see   4320
Wher dremes be somtyme—I sey nat alle—
Warnynge of thynges that shul after falle.
Looke of Egipte the kyng, daun Pharao,
His bakere and his butiller also,
Wher they ne felte noon effect in dremes.   4325
Whoso wol seken actes of sondry remes
May rede of dremes many a wonder thyng.
Lo Cresus, which that was of Lyde kyng,
Mette he nat that he sat upon a tree,
Which signified he sholde anhanged bee?   4330
Lo heere Andromacha, Ectores wyf,
That day that Ector sholde lese his lyf,
She dremed on the same nyght biforn
How that the lyf of Ector sholde be lorn,
If thilke day he wente into bataille.   4335
She warned hym, but it myghte nat availle;

He wente for to fighte natheles,
But he was slayn anon of Achilles.
But thilke tale is al to longe to telle,
And eek it is ny day, I may nat dwelle.   4340
Shortly I seye, as for conclusioun,
That I shal han of this avisioun
Adversitee; and I seye forthermoor,
That I ne telle of laxatyves no stoor,
For they been venymous, I woot it weel;   4345
I hem diffye, I love hem never a deel!
   Now lat us speke of myrthe, and stynte al
   this.
Madame Pertelote, so have I blis,
Of o thyng God hath sent me large grace;
For whan I se the beautee of youre face,   4350
Ye been so scarlet reed aboute youre yën,
It maketh al my drede for to dyen;
For al so siker as *In principio*,
Mulier est hominis confusio,—
Madame, the sentence of this Latyn is,   4355
'Womman is mannes joye and al his blis.'
For whan I feele a-nyght youre softe syde,
Al be it that I may nat on yow ryde,
For that oure perche is maad so narwe, allas!
I am so ful of joye and of solas,   4360
That I diffye bothe swevene and dreem."
And with that word he fley doun fro the beem,
For it was day, and eek his hennes alle,
And with a chuk he gan hem for to calle,
For he hadde founde a corn, lay in the yerd.   4365
Real he was, he was namoore aferd.
He fethered Pertelote twenty tyme,
And trad hire eke as ofte, er it was pryme.
He looketh as it were a grym leoun,
And on his toos he rometh up and doun;   4370

4303. lite, little. **4304. say,** saw. **4306. to kepe hym,** to be on his guard. **4308–9. litel tale hath he toold Of,** he attached little importance to. **4313. Macrobeus,** Macrobeus, author of a commentary on Cicero's *Somnium Scipionis*. See note to *PF* 31. **4315. Affermeth,** supports (the validity of). **4318. of,** concerning. **4320. Joseph,** who interpreted the dreams of Pharaoh and Paraoh's baker and butler; see *Genesis*, 40 and 41. **4321. Wher,** whether. **4324. butiller,** butler. **4326. actes of sondry remes,** the record of things done (*acta*) in various realms. **4328. Cresus.** See *MkT,* B 3917 ff. **4331. Andromacha,** Andromache, Hector's wife, who, according to Dares and later versions of the Troy story, had the dream which Chaucer describes. **4341. as for conclusioun,** in conclusion. **4344. ne telle . . . no stoor,** set no store by. **4346. never a deel,** not a particle. **4347. stynte al this,** stop all this (discussion). **4351. yën,** eyes. **4353. al so siker as,** just as sure as. *In principio* . . .**,** in the beginning, woman is man's confusion. Chauntecleer takes advantage of his wife's ignorance of Latin to mistranslate it. **4355. sentence,** meaning. **4362. fley,** flew. **4363. and eek his hennes alle.** They likewise flew down. **4365. lay,** (which) lay. **4366. Real,** regal. **4367. fethered,** covered with outspread feathers; trod. **4368. trad,** trod. **pryme,** 9 A.M.

Hym deigned nat to sette his foot to grounde.
He chukketh whan he hath a corn yfounde,
And to hym rennen thanne his wyves alle.
Thus roial, as a prince is in his halle,
Leve I this Chauntecleer in his pasture,   4375
And after wol I telle his aventure.
    Whan that the monthe in which the world
        bigan,
That highte March, whan God first maked man,
Was compleet, and passed were also,
Syn March bigan, thritty dayes and two,   4380
Bifel that Chauntecleer in al his pryde,
His sevene wyves walkynge by his syde,
Caste up his eyen to the brighte sonne,
That in the signe of Taurus hadde yronne   4384
Twenty degrees and oon, and somwhat moore,
And knew by kynde, and by noon oother loore,
That it was pryme, and crew with blisful stevene.
"The sonne," he seyde, "is clomben up on
    hevene
Fourty degrees and oon, and moore ywis.
Madame Pertelote, my worldes blis,   4390
Herkneth thise blisful briddes how they synge,
And se the fresshe floures how they sprynge;
Ful is myn herte of revel and solas!"

But sodeynly hym fil a sorweful cas,
For evere the latter ende of joye is wo.   4395
God woot that worldly joye is soone ago;
And if a rethor koude faire endite,
He in a cronycle saufly myghte it write
As for a sovereyn notabilitee.
Now every wys man, lat him herkne me;   4400
This storie is also trewe, I undertake,
As is the book of Launcelot de Lake,
That wommen holde in ful greet reverence.
Now wol I torne agayn to my sentence.
    A col-fox, ful of sly iniquitee,   4405
That in the grove hadde woned yeres three,
By heigh ymaginacioun forncast,
The same nyght thurghout the hegges brast
Into the yerd ther Chauntecleer the faire
Was wont, and eek his wyves, to repaire;   4410
And in a bed of wortes stille he lay,
Til it was passed undren of the day,
Waitynge his tyme on Chauntecleer to falle,
As gladly doon thise homycides alle
That in await liggen to mordre men.   4415
O false mordrour, lurkynge in thy den!
O newe Scariot, newe Genylon,
False dissymulour, o Greek Synon,

4372. **chukketh,** clucks. 4373. **rennen,** run. 4375. **pasture,** feeding. 4377. **the monthe . . .** According to medieval belief the world was created at the vernal equinox. 4380. **thritty dayes and two,** an elaborate way of dating Chauntecleer's adventure May 3: the thirty days of April and two of May had passed, although *Syn March bigan,* is confusing. The scribe of one MS (Harl. 7334) tried to avoid the difficulty by substituting *tway monthes* for *thritty dayes.* See note to l. 4384. It has been noticed several times that May 3 is the day that Palamon escapes from prison (*KnT,* A 1462) and that Pandarus took to his bed because of "a teene in love" and the next day broached the subject of Troilus' love to Criseyde (*TC* 2. 56). For a suggestion accounting for the date see note to *TC* 2. 56. 4384. **the signe of Taurus.** It has been calculated that the astronomical allusions here and in l. 4389 work out almost precisely to 9 A.M. on May 3. See Skeat's note to B 4045. 4386. **by kynde,** by nature, instinct. 4387. **crew,** crowed. **stevene,** voice. 4394. **fil,** befell. **cas,** chance, experience. 4395. **For evere the latter ende . . .** The same sentiment is expressed in *MLT,* B 421. 4396. **ago,** gone. 4397. **rethor,** rhetorician. 4402. **Launcelot de Lake,** the famous romance which Paolo and Francesca were reading when their love dawned. See Dante's *Inferno* (canto v), which may be the extent of Chaucer's knowledge of "the book." The reference has no point except as an ironical aside. 4404. **sentence,** subject. 4405. **col-fox,** a species of fox with black feet, ears, and tail and with some black in its fur. The animal which Chauntecleer saw in his dream had ears and tail tipped with black (cf. ll. 4093–4). 4406. **woned,** dwelt. 4407. **By heigh ymaginacioun forncast.** The interpretation of this line is uncertain. Manly takes it to mean "predestined by divine foresight," Robinson "by divine foreknowledge," and Tatlock "by decree of almighty Providence." This makes acceptable sense, but it must be admitted that there is no other instance (in Chaucer or in the *NED*) of *heigh ymaginacioun* used in this sense and the interpretation strains somewhat the most common meaning of *forncast.* Sisam, on the other hand, in his edition of the tale (Oxford, 1927) translates " 'foreseen by the exalted imagination'—referring to Chauntecleer's dream," and this interpretation is supported by V. M. Hamm (*MLN,* LXIX. 394–5), who traces the association of the imagination with prophetic vision through dreams back to Plato and points out that Chaucer's phrase has its closest parallel in Dante's *alta fantasia.* Taking the line to refer to Chauntecleer's dream puts the least strain on *forncast.* 4408. **brast,** burst. 4411. **wortes,** herbs. 4412. **undren,** properly *undern,* a word used for several different times of the day, 9 A.M., the middle of the forenoon, and the middle of the afternoon. Here the first of these seems most likely. 4413. **Waitynge,** watching. 4415. **liggen,** lie. 4417. **Scariot,** Judas Iscariot. **Genylon,** see note to B 1384. 4418. **Synon,** who suggested the wooden horse by which some Greeks got into Troy (Virgil, *Æneid,* II. 259).

That broghtest Troye al-outrely to sorwe!

O Chauntecleer, acursed be that morwe   4420

That thou into that yerd flaugh fro the
  bemes!

Thou were ful wel ywarned by thy dremes

That thilke day was perilous to thee;

But what that God forwoot moot nedes bee,

After the opinioun of certein clerkis.   4425

Witnesse on hym that any parfit clerk is,

That in scole is greet altercacioun

In this mateere, and greet disputisoun,

And hath been of an hundred thousand men.

But I ne kan nat bulte it to the bren   4430

As kan the hooly doctour Augustyn,

Or Boece, or the Bisshop Bradwardyn,

Wheither that Goddes worthy forwityng

Streyneth me nedely for to doon a thyng,—

"Nedely" clepe I symple necessitee;   4435

Or elles, if free choys be graunted me

To do that same thyng, or do it noght,

Though God forwoot it er that it was wroght;

Or if his wityng streyneth never a deel

But by necessitee condicioneel.   4440

I wol nat han to do of swich mateere;

My tale is of a cok, as ye may heere,

That took his conseil of his wyf, with sorwe,

To walken in the yerd upon that morwe

That he hadde met that dreem that I yow tolde.

Wommennes conseils been ful ofte colde;   4446

Wommannes conseil broghte us first to wo,

And made Adam fro Paradys to go,

Ther as he was ful myrie and wel at ese.

But for I noot to whom it myght displese,   4450

If I conseil of wommen wolde blame,

Passe over, for I seyde it in my game.

Rede auctours, where they trete of swich mateere,

And what they seyn of wommen ye may heere.

Thise been the cokkes wordes, and nat myne;

I kan noon harm of no womman divyne.   4456

    Faire in the soond, to bathe hire myrily,

Lith Pertelote, and alle hire sustres by,

Agayn the sonne, and Chauntecleer so free

Soong murier than the mermayde in the
  see;   4460

For Phisiologus seith sikerly

How that they syngen wel and myrily.

And so bifel that, as he caste his yë

Among the wortes on a boterflye,

He was war of this fox, that lay ful lowe.   4465

Nothyng ne liste hym thanne for to crowe,

But cride anon, "Cok! cok!" and up he sterte

As man that was affrayed in his herte.

For natureelly a beest desireth flee

Fro his contrarie, if he may it see,   4470

Though he never erst hadde seyn it with his yë.

    This Chauntecleer, whan he gan hym espye,

He wolde han fled, but that the fox anon

Seyde, "Gentil sire, allas! wher wol ye gon?

Be ye affrayed of me that am youre freend?

Now, certes, I were worse than a feend,   4476

If I to yow wolde harm or vileynye!

I am nat come youre conseil for t'espye,

But trewely, the cause of my comynge

4421. **flaugh,** flew. 4426. **Witnesse on hym that any . . .** Take as witness any finished scholar. 4427. **in scole,** in the schools (universities). **greet altercacioun,** over the problem of free will *vs.* predestination. 4428. **disputisoun,** disputation. 4430. **bulte,** bolt, sift. **bren,** bran. But Chaucer goes into the subject in *Troilus and Criseyde* (4. 958–1078). 4431. **Augustyn,** St. Augustine, bishop of Hippo (354–430), who discusses the question in his *De Libero Arbitrio* and, more briefly, in the *De Civitate Dei,* Book V, chap. 8–11. 4432. **Boece,** Boethius. **Bisshop Bradwardyn,** Thomas Bradwardine (*c.* 1290–1349), known as *doctor profundus.* His Oxford lectures were the basis of his most famous treatise, *De Causa Dei.* He died of the plague shortly after being consecrated Archbishop of Canterbury. 4434. **Streyneth me nedely,** constrains me of necessity. 4435. **symple necessitee,** as distinct from conditional necessity (l. 4440), which allowed for some exercise of free will. 4438. **forwoot,** has foreknowledge of. 4439. **wityng,** knowing. 4441. **of,** with. 4445. **met,** dreamed. 4446. **colde,** baneful. The proverb, which occurs in the *Proverbs of Alfred,* is thought to be of Norse origin. 4450. **noot,** know not. 4452. **in my game,** in jest. 4453. **auctours,** such as those represented in Jankyn's book. Cf. *WBT,* D 713. 4456. **I kan . . . divyne,** I cannot conceive of harm in any woman. 4457. **soond,** sand. 4459. **Agayn,** in. 4460. **Soong,** sang. 4461. **Phisiologus,** known in Middle English as the *Bestiary,* a collection of fanciful descriptions of creatures real and imaginary with a moral appended to each. In the Latin version (from a Greek original) each description originally began "Physiologus dicit" (the naturalist says). 4466. **Nothyng ne liste hym,** not at all did it please him. 4467. **sterte,** started. 4468. **affrayed,** frightened. 4469. **flee,** to flee. 4470. **contrarie,** adversary. 4471. **yë,** eye. 4477. **wolde,** intended, would (do). 4478. **conseil,** private affairs.

Was oonly for to herkne how that ye
    synge.   4480
For trewely, ye have as myrie a stevene
As any aungel hath that is in hevene.
Therwith ye han in musyk moore feelynge
Than hadde Boece, or any that kan synge.
My lord youre fader—God his soule blesse!—
And eek youre mooder, of hire gentillesse,   4486
Han in myn hous ybeen to my greet ese;
And certes, sire, ful fayn wolde I yow plese.
But, for men speke of syngyng, I wol seye,—
So moote I brouke wel myne eyen tweye,—
Save yow, I herde nevere man so synge   4491
As dide youre fader in the morwenynge.
Certes, it was of herte, al that he song.
And for to make his voys the moore strong,
He wolde so peyne hym that with bothe his
    yën   4495
He moste wynke, so loude he wolde cryen,
And stonden on his tiptoon therwithal,
And strecche forth his nekke long and smal.
And eek he was of swich discrecioun
That ther nas no man in no regioun   4500
That hym in song or wisdom myghte passe.
I have wel rad in 'Daun Burnel the Asse,'
Among his vers, how that ther was a cok,
For that a preestes sone yaf hym a knok
Upon his leg whil he was yong and nyce,   4505
He made hym for to lese his benefice.
But certeyn, ther nys no comparisoun

Bitwixe the wisedom and discrecioun
Of youre fader and of his subtiltee.
Now syngeth, sire, for seinte charitee;   4510
Lat se, konne ye youre fader countrefete?"
    This Chauntecleer his wynges gan to bete,
As man that koude his traysoun nat espie,
So was he ravysshed with his flaterie.
    Allas! ye lordes, many a fals flatour   4515
Is in youre courtes, and many a losengeour,
That plesen yow wel moore, by my feith,
Than he that soothfastnesse unto yow seith.
Redeth Ecclesiaste of flaterye;
Beth war, ye lordes, of hir trecherye.   4520
    This Chauntecleer stood hye upon his toos,
Strecchynge his nekke, and heeld his eyen cloos,
And gan to crowe loude for the nones.
And daun Russell the fox stirte up atones,
And by the gargat hente Chauntecleer,   4525
And on his bak toward the wode hym beer,
For yet ne was ther no man that hym sewed.
    O destinee, that mayst nat been eschewed!
Allas, that Chauntecleer fleigh fro the bemes!
Allas, his wyf ne roghte nat of dremes!   4530
And on a Friday fil al this meschaunce.
    O Venus, that art goddesse of plesaunce,
Syn that thy servant was this Chauntecleer,
And in thy servyce dide al his poweer,
Moore for delit than world to multiplye,   4535
Why woldestow suffre hym on thy day to
    dye?

4481. **myrie a stevene,** pleasing voice. 4484. **Boece.** Boethius wrote a treatise on music. 4487. **ese,** satisfaction. 4490. **brouke,** enjoy the use of. 4492. **morwenynge,** early morning. 4493. **of herte,** from his heart. 4497. **tiptoon,** tiptoes. 4499. **discrecioun,** discernment. 4502. **rad,** read. **Daun Burnel the Asse.** *Burnellus,* or *Speculum Stultorum,* a Latin satire by Nigel Wireker (*c.* 1180). Burnellus the ass, considering his tail too short, studies at Salerno and Paris but in the end is only able to say *ya*. The anecdote alluded to by the fox is of a cock that took revenge on a certain Gundulfus, about to become a priest, by not crowing at the usual time, causing him to be late for his ordination and thus to lose his benefice. 4503. **vers,** verses. 4505. **he,** *i.e.* the priest's son. **nyce,** foolish. 4508. **discrecioun,** sagacity. 4509. **his subtiltee,** his (the cock's) cleverness. 4511. **countrefete,** imitate. 4513. **traysoun,** treachery. 4514. **ravysshed with,** carried away by. 4515. **ye lordes.** The phrase here and in 4520 is somewhat different from the conventional *lordynges* and *lordes* (without *ye*), and seems like a rhetorical aside to those to whom it might apply. **flatour,** flatterer. 4516. **losengeour,** liar. 4519. **Ecclesiaste.** Skeat and most subsequent editors suggest the apocryphal book of *Ecclesiasticus,* but in it there is no actual discussion of flattery. Sisam, in his edition of the tale (Oxford, 1927), notes that *Ecclesiastes* being the work of Solomon, "it may stand for Solomon in any of his works, and refer to *Proverbs* 29:5, which is quoted in Chaucer's tale of Melibeus in the section on flattery." 4524. **daun Russell.** H. B. Hinckley, who believed that Chaucer knew a Teutonic version of *Reynard the Fox,* notes that the name *Russell* frequently occurs in Teutonic fox-epics. See *Notes on Chaucer* (Northampton, Mass., 1907), p. 151. In the Old French *Roman de Renart* Roussel is the name of the squirrel. **stirte,** started. **atones,** at once. 4525. **gargat,** throat. 4526. **beer,** bore. 4527. **sewed,** pursued. 4528. **eschewed,** avoided. 4529. **fleigh,** flew. 4530. **roghte of,** cared about. 4531. **Friday,** a day traditionally associated with bad luck, but also Venus's day. 4532. **plesaunce,** delight. 4533. **Syn,** since.

O Gaufred, deere maister soverayn,
That whan thy worthy kyng Richard was slayn
With shot, compleynedest his deeth so soore,
Why ne hadde I now thy sentence and thy
    loore,   4540
The Friday for to chide, as diden ye?
For on a Friday, soothly, slayn was he.
Thanne wolde I shewe yow how that I koude
    pleyne
For Chauntecleres drede and for his peyne.
    Certes, swich cry ne lamentacioun,   4545
Was nevere of ladyes maad whan Ylioun
Was wonne, and Pirrus with his streite swerd,
Whan he hadde hent kyng Priam by the berd,
And slayn hym, as seith us *Eneydos,*
As maden alle the hennes in the clos,   4550
Whan they had seyn of Chauntecleer the sighte.
But sovereynly dame Pertelote shrighte
Ful louder than dide Hasdrubales wyf,
Whan that hir housbonde hadde lost his lyf,
And that the Romayns hadde brend Cartage.
She was so ful of torment and of rage   4556
That wilfully into the fyr she sterte,
And brende hirselven with a stedefast herte.
    O woful hennes, right so criden ye,
As, whan that Nero brende the citee   4560
Of Rome, cryden senatoures wyves
For that hir husbondes losten alle hir lyves,—
Withouten gilt this Nero hath hem slayn.
Now wole I turne to my tale agayn.
    This sely wydwe and eek hir doghtres two
Herden thise hennes crie and maken wo,   4566

And out at dores stirten they anon,
And syen the fox toward the grove gon,
And bar upon his bak the cok away,
And cryden, "Out! harrow! and weyl-
    away!   4570
Ha! ha! the fox!" and after hym they ran,
And eek with staves many another man.
Ran Colle oure dogge, and Talbot and Gerland,
And Malkyn, with a dystaf in hir hand;
Ran cow and calf, and eek the verray hogges,
So fered for the berkyng of the dogges   4576
And shoutyng of the men and wommen eke,
They ronne so hem thoughte hir herte breke.
They yolleden as feendes doon in helle;
The dokes cryden as men wolde hem
    quelle;   4580
The gees for feere flowen over the trees;
Out of the hyve cam the swarm of bees.
So hydous was the noyse, a, *benedicitee!*
Certes, he Jakke Straw and his meynee
Ne made nevere shoutes half so shrille   4585
Whan that they wolden any Flemyng kille,
As thilke day was maad upon the fox.
Of bras they broghten bemes, and of box,
Of horn, of boon, in whiche they blewe and
    powped,
And therwithal they skriked and they
    howped.   4590
It semed as that hevene sholde falle.
Now, goode men, I prey yow herkneth alle:
    Lo, how Fortune turneth sodeynly
The hope and pryde eek of hir enemy!

4537. Gaufred, Geoffrey de Vinsauf, author of the *Nova Poetria,* a treatise on the art of poetry with examples by the author of the principles and devices he takes up. One of these examples is a lament for the death of Richard I. Richard was wounded with a poisoned arrow on a Friday, but died some days later. **4539. shot,** missile. **4540. ne hadde,** might I not have. **sentence and . . . loore,** insight and learning. **4543. pleyne,** lament. **4546. of,** by. **4547. Pirrus,** Pyrrhus, son of Achilles, who seized Priam by the hair (not beard) and killed him with his sword. See the *Æneid,* II. 469–553. **streite,** drawn. **4550. clos,** enclosure. **4552. sovereynly,** masterfully, powerfully. **shrighte,** shrieked. **4553. Hasdrubales wyf,** the wife of Hasdrubal, King of Carthage, defeated by Scipio in 146 B.C., whose suicide is also described in *FranklT,* F 1399–1404. The story could have been drawn from Jerome *Against Jovinian,* one of the works included in "Jankyn's book" (D 713). **4558. brende,** burned. **4561. senatoures wyves.** See the account of Nero in the *MkT* (B 3670) above. **4567. stirten,** started. **4568. syen,** saw. **4571. Ha! ha!,** a regular cry to frighten away wolves and other animals (Tatlock, *MLN,* XXIX. 143). **4573. Talbot and Gerland,** dogs' names. **4576. fered,** frightened. **4578. hem thoughte hir herte breke,** it seemed to them that their hearts would break. **4579. yolleden,** yelled. **4580. dokes,** ducks. **quelle,** kill. **4581. flowen,** flew. **4584. Jakke Straw.** In the Peasants' Revolt in 1381 Jack Straw and Wat Tyler were among the leaders. Contemporary accounts record the killing of many Flemings in London, where they had settled as weavers. When the uprising was put down Jack Straw and others were beheaded. **4587. was maad.** Chaucer is thinking of the uproar rather than the logical subject *shoutes.* **4588. bemes,** trumpets. **box,** boxwood. **4590. howped,** whooped.

This cok, that lay upon the foxes bak,   4595
In al his drede unto the fox he spak,
And seyde, "Sire, if that I were as ye,
Yet sholde I seyn, as wys God helpe me,
'Turneth agayn, ye proude cherles alle!
A verray pestilence upon yow falle!   4600
Now I am come unto the wodes syde;
Maugree youre heed, the cok shal heere abyde.
I wol hym ete, in feith, and that anon!' "
   The fox answerde, "In feith, it shal be don."
And as he spak that word, al sodeynly   4605
This cok brak from his mouth delyverly,
And heighe upon a tree he fleigh anon.
And whan the fox saugh that the cok was gon,
   "Allas!" quod he, "O Chauntecleer, allas!
I have to yow," quod he, "ydoon trespas,   4610
In as muche as I maked yow aferd
Whan I yow hente and broghte out of the yerd.
But, sire, I dide it in no wikke entente.
Com doun, and I shal telle yow what I mente;
I shal seye sooth to yow, God help me so!"   4615
   "Nay thanne," quod he, "I shrewe us bothe
      two.

And first I shrewe myself, bothe blood and
      bones,
If thou bigyle me any ofter than ones.
Thou shalt namoore, thurgh thy flaterye,
Do me to synge and wynke with myn yë;   4620
For he that wynketh, whan he sholde see,
Al wilfully, God lat him nevere thee!"
   "Nay," quod the fox, "but God yeve hym
      meschaunce,
That is so undiscreet of governaunce
That jangleth whan he sholde holde his pees."
   Lo, swich it is for to be recchelees   4626
And necligent, and truste on flaterye.
   But ye that holden this tale a folye,
As of a fox, or of a cok and hen,
Taketh the moralite, goode men.   4630
For seint Paul seith that al that writen is,
To oure doctrine it is ywrite, ywis;
Taketh the fruyt, and lat the chaf be stille.
Now, goode God, if that it be thy wille,
As seith my lord, so make us alle goode men,
And brynge us to his heighe blisse!
   Amen.   4636

Heere is ended the Nonnes Preestes Tale.

4598. **as wys God . . .**, as certainly as may God help me. **4602. Maugree**, in spite of. **4606. brak**, broke. **delyverly**, deftly, with agility. **4610. trespas**, wrong. **4612. hente**, seized. **4613. wikke**, evil. **4616. shrewe**, beshrew. **4622. wilfully**, of his own will. **lat**, let. **thee**, thrive. **4625. jangleth**, chatters, talks idly. **4626. recchelees**, careless. **4631. seint Paul seith**. *Rom.*, 15:4. **4632. doctrine**, instruction. **4633. fruyt.** Elsewhere in this semiproverbial comparison Chaucer uses the word *corn*, (Prologue to *LGW*, later version, l. 529). The word *fruyt* here is unusual. The comparison derives from *Matthew*, 3:12 (*Luke*, 3:17). In *Matthew*, 3:12 the Wyclifite Bible has *corne*, the Tyndale (1526) version *wheet;* in *Luke*, 3:17 the reverse is true. **4634. Now, goode God . . .** It is common in romances and minstrel narratives to close with an appeal for blessing, and the first three tales follow the practice. It is especially appropriate for the Nun's Priest to end his story in this way. **4635. my lord**, presumably the Nun's Priest's lord, who was the Bishop of London, but a marginal note in some MSS refers to the Archbishop of Canterbury.

EPILOGUE TO THE NUN'S PRIEST'S TALE

"Sire Nonnes Preest," oure Hooste seide anoon,
"I-blessed be thy breche, and every stoon!
This was a murie tale of Chauntecleer.
But by my trouthe, if thou were seculer,   4640
Thou woldest ben a trede-foul aright.
For if thou have corage as thou hast myght,
Thee were nede of hennes, as I wene,
Ya, moo than seven tymes seventene.   4644

See, whiche braunes hath this gentil preest,
So gret a nekke, and swich a large breest!
He loketh as a sperhauk with his yën;
Him nedeth nat his colour for to dyen
With brasile, ne with greyn of Portyngale.
Now, sire, faire falle yow for youre tale!"   4650
          And after that he, with ful merie chere,
Seide unto another, as ye shuln heere.

Group D (Fragment III)

The Wife of Bath's Tale

THE WIFE OF BATH'S PROLOGUE

The Prologe of the Wyves Tale of Bathe.

Experience, though noon auctoritee
Were in this world, is right ynogh for me
To speke of wo that is in mariage;
For, lordynges, sith I twelve yeer was of age,
Thonked be God that is eterne on lyve,   5

Housbondes at chirche dore I have had fyve,—
If I so ofte myghte have ywedded bee,—
And alle were worthy men in hir degree.
But me was toold, certeyn, nat longe agoon is,
That sith that Crist ne wente nevere but onis

4637. The Epilogue is not in the Ellesmere MS and is here printed from MS Dd. 4.24 in the Cambridge University Library. It is found in ten manuscripts and is certainly genuine, but is thought to have been later rejected by Chaucer. Lines 4641–2 are almost identical with lines 3135–6 of the Prologue to *The Monk's Tale.* The genuineness of the final two lines may be questioned. **4638. breche,** breech (part of the body). **stoon,** testicle. **4640. secular,** a layman. **4642. corage,** the will. **4645. whiche braunes,** what muscles. **4647. sperhauk,** sparrowhawk. **yën,** eyes. **4649. brasile,** a dyewood, originally imported from India, producing a bright red color used (among other things) for the rubrics of books. **greyn of Portyngale,** a red dye from the coccus, produced in Portugal. **4650. faire falle yow,** may it befall you happily.
    On **The Wife of Bath's Prologue** and the possibility that it was intended to introduce a "Marriage Group" see the introduction to *The Canterbury Tales*, especially pp. 234–5. An important source of the Wife of Bath's discourse was a collection of antifeminist tracts, of which the letter of St. Jerome *Adversus Jovinianum* was the most important. This was the book which Jankyn, her fifth husband, took great delight in and from which he occasionally read her certain passages, to her great annoyance (see ll. 669 ff.). For a penetrating study of the Wife of Bath and the structure of her *Prologue* see R. A. Pratt, "The Development of the Wife of Bath," in *Studies in Medieval Literature*, ed. MacEdward Leach (Philadelphia, 1961), pp. 45–79, and for the collection of antifeminist tracts the same author's "Jankyn's Book of Wikked Wyves," *Annuale Mediaevale*, III. 5–27.
    1. Experience, etc. The opening words of The Wife of Bath seem like an allusion to something that has gone before. Lawrence suggested that the lines point to B 4451 ff,. and this is possible, although the reference there is not explicitly to the "wo that is in mariage." The statement may be no more than an echo of *RR*, 12, 802–6, where *la veille* explains that her knowledge of love was not acquired in school, where one learns theory. *Mais je sai tout par la pratique: Esperiment m' en ont fait sage.* **auctoritee,** the written statement of an authority. **5. on lyve,** alive. **6. at chirche dore.** In the Middle Ages the marriage ceremony was performed at the entrance to the church, after which those present went inside for the Mass. See Rock, *The Church of Our Fathers*, IV. 200–4. **7. If I so ofte . . .,** if I could properly have been married so often. The meaning is validated by a passage in Jerome (see intro.) where the question is raised whether any husband after the first may properly be considered a husband.

To weddyng, in the Cane of Galilee, 11
That by the same ensample taughte he me
That I ne sholde wedded be but ones.
Herke eek, lo, which a sharp word for the nonès,
Biside a welle, Jhesus, God and man, 15
Spak in repreeve of the Samaritan:
"Thou hast yhad fyve housbondes," quod he,
"And that ilke man that now hath thee
Is noght thyn housbonde," thus seyde he certeyn.
What that he mente therby, I kan nat seyn; 20
But that I axe, why that the fifthe man
Was noon housbonde to the Samaritan?
How manye myghte she have in mariage?
Yet herde I nevere tellen in myn age
Upon this nombre diffinicioun. 25
Men may devyne and glosen, up and doun,
But wel I woot, expres, withoute lye,
God bad us for to wexe and multiplye;
That gentil text kan I wel understonde.
Eek wel I woot, he seyde myn housbonde 30
Sholde lete fader and mooder, and take to me.
But of no nombre mencioun made he,
Of bigamye, or of octogamye;
Why sholde men speke of it vileynye?
    Lo, heere the wise kyng, daun Salomon; 35
I trowe he hadde wyves mo than oon.
As wolde God it were leveful unto me
To be refresshed half so ofte as he!
Which yifte of God hadde he for alle his wyvys!
No man hath swich that in this world alyve is.
God woot, this noble kyng, as to my wit, 41

The firste nyght had many a myrie fit
With ech of hem, so wel was hym on lyve.
Yblessed be God that I have wedded fyve!
[Of whiche I have pyked out the beste, 44a
Bothe of here nether purs and of here cheste.
Diverse scoles maken parfyt clerkes,
And diverse practyk in many sondry werkes
Maketh the werkman parfyt sekirly;
Of fyve husbondes scoleiyng am I.] 44f
Welcome the sixte, whan that evere he shal.
For sothe, I wol nat kepe me chaast in al. 46
Whan myn housbonde is fro the world ygon,
Som Cristen man shal wedde me anon,
For thanne th'apostle seith that I am free
To wedde, a Goddes half, where it liketh me. 50
He seith that to be wedded is no synne;
Bet is to be wedded than to brynne.
What rekketh me, thogh folk seye vileynye
Of shrewed Lameth and his bigamye?
I woot wel Abraham was an hooly man, 55
And Jacob eek, as fer as ever I kan;
And ech of hem hadde wyves mo than two,
And many another holy man also.
Wher can ye seye, in any manere age,
That hye God defended mariage 60
By expres word? I pray yow, telleth me.
Or where comanded he virginitee?
I woot as wel as ye, it is no drede,
Th'apostel, whan he speketh of maydenhede,
He seyde that precept therof hadde he noon. 65
Men may conseille a womman to been oon,
But conseillyng is no comandement.
He putte it in oure owene juggement;

11. in the Cane, in Cana. Many of the arguments which the Wife of Bath advances are taken from the letter of St. Jerome (and the other texts) mentioned in the intro., and the pertinent passages are in many cases written in the margins of the Ellesmere and other manuscripts. 14. which, what. 15. Biside a welle. For the words between Christ and the woman of Samaria see John, 4: 6–26. 16. repreeve, reproof. 24. in myn age, in my lifetime. 26. devyne and glosen, conjecture and explain. 27. expres, expressly. 28. wexe, increase. 29. gentil, noble. 31. lete, leave. 33. bigamye, having two mates successively. In the discussion which follows, the Wife frequently (though not invariably) uses the word in this sense. 34. vileynye, reproach. 36. trowe, believe. 37. As wolde God, would God. leveful, permissible. 39. Which yifte, what a gift. 41. wit, understanding. 44a–f. These six lines are regarded by Manly as a late addition. They are omitted from the best manuscripts and break the nice continuity between lines 44 and 45. 44b. nether purs . . . cheste. There are obvious puns in both words. 44d. practyk, practice, experience. 44f. scoleiyng, studying, learning. 45. shal, i.e. comes along. 46. in al, at all (the reading of a number of manuscripts). 49. th'apostle, St. Paul; 1 Corinthians, 7:39. 50. a Goddes half, in God's name. 52. brynne, burn. 53. What rekketh me, what do I care. 54. shrewed, beshrewed, cursed. Lameth, Lamech, who had two wives; cf. Genesis, 4:19–24. 56. as fer as . . . I kan, as far as I know. 59. in any manere age, in any age whatever. 60. defended, forbade. 64. Th'apostle, St. Paul, as above. maydenhede, virginity. 65. precept, "commandment of the Lord."

For hadde God comanded maydenhede,
Thanne hadde he dampned weddyng with the
   dede. 70
And certes, if ther were no seed ysowe,
Virginitee, thanne wherof sholde it growe?
Poul dorste nat comanden, atte leeste,
A thyng of which his maister yaf noon heeste.
The dart is set up for virginitee: 75
Cacche whoso may, who renneth best lat see.
   But this word is nat taken of every wight,
But ther as God lust gyve it of his myght.
I woot wel that th'apostel was a mayde; 79
But nathelees, thogh that he wroot and sayde
He wolde that every wight were swich as he,
Al nys but conseil to virginitee.
And for to been a wyf he yaf me leve
Of indulgence; so is it no repreve
To wedde me, if that my make dye, 85
Withoute excepcioun of bigamye.
Al were it good no womman for to touche,—
He mente as in his bed or in his couche;
For peril is bothe fyr and tow t'assemble;
Ye knowe what this ensample may resemble. 90
This is al and som, he heeld virginitee
Moore parfit than weddyng in freletee.
Freletee clepe I, but if that he and she
Wolde leden al hir lyf in chastitee.
   I graunte it wel, I have noon envie, 95
Thogh maydenhede preferre bigamye.
It liketh hem to be clene, body and goost;
Of myn estaat I nyl nat make no boost.
For wel ye knowe, a lord in his houshold,
He hath nat every vessel al of gold; 100
Somme been of tree, and doon hir lord servyse.
God clepeth folk to hym in sondry wyse,
And everich hath of God a propre yifte,
Som this, som that, as hym liketh shifte.

Virginitee is greet perfeccioun, 105
And continence eek with devocioun,
But Crist, that of perfeccioun is welle,
Bad nat every wight he sholde go selle
Al that he hadde, and gyve it to the poore
And in swich wise folwe hym and his foore.
He spak to hem that wolde lyve parfitly; 111
And lordynges, by youre leve, that am nat I.
I wol bistowe the flour of al myn age
In the actes and in fruyt of mariage.
   Telle me also, to what conclusioun 115
Were membres maad of generacioun,
And of so parfit wys a wight ywroght?
Trusteth right wel, they were nat maad for
   noght.
Glose whoso wole, and seye bothe up and doun,
That they were maked for purgacioun 120
Of uryne, and oure bothe thynges smale
Were eek to knowe a femele from a male,
And for noon oother cause,—say ye no?
The experience woot wel it is noght so.
So that the clerkes be nat with me wrothe, 125
I sey this, that they maked ben for bothe,
This is to seye, for office, and for ese
Of engendrure, ther we nat God displese.
Why sholde men elles in hir bookes sette
That man shal yelde to his wyf hire dette? 130
Now wherwith sholde he make his paiement,
If he ne used his sely instrument?
Thanne were they maad upon a creature
To purge uryne, and eek for engendrure.
   But I seye noght that every wight is holde, 135
That hath swich harneys as I to yow tolde,
To goon and usen hem in engendrure.
Thanne sholde men take of chastitee no cure.
Crist was a mayde, and shapen as a man,
And many a seint, sith that the world bigan; 140

---

70. dampned, condemned. **71. ysowe,** sown. **75. dart,** *i.e.* prize. **77. taken of,** received, or accepted by. **78. ther as . . .** where it pleases God to give it. **82. Al nys but conseil,** it is all merely advice. **84. Of,** by. **repreve,** blameworthy matter. **85. To wedde me,** for me to marry. **make,** mate. **86. Withoute excepcioun of,** without being criticized for. **87. Al,** although. **91. al and som,** the sum and substance of it. **92. in freletee,** through frailty. **93. Freletee . . . but if that,** I call it frailty unless. **95. envie,** hard feelings. **96. preferre,** is considered preferable to. **97. goost,** soul. **101. tree,** wood. The comparison goes back to *2 Timothy*, 2:20. **104. shifte,** to provide. **110. foore,** track, footsteps; cf. *Matthew*, 19:21. **113. the flour of al myn age,** the best part of my life. **115. conclusioun,** end, purpose. **117. of so parfit wys a wight,** by so perfectly wise a person. **127. office,** natural function. **130. hire dette.** Cf. *1 Corinthians*, 7:3. **135. holde,** bound. **136. harneys,** equipment. **138. cure,** care.

Yet lyved they evere in parfit chastitee.
I nyl envye no virginitee.
Lat hem be breed of pured whete seed,
And lat us wyves hoten barly-breed;
And yet with barly-breed, Mark telle kan,   145
Oure Lord Jhesu refresshed many a man.
In swich estaat as God hath cleped us
I wol persevere; I nam nat precius.
In wyfhode I wol use myn instrument
As frely as my Makere hath it sent.   150
If I be daungerous, God yeve me sorwe!
Myn housbonde shal it have bothe eve and
    morwe,
Whan that hym list com forth and paye his
    dette.
An housbonde I wol have, I wol nat lette,
Which shal be bothe my dettour and my thral,
And have his tribulacioun withal   156
Upon his flessh, whil that I am his wyf.
I have the power durynge al my lyf
Upon his propre body, and noght he.
Right thus the Apostel tolde it unto me;   160
And bad oure housbondes for to love us weel.
Al this sentence me liketh every deel"—
Up stirte the Pardoner, and that anon:
"Now, dame," quod he, "by God and by seint
    John!
Ye been a noble prechour in this cas.   165
I was aboute to wedde a wyf; allas!
What sholde I bye it on my flessh so deere?
Yet hadde I levere wedde no wyf to-yeere!"
    "Abyde!" quod she, "my tale is nat bigonne.
Nay, thou shalt drynken of another tonne,   170
Er that I go, shal savoure wors than ale.
And whan that I have toold thee forth my tale

Of tribulacioun in mariage,
Of which I am expert in al myn age,   174
This is to seyn, myself have been the whippe,—
Than maystow chese wheither thou wolt sippe
Of thilke tonne that I shal abroche.
Be war of it, er thou to ny approche;
For I shal telle ensamples mo than ten.
'Whoso that nyl be war by othere men,   180
By hym shul othere men corrected be.'
The same wordes writeth Ptholomee;
Rede in his Almageste, and take it there."
    "Dame, I wolde praye yow, if youre wyl it
    were,"
Seyde this Pardoner, "as ye bigan,   185
Telle forth youre tale, spareth for no man,
And teche us yonge men of youre praktike."
    "Gladly," quod she, "sith it may yow like;
But that I praye to al this compaignye,
If that I speke after my fantasye,   190
As taketh not agrief of that I seye;
For myn entente nys but for to pleye."
    Now, sire, now wol I telle forth my tale.—
As evere moote I drynken wyn or ale,   194
I shal seye sooth, tho housbondes that I hadde,
As thre of hem were goode, and two were
    badde.
The thre men were goode, and riche, and olde;
Unnethe myghte they the statut holde
In which that they were bounden unto me.
Ye woot wel what I meene of this, pardee!   200
As help me God, I laughe whan I thynke,
How pitously a-nyght I made hem swynke!
And, by my fey, I tolde of it no stoor.
They had me yeven hir lond and hir tresoor;
Me neded nat do lenger diligence   205

142. envye, strive for. 143. breed, bread. pured, purified, sifted. 144. hoten, be called. 145. Mark, St. Mark, but actually *John*, 6:9. The reference is to the miracle of the loaves and the fishes. 148. precius, fastidious. 151. daungerous, difficult to approach. 154. lette, desist. 160. the Apostel, St. Paul; *1 Corinthians*, 7:4. 161. And bad . . . Cf. *Ephesians*, 5:25. 162. sentence, opinion. 163. Pardoner. See the note to A 669. Since the Pardoner would at best have been in minor orders, he would have been permitted at this time to marry. 167. What, why. 168. to-yeere, this year. 170. tonne, cask. 176. chese, choose. 177. abroche, open (*lit.* pierce). 180. Whoso . . . corrected be. The proverb (in Latin) is quoted in the margin of MS. Dd 4. 24. This and the proverb quoted below. (ll. 326–7) were doubtless in a manuscript of the *Almageste* of Ptolemy seen by Chaucer, since they occur in a series of apothegms attached to a brief account of Ptolemy at the beginning of the edition printed at Venice in 1515. See E. Flugel, *Anglia*, XVIII. 133–40. 181. corrected, reproved. 187. praktike, practical experience. 190. after my fantasye, according to my pleasure. 191. As taketh . . ., take not amiss what I say. 195. tho, those. 198. Unnethe, scarcely. 202. swynke, work. 203. fey, faith. I tolde . . . stoor, I took no account of it. 204. yeven, given.

To wynne hir love, or doon hem reverence.
They loved me so wel, by God above,
That I ne tolde no deyntee of hir love!
A wys womman wol bisye hire evere in oon
To gete hire love, ye, ther as she hath noon.   210
But sith I hadde hem hoolly in myn hond,
And sith they hadde me yeven al hir lond,
What sholde I taken keep hem for to plese,
But it were for my profit and myn ese?
I sette hem so a-werke, by my fey,   215
That many a nyght they songen 'weilawey!'
The bacon was nat fet for hem, I trowe,
That som men han in Essex at Dunmowe.
I governed hem so wel, after my lawe,
That ech of hem ful blisful was and fawe   220
To brynge me gaye thynges fro the fayre.
They were ful glad whan I spak to hem faire;
For, God it woot, I chidde hem spitously.
   Now herkneth hou I baar me proprely,
Ye wise wyves, that kan understonde.   225
Thus sholde ye speke and bere hem wrong on
     honde;
For half so boldely kan ther no man
Swere and lyen as a womman kan.
I sey nat this by wyves that been wyse,
But if it be whan they hem mysavyse.   230
A wys wyf, if that she kan hir good,
Shal beren hym on honde the cow is wood,
And take witnesse of hir owene mayde
Of hir assent; but herkneth how I sayde:
   'Sire olde kaynard, is this thyn array?   235
Why is my neighebores wyf so gay?
She is honoured over al ther she gooth;
I sitte at hoom, I have no thrifty clooth.

What dostow at my neighebores hous?
Is she so fair? artow so amorous?   240
What rowne ye with oure mayde? *Benedicite!*
Sire olde lecchour, lat thy japes be!
And if I have a gossib or a freend,
Withouten gilt, thou chidest as a feend,
If that I walke or pleye unto his hous!   245
Thou comest hoom as dronken as a mous,
And prechest on thy bench, with yvel preef!
Thou seist to me it is a greet meschief
To wedde a povre womman, for costage;
And if that she be riche, of heigh parage,   250
Thanne seistow that it is a tormentrie
To suffre hire pride and hire malencolie.
And if that she be fair, thou verray knave,
Thou seyst that every holour wol hire have;
She may no while in chastitee abyde,   255
That is assailled upon ech a syde.
   Thou seyst som folk desire us for richesse,
Somme for oure shap, and somme for oure fair-
     nesse,
And som for she kan either synge or daunce,
And som for gentillesse and daliaunce;   260
Som for hir handes and hir armes smale:
Thus goth al to the devel, by thy tale.
Thou seyst men may nat kepe a castel wal,
It may so longe assailed been over al.
   And if that she be foul, thou seist that she 265
Coveiteth every man that she may se,
For as a spaynel she wol on hym lepe,
Til that she fynde som man hire to chepe.
Ne noon so grey goos gooth ther in the lake
As, seistow, wol been withoute make.   270
And seyst it is an hard thyng for to welde

---

208. tolde no deyntee of, had no regard for. **209. evere in oon,** constantly. **213. What,** why. **taken keep,** take heed. **217. fet,** fetched. **218. Dunmowe.** At Dunmow in Essex (and elsewhere) a side of bacon was a prize which could be claimed by a couple who after a year could swear that they had not quarreled or regretted their marriage. **220. fawe,** fain. **223. spitously,** spitefully. **224. proprely,** well. **226. bere . . . on honde,** talk them down, prove them in the wrong. **229. by,** concerning. **230. hem mysavyse,** act inadvisedly. **231. kan hir good,** knows what is good for her. **232. Shal beren hym on honde,** argue him down. **the cow is wood,** the chough is mad. The situation is exemplified in *The Manciple's Tale,* of the bird that tells on the wife. **233. And take witnesse . . .,** and call upon the testimony of her own maid that she agrees. **235. kaynard,** sluggard. **thyn array,** your (idea of a proper) state of affairs. **237. over al ther,** everywhere where. **238. thrifty clooth,** suitable clothes. **241. rowne,** whisper. **243. gossib,** relation, acquaintance. **245. pleye,** amuse myself. **246. dronken as a mous.** See note to A 1261. **247. with yvel preef,** bad luck to you. **249. costage,** expense. **250. parage,** lineage. **252. malencolie,** an excess of black bile producing sullenness, anger, etc. **254. holour,** lecher. **256. ech a,** every. **260. daliaunce,** sociable behavior. **264. It may so longe . . .,** *i.e.* a castle wall cannot hold out if it is attacked everywhere for a long time. **268. hire to chepe,** to buy her. **270. make,** mate. **271. welde,** control.

A thyng that no man wole, his thankes, helde.
Thus seistow, lorel, whan thow goost to bedde;
And that no wys man nedeth for to wedde,
Ne no man that entendeth unto hevene.　275
With wilde thonder-dynt and firy levene
Moote thy welked nekke be tobroke!
　　Thow seyst that droppyng houses, and eek
　　　smoke,
And chidyng wyves maken men to flee
Out of hir owene hous; a! *benedicitee!*　280
What eyleth swich an old man for to chide?
　　Thow seyst we wyves wol oure vices hide
Til we be fast, and thanne we wol hem
　　shewe,—
Wel may that be a proverbe of a shrewe!
　　Thou seist that oxen, asses, hors, and houndes,
They been assayed at diverse stoundes;　286
Bacyns, lavours, er that men hem bye,
Spoones and stooles, and al swich housbondrye,
And so been pottes, clothes, and array;
But folk of wyves maken noon assay,　290
Til they be wedded; olde dotard shrewe!
And thanne, seistow, we wol oure vices shewe.
　　Thou seist also that it displeseth me
But if that thou wolt preyse my beautee,
And but thou poure alwey upon my face,　295
And clepe me "faire dame" in every place.
And but thou make a feeste on thilke day
That I was born, and make me fressh and gay;
And but thou do to my norice honour,
And to my chamberere withinne my bour,　300
And to my fadres folk and his allyes,—
Thus seistow, olde barel-ful of lyes!
　　And yet of oure apprentice Janekyn,
For his crisp heer, shynynge as gold so fyn,
And for he squiereth me bothe up and doun,　305

Yet hastow caught a fals suspecioun.
I wol hym noght, thogh thou were deed to-
　　morwe!
　　But tel me this: why hydestow, with sorwe, *may sorrow befall you.*
The keyes of thy cheste awey fro me?
It is my good as wel as thyn, pardee!　310
What, wenestow make an ydiot of oure dame?
Now by that lord that called is Seint Jame,
Thou shalt nat bothe, thogh that thou were
　　wood,
Be maister of my body and of my good;　314
That oon thou shalt forgo, maulgree thynd yën. *in spite of your eyes*
What helpeth it of me to enquere or spyen?
I trowe thou woldest loke *lock* me in thy chiste!
Thou sholdest seye, "Wyf, go where thee liste;
Taak youre disport, I wol nat leve no talys. *believe*
I knowe yow for a trewe wyf, dame Alys. *Alice*　320
We love no man that taketh kepe or charge *take heed or care*
Wher that we goon; we wol ben at oure large. *liberty*
　　Of alle men yblessed moot he be,
The wise astrologien, Daun Ptholome,
That seith this proverbe in his Almageste:　325
"Of alle men his wysdom is the hyeste
That rekketh nevere who hath the world in
　　honde." *in his control*
By this proverbe thou shalt understonde,
Have thou ynogh, what thar thee recche or *may care*
　　care *sorrow; woe*
How myrily that othere folkes fare?　330
For, certeyn, olde dotard, by youre leve,
Ye shul have queynte right ynogh at eve,
He is to greet a nygard that wolde werne *stingyers; forbid*
A man to lighte a candle at his lanterne;
He shal have never the lasse light, pardee.　335
Have thou ynogh, thee thar nat pleyne thee. *need not complain*
　　Thou seyst also, that if we make us gay

---

272. wole, his thankes, helde, wishes willingly to keep. The form *helde* is no doubt used for the rime. **273. lorel,** rogue. **275. entendeth unto,** aims at getting to. **276. levene,** lightning. **277. welked,** withered. **278. droppyng,** leaking. The three things that drive a man out of his house were a commonplace in the Middle Ages. It is an elaboration of *Proverbs,* 27:15. **283. fast,** secure (married). **286. assayed,** tested. **stoundes,** times. **287. lavours,** washbasins. **288. housbondrye,** housefurnishings. **289. array,** equipment, adornment. **299. norice,** nurse. **300. chamberere,** chambermaid. **301. allyes,** relatives. **302. lyes,** possibly a pun on *lies* and *lees,* as Skeat suggested. **304. crispe,** curly. **307. I wol hym noght,** I don't want him. **308. with sorwe,** (an imprecation) may sorrow befall you! **311. oure dame** the mistress of the house. She means herself. **313. wood,** mad. **314. good,** goods. **315. maugree thyne yën,** in spite of your eyes. **317. loke,** lock. **319. leve,** believe. **320. Alys,** Alice. **321. taketh kepe or charge,** takes heed or cares. **322. large,** liberty. **324. Daun Ptholome.** See note to D 180. **327. in honde,** in (his) control. **329. thar,** need. **332. queynte,** pudendum. **333. werne,** forbid. **336. thar nat pleyne,** need not complain.

With clothyng, and with precious array,

That it is peril of oure chastitee; 339

And yet, with sorwe! thou most enforce thee,

And seye thise wordes in the Apostles name:

"In habit maad with chastitee and shame

Ye wommen shul apparaille yow," quod he,

"And noght in tressed heer and gay perree,

As perles, ne with gold, ne clothes riche." 345

After thy text, ne after thy rubriche,

I wol nat wirche as muchel as a gnat.

    Thou seydest this, that I was lyk a cat;

Fo whoso wolde senge a cattes skyn,

Thanne wolde the cat wel dwellen in his in; 350

And if the cattes skyn be slyk and gay,

She wol nat dwelle in house half a day,

But forth she wole, er any day be dawed,

To shewe hir skyn, and goon a-caterwawed.

This is to seye, if I be gay, sire shrewe, 355

I wol renne out, my borel for to shewe.

    Sire olde fool, what helpeth thee to spyen?

Thogh thou preye Argus with his hundred yën

To be my warde-cors, as he kan best,

In feith, he shal nat kepe me but me lest; 360

Yet koude I make his berd, so moot I thee!

    Thou seydest eek that ther been thynges thre,

The whiche thynges troublen al this erthe,

And that no wight may endure the ferthe.

O leeve sire shrewe, Jhesu shorte thy lyf! 365

Yet prechestow and seyst an hateful wyf

Yrekened is for oon of thise meschances.

Been ther none othere maner resemblances

That ye may likne youre parables to,

But if a sely wyf be oon of tho? 370

Thou liknest eek wommenes love to helle,

To bareyne lond, ther water may nat dwelle.

Thou liknest it also to wilde fyr;

The moore it brenneth, the moore it hath desir

To consume every thyng that brent wole be. 375

Thou seyest, right as wormes shende a tree,

Right so a wyf destroyeth hire housbonde;

This knowe they that been to wyves bonde.'

    Lordynges, right thus, as ye have understonde,

Baar I stifly myne olde housbondes on honde

That thus they seyden in hir dronkenesse; 381

And al was fals, but that I took witnesse

On Janekyn, and on my nece also.

O Lord! the peyne I dide hem and the wo,

Ful giltelees, by Goddes sweete pyne! 385

For as an hors I koude byte and whyne.

I koude pleyne, and I was in the gilt,

Or elles often tyme hadde I been spilt.

Whoso that first to mille comth, first grynt;

I pleyned first, so was oure werre ystynt. 390

They were ful glade to excuse hem blyve

Of thyng of which they nevere agilte hir lyve.

Of wenches wolde I beren hem on honde,

Whan that for syk unnethes myghte they

    stonde.

    Yet tikled I his herte, for that he 395

Wende that I hadde of hym so greet chiertee!

I swoor that al my walkynge out by nyghte

Was for t'espye wenches that he dighte;

Under that colour hadde I many a myrthe.

For al swich wit is yeven us in oure byrthe; 400

Deceite, wepyng, spynnyng God hath yive

To wommen kyndely, whil that they may lyve.

---

340. **enforce,** reinforce, support with authority. 341. **the Apostles name,** St. Paul, *1 Timothy,* 2:9. 344. **perree,** precious stones, jewels. 346. **rubriche,** rubric, words written in red, such as a chapter heading, direction, etc. 349. **senge,** singe. 350. **dwellen in his in,** remain in its dwelling; *his* is the neuter pronoun. 353. **dawed,** dawned. 354. **a-caterwawed,** a-caterwauling. The *-ed* was originally a noun-ending. For a parallel case see *a-blakeberyed* (C 406), and for the historical development see note to F 1580. 355. **shrewe,** rascal. The word was used of both sexes. 356. **borel,** clothing. 359. **warde-cors,** bodyguard. 360. **but me lest,** unless I choose. 361. **make his berd,** deceive him. **so moot I thee,** so may I thrive. 364. **ferthe,** fourth. 365. **leeve,** dear. 367. **Yrekened,** held accountable. 370. **sely,** poor, unfortunate. **tho,** those. 373. **wilde fyr,** sometimes called Greek fire, a highly inflammable combination of saltpeter, sulphur, and other ingredients, used in sea warfare. 374. **brenneth,** burns. 375. **brent wole be,** can be burnt. 376. **shende,** injure, destroy. 380. **Baar I . . . on honde,** beat down by words or argument. 381. **That,** what. 385. **pyne,** suffering. 387. **in the gilt,** in the wrong. 388. **spilt,** undone. 389. **grynt,** grinds. 390. **werre ystynt,** war stopped. 391. **blyve,** quickly. 392. **agilte hir lyve,** were guilty in their life. 393. **beren hem on honde,** accuse them. 394. **for syk,** for (being) ill. **unnethes,** scarcely. 396. **Wende,** weened. **chiertee,** affection. 398. **dighte,** lay with. 399. **colour,** pretence. **myrthe,** pleasure, good time. 400. **in oure byrthe,** at our birth. 402. **kyndely,** by nature.

And thus of o thyng I avaunte me,
Atte ende I hadde the bettre in ech degree,
By sleighte, or force, or by som maner thyng,
As by continueel murmur or grucchyng.   406
Namely abedde hadden they meschaunce:
Ther wolde I chide, and do hem no plesaunce;
I wolde no lenger in the bed abyde,
If that I felte his arm over my syde,   410
Til he had maad his raunsoun unto me;
Thanne wolde I suffre hym do his nycetee.
And therfore every man this tale I telle,
Wynne whoso may, for al is for to selle;
With empty hand men may none haukes lure.
For wynnyng wolde I al his lust endure,   416
And make me a feyned appetit;
And yet in bacon hadde I nevere delit;
That made me that evere I wolde hem chide.
For thogh the pope hadde seten hem biside,   420
I wolde nat spare hem at hir owene bord;
For, by my trouthe, I quitte hem word for
    word.
As helpe me verray God omnipotent,
Though I right now sholde make my testament,
I ne owe hem nat a word that it nys quit.   425
I broghte it so aboute by my wit
That they moste yeve it up, as for the beste,
Or elles hadde we nevere been in reste.
For thogh he looked as a wood leoun,
Yet sholde he faille of his conclusioun.   430
    Thanne wolde I seye, 'Goode lief, taak keep
How mekely looketh Wilkyn, oure sheep!
Com neer, my spouse, lat me ba thy cheke!
Ye sholde been al pacient and meke,
And han a sweete spiced conscience,   435
Sith ye so preche of Jobes pacience.
Suffreth alwey, syn ye so wel kan preche;

And but ye do, certein we shal yow teche
That it is fair to have a wyf in pees.
Oon of us two moste bowen, doutelees;   440
And sith a man is moore resonable
Than womman is, ye moste been suffrable.
What eyleth yow to grucche thus and grone?
Is it for ye wolde have my queynte allone?
Wy, taak it al! lo, have it every deel!   445
Peter! I shrewe yow, but ye love it weel;
For if I wolde selle my bele chose,
I koude walke as fressh as is a rose;
But I wol kepe it for youre owene tooth.
Ye be to blame, by God! I sey yow sooth."   450
    Swiche manere wordes hadde we on honde.
Now wol I speken of my fourthe housbonde.
    My fourthe housbonde was a revelour;
This is to seyn, he hadde a paramour;
And I was yong and ful of ragerye,   455
Stibourne and strong, and joly as a pye.
How koude I daunce to an harpe smale,
And synge, ywis, as any nyghtyngale,
Whan I had dronke a draughte of sweete wyn!
Metellius, the foule cherl, the swyn,   460
That with a staf birafte his wyf hir lyf,
For she drank wyn, thogh I hadde been his wyf,
He sholde nat han daunted me fro drynke!
And after wyn on Venus moste I thynke,
For al so siker as cold engendreth hayl,   465
A likerous mouth moste han a likerous tayl.
In wommen vinolent is no defence,
This knowen lecchours by experience.
    But, Lord Crist! whan that it remembreth me
Upon my yowthe, and on my jolitee,   470
It tikleth me about myn herte roote.
Unto this day it dooth myn herte boote
That I have had my world as in my tyme.

---

403. avaunte me, boast. 404. in ech degree, at every step. 405. sleighte, cunning. 406. grucchyng, complaining. 407; Namely, especially. meschaunce, misfortune. 411. maad his raunsoun, paid the penalty. 412. nycetee, foolishness, lust. 414. al is for to selle, everything has its price. 416. wynnyng, gain, advantage. 418. bacon, in contrast with fresh meat. hence "old men." 422. quitte, requited, paid them back. 429. wood leoun, mad lion. 430. conclusioun, aim, purpose. 431. Goode lief, sweetheart. 432. Wilkyn, presumably the name of a pet sheep. 433. ba, kiss. 435. spiced conscience. nice disposition. 439. fair, well. 442. suffrable, patient. 446. shrewe, beshrew, curse. 447. bele chose, nice thing. 454. paramour, mistress. 455. ragerye, wantonness. 456. Stibourne, stubborn. pye, magpie. 460. Metellius. A marginal note in the Ellesmere MS refers to Valerius Maximus, lib. 6, cap. 3, where it is said that Egnatius Metellius clubbed his wife to death because she had drunk wine. 464. moste, must. 466. likerous, lecherous. 467. vinolent, under the influence of wine. is, there is. defence, resistence. 471. herte, heart's. 473. have had my world, enjoyed life.

But age, allas! that al wole envenyme,
Hath me biraft my beautee and my pith.   475
Lat go, farewel! the devel go therwith!
The flour is goon, ther is namoore to telle;
The bren, as I best kan, now moste I selle;
But yet to be right myrie wol I fonde.
Now wol I tellen of my fourthe housbonde.

    I seye, I hadde in herte greet despit   481
That he of any oother had delit.
But he was quit, by God and by Seint Joce!
I made hym of the same wode a croce;
Nat of my body, in no foul manere,   485
But certeinly, I made folk swich cheere
That in his owene grece I made hym frye
For angre, and for verray jalousye.
By God! in erthe I was his purgatorie,
For which I hope his soule be in glorie!   490
For, God it woot, he sat ful ofte and song,
Whan that his shoo ful bitterly hym wrong.
Ther was no wight, save God and he, that wiste,
In many wise, how soore I hym twiste.
He deyde whan I cam fro Jerusalem,   495
And lith ygrave under the roode beem,
Al is his tombe noght so curyus
As was the sepulcre of hym Daryus,
Which that Appelles wroghte subtilly;
It nys but wast to burye hym preciously.   500
Lat hym fare wel, God yeve his soule reste!
He is now in his grave and in his cheste.
    Now of my fifthe housbonde wol I telle.
God lete his soule nevere come in helle!
And yet was he to me the mooste shrewe;   505

That feele I on my ribbes al by rewe,
And evere shal unto myn endyng day.
But in oure bed he was so fresshe and gay,
And therwithal so wel koude he me glose,
Whan that he wolde han my *bele chose*,   510
That thogh he hadde me bete on every bon,
He koude wynne agayn my love anon.
I trowe I loved hym best, for that he
Was of his love daungerous to me.
We wommen han, if that I shal nat lye,   515
In this matere a queynte fantasye;
Wayte what thyng we may nat lightly have,
Therafter wol we crie al day and crave.
Forbede us thyng, and that desiren we;
Preesse on us faste, and thanne wol we fle.   520
With daunger oute we al oure chaffare;
Greet prees at market maketh deere ware,
And to greet cheep is holde at litel prys:
This knoweth every womman that is wys.   524
    My fifthe housbonde, God his soule blesse!
Which that I took for love, and no richesse,
He som tyme was a clerk of Oxenford,
And hadde left scole, and wente at hom to bord
With my gossib, dwellynge in oure toun;
God have hir soule! hir name was Alisoun.   530
She knew myn herte, and eek my privetee,
Bet than oure parisshe preest, so moot I thee!
To hire biwreyed I my conseil al.
For hadde myn housbonde pissed on a wal,
Or doon a thyng that sholde han cost his lyf,   535
To hire, and to another worthy wyf,
And to my nece, which that I loved weel,

---

475. pith, vigor. **478. bren,** bran. **479. fonde,** strive. **481. despit,** resentment. **483. quit,** requited, paid back. **Seint Joce,** a Breton saint, chosen probably for the rime. **484. croce,** staff (a stick to beat him with). **486. made . . . cheere,** showed people such hospitality. **492. Whan that,** at the same time that. **wrong,** pinched. The allusion is to a story, in the letter of St. Jerome (see introduction), of a certain Roman noble who was reproved by his friends for having divorced his rich and beautiful wife. Pointing to his shoe, he replied, "The shoe which you see looks new and elegant, but no one except me knows where it pinches." **494. twiste,** tortured. **495. fro Jerusalem,** where she had been on a pilgrimage; cf. A 463. **496. lith ygrave,** lies buried. **roode beem,** a beam supporting a large cross at the entrance to the choir. **497. Al,** although. **curyus,** elaborate. **498. Daryus,** A note in the margin of the Ellesmere MS gives as a reference "in Alexandro, libro sexto," and in the sixth book of the *Alexandreis,* by Gaultier de Chatillon, the tomb is described. It is there said to be the work of a Jewish artist named Apelles. **500. preciously,** in a costly manner. **501. Lat hym fare wel,** let him go, *i.e.* let's forget about him. **505. mooste shrewe,** greatest rascal. **506. by rewe,** in a row. **509. glose,** flatter, cajole. **514. daungerous,** grudging, cavalier. **516. queynte fantasye,** strange notion. **517. Wayte what,** whatever. See Derocquigny, *MLR,* III. 72, and Language, § 81. **518. al day,** continually. **521. With daunger,** sparingly, with reluctance. **oute,** set out. **chaffare,** wares. **522. prees,** crowd. **523. cheep,** bargain. **prys,** worth, esteem. **527. som tyme,** at one time. **529. gossib,** woman-friend. **531. privetee,** private affairs or thoughts. **532. thee,** thrive. **533. biwreyed,** betrayed, confided. **conseil,** secrets. confidences.

I wolde han toold his conseil every deel.
And so I dide ful often, God it woot,
That made his face often reed and hoot 540
For verray shame, and blamed hymself for he
Had toold to me so greet a pryvetee.

    And so bifel that ones in a Lente—
So often tymes I to my gossyb wente,
For evere yet I loved to be gay, 545
And for to walke in March, Averill, and May,
Fro hous to hous, to heere sondry talys—
That Jankyn clerk, and my gossyb dame Alys,
And I myself, into the feeldes wente.
Myn housbonde was at Londoun al that Lente;
I hadde the bettre leyser for to pleye, 551
And for to se, and eek for to be seye
Of lusty folk. What wiste I wher my grace
Was shapen for to be, or in what place?
Therfore I made my visitaciouns 555
To vigilies and to processiouns,
To prechyng eek, and to thise pilgrimages,
To pleyes of myracles, and to mariages,
And wered upon my gaye scarlet gytes. 559
Thise wormes, ne thise motthes, ne thise mytes,
Upon my peril, frete hem never a deel;
And wostow why? for they were used weel.
Now wol I tellen forth what happed me.
I seye that in the feeldes walked we,
Til trewely we hadde swich daliance, 565
This clerk and I, that of my purveiance
I spak to hym and seyde hym how that he,
If I were wydwe, sholde wedde me.
For certeinly, I sey for no bobance,
Yet was I nevere withouten purveiance 570
Of mariage, n' of othere thynges eek.

I holde a mouses herte nat worth a leek
That hath but oon hole for to sterte to,
And if that faille, thanne is al ydo.
I bar hym on honde he hadde enchanted
    me, 575
My dame taughte me that soutiltee.
And eek I seyde I mette of hym al nyght,
He wolde han slayn me as I lay upright,
And al my bed was ful of verray blood;
But yet I hope that he shal do me good, 580
For blood bitokeneth gold, as me was taught.
And al was fals; I dremed of it right naught,
But as I folwed ay my dames loore,
As wel of this as of othere thynges moore.
    But now, sire, lat me se, what I shal seyn? 585
A ha! by God, I have my tale ageyn.
    Whan that my fourthe housbonde was on
      beere,
I weep algate, and made sory cheere,
As wyves mooten, for it is usage,
And with my coverchief covered my visage, 590
But for that I was purveyed of a make,
I wepte but smal, and that I undertake.
    To chirche was myn housbonde born
      a-morwe
With neighebores, that for hym maden sorwe;
And Jankyn, oure clerk, was oon of tho. 595
As help me God! whan that I saugh hym go
After the beere, me thoughte he hadde a paire
Of legges and of feet so clene and faire,
That al myn herte I yaf unto his hoold.
He was, I trowe, a twenty wynter oold, 600
And I was fourty, if I shal seye sooth;
But yet I hadde alwey a coltes tooth.

---

541. and blamed. The subject _he_ is understood. **542. pryvetee**, confidential matter. **551. leyser**, leisure, opportunity. **552. seye**, seen. **553. Of lusty folk**, by pleasure-loving people. **What wiste I . . .** How did I know where my good fortune was destined to be found? **555. visitaciouns**, visits. **556. vigilies**, vigils, services on the eve of a festival. **processiouns**, _i.e._ as part of a religious ceremony. **558. pleyes of myracles**, miracle plays, properly saints' plays, but often any kind of religious plays. **559. wered upon**, wore; cf. _hadde upon_ (had on), D 1382. The construction is unusual, but is found also in D 1018. **gytes**, long cloaks; cf. A 3954. This is the most likely meaning; see Schultz-Gora, _Archiv_, CLV. 107–8. **560. mytes**, mites, insects. **561. Upon my peril**, probably to be understood in the same way as _Up peril of my soule_, E 2371. She saw to it that they never had a chance to eat her clothes. **562. they**, _i.e._ her scarlet gytes. **565. daliance.** The word may mean anything from conversation to intimacies. **566. of my purveiance**, _i.e._ by my foresight. **569. bobance**, boasting. **570. withouten purveiance**, without provision. **575. bar hym on honde**, led him to believe. **576. dame**, mother. **577. mette**, dreamed. **578. upright**, face up. **583. But as**, except as. Five manuscripts, including the Ellesmere, omit _as_, improving the sense but spoiling the meter. **587. on beere**, on his bier. **589. mooten**, must. **591. purveyed of**, provided with. **592. I undertake**, I assure you. **594. With**, by. **599. hoold**, keeping. **602. a coltes tooth**, the characteristics of youth, an inclination to wantonness.

Gat-tothed I was, and that bicam me weel;
I hadde the prente of seinte Venus seel.
As help me God! I was a lusty oon,   605
And faire, and riche, and yong, and wel bigon;
And trewely, as myne housbondes tolde me,
I hadde the beste *quoniam* myghte be.
For certes, I am al Venerien
In feelynge, and myn herte is Marcien.   610
Venus me yaf my lust, my likerousnesse,
And Mars yaf me my sturdy hardynesse;
Myn ascendent was Taur, and Mars therinne.
Allas! allas! that evere love was synne!
I folwed ay myn inclinacioun   615
By vertu of my constellacioun;
That made me I koude noght withdrawe
My chambre of Venus from a goode felawe.
Yet have I Martes mark upon my face,
And also in another privee place.   620
For God so wys be my savacioun,
I ne loved nevere by no discrecioun,
But evere folwede myn appetit,
Al were he short, or long, or blak, or whit;
I took no kepe, so that he liked me,   625
How poore he was, ne eek of what degree.
     What sholde I seye? but, at the monthes
       ende,
This joly clerk, Jankyn, that was so hende,
Hath wedded me with greet solempnytee;
And to hym yaf I al the lond and fee   630
That evere was me yeven therbifoore.

But afterward repented me ful soore;
He nolde suffre nothyng of my list.
By God! he smoot me ones on the lyst,
For that I rente out of his book a leef,   635
That of the strook myn ere wax al deef.
Stibourne I was as is a leonesse,
And of my tonge a verray jangleresse,
And walke I wolde, as I had doon biforn,   639
From hous to hous, although he had it sworn;
For which he often tymes wolde preche,
And me of olde Romayn geestes teche;
How he Symplicius Gallus lefte his wyf,
And hire forsook for terme of al his lyf,
Noght but for open-heveded he hir say   645
Lookynge out at his dore upon a day.
     Another Romayn tolde he me by name,
That, for his wyf was at a someres game
Withouten his wityng, he forsook hire eke.
And thanne wolde he upon his Bible seke   650
That ilke proverbe of Ecclesiaste
Where he comandeth, and forbedeth faste,
Man shal nat suffre his wyf go roule aboute.
Thanne wolde he seye right thus, withouten
     doute:
     'Whoso that buyldeth his hous al of salwes,
And priketh his blynde hors over the falwes,   656
And suffreth his wyf to go seken halwes,
Is worthy to been hanged on the galwes!'
But al for noght, I sette noght an hawe
Of his proverbes n' of his olde sawe,   660

---

603. Gat-tothed. See note to A 468. **604. seel,** birthmark. According to medieval writers on physiognomy everyone bore some mark according to the planet under whose influence he was born. The *seel* of Venus indicated lasciviousness. See Curry. *Chaucer and the Mediaeval Sciences,* p. 104. **606. wel bigon,** cheerful. **608. quoniam,** pudendum. **609. Venerien . . . Marcien,** under the influence of Venus and Mars. **611. lust,** desire. **likerousnesse,** lecherousness. **612. hardynesse,** boldness. **613. Myn ascendent was Taur . . .** At the time of her birth Mars was in the sign Taurus, which was rising above the horizon. Taurus is one of the mansions of Venus. **616. By vertu . . . constellacioun,** through the influence of my stars. **619. Martes,** Mars. **621. God so wys be,** may God so surely be. **624. blak, or whit,** brunette or blond. **625. I took no kepe,** I did not care. **626. degree,** rank. **628. hende,** pleasant. **630. fee,** landed property. **633. list,** desire. **634. lyst,** ear. **637. Stibourne,** untameable. **638. jangleresse,** noisy talker, scold. **640. had it sworn,** had sworn to the contrary. Cf. A 1089. **642. geestes,** stories. **643. Symplicius Gallus.** In Valerius Maximus, in whose *De Factis Dictisque Memorabilibus* the anecdote is found, the name is Sulpicius Gallus. **645. open-heveded,** bareheaded (*capite aperto* in Valerius). **say,** saw. **647. Another Romayn,** P. Sempronius Sophus; the incident is related in the same chapter of Valerius. **648. for,** because. **a someres game,** midsummer revels. On such revels in England, probably in part dramatic, see R. E. Parker, "Some Records of the *Somyr Play,*" *Stud. in Honor of John C. Hodges and Alwin Thaler* (1961), pp. 19–26. **649. wityng,** knowledge. **651. Ecclesiaste,** *Ecclesiasticus,* 25:25. **653. roule,** roam. **655. Whoso that buyldeth . . .** The four lines were apparently a popular jingle, since Skeat quotes them in very similar form from scraps of verse in Lansdowne MS 762 (15c.), printed in Wright and Halliwell, *Reliquiae Antiquae,* I. 233. **salwes,** branches of willow. **656. priketh,** spurs. **falwes,** plowed lands. **657. halwes,** shrines, *i.e.* go on pilgrimages.

Ne I wolde nat of hym corrected be.
I hate hym that my vices telleth me,
And so doo mo, God woot, of us than I.
This made hym with me wood al-outrely;
I nolde noght forbere hym in no cas.   665
    Now wol I seye yow sooth, by seint
      Thomas,
Why that I rente out of his book a leef,
For which he smoot me so that I was deef.
He hadde a book that gladly, nyght and day,
For his desport he wolde rede alway;   670
He cleped it Valerie and Theofraste,
At which book he lough alwey ful faste.
And eek ther was somtyme a clerk at Rome,
A cardinal, that highte Seint Jerome,
That made a book agayn Jovinian;   675
In which book eek ther was Tertulan,
Crisippus, Trotula, and Helowys,
That was abbesse nat fer fro Parys;
And eek the Parables of Salomon,
Ovides Art, and bookes many on,   680
And alle thise were bounden in o volume.
And every nyght and day was his custume,
Whan he hadde leyser and vacacioun
From oother worldly occupacioun,
To reden on this book of wikked wyves.   685
He knew of hem mo legendes and lyves
Than been of goode wyves in the Bible.
For trusteth wel, it is an inpossible
That any clerk wol speke good of wyves,
But if it be of hooly seintes lyves,   690

Ne of noon oother womman never the mo.
Who peyntede the leon, tel me who?
By God! if wommen hadde writen stories,
As clerkes han withinne hire oratories,
They wolde han writen of men moore wikked-
    nesse
Than al the mark of Adam may redresse.   696
The children of Mercurie and of Venus
Been in hir wirkyng ful contrarius;
Mercurie loveth wysdam and science,
And Venus loveth ryot and dispence.   700
And, for hire diverse disposicioun,
Ech falleth in otheres exaltacioun.
And thus, God woot, Mercurie is desolat
In Pisces, wher Venus is exaltat;
And Venus falleth ther Mercurie is reysed.   705
Therfore no womman of no clerk is preysed.
The clerk, whan he is oold, and may noght do
Of Venus werkes worth his olde sho,
Thanne sit he doun, and writ in his dotage
That wommen kan nat kepe hir mariage!   710
    But now to purpos, why I tolde thee
That I was beten for a book, pardee!
Upon a nyght Jankyn, that was oure sire,
Redde on his book, as he sat by the fire,
Of Eva first, that for hir wikkednesse   715
Was al mankynde broght to wrecchednesse,
For which that Jhesu Crist hymself was slayn,
That boghte us with his herte blood agayn.
Lo, heere expres of womman may ye fynde,
That womman was the los of al mankynde.   720

---

664. **wood,** enraged. **al-outrely,** completely. 665. **forbere,** spare. 671. **Valerie and Theofraste,** two of the authors included in the collection of antifeminist tracts mentioned in the intro. Valerie is Walter Map's "Epistola Valerii ad Rufinum ne Uxorem Ducat." Theofraste (Theophrastus) is the author of a *Liber de Nuptiis*, quoted at some length in St. Jerome's *Epistola adversus Jovinianum*. 672. **lough,** laughed. **faste,** vigorously. 674. **Seint Jerome,** *c.* 340–420; see previous note. 676. **Tertulan,** Tertullian (*c.* 160–*c.* 225), the author of several treatises in which chastity is exalted above marriage. 677. **Crisippus,** mentioned in the letter of Jerome, where Chaucer doubtless got the name. **Trotula,** considered by the Middle Ages to be a woman physician, author of a treatise on the diseases of women. Whether the attribution is correct or not, the treatise was well known. See G. L. Hamilton, *MP*, IV. 377–80. **Helowys,** Heloïse, wife of Abèlard, who later became head of a priory at Argenteuil, about six miles from Paris. 679. **Parables of Salomon,** the *Book of Proverbs*. 680. **Ovides Art,** the *Art of Love* (*Ars Amatoria*). 683. **vacacioun,** free time. 688. **an inpossible,** an impossibility. 692. **Who peyntede the leon . . . ?** In *Aesop's Fables* a man walking with a lion points out a representation of a man killing a lion. The lion replies that if lions were artists the scene represented might be different. 694. **oratories,** places for prayer. 696. **al the mark of Adam,** all in the image of Adam, all men. 697. **children of Mercurie . . .** Those born under the domination of Mercury. 698. **contrarius,** different. 700. **ryot,** wanton revels. 702. **Ech falleth . . .** In medieval astrology Mercury and Venus, being opposites, must each fall when the other is ascendant in a given sign. The example given for the exaltation of Venus is in Pisces, that for Mercury is in Virgo. 703. **desolat,** destitute of influence. 704. **exaltat.** Venus was in its exaltation when in the sign (Pisces) in which its influence was believed to be greatest. 705. **ther,** where. 706. **of,** by. 709. **sit . . . writ,** sits . . . writes. 713. **sire,** man of the house, husband. 720. **los,** *i.e.* the cause of loss.

Tho redde he me how Sampson loste his heres:
Slepynge, his lemman kitte it with hir sheres;
Thurgh which treson loste he bothe his yën.

Tho redde he me, if that I shal nat lyen,
Of Hercules and of his Dianyre,   725
That caused hym to sette hymself afyre.

No thyng forgat he the care and the wo
That Socrates hadde with his wyves two;
How Xantippa caste pisse upon his heed.
This sely man sat stille as he were deed;   730
He wiped his heed, namoore dorste he seyn,
But 'Er that thonder stynte, comth a reyn!'

Of Phasipha, that was the queene of Crete,
For shrewednesse, hym thoughte the tale swete;
Fy! spek namoore—it is a grisly thyng—   735
Of hire horrible lust and hir likyng.

Of Clitermystra, for hire lecherye,
That falsly made hire housbonde for to dye,
He redde it with ful good devocioun.

He tolde me eek for what occasioun   740
Amphiorax at Thebes loste his lyf.
Myn housbonde hadde a legende of his wyf,
Eriphilem, that for an ouche of gold
Hath prively unto the Grekes told
Wher that hir housbonde hidde hym in a place,
For which he hadde at Thebes sory grace.   746

Of Lyvia tolde he me, and of Lucye:
They bothe made hir housbondes for to dye;
That oon for love, that oother was for hate.
Lyvia hir housbonde, on an even late,   750
Empoysoned hath, for that she was his fo;
Lucia, likerous, loved hire housbonde so

That, for he sholde alwey upon hire thynke,
She yaf hym swich a manere love-drynke
That he was deed er it were by the morwe;   755
And thus algates housbondes han sorwe.

Thanne tolde he me how oon Latumyus
Compleyned unto his felawe Arrius
That in his gardyn growed swich a tree
On which he seyde how that his wyves thre
Hanged hemself for herte despitus.   761
'O leeve brother,' quod this Arrius,
'Yif me a plante of thilke blissed tree,
And in my gardyn planted shal it bee.'

Of latter date, of wyves hath he red   765
That somme han slayn hir housbondes in hir
  bed,
And lete hir lecchour dighte hire al the nyght,
Whan that the corps lay in the floor upright.
And somme han dryve nayles in hir brayn,
Whil that they slepte, and thus they han hem
  slayn.   770
Somme han hem yeve poysoun in hire drynke.
He spak moore harm than herte may bithynke;
And therwithal he knew of mo proverbes
Than in this world ther growen gras or herbes.
'Bet is,' quod he, 'thyn habitacioun   775
Be with a leoun or a foul dragoun,
Than with a womman usynge for to chyde.'
'Bet is,' quod he, 'hye in the roof abyde,
Than with an angry wyf doun in the hous;
They been so wikked and contrarious,   780
They haten that hir housbondes loven ay.'
He seyde, "a womman cast hir shame away,

721. heres, often used in the plur. where we use the collective *hair;* note the sing. pronoun *it* in the next line. See *Judges,* 16:15–20, although most of the examples are from Jerome. Chaucer tells the story of Samson at length in *The Monk's Tale* (B 3205–84). **722. Slepynge,** while he slept. **kitte,** cut. **723. yën,** eyes. **724. Tho,** then. **725. Hercules and . . . Dianyre.** See *The Monk's Tale* (B 3285–3332). **728. Socrates.** The story is best known to later times from Erasmus, but Chaucer found it in Jerome. **732. stynte,** stops. **733. Phasipha,** Pasiphaë, whose passion for a bull is related by Ovid, *Ars Amatoria,* I. 295–326, and briefly by Jerome. **734. shrewednesse,** evil disposition. **735. grisly,** horrible. **737. Clitermystra,** Clytemnestra, wife of Agamemnon. On her husband's return from Troy she murdered him with the help of her lover, Aegisthus. **741. Amphiorax,** Amphiaraus. See note to *TC* 2. 104–5. **743. ouche,** properly a clasp or brooch, but here the necklace for which Eryphile betrayed Amphiaraus. **747. Lyvia,** Livia, married to her cousin Drusus, poisoned him at the instigation of Sejanus in 23 A.D. **Lucye,** Lucia, or Lucilia, wife of Lucretius the poet, who poisoned her husband with a love-potion intended to revive his love. **752. likerous,** lecherous, passionate. **756. algates,** always. **757. Latumyus.** The name cannot be identified, but the story was told of various (equally unidentified) persons. Like the two previous examples, this anecdote was in the part of Jankyn's book called *Epistola Valerii ad Rufinum,* mentioned in the note to line 671. **761. despitus,** spiteful, angry. **762. leeve,** dear. **763. plante,** slip. **767. dighte,** lie with. **768. in the floor upright,** face up on the floor. **775. Bet is,** better it is. Cf. *Ecclesiasticus,* 25:16. **778. hye in the roof . . .** Cf. *Proverbs,* 21:9–10. **781. that,** that which. **782. cast,** casts. The proverb in Jerome is (rightly) attributed to Herodotus.

Whan she cast of hir smok;' and forthermo,
'A fair womman, but she be chaast also,
Is lyk a gold ryng in a sowes nose.' 785
Who wolde wene, or who wolde suppose,
The wo that in myn herte was, and pyne?
    And whan I saugh he wolde nevere fyne
To reden on this cursed book al nyght,'
Al sodeynly thre leves have I plyght 790
Out of his book, right as he radde, and eke
I with my fest so took hym on the cheke
That in oure fyr he fil bakward adoun.
And he up stirte as dooth a wood leoun,
And with his fest he smoot me on the heed, 795
That in the floor I lay as I were deed.
And whan he saugh how stille that I lay,
He was agast, and wolde han fled his way,
Til atte laste out of my swogh I breyde.
'O! hastow slayn me, false theef?' I seyde, 800
'And for my land thus hastow mordred me?
Er I be deed, yet wol I kisse thee.'
    And neer he cam, and kneled faire adoun,
And seyde, 'Deere suster Alisoun,
As help me God! I shal thee nevere smyte. 805

That I have doon, it is thyself to wyte.
Foryeve it me, and that I thee biseke!'
And yet eftsoones I hitte hym on the cheke,
And seyde, 'Theef, thus muchel am I wreke;
Now wol I dye, I may no lenger speke.' 810
But atte laste, with muchel care and wo,
We fille acorded by us selven two.
He yaf me al the bridel in myn hond,
To han the governance of hous and lond,
And of his tonge, and of his hond also; 815
And made hym brenne his book anon right tho.
And whan that I hadde geten unto me,
By maistrie, al the soveraynetee,
And that he seyde, 'Myn owene trewe wyf,
Do as thee lust the terme of al thy lyf; 820
Keep thyn honour, and keep eek myn estaat'—
After that day we hadden never debaat.
God helpe me so, I was to hym as kynde
As any wyf from Denmark unto Ynde,
And also trewe, and so was he to me. 825
I prey to God, that sit in magestee,
So blesse his soule for his mercy deere.
Now wol I seye my tale, if ye wol heere."

Biholde the wordes bitwene the Somonour and the Frere.

    The Frere lough, whan he hadde herd al this;
"Now dame," quod he, "so have I joye or blis,
This is a long preamble of a tale!" 831
And whan the Somonour herde the Frere gale,
"Lo," quod the Somonour, "Goddes armes
    two!
A frere wol entremette hym everemo.
Lo, goode men, a flye and eek a frere 835
Wol falle in every dyssh and eek mateere.
What spekestow of preambulacioun?
What! amble, or trotte, or pees, or go sit doun!
Thou lettest oure disport in this manere."

"Ye, woltow so, sire Somonour?" quod the
    Frere; 840
"Now, by my feith, I shal, er that I go,
Telle of a somonour swich a tale or two,
That alle the fok shal laughen in this place."
    "Now elles, Frere, I bishrewe thy face,"
Quod this Somonour, "and I bishrewe me, 845
But if I telle tales two or thre
Of freres, er I come to Sidyngborne,
That I shal make thyn herte for to morne,
For wel I woot thy pacience is gon." 849
    Oure Hoost cride "Pees! and that anon!"

783. **smok**, undergarment, chemise. 784. **A fair womman** . . . Cf. *Proverbs*, 11:22. 788. **fyne**, end. 790. **plyght**, plucked, torn. 791. **radde**, read. 792. **took**, struck. 794. **wood**, mad. 796. **in**, on. 799. **swogh**, swoon. **breyde**, started, came to. 803. **neer**, nearer. 806. **to wyte**, to blame. 807. **biseke**, beseech. 808. **eftsoones**, soon, immediately. 809. **wreke**, revenged. 812. **fille acorded**, fell into accord. 816. **And made**, and I made. **brenne**, burn. **tho**, then. 820. **lust**, it pleases. 829. **lough**, laughed. 832. **gale**, yelp. 834. **entremette**, meddle. 839. **lettest**, hinderest. 844. **elles**, otherwise. **bishrewe**, beshrew, curse. 847. **Sidyngborne**, Sittingbourne, about 40 m. from London.

And seyde, "Lat the womman telle hire tale.
Ye fare as folk that dronken ben of ale.
Do, dame, telle forth youre tale, and that is
    best."

"Al redy, sire," quod she, "right as yow lest,
If I have licence of this worthy Frere." 855
"Yis, dame," quod he, "tel forth, and I wol
    heere,"

Heere endeth the Wyf of Bathe hir Prologe.

THE WIFE OF BATH'S TALE

Here bigynneth the Tale of the Wyf of Bathe.

In th'olde dayes of the Kyng Arthour,
Of which that Britons speken greet honour,
Al was this land fulfild of fayerye.
The elf-queene, with hir joly compaignye, 860
Daunced ful ofte in many a grene mede.
This was the olde opinion, as I rede;
I speke of manye hundred yeres ago.
But now kan no man se none elves mo,
For now the grete charitee and prayeres 865
Of lymytours and othere hooly freres,
That serchen every lond and every streem,
As thikke as motes in the sonne-beem,
Blessynge halles, chambres, kichenes, boures,
Citees, burghes, castels, hye toures, 870
Thropes, bernes, shipnes, dayeryes—
This maketh that ther been no fayeryes.
For ther as wont to walken was an elf,
Ther walketh now the lymytour hymself

In undermeles and in morwenynges, 875
And seyth his matyns and his hooly thynges
As he gooth in his lymytacioun.
Wommen may go now saufly up and doun.
In every bussh or under every tree
Ther is noon oother incubus but he, 880
And he ne wol doon hem but dishonour.
    And so bifel that this kyng Arthour
Hadde in his hous a lusty bacheler,
That on a day cam ridynge fro ryver;
And happed that, allone as he was born, 885
He saugh a mayde walkynge hym biforn,
Of whiche mayde anon, maugree hir heed,
By verray force, he rafte hire maydenhed;
For which oppressioun was swich clamour
And swich pursute unto the kyng Arthour, 890
That dampned was this knyght for to be deed,
By cours of lawe, and sholde han lost his heed—

The Wife of Bath's Tale. The story of the knight and the loathly lady is found in various languages and in a variety of forms. Usually the lady is the victim of enchantment, from which she can be freed only by the love (sometimes a kiss) of the hero. The theme is combined in *The Wife of Bath's Tale* with that of the man whose life depends upon his being able to answer a certain question. The two motifs are likewise combined in a version, independent of Chaucer's, told by Gower in the *Confessio Amantis*, and in other versions, such as the English *Marriage of Sir Gawaine* and *The Weddynge of Sir Gawen and Dame Ragnell*. (All three texts are reprinted in *SA*.) Chaucer's immediate source is unknown. For a study of the various analogues see G. H. Maynadier, *The Wife of Bath's Tale: Its Sources and Analogues* (London, 1901) and Sigmund Eisner, *A Tale of Wonder: A Source Study of The Wife of Bath's Tale* (Wesford, 1957), where references to earlier discussions will be found.

As noted in the introduction to *The Shipman's Tale* Chaucer had originally intended that tale to be told by the Wife. The present story so aptly reinforces her philosophy of "sovereignty" that we can only applaud the substitution. It is likely that the tale was written at approximately the same time as the prologue.

866. lymytours. See note to A 209. **871. Thropes,** thorps, villages. **shipnes,** cowsheds. **873. ther as,** where. **875. under-meles,** later mornings. **morwenynges,** early mornings. **878. saufly,** safely. **880. incubus,** evil spirit or creature. **881. dishonour,** shame, as contrasted with the begetting upon them of devils. **884. fro ryver.** Hawking was usually pursued along a river. **887. maugree hir heed,** in spite of her head. **888. rafte,** bereft of. **889. oppressioun,** wrong. **890. pursute,** suing (for justice). **892. and sholde han,** and he must have.

Paraventure swich was the statut tho—
But that the queene and othere ladyes mo
So longe preyeden the kyng of grace,   895
Til he his lyf hym graunted in the place,
And yaf hym to the queene, al at hir wille,
To chese wheither she wolde hym save or spille.
   The queene thanketh the kyng with al hir
     myght,
And after this thus spak she to the knyght,   900
Whan that she saugh hir tyme, upon a day:
"Thou standest yet," quod she, "in swich array
That of thy lyf yet hastow no suretee.
I grante thee lyf, if thou kanst tellen me   904
What thyng is it that wommen moost desiren.
Be war, and keep thy nekke-boon from iren!
And if thou kanst nat tellen it anon,
Yet wol I yeve thee leve for to gon
A twelf-month and a day, to seche and leere
An answere suffisant in this mateere;   910
And suretee wol I han, er that thou pace,
Thy body for to yelden in this place."
   Wo was this knyght, and sorwefully he
     siketh;
But what! he may nat do al as hym liketh.
And at the laste he chees hym for to wende,   915
And come agayn, right at the yeres ende,
With swich answere as God wolde hym pur-
     veye;
And taketh his leve, and wendeth forth his
     weye.
   He seketh every hous and every place
Where as he hopeth for to fynde grace,   920
To lerne what thyng wommen loven moost;
But he ne koude arryven in no coost
Wher as he myghte fynde in this mateere
Two creatures accordynge in-feere.
Somme seyde wommen loven best richesse,   925
Somme seyde honour, somme seyde jolynesse,
Somme riche array, somme seyden lust a-bedde,

And oftetyme to be wydwe and wedde.
Somme seyde that oure hertes been moost esed
Whan that we been yflatered and yplesed.   930
He gooth ful ny the sothe, I wol nat lye.
A man shal wynne us best with flaterye;
And with attendance, and with bisynesse,
Been we ylymed, bothe moore and lesse.
   And somme seyn that we loven best   935
For to be free, and do right as us lest,
And that no man repreve us of oure vice,
But seye that we be wise, and no thyng nyce.
For trewely ther is noon of us alle,
If any wight wol clawe us on the galle,   940
That we nel kike, for he seith us sooth.
Assay, and he shal fynde it that so dooth;
For, be we never so vicious withinne,
We wol been holden wise and clene of synne.
   And somme seyn that greet delit han we   945
For to been holden stable, and eek secree,
And in o purpos stedefastly to dwelle,
And nat biwreye thyng that men us telle.
But that tale is nat worth a rake-stele.
Pardee, we wommen konne no thyng hele;   950
Witnesse on Myda,—wol ye heere the tale?
   Ovyde, amonges othere thynges smale,
Seyde Myda hadde, under his longe heres,
Growynge upon his heed two asses eres,   954
The whiche vice he hydde, as he best myghte,
Ful subtilly from every mannes sighte,
That, save his wyf, ther wiste of it namo.
He loved hire moost, and trusted hire also;
He preyde hire that to no creature
She sholde tellen of his disfigure.   960
   She swoor him, "Nay," for al this world to
     wynne,
She nolde do that vileynye or synne,
To make hir housbonde han so foul a name.
She nolde nat telle it for hir owene shame.
But nathelees, hir thoughte that she dyde,   965

---

894. **the queene,** Guinevere. 898. **chese,** choose. **spille,** destroy. 902. **array,** condition. 906. **iren,** _i.e._ the headsman's ax. 907. **anon,** immediately. 909. **leere,** learn. 913. **siketh,** sighs. 920. **grace,** favor. 922. **coost,** coast, region. 924. **in-feere,** together. 927. **lust,** pleasure. 934. **ylymed,** caught (as with birdlime). 937. **repreve,** reprove. 938. **nyce,** foolish. 940. **wol clawe us on the galle,** will scratch us on a sore spot. 941. **for . . . sooth,** because he speaks to us the truth. 946. **secree,** secret, capable of keeping a confidence. 947. **o purpos,** one purpose. 948. **biwreye,** betray. 949. **rake-stele,** rake handle. 950. **hele,** hide. 951. **Myda,** Midas. 954. **two asses eres,** as a punishment for his greed. 955. **vice,** blemish. 965. **dyde,** would die.

That she so longe sholde a conseil hyde;
Hir thoughte it swal so soore aboute hir herte
That nedely som word hire moste asterte;
And sith she dorste telle it to no man,
Doun to a mareys faste by she ran— 970
Til she cam there, hir herte was a-fyre—
And as a bitore bombleth in the myre,
She leyde hir mouth unto the water doun:
"Biwreye me nat, thou water, with thy soun,"
Quod she; "to thee I telle it and namo; 975
Myn housbonde hath longe asses erys two!
Now is myn herte al hool, now is it oute.
I myghte no lenger kepe it, out of doute."
Heere may ye se, thogh we a tyme abyde,
Yet out it moot; we kan no conseil hyde. 980
The remenant of the tale if ye wol heere,
Redeth Ovyde, and ther ye may it leere.

    This knyght, of which my tale is specially,
Whan that he saugh he myghte nat come therby,
This is to seye, what wommen love moost, 985
Withinne his brest ful sorweful was the goost.
But hoom he gooth, he myghte nat sojourne;
The day was come that homward moste he
    tourne.
And in his wey it happed hym to ryde,
In al this care, under a forest syde, 990
Wher as he saugh upon a daunce go
Of ladyes foure and twenty, and yet mo;
Toward the whiche daunce he drow ful yerne,
In hope that some wysdom sholde he lerne.
But certeinly, er he cam fully there, 995
Vanysshed was this daunce, he nyste where.
No creature saugh he that bar lyf,
Save on the grene he saugh sittynge a wyf—
A fouler wight ther may no man devyse.
Agayn the knyght this olde wyf gan ryse, 1000
And seyde, "Sire knyght, heer forth ne lith no
    wey.

Tel me what that ye seken, by youre fey!
Paraventure it may the bettre be;
Thise olde folk kan muchel thyng," quod she.
    "My leeve mooder," quod this knyght, "cer-
    teyn 1005
I nam but deed, but if that I kan seyn
What thyng it is that wommen moost desire.
Koude ye me wisse, I wolde wel quite youre
    hire."
    "Plight me thy trouthe heere in myn hand,"
    quod she,
"The nexte thyng that I requere thee, 1010
Thou shalt it do, if it lye in thy myght,
And I wol telle it yow er it be nyght."
    "Have heer my trouthe," quod the knyght,
    "I grante."
    "Thanne," quod she, "I dar me wel avante
Thy lyf is sauf; for I wol stonde therby, 1015
Upon my lyf, the queene wol seye as I.
Lat se which is the proudeste of hem alle,
That wereth on a coverchief or a calle,
That dar seye nat of that I shal thee teche.
Lat us go forth, withouten lenger speche." 1020
Tho rowned she a pistel in his ere,
And bad hym to be glad, and have no fere.
    Whan they be comen to the court, this
    knyght
Seyde he had holde his day, as he hadde hight,
And redy was his answere, as he sayde. 1025
Ful many a noble wyf, and many a mayde,
And many a wydwe, for that they been wise,
The queene hirself sittynge as a justise,
Assembled been, his answere for to heere;
And afterward this knyght was bode appeere.
    To every wight comanded was silence, 1031
And that the knyght sholde telle in audience
What thyng that worldly wommen loven best.
This knyght ne stood nat stille as doth a best,

---

967. swal, swelled. **soore,** sorely. **968. nedely,** of necessity. **asterte,** escape. **969. sith,** since. **970. mareys,** marsh. **972. bitore bombleth,** bittern booms. **980. moot,** must. **982. Redeth Ovyde.** In Ovid the story is told of Midas's barber, rather than his wife. **986. goost,** spirit. **993. drow,** drew. **yerne,** eagerly. **996. nyste,** knew not. **998. wyf,** woman. **999. devyse,** describe, picture. **1000. Agayn,** towards. **1001. heer forth . . .,** this road doesn't lead anywhere. **1004. kan,** know. **1008. quite youre hire,** repay you (*lit.* satisfy your payment). **1010. requere,** request. **1014. avante,** boast. **1018. wereth on,** wears, has on. **coverchief,** kerchief. **calle,** caul, hairnet. **1021. rowned,** whispered. **pistel,** epistle (short lesson). **1024. hight,** promised. **1030. bode appeere,** bidden to appear. **1034. best,** beast, dumb animal.

But to his questioun anon answerde   1035
With manly voys, that al the court it herde:
"My lige lady, generally," quod he,
"Wommen desiren to have sovereynetee
As wel over hir housbond as hir love,
And for to been in maistrie hym above.   1040
This is youre mooste desir, thogh ye me kille.
Dooth as yow list; I am heer at youre wille."
In al the court ne was ther wyf, ne mayde,
Ne wydwe, that contraried that he sayde,
But seyden he was worthy han his lyf.   1045
And with that word up stirte the olde wyf,
Which that the knyght saugh sittynge on the
     grene:
"Mercy," quod she, "my sovereyn lady queene!
Er that youre court departe, do me right.
I taughte this answere unto the knyght;   1050
For which he plighte me his trouthe there,
The firste thyng I wolde hym requere,
He wolde it do, if it lay in his myght.
Bifore the court thanne preye I thee, sir
     knyght,"
Quod she, "that thou me take unto thy wyf;
For wel thou woost that I have kept thy lyf.   1056
If I seye fals, sey nat, upon thy fey!"
     This knyght answerde, "Allas! and weylawey!
     I woot right wel that swich was my biheste.
For Goddes love, as chees a newe requeste!   1060
Taak al my good, and lat my body go."
     "Nay, thanne," quod she, "I shrewe us bothe
     two!
For thogh that I be foul, and oold, and poore,
I nolde for al the metal, ne for oore,
That under erthe is grave, or lith above,   1065
But if thy wyf I were, and eek thy love."
     "My love?" quod he, "nay, my dampna-
     cioun!
Allas! that any of my nacioun
Sholde evere so foule disparaged be!"
But al for noght; the ende is this, that he   1070

Constreyned was, he nedes moste hire wedde;
And taketh his olde wyf, and gooth to bedde.
     Now wolden som men seye, paraventure,
That for my necligence I do no cure
To tellen yow the joye and al th'array   1075
That at the feeste was that ilke day.
To which thyng shortly answere I shal:
I seye ther nas no joye ne feeste at al;
Ther nas but hevynesse and muche sorwe.
For prively he wedded hire on morwe,   1080
And al day after hidde hym as an owle,
So wo was hym, his wyf looked so foule.
     Greet was the wo the knyght hadde in his
     thoght,
Whan he was with his wyf abedde ybroght;
He walweth and he turneth to and fro.   1085
His olde wyf lay smylynge everemo,
And seyde, "O deere housbonde, benedicitee!
Fareth every knyght thus with his wyf as ye?
Is this the lawe of kyng Arthures hous?
Is every knyght of his so dangerous?   1090
I am youre owene love and eek youre wyf;
I am she which that saved hath youre lyf,
And, certes, yet ne dide I yow nevere unright;
Why fare ye thus with me this firste nyght?
Ye faren lyk a man had lost his wit.   1095
What is my gilt? For Goddes love, tel it,
And it shal been amended, if I may."
     "Amended?" quod this knyght, "allas! nay,
     nay!
It wol nat been amended nevere mo.
Thou art so loothly, and so oold also,   1100
And therto comen of so lough a kynde,
That litel wonder is thogh I walwe and wynde.
So wolde God myn herte wolde breste!"
     "Is this," quod she, "the cause of youre un-
     reste?"
     "Ye, certeinly," quod he, "no wonder is."
     "Now, sire," quod she, "I koude amende al
     this,   1106

1039. love, lover. 1045. han, to have. 1046. stirte, started. 1056. woost, knowest. kept, saved. 1059. biheste, promise. 1060. as chees, choose. 1061. good, property. 1065. grave, buried. 1068. nacioun, family. 1069. disparaged, degraded (by an unequal marriage). 1072. taketh, he takes. 1074. for my necligence . . ., through negligence I do not take the trouble. 1077. shortly, in brief. 1085. walweth, tosses. 1090. dangerous, distant, standoffish. 1101. lough, low. 1102. wynde, turn. 1103. breste, burst.

If that me liste, er it were dayes thre,
So wel ye myghte bere yow unto me.
  But, for ye speken of swich gentillesse
As is descended out of old richesse,   1110
That therfore sholden ye be gentil men,
Swich arrogance is nat worth an hen.
Looke who that is moost vertuous alway,
Pryvee and apert, and moost entendeth ay
To do the gentil dedes that he kan—   1115
Taak hym for the grettest gentil man.
Crist wole we clayme of hym oure gentillesse,
Nat of oure eldres for hire old richesse.
For thogh they yeve us al hir heritage,   1119
For which we clayme to been of heigh parage,
Yet may they nat biquethe, for no thyng,
To noon of us hir vertuous lyvyng,
That made hem gentil men ycalled be,
And bad us folwen hem in swich degree.
  Wel kan the wise poete of Florence,   1125
That highte Dant, speken in this sentence.
Lo, in swich maner rym is Dantes tale:
'Ful selde up riseth by his branches smale
Prowesse of man, for God, of his goodnesse,
Wole that of hym we clayme oure gentil-
    lesse';   1130
For of oure eldres may we no thyng clayme
But temporel thyng, that man may hurte and
    mayme.
  Eek every wight woot this as wel as I,
If gentillesse were planted natureelly
Unto a certeyn lynage doun the lyne,   1135
Pryvee and apert, thanne wolde they nevere
    fyne
To doon of gentillesse the faire office;
They myghte do no vileynye or vice.
  Taak fyr, and ber it in the derkeste hous

Bitwix this and the mount of Kaukasous,   1140
And lat men shette the dores and go thenne;
Yet wole the fyr as faire lye and brenne
As twenty thousand men myghte it biholde;
His office natureel ay wol it holde,
Up peril of my lyf, til that it dye.   1145
  Heere may ye se wel how that genterye
Is nat annexed to possessioun,
Sith folk ne doon hir operacioun
Alwey, as dooth the fyr, lo, in his kynde.   1149
For, God it woot, men may wel often fynde
A lordes sone do shame and vileynye;
And he that wole han pris of his gentrye,
For he was boren of a gentil hous,
And hadde his eldres noble and vertuous,
And nel hymselven do no gentil dedis,   1155
Ne folwen his gentil auncestre that deed is,
He nys nat gentil, be he duc or erl;
For vileyns synful dedes make a cherl.
For gentillesse nys but renomee   1159
Of thyne auncestres, for hire heigh bountee,
Which is a strange thyng to thy persone.
Thy gentillesse cometh fro God allone.
Thanne comth oure verray gentillesse of grace;
It was no thyng biquethe us with oure place.
  Thenketh hou noble, as seith Valerius,   1165
Was thilke Tullius Hostillius,
That out of poverte roos to heigh noblesse.
Reedeth Senek, and redeth eek Boece;
Ther shul ye seen expres that it no drede is
That he is gentil that dooth gentil dedis.   1170
And therfore, leeve housbonde, I thus conclude:
Al were it that myne auncestres were rude,
Yet may the hye God, and so hope I,
Grante me grace to lyven vertuously.
Thanne am I gentil, whan that I bigynne   1175

1108. So, so that. 1109. gentillesse, gentility, nobility. The ideas which follow were common in the Middle Ages, being found in Boethius, in the *Roman de la Rose*, in Dante (see below), etc. Cf. Vogt, *JEGP*, XXIV. 102–24. 1110. old richesse, inherited wealth. 1111. gentil, of superior position or quality. 1113. Looke who, whoever. See Lotspeich, *JEGP*, XXXVII. 1–2, and Language, § 81. 1117. wole, wishes (that). 1120. parage, rank. 1124. degree, state, condition. 1128. "Ful selde . . . ." The quotation is from *Purgatorio*, VII. 121–3, with some fusion of the wording of the *Convivio*. Cf. Lowes, *MP*, XIII. 19–33. 1136. fyne, cease. 1141. thenne, thence. 1142. lye, blaze. 1143. As, as if. 1144. His, its. 1145. Up, upon. 1146. genterye, gentility. 1148. ne doon hir operacioun, do not behave as they should. 1152. han pris of, be esteemed for. 1159. nys but renomee, is merely the renown. 1161. Which . . . persone, which has nothing to do with you. 1164. biquethe, bequeathed. place, position, rank. 1165. Valerius, Valerius Maximus, III, cap. 4. 1166. Tullius Hostillius, third legendary king of Rome (673–642 B.C.). 1168. Senek, Seneca. Boece, Boethius. 1169. expres, explicitly stated. drede, doubt. 1172. Al were it that, even if.

To lyven vertuously and weyve synne.

And ther as ye of poverte me repreeve,
The hye God, on whom that we bileeve,
In wilful poverte chees to lyve his lyf.
And certes every man, mayden, or wyf, 1180
May understonde that Jhesus, hevene kyng,
Ne wolde nat chese a vicious lyvyng.
Glad poverte is an honest thyng, certeyn;
This wole Senec and othere clerkes seyn.
Whoso that halt hym payd of his poverte, 1185
I holde hym riche, al hadde he nat a sherte.
He that coveiteth is a povre wight,
For he wolde han that is nat in his myght;
But he that noght hath, ne coveiteth have,
Is riche, although ye holde hym but a knave.
Verray poverte, it syngeth proprely; 1191
Juvenal seith of poverte myrily:
'The povre man, whan he goth by the weye,
Bifore the theves he may synge and pleye.'
Poverte is hateful good and, as I gesse, 1195
A ful greet bryngere out of bisynesse;
A greet amendere eek of sapience
To hym that taketh it in pacience.
Poverte is this, although it seme alenge,
Possessioun that no wight wol chalenge. 1200
Poverte ful ofte, whan a man is lowe,
Maketh his God and eek hymself to knowe.
Poverte a spectacle is, as thynketh me,
Thurgh which he may his verray freendes see.
And therfore, sire, syn that I noght yow greve,
Of my poverte namoore ye me repreve. 1206
    Now, sire, of elde ye repreve me;
And certes, sire, thogh noon auctoritee
Were in no book, ye gentils of honour
Seyn that men sholde an oold wight doon
    favour, 1210

And clepe hym fader, for youre gentillesse;
And auctours shal I fynden, as I gesse.
    Now ther ye seye that I am foul and old,
Than drede you noght to been a cokewold;
For filthe and eelde, also moot I thee, 1215
Been grete wardeyns upon chastitee.
But nathelees, syn I knowe youre delit,
I shal fulfille youre worldly appetit.
    Chese now," quod she, "oon of thise thynges
        tweye:
To han me foul and old til that I deye, 1220
And be to yow a trewe, humble wyf,
And nevere yow displese in al my lyf;
Or elles ye wol han me yong and fair,
And take youre aventure of the repair
That shal be to youre hous by cause of me, 1225
Or in som oother place, may wel be.
Now chese yourselven, wheither that yow
    liketh."
    This knyght avyseth hym and sore siketh,
But atte laste he seyde in this manere:
"My lady and my love, and wyf so deere, 1230
I put me in youre wise governance;
Cheseth youreself which may be moost ples-
    ance,
And moost honour to yow and me also.
I do no fors the wheither of the two;
For as yow liketh, it suffiseth me." 1235
    "Thanne have I gete of yow maistrie," quod
        she,
"Syn I may chese and governe as me lest?"
    "Ye, certes, wyf," quod he, "I holde it best."
    "Kys me," quod she, "we be no lenger
        wrothe;
For, by my trouthe, I wol be to yow bothe, 1240
This is to seyn, ye, bothe fair and good.

1176. weyve, shun. 1177. of poverte. Actually this is not one of the things the knight complains of. 1185. halt
hym payd of, holds himself satisfied with. 1186. al, although. 1189. coveiteth have, covets to have. 1190.
knave, one of mean estate. 1191. Verray, true. proprely. becomingly. 1192. Juvenal, *Sat.*, x. 21–22, but probably
through Dante, *Convivio*, IV. In any case, the idea was proverbial. myrily, cheerfully. 1195. hateful good. A marginal
gloss in the Ellesmere MS cites Secundus philosophus: *Paupertas est odibile bonum . . .* A collection of gnomic sayings
circulated in the Middle Ages under the name of Secundus. 1196. bryngere out of bisynesse, apparently translating
curarum remocio in the saying referred to. bisynesse, industry. 1199. alenge, wearisome. 1202. Maketh, understand *hym*.
1203. spectacle, eyeglass. Hoccleve, shortly after Chaucer's death uses the word (in the sing.) in this sense. The meaning
"something seen" is also possible, and this is the interpretation adopted by the *NED*. 1211. clepe, call. 1213. ther, whereas.
1214. Than, then. 1215. also moot I thee, as may I thrive. 1219. Chese, choose. 1224. aventure, chance. repair, frequenting. 1227. wheither, whichever. 1228. siketh, sighs. 1234. I do no fors . . . It doesn't matter to me which. 1236. gete, got.

I prey to God that I moote sterven wood,
But I to yow be also good and trewe
As evere was wyf, syn that the world was
      newe.
And but I be to-morn as fair to seene   1245
As any lady, emperice, or queene,
That is bitwixe the est and eke the west,
Dooth with my lyf and deth right as yow lest.
Cast up the curtyn, looke how that it is."
      And whan the knyght saugh verraily al this,
That she so fair was, and so yong therto,   1251
For joye he hente hire in his armes two,

His herte bathed in a bath of blisse.
A thousand tyme a-rewe he gan hire kisse,
And she obeyed hym in every thyng   1255
That myghte doon hym plesance or likyng.
      And thus they lyve unto hir lyves ende
In parfit joye; and Jhesu Crist us sende
Housbondes meeke, yonge, and fressh abedde,
And grace t' overbyde hem that we wedde; 1260
And eek I praye Jhesu shorte hir lyves
That wol nat be governed by hir wyves;
And olde and angry nygardes of dispence,
God sende hem soone verray pestilence!

Heere endeth the Wyves Tale of Bathe.

The Friar's Tale

THE FRIAR'S PROLOGUE

The Prologe of the Freres Tale.

This worthy lymytour, this noble Frere, 1265
He made alwey a maner louryng chiere
Upon the Somonour, but for honestee
No vileyns word as yet to hym spak he.
But atte laste he seyde unto the wyf,
"Dame," quod he, "God yeve yow right good
      lyf!
                                      1270
Ye han heer touched, also moot I thee,
In scole-matere greet difficultee.
Ye han seyd muche thyng right wel, I seye;
But, dame, heere as we ryde by the weye,
Us nedeth nat to speken but of game,   1275
And lete auctoritees, on Goddes name,

To prechyng and to scole eek of clergye.
But if it lyke to this compaignye,
I wol yow of a somonour telle a game.
Pardee, ye may wel knowe by the name   1280
That of a somonour may no good be sayd;
I praye that noon of you be yvele apayd.
A somonour is a rennere up and doun
With mandementz for fornicacioun,
And is ybet at every townes ende."   1285
      Oure Hoost tho spak, "A! sire, ye sholde be
      hende
And curteys, as a man of youre estaat;
In compaignye we wol have no debaat.

1242. **sterven wood,** die insane. 1245. **to-morn,** tomorrow. 1252. **hente,** took. 1254. **a-rewe,** in succession. 1260. **over-byde,** outlive. 1261. **shorte,** shorten. 1267. **Somonour.** On the duties of the summoner see note to A 623. **honestee,** propriety, proper behavior. 1268. **vileyns,** *i.e.* ill-mannered. 1272. **In scole-matere greet difficultee,** difficult scholastic questions. 1276. **lete,** leave. **auctoritees,** alluding to l. 1208 above and possibly to the Wife's opening words in her pro-logue. 1277. **clergye,** learning. 1279. **game,** something entertaining. 1280. **by the name,** from the word itself. 1282. **be yvele apayd,** be displeased, take offense. 1283. **rennere,** runner. 1284. **mandementz,** summonses. 1285. **ybet,** beaten. 1286. **hende,** polite, gracious.

Telleth youre tale, and lat the Somonour be."

"Nay," quod the Somonour, "lat hym seye
to me   1290

What so hym list; whan it comth to my lot,

By God! I shal hym quiten every grot.

I shal hym tellen which a greet honour

It is to be a flaterynge lymytour;

And eek of many another manere cryme   1295

Which nedeth nat rehercen at this tyme;

And his office I shal hym telle, ywis."

Oure Hoost answerde, "Pees, namoore of
this!"

And after this he seyde unto the Frere,   1299

"Tel forth youre tale, my leeve maister deere."

THE FRIAR'S TALE

Heere bigynneth the Freres Tale.

Whilom ther was dwellynge in my contree

An erchedekene, a man of heigh degree,

That boldely dide execucioun

In punysshynge of fornicacioun,

Of wicchecraft, and eek of bawderye,   1305

Of diffamacioun, and avowtrye,

Of chirche reves, and of testamentz,

Of contractes and of lakke of sacramentz,

Of usure, and of symonye also.

But certes, lecchours dide he grettest wo;   1310

They sholde syngen if that they were hent;

And smale tytheres weren foule yshent,

If any persoun wolde upon hem pleyne.

Ther myghte asterte hym no pecunyal peyne.

For smale tithes and for smal offrynge   1315

He made the peple pitously to synge.

For er the bisshop caughte hem with his hook,

They weren in the erchedeknes book.

Thanne hadde he, thurgh his jurisdiccioun,

Power to doon on hem correccioun.   1320

He hadde a somonour redy to his hond;

A slyer boye nas noon in Engelond;

For subtilly he hadde his espiaille,

That taughte hym wher that hym myghte
availle.

He koude spare of lecchours oon or two,   1325

To techen hym to foure and twenty mo.

For thogh this Somonour wood were as an hare,

1291. **hym list,** he pleases. 1292. **quiten every grot,** pay back every particle. 1293. **which,** what. 1297. **office,** employment. 1300. **leeve,** dear.

  The Friar's Tale. The basic plot of the Friar's Tale is found in several examples, but the victim is variously represented as a farmer, an unscrupulous lawyer, a harsh seneschal, etc. They prove the existence in popular literature of such a story as the Friar tells, but none can be considered an actual source. Much of the dialogue and characterization are apparently Chaucer's and the application of the story to a summoner may also be original with him. The *Tale* was probably written at much the same time as the Wife of Bath's *Prologue* and *Tale*, and is admirably integrated with the behavior of the Friar and the Summoner during the course of her self-revelation.

1301. **contree,** county, neighborhood. 1302. **erchedekene.** See note to A 623. Manly would identify the archdeacon with William de Ravenser, archdeacon of Lincoln, but the evidence is rather weak and he rightly does not press the identification. See *Some New Light on Chaucer*, pp. 102–22. 1305. **bawderye,** pandering. 1306. **avowtrye,** adultery. 1307. **Of chirche reves,** churchwardens. The construction depends upon *In punysshynge,* and the implication is in cases of laxness or corruption. **of testamentz.** Here (and with *contractes*) one must understand offenses in connection with these things. 1309. **usure,** lending for interest, forbidden by the church. **symonye,** the buying and selling of church offices. 1311. **syngen,** *i.e.* sing a sorrowful tune. **hent,** caught. 1312. **smale tytheres,** presumably those who cheated on their tithes. **foule yshent,** severely treated (put to shame). 1313. **persoun,** parson. **pleyne,** complain. 1314. **asterte,** escape. The archdeacon allowed no fine to escape him. 1317. **hook,** with reference to the shape of the bishop's crosier. 1320. **correccioun,** punishment. 1323. **subtilly,** craftily. **espiaille,** body of spies. 1326. **techen,** direct. 1327. **wood,** cf. "mad as a March hare."

To telle his harlotrye I wol nat spare;
For we been out of his correccioun.
They han of us no jurisdiccioun,   1330
Ne nevere shullen, terme of alle hir lyves.—
  "Peter! so been the wommen of the styves,"
Quod the Somonour, "yput out of my cure!"
  "Pees! with myschance and with mysaven-
    ture!"
Thus seyde oure Hoost, "and lat hym telle his
    tale.   1335
Now telleth forth, thogh that the Somonour
    gale;
Ne spareth nat, myn owene maister deere."—
  This false theef, this somonour, quod the
    Frere,
Hadde alwey bawdes redy to his hond,
As any hauk to lure in Engelond,   1340
That tolde hym al the secree that they knewe;
For hire acqueyntance was nat come of newe.
They weren his approwours prively.
He took hymself a greet profit therby;
His maister knew nat alwey what he wan.   1345
Withouten mandement a lewed man
He koude somne, on peyne of Cristes curs,
And they were glade for to fille his purs,
And make hym grete feestes atte nale.
And right as Judas hadde purses smale,   1350
And was a theef, right swich a theef was he;
His maister hadde but half his duetee.
He was, if I shal yeven hym his laude,

A theef, and eek a somnour, and a baude.
He hadde eek wenches at his retenue,   1355
That, wheither that sir Robert or sir Huwe,
Or Jakke, or Rauf, or whoso that it were
That lay by hem, they tolde it in his ere.
Thus was the wenche and he of oon assent;
And he wolde fecche a feyned mandement,   1360
And somne hem to chapitre bothe two,
And pile the man, and lete the wenche go.
Thanne wolde he seye, "Freend, I shal for thy
    sake
Do striken hire out of oure lettres blake;
Thee thar namoore as in this cas travaille.   1365
I am thy freend, ther I thee may availle."
Certeyn he knew of briberyes mo
Than possible is to telle in yeres two.
For in this world nys dogge for the bowe
That kan an hurt deer from an hool knowe   1370
Bet than this somnour knew a sly lecchour,
Or an avowtier, or a paramour.
And for that was the fruyt of al his rente,
Therfore on it he sette al his entente.
  And so bifel that ones on a day   1375
This somnour, evere waityng on his pray,
Rood for to somne an old wydwe, a ribibe,
Feynynge a cause, for he wolde brybe.
And happed that he saugh bifore hym ryde
A gay yeman, under a forest syde.   1380
A bowe he bar, and arwes brighte and kene;
He hadde upon a courtepy of grene,

1328. harlotrye, scurrility. **1329. out of**, outside of. Friars were not under the jurisdiction of bishops. They were governed by the general of their order. **1331. shullen**, shall. **terme of**, during the term of. **1332. styves**, stews, houses of prostitution. **1333. cure**, responsibility. **1336. gale**, yelp, cry out. **1339. bawdes**, bawds, go-betweens. The comparison is with the *lure* in hawking, which the *NED* defines as "An apparatus used by falconers to recall their hawks, constructed of a bunch of feathers to which is attached a long cord or thong, and from the interstices of which, during its training, the hawk is fed." The construction is elliptical: Such as (the devices used) to lure any hawk. **1341. secree**, secrets (collectively). **1342. of newe**, recently. **1343. approwours**, agents. **1346. mandement**, legal summons. **lewed**, ignorant. **1347. somne**, summon. **Cristes curs**, excommunication. **1349. atte nale**, for *atten ale*, at the alehouse. **1350. as Judas.** Cf. *John*, 12:6. **1352. duetee**, due, amount due. **1353. laude**, *lit.* praise, but here "his deserts." **1355. at his retenue**, among his following. **1359. of oon assent**, in collusion. **1361. chapitre**, meeting of the archdeacon's court. **1362. pile**, pluck, rob. **1364. Do striken hire out**, have her struck out. **1365. Thee thar**, you do not need (impers.). **travaille**, labor, go to any trouble. **1366. ther**, where. **1367. briberyes**, forms of extortion. The modern sense is a later development. **1369. dogge for the bowe**, "dog used to accompany an archer, to follow up a stricken deer." (Skeat). **1370. knowe.** Most editors adopt the reading *yknowe*, found in a single MS, to the improvement of the meter. But the variety of scribal emendations found in other MSS makes it certain that *knowe* was the reading of the archetype. **1372. avowtier**, adulterer. **1373. the fruyt of al his rente**, the best part of his income. **1376. waityng on**, on the lookout for. **1377. ribibe**, a kind of fiddle, here used contemptuously for an old woman. **1378. brybe**, rob, practice extortion. **1380. gay yeman**, carefree yeoman. **1382. courtepy**, short coat or cloak of coarse material.

An hat upon his heed with frenges blake.
"Sire," quod this somnour, "hayl, and wel
   atake!"   1384
"Welcome," quod he, "and every good felawe!
Wher rydestow, under this grene-wode shawe?"
Seyde this yeman, "wiltow fer to day?"
   This somnour hym answerde and seyde,
   "Nay;
Heere faste by," quod he, "is myn entente
To ryden, for to reysen up a rente   1390
That longeth to my lordes duetee."
   "Artow thanne a bailly?" "Ye," quod he.
He dorste nat, for verray filthe and shame
Seye that he was a somonour, for the name.
   "Depardieux," quod this yeman, "deere
   broother,   1395
Thou art a bailly, and I am another.
I am unknowen as in this contree;
Of thyn aqueyntance I wolde praye thee,
And eek of bretherhede, if that yow leste.
I have gold and silver in my cheste;   1400
If that thee happe to comen in oure shire,
Al shal be thyn, right as thou wolt desire."
   "Grantmercy," quod this somonour, "by my
   feith!"
Everych in ootheres hand his trouthe leith,
For to be sworne bretheren til they deye.   1405
In daliance they ryden forth and pleye.
   This somonour, which that was as ful of
   jangles,
As ful of venym been thise waryangles,
And evere enquerynge upon every thyng,
"Brother," quod he, "where is now youre dwel-
   lyng   1410

Another day if that I sholde yow seche?"
This yeman hym answerde in softe speche,
   "Brother," quod he, "fer in the north con-
   tree,
Where-as I hope som tyme I shal thee see.
Er we departe, I shal thee so wel wisse   1415
That of myn hous ne shaltow nevere mysse."
   "Now, brother," quod this somonour, "I
   yow preye,
Teche me, whil that we ryden by the weye,
Syn that ye been a baillif as am I,
Som subtiltee, and tel me feithfully   1420
In myn office how that I may moost wynne;
And spareth nat for conscience ne synne,
But as my brother tel me, how do ye."
   "Now, by my trouthe, brother deere," seyde
   he,
"As I shal tellen thee a feithful tale,   1425
My wages been ful streite and ful smale.
My lord is hard to me and daungerous,
And myn office is ful laborous,
And therfore by extorcions I lyve.
For sothe, I take al that men wol me yive.   1430
Algate, by sleyghte or by violence,
Fro yeer to yeer I wynne al my dispence.
I kan no bettre telle, feithfully."
   "Now certes," quod this Somonour, "so fare
   I.
I spare nat to taken, God it woot,   1435
But if it be to hevy or to hoot.
What I may gete in conseil prively,
No maner conscience of that have I.
Nere myn extorcioun, I myghte nat lyven,
Ne of swiche japes wol I nat be shryven.   1440

1383. **frenges**, bindings. The *Promp. Parv.* gives "frenge, or lyoure," which suggests a binding on the edge (see *NED, s.v. lear* 2) and this appears in illuminations. Cf. also *Manip. Vocab.*, "Frenge, lacinia." 1384. **wel atake**, well met (overtaken). 1386. **shawe**, grove. 1387. **fer**, far. 1390. **reysen up a rente**, collect certain income. 1391. **longeth**, pertains. **my lordes duetee**, what is due my lord. 1392. **bailly**, bailiff. 1394. **for the name**, because of the very name. 1395. *Depardieux*, by God. 1397. **as in**, in. **contree**, region. 1399. **bretherhede**, sworn brotherhood. The practice of taking an oath of complete loyalty was a very old one and generally involved the holding up or joining of hands. In its more solemn form of blood brotherhood the blood from small incisions in the hand was mingled. For a description of the swearing of brotherhood see the romance of *Amis and Amiloun*, ll. 145–56. 1407. **jangles**, idle talk. 1408. **waryangles**, shrikes, sometimes called butcherbirds. They impaled their prey on a thorn, and according to Giraldus Cambrensis the thorn was afterwards poisonous. See T. P. Harrison, *N & Q*, CXCIX. 189. 1411. **seche**, seek. 1413. **fer in the north contree**. Hell was often thought of as in the north. 1415. **wisse**, inform. 1420. **subtiltee**, crafty device. 1426. **streite**, narrow, limited. 1427. **daungerous**, demanding, hard to please. 1431. **Algate**, always. **sleyghte**, cunning, trick. 1432. **dispence**, expenditure. 1437. **in conseil**, in private, secretly. 1439. **Nere**, were it not for. 1440. **japes**, tricks. **wol I nat be shryven**, i.e. I will not be absolved (on condition of giving them up).

Stomak ne conscience ne knowe I noon;
I shrewe thise shrifte-fadres everychoon.
Wel be we met, by God and by Seint Jame!
But, leeve brother, tel me thanne thy name,"
Quod this somonour. In this meene while   1445
This yeman gan a litel for to smyle.

  "Brother," quod he, "wiltow that I thee telle?
I am a feend; my dwellyng is in helle,
And heere I ryde about my purchasyng,
To wite where men wol yeve me any thyng.
My purchas is th'effect of al my rente.   1451
Looke how thou rydest for the same entente
To wynne good, thou rekkest nevere how,
Right so fare I, for ryde wolde I now
Unto the worldes ende for a preye."   1455
  "A!" quod this somonour, "benedicite! what
    sey ye?
I wende ye were a yeman trewely.
Ye han a mannes shap as wel as I;
Han ye a figure thanne determinat
In helle, ther ye been in youre estat?"   1460
  "Nay, certeinly," quod he, "ther have we
    noon;
But whan us liketh, we kan take us oon,
Or elles make yow seme we been shape
Somtyme lyk a man, or lyk an ape,
Or lyk an angel kan I ryde or go.   1465
It is no wonder thyng thogh it be so;
A lowsy jogelour kan deceyve thee,
And pardee, yet kan I moore craft than he."
  "Why," quod this somonour, "ryde ye
    thanne or goon
In sondry shap, and nat alwey in oon?"   1470
  "For we," quod he, "wol us swiche formes
    make
As moost able is oure preyes for to take."

  "What maketh yow to han al this labour?"
  "Ful many a cause, leeve sire somonour,"
Seyde this feend, "but alle thyng hath tyme.
The day is short, and it is passed pryme,   1476
And yet ne wan I nothyng in this day.
I wol entende to wynnyng, if I may,
And nat entende oure wittes to declare.
For, brother myn, thy wit is al to bare   1480
To understonde, althogh I tolde hem thee.
But, for thou axest why labouren we—
For somtyme we been Goddes instrumentz,
And meenes to doon his comandementz,
Whan that hym list, upon his creatures,   1485
In divers art and in diverse figures.
Withouten hym we have no myght, certayn,
If that hym list to stonden ther-agayn.
And somtyme, at oure prayere, han we leve
Oonly the body and nat the soule greve;   1490
Witnesse on Job, whom that we diden wo.
And somtyme han we myght of bothe two,
This is to seyn, of soule and body eke.
And somtyme be we suffred for to seke
Upon a man, and doon his soule unreste,   1495
And nat his body, and al is for the beste.
Whan he withstandeth oure temptacioun,
It is a cause of his savacioun,
Al be it that it was nat oure entente
He sholde be sauf, but that we wolde hym
    hente.   1500
And somtyme be we servant unto man,
As to the erchebisshop Seint Dunstan,
And to the apostles servant eek was I."
  "Yet tel me," quod the somonour, "feith-
    fully,
Make ye yow newe bodies thus alway   1505
Of elementz?" The feend answerde, "Nay.

1441. **Stomak,** tender-heartedness. 1442. **shrewe,** beshrew, curse. **shrifte-fadres,** father-confessors. 1449. **purchasyng,** acquisition. 1450. **To wite wher,** to know whether. 1451. **purchas,** gain from begging. **th' effect . . .,** the sum and substance of my income. 1452. **Looke how,** just as. 1453. **rekkest,** carest. 1459. **figure . . . determinat,** definite shape. 1460. **ther,** where. **estat,** proper condition. 1463. **make yow seme,** make it seem to you. 1465. **go,** walk. 1468. **craft,** skill. 1471. **swiche formes make,** assume such shapes. 1476. **pryme,** nine o'clock. 1477. **wan,** won. 1478. **entende,** devote myself. 1479. **entende,** intend. **wittes,** plans. I will devote myself to getting gains, if I may, and (do) not intend to make known our plans (or devices). 1486. **figures,** shapes. 1488. **stonden ther-agayn,** oppose us. 1491. **Job.** See *Job,* 1:12 and 2:6. 1494. **to seke Upon,** attack. 1502. **Seint Dunstan.** St. Dunstan (924–988), archbishop of Canterbury, of whom several stories are told in which he subjected the devil to his will. See Sister M. Immaculate, *PQ,* xxi. 240–244. 1503. **the apostles servant.** In the *Legenda Aurea* such incidents are reported of Andrew Peter, James, Bartholomew, Thomas, etc. 1506. **Of elementz,** out of raw materials (earth, air, fire, water).

Somtyme we feyne, and somtyme we aryse
With dede bodyes, in ful sondry wyse,
And speke as renably and faire and wel
As to the Phitonissa dide Samuel.　　　　　　1510
(And yet wol som men seye it was nat he; ~I do not care about your theological ideas~
I do no fors of youre dyvynytee.) ~I am not joking~
But o thyng warne I thee, I wol nat jape,— ~at any rate~
Thou wolt algates wite how we been shape;
Thou shalt herafterwardes, my brother deere, ~where~ ~learn~
Come there thee nedeth nat of me to leere,　1516
For thou shalt, by thyn owene experience, ~know how to deliver lectures on this subject~
Konne in a chayer rede of this sentence
Bet than Virgile, while he was on lyve,
Or Dant also. Now lat us ryde blyve, ~quickly~　1520
For I wole holde compaignye with thee
Til it be so that thou forsake me."
　　"Nay," quod this somonour, "that shal nat
　　　bityde!
I am a yeman, knowen is ful wyde;
My trouthe wol I holde, as in this cas.　　　1525
For though thou were the devel Sathanas,
My trouthe wol I holde to my brother,
As I am sworn, and ech of us til oother,
For to be trewe brother in this cas;
And bothe we goon abouten oure purchas.　1530
Taak thou thy part, what that men wol thee
　　yive,
And I shal myn; thus may we bothe lyve.
And if that any of us have moore than oother,
Lat hym be trewe, and parte it with his
　　brother."　　　　　　　　　　　　　　1534
　　"I graunte," quod the devel, "by my fey."
And with that word they ryden forth hir wey.
And right at the entryng of the townes ende,

To which this somonour shoop hym for to
　　wende,
They saugh a cart that charged was with hey,
Which that a cartere droof forth in his wey. 1540
Deep was the wey, for which the carte stood.
The cartere smoot, and cryde as he were wood,
"Hayt, Brok! hayt, Scot! what spare ye for the
　　stones?
The feend," quod he, "yow fecche, body and
　　bones,
As ferforthly as evere were ye foled,　　　　1545
So muche wo as I have with yow tholed!
The devel have al, bothe hors and cart and
　　hey!"
　　This somonour seyde, "Heere shal we have a
　　　pley." ~sport~
And neer the feend he drough, as noght ne
　　were,
Ful prively, and rowned in his ere:　　　　　1550
"Herkne, my brother, herkne, by thy feith!
Herestow nat how that the cartere seith? ~seize~
Hent it anon, for he hath yeve it thee,
Bothe hey and cart, and eek his caples thre."
　　"Nay," quod the devel, "God woot, never a
　　　deel! ~Not a bit~　　　　　　　　　　1555
It is nat his entente, trust me weel.
Axe hym thyself, if thou nat trowest me;
Or elles stynt a while, and thou shalt see."
　　This cartere thakketh his hors upon the ~slaps~
　　　croupe, ~rump~　　　　　　　　　　　~lean forward~
And they bigonne to drawen and to stoupe.
"Heyt! now," quod he, "ther Jhesu Crist yow
　　blesse,　　　　　　　　　　　　　　　1561
And al his handwerk, bothe moore and lesse!

1507. feyne, assume a disguise. aryse With dede bodyes, enter into the bodies of the dead. 1509. renably, reasonably. 1510. Phitonissa. When Saul consulted the witch of Endor, where the Authorized Version speaks of "one that had a familiar spirit" (1 Chronicles, 10:13) the Vulgate has "pythonissam." At Saul's request she calls up Samuel, who foretells the defeat of Saul by the Philistines. (1 Samuel, 28:7–19). 1511. som men. Possibly an allusion to the argument of St. Eustathius (De Engastrimytho) that the apparition of Samuel was a hallucination in the mind of Saul. Views on the apparition are frequent in the early Fathers. See Cath. Encycl., x. 736, for references. 1512. I do no fors . . . I do not care about your theological ideas. 1513. I wol nat jape, I am not joking. 1514. algates, at any rate. 1516. there, where. leere, learn. 1518. Konne in a chayer rede . . ., know how to deliver lectures on this subject. 1519. Bet than Virgile, better than Virgil, referring to the visit of Æneas to the lower world, which fills book VI of the Æneid. 1520. blyve, quickly. 1530. purchas, acquisition. 1538. shoop hym, intended. 1539. charged. loaded. 1541. Deep, i.e. the ruts or mire. 1544. fecche, carry off. 1545. ferforthly, completely, surely. foled, foaled, born. 1546. tholed, suffered. 1548. a pley, sport. 1549. neer, nearer. as noght ne were, as if for no special reason. 1550. rowned, whispered. 1553. Hent, seize, take. yeve, given. 1554. caples, cart-horses. 1555. never a deel, not a bit. 1559. thakketh, slaps (lightly), pats. croupe, crupper, rump. 1560. stoupe, lean forward. 1561. ther, hortatory adverb. See Language, § 73.

That was wel twight, myn owene lyard boy.

I pray God save thee, and Seinte Loy!

Now is my cart out of the slow, pardee!" 1565

    "Lo, brother," quod the feend, "what tolde
        I thee?

Heere may ye se, myn owene deere brother,

The carl spak o thing, but he thoghte another.

Lat us go forth abouten oure viage;

Heere wynne I nothyng upon cariage." 1570

    Whan that they coomen somwhat out of
        towne,

This somonour to his brother gan to rowne:

"Brother," quod he, "heere woneth an old
    rebekke,

That hadde almoost as lief to lese hire nekke

As for to yeve a peny of hir good. 1575

I wole han twelf pens, though that she be wood,

Or I wol sompne hire unto oure office;

And yet, God woot, of hire knowe I no vice.

But for thou kanst nat, as in this contree, 1579

Wynne thy cost, taak heer ensample of me."

    This somonour clappeth at the wydwes gate.

"Com out," quod he, "thou olde virytrate!

I trowe thou hast som frere or preest with thee."

    "Who clappeth?" seyde this wyf, "benedicitee!

God save you, sire, what is youre sweete
    wille?" 1585

    "I have," quod he, "of somonce here a bille;

Up peyne of cursyng, looke that thou be

To-morn bifore the erchedeknes knee,

T'answere to the court of certeyn thynges."

    "Now, Lord," quod she, "Crist Jhesu, kyng
    of kynges, 1590

So wisly helpe me, as I ne may.

I have been syk, and that ful many a day.

I may nat go so fer," quod she, "ne ryde,

But I be deed, so priketh it in my syde.

May I nat axe a libel, sire somonour, 1595

And answere there by my procuratour

To swich thyng as men wole opposen me?"

    "Yis," quod this somonour, "pay anon, lat se,

Twelf pens to me, and I wol thee acquite.

I shal no profit han therby but lite; 1600

My maister hath the profit, and nat I.

Com of, and lat me ryden hastily;

Yif me twelf pens, I may no lenger tarye."

    "Twelf pens!" quod she, "now, lady Seinte
    Marie

So wisly help me out of care and synne, 1605

This wyde world thogh that I sholde wynne,

Ne have I nat twelf pens withinne myn hoold.

Ye knowen wel that I am povre and oold;

Kithe youre almesse on me, povre wrecche."

    "Nay thanne," quod he, "the foule feend me
    fecche 1610

If I th'excuse, though thou shul be spilt!"

    "Allas!" quod she, "God woot, I have no
    gilt."

    "Pay me," quod he, "or by the sweete seinte
    Anne,

As I wol bere awey thy newe panne

For dette which thou owest me of old. 1615

Whan that thou madest thyn housbonde coke-
    wold,

I payde at hoom for thy correccioun."

    "Thou lixt!" quod she, "by my savacioun,

Ne was I nevere er now, wydwe ne wyf,

Somoned unto youre court in al my lyf; 1620

Ne nevere I nas but of my body trewe!

Unto the devel blak and rough of hewe

Yeve I thy body and my panne also!"

    And whan the devel herde hire cursen so

1563. **twight,** pulled. **lyard,** gray or dappled gray. 1564. **Seinte Loy.** See note to A 120; used here because St. Loy was the patron saint of carters. 1565. **slow,** slough, mire. 1568. **carl,** fellow. 1569. **viage,** journey. 1570. **upon cariage,** in the way of payment due. *Cariage* was a feudal obligation to transport goods for an overlord, or payment in lieu of it. 1572. **rowne,** whisper. 1573. **woneth an old rebekke,** dwells an old crone (*lit.* fiddle). *Rebekke,* like *ribibe* in l. 1377, is a contemptuous term for an old woman. 1574. **lese,** lose. 1575. **yeve,** give. **good,** goods. 1578. **no vice,** nothing wrong. 1579. **for,** because. 1580. **Wynne thy cost,** make expenses. 1581. **clappeth,** knocks. 1582. **virytrate,** trot. This is the only instance of the word in *NED,* and the derivation is obscure. 1586. **somonce,** summons. 1587. **Up peyne of cursyng,** upon pain of excommunication. 1593. **go,** walk. 1594. **But I be deed,** without its killing me. 1595. **a libel,** a written copy of the charge. 1596. **procuratour,** proctor, proxy. 1597. **opposen,** bring against. 1600. **lite,** little. 1602. **Com of,** come on. **hastily,** without delay. 1607. **hoold,** house, tenement. 1609. **Kithe,** show. **almesse,** charity. 1616. **cokewold,** cuckold. 1617. **correccioun,** fine (Skeat). 1618. **lixt,** liest. **savacioun,** salvation.

Upon hir knees, he seyde in this manere,   1625
"Now, Mabely, myn owene mooder deere,
Is this youre wyl in ernest that ye seye?"
  "The devel," quod she, "so fecche hym er he deye,
And panne and al, but he wol hym repente!"
  "Nay, olde stot, that is nat myn entente,"
Quod this somonour, "for to repente me   1631
For any thyng that I have had of thee.
I wolde I hadde thy smok and every clooth!"
  "Now, brother," quod the devel, "be nat wrooth;
Thy body and this panne been myne by right.
Thou shalt with me to helle yet to-nyght,   1636
Where thou shalt knowen of oure privetee
Moore than a maister of dyvynytee."
And with that word this foule feend hym hente;   _seized_
Body and soule he with the devel wente   1640
Where as that somonours han hir heritage.
And God, that maked after his ymage
Mankynde, save and gyde us, alle and some,
And leve thise somonours goode men bicome!

Lordynges, I koude han toold yow, quod this Frere,   1645
Hadde I had leyser for this Somnour heere,
After the text of Crist, Poul, and John,
And of oure othere doctours many oon,
Swiche peynes that youre hertes myghte agryse,
Al be it so no tonge may it devyse,   1650
Thogh that I myghte a thousand wynter telle
The peynes of thilke cursed hous of helle.
But for to kepe us fro that cursed place,
Waketh, and preyeth Jhesu for his grace
So kepe us fro the temptour Sathanas.   1655
Herketh this word! beth war, as in this cas:
"The leoun sit in his awayt alway
To sle the innocent, if that he may."
Disposeth ay youre hertes to withstonde
The feend, that yow wolde make thral and bonde.   1660
He may nat tempte yow over youre myght,
For Crist wol be youre champion and knyght.
And prayeth that thise somonours hem repente
Of hir mysdedes, er that the feend hem hente!

Heere endeth the Freres Tale.

The Summoner's Tale

THE SUMMONER'S PROLOGUE

The Prologe of the Somonours Tale.

This Somonour in his styropes hye stood;
Upon this Frere his herte was so wood   1666
That lyk an aspen leef he quook for ire.   _trembled_
  "Lordynges," quod he, "but o thyng I desire;
I yow biseke that, of youre curteisye,

Syn ye han herd this false Frere lye,   1670
As suffreth me I may my tale telle.
This Frere bosteth that he knoweth helle,
And God it woot, that it is litel wonder;   _God Knows_ _little_
Freres and feendes been but lyte asonder.

1629. **but**, unless. 1630. **stot**, steer, obviously used contemptuously. 1633. **smok**, undershirt. **every clooth**, every bit of clothing. 1635. **by right**, because of the old woman's curse. 1637. **privetee**, private affairs. 1639. **hente**, seized. 1641. **heritage**, inheritance, what is allotted to them in the next world. 1644. **leve . . . bicome**, grant that these summoners may become good men. 1646. **leyser for**, permission of. 1647. **text**, the teaching. 1649. **agryse**, cause to shudder. 1650. **Al be it so**, even though. 1654. **Waketh**, watch. 1657. **in his awayt**, in wait, *Psalms*, 10:9. 1661. **over youre myght**, beyond your strength. 1664. **er . . . hente**, before the devil catches them. 1667. **quook**, trembled. 1673. **God it woot**, God knows. 1674. **lyte**, little.

For, pardee, ye han ofte tyme herd telle   1675
How that a frere ravysshed was to helle
In spirit ones by a visioun;
And as an angel ladde hym up and doun,
To shewen hym the peynes that ther were,
In al the place saugh he nat a frere;   1680
Of oother folk he saugh ynowe in wo.
Unto this angel spak the frere tho:
   'Now, sire,' quod he, 'han freres swich a grace
That noon of hem shal come to this place?'
   'Yis,' quod this angel, 'many a millioun!'
And unto Sathanas he ladde hym doun.   1686
'And now hath Sathanas,' seith he, 'a tayl
Brodder than of a carryk is the sayl.
Hold up thy tayl, thou Sathanas!' quod he;
'Shewe forth thyn ers, and lat the frere se   1690
Where is the nest of freres in this place!'

And er that half a furlong wey of space,
Right so as bees out swarmen from an hyve,
Out of the develes ers ther gonne dryve
Twenty thousand freres on a route,   1695
And thurghout helle swarmeden al aboute,
And comen agayn as faste as they may gon,
And in his ers they crepten everychon.
He clapte his tayl agayn and lay ful stille.
This frere, whan he looked hadde his fille   1700
Upon the tormentz of this sory place,
His spirit God restored, of his grace,
Unto his body agayn, and he awook.
But natheles, for fere yet he quook,
So was the develes ers ay in his mynde,   1705
That is his heritage of verray kynde.
God save yow alle, save this cursed Frere!
My prologe wol I ende in this manere.''

THE SUMMONER'S TALE

Heere bigynneth the Somonour his Tale.

Lordynges, ther is in Yorkshire, as I gesse,
A mersshy contree called Holdernesse,   1710
In which ther wente a lymytour aboute,
To preche, and eek to begge, it is no doute.
And so bifel that on a day this frere
Hadde preched at a chirche in his manere,
And specially, aboven every thyng,   1715
Excited he the peple in his prechyng
To trentals, and to yeve, for Goddes sake,
Wherwith men myghte hooly houses make,

Ther as divine servyce is honoured,
Nat ther as it is wasted and devoured,   1720
Ne ther it nedeth nat for to be yive,
As to possessioners, that mowen lyve,
Thanked be God, in wele and habundaunce.
"Trentals," seyde he, "deliveren fro penaunce
Hir freendes soules, as wel olde as yonge,—
Ye, whan that they been hastily ysonge,   1726
Nat for to holde a preest joly and gay;
He syngeth nat but o masse in a day.

1676. **ravysshed,** carried off. 1677. **by,** in. **visioun,** dream. 1678. **ladde,** led. 1688. **carryk,** carrack, a large sailing vessel.
1690. **ers,** ass. 1692. **half a furlong wey,** the time necessary to walk half a furlong, about 100 yards. 1694. **dryve,** rush.
1695. **on a route,** in a crowd. 1704. **quook,** quaked. 1706. **of verray kynde,** by nature.
   The Summoner's Tale. It is not surprising that so obscene a story as that told in *The Summoner's Tale* should not often
have been committed to writing. The nearest analogue which has been found is an Old French fabliau, *Li Dis de le Vescie
à Prestre* (The Tale of the Priest's Bladder), which will be found in *SA*. It is more likely to have been told orally, and Chaucer's
source was probably some version which he had heard. There is nothing to prevent us from believing that it was written
at the same time as *The Friar's Tale* and when the group introduced by *The Wife of Bath's Tale* was being composed.
   1710. **mersshy,** marshy. **contree,** district. **Holdernesse,** in southeast Yorkshire. 1711. **lymytour.** See note to A 209.
1716. **Excited,** exhorted. 1717. **trentals,** (the purchase of) thirty masses for the souls of the dead. 1719. **Ther as,** where.
1722. **possessioners,** the beneficed clergy. 1726. **hastily,** without delay. The Summoner makes the Friar suggest that it is
better to say all thirty masses as promptly as possible rather than to spread them over thirty days. 1727. **holde,** restrain.

Deliverteth out," quod he, "anon the soules!
Ful hard it is with flesshhook or with oules   1730
To been yclawed, or to brenne or bake.
Now spede yow hastily, for Cristes sake!"
And whan this frere had seyd al his entente,
With *qui cum patre* forth his wey he wente.
    Whan folk in chirche had yeve him what
        hem leste,   1735
He wente his wey, no lenger wholde he reste.
With scrippe and tipped staf, ytukked hye,
In every hous he gan to poure and prye,
And beggeth mele and chese, or elles corn.
His felawe hadde a staf tipped with horn,   1740
A peyre of tables al of yvory,
And a poyntel polysshed fetisly,
And wroot the names alwey, as he stood,
Of alle folk that yaf hym any good,
Ascaunces that he wolde for hem preye.   1745
"Yif us a busshel whete, malt, or reye,
A Goddes kechyl, or a trip of chese,
Or elles what yow lyst, we may nat cheese;
A Goddes halfpeny, or a masse peny,
Or yif us of youre brawn, if ye have eny;   1750
A dagon of youre blanket, leeve dame,
Oure suster deere,—lo! heere I write youre
    name,—
Bacon or boef, or swich thyng as ye fynde."
    A sturdy harlot wente ay hem bihynde,
That was hir hostes man, and bar a sak,   1755
And what men yaf hem, leyde it on his bak.
And whan that he was out at dore, anon
He planed awey the names everichon
That he biforn had writen in his tables;

He served hem with nyfles and with fables. 1760
    "Nay, ther thou lixt, thou Somonour!" quod
        the Frere.
    "Pees," quod oure Hoost, "for Cristes
        mooder deere!
Tel forth thy tale, and spare it nat at al."
    "So thryve I," quod this Somonour, "so I
        shal!"
    So longe he wente, hous by hous, til he   1765
Cam til an hous ther he was wont to be
Refresshed moore than in an hundred placis.
Syk lay the goode man whos that the place is;
Bedrede upon a couche lowe he lay.
"*Deus hic!*" quod he, "o Thomas, freend, good
        day!"   1770
Seyde this frere, curteisly and softe.
"Thomas," quod he, "God yelde yow! ful ofte
Have I upon this bench faren ful weel;
Heere have I eten many a myrie meel."
And fro the bench he droof awey the cat,   1775
And leyde adoun his potente and his hat,
And eek his scrippe, and sette hym softe adoun.
His felawe was go walked into toun
Forth with his knave, into that hostelrye
Where as he shoop hym thilke nyght to lye. 1780
    "O deere maister," quod this sike man,
"How han ye fare sith that March bigan?
I saugh yow noght this fourtenyght or moore."
"God woot," quod he, "laboured I have ful
        soore,
And specially, for thy savacioun   1785
Have I seyd many a precious orisoun,
And for oure othere freendes, God hem blesse!

1730. oules, hooks. **1734. *qui cum patre*,** a formula referring to Christ's being with the Father in heaven. **1735. what hem leste,** what it pleased them to give him. **1737. scrippe,** wallet. **tipped staf,** a staff tipped with metal and carried as a symbol of his office. Cf. mod. *tipstaff.* **ytukked hye,** his robe tied with his ceinture of rope. **1740. His felawe.** The friars often went about in pairs. **1741. A peyre of tables.** Two folding tablets held together by strings or wires passing through holes at the side. The inner surfaces were sunk below the level of the rim and coated with wax. See E. M. Thompson, *An Introduction to Greek and Latin Palaeography* (Oxford, 1912), pp. 14–20. **1742. poyntel,** stylus, with which to write on the wax. **fetisly,** carefully. **1744. good,** goods. **1745. Ascaunces,** as if. **1747. A Goddes kechyl,** a little cake given in charity. **trip,** morsel. **1748. cheese,** choose. **1749. masse peny,** penny for saying mass. **1750. brawn,** flesh of the boar (or of swine). **1751. dagon,** piece. The *Prompt. Parv.* lists *Dagge of clothe.* **blanket,** undyed woolen cloth, blanket. The suggestion of J. G. Southworth (*Explicator,* XI, No. 29) that the word be taken in the sense of "a less expensive cut of meat" would be attractive but for the fact that the word is not recorded in this sense in either OF. or ME. **leeve dame,** dear lady. **1754. harlot,** fellow, rogue. **1755. hostes man.** The meaning appears to be "servant." Skeat explains it as "servant to the guests at the convent," but this appears to be a guess. **1758. planed,** smoothed. **1760. nyfles,** trifles, fictitious tales. **1766. ther,** where. **1769. Bedrede,** bedridden. **1770. *Deus hic,*** God be here. **1772. yelde,** reward. **1776. potente,** staff. **1778. was go walked,** had gone walking. **1780. shoop hym,** intended.

I have to day been at youre chirche at messe,
And seyd a sermon after my symple wit,
Nat al after the text of hooly writ; 1790
For it is hard to yow, as I suppose,
And therfore wol I teche yow al the glose.
Glosynge is a glorious thyng, certeyn,
For lettre sleeth, so as we clerkes seyn.
There have I taught hem to be charitable, 1795
And spende hir good ther it is resonable;
And there I saugh oure dame,—a! where is she?"
"Yond in the yerd I trowe that she be,"
Seyde this man, "and she wol come anon."
"Ey, maister, welcome be ye, by Seint
John!" 1800
Seyde this wyf, "how fare ye, hertely?"
The frere ariseth up ful curteisly,
And hire embraceth in his armes narwe,
And kiste hire sweete, and chirketh as a sparwe
With his lyppes: "Dame," quod he, "right
weel, 1805
As he that is youre servant every deel,
Thanked be God, that yow yaf soule and lyf!
Yet saugh I nat this day so fair a wyf
In al the chirche, God so save me!"
"Ye, God amende defautes, sire," quod she.
"Algates, welcome be ye, by my fey!" 1811
"Graunt mercy, dame, this have I founde alwey.
But of youre grete goodnesse, by youre leve,
I wolde prey yow that ye nat yow greve,
I wole with Thomas speke a litel throwe. 1815
Thise curatz been ful necligent and slowe
To grope tendrely a conscience
In shrift; in prechyng is my diligence,
And studie in Petres wordes and in Poules.
I walke, and fisshe Cristen mennes soules, 1820

To yelden Jhesu Crist his propre rente;
To sprede his word is set al myn entente."
"Now, by your leve, o deere sire," quod she,
"Chideth him weel, for seinte Trinitee!
He is as angry as a pissemyre, 1825
Though that he have al that he kan desire,
Though I hym wrye a-nyght and make hym
warm,
And over hym leye my leg outher myn arm,
He groneth lyk oure boor, lith in oure sty.
Oother desport right noon of hym have I; 1830
I may nat plese hym in no maner cas."
"O Thomas, je vous dy, Thomas! Thomas!
This maketh the feend; this moste ben amended.
Ire is a thyng that hye God defended,
And therof wol I speke a word or two." 1835
"Now, maister," quod the wyf, "er that I go,
What wol ye dyne? I wol go theraboute."
"Now, dame," quod he, "now je vous dy sanz
doute,
Have I nat of a capon but the lyvere,
And of youre softe breed nat but a shyvere, 1840
And after that a rosted pigges heed—
But that I nolde no beest for me were deed—
Thanne hadde I with yow hoomly suffisaunce.
I am a man of litel sustenaunce;
My spirit hath his fostryng in the Bible. 1845
The body is ay so redy and penyble
To wake, that my stomak is destroyed.
I prey yow, dame, ye be nat anoyed,
Though I so freendly yow my conseil shewe.
By God! I wolde nat telle it but a fewe." 1850
"Now, sire," quod she, "but o word er I go.
My child is deed withinne thise wykes two,
Soone after that ye wente out of this toun."

1792. glose, interpretation. 1793. glosynge, interpretation, but possibly with the additional meaning "specious talk." 1794. For lettre sleeth. Cf. *2 Corinthians*, 3:6: for the letter killeth, but the spirit giveth life. 1804. sweete, sweetly. Kissing was a normal form of greeting. chirketh, chirps. 1810. defautes, faults, defects. 1811. Algates, at any rate. fey, faith. 1812. Graunt mercy, many thanks. 1815. throwe, while. 1817. grope, search. 1821. rente, due. 1825. pissemyre, ant. 1827. wrye, cover. 1828. outher, or. 1829. boor, lith, pig, that lies. 1831. in no maner cas, under any circumstances. 1832. *je vous dy,* I tell you. The French phrases that the Friar drops are intended either as a compliment to Thomas and his wife or are meant to impress them. 1833. This maketh the feend, this is the work of the devil. 1834. Ire, wrath, one of the seven deadly sins, usually third in the list. defended, forbade. 1837. What wol ye dyne? What will you have for dinner? 1838. *sanz doute,* without doubt. 1840. nat but, nothing but. shyvere, sliver. 1842. I nolde . . ., I would not have any animal killed for me. 1846. penyble, constant in endeavor. 1847. To wake, keeping vigils. stomak, appetite. 1852. is deed, died.

"His deeth saugh I by revelacioun,"
Seyde this frere, "at hoom in oure dortour.   1855
I dar wel seyn that, er that half an hour
After his deeth, I saugh hym born to blisse
In myn avisioun, so God me wisse!
So dide oure sexteyn and oure fermerer,
That han been trewe freres fifty yeer;   1860
They may now—God be thanked of his
    loone!—
Maken hir jubilee and walke allone.
And up I roos, and al oure covent eke,
With many a teere trillyng on my cheke,
Withouten noyse or claterynge of belles;   1865
Te Deum was oure song, and nothyng elles,
Save that to Crist I seyde an orisoun,
Thankynge hym of his revelacioun.
For, sire and dame, trusteth me right weel,
Oure orisons been moore effectueel,   1870
And moore we seen of Cristes secree thynges,
Than burel folk, although they weren kynges.
We lyve in poverte and in abstinence,
And burell folk in richesse and despence
Of mete and drynke, and in hir foul delit.   1875
We han this worldes lust al in despit.
Lazar and Dives lyveden diversly,
And diverse gerdon hadden they therby.
Whoso wol preye, he moot faste and be clene,
And fatte his soule, and make his body lene.   1880
We fare as seith th'apostle; clooth and foode
Suffisen us, though they be nat ful goode.
The clennesse and the fastynge of us freres
Maketh that Crist accepteth oure preyeres.
    Lo, Moyses fourty dayes and fourty nyght
Fasted, er that the heighe God of myght   1886
Spak with hym in the mountain of Synay.

With empty wombe, fastynge many a day,
Receyved he the lawe that was writen
With Goddes fynger; and Elye, wel ye witen,
In mount Oreb, er he hadde any speche   1891
With hye God, that is oure lyves leche,
He fasted longe, and was in contemplaunce.
    Aaron, that hadde the temple in governaunce,
And eek the othere preestes everichon,   1895
Into the temple whan they sholde gon
To preye for the peple, and do servyse,
They nolden drynken in no maner wyse
No drynke which that myghte hem dronke
    make,
But there in abstinence preye and wake,   1900
Lest that they deyden. Taak heede what I seye!
But they be sobre that for the peple preye,
War that I seye—namoore, for it suffiseth.
Oure Lord Jhesu, as hooly writ devyseth,
Yaf us ensample of fastynge and preyeres.   1905
Therfore we mendynantz, we sely freres,
Been wedded to poverte and continence,
To charite, humblesse, and abstinence,
To persecucioun for rightwisnesse,
To wepynge, misericorde, and clennesse.   1910
And therfore may ye se that oure preyeres—
I speke of us, we mendynantz, we freres—
Been to the hye God moore acceptable
Than youres, with youre feestes at the table.
Fro Paradys first, if I shal nat lye,   1915
Was man out chaced for his glotonye;
And chaast was man in Paradys, certeyn.
    But herkne now, Thomas, what I shal seyn.
I ne have no text of it, as I suppose,
But I shal fynde it in a maner glose,   1920
That specially oure sweete Lord Jhesus

1855. dortour, dormitory. **1856. er that . . .,** before half an hour (had passed). **1858. me wisse,** guide me. **1859. sexteyn,** sacristan. **fermerer,** officer in charge of the infirmary. **1861. loone,** gift, grace. **1862. and walke allone.** This seems to indicate that traveling alone (rather than in pairs or groups) was a privilege granted to one who celebrated his fiftieth anniversary as a friar. **1863. covent,** convent. **1864. trillyng,** flowing. Some MSS. (including Ellesmere) read *triklyng.* **1866. *Te Deum*,** *Te Deum laudamus* (we praise thee, O Lord), the opening words and familiar title of a hymn regularly sung at the close of Matins and occasionally at other times. **1872. burel folk,** secular people. *Burel* is a type of coarse woolen cloth. **1877. Lazar,** Lazarus. Cf. *Luke,* 16:19–31. **1878. gerdon,** reward. **1881. as seith th' apostle.** Cf. *1 Timothy,* 6:8. **1885. Lo, Moyses.** Cf. *Exodus,* 34:28. **1890. Elye,** Elijah. Cf. *1 Kings,* 19:8. **1891. Oreb,** Horeb. **1893. contemplaunce,** contemplation. **1894. Aaron.** Cf. *Leviticus,* 10:8–11. **1897. do servyse,** perform their rites. **1903. War,** beware. **that,** what. **1904. devyseth,** relates. **1905. Yaf,** gave. **1906. mendynantz,** mendicants. **sely,** simple. **1910. misericorde,** mercy. **clennesse,** purity. **1917. chaast,** chaste. **1919. text,** biblical passage. **1920. a maner glose,** a kind of commentary.

Spak this by freres, whan he seyde thus:
'Blessed be they that povere in spirit been.'
And so forth al the gospel may ye seen,
Wher it be likker oure professioun,   1925
Or hirs that swymmen in possessioun.
Fy on hire pompe and on hire glotonye!
And for hir lewednesse I hem diffye.
   Me thynketh they been lyk Jovinyan,
Fat as a whale, and walkynge as a swan,   1930
Al vinolent as botel in the spence.
Hir preyere is of ful greet reverence,
Whan they for soules seye the psalm of Davit;
Lo, 'buf!' they seye, '*cor meum eructavit*!'
Who folweth Cristes gospel and his foore,   1935
But we that humble been, and chaast, and poore,
Werkeris of Goddes word, nat auditours?
Therfore, right as an hauk up at a sours
Up springeth into th'eir, right so prayeres
Of charitable and chaste bisy freres   1940
Maken hir sours to Goddes eres two.
Thomas! Thomas! so moote I ryde or go,
And by that lord that clepid is Seint Yve,
Nere thou oure brother, sholdestou nat thryve.
In oure chapitre praye we day and nyght   1945
To Crist, that he thee sende heele and myght
Thy body for to weelden hastily."
   "God woot," quod he, "no thyng therof
     feele I!
As help me Crist, as I in fewe yeres,
Have spended upon diverse manere freres   1950
Ful many a pound; yet fare I never the bet.

Certeyn, my good have I almoost biset.
Farwel, my gold, for it is al ago!"
   The frere answerde, "O Thomas, dostow so?
What nedeth yow diverse freres seche?   1955
What nedeth hym that hath a parfit leche
To sechen othere leches in the toun?
Youre inconstance is youre confusioun.
Holde ye thanne me, or elles oure covent,
To praye for yow been insufficient?   1960
Thomas, that jape nys nat worth a myte.
Youre maladye is for we han to lyte.
A! yif that covent half a quarter otes!
A! yif that covent foure and twenty grotes!
A! yif that frere a peny, and lat hym go!   1965
Nay, nay, Thomas, it may no thyng be so!
What is a ferthyng worth parted in twelve?
Lo, ech thyng that is oned in himselve
Is moore strong than whan it is toscatered.
Thomas, of me thou shalt nat been yflatered;
Thou woldest han oure labour al for noght.   1971
The hye God, that al this world hath wroght,
Seith that the werkman worthy is his hyre.
Thomas, noght of youre tresor I desire
As for myself, but that al oure covent   1975
To preye for yow is ay so diligent,
And for to buylden Cristes owene chirche.
Thomas, if ye wol lernen for to wirche,
Of buyldynge up of chirches may ye fynde,
If it be good, in Thomas lyf of Inde.   1980
Ye lye heere ful of anger and of ire,
With which the devel set youre herte afyre,

1922. by freres, concerning friars. **1923. povere,** poor. Cf. *Matthew*, 5:3. **1925. Wher it be likker,** whether it be more like. **professioun,** vow, what we profess. **1926. hirs,** theirs, referring to the beneficed clergy. See l. 1722. **1928. lewednesse,** unintelligent attitude (in resenting the intrusion of friars in their parishes). **1929. Jovinyan.** Jerome, in the treatise which Chaucer used so frequently in *The Wife of Bath's Prologue*, speaks of Jovinian as fat and walking like a bridegroom (Lib. I, cap. 40). *Swan* is better for the rime than for the comparison. **1931. vinolent . . .,** as full of wine as a bottle in the buttery. **1934. buf,** an interjection representing the sound of belching. *cor meum eructavit,* the opening words of Psalm 45, "My heart has uttered (a good word)." But the Summoner plays sarcastically on the literal meaning of *eructare,* to belch. **1935. foore,** track, trace **1937. auditours,** hearers. Cf. *James*, 1:22. **1938. at a sours,** with a swoop. **1942. ryde or go,** ride or walk, a common phrase. **1943. Seint Yve.** See note to B 1417, with which the present line is identical. **1944. Nere thou oure brother,** if you were not our brother. Thomas had apparently received a "letter of fraternity" which enrolled him as a confrere of the Friar's house. See A. G. Little, *The Grey Friars in Oxford,* p. 90, and cf. l. 2128 below. **1946. heele and myght,** health and strength. **1947. weelden hastily,** quickly have the use of. **1952. good,** property. **biset,** used up. **1956. leche,** physician. **1958. confusioun,** undoing. **1961. jape,** foolish notion. **myte,** small copper coin, farthing. **1962. for,** because. **1963. A! yif that covent . . .,** Oh, give that convent. The friar is mimicking statements such as Thomas might have made. **1968. oned,** united. **1969. toscatered,** scattered about. **1978. to wirche,** to do something useful. **1980. in Thomas lyf of Inde,** in the life of St. Thomas of India. Most versions of the legend of St. Thomas follow the account in the *Legenda Aurea,* which does not mention his building churches, but the *South English Legendary* adds "Churchen he rerde meny on" (ed. C. D' Evelyn and A. J. Mill in the EETS, 236), l. 175. **1982. set,** sets.

And chiden heere the sely innocent,
Youre wyf, that is so meke and pacient.   1984
And therfore, Thomas, trowe me if thee leste,
Ne stryve nat with thy wyf, as for thy beste;
And ber this word awey now, by thy feith,
Touchynge swich thyng, lo, what the wise seith:
'Withinne thyn hous ne be thou no leoun;
To thy subgitz do noon oppressioun,   1990
Ne make thyne aqueyntance nat for to flee.'
And, Thomas, yet eftsoones I charge thee,
Be war from hire that in thy bosom slepeth;
War fro the serpent that so slily crepeth
Under the gras, and styngeth subtilly.   1995
Be war, my sone, and herkne paciently,
That twenty thousand men han lost hir lyves
For stryvyng with hir lemmans and hir wyves.
Now sith ye han so hooly meke a wyf,
What nedeth yow, Thomas, to maken stryf?
Ther nys, ywys, no serpent so cruel,   2001
Whan man tret on his tayl, ne half so fel,
As womman is, whan she hath caught an ire;
Vengeance is thanne al that they desire.
Ire is a synne, oon of the grete of sevene,   2005
Abhomynable unto the God of hevene;
And to hymself it is destruccioun.
This every lewed viker or persoun
Kan seye, how ire engendreth homycide.
Ire is, in sooth, executour of pryde.   2010
I koude of ire seye so muche sorwe,
My tale sholde laste til to-morwe.
And therfore preye I God, bothe day and nyght,
An irous man, God sende hym litel myght!
It is greet harm and certes greet pitee   2015

To sette an irous man in heigh degree.
    Whilom ther was an irous potestat,
As seith Senek, that, durynge his estaat,
Upon a day out ryden knyghtes two,
And as Fortune wolde that it were so,   2020
That oon of hem cam hoom, that oother noght.
Anon the knyght bifore the juge is broght,
That seyde thus, 'Thou hast thy felawe slayn,
For which I deme thee to the deeth, certayn.'
And to another knyght comanded he,   2025
'Go lede hym to the deeth, I charge thee.'
And happed, as they wente by the weye
Toward the place ther he sholde deye,
The knyght cam which men wenden had be
    deed.
Thanne thoughte they it were the beste reed   2030
To lede hem bothe to the juge agayn.
They seiden, 'Lord, the knyght ne hath nat slayn
His felawe; heere he standeth hool alyve.'
'Ye shul be deed,' quod he, 'so moot I thryve!
That is to seyn, bothe oon, and two, and thre!'
And to the firste knyght right thus spak he,   2036
'I dampned thee; thou most algate be deed.
And thou also most nedes lese thyn heed,
For thou art cause why thy felawe deyth.'   2039
And to the thridde knyght right thus he seith,
'Thou hast nat doon that I comanded thee.'
And thus he dide doon sleen hem alle thre.
    Irous Cambises was eek dronkelewe,
And ay delited hym to been a shrewe.
And so bifel, a lord of his meynee,   2045
That loved vertuous moralitee,
Seyde on a day bitwix hem two right thus:

1986. as for thy beste, for your own good. **1988. the wise,** i.e, Jesus, son of Sirach, author of the book of *Ecclesiasticus.*
1989. ne be thou no leoun . . . *Ecclesiasticus,* 4:35 (Douai vers.): Be not as a lion in thy house, terrifying them of thy
household and oppressing them that are under thee. **1992. eftsoones,** again. **1993. Be war from hire . . .,** beware of her
. . . If this admonition seems strange after the friar has just praised the wife's meekness and patience, it must be remembered that the theme of the friar's discourse is Ire (Wrath) and he argues that in addition to the fact that Thomas has no
reason to be angry with his wife, as she says he is (ll. 1825 ff.), he should beware of arousing a woman's resentment and
possible revenge. After this he proceeds to a more general treatment of the sin of Wrath. Lines 1993–2004 contain
reminiscences of the long discourse of Genius, against trusting secrets to one's wife. in *RR,* 16323 ff. **2002. tret,** treadeth.
fel, fierce, ruthless. **2005. oon of the grete . . .** One of the main sins among the seven deadly sins (Pride, Envy, Wrath,
Sloth, Avarice, Gluttony, Lechery). **2007. to hymself,** to a man himself. **2008. lewed,** ignorant, common. **2017.
potestat,** ruler, magistrate. **2018. Senek.** One of the so-called *Dialogues* of Seneca is called *De Ira,* where all three anecdotes
which follow are found. The pertinent passages are in *SA.* **his estaat,** term of office. **2019. ryden,** rode. **2024. deme,** condemn. **2028. ther,** where. **2029. wenden,** thought, supposed. **2038. lese,** lose. **2043. dronkelewe,** given to drunkenness.
2044. shrewe, rascal. **2045. meynee,** household, following.

'A Lord is lost, if he be vicius;
And dronkenesse is eek a foul record
Of any man, and namely in a lord   2050
Ther is ful many an eye and many an ere
Awaityng on a lord, and he noot where.
For Goddes love, drynk moore attemprely!
Wyn maketh man to lesen wrecchedly
His mynde and eek his lymes everichon.'   2055
    'The revers shaltou se,' quod he, 'anon,
And preve it by thyn owene experience,
That wyn ne dooth to folk no swich offence.
Ther is no wyn bireveth me my myght
Of hand ne foot, ne of myne eyen sight.'   2060
And for despit he drank ful muchel moore,
An hondred part, than he hadde don bifoore;
And right anon this irous, cursed wrecche
Leet this knyghtes sone bifore hym fecche,
Comandynge hym he sholde bifore hym stonde.
And sodeynly he took his bowe in honde,   2066
And up the streng he pulled to his ere,
And with an arwe he slow the child right there.
'Now wheither have I a siker hand or noon?'
Quod he; 'is al my myght and mynde agon?
Hath wyn byreved me myn eyen sight?'   2071
What sholde I telle th'answere of the knyght?
His sone was slayn, ther is namoore to seye.
Beth war, therfore, with lordes how ye pleye.
Syngeth *Placebo*, and 'I shal, if I kan,'   2075
But if it be unto a povre man.
To a povre man men sholde his vices telle,
But nat to a lord, thogh he sholde go to helle.
    Lo irous Cirus, thilke Percien,
How he destroyed the ryver of Gysen,   2080
For that an hors of his was dreynt therinne,
Whan that he wente Babiloigne to wynne.

He made that the ryver was so smal
That wommen myghte wade it over al.
Lo, what seyde he that so wel teche kan?   2085
'Ne be no felawe to an irous man,
Ne with no wood man walke by the weye,
Lest thee repente;' I wol no ferther seye.
    Now, Thomas, leeve brother, lef thyn ire;
Thou shalt me fynde as just as is a squyre.   2090
Hoold nat the develes knyf ay at thyn herte—
Thyn angre dooth thee al to soore smerte—
But shewe to me al thy confessioun."
    "Nay," quod the sike man, "by Seint Sy-
        moun!
I have be shryven this day at my curat.   2095
I have hym toold hoolly al myn estat;
Nedeth namoore to speken of it," seith he,
"But if me list, of myn humylitee."
    "Yif me thanne of thy gold, to make oure
        cloystre,"
Quod he, "for many a muscle and many an
        oystre,   2100
Whan othere men han ben ful wel at eyse,
Hath been oure foode, oure cloystre for to reyse.
And yet, God woot, unnethe the fundement
Parfourned is, ne of oure pavement
Nys nat a tyle yet withinne oure wones.   2105
By God! we owen fourty pound for stones.
    Now help, Thomas, for hym that harwed
        helle!
For elles moste we oure bookes selle.
And if yow lakke oure predicacioun,
Thanne goth the world al to destruccioun.   2110
For whoso wolde us fro this world bireve,
So God me save, Thomas, by youre leve,
He wolde bireve out of this world the sonne.

2048. **vicius,** given to vice. 2049. **foul record,** shameful reputation. 2050. **namely,** especially. 2052. **Awaityng,** watching, spying upon. **noot,** does not know. 2053. **attemprely,** moderately. 2054. **lesen,** lose. 2055. **lymes,** *i.e.* control of his limbs. 2056. **revers,** reverse. 2062. **An hondred part,** a hundred times (more). 2064. **Leet . . . fecche,** caused to be brought. 2068. **slow,** slew. **child,** young man. 2069. **wheither have I,** do I have. *Wheither* may introduce a direct question. **siker,** sure, steady. 2075. ***Placebo,*** I will please, the beginning of *Psalms,* 114:9 in the Vulgate, widely known because of its use as an antiphon in the Office of the Dead. 2076. **But if,** unless. 2079. **Cirus,** Cyrus. He is said to have destroyed a river by diverting it into many small channels. 2080. **Gysen,** a corruption of Gyndes (not due to Chaucer), a river which cannot be definitely identified. See F. P. Magoun, *Mediaeval Stud.,* xv. 119. 2081. **dreynt,** drowned. 2083. **made that . . . was,** caused to become. 2085. **he,** Solomon. 2086. **Ne be no felawe . . .** Cf. *Proverbs,* 22:24–5. 2087. **wood,** mad. 2090. **squyre,** carpenter's square. 2095. **at,** by, at the hands of. 2096. **estat,** condition. 2103. **unnethe the fundement,** scarcely the foundation. 2104. **Parfourned,** completed. 2105. **wones,** habitation. 2107. **harwed,** harrowed. 2109. **predicacioun,** preaching. 2111. **bireve,** remove.

For who kan teche and werchen as we konne?
And that is nat of litel tyme," quod he,   2115
"But syn Elye was, or Elise,
Han freres been, that fynde I of record,
In charitee, ythanked be oure Lord!
Now Thomas, help, for seinte charitee!"
And doun anon he sette hym on his knee.   2120
    This sike man wax wel ny wood for ire;
He wolde that the frere had been on fire,
With his false dissymulacioun.
"Swich thyng as is in my possessioun,"   2124
Quod he, "that may I yeven, and noon oother.
Ye sey me thus, how that I am youre brother?"
    "Ye, certes," quod the frere, "trusteth weel.
I took oure dame oure lettre with oure seel."
    "Now wel," quod he, "and somwhat shal I yive
Unto youre hooly covent whil I lyve;   2130
And in thyn hand thou shalt it have anon,
On this condicion, and oother noon,
That thou departe it so, my deere brother,
That every frere have also muche as oother.
This shaltou swere on thy professioun,   2135
Withouten fraude or cavillacioun."
    "I swere it," quod this frere, "by my feith!"
And therwithal his hand in his he leith,
"Lo, heer my feith; in me shal be no lak."
    "Now thanne, put in thyn hand doun by my bak,"   2140
Seyde this man, "and grope wel bihynde.
Bynethe my buttok ther shaltow fynde
A thyng that I have hyd in pryvetee."
    "A!" thoghte this frere, "that shal go with me!"
And doun his hand he launcheth to the clifte,
In hope for to fynde there a yifte.   2146

And whan this sike man felte this frere
Aboute his tuwel grope there and heere,
Amydde his hand he leet the frere a fart,
Ther nys no capul, drawynge in a cart,   2150
That myghte have lete a fart of swich a soun.
    The frere up stirte as dooth a wood leoun,—
"A! false cherl!" quod he, "for Goddes bones!
This hastow for despit doon for the nones.
Thou shalt abye this fart, if that I may!"   2155
    His meynee, whiche that herden this affray,
Cam lepynge in and chaced out the frere;
And forth he gooth, with a ful angry cheere,
And fette his felawe, ther as lay his stoor.
He looked as it were a wilde boor;   2160
He grynte with his teeth, so was he wrooth.
A sturdy paas doun to the court he gooth,
Wher as ther woned a man of greet honour,
To whom that he was alwey confessour.
This worthy man was lord of that village.   2165
This frere cam as he were in a rage,
Where as this lord sat etyng at his bord;
Unnethes myghte the frere speke a word,
Til atte laste he seyde, "God yow see!"   2169
    This lord gan looke, and seide, "Benedicitee!
What, frere John, what maner world is this?
I se wel that som thyng ther is amys;
Ye looken as the wode were ful of thevys.
Sit doun anon, and tel me what youre grief is,
And it shal been amended, if I may."   2175
    "I have," quod he, "had a despit this day,
God yelde yow, adoun in youre village,
That in this world is noon so povre a page
That he nolde have abhomynacioun
Of that I have receyved in youre toun.   2180
And yet ne greveth me nothyng so soore,
As that this olde cherl with lokkes hoore

2115. **is nat of litel tyme,** has not been for a short period of time. 2116. **syn Elye was, or Elise,** since the time of Elijah, or Elisha. The Carmelites claimed that their founder was Elijah, who vanquished the prophets of Baal on Mount Carmel, and his successor Elisha, who lived on the sacred mountain. It would thus appear that the friar was a Carmelite. 2122. **had been on fire,** *i.e.* like the sacrifice by which Elijah triumphed over the prophets of Baal. 2123. **false dissymulacioun,** hypocrisy, false pretences. 2128. **took,** carried. See note to l. 1944 above. 2133. **departe it,** divide it up. 2135. **professioun,** oath, the vow which he took on entering his order. 2136. **cavillacioun,** cavilling. 2144. **that shal go with me,** that is agreeable to me. 2145. **clifte,** cleft. 2148. **tuwel,** rectum. 2150. **capul,** horse. 2155. **abye,** pay for. 2156. **meynee,** household. 2159. **fette,** fetched. **ther as,** *i.e.* with whom. **stoor,** store (what he had collected). 2161. **grynte,** gnashed (see *NED s.v. grint*), but the reading in the MSS varies greatly: *grinth, gryndeth, grynted, grynt,* etc. 2162. **sturdy,** furious. **court,** manor-house; cf. Hampton *Court.* 2163. **woned,** lived. 2169. **see,** watch over (a common form of greeting). 2174. **grief,** grievance. 2176. **despit,** insult, indignity. 2177. **yelde,** reward.

Blasphemed hath oure hooly covent eke."
  "Now, maister," quod this lord, "I yow
      biseke,—"
  "No maister, sire," quod he, "but servitour,
Thogh I have had in scole that honour.   2186
God liketh nat that 'Raby' men us calle,
Neither in market ne in youre large halle."
  "No fors," quod he, "but tel me al youre
      grief."
  "Sire," quod this frere, "an odious meschief
This day bityd is to myn ordre and me,   2191
And so, *per consequens*, to ech degree
Of hooly chirche, God amende it soone!"
  "Sire," quod the lord, "ye woot what is to
      doone.
Distempre yow noght, ye be my confessour;
Ye been the salt of the erthe and the savour. 2196
For Goddes love, youre pacience ye holde!
Tel me youre grief"; and he anon hym tolde,
As ye han herd biforn, ye woot wel what.
  The lady of the hous ay stille sat   2200
Til she had herd what the frere sayde.
"Ey, Goddes mooder," quod she, "Blisful
      mayde!
Is ther oght elles? telle me feithfully."
  "Madame," quod he, "how thynke ye
      herby?"
  "How that me thynketh?" quod she, "so
      God me speede,   2205
I seye, a cherl hath doon a cherles dede.
What shold I seye? God lat hym nevere thee!
His sike heed is ful of vanytee;
I holde hym in a manere frenesye."
  "Madame," quod he, "by God, I shal nat lye,
But I on oother wyse may be wreke,   2211
I shal disclaundre hym over al ther I speke,
This false blasphemour, that charged me

To parte that wol nat departed be,
To every man yliche, with meschaunce!"   2215
  The lord sat stille as he were in a traunce,
And in his herte he rolled up and doun,
"How hadde this cherl ymaginacioun
To shewe swich a probleme to the frere?   2219
Nevere erst er now herde I of swich mateere.
I trowe the devel putte it in his mynde.
In ars-metrik shal ther no man fynde,
Biforn this day, of swich a questioun.
Who sholde make a demonstracioun
That every man sholde have yliche his part   2225
As of the soun or savour of a fart?
O nyce, proude cherl, I shrewe his face!
Lo, sires," quod the lord, "with harde grace!
Who evere herde of swich a thyng er now?
To every man ylike, tel me how?   2230
It is an inpossible, it may nat be.
Ey, nyce cherl, God lete him nevere thee!
The rumblynge of a fart, and every soun,
Nis but of eir reverberacioun,
And evere it wasteth litel and litel awey.   2235
Ther is no man kan deemen, by my fey,
If that it were departed equally.
What, lo, my cherl, lo, yet how shrewedly
Unto my confessour to-day he spak!
I holde hym certeyn a demonyak!   2240
Now ete youre mete, and lat the cherl go pleye;
Lat hym go honge hymself a devel weye!"

The wordes of the lordes squier and his kervere for departynge of the fart on twelve.

  Now stood the lordes squier at the bord,
That karf his mete, and herde word by word
Of alle thynges whiche I have yow sayd.   2245

2186. in scole, *i.e.* he had earned the title of Master in the schools. **2187. Raby,** Rabbi, an allusion to *Matthew,* 23:7, where Jesus says the scribes and the Pharisses love "greetings in the markets, and to be called of men, Rabbi, Rabbi." **2189. No fors,** no matter. **2190. meschief,** wrong. **2195. Distempre yow noght,** do not lose your temper. **2207. thee,** thrive. **2208. vanytee,** foolish ideas. **2209. in a manere frenesye,** in a kind of frenzy. **2211. But,** unless. **wreke,** revenged. **2212. disclaundre,** disgrace. **over al ther,** everywhere where. **2214. that,** that which **2215. yliche,** equally. **with meschaunce**! curse him! **2217. rolled up and doun,** turned over. **2219. shewe,** present. **2222. ars-metrik,** arithmetic, but the obscene pun is evident. **2227. nyce,** foolish. **2228. with harde grace!** May God show him disfavor; bad luck to him! **2231. an inpossible,** an impossibility. **2242. a devel weye,** and go to the devil (but like many oaths, this one is hardly translatable).

"My lord," quod he, "be ye nat yvele apayd,
I koude telle, for a gowne-clooth,
To yow, sire frere, so ye be nat wrooth,
How that this fart sholde evene ydeled be
Among youre covent, if it lyked me."   2250
  "Tel," quod the lord, "and thou shalt have
    anon
A gowne-clooth, by God and by Seint John!"
  "My lord," quod he, "whan that the weder
    is fair,
Withouten wynd or perturbynge of air,   2254
Lat brynge a cartwheel heere into this halle;
But look that it have his spokes alle,—
Twelve spokes hath a cartwheel comunly.
And bryng me thanne twelve freres, woot ye
  why?
For thrittene is a covent, as I gesse.   2259
Youre confessour heere, for his worthynesse,
Shal parfourne up the nombre of his covent.
Thanne shal they knele doun, by oon assent,
And to every spokes ende, in this manere,
Ful sadly leye his nose shal a frere.
Youre noble confessour—there God hym
  save!—   2265
Shal holde his nose upright under the nave.
Thanne shal this cherl, with bely stif and toght
As any tabour, hyder been ybroght;

And sette hym on the wheel right of this cart,
Upon the nave, and make hym lete a fart.   2270
And ye shul seen, up peril of my lyf,
By preeve which that is demonstratif,
That equally the soun of it wol wende,
And eke the stynk, unto the spokes ende,
Save that this worthy man, youre confessour,
By cause he is a man of greet honour,   2276
Shal have the first fruyt, as resoun is.
The noble usage of freres yet is this,
The worthy men of hem shul first be served;
And certeinly he hath it weel disserved.   2280
He hath to-day taught us so muche good
With prechyng in the pulpit ther he stood,
That I may vouchesauf, I sey for me,
He hadde the firste smel of fartes thre;
And so wolde al his covent hardily,   2285
He bereth hym so faire and hoolily."
  The lord, the lady, and ech man, save the
    frere,
Seyde that Jankyn spak, in this matere,
As wel as Euclide or Protholomee.
Touchynge the cherl, they seyde, subtiltee   2290
And heigh wit made hym speken as he spak;
He nys no fool, ne no demonyak.
And Jankyn hath ywonne a newe gowne.—
My tale is doon; we been almoost at towne.

Heere endeth the Somonours Tale.

2246. **yvele apayd,** displeased. 2247. **gowne-clooth,** cloth for a gown. 2249. **ydeled,** divided. 2259. **thrittene is a covent.** In theory, the ideal convent consisted of twelve monks or friars plus the abbot or superior, in imitation of the twelve apostles. 2261. **parfourne up,** complete. 2264. **sadly,** firmly. 2266. **nave,** hub. 2272. **demonstratif,** demonstrable. 2289. **Protholomee,** a common error for Ptolemy. 2294. **almoost at towne.** Cf. the Summoner's statement at D 847.

Group E (Fragment IV)

The Clerk's Tale

THE CLERK'S PROLOGUE

Heere folweth the Prologe of the Clerkes Tale of Oxenford.

"Sire Clerk of Oxenford," oure Hooste
    sayde,
"Ye ryde as coy and stille as dooth a mayde
Were newe spoused, sittynge at the bord;
This day ne herde I of youre tonge a word.
I trowe ye studie aboute som sophyme;   5
But Salomon seith 'every thyng hath tyme.'
    For Goddes sake, as beth of bettre cheere!
It is no tyme for to studien heere.
Telle us som myrie tale, by youre fey!
For what man that is entred in a pley,   10
He nedes moot unto the pley assente.
But precheth nat, as freres doon in Lente,
To make us for oure olde synnes wepe,
Ne that thy tale make us nat to slepe.
    Telle us som murie thyng of aventures.   15
Youre termes, youre colours, and youre figures,
Keepe hem in stoor til so be that ye endite
Heigh style, as whan that men to kynges write.
Speketh so pleyn at this tyme, we yow preye,
That we may understonde what ye seye."   20
    This worthy clerk benignely answerde:
"Hooste," quod he, "I am under youre yerde;

Ye han of us as now the governance,
And therfore wol I do yow obeisance,
As fer as resoun axeth, hardily.   25
I wol yow telle a tale which that I
Lerned at Padowe of a worthy clerk,
As preved by his wordes and his werk.
He is now deed and nayled in his cheste,
I prey to God so yeve his soule reste!   30
    Fraunceys Petrak, the lauriat poete,
Highte this clerk, whos rethorike sweete
Enlumyned al Ytaille of poetrie,
As Lynyan dide of philosophie,
Or lawe, or oother art particuler;   35
But deeth, that wol nat suffre us dwellen heer,
But as it were a twynklyng of an yë,
Hem bothe hath slayn, and alle shul we dye.
    But forth to tellen of this worthy man
That taughte me this tale, as I bigan,   40
I seye that first with heigh stile he enditeth,
Er he the body of his tale writeth,
A prohemye, in the which discryveth he
Pemond, and of Saluces the contree,
And speketh of Apennyn, the hilles hye,   45

1. Oxenford, Oxford. **2. coy,** quiet. **5. sophyme,** sophism, specious argument. **6. Salomon seith.** *Eccles.,* 3:1: To every thing there is a season. **7. as beth,** be. **11. moot unto the pley assente,** must abide by the rules of the game. The proverb is No. 1914 in Morawski, and other examples in French and German are cited in Singer, II. 61. **16. termes,** technical language, such as was associated with the schools. **colours . . . figures.** These are terms employed in medieval rhetoric and not always sharply distinguished, but in general *colours* refers to figures of speech (metaphor, simile, etc.), *figures* to patterns of thought (the *figurae sententiarum* of Geoffrey de Vinsauf, such as antithesis, personification, and the like), or the easier rhetorical devices (*figurae verborum,* such as repetition, balanced clauses, rhetorical questions, and many others). See also the notes to *HF* 858–9. **22. yerde,** stick, rule. **24. obeisance,** obedience. **27. Padowe,** Padua. **28. preved,** proved. **31. Petrak,** Petrarch (1304–1374). The Clerk's statement has caused some to believe that Chaucer himself had met Petrarch. See the life of Chaucer, above, p. xiv. **32. Highte,** was named. **33. of poetrie,** in respect to poetry. **34. Lynyan,** Giovanni di Lignano (d. 1383), professor of canon law at Bologna. See A. S. Cook, *Romanic Rev.,* VIII. 353–82. **43. prohemye,** intro- duction. The reference is to the first part of Petrarch's narrative, which serves to introduce the story proper. **44. Pemond,** Piedmont. **Saluces,** Saluzzo. **45. Apennyn,** the Apennines.

That been the boundes of West Lumbardye,
And of Mount Vesulus in special,
Where as the Poo out of a welle smal
Taketh his firste spryngyng and his sours,
That estward ay encresseth in his cours   50
To Emele-ward, to Ferrare, and Venyse;

The which a long thyng were to devyse.
And trewely, as to my juggement,
Me thynketh it a thyng impertinent,
Save that he wole conveyen his mateere;   55
But this his tale, which that ye may heere."

THE CLERK'S TALE

Heere bigynneth the Tale of the Clerk of Oxenford.

Ther is right at the west syde of Ytaille,
Doun at the roote of Vesulus the colde,
A lusty playne, habundant of vitaille,
Where many a tour and toun thou mayst bi-
    holde,   60
That founded were in tyme of fadres olde,
And many another delitable sighte,
And Saluces this noble contree highte.

A markys whilom lord was of that lond,
As were his worthy eldres hym bifore;   65
And obeisant, ay redy to his hond,
Were alle his liges, bothe lasse and moore.
Thus in delit he lyveth, and hath doon yoore,
Biloved and drad, thurgh favour of Fortune,
Bothe of his lordes and of his commune.   70

Therwith he was, to speke as of lynage,
The gentilleste yborn of Lumbardye,
A fair persone, and strong, and yong of age,
And ful of honour and of curteisye;
Discreet ynogh his contree for to gye,   75
Save in somme thynges that he was to blame;
And Walter was this yonge lordes name.

I blame hym thus, that he considered noght
In tyme comynge what myghte hym bityde,
But on his lust present was al his thoght,   80
As for to hauke and hunte on every syde.
Wel ny alle othere cures leet he slyde,
And eek he nolde—and that was worst of
    alle—
Wedde no wyf, for noght that may bifalle.

47. Mount Vesulus, Monte Viso. **48. welle,** spring. **51. Emele-ward** . . . Emilia . . . Ferrara . . . Venice. **52. devyse,** describe. **55. conveyen,** set on its way.
   The Clerk's Tale. The story of Patient Griselda was told by Boccaccio as the closing story of the *Decameron*, but Boccaccio's Italian was turned into Latin by Petrarch and it is from Petrarch that the Clerk tells us he obtained it. Petrarch's narrative was twice translated into French, once by Philippe de Mézières and once by a translator whose name we do not know. It has been shown by J. Burke Severs, in *The Literary Relationships of Chaucer's Clerkes Tale* (New Haven, 1942), that Chaucer used both the Latin original and the anonymous French version. The two texts can be read in *SA*, where they are edited with an introduction by Professor Severs.
   The incredible resignation with which Griselde submits to the cruelties and the indignities which her husband inflicts upon her is more understandable in the light of medieval attitudes, but even in the fourteenth century, as the Clerk admits, Griseldes were rare. The happy outcome of the story—Griselde's sudden restoration to prosperity—contrasts with the medieval notion of tragedy, exemplified in the various parts of *The Monk's Tale*, and it doubtless appealed to the medieval listener as an antidote to the malign operations of Fortune, of which there seemed to be so many more examples. Even to those who acknowledged its incredibility it had a strong appeal as a symbol of womanly nobility and Christian fortitude. Chaucer has enhanced this appeal by many touches which he has added to the characterization of Griselde and which, even if we deplore her lack of spirit, arouse our pity.
   It is probable that the story was originally independent of *The Canterbury Tales*. It is in the same stanza form as the *Troilus*, although the Clerk's introduction is in couplets. The reference to Lignano (l. 38) as dead places it after 1383.
58. roote, foot. **Vesulus the colde.** Monte Viso, in the Italian Alps, has an elevation of over 12,000 ft. **59. lusty,** pleasant. **63. contree,** district. **64. markys,** marquis. **69. drad,** dreaded. **75. gye,** govern. **80. lust present,** immediate pleasure. **82. cures,** cares. responsibilities.

Oonly that point his peple bar so soore   85
That flokmeele on a day they to hym wente,
And oon of hem, that wisest was of loore—
Or elles that the lord best wolde assente
That he sholde telle hym what his peple mente,
Or elles koude he shewe wel swich mateere—
He to the markys seyde as ye shul heere: 91

"O noble markys, youre humanitee
Asseureth us and yeveth us hardinesse,
As ofte as tyme is of necessitee,
That we to yow mowe telle oure hevynesse.   95
Accepteth, lord, now of youre gentillesse,
That we with pitous herte unto yow pleyne,
And lat youre eres nat my voys desdeyne.

"Al have I noght to doone in this mateere
Moore than another man hath in this place,   100
Yet for as muche as ye, my lord so deere,
Han alwey shewed me favour and grace
I dar the bettre aske of yow a space
Of audience, to shewen oure requeste,
And ye, my lord, to doon right as yow leste.

"For certes, lord, so wel us liketh yow   106
And al youre werk, and evere han doon, that we
Ne koude nat us self devysen how
We myghte lyven in moore felicitee,
Save o thyng, lord, if it youre wille be,   110
That for to been a wedded man yow leste;
Thanne were youre peple in sovereyn hertes reste.

✳ "Boweth youre nekke under that blisful yok
Of soveraynetee, noght of servyse,   114
Which that men clepe spousaille or wedlok;
And thenketh, lord, among youre thoghtes wyse
How that oure dayes passe in sondry wyse;

For thogh we slepe, or wake, or rome, or ryde,
Ay fleeth the tyme; it nyl no man abyde.   119

"And thogh youre grene youthe floure as yit,
In crepeth age alwey, as stille as stoon,
And deeth manaceth every age, and smyt
In ech estaat, for ther escapeth noon;
And al so certein as we knowe echoon
That we shul deye, as uncerteyn we alle   125
Been of that day whan deeth shal on us falle.

"Accepteth thanne of us the trewe entente,
That nevere yet refuseden thyn heeste,
And we wol, lord, if that ye wole assente,
Chese yow a wyf, in short tyme atte leeste,   130
Born of the gentilleste and of the meeste
Of al this land, so that it oghte seme
Honour to God and yow, as we kan deeme.

"Delivere us out of al this bisy drede,
And taak a wyf, for hye Goddes sake!   135
For if it so bifelle, as God forbede,
That thurgh youre deeth youre lynage sholde slake,
And that a straunge successour sholde take
Youre heritage, O, wo were us alyve!
Wherfore we pray you hastily to wyve."   140

Hir meeke preyere and hir pitous cheere
Made the markys herte han pitee.
"Ye wol," quod he, "myn owene peple deere,
To that I nevere erst thoughte streyne me.
I me rejoysed of my liberte,   145
That seelde tyme is founde in mariage;
Ther I was free, I moot been in servage.

"But nathelees I se youre trewe entente,
And truste upon youre wit, and have doon ay;
Wherfore of my free wyl I wole assente   150

---

85. bar so soore, took so hard. **86. flokmeele,** in a flock. **92. humanitee,** benevolence. **93. yeveth us hardinesse,** makes us bold. **94. As ofte . . . necessitee,** as often as is necessary. **99. Al,** although. **103. a space Of audience,** a (period of) hearing. **105. as yow leste,** as you please. **106. us liketh,** it pleases us. **108. us self,** ourselves. **115. spousaille,** marriage. **122. manaceth,** menaces. **smyt,** smites. **130. Chese,** choose. **134. bisy drede,** anxiety. **137. slake,** come to an end. **144. streyne me,** to constrain myself. **147. Ther,** where. **149. wit,** judgment.

To wedde me, as soone as evere I may.
But ther as ye han profred me to-day
To chese me a wyf, I yow relesse
That choys, and prey yow of that profre cesse.

"For God it woot, that children ofte been 155
Unlyk hir worthy eldres hem bifore;
Bountee comth al of God, nat of the streen
Of which they been engendred and ybore.
I truste in Goddes bountee, and therfore
My mariage and myn estaat and reste 160
I hym bitake; he may doon as hym leste.

"Lat me allone in chesynge of my wyf,—
That charge upon my bak I wole endure.
But I yow preye, and charge upon youre lyf,
That what wyf that I take, ye me assure 165
To worshipe hire, whil that hir lyf may dure,
In word and werk, bothe heere and every-
    wheere,
As she an emperoures doghter weere.

"And forthermoore, this shal ye swere,
    that ye
Agayn my choys shul neither grucche ne
    stryve; 170
For sith I shal forgoon my libertee
At youre requeste, as evere moot I thryve,

Ther as myn herte is set, ther wol I wyve;
And but ye wole assente in swich manere, 174
I prey yow, speketh namoore of this matere."

With hertely wyl they sworen and assenten
To al this thyng, ther seyde no wight nay;
Bisekynge hym of grace, er that they wenten,
That he wolde graunten hem a certein day
Of his spousaille, as soone as evere he may; 180
For yet alwey the peple somwhat dredde,
Lest that the markys no wyf wolde wedde.

He graunted hem a day, swich as hym leste,
On which he wolde be wedded sikerly,
And seyde he dide al this at hir requeste. 185
And they, with humble entente, buxomly,
Knelynge upon hir knees ful reverently,
Hym thonken alle; and thus they han an ende
Of hire entente, and hoom agayn they wende.

And heerupon he to his officeres 190
Comaundeth for the feste to purveye,
And to his privee knyghtes and squieres
Swich charge yaf as hym liste on hem leye;
And they to his comandement obeye,
And ech of hem dooth al his diligence 195
To doon unto the feeste reverence.

Explicit prima pars.

Incipit secunda pars.

Noght fer fro thilke paleys honurable,
Wher as this markys shoop his mariage,
There stood a throop, of site delitable,
In which that povre folk of that village 200
Hadden hir beestes and hir herbergage,
And of hire labour tooke hir sustenance,
After that the erthe yaf hem habundance.

Amonges thise povre folk ther dwelte a man
Which that was holden povrest of hem alle;

But hye God somtyme senden kan 206
His grace into a litel oxes stalle;
Janicula men of that throop hym calle.
A doghter hadde he, fair ynogh to sighte,
And Grisildis this yonge mayden highte. 210

But for to speke of vertuous beautee,
Thanne was she oon the faireste under sonne;
For povreliche yfostred up was she,
No likerous lust was thurgh hire herte yronne.

---

157. Bountee, goodness. **streen,** lineage. **161. bitake,** commit. **163. charge,** burden. **168. As,** as if. **173. Ther as,** wherever. **176. hertely,** sincere. **178. of,** by his. **181. dredde,** dreaded. **184. sikerly,** assuredly. **186. buxomly,** obediently. **191. purveye,** provide, prepare. **192. privee,** personal, intimate. **196. reverence,** honor. **198. shoop,** planned to have. **199. throop,** village. **201. herbergage,** lodging, abode. **203. After that,** according as. **212. oon the faireste,** one of the fairest; see Language, § 50. **214. likerous lust,** desire for luxuries.

Wel ofter of the welle than of the tonne   215
She drank, and for she wolde vertu plese,
She knew wel labour, but noon ydel ese.

But thogh this mayde tendre were of age,
Yet in the brest of hire virginitee
Ther was enclosed rype and sad corage;   220
And in greet reverence and charitee
Hir olde povre fader fostred shee.
A fewe sheep, spynnynge, on feeld she kepte;
She wolde noght been ydel til she slepte.

And whan she homward cam, she wolde
     brynge   225
Wortes or othere herbes tymes ofte,
The whiche she shredde and seeth for hir lyv-
     ynge,
And made hir bed ful harde and nothyng softe;
And ay she kepte hir fadres lyf on-lofte
With everich obeisaunce and diligence   230
That child may doon to fadres reverence.

Upon Grisilde, this povre creature,
Ful ofte sithe this markys sette his yë
As he on huntyng rood paraventure;
And whan it fil that he myghte hire espye,   235
He noght with wantowne lookyng of folye
His eyen caste on hire, but in sad wyse
Upon hir chiere he wolde hym ofte avyse,

Commendynge in his herte hir womman-
     hede,
And eek hir vertu, passynge any wight   240
Of so yong age, as wel in chiere as dede.
For thogh the peple have no greet insight
In vertu, he considered ful right

Hir bountee, and disposed that he wolde   244
Wedde hire oonly, if evere he wedde sholde.

The day of weddyng cam, but no wight kan
Telle what womman that it sholde be;
For which merveille wondred many a man,
And seyden, whan they were in privetee,
"Wol nat oure lord yet leve his vanytee?   250
Wol he nat wedde? allas, allas, the while!
Why wole he thus hymself and us bigile?"

But nathelees this markys hath doon make
Of gemmes, set in gold and in asure,
Brooches and rynges, for Grisildis sake;   255
And of hir clothyng took he the mesure
By a mayde lyk to hire stature,
And eek of othere aornementes alle
That unto swich a weddyng sholde falle.

The time of undren of the same day   260
Approcheth, that this weddyng sholde be;
And al the paleys put was in array,
Bothe halle and chambres, ech in his degree;
Houses of office stuffed with plentee
Ther maystow seen, of deyntevous vitaille . 265
That may be founde as fer as last Ytaille.

This roial markys, richely arrayed,
Lordes and ladyes in his compaignye,
The whiche that to the feeste weren yprayed,
And of his retenue the bachelrye,   270
With many a soun of sondry melodye,
Unto the village of the which I tolde,
In this array the righte wey han holde.

Grisilde of this, God woot, ful innocent,
That for hire shapen was al this array,   275

---

215. welle, spring. **tonne,** wine cask. **220. rype and sad corage,** mature and sober spirit. **222. fostred,** took care of. **223. spynnynge,** while she was spinning. **226. Wortes,** herbs. **227. shredde,** cut up. **seeth,** boiled. **lyvynge,** sustenance. **229. on-lofte,** aloft; *i.e.* she kept him alive. **233. ofte sithe,** oftentimes. **234. paraventure,** perchance. **235. it fil,** it happened. **237. in sad wyse,** soberly. **238. hym . . . avyse,** reflect. **242. the peple . . . vertu,** the common people are not quick to recognize virtue. **244. bountee,** goodness. **disposed,** made up his mind. **250. vanytee,** foolish behavior. **253. hath doon make,** has caused to be made. **254. asure,** blue (enamel). **258. aornementes,** adornments. **259. sholde falle,** were appropriate. **260. undren,** undern (here about 9 A.M.). **264. Houses of office,** service buildings (kitchen, etc.), often separated from the manor house. **265. deyntevous vitaille,** choice or rare foodstuff. **266. as fer as last Ytaille,** as far as Italy reaches. **269. yprayed,** invited. **270. bachelrye,** company of young men or young knights. **273. In this array,** thus assembled. **275. shapen,** constituted. **array,** assembly.

To fecchen water at a welle is went,
And cometh hoom as soone as ever she may;
For wel she hadde herd seyd that thilke day
The markys sholde wedde, and if she myghte,
She wolde fayn han seyn som of that sighte.   280

She thoghte, "I wole with othere maydens
        stonde,
That been my felawes, in oure dore and se
The markysesse, and therfore wol I fonde
To doon at hoom, as soone as it may be,
The labour which that longeth unto me;   285
And thanne I may at leyser hire biholde,
If she this wey unto the castel holde."

And as she wolde over hir thresshfold gon,
The markys cam, and gan hire for to calle;
And she set doun hir water pot anon,   290
Biside the thresshfold, in an oxes stalle,
And doun upon hir knes she gan to falle,
And with sad contenance kneleth stille,
Til she had herd what was the lordes wille.

This thoghtful markys spak unto this mayde
Ful sobrely, and seyde in this manere: 296
"Where is youre fader, O Grisildis?" he sayde.
And she with reverence, in humble cheere,
Answerde, "Lord, he is al redy heere."
And in she gooth withouten lenger lette,   300
And to the markys she hir fader fette.

He by the hand thanne took this olde man,
And seyde thus, whan he hym hadde asyde:
"Janicula, I neither may ne kan
Lenger the plesance of myn herte hyde.   305
If that thou vouchesauf, what so bityde,
Thy doghter wol I take, er that I wende,
As for my wyf, unto hir lyves ende.

"Thou lovest me, I woot it wel certeyn,
And art my feithful lige man ybore;   310
And al that liketh me, I dar wel seyn
It liketh thee, and specially therfore
Tel me that poynt that I have seyd bifore,
If that thou wolt unto that purpos drawe,
To take me as for thy sone-in-lawe."   315

This sodeyn cas this man astonyed so
That reed he wax; abayst and al quakynge
He stood; unnethes seyde he wordes mo,
But oonly thus: "Lord," quod he, "my willynge
Is as ye wole, ne ayeyns youre likynge   320
I wol no thyng, ye be my lord so deere;
Right as yow lust, governeth this mateere."

"Yet wol I," quod this markys softely,
"That in thy chambre I and thou and she
Have a collacioun, and wostow why?   325
For I wol axe if it hire wille be
To be my wyf, and reule hire after me.
And al this shal be doon in thy presence;
I wol noght speke out of thyn audience."

And in the chambre, whil they were aboute
Hir tretys, which as ye shal after heere,   331
The peple cam unto the hous withoute,
And wondred hem in how honeste manere
And tentifly she kepte hir fader deere.
But outrely Grisildis wondre myghte,   335
For nevere erst ne saugh she swich a sighte.

No wonder is thogh that she were astoned
To seen so greet a gest come in that place;
She nevere was to swiche gestes woned,
For which she looked with ful pale face.   340
But shortly forth this matere for to chace,
Thise arn the wordes that the markys sayde
To this benigne, verray, feithful mayde.

---

283. **markysesse**, marchioness. **fonde**, strive. 293. **sad**, sober. 296. **sobrely**, quietly. 298. **cheere**, mood, manner. 300.
lette, delay. 301. **fette**, fetched. 303. **hadde**, had taken. 305. **plesance**, desire. 316. **cas**, situation, occurrence. **astonyed**,
astonished. 317. **abayst**. abashed. 318. **unnethes**, scarcely. 322. **yow lust**, it pleases you. 325. **collacioun**, conference.
327. **reule hire after me**, govern herself according to my will. 329. **audience**, hearing. 331. **tretys**, negotiation. 333.
wondred hem, marveled. **honeste**, virtuous. 334. **tentifly**, attentively. 335. **outrely**, truly, indeed. 336. **erst**, before.
338. **gest**, company. 339. **gestes**, companies, guests. **woned**, accustomed. 341. **forth . . . chace**, pursue.

"Grisilde," he seyde, "ye shal wel understonde
It liketh to youre fader and to me   345
That I yow wedde, and eek it may so stonde,
As I suppose, ye wol that it so be.
But thise demandes axe I first," quod he,
"That, sith it shal be doon in hastif wyse,
Wol ye assente, or elles yow avyse?   350

     "I seye this, be ye redy with good herte
To al my lust, and that I frely may,
As me best thynketh, do yow laughe or smerte,
And nevere ye to grucche it, nyght ne day?
And eek whan I sey 'ye,' ne sey nat 'nay,'   355
Neither by word ne frownyng contenance?
Swere this, and heere I swere oure alliance."

     Wondrynge upon this word, quakynge for
          drede,
She seyde, "Lord, undigne and unworthy
Am I to thilke honour that ye me beede,   360
But as ye wole yourself, right so wol I.
And heere I swere that nevere willyngly,
In werk ne thoght, I nyl yow disobeye,
For to be deed, though me were looth to deye."

     "This is ynogh, Grisilde myn," quod he.   365
And forth he gooth, with a ful sobre cheere,
Out at the dore, and after that cam she,
And to the peple he seyde in this manere:
"This is my wyf," quod he, "that standeth
          heere.
Honoureth hire and loveth hire, I preye,   370
Whoso me loveth; ther is namoore to seye."

     And for that no thyng of hir olde geere
She sholde brynge into his hous, he bad
That wommen sholde dispoillen hire right
          theere;

Of which thise ladyes were nat right glad   375
To handle hir clothes, wherinne she was clad.
But natheles, this mayde bright of hewe
Fro foot to heed they clothed han al newe.

     Hir heris han they kembd, that lay untressed
Ful rudely, and with hir fyngres smale   380
A corone on hire heed they han ydressed,
And sette hire ful of nowches grete and smale.
Of hire array what sholde I make a tale?
Unnethe the peple hir knew for hire fairnesse,
Whan she translated was in swich richesse.   385

     This markys hath hire spoused with a ryng
Broght for the same cause, and thanne hire
          sette
Upon an hors, snow-whit and wel amblyng,
And to his paleys, er he lenger lette,   389
With joyful peple that hire ladde and mette,
Conveyed hire, and thus the day they spende
In revel, til the sonne gan descende.

     And shortly forth this tale for to chace,
I seye that to this newe markysesse
God hath swich favour sent hire of his grace,
That it ne semed nat by liklynesse   396
That she was born and fed in rudenesse,
As in a cote or in an oxe-stalle,
But norissed in an emperoures halle.

     To every wight she woxen is so deere   400
And worshipful that folk ther she was bore,
And from hire birthe knew hire yeer by yeere,
Unnethe trowed they,—but dorste han swore—
That to Janicle, of which I spak bifore,
She doghter were, for, as by conjecture,   405
Hem thoughte she was another creature.

---

349. in hastif wyse, without delay. **352. lust,** desire. **353. As me best thynketh,** as seems best to me. **354. grucche it,** begrudge it, complain about it. **358. quakynge for drede,** trembling from fear. **359. undigne,** unworthy. **360. beede,** offer. **372. geere,** clothing. **374. dispoillen,** strip, undress. **379. untressed,** loose (not braided). **381. corone,** nuptial garland, The name of such a garland was *paste* (see *NED*, s.v. *paste*, sense 7), although the word is not recorded so early as Chaucer. In *Dives et Pauper* we are told, "Thre ornamentes longe principally to a wyfe: a rynge on her fynger, a broche on her breste, and a garlonde on her hede." (Quoted in Rock, *The Church of Our Fathers*, IV. 202). **ydressed,** set. **382. nowches,** brooches, ornaments. **384. Unnethe,** scarcely. **397. born and fed,** born and raised. **398. cote,** humble cottage. **400. woxen,** grown.

For though that evere vertuous was she,
She was encressed in swich excellence
Of thewes goode, yset in heigh bountee,
And so discreet and fair of eloquence, 410
So benigne and so digne of reverence,
And koude so the peples herte embrace,
That ech hire lovede that looked on hir face.

Noght oonly of Saluces in the toun
Publiced was the bountee of hir name, 415
But eek biside in many a regioun,
If oon seide wel, another seyde the same;
So spradde of hire heighe bountee the fame
That men and wommen, as wel yonge as olde,
Goon to Saluce, upon hire to biholde. 420

Thus Walter lowely—nay, but roially—
Wedded with fortunat honestetee,
In Goddes pees lyveth ful esily
At hoom, and outward grace ynogh had he;
And for he saugh that under low degree 425
Was ofte vertu hid, the peple hym heelde
A prudent man, and that is seyn ful seelde.

Nat oonly this Grisildis thurgh hir wit

Koude al the feet of wyfly hoomlinesse,
But eek, whan that the cas required it, 430
The commune profit koude she redresse.
Ther nas discord, rancour, ne hevynesse
In al that land, that she ne koude apese,
And wisely brynge hem alle in reste and ese.

Though that hire housbonde absent were,
anon 435
If gentil men or othere of hire contree
Were wrothe, she wolde bryngen hem aton;
So wise and rype wordes hadde she,
And juggementz of so greet equitee,
That she from hevene sent was, as men
wende, 440
Peple to save and every wrong t'amende.

Nat longe tyme after that this Grisild
Was wedded, she a doghter hath ybore.
Al had hire levere have born a knave child,
Glad was this markys and the folk therfore;
For though a mayde child coome al bifore, 446
She may unto a knave child atteyne
By liklihede, syn she nys nat bareyne.

Explicit secunda pars.

Incipit tercia pars.

Ther fil, as it bifalleth tymes mo,
Whan that this child had souked but a
throwe, 450
This markys in his herte longeth so
To tempte his wyf, hir sadnesse for to knowe,
That he ne myghte out of his herte throwe
This merveillous desir his wyf t'assaye;
Nedelees, God woot, he thoghte hire for
t'affraye. 455

He hadde assayed hire ynogh bifore,
And foond hire evere good; what neded it
Hire for to tempte, and alwey moore and
moore,
Though som men preise it for a subtil wit?
But as for me, I seye that yvele it sit 460
To assaye a wyf whan that it is no nede,
And putten hire in angwyssh and in drede.

409. **thewes**, qualities (of mind). 412. **embrace**, bind, draw (to herself). 415. **Publiced**, disseminated, noised abroad. 416. **eek biside**, moreover. 421. **lowely**, humbly. 422. **fortunat**, marked by good fortune. **honestetee**, honor. 424. **outward**, outside (his house). 427. **seyn**, seen. 429. **Koude**, knew. **feet**, feat, art. **wyfly hoomlinesse**, a woman's domestic duties. This is an unusual use of *hoomlinesse*, but both the Latin and the French of Chaucer's sources indicate that this is the meaning intended. 431. **commune profit . . . redresse**, promote the general welfare. 433. **apese**, pacify. 435. **anon**, straightway, is to be construed with *wolde bryngen*. 437. **aton**, in agreement. 444. **Al had hire . . .**, although it would have been more agreeable to her to have borne a male child. 450. **a throwe**, a little while. 452. **tempte**, test. **sadnesse**, steadfastness. 454. **t'assaye**, to put to the test. 455. **Nedelees**, unnecessarily. **affraye**, frighten. 459. **a subtil wit**, a clever idea. 460. **yvele it sit**, it is unbecoming.

For which this markys wroghte in this man-
 ere:
He cam allone a-nyght, ther as she lay, 464
With stierne face and with ful trouble cheere,
And seyde thus: "Grisilde," quod he, "that day
That I yow took out of youre povere array,
And putte yow in estaat of heigh noblesse,—
Ye have nat that forgeten, as I gesse?

"I seye, Grisilde, this present dignitee, 470
In which that I have put yow, as I trowe,
Maketh yow nat foryetful for to be
That I yow took in povre estaat ful lowe,
For any wele ye moot yourselven knowe. 474
Taak heede of every word that y yow seye;
Ther is no wight that hereth it but we tweye.

"Ye woot youreself wel how that ye cam
 heere
Into this hous, it is nat longe ago;
And though to me that ye be lief and deere,
Unto my gentils ye be no thyng so. 480
They seyn, to hem it is greet shame and wo
For to be subgetz and been in servage
To thee, that born art of a smal village.

"And namely sith thy doghter was ybore
Thise wordes han they spoken, doutelees. 485
But I desire, as I have doon bifore,
To lyve my lyf with hem in reste and pees.
I may nat in this caas be recchelees;
I moot doon with thy doghter for the beste,
Nat as I wolde, but as my peple leste. 490

"And yet, God woot, this is ful looth to me;
But nathelees withoute youre wityng
I wol nat doon; but this wol I," quod he,
"That ye to me assente as in this thyng. 494
Shewe now youre pacience in youre werkyng,

That ye me highte and swore in youre village
That day that maked was oure mariage."

Whan she had herd al this, she noght ameved
Neither in word, or chiere, or contenaunce;
For, as it semed, she was nat agreved. 500
She seyde, "Lord, al lyth in youre plesaunce.
My child and I, with hertely obeisaunce,
Been youres al, and ye mowe save or spille
Youre owene thyng; werketh after youre wille.

"Ther may no thyng, God so my soule save,
Liken to yow that may displese me; 506
Ne I desire no thyng for to have,
Ne drede for to leese, save oonly yee.
This wyl is in myn herte, and ay shal be;
No lengthe of tyme or deeth may this deface,
Ne chaunge my corage to another place." 511

Glad was this markys of hire answeryng,
But yet he feyned as he were nat so;
Al drery was his cheere and his lookyng,
Whan that he sholde out of the chambre go.
Soone after this, a furlong wey or two, 516
He prively hath toold al his entente
Unto a man, and to his wyf hym sente.

A maner sergeant was this privee man, 519
The which that feithful ofte he founden hadde
In thynges grete, and eek swich folk wel kan
Doon execucioun in thynges badde.
The lord knew wel that he hym loved and
 dradde;
And whan this sergeant wiste his lordes wille,
Into the chambre he stalked hym ful stille. 525

"Madame," he seyde, "ye moote foryeve it
 me,
Though I do thyng to which I am constreyned.

---

464. **ther as**, where. 465. **trouble**, troubled. 467. **array**, estate. 480. **gentils**, gentlefolk. 484. **namely**, especially. 488. **recchelees**, indifferent. 490. **leste**, it pleases. 492. **wityng**, knowledge. 493. **doon**, act. 496. **highte**, promised. 498. **ameved**, changed. 502. **hertely**, sincere. **obeisaunce**, obedience. 503. **spille**, destroy. 508. **leese**, lose. 511. **corage**, heart. 516. **a furlong wey**, the time necessary to walk a furlong (an eighth of a mile). 519. **sergeant**, servant, or (more probable here) an officer employed in the enforcement of the law. **privee**, confidential. 523. **dradde**, feared. 525. **stalked**, crept (went quietly).

Ye been so wys that ful wel knowe ye
That lordes heestes mowe nat been yfeyned;
They mowe wel been biwailled or compleyned,
But men moote nede unto hire lust obeye,   531
And so wol I; ther is namoore to seye.

"This child I am comanded for to take,"—
And spak namoore, but out the child he hente
Despitously, and gan a cheere make   535
As though he wolde han slayn it er he wente.
Grisildis moot al suffre and al consente;
And as a lamb she sitteth meke and stille,
And leet this crueel sergeant doon his wille.

Suspecious was the diffame of this man,   540
Suspect his face, suspect his word also;
Suspect the tyme in which he this bigan.
Allas! hir doghter that she loved so,
She wende he wolde han slawen it right tho.
But nathelees she neither weep ne syked,   545
Conformynge hire to that the markys lyked.

But atte laste to speken she bigan,
And mekely she to the sergeant preyde,
So as he was a worthy gentil man,
That she moste kisse hire child er that it deyde.
And in hir barm this litel child she leyde   551
With ful sad face, and gan the child to blisse,
And lulled it, and after gan it kisse.

And thus she seyde in hire benigne voys,
"Fareweel my child! I shal thee nevere see.   555
But sith I thee have marked with the croys
Of thilke Fader—blessed moote he be!—
That for us deyde upon a croys of tree,
Thy soule, litel child, I hym bitake,
For this nyght shaltow dyen for my sake."   560

I trowe that to a norice in this cas
It had been hard this reuthe for to se;
Wel myghte a mooder thanne han cryd "allas!"
But nathelees so sad stidefast was she
That she endured al adversitee,   565
And to the sergeant mekely she sayde,
"Have heer agayn youre litel yonge mayde.

"Gooth now," quod she, "and dooth my
    lordes heeste;
But o thyng wol I prey yow of youre grace,
That, but my lord forbad yow, atte leeste   570
Burieth this litel body in som place
That beestes ne no briddes it torace."
But he no word wol to that purpos seye,
But took the child and wente upon his weye.

This sergeant cam unto his lord ageyn,   575
And of Grisildis wordes and hire cheere
He tolde hym point for point, in short and
    pleyn,
And hym presenteth with his doghter deere.
Somwhat this lord hadde routhe in his manere,
But nathelees his purpos heeld he stille,   580
As lordes doon, whan they wol han hir wille;

And bad this sergeant that he pryvely
Sholde this child ful softe wynde and wrappe,
With alle circumstances tendrely,
And carie it in a cofre or in a lappe;   585
But, upon peyne his heed of for to swappe,
That no man sholde knowe of his entente,
Ne whenne he cam, ne whider that he wente;

But at Boloigne to his suster deere,
That thilke tyme of Panik was countesse,   590
He sholde it take, and shewe hire this mateere,

---

529. **heestes**, commands. **yfeyned**, avoided. 531. **lust**, pleasure, will. 534. **hente**, seized. 535. **gan a cheere make**, assumed an appearance. 540. **Suspecious**, arousing suspicion. **diffame**, evil reputation. 541. **Suspect**, ominous. 544. **tho**, then. 545. **weep**, wept. **syked**, sighed. 550. **moste**, might. 551. **barm**, bosom. 558. **tree**, wood. 559. **bitake**, commit. 561. **norice**, nurse. 564. **sad**, quietly. 572. **torace**, tear to pieces. 577. **in short and pleyn**, briefly and clearly (or fully). The senses of *pleyn* (clear, full) are often indistinguishable. 579. **Somwhat**, to some extent. 585. **lappe**, piece of cloth. 586. **swappe**, strike off, *i.e.* of having his head struck off. 588. **whenne**, whence. 589. **Boloigne**, Bologna. 590. **Panik**, not identified. It represents *Panago* in Boccaccio, *Panico* in Petrarch, *Paniquo* in *Le Livre de Griseldis*. 591. **shewe hire this mateere**, explain the matter to her.

Bisekynge hire to doon hire bisynesse
This child to fostre in alle gentillesse;
And whos child that it was he bad hire hyde
From every wight, for oght that may bityde.

The sergeant gooth, and hath fulfild this
thyng; 596
But to this markys now retourne we.
For now gooth he ful faste ymaginyng
If by his wyves cheere he myghte se,
Or by hire word aperceyve, that she 600

Were chaunged; but he nevere hire koude fynde
But evere in oon ylike sad and kynde.

As glad, as humble, as bisy in servyse,
And eek in love, as she was wont to be,
Was she to hym in every maner wyse; 605
Ne of hir doghter noght a word spak she.
Noon accident, for noon adversitee,
Was seyn in hire, ne nevere hir doghter name
Ne nempned she, in ernest nor in game. 609

Explicit tercia pars.

Sequitur pars quarta.

In this estaat ther passed been foure yeer
Er she with childe was, but, as God wolde,
A knave child she bar by this Walter,
Ful gracious and fair for to biholde.
And whan that folk it to his fader tolde,
Nat oonly he, but al his contree merye 615
Was for this child, and God they thanke and
herye.

Whan it was two yeer old, and fro the brest
Departed of his norice, on a day
This markys caughte yet another lest
To tempte his wyf yet ofter, if he may. 620
O nedelees was she tempted in assay!
But wedded men ne knowe no mesure,
Whan that they fynde a pacient creature.

"Wyf," quod this markys, "ye han herd er
this,
My peple sikly berth oure mariage; 625
And namely sith my sone yboren is,
Now is it worse than evere in al oure age.
The murmur sleeth myn herte and my corage,
For to myne eres comth the voys so smerte
That it wel ny destroyed hath myn herte. 630

"Now sey they thus: 'Whan Walter is agon,
Thanne shal the blood of Janicle succede
And been oure lord, for oother have we noon.'
Swiche wordes seith my peple, out of drede.
Wel oughte I of swich murmur taken heede;
For certeinly I drede swich sentence, 636
Though they nat pleyn speke in myn audience.

"I wolde lyve in pees, if that I myghte;
Wherfore I am disposed outrely,
As I his suster servede by nyghte, 640
Right so thenke I to serve hym pryvely.
This warne I yow, that ye nat sodeynly
Out of youreself for no wo sholde outreye;
Beth pacient, and therof I yow preye."

"I have," quod she, "seyd thus, and evere
shal: 645
I wol no thyng, ne nyl no thyng, certayn,
But as yow list. Naught greveth me at al,
Though that my doughter and my sone be
slayn,—
At youre comandement, this is to sayn. 649
I have noght had no part of children tweyne
But first siknesse, and after, wo and peyne.

593. **gentillesse,** gentle breeding. 595. **bityde,** happen. 602. **evere in oon ylike;** uniformly. **sad,** steadfast. 607. **accident,** accidental sign. 608. **doghter,** the uninflected genitive, as in OE. 609. **nempned,** named. **in ernest nor in game,** under any circumstance. 616. **herye,** praise. 619. **lest,** desire. 620. **tempte,** test, as in l. 452. 625. **sikly berth,** bear ill, dislike. 627. **age,** lifetime. 628. **corage,** spirit. 629. **smerte,** sharply. 634. **out of drede,** without doubt. 636. **sentence,** opinion 637. **audience,** hearing. 643. **outreye,** go to excess. 650. **part,** possession, enjoyment.

"Ye been oure lord, dooth with youre owene
    thyng
Right as yow list; axeth no reed at me.
For as I lefte at hoom al my clothyng,
Whan I first cam to yow, right so," quod she,
"Lefte I my wyl and al my libertee,   656
And took youre clothyng; wherfore I yow
    preye,
Dooth youre plesaunce, I wol youre lust obeye.

"And certes, if I hadde prescience   659
Youre wyl to knowe, er ye youre lust me tolde,
I wolde it doon withouten necligence;
But now I woot youre lust, and what ye wolde,
Al youre plesance ferme and stable I holde;
For wiste I that my deeth wolde do yow ese,
Right gladly wolde I dyen, yow to plese.   665

"Deth may noght make no comparisoun
Unto youre love." And whan this markys say
The constance of his wyf, he caste adoun
His eyen two, and wondreth that she may
In pacience suffre al this array;   670
And forth he goth with drery contenance,
But to his herte it was ful greet plesance.

This ugly sergeant, in the same wyse
That he hire doghter caughte, right so he,
Or worse, if men worse kan devyse,   675
Hath hent hire sone, that ful was of beautee.
And evere in oon so pacient was she
That she no chiere maade of hevynesse,
But kiste hir sone, and after gan it blesse;

Save this, she preyde hym that, if he
    myghte,   680
Hir litel sone he wolde in erthe grave,
His tendre lymes, delicaat to sighte,
Fro foweles and fro beestes for to save,

But she noon answere of hym myghte have.
He wente his wey, as hym no thyng ne roghte;
But to Boloigne he tendrely it broghte.   686

This markys wondred, evere lenger the
    moore,
Upon hir pacience, and if that he
Ne hadde soothly knowen therbifoore
That parfitly hir children loved she,   690
He wolde have wend that of som subtiltee,
And of malice, or for crueel corage,
That she hadde suffred this with sad visage.

But wel he knew that next hymself, certayn,
She loved hir children best in every wyse.   695
But now of wommen wolde I axen fayn
If thise assayes myghte nat suffise?
What koude a sturdy housbonde moore devyse
To preeve hir wyfhod and hir stedefastnesse,
And he continuynge evere in sturdinesse?   700

But ther been folk of swich condicioun
That whan they have a certein purpos take,
They kan nat stynte of hire entencioun,
But, right as they were bounden to a stake,
They wol nat of that firste purpos slake.   705
Right so this markys fulliche hath purposed
To tempte his wyf as he was first disposed.

He waiteth if by word or contenance
That she to hym was changed of corage;
But nevere koude he fynde variance.   710
She was ay oon in herte and in visage;
And ay the forther that she was in age,
The moore trewe, if that it were possible,
She was to hym in love, and moore penyble.

For which it semed thus, that of hem two 715
Ther nas but o wyl; for, as Walter leste,

---

653. **axeth no reed at me,** do not consult my wishes. 659. **prescience,** foreknowledge. 666. **Deth . . . love,** *i.e.* death is a small thing in comparison with your love. 667. **say,** saw. 670. **array,** arrangement, "business." 675. **Or worse.** The phrase is alternative to *in the same wyse.* **devyse,** imagine. 677. **evere in oon,** uniformly, constantly. 679. **blesse,** make the sign of the cross over it. 681. **grave,** bury. 682. **delicaat,** delightful. 691. **subtiltee,** guile. 693. **sad,** composed, steadfast. 697. **assayes,** tests. 700. **sturdinesse,** harshness. 702. **a certein purpos take,** resolved to do something. 703. **stynte of,** cease from. 704. **bounden to a stake.** This is sometimes taken as an allusion to bear-baiting, but the comparison is sufficiently vivid as conveying fixity of purpose. 705. **slake,** weaken, desist (from). 708. **waiteth,** watches (to see). 709. **of corage,** in heart. 714. **penyble,** painstaking. 716. **leste,** wished.

The same lust was hire plesance also.
And, God be thanked, al fil for the beste.
She shewed wel, for no worldly unreste
A wyf, as of hirself, nothing ne sholde   720
Wille in effect, but as hir housbonde wolde.

The sclaundre of Walter ofte and wyde
          spradde,
That of a crueel herte he wikkedly,
For he a povre womman wedded hadde,
Hath mordred bothe his children prively.   725
Swich murmur was among hem comunly.
No wonder is, for to the peples ere
Ther cam no word, but that they mordred
          were.

For which, where as his peple therbifore
Hadde loved hym wel, the sclaundre of his
          diffame   730
Made hem that they hym hatede therfore.
To been a mordrere is an hateful name;
But nathelees, for ernest ne for game,
He of his crueel purpos nolde stente;
To tempte his wyf was set al his entente.   735

Whan that his doghter twelve yeer was of
          age,
He to the court of Rome, in subtil wyse
Enformed of his wyl, sente his message,
Comaundynge hem swiche bulles to devyse
As to his crueel purpos may suffyse,   740
How that the pope, as for his peples reste,
Bad hym to wedde another, if hym leste.

I seye, he bad they sholde countrefete
The popes bulles, makynge mencioun
That he hath leve his firste wyf to lete,   745

As by the popes dispensacioun,
To stynte rancour and dissencioun
Bitwixe his peple and hym; thus seyde the
          bulle,
The which they han publiced atte fulle.

The rude peple, as it no wonder is,   750
Wenden ful wel that it hadde be right so;
But whan thise tidynges came to Grisildis,
I deeme that hire herte was ful wo.
But she, ylike sad for everemo,
Disposed was, this humble creature,   755
The adversitee of Fortune al t'endure,

Abidynge evere his lust and his plesance,
To whom that she was yeven herte and al,
As to hire verray worldly suffisance.
But shortly if this storie I telien shal,   760
This markys writen hath in special
A lettre in which he sheweth his entente,
And secreely he to Boloigne it sente.

To the Erl of Panyk, which that hadde tho
Wedded his suster, preyde he specially   765
To bryngen hoom agayn his children two
In honourable estaat al openly.
But o thyng he hym preyede outrely,
That he to no wight, though men wolde en-
          quere,
Sholde nat telle whos children that they
          were,   770

But seye, the mayden sholde ywedded be
Unto the Markys of Saluce anon.
And as this erl was preyed, so dide he;
For at day set he on his wey is goon

717. **lust,** desire. 718. **fil,** happened. 719. **for no worldly unreste,** because of any worldly distress. 720. **A wyf . . . wolde,** a wife, so far as she is concerned, should wish nothing in fact but what her husband wished. 722. **sclaundre,** evil reputation. 723. **of,** because of. 726. **hem.** The pronoun anticipates the next line. 733. **for ernest ne for game,** under no circumstances. 734. **stente,** cease; cf. l. 703. 737. **in subtil wyse Enformed of his wyl,** secretly informed of his intention. 738. **message,** messenger. 742. **if hym leste,** if it pleased him to. 745. **lete,** leave. 747. **To stynte,** to put an end to. 751. **Wenden,** supposed. 754. **ylike sad,** uniformly steadfast. 757. **his lust . . . plesance,** his desires and what was pleasing to him. 759. **verray,** true. 764. **tho,** then. 768. **outrely,** emphatically. 772. **Saluce,** Saluzzo. Girls were frequently married at twelve; cf. the Wife of Bath (D 4). **anon,** immediately. 774. **at day set,** at the appointed time.

Toward Saluce, and lordes many oon 775
In riche array, this mayden for to gyde,
Hir yonge brother ridynge hire bisyde.

Arrayed was toward his mariage
This fresshe mayde, ful of gemmes cleere;

Hir brother, which that seven yeer was of age,
Arrayed eek ful fressh in his manere. 781
And thus in greet noblesse and with glad
    cheere,
Toward Saluces shapynge hir journey,
Fro day to day they ryden in hir wey.

Explicit quarta pars.

Sequitur pars quinta.

Among al this, after his wikke usage, 785
This markys, yet his wyf to tempte moore
To the outtreste preeve of hir corage,
Fully to han experience and loore
If that she were as stidefast as bifoore,
He on a day, in open audience, 790
Ful boistously hath seyd hire this sentence:

"Certes, Grisilde, I hadde ynogh plesance
To han yow to my wyf for youre goodnesse,
As for youre trouthe and for youre obeisance,
Noght for youre lynage, ne for youre richesse;
But now knowe I in verray soothfastnesse 796
That in greet lordshipe, if I wel avyse,
Ther is greet servitude in sondry wyse.

"I may nat doon as every plowman may.
My peple me constreyneth for to take 800
Another wyf, and crien day by day;
And eek the pope, rancour for to slake,
Consenteth it, that dar I undertake;
And trewely thus muche I wol yow seye,
My newe wyf is comynge by the weye. 805

"Be strong of herte, and voyde anon hir
    place,
And thilke dowere that ye broghten me,
Taak it agayn; I graunte it of my grace.

Retourneth to youre fadres hous," quod he;
"No man may alwey han prosperitee. 810
With evene herte I rede yow t'endure
The strook of Fortune or of aventure."

And she agayn answerde in pacience,
"My lord," quod she, "I woot, and wiste alway,
How that bitwixen youre magnificence 815
And my poverte no wight kan ne may
Maken comparisoun; it is no nay.
I ne heeld me nevere digne in no manere
To be youre wyf, no, ne youre chamberere.

"And in this hous, ther ye me lady maade—
The heighe God take I for my witnesse, 821
And also wysly he my soule glaade—
I nevere heeld me lady ne maistresse,
But humble servant to youre worthynesse,
And evere shal, whil that my lyf may dure, 825
Aboven every worldly creature.

"That ye so longe of youre benignitee
Han holden me in honour and nobleye,
Where as I was noght worthy for to bee,
That thonke I God and yow, to whom I preye
Foryelde it yow; ther is namoore to seye. 831
Unto my fader gladly wol I wende,
And with hym dwelle unto my lyves ende.

---

776. **gyde,** conduct. 778. **Arrayed,** adorned. **toward,** (in preparation) for. 782. **noblesse,** splendor. 785. **Among,** along with. **wikke,** wicked. 787. **outtreste preeve of hir corage,** uttermost test of her spirit. 788. **experience and loore,** first-hand knowledge. 790. **open audience,** open assembly, publicly. 791. **boistously,** loudly. 792. **hadde ynogh plesance,** was sufficiently pleased. 798. **greet servitude,** *i.e.* a great lord is under various kinds of restraint. 800. **constreyneth,** urge, compel. 801. **crien,** cry out. 802. **slake,** lessen. 803. **undertake,** allege. 806. **voyde anon,** vacate immediately. 811. **evene herte,** even temper. 812. **aventure,** misfortune. 817. **it is no nay,** it cannot be denied. 818. **digne,** worthy. 819. **chamberere,** chambermaid. 820. **ther,** where. 822. **also wysly . . .,** as surely as (I hope) he may gladden my soul. 823. **heeld me,** considered myself. 825. **dure,** last. 826. **Aboven every,** more than to any other. 828. **nobleye,** noble estate. 831. **Foryelde it yow,** requite you for it.

"Ther I was fostred of a child ful smal,
Til I be deed my lyf ther wol I lede,   835
A wydwe clene in body, herte, and al.
For sith I yaf to yow my maydenhede,
And am youre trewe wyf, it is no drede,
God shilde swich a lordes wyf to take
Another man to housbonde or to make!   840

"And of youre newe wyf God of his grace
So graunte yow wele and prosperitee!
For I wol gladly yelden hire my place,
In which that I was blisful wont to bee.
For sith it liketh yow, my lord," quod shee, 845
"That whilom weren al myn hertes reste,
That I shal goon, I wol goon whan yow leste.

"But ther as ye me profre swich dowaire
As I first broghte, it is wel in my mynde   849
It were my wrecched clothes, nothyng faire,
The whiche to me were hard now for to fynde.
O goode God! how gentil and how kynde
Ye semed by youre speche and youre visage
The day that maked was oure mariage!

"But sooth is seyd—algate I fynde it trewe,
For in effect it preeved is on me—   856
Love is noght oold as whan that it is newe.
But certes, lord, for noon adversitee,
To dyen in the cas, it shal nat bee
That evere in word or werk I shal repente 860
That I yow yaf myn herte in hool entente.

"My lord, ye woot that in my fadres place
Ye dide me streepe out of my povre weede,
And richely me cladden, of youre grace.
To yow broghte I noght elles, out of drede, 865
But feith, and nakednesse, and maydenhede;
And heere agayn your clothyng I restoore,
And eek your weddyng ryng, for everemore.

"The remenant of youre jueles redy be
Inwith youre chambre, dar I saufly sayn. 870
Naked out of my fadres hous," quod she,
"I cam, and naked moot I turne agayn.
Al youre plesance wol I folwen fayn;
But yet I hope it be nat youre entente 874
That I smoklees out of youre paleys wente.

"Ye koude nat doon so dishonest a thyng,
That thilke wombe in which youre children leye
Sholde biforn the peple, in my walkyng,
Be seyn al bare; wherfore I yow preye,
Lat me nat lyk a worm go by the weye. 880
Remembre yow, myn owene lord so deere,
I was youre wyf, though I unworthy weere.

"Wherfore, in gerdon of my maydenhede,
Which that I broghte, and noght agayn I bere,
As voucheth sauf to yeve me, to my meede,
But swich a smok as I was wont to were, 886
That I therwith may wrye the wombe of here
That was youre wyf. And heer take I my leeve
Of yow, myn owene lord, lest I yow greve."

"The smok," quod he, "that thou hast on thy bak, 890
Lat it be stille, and bere it forth with thee."
But wel unnethes thilke word he spak,
But wente his wey, for routhe and for pitee.
Biforn the folk hirselven strepeth she,
And in hir smok, with heed and foot al bare, 895
Toward hir fader hous forth is she fare.

The folk hire folwe, wepynge in hir weye,
And Fortune ay they cursen as they goon;
But she fro wepyng kepte hire eyen dreye,
Ne in this tyme word ne spak she noon. 900
Hir fader, that this tidynge herde anoon,

834. **of a child,** as a child. 838. **drede,** doubt. 839. **shilde . . . to take,** protect from taking. 840. **make,** mate. 842. **wele,** happiness. 848. **dowaire,** dowry. 855. **algate,** in any case. 857. **Love is noght oold,** love is not the same when it is old as when it is new. 859. **To dyen in the cas,** even though I should die in this case. 863. **dide me streepe,** had me stripped. 870. **Inwith,** within. 875. **smoklees,** without a smock (undergarment). 876. **dishonest,** shameful. 883. **gerdon,** reward. 884. **agayn I bere,** I carry back. 885. **As voucheth sauf,** vouchsafe. For horatory *as* see Language, § 73. **meede,** reward. 887. **wrye,** cover. **here,** her. 896. **fader,** father's. **fare,** fared, gone.

Curseth the day and tyme that Nature
Shoop hym to been a lyves creature.

For out of doute this olde poure man
Was evere in suspect of hir mariage;　　　905
For evere he demed, sith that it bigan,
That whan the lord fulfild hadde his corage,
Hym wolde thynke it were a disparage
To his estaat so lowe for t'alighte,
And voyden hire as soone as ever he myghte.

Agayns his doghter hastiliche goth he,　　911
For he by noyse of folk knew hire comynge,
And with hire olde coote, as it myghte be
He covered hire, ful sorwefully wepynge.
But on hire body myghte he it nat brynge,　915
For rude was the clooth, and moore of age
By dayes fele than at hire mariage.

Thus with hire fader, for a certeyn space,
Dwelleth this flour of wyfly pacience,

That neither by hire wordes ne hire face,　920
Biforn the folk, ne eek in hire absence,
Ne shewed she that hire was doon offence;
Ne of hire heighe estaat no remembraunce
Ne hadde she, as by hire contenaunce.

No wonder is, for in hire grete estaat　　925
Hire goost was evere in pleyn humylitee;
No tendre mouth, noon herte delicaat,
No pompe, no semblant of roialtee,
But ful of pacient benyngnytee,
Discreet and pridelees, ay honurable,　　930
And to hire housbonde evere meke and stable.

✳ Men speke of Job, and moost for his humblesse,
As clerkes, whan hem list, konne wel endite,
Namely of men, but as in soothfastnesse,
Though clerkes preise wommen but a lite,　935
Ther kan no man in humblesse hym acquite
As womman kan, ne kan been half so trewe
As wommen been, but it be falle of newe.

[Pars sexta].

Fro Boloigne is this Erl of Panyk come,
Of which the fame up sprang to moore and lesse,
And to the peples eres, alle and some,　　941
Was kouth eek that a newe markysesse
He with hym broghte, in swich pompe and
　　richesse
That nevere was ther seyn with mannes yë
So noble array in al West Lumbardye.　　945

The markys, which that shoop and knew al
　　this,
Er that this erl was come, sente his message
For thilke sely povre Grisildis;
And she with humble herte and glad visage,
Nat with no swollen thoght in hire corage,　950

Cam at his heste, and on hire knees hire sette,
And reverently and wisely she hym grette.

"Grisilde," quod he, "my wyl is outrely,
This mayden, that shal wedded been to me,
Received be to-morwe as roially　　　　955
As it possible is in myn hous to be,
And eek that every wight in his degree
Have his estaat, in sittyng and servyse
And heigh plesaunce, as I kan best devyse.

"I have no wommen suffisaunt, certayn,　960
The chambres for t'arraye in ordinaunce
After my lust, and therfore wolde I fayn
That thyn were al swich manere governaunce.

903. **a lyves creature,** a living creature. 905. **in suspect,** suspicious. 907. **corage,** will, desire. 908. **Hym wolde thynke,** it would seem to him. 909. **alighte,** descend. 910. **voyden,** get rid of. 911. **Agayns,** toward, to meet. 913. **as it myghte be,** such as it was. 917. **fele,** many. 918. **space,** space of time. 919. **wyfly,** womanly. wifely. 921. **hire,** their, 922, **hire . . . offence,** any wrong had been done to her. 924. **as by,** *i.e.* to judge by. 926. **goost,** spirit. **pleyn,** full. 927. **delicaat,** self-indulgent. 928. **semblant,** appearance. 930. **ay,** ever. 934. **Namely,** especially. 936. **humblesse,** humility. 938. **but it be falle of newe,** unless very recently. 940. **fame,** rumor, report. 941. **alle and some,** all and sundry. 946. **shoop,** arranged. 947. **message,** messenger. 948. **sely,** simple (in a good sense). 953. **outrely,** utterly. 958. **in sittyng,** at the table. 961. **in ordinaunce,** properly. 962. **After my lust,** according to my desire.

Thou knowest eek of old al my plesaunce;
Thogh thyn array be badde and yvel biseye,   965
Do thou thy devoir at the leeste weye."

"Nat oonly, lord, that I am glad," quod she,
"To doon youre lust, but I desire also
Yow for to serve and plese in my degree
Withouten feyntyng, and shal everemo;   970
Ne nevere, for no wele ne no wo,
Ne shal the goost withinne myn herte stente
To love yow best with al my trewe entente."

And with that word she gan the hous to
    dighte,
And tables for to sette, and beddes make;   975
And peyned hire to doon al that she myghte,
Preyynge the chambereres, for Goddes sake,
To hasten hem, and faste swepe and shake;
And she, the mooste servysable of alle,
Hath every chambre arrayed and his halle.   980

Abouten undren gan this erl alighte,
That with hym broghte thise noble children
    tweye,
For which the peple ran to seen the sighte
Of hire array, so richely biseye;
And thanne at erst amonges hem they seye   985
That Walter was no fool, thogh that hym leste
To chaunge his wyf, for it was for the beste.

For she is fairer, as they deemen alle,
Than is Grisilde, and moore tendre of age,
And fairer fruyt bitwene hem sholde falle,   990
And moore plesant, for hire heigh lynage.
Hir brother eek so fair was of visage

That hem to seen the peple hath caught ples-
    aunce,
Commendynge now the markys governaunce.

"O stormy peple! unsad and evere untrewe!
Ay undiscreet and chaungynge as a vane!   996
Delitynge evere in rumbul that is newe,
For lyk the moone ay wexe ye and wane!
Ay ful of clappyng, deere ynogh a jane!
Youre doom is fals, youre constance yvele
    preeveth;   1000
A ful greet fool is he that on yow leeveth."

Thus seyden sadde folk in that citee,
Whan that the peple gazed up and doun;
For they were glad, right for the noveltee,
To han a newe lady of hir toun.   1005
Namoore of this make I now mencioun,
But to Grisilde agayn wol I me dresse,
And telle hir constance and hir bisynesse.

Ful bisy was Grisilde in every thyng
That to the feeste was apertinent.   1010
Right noght was she abayst of hire clothyng,
Thogh it were rude and somdeel eek torent;
But with glad cheere to the yate is went
With oother folk, to greete the markysesse,
And after that dooth forth hire bisynesse.   1015

With so glad chiere his gestes she receyveth,
And konnyngly, everich in his degree,
That no defaute no man aperceyveth,
But ay they wondren what she myghte bee
That in so povre array was for to see,   1020
And koude swich honour and reverence,
And worthily they preisen hire prudence.

---

965. **yvel biseye,** ill-looking. 966. **devoir,** duty. **at the leeste weye,** leastwise, at least. 970. **feyntyng,** weariness. 972. **stente,** cease. 974. **dighte,** prepare. 977. **chambereres,** chambermaids. 979. **servysable,** hard-working. 981. **undren,** 9 A.M. 984. **richely biseye,** rich looking. 985. **at erst,** finally. **seye,** saw. 993. **hath caught plesaunce,** have become pleased. 995. **unsad,** unstable. This stanza is Chaucer's addition, and could well represent his memory of and attitude toward the Peasants' Revolt of 1381. 996. **vane,** weathercock. 997. **rumbul,** tumult. 999. **clappyng,** chattering. **deere ynogh a jane,** dear at any price. A *jane* was a Genoese coin worth a half-penny. Cf. *Sir Thopas* (B 1925). 1000. **doom,** judgment. **youre constance . . .,** your constancy proves to be bad. 1001. **leeveth,** believes. 1002. **Thus seyden sadde folk . . .** The contrast is between steadfast folk and *the people*, who welcomed novelty. 1007. **me dresse,** address myself. 1011. **abayst of,** embarrassed by. 1012. **torent,** torn, tattered. 1013. **yate,** gate. 1015. **dooth forth,** continues, goes on with. 1021. **koude,** knew, exemplified. **honour and reverence,** worthiness and dignity. 1022. **worthily,** deservedly.

In al this meene while she ne stente
This mayde and eek hir brother to commende
With al hir herte, in ful benynge entente,   1025
So wel that no man koude hir pris amende.
But atte laste, whan that thise lordes wende
To sitten doun to mete, he gan to calle
Grisilde, as she was bisy in his halle.   1029

"Grisilde," quod he, as it were in his pley,
"How liketh thee my wyf, and hire beautee?"
"Right wel," quod she, "my lord; for, in good
    fey,
A fairer saugh I nevere noon than she.
I prey to God yeve hire prosperitee;
And so hope I that he wol to yow sende   1035
Plesance ynogh unto youre lyves ende.

"O thyng biseke I yow, and warne also,
That ye ne prikke with no tormentynge
This tendre mayden, as ye han doon mo;
For she is fostred in hire norissynge   1040
Moore tendrely, and, to my supposynge,
She koude nat adversitee endure
As koude a povre fostred creature."

And whan this Walter saugh hire pacience,
Hir glade chiere, and no malice at al,   1045
And he so ofte had doon to hire offence,
And she ay sad and constant as a wal,
Continuynge evere hire innocence overal,
This sturdy markys gan his herte dresse
To rewen upon hire wyfly stedfastnesse.   1050

"This is ynogh, Grisilde myn," quod he;
"Be now namoore agast ne yvele apayed.
I have thy feith and thy benyngnytee,
As wel as evere womman was, assayed,
In greet estaat, and povreliche arrayed.   1055
Now knowe I, dere wyf, thy stedfastnesse,"—
And hire in armes took and gan hire kesse.

And she for wonder took of it no keep;
She herde nat what thyng he to hire seyde;
She ferde as she had stert out of a sleep,   1060
Til she out of hir mazednesse abreyde.
"Grisilde," quod he, "by God, that for us deyde,
Thou art my wyf, ne noon oother I have,
Ne nevere hadde, as God my soule save!

"This is thy doghter, which thou hast sup-
    posed   1065
To be my wyf; that oother feithfully
Shal be myn heir, as I have ay disposed;
Thou bare hym in thy body trewely.
At Boloigne have I kept hem prively;   1069
Taak hem agayn, for now maystow nat seye
That thou hast lorn noon of thy children tweye.

"And folk that ootherweys han seyd of me,
I warne hem wel that I have doon this deede
For no malice, ne for no crueltee,   1074
But for t'assaye in thee thy wommanheede,
And nat to sleen my children—God forbeede!—
But for to kepe hem pryvely and stille,
Til I thy purpos knewe and al thy wille."

Whan she this herde, aswowne doun she
    falleth
For pitous joye, and after hire swownynge   1080
She bothe hire yonge children to hire calleth,
And in hire armes, pitously wepynge,
Embraceth hem, and tendrely kissynge
Ful lyk a mooder, with hire salte teeres
She bathed bothe hire visage and hire heeres.

O which a pitous thyng it was to se   1086
Hir swownyng, and hire humble voys to heere!
"Grauntmercy, lord, God thanke it yow," quod
    she,
"That ye han saved me my children deere!   1089

1026. pris, praise. **1028. he,** *i.e.* Walter. **1030. in his pley,** in jest. **1031. liketh,** pleases. **1036. Plesance,** happiness.
1037. O, one. **biseke,** beseech. **1039. doon mo,** *i.e.* done to others. **1047. sad,** steadfast. **1048. innocence,** blameless
character. **overal,** everywhere. **1049. dresse,** prepare. **1052. yvele apayed,** displeased. **1057. kesse,** kiss. The form is
Kentish; see Language, § 8. **1058. keep,** heed. **1060. stert,** started, awakened suddenly. **1061. abreyde,** awoke (suddenly). **1067. ay disposed,** always intended. **1073. warne hem,** bid them take heed. **1079. Whan she this herde.** The next
four stanzas are almost entirely Chaucer's addition. **1086. which a,** what a. **1088. Grauntmercy,** great thank(s). **God
thanke it yow,** may God reward you for it.

Now rekke I nevere to been deed right heere;
Sith I stonde in youre love and in youre grace,
No fors of deeth, ne whan my spirit pace!

      "O tendre, o deere, o yonge children myne!
Youre woful mooder wende stedfastly
That crueel houndes or som foul vermyne   1095
Hadde eten yow; but God, of his mercy,
And youre benyngne fader tendrely
Hath doon yow kept,"—and in that same
      stounde
Al sodeynly she swapte adoun to grounde.

      And in hire swough so sadly holdeth she   1100
Hire children two, whan she gan hem t'em-
      brace,
That with greet sleighte and greet difficultee
The children from hire arm they gonne arace.
O many a teere on many a pitous face
Doun ran of hem that stooden hire bisyde;   1105
Unnethe abouten hire myghte they abyde.

      Walter hire gladeth, and hire sorwe slaketh;
She riseth up, abaysed, from hire traunce,
And every wight hire joye and feeste maketh
Til she hath caught agayn hire contenaunce.
Walter hire dooth so feithfully plesaunce   1111
That it was deyntee for to seen the cheere
Bitwixe hem two, now they been met yfeere.

      Thise ladyes, whan that they hir tyme say,
Han taken hire and into chambre gon,   1115
And strepen hire out of hire rude array,
And in a clooth of gold that brighte shoon,
With a coroune of many a riche stoon
Upon hire heed, they into halle hire broghte,
And ther she was honored as hire oghte.   1120

      Thus hath this pitous day a blisful ende,
For every man and womman dooth his myght
This day in murthe and revel to dispende
Til on the welkne shoon the sterres lyght.
For moore solempne in every mannes syght   1125
This feste was, and gretter of costage,
Than was the revel of hire mariage.

      Ful many a yeer in heigh prosperitee
Lyven thise two in concord and in reste,
And richely his doghter maryed he   1130
Unto a lord, oon of the worthieste
Of al Ytaille; and thanne in pees and reste
His wyves fader in his court he kepeth,
Til that the soule out of his body crepeth.

      His sone succedeth in his heritage   1135
In reste and pees, after his fader day,
And fortunat was eek in mariage,
Al putte he nat his wyf in greet assay.
This world is nat so strong, it is no nay,
As it hath been in olde tymes yoore,   1140
And herkneth what this auctour seith therfoore.

✳ This storie is seyd, nat for that wyves sholde
Folwen Grisilde as in humylitee,
For it were inportable, though they wolde;
But for that every wight, in his degree,   1145
Sholde be constant in adversitee
As was Grisilde; therfore Petrak writeth
This storie, which with heigh stile he enditeth.

      For, sith a womman was so pacient
Unto a mortal man, wel moore us oghte   1150
Receyven al in gree that God us sent;
For greet skile is he preeve that he wroghte.
But he ne tempteth no man that he boghte,

1090. **rekke I nevere . . .,** I do not care if I die right here. 1092. **No fors of deeth,** death does not matter. 1094. **wende stedfastly,** constantly supposed. 1098. **doon yow kept,** caused you to be preserved; cf. Language, § 68. **stounde,** time, moment. 1099. **swapte,** flopped. 1100. **swough,** swoon. **sadly,** firmly. 1102. **sleighte,** ingenuity. 1103. **arace,** extricate. 1105. **bisyde,** round about. 1106. **Unnethe,** scarcely. 1108. **abaysed,** disconcerted. 1112. **deyntee,** a delight. **cheere,** gladness. 1113. **yfeere,** together. 1114. **Thise,** the. **say,** saw. 1116. **strepen,** strip. 1120. **hire oghte,** was due her. 1124. **on the welkne,** in the sky. 1125. **solempne,** sumptuous. 1126. **costage,** cost. 1136. **fader,** father's. 1138. **Al,** although. 1139. **it is no nay,** it cannot be denied. 1144. **inportable,** intolerable. 1151. **in gree,** with good will, without complaint. **sent,** sends. 1152. **greet skile is,** it is most reasonable (that), **preeve,** test. **that,** what. 1153. **tempteth,** here used in the modern sense. **boghte,** redeemed.

As seith Seint Jame, if ye his pistel rede;
He preeveth folk al day, it is no drede, 1155

And suffreth us, as for oure exercise,
With sharpe scourges of adversitee
Ful ofte to be bete in sondry wise;
Nat for to knowe oure wyl, for certes he,
Er we were born, knew al oure freletee; 1160
And for oure beste is al his governaunce.
Lat us thanne lyve in vertuous suffraunce.

But o word, lordynges, herkneth er I go:
It were ful hard to fynde now-a-dayes
In al a toun Grisildis thre or two; 1165

For if that they were put to swiche assayes,
The gold of hem hath now so badde alayes
With bras, that thogh the coyne be fair at yë,
It wolde rather breste a-two than plye.

For which heere, for the Wyves love of
      Bathe— 1170
Whos lyf and al hire secte God mayntene
In heigh maistrie, and elles were it scathe—
I wol with lusty herte, fressh and grene,
Seyn yow a song to glade yow, I wene;
And lat us stynte of ernestful matere. 1175
Herkneth my song that seith in this manere:

Lenvoy de Chaucer.

Grisilde is deed, and eek hire pacience,
And bothe atones buryed in Ytaille;
For which I crie in open audience,
No wedded man so hardy be t'assaille 1180
His wyves pacience in trust to fynde
Grisildis, for in certein he shal faille.

O noble wyves, ful of heigh prudence,
Lat noon humylitee youre tonge naille,
Ne lat no clerk have cause or diligence 1185
To write of yow a storie of swich mervaille
As of Grisildis pacient and kynde,
Lest Chichevache yow swelwe in hire entraille!

Folweth Ekko, that holdeth no silence,
But evere answereth at the countretaille. 1190

Beth nat bidaffed for youre innocence,
But sharply taak on yow the governaille.
Emprenteth wel this lessoun in youre mynde,
For commune profit sith it may availle.

Ye archewyves, stondeth at defense, 1195
Syn ye be strong as is a greet camaille;
Ne suffreth nat that men yow doon offense.
And sklendre wyves, fieble as in bataille,
Beth egre as is a tygre yond in Ynde;
Ay clappeth as a mille, I yow consaille. 1200

Ne dreed hem nat, doth hem no reverence,
For though thyn housbonde armed be in maille,
The arwes of thy crabbed eloquence
Shal perce his brest, and eek his aventaille.

1154. Seint Jame. *James,* 1:13: for God cannot be tempted with evil, neither tempteth he any man. 1155. preeveth, tests. drede, doubt. 1156. excercise, discipline. 1162. suffraunce, patience. This is the end of the story in Chaucer's sources, Petrarch's version and its French derivative. The next two stanzas were clearly written at the time the tale was assigned to the Clerk and fitted into the so-called Marriage Group. 1167. alayes, alloys. 1168. at yë, to the eye. 1169. breste, break. plye, bend. 1171. secte, sex; cf. Kökeritz, *PQ,* XXVI. 147–51. It may also mean "kind of person." 1172. were it scathe, it would be a pity. 1177. Grisilde is deed. The lyric which here follows is a metrical *tour de force*; it will be noticed that only three rimes are employed in the six stanzas. In the manuscripts it is regularly introduced by the words "Lenvoy de Chaucer," which may be a remnant of the pre-*Canterbury Tales* form of the Griselda narrative. In any case the rubric is to be taken as indicating that the stanzas which follow are Chaucer's addition, not that the Clerk is no longer speaking. 1178. atones, at one time, together. 1181. in trust to, trusting to. 1182. in certein, certainly. 1184. naille, *i.e.* restrain. 1187. Grisildis, Griselde. 1188. Chichevache. The word in OF. means "lean cow" and is the name of a cow that fed only on patient wives. The satirical story, originally French, is told in Lydgate's *Bycorne and Chichevache.* swelwe, swallow. 1189. Ekko, Echo. 1190. at the countretaille, in reply. The *countretaille* was the half of a tally which corresponded to the other half when the tally had been split. 1191. bidaffed, made a fool of. 1195. In one group of MSS this stanza comes at the end of the Envoy. stondeth at defense, be on guard. 1196. camaille, camel. 1198. sklendre, slender, frail. as in, in. 1199. egre, sharp, fierce. 1200. clappeth, clatter. 1204. aventaille, a wide band of chain mail protecting the lower part of the face, the neck, and the upper chest.

In jalousie I rede eek thou hym bynde, 1205
And thou shalt make hym couche as doth a
    quaille.

  If thou be fair, ther folk been in presence,
Shewe thou thy visage and thyn apparaille;

If thou be foul, be fre of thy dispence;
To gete thee freendes ay do thy travaille; 1210
Be ay of chiere as light as leef on lynde,
And lat hym care, and wepe, and wrynge, and
    waille!

Heere endeth the Tale of the Clerk of Oxenford.

The Merchant's Tale

THE MERCHANT'S PROLOGUE

The Prologe of the Marchantes Tale.

"Wepyng and waylyng, care and oother
    sorwe
I knowe ynogh, on even and a-morwe," 1214
Quod the Marchant, "and so doon othere mo
That wedded been. I trowe that it be so,
For wel I woot it fareth so with me.
I have a wyf, the worste that may be;
For thogh the feend to hire ycoupled were,
She wolde hym overmacche, I dar wel swere.
What sholde I yow reherce in special 1221
Hir hye malice? She is a shrewe at al.
Ther is a long and large difference
Bitwix Grisildis grete pacience

And of my wyf the passyng crueltee. 1225
Were I unbounden, also moot I thee!
I wolde nevere eft comen in the snare.
We wedded men lyve in sorwe and care.
Assaye whoso wole, and he shal fynde
That I seye sooth, by Seint Thomas of Ynde,
As for the moore part, I sey nat alle. 1231
God shilde that it sholde so bifalle!
  A! goode sire Hoost, I have ywedded bee
Thise monthes two, and moore nat, pardee;
And yet, I trowe, he that al his lyve 1235
Wyflees hath been, though that men wolde him
    ryve

1206. couche, cower. **1207. ther,** where. **1208. apparaille,** apparel. **1209. dispence,** spending. **1211. lynde,** linden-tree. Following the *Envoy* in one large group of manuscripts a stanza is found introduced by the rubric **Bihoold the murye wordes of the Hoost:**

> This worthy Clerk, whan ended was his tale,
> Oure Hooste seyde, and swoor, "By Goddes bones,
> Me were levere than a barel ale
> My wyf at hoom had herd this legende ones!
> This is a gentil tale for the nones,
> As to my purpos, wiste ye my wille;
> But thyng that wol nat be, lat it be stille.

These lines may have been intended at one time to form the endlink (or the beginning of one) to *The Clerk's Tale,* but were canceled when Chaucer wrote the Prologue to *The Merchant's Tale.* **1213. Wepyng and waylyng . . .** The Merchant catches up the closing words of the Clerk. **1219. feend,** devil. **1221. What,** why. **1222. at al,** in every respect. We use the expression generally in the negative. **1225. passyng,** extreme. **1226. thee,** thrive. **1227. eft,** again. **1232. shilde,** forbid. **1236. ryve,** pierce.

Unto the herte, ne koude in no manere
Tellen so muchel sorwe as I now heere
Koude tellen of my wyves cursednesse!"
  "Now," quod oure Hoost, "Marchaunt, so
    God yow blesse, 1240

Syn ye so muchel knowen of that art.
Ful hertely, I pray yow telle us part."
  "Gladly," quod he, "but of myn owene
    soore,
For soory herte, I telle may namoore."

THE MERCHANT'S TALE

Heere bigynneth the Marchantes Tale.

Whilom ther was dwellynge in Lumbardye
A worthy knyght, that born was of Pavye, 1246
In which he lyved in greet prosperitee;
And sixty yeer a wyflees man was hee,
And folwed ay his bodily delyt
On wommen, ther as was his appetyt, 1250
As doon thise fooles that been seculeer.
And whan that he was passed sixty yeer,
Were it for hoolynesse or for dotage,
I kan nat seye, but swich a greet corage
Hadde this knyght to been a wedded man 1255
That day and nyght he dooth al that he kan
T'espien where he myghte wedded be,
Preyinge oure Lord to graunten him that he
Mighte ones knowe of thilke blisful lyf
That is bitwixe an housbonde and his wyf, 1260

And for to lyve under that hooly boond
With which that first God man and womman
  bond.
"Noon oother lyf," seyde he, "is worth a bene;
For wedlok is so esy and so clene,
That in this world it is a paradys." 1265
Thus seyde this olde knyght, that was so wys.
  And certeinly, as sooth as God is kyng,
To take a wyf it is a glorious thyng,
And namely whan a man is oold and hoor;
Thanne is a wyf the fruyt of his tresor. 1270
Thanne sholde he take a yong wyf and a feir,
On which he myghte engendren hym an heir,
And lede his lyf in joye and in solas,
Where as thise bacheleris synge "allas,"
Whan that they fynden any adversitee 1275

1241. art, subject.

  The Merchant's Tale. The story which the Merchant tells is found in many versions, but, as is the case with other fabliaux in *The Canterbury Tales*, we do not have its immediate source. A number of the more important analogues are printed in *SA*. In the long introduction to the pear-tree episode Chaucer has woven together bits from Jerome's treatise *Against Jovinian*, the *Roman de la Rose*, Deschamps' long poem called *Le Miroir de Mariage*, and elsewhere. In it there are so many ideas and phrases in common with *The Wife of Bath's Prologue* that one can hardly doubt that the two were written at much the same time.
  The long passage (ll. 1267–1392) in which the Merchant, speaking in his own person, defends marriage both for the many blessings which a wife brings to her husband and as a sacrament of the Church, defies Theophrastus and his cynical views, and supports his argument with Biblical examples, seems very strange coming from a man who has just told the company of his own disastrous experience in wedlock, not two months old. Those who believe that the tale was always intended for the Merchant consider these lines ironic. On the other hand, Manly noted (*The Canterbury Tales*, p. 596), "The Tale itself can hardly have been originally composed with the Merchant in mind as the narrator" and that "there are several lines which indicate that the narrator belonged to the clergy (ll. 1251, 1322, 1384, 1390 and 2055)." This is the view of the present writer, who believes that the tale was originally written for the Friar and was transferred to the Merchant when Chaucer came across a story to which the Summoner could retaliate (see "The Original Teller of the Merchant's Tale," *MP*, xxxv. 15–26). It is only fair to add that Mrs. Dempster has defended her own view (that the Merchant's words are ironical) in *MP*, xxxvi. 1–8.
  1246. Pavye, Pavia, a city some 20 miles south of Milan. **1251. seculeer,** of the laity, as opposed to the clergy. **1254. corage,** heart, desire. **1259. thilke blisful lyf.** This is the old knight's opinion, not the Merchant's. **1267. And certeinly . . .** At this point the narrator, it appears, begins to speak in his own person. **1269. namely,** especially. **hoor,** hoar. **1270. the fruyt,** the best part.

In love, which nys but childyssh vanytee.
And trewely it sit wel to be so,
That bacheleris have often peyne and wo;
On brotel ground they buylde, and brotelnesse
They fynde, whan they wene sikernesse.   1280
They lyve but as a bryd or as a beest,
In libertee, and under noon arreest,
Ther as a wedded man in his estaat
Lyveth a lyf blisful and ordinaat,
Under this yok of mariage ybounde.   1285
Wel may his herte in joye and blisse habounde,
For who kan be so buxom as a wyf?
Who is so trewe, and eek so ententyf
To kepe hym, syk and hool, as is his make?
For wele or wo she wole hym nat forsake;   1290
She nys nat wery hym to love and serve,
Thogh that he lye bedrede, til he sterve.
And yet somme clerkes seyn it nys nat so,
Of whiche he Theofraste is oon of tho.
What force though Theofraste liste lye?   1295
"Ne take no wyf," quod he, "for housbondrye,
As for to spare in houshold thy dispence.
A trewe servant dooth moore diligence
Thy good to kepe, than thyn owene wyf,
For she wol clayme half part al hir lyf.   1300
And if that thou be syk, so God me save,
Thy verray freendes, or a trewe knave,
Wol kepe thee bet than she that waiteth ay
After thy good and hath doon many a day.
And if thou take a wyf unto thyn hoold,   1305
Ful lightly maystow been a cokewold."
This sentence, and an hundred thynges worse,

Writeth this man, ther God his bones corse!
But take no kep of al swich vanytee;
Deffie Theofraste, and herke me.   1310
A wyf is Goddes yifte verraily;
Alle othere manere yiftes hardily,
As londes, rentes, pasture, or commune,
Or moebles, alle been yiftes of Fortune,
That passen as a shadwe upon a wal.   1315
But drede nat, if pleynly speke I shal,
A wyf wol laste, and in thyn hous endure,
Wel lenger than thee list, paraventure.
Mariage is a ful greet sacrement.
He which that hath no wyf, I holde hym shent;
He lyveth helplees and al desolat,—   1321
I speke of folk in seculer estaat.
And herke why, I sey nat this for noght,
That womman is for mannes help ywroght.
The hye God, whan he hadde Adam maked,
And saugh him al allone, bely-naked,   1326
God of his grete goodnesse seyde than,
"Lat us now make an help unto this man
Lyk to hymself"; and thanne he made him Eve.
Heere may ye se, and heerby may ye preve,   1330
That wyf is mannes help and his confort,
His paradys terrestre, and his disport.
So buxom and so vertuous is she,
They moste nedes lyve in unitee.
O flessh they been, and o flessh, as I gesse,   1335
Hath but oon herte, in wele and in distresse.
A wyf! a, Seinte Marie, *benedicite!*
How myghte a man han any adversitee
That hath a wyf? Certes, I kan nat seye.

1276. vanytee, foolishness. **1277. it sit wel,** it is fitting. **1279. brotel,** fragile, unsafe. **brotelnesse,** insecurity. **1280. wene sikernesse,** think (to find) security. **1281. bryd,** bird. **1282. arreest,** restraint. **1283. Ther as,** whereas. **1284. ordinaat,** well ordered. **1287. buxom,** obedient, obliging. **1288. ententyf,** attentive. **1289. make,** mate. **1292. bedrede,** bedridden. **sterve,** die. **1294. Theofraste.** Theophrastus. His *Liber Aureolus de Nuptiis* is now lost, but a part of it is quoted by Jerome in his treatise against Jovinian (Bk i, ch. 47). It is a violent argument against marriage. **tho,** those. **1295. What force,** what matter. **1296. housbondrye,** economy. **1297. dispence,** expenditure. **1299. good,** goods. **1302. knave,** male servant. **1305. hoold,** keeping. **1306. cokewold,** cuckold. **1307. sentence,** opinion. **1308. ther,** hortatory *ther;* see Language, § 73. **corse,** curse. **1309. kep,** heed. **vanytee,** nonsense. **1312. hardily,** certainly. **1313. commune,** common, rights shared with other tenants on a manor, such as grazing one's beasts on uncultivated land, fishing, cutting wood, etc. These naturally had economic value. **1314. moebles,** movable goods, personal property. **1318. Wel lenger than thee list.** Much of the passage is taken from Albertano of Brescia's *Liber de Amore et Dilectione Dei,* but this line is Chaucer's addition. For the pertinent passages in Albertano see Koeppel, *Archiv,* LXXXVI. 40–1. **1319. sacrement.** Marriage is one of the seven sacraments of the Church. **1320. shent,** ruined, lost. **1321. al desolat,** completely lonely. **1322. in seculer estaat.** In this parenthetical remark the narrator is careful to indicate that his advocating of marriage does not apply to the clergy. Cf. l. 1251. **1330. preve,** prove. **1332. paradys terrestre,** earthly paradise. **disport,** delight. **1335. O flessh they been.** Cf. *Ephesians,* 5:31: and they two shall be one flesh (also *Matthew,* 19:5 and *Mark,* 10:8). **1339. Certes,** certainly.

The blisse which that is bitwixe hem tweye
Ther may no tonge telle, or herte thynke. 1341
If he be povre, she helpeth hym to swynke;
She kepeth his good, and wasteth never a deel;
Al that hire housbonde lust, hire liketh weel;
She seith nat ones "nay," whan he seith
  "ye." 1345
"Do this," seith he; "Al redy, sire," seith she.
O blisful ordre of wedlok precious,
Thou art so murye, and eek so vertuous,
And so commended and approved eek
That every man that halt hym worth a leek,
Upon his bare knees oughte al his lyf 1351
Thanken his God that hym hath sent a wyf,
Or elles preye to God hym for to sende
A wyf, to laste unto his lyves ende.
For thanne his lyf is set in sikernesse; 1355
He may nat be deceyved, as I gesse,
So that he werke after his wyves reed.
Thanne may he boldely beren up his heed,
They been so trewe, and therwithal so wyse;
For which, if thou wolt werken as the wyse,
Do alwey so as wommen wol thee rede. 1361
  Lo, how that Jacob, as thise clerkes rede,
By good conseil of his mooder Rebekke,
Boond the kydes skyn aboute his nekke,
For which his fadres benysoun he wan. 1365
  Lo Judith, as the storie eek telle kan,
By wys conseil she Goddes peple kepte,
And slow hym Olofernus, whil he slepte.
  Lo Abigayl, by good conseil, how she
Saved hir housbonde Nabal, whan that he 1370
Sholde han be slayn; and looke, Ester also
By good conseil delyvered out of wo

The peple of God, and made hym Mardochee
Of Assuere enhaunced for to be.
  Ther nys no thyng in gree superlatyf, 1375
As seith Senek, above an humble wyf.
  Suffre thy wyves tonge, as Catoun bit;
She shal comande, and thou shalt suffren it,
And yet she wole obeye of curteisye.
A wyf is kepere of thyn housbondrye; 1380
Wel may the sike man biwaille and wepe,
Ther as ther nys no wyf the hous to kepe.
I warne thee, if wisely thou wolt wirche,
Love wel thy wyf, as Crist loved his chirche.
If thou lovest thyself, thou lovest thy wyf; 1385
No man hateth his flessh, but in his lyf
He fostreth it, and therfore bidde I thee,
Cherisse thy wyf, or thou shalt nevere thee.
Housbonde and wyf, what so men jape or
  pleye,
Of worldly folk holden the siker weye; 1390
They been so knyt ther may noon harm bityde,
And namely upon the wyves syde.
For which this Januarie, of whom I tolde,
Considered hath, inwith his dayes olde,
The lusty lyf, the vertuous quyete, 1395
That is in mariage hony-sweete;
And for his freendes on a day he sente,
To tellen hem th'effect of his entente.
  With face sad his tale he hath hem toold.
He seyde, "Freendes, I am hoor and oold, 1400
And almoost, God woot, on my pittes brynke;
Upon my soule somwhat moste I thynke.
I have my body folily despended;
Blessed be God that it shal been amended!
For I wol be, certeyn, a wedded man, 1405

1342. **swynke**, work. 1343. **kepeth his good**, looks after his possessions. 1348. **murye**, pleasant. 1355. **sikernesse**, security. 1357. **So that**, provided. 1361. **rede**, counsel. 1363. **Rebekke**, etc. The examples of Rebecca, Judith, Abigail, and Esther are cited also in the *Melibeus* (which is not included in the present volume). Chaucer took them from Albertano of Brescia. See the article of Koeppel referred to in the note to l. 1318. For the Biblical stories see *Genesis*, 27:1–29; the apocryphal book of *Judith*, chap. 11–13; *1 Samuel*, 25:1–35; *Esther*, 7:1–10. 1375. **in gree superlatyf**, in the highest favor, more to be desired. 1377. **bit**, bids. The reference is to the *Distichs of Cato*, but is also taken at second hand from Albertano of Brescia. 1380. **housbondrye**, possessions (household goods, farm produce, etc.). 1384. **Love wel thy wyf . . .** Cf. the epistle of St. Paul (*Ephesians*, 5:25): Husbands, love your wives, even as Christ also loved the church. 1385. **If thou lovest thyself . . .** Cf. *Ephesians*, 5:28: He that loveth his wife loveth himself. 1386. **No man hateth . . .** Cf. *Ephesians*, 5:29: For no man ever yet hated his own flesh; but nourisheth and cherisheth it. 1388. **thee**, thrive. 1389. **what so**, however. 1390. **Of worldly folk.** See note to l. 1322. **siker**, surer. 1391. **bityde**, happen. 1393. **For which this Januarie, of whom I tolde.** Further evidence that the narrator has been speaking in his own person. 1394. **inwith**, within, in. 1395. **lusty**, enjoyable. 1398. **effect**, substance. 1399. **sad**, composed. 1403. **folily**, foolishly.

And that anoon in al the haste I kan.
Unto som mayde fair and tendre of age,
I prey yow, shapeth for my mariage
Al sodeynly, for I wol nat abyde;
And I wol fonde t'espien, on my syde,   1410
To whom I may be wedded hastily.
But forasmuche as ye been mo than I,
Ye shullen rather swich a thyng espyen
Than I, and where me best were to allyen.
    But o thyng warne I yow, my freendes deere,
I wol noon oold wyf han in no manere.   1416
She shal nat passe twenty yeer, certayn;
Oold fissh and yong flessh wolde I have ful fayn.
Bet is," quod he, "a pyk than a pykerel,
And bet than old boef is the tendre veel.   1420
I wol no womman thritty yeer of age;
It is but bene-straw and greet forage.
And eek thise olde wydwes, God it woot,
They konne so muchel craft on Wades boot,
So muchel broken harm, whan that hem
    leste,   1425
That with hem sholde I nevere lyve in reste.
For sondry scoles maken sotile clerkis;
Womman of manye scoles half a clerk is.
But certeynly, a yong thyng may men gye,
Right as men may warm wex with handes plye.
Wherfore I sey yow pleynly, in a clause,   1431
I wol noon oold wyf han right for this cause.
For if so were I hadde swich myschaunce,
That I in hire ne koude han no plesaunce,
Thanne sholde I lede my lyf in avoutrye,   1435
And go streight to the devel, whan I dye.
Ne children sholde I none upon hire geten;
Yet were me levere houndes had me eten,
Than that myn heritage sholde falle

In straunge hand, and this I telle yow alle.   1440
I dote nat, I woot the cause why
Men sholde wedde, and forthermoore woot I,
Ther speketh many a man of mariage
That woot namoore of it than woot my page,
For whiche causes man sholde take a wyf.   1445
If he ne may nat lyven chaast his lyf,
Take hym a wyf with greet devocioun,
By cause of leveful procreacioun
Of children, to th'onour of God above,
And nat oonly for paramour or love;   1450
And for they sholde leccherye eschue,
And yelde hir dette whan that it is due;
Or for that ech of hem sholde helpen oother
In meschief, as a suster shal the brother,
And lyve in chastitee ful holily.   1455
But sires, by youre leve, that am nat I.
For, God be thanked! I dar make avaunt,
I feele my lymes stark and suffisaunt
To do al that a man bilongeth to;
I woot myselven best what I may do.   1460
Though I be hoor, I fare as dooth a tree
That blosmeth er that fruyt ywoxen bee;
And blosmy tree nys neither drye ne deed.
I feele me nowhere hoor but on myn heed;
Myn herte and alle my lymes been as grene   1465
As laurer thurgh the yeer is for to sene.
And syn that ye han herd al myn entente,
I prey yow to my wyl ye wole assente."
    Diverse men diversely hym tolde
Of mariage manye ensamples olde.   1470
Somme blamed it, somme preysed it, certeyn;
But atte laste, shortly for to seyn,
As alday falleth altercacioun
Bitwixen freendes in disputisoun,

1409. **Al sodeynly,** at once. 1410. **fonde,** strive. 1413. **rather,** sooner. 1418. **Oold,** *i.e.* fully grown. The expression, which comes from Albertano, is proverbial. 1419. **pyk . . . pykerel.** A pickerel is a young pike. 1422. **greet forage,** a lot of dry fodder. 1424. **Wades boot.** Although Wade was a famous hero (see note to *TC* 3. 614), the significance of the allusion escapes us. **boot,** boat. 1425. **broken harm.** Skeat's interpretation "petty annoyances" is plausible; Cassidy (*MLN,* LVIII. 23–7) suggests construing *broken* as an infinitive, with the sense "to make use of." 1427. **For sondry scoles . . .** The line is almost the same as D 44c, and the other half of the couplet may be read in the light of that passage. The meaning is that women are on the way to being learned in many schools of practical experience. 1429. **gye,** guide. 1430. **plye,** bend, mould. 1431. **in a clause,** in a few words. 1435. **avoutrye,** adultery. 1445. **whiche,** what. 1448. **leveful,** permissible, lawful. 1450. **paramour,** passion. 1454. **meschief,** misfortune. 1456. **But sires . . .** Cf. *WBProl.,* D 112. 1457. **make avaunt,** boast. 1458. **stark,** strong. 1463. **blosmy,** full of blossoms. 1466. **laurer,** laurel. 1473. **alday falleth,** continually happens.

Ther fil a stryf bitwixe his bretheren two, 1475
Of whiche that oon was cleped Placebo,
Justinus soothly called was that oother.
    Placebo seyde, "O Januarie, brother,
Ful litel nede hadde ye, my lord so deere,
Conseil to axe of any that is heere, 1480
But that ye been so ful of sapience
That yow ne liketh, for youre heighe prudence,
To weyven fro the word of Salomon.
This word seyde he unto us everychon:
'Wirk alle thyng by conseil,' thus seyde he, 1485
'And thanne shaltow nat repente thee.'
But though that Salomon spak swich a word,
Myn owene deere brother and my lord,
So wysly God my soule brynge at reste,
I holde youre owene conseil is the beste. 1490
For, brother myn, of me taak this motyf,
I have now been a court-man al my lyf,
And God it woot, though I unworthy be,
I have stonden in ful greet degree
Abouten lordes of ful heigh estaat; 1495
Yet hadde I nevere with noon of hem debaat.
I nevere hem contraried, trewely;
I woot wel that my lord kan moore than I.
With that he seith, I holde it ferme and stable;
I seye the same, or elles thyng semblable. 1500
A ful greet fool is any conseillour
That serveth any lord of heigh honour,
That dar presume, or elles thenken it,
That his conseil sholde passe his lordes wit.
Nay, lordes been no fooles, by my fay! 1505
Ye han youreselven shewed heer to-day
So heigh sentence, so holily and weel,
That I consente and conferme everydeel
Youre wordes alle and youre opinioun.

By God, ther nys no man in al this toun, 1510
Ne in Ytaille, that koude bet han sayd!
Crist halt hym of this conseil ful wel apayd.
And trewely, it is an heigh corage
Of any man that stapen is in age
To take a yong wyf; by my fader kyn, 1515
Youre herte hangeth on a joly pyn!
Dooth now in this matiere right as yow leste,
For finally I holde it for the beste."
    Justinus, that ay stille sat and herde,
Right in this wise he to Placebo answerde: 1520
"Now, brother myn, be pacient, I preye,
Syn ye han seyd, and herkneth what I seye.
Senek, amonges othere wordes wyse,
Seith that a man oghte hym right wel avyse
To whom he yeveth his lond or his catel. 1525
And syn I oghte avyse me right wel
To whom I yeve my good awey fro me,
Wel muchel moore I oghte avysed be
To whom I yeve my body for alwey.
I warne yow wel, it is no childes pley 1530
To take a wyf withouten avysement.
Men moste enquere, this is myn assent,
Wher she be wys, or sobre, or dronkelewe,
Or proud, or elles ootherweys a shrewe,
A chidestere, or wastour of thy good, 1535
Or riche, or poore, or elles mannyssh wood.
Al be it so that no man fynden shal
Noon in this world that trotteth hool in al,
Ne man, ne beest, swich as men koude devyse;
But nathelees it oghte ynough suffise 1540
With any wyf, if so were that she hadde
Mo goode thewes than hire vices badde;
And al this axeth leyser for t'enquere.
For, God it woot, I have wept many a teere

1476. cleped, named. **1483. weyven fro,** abandon. **Salomon.** Not Solomon, but *Ecclesiasticus*, 32:24. **1489. wysly,** surely. **1491. motyf,** argument, thought. **1492. court-man,** courtier. **1494. degree,** rank. **1499. With that,** as to what. **1507. holily,** virtuously. **1512. halt,** holds. **wel apayd,** satisfied, pleased. **1513. corage,** spirit. **1514. stapen,** advanced (*lit.* stepped). **1515. fader,** father's. **1516. hangeth on a joly pyn,** is lively or merry; an idiomatic expression, the semantic development of which is not clear. **1523. Senek,** Seneca. The saying is also attributed to Cato, but Koeppel showed (*Anglia*, XIII. 183) that it occurs in more nearly Chaucer's form in Valerius Maximus. It is also found in Walter Map (*Ad Rufinum*), and in view of Chaucer's use of this epistle elsewhere this seems the most likely place for him to have got it. **1525. catel,** property. **1527. good,** goods. **1532. assent,** opinion. **1533. Wher,** whether. **dronkelewe,** given to drunkenness. **1535. chidestere,** scolding woman. **1536. mannyssh wood,** humanly (naturally) mad; but Utley's suggestion "man-crazy" (*MLN*, LIII. 359–62) is not impossible. **1538. trotteth . . .,** trots perfectly in all respects. The image was probably suggested by a passage in the *Miroir de Mariage*, which Chaucer is here condensing, in which choosing a wife is compared to buying a horse (l. 1562: *ilz troteront dessus la monstre*). **1539. devyse,** imagine. **1542. thewes,** qualities.

Ful pryvely, syn I have had a wyf.   1545
Preyse whoso wole a wedded mannes lyf,
Certein I fynde in it but cost and care
And observances, of alle blisses bare.
And yet, God woot, my neighebores aboute,
And namely of wommen many a route,   1550
Seyn that I have the mooste stedefast wyf,
And eek the mekeste oon that bereth lyf;
But I woot best where wryngeth me my sho.
Ye mowe, for me, right as yow liketh do;
Avyseth yow—ye been a man of age—   1555
How that ye entren into mariage,
And namely with a yong wyf and a fair.
By hym that made water, erthe, and air,
The yongeste man that is in al this route
Is bisy ynough to bryngen it aboute   1560
To han his wyf allone. Trusteth me,
Ye shul nat plesen hire fully yeres thre,—
This is to seyn, to doon hire ful plesaunce.
A wyf axeth ful many an observaunce.
I prey yow that ye be nat yvele apayd.   1565
   "Wel," quod this Januarie, "and hastow
      sayd?
Straw for thy Senek, and for thy proverbes!
I counte nat a panyer ful of herbes
Of scole-termes. Wyser men than thow,
As thou hast herd, assenteden right now   1570
To my purpos. Placebo, what sey ye?"
   "I seye it is a cursed man," quod he,
"That letteth matrimoigne, sikerly."
And with that word they rysen sodeynly,
And been assented fully that he sholde   1575
Be wedded whanne hym liste, and where he
   wolde.
   Heigh fantasye and curious bisynesse
Fro day to day gan in the soule impresse
Of Januarie aboute his mariage.
Many fair shap and many a fair visage   1580
Ther passeth thurgh his herte nyght by nyght,

As whoso tooke a mirour, polisshed bryght,
And sette it in a commune market-place,
Thanne sholde he se ful many a figure pace
By his mirour; and in the same wyse   1585
Gan Januarie inwith his thoght devyse
Of maydens whiche that dwelten hym bisyde.
He wiste nat wher that he myghte abyde.
For if that oon have beaute in hir face,
Another stant so in the peples grace   1590
For hire sadnesse and hire benyngnytee
That of the peple grettest voys hath she;
And somme were riche, and hadden badde
   name.
But nathelees, bitwixe ernest and game,
He atte laste apoynted hym on oon,   1595
And leet alle othere from his herte goon,
And chees hire of his owene auctoritee;
For love is blynd alday, and may nat see.
And whan that he was in his bed ybroght,
He purtreyed in his herte and in his thoght   1600
Hir fresshe beautee and hir age tendre,
Hir myddel smal, hire armes longe and sklen-
   dre,
Hir wise governaunce, hir gentillesse,
Hir wommanly berynge, and hire sadnesse.
And whan that he on hire was conde-
   scended,   1605
Hym thoughte his choys myghte nat ben
   amended.
For whan that he hymself concluded hadde,
Hym thoughte ech oother mannes wit so badde
That inpossible it were to repplye
Agayn his choys, this was his fantasye.   1610
His freendes sente he to, at his instaunce,
And preyed hem to doon hym that plesaunce,
That hastily they wolden to hym come;
He wolde abregge hir labour, alle and some.
Nedeth namoore for hym to go ne ryde;   1615
He was apoynted ther he wolde abyde.

1548. observances, obligations. **1550. of wommen many a route,** a lot of women. **1553. But I woot best . . .** Cf. D 492. **1554. for me,** as far as I am concerned. **1559. route,** company. **1564. observaunce,** attention. **1565. yvele apayd,** displeased. **1568. panyer,** basket. **1573. letteth,** hinders. **1577. curious bisynesse,** eager attention. **1578. impresse,** crowd. **1586. inwith,** within. **1587. hym bisyde,** nearby. **1591. sadnesse,** steadfastness. **benyngnytee,** graciousness. **1597. chees,** chose. **auctoritee,** judgment. **1598. alday,** always. **1600. purtreyed,** pictured. **1605. condescended,** agreed, settled (upon). **1615. go ne ryde,** walk nor ride (a stock phrase). **1616. was apoynted,** had made up his mind.

Placebo cam, and eek his freendes soone,
And alderfirst he bad hem alle a boone,
That noon of hem none argumentes make
Agayn the purpos which that he hath take, 1620
Which purpos was plesant to God, seyde he,
And verray ground of his prosperitee.

He seyde ther was a mayden in the toun,
Which that of beautee hadde greet renoun,
Al were it so she were of smal degree; 1625
Suffiseth hym hir yowthe and hir beautee.
Which mayde, he seyde, he wolde han to his
      wyf,
To lede in ese and hoolynesse his lyf;
And thanked God that he myghte han hire al,
That no wight his blisse parten shal. 1630
And preyde hem to laboure in this nede,
And shapen that he faille nat to spede;
For thanne, he seyde, his spirit was at ese.
"Thanne is," quod he, "no thyng may me dis-
      plese,
Save o thyng priketh in my conscience, 1635
The which I wol reherce in youre presence.

I have," quod he, "herd seyd, ful yoore ago,
Ther may no man han parfite blisses two,—
This is to seye, in erthe and eek in hevene.
For though he kepe hym fro the synnes sevene,
And eek from every branche of thilke tree, 1641
Yet is ther so parfit felicitee
And so greet ese and lust in mariage,
That evere I am agast now in myn age
That I shal lede now so myrie a lyf, 1645
So delicat, withouten wo and stryf,
That I shal have myn hevene in erthe heere.
For sith that verray hevene is boght so deere
With tribulacioun and greet penaunce,
How sholde I thanne, that lyve in swich ples-
      aunce 1650

As alle wedded men doon with hire wyvys,
Come to the blisse ther Crist eterne on lyve ys?
This is my drede, and ye, my bretheren tweye,
Assoilleth me this questioun, I preye."

Justinus, which that hated his folye, 1655
Answerde anon right in his japerye;
And for he wolde his longe tale abregge,
He wolde noon auctoritee allegge,
But seyde, "Sire, so ther be noon obstacle
Oother than this, God of his hygh myracle 1660
And of his mercy may so for yow wirche
That, er ye have youre right of hooly chirche,
Ye may repente of wedded mannes lyf,
In which ye seyn ther is no wo ne stryf.
And elles, God forbede but he sente 1665
A wedded man hym grace to repente
Wel ofte rather than a sengle man!
And therfore, sire—the beste reed I kan—
Dispeire yow noght, but have in youre mem-
      orie,
Paraunter she may be youre purgatorie! 1670
She may be Goddes meene and Goddes
      whippe;
Thanne shal youre soule up to hevene skippe
Swifter than dooth an arwe out of a bowe.
I hope to God, herafter shul ye knowe
That ther nys no so greet felicitee 1675
In mariage, ne nevere mo shal bee,
That yow shal lette of youre savacioun,
So that ye use, as skile is and resoun,
The lustes of youre wyf attemprely,
And that ye plese hire nat to amorously, 1680
And that ye kepe yow eek from oother synne.
My tale is doon, for my wit is thynne.
Beth nat agast herof, my brother deere,
But lat us waden out of this mateere.
The Wyf of Bathe, if ye han understonde, 1685

1618. **bad hem . . . a boone,** asked them a favor. 1622. **verray,** true. 1625. **Al,** although. **smal degree,** humble station. 1630. **parten,** share. 1632. **shapen,** arrange. 1637. **ful yoore ago,** long ago. 1640. **synnes sevene,** the seven deadly sins. 1641. **of thilke tree.** Each sin had many branches, together arranged in the form of a tree. 1646. **delicat,** delightful. 1652. **on lyve,** alive. 1654. **Assoilleth,** clear up, solve. 1656. **japerye,** joking, mockery. 1660. **myracle,** miraculous power. 1661. **wirche,** work, bring about. 1662. **er . . . hooly chirche,** *i.e.* before you die. 1665. **God forbede but he sente,** God forbid that he should not send. 1670. **Paraunter,** peradventure. Cf. the Wife of Bath's statement (D 489): *in erthe I was his purgatorie.* 1671. **meene,** instrument. 1677. **lette of,** keep from. 1678. **So that,** provided. **skile,** reason. 1679. **attemprely,** in moderation. 1685. Chaucer forgets that Justinus could not have heard the Wife of Bath's discourse.

Of mariage, which we have on honde,
Declared hath ful wel in litel space.
Fareth now wel, God have yow in his grace."
   And with this word this Justyn and his
      brother
Han take hir leve, and ech of hem of
   oother.   1690
For whan they saugh that it moste nedes be,
They wroghten so, by sly and wys tretee,
That she, this mayden, which that Mayus
   highte,
As hastily as evere that she myghte,
Shal wedded be unto this Januarie.   1695
I trowe it were to longe yow to tarie,
If I yow tolde of every scrit and bond
By which that she was feffed in his lond,
Or for to herknen of hir riche array.
But finally ycomen is the day   1700
That to the chirche bothe be they went
For to receyve the hooly sacrement.
Forth comth the preest, with stole aboute his
   nekke,
And bad hire be lyk Sarra and Rebekke
In wysdom and in trouthe of mariage;   1705
And seyde his orisons, as is usage,
And croucheth hem, and bad God sholde hem
   blesse,
And made al siker ynogh with hoolynesse.
   Thus been they wedded with solempnitee,
And at the feeste sitteth he and she   1710
With othere worthy folk upon the deys.
Al ful of joye and blisse is the paleys,
And ful of instrumentz and of vitaille,
The mooste deyntevous of al Ytaille.
Biforn hem stoode instrumentz of swich soun

That Orpheus, ne of Thebes Amphioun,   1716
Ne maden nevere swich a melodye.
At every cours thanne cam loud mynstralcye,
That nevere tromped Joab for to heere,
Nor he Theodomas yet half so cleere,   1720
At Thebes, whan the citee was in doute.
Bacus the wyn hem shenketh al aboute,
And Venus laugheth upon every wight,
For Januarie was bicome hir knyght,
And wolde bothe assayen his corage   1725
In libertee, and eek in mariage;
And with hire fyrbrond in hire hand aboute
Daunceth biforn the bryde and al the route.
And certeinly, I dar right wel seyn this,
Ymeneus, that god of weddyng is,   1730
Saugh nevere his lyf so myrie a wedded man.
Hoold thou thy pees, thou poete Marcian,
That writest us that ilke weddyng murie
Of hire Philologie and hym Mercurie,
And of the songes that the Muses songe!   1735
To smal is bothe thy penne, and eek thy tonge,
For to descryven of this mariage.
Whan tendre youthe hath wedded stoupyng
   age,
Ther is swich myrthe that it may nat be writen.
Assayeth it youreself, thanne may ye witen
If that I lye or noon in this matiere.   1741
   Mayus, that sit with so benyngne a chiere,
Hire to biholde it semed fayerye.
Queene Ester looked nevere with swich an yë
On Assuer, so meke a look hath she.   1745
I may yow nat devyse al hir beautee.
But thus muche of hire beautee telle I may,
That she was lyk the brighte morwe of May,
Fulfild of alle beautee and plesaunce.

1692. wroghten, brought it about. **sly,** skillful. **tretee,** negotiation. **1693. Mayus,** the masculine name of the month is probably used for the sake of the meter. **1697. scrit,** writing, deed. **1698. feffed,** enfeoffed, put in possession of. **1704. Sarra and Rebekke.** In the course of the marriage ceremony the priest prays, "May she be amiable to her husband as Rachel, wise as Rebecca, long-lived and faithful as Sarah." **1707. croucheth,** makes the sign of the cross. **1708. hoolynesse,** religious ceremony. **1711. deys,** dais. **1714. deyntevous,** delicious. **1716. Orpheus.** See note to *BD* 569. **Amphioun,** while the walls of Thebes were being built Amphion played his lyre so marvellously that the stones moved into place of their own accord. **1718. cours,** course of the meal. **1719. Joab . . . Theodomas.** See note to *HF* 1245. **1721. in doute,** in danger (*lit.* fear), when the city was besieged. **1722. Bacus,** Bacchus, the god of wine. **shenketh,** pours. **1726. In libertee,** unmarried. **1727. fyrbrond,** torch. **1730. Ymeneus,** Hymen, who generally carried the bridal torch, but in giving it to Venus Chaucer was following *RR*, 3424–6. **1731. his lyf,** in his life. **1732. Marcian,** Martianus Capella, whose treatise on the seven liberal arts is entitled *De Nuptiis Philologiae et Mercurii* (5th c.). **1741. or noon,** or no. **1743. fayerye,** enchantment, illusion. **1744. Queene Ester . . . Assuer.** Queen Esther . . . Ahasuerus; *Esther,* 5:2. **1746. devyse,** describe.

This Januarie is ravysshed in a traunce 1750
At every tyme he looked on hir face;
But in his herte he gan hire to manace
That he that nyght in armes wolde hire streyne
Harder than evere Parys dide Eleyne.
But nathelees yet hadde he greet pitee 1755
That thilke nyght offenden hire moste he,
And thoughte, "Allas! O tendre creature,
Now wolde God ye myghte wel endure
Al my corage, it is so sharp and keene!
I am agast ye shul it nat susteene. 1760
But God forbede that I dide al my myght!
Now wolde God that it were woxen nyght,
And that the nyght wolde lasten everemo.
I wolde that al this peple were ago."
And finally he dooth al his labour, 1765
As he best myghte, savynge his honour,
To haste hem fro the mete in subtil wyse.

The tyme cam that resoun was to ryse;
And after that men daunce and drynken faste,
And spices al aboute the hous they caste, 1770
And ful of joye and blisse is every man,—
Al but a squyer, highte Damyan,
Which carf biforn the knyght ful many a day.
He was so ravysshed on his lady May 1774
That for the verray peyne he was ny wood.
Almoost he swelte and swowned ther he stood,
So soore hath Venus hurt hym with hire brond,
As that she bar it daunsynge in hire hond;
And to his bed he wente hym hastily.
Namoore of hym as at this tyme speke I, 1780
But there I lete hym wepe ynogh and pleyne,
Til fresshe May wol rewen on his peyne.

O perilous fyr, that in the bedstraw bredeth!
O famulier foo, that his servyce bedeth!

O servant traytour, false hoomly hewe, 1785
Lyk to the naddre in bosom sly untrewe,
God shilde us alle from youre aqueyntaunce!
O Januarie, dronken in plesaunce
In mariage, se how thy Damyan,
Thyn owene squier and thy borne man, 1790
Entendeth for to do thee vileynye.
God graunte thee thy hoomly fo t'espye!
For in this world nys worse pestilence
Than hoomly foo al day in thy presence. 1794

Parfourned hath the sonne his ark diurne;
No lenger may the body of hym sojurne
On th'orisonte, as in that latitude.
Night with his mantel, that is derk and rude,
Gan oversprede the hemysperie aboute;
For which departed is this lusty route 1800
Fro Januarie, with thank on every syde.
Hoom to hir houses lustily they ryde,
Where as they doon hir thynges as hem leste,
And whan they sye hir tyme, goon to reste.
Soone after that, this hastif Januarie 1805
Wolde go to bedde, he wolde no lenger tarye.
He drynketh ypocras, clarree, and vernage
Of spices hoote, t'encreessen his corage;
And many a letuarie hath he ful fyn,
Swiche as the cursed monk, daun Constantyn,
Hath writen in his book De Coitu; 1811
To eten hem alle he nas no thyng eschu.
And to his privee freendes thus seyde he:
"For Goddes love, as soone as it may be,
Lat voyden al this hous in curteys wyse." 1815
And they han doon right as he wol devyse.
Men drynken, and the travers drawe anon.
The bryde was broght abedde as stille as stoon;
And whan the bed was with the preest yblessed,

1752. **manace,** threaten. 1753. **streyne,** clasp. 1754. **Parys . . . Eleyne,** Paris . . . Helen. 1756. **offenden,** give pain to. 1759. **corage,** desire. 1760. **agast,** afraid. 1762. **woxen,** grown, become. 1765. **dooth al his labour,** makes every effort. 1767. **the mete,** the wedding feast. 1769. **men,** the impers. pron., they. 1772. **highte,** named. 1773. **carf,** carved. 1774. **ravysshed,** enraptured. 1775. **wood,** mad. 1776. **swelte,** perished. 1784. **famulier,** of one's own household. **bedeth,** offers. 1785. **hoomly hewe,** domestic servant. 1786. **naddre,** adder. 1791. **vileynye,** wrong. 1795. **Parfourned,** completed. **diurne,** daily. 1797. **orisonte,** horizon. 1799. **hemysperie,** hemisphere. 1800. **lusty route,** joyful company. 1803. **hir thynges . . . leste,** whatever they pleased. 1804. **sye,** saw. 1805. **hastif,** eager, impatient. 1807. **ypocras,** spiced wine. **clarree,** spiced wine sweetened with honey and strained. **vernage,** a sweet Italian wine. See note to B 1261. 1808. **corage,** desire. 1809. **letuarie,** electuary, a medicine mixed with syrup. 1810. **daun,** don, a familiar title for a monk. **Constantyn,** see note to A 433. 1811. *De Coitu.* The treatise, according to Skeat, is printed in the Basel, 1536, edition of his works. For an account of it see the article of M. Bassan cited in the note to A 433. 1812. **eschu,** loath. 1815. **Lat voyden,** do clear out. 1817. **travers,** curtain forming a screen. 1819. **with,** by.

Out of the chambre hath every wight hym
   dressed;   1820
And Januarie hath faste in armes take
His fresshe May, his paradys, his make.
He lulleth hire, he kisseth hire ful ofte;
With thikke brustles of his berd unsofte,
Lyk to the skyn of houndfyssh, sharp as brere—
For he was shave al newe in his manere—   1826
He rubbeth hire aboute hir tendre face,
And seyde thus, "Allas! I moot trespace
To yow, my spouse, and yow greetly offende,
Er tyme come that I wil doun descende.   1830
But nathelees, considereth this," quod he,
"Ther nys no werkman, whatsoevere he be,
That may bothe werke wel and hastily;
This wol be doon at leyser parfitly.
It is no fors how longe that we pleye;   1835
In trewe wedlok coupled be we tweye;
And blessed be the yok that we been inne,
For in oure actes we mowe do no synne.
A man may do no synne with his wyf,
Ne hurte hymselven with his owene knyf;   1840
For we han leve to pleye us by the lawe."
Thus laboureth he til that the day gan dawe;
And thanne he taketh a soppe in fyn clarree,
And upright in his bed thanne sitteth he,
And after that he sang ful loude and cleere,   1845
And kiste his wyf, and made wantown cheere.
He was al coltissh, ful of ragerye,
And ful of jargon as a flekked pye.
The slakke skyn aboute his nekke shaketh,   1849
Whil that he sang, so chaunteth he and craketh.
But God woot what that May thoughte in hir
   herte,
Whan she hym saugh up sittynge in his sherte,
In his nyght-cappe, and with his nekke lene;
She preyseth nat his pleyyng worth a bene.

Thanne seide he thus, "My reste wol I take;
Now day is come, I may no lenger wake."   1856
And doun he leyde his heed, and sleep til
   pryme.
And afterward, whan that he saugh his tyme,
Up ryseth Januarie; but fresshe May
Heeld hire chambre unto the fourthe day,   1860
As usage is of wyves for the beste.
For every labour somtyme moot han reste,
Or elles longe may he nat endure;
This is to seyn, no lyves creature,
Be it of fyssh, or bryd, or beest, or man.   1865
   Now wol I speke of woful Damyan,
That langwissheth for love, as ye shul heere;
Therfore I speke to hym in this manere:
I seye, "O sely Damyan, allas!
Andswere to my demaunde, as in this cas.   1870
How shaltow to thy lady, fresshe May,
Telle thy wo? She wole alwey seye nay.
Eek if thou speke, she wol thy wo biwreye.
God be thyn help! I kan no bettre seye."
   This sike Damyan in Venus fyr   1875
So brenneth that he dyeth for desyr,
For which he putte his lyf in aventure.
No lenger myghte he in this wise endure,
But prively a penner gan he borwe,
And in a lettre wroot he al his sorwe,   1880
In manere of a compleynt or a lay,
Unto his faire, fresshe lady May;
And in a purs of sylk, heng on his sherte
He hath it put, and leyde it at his herte.
   The moone, that at noon was thilke day   1885
That Januarie hath wedded fresshe May
In two of Tawr, was into Cancre glyden;
So longe hath Mayus in hir chambre abyden,
As custume is unto thise nobles alle.
A bryde shal nat eten in the halle   1890

1820. hym dressed, betaken himself. **1823. lulleth,** soothes. **1825. houndfyssh,** dogfish, a kind of small shark. **brere,** briar. **1828–9. trespace To,** commit offense against. **1834. wol,** must. **1835. It is no fors,** it does not matter. **1841. pleye us,** enjoy ourselves. **1843. soppe,** a piece of bread soaked in wine. **1846. made wantown cheere,** behaved amorously. **1847. ragerye,** wantonness. **1848. jargon,** chatter. **flekked pye,** spotted magpie. **1850. chaunteth,** sings. **craketh,** croaks. **1854. preyseth,** values. **1857. sleep,** slept. **pryme,** 9 A.M. **1862. labour.** The Lincoln MS reads *laborer*, which would give an antecedent for *he* in the next line, but the evidence is overwhelmingly in favor of the reading in the text. **moot,** must. **1864. lyves,** living. **1869. sely,** poor. **1873. biwreye,** betray. **1876. brenneth,** burns. **1877. in aventure,** in jeopardy. **1879. penner,** a case containing pens. **1881. a compleynt or a lay,** types of short poem. **1883. heng,** which hung. **1887. two of Tawr,** the second degree of Taurus. **was into Cancre glyden,** had passed into Cancer.

Til dayes foure, or thre dayes atte leeste,
Ypassed been; thanne lat hire go to feeste.
The fourthe day compleet fro noon to noon,
Whan that the heighe masse was ydoon,
In halle sit this Januarie and May,   1895
As fressh as is the brighte someres day.
And so bifel how that this goode man
Remembred hym upon this Damyan,
And seyde, "Seynte Marie! how may this be,
That Damyan entendeth nat to me?   1900
Is he ay syk, or how may this bityde?"
His squieres, whiche that stooden ther bisyde,
Excused hym by cause of his siknesse,
Which letted hym to doon his bisynesse;   1904
Noon oother cause myghte make hym tarye.
    "That me forthynketh," quod this Januarie.
    "He is a gentil squier, by my trouthe!
If that he deyde, it were harm and routhe.
He is as wys, discreet, and as secree
As any man I woot of his degree,   1910
And therto manly, and eek servysable,
And for to been a thrifty man right able.
But after mete, as soone as evere I may,
I wol myself visite hym, and eek May,
To doon hym al the confort that I kan."   1915
And for that word hym blessed every man,
That of his bountee and his gentillesse
He wolde so conforten in siknesse
His squier, for it was a gentil dede.   1919
"Dame," quod this Januarie, "taak good hede,
At after-mete ye with youre wommen alle,
Whan ye han been in chambre out of this halle,
That alle ye go se this Damyan.
Dooth hym disport—he is a gentil man;
And telleth hym that I wol hym visite,   1925
Have I no thyng but rested me a lite;
And spede yow faste, for I wole abyde
Til that ye slepe faste by my syde."
And with that word he gan to hym to calle

A squier, that was marchal of his halle,   1930
And tolde hym certeyn thynges, what he wolde.
    This fresshe May hath streight hir wey
        yholde,
With alle hir wommen, unto Damyan.
Doun by his beddes syde sit she than,
Confortynge hym as goodly as she may.   1935
This Damyan, whan that his tyme he say,
In secree wise his purs and eek his bille,
In which that he ywriten hadde his wille,
Hath put into hire hand, withouten moore,
Save that he siketh wonder depe and soore,   1940
And softely to hire right thus seyde he:
"Mercy! and that ye nat discovere me,
For I am deed if that this thyng be kyd."
This purs hath she inwith hir bosom hyd,
And wente hire wey; ye gete namoore of me.
But unto Januarie ycomen is she,   1946
That on his beddes syde sit ful softe.
He taketh hire, and kisseth hire ful ofte,
And leyde hym doun to slepe, and that anon.
She feyned hire as that she moste gon   1950
Ther as ye woot that every wight moot neede;
And whan she of this bille hath taken heede,
She rente it al to cloutes atte laste,
And in the pryvee softely it caste.
    Who studieth now but faire fresshe May?
Adoun by olde Januarie she lay,   1956
That sleep til that the coughe hath hym
        awaked.
Anon he preyde hire strepen hire al naked;
He wolde of hire, he seyde, han som plesaunce,
And seyde hir clothes dide hym encombraunce,
And she obeyeth, be hire lief or looth.   1961
But lest that precious folk be with me wrooth,
How that he wroghte, I dar nat to yow telle,
Or wheither hire thoughte it paradys or helle.
But heere I lete hem werken in hir wyse   1965
Til evensong rong, and that they moste aryse.

1893. fro noon to noon, from noon to the hour of nones (three o'clock). **1900. entendeth,** attends. **1901. bityde,** happen. **1904. letted,** prevented. **1906. That me forthynketh,** I am sorry. **1909. secree,** discreet (able to keep a secret). **1913. mete,** dinner. **1917. bountee,** goodness. **1921. after-mete,** the period after a meal, generally after dinner. **1924. Dooth hym disport,** cheer him up. **1930. marchal of his halle.** See note to A 752. **1934. sit,** sits. **1936. say,** saw. **1939. withouten moore,** without more ado. **1940. siketh,** sighs. **wonder,** wonderfully. **1942. discovere,** betray. **1943. kyd,** known. **1952. bille,** writing. **1953. cloutes,** pieces. **1957. sleep,** slept. **1962. precious,** prudish. **1964. hire thoughte it,** it seemed to her. **1966. evensong,** *i.e.* the bell for evensong.

Were it by destynee or aventure,
Were it by influence or by nature,
Or constellacioun, that in swich estaat
The hevene stood, that tyme fortunaat   1970
Was for to putte a bille of Venus werkes—
For alle thyng hath tyme, as seyn thise
    clerkes—
To any womman, for to gete hire love,
I kan nat seye; but grete God above,
That knoweth that noon act is causelees,   1975
He deme of al, for I wole holde my pees.
But sooth is this, how that this fresshe May
Hath take swich impressioun that day
Of pitee of this sike Damyan,
That from hire herte she ne dryve kan   1980
The remembrance for to doon hym ese.
"Certeyn," thoghte she, "whom that this thyng
    displese,
I rekke noght, for heere I hym assure
To love hym best of any creature,   1984
Though he namoore hadde than his sherte."
Lo, pitee renneth soone in gentil herte!
Heere may ye se how excellent franchise
In wommen is, whan they hem narwe avyse.
Som tyrant is, as ther be many oon,
That hath an herte as hard as any stoon,   1990
Which wolde han let hym sterven in the place
Wel rather than han grauntted hym hire grace;
And hem rejoysen in hire crueel pryde,
And rekke nat to been an homycide.
This gentil May, fulfilled of pitee,   1995
Right of hire hand a lettre made she,
In which she graunteth hym hire verray grace.
Ther lakketh noght, oonly but day and place,
Wher that she myghte unto his lust suffise;
For it shal be right as he wole devyse.   2000
And whan she saugh hir tyme, upon a day,

To visite this Damyan gooth May,
And sotilly this lettre doun she threste
Under his pilwe, rede it if hym leste.
She taketh hym by the hand, and harde hym
    twiste   2005
So secrely that no wight of it wiste,
And bad hym been al hool, and forth she wente
To Januarie, whan that he for hire sente.
Up riseth Damyan the nexte morwe;
Al passed was his siknesse and his sorwe.   2010
He kembeth hym, he preyneth hym and pyk-
    eth,
He dooth al that his lady lust and lyketh;
And eek to Januarie he gooth as lowe
As evere dide a dogge for the bowe.
He is so plesant unto every man   2015
(For craft is al, whoso that do it kan)
That every wight is fayn to speke hym good;
And fully in his lady grace he stood.
Thus lete I Damyan aboute his nede,
And in my tale forth I wol procede.   2020
    Somme clerkes holden that felicitee
Stant in delit, and therfore certeyn he,
This noble Januarie, with al his myght,
In honest wyse, as longeth to a knyght,
Shoop hym to lyve ful deliciously.   2025
His housynge, his array, as honestly
To his degree was maked as a kynges.
Amonges othere of his honeste thynges,
He made a gardyn, walled al with stoon;
So fair a gardyn woot I nowher noon.   2030
For, out of doute, I verraily suppose
That he that wroot the Romance of the Rose
Ne koude of it the beautee wel devyse;
Ne Priapus ne myghte nat suffise,
Though he be god of gardyns, for to telle   2035
The beautee of the gardyn and the welle,

1967. aventure, chance. **1971. bille of,** plea for. **1976. He deme,** may he judge. **1978, impressioun,** feeling. **1987. franchise,** generosity. **1988. narwe avyse,** consider carefully. **1989. tyrant,** *i.e.* hard-hearted woman. **1991. sterven,** die. **1999. unto his lust suffise,** satisfy his desire. **2000. devyse,** arrange. **2003. sotilly,** cunningly. **threste,** thrust. **2005. twiste,** squeezed. **2011. preyneth,** preens. **pyketh,** makes himself neat and clean. **2012. lust,** desires. **2013. lowe,** docilely, obediently. **2014. a dogge for the bowe,** a hunting dog. Cf. D 1369–70. **2018. lady,** lady's. **2019. lete,** let go. **2022. Stant in delit,** consists of, or depends upon, pleasure, referring to the Epicurean philosophy. **2025. deliciously,** sumptuously. **2026. honestly . . .,** worthily for his rank. **2032. he that wroot,** Guillaume de Lorris, who wrote the first part of the *Roman de la Rose,* the setting of, which is a beautiful garden. **2033. devyse,** describe. **2034. Priapus,** god of fruitfulness, including the produce of gardens. **2036. welle,** spring.

That stood under a laurer alwey grene.
Ful ofte tyme he Pluto and his queene,
Proserpina, and al hire fayerye,
Disporten hem and maken melodye   2040
Aboute that welle, and daunced, as men tolde.
   This noble knyght, this Januarie the olde,
Swich deyntee hath in it to walke and pleye,
That he wol no wight suffren bere the keye
Save he hymself; for of the smale wyket   2045
He baar alwey of silver a clyket,
With which, whan that hym leste, he it un-
   shette.
And whan he wolde paye his wyf hir dette
In somer seson, thider wolde he go,   2049
And May his wyf, and no wight but they two;
And thynges whiche that were nat doon
   abedde,
He in the gardyn parfourned hem and spedde.
And in this wyse, many a murye day,
Lyved this Januarie and fresshe May.
But worldly joye may nat alwey dure   2055
To Januarie, ne to no creature.
   O sodeyn hap! o thou Fortune unstable!
Lyk to the scorpion so deceyvable,
That flaterest with thyn heed whan thou wolt
   stynge;
Thy tayl is deeth, thurgh thyn envenymynge.
O brotil joye! o sweete venym queynte!   2061
O monstre, that so subtilly kanst peynte
Thy yiftes under hewe of stidefastnesse,
That thou deceyvest bothe moore and lesse!
Why hastow Januarie thus deceyved,   2065
That haddest hym for thy fulle freend re-
   ceyved?
And now thou hast biraft hym bothe his yën,
For sorwe of which desireth he to dyen.
   Allas! this noble Januarie free,
Amydde his lust and his prosperitee,   2070

Is woxen blynd, and that al sodeynly.
He wepeth and he wayleth pitously;
And therwithal the fyr of jalousie,
Lest that his wyf sholde falle in som folye,
So brente his herte that he wolde fayn   2075
That som man bothe hire and hym had slayn.
For neither after his deeth, nor in his lyf,
Ne wolde he that she were love ne wyf,
But evere lyve as wydwe in clothes blake,
Soul as the turtle that lost hath hire make. 2080
But atte laste, after a month or tweye,
His sorwe gan aswage, sooth to seye;
For whan he wiste it may noon oother be,
He paciently took his adversitee,
Save, out of doute, he may nat forgoon   2085
That he nas jalous everemoore in oon;
Which jalousye it was so outrageous,
That neither in halle, n'yn noon oother hous,
Ne in noon oother place, neverthemo,
He nolde suffre hire for to ryde or go,   2090
But if that he had hond on hire alway;
For which ful ofte wepeth fresshe May,
That loveth Damyan so benyngnely
That she moot outher dyen sodeynly,
Or elles she moot han hym as hir leste.   2095
She wayteth whan hir herte wolde breste.
   Upon that oother syde Damyan
Bicomen is the sorwefulleste man
That evere was; for neither nyght ne day
Ne myghte he speke a word to fresshe May,
As to his purpos, of no swich mateere,   2101
But if that Januarie moste it heere,
That hadde an hand upon hire everemo.
But nathelees, by writyng to and fro,
And privee signes, wiste he what she mente,
And she knew eek the fyn of his entente.   2106
   O Januarie, what myghte it thee availle,
Thogh thou myghtest se as fer as shippes saille?

2037. laurer, laurel. 2038. Pluto . . . Proserpina. See note to HF 449. 2039. fayerye, band of nymphs. 2043. deyntee, delight. 2046. clyket, small key. 2047. unshette, unlocked, opened. 2055. dure, last. 2058. scorpion. See note to BD 636. 2061. brotil, fragile. queynte, cunning. 2067. biraft, deprived of. 2070. lust, pleasure. 2071. woxen, waxed, become. 2075. brente, burnt. 2078. love, sweetheart. 2080. Soul, solitary, single. turtle, turtle-dove. make, mate. 2083. noon oother, not otherwise. 2085. forgoon, cease from. 2086. everemoore in oon, constantly. 2090. ryde or go, ride or walk. 2093. benyngnely, gently, graciously. 2095. as hir leste, as she wished. 2096. wayteth, expects the time. 2106. fyn, end, aim.

For as good is blynd deceyved be
As to be deceyved whan a man may se.   2110

   Lo, Argus, which that hadde an hondred yën,
For al that evere he koude poure or pryen,
Yet was he blent, and, God woot, so been mo,
That wenen wisly that it be nat so.
Passe over is an ese, I sey namoore.   2115

   This fresshe May, that I spak of so yoore,
In warm wex hath emprented the clyket,
That Januarie bar of the smale wyket,
By which into his gardyn ofte he wente;
And Damyan, that knew al hire entente,   2120
The cliket countrefeted pryvely.
Ther nys namoore to seye, but hastily
Som wonder by this clyket shal bityde,
Which ye shul heeren, if ye wole abyde.   2124

   O noble Ovyde, ful sooth seystou, God woot,
What sleighte is it, thogh it be long and hoot,
That Love nyl fynde it out in som manere?
By Piramus and Tesbee may men leere;
Thogh they were kept ful longe streite overal,
They been accorded, rownynge thurgh a
    wal,   2130
Ther no wight koude han founde out swich a
    sleighte.

   But now to purpos: er that dayes eighte
Were passed, er the month of Juyl, bifil
That Januarie hath caught so greet a wil,   2134
Thurgh eggyng of his wyf, hym for to pleye
In his gardyn, and no wight but they tweye,
That in a morwe unto his May seith he:
"Rys up, my wyf, my love, my lady free!
The turtles voys is herd, my dowve sweete;
The wynter is goon with alle his reynes
    weete.   2140
Com forth now, with thyne eyen columbyn!
How fairer been thy brestes than is wyn!

The gardyn is enclosed al aboute;
Com forth, my white spouse! out of doute
Thou hast me wounded in myn herte, O wyf!
No spot of thee ne knew I al my lyf.   2146
Com forth, and lat us taken oure disport;
I chees thee for my wyf and my confort."

   Swiche olde lewed wordes used he.
On Damyan a signe made she,   2150
That he sholde go biforn with his cliket.
This Damyan thanne hath opened the wyket,
And in he stirte, and that in swich manere
That no wight myghte it se neither yheere,
And stille he sit under a bussh anon.   2155

   This Januarie, as blynd as is a stoon,
With Mayus in his hand, and no wight mo,
Into his fresshe gardyn is ago,
And clapte to the wyket sodeynly.
   "Now wyf," quod he, "heere nys but thou
    and I,   2160
That art the creature that I best love.
For by that Lord that sit in hevene above,
Levere ich hadde to dyen on a knyf,
Than thee offende, trewe deere wyf!
For Goddes sake, thenk how I thee chees,   2165
Noght for no coveitise, doutelees,
But oonly for the love I had to thee.
And though that I be oold, and may nat see,
Beth to me trewe, and I wol telle yow why.
Thre thynges, certes, shal ye wynne therby:
First, love of Crist, and to youreself honour,
And al myn heritage, toun and tour;   2172
I yeve it yow, maketh chartres as yow leste;
This shal be doon to-morwe er sonne reste,
So wisly God my soule brynge in blisse.   2175
I prey yow first, in covenant ye me kisse;
And though that I be jalous, wyte me noght.
Ye been so depe enprented in my thoght

2113. **blent**, deceived. 2114. **wenen wisly**, are confident. 2115. **Passe over is an ese**, what you don't know won't hurt you. 2117. **wex**, wax. 2126. **sleighte**, trick. 2127. **That Love nyl fynde it out.** Ovid, *Metam*, IV. 68: *Quid non sentit amor?* It is in the story of Pyramus and Thisbe. 2129. **kept . . . streite overal**, guarded strictly in every way. 2130. **rownynge**, whispering. 2133. **Juyl.** I keep the reading of the MSS, and understand the phrase *er the month of Juyl* to mean "before the month of July," therefore "before eight days in June had passed." **bifil**, it happened. 2137. **in a morwe**, one morning. 2141. **eyen columbyn**, dove's eyes. Cf. the *Song of Solomon*, 1:15. January's speech is full of echoes of Solomon's imagery, but the passages are also quoted by Jerome (*Against Jovinian*, I. 30), who bends them to his purpose. 2144. **white**, clothed in white. 2146. **spot**, blemish. 2148. **chees**, choose. 2153. **stirte**, went quickly. 2158. **ago**, gone. 2162. **sit**, sits. 2173. **chartres**, charters, by which property was conveyed. 2174. **sonne reste**, sunset. 2175. **wisly**, surely. 2177. **wyte**, blame.

That, whan that I considere youre beautee,
And therwithal the unlikly elde of me,　　2180
I may nat, certes, though I sholde dye,
Forbere to been out of youre compaignye
For verray love; this is withouten doute.
Now kys me, wyf, and lat us rome aboute."
　This fresshe May, whan she thise wordes
　　　herde,　　2185
Benyngnely to Januarie answerde,
But first and forward she bigan to wepe.
"I have," quod she, "a soule for to kepe
As wel as ye, and also myn honour,
And of my wyfhod thilke tendre flour,　　2190
Which that I have assured in youre hond,
Whan that the preest to yow my body bond;
Wherfore I wole answere in this manere,
By the leve of yow, my lord so deere:
I prey to God that nevere dawe the day　　2195
That I ne sterve, as foule as womman may,
If evere I do unto my kyn that shame,
Or elles I empeyre so my name,
That I be fals; and if I do that lakke,
Do strepe me and put me in a sakke,　　2200
And in the nexte ryver do me drenche.
I am a gentil womman and no wenche.
Why speke ye thus? but men been evere un-
　　　trewe,
And wommen have repreve of yow ay newe.
Ye han noon oother contenance, I leeve,　　2205
But speke to us of untrust and repreeve."
　And with that word she saugh wher Damyan
Sat in the bussh, and coughen she bigan,
And with hir fynger signes made she
That Damyan sholde clymbe upon a tree,　　2210
That charged was with fruyt, and up he wente.
For verraily he knew al hire entente,

And every signe that she koude make,
Wel bet than Januarie, hir owene make;
For in a lettre she hadde toold hym al　　2215
Of this matere, how he werchen shal.
And thus I lete hym sitte upon the pyrie,
And Januarie and May romynge ful myrie.
　Bright was the day, and blew the firmament;
Phebus hath of gold his stremes doun ysent,
To gladen every flour with his warmnesse.　2221
He was that tyme in Geminis, as I gesse,
But litel fro his declynacion
Of Cancer, Jovis exaltacion.
And so bifel, that brighte morwe-tyde,　　2225
That in that gardyn, in the ferther syde,
Pluto, that is kyng of Fayerye,
And many a lady in his compaignye,
Folwynge his wyf, the queene Proserpyna,
Which that he ravysshed out of Ethna　　2230
Whil that she gadered floures in the mede—
In Claudyan ye may the stories rede,
How in his grisely carte he hire fette—
This kyng of Fairye thanne adoun hym sette
Upon a bench of turves, fressh and grene,　2235
And right anon thus seyde he to his queene:
　"My wyf," quod he, "ther may no wight
　　　seye nay;
Th'experience so preveth every day
The tresons whiche that wommen doon to man.
Ten hondred thousand stories tellen I kan　2240
Notable of youre untrouthe and brotilnesse.
O Salomon, wys, and richest of richesse,
Fulfild of sapience and of worldly glorie,
Ful worthy been thy wordes to memorie
To every wight that wit and reson kan.　　2245
Thus preiseth he yet the bountee of man:
'Amonges a thousand men yet foond I oon,

2191. **assured,** trusted. 2196. **sterve,** die. **foule,** wretchedly. 2198. **elles,** otherwise. **empeyre,** injure. 2199. **lakke,** misdeed. 2201. **do me drenche,** have me drowned. 2203. **Why speke ye thus?** Cf. esp. l. 2169. 2204. **repreve of yow,** reproof from you. 2205-6. The only constant behavior of you men, I believe, is speaking to us of distrust and reproach. 2211. **charged,** loaded. 2217. **pyrie,** pear tree. 2222. **Geminis,** the sign of the zodiac, Gemini. 2223. **declynacion.** The sun was in its declination on entering Cancer, at which time Jupiter was in Cancer. "The 'exaltation' of a planet was the sign in which it was . . . supposed to exercise its greatest power." (Skeat). 2230. **ravysshed,** carried off. **Ethna,** the valley of Etna in Sicily. The MSS show great confusion in this line. The reading here adopted, that of Harl. MS. 7335 and the Paris MS, has the virtue of being close to Claudian (see l. 2232) and, what is more important, of giving meaning to l. 2231. 2232. **Claudyan,** Claudian (c. 400), author of *De Raptu Proserpinae*. 2233. **grisely carte,** terrible chariot. 2235. **a bench of turves.** As explained in the note to *LGW* 203. 2241. **brotilnesse,** frailty. 2245. **wit and reson kan,** has intelligence and reason. 2246. **bountee,** goodness. 2247. **Amonges a thousand men . . .** Cf. *Ecclesiastes*, 7:28.

But of wommen alle foond I noon.'
 Thus seith the kyng that knoweth youre
  wikkednesse.
And Jhesus, *filius Syrak*, as I gesse,   2250
Ne speketh of yow but seelde reverence.
A wylde fyr and corrupt pestilence
So falle upon youre bodyes yet to-nyght!
Ne se ye nat this honurable knyght,
By cause, allas! that he is blynd and old, 2255
His owene man shal make hym cokewold.
Lo, where he sit, the lechour, in the tree!
Now wol I graunten, of my magestee,
Unto this olde, blynde, worthy knyght
That he shal have ayeyn his eyen syght, 2260
Whan that his wyf wold doon hym vileynye.
Thanne shal he knowen al hire harlotrye,
Bothe in repreve of hire and othere mo."
 "Ye shal?" quod Proserpyne, "wol ye so?
Now by my moodres sires soule I swere 2265
That I shal yeven hire suffisant answere,
And alle wommen after, for hir sake;
That, though they be in any gilt ytake, 2268
With face boold they shulle hemself excuse,
And bere hem doun that wolden hem accuse.
For lakke of answere noon of hem shal dyen.
Al hadde man seyn a thyng with bothe his yën,
Yit shul we wommen visage it hardily,
And wepe, and swere, and chyde subtilly,
So that ye men shul been as lewed as gees. 2275
What rekketh me of youre auctoritees?
 I woot wel that this Jew, this Salomon,
Foond of us wommen fooles many oon.
But though that he ne foond no good womman,
Yet hath ther founde many another man 2280
Wommen ful trewe, ful goode, and vertuous.
Witnesse on hem that dwelle in Cristes hous;

With martirdom they preved hire constance.
The Romayn geestes eek maken remembrance
Of many a verray, trewe wyf also.   2285
But, sire, ne be nat wrooth, al be it so,
Though that he seyde he foond no good
 womman,
I prey yow take the sentence of the man;
He mente thus, that in sovereyn bontee
Nis noon but God, but neither he ne she. 2290
 Ey! for verray God, that nys but oon,
What make ye so muche of Salomon?
What though he made a temple, Goddes hous?
What though he were riche and glorious?
So made he eek a temple of false goddis. 2295
How myghte he do a thyng that moore for-
 bode is?
Pardee, as faire as ye his name emplastre,
He was a lecchour and an ydolastre,
And in his elde he verray God forsook;
And if that God ne hadde, as seith the book, 2300
Yspared him for his fadres sake, he sholde
Have lost his regne rather than he wolde.
I sette right noght, of al the vileynye
That ye of wommen write, a boterflye!
I am a womman, nedes moot I speke, 2305
Or elles swelle til myn herte breke.
For sithen he seyde that we been jangleresses,
As evere hool I moote brouke my tresses,
I shal nat spare, for no curteisye, 2309
To speke hym harm that wolde us vileynye."
 "Dame," quod this Pluto, "be no lenger
  wrooth;
I yeve it up! but sith I swoor myn ooth
That I wolde graunten hym his sighte ageyn,
My word shal stonde, I warne yow certeyn.
I am a kyng, it sit me noght to lye." 2315

2250. Jhesus, *filius Syrak*, the supposed author of *Ecclesiasticus*. **2251. Ne speketh . . .,** but seldom expresses respect for you. **2252. wylde fyr,** erysipelas. Cf. A 4172. **corrupt,** rotting. **2257. sit,** sits. **2261. vileynye,** outrage. **2263. repreve,** reproof. **2272. Al hadde man,** even if one had. **2273. visage it hardily,** face it out boldly. **2275. lewed,** foolish. **2276. rekketh me,** do I care. **2283. preved,** proved. **2284. The Romayn geestes,** Roman history, rather than the *Gesta Romanorum*. **2285. verray,** faithful. **2288. sentence,** meaning. **2289. sovereyn bontee,** absolute goodness. **2291. that nys . . .,** that is the one and only God. **2292. What,** why. **2295. of,** for. Cf. *1 Kings,* 11:7–8. **2296. forbode,** forbidden. **2297. emplastre,** plaster over (to improve the appearance). **2298. ydolastre,** idolater. **2299. elde,** old age. **2300. as seith the book.** *1 Kings,* 11:11–13. **2302. regne,** kingdom. **rather,** sooner. **2304. ye,** ye men. **2305. moot,** must. **2307. jangler- esses,** great talkers. **2308. As evere hool . . .** As ever I hope to keep (*brouke*) my tresses whole. **2310. that wolde us vileynye,** would do us shame. **2315. it sit me noght . . .,** it is not fitting that I should break my word.

"And I," quod she, "a queene of Fayerye!
Hir answere shal she have, I undertake.
Lat us namoore wordes heerof make;
For sothe, I wol no lenger yow contrarie."
　Now lat us turne agayn to Januarie,　　2320
That in the gardyn with his faire May
Syngeth ful murier than the papejay,
"Yow love I best, and shal, and oother noon."
So longe aboute the aleyes is he goon,
Til he was come agayns thilke pyrie　　2325
Where as this Damyan sitteth ful myrie
An heigh among the fresshe leves grene.
　This fresshe May, that is so bright and
　　sheene,
Gan for to syke, and seyde, "Allas, my syde!
Now sire," quod she, "for aught that may
　　bityde,　　2330
I moste han of the peres that I see,
Or I moot dye, so soore longeth me
To eten of the smale peres grene.
Help, for hir love that is of hevene queene!
I telle yow wel, a womman in my plit　　2335
May han to fruyt so greet an appetit
That she may dyen, but she of it have."
　"Allas!" quod he, "that I ne had heer a knave
That koude clymbe! Allas, allas," quod he,
"For I am blynd!" "Ye, sire, no fors," quod
　　she;　　2340
"But wolde ye vouchesauf, for Goddes sake,
The pyrie inwith youre armes for to take,
For wel I woot that ye mystruste me,
Thanne sholde I clymbe wel ynogh," quod she,
"So I my foot myghte sette upon youre
　　bak."　　2345
　"Certes," quod he, "theron shal be no lak,
Mighte I yow helpen with myn herte blood."
He stoupeth doun, and on his bak she stood,
And caughte hire by a twiste, and up she
　　gooth—

Ladyes, I prey yow that ye be nat wrooth;
I kan nat glose, I am a rude man—　　2351
And sodeynly anon this Damyan
Gan pullen up the smok, and in he throng.
　And whan that Pluto saugh this grete wrong,
To Januarie he gaf agayn his sighte,　　2355
And made hym se as wel as evere he myghte.
And whan that he hadde caught his sighte
　　agayn,
Ne was ther nevere man of thyng so fayn,
But on his wyf his thoght was everemo.
Up to the tree he caste his eyen two,　　2360
And saugh that Damyan his wyf had dressed
In swich manere it may nat been expressed,
But if I wolde speke uncurteisly;
And up he yaf a roryng and a cry,　　2364
As dooth the mooder whan the child shal dye:
"Out! help; allas! harrow!" he gan to crye,
"O stronge lady stoore, what dostow?"
　And she answerde, "Sire, what eyleth yow?
Have pacience and resoun in youre mynde!
I have yow holpe on bothe youre eyen blynde.
Up peril of my soule, I shal nat lyen,　　2371
As me was taught, to heele with youre yën,
Was no thyng bet, to make yow to see,
Than strugle with a man upon a tree.
God woot, I dide it in ful good entente."　　2375
　"Strugle!" quod he, "ye, algate in it wente!
God yeve yow bothe on shames deth to dyen!
He swyved thee, I saugh it with myne yën,
And elles be I hanged by the hals!"
　"Thanne is," quod she, "my medicyne fals;
For certeinly, if that ye myghte se,　　2381
Ye wolde nat seyn thise wordes unto me.
Ye han som glymsyng, and no parfit sighte."
　"I se," quod he, "as wel as evere I myghte,
Thonked be God! with bothe myne eyen two,
And by my trouthe, me thoughte he dide thee
　　so."　　2386

2319. contrarie, oppose, contradict. 2322. murier, more merrily. papejay, popinjay. 2324. aleyes, garden paths. 2325. agayns, in front of. 2327. An heigh, on high. 2329. syke, sigh. 2335. plit, condition. 2338. knave, servant. 2340. no fors, no matter. 2342. inwith, within. 2349. twiste, branch. 2351. glose, use fair words. 2353. throng, thrust. 2361. dressed, addressed. 2363. uncurteisly, vulgarly. 2365. mooder, mother. 2367. stoore, bold, impudent (*lit.* great, strong). 2370. holpe, helped. 2371. Up, upon. 2376. algate, nevertheless. 2377. on shames deth, by a shameful death. 2378. swyved, had intercourse with. 2379. hals, neck. 2382. seyn, say. 2383. glymsyng, fleeting vision.

"Ye maze, maze, goode sire," quod she;
"This thank have I for I have maad yow see.
Allas," quod she, "that evere I was so kynde!"
　"Now, dame," quod he, "lat al passe out of
　　mynde. 2390
Com doun, my lief, and if I have myssayd,
God helpe me so, as I am yvele apayd.
But, by my fader soule, I wende han seyn
How that this Damyan hadde by thee leyn, 2394
And that thy smok hadde leyn upon his brest."
　"Ye, sire," quod she, "ye may wene as yow
　　lest.
But, sire, a man that waketh out of his sleep,
He may nat sodeynly wel taken keep
Upon a thyng, ne seen it parfitly,
Til that he be adawed verraily. 2400
Right so a man that longe hath blynd ybe,

Ne may nat sodeynly so wel yse,
First whan his sighte is newe come ageyn,
As he that hath a day or two yseyn.
Til that youre sighte ysatled be a while, 2405
Ther may ful many a sighte yow bigile.
Beth war, I prey yow; for, by hevene kyng,
Ful many a man weneth to seen a thyng,
And it is al another than it semeth.
He that mysconceyveth, he mysdemeth." 2410
And with that word she leep doun fro the tree.
　This Januarie, who is glad but he?
He kisseth hire, and clippeth hire ful ofte,
And on hire wombe he stroketh hire ful softe,
And to his palays hoom he hath hire lad. 2415
Now, goode men, I pray yow to be glad.
Thus endeth heere my tale of Januarie;
God blesse us, and his mooder Seinte Marie!

Heere is ended the Marchantes Tale of Januarie.

EPILOGUE TO THE MERCHANT'S TALE

　"Ey! Goddes mercy!" seyde oure Hoost tho,
"Now swich a wyf I pray God kepe me fro!
Lo, whiche sleightes and subtilitees 2421
In wommen been! for ay as bisy as bees
Been they, us sely men for to deceyve,
And from a sooth evere wol they weyve;
By this Marchauntes tale it preveth weel. 2425
But doutelees, as trewe as any steel
I have a wyf, though that she povre be,
But of hir tonge, a labbyng shrewe is she,
And yet she hath an heep of vices mo;

Therof no fors! lat alle swiche thynges go. 2430
But wyte ye what? In conseil be it seyd,
Me reweth soore I am unto hire teyd.
For, and I sholde rekenen every vice
Which that she hath, ywis I were to nyce;
And cause why, it sholde reported be 2435
And toold to hire of somme of this meynee,—
Of whom, it nedeth nat for to declare,
Syn wommen konnen outen swich chaffare;
And eek my wit suffiseth nat therto,
To tellen al, wherfore my tale is do." 2440

2387. **maze,** are bewildered, rave. 2391. **lief,** dear. 2392. **yvele apayd,** sorry. 2393. **wende han seyn,** thought to have seen. 2396. **as yow lest,** as you please. 2398. **keep,** heed. 2400. **adawed verraily,** truly awake. 2405. **ysatled,** settled. 2406. **bigile,** deceive. 2407. **hevene,** heaven's. 2410. **mysdemeth,** misjudges. 2411. **leep,** leaped. 2413. **clippeth,** embraces. 2415. **lad,** led. 2419. **tho,** then. 2420. **swich,** such. 2421. **whiche,** what. **sleightes,** tricks. 2423. **sely,** simple. 2424. **sooth,** truth. **weyve,** turn aside. 2425. **preveth,** proves. 2428. **labbyng,** blabbing. 2430. **no fors,** no matter. 2431. **wyte ye what?** do you know what? **conseil,** confidence. 2433. **and,** if. 2434. **nyce,** foolish. 2436. **of,** by. **meynee,** company. 2437. **Of whom,** by whom. 2438. **Syn,** since. **outen,** set out, expose to view. **chaffare,** wares. Cf. D 521.

Group F (Fragment V)

The Squire's Tale

THE PROLOGUE OF THE SQUIRE'S TALE

"Squier, com neer, if it youre wille be,
And sey somwhat of love; for certes ye
Konnen theron as muche as any man."
　"Nay, sire," quod he, "but I wol seye as I kan

With hertly wyl; for I wol nat rebelle　　　5
Agayn youre lust; a tale wol I telle.
Have me excused if I speke amys;
My wyl is good, and lo, my tale is this."

THE SQUIRE'S TALE

Heere bigynneth the Squieres Tale.

　At Sarray, in the land of Tartarye,
Ther dwelte a kyng that werreyed Russye,　10
Thurgh which ther dyde many a doughty man.
This noble kyng was cleped Cambyuskan,
Which in his tyme was of so greet renoun

That ther was nowher in no regioun
So excellent a lord in alle thyng.　　　15
Hym lakked noght that longeth to a kyng.
As of the secte of which that he was born
He kepte his lay, to which that he was sworn;

1-8. These uninspired lines are frequently written in the MSS as the concluding lines of *The Merchant's Epilogue.*
　The Squire's Tale. The charming story which the Squire begins to tell is one of those Eastern tales of magic which we associate with the *Arabian Nights.* The scene is laid in Tartary. The three magical objects are a mechanical horse, which by the turning of a pin can carry the rider wherever he wishes to go, a ring which enables its owner to understand the language of birds, and a mirror which can give warning of threatened invasion or the approach of an enemy. All of these magical elements can be found elsewhere. Such a mirror is described in the *Epistola* of the fabulous Asiatic monarch Prester John, and a similar magic horse, except that it is made of ebony, occurs in the Old French romance of *Cléomadès,* by Adenès le Roi. Rings which enable the possessor to understand the language of birds are unusual, but one has been found in a late German folktale, and of course human beings who understand birds occur frequently in fairy tales, For all these elements, and for Eastern analogues to the falcon's story, which Professor Braddy has called attention to, the reader must be referred to Professor H. S. V. Jones's chapter in *SA* (with the references there given) and to W. A. Clouston's *On the Magical Elements in Chaucer's Squire's Tale* (1890, Chaucer Soc., 2nd Ser., No. 26).
　Chaucer's acquaintance with the *Epistola Presbyteri Johannis* and the *Cléomadès* have not been proved and to the present writer remains doubtful. The fact that the various elements of the plot are not found combined elsewhere has led some scholars to believe that Chaucer may have been combining hints and themes from various sources. It is not, however, his usual practice to invent new plots. The incompleteness of the story makes judgement difficult, but in what we have the various strands are nicely woven together and the closing lines of Part II indicate briefly what is to follow. Perhaps it is better to accept the remark "as the storie telleth us" (l. 655), conventional as it is, at its face value and to believe that he had a written source now lost or was retelling a story that he had once heard. The date at which he wrote the tale is equally difficult to determine, and in the complete absence of evidence it is useless to speculate.
　9. Sarray, Tzarev, in southeastern Russia, a little north of the Caspian Sea **10. werreyed,** made war on **12. Cambyuskan.** The name is generally equated with Gengis Khan, but the invasion of Russia (1224) was by his grandson Batu Khan. **17. secte,** religion **18. his lay,** its law.

And therto he was hardy, wys, and riche,
And pitous and just, alwey yliche; 20
Sooth of his word, benigne, and honurable;
Of his corage as any centre stable;
Yong, fressh, and strong, in armes desirous
As any bacheler of al his hous.
A fair persone he was and fortunat, 25
And kepte alwey so wel roial estat
That there was nowher swich another man.
   This noble kyng, this Tartre Cambyuskan,
Hadde two sones on Elpheta his wyf,
Of whiche the eldeste highte Algarsyf, 30
That oother sone was cleped Cambalo.
A doghter hadde this worthy kyng also,
That yongest was, and highte Canacee.
But for to telle yow al hir beautee,
It lyth nat in my tonge, n'yn my konnyng; 35
I dar nat undertake so heigh a thyng.
Myn Englissh eek is insufficient.
It moste been a rethor excellent,
That koude his colours longynge for that art,
If he sholde hire discryven every part. 40
I am noon swich, I moot speke as I kan.
   And so bifel that whan this Cambyuskan
Hath twenty wynter born his diademe,
As he was wont fro yeer to yeer, I deme,
He leet the feeste of his nativitee 45
Doon cryen thurghout Sarray his citee,
The laste Idus of March, after the yeer.
Phebus the sonne ful joly was and cleer;
For he was neigh his exaltacioun
In Martes face, and in his mansioun 50
In Aries, the colerik hoote signe.
Ful lusty was the weder and benigne,

For which the foweles, agayn the sonne sheene,
What for the sesoun and the yonge grene,
Ful loude songen hire affecciouns. 55
Hem semed han geten hem protecciouns
Agayn the swerd of wynter, keene and coold.
   This Cambyuskan, of which I have yow
     toold,
In roial vestiment sit on his deys,
With diademe, ful heighe in his paleys, 60
And halt his feeste so solempne and so ryche
That in this world ne was ther noon it lyche;
Of which if I shal tellen al th'array,
Thanne wolde it occupie a someres day;
And eek it nedeth nat for to devyse 65
At every cours the ordre of hire servyse.
I wol nat tellen of hir strange sewes,
Ne of hir swannes, ne of hire heronsewes.
Eek in that lond, as tellen knyghtes olde,
Ther is som mete that is ful deynte holde, 70
That in this lond men recche of it but smal;
Ther nys no man that may reporten al.
I wol nat taryen yow, for it is pryme,
And for it is no fruyt, but los of tyme;
Unto my firste I wole have my recours. 75
   And so bifel that after the thridde cours,
Whil that this kyng sit thus in his nobleye,
Herknynge his mynstralles hir thynges pleye
Biforn hym at the bord deliciously,
In at the halle dore al sodeynly 80
Ther cam a knyght upon a steede of bras,
And in his hand a brood mirour of glas,
Upon his thombe he hadde of gold a ryng,
And by his syde a naked swerd hangyng;
And up he rideth to the heighe bord. 85

---

20. **alwey yliche,** consistently. 22. **corage,** heart, spirit. **centre,** the center around which anything revolves. 23. **desirous,** eager. 24. **bacheler,** young knight. 25. **fortunat,** favored by fortune. 30. **highte,** was named. 31. **cleped,** called. 38. **rethor,** rhetorician. 39. **colours,** figures of speech and other rhetorical devices. **longynge for,** pertaining to. 44. **deme,** suppose. 45. **leet . . . Doon cryen,** caused to be proclaimed. 47. **The laste Idus,** the last of the days from nones to the ides (March 15), which were designated as days of the ides, therefore the day itself. **after,** according to, in that year. 49. **exaltacioun.** The sun had its exaltation, and was of greatest influence, in the sign Ares. Each planet had its house or mansion in one of the signs, and the sun's mansion was in Ares. The first third (10 degrees) of a sign was the first "face" of that sign, and the first face of Ares was called the face of Mars. 51. **the colerik hoote signe.** Each sign had its special qualities, and Aries was designated as hot and choleric (inducing passion). 52. **lusty,** pleasant. 53. **agayn,** toward, with respect to. 54. **What for,** what with. 59. **sit,** sits. 61. **halt,** holds. **solempne,** sumptuous. 63. **array,** arrangement, here the courses of a dinner. 67. **sewes,** broths. 68. **heronsewes,** young herons. 70. **holde,** held, considered. 73. **taryen,** delay. **pryme,** 9 A.M. 74. **no fruyt,** not profitable. 75. **my firste,** my first topic. **wole . . . recours,** will return. 77. **nobleye,** royal splendor. 80. **In at the halle dore.** For a knight riding into a hall cf. *Sir Gawain and the Green Knight.* 83. **Upon his thombe.** Rings were often worn on the thumb. 85. **bord,** table.

In al the halle ne was ther spoken a word
For merveille of this knyght; hym to biholde
Ful bisily they wayten, yonge and olde.

    This strange knyght, that cam thus sodeynly,
Al armed, save his heed, ful richely,   90
Saleweth kyng and queene and lordes alle,
By ordre, as they seten in the halle,
With so heigh reverence and obeisaunce,
As wel in speche as in his contenaunce,
That Gawayn, with his olde curteisye,   95
Though he were comen ayeyn out of Fairye,
Ne koude hym nat amende with a word.
And after this, biforn the heighe bord,
He with a manly voys seide his message,
After the forme used in his langage,   100
Withouten vice of silable or of lettre;
And, for his tale sholde seme the bettre,
Accordant to his wordes was his cheere,
As techeth art of speche hem that it leere.
Al be it that I kan nat sowne his stile,   105
Ne kan nat clymben over so heigh a style,
Yet seye I this, as to commune entente,
Thus muche amounteth al that evere he mente,
If it so be that I have it in mynde.

    He seyde, "The kyng of Arabe and of Inde,
My lige lord, on this solempne day   111
Saleweth yow, as he best kan and may,
And sendeth yow, in honour of youre feeste,
By me, that am al redy at youre heeste,
This steede of bras, that esily and weel   115
Kan in the space of o day natureel—
This is to seyn, in foure and twenty houres—
Wher so yow lyst, in droghte or elles shoures,
Beren youre body into every place
To which youre herte wilneth for to pace;   120
Withouten wem of yow, thurgh foul or fair;
Or, if yow lyst to fleen as hye in the air

As dooth an egle whan hym list to soore,
This same steede shal bere yow evere moore,
Withouten harm, til ye be ther yow leste,   125
Though that ye slepen on his bak or reste,
And turne ayeyn with writhyng of a pyn.
He that it wroghte koude ful many a gyn.
He wayted many a constellacioun
Er he had doon this operacioun,   130
And knew ful many a seel and many a bond.

    This mirour eek, that I have in myn hond,
Hath swich a myght that men may in it see
Whan ther shal fallen any adversitee
Unto youre regne or to youreself also,   135
And openly who is youre freend or foo.

    And over al this, if any lady bright
Hath set hire herte on any maner wight,
If he be fals, she shal his tresoun see,
His newe love, and al his subtiltee,   140
So openly that ther shal no thyng hyde.
Wherfore, ageyn this lusty someres tyde,
This mirour and this ryng, that ye may see,
He hath sent to my lady Canacee,
Youre excellente doghter that is heere.   145

    The vertu of the ryng, if ye wol heere,
Is this, that if hire lust it for to were
Upon hir thombe, or in hir purs it bere,
Ther is no fowel that fleeth under the hevene
That she ne shal wel understonde his stevene, 150
And knowe his menyng openly and pleyn,
And answere hym in his langage ageyn;
And every gras that groweth upon roote
She shal eek knowe, and whom it wol do boote,
Al be his woundes never so depe and wyde. 155

    This naked swerd, that hangeth by my syde,
Swich vertu hath that, what man so ye smyte,
Thurgh out his armure it wole kerve and byte,
Were it as thikke as is a branched ook;   159

---

88. bisily, intently. **wayten,** watch. **91. Saleweth,** greets. **92. seten,** sat. **94. contenaunce,** bearing. **95. Gawayn.** Gawain is often a model of knightly behavior in medieval romances. **101. vice,** fault. **102. for,** in order that. **104. leere,** teach. **105. sowne,** imitate the sound of. **106. style,** set of steps over a fence. **107. commune entente,** general purport. **108. Thus muche amounteth,** amounts to this. **110. Arabe,** Arabia. **111. solempne,** important. **114. heeste,** command. **116. o day natureel,** one 24-hour day, in contrast with the day *artificial* (from sunrise to sunset). **121. wem of,** harm to. **122. fleen,** fly. **125. ther,** where. **127. turne,** return. **writhyng,** twisting. **128. koude,** knew. **gyn,** craft, device. **129. wayted,** watched until the stars were favorable. **131. seel . . . bond.** Seals were employed in magic and it is supposed that *bond* is used in a somewhat synonymous sense. **135. regne,** kingdom **141. hyde,** lie concealed. **147. hire lust,** it pleases her. **149. fleeth,** flies. **150. stevene,** language. **153. gras,** herb. **154. boote,** good, remedy.

And what man that is wounded with the strook
Shal never be hool til that yow list, of grace,
To stroke hym with the plat in thilke place
Ther he is hurt; this is as muche to seyn,
Ye moote with the platte swerd ageyn
Stroke hym in the wounde, and it wol close, 165
This is a verray sooth, withouten glose;
It failleth nat whils it is in youre hoold."
    And whan this knyght hath thus his tale
        toold,
He rideth out of halle, and doun he lighte.
His steede, which that shoon as sonne brighte,
Stant in the court, stille as any stoon.   171
This knyght is to his chambre lad anoon,
And is unarmed, and to mete yset.
    The presentes been ful roially yfet,—
This is to seyn, the swerd and the mirour, 175
And born anon into the heighe tour
With certeine officers ordeyned therfore;
And unto Canacee this ryng is bore
Solempnely, ther she sit at the table.
But sikerly, withouten any fable,   180
The hors of bras, that may nat be remewed,
It stant as it were to the ground yglewed.
Ther may no man out of the place it dryve
For noon engyn of wyndas or polyve;
And cause why? for they kan nat the craft. 185
And therfore in the place they han it laft,
Til that the knyght hath taught hem the manere
To voyden hym, as ye shal after heere.
    Greet was the prees that swarmeth to and fro
To gauren on this hors that stondeth so;   190
For it so heigh was, and so brood and long,
So wel proporcioned for to been strong,
Right as it were a steede of Lumbardye;

Therwith so horsly, and so quyk of yë,
As it a gentil Poilleys courser were.   195
For certes, fro his tayl unto his ere,
Nature ne art ne koude hym nat amende
In no degree, as al the peple wende.
But everemoore hir mooste wonder was
How that it koude gon, and was of bras;   200
It was of Fairye, as the peple semed.
Diverse folk diversely they demed;
As many heddes, as manye wittes ther been.
They murmureden as dooth a swarm of been,
And maden skiles after hir fantasies,   205
Rehersynge of thise olde poetries,
And seyden it was lyk the Pegasee,
The hors that hadde wynges for to flee;
Or elles it was the Grekes hors Synoun,
That broghte Troie to destruccioun,   210
As men in thise olde geestes rede.
"Myn herte," quod oon, "is everemoore in
        drede;
I trowe som men of armes been therinne,
That shapen hem this citee for to wynne.
It were right good that al swich thyng were
        knowe."   215
Another rowned to his felawe lowe,
And seyde, "He lyeth, for it is rather lyk
An apparence ymaad by som magyk,
As jogelours pleyen at thise feestes grete."
Of sondry doutes thus they jangle and trete, 220
As lewed peple demeth comunly
Of thynges that been maad moore subtilly
Than they kan in hir lewednesse comprehende;
They demen gladly to the badder ende.
    And somme of hem wondred on the mirour,
That born was up into the maister-tour,   226

162. **plat**, flat. **163. Ther**, where. **164. moote**, may. **166. glose**, deceit. **167. hoold**, possession. **169. lighte**, alights. **171. stant**, stands. **172. lad**, led. **174. yfet**, fetched. **177. With**, by. **ordeyned**, appointed. **180. sikerly**, certainly. **181. remewed**, removed. **184. engyn of wyndas or polyve**, contrivance of windlass or pulley. **185. kan nat the craft**, don't know the device. **186. laft**, left. **188. voyden**, remove, get rid of. **189. prees**, press, crowd. **190. gauren**, stare. **193. Lumbardye.** Lombardy was well known for its horses. **194. horsly**, horse-like, as a horse should be. **195. Poilleys courser**, riding horse of Apulia. **199. hir**, their. **201. the peple semed**, it seemed to the people. **205. skiles**, reasons, arguments. **207. Pegasee**, Pegasus. **208. flee**, fly. **209. the Grekes hors Synoun**, the horse of the Greek Sinon. For the construction see *BD* 282 and Language, § 56. For Sinon see *HF* 151–5 and B 4418. **211. geestes**, histories, stories. **213. som men of armes been therinne**, as in the Trojan horse. **214. shapen hem**, plan. **216. rowned**, whispered. **218. apparence**, apparition. **219. jogelours**, jugglers, minstrels. **pleyen**, perform. **220. jangle**, chatter. **trete**, talk, discuss. **221. lewed**, unlearned. **223. lewednesse**, ignorance. **224. They demen . . .** They put the worst interpretation on things. **225. on**, at, about.

Hou men myghte in it swiche thynges se.
　Another answerde, and seyde it myghte wel
　　be
Naturelly, by composiciouns
Of anglis and of slye reflexiouns,　　　　　　230
And seyden that in Rome was swich oon.
They speken of Alocen, and Vitulon,
And Aristotle, that writen in hir lyves
Of queynte mirours and of perspectives,
As knowen they that han hir bookes herd.　235
　And oother folk han wondred on the swerd
That wolde percen thurghout every thyng,
And fille in speche of Thelophus the kyng,
And of Achilles with his queynte spere,
For he koude with it bothe heele and dere,　240
Right in swich wise as men may with the swerd
Of which right now ye han youreselven herd.
They speken of sondry hardyng of metal,
And speke of medicynes therwithal,
And how and whanne it sholde yharded be,　245
Which is unknowe, algates unto me.
　Tho speeke they of Canacees ryng,
And seyden alle that swich a wonder thyng
Of craft of rynges herde they nevere noon,
Save that he Moyses and kyng Salomon　　250
Hadde a name of konnyng in swich art.
Thus seyn the peple, and drawen hem apart.
But natheless somme seiden that it was
Wonder to maken of fern-asshen glas,
And yet nys glas nat lyk asshen of fern;　　255

But, for they han knowen it so fern,
Therfore cesseth hir janglyng and hir wonder.
As soore wondren somme on cause of thonder,
On ebbe, on flood, on gossomer, and on myst,
And alle thyng, til that the cause is wyst.　　260
Thus jangle they, and demen, and devyse,
Til that the kyng gan fro the bord aryse.
　Phebus hath laft the angle meridional,
And yet ascendynge was the beest roial,
The gentil Leon, with his Aldiran,　　　　265
Whan that this Tartre kyng, this Cambyuskan,
Roos fro his bord, ther as he sat ful hye.
Toforn hym gooth the loude mynstralcye,
Til he cam to his chambre of paramentz,
Ther as they sownen diverse instrumentz,　270
That it is lyk an hevene for to heere.
Now dauncen lusty Venus children deere,
For in the Fyssh hir lady sat ful hye,
And looketh on hem with a freendly yё.
　This noble kyng is set upon his trone.　　275
This strange knyght is fet to hym ful soone,
And on the daunce he gooth with Canacee.
Heere is the revel and the jolitee
That is nat able a dul man to devyse.
He most han knowen love and his servyse,　280
And been a feestlych man as fressh as May,
That sholde yow devysen swich array.
　Who koude telle yow the forme of daunces
So unkouthe and swiche fresshe contenaunces,
Swich subtil lookyng and dissymulynges　285

---

229. composiciouns, combinations. **230. slye,** skilfully contrived. **231. in Rome was swich oon.** In various medieval works, such as *The Seven Sages*, Virgil is said to have set up a mirror in Rome by which an enemy might be seen thirty miles away. **232. Alocen,** Alhazen, an Arabian scientist, author of a work on optics. **Vitulon,** a Polish mathematician, who translated Alhazen's work into Latin. **233. writen,** wrote. **lyves,** lifetimes. **234. perspectives,** telescopes. **238. fille,** fell. **Thelophus,** Telephus, king of Mysia, who was married to a daughter of Priam and was wounded by Achilles while opposing the landing of the Greeks at Troy. His wound was healed with rust from Achilles' spear. **240. dere,** injure. **243. hardyng,** tempering. **246. algates,** at any rate. **250. Moyses . . .** Both Moses and Solomon in the Middle Ages were credited with magical rings. See Clouston, *On the Magical Elements in Chaucer's Squire's Tale*, pp. 334–41. **251. a name of,** a reputation for. **254. fern-asshen,** presumably the ashes from burnt ferns, but this is the only instance of the word now known. **256. fern,** long ago. **259. gossomer,** gossamer, cobwebs. **260. wyst,** known. **263. angle meridional,** that part of the heavens covering the 30° east of the meridian which the sun would pass through by noon. The time was therefore past noon. **264. beest roial,** the lion, and here the sign Leo, which in the latitude of London on March 15 in Chaucer's day would be rising (*ascendynge*) above the horizon, and continue rising for over two hours. **265. Aldiran,** There is some doubt about the meaning of this word, but it is generally taken to refer to one of the stars in Leo or to the twin stars Castor and Pollux. **269. chambre of paramentz,** presence chamber. **270. sownen,** sound. **272. Venus children,** lovers. **273. the Fyssh,** Pisces, which was the 'exaltation' of Venus, the mansion in which she exerted the greatest influence. **hir lady,** their lady, Venus. **sat ful hye,** *i.e.* because she was in her exaltation. **275. trone,** throne. **276. fet,** fetched. **277. on,** in. **279. devyse,** describe. **281. feestlych,** given to festivity. **282. array,** "matters," "business." **284. unkouthe,** strange, unfamiliar.

For drede of jalouse mennes aperceyvynges?
No man but Launcelot, and he is deed.
Therfore I passe of al this lustiheed;
I sey namoore, but in this jolynesse
I lete hem, til men to the soper dresse.   290
   The styward bit the spices for to hye,
And eek the wyn, in al this melodye.
The usshers and the squiers been ygoon,
The spices and the wyn is come anoon.
They ete and drynke; and whan this hadde an
   ende,   295
Unto the temple, as reson was, they wende.
The service doon, they soupen al by day.
What nedeth yow rehercen hire array?
Ech man woot wel that at a kynges feeste
Hath plentee to the meeste and to the leeste,   300
And deyntees mo than been in my knowyng.
At after-soper gooth this noble kyng
To seen this hors of bras, with al a route
Of lordes and of ladyes hym aboute.   304
   Swich wondryng was ther on this hors of
   bras
That syn the grete sege of Troie was,
Theras men wondreden on an hors also,
Ne was ther swich a wondryng as was tho.
But fynally the kyng axeth this knyght
The vertu of this courser and the myght,   310
And preyde hym to telle his governaunce.
   This hors anoon bigan to trippe and daunce,
Whan that this knyght leyde hand upon his
   reyne,
And seyde, "Sire, ther is namoore to seyne,
But, whan yow list to ryden anywhere,   315
Ye mooten trille a pyn, stant in his ere,

Which I shal telle yow bitwix us two.
Ye moote nempne hym to what place also,
Or to what contree, that yow list to ryde.
And whan ye come ther as yow list abyde,   320
Bidde hym descende, and trille another pyn,
For therin lith th'effect of al the gyn,
And he wol doun descende and doon youre
   wille,
And in that place he wol abyden stille.
Though al the world the contrarie hadde
   yswore,   325
He shal nat thennes been ydrawe ne ybore.
Or, if yow liste bidde hym thennes goon,
Trille this pyn, and he wol vanysshe anoon
Out of the sighte of every maner wight,
And come agayn, be it by day or nyght,   330
Whan that yow list to clepen hym ageyn
In swich a gyse as I shal to yow seyn
Bitwixe yow and me, and that ful soone.
Ride whan yow list, ther is namoore to
   doone."
   Enformed whan the kyng was of that
   knyght,
And hath conceyved in his wit aright   336
The manere and the forme of al this thyng,
Ful glad and blithe, this noble doughty kyng
Repeireth to his revel as biforn.
The brydel is unto the tour yborn   340
And kept among his jueles leeve and deere.
The hors vanysshed, I noot in what manere,
Out of hir sighte; ye gete namoore of me.
But thus I lete in lust and jolitee
This Cambyuskan his lordes festeiynge,   345
Til wel ny the day bigan to sprynge.

Explicit prima pars.

288. **of,** over. **lustiheed,** jollity. 290. **dresse,** prepare to go. 291. **bit,** bids. **hye,** (them) hurry (with). 299. Some MSS (including Ellesmere) omit *at,* whereby *feeste* becomes the subject of *Hath,* but this leaves the line short by a syllable. It seems better to accept Skeat's interpretation of *hath* as equivalent to F. *il y a,* which in OF. is sometimes simply *a.* 302. **after-soper,** a period of time, not sharply defined, after supper. Supper was generally toward evening and people went to bed soon afterwards. Here the company dance until time for supper. They eat and drink, "and whan this hadde an ende" they go to the temple. After the service "they soupen al by day." Since it is still daylight, they go to inspect the horse. 303. **al a route,** a whole company. 306. **syn,** since. 307. **Theras,** where. 308. **tho,** then. 311. **his governaunce,** how it was managed. 316. **trille,** turn. **stant,** (which) stands. 318. **nempne,** name, mention. 320. **ther as,** where. 322. **effect,** efficacy. **gyn,** contrivance. 326. **ydrawe ne ybore,** drawn or carried. 331. **clepen,** call. 332. **gyse,** manner. 335. **of,** by. 340. **The brydel.** Removing the bridle caused the horse to vanish, or become invisible. 341. **leeve,** lief, precious. 342. **noot,** know not. 343. **hir,** their. 345. **festeiynge,** making festivity.

Sequitur pars secunda.

The norice of digestioun, the sleep,
Gan on hem wynke and bad hem taken keep
That muchel drynke and labour wolde han
    reste;
And with a galpyng mouth hem alle he keste,
And seyde that it was tyme to lye adoun,   351
For blood was in his domynacioun.
"Cherisseth blood, natures freend," quod he.
They thanken hym galpynge, by two, by thre,
And every wight gan drawe hym to his reste,   355
As sleep hem bad; they tooke it for the beste.
    Hire dremes shul nat now been toold for me;
Ful were hire heddes of fumositee,
That causeth dreem of which ther nys no charge,
They slepen til that it was pryme large,   360
The mooste part, but it were Canacee.
She was ful mesurable, as wommen be;
For of hir fader hadde she take leve
To goon to reste soone after it was eve.
Hir liste nat appalled for to be,   365
Ne on the morwe unfeestlich for to se,
And slepte hire firste sleep, and thanne awook.
For swich a joye she in hir herte took
Bothe of hir queynte ryng and hire mirour,
That twenty tyme she changed hir colour;   370
And in hire sleep, right for impressioun
Of hire mirour, she hadde a visioun.
Wherfore, er that the sonne gan up glyde,
She cleped on hir maistresse hire bisyde,
And seyde that hire liste for to ryse.   375
    Thise olde wommen that been gladly wyse,
As is hire maistresse, answerde hire anon,
And seyde, "Madame, whider wil ye goon

Thus erly, for the folk been alle on reste?"
    "I wol," quod she, "arise, for me leste   380
No lenger for to slepe, and walke aboute."
    Hire maistresse clepeth wommen a greet
    route,
And up they rysen, wel a ten or twelve;
Up riseth fresshe Canacee hirselve,
As rody and bright as dooth the yonge sonne, 385
That in the Ram is foure degrees up ronne—
Noon hyer was he whan she redy was—
And forth she walketh esily a pas,
Arrayed after the lusty seson soote
Lightly, for to pleye and walke on foote,   390
Nat but with fyve or sixe of hir meynee;
And in a trench forth in the park gooth she.
    The vapour which that fro the erthe glood
Made the sonne to seme rody and brood;
But nathelees it was so fair a sighte   395
That it made alle hire hertes for to lighte,
What for the seson and the morwenynge,
And for the foweles that she herde synge.
For right anon she wiste what they mente,
Right by hir song, and knew al hire entente, 400
    The knotte why that every tale is toold,
If it be taried til that lust be coold
Of hem that han it after herkned yoore,
The savour passeth ever lenger the moore,
For fulsomnesse of his prolixitee;   405
And by the same resoun, thynketh me,
I sholde to the knotte condescende,
And maken of hir walkyng soone an ende.
    Amydde a tree, for drye as whit as chalk,
As Canacee was pleyyng in hir walk,   410

---

347. norice, nurse. **350. galpyng**, yawning. **keste**, kissed. The form is Kentish; see Language, §8. **352. For blood . . .,** Blood (as one of the humors) was supposed to be in domination from 8 P.M. to 3 A.M., or, according to other authorities, from midnight until 6 A.M. **353. Cherisseth**, take good care of. **357. for**, by. **358. fumositee**, fumes arising from wine drinking. Dame Pertelote in the *NPT*, B 4113 ff. discourses on the causes of dreams. **359. charge**, significance. **360. pryme large**, well into the period of prime, which ended at 9 A.M. **361. but it were**, except. **362. mesurable**, moderate. **365. appalled**, made pale, tired. **366. unfeestlich**, unfestive. **369. queynte**, curious. **371. impressioun**, the effect produced (by). **376. glady wyse . . .,** are glad to know all that is in their mistress's mind. **382. clepeth**, calls. **386. up ronne**, *i.e.* has risen four degrees above the horizon; very soon after sunrise. **388. esily a pas**, at an easy pace. **389. soote**, sweet. **391. Nat but with**, with only. **392. trench**, path through the shrubbery or the trees. **393. glood**, glided. **396. lighte**, feel light. **397. morwenynge**, early morning. **401. knotte**, main point. **402. taried**, delayed. **lust**, desire, interest. **403. yoore**, for a while. **405. his**, its. **407. condescende**, get down. **409. drye**, dryness; sometimes printed *fordrye* (dried up), but the past part. is usually *fordryed*. For the construction cf. *for old* (A 2142), *for blak* (A 2144), *for syk* (D 394).

Ther sat a faucon over hire heed ful hye,
That with a pitous voys so gan to crye
That all the wode resouned of hire cry.
Ybeten hadde she hirself so pitously
With bothe hir wynges, til the rede blood   415
Ran endelong the tree ther-as she stood.
And evere in oon she cryde alwey and shrighte,
And with hir beek hirselven so she prighte,
That ther nys tygre, ne noon so crueel beest,
That dwelleth outher in wode or in forest,   420
That nolde han wept, if that he wepe koude,
For sorwe of hire, she shrighte alwey so loude.
For ther nas nevere yet no man on lyve,
If that I koude a faucon wel discryve,
That herde of swich another of fairnesse,   425
As wel of plumage as of gentillesse
Of shap, of al that myghte yrekened be.
A faucon peregryn thanne semed she
Of fremde land; and everemoore, as she stood,
She swowneth now and now for lakke of blood,
Til wel neigh is she fallen fro the tree.   431
      This faire kynges doghter, Canacee,
That on hir fynger baar the queynte ryng,
Thurgh which she understood wel every thyng
That any fowel may in his leden seyn,   435
And koude answeren hym in his ledene ageyn,
Hath understonde what this faucon seyde,
And wel neigh for the routhe almoost she
      deyde.
And to the tree she gooth ful hastily,
And on this faukon looketh pitously,   440
And heeld hir lappe abrood, for wel she wiste
The faukon moste fallen fro the twiste,
Whan that it swowned next, for lakke of blood.
A longe while to wayten hire she stood,
Til atte laste she spak in this manere   445
Unto the hauk, as ye shal after heere:

      "What is the cause, if it be for to telle,
That ye be in this furial pyne of helle?"
Quod Canacee unto this hauk above.
"Is this for sorwe of deeth or los of love?   450
For, as I trowe, thise been causes two
That causen moost a gentil herte wo;
Of oother harm it nedeth nat to speke.
For ye yourself upon yourself yow wreke,
Which proveth wel that outher ire or drede   455
Moot been enchesoun of youre cruel dede,
Syn that I see noon oother wight yow chace.
For love of God, as dooth youreselven grace,
Or what may been youre help? for west nor est
Ne saugh I nevere er now no bryd ne beest   460
That ferde with hymself so pitously.
Ye sle me with youre sorwe verraily,
I have of yow so greet compassioun.
For Goddes love, com fro the tree adoun;
And as I am a kynges doghter trewe,   465
If that I verraily the cause knewe
Of youre disese, if it lay in my myght,
I wolde amenden it er that it were nyght,
As wisly helpe me grete God of kynde!
And herbes shal I right ynowe yfynde   470
To heele with youre hurtes hastily."
      Tho shrighte this faucon yet moore pitously
Than ever she dide, and fil to grounde anon,
And lith aswowne, deed and lyk a stoon,
Til Canacee hath in hire lappe hire take   475
Unto the tyme she gan of swough awake.
And after that she of hir swough gan breyde,
Right in hir haukes ledene thus she seyde:
"That pitee renneth soone in gentil herte,
Feelynge his similitude in peynes smerte,   480
Is preved alday, as men may it see,
As wel by werk as by auctoritee;
For gentil herte kitheth gentillesse.

416. **endelong,** along. 417. **evere in oon,** constantly, uniformly. **shrighte,** shrieked. 418. **prighte,** pricked. 420. **outher,** either. 423. **on lyve,** alive. 426. **gentillesse,** gracefulness, beauty. 428. **faucon peregryn,** *lit.* pilgrim falcon. Editors from Tyrwhitt down have quoted the *Tresor* of Brunetto Latini to the effect that the bird is so called because its nest is never found. 429. **fremde,** foreign. 430. **now and now,** now and again. 435. **leden,** language. 441. **lappe,** any part of a garment hanging loose. 442. **moste,** must. **twiste,** branch. 444. **wayten,** watch. 447. **if . . . telle,** if it may be told. 448. **furial pyne,** furious pain. 454. **yow wreke,** avenge yourself. 455. **outher ire or drede,** either anger or anxiety. 456. **Moot,** must. **enchesoun,** cause. 458. **as dooth youreselven grace,** have mercy on yourself. 467. **disese,** distress. 469. **As wisly . . .,** as certainly may the great God of nature help me. 471. **hastily,** quickly. 476. **swough,** swoon. 477. **breyde,** come out of. 480. **his similitude,** its counterpart. 482. **werk,** experience. 483. **kitheth,** shows.

I se wel that ye han of my distresse
Compassion, my faire Canacee,   485
Of verray wommanly benignytee
That Nature in youre principles hath set.
But for noon hope for to fare the bet,
But for to obeye unto youre herte free,
And for to maken othere be war by me,   490
As by the whelp chasted is the leoun,
Right for that cause and that conclusioun,
Whil that I have a leyser and a space,
Myn harm I wol confessen er I pace."

    And evere, whil that oon hir sorwe tolde,   495
That oother weep as she to water wolde,
Til that the faucon bad hire to be stille,
And, with a syk, right thus she seyde hir wille:
    "Ther I was bred—allas, that ilke day!—
And fostred in a roche of marbul gray   500
So tendrely that no thyng eyled me,
I nyste nat what was adversitee,
Til I koude flee ful hye under the sky.
Tho dwelte a tercelet me faste by,
That semed welle of alle gentillesse;   505
Al were he ful of treson and falsnesse,
It was so wrapped under humble cheere,
And under hewe of trouthe in swich manere,
Under plesance, and under bisy peyne,
That no wight koude han wend he koude feyne,
So depe in greyn he dyed his coloures.   511
Right as a serpent hit hym under floures
Til he may seen his tyme for to byte,
Right so this god of loves ypocryte
Dooth so his cerymonyes and obeisaunces,   515
And kepeth in semblaunt alle his observaunces
That sownen into gentillesse of love.

As in a toumbe is al the faire above,
And under is the corps, swich as ye woot,
Swich was this ypocrite, bothe coold and hoot.
And in this wise he served his entente,   521
That, save the feend, noon wiste what he
    mente,
Til he so longe hadde wopen and compleyned,
And many a yeer his service to me feyned,
Til that myn herte, to pitous and to nyce,   525
Al innocent of his corouned malice,
For fered of his deeth, as thoughte me,
Upon his othes and his seuretee,
Graunted hym love upon this condicioun,
That everemoore myn honour and renoun   530
Were saved, bothe privee and apert;
This is to seyn, that after his desert,
I yaf hym al myn herte and al my thoght—
God woot and he, that ootherwise noght—
And took his herte in chaunge of myn for ay.   535
But sooth is seyd, goon sithen many a day,
'A trewe wight and a theef thenken nat oon.'
And whan he saugh the thyng so fer ygoon
That I hadde graunted hym fully my love,
In swich a gyse as I have seyd above,   540
And yeven hym my trewe herte as free
As he swoor he yaf his herte to me;
Anon this tigre, ful of doublenesse,
Fil on his knees with so devout humblesse,
With so heigh reverence, and, as by his cheere,
So lyk a gentil lovere of manere,   546
So ravysshed, as it semed, for the joye,
That nevere Jason ne Parys of Troye—
Jason? certes, ne noon oother man
Syn Lameth was, that alderfirst bigan   550

---

491. chasted, chastised. The allusion is to the practice of beating a dog in front of a lion, and to the proverb that resulted. Cf. *Othello,* II. iii. 272: even so as one would beat his offenceless dog to affright an imperious lion. **492. conclusioun,** end, purpose. **496. weep,** wept. **wolde,** would turn. **499. Ther,** where. It is likely that the bird is a princess temporarily transformed into a falcon. **500. roche,** rock. **503. flee,** fly. **504. Tho,** then. **tercelet,** male falcon. **505. welle,** source. **506. Al were he,** although he was. **509. plesance,** pleasant manner. **bisy peyne,** attentiveness, attentions. **511. in greyn,** in a fast color, hence, in the very fiber. **coloures,** outward appearances. **512. hit,** hides. **516. in semblaunt,** seemingly. **517. sownen into,** are appropriate to. **gentillesse of,** nobility in. **520. bothe coold and hoot,** under all circumstances. **521. entente,** purpose. **523. wopen,** wept. **525. to nyce,** too foolish. **526. corouned,** consecrated, sovereign. **527. For fered,** for fear. **as thoughte me,** as it seemed to me. **532. after,** according to. **534. that ootherwise noght,** that I gave him my heart on no other condition. **535. chaunge,** exchange. **536. goon,** ago; see note to A 1521. **sithen,** since. **537. trewe wight,** honest man. **nat oon,** not alike. **540. gyse,** manner. **546. of manere,** in behavior. **547. ravysshed,** carried away, beside himself. **548. Jason,** who deserted Media for Creusa. **Parys,** Paris, who deserted Oenone for Helen. **550. Syn Lameth,** since Lameth. **alderfirst,** first of all. Lameth, according to *Genesis,* 4:19, took two wives.

To loven two, as writen folk biforn—
Ne nevere, syn the firste man was born,
Ne koude man, by twenty thousand part,
Countrefete the sophymes of his art,
Ne were worthy unbokelen his galoche, 555
Ther doublenesse or feynyng sholde approche,
Ne so koude thonke a wight as he dide me!
His manere was an hevene for to see
Til any womman, were she never so wys,
So peynted he and kembde at point-devys 560
As wel his wordes as his contenaunce.
And I so loved hym for his obeisaunce,
And for the trouthe I demed in his herte,
That if so were that any thyng hym smerte,
Al were it never so lite, and I it wiste, 565
Me thoughte I felte deeth myn herte twiste.
And shortly, so ferforth this thyng is went,
That my wyl was his willes instrument;
This is to seyn, my wyl obeyed his wyl
In alle thyng, as fer as reson fil, 570
Kepynge the boundes of my worship evere.
Ne nevere hadde I thyng so lief, ne levere,
As hym, God woot! ne nevere shal namo.
    This laste lenger than a yeer or two,
That I supposed of hym noght but good. 575
But finally, thus atte laste it stood,
That Fortune wolde that he moste twynne
Out of that place which that I was inne.
Wher me was wo, that is no questioun;
I kan nat make of it discripsioun; 580
For o thyng dar I tellen boldely,
I knowe what is the peyne of deeth therby;
Swich harm I felte for he ne myghte bileve.
So on a day of me he took his leve,
So sorwefully eek that I wende verraily 585
That he had felt as muche harm as I,

Whan that I herde hym speke, and saugh his
   hewe.
But nathelees, I thoughte he was so trewe,
And eek that he repaire sholde ageyn
Withinne a litel while, sooth to seyn; 590
And resoun wolde eek that he moste go
For his honour, as ofte it happeth so,
That I made vertu of necessitee,
And took it wel, syn that it moste be.
As I best myghte, I hidde fro hym my sorwe, 595
And took hym by the hond, Seint John to
   borwe,
And seyde hym thus: 'Lo, I am youres al;
Beth swich as I to yow have been and shal.'
What he answerde, it nedeth noght reherce;
Who kan sey bet than he, who kan do werse? 600
Whan he hath al wel seyd, thanne hath he doon.
'Therfore bihoveth hire a ful long spoon
That shal ete with a feend,' thus herde I seye.
So atte laste he moste forth his weye,
And forth he fleeth til he cam ther hym leste. 605
Whan it cam hym to purpos for to reste,
I trowe he hadde thilke text in mynde,
That 'alle thyng, repeirynge to his kynde,
Gladeth hymself;' thus seyn men, as I gesse.
Men loven of propre kynde newefangelnesse,
As briddes doon that men in cages fede. 611
For though thou nyght and day take of hem
   hede,
And strawe hir cage faire and softe as silk,
And yeve hem sugre, hony, breed and milk,
Yet right anon as that his dore is uppe, 615
He with his feet wol spurne adoun his cuppe,
And to the wode he wole, and wormes ete;
So newefangel been they of hire mete,
And loven novelries of propre kynde;

---

554. **sophymes**, deceits. 555. **unbokelen his galoche**, unbuckle his shoe; cf. *Mark*, 1:7. 556. **Ther**, where. **approche**, be involved. 557. **thonke**, thank. 559. **Til**, to. 560. **kembde**, combed. **at point-devys**, precisely, carefully. 561. **contenaunce**, demeanor. 562. **obeisaunce**, marks of respect. 567. **so ferforth**, so far, to such an extent. 571. **worship**, honor. 572. **so lief, ne levere**, so dear, nor dearer. 574. **laste**, lasted. 577. **twynne**, depart. 579. **Wher**, whether. 583. **for**, because. **bileve**, remain. 585. **verraily**, verily. 586. **harm**, sorrow. 589. **repaire**, return. 591. **wolde**, wished, required. 596. **to borwe**, as a pledge. 600. **Who kan . .** , who can talk better and act worse? 602. **a ful long spoon**. A common proverb. 603. **feend**, devil. 608. **alle thyng, repeirynge . . .** The sentiment, which comes from Boethius (III, met. 2), is translated by Chaucer "alle thynges rejoysen hem of hir retornynge ayen to hir nature." 610. **of propre kynde**, by their nature. 611. **As briddes doon**. The comparison comes from the same passage in Boethius. 613. **strawe**, strew. 615. **anon as**, as soon as. 616. **spurne adoun**, kick over (down). 619. **novelries**, new things.

No gentillesse of blood ne may hem bynde. 620
  So ferde this tercelet, allas the day!
Though he were gentil born, and fressh and gay,
And goodlich for to seen, and humble and free,
He saugh upon a tyme a kyte flee,
And sodeynly he loved this kyte so   625
That al his love is clene fro me ago;
And hath his trouthe falsed in this wyse.
Thus hath the kyte my love in hire servyse,
And I am lorn withouten remedie!"
And with that word this faucon gan to crie, 630
And swowned eft in Canacees barm.
  Greet was the sorwe for the haukes harm
That Canacee and alle hir wommen made;
They nyste hou they myghte the faucon glade.
But Canacee hom bereth hire in hir lappe,   635
And softely in plastres gan hire wrappe,
Ther as she with hire beek hadde hurt hirselve.
Now kan nat Canacee but herbes delve
Out of the ground, and make salves newe
Of herbes preciouse and fyne of hewe,   640
To heelen with this hauk. Fro day to nyght
She dooth hire bisynesse and al hire myght,
And by hire beddes heed she made a mewe,
And covered it with veluettes blewe,
In signe of trouthe that is in wommen sene. 645
And al withoute, the mewe is peynted grene,
In which were peynted alle thise false fowles,
As ben thise tidyves, tercelettes, and owles;

Right for despit were peynted hem bisyde,
Pyes, on hem for to crie and chyde.   650
  Thus lete I Canacee hir hauk kepyng;
I wol namoore as now speke of hir ryng,
Til it come eft to purpos for to seyn
How that this faucon gat hire love ageyn
Repentant, as the storie telleth us,   655
By mediacioun of Cambalus,
The kynges sone, of which that I yow tolde.
But hennesforth I wol my proces holde
To speke of aventures and of batailles,
That nevere yet was herd so grete mervailles. 660
  First wol I telle yow of Cambyuskan,
That in his tyme many a citee wan;
And after wol I speke of Algarsif,
How that he wan Theodora to his wif,
For whom ful ofte in greet peril he was,   665
Ne hadde he been holpen by the steede of bras;
And after wol I speke of Cambalo,
That faught in lystes with the bretheren two
For Canacee er that he myghte hire wynne.
And ther I lefte I wol ayeyn bigynne.   670

Explicit secunda pars.

Incipit pars tercia.

Appollo whirleth up his chaar so hye,
Til that the god Mercurius hous, the slye—
.   .   .   .

Heere folwen the wordes of the Frankeleyn to the Squier, and the wordes of the Hoost to the Frankeleyn.

"In feith, Squier, thow hast thee wel yquit
And gentilly. I preise wel thy wit,"
Quod the Frankeleyn, "considerynge thy
  yowthe,   675
So feelyngly thou spekest, sire, I allow the!

As to my doom, ther is noon that is heere
Of eloquence that shal be thy peere,
If that thou lyve; God yeve thee good chaunce,
And in vertu sende thee continuaunce!   680
For of thy speche I have greet deyntee.

624. **flee,** fly. 629. **lorn,** lost. 631. **eft,** again. **barm,** lap. 634. **nyste,** did not know. 636. **plastres,** plasters. 637. **Ther as,** where. 638. **kan nat . . . but,** can only. 644. **blewe,** the symbol of constancy, whereas green (cf. l. 646) symbolized inconstancy. 648. **tidyves.** See *LGW* 154, where the *tydif* is mentioned as a false bird. 650. **Pyes,** magpies. 651. **lete,** leave. 658. **proces holde,** keep to my subject (argument). 666. **holpen,** helped. 667. **Cambalo,** hardly the same as the Cambalus of l. 656 unless we take *wynne* in the sense of "reach, get to." 671. **Appollo.** The sun whirls his chariot up until he enters the mansion (*hous*) of Mercury, which was the sign Gemini. This is another way of saying that two months had passed. 676. **allow,** commend. 677. **doom,** judgment. 679. **chaunce,** fortune. 681. **deyntee,** pleasure.

I have a sone, and by the Trinitee,
I hadde levere than twenty pound worth lond,
Though it right now were fallen in myn hond,
He were a man of swich discrecioun   685
As that ye been! Fy on possessioun,
But if a man be vertuous withal!
I have my sone snybbed, and yet shal,
For he to vertu listeth nat entende;
But for to pleye at dees, and to despende   690
And lese al that he hath, is his usage.
And he hath levere talken with a page
Than to comune with any gentil wight
Where he myghte lerne gentillesse aright."
  "Straw for youre gentillesse!" quod oure
    Hoost.   695

"What, Frankeleyn! pardee, sire, wel thou
  woost
That ech of yow moot tellen atte leste
A tale or two, or breken his biheste."
  "That knowe I wel, sire," quod the Frank-
    eleyn.
"I prey yow, haveth me nat in desdeyn,   700
Though to this man I speke a word or two."
  "Telle on thy tale withouten wordes mo."
  "Gladly, sire Hoost," quod he, "I wole obeye
Unto your wyl; now herkneth what I seye.
I wol yow nat contrarien in no wyse   705
As fer as that my wittes wol suffyse.
I prey to God that it may plesen yow;
Thanne woot I wel that it is good ynow."

The Franklin's Tale

THE FRANKLIN'S PROLOGUE

The Prologe of the Frankeleyns Tale.

  Thise olde gentil Britouns in hir dayes
Of diverse aventures maden layes,   710
Rymeyed in hir firste Briton tonge;
Whiche layes with hir instrumentz they songe,
Or elles redden hem for hir plesaunce,
And oon of hem have I in remembraunce,
Which I shal seyn with good wyl as I kan.   715
  But, sires, by cause I am a burel man,
At my bigynnyng first I yow biseche,
Have me excused of my rude speche.

I lerned nevere rethorik, certeyn;
Thyng that I speke, it moot be bare and pleyn.
I sleep nevere on the Mount of Pernaso,   721
Ne lerned Marcus Tullius Scithero.
Colours ne knowe I none, withouten drede,
But swiche colours as growen in the mede,
Or elles swiche as men dye or peynte.   725
Colours of rethoryk been me to queynte;
My spirit feeleth noght of swich mateere.
But if yow list, my tale shul ye heere.

683. **twenty pound worth lond,** land which would yield £20 a year in income. 685. **discrecioun,** prudence, good sense. 688. **snybbed,** reproved. 689. **entende,** incline. 690. **dees,** dice. 691. **lese,** lose. 697. **atte leste,** at least. 698. **biheste,** promise. 700. **haveth . . . desdeyn,** do not be offended with me. 709. **Britouns,** Bretons, people of Brittany. 711. **Rymeyed,** rimed. **firste,** original. 716. **burel,** plain. 721. **Pernaso,** Parnassus. 722. **Scithero,** Cicero. 723. **Colours,** *i.e.* colors of rhetoric, figures of speech, rhetoric devices, but of course the Franklin is punning on the word *colours* in this and the next line. 726. **queynte,** strange, unfamiliar.

THE FRANKLIN'S TALE

Heere bigynneth the Frankeleyns Tale.

In Armorik, that called is Britayne,
Ther was a knyght that loved and dide his
    payne   730
To serve a lady in his beste wise;
And many a labour, many a greet emprise
He for his lady wroghte, er she were wonne.
For she was oon the faireste under sonne,
And eek therto comen of so heigh kynrede   735
That wel unnethes dorste this knyght, for drede,
Telle hire his wo, his peyne, and his distresse.
But atte laste she, for his worthynesse,
And namely for his meke obeysaunce,
Hath swich a pitee caught of his penaunce   740
That pryvely she fil of his accord
To take hym for hir housbonde and hir lord,

Of swich lordshipe as men han over hir wyves.
And for to lede the moore in blisse hir lyves,
Of his free wyl he swoor hire as a knyght   745
That nevere in al his lyf he, day ne nyght,
Ne sholde upon hym take no maistrie
Agayn hir wyl, ne kithe hire jalousie,
But hire obeye, and folwe hir wyl in al,
As any lovere to his lady shal,   750
Save that the name of soveraynetee,
That wolde he have for shame of his degree.
   She thanked hym, and with ful greet hum-
    blesse
She seyde, "Sire, sith of youre gentillesse
Ye profre me to have so large a reyne,   755
Ne wolde nevere God bitwixe us tweyne,

The Franklin's Tale. The story which the Franklin tells is by his own statement a Breton lay. This is a short romance suitable for singing or recitation at a single sitting. The most famous are the lays of Marie de France, which are in French, but we have a number of examples of the type in Middle English. Some of them are not distinguishable from other short English romances, in subject matter or treatment, except that the scene is Brittany, or they claim to be Breton lays and indeed are based in some cases on existing Breton lays in French. In the Middle English *Lai le Freine* we are told that such lays are mostly of love and many of "fairy." *The Franklin's Tale* is of both. It is thus possible that its source may have been a French lay now lost, and that is the opinion of some scholars.

In the absence of such a source and of any evidence (other than the Franklin's statement) that such a Breton lay ever existed, other students of Chaucer have concluded that Chaucer based his tale on an episode in Boccaccio's *Filocolo*, a long prose romance telling the story known in English as *Floris and Blancheflour*. The episode is one in a series posing *questioni d'amore*, problems of love which offer interesting topics for discussion. The skeleton of the plot is the same as that of *The Franklin's Tale*, and the question in both is the same,—which of the three characters (husband, lover, magician) performed the most generous act? In the *Filocolo* the miracle consists in making a garden produce with summer abundance in January. Boccaccio used the episode again in the *Decameron* (x. 5). The scene, of course, is not laid in Brittany. It is not impossible that Boccaccio was adapting a Breton lay, but the story belongs to a type of folktale widely known in the East, which students of folktales call "the damsel's rash promise." In any case, Chaucer is supposed to have taken the names of at least two of his characters (Arveragus and Aurelius) from the *Historia Regum Britanniae* of Geoffrey of Monmouth. Dorigen's long lament, in which she recalls many women who preferred to die rather than sacrifice their virtue, was certainly not in Chaucer's source, whatever that source was. All the examples are drawn from St. Jerome's treatise against Jovinian, which Chaucer made so much use of in the prologue to *The Wife of Bath's Tale* and elsewhere. For the pertinent passages of the *Filocolo*, Geoffrey of Monmouth, and Jerome as well as selected quotations from other Breton lays, the reader may consult *SA*, where an excellent bibliography of previous scholarship is given.

The association of the *Tale* with the larger discussion of marriage (the so-called Marriage Group) and the use of Jerome's treatise suggest that it was written at the time this discussion was conceived. The passage in which he draws upon Jerome could, of course, be a later addition, but the resemblances to small details in the *Teseida* which have been advanced are not such as to require us to put *The Franklin's Tale* back in the period when Chaucer was writing the *Palamon and Arcite.* While it is impossible to be dogmatic, it is perhaps safest to assign *The Franklin's Tale* to the period of *The Canterbury Tales* in general and of the Marriage Group in particular.

729. Armorik, Armorica (Brittany). **732. emprise,** undertaking. **734. oon the faireste,** one of the fairest. **739. namely,** especially. **obeysaunce,** marks of respect. **740. penaunce,** distress. **741. fil of his accord,** came to agreement with him. **748. kithe,** show. **752. for shame of . . .,** lest it should reflect upon his rank. **755. profre me,** offer me (the privilege). **so large a reyne,** so free a rein. **756. Ne wolde nevere God . . .,** would that God grant that there should never be, through fault of mine, either war or strife between us.

As in my gilt, were outher werre or stryf.
Sire, I wol be youre humble trewe wyf;
Have heer my trouthe, til that myn herte
  breste."
Thus been they bothe in quiete and in reste. 760
  For o thyng, sires, saufly dar I seye,
That freendes everych oother moot obeye,
If they wol longe holden compaignye.
Love wol nat been constreyned by maistrye.
Whan maistrie comth, the God of Love anon
Beteth his wynges, and farewel, he is gon! 766
Love is a thyng as any spirit free.
Wommen, of kynde, desiren libertee,
And nat to been constreyned as a thral;
And so doon men, if I sooth seyen shal. 770
Looke who that is moost pacient in love,
He is at his avantage al above.
Pacience is an heigh vertu, certeyn,
For it venquysseth, as thise clerkes seyn,
Thynges that rigour sholde nevere atteyne. 775
For every word men may nat chide or pleyne.
Lerneth to suffre, or elles, so moot I goon,
Ye shul it lerne, wher so ye wole or noon;
For in this world, certein, ther no wight is
That he ne dooth or seith somtyme amys. 780
Ire, siknesse, or constellacioun,
Wyn, wo, or chaungynge of complexioun
Causeth ful ofte to doon amys or speken.
On every wrong a man may nat be wreken.
After the tyme moste be temperaunce 785
To every wight that kan on governaunce.
And therfore hath this wise, worthy knyght,
To lyve in ese, suffrance hire bihight,
And she to hym ful wisly gan to swere
That nevere sholde ther be defaute in here. 790
  Heere may men seen an humble, wys accord;
Thus hath she take hir servant and hir lord,—

Servant in love, and lord in mariage.
Thanne was he bothe in lordshipe and servage.
Servage? nay, but in lordshipe above, 795
Sith he hath bothe his lady and his love;
His lady, certes, and his wyf also,
The which that lawe of love acordeth to.
And whan he was in this prosperitee,
Hoom with his wyf he gooth to his contree, 800
Nat fer fro Pedmark, ther his dwellyng was,
Where as he lyveth in blisse and in solas.
  Who koude telle, but he hadde wedded be,
The joye, the ese, and the prosperitee
That is bitwixe an housbonde and his wyf? 805
A yeer and moore lasted this blisful lyf,
Til that the knyght of which I speke of thus,
That of Kayrrud was cleped Arveragus,
Shoop hym to goon and dwelle a yeer or tweyne
In Engelond, that cleped was eek Briteyne, 810
To seke in armes worship and honour;
For al his lust he sette in swich labour;
And dwelled there two yeer, the book seith
  thus.
  Now wol I stynten of this Arveragus,
And speken I wole of Dorigen his wyf, 815
That loveth hire housbonde as hire hertes lyf.
For his absence wepeth she and siketh,
As doon thise noble wyves whan hem liketh.
She moorneth, waketh, wayleth, fasteth, pleyn-
  eth;
Desir of his presence hire so destreyneth 820
That al this wyde world she sette at noght.
Hire freendes, whiche that knewe hir hevy
  thoght,
Conforten hire in al that ever they may.
They prechen hire, they telle hire nyght and day
That causelees she sleeth hirself, allas! 825
And every confort possible in this cas

759. breste, break, burst. **762. everych oother,** each other. **obeye,** yield to. **768. of kynde,** by nature. **771. Looke who,** whoever. **772. al above,** above all others. **775. rigour,** harshness, severity. **778. wher so,** whether. **781. constellacioun** his stars. **782. complexioun,** the combination of the four humors (hot, cold, moist, dry) in the body, from which the temperament of a person resulted. **784. wreken,** revenged. **785. After,** according to. **temperaunce,** moderation. **786. kan on governaunce,** knows how to govern himself. **788. bihight,** pledged. **789. wisely,** certainly. **790. here,** her. **795. above,** on high; cf. *God above.* **801. Pedmark,** Penmark, on the coast of Finistère, the westernmost *département* of Brittany. **ther,** where. **803. but,** unless. **808. Kayrrud.** The name corresponds to the modern Kerru, but no place of this name is known near Penmark. **cleped,** named. **809. Shoop hym,** arranged. **811. worship,** renown. **812. al his lust he sette,** he set his heart on. **814. stynten,** leave off. **of,** concerning. **817. siketh,** sighs. **818. hem liketh,** it pleases them to. **820. destreyneth,** oppresses.

They doon to hire with al hire bisynesse,
Al for to make hire leve hire hevynesse.

By proces, as ye knowen everichoon,
Men may so longe graven in a stoon　　　830
Til som figure therinne emprented be.
So longe han they conforted hire, til she
Receyved hath, by hope and by resoun,
The emprentyng of hire consolacioun,
Thurgh which hir grete sorwe gan aswage;　835
She may nat alwey duren in swich rage.

And eek Arveragus, in al this care,
Hath sent hire lettres hoom of his welfare,
And that he wol come hastily agayn;
Or elles hadde this sorwe hir herte slayn.　840

Hire freendes sawe hir sorwe gan to slake,
And preyde hire on knees, for Goddes sake,
To come and romen hire in compaignye,
Awey to dryve hire derke fantasye.
And finally she graunted that requeste,　　845
For wel she saugh that it was for the beste.

Now stood hire castel faste by the see,
And often with hire freendes walketh shee,
Hire to disporte, upon the bank an heigh,
Where as she many a ship and barge seigh　850
Seillynge hir cours, where as hem liste go.
But thanne was that a parcel of hire wo,
For to hirself ful ofte, "Allas!" seith she,
"Is ther no ship, of so manye as I se,
Wol bryngen hom my lord? Thanne were myn
　　herte　　　　　　　　　　　　　　　　　855
Al warisshed of his bittre peynes smerte."

Another tyme ther wolde she sitte and
　　thynke,
And caste hir eyen dounward fro the brynke.
But whan she saugh the grisly rokkes blake,
For verray feere so wolde hir herte quake　860
That on hire feet she myghte hire noght sustene.
Thanne wolde she sitte adoun upon the grene,
And pitously into the see biholde,

And seyn right thus, with sorweful sikes colde:
"Eterne God, that thurgh thy purveiaunce
Ledest the world by certein governaunce,　　866
In ydel, as men seyn, ye no thyng make.
But, Lord, thise grisly feendly rokkes blake,
That semen rather a foul confusioun
Of werk than any fair creacioun　　　　　870
Of swich a parfit wys God and a stable,
Why han ye wroght this werk unresonable?
For by this werk, south, north, ne west, ne eest,
Ther nys yfostred man, ne bryd, ne beest;
It dooth no good, to my wit, but anoyeth.　875
Se ye nat, Lord, how mankynde it destroyeth?
An hundred thousand bodyes of mankynde
Han rokkes slayn, al be they nat in mynde,
Which mankynde is so fair part of thy werk
That thou it madest lyk to thyn owene merk.
Thanne semed it ye hadde a greet chiertee　881
Toward mankynde; but how thanne may it bee
That ye swiche meenes make it to destroyen,
Whiche meenes do no good, but evere anoyen?
I woot wel clerkes wol seyn as hem leste,　885
By argumentz, that al is for the beste,
Though I ne kan the causes nat yknowe.
But thilke God that made wynd to blowe
As kepe my lord! this my conclusion.
To clerkes lete I al disputison.　　　　　890
But wolde God that alle thise rokkes blake
Were sonken into helle for his sake!
Thise rokkes sleen myn herte for the feere."
Thus wolde she seyn, with many a pitous teere.

Hire freendes sawe that it was no disport　895
To romen by the see, but disconfort,
And shopen for to pleyen somwher elles.
They leden hire by ryveres and by welles,
And eek in othere places delitables;
They dauncen, and they pleyen at ches and
　　tables.　　　　　　　　　　　　　　　　900
So on a day, right in the morwe-tyde,

---

829. **By proces,** in the course of time. 830. **graven,** engrave, scratch. 834. **hire,** their. 836. **rage,** distress. 839. **hastily,** quickly, soon. 843. **romen hire,** go for a walk. 844. **derke fantasye,** dismal mood. 850. **barge,** cargo vessel with sails. **seigh,** saw. 852. **parcel,** part. 856. **warisshed,** cured. **his,** its. 864. **sikes,** sighs. 865. **purveiaunce,** providence. 867. **In ydel,** in vain. 874. **yfostred,** helped, promoted. 880. **merk,** image. 881. **chiertee,** affection. 889. **As kepe,** keep. **this,** this is. 890. **lete,** leave. **disputison,** disputation. 897. **shopen,** arranged. 898. **welles,** small streams. 900. **tables,** backgammon.

Unto a gardyn that was ther bisyde,
In which that they hadde maad hir ordinaunce
Of vitaille and of oother purveiaunce,
They goon and pleye hem al the longe day.   905
And this was on the sixte morwe of May,
Which May hadde peynted with his softe
    shoures
This gardyn ful of leves and of floures;
And craft of mannes hand so curiously
Arrayed hadde this gardyn, trewely,   910
That nevere was ther gardyn of swich prys,
But if it were the verray paradys.
The odour of floures and the fresshe sighte
Wolde han maked any herte lighte
That evere was born, but if to greet siknesse, 915
Or to greet sorwe, helde it in distresse;
So ful it was of beautee with plesaunce.
At after-dyner gonne they to daunce,
And synge also, save Dorigen allone,
Which made alwey hir compleint and hir
    moone,   920
For she ne saugh hym on the daunce go
That was hir housbonde and hir love also.
But nathelees she moste a tyme abyde,
And with good hope lete hir sorwe slyde.
    Upon this daunce, amonges othere men,   925
Daunced a squier biforn Dorigen,
That fressher was and jolyer of array,
As to my doom, than is the monthe of May.
He syngeth, daunceth, passynge any man
That is, or was, sith that the world bigan.   930
Therwith he was, if men sholde hym discryve,
Oon of the beste farynge man on lyve;
Yong, strong, right vertuous, and riche, and
    wys,
And wel biloved, and holden in greet prys.
And shortly, if the sothe I tellen shal,   935

Unwityng of this Dorigen at al,
This lusty squier, servant to Venus,
Which that ycleped was Aurelius,
Hadde loved hire best of any creature
Two yeer and moore, as was his aventure,   940
But nevere dorste he tellen hire his grevaunce.
Withouten coppe he drank al his penaunce.
He was despeyred; no thyng dorste he seye,
Save in his songes somwhat wolde he wreye
His wo, as in a general compleynyng;   945
He seyde he lovede, and was biloved no thyng.
Of swich matere made he manye layes,
Songes, compleintes, roundels, virelayes,
How that he dorste nat his sorwe telle,
But langwissheth as a furye dooth in helle;   950
And dye he moste, he seyde, as dide Ekko
For Narcisus, that dorste nat telle hir wo.
In oother manere than ye heere me seye,
Ne dorste he nat to hire his wo biwreye,
Save that, paraventure, somtyme at daunces, 955
Ther yonge folk kepen hir observaunces,
It may wel be he looked on hir face
In swich a wise as man that asketh grace;
But nothyng wiste she of his entente.
Nathelees it happed, er they thennes wente,   960
By cause that he was hire neighebour,
And was a man of worship and honour,
And hadde yknowen hym of tyme yoore,
They fille in speche; and forthe, moore and
    moore,
Unto his purpos drough Aurelius,   965
And whan he saugh his tyme, he seyde thus:
"Madame," quod he, "by God that this world
    made,
So that I wiste it myghte youre herte glade,
I wolde that day that youre Arveragus
Wente over the see, that I, Aurelius,   970

903. **ordinaunce,** arrangement. 904. **purveiaunce,** provision. 909. **curiously,** skilfully. 910. **Arrayed,** arranged, laid out. 912. **verray paradys,** Paradise itself. 918. **after-dyner,** late forenoon. See note to B 1445. **gonne,** began. 932. **of the . . . man.** See Language, § 50. **beste farynge,** most attractive. 934. **prys,** esteem. 942. **Withouten coppe,** without satisfaction. The expression *to drink without the cup* occurs twice in *The Tale of Beryn* (ll. 306, 460) and in both instances means to be cheated out of one's expectation; to go without satisfaction. 944. **wreye,** betray. 948. **roundels,** a short lyric form (originally French); see note to *PF* 675 and for an example ll. 680–92 of that poem. The *virelay* also is a variable form, but the basic feature seems to have been stanzas of the type *aaabaaab* with a refrain. 951. **Ekko,** Echo; see note to *BD* 735. 954. **biwreye,** reveal. 963. **hadde.** The subject *she* must be supplied (from *hire*, l. 961). 964. **fille in,** fell into. 965. **drough,** drew.

Hadde went ther nevere I sholde have come
  agayn.
For wel I woot my servyce is in vayn;
My gerdon is but brestyng of myn herte.
Madame, reweth upon my peynes smerte;
For with a word ye may me sleen or save. 975
Heere at youre feet God wolde that I were
  grave!
I ne have as now no leyser moore to seye;
Have mercy, sweete, or ye wol do me deye!"
She gan to looke upon Aurelius: 979
"Is this youre wyl," quod she, "and sey ye thus?
Nevere erst," quod she, "ne wiste I what ye
  mente.
But now, Aurelie, I knowe youre entente,
By thilke God that yaf me soule and lyf,
Ne shal I nevere been untrewe wyf
In word ne werk, as fer as I have wit; 985
I wol been his to whom that I am knyt.
Taak this for fynal answere as of me.
But after that in pley thus seyde she:
  "Aurelie," quod she, "by heighe God above,
Yet wolde I graunte yow to been youre love, 990
Syn I yow se so pitously complayne.
Looke what day that endelong Britayne
Ye remoeve alle the rokkes, stoon by stoon,
That they ne lette ship ne boot to goon,—
I seye, whan ye han maad the coost so clene 995
Of rokkes that ther nys no stoon ysene,
Thanne wol I love yow best of any man,
Have heer my trouthe, in al that evere I kan."
  "Is ther noon oother grace in yow?" quod he.
"No, by that Lord," quod she, "that maked
  me! 1000
For wel I woot that it shal never bityde.
Lat swiche folies out of youre herte slyde.
What deyntee sholde a man han in his lyf
For to go love another mannes wyf,
That hath hir body whan so that hym liketh?"

Aurelius ful ofte soore siketh; 1006
Wo was Aurelie whan that he this herde,
And with a sorweful herte he thus answerde:
  "Madame," quod he, "this were an inpos-
  sible!
Thanne moot I dye of sodeyn deth horrible."
And with that word he turned hym anon. 1011
Tho coome hir othere freendes many oon,
And in the aleyes romeden up and doun,
And nothyng wiste of this conclusioun,
But sodeynly bigonne revel newe 1015
Til that the brighte sonne loste his hewe;
For th' orisonte hath reft the sonne his lyght,—
This is as muche to seye as it was nyght!
And hoom they goon in joye and in solas,
Save oonly wrecche Aurelius, allas! 1020
He to his hous is goon with sorweful herte.
He seeth he may nat fro his deeth asterte;
Hym semed that he felte his herte colde.
Up to the hevene his handes he gan holde,
And on his knowes bare he sette hym doun, 1025
And in his ravyng seyde his orisoun.
For verray wo out of his wit he breyde.
He nyste what he spak, but thus he seyde;
With pitous herte his pleynt hath he bigonne
Unto the goddes, and first unto the sonne: 1030
  He seyde, "Appollo, god and governour
Of every plaunte, herbe, tree, and flour,
That yevest, after thy declinacioun,
To ech of hem his tyme and his sesoun,
As thyn herberwe chaungeth lowe or heighe,
Lord Phebus, cast thy merciable eighe 1036
On wrecche Aurelie, which that am but lorn.
Lo, lord! my lady hath my deeth ysworn
Withoute gilt, but thy benignytee
Upon my dedly herte have som pitee. 1040
For wel I woot, lord Phebus, if yow lest,
Ye may me helpen, save my lady, best.
Now voucheth sauf that I may yow devyse

---

971. **ther,** whence. 973. **gerdon,** reward. **brestyng,** bursting. 976. **grave,** buried. 981. **Nevere erst,** never before. 983. **yaf,** gave. 992. **Looke what,** whatever. **endelong Britayne,** along Brittany. 994. **lette,** prevent. 996. **ysene,** visible. 998. **in al that evere I kan,** to the best of my ability. 1001. **bityde,** happen. 1003. **deyntee,** pleasure. 1006. **siketh,** sighs. 1010. **moot,** may. 1013. **aleyes,** walks. 1017. **orisonte,** horizon. 1020. **wrecche,** wretched. 1022. **asterte,** escape. 1023. **colde,** grow cold. 1025. **knowes,** knees. 1026. **orisoun,** prayer. 1027. **breyde,** started suddenly. 1033. **yevest,** givest. **after,** according to. **declinacion,** distance above (or below) the equator. 1035. **herberwe,** 'house,' position in the zodiac. 1036. **eighe,** eye. 1037. **lorn,** lost. 1040. **dedly,** deathly, dying. 1043. **devyse,** describe, explain.

How that I may been holpen and in what
    wyse.
    Youre blisful suster, Lucina the sheene, 1045
That of the see is chief goddesse and queene
(Though Neptunus have deitee in the see,
Yet emperisse aboven hym is she),
Ye knowen wel, lord, that right as hir desir
Is to be quyked and lighted of youre fir, 1050
For which she folweth yow ful bisily,
Right so the see desireth naturelly
To folwen hire, as she that is goddesse
Bothe in the see and ryveres moore and lesse.
Wherfore, lord Phebus, this is my requeste—
Do this miracle, or do myn herte breste— 1056
That now next at this opposicioun
Which in the signe shal be of the Leoun,
As preieth hire so greet a flood to brynge 1059
That fyve fadme at the leeste it oversprynge
The hyeste rokke in Armorik Briteyne;
And lat this flood endure yeres tweyne.
Thanne certes to my lady may I seye,
'Holdeth youre heste, the rokkes been aweye.'
    Lord Phebus, dooth this miracle for me. 1065
Preye hire she go no faster cours than ye;
I seye, preyeth youre suster that she go
No faster cours than ye thise yeres two.
Thanne shal she been evene atte fulle alway,
And spryng flood laste bothe nyght and day.
And but she vouchesauf in swich manere 1071
To graunte me my sovereyn lady deere,
Prey hire to synken every rok adoun
Into hir owene dirke regioun
Under the ground, ther Pluto dwelleth inne,
Or nevere mo shal I my lady wynne. 1076
Thy temple in Delphos wol I barefoot seke.

Lord Phebus, se the teeris on my cheke,
And of my peyne have som compassioun."
And with that word in swowne he fil adoun,
And longe tyme he lay forth in a traunce. 1081
    His brother, which that knew of his pen-
    aunce,
Up caughte hym, and to bedde he hath hym
    broght.
Dispeyred in this torment and this thoght
Lete I this woful creature lye; 1085
Chese he, for me, wheither he wol lyve or dye.
    Arveragus, with heele and greet honour,
As he that was of chivalrie the flour,
Is comen hoom, and othere worthy men.
O blisful artow now, thou Dorigen, 1090
That hast thy lusty housbonde in thyne armes,
The fresshe knyght, the worthy man of armes,
That loveth thee as his owene hertes lyf.
No thyng list hym to been ymaginatyf,
If any wight hadde spoke, whil he was oute, 1095
To hire of love; he hadde of it no doute.
He noght entendeth to no swich mateere,
But daunceth, justeth, maketh hire good cheere;
And thus in joye and blisse I lete hem dwelle,
And of the sike Aurelius wol I telle. 1100
    In langour and in torment furyus
Two yeer and moore lay wrecche Aurelyus,
Er any foot he myghte on erthe gon;
Ne confort in this tyme hadde he noon,
Save of his brother, which that was a clerk.
He knew of al this wo and al this werk; 1106
For to noon oother creature, certeyn,
Of this matere he dorste no word seyn.
Under his brest he baar it moore secree
Than evere dide Pamphilus for Galathee. 1110

1045. Lucina, the goddess of light, here applied to Diana and the moon. **1057. opposicioun.** The highest tides occur when the sun and moon are in conjunction (in the same sign of the zodiac) or in opposition (in opposite signs). Aurelius asks Phoebus to perform the desired miracle the next time he is in Leo (his house) because then his power is greatest (and when the moon will be in Aquarius). This will be in about three months. **1059. As preieth,** pray. **1060. oversprynge,** leap over, *i.e.* be higher than the highest rock. **1062. yeres tweyne.** The miracle would consist in having the sun and moon remain in opposition for two years, so that the rocks would remain under water for an equal length of time. **1064. Holdeth youre heste,** keep your promise. **1069. atte fulle,** *i.e.,* full moon. **1070. laste,** depends on *shal*. **1074. hir owene dirke regioun.** Lucina is also identified with Proserpina, queen of the lower world. **1077. Delphos,** Delphi. **1082. penaunce,** distress. **1084. Dispeyred,** in despair. **1085. Lete,** leave. **1086. Chese he,** let him choose. **for me,** as far as I am concerned. **1087. heele,** health. **1094. ymaginatyf,** given to imagining. **1095. If,** whether. **1096. doute,** fear. **1097. He noght entendeth,** he pays no attention. **1110. Pamphilus.** The allusion is to the lover in a twelfth-century Latin dialogue of this name, in which the lover with the help of a *vieille* seduces a young woman. The text can be most conveniently read in G. Cohen, La "Comédie" latine en France au XIIᵉ siècle (2v, 1931), II. 167–223.

His brest was hool, withoute for to sene,
But in his herte ay was the arwe kene.
And wel ye knowe that of a sursanure
In surgerye is perilous the cure,
But men myghte touche the arwe, or come
   therby.   1115
His brother weep and wayled pryvely,
Til atte laste hym fil in remembraunce,
That whiles he was at Orliens in Fraunce,
As yonge clerkes, that been lykerous
To reden artes that been curious,   1120
Seken in every halke and every herne
Particuler sciences for to lerne—
He hym remembred that, upon a day,
At Orliens in studie a book he say
Of magyk natureel, which his felawe,   1125
That was that tyme a bacheler of lawe,
Al were he ther to lerne another craft,
Hadde prively upon his desk ylaft;
Which book spak muchel of the operaciouns
Touchynge the eighte and twenty mansiouns
That longen to the moone, and swich folye   1131
As in oure dayes is nat worth a flye,—
For hooly chirches feith in oure bileve
Ne suffreth noon illusioun us to greve.
And whan this book was in his remembraunce,
Anon for joye his herte gan to daunce,   1136
And to hymself he seyde pryvely:
"My brother shal be warisshed hastily;
For I am siker that ther be sciences
By whiche men make diverse apparences,   1140
Swiche as thise subtile tregetoures pleye.
For ofte at feestes have I wel herd seye
That tregetours, withinne an halle large,
Have maad come in a water and a barge,
And in the halle rowen up and doun.   1145

Somtyme hath semed come a grym leoun;
And somtyme floures sprynge as in a mede;
Somtyme a vyne, and grapes white and rede;
Somtyme a castel, al of lym and stoon;
And whan hem lyked, voyded it anon.   1150
Thus semed it to every mannes sighte.
   Now thanne conclude I thus, that if I myghte
At Orliens som oold felawe yfynde
That hadde thise moones mansions in mynde,
Or oother magyk natureel above,   1155
He sholde wel make my brother han his love.
For with an apparence a clerk may make,
To mannes sighte, that alle the rokkes blake
Of Britaigne weren yvoyded everichon,   1159
And shippes by the brynke comen and gon,
And in swich forme enduren a wowke or two.
Thanne were my brother warisshed of his wo;
Thanne moste she nedes holden hire biheste,
Or elles he shal shame hire atte leeste."
   What sholde I make a lenger tale of this?   1165
Unto his brotheres bed he comen is,
And swich confort he yaf hym for to gon
To Orliens that he up stirte anon,
And on his wey forthward thanne is he fare
In hope for to been lissed of his care.   1170
   Whan they were come almoost to that citee,
But if it were a two furlong or thre,
A yong clerk romynge by hymself they mette,
Which that in Latyn thriftily hem grette,
And after that he seyde a wonder thyng: 1175
"I knowe," quod he, "the cause of youre com-
   yng."
And er they ferther any foote wente,
He tolde hem al that was in hire entente.
   This Briton clerk hym asked of felawes   1179
The whiche that he had knowe in olde dawes,

1111. withoute for to sene, to all outward appearance. **1112. But in his herte.** This echoes the opening line of *Pamphilus:* Vulneror et clausum porto sub pectore telum. **1113. sursanure,** a wound only superficially healed over. **1115. But,** unless. **1116. weep,** wept. **1118. Orliens,** Orléans, famous in the Middle Ages for its university. **1119. lykerous,** eager. **1120. curious,** recondite, occult, **1121. halke . . . herne,** nook and corner. **1122. Particuler,** out-of-the-way, known to only a few. **1124. studie,** place of study, study hall. **say,** saw. **1127. Al were he,** even though he was. **1130. mansiouns,** the 28 parts into which the path of the moon among the stars was divided. **1131. longen,** belong. **1133. bileve,** belief. **1134. illusioun,** deception, practices intended to deceive. **1138. warisshed,** cured. **1141. tregetoures,** magicians. **1144. water,** body of water. **1149. lym,** lime. **1150. voyded it,** made it vanish. **anon,** immediately. **1154. thise moones mansions,** these mansions of the moon. **1157. apparence,** illusion. **1159. yvoyded,** made to disappear. **1160. brynke,** coast. **1161. wowke,** week. **1165. What,** why. **1167. confort,** encouragement. **1168. stirte,** leaped. **1169. fare,** gone. **1170. lissed,** eased. **1174. thriftily,** in a seemly manner. **hem grette,** greeted them. **1180. dawes,** days.

And he answerde hym that they dede were,
For which he weep ful ofte many a teere.

    Doun of his hors Aurelius lighte anon,
And with this magicien forth is he gon   1184
Hoom to his hous, and maden hem wel at ese.
Hem lakked no vitaille that myghte hem plese.
So wel arrayed hous as ther was oon
Aurelius in his lyf saugh nevere noon.

    He shewed hym, er he wente to sopeer,
Forestes, parkes ful of wilde deer;   1190
Ther saugh he hertes with hir hornes hye,
The gretteste that evere were seyn with yë.
He saugh of hem an hondred slayn with
    houndes,
And somme with arwes blede of bittre woundes.
He saugh, whan voyded were thise wilde deer,
Thise fauconers upon a fair ryver,   1196
That with hir haukes han the heron slayn.

    Tho saugh he knyghtes justyng in a playn;
And after this he dide hym swich plesaunce
That he hym shewed his lady on a daunce,   1200
On which hymself he daunced, as hym
    thoughte.
And whan this maister that this magyk
    wroughte
Saugh it was tyme, he clapte his handes two,
And farewel! al oure revel was ago.   1204
And yet remoeved they nevere out of the hous,
Whil they saugh al this sighte merveillous,
But in his studie, ther as his bookes be,
They seten stille, and no wight but they thre.

    To hym this maister called his squier,
And seyde hym thus: "Is redy oure soper?   1210
Almoost an houre it is, I undertake,
Sith I yow bad oure soper for to make,
Whan that thise worthy men wenten with me
Into my studie, ther as my bookes be."

    "Sire," quod this squier, "whan it liketh yow,
It is al redy, though ye wol right now."   1216

    "Go we thanne soupe," quod he, "as for the
    beste.
Thise amorous folk somtyme moote han hir
    reste."

    At after-soper fille they in tretee
What somme sholde this maistres gerdon be,
To remoeven alle the rokkes of Britayne,   1221
And eek from Gerounde to the mouth of Sayne.

    He made it straunge, and swoor, so God hym
    save,
Lasse than a thousand pound he wolde nat have,
Ne gladly for that somme he wolde nat goon.
Aurelius, with blisful herte anoon,   1226
Answerde thus: "Fy on a thousand pound!
This wyde world, which that men seye is
    round,
I wolde it yeve, if I were lord of it.
This bargayn is ful dryve, for we been knyt. 1230
Ye shal be payed trewely, by my trouthe!
But looketh now, for no necligence or slouthe
Ye tarie us heere no lenger than to-morwe."

    "Nay," quod this clerk, "have heer my feith
    to borwe."

    To bedde is goon Aurelius whan hym leste,
And wel ny al that nyght he hadde his reste. 1236
What for his labour and his hope of blisse,
His woful herte of penaunce hadde a lisse.

    Upon the morwe, whan that it was day,
To Britaigne tooke they the righte way,   1240
Aurelius and this magicien bisyde,
And been descended ther they wolde abyde.
And this was, as thise bookes me remembre,
The colde, frosty seson of Decembre.

    Phebus wax old, and hewed lyk latoun,   1245
That in his hoote declynacioun
Shoon as the burned gold with stremes brighte;
But now in Capricorn adoun he lighte,
Where as he shoon ful pale, I dar wel seyn.
The bittre frostes, with the sleet and reyn,   1250

1182. weep, wept. **1185. maden hem,** (they) made themselves. **1201. hym thoughte,** it seemed to him. **1219. after-soper,** see note to F 302. **tretee,** negotiation. **1220. gerdon,** reward. **1222. Gerounde,** the river Gironde. **Sayne,** Seine. **1223. He made it straunge,** he made it difficult, was reluctant. **1230. dryve,** driven. **knyt,** agreed. **1234. to borwe,** as a pledge. **1238. lisse,** alleviation. **1240. righte,** direct. **1245. laton,** brass. **1246. his hoote declynacioun.** See note to l. 1033. His hot declination would be when he was north of the equator and especially at the highest point (in the sign of Cancer), but now he is in Capricorn (the opposite sign). **1247. burned,** burnished.

Destroyed hath the grene in every yerd.
Janus sit by the fyr, with double berd,
And drynketh of his bugle horn the wyn;
Biforn hym stant brawen of the tusked swyn,
And "Nowel" crieth every lusty man.   1255
    Aurelius, in al that evere he kan,
Dooth to this maister chiere and reverence,
And preyeth hym to doon his diligence
To bryngen hym out of his peynes smerte,
Or with a swerd that he wolde slitte his
    herte.   1260
    This subtil clerk swich routhe had of this man
That nyght and day he spedde hym that he kan
To wayten a tyme of his conclusioun;
This is to seye, to maken illusioun,
By swich an apparence or jogelrye—   1265
I ne kan no termes of astrologye—
That she and every wight sholde wene and seye
That of Britaigne the rokkes were aweye,
Or ellis they were sonken under grounde.
So atte laste he hath his tyme yfounde   1270
To maken his japes and his wrecchednesse
Of swich a supersticious cursednesse.
His tables Tolletanes forth he brought,
Ful wel corrected, ne ther lakked nought,
Neither his collect ne his expans yeeris,   1275
Ne his rootes, ne his othere geeris,
As been his centris and his argumentz

And his proporcioneles convenientz
For his equacions in every thyng.
And by his eighte speere in his wirkyng   1280
He knew ful wel how fer Alnath was shove
Fro the heed of thilke fixe Aries above,
That in the ninthe speere considered is;
Ful subtilly he kalkuled al this.   1284
    Whan he hadde founde his firste mansioun,
He knew the remenaunt by proporcioun,
And knew the arisyng of his moone weel,
And in whos face, and terme, and everydeel;
And knew ful weel the moones mansioun
Acordaunt to his operacioun,   1290
And knew also his othere observaunces
For swiche illusiouns and swiche meschaunces
As hethen folk useden in thilke dayes.
For which no lenger maked he delayes,
But thurgh his magik, for a wyke or tweye, 1295
It semed that alle the rokkes were aweye.
    Aurelius, which that yet despeired is
Wher he shal han his love or fare amys,
Awaiteth nyght and day on this myracle;   1299
And whan he knew that ther was noon obstacle,
That voyded were thise rokkes everychon,
Doun to his maistres feet he fil anon,
And seyde, "I woful wrecche, Aurelius,
Thanke yow, lord, and lady myn Venus,
That me han holpen fro my cares colde."   1305

1251. yerd, yard. **1252. Janus,** from whom January takes its name; *with double berd* refers to the fact that Janus looks in two directions. **1253. bugle horn,** drinking vessel made from the horn of a bugle or wild ox. These lines refer to the Christmas season associated with wine and the wild boar. **1254. brawen,** meat. **1255. Nowel,** Noel. **1262. spedde hym,** hastened. **that he kan,** as well as he could. **1263. wayten,** watch for (a time when the heavens were propitious). **of,** for. **conclusioun,** accomplishment. **1265. jogelrye,** magic. (*lit.* jugglery). **1266. kan,** know. **1271. japes,** tricks. **1273. tables Tolletanes,** Tabulae Toletanae, astronomical tables compiled in the thirteenth century by order of Alphonso X of Castile. They were calculated for the city of Toledo, hence their name. The parade of astrological learning which follows is not characteristic of Breton lais. **1275. collect . . . expans yeeris,** Chaucer in his *Astrolabe* says that in calculating the movement of a planet periods of 1 to 20 years are called *anni expansi* and from 20 to 3000 *anni collecti*. **1276. rootes,** data from which other figures can be arrived at by the use of the tables. **geeris,** equipment. **1277. centris . . . argumentz . . . proporcioneles convenientz . . . equacions.** These technical terms of astrology (which I do not pretend to comprehend) are dealt with in the *NED* and in the notes of Skeat, Robinson, Hinckley, etc. They need not be explained at second-hand here. It is doubtful whether the Franklin could have explained them or Chaucer's audience have understood them, but they serve to make more impressive the clerk from Orléan's magic. **1280. eighte speere,** eighth sphere, in which the fixed stars were supposed to be set. **1281. Alnath . . .** I cannot do better than quote Skeat's note: "*Alnath* is still a name for the bright star α Arietis, . . . which was necessarily situated in the eighth sphere. But the head of the *fixed* Aries, or the true equinoctial point, was in the ninth sphere above it." The precession of the equinoxes could be calculated by observing the distances between these two points. **1285. his firste mansioun,** *i.e.* the moon's. **1286. the remenaunt,** the rest. **1288. in whos face.** Each sign of the zodiac was divided into thirds, known as "faces," and each face was assigned to a planet. **terme,** another division of a sign (generally containing five divisions of unequal size), also assigned to the different planets. **1290. Acordaunt to,** suitable for. **1292. meschaunces,** wickednesses. **1295. wyke,** week. **1298. Wher,** whether.

And to the temple his wey forth hath he holde,
Where as he knew he sholde his lady see.
And whan he saugh his tyme, anon-right hee,
With dredful herte and with ful humble cheere,
Salewed hath his sovereyn lady deere: 1310

"My righte lady," quod this woful man,
"Whom I moost drede and love as I best kan,
And lothest were of al this world displese,
Nere it that I for yow have swich disese   1314
That I moste dyen heere at youre foot anon,
Noght wolde I telle how me is wo bigon.
But certes outher moste I dye or pleyne;
Ye sle me giltelees for verray peyne.
But of my deeth thogh that ye have no routhe,
Avyseth yow er that ye breke youre trouthe.
Repenteth yow, for thilke God above,   1321
Er ye me sleen by cause that I yow love.
For, madame, wel ye woot what ye han hight—
Nat that I chalange any thyng of right
Of yow, my sovereyn lady, but youre grace—
But in a gardyn yond, at swich a place,   1326
Ye woot right wel what ye bihighten me;
And in myn hand youre trouthe plighten ye
To love me best—God woot, ye seyde so,
Al be that I unworthy am therto.   1330
Madame, I speke it for the honour of yow
Moore than to save myn hertes lyf right now,—
I have do so as ye comanded me;
And if ye vouchesauf, ye may go see.   1334
Dooth as yow list; have youre biheste in mynde,
For, quyk or deed, right there ye shal me fynde.
In yow lith al to do me lyve or deye,—
But wel I woot the rokkes been aweye."

He taketh his leve, and she astoned stood;
In al hir face nas a drope of blood.   1340
She wende nevere han come in swich a trappe.

"Allas," quod she, "that evere this sholde
          happe!
For wende I nevere by possibilitee
That swich a monstre or merveille myghte be!
It is agayns the proces of nature."   1345
And hoom she goth a sorweful creature;
For verray feere unnethe may she go.
She wepeth, wailleth, al a day or two,
And swowneth, that it routhe was to see.
But why it was to no wight tolde shee,   1350
For out of towne was goon Arveragus.
But to hirself she spak, and seyde thus,
With face pale and with ful sorweful cheere,
In hire compleynt, as ye shal after heere:

"Allas," quod she, "on thee, Fortune, I
          pleyne,   1355
That unwar wrapped hast me in thy cheyne,
Fro which t'escape woot I no socour,
Save oonly deeth or elles dishonour;
Oon of thise two bihoveth me to chese.
But nathelees, yet have I levere to lese   1360
My lif than of my body to have a shame,
Or knowe myselven fals, or lese my name;
And with my deth I may be quyt, ywis.
Hath ther nat many a noble wyf er this,
And many a mayde, yslayn hirself, allas!   1365
Rather than with hir body doon trespas?
Yis, certes, lo, thise stories beren witnesse:
Whan thritty tirauntz, ful of cursednesse,
Hadde slayn Phidon in Atthenes atte feste,
They comanded his doghtres for t'areste,   1370
And bryngen hem biforn hem in despit,
Al naked, to fulfille hir foul delit,
And in hir fadres blood they made hem daunce
Upon the pavement, God yeve hem mys-
          chaunce!

1308. **anon-right**, right away. 1310. **Salewed**, saluted. 1314. **disese**, distress. 1317. **outher**, either. 1318. **Ye sle me**, you are killing me. 1323. **hight**, promised. 1324. **chalange . . . of right**, claim as a right. 1327. **bihighten**, promised. 1328. **plighten**, plighted. 1335. **biheste**, promise. 1337. **do**, make. 1339. **astoned**, stunned. 1344. **monstre**, extraodinary thing. 1347. **unnethe**, scarcely. 1356. **unwar**, unexpectedly. 1359. **chese**, choose. 1360. **have I levere**, I would rather. **lese**, lose. 1362. **name**, good name. 1363. **quyt**, released. 1367. **thise stories**. The examples which follow are all taken from Jerome's treatise against Jovinian (Bk I, ch. 41-46), mentioned in the introductory note. Lists of this sort are frequent in Chaucer's poetry and are in accordance with the teachings of medieval rhetoric. Machaut made them fashionable, but they are in no wise characteristic of the Breton lai and in the present instance are prolonged beyond artistic limits. 1368. **thritty tirauntz.** The Thirty Tyrants in Athens were overthrown by Thrasybulus in 403 B.C. 1370. **They comanded . . .**, *men* understood. 1371. **in despit,** for malice.

For which thise woful maydens, ful of drede,
Rather than they wolde lese hir maydenhede,
They prively been stirt into a welle,　　　1377
And dreynte hemselven, as the bookes telle.

They of Mecene leete enquere and seke
Of Lacedomye fifty maydens eke,　　　1380
On whiche they wolden doon hir lecherye.
But was ther noon of al that compaignye
That she nas slayn, and with a good entente
Chees rather for to dye than assente
To been oppressed of hir maydenhede.　　　1385
Why sholde I thanne to dye been in drede?
Lo, eek, the tiraunt Aristoclides,
That loved a mayden, heet Stymphalides,
Whan that hir fader slayn was on a nyght,
Unto Dianes temple goth she right,　　　1390
And hente the ymage in hir handes two,
Fro which ymage wolde she nevere go.
No wight ne myghte hir handes of it arace
Til she was slayn, right in the selve place.

Now sith that maydens hadden swich despit
To been defouled with mannes foul delit,　　　1396
Wel oghte a wyf rather hirselven slee
Than be defouled, as it thynketh me.
What shal I seyn of Hasdrubales wyf,
That at Cartage birafte hirself hir lyf?　　　1400
For whan she saugh that Romayns wan the
　　　toun,
She took hir children alle, and skipte adoun
Into the fyr, and chees rather to dye
Than any Romayn dide hire vileynye.

Hath nat Lucresse yslayn hirself, allas!　　　1405
At Rome, whan that she oppressed was
Of Tarquyn, for hire thoughte it was a shame
To lyven whan that she had lost hir name?
The sevene maydens of Milesie also　　　1409
Han slayn hemself, for verrey drede and wo,
Rather than folk of Gawle hem sholde oppresse.
Mo than a thousand stories, as I gesse,
Koude I now telle as touchynge this mateere.
Whan Habradate was slayn, his wyf so deere
Hirselven slow, and leet hir blood to glyde　　　1415
In Habradates woundes depe and wyde,
And seyde, 'My body, at the leeste way,
Ther shal no wight defoulen, if I may.'

What sholde I mo ensamples heerof sayn,
Sith that so manye han hemselven slayn　　　1420
Wel rather than they wolde defouled be?
I wol conclude that it is bet for me
To sleen myself than been defouled thus.
I wol be trewe unto Arveragus,
Or rather sleen myself in som manere,　　　1425
As dide Demociones doghter deere
By cause that she wolde nat defouled be.
O Cedasus, it is ful greet pitee
To reden how thy doghtren deyde, allas!
That slowe hemself for swich a manere cas.　　　1430
As greet a pitee was it, or wel moore,
The Theban mayden that for Nichanore
Hirselven slow, right for swich manere wo.
Another Theban mayden dide right so;　　　1434
For oon of Macidonye hadde hire oppressed,

1377. been stirt, have leaped. **welle,** spring. **1378. dreynte,** drowned. **1379. Mecene,** Messene, in the southwest part of the Peloponnesus. **1380. Lacedomye,** Lacedaemonia (Sparta). Messene and Sparta were accustomed to exchange virgins in connection with certain religious rites, as Jerome tells us. **1383. entente,** will. **1385. oppressed,** ravished. **1387. Aristoclides,** tyrant of Orchomenos in Arcadia. **1388. heet,** called. **Stymphalides.** Jerome says *virginem Stymphalidem,* a virgin of Stymphalus. Chaucer apparently mistook the adjective for the name of the virgin. **1391. hente,** took. **1393. arace,** tear away. **1394. selve,** same. **1395. hadden . . . despit,** scorned. **1399. Hasdrubales wyf.** When Hasdrubal surrendered himself to Scipio his wife threw herself and her children into the flames which destroyed the city. **1404. dide,** should do. **1405. Lucresse.** See note to *BD* 1082. **1406. oppressed . . . of.** Cf l. 1385. **1407. hire thoughte,** it seemed to her. **1409. Milesie,** Miletus, in Asia Minor. **1411. folk of Gawle,** The Galatians, who sacked the city in 276 B.C. (Magoun, *Mediaeval Stud.,* xv. 118, 124). **1414. Habradate.** Jerome cites Xenophon's *Cyropaedia,* where the story is told in Bk. VII. **1415. leet,** caused. **1426. Demociones doghter.** Jerome calls Demotion head of the Areopagites. His daughter was betrothed to Leosthenes, and when he died in the siege of Lamia (322 B.C.) she killed herself. **1428. Cedasus,** Scedasus of Bœotia. Jerome tells the story which Dorigen finds so painful to read. The two daughters, having given hospitality to two youths, were violated by them, whereupon the daughters killed each other. **1429. doghtren,** daughters. **1432. The Theban mayden.** Nicanor, having captured Thebes, fell in love with a captured virgin, but she killed herself rather than submit to his embraces. **1434. Another Theban mayden.** Jerome gives no names, but says that the maiden was violated by a Macedonian. Hiding her grief, she watched her opportunity, killed him in his sleep, and then stabbed herself with the same sword. **1435. oppressed,** ravished.

She with hire deeth hir maydenhede redressed.
What shal I seye of Nicerates wyf,
That for swich cas birafte hirself hir lyf?
How trewe eek was to Alcebiades
His love, that rather for to dyen chees   1440
Than for to suffre his body unburyed be.
Lo, which a wyf was Alceste," quod she.
"What seith Omer of goode Penalopee?
Al Grece knoweth of hire chastitee.
Pardee, of Laodomya is writen thus,   1445
That whan at Troie was slayn Protheselaus,
No lenger wolde she lyve after his day.
The same of noble Porcia telle I may;
Withoute Brutus koude she nat lyve,
To whom she hadde al hool hir herte yive.   1450
The parfit wyf hod of Arthemesie
Honured is thurgh al the Barbarie.
O Teuta, queene! thy wyfly chastitee
To alle wyves may a mirour bee.
The same thyng I seye of Bilyea,   1455
Of Rodogone, and eek Valeria."
    Thus pleyned Dorigen a day or tweye,
Purposynge evere that she wolde deye.
But nathelees, upon the thridde nyght,   1459
Hoom cam Arveragus, this worthy knyght,
And asked hire why that she weep so soore;

And she gan wepen ever lenger the moore.
"Allas," quod she, "that evere was I born!
Thus have I seyd," quod she, "thus have I
    sworn"—
And toold hym al as ye han herd bifore;   1465
It nedeth nat reherce it yow namoore.
This housbonde, with glad chiere, in freendly
    wyse
Answerde and seyde as I shal yow devyse:
"Is ther oght elles, Dorigen, but this?"
    "Nay, nay," quod she, "God helpe me so as
        wys!   1470
This is to muche, and it were Goddes wille."
    "Ye, wyf," quod he, "lat slepen that is stille.
It may be wel, paraventure, yet to day.
Ye shul youre trouthe holden, by my fay!
For God so wisly have mercy upon me,   1475
I hadde wel levere ystiked for to be
For verray love which that I to yow have,
But if ye sholde youre trouthe kepe and save.
Trouthe is the hyeste thyng that man may
    kepe"—
But with that word he brast anon to wepe,   1480
And seyde, "I yow forbede, up peyne of deeth,
That nevere, whil thee lasteth lyf ne breeth,
To no wight telle thou of this aventure,—

1436. **redressed,** compensated for. 1437. **Nicerates wyf.** Niceratus, son of Nicias, the Athenian leader who made peace with Sparta in 423 B.C. In 404 B.C. Athens surrendered to the Spartan general Lysander, after which the Thirty Tyrants obtained control of the city. According to Jerome, the wife of Niceratus killed herself rather than submit to the lust of the tyrants. 1439. **Alcebiades,** Alcibiades, friend of Socrates, was murdered at the instigation of Lysander and the Thirty Tyrants. His mistress, in defiance of his enemies, buried the body. Plutarch gives her name as Timandra. 1440. **chees,** chose. 1442. **which a,** what a. **Alceste,** Alcestis. See *LGW* 510–16. 1443. **Omer,** Homer. Chaucer, of course, knew Homer only as a name. **Penalopee.** While her husband was engaged in the siege of Troy Penelope put off many suitors, telling them she must first finish a robe she was weaving for the king, his father. At night she unraveled all she had woven during the day. 1445. **Laodomya,** Laodamia. After the death of her husband Protesilaus the gods granted her prayer to be allowed to speak with him for three hours. When he died a second time Laodamia died with him. 1448. **Porcia.** After the death of Brutus she is said to have eluded those who watched her and to have choked herself with burning charcoal snatched from the fire. 1451. **Arthemesie,** Artemisia, queen of Caria, who built for her husband a tomb, says Jerome, "so great that even to the present day all costly sepulchres are called after his name *mausoleums*." 1452. **Barbarie,** heathendom. 1453. **Teuta.** Jerome merely says she was queen of the Illyrians and owed her successes at home and her victories over the Romans to her marvellous chastity. 1455. **Bilyea,** Bilia, wife of Gaius Duilius, who won Rome's first naval victory (260 B.C.). The story which Jerome tells to prove her fidelity to her husband is that when he asked her angrily why she did not tell him that his breath was bad, she replied that she supposed all men had bad breath. 1456. **Rodogone,** Rhodogune, daughter of Darius, killed her nurse because she urged her to marry again. **Valeria.** Jerome has apparently confused two persons of the name. He calls her wife of Servius, but this Valeria married again. On the other hand, Valeria the daughter of Diocletian, after the death of her husband Galerius, rejected the advances of his successor. A full account of the indignities which she suffered for her constancy, her exile and eventual execution, is in Gibbon, *Decline and Fall*, ch. 14. 1457. **pleyned,** complained. 1461. **weep,** wept. **soore,** bitterly. 1462. **lenger,** longer. 1468. **devyse,** relate. 1470. **so as wys,** as certainly (may God help me). 1471. **and,** if, *i.e.* if God allow me to say so. 1472. **lat slepen.** Cf. "let sleeping dogs lie." 1474. **trouthe,** troth, pledge. 1475. **God so wisly,** may God so surely. 1476. **ystiked,** stabbed. 1478. **But if,** than , . . not. 1480. **brast . . . to wepe,** burst into weeping. *Wepe* may be either a noun or *to wepe* an infinitive where we use the present participle. See Language, § 67. 1481. **up,** upon.

As I may best, I wol my wo endure,—
Ne make no contenance of hevynesse,   1485
That folk of yow may demen harm or gesse."
    And forth he cleped a squier and a mayde:
"Gooth forth anon with Dorigen," he sayde,
"And bryngeth hire to swich a place anon."
They take hir leve, and on hir wey they gon,
But they ne wiste why she thider wente.   1491
He nolde no wight tellen his entente.
    Paraventure an heep of yow, ywis,
Wol holden hym a lewed man in this
That he wol putte his wyf in jupartie.   1495
Herkneth the tale er ye upon hire crie.
She may have bettre fortune than yow semeth;
And whan that ye han herd the tale, demeth.
    This squier, which that highte Aurelius,
On Dorigen that was so amorus,   1500
Of aventure happed hire to meete
Amydde the toun, right in the quykkest strete,
As she was bown to goon the wey forth right
Toward the gardyn ther as she had hight.
And he was to the gardyn-ward also;   1505
For wel he spyed whan she wolde go
Out of hir hous to any maner place.
But thus they mette, of aventure or grace,
And he saleweth hire with glad entente,
And asked of hire whiderward she wente;   1510
And she answerde, half as she were mad,
"Unto the gardyn, as myn housbonde bad,
My trouthe for to holde, allas! allas!"
    Aurelius gan wondren on this cas,
And in his herte hadde greet compassioun   1515
Of hire and of hire lamentacioun,
And of Arveragus, the worthy knyght,
That bad hire holden al that she had hight,
So looth hym was his wyf sholde breke hir
    trouthe;
And in his herte he caughte of this greet routhe,

Considerynge the beste on every syde,   1521
That fro his lust yet were hym levere abyde
Than doon so heigh a cherlyssh wrecchednesse
Agayns franchise and alle gentillesse;
For which in fewe wordes seyde he thus: 1525
    "Madame, seyth to youre lord Arveragus,
That sith I se his grete gentillesse
To yow, and eek I se wel youre distresse,
That him were levere han shame (and that were
    routhe)
Than ye to me sholde breke thus youre trouthe,
I have wel levere evere to suffre wo   1531
Than I departe the love bitwix yow two.
I yow relesse, madame, into youre hond
Quyt every serement and every bond
That ye han maad to me as heerbiforn,   1535
Sith thilke tyme which that ye were born.
My trouthe I plighte, I shal yow never repreve
Of no biheste, and heere I take my leve,
As of the treweste and the beste wyf
That evere yet I knew in al my lyf.   1540
But every wyf be war of hire biheeste!
On Dorigen remembreth, atte leeste.
Thus kan a squier doon a gentil dede
As wel as kan a knyght, withouten drede."
    She thonketh hym upon hir knees al bare, 1545
And hoom unto hir housbonde is she fare,
And tolde hym al, as ye han herd me sayd;
And be ye siker, he was so weel apayd
That it were inpossible me to wryte.
What sholde I lenger of this cas endyte?   1550
    Arveragus and Dorigen his wyf
In sovereyn blisse leden forth hir lyf.
Nevere eft ne was ther angre hem bitwene.
He cherisseth hire as though she were a queene,
And she was to hym trewe for everemoore. 1555
Of thise two folk ye gete of me namoore.
    Aurelius, that his cost hath al forlorn,

1487. **cleped**, called. 1494. **lewed**, foolish. 1495. **jupartie**, jeopardy. 1496. **upon hire crie**, cry out against her. 1497. **yow semeth**, it seems to you, you suppose. 1498. **demeth**, judge. 1502. **quykkest**, busiest (liveliest). 1503. **bown**, ready. 1504. **hight**, promised. 1506. **spyed**, kept watch. 1508. **of aventure or grace**, by chance or good fortune. 1509. **entente**, mood; **with glad entente**, pleasantly, cheerfully. 1514. **cas**, matter. 1518. **hight**, promised. 1522. **lust**, desire. **abyde**, desist, refrain. 1524. **franchise**, nobility, generosity. 1532. **departe**, divide. 1534. **serement**, oath. A great many manuscripts read *surement*. 1537. **repreve**, reproach. 1538. **Of**, for. **biheste**, promise. 1544. **drede**, doubt. 1546. **fare**, gone. 1548. **apayd**, satisfied. 1549. **me to wryte.** This is Chaucer the writer, who forgets momentarily that the Franklin is telling a story to fellow-pilgrims. 1553. **angre**, trouble. 1557. **cost**, expense. **forlorn**, lost.

Curseth the tyme that evere he was born:
"Allas," quod he, "allas, that I bihighte
Of pured gold a thousand pound of wighte 1560
Unto this philosophre! How shal I do?
I se namoore but that I am fordo.
Myn heritage moot I nedes selle,
And been a beggere; heere may I nat dwelle,
And shamen al my kynrede in this place, 1565
But I of hym may gete bettre grace.
But nathelees, I wole of hym assaye,
At certeyn dayes, yeer by yeer, to paye,
And thanke hym of his grete curteisye.
My trouthe wol I kepe, I wol nat lye." 1570
With herte soor he gooth unto his cofre,
And broghte gold unto this philosophre,
The value of fyve hundred pound, I gesse,
And hym bisecheth, of his gentillesse,
To graunte hym dayes of the remenaunt; 1575
And seyde, "Maister, I dar wel make avaunt,
I failled nevere of my trouthe as yit.
For sikerly my dette shal be quyt
Towardes yow, howevere that I fare
To goon a-begged in my kirtle bare. 1580
But wolde ye vouchesauf, upon seuretee,
Two yeer or thre for to respiten me,
Thanne were I wel; for elles moot I selle
Myn heritage; ther is namoore to telle."
This philosophre sobrely answerde, 1585
And seyde thus, whan he thise wordes herde:
"Have I nat holden covenant unto thee?"
"Yes, certes, wel and trewely," quod he.
"Hastow nat had thy lady as thee liketh?"
"No, no," quod he, and sorwefully he siketh.
"What was the cause? tel me if thou kan."
Aurelius his tale anon bigan, 1592

And tolde hym al, as ye han herd bifoore;
It nedeth nat to yow reherce it moore.
He seide, "Arveragus, of gentillesse, 1595
Hadde levere dye in sorwe and in distresse
Than that his wyf were of hir trouthe fals."
The sorwe of Dorigen he tolde hym als;
How looth hire was to been a wikked wyf, 1599
And that she levere had lost that day hir lyf,
And that hir trouthe she swoor thurgh inno-
cence,
She nevere erst hadde herd speke of apparence.
"That made me han of hire so greet pitee;
And right as frely as he sente hire me,
As frely sente I hire to hym ageyn. 1605
This al and som; ther is namoore to seyn."
This philosophre answerde, "Leeve brother,
Everich of yow dide gentilly til oother.
Thou art a squier, and he is a knyght;
But God forbede, for his blisful myght, 1610
But if a clerk koude doon a gentil dede
As wel as any of yow, it is no drede!
Sire, I releesse thee thy thousand pound,
As thou right now were cropen out of the
ground,
Ne nevere er now ne haddest knowen me. 1615
For, sire, I wol nat taken a peny of thee
For al my craft, ne noght for my travaille.
Thou hast ypayed wel for my vitaille.
It is ynogh, and farewel, have good day!" 1619
And took his hors, and forth he goth his way.
Lordynges, this question, thanne, wol I aske
now,
Which was the mooste fre, as thynketh yow?
Now telleth me, er that ye ferther wende.
I kan namoore; my tale is at an ende.

Heere is ended the Frankeleyns Tale.

1559. **bihighte**, promised. 1560. **pured**, refined. **of wighte**, by weight. 1562. **fordo**, ruined. 1566. **But**, unless. 1567. **of hym assaye**, make trial of him, try to arrange. 1575. **dayes**, time in which to pay. 1577. **trouthe**, pledge. 1580. **To goon a-begged**, to go a-begging. The form is properly *a-beggeth, on beggeth* (noun), corresponding to OE *-aþ, -oþ* (*on fiscaþe, on huntoþe*, in King Alfred's trans. of Orosius). For other examples see Skeat's note to the line. Forms like *beggeth* were in time confused with, or assimilated to, the past participle, and by analogy other past participles were used in the same way. Cf. *a-blakeberyed* (C 406) and *a-caterwawed* (D 354). 1581. **seuretee**, surety, collateral. 1582. **respiten**, grant an extension of time. 1585. **sobrely**, quietly. 1590. **siketh**, sighs. 1598. **als**, also. 1602. **apparence**, illusion. 1606. **This al and som**, this is the whole story. 1607. **Leeve**, dear. 1608. **Everich**, each. 1611. **But if . .** , if a clerk could not. 1612. **drede**, doubt. 1614. **As**, as if. **cropen**, crept. 1622. **fre**, generous, noble.

Group C (Fragment VI)

The Physician's Tale

Heere folweth the Phisiciens Tale.

Ther was, as telleth Titus Livius,
A knyght that called was Virginius,
Fulfild of honour and of worthynesse,
And strong of freendes, and of greet richesse.
This knyght a doghter hadde by his wyf; 5
No children hadde he mo in al his lyf.
Fair was this mayde in excellent beautee
Aboven every wight that man may see;
For Nature hath with sovereyn diligence
Yformed hire in so greet excellence, 10
As though she wolde seyn, "Lo! I, Nature,
Thus kan I forme and peynte a creature,
Whan that me list; who kan me countrefete?
Pigmalion noght, though he ay forge and bete,
Or grave, or peynte, for I dar wel seyn, 15
Apelles, Zanzis, sholde werche in veyn
Outher to grave, or peynte, or forge, or bete,
If they presumed me to countrefete.
For He that is the formere principal
Hath maked me his vicaire general, 20

To forme and peynten erthely creaturis
Right as me list, and ech thyng in my cure is
Under the moone, that may wane and waxe;
And for my werk right no thyng wol I axe;
My lord and I been ful of oon accord. 25
I made hire to the worship of my lord;
So do I alle myne othere creatures,
What colour that they han, or what figures."
Thus semeth me that Nature wolde seye.
This mayde of age twelve yeer was and
          tweye, 30
In which that Nature hadde swich delit.
For right as she kan peynte a lilie whit,
And reed a rose, right with swich peynture
She peynted hath this noble creature,
Er she were born, upon hir lymes fre, 35
Where as by right swiche colours sholde be;
And Phebus dyed hath hire tresses grete
Lyk to the stremes of his burned heete.
And if that excellent was hire beautee,

The Physician's Tale. All treatments of the Appius and Virginia story in the Middle Ages go back to the account in Livy's great Roman history, *Ab urbe condita*. It was retold in rather bare outline in the *Roman de la Rose*, and Chaucer's contemporary, the poet Gower, told it in the *Confessio Amantis*. Chaucer's poem owes nothing to Gower's treatment. That he knew the account in the *Roman de la Rose* goes without saying. The question is whether he had read Livy in the original, and it is not easily answered; the differences between *The Physician's Tale* and Livy are more noticeable than the occasional similarities. Two long passages (ll. 35–120 and 207–53) in *The Physician's Tale* are Chaucer's own additions, and if we subtract them from the Physician's narrative, only about 150 lines remain. Unless new evidence is produced, we must be content to say that he told the story on the basis of the account in the *Roman de la Rose*, but may have derived certain details from Livy at first- or second-hand.
   It is quite clear that the tale was not originally composed for *The Canterbury Tales*. The long and inappropriate digression on the responsibilities of governesses and parents for the proper surveillance of the young suggests that Chaucer was moved to write the poem by some actual circumstances with which he was familiar. Its assignment to the Physician is not especially appropriate.
1. Titus Livius, Livy, the Roman historian (59 B.C.–17 A.D.). From what has just been said the mention of him here is not to be taken as proof that Chaucer based his tale directly on the Latin, but rather as an example of the tendency of medieval poets to allege ancient authority for what they related. **8. wight,** creature. **13. countrefete,** successfully imitate, match. **14. Pigmalion,** Pygmalion, who fell in love with an ivory image he had carved, and, after Venus had given life to the maiden, married her. Cf. Ovid, *Metam.*, x. 243–97. **16. Apelles.** See note to D 498. **Zanzis,** Zeuxis, a celebrated Greek painter *c.* 400 B.C. **17. Outher,** either. **19. formere,** creator. **22. cure,** care. **25. ful,** fully. **28. figures,** shapes. **38. burned,** burnished, shining; **burned heete,** sunshine.

A thousand foold moore vertuous was she.   40
In hire ne lakked no condicioun
That is to preyse, as by discrecioun.
As wel in goost as body chast was she;
For which she floured in virginitee
With alle humylitee and abstinence,   45
With alle attemperaunce and pacience,
With mesure eek of beryng and array.
Discreet she was in answeryng alway;
Though she were wis as Pallas, dar I seyn,
Hir facound eek ful wommanly and pleyn,   50
No countrefeted termes hadde she
To seme wys; but after hir degree
She spak, and alle hire wordes, moore and lesse,
Sownynge in vertu and in gentillesse.   54
Shamefast she was in maydens shamefastnesse,
Constant in herte, and evere in bisynesse
To dryve hire out of ydel slogardye.
Bacus hadde of hir mouth right no maistrie;
For wyn and youthe dooth Venus encresse,
As men in fyr wol casten oille or greesse.   60
And of hir owene vertu, unconstreyned,
She hath ful ofte tyme syk hire feyned,
For that she wolde fleen the compaignye
Where likly was to treten of folye,
As is at feestes, revels, and at daunces,   65
That been occasions of daliaunces.
Swich thynges maken children for to be
To soone rype and boold, as men may se,
Which is ful perilous, and hath been yoore.
For al to soone may she lerne loore   70
Of booldnesse, whan she woxen is a wyf.
    And ye maistresses, in youre olde lyf,
That lordes doghtres han in governaunce,
Ne taketh of my wordes no displesaunce.
Thenketh that ye been set in governynges   75

Of lordes doghtres, oonly for two thynges:
Outher for ye han kept youre honestee,
Or elles ye han falle in freletee,
And knowen wel ynough the olde daunce,
And han forsaken fully swich meschaunce   80
For everemo; therfore, for Cristes sake,
To teche hem vertu looke that ye ne slake.
    A theef of venysoun, that hath forlaft
His likerousnesse and al his olde craft,
Kan kepe a forest best of any man.   85
Now kepeth wel, for if ye wole, ye kan.
Looke wel that ye unto no vice assente,
Lest ye be dampned for youre wikke entente;
For whoso dooth, a traitour is, certeyn.
And taketh kepe of that that I shal seyn: 90
Of alle tresons sovereyn pestilence
Is whan a wight bitrayseth innocence.
    Ye fadres and ye moodres eek also,
Though ye han children, be it oon or mo,
Youre is the charge of al hir surveiaunce,   95
Whil that they been under youre governaunce.
Beth war, that by ensample of youre lyvynge,
Or by youre necligence in chastisynge,
That they ne perisse; for I dar wel seye,
If that they doon, ye shul it deere abeye.   100
Under a shepherde softe and necligent
The wolf hath many a sheep and lamb torent.
Suffiseth oon ensample now as heere,
For I moot turne agayn to my matere.
    This mayde, of which I wol this tale expresse,
So kepte hirself hir neded no maistresse;   106
For in hir lyvyng maydens myghten rede,
As in a book, every good word or dede
That longeth to a mayden vertuous,
She was so prudent and so bountevous.   110
For which the fame out sprong on every syde,

---

42. discrecioun, discernment. **43. goost**, soul, spirit. **47. mesure**, moderation. **49. Pallas**, Minerva, goddess of wisdom. **50. facound**, manner of speaking. **51. countrefeted**, false, pretentious. **52. degree**, station. **54. Sownynge in**, conducing to, appropriate to. **55. Shamefast**, modest. **57. slogardye**, slothfulness. **58. Bacus**, Bacchus, god of wine. **59. Venus**, i.e. passion. **64. Where likly was . . .** Where it was likely to concern folly. **66. daliaunces**, wanton toying. **69. yoore**, for a long time. **71. woxen is a wyf**, has grown to be a woman. **72. ye maistresses**, you governesses. See intro. **olde lyf**, old age, maturity. **77. honestee**, virtue. **78. falle in freletee**, have sinned. **79. the olde daunce**, i.e. love-making. **80. meschaunce**, misconduct. **82. slake**, grow slack. **83. theef of venysoun**, poacher. **forlaft**, given up. **84. likerousnesse**, appetite. **85. kepe**, guard. **88. wikke**, wicked. **entente**, inclination. **90. kep**, heed. **91. sovereyn**, the greatest. **92. wight**, person. **bitrayseth**, betrays. **95. surveiaunce**, surveillance. **99. perisse**, perish. **100. abeye**, pay for. **102. torent**, torn to pieces. **104. moot**, must. **110. bountevous**, full of goodness.

Bothe of hir beautee and hir bountee wyde,
That thurgh that land they preised hire echone
That loved vertu, save Envye allone,
That sory is of oother mennes wele,   115
And glad is of his sorwe and his unheele.
(The doctour maketh this descripcioun.)

This mayde upon a day wente in the toun
Toward a temple, with hire mooder deere,
As is of yonge maydens the manere.   120
Now was ther thanne a justice in that toun,
That governour was of that regioun.
And so bifel this juge his eyen caste
Upon this mayde, avysynge hym ful faste,
As she cam forby ther as this juge stood.   125
Anon his herte chaunged and his mood,
So was he caught with beautee of this mayde,
And to hymself ful pryvely he sayde,
"This mayde shal be myn, for any man!"

Anon the feend into his herte ran,   130
And taughte hym sodeynly that he by slyghte
The mayden to his purpos wynne myghte.
For certes, by no force ne by no meede,
Hym thoughte, he was nat able for to speede;
For she was strong of freendes, and eek she   135
Confermed was in swich soverayn bountee,
That wel he wiste he myghte hire nevere wynne
As for to make hire with hir body synne.
For which, by greet deliberacioun,
He sente after a cherl, was in the toun,   140
Which that he knew for subtil and for boold.
This juge unto this cherl his tale hath toold
In secree wise, and made hym to ensure
He sholde telle it to no creature,
And if he dide, he sholde lese his heed.   145
Whan that assented was this cursed reed,
Glad was this juge, and maked him greet
  cheere,

And yaf hym yiftes preciouse and deere.
Whan shapen was al hire conspiracie
Fro point to point, how that his lecherie   150
Parfourned sholde been ful subtilly,
As ye shul heere it after openly,
Hoom gooth the cherl, that highte Claudius.
This false juge, that highte Apius—
So was his name, for this is no fable,   155
But knowen for historial thyng notable;
The sentence of it sooth is, out of doute—
This false juge gooth now faste aboute
To hasten his delit al that he may.
And so bifel soone after, on a day,   160
This false juge, as telleth us the storie,
As he was wont, sat in his consistorie,
And yaf his doomes upon sondry cas.
This false cherl cam forth a ful greet pas,
And seyde, "Lord, if that it be youre wille, 165
As dooth me right upon this pitous bille,
In which I pleyne upon Virginius;
And if that he wol seyn it is nat thus,
I wol it preeve, and fynde good witnesse,
That sooth is that my bille wol expresse."   170

The juge answerde, "Of this, in his absence,
I may nat yeve diffynytyve sentence.
Lat do hym calle, and I wol gladly heere;
Thou shalt have al right, and no wrong heere."

Virginius cam to wite the juges wille,   175
And right anon was rad this cursed bille;
The sentence of it was as ye shul heere:

"To yow, my lord, sire Apius so deere,
Sheweth youre povre servant Claudius
How that a knyght, called Virginius,   180
Agayns the lawe, agayn al equitee,
Holdeth, expres agayn the wyl of me,
My servant, which that is my thral by right,
Which fro myn hous was stole upon a nyght,

---

112. bountee, goodness. **113. echone,** each one. **115. wele,** welfare. **116. unheele,** misfortune. **117. The doctour.** St. Augustine (Doctor Ecclesiae), in a commentary on *Psalms* 104:25 (Migne, *PL,* xxxvii. 1399). **125. forby ther as,** past the place where. **129. for,** in spite of. **130. feend,** devil. **131. slyghte,** sleight, trickery. **133. meede,** bribery. **140. cherl,** fellow, retainer. **141. for,** as being. **143. ensure,** give assurance. **146. reed,** counsel, plan. **147. maked him greet cheere,** was very friendly to him. **148. yiftes,** gifts. **152. after,** later. **153. highte,** was named. **156. historial,** historical. **157. sentence,** substance. **sooth,** true. **162. consistorie,** court of justice. **163. doomes,** judgments. **cas,** cases. **164. a ful greet pas,** at a great rate. **166. As dooth,** do (horatory *as*). **pitous,** deserving pity. **bille,** bill of complaint. **169. preeve,** prove. **173. Lat do hym calle,** have him summoned. **175. wite,** know, learn. **176. rad,** read. **179. povre,** poor. **183. thral,** slave.

Whil that she was ful yong; this wol I preeve 185
By witnesse, lord, so that it nat yow greeve.
She nys his doghter nat, what so he seye.
Wherfore to yow, my lord the juge, I preye,
Yeld me my thral, if that it be youre wille."
Lo, this was al the sentence of his bille. 190
   Virginius gan upon the cherl biholde,
But hastily, er he his tale tolde,
And wolde have preeved it as sholde a knyght,
And eek by witnessyng of many a wight,
That al was fals that seyde his adversarie, 195
This cursed juge wolde no thyng tarie,
Ne heere a word moore of Virginius,
But yaf his juggement, and seyde thus:
   "I deeme anon this cherl his servant have;
Thou shalt no lenger in thyn hous hir save. 200
Go bryng hire forth, and put hire in oure
   warde.
The cherl shal have his thral, this I awarde."
   And whan this worthy knyght Virginius,
Thurgh sentence of this justice Apius,
Moste by force his deere doghter yiven 205
Unto the juge, in lecherie to lyven,
He gooth hym hoom, and sette him in his halle,
And leet anon his deere doghter calle,
And with a face deed as asshen colde
Upon hir humble face he gan biholde, 210
With fadres pitee stikynge thurgh his herte,
Al wolde he from his purpos nat converte.
   "Doghter," quod he, "Virginia, by thy name,
Ther been two weyes, outher deeth or shame,
That thou most suffre; allas, that I was bore!
For nevere thou deservedest wherfore 216
To dyen with a swerd or with a knyf.
O deere doghter, endere of my lyf,
Which I have fostred up with swich plesaunce
That thou were nevere out of my remem-
   braunce! 220
O doghter, which that art my laste wo,

And in my lyf my laste joye also,
O gemme of chastitee, in pacience
Take thou thy deeth, for this is my sentence.
For love, and nat for hate, thou most be
   deed; 225
My pitous hand moot smyten of thyn heed.
Allas, that evere Apius the say!
Thus hath he falsly jugged the to-day"—
And tolde hire al the cas, as ye bifore
Han herd; nat nedeth for to telle it moore. 230
   "O mercy, deere fader!" quod this mayde,
And with that word she bothe hir armes layde
Aboute his nekke, as she was wont to do.
The teeris bruste out of hir eyen two,
And seyde, "Goode fader, shal I dye? 235
Is ther no grace, is ther no remedye?"
   "No, certes, deere doghter myn," quod he.
   "Thanne yif me leyser, fader myn," quod
   she,
"My deeth for to compleyne a litel space;
For, pardee, Jepte yaf his doghter grace 240
For to compleyne, er he hir slow, allas!
And, God it woot, no thyng was hir trespas,
But for she ran hir fader first to see,
To welcome hym with greet solempnitee."
And with that word she fil aswowne anon, 245
And after, whan hir swownyng is agon,
She riseth up, and to hir fader sayde,
"Blissed be God, that I shal dye a mayde!
Yif me my deeth, er that I have a shame;
Dooth with youre child youre wyl, a Goddes
   name!" 250
   And with that word she preyed hym ful ofte
That with his swerd he shulde smyte softe;
And with that word aswowne doun she fil.
Hir fader, with ful sorweful herte and wil,
Hir heed of smoot, and by the top it hente, 255
And to the juge he gan it to presente,
As he sat yet in doom in consistorie.

186. **so that,** provided. 200. **save,** keep. 201. **warde,** keeping. 208. **leet anon,** caused immediately. 209. **asshen,** ashes. 211. **stikynge,** piercing. 212. **Al,** although. **converte,** turn aside. 226. **moot,** must. 227. **say,** saw. 234. **bruste,** burst. 238. **yif,** give. **leyser,** time. 240. **Jepte,** Jephtha, who had promised to sacrifice the first one who came out of his house if God would grant him victory over the Ammonites. His only daughter was the one who came out to meet him. He granted her two months of respite before keeping his vow. Cf. *Judges,* 11:30–9. Virginia's allusion is not only a little surprising, but hardly bears out the description of the physician in the *General Prologue* (His studie was but litel on the Bible). 257. **doom,** judgment.

And whan the juge it saugh, as seith the storie,
He bad to take hym and anhange hym faste;
But right anon a thousand peple in thraste,   260
To save the knyght, for routhe and for pitee,
For knowen was the false iniquitee.
The peple anon had suspect in this thyng,
By manere of the cherles chalangyng,
That it was by the assent of Apius;   265
They wisten wel that he was lecherus.
For which unto this Apius they gon,
And caste hym in a prisoun right anon,
Ther as he slow hymself; and Claudius,
That servant was unto this Apius,   270
Was demed for to hange upon a tree,
But that Virginius, of his pitee,
So preyde for hym that he was exiled;

And elles, certes, he had been bigyled.
The remenant were anhanged, moore and
    lesse,   275
That were consentant of this cursednesse.
    Heere may men seen how synne hath his
        merite.
Beth war, for no man woot whom God wol
    smyte
In no degree, ne in which manere wyse
The worm of conscience may agryse   280
Of wikked lyf, though it so pryvee be
That no man woot therof but God and he.
For be he lewed man, or ellis lered,
He noot how soone that he shal been afered.
Therfore I rede yow this conseil take: 285
Forsaketh synne, er synne yow forsake.

Heere endeth the Phisiciens Tale.

The Physician-Pardoner Link

The wordes of the Hoost to the Phisicien and the Pardoner.

Oure Hooste gan to swere as he were wood;
"Harrow!" quod he, "by nayles and by blood!
This was a fals cherl and a fals justise.
As shameful deeth as herte may devyse   290
Come to thise juges and hire advocatz!
Algate this sely mayde is slayn, allas!
Allas, to deere boughte she beautee!
Wherfore I seye al day that men may see
That yiftes of Fortune and of Nature   295
Been cause of deeth to many a creature.
Hire beautee was hir deth, I dar wel sayn.

Allas, so pitously as she was slayn!
Of bothe yiftes that I speke of now
Men han ful ofte moore for harm than prow.
But trewely, myn owene maister deere,   301
This is a pitous tale for to heere.
But nathelees, passe over, is no fors.
I pray to God so save thy gentil cors,
And eek thyne urynals and thy jurdones,   305
Thyn ypocras, and eek thy galiones,
And every boyste ful of thy letuarie;
God blesse hem, and oure lady Seinte Marie!

260. **thraste,** thrust. 263. **suspect,** suspicion. 264. **manere,** reason. 271. **demed,** condemned. 272. **of his pitee,** out of pity for him. 274. **bigyled,** betrayed. 277. **his merite,** its desert. 279. **in which manere wyse,** in what way. 280. **agryse,** shudder. 281. **Of,** because of. 283. **lewed . . . lered,** unlearned . . . learned. 284. **noot,** knows not. **afered,** afraid (at the approach of death). 286. **Forsaketh . . .,** give up sin before sin gives you up (before you die). 287. **wood,** mad. 288. **Harrow!** A common ejaculation, of obscure origin. **by nayles and by blood.** Swearing was often by circumstances associated with the Crucifixion. 291. **advocatz.** The *t* was silent, and the word was often spelled -*cas*. 292. **Algate,** in any case. **sely,** simple. 294. **al day,** constantly, continually. 300. **for,** tending to. Many MSS omit *for*. **prow,** profit. 303. **is no fors,** it can't be helped. 304. **cors,** body, person. 305. **urynals,** here the glass vessels for collecting specimens of urine. **jurdones,** a kind of flask used by physicians. 306. **ypocras, galiones,** beverages named after Hippocrates and Galen, famous physicians. No other instance of the latter word is known. 307. **boyste,** flask. **letuarie,** medicine with a syrop base.

So moot I theen, thou art a propre man,
And lyk a prelat, by Seint Ronyan!   310
Seyde I nat wel? I kan nat speke in terme;
But wel I woot thou doost myn herte to erme,
That I almoost have caught a cardynacle.
By corpus bones! but I have triacle,
Or elles a draughte of moyste and corny ale,   315
Or but I heere anon a myrie tale,
Myn herte is lost for pitee of this mayde.
Thou beel amy, thou Pardoner," he sayde,
"Telle us som myrthe or japes right anon."

"It shal be doon," quod he, "by Seint Ron-
      yon!   320
But first," quod he, "heere at this alestake
I wol bothe drynke, and eten of a cake."
   But right anon thise gentils gonne to crye,
"Nay, lat hym telle us of no ribaudye!   324
Telle us som moral thyng, that we may leere
Som wit, and thanne wol we gladly heere."
   "I graunte, ywis," quod he, "but I moot
      thynke
Upon som honest thyng while that I drynke."

The Pardoner's Tale

THE PARDONER'S PROLOGUE

Heere folweth the Prologe of the Pardoners Tale.

Radix malorum est Cupiditas. Ad Thimotheum, 6⁰.

"Lordynges," quod he, "in chirches whan I
      preche,
I peyne me to han an hauteyn speche,   330
And rynge it out as round as gooth a belle,
For I kan al by rote that I telle.

My theme is alwey oon, and evere was—
Radix malorum est Cupiditas.
   First I pronounce whennes that I come,   335
And thanne my bulles shewe I, alle and some.
Oure lige lordes seel on my patente,

309. **So moot I theen,** as I may (hope to) thrive. **propre,** handsome. 310. **Seint Ronyan,** supposed to be a Scottish saint familiar in the title of Scott's novel, *St. Ronan's Well.* Others have seen in the oath an obscene pun. 311. **in terme,** in learned language. 312. **erme,** grieve. 313. **cardynacle,** the Host's mistake for *cardiacle,* a pain about the heart. 314. **By corpus bones,** further evidence, as Skeat points out, of the Host's ignorance, who mixes two oaths, *by corpus Domini* and *by Christes bones.* **triacle,** salve. 315. **moyste,** musty, often applied to ale that is very old. **corny,** full-bodied, tasting of corn or malt. 318. **beel amy,** *bel ami,* fair friend. 319. **myrthe,** entertaining story. **japes,** humorous matters. **right anon,** right away. 321. **alestake,** a projecting pole hung with a garland, the regular sign of an alehouse. 324. **ribaudye,** ribaldry. 325. **leere,** learn. 326. **wit,** wisdom.

The Pardoner's Tale and the preceding *Prologue* are admirably integrated. There is no reason to doubt that they were written at the same time and for *The Canterbury Tales.*
   The story proper is widespread and is probably of Eastern origin. However, it is found in collections of *novelle* and of *exempla* (illustrative stories for use in sermons) which circulated in western Europe prior to Chaucer's tale, and his source was doubtless one or more of these. The exact version has not been found. Into the basic framework of the story Chaucer has woven much from his own imagination and reading. The analogues nearest to Chaucer's version as well as some of the sources of the material which he has used in the *Prologue* are reprinted in *SA.* This story of the three rioters, whose reckless-ness and lack of faith even to one another results in the death of them all, is one of the finest narratives in the whole of *The Canterbury Tales.* A perceptive analysis of the action, by E. W. Stockton, will be found in *Tennessee Stud. in Lit.,* Vol. VI. 330. **hauteyn,** lofty. 332. **kan,** know. 333. **theme,** text. 334. *Radix malorum.* 1 *Timothy,* 6:10. The appropriateness of the Pardoner's text, "The love of money is the root of all evil," needs no comment. 335. **whennes that I come.** Cf. A 687. 336. **bulles.** Cf. note to A 669. **alle and some,** each and all. 337. **Oure lige lordes seel . . .** His patent bore the seal of the bishop.

That shewe I first, my body to warente,
That no man be so boold, ne preest ne clerk,
Me to destourbe of Cristes hooly werk.   340
And after that thanne telle I forth my tales;
Bulles of popes and of cardynales,
Of patriarkes and bisshopes I shewe,
And in Latyn I speke a wordes fewe,
To saffron with my predicacioun,   345
And for to stire hem to devocioun.
Thanne shewe I forth my longe cristal stones,
Ycrammed ful of cloutes and of bones,—
Relikes been they, as wenen they echoon.
Thanne have I in latoun a sholder-boon   350
Which that was of an hooly Jewes sheep.
'Goode men,' I seye, 'taak of my wordes keep;
If that this boon be wasshe in any welle,
If cow, or calf, or sheep, or oxe swelle
That any worm hath ete, or worm ystonge,   355
Taak water of that welle and wassh his tonge,
And it is hool anon; and forthermoor,
Of pokkes and of scabbe, and every soor
Shal every sheep be hool that of this welle
Drynketh a draughte. Taak kepe eek what I
    telle: 360
If that the good-man that the beestes oweth
Wol every wyke, er that the cok hym croweth,
Fastynge, drynken of this welle a draughte,
As thilke hooly Jew oure eldres taughte,
His beestes and his stoor shal multiplie.   365
    And, sires, also it heeleth jalousie;
For though a man be falle in jalous rage,
Lat maken with this water his potage,
And nevere shal he moore his wyf mystriste,
Though he the soothe of hir defaute wiste,   370
Al had she taken preestes two or thre.
    Heere is a miteyn eek, that ye may se.
He that his hand wol putte in this mitayn,

He shal have multipliyng of his grayn,
Whan he hath sowen, be it whete or otes,   375
So that he offre pens, or elles grotes.
    Goode men and wommen, o thyng warne I
        yow:
If any wight be in this chirche now
That hath doon synne horrible, that he
Dar nat, for shame, of it yshryven be,   380
Or any womman, be she yong or old,
That hath ymaad hir housbonde cokewold,
Swich folk shal have no power ne no grace
To offren to my relikes in this place.   384
And whoso fyndeth hym out of swich blame,
They wol come up and offre in Goddes name,
And I assoille hem by the auctoritee
Which that by bulle ygraunted was to me.'
    By this gaude have I wonne, yeer by yeer,
An hundred mark sith I was pardoner.   390
I stonde lyk a clerk in my pulpet,
And whan the lewed peple is doun yset,
I preche so as ye han herd bifoore,
And telle an hundred false japes moore.   394
Thanne peyne I me to strecche forth the nekke,
And est and west upon the peple I bekke,
As dooth a dowve sittynge on a berne.
Myne handes and my tonge goon so yerne
That it is joye to se my bisynesse.
Of avarice and of swich cursednesse   400
Is al my prechyng, for to make hem free
To yeven hir pens, and namely unto me.
For myn entente is nat but for to wynne,
And nothyng for correccioun of synne.   404
I rekke nevere, whan that they been beryed,
Though that hir soules goon a-blakeberyed!
For certes, many a predicacioun
Comth ofte tyme of yvel entencioun;
Som for plesance of folk and flaterye,

---

338. my body, myself. **warente,** guarantee, protect. **339. ne preest ne clerk.** An allusion to the resentment of the parish clergy towards the pardoners; cf. A 703–4. **343. patriarkes,** usually applied to the heads of the Eastern Church, but also of certain dioceses in the West (Venice, Lisbon). **345. saffron,** color, adorn. **347. cristal stones,** crystal or glass cases. **348. cloutes,** rags. **349. as . . . echoon,** as each one thinks. **350. latoun,** a metal resembling brass. **352. keep,** heed. **353. wasshe,** washed. **welle,** spring. **355. worm,** snake. **361. oweth,** owns. **362. wyke,** week. **364. thilke hooly Jew,** Jacob; Cf. *Genesis,* 30:37–43. **365. stoor,** stock. **371. Al,** although. **376. So that,** provided. **387. assoille,** absolve. **389. gaude,** trick. **390. mark,** a mark was 13*s.* 4*d.* (two-thirds of a pound). **sith,** since. **392. lewed,** ignorant. **394. japes,** tales. **396. bekke,** nod. **397. berne,** barn. **398. yerne,** eagerly, briskly. **402. namely,** especially. **404. correccioun,** amendment. **406. a-blakeberyed,** a-blackberrying, wandering aimlessly. For the constr. see note to F 1580. **409. plesance,** the pleasing.

To been avaunced by ypocrisye,   410
And som for veyne glorie, and som for hate.
For whan I dar noon oother weyes debate,
Thanne wol I stynge hym with my tonge smerte
In prechyng, so that he shal nat asterte
To been defamed falsly, if that he   415
Hath trespased to my bretheren or to me.
For though I telle noght his propre name,
Men shal wel knowe that it is the same,
By signes, and by othere circumstances.
Thus quyte I folk that doon us displesances;   420
Thus spitte I out my venym under hewe
Of hoolynesse, to semen hooly and trewe.
    But shortly myn entente I wol devyse:
I preche of no thyng but for coveityse.
Therfore my theme is yet, and evere was,   425
Radix malorum est Cupiditas.
Thus kan I preche agayn that same vice
Which that I use, and that is avarice.
But though myself be gilty in that synne,
Yet kan I maken oother folk to twynne   430
From avarice, and soore to repente.
But that is nat my principal entente;
I preche nothyng but for coveitise.
Of this mateere it oghte ynogh suffise.
    Thanne telle I hem ensamples many oon   435

Of olde stories longe tyme agoon.
For lewed peple loven tales olde;
Swiche thynges kan they wel reporte and holde.
What, trowe ye, that whiles I may preche,
And wynne gold and silver for I teche,   440
That I wol lyve in poverte wilfully?
Nay, nay, I thoghte it nevere, trewely!
For I wol preche and begge in sondry landes;
I wol nat do no labour with myne handes,
Ne make baskettes, and lyve therby,   445
By cause I wol nat beggen ydelly.
I wol noon of the apostles countrefete;
I wol have moneie, wolle, chese, and whete,
Al were it yeven of the povereste page,
Or of the povereste wydwe in a village,   450
Al sholde hir children sterve for famyne.
Nay, I wol drynke licour of the vyne,
And have a joly wenche in every toun.
But herkneth, lordynges, in conclusioun:
Youre likyng is that I shal telle a tale.   455
Now have I dronke a draughte of corny ale,
By God, I hope I shal yow telle a thyng
That shal by reson been at youre likyng.
For though myself be a ful vicious man,
A moral tale yet I yow telle kan,   460
Which I am wont to preche for to wynne.
Now hoold youre pees! my tale I wol bigynne."

412. debate, argue. 413. hym. Though there is no antecedent, the lines that follow show that the Pardoner has in mind any one who proves hard to persuade. smerte, smartly. 414. asterte To been, escape from being. 416. trespased, done wrong. my bretheren, fellow-pardoners. 420. quyte, pay back. 423. devyse, describe, explain. 427. agayn, against. 430. twynne, separate (themselves), depart. 435. ensamples, examples, exempla, stories used to point a moral in preaching. 440. for I teche, because I teach poverty. 441. wilfully, voluntarily. 445. baskettes, (three syllables). From Piers Plowman (C XVIII. 17–18) it seems that St. Paul was believed to have earned his living, after preaching, by making baskets (panyeres). But the idea is probably due to confusion with Paul the Hermit. In the Vitae Patrum (the life of Paul the Hermit by St. Jerome) Paul occupied himself making baskets; cf. PL, XXIII. 28. 446. idelly, in vain. 447. countrefete, imitate. 449. Al, although. povereste, poorest. 451. sterve for famyne, die of starvation. 458. by reson, with good reason.

THE PARDONER'S TALE

Heere bigynneth the Pardoners Tale.

In Flaundres whilom was a compaignye
Of yonge folk that haunteden folye,
As riot, hasard, stywes, and tavernes,   465
Where as with harpes, lutes, and gyternes,
They daunce and pleyen at dees bothe day and
    nyght,
And eten also and drynken over hir myght,
Thurgh which they doon the devel sacrifise
Withinne that develes temple, in cursed wise,
By superfluytee abhomynable.   471
Hir othes been so grete and so dampnable
That it is grisly for to heere hem swere.
Oure blissed Lordes body they totere,—
Hem thoughte that Jewes rente hym noght
    ynough;   475
And ech of hem at otheres synne lough.
And right anon thanne comen tombesteres
Fetys and smale, and yonge frutesteres,
Syngeres with harpes, baudes, wafereres,
Whiche been the verray develes officeres   480
To kyndle and blowe the fyr of lecherye,
That is annexed unto glotonye.
The hooly writ take I to my witnesse
That luxurie is in wyn and dronkenesse.
Lo, how that dronken Looth, unkyndely,   485
Lay by his doghtres two, unwityngly;
So dronke he was, he nyste what he wroghte.
Herodes, whoso wel the stories soghte,
Whan he of wyn was repleet at his feeste,
Right at his owene table he yaf his heeste   490

To sleen the Baptist John, ful giltelees.
    Senec seith a good word doutelees;
He seith he kan no difference fynde
Bitwix a man that is out of his mynde
And a man which that is dronkelewe,   495
But that woodnesse, yfallen in a shrewe,
Persevereth lenger than dooth dronkenesse.
O glotonye, ful of cursednesse!
O cause first of oure confusioun!
O original of oure dampnacioun,   500
Til Crist hadde boght us with his blood agayn!
Lo, how deere, shortly for to sayn,
Aboght was thilke cursed vileynye!
Corrupt was al this world for glotonye.
    Adam oure fader, and his wyf also,   505
Fro Paradys to labour and to wo
Were dryven for that vice, it is no drede.
For whil that Adam fasted, as I rede,
He was in Paradys; and whan that he
Eet of the fruyt deffended on the tree,   510
Anon he was out cast to wo and peyne.
O glotonye, on thee wel oghte us pleyne!
O, wiste a man how manye maladyes
Folwen of excesse and of glotonyes,
He wolde been the moore mesurable   515
Of his diete, sittynge at his table.
Allas! the shorte throte, the tendre mouth,
Maketh that est and west and north and south,
In erthe, in eir, in water, men to swynke
To gete a glotoun deyntee mete and drynke! 520

---

465. hasard, gambling with dice. **stywes,** houses of ill fame. **466. gyternes,** musical instruments like a guitar. **467. dees,** dice. **470. that develes temple,** the tavern. **473. grisly,** horrible. **474. totere,** tear to pieces (swearing by the parts of Christ's body). **475. Hem thoughte,** it seemed to them. **476. lough,** laughed. **477. tombesteres,** female acrobats or dancers. **478. Fetys,** shapely, pretty. **frutesteres,** fruit-sellers (female). **479. wafereres,** makers and sellers of wafers and cakes. **482. annexed unto,** joined to. **483. The hooly writ.** *Ephesians,* 5: 18: And be not drunk with wine, wherein is luxury (Douai version). **484. luxurie,** lechery. **485. Looth,** Lot; cf. *Genesis,* 19 30–8. **unkyndely,** unnaturally. **487. he nyste . . .,** he didn't know what he was doing. **488. Herodes,** Herod; cf. *Matthew,* 14: 1–12. **soghte,** should seek. **490. yaf his heeste,** gave his command. **492. Senec,** Seneca (*Letters,* Epis. 83). **495. dronkelewe,** drunken. **496. woodnesse,** madness. **shrewe,** an evil or worthless person of either sex. **503. vileynye,** wrong-doing, sin. **504. Corrupt,** infected with evil. **for,** on account of. **507. drede,** doubt. **510. deffended,** forbidden. **512. pleyne,** complain. **519. swynke,** labor. **520. deyntee,** choice, rare.

Of this matiere, o Paul, wel kanstow trete:
"Mete unto wombe, and wombe eek unto
    mete,
Shal God destroyen bothe," as Paulus seith.
Allas! a foul thyng is it, by my feith,
To seye this word, and fouler is the dede,   525
Whan man so drynketh of the white and rede
That of his throte he maketh his pryvee,
Thurgh thilke cursed superfluitee.
    The apostel wepyng seith ful pitously,
"Ther walken manye of whiche yow toold
    have I—   530
I seye it now wepyng, with pitous voys—
That they been enemys of Cristes croys,
Of whiche the ende is deeth; wombe is hir
    god!"
O wombe! O bely! O stynkyng cod,
Fulfilled of donge and of corrupcioun!   535
At either ende of thee foul is the soun.
How greet labour and cost is thee to fynde!
Thise cookes, how they stampe, and streyne,
    and grynde,
And turnen substaunce into accident,
To fulfille al thy likerous talent!   540
Out of the harde bones knokke they
The mary, for they caste noght awey
That may go thurgh the golet softe and swoote.
Of spicerie of leef, and bark, and roote
Shal been his sauce ymaked by delit,   545
To make hym yet a newer appetit.
But, certes, he that haunteth swiche delices
Is deed, whil that he lyveth in tho vices.
    A lecherous thyng is wyn, and dronkenesse
Is ful of stryvyng and of wrecchednesse.   550
O dronke man, disfigured is thy face,
Sour is thy breeth, foul artow to embrace,

And thurgh thy dronke nose semeth the soun
As though thou seydest ay "Sampsoun, Samp-
    soun!"
And yet, God woot, Sampsoun drank nevere no
    wyn.   555
Thou fallest as it were a styked swyn;
Thy tonge is lost, and al thyn honeste cure;
For dronkenesse is verray sepulture
Of mannes wit and his discrecioun.
In whom that drynke hath dominacioun   560
He kan no conseil kepe, it is no drede.
Now kepe yow fro the white and fro the
    rede,
And namely fro the white wyn of Lepe,
That is to selle in Fysshstrete or in Chepe.
This wyn of Spaigne crepeth subtilly   565
In othere wynes, growynge faste by,
Of which ther ryseth swich fumositee
That whan a man hath dronken draughtes thre,
And weneth that he be at hoom in Chepe,
He is in Spaigne, right at the toune of Lepe,—
Nat at the Rochele, ne at Burdeux toun;   571
And thanne wol he seye "Sampsoun, Samp-
    soun!"
    But herkneth, lordynges, o word, I yow
    preye,
That alle the sovereyn actes, dar I seye,
Of victories in the Olde Testament,   575
Thurgh verray God, that is omnipotent,
Were doon in abstinence and in preyere.
Looketh the Bible, and ther ye may it leere.
    Looke, Attilla, the grete conquerour,   579
Deyde in his sleep, with shame and dishonour,
Bledynge ay at his nose in dronkenesse.
A capitayn sholde lyve in sobrenesse.
And over al this, avyseth yow right wel

521. **Paul.** Cf. *1 Corinthians*, 6: 13. 522. **wombe**, belly. 529. **The apostel**, St. Paul cf. *Philippians*, 3: 18–9. 534. **cod**, bag, here the stomach. 535. **corrupcioun**, decomposed matter. 537. **fynde**, provide for. 538. **stampe**, pound. 539. **substaunce into accident**, terms of scholastic philosophy, implying here an attempt to disguise the real character of a thing by changing its appearance. **540. likerous talent**, lecherous (gluttonous) inclination. 542. **mary**, marrow. 543. **softe and swoote**, softly and sweetly. 545. **by**, with respect to. 547. **delices**, delights. 548: **tho**, those. 553. **soun**, sound. 557. **honeste cure**, efforts toward decency. 561. **drede**, doubt. 563. **namely**, especially. **Lepe**, near Cadiz. 564. **to selle**, for sale. **Fysshstrete**, Fish Street, running into Thames Street, where Chaucer's father lived. **Chepe**, Cheapside, well known for its taverns. 565. **crepeth subtilly.** Chaucer hints that Spanish wine, being cheaper, was sometimes mixed with the French wine of Rochelle and Bordeaux. 567. **fumositee**, the vapor from wine, that was supposed to go to the head. 571. **the Rochele**, La Rochelle. According to Skeat, this means that he doesn't know where he is. 574. **sovereyn actes**, major accomplishments. 578. **leere**, learn.

What was comaunded unto Lamuel—
Nat Samuel, but Lamuel, seye I;   585
Redeth the Bible, and fynde it expresly
Of wyn-yevyng to hem that han justise.
Namoore of this, for it may wel suffise.

And now that I have spoken of glotonye,
Now wol I yow deffenden hasardrye.   590
Hasard is verray mooder of lesynges,
And of deceite, and cursed forswerynges,
Blaspheme of Crist, manslaughtre, and wast also
Of catel and of tyme; and forthermo,
It is repreeve and contrarie of honour   595
For to ben holde a commune hasardour.
And ever the hyer he is of estaat,
The moore is he yholden desolaat.
If that a prynce useth hasardrye,
In alle governaunce and policye   600
He is, as by commune opinioun,
Yholde the lasse in reputacioun.

Stilboun, that was a wys embassadour,
Was sent to Corynthe, in ful greet honour,
Fro Lacidomye, to make hire alliaunce.   605
And whan he cam, hym happede, par chaunce,
That alle the gretteste that were of that lond,
Pleyynge atte hasard he hem fond.
For which, as soone as it myghte be,
He stal hym hoom agayn to his contree,   610
And seyde, "Ther wol I nat lese my name,
Ne I wol nat take on me so greet defame,
Yow for to allie unto none hasardours.
Sendeth othere wise embassadours;
For, by my trouthe, me were levere dye   615
Than I yow sholde to hasardours allye.
For ye, that been so glorious in honours,
Shul nat allyen yow with hasardours

As by my wyl, ne as by my tretee."
This wise philosophre, thus seyde hee.   620
    Looke eek that to the kyng Demetrius
The kyng of Parthes, as the book seith us,
Sente him a paire of dees of gold in scorn,
For he hadde used hasard ther-biforn;
For which he heeld his glorie or his renoun   625
At no value or reputacioun.
Lordes may fynden oother maner pley
Honeste ynough to dryve the day awey.
    Now wol I speke of othes false and grete
A word or two, as olde bookes trete.   630
Gret sweryng is a thyng abhominable,
And fals sweryng is yet moore reprevable.
The heighe God forbad sweryng at al—
Witnesse on Mathew; but in special
Of sweryng seith the hooly Jeremye,   635
"Thou shalt swere sooth thyne othes, and nat
    lye,
And swere in doom, and eek in rightwisnesse";
But ydel sweryng is a cursednesse.
Bihoold and se that in the firste table
Of heighe Goddes heestes honurable,   640
Hou that the seconde heeste of hym is this:
"Take nat my name in ydel or amys."
Lo, rather he forbedeth swich sweryng
Than homycide or many a cursed thyng;
I seye that, as by ordre, thus it stondeth;   645
This knoweth, that his heestes understondeth,
How that the seconde heeste of God is that.
And forther over, I wol thee telle al plat,
That vengeance shal nat parten from his hous
That of his othes is to outrageous.   650
"By Goddes precious herte," and "By his
    nayles,"

---

584. Lamuel, Lemuel; cf. *Proverbs*, 31: 4–5: It is not for kings, O Lemuel, it is not for kings to drink wine . . . lest they drink, and forget the law . . .. **587. Of,** concerning. **han justise,** *i.e.*, have responsibility for rendering justice. **590. deffenden hasardrye,** forbid gambling. **591. lesynges,** lies. **594. catel,** goods, property. **595. repreeve,** reproof. **598. desolaat,** abandoned. **603. Stilboun.** The anecdote is told by John of Salisbury in the *Polycraticus* (I. 5), where the ambassador is named Chilon. **605. Lacidomye,** Lacedaemon. **608. hasard,** dice. **611. lese,** lose. **621. Demetrius,** one of the kings of the Parthians, whose story is also in the *Polycraticus*, where it follows immediately the previous anecdote. **623. dees,** dice. **634. Mathew.** Cf. *Matthew*, 5:34: But I say unto you, Swear not at all . . . **635. Jeremye,** Jeremiah. The quotation is from *Jeremiah*, 4:2. **637. doom,** judgment. **638. cursednesse,** wickedness. **639. the firste table,** the stone tablet containing the first five of the Ten Commandments (*Goddes heestes*). **641. the seconde heeste.** The second commandment is now the third. Formerly the first and second commandments were combined, and the tenth was divided. **643. rather,** earlier (in the list) than homicide. **646. knoweth.** *He* or *man* is understood. **648. forther over,** furthermore. **al plat,** flatly. **649. parten,** depart. Cf. *Ecclesiasticus*, 23: 11.

And "By the blood of Crist that is in Hayles,
Sevene is my chaunce, and thyn is cynk and
    treye!"
"By Goddes armes, if thou falsly pleye,   654
This daggere shal thurghout thyn herte go!"—
This fruyt cometh of the bicched bones two:
Forsweryng, ire, falsnesse, homycide.
Now, for the love of Crist, that for us dyde,
Lete youre othes, bothe grete and smale.
But, sires, now wol I telle forth my tale.   660
    Thise riotoures thre of whiche I telle,
Longe erst er prime rong of any belle,
Were set hem in a taverne for to drynke,
And as they sat, they herde a belle clynke
Biforn a cors, was caried to his grave.   665
That oon of hem gan callen to his knave:
"Go bet," quod he, "and axe redily
What cors is this that passeth heer forby;
And looke that thou reporte his name weel."
    "Sire," quod this boy, "it nedeth never-a-
    deel;   670
It was me toold er ye cam heer two houres.
He was, pardee, an old felawe of youres;
And sodeynly he was yslayn to-nyght,
Fordronke, as he sat on his bench upright.
Ther cam a privee theef men clepeth Deeth,   675
That in this contree al the peple sleeth,
And with his spere he smoot his herte atwo,
And wente his wey withouten wordes mo.
He hath a thousand slayn this pestilence.
And, maister, er ye come in his presence,   680
Me thynketh that it were necessarie
For to be war of swich an adversarie.
Beth redy for to meete hym everemoore;
Thus taughte me my dame; I sey namoore."
"By seinte Marie!" seyde this taverner,   685

"The child seith sooth, for he hath slayn this
    yeer,
Henne over a mile, withinne a greet village,
Bothe man and womman, child, and hyne, and
    page;
I trowe his habitacioun be there.
To been avysed greet wysdom it were,   690
Er that he dide a man a dishonour."
    "Ye, Goddes armes!" quod this riotour,
"Is it swich peril with hym for to meete?
I shal hym seke by wey and eek by strete,
I make avow to Goddes digne bones!   695
Herkneth, felawes, we thre been al ones;
Lat ech of us holde up his hand til oother,
And ech of us bicomen otheres brother,
And we wol sleen this false traytour Deeth.
He shal be slayn, he that so manye sleeth,   700
By Goddes dignitee, er it be nyght!"
    Togidres han thise thre hir trouthes plight
To lyve and dyen ech of hem for oother,
As though he were his owene ybore brother.
And up they stirte, al dronken in this rage,   705
And forth they goon towardes that village
Of which the taverner hadde spoke biforn.
And many a grisly ooth thanne han they
    sworn,
And Cristes blessed body they torente—   709
Deeth shal be deed, if that they may hym hente!
    Whan they han goon nat fully half a mile,
Right as they wolde han troden over a stile,
An oold man and a povre with hem mette.
This olde man ful mekely hem grette,
And seyde thus, "Now, lordes, God yow see!"
    The proudeste of thise riotoures three   716
Answerde agayn, "What, carl, with sory
    grace!

652. **Hayles,** the abbey of Hales in Gloucestershire, which was believed to have some of Christ's blood. 653. **Sevene is my chaunce,** *i.e.* in the game of hazard or craps. **cynk and treye,** five and three; 656. **bicched bones,** cursed dice. 659. **Lete,** leave. 662. **erst er,** *lit.* first before. **prime,** the canonical hour, here probably about 6 A.M., announced by the ringing of a bell. 664. **belle,** a hand-bell, later called a *lych bell,* carried beside the corpse in funerals. In the Bayeux tapestry two men with bells are shown beside the body at the burial of Edward the Confessor. 665. **cors,** body, corpse. **his,** its. 666. **knave,** boy, servant. 667. **Go bet,** go better (quickly), originally a hunting cry to the dogs. **axe,** ask. **redily,** promptly, but often used as a mere intensive. 668. **forby,** by. 669. **weel,** well. 670. **it nedeth . . .,** it is not at all necessary. 672. **felawe,** friend, companion. 673. **to-nyght,** last night. 674. **Fordronke,** very drunk. 679. **this pestilence,** during the present plague. 687. **Henne,** hence. 688. **hyne,** hind, laborer. 690. **avysed,** forewarned. 695. **digne,** worthy. 696. **ones,** of one mind. 697. **til,** to. 701. **dignitee,** worthiness. 702. **Togidres,** together. On the swearing of brotherhood see the note to A 1132. 705. **stirte,** sprang. 710. **hente,** catch. 713. **povre,** poor. 714. **grette,** greeted. 715. **God yow see,** *i.e.* God be with you. 717. **with sory grace**! an exclamation of impatience.

Why artow al forwrapped save thy face?
Why lyvestow so longe in so greet age?"

   This olde man gan looke in his visage, 720
And seyde thus: "For I ne kan nat fynde
A man, though that I walked into Ynde,
Neither in citee ne in no village,
That wolde chaunge his youthe for myn age;
And therfore moot I han myn age stille, 725
As longe tyme as it is Goddes wille.
Ne Deeth, allas, ne wol nat han my lyf!
Thus walke I, lyk a restelees kaityf,
And on the ground, which is my moodres gate,
I knokke with my staf, bothe erly and late, 730
And seye, 'Leeve mooder, leet me in!
Lo, how I vanysshe, flessh, and blood, and
   skyn!
Allas! whan shul my bones been at reste?
Mooder, with yow wolde I chaunge my cheste
That in my chambre longe tyme hath be, 735
Ye, for an heyre clowt to wrappe in me!'
But yet to me she wol nat do that grace,
For which ful pale and welked is my face.

   But, sires, to yow it is no curteisye
To speken to an old man vileynye, 740
But he trespasse in word, or elles in dede.
In Hooly Writ ye may yourself wel rede:
'Agayns an oold man, hoor upon his heed,
Ye sholde arise;' wherfore I yeve yow reed,
Ne dooth unto an oold man noon harm
   now, 745
Namoore than that ye wolde men did to yow
In age, if that ye so longe abyde.
And God be with yow, where ye go or ryde!
I moot go thider as I have to go."

   "Nay, olde cherl, by God, thou shalt nat so,"
Seyde this oother hasardour anon; 751
"Thou partest nat so lightly, by Seint John!

Thou spak right now of thilke traytour Deeth,
That in this contree alle oure freendes sleeth.
Have heer my trouthe, as thou art his espye,
Telle where he is, or thou shalt it abye, 756
By God, and by the hooly sacrement!
For soothly thou art oon of his assent
To sleen us yonge folk, thou false theef!" 759

   "Now, sires," quod he, "if that yow be so leef
To fynde Deeth, turne up this croked wey,
For in that grove I lafte hym, by my fey,
Under a tree, and there he wole abyde;
Noght for youre boost he wole him no thyng
   hyde.
Se ye that ook? Right there ye shal hym
   fynde. 765
God save yow, that boghte agayn mankynde,
And yow amende!" Thus seyde this olde man;
And everich of thise riotoures ran
Til he cam to that tree, and ther they founde
Of floryns fyne of gold ycoyned rounde 770
Wel ny an eighte busshels, as hem thoughte.
No lenger thanne after Deeth they soughte,
But ech of hem so glad was of that sighte,
For that the floryns been so faire and brighte,
That doun they sette hem by this precious
   hoord. 775
The worste of hem, he spak the firste word.
   "Bretheren," quod he, "taak kepe what I
   seye;
My wit is greet, though that I bourde and
   pleye.
This tresor hath Fortune unto us yiven,
In myrthe and joliftee oure lyf to lyven, 780
And lightly as it comth, so wol we spende.
Ey! Goddes precious dignitee! who wende
To-day that we sholde han so fair a grace?
But myghte this gold be caried fro this place

---

718. **forwrapped,** wrapped up completely. 722. **Ynde,** India. 725. **moot,** must. 728. **kaityf,** wretch (*orig.* captive). 731. **Leeve,** dear. 732. **vanysshe,** waste away. 734. **cheste,** *i.e.,* for clothes, here referring to the contents. 736. **heyre clowt,** piece of haircloth (for burial). **to wrappe in me,** to wrap me in. 738. **welked,** withered. 740. **vileynye,** rudeness. 741. **But,** unless. 742. **In Hooly Writ.** *Leviticus,* 19:32. 744. **yeve yow reed,** give you advice. 748. **where ye go,** whether ye walk. 755. **espye,** spy. 756. **abye,** pay for. 758. **oon of his assent,** in league together. 760. **leef,** agreeable. 765. **ook.** In the ritual known as "burying Death," described in Fraser's *Golden Bough,* an effigy of Death is buried under an oak tree. See F. H. Candelaria, *MLN,* LXXI. 321–2. 770. **floryns,** gold coins (with a value of about 3 shillings), named from the flower (lily) stamped on them, but orig. minted at Florence. The word is often loosely used for money in general. 772. **thanne,** then. 777. **taak kepe,** take heed. 778. **bourde,** jest. 782. **wende,** would have thought.

Hoom to myn hous, or elles unto youres— 785
For wel ye woot that al this gold is oures—
Thanne were we in heigh felicitee.
But trewely, by daye it may nat bee.
Men wolde seyn that we were theves stronge,
And for oure owene tresor doon us honge. 790
This tresor moste ycaried be by nyghte
As wisely and as slyly as it myghte.
Wherfore I rede that cut among us alle
Be drawe, and lat se wher the cut wol falle;
And he that hath the cut with herte blithe 795
Shal renne to the towne, and that ful swithe,
And brynge us breed and wyn ful prively.
And two of us shul kepen subtilly
This tresor wel; and if he wol nat tarie,
Whan it is nyght, we wol this tresor carie, 800
By oon assent, where as us thynketh best."
That oon of hem the cut broghte in his fest,
And bad hem drawe, and looke where it wol
falle;
And it fil on the yongeste of hem alle,
And forth toward the toun he wente anon. 805
And also soone as that he was gon,
That oon of hem spak thus unto that oother:
"Thow knowest wel thou art my sworne
brother;
Thy profit wol I telle thee anon.
Thou woost wel that oure felawe is agon. 810
And heere is gold, and that ful greet plentee,
That shal departed been among us thre.
But nathelees, if I kan shape it so
That it departed were among us two,
Hadde I nat doon a freendes torn to thee?" 815
That oother answerde, "I noot hou that may
be.
He woot wel that the gold is with us tweye;
What shal we doon? What shal we to hym
seye?"

"Shal it be conseil?" seyde the firste shrewe,
"And I shal tellen in a wordes fewe 820
What we shal doon, and brynge it wel aboute."
"I graunte," quod that oother, "out of doute,
That, by my trouthe, I wol thee nat biwreye."
"Now," quod the firste, "thou woost wel we
be tweye,
And two of us shul strenger be than oon. 825
Looke whan that he is set, that right anoon
Arys as though thou woldest with hym pleye,
And I shal ryve hym thurgh the sydes tweye
Whil that thou strogelest with hym as in game,
And with thy daggere looke thou do the same;
And thanne shal al this gold departed be, 831
My deere freend, bitwixen me and thee.
Thanne may we bothe oure lustes all fulfille,
And pleye at dees right at oure owene wille."
And thus acorded been thise shrewes tweye
To sleen the thridde, as ye han herd me seye. 836
This yongeste, which that wente to the toun,
Ful ofte in herte he rolleth up and doun
The beautee of thise floryns newe and brighte.
"O Lord!" quod he, "if so were that I myghte
Have al this tresor to myself allone, 841
Ther is no man that lyveth under the trone
Of God that sholde lyve so murye as I!"
And atte laste the feend, oure enemy, 844
Putte in his thought that he sholde poyson beye,
With which he myghte sleen his felawes tweye;
For-why the feend foond hym in swich lyvynge
That he hadde leve hym to sorwe brynge.
For this was outrely his fulle entente,
To sleen hem bothe, and nevere to repente. 850
And forth he gooth, no lenger wolde he tarie,
Into the toun, unto a pothecarie,
And preyde hym that he hym wolde selle
Som poyson, that he myghte his rattes quelle;
And eek ther was a polcat in his hawe, 855

---

790. doon us honge, have us hanged. **793. rede,** advise. **cut,** lots. The casting of lots was by means of straws or sticks of different length. Some MSS read *strawe* in l. 802. **796. renne,** run. **swithe,** quickly. **798. kepen,** guard. **802. That oon,** the one, one. **fest,** fist, hand. **805. anon,** immediately. **806. also,** as. **809. Thy profit,** what is to your advantage. **814. departed,** divided **819. conseil,** a secret. **shrewe,** rascal. **823. biwreye,** betray. **824. woost,** knowest. **826. Looke whan.** The expression sometimes means "whenever," but not always. **828. ryve,** pierce, stab. **833. lustes,** desires. **842. trone Of God,** throne of God, heaven. **843. murye,** merry. **844. feend,** devil. **845. beye,** buy. **847. lyvynge,** way of life. **848. leve,** leave, permission. **854. quelle,** kill. **855. hawe,** yard.

That, as he seyde, his capouns hadde yslawe,
And fayn he wolde wreke hym, if he myghte,
On vermyn that destroyed hym by nyghte.

    The pothecarie answerde, "And thou shalt have
A thyng that, also God my soule save,   860
In al this world ther is no creature,
That eten or dronken hath of this confiture
Noght but the montance of a corn of whete,
That he ne shal his lif anon forlete;
Ye, sterve he shal, and that in lasse while   865
Than thou wold goon a paas nat but a mile,
This poysoun is so strong and violent."

    This cursed man hath in his hond yhent
This poysoun in a box, and sith he ran
Into the nexte strete unto a man,   870
And borwed [of] hym large botels thre;
And in the two his poyson poured he;
The thridde he kepte clene for his drynke.
For al the nyght he shoop hym for to swynke
In cariynge of the gold out of that place.   875
And whan this riotour, with sory grace,
Hadde filled with wyn his grete botels thre,
To his felawes agayn repaireth he.

    What nedeth it to sermone of it moore?   879
For right as they hadde cast his deeth bifoore,
Right so they han hym slayn, and that anon.
And whan that this was doon, thus spak that oon:
"Now lat us sitte and drynke, and make us merie,
And afterward we wol his body berie."   884
And with that word it happed hym, par cas,
To take the botel ther the poyson was,
And drank, and yaf his felawe drynke also,
For which anon they storven bothe two.

    But certes, I suppose that Avycen
Wroot nevere in no canon, ne in no fen,   890
Mo wonder signes of empoisonyng
Than hadde thise wrecches two, er hir endyng.
Thus ended been thise homycides two,
And eek the false empoysonere also.

    O cursed synne of alle cursednesse!   895
O traytours homycide, O wikkednesse!
O glotonye, luxurie, and hasardrye!
Thou blasphemour of Crist with vileynye
And othes grete, of usage and of pride!
Allas! mankynde, how may it bitide   900
That to thy creatour, which that the wroghte,
And with his precious herte-blood thee boghte,
Thou art so fals and so unkynde, allas?

    Now, goode men, God foryeve yow youre trespas,
And ware yow fro the synne of avarice!   905
Myn hooly pardoun may yow alle warice,
So that ye offre nobles or sterlynges,
Or elles silver broches, spoones, rynges.
Boweth youre heed under this hooly bulle!   909
Cometh up, ye wyves, offreth of youre wolle!
Youre names I entre heer in my rolle anon;
Into the blisse of hevene shul ye gon.
I yow assoille, by myn heigh power,
Yow that wol offre, as clene and eek as cleer
As ye were born.—And lo, sires, thus I preche.
And Jhesu Crist, that is oure soules leche,   916
So graunte yow his pardoun to receyve,
For that is best; I wol yow nat deceyve.

    But, sires, o word forgat I in my tale:
I have relikes and pardoun in my male,   920
As faire as any man in Engelond,
Whiche were me yeven by the popes hond.
If any of yow wole, of devocioun,

---

856. **yslawe**, killed. 858. **vermyn**, objectionable animals. **destroyed**, were ruining. 860. **also**, as. 862. **confiture**, preparation. 863. **montance of a corn**, amount of a grain. 864. **anon forlete**, yield up immediately. 865. **sterve**, die. 866. **a paas**, at a walk. 868. **yhent**, taken. 874. **shoop hym**, planned. **swynke**, labor. 876. **with sory grace**, a curse upon him. 879. **sermone**, preach, speak. 885. **par cas**, by chance. 886. **ther**, where. 888. **storven**, died. 889. **Avycen**. Avicenna, an Arabic physician (d. 1037), also mentioned in A 432. 890. **canon**. Avicenna's most famous work was the *Book of the Canon in Medicine*. **fen**, the designation of each chapter in his book (Arabic *fann*, a part of a science). 891. **signes**, symtoms. 896. **traytours**, traitorous. 897. **luxurie**, lechery. 898. **vileynye**, wicked speech. 899. **usage**, habit. 905. **ware yow**, beware. 906. **warice**, cure. 907. **So that**, provided. **nobles**, gold coins of about the diameter of a half crown or a U.S. half dollar, although much thinner. **sterlynges**, silver pennies. 910. **wolle**, wool. Offerings in kind were common. 913. **assoille**, absolve. 916. **leche**, physician. 919. **sires**. From here on the Pardoner is addressing his fellow-pilgrims. 920. **male**, bag. 922. **yeven**, given.

Offren, and han myn absolucioun,

Com forth anon, and kneleth heere adoun,   925

And mekely receyveth my pardoun;

Or elles taketh pardoun as ye wende,

Al newe and fressh at every miles ende,

So that ye offren, alwey newe and newe,

Nobles or pens, whiche that be goode and trewe.

It is an honour to everich that is heer   931

That ye mowe have a suffisant pardoneer

T'assoille yow, in contree as ye ryde,

For aventures whiche that may bityde.

Paraventure ther may fallen oon or two   935

Doun of his hors, and breke his nekke atwo.

Looke which a seuretee is it to yow alle

That I am in youre felaweship yfalle,

That may assoille yow, bothe moore and lasse,

Whan that the soule shal fro the body passe.   940

I rede that oure Hoost heere shal bigynne,

For he is moost enveluped in synne.

Com forth, sire Hoost, and offre first anon,

And thou shalt kisse the relikes everychon,

Ye, for a grote! Unbokele anon thy purs."   945

"Nay, nay!" quod he, "thanne have I Cristes

     curs!

Lat be," quod he, "it shal nat be, so theech!

Thou woldest make me kisse thyn olde breech,

And swere it were a relyk of a seint,   949

Though it were with thy fundement depeint!

But, by the croys which that Seint Eleyne

     fond,

I wolde I hadde thy coillons in myn hond

In stide of relikes or of seintuarie.

Lat kutte hem of, I wol thee helpe hem carie;

They shul be shryned in an hogges toord!"   955

     This Pardoner answerde nat a word;

So wrooth he was, no word ne wolde he seye.

     "Now," quod oure Hoost, "I wol no lenger

     pleye

With thee, ne with noon oother angry man."

But right anon the worthy Knyght bigan,   960

Whan that he saugh that al the peple lough,

"Namoore of this, for it is right ynough!

Sire Pardoner, be glad and myrie of cheere;

And ye, sire Hoost, that been to me so deere,

I prey yow that ye kisse the Pardoner.   965

And Pardoner, I prey thee, drawe thee neer,

And, as we diden, lat us laughe and pleye."

Anon they kiste, and ryden forth hir weye.

Heere is ended the Pardoners Tale.

927. **wende**, *i.e*, ride along. 929. **newe and newe**, ever anew. 931. **honour**, privilege. 932. **mowe**, may. 933. **assoille yow**, give you absolution. 934. **aventures**, chances, accidents. **bityde**, happen. 937. **which a**, what a. 939. **assoille**, here the final rites of the Church. 945. **grote**, groat, a silver coin worth four pence. 947. **so theech**, *so thee ich*, so may I thrive. 948. **breech**, a short undergarment, mod. "shorts." 950. **fundement**, rectum. **depeint**, stained. 951. **Seint Eleyne**, St. Helena. The Invention of the Cross (finding of the cross by St. Helena) is commemorated by the Church on May 3. 952. **coillons**, testicles. 953. **seintuarie**, box containing relics. 961. **lough**, laughed. 968. **ryden**, rode.

Group G (Fragment VIII)

The Second Nun's Tale

THE SECOND NUN'S PROLOGUE

The Prologe of the Seconde Nonnes Tale.

The ministre and the norice unto vices,
Which that men clepe in Englissh ydelnesse,
That porter of the gate is of delices,
To eschue, and by hire contrarie hire op-
    presse,
That is to seyn, by leveful bisynesse,   5
Wel oughten we to doon al oure entente,
Lest that the feend thurgh ydelnesse us hente.

For he that with his thousand cordes slye
Continuelly us waiteth to biclappe,
Whan he may man in ydelnesse espye,   10
He kan so lightly cacche hym in his trappe,
Til that a man be hent right by the lappe,
He nys nat war the feend hath hym in honde.
Wel oghte us werche, and ydelnesse with-
    stonde.

And though men dradden nevere for to dye,   15
Yet seen men wel by resoun, doutelees,
That ydelnesse is roten slogardye,
Of which ther nevere comth no good
    n'encrees,
And syn that slouthe hire holdeth in a lees
Oonly to slepe, and for to ete and drynke,   20
And to devouren al that othere swynke,

And for to putte us fro swich ydelnesse,
That cause is of so greet confusioun,
I have heer doon my feithful bisynesse
After the legende, in translacioun   25
Right of thy glorious lif and passioun,
Thou with thy gerland wroght with rose and
    lilie,—
Thee meene I, mayde and martyr, Seint Cecilie.

The Second Nun's Prologue and Tale. The Prioress's traveling companion, the Second Nun, appropriately relates the legend of St. Cecilia. Yet it was clearly not written for her or indeed for *The Canterbury Tales*. Not only has the tell-tale "unworthy sone of Eve" (l. 62) been left to startle the reader when it falls from the lips of a nun, but the legend proper is preceded by an elaborate prologue more suitable for an independent piece. Prologue and tale are in the stanza form of the *Troilus* and the whole work was doubtless a poem which Chaucer had written on another occasion and which he had on hand when he started putting together *The Canterbury Tales*. Fortunately there was a pilgrim to whom it could most fittingly be assigned.

The final section of the prologue and the earlier part of the tale (to l. 357) are a faithful translation of the account in the *Legenda Aurea* of Jacobus de Voragine as we know it in Graesse's edition. For the rest Chaucer seems to have drawn upon a somewhat fuller narrative, of which we have independent texts, but which may have been in the particular manuscript of the *Legenda Aurea* which he used. On this and other lesser points the student may consult G. H. Gerould's chapter in *SA*.

1. norice, nurse. **2. clepe**, call. **3. delices**, delights. The line is reminiscent of the *RR* (ll. 513–93) where Idleness, in answer to the lover's knock, opens the gate into a garden which belongs to Delight. **4. oppresse**, overcome. **5. leveful**, permissible. **7. feend**, devil. **hente**, seize. **8. cordes slye**, *i.e.* his net. **9. waiteth**, lies in wait. **biclappe**, trap. **12. lappe**, flap of a garment. **14. werche**, work. **15. though men dradden nevere**, even if men did not fear. **17. slogardye**, sloth. **19. hire**, ydelnesse. **lees**, leash. **21. swynke**, labor for. **25. legende**, the life of a saint. The reference here may also be to the best-known collection of legends, the *Legenda Aurea*. See introduction. **26. passioun**, suffering and death. **27. rose and lilie**, symbols of divine love and purity.

Invocacio ad Mariam

And thow that flour of virgines art alle,
Of whom that Bernard list so wel to write,   30
To thee at my bigynnyng first I calle;
Thou confort of us wrecches, do me endite
Thy maydens deeth, that wan thurgh hire
     merite
The eterneel lyf, and of the feend victorie,
As man may after reden in hire storie.   35

Thow Mayde and Mooder, doghter of thy
     Sone,
Thow welle of mercy, synful soules cure,
In whom that God for bountee chees to wone,
Thow humble, and heigh over every creature,
Thow nobledest so ferforth oure nature,   40
That no desdeyn the Makere hadde of kynde
His Sone in blood and flessh to clothe and
     wynde.

Withinne the cloistre blisful of thy sydis
Took mannes shap the eterneel love and pees,
That of the tryne compas lord and gyde is,   45
Whom erthe and see and hevene, out of relees,
Ay heryen; and thou, Virgine wemmelees,
Baar of thy body—and dweltest mayden
     pure—
The Creatour of every creature.

Assembled is in thee magnificence   50
With mercy, goodnesse, and with swich pitee
That thou, that art the sonne of excellence
Nat oonly helpeth hem that preyen thee,
But often tyme, of thy benygnytee,
Ful frely, er that men thyn help biseche,   55
Thou goost biforn, and art hir lyves leche.

Now help, thow meeke and blisful faire mayde,
Me, flemed wrecche, in this desert of galle;
Thynk on the womman Cananee, that sayde
That whelpes eten somme of the crommes alle
That from hir lordes table been yfalle;   61
And though that I, unworthy sone of Eve,
Be synful, yet accepte my bileve.

And, for that feith is deed withouten werkis,
So for to werken yif me wit and space,   65
That I be quit fro thennes that most derk is!
O thou, that art so fair and ful of grace,
Be myn advocat in that heigh place
Theras withouten ende is songe "Osanne,"
Thow Cristes mooder, doghter deere of Anne!

And of thy light my soule in prison lighte,   71
That troubled is by the contagioun
Of my body, and also by the wighte
Of erthely lust and fals affeccioun;
O havene of refut, o salvacioun   75
Of hem that been in sorwe and in distresse,
Now help, for to my werk I wol me dresse.

Yet preye I yow that reden that I write,
Foryeve me that I do no diligence
This ilke storie subtilly to endite,   80
For bothe have I the wordes and sentence
Of hym that at the seintes reverence
The storie wroot, and folwen hire legende,
And pray yow that ye wole my werk amende.

*Interpretacio nominis Cecilie quam ponit
Frater Jacobus Januensis in Legenda*

First wolde I yow the name of Seinte Cecilie   85
Expowne, as men may in hir storie see.

---

30. Bernard, St. Bernard of Clairvaux (1090–1153). **33. Thy maydens deeth.** St. Bernard was noted for his devotion to the Virgin. One of Fra Lippo Lippi's finest paintings, in the church of La Badia in Florence, depicts the Virgin appearing before St. Bernard as he writes. **35. storie**, saint's legend. **38. bountee . . . wone**, goodness chose to dwell. **41. kynde**, nature. **45. tryne compas**, threefold world,—heaven, earth, and sea (Skeat). **46. out of relees**, without ceasing. **47. heryen**, glorify. **wemmelees**, spotless. **48. Baar**, bore. **dweltest**, didst remain. **52. sonne**, sun. **56. leche**, physician. **58. flemed wrecche**, banished exile. **galle**, bitterness. **59. womman Cananee**, woman of Canaan; cf. *Matthew*, 15:22–7. **60. whelpes**, dogs. **62. sone**. See Introduction. **66. quit**, released. **73. wighte**, weight. **74. lust**, desire. **75. refut**, refuge. **77. me dresse**, address myself. **78. that**, what. **81. sentence**, meaning, substance. **82. at the seintes reverence**, in reverence of the saint. **84. *Interpretacio* . . .** The various interpretations of the name Cecilia are, as the rubric says, taken from the opening paragraph of Jacobus Januensis (of Genoa), better known as Jacobus de Voragine, in the *Legenda Aurea*. **86. Expowne**, expound.

It is to seye in Englissh "hevenes lilie,"
For pure chaastnesse of virginitee;
Or, for she whitnesse hadde of honestee,
And grene of conscience, and of good fame   90
The soote savour, "lilie" was hir name.

Or Cecilie is to seye "the wey to blynde,"
For she ensample was by good techynge;
Or elles Cecile, as I writen fynde,
Is joyned, by a manere conjoynynge   95
Of "hevene" and "Lia"; and heere, in figur-
ynge,
The "hevene" is set for thoght of hoolynesse,
And "Lia" for hire lastynge bisynesse.

Cecile may eek be seyd in this manere,
"Wantynge of blyndnesse," for hir grete light
Of sapience, and for hire thewes cleere;   101
Or elles, loo, this maydens name bright
Of "hevene" and "leos" comth, for which by
right

Men myghte hire wel "the hevene of peple"
calle,
Ensample of goode and wise werkes alle.   105

For "leos" "peple" in Englissh is to seye,
And right as men may in the hevene see
The sonne and moone and sterres every weye,
Right so men goostly in this mayden free
Seyen of feith the magnanymytee,   110
And eek the cleernesse hool of sapience,
And sondry werkes, brighte of excellence.

And right so as thise philosophres write
That hevene is swift and round and eek bren-
nynge,
Right so was faire Cecilie the white   115
Ful swift and bisy evere in good werkynge,
And round and hool in good perseverynge,
And brennynge evere in charite ful brighte.
Now have I yow declared what she highte.

Explicit.

THE SECOND NUN'S TALE

Here bigynneth the Seconde Nonnes Tale of the lyf of Seinte Cecile.

This mayden bright Cecilie, as hir lif
seith,   120
Was comen of Romayns, and of noble kynde,
And from hir cradel up fostred in the feith
Of Crist, and bar his gospel in hir mynde.
She nevere cessed, as I writen fynde,
Of hir preyere, and God to love and drede,   125
Bisekynge hym to kepe hir maydenhede.

And whan this mayden sholde unto a man
Ywedded be, that was ful yong of age,

Which that ycleped was Valerian,
And day was comen of hir marriage,   130
She, ful devout and humble in hir corage,
Under hir robe of gold, that sat ful faire,
Hadde next hire flessh yclad hire in an haire.

And whil the organs maden melodie,
To God allone in herte thus sang she: 135
"O Lord, my soule and eek my body gye
Unwemmed, lest that it confounded be."
And, for his love that dyde upon a tree,

89. **whitnesse,** whiteness. 91. **soote,** sweet. 92. **the wey to blynde,** a translation of *caecis via*, a path for the blind.
96. **Lia,** the Latin spelling of Leah, symbol of the active life. See *Genesis,* 29:32–5, etc. **in figurynge,** figuratively. 101.
sapience, wisdom. **thewes,** mental or moral qualities, virtues. 103. **leos,** Greek λεώς, people. 106. **seye,** say. 110. **Seyen,**
saw. 114. **brennynge,** burning. 119. **highte,** was named. 124. **cessed,** ceased. 126. **Bisekynge,** beseeching. 129. **ycleped,**
called. 131. **corage,** heart. 133. **haire,** haircloth shirt 136. **gye,** guide. 137. **Unwemmed,** unstained.

Every seconde and thridde day she faste,
Ay biddynge in hire orisons ful faste.　　　140

The nyght cam, and to bedde moste she gon
With hire housbonde, as ofte is the manere,
And pryvely to hym she seyde anon,
"O sweete and wel biloved spouse deere,
Ther is a conseil, and ye wolde it heere,　　　145
Which that right fayn I wolde unto yow seye,
So that ye swere ye shul it nat biwreye."

　　Valerian gan faste unto hire swere
That for no cas, ne thyng that myghte be,
He sholde nevere mo biwreyen here;　　　150
And thanne at erst to hym thus seyde she:
"I have an aungel which that loveth me,
That with greet love, wher so I wake or sleepe,
Is redy ay my body for to kepe.

"And if that he may feelen, out of drede,　　　155
That ye me touche, or love in vileynye,
He right anon wol sle yow with the dede,
And in youre yowthe thus ye shullen dye;
And if that ye in clene love me gye,　　　159
He wol yow loven as me, for youre clennesse,
And shewen yow his joye and his brightnesse."

　　Valerian, corrected as God wolde,
Answerde agayn, "If I shal trusten thee,
Lat me that aungel se, and hym biholde;
And if that it a verray angel bee,　　　165
Thanne wol I doon as thou hast prayed me;
And if thou love another man, for sothe
Right with this swerd thanne wol I sle yow
　　bothe."

Cecile answerde anon-right in this wise:
"If that yow list, the angel shul ye see,　　　170

So that ye trowe on Crist and yow baptize.
Gooth forth to Via Apia," quod shee,
"That fro this toun ne stant but miles three,
And to the povre folkes that ther dwelle,
Sey hem right thus, as that I shal yow telle.　　　175

"Telle hem that I, Cecile, yow to hem sente,
To shewen yow the goode Urban the olde,
For secree nedes and for good entente.
And whan that ye Seint Urban han biholde,
Telle hym the wordes whiche that I to yow
　　tolde;　　　180
And whan that he hath purged yow fro synne,
Thanne shul ye se that angel, er ye twynne."

　　Valerian is to the place ygon,
And right as hym was taught by his lernynge,
He foond this hooly olde Urban anon　　　185
Among the seintes buryeles lotynge.
And he anon, withouten tariynge,
Dide his message; and whan that he it tolde,
Urban for joye his handes gan up holde.

The teeris from his eyen leet he falle.　　　190
"Almyghty Lord, o Jhesu Crist," quod he,
"Sowere of chaast conseil, hierde of us alle,
The fruyt of thilke seed of chastitee
That thou hast sowe in Cecile, taak to thee!
Lo, lyk a bisy bee, withouten gile,　　　195
Thee serveth ay thyn owene thral Cecile.

"For thilke spouse that she took but now
Ful lyk a fiers leoun, she sendeth heere,
As meke as evere was any lomb, to yow!"
And with that word anon ther gan appeere　　　200
An oold man, clad in white clothes cleere,
That hadde a book with lettre of gold in honde,
And gan bifore Valerian to stonde.

---

139. **faste,** fasted. 145. **conseil,** secret. 147. **biwreye,** betray. 151. **at erst,** for the first time, finally. 153. **wher so,** whether. 155. **drede,** doubt. 156. **in vileynye,** shamefully. 159. **gye,** lead, govern. 162. **corrected,** set right, admonished. 165. **verray,** true. 167-8. The rime *sothe: bothe* is imperfect. See note to BD 514. 169. **anon-right,** immediately. 171. **yow baptize,** have yourself baptized. 172. **to Via Apia,** The Via Appia, or Appian Way, is a road leading out of Rome to the south. Chaucer mistranslates the Latin, which says he is to go along the Appian Way to the third milestone. 178. **secree,** secret. 179. **Urban,** Pope Urban I (222–30). 182. **twynne,** depart. 184. **by his lernynge,** in his instructions. 186. **seintes buryeles,** sepulchres of the saints, the catacombs. **lotynge,** lying hid. 192. **hierde,** shepherd. 194. **sowe,** sown. 201. **cleere,** bright, shining.

Valerian as deed fil doun for drede   204
Whan he hym saugh, and he up hente hym tho,
And on his book right thus he gan to rede:
"O Lord, o feith, o God, withouten mo,
O Cristendom, and Fader of alle also,
Aboven alle and over alle everywhere."
Thise wordes al with gold ywriten were.   210

Whan this was rad, thanne seyde this olde man,
"Leevestow this thyng or no? Sey ye or nay."
"I leeve al this thyng," quod Valerian,
"For sother thyng than this, I dar wel say,
Under the hevene no wight thynke may."   215
Tho vanysshed this olde man, he nyste where,
And Pope Urban hym cristened right there.

Valerian gooth hoom and fynt Cecilie
Withinne his chambre with an angel stonde.
This angel hadde of roses and of lilie   220
Corones two, the whiche he bar in honde;
And first to Cecile, as I understonde,
He yaf that oon, and after gan he take
That oother to Valerian, hir make.   224

"With body clene and with unwemmed thoght
Kepeth ay wel thise corones," quod he;
"Fro paradys to yow have I hem broght,
Ne nevere mo ne shal they roten bee,
Ne lese hir soote savour, trusteth me;
Ne nevere wight shal seen hem with his yë,   230
But he be chaast and hate vileynye.

"And thow, Valerian, for thow so soone
Assentedest to good conseil also,
Sey what thee list, and thou shalt han thy boone."
"I have a brother," quod Valerian tho,   235
"That in this world I love no man so.
I pray yow that my brother may han grace
To knowe the trouthe, as I do in this place."

The angel seyde, "God liketh thy requeste,
And bothe, with the palm of martirdom,   240
Ye shullen come unto his blisful feste."
And with that word Tiburce his brother coom.
And whan that he the savour undernoom,
Which that the roses and the lilies caste,
Withinne his herte he gan to wondre faste,   245

And seyde, "I wondre, this tyme of the yeer,
Whennes that soote savour cometh so
Of rose and lilies that I smelle heer.
For though I hadde hem in myne handes two,
The savour myghte in me no depper go.   250
The sweete smel that in myn herte I fynde
Hath chaunged me al in another kynde."

Valerian seyde: "Two corones han we,
Snow white and rose reed, that shynen cleere,
Whiche that thyne eyen han no myght to see;
And as thou smellest hem thurgh my preyere,
So shaltow seen hem, leeve brother deere,   257
If it so be thou wolt, withouten slouthe,
Bileve aright and knowen verray trouthe."

Tiburce answerde, "Seistow this to me   260
In soothnesse, or in dreem I herkne this?"
"In dremes," quod Valerian, "han we be
Unto this tyme, brother myn, ywis.
But now at erst in trouthe oure dwellyng is."
"How woostow this?" quod Tiburce, "and in
      what wyse?"   265
Quod Valerian, "That shal I thee devyse.

"The aungel of God hath me the trouthe
      ytaught
Which thou shalt seen, if that thou wolt reneye
The ydoles and be clene, and elles naught."
And of the myracle of thise corones tweye   270
Seint Ambrose in his preface list to seye;

205. **hente,** took. **tho,** then. 207. **O Lord, o feith, etc.,** One Lord, one faith, etc. 212. **Leevestow,** believest thou. **Sey ye,** say yea. 214. **sother,** truer. 218. **fynt,** finds. 224. **make,** mate. 225. **unwemmed,** unblemished. 228. **roten,** rotten. 229. **lese,** lose. **soote,** sweet. 231. **vileynye,** wickedness. 242. **coom,** came. 243. **undernoom,** perceived. 250. **depper,** deeper. 252. **in,** into. 255. **eyen,** eyes. 257. **leeve,** dear. 266. **devyse,** explain. 268. **reneye,** renounce. 269. **elles,** otherwise. 271. **preface,** a liturgical term; a chant intoned by the celebrant at the beginning of the central part of the Mass (the Consecration). The Ambrosian rite, which is here referred to, was the liturgy of Milan. St. Ambrose was bishop of Milan, 374–397. **list to seye,** pleases to tell.

Solempnely this noble doctour deere
Commendeth it, and seith in this manere:

"The palm of martirdom for to receyve,
Seinte Cecile, fulfild of Goddes yifte,   275
The world and eek hire chambre gan she
  weyve;
Witnesse Tyburces and Valerians shrifte,
To whiche God of his bountee wolde shifte
Corones two of floures wel smellynge,   279
And made his angel hem the corones brynge.

The mayde hath broght thise men to blisse
  above;
The world hath wist what it is worth, certeyn,
Devocioun of chastitee to love."
Tho shewed hym Cecile al open and pleyn
That alle ydoles nys but a thyng in veyn,   285
For they been dombe, and therto they been deve,
And charged hym his ydoles for to leve.

"Whoso that troweth nat this, a beest he is,"
Quod tho Tiburce, "if that I shal nat lye."
And she gan kisse his brest, that herde this,   290
And was ful glad he koude trouthe espye.
"This day I take thee for myn allye,"
Seyde this blisful faire mayde deere,
And after that, she seyde as ye may heere: 294

"Lo, right so as the love of Crist," quod she,
"Made me thy brotheres wyf, right in that wise
Anon for myn allye heer take I thee,
Syn that thou wolt thyne ydoles despise.
Go with thy brother now, and thee baptise,
And make thee clene, so that thou mowe bi-
  holde   300
The angeles face of which thy brother tolde."

Tiburce answerde and seyde, "Brother deere,
First tel me whider I shal, and to what man?"

"To whom?" quod he, "com forth with right
  good cheere,
I wol thee lede unto the Pope Urban."   305
"Til Urban? brother myn Valerian,"
Quod tho Tiburce, "woltow me thider lede?
Me thynketh that it were a wonder dede.

"Ne menestow nat Urban," quod he tho,
"That is so ofte dampned to be deed,   310
And woneth in halkes alwey to and fro,
And dar nat ones putte forth his heed?
Men sholde hym brennen in a fyr so reed
If he were founde, or that men myghte hym
  spye,
And we also, to bere hym compaignye;   315

"And whil we seken thilke divinitee
That is yhid in hevene pryvely,
Algate ybrend in this world shul we be!"
To whom Cecile answerde boldely,
"Men myghten dreden wel and skilfully   320
This lyf to lese, myn owene deere brother,
If this were lyvynge oonly and noon oother.

"But ther is bettre lif in oother place,   323
That nevere shal be lost, ne drede thee noght,
Which Goddes Sone us tolde thurgh his grace.
That Fadres Sone hath alle thyng ywroght,
And al that wroght is with a skilful thoght,
The Goost, that fro the Fader gan procede,
Hath sowled hem, withouten any drede.   329

By word and by myracle heigh Goddes Sone,
Whan he was in this world, declared heere
That ther was oother lyf ther men may wone."
To whom answerde Tiburce, "O suster deere,
Ne seydestow right now in this manere,
Ther nys but o God, lord in soothfastnesse?   335
And now of three how maystow bere wit-
  nesse?"

---

276. weyve, put aside, give up. **277. shrifte,** confession. **278. shifte,** assign. **282. wist,** come to know. **285. nys but,** are nothing but. The form is influenced by *thyng*. **286. deve,** deaf. **299. thee baptise,** be baptised. **300. mowe,** may. **310. dampned,** condemned. **311. halkes,** nooks, hiding-places. **313. brennen,** burn. **315. And we also.** The constr. is elliptical. The meaning is, "We also would be burnt." **318. Algate,** all the same. **320. skilfully,** reasonably. **321. lese,** lose. **322. lyvynge oonly,** the only life. **327. wroght . . . thoght,** is endowed with reason. **328. Goost,** Holy Ghost. **329. sowled,** animated. **hem,** all created things. **332. ther,** where. **wone,** dwell. **335. o God,** one God.

"That shal I telle," quod she, "er I go.
Right as a man hath sapiences three,
Memorie, engyn, and intellect also,
So in o beynge of divinitee,   340
Thre persones may ther right wel bee."
Tho gan she hym ful bisily to preche
Of Cristes come, and of his peynes teche,

And manye pointes of his passioun;
How Goddes Sone in this world was withholde
To doon mankynde pleyn remissioun,   346
That was ybounde in synne and cares colde;
Al this thyng she unto Tiburce tolde.
And after this, Tiburce in good entente
With Valerian to Pope Urban he wente,   350

That thanked God, and with glad herte and
    light
He cristned hym, and made hym in that place
Parfit in his lernynge, Goddes knyght.
And after this, Tiburce gat swich grace
That every day he saugh, in tyme and space,   355
The aungel of God; and every maner boone
That he God axed, it was sped ful soone.

    It were ful hard by ordre for to seyn
How manye wondres Jhesus for hem wroghte;
But atte laste, to tellen short and pleyn,   360
The sergeantz of the toun of Rome hem soghte,
And hem biforn Almache, the prefect, broghte,
Which hem apposed, and knew al hire entente,
And to the ymage of Juppiter hem sente,

And seyde, "Whoso wol nat sacrifise,   365
Swap of his heed; this my sentence heer."
Anon thise martirs that I yow devyse,
Oon Maximus, that was an officer

Of the prefectes, and his corniculer,
Hem hente, and whan he forth the seintes
    ladde,   370
Hymself he weep for pitee that he hadde.

Whan Maximus had herd the seintes loore,
He gat hym of the tormentoures leve,
And ladde hem to his hous withoute moore,
And with hir prechyng, er that it were eve,   375
They gonnen fro the tormentours to reve,
And fro Maxime, and fro his folk echone,
The false feith, to trowe in God allone.

    Cecile cam, whan it was woxen nyght,
With preestes that hem cristned alle yfeere;   380
And afterward, whan day was woxen light,
Cecile hem seyde with a ful stedefast cheere,
"Now, Cristes owene knyghtes leeve and deere,
Cast alle awey the werkes of derknesse,
And armeth yow in armure of brightnesse.   385

"Ye han for sothe ydoon a greet bataille,
Youre cours is doon, youre feith han ye con-
    served.
Gooth to the corone of lif that may nat faille;
The rightful Juge, which that ye han served,
Shal yeve it yow, as ye han it deserved."   390
And whan this thyng was seyd as I devyse,
Men ledde hem forth to doon the sacrefise.

But whan they weren to the place broght
To tellen shortly the conclusioun,
They nolde encense ne sacrifise right noght,   395
But on hir knees they setten hem adoun
With humble herte and sad devocioun,
And losten bothe hir hevedes in the place.
Hir soules wenten to the Kyng of grace.

---

338. **sapiences three,** three qualities of mind. 339. **engyn,** imagination. 343. **come,** coming, incarnation. 345. **withholde,** retained, employed. 346. **pleyn,** full. 352-3. **made hym . . . Goddes knyght,** by administering the sacrament of Confirmation. See C. A. Reilly, *MLN,* LXIX. 37–39. 362. **Almache,** called Almachius in the *Legenda Aurea.* 363. **apposed,** questioned. 366. **Swap of,** strike off. 369. **corniculer,** a subordinate officer, named from the horn-shaped ornament on his helmet, awarded for bravery. 370. **hente,** seized. 371. **weep,** wept. 372. **loore,** teaching. 373. **leve,** leave, permission. 374. **withoute moore,** without more ado. 375. **with hir,** by their. 376. **reve,** take away. 380. **yfeere,** together. 386. **Ye han for sothe . . .,** a paraphrase of *2 Timothy,* 4:7–8. 391. **devyse,** relate. 395. **encense,** burn incense. 397. **sad,** steadfast. 398. **hevedes,** heads.

This Maximus, that saugh this thyng bityde,
With pitous teeris tolde it anon-right,   401
That he hir soules saugh to hevene glyde
With aungels ful of cleernesse and of light,
And with his word converted many a wight;
For which Almachius dide hym so tobete   405
With whippe of leed, til he his lif gan lete.

   Cecile hym took and buryed hym anon
By Tiburce and Valerian softely
Withinne hire buriyng place, under the stoon;
And after this, Almachius hastily   410
Bad his ministres fecchen openly
Cecile, so that she myghte in his presence
Doon sacrifice, and Juppiter encense.

But they, converted at hir wise loore,
Wepten ful soore, and yaven ful credence   415
Unto hire word, and cryden moore and moore,
"Crist, Goddes Sone, withouten difference,
Is verray God—this is al oure sentence—
That hath so good a servant hym to serve.
This with o voys we trowen, thogh we
   sterve!"   420

   Almachius, that herde of this doynge,
Bad fecchen Cecile, that he myghte hire see,
And alderfirst, lo! this was his axynge.
"What maner womman artow?" tho quod he.
"I am a gentil womman born," quod she.   425
"I axe thee," quod he, "though it thee greeve,
Of thy religioun and of thy bileeve."

   "Ye han bigonne youre questioun folily,"
Quod she, "that wolden two answeres conclude
In o demande; ye axed lewedly."   430
Almache answerde unto that similitude,
"Of whennes comth thyn answeryng so rude?"

"Of whennes?" quod she, whan that she was
   freyned,
"Of conscience and of good feith unfeyned."

   Almachius seyde, "Ne takestow noon heede
Of my power?" And she answerde hym
   this: 436
"Youre myght," quod she, "ful litel is to
   dreede,
For every mortal mannes power nys
But lyk a bladdre ful of wynd, ywys.
For with a nedles poynt, whan it is blowe,   440
May al the boost of it be leyd ful lowe."

   "Ful wrongfully bigonne thow," quod he,
"And yet in wrong is thy perseveraunce.
Wostow nat how oure myghty princes free
Han thus comanded and maad ordinaunce,   445
That every Cristen wight shal han penaunce
But if that he his Cristendom withseye,
And goon al quit, if he wole it reneye?"

   "Yowre princes erren, as youre nobleye
   dooth,"
Quod tho Cecile, "and with a wood sentence
Ye make us gilty, and it is nat sooth.   451
For ye, that knowen wel oure innocence,
For as muche as we doon a reverence
To Crist, and for we bere a Cristen name,
Ye putte on us a cryme, and eek a blame.   455

But we that knowen thilke name so
For vertuous, we may it nat withseye."
Almache answerde, "Chees oon of thise two:
Do sacrifice, or Cristendom reneye,   459
That thou mowe now escapen by that weye."
At which the hooly blisful faire mayde
Gan for to laughe, and to the juge sayde:

---

400. **bityde,** happen. 401. **anon-right,** at once. 403. **cleernesse,** brightness. 406. **whippe of leed,** thongs tipped with lead. **gan lete,** gave up. 409. **hire,** their. 413. **encense,** burn incense to. 414. **at,** by. **loore,** teaching. 415. **yaven,** gave. 418. **sentence,** opinion. 420. **sterve,** die. 423. **alderfirst,** first of all. 428. **folily,** foolishly. 429. **conclude,** include. 430. **o demande,** one question. **lewedly,** ignorantly. 431. **similitude,** comparison, parable. 433. **freyned,** asked. 440. **blowe,** blown up. 441. **boost,** pride, ostentation. 446. **han penaunce,** suffer punishment, pay the penalty for his belief. 447. **But if,** unless. **withseye,** renounce. 448. **it reneye,** renounce his sin. 449. **nobleye,** nobility, nobles. 450. **wood,** mad, unreasonable. 458. **Chees,** choose. 460. **mowe,** mayest.

"O juge, confus in thy nycetee,
Woltow that I reneye innocence,
To make me a wikked wight?" quod shee.   465
"Lo, he dissymuleth heere in audience;
He stareth, and woodeth in his advertence!"
To whom Almachius, "Unsely wrecche,
Ne woostow nat how fer my myght may
    strecche?

"Han noght oure myghty princes to me yiven,
Ye, bothe power and auctoritee   471
To maken folk to dyen or to lyven?
Why spekestow so proudly thanne to me?"
"I speke noght but stedfastly," quod she;
"Nat proudly, for I seye, as for my syde,   475
We haten deedly thilke vice of pryde.

"And if thou drede nat a sooth to heere,
Thanne wol I shewe al openly, by right,
That thou hast maad a ful gret lesyng heere.
Thou seyst thy princes han thee yeven myght
Bothe for to sleen and for to quyken a wight;
Thou, that ne mayst but oonly lyf bireve,   482
Thou hast noon oother power ne no leve.

"But thou mayst seyn thy princes han thee
    maked
Ministre of deeth; for if thou speke of mo,   485
Thou lyest, for thy power is ful naked."
"Do wey thy booldnesse," seyde Almachius
    tho,
"And sacrifice to oure goddes, er thou go!
I recche nat what wrong that thou me profre,
For I kan suffre it as a philosophre;   490

"But thilke wronges may I nat endure
That thou spekest of oure goddes heere," quod
    he.
Cecile answerde, "O nyce creature!

Thou seydest no word syn thou spak to me
That I ne knew therwith thy nycetee;   495
And that thou were, in every maner wise,
A lewed officer and a veyn justise.

"Ther lakketh no thyng to thyne outter yën
That thou n'art blynd; for thyng that we seen
    alle
That it is stoon,—that men may wel espyen,—
That ilke stoon a god thow wolt it calle.   501
I rede thee, lat thyn hand upon it falle,
And taste it wel, and stoon thou shalt it fynde,
Syn that thou seest nat with thyne eyen blynde.

"It is a shame that the peple shal   505
So scorne thee, and laughe at thy folye;
For communly men woot it wel overal
That myghty God is in his hevenes hye;
And thise ymages, wel thou mayst espye,
To thee ne to hemself mowen noght profite,
For in effect they been nat worth a myte."   511

Thise wordes and swiche othere seyde she,
And he weex wrooth, and bad men sholde hir
    lede
Hom til hir hous, and "In hire hous," quod he,
"Brenne hire right in a bath of flambes rede."
And as he bad, right so was doon the dede;   516
For in a bath they gonne hire faste shetten,
And nyght and day greet fyr they under
    betten.

The longe nyght, and eek a day also,
For al the fyr, and eek the bathes heete,   520
She sat al coold, and feelede no wo.
It made hire nat a drope for to sweete.
But in that bath hir lyf she moste lete,
For he Almachius, with ful wikke entente,
To sleen hire in the bath his sonde sente.   525

463. **confus,** confounded. **nycetee,** folly. 466. **dissymuleth,** dissembles. **in audience,** publicly. 467. **woodeth,** rages. **advertence,** mind. 468. **Unsely,** unhappy. 474. **stedfastly,** confidently. 479. **lesyng,** falsehood. 480. **yeven,** given. 481. **quyken,** make live. 486. **ful naked,** completely lacking. 495. **nycetee,** foolishness. 497. **lewed,** ignorant. **veyn,** worthless. 498. **Ther lakketh . . .,** you are nothing less than blind. 503. **taste,** test. 507. **overal,** everywhere. 510. **mowen,** may. 513. **weex,** waxed. 515. **flambes,** flames. 517. **bath,** chamber for bathing. **shetten,** shut. 518. **betten,** kindled. 523. **lete,** give up. 524. **wikke,** wicked. 525. **sonde,** messenger, emissary.

Thre strokes in the nekke he smoot hire tho,
The tormentour, but for no maner chaunce
He myghte noght smyte al hir nekke atwo;
And for ther was that tyme an ordinaunce
That no man sholde doon man swich penaunce
The ferthe strook to smyten, softe or soore,   531
This tormentour ne dorste do namoore,

But half deed, with hir nekke ycorven there,
He lefte hir lye, and on his wey he went.
The Cristen folk, which that aboute hire were,
With sheetes han the blood ful faire yhent.   536
Thre dayes lyved she in this torment,
And nevere cessed hem the feith to teche
That she hadde fostred; hem she gan to preche,

And hem she yaf hir moebles and hir thyng,   540
And to the Pope Urban bitook hem tho,
And seyde, "I axed this of hevene kyng,
To han respit thre dayes and namo,
To recomende to yow, er that I go,
Thise soules, lo! and that I myghte do werche
Heere of myn hous perpetuelly a cherche."   546

   Seint Urban, with his deknes, prively
The body fette, and buryed it by nyghte
Among his othere seintes honestly.
Hir hous the chirche of Seinte Cecilie highte;   550
Seint Urban halwed it, as he wel myghte;
In which, into this day, in noble wyse,
Men doon to Crist and to his seinte servyse.

Heere is ended the Seconde Nonnes Tale.

The Canon's Yeoman's Tale

THE CANON'S YEOMAN'S PROLOGUE

The Prologe of the Chanouns Yemannes Tale.

   Whan ended was the lyf of Seinte Cecile,
Er we hadde riden fully fyve mile,   555
At Boghtoun under Blee us gan atake
A man that clothed was in clothes blake,
And under-nethe he hadde a whyt surplys.
His hakeney, that was al pomely grys,
So swatte that it wonder was to see;   560
It semed as he had priked miles three.
The hors eek that his yeman rood upon

So swatte that unnethe myghte it gon.
Aboute the peytrel stood the foom ful hye;
He was of foom al flekked as a pye.   565
A male tweyfoold upon his croper lay;
It semed that he caried lite array.
Al light for somer rood this worthy man,
And in myn herte wondren I bigan
What that he was, til that I understood   570
How that his cloke was sowed to his hood;

527. **for no maner chaunce,** under no circumstances. 528. **atwo,** in two. 530. **penaunce,** injury. 533. **ycorven,** cut. 536. **yhent,** caught. 540. **moebles,** furnishings, goods. 541. **bitook,** commended. 542. **seyde,** reported. 545. **do werche,** have made. 547. **deknes,** deacons. 548. **fette,** fetched. 549. **honestly,** fittingly, honorably. 550. **highte,** was named. 556. **Boghtoun under Blee,** Boughton under the Blean forest is five miles beyond Ospring, where travelers between London and Canterbury frequently stopped and where the pilgrims had presumably spent the night; cf. ll. 588–9. **atake,** overtake. 559. **pomely grys,** dappled gray. 560. **swatte,** sweat. 561. **priked,** spurred, ridden hard. 562. **yeman,** yeoman, servant. 563. **unnethe,** scarcely. 564. **peytrel,** part of the harness covering the breast, originally the breastplate of the horse's armor. 565. **pye,** magpie. 566. **male tweyfoold,** double bag or leather wallet. **his croper,** its hind-quarters. 567. **lite array,** little equipment, clothing. 571. **sowed,** sewed.

For which, whan I hadde longe avysed me,
I demed hym som chanoun for to be.
His hat heeng at his bak doun by a laas,
For he hadde riden moore than trot or paas;
He hadde ay priked lik as he were wood.　　576
A clote-leef he hadde under his hood
For swoot, and for to kepe his heed from heete.
But it was joye for to seen hym swete!
His forheed dropped as a stillatorie,　　580
Were ful of plantayne and of paritorie.
And whan that he was come, he gan to crye,
"God save," quod he, "this joly compaignye!
Faste have I priked," quod he, "for youre sake,
By cause that I wolde yow atake,　　585
To riden in this myrie compaignye."
His yeman eek was ful of curteisye,
And seyde, "Sires, now in the morwe-tyde
Out of youre hostelrie I saugh yow ryde,　　589
And warned heer my lord and my soverayn,
Which that to ryden with yow is ful fayn
For his desport; he loveth daliaunce."

　　"Freend, for thy warnyng God yeve thee
　　　good chaunce!"
Thanne seyde oure Hoost, "for certein it wolde
　　seme
Thy lord were wys, and so I may wel deme.　　595
He is ful jocunde also, dar I leye!
Can he oght telle a myrie tale or tweye,
With which he glade may this compaignye?"

　　"Who, sire? my lord? ye, ye, withouten lye,
He kan of murthe and eek of jolitee　　600
Nat but ynough; also, sire, trusteth me,
And ye hym knewe as wel as do I,
Ye wolde wondre how wel and craftily
He koude werke, and that in sondry wise.

He hath take on hym many a greet emprise,　　605
Which were ful hard for any that is heere
To brynge aboute, but they of hym it leere.
As hoomly as he rit amonges yow,
If ye hym knewe, it wolde be for youre prow.
Ye wolde nat forgoon his aqueyntaunce　　610
For muchel good, I dar leye in balaunce
Al that I have in my possessioun.
He is a man of heigh discrecioun;
I warne yow wel, he is a passyng man."
　　"Wel," quod oure Hoost, "I pray thee, tel me
　　　than,　　615
Is he a clerk, or noon? telle what he is."

　　"Nay, he is gretter than a clerk, ywis,"
Seyde this Yeman, "and in wordes fewe,
Hoost, of his craft somwhat I wol yow shewe.

　　I seye, my lord kan swich subtilitee—　　620
But al his craft ye may nat wite at me,
And somwhat helpe I yet to his wirkyng—
That al this ground on which we been ridyng,
Til that we come to Caunterbury toun,
He koude al clene turne it up so doun,　　625
And pave it al of silver and of gold."

　　And whan this Yeman hadde this tale ytold
Unto oure Hoost, he seyde, "Benedicitee!
This thyng is wonder merveillous to me,
Syn that thy lord is of so heigh prudence,　　630
By cause of which men sholde hym reverence,
That of his worshipe rekketh he so lite.
His oversloppe nys nat worth a myte,
As in effect, to hym, so moot I go!
It is al baudy and totore also.　　635
Why is thy lord so sluttissh, I the preye,
And is of power bettre clooth to beye,
If that his dede accorde with thy speche?

---

572. avysed me, reflected. 573. chanoun, canon. There were two types of ecclesiastic known as canons: regular canons and secular canons. Regular canons lived a communal life, much like that of monks, under the Augustinian rule. Secular canons at this time were sometimes regular canons that had been given episcopal permission to have the cure of souls and to serve parish churches. There were also secular canons who served cathedral churches and constituted the body of clergy surrounding a bishop. The canon here described seems to belong to one of the latter classes, but is perhaps a renegade (cf. ll. 656–62). 574. laas, cord. 575. paas, amble. 576. wood, mad. 577. clote-leef, leaf of the burdock (which was large). 578. swoot, sweat, *i.e.*, on account of the heat. 579. swete, sweat. 580. stillatorie, apparatus for distillation, a still. 581. Were, as if it were, which might have been. paritorie, pellitory, an herb. 592. daliaunce, conversation, companionship. 596. leye, wager. 597. oght, in any way. 601. Nat but, quite. 602. And, if. 605. emprise, undertaking. 607. leere, learn. 608. rit, rides. 609. prow, profit. 614. passyng, excellent. 620. kan swich subtilitee, knows such intricate matters. 621. wite at me, know from me. 625. up so doun, upside down. 632. worshipe, honor, appearance. 633. oversloppe, robe, outer garment. 634. As in effect, to hym, generally speaking, for a man like him, upon my word (so may I walk). 635. baudy, dirty. totore, tattered. 636. sluttissh, slovenly.

Telle me that, and that I thee biseche."

   "Why?" quod this Yeman, "wherto axe ye
     me?   640

God help me so, for he shal nevere thee!
(But I wol nat avowe that I seye,
And therfore keep it secree, I yow preye.)
He is to wys, in feith, as I bileeve.
That that is overdoon, it wol nat preeve   645
Aright, as clerkes seyn; it is a vice.
Wherfore in that I holde hym lewed and nyce.
For whan a man hath over-greet a wit,
Ful oft hym happeth to mysusen it.   649
So dooth my lord, and that me greveth soore;
God it amende! I kan sey yow namoore."

   "Ther-of no fors, good Yeman," quod oure
     Hoost;
"Syn of the konnyng of thy lord thow woost,
Telle how he dooth, I pray thee hertely,
Syn that he is so crafty and so sly.   655
Where dwelle ye, if it to telle be?"

   "In the suburbes of a toun," quod he,
"Lurkynge in hernes and in lanes blynde,
Whereas thise robbours and thise theves by
     kynde
Holden hir pryvee fereful residence,   660
As they that dar nat shewen hir presence;
So faren we, if I shal seye the sothe."

   "Now," quod oure Hoost, "yit lat me talke
     to the.
Why artow so discoloured of thy face?"

   "Peter!" quod he, "God yeve it harde grace,
I am so used in the fyr to blowe   666
That it hath chaunged my colour, I trowe.
I am nat wont in no mirour to prie,
But swynke soore and lerne multiplie.
We blondren evere and pouren in the fir,   670
And for al that we faille of oure desir,

For evere we lakken oure conclusioun.
To muchel folk we doon illusioun,
And borwe gold, be it a pound or two,
Or ten, or twelve, or manye sommes mo,   675
And make hem wenen, at the leeste weye,
That of a pound we koude make tweye.
Yet is it fals, but ay we han good hope
It for to doon, and after it we grope.
But that science is so fer us biforn,   680
We mowen nat, although we hadden it sworn,
It overtake, it slit awey so faste.
It wole us maken beggers atte laste."

   Whil this Yeman was thus in his talkyng,
This Chanoun drough hym neer, and herde al
     thyng   685
Which that this Yeman spak, for suspecioun
Of mennes speche evere hadde this Chanoun.
For Catoun seith that he that gilty is
Demeth alle thyng be spoke of hym, ywis.
That was the cause he gan so ny hym drawe 690
To his Yeman, to herknen al his sawe.
And thus he seyde unto his Yeman tho:
"Hoold thou thy pees, and spek no wordes mo,
For if thou do, thou shalt it deere abye.   694
Thou sclaundrest me heere in this compaignye,
And eek discoverest that thou sholdest hyde."

   "Ye," quod oure Hoost, "telle on, what so
     bityde.
Of al his thretyng rekke nat a myte!"

   "In feith," quod he, "namoore I do but lyte."
And whan this Chanon saugh it wolde nat
     bee,   700
But his Yeman wolde telle his pryvetee,
He fledde awey for verray sorwe and shame.

   "A!" quod the Yeman, "heere shal arise
     game;
Al that I kan anon now wol I telle.

---

641. thee, thrive. This is presumably an aside to the Host. **642. avowe that I seye,** say openly what I tell you. **645. preeve,** turn out. **647. lewed and nyce,** ignorant and foolish. **652. no fors,** no matter. **658. hernes,** nooks. **lanes blynde,** obscure alleys. **659. thise,** the generalizing demonstrative (your robbers and your thieves). **by kynde,** by their nature. **665. God yeve it harde grace,** an imprecation such as "Curse the luck!" **668. prie,** peer. **669. multiplie,** to multiply, to make more gold from base metals and a little gold. **670. blondren,** blunder, proceed confusedly. **pouren,** stare. **672. conclusioun,** desired result. **680. so fer us biforn,** so far ahead of us. **682. slit,** slides. **685. drough,** drew. **688. Catoun,** the *Distichs of Cato*, I. 17; cf. note to A 3227. **691. al his sawe,** all that he said. **694. abye,** pay for. **696. discoverest,** disclosest. **that,** what. **697. bityde,** happen. **698. thretyng,** threatening. **699. lyte,** little. **701. pryvetee,** private affairs. **704. kan,** know.

Syn he is goon, the foule feend hym
    quelle!   705
For nevere heerafter wol I with hym meete
For peny ne for pound, I yow biheete.
He that me broghte first unto that game,
Er that he dye, sorwe have he and shame!
For it is ernest to me, by my feith;   710
That feele I wel, what so any man seith.

And yet, for al my smert and al my grief,
For al my sorwe, labour, and meschief,
I koude nevere leve it in no wise.
Now wolde God my wit myghte suffise   715
To tellen al that longeth to that art!
But nathelees yow wol I tellen part.
Syn that my lord is goon, I wol nat spare;
Swich thyng as that I knowe, I wol declare.

Heere endeth the Prologe of the Chanouns Yemannes Tale.

THE CANON'S YEOMAN'S TALE

Heere bigynneth the Chanouns Yeman his Tale.

With this Chanoun I dwelt have seven yeer,
And of his science am I never the neer.   721
Al that I hadde I have lost therby,
And, God woot, so hath many mo than I.
Ther I was wont to be right fressh and gay
Of clothyng and of oother good array,   725

Now may I were an hose upon myn heed;
And wher my colour was bothe fressh and reed,
Now is it wan and of a leden hewe—
Whoso it useth, soore shal he rewe!—
And of my swynk yet blered is myn yë   730
Lo! which avantage is to multiplie!

705. **quelle**, kill. 707. **biheete**, promise. 710. **ernest**, serious. 716. **longeth**, pertains.

The Canon's Yeoman's Tale presents rather more problems than most of the other tales. Many of the technical terms used in the description of alchemy and its processes are not well understood and some are used in a number of different senses in medieval alchemical treatises. The student who wishes a useful introduction to the subject may consult Arthur J. Hopkins, *Alchemy, Child of Greek Philosophy* (New York, 1934). No general source for the Yeoman's remarks is known, and they were probably put together by Chaucer from his reading in the subject and possibly his acquaintance with practitioners and their victims. Extracts from treatises which he mentions by name and other briefer items with which he may have been familiar are gathered together in *SA*, with a useful background statement by John W. Spargo. The superb little by-play by which the Canon and his Yeoman join the group of pilgrims raises its own small question. When the Yeoman talks too freely about his master's affairs the Canon rides off in shame while the Yeoman remains with the company and tells one of the tales. Neither the Canon nor his Yeoman is mentioned in *The General Prologue*. Kittredge was of the opinion that the omission was deliberate and that Chaucer planned from the very beginning this realistic and very effective incident. This may well be doubted. It is just as likely that Chaucer, after writing much of what we have of *The Canterbury Tales*, noticed that the company described in *The General Prologue* was short one pilgrim and, having become interested in the frauds of alchemists, adopted this device for introducing the subject and at the same time correcting the earlier oversight. There is finally the question whether all of *The Canon's Yeoman's Tale* was originally composed for *The Canterbury Tales*. Manly observed (Manly-Rickert, IV. 521) that the story proper, called *Pars Secunda* in the MSS, may have been written originally for some special occasion, and ll. 992 ff. lend color to this suggestion. On the possiblity that Chaucer may have had in mind a particular canon, as originally suggested by H. G. Richardson (*Trans. Royal Hist. Soc.*, 4 Ser., v. 28–70), the student may consult Manly's discussion in *Some New Light on Chaucer*, pp. 242–6. It has been more than once suggested that Chaucer's intimate acquaintance with this fantastic science and his vigorous denunciation of it may have resulted from some experience in which he was himself the victim. In any case, there is one opinion on which students of Chaucer are quite in agreement, that *The Canon's Yeoman's Tale* belongs to a very late stage in the composition of *The Canterbury Tales*, and that the introductory device by which it is brought into the framework is one of the most effective and memorable of incidents which make up the drama of the pilgrimage.

721. **of**, from. **never the neer**, no better off (nearer to my purpose). 724. **Ther**, whereas. 726. **hose**, stocking. 729. **rewe**, repent (of it). 730. **swynk**, labor. **blered**, bleared, but the phrase probably means "I have been cheated," as it commonly does. Here a pun is probably intended. 731. **which**, what. **to multiplie**. See note to l. 669.

That slidynge science hath me maad so bare
That I have no good, wher that evere I fare;
And yet I am endetted so therby,
Of gold that I have borwed, trewely,   735
That whil I lyve I shal it quite nevere.
Lat every man be war by me for evere!
What maner man that casteth hym therto,
If he continue, I holde his thrift ydo.
For so helpe me God, therby shal he nat
    wynne,   740
But empte his purs, and make his wittes thynne.
And whan he, thurgh his madnesse and folye,
Hath lost his owene good thurgh jupartye,
Thanne he exciteth oother folk therto,
To lesen hir good, as he hymself hath do.   745
For unto shrewes joye it is and ese
To have hir felawes in peyne and disese.
Thus was I ones lerned of a clerk.
Of that no charge, I wol speke of oure werk.

    Whan we been there as we shul exercise   750
Oure elvysshe craft, we semen wonder wise,
Oure termes been so clergial and so queynte.
I blowe the fir til that myn herte feynte.
What sholde I tellen ech proporcion
Of thynges whiche that we werche upon—   755
As on fyve or sixe ounces, may wel be,
Of silver, or som oother quantitee—
And bisye me to telle yow the names
Of orpyment, brent bones, iren squames,
That into poudre grounden been ful smal;   760
And in an erthen pot how put is al,
And salt yput in, and also papeer,

Biforn thise poudres that I speke of heer;
And wel ycovered with a lampe of glas;
And of muche oother thyng which that ther
    was;   765
And of the pot and glasses enlutyng,
That of the eyr myghte passe out nothyng;
And of the esy fir, and smart also,
Which that was maad, and of the care and wo
That we hadde in oure matires sublymyng,   770
And in amalgamyng and calcenyng
Of quyksilver, yclept mercurie crude?
For alle oure sleightes we kan nat conclude.
Oure orpyment and sublymed mercurie,
Oure grounden litarge eek on the porfurie,   775
Of ech of thise of ounces a certeyn—
Noght helpeth us, oure labour is in veyn.
Ne eek oure spirites ascencioun,
Ne oure materes that lyen al fix adoun,
Mowe in oure werkyng no thyng us availle,   780
For lost is al oure labour and travaille;
And al the cost, a twenty devel waye,
Is lost also, which we upon it laye.

    Ther is also ful many another thyng
That is unto oure craft apertenyng.   785
Though I by ordre hem nat reherce kan,
By cause that I am a lewed man,
Yet wol I telle hem as they come to mynde,
Thogh I ne kan nat sette hem in hir kynde:
As boole armonyak, verdegrees, boras,   790
And sondry vessels maad of erthe and glas,
Oure urynals and oure descensories,
Violes, crosletz, and sublymatories,

---

732. slidynge, slippery, uncertain. **735. Of,** for. **736. quite,** repay. **738. casteth hym,** devotes himself. **739. ydo,** ended. **741. empte,** empty. **743. jupartye,** risk. **744. exciteth,** causes. **746. shrewes,** rascals. **747. disese,** trouble. **748. lerned of,** taught by. **749. no charge,** no matter. **750. there as,** where. **751. elvysshe,** weird, strange. **752. so clergial and so queynte,** so learned and so strange. **754. What,** why. **755. werche,** work. **759. orpyment,** trisulphide of arsenic. **brent,** burned. **squames,** scales. **760. poudre,** powder. **762. papeer,** presumably paper for lining the pot. The form and accentuation are app. dictated by the rime. **764. lampe,** sheet (OF. *lame* with intrusive *p*.). **766. enlutyng,** sealing up (with lute or clay cement). **767. eyr,** vapor. **768. esy,** gentle, moderate. **smart,** brisk. **770. sublymyng,** sublimation, vaporizing. **771. amalgamyng,** combining with quicksilver. **calcenyng,** oxidizing. **772. yclept,** called. **773. sleightes,** clever devices. **conclude,** obtain the desired result. **775. litarge,** litharge (protoxide of lead). **on the porfurie,** in the mortar (made of porphyry); to be construed with *grounden.* **776. a certeyn,** a certain number. **778. spirites ascencioun,** vapors arising from the four spirits, which, as explained in ll. 822–4, were mercury, arsenic (*orpyment*), sal ammoniac, and sulphur (*brymstoon*). **779. al fix adoun,** at the bottom in a fixed (solid) state. **786. by ordre,** in order. **787. lewed,** ignorant. **789. sette hem in hir kynde,** classify them. **790. boole armonyak,** a fine red clay. **verdegrees,** verdigris, copper acetate. **boras,** borax. **792. urynals,** in alchemy, glass vessels for making solutions. In the 18th c. they are described as oblong. **descensories,** retorts. **793. Violes,** vials. **crosletz,** crucibles. **sublymatories,** vessels used for vaporizing solids.

Cucurbites and alambikes eek,
And othere swiche, deere ynough a leek.   795
Nat nedeth it for to reherce hem alle,—
Watres rubifiyng, and boles galle,
Arsenyk, sal armonyak, and brymstoon;
And herbes koude I telle eek many oon,
As egremoyne, valerian, and lunarie,   800
And othere swiche, if that me liste tarie;
Oure lampes brennyng bothe nyght and day,
To brynge aboute oure purpos, if we may;
Oure fourneys eek of calcinacioun,
And of watres albificacioun;   805
Unslekked lym, chalk, and gleyre of an ey,
Poudres diverse, asshes, donge, pisse, and cley,
Cered pokets, sal peter, vitriole,
And diverse fires maad of wode and cole;
Sal tartre, alkaly, and sal preparat,   810
And combust materes and coagulat;
Cley maad with hors or mannes heer, and
    oille
Of tartre, alum glas, berme, wort, and argoille,
Resalgar, and oure materes enbibyng,
And eek of oure materes encorporyng,   815
And of oure silver citrinacioun,
Oure cementyng and fermentacioun,
Oure yngottes, testes, and many mo.
    I wol yow telle, as was me taught also,
The foure spirites and the bodies sevene,   820
By ordre, as ofte I herde my lord hem nevene.
    The firste spirit quyksilver called is,
The seconde orpyment, the thridde, ywis,
Sal armonyak, and the ferthe brymstoon.

The bodyes sevene eek, lo! hem heere anoon:
Sol gold is, and Luna silver we threpe,   826
Mars iren, Mercurie quyksilver we clepe,
Saturnus leed, and Juppiter is tyn,
And Venus coper, by my fader kyn!
    This cursed craft whoso wole exercise,   830
He shal no good han that hym may suffise;
For al the good he spendeth theraboute
He lese shal; therof have I no doute.
Whoso that listeth outen his folie,
Lat hym come forth and lerne multiplie;   835
And every man that oght hath in his cofre,
Lat hym appiere, and wexe a philosophre.
Ascaunce that craft is so light to leere?
Nay, nay, God woot, al be he monk or frere,
Preest or chanoun, or any oother wyght,   840
Though he sitte at his book bothe day and
    nyght
In lernyng of this elvysshe nyce loore,
Al is in veyn, and parde! muchel moore.
To lerne a lewed man this subtiltee—
Fy! spek nat therof, for it wol nat bee;   845
And konne he letterure, or konne he noon,
As in effect, he shal fynde it al oon.
For bothe two, by my savacioun,
Concluden in multiplicacioun
Ylike wel, whan they han al ydo;   850
This is to seyn, they faillen bothe two.
    Yet forgat I to maken rehersaille
Of watres corosif, and of lymaille,
And of bodies mollificacioun,
And also of hire induracioun;   855

794. **Cucurbites,** pear-shaped retorts used in distillation. 795. **deere ynough a leek,** dear at any price. 797. **rubifiyng,** reddening, a chemical process, supposed to be preliminary to making gold. A passage describing it may be found by those interested in *The Boke of Quinte Essence,* quoted by Skeat. **boles,** bull's. 800. **egremoyne,** agrimony. **lunarie,** moonwort; honesty. 805. **albificacioun,** whitening, a process producing white water, a liquid used in making silver. 806. **gleyre of an ey,** the white of an egg. 808. **Cered pokets,** explained by Skeat as small bags coated or impregnated with wax, an explanation which hardly fits the context, but see note to l. 818. **sal peter,** saltpeter, rock-salt. **vitriole,** sulphuric acid. 810. **Sal tartre,** salt of tartar. **sal preparat,** ordinary salt. 811. **combust,** burnt. **coagulat,** coagulated, congealed. 813. **alum glas,** rock alum. **berme,** yeast. **wort,** unfermented beer. **argoille,** tartar which forms on a wine cask. 814. **Resalgar,** an arsenic compound (ratsbane). **materes enbibyng,** moistening materials. 815. **encorporyng,** incorporating. 816. **citrinacioun,** a stage of the process in which the mixture assumes a citron color. 817. **cementyng,** fusing by means of heat. 818. **testes,** crucibles. In the above jumbled collection of technical terms—substances, processes, apparatus—the Yeoman is doubtless repeating words and expresssions which he has heard, but does not understand, in order to give the impression that alchemy is a very recondite subject. 820. **foure spirites.** See note to l. 778. 826. **threpe,** assert, maintain. 827. **clepe,** call. 834. **outen,** display. 837. **appiere,** come forward (into view). **wexe,** become (grow). 838. **Ascaunce,** as if. **leere,** learn. 842. **elvysshe nyce,** mysterious (and) foolish. 844. **lerne,** teach. 846. **konne . . . noon,** whether he be learned or not. 847. **al oon,** all the same. 848. **savacioun,** salvation. 853. **lymaille,** metal filings. 854. **mollificacioun,** softening. 855. **induracioun,** hardening.

Oilles, ablucions, and metal fusible,—
To tellen al wolde passen any bible
That owher is; wherfore, as for the beste,
Of alle thise names now wol I me reste.
For, as I trowe, I have yow toold ynowe   860
To reyse a feend, al looke he never so rowe.
   A! nay! lat be! the philosophres stoon,
Elixer clept, we sechen faste echoon;
For hadde we hym, thanne were we siker ynow.
But unto God of hevene I make avow,   865
For al oure craft, whan we han al ydo,
And al oure sleighte, he wol nat come us to.
He hath ymaad us spenden muchel good,
For sorwe of which almoost we wexen wood,
But that good hope crepeth in oure herte,   870
Supposynge evere, though we sore smerte,
To be releeved by hym afterward.
Swich supposyng and hope is sharp and hard;
I warne yow wel, it is to seken evere.   874
That futur temps hath maad men to dissevere,
In trust therof, from al that evere they hadde.
Yet of that art they kan nat wexen sadde,
For unto hem it is a bitter sweete,—
So semeth it,—for nadde they but a sheete,
Which that they myghte wrappe hem inne
      a-nyght,   880
And a brat to walken inne by daylyght,
They wolde hem selle and spenden on this craft.
They kan nat stynte til no thyng be laft.
And everemoore, where that evere they goon,
Men may hem knowe by smel of brymstoon.
For al the world they stynken as a goot;   886
Hir savour is so rammyssh and so hoot
That though a man from hem a mile be,
The savour wole infecte hym, trusteth me.
And thus by smellyng, and threedbare array,
If that men liste, this folk they knowe may.   891
And if a man wole aske hem pryvely

Why they been clothed so unthriftily,
They right anon wol rownen in his ere,
And seyn that if that they espied were,   895
Men wolde hem slee by cause of hir science.
Lo, thus this folk bitrayen innocence!
   Passe over this; I go my tale unto.
Er that the pot be on the fir ydo,
Of metals with a certeyn quantitee,   900
My lord hem trempeth, and no man but he—
Now he is goon, I dar seyn boldely—
For, as men seyn, he kan doon craftily.
Algate I woot wel he hath swich a name,
And yet ful ofte he renneth in a blame.   905
And wite ye how? ful ofte it happeth so,
The pot tobreketh, and farewel, al is go!
Thise metals been of so greet violence,
Oure walles mowe nat make hem resistence,
But if they weren wroght of lym and stoon; 910
They percen so, and thurgh the wal they goon.
And somme of hem synken into the ground—
Thus han we lost by tymes many a pound—
And somme are scatered al the floor aboute;
Somme lepe into the roof. Withouten doute,
Though that the feend noght in oure sighte
      hym shewe,   916
I trowe he with us be, that ilke shrewe!
In helle, where that he lord is and sire,
Nis ther moore wo, ne moore rancour ne ire.
Whan that oure pot is broke, as I have sayd, 920
Every man chit, and halt hym yvele apayd.
   Somme seyde it was long on the fir makyng;
Somme seyde nay, it was on the blowyng,—
Thanne was I fered, for that was myn office.
"Straw!" quod the thridde, "ye been lewed and
      nyce.   925
It was nat tempred as it oghte be."
"Nay," quod the fourthe, "stynt and herkne
      me.

857. **bible,** book. 858. **owher,** anywhere. 861. **rowe,** rough. 863. **clept,** called. 864. **siker,** sure, safe. 874. **evere,** forever. 875. **temps,** time (expectation). **dissevere,** part. 877. **wexen sadde,** have their fill. 879. **nadde,** even if they did not have. 881. **brat,** rag (*lit.* coarse cloth or a cloak made of it). 883. **stynte,** leave off. 887. **savour,** odor. **rammyssh,** ramlike. **hoot,** intense. 894. **rownen,** whisper. 895. **espied,** perceived. 899. **ydo,** put. 901. **trempeth,** mixes. 903. **kan doon craftily,** is skillful. 904. **Algate,** at any rate. 905. **renneth in a blame,** runs into blame. 907. **tobreketh,** breaks in pieces. **go,** gone. 913. **by tymes,** at times. 916. **feend,** the Devil. 917. **that ilke shrewe,** the rascal himself. 921. **chit,** chides. **yvele apayd,** dissatisfied. 922-3. **Somme . . . Somme,** one . . . another. **long on,** on account of (the way the fire was made). 924. **fered,** afraid. 926. **tempred,** mixed in proper proportions. 927. **stynt,** stop (talking).

By cause oure fir ne was nat maad of beech,
That is the cause, and oother noon, so theech!"
I kan nat telle wheron it was along,   930
But wel I woot greet strif is us among.
　　"What," quod my lord, "ther is namoore to
　　doone;
Of thise perils I wol be war eftsoone.
I am right siker that the pot was crased.
Be as be may, be ye no thyng amased;   935
As usage is, lat swepe the floor as swithe,
Plukke up youre hertes, and beeth glad and
　　blithe."
　　The mullok on an heep ysweped was,
And on the floor ycast a canevas,
And al this mullok in a syve ythrowe,   940
And sifted, and ypiked many a throwe.
　　"Pardee," quod oon, "somwhat of oure
　　metal
Yet is ther heere, though that we han nat al.
Although this thyng myshapped have as now,
Another tyme it may be wel ynow.   945
Us moste putte oure good in aventure.
A marchant, pardee, may nat ay endure,
Trusteth me wel, in his prosperitee.

Somtyme his good is drowned in the see,
And somtyme comth it sauf unto the londe."   950
　　"Pees!" quod my lord, "the nexte tyme I wol
　　fonde
To bryngen oure craft al in another plite,
And but I do, sires, lat me han the wite.
Ther was defaute in somwhat, wel I woot."
　　Another seyde the fir was over-hoot,—   955
But, be it hoot or coold, I dar seye this,
That we concluden everemoore amys.
We faille of that which that we wolden have,
And in oure madnesse everemoore we rave.
And whan we been togidres everichoon,   960
Every man semeth a Salomon.
But al thyng which that shyneth as the gold
Nis nat gold, as that I have herd it told;
Ne every appul that is fair at yё
Ne is nat good, what so men clappe or crye.   965
Right so, lo, fareth it amonges us:
He that semeth the wiseste, by Jhesus!
Is moost fool, whan it cometh to the preef;
And he that semeth trewest is a theef.
That shul ye knowe, er that I fro yow wende,
By that I of my tale have maad an ende.   971

Explicit prima pars.

Et sequitur pars secunda.

Ther is a chanoun of religioun
Amonges us, wolde infecte al a toun,
Thogh it as greet were as was Nynyvee,
Rome, Alisaundre, Troye, and othere three.   975
His sleightes and his infinite falsnesse
Ther koude no man writen, as I gesse,
Though that he myghte lyve a thousand yeer.
In al this world of falshede nis his peer;
For in his termes he wol hym so wynde,   980
And speke his wordes in so sly a kynde,
Whanne he commune shal with any wight,

That he wol make hym doten anon-right,
But it a feend be, as hymselven is.
Ful many a man hath he bigiled er this,   985
And wole, if that he lyve may a while;
And yet men ride and goon ful many a mile
Hym for to seke and have his aqueyntaunce,
Noght knowynge of his false governaunce.
And if yow list to yeve me audience,   990
I wol it tellen heere in youre presence.
　　But worshipful chanons religious,
Ne demeth nat that I sclaundre youre hous,

929. **so theech,** so may I thrive. 930. **wheron it was along,** what it was on account of. 933. **be war eftsoone,** soon guard against. 934. **crased,** cracked. 936. **as swithe,** without more ado (*lit.* quickly). 938. **mullok,** rubbish, refuse. 941. **ypiked,** sorted. **many a throwe,** many a time. 951. **fonde,** endeavor. 952. **plite,** condition. 953. **wite,** blame. 964. **at yё,** to the eye. 965. **clappe,** chatter. 968. **preef,** proof. 973. **wolde,** (who) would. **al a toun,** a whole town. 976. **sleightes,** deceits. 977. **writen,** possibly a slip, possibly evidence that the tale was not originally written for the *CT.* 979. **of,** in respect of. 980. **wynde,** involve. 981. **so sly a kynde,** so skilful a way. 983. **doten,** behave foolishly. **anon-right,** right away. 987. **goon,** walk. 989. **governaunce,** behavior. 990. **yeve,** give. 993. **sclaundre,** defame, reproach.

Although that my tale of a chanoun bee.
Of every ordre som shrewe is, pardee, 995
And God forbede that al a compaignye
Sholde rewe o singuleer mannes folye.
To sclaundre yow is no thyng myn entente,
But to correcten that is mys I mente.
This tale was nat oonly toold for yow, 1000
But eek for othere mo; ye woot wel how
That among Cristes apostelles twelve
Ther nas no traytour but Judas hymselve.
Thanne why sholde al the remenant have a
    blame
That giltlees were? By yow I seye the same, 1005
Save oonly this, if ye wol herkne me:
If any Judas in youre covent be,
Remoeveth hym bitymes, I yow rede,
If shame or los may causen any drede.
And beeth no thyng displesed, I yow preye, 1010
But in this cas herkeneth what I shal seye.
    In Londoun was a preest, an annueleer,
That therinne dwelled hadde many a yeer,
Which was so plesaunt and so servysable
Unto the wyf, where as he was at table, 1015
That she wolde suffre hym no thyng for to paye
For bord ne clothyng, wente he never so gaye;
And spendyng silver hadde he right ynow.
Therof no fors; I wol procede as now,
And telle forth my tale of the chanoun 1020
That broghte this preest to confusioun.
    This false chanoun cam upon a day
Unto this preestes chambre, wher he lay,
Bisechynge hym to lene hym a certeyn
Of gold, and he wolde quite it hym ageyn. 1025
"Leene me a marc," quod he, "but dayes three,
And at my day I wol it quiten thee.
And if so be that thow me fynde fals,
Another day do hange me by the hals!"

This preest hym took a marc, and that as
    swithe, 1030
And this chanoun hym thanked ofte sithe,
And took his leve, and wente forth his weye,
And at the thridde day broghte his moneye,
And to the preest he took his gold agayn,
Wherof this preest was wonder glad and fayn.
    "Certes," quod he, "no thyng anoyeth me
To lene a man a noble, or two, or thre, 1037
Or what thyng were in my possessioun,
Whan he so trewe is of condicioun
That in no wise he breke wole his day; 1040
To swich a man I kan never seye nay."
    "What!" quod this chanoun, "sholde I be
    untrewe?
Nay, that were thyng yfallen al of newe.
Trouthe is a thyng that I wol evere kepe
Unto that day in which that I shal crepe 1045
Into my grave, and ellis God forbede.
Bileveth this as siker as your Crede.
God thanke I, and in good tyme be it sayd,
That ther was nevere man yet yvele apayd
For gold ne silver that he to me lente, 1050
Ne nevere falshede in myn herte I mente.
And sire," quod he, "now of my pryvetee,
Syn ye so goodlich han been unto me,
And kithed to me so greet gentillesse,
Somwhat to quyte with youre kyndenesse 1055
I wol yow shewe, and if yow list to leere,
I wol yow teche pleynly the manere
How I kan werken in philosophie.
Taketh good heede, ye shul wel seen at yë
That I wol doon a maistrie er I go." 1060
    "Ye," quod the preest, "ye, sire, and wol
    ye so?
Marie! therof I pray yow hertely."
    "At youre comandement, sire, trewely,"

997. rewe, feel remorse for. singuleer, individual. 999. that is mys, what is wrong. 1007. in youre covent, See intro. 1009. If shame . . ., i.e. if you have any fear of shame or loss. 1012. annueleer, one whose function was to sing annivers-ary masses for the dead, on the days when the various benefactors died. 1015. wyf . . . table, woman with whom he took his meals. 1018. spendyng silver, money to spend. 1019. no fors, no matter. 1023. lay, lodged. 1024. lene, lend. a certeyn, a certain sum. 1025. quite, repay. 1026. Leene, lend. marc. A mark was 13s. 4d (two-thirds of a pound). 1029. hals, neck. 1030. took, brought. as swithe, promptly. 1031. ofte sithe, many times. 1037. noble, a gold coin; see note to A 3256. 1039. condicioun, moral nature. 1043. that were . . . newe, that would be something I have never done. 1048. and in good tyme . . ., and fortunately I am able to say it. 1049. yvele apayd, dissatisfied. 1052. pryvetee, secret. 1053. Syn, since. 1054. kithed, manifested. 1055. to quyte with, with which to repay. 1056. leere, learn. 1059. at yë, plainly. 1060. doon a maistrie, give a masterly demonstration.

Quod the chanoun, "and ellis God forbeede!"
　　Loo, how this theef koude his service beede!
Ful sooth it is that swich profred servyse　　1066
Stynketh, as witnessen thise olde wyse,
And that, ful soone I wol it verifie
In this chanoun, roote of al trecherie,　　1069
That everemoore delit hath and gladnesse—
Swiche feendly thoghtes in his herte impresse—
How Cristes peple he may to meschief brynge.
God kepe us from his false dissymulynge!
　　Noght wiste this preest with whom that he
　　　delte,
Ne of his harm comynge he no thyng felte.　1075
O sely preest! o sely innocent!
With coveitise anon thou shalt be blent!
O gracelees, ful blynd is thy conceite,
No thyng ne artow war of the deceite
Which that this fox yshapen hath to thee!　1080
His wily wrenches thou ne mayst nat flee.
Wherfore, to go to the conclusioun,
That refereth to thy confusioun,
Unhappy man, anon I wol me hye
To tellen thyn unwit and thy folye,　　1085
And eek the falsnesse of that oother wrecche,
As ferforth as that my konnyng wol strecche.
　　This chanoun was my lord, ye wolden weene?
Sire hoost, in feith, and by the hevenes queene,
It was another chanoun, and nat hee,　　1090
That kan an hundred foold moore subtiltee.
He hath bitrayed folkes many tyme;
Of his falsnesse it dulleth me to ryme.
Evere whan that I speke of his falshede,
For shame of hym my chekes wexen rede.　1095
Algates they bigynnen for to glowe,
For reednesse have I noon, right wel I knowe,
In my visage; for fumes diverse
Of metals, whiche ye han herd me reherce,
Consumed and wasted han my reednesse.　1100

Now taak heede of this chanons cursednesse!
　　"Sire," quod he to the preest, "lat youre man
　　　gon
For quyksilver, that we it hadde anon;
And lat hym bryngen ounces two or three;
And whan he comth, as faste shal ye see　　1105
A wonder thyng, which ye saugh nevere er
　　　this."
　　"Sire," quod the preest, "it shal be doon,
　　　ywis."
He bad his servant fecchen hym this thyng,
And he al redy was at his biddyng,
And wente hym forth, and cam anon agayn
With this quyksilver, shortly for to sayn,　　1111
And took thise ounces thre to the chanoun;
And he hem leyde faire and wel adoun,
And bad the servant coles for to brynge,
That he anon myghte go to his werkynge.　　1115
　　The coles right anon weren yfet,
And this chanoun took out a crosselet
Of his bosom, and shewed it to the preest.
"This instrument," quod he, "which that thou
　　　seest,
Taak in thyn hand, and put thyself therinne　1120
Of this quyksilver an ounce, and heer bigynne,
In name of Crist, to wexe a philosofre.
Ther been ful fewe to whiche I wolde profre
To shewen hem thus muche of my science.
For ye shul seen heer, by experience,　　1125
That this quyksilver I wol mortifye
Right in youre sighte anon, withouten lye,
And make it as good silver and as fyn
As ther is any in youre purs or myn,
Or elleswhere, and make it malliable;　　1130
And elles holdeth me fals and unable
Amonges folk for evere to appeere.
I have a poudre heer, that coste me deere,
Shal make al good, for it is cause of al　　1134

1064. ellis, otherwise. 1065. beede, offer. 1066. profred servyse Stynketh. The proverb "Proffered service stinks."
1071. feendly, devilish. impresse, press in, throng. 1073. dissymulynge, dissembling. 1075. his harm comynge, his
coming harm. 1076. sely, simple, foolish. 1077. coveitise, covetousness. blent, blinded. 1078. conceite, judgment.
1081. wrenches, stratagems. 1085. unwit, imprudence, stupidity. 1091. kan, knows. subtiltee, craftiness. 1093. dulleth,
depresses. 1096. Algates, at any rate. 1100. han, have. 1102. lat . . . gon, send. 1103. hadde, might have. anon,
immediately. 1107. ywis, certainly. 1112. took, brought. 1116. yfet, fetched. 1117. crosselet, crucible. 1126. mortifye,
a chemical term meaning to change the form of a substance, as when quicksilver is treated to congeal and harden it. 1131.
unable, unworthy.

My konnyng, which that I yow shewen shal.
Voyde youre man, and lat hym be theroute,
And shette the dore, whils we been aboute
Oure pryvetee, that no man us espie,
Whils that we werke in this philosophie."
    Al as he bad fulfilled was in dede.   1140
This ilke servant anonright out yede
And his maister shette the dore anon,
And to hire labour spedily they gon.
    This preest, at this cursed chanons biddyng,
Upon the fir anon sette this thyng,   1145
And blew the fir, and bisyed hym ful faste.
And this chanoun into the crosselet caste
A poudre, noot I wherof that it was
Ymaad, outher of chalk, outher of glas,
Or somwhat elles, was nat worth a flye,   1150
To blynde with this preest; and bad hym hye
The coles for to couchen al above
The crosselet. "For in tokenyng I thee love,"
Quod this chanoun, "thyne owene handes two
Shul werche al thyng which that shal heer be
    do."   1155
    "Graunt mercy," quod the preest, and was
    ful glad,
And couched coles as that the chanoun bad.
And while he bisy was, this feendly wrecche,
This false chanoun—the foule feend hym
    fecche!—
Out of his bosom took a bechen cole,   1160
In which ful subtilly was maad an hole,
And therinne put was of silver lemaille
An ounce, and stopped was, withouten faille,
This hole with wex, to kepe the lemaille in.
And understondeth that this false gyn   1165
Was nat maad ther, but it was maad bifore;
And othere thynges I shal tellen moore
Herafterward, whiche that he with hym
    broghte.

Er he cam there, hym to bigile he thoghte,
And so he dide, er that they wente atwynne;
Til he had terved hym, koude he nat blynne.
It dulleth me whan that I of hym speke.   1172
On his falshede fayn wolde I me wreke,
If I wiste how, but he is heere and there;
He is so variaunt, he abit nowhere.   1175
    But taketh heede now, sires, for Goddes
    love!
He took his cole of which I spak above,
And in his hand he baar it pryvely.
And whiles the preest couched bisily
The coles, as I tolde yow er this,   1180
This chanoun seyde, "Freend, ye doon amys.
This is nat couched as it oghte be;
But soone I shal amenden it," quod he.
"Now lat me medle therwith but a while,
For of yow have I pitee, by Seint Gile!   1185
Ye been right hoot; I se wel how ye swete.
Have heere a clooth, and wipe awey the wete."
And whiles that the preest wiped his face,
This chanoun took his cole—with sory grace!—
And leyde it above upon the myddeward   1190
Of the crosselet, and blew wel afterward,
Til that the coles gonne faste brenne.
    "Now yeve us drynke," quod the chanoun
    thenne;
"As swithe al shal be wel, I undertake.
Sitte we doun, and lat us myrie make."   1195
And whan that this chanounes bechen cole
Was brent, al the lemaille out of the hole
Into the crosselet fil anon adoun;
And so it moste nedes, by resoun,
Syn it so evene aboven it couched was.   1200
But therof wiste the preest nothyng, alas!
He demed alle the coles yliche good;
For of that sleighte he nothyng understood.
And whan this alkamystre saugh his tyme,

1136. **Voyde,** send away. 1141. **yede,** went. 1148. **noot I,** I know not. 1149. **outher . . . outher,** either . . . or. 1152. **couchen,** lay. 1153. **in tokenyng,** as an evidence that. 1155. **werche al thyng,** do everything. 1157. **as that,** as. 1160. **bechen cole,** charcoal of beechwood. 1161. **subtilly,** craftily. 1162. **lemaille,** filings. 1164. **wex,** wax. 1165. **gyn,** contrivance. 1169. **bigile,** cheat. 1170. **wente atwynne,** separated. 1171. **terved,** skinned. **blynne,** cease. 1172. **dulleth,** depresses. 1173. **me wreke,** avenge myself. 1175. **variaunt,** shifty. **abit,** abides. 1185. **Seint Gile,** St. Giles (St. Aegidius). 1189. **with sory grace,** bad luck to him. 1194. **As swithe,** soon (quickly). 1200. **evene,** directly. 1202. **yliche good,** equally good, all alike. 1203. **sleighte,** trickery. 1204. **alkamystre,** alchemist.

"Ris up," quod he, "sire preest, and stondeth
   by me;   1205
And for I woot wel ingot have ye noon,
Gooth, walketh forth, and bryng us a chalk
   stoon;
For I wol make it of the same shap
That is an ingot, if I may han hap.
And bryngeth eek with yow a bolle or a panne
Ful of water, and ye shul se wel thanne   1211
How that oure bisynesse shal thryve and preeve.
And yet, for ye shul han no mysbileeve
Ne wrong conceite of me in youre absence,
I ne wol nat been out of youre presence,   1215
But go with yow, and come with yow ageyn."
The chambre dore, shortly for to seyn,
They opened and shette, and wente hir weye.
And forth with hem they carieden the keye,
And coome agayn withouten any delay.   1220
What sholde I tarien al the longe day?
He took the chalk, and shoop it in the wise
Of an ingot, as I shal yow devyse.

   I seye, he took out of his owene sleeve
A teyne of silver—yvele moot he cheeve!— 1225
Which that ne was nat but an ounce of weighte.
And taaketh heede now of his cursed sleighte!

   He shoop his ingot, in lengthe and in breede
Of this teyne, withouten any drede,
So slyly that the preest it nat espide,   1230
And in his sleve agayn he gan it hide,
And fro the fir he took up his mateere,
And in th'yngot putte it with myrie cheere,
And in the water-vessel he it caste,
Whan that hym luste, and bad the preest as
   faste,   1235
"Loke what ther is, put in thyn hand and grope.
Thow fynde shalt ther silver, as I hope."
What, devel of helle! sholde it elles be?
Shaving of silver silver is, pardee!
He putte his hand in and took up a teyne   1240

Of silver fyn, and glad in every veyne
Was this preest, whan he saugh that it was so.
"Goddes blessyng, and his moodres also,
And alle halwes, have ye, sire chanoun,"
Seyde the preest, "and I hir malisoun,   1245
But, and ye vouchesauf to techen me
This noble craft and this subtilitee,
I wol be youre in al that evere I may."

   Quod the chanoun, "Yet wol I make assay
The seconde tyme, that ye may taken heede
And been expert of this, and in youre neede 1251
Another day assaye in myn absence
This disciplyne and this crafty science.
Lat take another ounce," quod he tho,
"Of quyksilver, withouten wordes mo,   1255
And do therwith as ye han doon er this
With that oother, which that now silver is."

   This preest hym bisieth in al that he kan
To doon as this chanoun, this cursed man,
Comanded hym, and faste he blew the fir,   1260
For to come to th'effect of his desir.
And this chanon, right in the meene while,
Al redy was this preest eft to bigile,
And for a contenaunce in his hand he bar
An holwe stikke—taak kepe and be war!— 1265
In the ende of which an ounce, and namoore,
Of silver lemaille put was, as bifore
Was in his cole, and stopped with wex weel
For to kepe in his lemaille every deel.
And whil this preest was in his bisynesse, 1270
This chanoun with his stikke gan hym dresse
To hym anon, and his poudre caste in
As he dide er—the devel out of his skyn
Hym terve, I pray to God, for his falshede!
For he was evere fals in thoght and dede—
And with this stikke, above the crosselet, 1276
That was ordeyned with that false jet
He stired the coles til relente gan
The wex agayn the fir, as every man,

1206. ingot, mold. **1209. hap,** good fortune. **1210. bolle,** bowl. **1212. preeve,** prove (successful). **1221. What,** why.
1225. teyne, properly a small rod, but from ll. 1317–24 it appears to have been flat. **yvele . . . cheeve,** may he come to a
bad end. **1227. sleighte,** trick. **1228. shoop,** shaped. **1229. drede,** doubt. **1235. as faste,** quickly. **1236. grope,** feel around.
1241. in every veyne, in every part of his body. **1244. halwes,** saints. **1245. malisoun,** curse. **1246. But,** unless. **and,** if.
1248. youre, yours. **1253. crafty,** ingenious. **1263. eft,** again. **1264. for a contenaunce,** for appearance's sake. **1265. kepe,**
heed. **1271. hym dresse,** direct himself, go. **1274. terve,** flay. **1277. ordeyned,** equipped. **jet,** device. **1278. relente,** to
melt. **1279. agayn,** in the presence of.

But it a fool be, woot wel it moot nede,   1280
And al that in the stikke was out yede,
And in the crosselet hastily it fel.

Now, gode sires, what wol ye bet than wel?
Whan that this preest thus was bigiled ageyn,
Supposynge noght but treuthe, sooth to seyn,
He was so glad that I kan nat expresse   1286
In no manere his myrthe and his gladnesse;
And to the chanoun he profred eftsoone
Body and good. "Ye," quod the chanoun soone,
"Though povre I be, crafty thou shalt me fynde.
I warne thee, yet is ther moore bihynde.   1291
Is ther any coper herinne?" seyde he.
    "Ye," quod the preest, "sire, I trowe wel ther
        be."
    "Elles go bye us som, and that as swithe;
Now, goode sire, go forth thy wey and hy
        the."   1295
    He wente his wey, and with the coper cam,
And this chanon it in his handes nam,
And of that coper weyed out but an ounce.
    Al to symple is my tonge to pronounce,
As ministre of my wit, the doublenesse   1300
Of this chanoun, roote of alle cursednesse!
He semed freendly to hem that knewe hym
        noght,
But he was feendly bothe in werk and thoght.
It weerieth me to telle of his falsnesse,
And nathelees yet wol I it expresse,   1305
To th'entente that men may be war therby,
And for noon oother cause, trewely.
    He putte this ounce of coper in the crosselet,
And on the fir as swithe he hath it set,
And caste in poudre, and made the preest to
        blowe,   1310
And in his werkyng for to stoupe lowe,
As he dide er,—and al nas but a jape;
Right as hym liste, the preest he made his ape!
And afterward in the ingot he it caste,

And in the panne putte it at the laste   1315
Of water, and in he putte his owene hand,
And in his sleve (as ye biforen-hand
Herde me telle) he hadde a silver teyne.
He slyly took it out, this cursed heyne,
Unwityng this preest of his false craft,   1320
And in the pannes botme he hath it laft;
And in the water rombled to and fro,
And wonder pryvely took up also
The coper teyne, noght knowynge this preest,
And hidde it, and hym hente by the breest,
And to hym spak, and thus seyde in his game:
"Stoupeth adoun, by God, ye be to blame!   1327
Helpeth me now, as I dide yow whileer;
Putte in youre hand, and looketh what is theer."
    This preest took up this silver teyne anon, 1330
And thanne seyde the chanoun, "Lat us gon
With thise thre teynes, whiche that we han
        wroght,
To som goldsmyth, and wite if they been oght.
For, by my feith, I nolde, for myn hood,
But if that they were silver fyn and good,   1335
And that as swithe preeved it shal bee."
    Unto the goldsmyth with thise teynes three
They wente, and putte thise teynes in assay
To fir and hamer; myghte no man seye nay,
But that they weren as hem oghte be.   1340
    This sotted preest, who was gladder than he?
Was nevere brid gladder agayn the day,
Ne nyghtyngale, in the sesoun of May,
Was nevere noon that luste bet to synge;
Ne lady lustier in carolynge,   1345
Or for to speke of love and wommanhede,
Ne knyght in armes to doon an hardy dede,
To stonden in grace of his lady deere,
Than hadde this preest this soory craft to leere.
And to the chanoun thus he spak and seyde: 1350
"For love of God, that for us alle deyde,
And as I may deserve it unto yow,

1281. yede, went. 1283. what . . . wel, what better than well do you want. 1288. eftsoone, again. 1289. good, possessions. 1290. crafty, clever. 1294. as swithe, quickly. 1297. nam, took. 1304. weerieth, wearies. 1312. nas but, was nothing but. jape, trick. 1318. teyne, cf. l. 1225. 1319. heyne, wretch. 1320. Unwityng this preest, this priest not knowing. 1322. rombled, felt around. 1324. noght knowynge this preest, without the priest's knowledge. 1325. hente, took. 1328. whileer, a while ago. 1341. sotted, foolish. 1345. lustier, happier. carolynge. See note to BD 849.

What shal this receite coste? telleth now!"
  "By oure Lady," quod this chanon, "it is
    deere,
I warne yow wel; for save I and a frere,   1355
In Engelond ther kan no man it make."
  "No fors," quod he, "now, sire, for Goddes
    sake,
What shal I paye? telleth me, I preye."
  "Ywis," quod he, "it is ful deere, I seye.
Sire, at o word, if that thee list it have,   1360
Ye shul paye fourty pound, so God me save!
And nere the freendshipe that ye dide er this
To me, ye sholde paye moore, ywis."
  This preest the somme of fourty pound anon
Of nobles fette, and took hem everichon   1365
To this chanoun, for this ilke receit.
Al his werkyng nas but fraude and deceit.
  "Sire preest," he seyde, "I kepe han no loos
Of my craft, for I wolde it kept were cloos;
And, as ye love me, kepeth it secree.   1370
For, and men knewen al my soutiltee,
By God, they wolden han so greet envye
To me, by cause of my philosophye,
I sholde be deed; ther were noon oother weye."
  "God it forbeede," quod the preest, "what
    sey ye?   1375
Yet hadde I levere spenden al the good
Which that I have, and elles wexe I wood,
Than that ye sholden falle in swich mescheef."
  "For youre good wyl, sire, have ye right
    good preef,"   1379
Quod the chanoun, "and farwel, grant mercy!"
He wente his wey, and never the preest hym sy

After that day; and whan that this preest
  shoolde
Maken assay, at swich tyme as he wolde,
Of this receit, farwel! it wolde nat be.
Lo, thus byjaped and bigiled was he!   1385
Thus maketh he his introduccioun,
To brynge folk to hir destruccioun.
  Considereth, sires, how that, in ech estaat,
Bitwixe men and gold ther is debaat
So ferforth that unnethes is ther noon.   1390
This multiplying blent so many oon
That in good feith I trowe that it bee
The cause grettest of swich scarsetee.
Philosophres speken so mystily
In this craft that men kan nat come therby,   1395
For any wit that men han now-a-dayes.
They mowe wel chiteren as doon thise jayes,
And in hir termes sette hir lust and peyne,
But to hir purpos shul they nevere atteyne.
A man may lightly lerne, if he have aught,   1400
To multiplie, and brynge his good to naught!
  Lo! swich a lucre is in this lusty game,
A mannes myrthe it wol turne unto grame,
And empten also grete and hevye purses,
And maken folk for to purchacen curses   1405
Of hem that han hir good therto ylent.
O! fy, for shame! they that han been brent,
Allas! kan they nat flee the fires heete?
Ye that it use, I rede ye it leete,
Lest ye lese al; for bet than nevere is late.   1410
Nevere to thryve were to long a date.
Though ye prolle ay, ye shul it nevere fynde.
Ye been as boold as is Bayard the blynde,

1353. receite, recipe. 1357. No fors, no matter. 1362. nere, were it not (for). 1365. fette, fetched. took, brought. 1367. nas but, was nothing but. 1368. I kepe han no loos, I care to have no fame. 1371. and, if. soutiltee, skill. 1372. envye, ill-will. 1376. good, property. 1377. wood, mad. 1378. mescheef, misfortune. 1379. preef, issue, result, fortune. 1380. grant mercy, many thanks. 1381. sy, saw. 1385. byjaped and bigiled, tricked and fooled. 1386. maketh . . . introduccioun, prepares the way. 1388. in ech estaat . . ., in all ranks of society there is such a contest between men and gold (such an effort of all men to win gold) that there is scarcely any (gold to be won). 1391. multiplying. See note to l. 669 above. blent, blinds. The idea is that so many people are taken in by the alchemists and have lost what gold they had that the metal has become scarce. 1394. Philosophres, alchemists. 1395. kan nat come therby, can not get head or tail of it. 1397. chiteren, chatter. 1398. in hir termes . . ., set their heart on technical terms. 1399. to hir purpos . . . atteyne, they shall never succeed in their endeavor. 1400. A man . . . A man, if he has any wealth, may easily learn his lesson in alchemy and lose everything. 1402. lucre, profit. lusty, pleasant. 1403. grame, sorrow. 1404. empten, empty. 1407. brent, burnt. 1409. rede, advise. leete, give up. 1410. for bet . . ., better late than never. 1411. were . . . date, would be too long a time. 1412. prolle ay, prowl around forever. 1413. Bayard, the name of a horse in several chansons de geste, especially in *Renaud de Montauban*, from which it apparently passed into popular tradition. The rashness of blind Bayard was proverbial, as several references in Skeat show.

That blondreth forth, and peril casteth noon.
He is as boold to renne agayn a stoon   1415
As for to goon bisides in the weye.
So faren ye that multiplie, I seye.
If that youre eyen kan nat seen aright,
Looke that youre mynde lakke noght his sight.
For though ye looken never so brode and stare,
Ye shul nothyng wynne on that chaffare,   1421
But wasten al that ye may rape and renne.
Withdraweth the fir, lest it to faste brenne;
Medleth namoore with that art, I mene,   1424
For if ye doon, youre thrift is goon ful clene.
And right as swithe I wol yow tellen heere
What philosophres seyn in this mateere.
    Lo, thus seith Arnold of the Newe Toun,
As his Rosarie maketh mencioun;
He seith right thus, withouten any lye: 1430
"Ther may no man mercurie mortifie
But it be with his brother knowlechyng."
How [be] that he which that first seyde this thyng
Of philosophres fader was, Hermes—
He seith how that the dragon, doutelees,   1435
Ne dyeth nat, but if that he be slayn
With his brother; and that is for to sayn,
By the dragon, Mercurie, and noon oother
He understood, and brymstoon by his brother,
That out of Sol and Luna were ydrawe.   1440
"And therfore," seyde he,—taak heede to my
    sawe—
"Lat no man bisye hym this art for to seche,
But if that he th'entencioun and speche

Of philosophres understonde kan;
And if he do, he is a lewed man.   1445
For this science and this konnyng," quod he,
"Is of the secree of secrees, pardee."
    Also ther was a disciple of Plato,
That on a tyme seyde his maister to,
As his book Senior wol bere witnesse,   1450
And this was his demande in soothfastnesse:
"Telle me the name of the privee stoon?"
    And Plato answerde unto hym anoon,
"Take the stoon that Titanos men name."
    "Which is that?" quod he. "Magnasia is the
    same,"   1455
Seyde Plato. "Ye, sire, and is it thus?
This is *ignotum per ignocius.*
What is Magnasia, good sire, I yow preye?"
    "It is a water that is maad, I seye,
Of elementes foure," quod Plato.   1460
    "Telle me the roote, good sire," quod he tho,
"Of that water, if it be youre wille."
    "Nay, nay," quod Plato, "certein, that I nylle.
The philosophres sworn were everychoon
That they sholden discovere it unto noon,   1465
Ne in no book it write in no manere.
For unto Crist it is so lief and deere
That he wol nat that it discovered bee,
But where it liketh to his deitee
Men for t'enspire, and eek for to deffende   1470
Whom that hym liketh; lo, this is the ende."
    Thanne conclude I thus, sith that God of
    hevene

1414. casteth, takes into account, perceives. **1415. agayn,** against. **1416. goon bisides,** go around an obstacle. **1418. eyen,** eyes. **1420. brode,** with open eyes. **1421. chaffare,** business. **1422. rape and renne,** snatch and catch. The alliterative phrase is of uncertain origin. **1424. mene,** say. **1425. as swithe,** quickly. **1426. as swithe,** quickly. **1428. Arnold of the Newe Toun,** Arnoldus de Villa Nova. (d. 1314), author of a treatise on alchemy entitled *Rosarium Philosophorum.* **1431. mortifie.** See note to l. 1126 above. **1432. his brother knowlechyng,** with the knowledge (collaboration?) of its brother. The brother of mercury was sulphur or brimstone. **1434. Hermes,** Hermes Trismegistus, supposed to have been the author of numerous works on alchemy. **1436. slayn,** a synonym for "mortified," *i.e.* mercury can be transmuted (see note to l. 1126) into a solid state only by means of sulphur. Arnoldus says "mercurius nunquam moritur id est congelatur nisi cum fratre suo . . ." The figurative language of these lines is part of the mystification indulged in by alchemical writers, but we still use such figurative expressions (a metal is *attacked* by acid). The use of *dragon* here is not obvious. It is also taken from Arnoldus. Cf. Lowes. *MLN,* xxviii. 229. **1437. With,** by. **1440. Sol and Luna,** symbols of gold and silver. **1442. seche,** pursue. **1443. entencioun,** meaning. **speche,** language. **1445. lewed,** foolish. **1447. secree of secrees,** secret of secrets. **1450. Senior.** The full title is *Senior Zadith Tabula Chemica.* It is the work of an Arabic alchemist of the tenth century. The story of Plato which follows is there attributed to Solomon. The pertinent passage is printed in *SA.* **1452. privee stoon,** secret (philosopher's) stone. **1457. *ignotum per ignocius,*** (to explain) the unknown by the more unknown. **1459. water,** liquid. **1461. roote,** essential part. **tho,** then. **1463. nylle,** will not. **1469. But where it liketh . . .,** except where it pleases His deity to impart knowledge to men, and also to deny it to whomever it pleases Him to.

Ne wil nat that the philosophres nevene
How that a man shal come unto this stoon,
I rede, as for the beste, lete it goon.   1475
For whoso maketh God his adversarie,
As for to werken any thyng in contrarie

Of his wil, certes, never shal he thryve,
Thogh that he multiplie terme of his lyve.
And there a poynt; for ended is my tale.   1480
God sende every trewe man boote of his
    bale!

Heere is ended the Chanouns Yemannes Tale.

Group H (Fragment IX)

The Manciple's Tale

THE MANCIPLE'S PROLOGUE

Heere folweth the Prologe of the Maunciples Tale.

Woot ye nat where ther stant a litel toun
Which that ycleped is Bobbe-up-and-doun,
Under the Blee, in Caunterbury weye?
Ther gan oure Hooste for to jape and pleye,
And seyde, "Sires, what! Dun is in the myre! 5
Is ther no man, for preyere ne for hyre,
That wole awake oure felawe al bihynde?
A theef myghte hym ful lightly robbe and
    bynde.
See how he nappeth! see how, for cokkes bones,
That he wol falle fro his hors atones!   10
Is that a cook of Londoun, with meschaunce?
Do hym come forth, he knoweth his penaunce;
For he shal telle a tale, by my fey,
Although it be nat worth a botel hey.

Awake, thou Cook," quod he, "God yeve thee
    sorwe!   15
What eyleth thee to slepe by the morwe?
Hastow had fleen al nyght, or artow dronke?
Or hastow with som quene al nyght yswonke,
So that thow mayst nat holden up thyn heed?"
    This Cook, that was ful pale and no thyng
        reed,   20
Seyde to oure Hoost, "So God my soule blesse,
As ther is falle on me swich hevynesse,
Noot I nat why, that me were levere slepe
Than the best galon wyn in Chepe."
    "Wel," quod the Maunciple," if it may doon
        ese   25
To thee, sire Cook, and to no wight displese,

1473. nevene, name, tell. **1479. terme of,** the whole period of. **1480. poynt,** period, full stop. **1481. boote of his bale,** help out of his trouble. **1. Woot ye,** know ye. **stant,** stands. **2. ycleped,** called. **Bobbe-up-and-doun,** supposed to be a humorous corruption of Harbledown. **3. Blee,** the Blean forest. **in Caunterbury weye,** on the Canterbury road. **4. jape,** joke. **5. Dun is in the myre,** a popular saying, originating in a country game. A large log was set down in the middle of a room. With the announcement "Dun is in the mire" two players tried to move it; if they failed, a third joined them, etc. *Dun* was a popular name for a horse. The game is described in Brand's *Popular Antiquities.* The Host means that it is time to start the entertainment. **9. for cokkes bones,** a euphemistic equivalent of "for God's bones." **10. atones,** at once. **11. with meschaunce,** bad luck to him. **12. Do hym,** make him. **14 a botel hey,** a small bundle of hay. **17. fleen,** fleas. **18. quene,** quean, harlot. **yswonke,** labored. **23. Noot I,** I know not. **24. Chepe,** Cheapside. **25. Maunciple.** See note to A 567.

Which that heere rideth in this compaignye,
And that oure Hoost wole, of his curteisye,
I wol as now excuse thee of thy tale.
For, in good feith, thy visage is ful pale,   30
Thyne eyen daswen eek, as that me thynketh,
And, wel I woot, thy breeth ful soure stynketh:
That sheweth wel thou art nat wel disposed.
Of me, certeyn, thou shalt nat been yglosed.
See how he ganeth, lo! this dronken wight,   35
As though he wolde swolwe us anonright.
Hoold cloos thy mouth, man, by thy fader kyn!
The devel of helle sette his foot therin!
Thy cursed breeth infecte wole us alle.
Fy, stynkyng swyn! fy, foule moote thee falle!
A! taketh heede, sires, of this lusty man.   41
Now, sweete sire, wol ye justen atte fan?
Therto me thynketh ye been wel yshape!
I trowe that ye dronken han wyn ape,
And that is whan men pleyen with a straw."   45
And with this speche the Cook wax wrooth
     and wraw,
And on the Manciple he gan nodde faste
For lakke of speche, and doun the hors hym
     caste,
Where as he lay, til that men hym up took.
This was a fair chyvachee of a cook!   50
Allas! he nadde holde hym by his ladel!
And er that he agayn were in his sadel,
Ther was greet showvyng bothe to and fro
To lifte hym up, and muchel care and wo,
So unweeldy was this sory palled goost.   55
And to the Manciple thanne spak oure Hoost:
     "By cause drynke hath dominacioun

Upon this man, by my savacioun,
I trowe he lewedly telle wolde his tale.
For, were it wyn, or oold or moysty ale,   60
That he hath dronke, he speketh in his nose,
And fneseth faste, and eek he hath the pose.
     He hath also to do moore than ynough
To kepen hym and his capul out of the slough;
And if he falle from his capul eftsoone,   65
Thanne shal we alle have ynogh to doone
In liftyng up his hevy dronken cors.
Telle on thy tale; of hym make I no fors.
     But yet, Manciple, in feith thou art to nyce,
Thus openly repreve hym of his vice.   70
Another day he wole, peraventure,
Reclayme thee and brynge thee to lure;
I meene, he speke wole of smale thynges,
As for to pynchen at thy rekenynges,
That were nat honeste, if it cam to preef."   75
     "No," quod the Manciple, "that were a greet
     mescheef!
So myghte he lightly brynge me in the snare.
Yet hadde I levere payen for the mare
Which he rit on, than he sholde with me stryve.
I wol nat wratthen hym, also moot I thryve!   80
That that I spak, I seyde it in my bourde.
And wite ye what? I have heer in a gourde
A draghte of wyn, ye, of a ripe grape,
And right anon ye shul seen a good jape.
This Cook shal drynke therof, if I may.   85
Up peyne of deeth, he wol nat seye me nay."
     And certeynly, to tellen as it was,
Of this vessel the Cook drank faste, allas!
What neded hym? he drank ynough biforn.

---

31. **daswen,** are dazed. 33. **nat wel disposed,** indisposed. 34. **yglosed,** flattered. 35. **ganeth,** yawns. 37. **fader,** father's. 40. **foule moote thee falle,** may evil befall thee; *lit.* may it evilly befall thee. 41. **lusty.** While the sense may be "lustful" (as *NED* takes it), the lines that follow suggest that the Manciple is here sarcastic and that *lusty* means "lively, agreeable." 42. **justen atte fan,** an allusion to the sport of riding toward and striking a vane or quintain and passing beyond before the other end had swung around and struck the rider. Of course, the drunken Cook could not have performed the feat successfully. 44. **wyn ape,** ape-wine, wine that makes a monkey of the drinker. For the origin of the notion in Rabbinical tradition see Skeat's note. 45. **pleyen with a straw,** as a monkey or kitten might play with a straw. 46. **wraw,** angry. 50. **chyvachee . . .,** a fine example of a cook's horsemanship. 51. **Allas . . .,** it is too bad that he hadn't stuck to his ladle. 55. **palled,** incapacitated. 59. **lewedly,** ignorantly, badly. 60. **moysty,** old; see note to C 315. 62. **fneseth,** puffs. **pose,** cold in the head. 64. **capul,** nag. 65. **eftsoone,** again. 67. **cors,** body, carcass. 68. **make I no fors,** I take no account. 69. **nyce,** foolish. 72. **Reclayme . . . lure.** The metaphor is from hawking. *To reclaim* is to call back the hawk to the fist by means of a lure (see note to D 1339). The Host means he will set a snare for him, get him in his power. 74. **pynchen at thy rekenynges,** find fault with your accounts. 75. **honeste,** fitting, desirable. The Host slyly implies that the Manciple's accounts would not stand close inspection. 79. **rit,** rides. 80. **wratthen,** make angry. 81. **bourde,** jesting. 82. **wite ye,** do you know. 84. **jape,** joke. 86. **Up,** upon.

And whan he hadde pouped in this horn,　　90
To the Manciple he took the gourde agayn;
And of that drynke the Cook was wonder fayn,
And thanked hym in swich wise as he koude.
　Thanne gan oure Hoost to laughen wonder
　　loude,
And seyde, "I se wel it is necessarie,　　95
Where that we goon, good drynke with us
　carie;

For that wol turne rancour and disese
T'acord and love, and many a wrong apese.
　O thou Bacus, yblessed be thy name,
That so kanst turnen ernest into game!　　100
Worship and thank be to thy deitee!
Of that mateere ye gete namoore of me.
Telle on thy tale, Manciple, I thee preye."
　"Wel, sire," quod he, "now herkneth what I
　seye."

THE MANCIPLE'S TALE

Heere bigynneth the Maunciples Tale of the Crowe.

Whan Phebus dwelled heere in this erthe
　adoun,　　105
As olde bookes maken mencioun,
He was the mooste lusty bachiler
In al this world, and eek the beste archer.
He slow Phitoun, the serpent, as he lay
Slepynge agayn the sonne upon a day;　　110
And many another noble worthy dede
He with his bowe wroghte, as men may rede.
　Pleyen he koude on every mynstralcie,
And syngen, that it was a melodie
To heeren of his cleere voys the soun.　　115
Certes the kyng of Thebes, Amphioun,
That with his syngyng walled that citee,
Koude nevere syngen half so wel as hee.
Therto he was the semelieste man
That is or was, sith that the world bigan.　　120
What nedeth it his fetures to discryve?
For in this world was noon so fair on-lyve.
He was therwith fulfild of gentillesse,
Of honour, and of parfit worthynesse.
　This Phebus, that was flour of bachilrie,　　125

As wel in fredom as in chivalrie,
For his desport, in signe eek of victorie
Of Phitoun, so as telleth us the storie,
Was wont to beren in his hand a bowe.　　129
　Now hadde this Phebus in his hous a crowe
Which in a cage he fostred many a day,
And taughte it speke, as men teche a jay.
Whit was this crowe as is a snow-whit swan,
And countrefete the speche of every man
He koude, whan he sholde telle a tale.　　135
Therwith in al this world no nyghtyngale
Ne koude, by an hondred thousand deel,
Syngen so wonder myrily and weel.
　Now hadde this Phebus in his hous a wyf
Which that he lovede moore than his lyf,　　140
And nyght and day dide evere his diligence
Hir for to plese, and doon hire reverence,
Save oonly, if the sothe that I shal sayn,
Jalous he was, and wolde have kept hire fayn.
For hym were looth byjaped for to be,　　145
And so is every wight in swich degree;
But al in ydel, for it availleth noght.

90. **pouped in his horn,** *lit.* blown; taken a gulp. **91. took,** handed. **99. Bacus,** Bacchus.
　The Manciple's Tale. The story of the tell-tale bird is a widespread folktale, but Chaucer's principal source is Ovid (*Metam.*, ii. 531–632) or a version derived from his. The narrative thread has been amplified by a number of sententious passages. The date of composition is very uncertain.
105. Phebus, Apollo. **109. Phitoun,** the Python. **113. mynstralcie,** musical instrument. **114. melodie,** sweet music. **116. Amphioun.** See E 1716. **119. semelieste,** handsomest. **122. on-lyve,** alive. **125. bachilrie,** young manhood. **126. fredom,** liberality. **chivalrie,** knightly accomplishments. **127. desport,** amusement. **128. Of,** over. **134. countrefete,** imitate. **137. thousand deel,** thousandth part. **142. doon hire reverence,** show her respect. **144. kept,** guarded. **145. byjaped,** tricked. **146. in swich degree,** in such a situation. **147. in ydel,** in vain.

A good wyf, that is clene of werk and thoght,
Sholde nat been kept in noon awayt, certayn;
And trewely, the labour is in vayn   150
To kepe a shrewe, for it wol nat bee.
This holde I for a verray nycetee,
To spille labour for to kepe wyves:
Thus writen olde clerkes in hir lyves.
    But now to purpos, as I first bigan: 155
This worthy Phebus dooth al that he kan
To plesen hire, wenynge by swich plesaunce,
And for his manhede and his governaunce,
That no man sholde han put hym from hir
    grace.
But God it woot, ther may no man embrace
As to destreyne a thyng which that nature   161
Hath natureelly set in a creature.
    Taak any bryd, and put it in a cage,
And do al thyn entente and thy corage
To fostre it tendrely with mete and drynke   165
Of alle deyntees that thou kanst bithynke,
And keep it al so clenly as thou may,
Although his cage of gold be never so gay,
Yet hath this brid, by twenty thousand foold,
Levere in a forest, that is rude and coold,   170
Goon ete wormes and swich wrecchednesse.
For evere this brid wol doon his bisynesse
To escape out of his cage, if he may.
His libertee this brid desireth ay.   174
    Lat take a cat, and fostre hym wel with milk
And tendre flessh, and make his couche of silk,
And lat hym seen a mous go by the wal,
Anon he weyveth milk and flessh and al,
And every deyntee that is in that hous,
Swich appetit hath he to ete a mous.   180
Lo, heere hath lust his dominacioun,
And appetit fleemeth discrecioun.
    A she-wolf hath also a vileyns kynde.
The lewedeste wolf that she may fynde,
Or leest of reputacioun, wol she take,   185
In tyme whan hir lust to han a make.

Alle thise ensamples speke I by thise men
That been untrewe, and nothyng by wommen.
For men han evere a likerous appetit
On lower thyng to parfourne hire delit   190
Than on hire wyves, be they never so faire,
Ne never so trewe, ne so debonaire.
Flessh is so newefangel, with meschaunce,
That we ne konne in nothyng han plesaunce
That sowneth into vertu any while.   195
    This Phebus, which that thoghte upon no
        gile,
Deceyved was, for al his jolitee.
For under hym another hadde shee,
A man of litel reputacioun,
Nat worth to Phebus in comparisoun.   200
The moore harm is, it happeth ofte so,
Of which ther cometh muchel harm and wo.
    And so bifel, whan Phebus was absent,
His wyf anon hath for hir lemman sent.   204
Hir lemman? Certes, this is a knavyssh speche!
Foryeveth it me, and that I yow biseche.
    The wise Plato seith, as ye may rede,
The word moot nede accorde with the dede.
If men shal telle proprely a thyng,
The word moost cosyn be to the werkyng.   210
I am a boystous man, right thus seye I,
Ther nys no difference, trewely,
Bitwixe a wyf that is of heigh degree,
If of hir body dishonest she bee,
And a povre wenche, oother than this—   215
If it so be they werke bothe amys—
But that the gentile, in estaat above,
She shal be cleped his lady, as in love;
And for that oother is a povre womman,   219
She shal be cleped his wenche or his lemman.
And, God it woot, myn owene deere brother,
Men leyn that oon as lowe as lith that oother.
    Right so bitwixe a titlelees tiraunt
And an outlawe, or a theef erraunt,
The same I seye, ther is no difference.   225

149. in . . . awayt, under watch. 152. verray nycetee, true folly. 153. spille, waste. 158. governaunce, behavior. 160. embrace, clasp. 161. As to, so as to. destreyne, constrain. 164. corage, inclination. 172. doon his bisynesse, exert itself. 178. weyveth, abandons. 181. lust, desire. 182. fleemeth, puts to flight. 183. vileyns kynde, villein's nature. 186. hir lust, she desires. make, mate. 189. likerous, lecherous. 193. newefangel, eager for novelty. with meschaunce, a curse upon it. 195. sowneth into, conduces to. 197. jolitee, cheerfulness, good qualities. 200. Nat worth, unworthy. 204. lemman, paramour. 210. werkyng, deed. 211. boystous, plain, rude. 214. dishonest, lewd, immoral. 222. leyn, set. lith, lies. 223. titlelees, without title or claim, usurping. 224. erraunt, wandering, arrant.

To Alisaundre was toold this sentence,
That, for the tirant is of gretter myght,
By force of meynee, for to sleen dounright,
And brennen hous and hoom, and make al
    playn,
Lo, therfore is he cleped a capitayn;   230
And for the outlawe hath but smal meynee,
And may nat doon so greet an harm as he,
Ne brynge a contree to so greet mescheef,
Men clepen hym an outlawe or a theef.
But, for I am a man noght textueel,   235
I wol noght telle of textes never a deel;
I wol go to my tale, as I bigan.
Whan Phebus wyf had sent for hir lemman,
Anon they wroghten al hire lust volage.   239
    The white crowe, that heeng ay in the cage,
Biheeld hire werk, and seyde never a word.
And whan that hoom was come Phebus, the
    lord,
This crowe sang "Cokkow! cokkow!
    cokkow!"
"What, bryd!" quod Phebus, "what song
    syngestow?
Ne were thow wont so myrily to synge   245
That to myn herte it was a rejoysynge
To heere thy voys? Allas! what song is this?"
    "By God!" quod he, "I synge nat amys.
Phebus," quod he, "for al thy worthynesse,
For al thy beautee and thy gentilesse,   250
For al thy song and al thy mynstralcye,
For al thy waityng, blered is thyn yë
With oon of litel reputacioun,
Noght worth to thee, as in comparisoun,   254
The montance of a gnat, so moote I thryve!
For on thy bed thy wyf I saugh hym swyve."
    What wol ye moore? The crowe anon hym
    tolde,

By sadde tokenes and by wordes bolde,
How that his wyf had doon hire lecherye,
Hym to greet shame and to greet vileynye;   260
And tolde hym ofte he saugh it with his yën.
    This Phebus gan aweyward for to wryen,
And thoughte his sorweful herte brast atwo.
His bowe he bente, and sette therinne a flo,
And in his ire his wyf thanne hath he slayn.   265
This is th'effect, ther is namoore to sayn;
For sorwe of which he brak his mynstralcie,
Bothe harpe, and lute, and gyterne, and sautrie;
And eek he brak his arwes and his bowe,
And after that thus spak he to the crowe: 270
    "Traitour," quod he, "with tonge of scor-
    pioun,
Thou hast me broght to my confusioun;
Allas, that I was wroght! why nere I deed?
O deere wyf! o gemme of lustiheed!
That were to me so sad and eek so trewe,   275
Now listow deed, with face pale of hewe,
Ful giltelees, that dorste I swere, ywys!
O rakel hand, to doon so foule amys!
O trouble wit, o ire recchelees,
That unavysed smyteth giltelees!   280
O wantrust, ful of fals suspecioun,
Where was thy wit and thy discrecioun?
O every man, be war of rakelnesse!
Ne trowe no thyng withouten strong witnesse.
Smyt nat to soone, er that ye witen why,   285
And beeth avysed wel and sobrely
Er ye doon any execucioun
Upon youre ire for suspecioun.
Allas! a thousand folk hath rakel ire
Fully fordoon, and broght hem in the mire.   290
Allas! for sorwe I wol myselven slee!"
And to the crowe, "O false theef!" seyde he,
"I wol thee quite anon thy false tale.

---

226. Alisaundre. The story of Alexander occurs frequently in medieva literature. **227. for,** because. **gretter,** greater. **228. meynee,** body of followers. **229. brennen,** burn. **make al playn,** level everything to the ground. **230. cleped,** called. **235. textueel,** book-learned. **236. textes,** authorities. **239. volage,** giddy, inconstant. **240. heeng,** hung. **241. hire,** their. **252. waityng,** watching. **blered is thyn yë,** you have been hoodwinked. **255. montance,** amount, value. **moote,** may. **256. swyve,** have intercourse with. **258. sadde,** sufficient. **261. yën,** eyes. **262. wryen,** turn. **263. brast,** would burst. **264. flo,** arrow. **267. mynstralcie,** collection of musical instruments. **268. gyterne,** type of guitar. **sautrie,** psaltery. See note to A 296. **273. why nere I deed,** why might I not be dead. **274. lustiheed,** delight. **275. sad,** constant. **276. listow,** lyest thou. **278. rakel** rash. **279. trouble wit,** troubled mind. **281. wantrust,** distrust. **283. rakelnesse,** rashness. **285. witen,** know. **287. doon . . . execucion Upon youre ire,** give effect to your anger. **290. fordoon,** ruined. **293. quite anon,** requite immediately.

Thou songe whilom lyk a nyghtyngale;
Now shaltow, false theef, thy song forgon,   295
And eek thy white fetheres everichon,
Ne nevere in al thy lif ne shaltou speke.
Thus shal men on a traytour been awreke;
Thou and thyn ofspryng evere shul be blake,
Ne nevere sweete noyse shul ye make,   300
But evere crie agayn tempest and rayn,
In tokenynge that thurgh thee my wyf is slayn."
And to the crowe he stirte, and that anon,
And pulled his white fetheres everychon,   304
And made hym blak, and refte hym al his song,
And eek his speche, and out at dore hym slong
Unto the devel, which I hym bitake;
And for this caas been alle crowes blake.

Lordynges, by this ensample I yow preye,
Beth war, and taketh kepe what that ye seye:
Ne telleth nevere no man in youre lyf   311
How that another man hath dight his wyf;
He wol yow haten mortally, certeyn.
Daun Salomon, as wise clerkes seyn,
Techeth a man to kepen his tonge weel.   315
But, as I seyde, I am noght textueel.
But nathelees, thus taughte me my dame:
"My sone, thenk on the crowe, a Goddes name!
My sone, keep wel thy tonge, and keep thy
    freend.
A wikked tonge is worse than a feend;   320
My sone, from a feend men may hem blesse.
My sone, God of his endelees goodnesse
Walled a tonge with teeth and lippes eke,
For man sholde hym avyse what he speeke.
My sone, ful ofte, for to muche speche   325
Hath many a man been spilt, as clerkes teche;
But for litel speche avysely
Is no man shent, to speke generally.

My sone, thy tonge sholdestow restreyne   329
At alle tymes, but whan thou doost thy peyne
To speke of God, in honour and preyere.
The firste vertu, sone, if thou wolt leere,
Is to restreyne and kepe wel thy tonge;
Thus lerne children whan that they been yonge.
My sone, of muchel spekyng yvele avysed,   335
Ther lasse spekyng hadde ynough suffised,
Comth muchel harm; thus was me toold and
    taught.
In muchel speche synne wanteth naught.
Wostow wherof a rakel tonge serveth?
Right as a swerd forkutteth and forkerveth   340
An arm a-two, my deere sone, right so
A tonge kutteth freendshipe al a-two.
A janglere is to God abhomynable.
Reed Salomon, so wys and honurable;
Reed David in his psalmes, reed Senekke.   345
My sone, spek nat, but with thyn heed thou
    bekke.
Dissimule as thou were deef, if that thou heere
A janglere speke of perilous mateere.
The Flemyng seith, and lerne it if thee leste,
That litel janglyng causeth muchel reste.   350
My sone, if thou no wikked word hast seyd,
Thee thar nat drede for to be biwreyd;
But he that hath mysseyd, I dar wel sayn,
He may by no wey clepe his word agayn.   354
Thyng that is seyd is seyd, and forth it gooth,
Though hym repente, or be hym nevere so looth.
He is his thral to whom that he hath sayd
A tale of which he is now yvele apayd.
My sone, be war, and be noon auctour newe
Of tidynges, wheither they been false or trewe.
Wherso thou come, amonges hye or lowe,   361
Kepe wel thy tonge, and thenk upon the crowe."

Heere is ended the Maunciples Tale of the Crowe.

298. awreke, avenged. **299. blake,** black. **300. noyse,** sound. **301. agayn,** before, in anticipation of. **303. stirte,** sprang. **305. refte hym,** deprived him of. **306. slong,** slung. **307. which I hym bitake,** to whom I commit him. **310. kepe,** heed. **312. dight,** lain with. **317. dame,** mother. **318. a,** in. **321. blesse,** cross themselves. **327. avysely,** advisedly. **328. shent,** disgraced. **330. peyne,** exertion. **332. leere,** learn. Much of this whole moralizing passage echoes the *Distichs of Cato* and its glosses, which Chaucer doubtless became familiar with as a schoolboy. Cf. R. Hazelton, "Chaucer and Cato," *Speculum,* xxxv. 357–80. **335. yvele avysed,** ill advised. **336. Ther,** where. **338. wanteth naught,** is not wanting. **339. Wostow,** knowest thou. **340. forkutteth, forkerveth.** The prefix *for-* is intensive. **346. bekke,** nod. **347. Dissimule,** dissemble. **348. janglere,** a loud or quarrelsome talker. **349. The Flemyng,** the Flemish man. **352. thar,** need. **biwreyd,** betrayed. **354. clepe,** recall. **358. yvele apayd,** displeased. **359. auctour,** author.

Group I (Fragment X)

The Parson's Prologue

Heere folweth the Prologe of the Persouns Tale.

By that the Maunciple hadde his tale al
    ended,
The sonne fro the south lyne was descended
So lowe that he nas nat, to my sighte,
Degreës nyne and twenty as in highte.
Foure of the clokke it was tho, as I gesse,   5
For ellevene foot, or litel moore or lesse,
My shadwe was at thilke tyme, as there,
Of swiche feet as my lengthe parted were
In sixe feet equal of proporcioun.
Therwith the moones exaltacioun,   10
I meene Libra, alwey gan ascende,
As we were entryng at a thropes ende;
For which oure Hoost, as he was wont to gye,
As in this caas, oure joly compaignye,
Seyde in this wise: "Lordynges everichoon,   15
Now lakketh us no tales mo than oon.
Fulfilled is my sentence and my decree;
I trowe that we han herd of ech degree;
Almoost fulfild is al myn ordinaunce.
I pray to God, so yeve hym right good
    chaunce,

That telleth this tale to us lustily.   21
  Sire preest," quod he, "artow a vicary?
Or arte a person? sey sooth, by thy fey!
Be what thou be, ne breke thou nat oure pley;
For every man, save thou, hath toold his tale.   25
Unbokele, and shewe us what is in thy male;
For, trewely, me thynketh by thy cheere
Thou sholdest knytte up wel a greet mateere.
Telle us a fable anon, for cokkes bones!"
  This Persoun answerde, al atones,   30
"Thou getest fable noon ytoold for me;
For Paul, that writeth unto Thymothee,
Repreveth hem that weyven soothfastnesse,
And tellen fables and swich wrecchednesse.
Why sholde I sowen draf out of my fest,   35
Whan I may sowen whete, if that me lest?
For which I seye, if that yow list to heere
Moralitee and vertuous mateere,
And thanne that ye wol yeve me audience,
I wol ful fayn, at Cristes reverence,   40
Do yow plesaunce leefful, as I kan.
But trusteth wel, I am a Southren man,

---

1. Maunciple. Since the Manciple's short tale is told early in the morning (cf. H 16) and it is now late afternoon (l. 5), the word *Maunciple* presents obvious difficulties. In the Hengwrt MS it is written over an erasure. Other MSS have *Yeman, Marchaunt, Frankelyn*. All readings are due to early scribe-editors and it is useless to try to draw conclusions from them as to Chaucer's intention. **2. south lyne,** another name for the meridian, which passes through the north and south points of the horizon. The sun passes the meridian at noon and has descended, according to l. 4, until it is only 29° above the western horizon. The time was then, as l. 5 says, four o'clock and an object six feet high would cast a shadow eleven feet. **5. tho,** then. **7. as there,** in that location. **8. Of swiche feet.** This does not mean that Chaucer was six feet tall, but that if his own height were divided into six equal parts, his shadow would extend a distance of eleven such parts. **10. the moones exaltacioun.** This is a difficult passage, since Libra is not the exaltation of the moon but of Saturn. (The exaltation of a planet is that sign in which it exerts its greatest influence.) The moon's exaltation was really Taurus. Either Chaucer or an early scribe made a mistake. **11. alwey gan ascende,** kept steadily ascending (above the horizon). **12. a thropes ende,** the end of a village. **13. gye,** direct. **16. Now lakketh us . . .** The Host is, of course, speaking in anticipation of the completion of tales which were never written. Moreover, the original plan set forth in *The General Prologue* has given place to a single tale from each pilgrim. Cf. l. 25 below. **18. of,** from. **degree,** rank. He is speaking of the various classes to which the pilgrims belonged. **20. chaunce,** fortune. **21. lustily,** pleasantly, for our pleasure. **22. vicary,** vicar. **23. person,** parson. **26. male,** bag. **31. for,** by. **33. weyven,** abandon. **35. draf,** chaff. **fest,** fist. **41. plesaunce leefful,** lawful pleasure.

I kan nat geeste 'rum, ram, ruf,' by lettre,
Ne, God woot, rym holde I but litel bettre;
And therfore, if yow list—I wol nat glose— 45
I wol yow telle a myrie tale in prose
To knytte up al this feeste, and make an ende.
And Jhesu, for his grace, wit me sende
To shewe yow the wey, in this viage,
Of thilke parfit glorious pilgrymage 50
That highte Jerusalem celestial.
And if ye vouche sauf, anon I shal
Bigynne upon my tale, for which I preye
Telle youre avys, I kan no bettre seye.

But nathelees, this meditacioun
I putte it ay under correccioun 55
Of clerkes, for I am nat textueel;
I take but the sentence, trusteth weel.
Therfore I make protestacioun

That I wol stonde to correccioun." 60
Upon this word we han assented soone,
For, as it seemed, it was for to doone,
To enden in som vertuous sentence,
And for to yeve hym space and audience;
And bade oure Hoost he sholde to hym
seye 65
That alle we to telle his tale hym preye.
Oure Hoost hadde the wordes for us alle:
"Sire preest," quod he, "now faire yow
bifalle!
Telleth," quod he, "youre meditacioun.
But hasteth yow, the sonne wole adoun; 70
Beth fructuous, and that in litel space,
And to do wel God sende yow his grace!
Sey what yow list, and we wol gladly heere."
And with that word he seyde in this manere.

[The "myrie tale in prose" which the Parson promises is actually a treatise or sermon on Penitence and the Seven Deadly Sins. Since the present volume is limited to Chaucer's poetry, it is not included. In all the manuscripts that are not incomplete at the end it is followed by what has come to be known as Chaucer's *Retraction*. In it the poet expresses regret for those of his writings that he considered "worldly vanities" and prays for forgiveness. Its genuineness has been questioned, but there seems to be no good reason for rejecting it. It was obviously written near the end of his life and is far from being without parallel in the literature of the Middle Ages and of later times. Since it is short and of considerable interest, it is here printed. For an excellent survey of critical opinion on the *Retraction* see the article of James D. Gordon in *Studies in Medieval Literature*, ed. MacEdward Leach (Philadelphia, 1961), pp. 81–96.]

43. geeste 'rum, ram, ruf,' tell a tale in alliterative verse, which was at this time experiencing a revival in the North, and to a lesser extent in the West. The reason for the Parson's remark is not obvious, since none of the preceding tales are in this form. Chaucer might have planned a tale to precede *The Parson's Tale* which would have used or parodied the measure, but since the Parson holds rime but little better he may be merely contrasting the two current types of verse with prose. **45. glose,** mince words. **54. avys,** opinion, assent. **57. textueel,** learned in authorities. **58. sentence,** meaning. **62. for to doone,** the thing to do. **65. bade,** we bade. **71. fructuous,** fruitful. **73–4. Sey what yow list . . .** In all the MSS these two lines follow l. 68, but are here shifted in accordance with Manly's suggestion (*Cant. Tales*, p. 656). They may originally have been added in the margin.

Chaucer's Retraction

Heere taketh the makere of this book his leve.

Now preye I to hem alle that herkne this litel tretys or rede, that if ther be any thyng in it that liketh hem, that therof they thanken oure Lord Jhesu Crist, of whom procedeth al wit and al goodnesse. And if ther be any thyng that displese hem, I preye hem also that they arrette it to the defaute of myn unkonnynge, and nat to my wyl, that wolde ful fayn have seyd bettre if I hadde had konnynge. For oure book seith, "Al that is writen is writen for oure doctrine," and that is myn entente. Wherfore I biseke yow mekely, for the mercy of God, that ye preye for me that Crist have mercy on me and foryeve me my giltes; and namely of my translacions and enditynges of worldly vanitees, the whiche I revoke in my retracciouns: as is the book of Troilus; the book also of Fame; the book of the xxv. Ladies; the book of the Duchesse; the book of Seint Valentynes day of the Parlement of Briddes; the tales of Caunterbury, thilke that sownen into synne; the book of the Leoun; and many another book, if they were in my remembrance, and many a song and many a leccherous lay; that Crist for his grete mercy foryeve me the synne. But of the translacioun of Boece de Consolacione, and othere bookes of legendes of seintes, and omelies, and moralitee, and devocioun, that thanke I oure Lord Jhesu Crist and his blisful mooder, and alle the seintes of hevene, bisekynge hem that they from hennes forth unto my lyves ende sende me grace to biwayle my giltes, and to studie to the salvacioun of my soule; and graunte me grace of verray penitence, confessioun and satisfaccioun to doon in this present lyf, thurgh the benigne grace of hym that is kyng of kynges and preest over alle preestes, that boghte us with the precious blood of his herte; so that I may been oon of hem at the day of doome that shulle be saved. *Qui cum patre et Spiritu Sancto vivit et regnat Deus per omnia secula. Amen.*

Heere is ended the book of the tales of Caunterbury, compiled by Geffrey Chaucer, of whos soule Jhesu Crist have mercy. Amen.

Short Poems

TO ROSEMOUNDE

A Balade

Madame, ye ben of al beaute shryne
As fer as cercled is the mapemounde,
For as the cristall glorious ye shyne,
And lyke ruby ben your chekes rounde.
Therwith ye ben so mery and so jocounde   5
That at a revell whan that I se you daunce,
It is an oynement unto my wounde,
Thogh ye to me ne do no daliaunce.

For thogh I wepe of teres ful a tyne,
Yet may that wo myn herte nat confounde;   10
Your semy voys, that ye so small out-twyne,
Maketh my thoght in joy and blys habounde.
So curtaysly I go, with love bounde,

That to myself I sey, in my penaunce,
"Suffyseth me to love you, Rosemounde,   15
Thogh ye to me ne do no daliaunce."

Nas never pyk walwed in galauntyne
As I in love am walwed and ywounde,
For which ful ofte I of myself devyne
That I am trewe Tristam the secounde.   20
My love may not refreyde nor affounde;
I brenne ay in amorous plesaunce.
Do what you lyst, I wyl your thral be founde,
Thogh ye to me ne do no daliaunce.

TREGENTIL————CHAUCER.

CHAUCERS WORDES UNTO ADAM, HIS OWNE SCRIVEYN

Adam scriveyn, if ever it thee bifalle
Boece or Troylus for to wryten newe,
Under thy long lokkes thou most have the
    scalle,

But after my makyng thou wryte more trewe;
So ofte a daye I mot thy werk renewe,   5
It to correcte and eke to rubbe and scrape;
And al is thorugh thy negligence and rape.

To Rosemounde. This little poem is one of the many "balades, roundels, virelayes" which Alceste in *The Legend of Good Women* says that Chaucer wrote. It is a courtly love lyric to an unknown lady, written, however, in a rather bantering mood. It is quite likely an early piece, as is generally thought. For a useful commentary on the text see H. Kökeritz. *MLN*, LXIII. 310–18. **2. mapemounde.** Early maps of the world were often enclosed in an oval or circular form. **8. do no daliaunce,** pay no attention, show no favor. **9. tyne,** tub, vat. **11. semy,** thin, delicate. **small,** quietly, slightly. The MS reads *fynall*, an easy scribal blunder. **out-twyne,** give utterance to, *lit.* twist out. **17. pyk,** pike. **walwed,** immersed. **galauntyne,** a kind of sauce, made of wine, vinegar, and spices, thickened with bread and boiled. See recipe in *EETS* 91, p. 101. **20. Tristam,** Tristan, the lover of Iseult. **21. refreyde nor affounde,** cool nor grow cold. **22. brenne,** burn. In the unique MS *an* is inserted above the line between *in* and *amorous*.

Chaucers Wordes unto Adam. 3. scalle, a skin disease, esp. of the scalp. **4. makyng,** composing. **7. rape,** haste.

GENTILESSE

Moral Balade of Chaucier

The firste stok, fader of gentilesse—
What man that claymeth gentil for to be
Must folowe his trace, and alle his wittes dresse
Vertu to sewe, and vyces for to flee.
For unto vertu longeth dignitee,
And nought the revers, saufly dar I deme,
Al were he mytre, croune, or diademe.

This firste stok was ful of rightwisnesse,
Trewe of his word, sobre, pitous, and free,
Clene of his gooste, and loved besinesse,   10
Ageinst the vyce of slouthe, in honestee;

And, but his heir love vertu, as dide he,
He is nought gentil, thogh he riche seme,
Al were he mytre, croune, or diademe.

Vyce may wel be heir to old richesse;   15
But ther may no man, as men may wel see,
Bequethe his heir his vertuous noblesse—
That is appropred unto no degree
But to the firste fader in magestee,
That maketh hem his heyres that him queme—   20
Al were he mytre, croune, or diademe.   21

TRUTH

Balade de Bon Conseyl

Fle fro the prees, and dwelle with sothfastnesse,
Suffise unto thy good, though it be smal;
For hord hath hate, and clymbyng tykelnesse,
Prees hath envye, and wele blent over-al;
Savour no more than thee bihove shal;   5
Reule wel thyself, that other folk canst rede;
And trouthe thee shal delivere, it is no drede.

Tempest thee nought al croked to redresse,
In trust of hir that turneth as a bal:
Gret reste stant in litel besynesse;   10
Be war also to spurne ayeyns an al;
Stryve not, as doth the crokke with the wal.
Daunte thyself, that dauntest otheres dede;
And trouthe thee shal delivere, it is no drede.

Gentilesse. The theme of this little poem, the nature of true nobility, is found also in the curtain-lecture delivered by the old woman in *The Wife of Bath's Tale* (D 1109 ff) and goes back to Boethius. **1. The firste stok,** God or Christ. **3. trace,** path, footsteps. **4. sewe,** follow. **5. longeth dignitee,** worthiness pertains. **7. Al were,** Although he wear. **10. gooste,** spirit. **15. old richesse,** inherited wealth. **18. appropred . . .,** made the peculiar possession of no single rank. **20. queme,** please.

Truth. The punning references to *beste* and *Vache* (cow) were explained by Edith Rickert (*MP,* XI. 209–25) as directed toward Sir Philip la Vache (1346–1408), married to the daughter of Chaucer's friend, Sir Lewis Clifford, and associated with many other acquaintances of the poet. Although Vache acquired considerable wealth and was unusually fortunate in his official employment, he may have experienced a minor set-back around 1386–90. If the circumstances of this brief period occasioned the poem, they may suggest its approximate date, but a number of allusions are not explained by what we know of Vache's life. The text is based on B.M. Add. MS 10,340, the only one of the twenty-two MSS containing the Envoy. **1. prees,** competitive crowd. **2. Suffise unto . . .,** be satisfied with your possessions. This is a rare use of the verb. The Add. MS reads *Suffise thin owen thing.* **3. tykelnesse,** insecurity. **4. wele,** prosperity. **blent,** blinds. **over-al,** everywhere. **5. Savour,** have a taste for. **6. rede,** counsel. **7. And trouthe thee shal delivere.** Cf. *John,* 8:32. **drede,** doubt. **8. Tempest thee . . .** Be not violently moved to redress all that is not straight. **9. hir,** the goddess Fortune. **11. spurne,** kick. **al,** awl. **13. Daunte,** control.

That thee is sent, receyve in buxumnesse; 15
The wrastling for this world axeth a fal.
Here is non home, here nis but wyldernesse:
Forth, pilgrym, forth! Forth, beste, out of thy
    stal!
Know thy contree, look up, thank God of al;
Hold the heye wey, and lat thy gost thee
    lede; 20
And trouthe thee shal delivere, it is no drede.

Envoy

Therfore, thou Vache, leve thine old wrechede-
    nesse;
Unto the world leve now to be thral;
Crie him mercy, that of his hye godnesse
Made thee of nought, and in especial 25
Draw unto him, and pray in general
For thee, and eek for other, hevenlych mede;
And trouthe thee shal delivere, it is no drede.

LAK OF STEDFASTNESSE

Balade

Somtyme the world was so stedfast and
    stable
That mannes word was obligacioun;
And now it is so fals and deceivable
That word and dede, as in conclusioun,
Ben nothing lyk, for turned up so doun 5
Is al this world for mede and wilfulnesse,
That al is lost for lak of stedfastnesse.

What maketh this world to be so variable
But lust that folk have in dissensioun?
For among us now a man is holde unable, 10
But if he can, by som collusioun,
Do his neighbour wrong or oppressioun.
What causeth this but wilful wrecchednesse,
That al is lost for lak of stedfastnesse?

Trouthe is put doun, resoun is holden fable; 15
Vertu hath now no dominacioun;
Pitee exyled, no man is merciable;
Through covetyse is blent discrecioun.
The world hath mad a permutacioun
Fro right to wrong, fro trouthe to fikelnesse, 20
That al is lost for lak of stedfastnesse.

Lenvoy to King Richard

O prince, desire to be honourable,
Cherish thy folk and hate extorcioun!
Suffre nothing that may be reprevable
To thyn estat don in thy regioun. 25
Shew forth thy swerd of castigacioun,
Dred God, do law, love trouthe and worthinesse,
And wed thy folk ageyn to stedfastnesse.

15. That, that which. **buxumnesse,** humility. **16. axeth,** asks. **19. thy contree,** thy proper sphere. **20. gost,** moral sense, conscience. **23. leve,** cease. **27. mede,** reward. It has been suggested that *mede* be interpreted here as "meadow" as a continuation of the punning references mentioned above. See J. F. Ragan, *MLN,* LXVIII. 534.

    Lak of Stedfastnesse. The theme of this, as of several of Chaucer's short poems, is quite conventional. Only the *Lenvoy to King Richard* gives it a more personal quality. Shirley says it was written in Chaucer's last years, but it would be at least as applicable to the period of vigorous opposition to Richard's favorites (1386–88) or the moment when he asserted his right to rule in his own name (1389). **4. as in conclusioun,** as things turn out. **5. up so doun,** upside down. **6. mede,** bribery. **10. unable,** lacking in ability. **13. wrecchednesse,** baseness. **18. blent,** blinded. **24. Suffre . . . don,** suffer to be done.

LENVOY DE CHAUCER A SCOGAN

Tobroken been the statutz hye in hevene
That creat were eternally to dure,
Syth that I see the bryghte goddis sevene
Mowe wepe and wayle, and passioun
    endure,
As may in erthe a mortal creature.   5
Allas, fro whennes may thys thing procede,
Of which errour I deye almost for drede?

By word eterne whilom was yshape
That fro the fyfte sercle, in no manere,
Ne myghte a drope of teeres doun escape.   10
But now so wepith Venus in hir spere
That with hir teeres she wol drenche us here.
Allas! Scogan, this is for thyn offence;
Thow causest this diluge of pestilence.

Hastow not seyd, in blaspheme of the
    goddes.   15
Thurgh pride, or thrugh thy grete rekelnesse,
Swich thing as in the lawe of love forbode is,
That, for thy lady sawgh nat thy distresse,
Therfore thow yave hir up at Michelmesse?
Allas! Scogan, of olde folk ne yonge   20
Was never erst Scogan blamed for his tonge.

Thow drowe in skorn Cupide eke to record
Of thilke rebel word that thou hast spoken,
For which he wol no lenger be thy lord.
And, Scogan, though his bowe be nat
    broken,
He wol nat with his arwes been ywroken   26
On the, ne me, ne noon of oure figure;
We shul of him have neyther hurt ne cure.

Now certes, frend, I drede of thyn unhap,
Lest for thy gilt the wreche of Love procede   30
On alle hem that ben hoor and rounde of
    shap,
That ben so lykly folk in love to spede.
Than shal we for oure labour han no mede;
But wel I wot, thow wolt answere and saye:
"Lo, olde Grisel lyst to ryme and playe!"   35

Nay, Scogan, say not so, for I m'excuse—
God helpe me so!—in no ryme, dowteles,
Ne thynke I never of slepe to wake my muse,
That rusteth in my shethe stille in pees.
While I was yong, I put hir forth in prees;   40
But al shal passe that men prose or ryme;
Take every man hys turn, as for his tyme.

Lenvoy de Chaucer a Scogan. Henry Scogan was a younger contemporary of Chaucer's, a courtier, and a poet in a small way. The little *jeu d' esprit* addressed to him is a verse epistle. Chaucer chides him for a breach of the courtly love code—renouncing his lady because she will not pity his distress, possibly in the spirit of George Wither. The present torrential rains are Venus's tears. We are both past the time of young love. At our age there is no need to fear Cupid's arrows, but he may take vengeance on us in our poetry, spelling the end of reward. As for me, my muse is rusting in its sheath. There was a time when this wasn't so, but all things pass away. Scogan, you are at the stream's head—at court; I am at the end of that stream, "forgotten in solitary wilderness"—in Greenwich. Remember what Cicero said about friendship. Put in a good word for me, if the opportunity presents itself, And never again commit an act in defiance of love. The poem is generally dated 1393, a year marked by heavy rains and floods. **1. Tobroken been . . .** The laws of heaven have been broken. **2. dure,** endure, last. **3. goddis sevene,** the gods identified with the seven planets. **6. Allas, fro whennes . . .,** *i.e.* what fault has brought about this situation? **7. errour,** anomaly. **8. eterne,** eternal. **yshape,** established. **9. fyfte sercle,** the circle of Venus. **11. spere,** sphere. **14. diluge of pestilence,** pestilential dèluge. **16. rekelnesse,** rashness. **18. for,** because. **19. yave,** gave. **20. of,** by. **21. erst,** before. **22. drowe,** drew. **to record,** as a witness. **26. ywroken,** revenged. **28. hurt ne cure.** Cupid's arrows could either hurt or heal. **29. drede of thyn unhap,** am frightened by thy mishap. **30. wreche,** vengeance. **32. lykly,** suitable. **33. mede,** reward. **35. olde Grisel,** old Gray-head. **38. of,** from. **40. in prees,** in the crowd.

Envoy

Scogan, that knelest at the stremes hed
Of grace, of alle honour and worthynesse,
In th'ende of which streme I am dul as ded,　　45

Forgete in solytarie wildernesse,—
Yet, Scogan, thenke on Tullius kyndenesse;
Mynne thy frend, there it may fructyfye!
Farewel, and loke thow never eft Love dyffye.

LENVOY DE CHAUCER A BUKTON

My maister Bukton, whan of Criste our kynge
Was axed what is trouthe or sothfastnesse,
He nat a word answerde to that axinge,
As who saith, 'No man is al trewe," I gesse.
And therfore, though I highte to expresse　　5
The sorwe and wo that is in mariage,
I dar not writen of it no wikkednesse,
Lest I myself falle eft in swich dotage.

I wol nat seyn how that hyt is the cheyne
Of Sathanas, on which he gnaweth evere;　　10
But I dar seyn, were he out of his peyne,
As by his wille he wolde be bounde nevere.
But thilke doted fool that eft hath levere
Ycheyned be than out of prisoun crepe,
God lete him never fro his wo dissevere,　　15
Ne no man him bewayle, though he wepe!

But yet, lest thow do worse, take a wyf;
Bet ys to wedde than brenne in worse wise.
But thow shal have sorwe on thy flessh, thy lyf,
And ben thy wives thral, as seyn these wise;　　20
And yf that hooly writ may nat suffyse,
Experience shal the teche, so may happe,
That the were lever to be take in Frise
Than eft to falle of weddynge in the trappe.

Envoy

This lytel writ, proverbes, or figure　　25
I sende yow, take kepe of hyt, I rede;
Unwise is he that kan no wele endure.
If thow be siker, put the nat in drede.
The Wyf of Bathe I pray yow that ye rede
Of this matere that we have on honde.　　30
God graunte yow your lyf frely to lede
In fredam; for ful hard is to be bonde.

43. the stremes hed. A marginal gloss in all three MSS reads "Windsor." **46. Forgete,** forgotten. **solytarie wilder-nesse.** A marginal gloss in the MSS indicates that this refers to Greenwich, where Chaucer was probably living at this time. **47. Tullius kyndenesse.** It has been suggested that the reference is to Tullus Hostilius, the third legendary king of Rome, who was celebrated for his friendship to the poor and who is called Tullius Hostillius in *WBT* (D 1166), but it seems on the whole more likely that Chaucer is thinking of Cicero's *De Amicitia,* referred to in *RR,* 5405–17. The render-ing of this passage in the English *Romaunt* (ll. 5285 ff.) fits the present allusion even better. **48. Mynne,** remember. **fructyfye,** bear fruit. **49. eft,** again.

Lenvoy de Chaucer a Bukton. The occasion that called forth this whimsical little poem was the intended marriage of one of Chaucer's friends. The allusion to Friesland helps to fix the date. According to Froissart the Frisians were accustomed to exchange their prisoners, but any that could not be exchanged were put to death. An expedition against Friesland was being organized in England in August 1396, which would give point to the statement that being taken prisoner in Friesland might prove preferable to the experience of marriage. Of the Buktons known to have been in England at this time, two have been advanced as the subject of the poem—Robert Bukton of Suffolk and Sir Peter Bukton of Yorkshire. Both were cour-tiers and both appear rather frequently in the records. Of the two, Sir Peter Bukton was more often associated with Chaucer's circle of friends and with the house of Lancaster. In 1396 he would have been forty-six years old. For the fullest discussion of the two candidates see E. P. Kuhl, *PMLA,* xxxviii. 115–32. It should be pointed out that the emphasis on the woes of marriage is not to be taken too seriously. As Kittredge observed (*Chaucer and his Poetry,* p. 34), "The thing may well have been read at a farewell dinner, amidst the inextinguishable laughter of the blessed bachelors." **5. highte,** promised. **8. Lest I . . .** Chaucer's wife had died in 1387. **eft,** again. **12. As by his wille,** willingly. **13. hath levere,** would rather. **15. dissevere,** part from. **16. bewayle,** feel sorry for. **18. Bet ys to wedde . . .** Cf. "for it is better to marry than to burn" (*1 Corinthians,* 7:9). **22. so may happe,** as it may happen. **23. to be take in Frise,** *i.e.* taken prisoner in Friesland. See introductory note. **25. proverbes,** collection of proverbs. **figure,** presentation. **26. kepe,** heed. **rede,** advise. **27. wele,** prosperity. **29. The Wyf of Bathe.** This is interesting evidence that although the *CT* was still unfinished, *The Wife of Bath's Prologue* was already in circulation and could be read. On the date of the Marriage Group see the introduction to *CT* (pp. 234–5). In 1396 it was relatively new and yet apparently well known. **32. bonde,** a slave.

THE COMPLAYNT OF CHAUCER TO HIS PURSE

To yow, my purse, and to noon other wight
Complayne I, for ye be my lady dere!
I am so sory, now that ye been lyght;
For certes, but ye make me hevy chere,
Me were as leef be layd upon my bere;   5
For which unto your mercy thus I crye:
Beth hevy ageyn, or elles mot I dye!

Now voucheth sauf this day, or hyt be nyght,
That I of yow the blisful soun may here,
Or see your colour lyk the sonne bryght,   10
That of yelownesse hadde never pere.
Ye be my lyf, ye be myn hertes stere,
Quene of comfort and of good companye:
Beth hevy ageyn, or elles moot I dye!

Now purse, that ben to me my lyves lyght   15
And saveour, as doun in this worlde here,
Out of this toune helpe me thurgh your myght,
Syn that ye wole nat ben my tresorere;
For I am shave as nye as any frere.
But yet I pray unto your curtesye: 20
Beth hevy agen, or elles moot I dye!

Lenvoy de Chaucer

O conquerour of Brutes Albyoun,
Which that by lyne and free eleccioun
Been verray kyng, this song to yow I sende;
And ye, that mowen alle oure harmes amende,
Have mynde upon my supplicacioun!   26

The Complaynt . . . to his Purse. This charming little complaint with its appeal to Henry IV in the Envoy is not without parallels in Machaut, Deschamps, and other French poets. It is couched in the form of a love poem, the poet's purse being represented as his "lady dere." While the first three stanzas might have been written at almost any time, the Envoy can be dated quite soon after the acceptance by Parliament of John of Gaunt's son as king. This was on Sept. 30, 1399. The poet had not long to wait. The answer came on Oct. 13, (not Oct. 3, as usually stated) in the form of a grant of forty marks a year. **7. mot,** must. **10. your colour,** of gold. **12. stere,** rudder. **17. Out of this toune.** After receiving the grant Chaucer leased a house in the suburb of Westminster. **22. O conquerour.** Early in 1399 when John of Gaunt died, Richard II seized his lands, which should have passed to Gaunt's son Henry, because the latter had been exiled the year before. Henry returned to England at the head of a small force; with the support of a large part of the nobility he captured the king, imprisoned him in the tower, and forced him to abdicate. **Brutes Albyoun,** Albion (England), supposedly founded by the legendary Brutus. **23. by lyne,** Henry was the grandson of Edward III. **free eleccioun,** the action of Parliament. **24. verray,** true. **25. mowen,** may.

GLOSSARY

GLOSSARY

THE GLOSSARY includes all words that have become obsolete or are used in senses not obvious from their modern use. Where words are included because of meanings no longer current, the modern meaning has not necessarily been noted.

The entry word represents with few exceptions the commonest spelling in the texts. Cross-references have been added where it seemed necessary. This is the period when a final *-e* from the oblique cases, especially the dative, was being added to the nominative form of nouns indiscriminately. If the only instances of a word in the text have such an inorganic *-e* (*e.g. tyde*), it is so entered in the Glossary. Where forms with and without the vowel occur they are entered like the noun *soor(e)*. Likewise adjectives which occur only in the weak or definite form with inflectional *-e* (*stoure, streite, sweynte*) are entered under the spelling found in the text, generally with a label. Infinitives are entered under the form actually found, with or without final *-n*—*dispende, dispoillen, disporte(n)*. For all such matters the student is referred to the section of the introduction on Language.

Dialectal and spelling variants likely to trouble the student have usually been recorded with a cross-reference to the main entry, but in a few instances have been given separate entry (*lest, list*) because of the number and variety of uses. Common spelling variants like *aunce—ance, aunt—ant, aunde—ande, aunge—ange, ioun—ion, ye—ie* are disregarded.

Grammatical labels such as *n* (noun), *v* (verb), *pp* (past participle) require no explanation. In those cases where for brevity the label *pt s* (preterite singular) is used, it is to be assumed that the first or third person is meant. Line references are given in sufficient number to enable the student to examine the form or meaning in context. Where the references record only a small fraction of the instances that occur this is indicated by "etc."

The following symbols are used: BD (*Book of the Duchess*), HF (*Hous of Fame*), PF (*Parlement of Foules*), TC (*Troilus and Criseyde*), LGW (*Legend of Good Women*), Adam (*Chaucer's Words unto Adam*), Buk (*Lenvoy de Chaucer a Bukton*), Gent (*Gentilesse*), Lak (*Lak of Stedfastnesse*), Purse (*Complaynt of Chaucer to his Purse*), Rosem (*To Rosemounde*), Scogan (*Lenvoy de Chaucer a Scogan*). References to *The Canterbury Tales* are by Group and line, *e.g.* A 26, F 310.

The student may be reminded that the prefix *be-* is usually spelled *bi-* in Middle English (*bifalle, bigynne, bileve*, etc.).

GLOSSARY

A

a *indef art* a BD 36, etc.; **al a** a whole E 1165.

a *prep* on A 3516, B 1370, D 50; in A 2934; **a sooth** in truth TC 5.1295; **a Goddes name** A 854, H 318. See **a-morwe, a-nyght**.

aas *n* ace, one (in dice) B 3851.

abate *v* bring down, destroy B 3780.

abaved *ppl adj* abashed BD 614.

abaysed *pp* disconcerted E 1108; startled TC 3.1233; **abayst** abashed TC 3.94, E 317; embarrassed E 1011.

abedde *adv* in bed TC 3.693, B 1367, D 407.

abegge *v* pay for it A 3938.

a-begged a-begging F 1580.

abet *n* abetting TC 2.357.

abeye *v* pay for C 100. See **abyen**.

abit see **abyden**.

a-blakeberyed a-blackberrying, wandering aimlessly C 406.

able *adj* able BD 786; ready BD 779; fit LGW 320, A 167.

abood, abod *n* delay A 965, TC 5.1307.

abood see **abyden**.

aboughte see **abyen**.

aboute *adv* about, around A 621; round about A 488; in turn A 890; **been aboute** undertake, engage in A 1142.

aboute(n) *prep* about, around A 158, E 1106, etc.

above *prep* above PF 394, A 1962.

above *adj & adv* above, on high A 1599, F 795, 989.

aboven *prep* above A 53, etc.

abregge *v* abridge, shorten TC 3.262, 295, A 2999, E 1657.

abreyde *v* start (from sleep), wake up TC 5.520; come to HF 559, TC 3.1113; **abreyd, abrayd** *str pt s* HF 110, B 192; **abreyde** *later pt s* TC 1.724, B 4198, E 1061.

abroche *v* pierce, open D 177.

abrood *adv* spread out F 441.

abusioun *n* deception B 214; absurdity, outrage TC 4.990, 1060.

abyden, abi- *v* wait, await TC 5.1155, A 927; remain TC 1.474; desist, refrain F 1522; **abideth, abit** *3 s* remains TC 2.987, G 1175; waits for TC 1.1091; **abod** *pt s* awaited TC 4.156; stopped HF 1602; experienced BD 247; **abood** waited

LGW 309; **abiden** *pp* TC 2.935, A 2982; **abyd** *imp s* wait A 3129; **abydeth** *imp pl* wait B 1175.

abye(n) *v* pay for A 4393, B 2012; **aboughte** *pt s* suffered A 2303; **aboughte** *pt pl* paid for, purchased TC 5.1756; **aboght** *pp* redeemed A 3100; atoned for C 503.

a-caterwawed a-caterwauling D 354.

accesse *n* attack (of illness), fever TC 2.1315, 1543, 1578.

accident *n* occurrence, circumstance TC 3.918; accidental sign E 607; appearance C 539; the non-essential, the uncertain TC 4.1505.

accomplice *v* accomplish A 2864.

accordant *adj* corresponding F 103. See **acordaunt**.

accusement *n* disclosure, betrayal TC 4.556.

accusour *n* accuser, blamer LGW 353; betrayer, revealer TC 3.1450.

achaat *n* purchase A 571.

achatours *n pl* buyers, purchasing agents A 568.

ache *n* ache; **ache of hed** TC 4.728.

achekkked *pp* checked HF 2093.

acheve *v* achieve TC 4.79; **acheved** *pt s* HF 463; **acheved** *pp* HF 1738, TC 2.1392.

acloyeth *3 s* overburdens PF 517.

a-compas *adv* in a circle LGW 300.

acord *n* agreement LGW 159, A 3082; arrangement A 838; **of acord** in agreement PF 381; **of oon acord** in complete agreement C 25; in harmony BD 305, LGW 169.

acordaunt *adj* according A 37; suitable F 1290; in harmony (with) PF 203, A 3363.

acorde, acc- *v* accord, agree PF 608, TC 4.1519, H 208; harmonize TC 5.446; **acorde** *1 s* grant LGW 3; **acorden** *pl* agree B 2137; **acorded** *pt s* B 1504; **acordeden** *pt pl* LGW 168; **acorded** *pp* A 818.

acorse *v* curse TC 3.1072, 4.839.

acoye *v* quiet, tame TC 5.782.

acquitance *n* release A 4411.

acquite *v* acquit D 1599; **hym a.** acquit himself; **aquite** *imp s* require TC 2.1200.

actes *n pl* acts, actions, deeds HF 347, C 574, D 114, E 1838; records B 4326.

acused, acc- *pt s* blamed, condemned TC 2.1081, A 1765.

acustumaunce *n* habit HF 28; **hadde of a.** was accustomed B 3701.

adamant *n* adamant (hard stone) A 1990; **adamauntes** loadstones PF 148.

adawe *v* awake, come to TC 3.1120; **adawed** *pp* awake E 2400.

a-day *adv phr* by day TC 1.1075, 2.60.

adoun *adv* down BD 13, etc.; below HF 889, G 779, H 105.

adrad, adred *ppl adj* afraid BD 493, HF 928, A 605.

advertence *n* attention HF 709, TC 4.698; consideration TC 5.1258; mind G 467.

advocacies *n pl* charges TC 2.1469.

afer *adv* afar HF 1215, TC 1.313, LGW 212.

a-fere *adv* afire, on fire TC 1.229 (Kentish form).

afered, aferd *pp & adj* frightened A 4095, B 1590, C 284; afraid TC 1.974, 3.482, A 628, 1518, B 4611.

affeccioun *n* state of mind, emotion A 3611; love, passion B 586; **affeccioun of hoolynesse** religious feeling A 1158.

affectis *n pl* desires TC 3.1391.

afferme *v* affirm TC 2.1588; **affermeth** *3 s* supports B 4315. **affermed** *pp* decreed A 2349.

affiance *n* good faith B 1330.

affounde *v* grow cold Rosem 21.

affray *n* disturbance, commotion B 3273, D 2156; alarm B 1137; fright HF 553.

affraye *v* frighten E 455; **affrayed** *pp* frightened, afraid B 1590, 4468, 4475; startled BD 296.

affyle, -ile *v* make smooth TC 2.1681, A 712.

aforyeyn *prep* opposite TC 2.1188.

afright *pp* frightened B 4085.

after, -ir *prep* after A 731, etc.: according to, in accordance with TC 5.376, A 125; for A 525, B 467; to F 403; **as after** according to B 1847; **after me** according to my will E 327; **after oon** of one quality, alike A 341, 1781.

after *adv* afterwards, later TC 1.4, C 152; in the future TC 5.986.

after *conj* after TC 4.935, A 3357; as, according as LGW 575; **after as** according as PF 216; **after that**

after TC 4.1276, A 2522, D 1853, E 442; according as TC 2.1347, E 203.

after-dyner *n* the period after dinner, i.e. late forenoon B 1445, F 918.

after-mete *n* the period after dinner E 1921.

after-soper *n* the period after supper F 302, 1219.

a-game *adv* in jest TC 3.636, 648. See **game.**

agast *ppl adj* afraid A 4267, E 1760.

agaste *v* frighten, terrify TC 2.901, B 4278; **agaste** *pt s* B 3395; *pt s refl* was frightened A 2424; **agast** *pp* HF 557, A 2931, B 4079, D 798. See **agast** *ppl adj.*

agayn, ayeyn *adv* again A 892; in return A 4274.

agaynes, agayns, ayeyns, ayens *prep* meanings as under **ageyn:** (1) LGW 344, Truth 11; (2) BD 16; (3) B 999, E 911; (4) B 3702, E 2325; (5) PF 342.

agaynward *adv* back again B 441. Cf. **ayeynward.**

age *n* age A 82, etc.; old age TC 2.395, C 747; lifetime HF 1986, D 24, E 627; maturity E 1555; **ages** *pl* periods (of time) TC 2.27, B 3177.

ageyn, ayeyn, ayein *prep* (1) against (in opposition to) LGW 189, A 66, E 170; (2) against (contrary to) A 2451, C 181; (3) towards (in the direction of) A 2680, D 1000; **agayn the day** towards morning B 4268; (4) in front of, in the presence of (the sun, etc.) PF 443, TC 5.1239, LGW 48; (5) in anticipation of F 142, G 1342.

agilten *v* do wrong, offend, sin LGW 436; **agylte(e)** *pt s* HF 329, TC 3.840; **agilte** *pt pl* D 392; **agilt** *pp* LGW 463, TC 5.1684.

agon, ago, agoon *pp* (of **agon**) gone PF 465, A 2336; gone away A 1276; past A 1782, 2784.

agonye *n* fit A 3452.

a-greef, agref, agrief *adv* amiss, unkindly; **take a-greef** PF 543, TC 3.862, D 191.

agreën *v* please, be pleased, consent TC 3.131; **agre(e)** *pr s subj* PF 409, TC 1.409.

agreved *pp* injured A 4181.

agroos see **agryse.**

agryse *v* shudder HF 210, B 614; tremble TC 2.1435; cause to shudder D 1649; **agroos** *pt s* was frightened TC 2.930.

aiel *n* grandfather, forefather A 2477.

aile see **eyle.**

ake *v* ache HF 632, TC 2.549; **ake(n)** *pr pl* TC 3.1561, B 2113.

aketoun *n* quilted vest worn under hauberk B 2050.

al *n* awl Truth 11. See **oules.**

al, alle *adj* all BD 99, 300, PF 131, TC 5.498, B 907, 4414; **al a** a whole A 584, F 1348, G 996; **alle thyng** every thing BD 141, 1264, HF 1837, TC 1.237, D 1475; **at al** (*positively*) in any way, entirely C 633, E 1222; (*negatively*) in any way, at all B 1360, D 1078, 1763.

al *pron* all, everything BD 116, TC 1.544, A 319; **al and al** everything BD 1003; **alle and some** one and all, each and all TC 5.883, A 2187, B 263, E 941; **al and som** the sum and substance, the whole matter, everything PF 650, TC 2.363, F 1606. See **alder-, aller.**

al *adv* all, quite, entirely TC 1.93, 898, A 683, D 1480; completely PF 432, B 3215; solely TC 5.14; **al atanes** (*Northern*) right away A 4074.

al *conj* (*with inverted word order*) although, even if HF 1740, PF 8, TC 1.17, A 297, D 624.

alabastre *n* alabaster A 190.

alambikes *n pl* alembics G 794. Cf. **lambic.**

alauntz *n pl* wolf-hounds, very large hunting dogs A 2148.

alayes *n pl* alloys E 1167.

albificacioun *n* whitening G 805 (see note).

alday *adv* continually, constantly TC 1.106, 2.457, A 1168; always B 1702, E 1598. Also **al-day.**

alderbest *adj* best of all BD 907; **alderbeste** BD 246, 1279, TC 3.1597.

alderbest *adv* best of all BD 87, TC 1.1008, A 710.

alderfayreste *adj* fairest of all BD 1050.

alderfirst, altherfirst *adv* first of all HF 1368, TC 1.1069, F 550, G 423.

alderfirste, altherferste *adj* first of all BD 1173, TC 3.97.

alderlest *adv* least of all TC 1.604.

alderlevest *adj* dearest of all TC 3.239, 5.576.

aldermost, aldirmost *adv* most of all TC 1.152, 248, 1003.

aldernext *adv* nearest of all, very near PF 244.

alderwisest *adj* wisest of all TC 1.247.

ale *n* ale A 341, 382; **atte nale** at the alehouse D 1349.

alegge see **allegge.**

alenge *adj* wearisome, ong B 1412, D 1199.

alestake *n* a projecting pole hung with a garland, the regular sign of an alehouse A 667, C 321.

aleye *n* alley B 1758; **aleyes** *pl* garden

paths, walks TC 2.820, E 2324, F 1013.

algate *adv* in any case, at any rate BD 887, TC 5.1071, C 292; always LGW 361, A 571, B 1201; at all cost HF 943; nevertheless LGW 238, E 2376; of course D 588.

algates *adv* at any rate BD 1171, TC 3.24, D 1811; under any circumstances LGW 594; always, in all cases D 756; assuredly D 1514; nevertheless B 520.

al-if *conj* even if TC 3.398.

alighte *v* alight E 981; descend E 909; **alighte** *pt s* alighted TC 5.189, 1017, A 983, B 1660; *pt pl* TC 5.513; **alight, alyght** *pp* A 722, 2189.

alkamystre *n* alchemist G 1204.

allegge *v* adduce, cite TC 3.297, A 3000, E 1658; **alegge** *1 s* HF 314.

aller, alder *gen pl* of **al** of all; **hir aller** of them all A 586; **oure aller, our alder** of us all A 799, 823, LGW 298.

alleskynnes *adj* of all kinds HF 1530.

alliaunce, alliance *n* alliance TC 3.1746, A 2973; union (by marriage) E 357; kinship B 1329.

allow *pr 1 s* commend F 676.

allye *n* ally, kinsman G 292, 297; relative B 3593; **allyes** relatives D 301.

allye(n), allie *v* ally C 613, 616; enter into alliance A 3945, E 1414; **allied** *pp* allied TC 1.87; possessed of allies B 3720.

almesse *n* alms B 168; charity D 1609.

almest *adv* almost B 1948.

almost, almoost *adv* almost HF 650, A 155, etc.

aloes see **ligne aloes.**

along (on) *adj* on account of TC 2.1001, 3.783, G 930.

aloonly *adv* solely TC 5.1779.

alose *v* praise, commend TC 4.1473.

al-outrely, al-outerly, al-utterly *adv* completely, absolutely BD 1244, HF 296, TC 1.382.

als *adv* also HF 2071, TC 2.726; as A 170, 4177. See **also, as.**

also, al so *adv* also BD 728, A 64; **also . . . as** as . . . as HF 656, TC 3.1388, A 730, **al so . . . that** so . . . that A 3104. See **als, as** *adv*; **as** *expletive particle.*

also *conj* as HF 629, B 2112, C 860.

alswa *adv* also A 4085.

altherfastest *adj* very fast HF 2131.

altherferste see **alderfirste.**

altherfirst see **alderfirst.**

alum glas *n* rock alum G 813.

al-utterly see **al-outrely.**

alwey, alway *adv* always BD 15, TC 5.142, LGW 103, A 185, 275, E 2037; all the time F 422.

amadrides *n pl* hamadryads A 2928.

amalgamyng *n* combining with quicksilver G 771.

amayed *pp* dismayed TC 1.648, 4.641.

ambages *n pl* circumlocutions, ambiguities TC 5.897.

ambes as *n pl* double aces B 124.

ambil *n* an ambling pace B 2075.

amblere *n* saddle horse A 469.

amendement *n* reparation A 4185.

amenden *v* correct, reform TC 5.1613 E 441, Purse 25; **amende** *3 s subj* C 767, D 1810; **amended** *pp* A 190, D 1833; improve, cause improvement TC 3.422, A 3066; **amende** *1 s* TC 2.854; **amended** *pt s* BD 1102; *pp* B 3444; remedy BD 551, TC 5.138; **amende** *3 s subj* D 2193; **amended** *pp* B 1619, D 1097; improve upon A 2196, E 1026; *pp* B 4048, E 1606; make amends TC 2.245.

ameved *pt 3 s* changed E 498.

among *prep* among BD 60, HF 1687; between C 814; along with TC 5.1548, E 785; during TC 3.860.

among *adv* round about BD 298; all the while TC 3.1816.

amonges *prep* amongst A 759, etc.

a-morwe *adv* in the (early) morning BD 1103, A 822; the next day A 1621, D 593.

amounteth *3 s* amounts to F 108; means A 2362, 3901, B 569.

amphibologyes *n pl* ambiguities TC 4.1406.

amy *n* friend; **beel amy** good friend C 318.

amydde *prep* amid BD 165, etc.

amyddes *prep* amidst B 3919; **amyddes of** amidst HF 845; in the middle of A 2009.

amyddes *adv* in the midst PF 277.

amys *adv* amiss BD 1141; wrong, wrongly HF 269, 596, A 3181; badly TC 1.491; F 1298.

an *indef art* an BD 4, etc.

an *prep* on; **an heigh** on high A 1065, E 2327.

ancle *n* ankle A 1660.

and *conj* if TC 1.125, 695, B 3140, etc.

angle *n* astronomical term B 304; **angle meridional** F 263; **anglis** *pl* angles F 230. See notes to B 301 and F 263.

angre *n* anger A 3745, etc.; trouble F 1553; a feeling or fit of anger TC 1.563.

anhange *v* hang C 259; **anhanged** *pp* hanged B 3945, C 275; **anhonged** TC 2.1620.

anlaas *n* broad, two-edged dagger A 357.

annexed *pp* joined C 482, D 1147.

annueleer *n* a priest supported to sing *annuals* or anniversary masses for the dead G 1012.

annunciat *pp* announced, foretold B 3205.

anon, anoon *adv* immediately BD 80, A 32, etc.; **anon as that** as soon as F 615.

anon-rightes *adv* immediately A 3480.

anon-ryght, anon-right, anoon-ryght *adv* immediately B 354, 536, etc.

anoy *n* annoyance, vexation TC 4.845, B 1320.

anoyen *v* annoy, vex TC 4.1304, B 492, F 884; **anoyeth** *3 s* causes harm F 875; **anoyeth** *impers* it annoys G 1036; **anoyeth** *imp pl* B 494; **anoyed** *pp* D 1848.

antiphoner *n* liturgical book (of antiphons) B 1709.

anvelt *n* anvil BD 1165.

a-nyght *adv* at night HF 42, A 1042, etc.

any-thyng *adv* at all TC 1.848.

aornementes *n pl* adornments E 258.

a-paas see **a pas.**

apaire *v* suffer harm, deteriorate HF 756; **appaire** *1 pl* TC 2.329. See **apeyren.**

apalled *pp* grown dim A 3053; enfeebled B 1292; pale, tired F 365.

a pas, a-paas *adv* at a walk, slowly TC 2.627, A 2217, C 866; apace, quickly HF 1051, TC 4.465; **esily a pas** at an easy pace F 388. See **paas.**

apayed *pp* satisfied, pleased TC 3.421, 5.1249; **apayd** A 1868, E 1512; **appayed** TC 1.649; **yvele apayed** ill pleased, displeased TC 4.642, LGW 80, B 1580; sorry E 2392.

ape *n* ape HF 1212; fool A 3389, G 1313; **Goddes apes** natural-born fools TC 1.913; **putte in the mannes hood an ape** made a fool of the man B 1630. See **wyn ape.**

aperceyve *v* perceive TC 4.656, E 600.

aperceyvynges *n pl* noticing, taking notice F 286.

apert *adv* openly HF 717, D 1114, 1136, F 531.

apertenaunt *adj* belonging (to) B 3505: **apertinent** appropriate E 1010.

apertenyng *part* belonging G 785.

apese *v* appease, pacify TC 3.110, E 433; quiet TC 3.887, 5.117; assuage H 98; **apaisen** *2 pl* TC 3.22; **apesed** *pp* TC 1.250, 940.

apeyren *v* injure A 3147; **apeired** *pp* TC 1.38. See **apaire.**

apiked *pp* cleaned, adorned A 365.

apoynte *v* set a time, say definitely TC 5.1620; **a hire** *refl* decide, determine TC 2.691; **apoynteden hym** *pt 3 s refl* decided E 1595; **apoynteden** *pt 3 pl* determined TC 3.454; **was apoynted** was determined, had decided E 1616.

appaire see **apaire.**

apparaille *n* apparel E 1208.

apparaillen *v* clothe D 343; prepare B 3797.

apparaillynge *n* preparation A 2913.

apparence *n* appearance HF 265; apparition, illusion F 218, 1157, 1602; *pl* F 1140.

appere, apere, appeere, appiere *v* HF 190, PF 42, TC 2.909, A 2346, G 200; come forward into view G 837.

apperen *v* be the peer of LGW 273.

appetit *n* desire A 1680; *pl* A 1670, B 3390.

apposed *pt 3 s* questioned G 363.

appreved *pp* approved E 1349; tried and true LGW 21.

approche(n) *v* approach HF 1521, TC 5.1; be involved F 556.

appropred *pp* made the peculiar possession of Gent 18.

approwours *n pl* agents D 1343.

aqueynte *v* acquaint BD 532; **aqueynteden** *pt 3 pl* became acquainted HF 250; **aqueynted** *pp* B 1219.

aquite see **acquite.**

arace *v* root out TC 5.954; extricate E 1103; tear away F 1393; **arace** *3 s subj* root out TC 3.1015.

aray see **array.**

araye see **arraye.**

archewyves *n pl* master-wives E 1195.

arede *v* explain, foretell TC 4.1570; guess, conjecture TC 2.132, 4.1112; interpret BD 289.

arest *n* arrest, detention A 1310; seizure B 4090; restraint LGW 397, E 1282; hook-like rest for lance, attached to breastplate A 2602.

areste, arresten *v* stop, arrest A 827, B 4210, F 1370.

arette *2 pl* impute, attribute A 726; **aretted** *pp* A 2729.

a-rewe *adv* in succession D 1254.

argoille *n* tartar (on a wine cask) G 813.

argumenten *3 pl* argue B 212; **argumented** *pt 3 s* TC 1.377.

aright, aryght *adv* rightly, truly, well HF 50, LGW 67, A 189, etc.; successfully TC 4.1463; straight, in a straight line A 4254; quickly TC 3.462; **preven a.** turn out well G 646.

arisyng *n* rising F 1287.

armee *n* armed expedition A 60.

armes *n pl* weapons; **men of armes** F 213; **god of armes**, Mars A 2159; deeds of arms, prowess HF 144, 1411, TC 1.58; coat-of-arms HF 1331, A 2891; **in oon armes** in identical coats of armes A 1012.

arm-greet *adj* as thick as the arm A 2145.

armonyak *adj* Armenian, ammoniac. See **booe a., sal a.**

armonye *n* harmony BD 313, HF 1396; harmony, music TC 5.1812.

armypotente *adj* strong in arms A 1982, 2441.

arn *3 pl* are HF 1008, TC 1.1006, 4.972, 5.1374, E 342.

a-roume *adv* at large HF 540.

a-rowe *adv* in turn HF 1835; in a row LGW 554.

array, earlier **aray** *n* preparation, arrangements, order TC 3.536, A 3630, B 299, E 262; assembly E 373, 375; festivities D 1075, F 63, 282; accouterment, equipment A 73, B 3493, D 289: furnishings A 2199, B 1437, E 2026; attire, clothes, clothing and other necessities A 330, 716, B 1244, E 965, G 567; **of greet array** richly adorned, splendid B 3272; condition A 934, B 972, E 670; estate E 467; behavior D 235; appearance B 775.

arraye, arraie, earlier **araye** *v* prepare, arrange E 961; clothe, adorn B 1202, 1396, **hym arraieth** *3 s* arrays himself, dresses fastidiously A 3689; **arrayed** *pt 3 s* prepared B 1098; adorned A 2090; **arrayed** *pp* prepared, made ready B 252, 4227; provided A 2046; **wel a.** in fine condition (ironical) A 1801; appointed E 980, F 1187; arranged A 2867; planned, laid out F 910; destined TC 2.200; clothed, dressed, adorned TC 1.167, 2.1187, 3.423, A 1389, E 262; clad F 389.

arrette(d) see **arette.**

arryvage *n* landing HF 223.

ars-metrike *n* arithmetic A 1898, D 2222.

art *n* skill, craft, craftsmanship HF 335, TC 2.11, 257; principles governing an activity which involves knowledge or skill, as **art of medicyne** TC 1.659; **art of speche** F 104; **art of songe** BD 1168; **art poetical** HF 1095; **loves art** TC 3.1333; learning, the learning of the schools, esp. the trivium A 3191, 4056, 4122; science, field of a profession E 35, F 1120, G 716; subject E 1241; plan, method, means TC 1.927, 4.1266, A 2445.

arten *v* induce TC 1.388.

artificial *adj* **a. day** the period between sunrise and sunset B 2.

artow art thou HF 1872, etc.

arwe *n* arrow TC 2.641, etc.; **arwes** *pl* PF 212, etc.

aryse, arise *v* arise HF 209, F 380; be raised TC 4.1480; **ariseth, arist** *3 s* B 265, 1265; **arisen** *pt pl* TC 2.1598; **arise, arisen** *pp* TC 2.1462, A 1041; **arys** *imp s* A 1045, B 4206, C 827; **ariseth** *imp pl* TC 2.221.

aryvayle *n* landing HF 451.

as *conj* as, since BD 12, 35, 73, etc.; **as hyt** which BD 1323; as if HF 546, TC 3.64, A 81, etc.; that D 196; (in comparisons) **greye as glas** A 152, **wis as Pallas** C 49, **as red as rose** LGW 112; **as if** whether TC 3.578; **as that** as PF 95, B 3473; **as that me thynketh** as it seems to me H 31; **as thogh that** as if LGW 371; **as who sayth** as if to say BD 558, TC 1.1011, Buk 4; as one might say TC 3.268; **as wheither** whether TC 5.1300; **so as, ther as** as A 39, A 34; as . . . as TC 1.123, E 2356, F 203; **as ferforth as** as far as TC 4.891, B 19, 1099; the same as if TC 1.121; **as shortly as** as briefly as PF 34; **as wel . . . as** both . . . and A 49, B 1000–1; **also . . . as** as . . . as HF 656, D 2134; **so . . . as** A 321, B 1258, F 854; **swich as, swich . . . as** such as, such . . . as TC 1.34, D 147, E 183, F 519.

as *adv* (and adverbial uses) as, so B 1882, Purse 5; very, to the greatest possible extent: **as faste** very soon, very quickly TC 2.898, 1358, G 1235; **as swithe, as swythe** quickly, immediately PF 623, B 637, G 1194.

as + *prep:* **as after** according to B 3555; **as by** in view of A 244; judging by E 924; **as for** for TC 5.1691; **as for the tyme** for the present B 714; **as in** in TC 3.489, B 3688; **as in my gylt** through fault of mine TC 2.244; **as of** concerning PF 26; **as of so litel space** considering the shortness of the time A 87; **as to** according to PF 547, TC 1.100, F 107.

as + *adv:* **as now, as nowthe** now, at present, at this time HF 56, A 462, 2264; for the present A 885, G 1019; on the present occasion G 944; **as paramours** passionately, in the manner of a lover TC 5.158; **as tho** then TC 5.227, at that time TC 3.922; **as yit** yet HF 599, TC 5.105, E 120.

as + *infin:* **as to speke of** speaking of TC 5.974.

as + *part:* **as touchyng** TC 3.42.

as *rel adv:* **ther as** where A 34, 2810.

as *rel pron* as D 270.

as *prep* like, as BD 779, HF 791, 1004, TC 3.1200, 4.447, 595, 626, Rosem 3.

as *expletive particle*, introducing (*a*) an imperative, (*b*) a hortatory subjunctive of wish, imprecation, etc. See Language § 73. (*a*) **as beth nat wroth** be not angry TC 5.145; **as lene it me** lend it to me A 3777; **as keepe me** A 2302; **also** (= **as**) **God your soule blesse** HF 1612; (*b*) **as wolde God** would God TC 3.1387, 5.523; **as go we** let us go TC 5.523.

ascaunce *conj* as if G 838.

ascaunces *conj* as if D 1745; as if to say TC 1.205, 292.

ascende *v* ascend, rise above the horizon I 11; **ascendynge** *pr part* rising in the east F 264; **ascended** *pp* B 4047.

ascendent *n* ascendant, horoscope A 417 (see note), D 613; **ascendentes** *pl* HF 1268; **ascendent tortuous** B 302 (see note).

ascry *n* outcry, shout TC 2.611.

aseuraunce *n* assurance TC 5.1259; **maken assurance** assure (me) B 341.

ashamed *pp* put to shame, disgraced A 2667; reluctant TC 2.1047; **for pur ashamed** for very shame TC 2.656.

asken *v* ask B 101; **aske** *1 s* request PF 648, A 2420; **asketh** *3 s* demands TC 1.339; **aske** *2 s subj* ask B 102; *3 s subj* may ask BD 32. See **axen.**

askyng *n* request HF 1700.

aslake *v* grow less A 3553; **aslaked** *pp* moderated, allayed A 1760.

asonder, ysonder *adv* apart, asunder BD 425, TC 3.660, A 491; apart in character D 1674.

asp(e) *n* aspen (tree) PF 180, A 2921; **aspes** *gen s* TC 3.1200.

aspect *n* relative position of heavenly bodies A 1087; *pl* TC 2.682, 3.716.

aspen leef *n* aspen leaf D 1667.

aspre *adj* bitter TC 4.827, 847.

aspye, aspie(n) *v* catch sight of TC 3.573; see, notice HF 1689, PF 194, TC 2.649; observe TC 2.775; **aspide, aspyed** *pt s* caught sight of TC 2.1252, 5.539; noticed, saw HF 1320, TC 3.85; looked closely HF 1128; **aspied** *pp* seen, discovered TC 1.85, 3.524. See **espyen, spyen.**

assaut *n* assault A 989.

assay *n* trial BD 552, D 290; attempt, experiment PF 2, TC 4.1508, G 1249; **in a.** as a test E 621; to the test G 1338; **in greet a.** to a severe test E 1138; **assayes** *pl* tests E 697.

assaye(n), **assay**, **asay** *v* try, attempt PF 257, TC 5. 783, G 1253; **asaieth** *3 s* TC 5.784; **assaye** *pr subj* let him try E 1229; **assay** *imp s* D 942; **assayeth** *imp pl* E 1740; test BD 346, E 1725; **assayinge** *part* TC 5.760; **assayed** *pp* TC 4.639, D 286; experienced TC 1.646; put to the test BD 574, E 454; try (to find out) LGW 487; try (to make love to) TC 1.928, 5.788; try to arrange F 1567.

assege *n* siege TC 1.464, 2.107; besieging force TC 2.123, 4.62.

assegeden *pt pl* besieged TC 1.60; **asseged** *pp* A 881.

assent *n* consent A 852, B 35, C 265; opinion TC 4.933, E 1532; will A 3075; **of oon assent** in collusion D 1359; **of his assent** in collusion with him C 758; **of thyn assent** complying with thee TC 4.535; **by oon assent** with one accord PF 557, TC 4.346, A 777, **by noon assent** by any agreement A 945; **so it were hire assent** if she agreed TC 4.554.

assente *v* assent TC 2.356, E 1468; **assentedest** didst assent G 233; **assenteden** *pt pl* E 1570; **assented** *pp* PF 526, I 61; consent E 11, 88, F 1384; **assente** *3 s subj* TC 2.335; **assented** *pt s* TC 1.1009; **assentynge** *part* B 342; agree, agree to, agree upon TC 2.1300, A 374; reach a decision TC 1.391; **assenten** *3 pl* agree B 344; **assente** *2 pl subj* E 494; **assented** *pp* agreed, agreed upon C 146, E 1575.

assh(e) *n* ash tree PF 176, A 2922.

asshen *n pl* ashes TC 2.539, A 1302, etc.; **asshes** G 807.

asshen of fern see **fern-asshen.**

asshy *adj* covered with ashes A 2883.

assise *n* assize, county court A 314.

assoille(n) *v* give absolution to C 933, 939; release from TC 5.1453; **assoille** *1 s* absolve C 387, 913; **assoilleth** *imp pl* clear up, solve E 1654.

assoillyng *n* absolution A 661.

assure *v* assure PF 448, B 1231; feel secure TC 5.1624; acquire confidence TC 5.870; **assure** *1 s* promise E 1983; *2 pl subj* promise E 165; **asseureth** *3 s* assures; **assureth** *3 s* gives assurance; **assuren** *3 pl* confirm, seal (covenant) A 1924; **assure**

imp s trust TC 1.680; **assured** *pt 3 s* confirmed B 3378; *pp* confident, assured HF 581, TC 3.1395; self-possessed TC 1.182; entrusted E 2191.

asterte *v* escape, escape from BD 1154, A 1595, F 1022; **asterte** *3 s subj* TC 5.1343; *pt s* TC 1.1050, 3.97; **asterte**, **asterted** *pt subj* might escape B 437, 475; **astert** *pp* A 1592.

astone, **astonie** *v* astonish; **astonyeth** *3 s* bewilders HF 1174; is astonished PF 5; **astonyed** *pt s* E 316; **astoned**, **astonyed** *pp* astonished HF 549, TC 1.274, E 337; bewildered PF 142, TC 2.603; dumbfounded TC 5.1728; stunned TC 3.1089, F 1339.

astored *pp* supplied, stocked A 609.

astrelabie *n* astrolabe A 3209.

astrologien *n* astronomer D 324.

astromye *n* mispronunciation of **astronomye** A 3451, 3457.

astronomye *n* astrology TC 4.115, A 414.

asure *n* lapis lazuli B 4052; blue (presumably blue enamel) TC 3.1370, E 254.

aswage *v* lessen TC 4.255, B 3834, E 2082, F 835.

asweved *pp* bewildered HF 549.

aswowne *adv* in a swoon, unconscious BD 123, TC 3.1092, A 3823.

asyde, –ide *adv* aside BD 558, A 896, etc.; sidelong BD 862.

at *prep* at A 20, 23, etc.; against A 4280 (**sporned at a stoon** kicked against, tripped over a stone); by D 2095, G 414; for LGW 375, A 2150, I 40; from LGW 477, G 621; in TC 5.848; **at alle degrees** in all respects A 3724; **at regard of** in comparison with HF 1723; **at the beste** in the best manner, very well A 749; of TC 2.984, 3.211, 4.555; to A 2226, B 1975; **at ye, at eye** to the eye E 1168, G 964; with your own eye A 3016, G 1059; with one's own eye LGW 100.

atake *v* overtake G 556, 585; **wel atake** *pp* wel met (overtaken) D 1384.

atanes *adv* at once (Northern) A 4074.

atempre, **attempre(e)** *adj* mild, temperate BD 341, PF 204, TC 1.953, B 4028.

atemprely, **att-** *adv* temperately, moderately B 1452, D 2053; in moderation E 1679.

athynken *v* (impersonal) cause regret TC 5.878; **m'athinketh** I regret TC 1.1050; **m'athynketh** A 3170.

atir, atyr *n* attire TC 1.181; clothes PF 225.

aton *adv* in accord TC 3.565, A 4197, E 437.

atones, att- *adv* at once (at one time) TC 1.804, LGW 294, A 765; all together E 1178; immediately A 3280, B 670, H 10; once and for all TC 5.41.

atrede *v* outwit TC 4.1456, A 2449.

atrenne *v* outrun TC 4.1456, A 2449.

attamed *pp* begun B 4008.

atte contract. of **at the** HF 821, A 125, B 1563, C 608; **atte beste** in the best manner possible A 29, 4147; **atte ende** at the end D 404; **atte fulle** fully A 651, B 203; **atte laste, atte last** HF 955, 1320; **atte leeste** at least A 1121, B 38; **atte nale** at the alehouse D 1349.

attemperaunce *n* temperance C 46.

attempre see **atempre.**

attemprely see **atemprely.**

atthamaunt *n* adamant A 1305.

attones see **atones.**

attricioun *n* a mild form of contrition TC 1.557.

atweyne *adv* in two BD 1193.

atwixe, atwixen *prep* between TC 4.821, 5.472, 886.

a-two, atwo *adv* in two TC 3.1475, 5.180, A 3569, etc.

atwynne *adv* apart TC 3.1666, A 3589; **wente atwynne** separated G 1170.

auctorite(e), autorite *n* authority PF 506, TC 1.65, A 3000, etc.; judgment E 1597.

auctour *n* author HF 314, TC 1.394, etc.; creator TC 3.1016, 1765; originator H 359.

audience *n* hearing PF 308, TC 4.70, B 673; audience B 3991; **in audience, in open audience** in open meeting, publicly D 1032, G 466, E 790.

auditour *n* auditor, overseer A 594; **auditours** *pl* hearers D 1937.

aught *pron* anything HF 993, TC 1.578, A 389, etc. See **oght.**

aught *adv* in any way TC 1.383, B 1034, etc. See **oght.**

augrym stones *n pl* small stones used in calculations A 3210.

augurye *n* divination TC 4.116, 5.380.

auncestre *n* ancestor PF 41, D 1156; *pl* D 1160, 1172.

auncetrye *n* ancestry A 3982.

aungel *n* angel PF 191, etc.

aungelik *adj* angelic TC 1.102.

aungelyke *adv* like an angel LGW 236.

auntre *v* venture A 4209; **auntred hym** *pt s* took a chance A 4205.

auntrous *adj* adventurous A 2099.

autentyk *adj* authentic BD 1086.

auter *n* altar PF 249, TC 5.1466, A 1905, etc.

availle, avaylle, avaylen *v* help TC 1.756, 2.1430, B 3950, D 1366; **avayleth** *3 s* HF 363; be profitable HF 1749, TC 2.1439, E 1194; **avayle** *3 pl* are profitable PF 538; be worth, do any good TC 5.1850, B 4336; avail, profit (*impers*) D 1324, E 2107; **avaylleth, availleth** *3 s* it avails TC 1.604, A 3040, B 589; advance (a cause) TC 1.20; be sufficient A 2401.

avale(n) *v* descend TC 3.626; doff A 3122.

avantage, avaun- *n* advantage A 1293, 2447; **at his a.** in a better condition F 772; **to doon his a.** to profit himself B 729.

avaunce *v* advance, cause to prosper HF 640, TC 1.518, 5.1435; profit one A 246; benefit TC 1.47; **avaunced** *pp* benefitted C 410.

avaunt, avant *n* boast TC 1.1050; **make avaunt** boast TC 2.727, A 277, E 1457; **avantes** *pl* TC 3.289.

avauntage see **avantage.**

avaunte, avante *v* boast (*refl*) D 1014; *1 s* PF 470, D 403; *3 pl* TC 3.318; extol, flatter HF 1788.

avauntour, avantour *n* boaster PF 430, TC 2.724, B 4107.

avauntyng *n* boasting A 3884.

aventaille *n* ventail, wide band of chain-mail protecting lower part of face, the neck, and upper chest TC 5.1558, E 1204.

aventure *n* chance TC 1.568, A 1186; **be, by, of, par aventure** by chance HF 1297, A 25, 844, F 1501, 1508, B 1205; **in aventure** uncertain TC 1.784; fortune HF 1052, TC 1.368, A 2357; *pl* HF 1631; fate, (one's) lot TC 1.1092, 2.742, B 465; adventure, experience TC 1.35, 3.1217, B 4376, F 1483; *pl* A 795, C 15; misfortune LGW 657, B 1151, E 812; accident A 2703; *pl* C 934; **on aventure** in case anything happens TC 5.298; **in aventure** in jeopardy: **putte in a.** risk G 946, risked E 1877.

avise see **avyse.**

avisioun, avys- *n* vision HF 7, 104, B 4304, D 1858; *pl* HF 48, TC 5.374.

avouterye, avoutrye, avowtrye *n* adultery PF 361, D 1306, E 1435.

avow(e) *n* vow BD 93, A 2237, B 334.

avowe *v* avow, assert TC 3.855, G 642.

avowtier *n* adulterer D 1372.

avoy *interj* alas, fie B 4098.

avys *n* consideration TC 3.453, 4.416, A 786; opinion A 1868, I 54; advice, counsel TC 1.620, A 3076.

avyse, avise *v* consider, take counsel, reflect on (often *refl*) PF 648, TC 1.364, 2.1215, B 664, E 238; contemplate TC 5.1814; **avyse** *1 s* E 797; **avise** *2 s subj* LGW 509; **avyseth** *3 s* B 1266, D 1228; **avyse** *3 pl* E 1988; **avysed** *pt s* TC 2.1726; **avise, avyse** *imp s* LGW 335, A 4188; **avyseth (yow)** *imp pl* TC 2.1730, A 3185; **avysed** *pp* TC 2.1177; **was a.** had considered TC 2.605; **am a.** have come to a conclusion TC 4.1262; **sodeynly a.** by a sudden resolution TC 3.1186; **to been a.** to be forewarned C 690; **be wel a.** be careful, be cautious, take heed A 3584, 4333, E 1528; **beeth a. wel** consider carefully! H 286; **yvele a.** ill-considered H 335; **avise** *1 s* advise BD 697; **avysed** *pp* TC 2.1695; **avyse** *v* contemplate TC 5.1814; *2 pl* observe, stare at TC 2.276.

avysely *adv* advisedly H 327.

avysement, avi- *n* consideration, reflection TC 2.343, LGW 407, E 1531; deliberation PF 555, TC 4.936; contemplation TC 5.1811.

await, awayt *n* waiting, watching: **in await** in ambush B 4415, D 1657; under surveillance, with a watchful eye on B 3915, H 149; with watchfulness, cautiously TC 3.457; **withouten a.** without delay TC 3.579.

awaite *v* wait, watch; **awaiteth** *3 s* B 1776, F 1299; **awaityng** *part* watching, spying upon D 2052.

awake *v* awake TC 2.70, A 4215; come to F 476; **awaketh** *3 s* TC 2.810; **awaked** *pt s* A 2523; **awak, awake** *imp s* BD 179, HF 556, TC 1.729, A 3478, H 15; **awaketh** *imp pl* BD 183, A 3700.

awake(n) *v* awaken TC 1.564, H 7; **awaked** *pp* E 1957.

awe *n* fear, awe, veneration TC 1.1006, 4.620, A 654, B 3749.

awen *adj* own (Northern) A 4239.

a-wepe *adv* a-weeping, in tears TC 2.408.

a-werke *adv* to work; **sette hem . . . awerke** "made them sweat" D 215; **yset a-werk** imposed upon, duped A 4337.

awey(e), away *adv* away BD 49, etc.; gone TC 2.123, LGW 25, B 609.

aweyward *adv* away H 262.

awhaped *pp* disconcerted, bewildered TC 1.316, LGW 132.

awreke *pp* avenged H 298.

awroken *pp* avenged A 3752. Cf. **awreke.**

axe(n) *v* BD 30, 1276, TC 2.147, B 1584, E 326; **axe at** ask of TC 2.894, 3.1682; **axe** *1 s* A 1347, D 21, E 348; **axest** *2 s* D 1482; **axeth** *3 s* E 25, F 309, Truth 16; requires TC 2.227, 1071, E 1543; **axe** *2 pl* G 640; **axed, axede** *pt* BD 185, HF 50, TC 3.569, A 3661; **axed** *pt subj* A 3413; **axe** *imp s* A 3557, C 667; **axeth** *imp pl* E 653; **axed** *pp* HF 1766, TC 4.149, Buk 2. See **asken.**

axyng *n* request HF 1541, A 1826; **axynge, axing** question G 423, Buk 3.

ay *adv* ever, always TC 1.449, A 63, E 149, H 174, etc.

ayens see **agaynes.**

ayerissh see **eyryssh.**

ayeyn, -ein see **ageyn.**

ayeynward *adv* back again TC 3.750, 4.1581; on the other hand TC 4.1027. Cf. **agaynward.**

B

ba *v* kiss D 433.

babewynnes *n pl* grotesque carvings, gargoyles HF 1189.

bacheler *n* young knight A 3085, D 883, F 24; aspirant to knighthood A 80; **bachiler** young man H 107; **bacheleris** unmarried men E 1274, 1278; **bacheler of lawe** bachelor of law F 1126.

bachelrye *n* company of young men or young knights E 270; **bachilrie** young manhood H 125.

bacon, -oun *n* bacon B 4035; smoked pork D 418 (see note); pork, side of pork D 217, 1735.

bad see **bidden.**

badder *adj* worse F 224.

baggepipe *n* bagpipe A 565.

baggeth *3 s* squints BD 623.

bailly *n* bailiff D 1392, 1396; **bailif** A 603, D 1419.

baiten, bayte *v* feed TC 1.192, B 466; **baiteth** *3 s* B 2103.

bake mete *n* pie made with meat or fish A 343 (see note).

balade *n* balade, a French lyric form LGW 270, 539; **balades** *pl* LGW 423 (see note).

balaunce, -ance *n* balance, scale B 3776; **in balaunce** in suspense BD 1021; in jeopardy TC 2.466, 4.1560, G 611.

bale *n* sorrow, trouble BD 535, TC 4.739, G 1481; **for bote ne bale** for good nor evil BD 227.

balke *n* beam A 3920; *pl* A 3626.

balled *adj* bald A 198, 2518.

bane *n* death, bane HF 408, TC 2.320, A 1097, etc.

baner *n* banner A 966, 976, 978, etc.

banes *n pl* bones (Northern) A 4073.

baptize *v refl* be baptized G 171, 229.

bar, baar see **beren** *v.*

barbe *n* a pleated covering for the throat (or chin) and the chest, worn by widows and nuns TC 2.110.

Barbre *adj* Barbary, heathen B 281.

bare *adj* bare, uncovered A 1758, E 1351; bareheaded A 683; empty A 4390; lacking, completely without TC 4.1168, 5.1547, D 1480; insufficient TC 1.662; mere TC 3.1099, LGW 405, F 1580; unadorned F 720; destitute G 732.

bareyne *adj* barren, sterile B 68, D 372, E 448; completely without A 1244.

bargayn *n* business agreement F 1230; *pl* money-lending transactions A 282.

barge *n* ship, sailing vessel of medium size LGW 621, A 410, F 850.

barly-breed *n* barley bread D 144, 145.

barm *n* bosom, lap B 3256, 3630, E 551, F 631.

barmclooth *n* apron A 3236.

baroun *n* baron TC 4.33, 190.

barred *pp* striped A 3235.

barres *n pl* metal bars on a girdle A 329 (see note).

bataille *n* battle A 879, etc; *pl* HF 454, A 61; **god . . . of bataylle** god of war HF 1447, TC 2.630.

batailled *pp* crenelated B 4050.

bath *n* bath D 1253, G 515; Roman bath B 3699; chamber for bathing G 517, 523, 525.

bathe *pron* both (Northern) A 4087, 4112, 4191.

baude *n* bawd TC 2.353, D 1354; **bawdes** *pl* D 1339; **baudes** harlots C 479.

bauderye *n* act of a bawd TC 3.397; **bawderye** pandering D 1305; **Bauderie** Mirth, Gaiety A 1926.

baudy *adj* dirty G 635.

bawdryk *n* baldric A 116 (see note).

bawme *n* balm, an aromatic resin HF 1686; fragrance TC 2.53.

be *prep* by BD 1331, HF 2, 48, etc. See **by.**

be see **ben.**

be- see **bi-.**

beau sir *n* fair sir HF 643.

bechen *adj* of beech wood G 1160, 1196.

become see **bicomen.**

bede, beede *v* offer, proffer HF 32, TC 4.1105, 5.185, G 1065; **bedeth** *3 s* E 1784; **beede** *2 pl* E 360; **bade**
pt pl directed I 65; **bede, bode, boden** *pp* bidden, commanded BD 194, TC 3.691, LGW 366, D 1030.

bedrede *pp* bedridden D 1769, E 1292.

bee *n* bee G 195; **been** *pl* HF 1522, TC 2.193; **bees** *pl* B 4582, D 1693, E 2422.

beel(e), bele *adj* fair HF 1796, TC 2.288; **beel amy** fair friend C 318; **beele cheere** hospitality B 1599; **bele chose** pudendum D 447, 510.

been see **bee.**

beer see **beren.**

beere, bere *n* bier HF 1744, TC 2.1638, A 2871, D 587, Purse 5, etc.

beest, best(e) *n* beast, animal BD 159, HF 1003, LGW 113, A 1309, etc.

befalle see **bifalle.**

befil see **bifalle.**

beforn see **biforn.**

beggestere *n* beggar A 242 (the ending was originally feminine, as in *spinster*).

behette see **bihote.**

behewe *pp* carved HF 1306.

behighte(n) see **bihote.**

behoteth see **bihote.**

bekke *v* nod; *1 s* C 396; *2 s subj* H 346; **bekked on** nodded to TC 2.1260.

bele see **beele.**

belle *n* bell BD 1322, etc.; **bere the b.** be the first, take the prize TC 3.198; **my b. shal be ronge** TC 5.1062 (see note).

bely *n* belly C 534, D 2267.

bely-naked *adj* belly-naked, completely naked, E 1326.

beme *n* trumpet HF 1240; *pl* B 4588.

ben, bee(n) *v* be PF 465, 637, E 859; **am** *1 s* HF 588, etc.; **is** *1 s* (Northern) A 4031, 4045, 4202; **art** *2 s* PF 683, E 310; **arte** *2 s* (*interr*) TC 5.1165, I 23; **artow** art thou HF 1872, TC 1.731; **is** *2 s* (Northern) A 4089; **is, ys** *3 s* HF 76, 775; **ar, are, be(n), been** *pl* TC 2.113, 235, A 4110, 4045, B 118; **be, bee** *pr subj* PF 432, TC 1.890; **be** *2 pl subj* TC 2.584, D 1848; **was** *pt 1 & 3 s* BD 387, HF 82; **were** *pt 2 s* B 366; **were, weren, wern** *pt pl* BD 1289, A 28, 29, D 1457; **were, wer, weere** *pt s subj* LGW 107, A 148, B 366, E 168; **be** *imp s* E 1209; **beth, beeth** *imp pl* TC 5.1785, B 1397; **been** *pp* A 199, etc.; **iben, ybe, ybee(n)** *pp* HF 1138, LGW 6, 289, B 4487; **be** *pp* BD 530, 1064; **be as be may** be it as it may B 1012; **be what she be** be she whoever she may TC 1.679; **been lik** likely to be A 3226, B 3319.

bench *n* bench C 674, D 247; mound of turf E 2235; table or counter B 1548.

benched *pp* provided with benches TC 2.822 (see note); provided with mounds of turf LGW 204.

bende *v* bend; turn TC 2.1250; **bende** *3 s subj* TC 2.1378; **bente** *pt 3 s* H 264; **benten** *pt 3 pl* bent TC 2.861; **bent, bente** *pp* bent TC 4.40; arched A 3246; crescent TC 3.624.

bendiste *interj* benedicite TC 1.780.

bene-straw *n* bean straw E 1422.

benigne, -nygne, -nyngne *adj* gentle, kind, gracious BD 918, LGW 243, E 1025.

benignely, -nygnely, -nyngnely *adv* gently, graciously PF 370, E 21, 2093, 2186.

benignytee, benyng- *n* benignity, graciousness, kindness TC 1.40, B 446, E 1591; **benignites** *pl* TC 5.1859.

bente *n* grassy slope A 1981.

benyson *n* blessing E 1365.

ber *n* pillowcase BD 254.

berd *n* beard BD 456, A 270, 689; **in the berd** resolutely, face to face TC 4.41; **make a berd** fool, get the better of A 4096; **make his berd** deceive him D 361; hence **A berd!** a trick! A 3742.

bere see **beere.**

bere, beer(e) *n* bear TC 3.1780, 4.1453, A 1640; **beres** *gen & pl* HF 1589, A 2018, 2142; **eyther Bere** the constellation Ursa Major or Ursa Minor HF 1004.

bere(n) *v* bear, carry BD 64, F 119; *refl* conduct oneself D 1108; **bere** *pr s* B 1127, E 884; **bere, beren** *pr pl* BD 894, F 1367, G 454; **bere** *3 subj* may carry A 2547; may pierce A 2256; **bere, bare** *pt 2 s* bore E 1068; gave birth to TC 4.763; **beer** *pt 3 s* bore LGW 216, A 3692; gave birth to B 722; **bar, baar** *pt 3 s* bore, carried BD 196, A 105, B 626; wore A 3265; **bar hym** *pt 3 s refl* conducted himself TC 3.490; bore, gave birth to B 1652, G 48; **baren** *pt 1 pl refl* conducted ourselves A 721; **beren** *pt 3 pl* bore HF 1332; **ber, bere** *imp s* bear, carry A 3397, D 1139, E 891; **ber** *imp pl* TC 2.1141; **born, bore, boren** *pp* born, borne BD 1301, A 1073, D 1153; **yborn, ybore(n)** *pp* born, borne A 378, 1019, E 158; **borne** *pp as def adj* E 1790; **bere the belle** do the better TC 3.198; **sikly berth** endures with ill feeling E 625; **hym beer** betook himself B 4526; **beren (berth, bar) . . . on honde**

accuse, accuse falsely B 620, D 226, 380, 393, TC 3.1154; assert, make (someone) believe TC 4.1404, D 232, 575.

berie see **burien.**

berkyng *n* barking B 4576.

berme *n* yeast G 813.

berne *n* barn A 3258, B 3759, C 397; **bernes** *pl* B 1256, D 871.

beseke see **biseke.**

besette see **bisette.**

beseye see **biseye.**

besily see **bisily.**

best, beste see **beest.**

beste farynge *adj* handsomest, most attractive F 932.

bestialite *n* animal nature TC 1.735.

besy see **bisy.**

besynesse see **bisynesse.**

bet *adj* better HF 108, TC 1.257 A 3716, etc.

bet *adv* better BD 667, HF 13, A 242, etc,; **go bet** go with full speed BD 136, C 667.

bete, beete *v* kindle A 2253, 2292; mend A 3927; assuage TC 1.665; **betten** *pt pl* kindled G 518; **bete** *imp pl* assuage TC 4.928.

bete *v* beat, flap (the wings) HF 570, TC 3.1416, B 4512, C 17; **bet** *pt s* TC 4.752; **beete, bette** *pt pl* A 4308, 4316; **bet** *imp s* TC 1.932; **bete, beten** *pp* B 1732, D 511, 712, E 1158; **ybet, ybete, ybeten** *pp* HF 1041, TC 1.741, D 1285; **ybete** *pp* embroidered or woven A 979; **gold-ybete** embroidered or interwoven with gold threads TC 2.1229.

beth see **ben.**

bethynke, bethoghte see **bithynken.**

betraysed see **bitrayseth.**

bewared *pp* expended TC 1.636.

bewreye see **biwreyen.**

bewrye (properly **bewreye**) *v* betray PF 348.

beye see **byen.**

bibbed *pp* imbibed A 4162.

bible *n* the Bible BD 987, A 438; book HF 1334, G 857.

bibledde *pp* covered with blood A 2002.

biblotte *imp s* blot TC 2.1027.

bicched bones *n pl* dice C 656.

biclappe *v* catch, trap G 9.

bicome(n) be- *v* become BD 115, C 697, D 1644; **bicam, bicom** *pt s* BD 243, TC 1.1079; **bicome, bicomen, become** *pp* BD 767, E 1724, 2098; **wher bycometh it** what becomes of it TC 2.795; **wher he become** what becomes of him TC 2.1151; **bicam me** was becoming to me D 603.

bidaffed *pp* made a fool of E 1191.

bidden, byd *v* request, beseech, beg, pray BD 1027, TC 2.118; **biddest** *2 s* TC 4.456; **biddeth, bit** *3 s* TC 1.40, A 187, F 291; **bad** *pt 3 s* BD 187, E 1618; **bid** *imp s* HF 808, TC 3.342 (pray); **biddeth** *imp pl* pray TC 1.36; **bidde** *pp* B 440; the *pp* is usually replaced by the *pp* of **bede,** q.v.; **I bidde wisshe** I intend to wish TC 2.406 (see note).

bide see **byde.**

bifalle, by-, be-, bifelle *v* befall, happen HF 101, TC 1.236; **bifel, befil** *pt s* BD 66, A 19; **bifalle** *pp* A 795, B 726.

bifallyng, by- *n* happening TC 4.1018, 1076.

bifelle see **bifalle.**

bifor(e) by- *prep* before TC 5.1122, A 450, etc.

bifore, bifoore *adv* before C 229, 393; **al b.** first of all A 377, E 446.

biforen-hand *adv* beforehand G 1317.

biforn, by- *adv* before, previously PF 107, A 572, F 551; in advance B 1184, 1668; ahead A 572; **(al) byforn** in front TC 1.221, A 590.

biforn, biforen, by-, be- *prep* before HF 60, TC 1.110, 4.979, A 100.

bigete(n) *pp* begotten TC 1.977, B 3138, 3199.

bigon, by-, begoon *pp* of **bigo: wel bigon** happy, cheerful PF 171, D 606; fortunate TC 2.294; **wo b.** woe begone, in distress TC 3.117, B 918; **wors b.** worse beset TC 5.1328; **sorwfully b.** overwhelmed TC 1.114.

bigyle, -ile *v* cheat, deceive, delude TC 1.716, 2.270, E 2406, G 1169; **bigyle** *2 s subj* B 4618; **bigyled** *pp* A 4321, G 1385; betrayed C 274.

bigynne, by-, be- *v* PF 392, TC 1.389, 2.874, A 42; **begynne** *2 s subj* LGW 566; **bigynnen** *3 pl* G 1096; **bigan, bygan, began** *pt 1 & 3 s* BD 80, HF 100, PF 118, TC 1.353, A 44, 2482; **bigonne** *pt 2 s* G 442; **bigonne, begunne, began** *pt pl* HF 1220, PF 561, TC 2.512, D 1560, F 1015; **bigynne** *imp s* G 1121; **bigonne, bygonne, begonne** *pp* TC 2.48, LGW 196, 229, A 52.

biheete see **bihote.**

biheste, by-, biheeste *n* promise TC 2.359, 3.315, B 37.

biholde, be- *v* look, look at, behold HF 532, 1112, LGW 1301, 1363; **biheld, byheld, biheeld, beheld** *pt s* HF 481, TC 2.275, 1606, H 241; **behelden** *pt pl* TC 1.177; **byhelde** *pt 3 s subj* TC 2.378; **behold** *imp s* HF 926; **biholde** *pp* HF 1285, G 179.

bihote, biheete *1 s* promise A 1854, G 707; **behoteth** *3 s* BD 621; **byheete** *2 pl* TC 1.539; **behette** *pt s* PF 436; **bihighte, behighte** *pt s* TC 5.510, 1204, F 1559; **bihighten, behighten** *pt 2 pl* TC 5.496, F 1327; **bihyghte** *pt 3 pl* TC 3.319; **bihight, bihyght** *pp* TC 5.354, 1104, F 788.

bihove *v* befit Truth 5; **behoveth, byhoveth** *3 s (impers)* behoves, is necessary TC 1.858, F 602, 1359; **boes** *3 s* A 4027 (Northern).

bihovely *adj* profitable TC 2.261.

bihynde, be- *adv* behind BD 890, HF 238, 2150, A 3239, 4164.

bihynde, by-, be- *prep* behind BD 428, HF 977, 1214, LGW 282, 643, A 1050, 2143.

biknowe *v* acknowledge, confess A 1556, B 886; **biknewe** *pt 3 pl* B 4251.

bilden, buylden *v* build HF 1133, D 1977; **buyldeth, bilt** *3 s* D 655, HF 1135; **buylde** *3 pl* E 1279; **bulte** *pt s* A 1548.

biles see **byle.**

bileve, by- *n* religious belief, creed, faith TC 5.593, A 3456, F 1133, G 63, 427.

bileve¹ be- *v* believe HF 990, LGW 27, A 3162, B 574, G 259; **bileeve** *1 s* G 644; *1 pl* D 1178; **bileve** *imp s* TC 2.1502; **bileveth** *imp pl* G 1047.

bileve² see **bleven.**

bille *n* bill of complaint, petition C 166; plea E 1971; bill, summons D 1586; letter E 1937, TC 2.1130.

bilongeth *3 s* belongs B 3820, E 1459.

biloved *pp* beloved TC 1.131, A 215, etc.

bilynne *v* cease TC 3.1365. See **blynne.**

biquethe, by- *v* bequeath D 1121, Gent 17; *1 s* TC 4.786, A 2768; **biquethe** *pp* D 1164.

biraft(e) see **bireve.**

bireve, by- *v* take away, remove, deprive (of) TC 1.685, D 2111, G 482; **bireveth** *3 s* D 2059; **birafte, berafte** PF 87, B 83, D 461; **biraft, byraft** *pp* TC 3.1340, 4.228, A 1361; **bireved** D 2071.

biseche, be- *v* beseech BD 1132, 1224, TC 1.1062, 2.1007; **besechen** *3 pl* HF 1554; **biseche** *3 s subj* G 55; **bisoghte, bisoughte** *pt 3 s* B 516, 1094; **bysoughte** *pt 1 s subj* TC 1.769; **bisoughtest** *pt 2 s* TC 5.1734; **besoughte(n)** *pt pl* HF 1706, LGW 155; **bisechyng(e)** *part* TC 5.1585, B 379, G 1024. See **biseke.**

biseke *v* beseech TC 3.77, 4.131; **biseke, biseeke** *1 s* B 3174, D 807; **beseke(n)** *1 pl* TC 2.1674, A 918; **bisekynge** *part* E 178, 592. See **biseche.**

bisemare *n* contemptuous behavior A 3965.

bisette, be- *v* employ, occupy, bestow BD 772; **bisette, besette** *pt s* BD 1096, A 279, B 1565; **biset, byset** *pp* employed TC 3.1413, A 3299; bestowed, set BD 863, TC 1.521, 2.834; planned A 3012; used up D 1952; **yvel biset** ill bestowed A 3715; **wel biset** fitting PF 598.

biseye, be- *pp* provided BD 829; **goodly biseyn** handsome TC 2.1262; **richely biseye** rich-looking E 984; **yvel biseye** ill-looking E 965.

bishet *pp* shut up TC 3.602.

bishrewe *1 s* beshrew, curse D 844; *refl* D 845.

biside, bisyde, be- *adv* besides, also A 967, B 2061, F 1241; hard by, nearby B 1796; aside, away TC 3.1781; **eek b.** moreover E 416; **ther b.** near there, nearby BD 1316, TC 2.76, B 398.

biside, bisyde, be- *prep* beside PF 211, B 3937, D 420; near A 445, 620, E 291; without HF 2105, TC 2.734, 3.622.

bisides *adv* along G 1416.

bisides *prep:* **hym bisides** near at hand A 402.

bisily, be- *adv* busily HF 16, PF 74, A 301; intently F 88; without delay TC 3.1153; **bisyly** zealously TC 1.771.

bismotered *pp* soiled, stained A 76.

bisoghte, -oughte see **biseche.**

bistad *pp* beset by enemies, in trouble B 649.

bistowe *v* bestow A 3981, D 113; **bistowed** *pp* placed TC 1.967, 3.1271; spent B 1609, 1610.

bistrood *pt s* bestrode B 2093.

bisy, besy, busy *adj* busy HF 1472, A 321, etc.; eager BD 1265; intense A 2320; anxious, worried TC 3.1381; **b. cure** diligent attention, effort PF 369, TC 3.1042, A 2853, B 188; **b. drede** anxiety TC 4.1645, E 134; **b. gost** eager spirit LGW 103; **b. hevynesse** disquiet PF 89; **b. peyne** attentiveness F 509; **b. thoght** anxiety B 779; **in a bysi wyse** attentively TC 2.274.

bisye *v refl* exert oneself, occupy oneself D 209, G 758, 1442; **bisyed** *pt s* G 1146; **besyede** *pt pl* PF 192.

bisynesse, by-, be- *n* state of being

busy, activity, toil PF 86, TC 3.1413, A 3654; task, enterprise TC 1.1042, B 1415, E 1015; diligence, industry, TC 3.165, D 1196; endeavor TC 3.1610, A 520, G 24; attention D 993, E 1577; eagerness Truth 10; *pl* occupations TC 2.1174; **doon (dide) . . . b.** exert oneself BD 1156, TC 1.795, A 1007.

bit see **bidden.**

bitake *v* commit, commend: *1 s* A 3750, E 161, 559; consign H 307; **bitook** *pt s* commended G 541.

biteche *1 s* consign to B 2114.

bithynke(n), be- *v* think, imagine PF 483, D 772, H 166; consider TC 1.982; **bethenke** *1 s* BD 698; **bithoghte, bythought** *pt s* BD 1183, TC 1.545, A 4403; **bethenke** *imp s* BD 1304; **bithought, bythoght** *pp* TC 2.225, A 767.

bitok(e)neth *3 s* betokens, represents TC 5.1513, B 3942, D 581.

bitore *n* bittern, heron D 972.

bitrayen, bytraien *3 pl* betray LGW 486, G 897; betrayed *pt s* HF 294, 407; **bitrayed, betrayed** *pp* LGW 137, G 1092.

bitrayseth *3 s* betrays C 92; **bytraise** *3 pl* TC 5.1783; **betraysed** *pt s* betrayed BD 1120; **bitraised, bitraysed** *pp* TC 4.1648, B 3570.

bittre, bitter *adj* bitter TC 1.385, A 1280, G 878, etc.

bitwene, bytweene *prep* between HF 2028, TC 2.1706, etc.

bitwene, by- *adv* in between TC 2.823, 5.1086.

bitwixe(n), bitwix *prep* between A 277, 880, 1632, etc.; **betwixen,** etc. BD 156, PF 40, etc.

bityde(n) *v* happen, take place TC 2.623, C 934; **bitide** C 900; **bitit** *3 s* TC 2.48, 5.345; **bityde** *3 s subj* E 306; **bitidde** *pt s* TC 2.55; **bitid, bityd, betyd** *pp* HF 384, TC 3.288, D 2191; **bityde what bityde** come what may TC 5.750, B 2064.

biwaille(n) *v* bewail TC 5.639, B 26; **bywaille** TC 1.755; **bewaille** TC 4.272; **bewayle** feel sorry for Buk 16; **bywayling(e)** *part* TC 1. 547, 4.1251; **biwailled, bewayled** *pp* BD 1247, E 530.

biwreye(n), by- *v* reveal TC 2.1370, A 2229; **bewreye** 3.377; betray B 1323, C 823, P 948, G 150; **biwreyest** *2 s* B 773, 4241; **biwreyed** *pt s* D 533; **biwreye** *imp s* D 974; **biwreyd** *pp* H 352.

biyonde *prep* beyond B 1909.

blak *adj* black BD 253, TC 1.170, etc.; brunette D 624; **blake** *pl & wk* TC 3.1429, A 557, 899, etc.

blak *n* black BD 445, TC 1.642, A 294; blackness A 2144.

blaked *pp* blackened B 3321.

blanket *n* undyed woolen cloth, blanket D 1751.

blankmanger *n* a kind of rice pudding A 387 (see note).

blase *n* blaze TC 4.184.

blasen *v* blow (on a horn) HF 1802.

blaspheme *n* blasphemy C 593 Scogan 15.

blasphemour *n* blasphemer C 898, D 2213.

blaste *v* blow a blast HF 1866.

blaunche fevere *n* love-sickness TC 1.916.

blede *v* bleed TC 1.502; **bledde** *pt* TC 2.950, A 145.

blende *v* blind, deceive TC 2.1496; **blent** *3 s* PF 600, TC 4.5; **blente** *pt s* TC 5.1195; **blent, yblent** *pp* BD 647, TC 2.1743, A 3808, E 2113.

blere *v* blear; **blere hir ye** blear their eye, get the better of them A 4049; **bleryng of a proud milleres ye,** getting the better of . . . A 3865; **blered** *pp:* **blered is myn ye** I have been cheated G 730; **blered is thyn ye** you have been hoodwinked H 252.

blesse(n) *v* bless A 3448, B 1146; *refl* make the sign of the cross H 321; **blesseth hire** crosses herself B 449; **blesse** *3 s subj* guard, save TC 1.436; **blessed, yblessed** *pp* LGW 145, D 44, H 99. See **blisseth.**

bleve(n), bileve *v* remain TC 3.623, 4.539, 1357, F 583.

blew *adj* blue A 564, etc.

bleynte *pt s* (of **blenche**) turned away TC 3.1346; turned pale A 1078.

blisful, blys- *adj* happy, fortunate PF 48, TC 2.422, etc.; beatified, blessed A 17; beautiful, pleasing A 3247, B 172.

blisse *v* bless E 552.

blisseth *3 s:* **she blisseth hire** she crosses herself B 868; **blissed** *pp & adj* blessed C 248, 474, D 763. See **blessen.**

blody, bloody *adj* bloody TC 2.203, B 4205; bloodcurdling HF 1239, A 2512.

blondreth *3 s* blunders G 1414; **blondren** *1 pl* G 670.

bloo *adj* lead-colored HF 1647.

blosme *n* blossom A 3324; **blosmes** *pl* LGW 143, 157.

blosmy *adj* covered with blossoms PF 183, TC 2.821, E 1463.

blowe *v* blow A 565, etc.; **blowen** *pp* announced by trumpets A 2241; **blowe** *pp* inflated G 440; **yblowe,**

iblowe *pp* spread abroad HF 1139, TC 1.384, 530.

blynd *adj* blind TC 1.628, etc.; **lanes blynde** dark lanes G 658.

blynne *v* cease G 1171. See **bilynne**.

blythely *adv* gladly BD 749, 755.

blyve *adv* quickly, soon BD 152, TC 1.595; **as b., also b.** immediately, as soon as possible BD 1277, TC 1.965, 4.174, LGW 435.

bobance *n* boastfulness D 569.

bocher *n* butcher A 2025.

bode *n* omen, warning PF 343.

body *n* body HF 981, etc.; person B 1185; **bodyes** *pl* A 942.

boef *n* beef D 1753, E 1420.

boes see **bihove**.

boghte see **byen**.

boidekyn *n* dagger A 3960; **boydekyns** *pl* B 3892, 3897.

boistously *adv* E 791. Cf. **boystous**.

bokeler *n* buckler A 112, 471, 558, 3266, 4019; **bokeleer** A 668.

bokelynge *part* buckling A 2503.

boket *n* bucket A 1533.

boldnesse, boold- *n* boldness C 71, G 487; assurance BD 617.

bole *n* bull TC 3,723, 4.239; **Bole,** the sign Taurus TC 2.55; **boles** *gen s* G 797; *pl* A 2139, B 4125.

bolle *n* bowl G 1210.

bolt *n* crossbow-bolt A 3264; **b. upright** straight as an arrow, stretched out on the back A 4265, B 1506.

bombleth *3 s* makes a booming noise D 972.

bon hostell *exclam* good hospitality HF 1022.

bond, boond *n* something that binds, cord, fetter TC 3.1358, B 3262, F 131 (see note); obligation, bond, covenant, promise PF 438, A 1604, B 1558, F 1534; marriage contract A 3094; deed E 1697; binding force TC 3.1261, 1766, LGW 89; **bittre bondes** *pl* mental anguish TC 3.1116.

bond, boond see **bynde**.

bonde *n* serf, villein, slave TC 1.840, D 1660, Buk 32; a person subject to another TC 2.1223, B 3460, D 378.

bone, boone *n* request, petition, boon BD 129, HF 1537, PF 643, E 1618.

bood see **byde**.

boole armonyak *n* Armenian bole, a fine red clay G 790.

boon, bon *n* bone BD 940, TC 2.926; **bones** *pl* A 546; **fel and bones** skin and bones TC 1.91; **bicched bones** dice C 656.

boor *n* boar TC 3.721; male pig D 1829.

boos *n* boss A 3266.

boost *n* loud or threatening talk

A 4001, C 764; boast, boastful speech B 401; pride, ostentation B 3289, G 441.

boot *n* boat TC 2.3, E 1424, F 994.

boot see **byten**.

boot(e), bote *n* remedy, boot HF 32, TC 1.352, 3.61, A 424, etc.

booteles *adj* without remedy TC 1.782.

bootes *n pl* boots A 203, 273.

boras *n* borax A 630, G 790.

bord *n* plank, board BD 74, A 3440; table B 430, F 85; **to b.** at table A 3188; **hadde the b. bigonne** occupied the place of honor at the table A 52; **into shippes b.** on board ship A 3585.

bore *n* hole TC 3.1453.

borel *n* clothing D 356. See **burel**.

borneth *3 s* attends to, *lit.* burnishes TC 1.327. Cf. **burned**.

borwe, borugh *n* pledge TC 1.1038, F 596; **to b.** in pledge, as a pledge TC 5.1664, A 1622, F 1234.

borwe *v* borrow TC 1.488, A 4417.

bote see **boote**.

botel[1] *n* bottle C 886, D 1931; **botels, botelles** *pl* C 871, 877.

botel[2] *n* bundle: **botel hey** bundle of hay H 14.

boterflye *n* butterfly B 3980, 4464, E 2304.

both(e) *pron, adj & conj* both HF 676, A 1797, 1839, etc.; **oure bothe** of us both TC 1.972; **hire bothe** of them both TC 3.453; **youre bother** of you both TC 4.168.

bother see **bothe**.

botiller, but- *n* butler HF 592, B 4324.

botme *n* bottom TC 1.297, etc.

botmeles *adj* bottomless, empty TC 5.1431.

bouk *n* trunk of the body A 2746.

bountee *n* goodness BD 1198, etc.; worth, excellence B 3304.

bountevous *adj* full of goodness, virtuous, kind TC 1.883, C 110.

bour *n* bower, bed-chamber HF 1186, B 1932; **boures** *pl* PF 304, A 3367.

bourde *n* jesting H 81.

bourde *v* joke: *1 s* C 778; **wel bourded** *pp* what a joke! PF 589.

bow, bough *n* bough PF 190, A 1980; **bowes** *pl* PF 183, A 1642.

bown *adj* ready, prepared F 1503.

box *n* box tree, boxwood A 2922, B 4588; box, container B 745; cashbox A 4390.

boxtree, boxtre *n* box tree, boxwood PF 178, A 1302.

boy, boye *n* boy B 1752; rascal D 1322.

boydekyns see **boidekyn**.

boyste *n* box, flask C 307; **boystes** *pl* HF 2129.

boystous *adj* plain, rude HF 211. Cf. **boistously**.

bracer *n* guard for the forearm against the bowstring A 111.

bragot *n* a drink A 3261 (see note).

brak see **breken**.

bras *n* brass HF 142, etc.

brasile *n* a dyewood B 4649 (see note).

brast(e) see **bresten**.

brat *n* rag, coarse cloth or garment G 881.

braunche *n* branch PF 612, etc.; species TC 3.132.

brawn, brawen *n* muscle A 546; *pl* A 2135; meat, flesh, flesh of the boar D 1750, F 1254.

brayde see **breyde**.

breche, breech *n* breech (part of body) B 4638; short undergarment, shorts B 2049, C 948.

brede[1] *n* roast meat HF 1222.

brede[2]**, breede** *n* breadth BD 956, A 1970, G 1228; space TC 1.179; **on b.** abroad TC 1.530.

breed, bred *n* bread BD 94, TC 2.444, etc.

breem, *n* bream, carp A 350.

breeth, breth *n* breath TC 1.801, A 5, etc.

breke(n) *v* break TC 3.1299, A 551, F 698; cut short, interrupt TC 2.1600, 5.1032; **brak** *pt s* broke BD 71, A 1468; **breeke, breke** *pt s subj* would break B 4578, E 2306; **brek** *imp* B 3390, 3117; **broke, broken** TC 1.89, G 920; **broken** *ppl adj* fragmentary E 1425 (see note).

brekers *n pl* breakers PF 78.

brekke *n* blemish BD 940.

brembul *n* bramble B 1936.

breme *adj* fierce TC 4.184.

breme *adv* fiercely A 1699.

bren *n* bran A 4053, A 4430, D 478.

brend see **brennen**.

brenne(n) *v* burn, be burnt TC 1.91, A 2867, D 816; **brynne** D 52; **brende, brente** *pt* HF 954, A 2403, B 289; **brennyng(e)** *part* A 2338, G 802; **brent, brend, ybrent, ybrend** *pp* TC 4.77, A 946, D 375; **brend gold** refined, pure gold A 2162.

brennynge *n* burning A 996, 2338.

brennyngly *adv* hotly TC 1.607; fervently A 1564.

brere *n* briar E 1825; *pl* A 1532.

brest *n* breast TC 1.932, A 115, etc.; *pl* BD 956, TC 3.1250.

brest boon *n* breastbone A 2710.

breste(n) *v* burst, break HF 2018, TC 4.373, A 1980, D 1103; crush, overwhelm TC 3.1434; **brast** *pt s* B 4408; **bruste, broste** *pt pl* TC 2.326, B 671, C 234; **breste** *3 s subj* may break F 759; **braste, brast, brest** *pt subj* would burst BD 1193. TC 2.1008, 530, H 263; **brosten** *pp* burst TC 2.976; broken A 3829.

brestyng *n* bursting, breaking F 973.

bretful, bret-ful *adj* brimful HF 2123, A 687, 2164.

bretherhed(e) *n* brotherhood B 1232, D 1399; gild, fraternity A 511.

brew *pt 3 s* brewed, plotted B 3575.

brewhous *n* brewhouse, alehouse A 3334.

breyde *v* move suddenly, start, dart; awake, come to TC 4.230, F 477; **breyde, brayde** *pt s* A 4285, D 799, F 1027; pulled, took HF 1678, B 837.

briberyes *n pl* extortions D 1367.

brid see **bryd**.

brigge *n* bridge A 3922.

bright, bryght *adj* bright BD 821, HF 503, etc.; *as n* brightness TC 2.864.

brighte, bryghte *adv* brightly HF 1015, TC 2.764, B 11.

brike *n* trap B 3580.

brocage *n* the use of agents A 3375 (see note).

broche, brooch *n* brooch HF 1740, A 160, etc.

brodder *adj* broader D 1688.

brode *adv* broadly HF 1683, A 739; plainly TC 5.1017; with open eyes G 1420.

brode see **brood**.

brokkynge *part* trilling, quavering A 3377.

bromes *n pl* broom bushes HF 1226.

brond *n* brand (burning wood), firebrand B 2095, 3224, E 1777; **brondes** *pl* A 2338.

brood, brod(e) *adj* HF 792, A 155; **brode** *pl & def* A 2136, 3024.

broste, brosten see **bresten**.

brotel, -il *adj* brittle, fragile, insecure TC 3.820, E 1279, 2061.

brotelnesse *n* fragility, insecurity TC 5.1832, E 1279; **brotilnesse** frailty E 2241.

brother *n* brother HF 795, etc.; **brother** *gen s* brother's A 3084, B 3593; blood brother A 1131; **breth(e)ren** *pl* TC 1.471, C 416.

brouded see **broyden**.

brouke *v* keep, enjoy the use of B 4490, E 2308; **browke** *1 s subj* may I keep HF 273; **browken** *3 pl subj* may they enjoy LGW 194.

broun *adj* brown BD 857, etc.

browdynge *n* embroidery A 2498.

broyded *pp* braided A 1049.

broyden *pp* embroidered A 3238; **brouded** ornamented B 3659.

bruste see **bresten**.

brustles *n pl* bristles A 556, E 1824.

brybe *v* steal A 4417; practise extortion D 1378.

bryd, brid(d) *n* bird HF 1003, TC 3.10, A 3699; **bryddes, briddes** *pl* PF 190, TC 2.921.

bryde *n* bride E 1728, etc.

brydel, bri- *n* bridle TC 1.953, A 169, etc.

brymstoon *n* brimstone A 629, G 798.

brynge(n), bringe *v* bring HF 1573, A 602, B 3623, etc.; **brynges** *2 s* HF 1908; **brynge** *3 s subj* may bring TC 1.31; **broughte, broghte, broght** *pt 3 s* HF 2029, TC 2.914, LGW 516, A 566; **brynge** *imp s* TC 2.1132; **bryngeth** *imp pl* B 3384, F 1489; **brought, broght, ybrought, ybroght** *pp* LGW 599, A 1111, 1490, 2697; **made . . . broght** caused to be brought HF 155; **forth brynge,** bring up, rear, PF 192, 613.

bryngere *n* one who brings D 1196.

brynke *n* brink E 1401; coast F 858, 1160.

brynne see **brennen**.

bugle horn *n* drinking vessel made from the horn of a bugle or wild ox F 1253.

buk(ke) *n* buck (in its sixth year) PF 195, B 1946; *pl* BD 429; **may blowe the bukkes horn** may go whistle A 3387.

bulle *n* papal decree C 388, 909, E 748; **bulles** *pl* C 336, 342, E 739, 744.

bulte *v* bolt, separate the bran B 4430.

bulte see **bilden**.

burdoun *n* bass A 673 (see note); **burdon** bass accompaniment A 4165.

burel *adj* plain F 716; (like those wearing borel or coarse clothing) **borel men** laymen B 3145; **burrel(l) folk** lay folk D 1872, 1874.

burgeys *n* burgess TC 4.345, A 369, 754.

burghes *n pl* towns, boroughs D 870.

burien, -ye, berie *v* bury B 1828, C 884, D 500; **bury** *2 pl subj* BD 207; **buryed** *pt s* G 407, 548; **burieth** *imp pl* E 571; **beryed** *pp* C 405; **buryed** *pp* E 1178; **yburyed, iburied** *pp* A 946, TC 2.1311.

burned *pp* burnished, polished, shining HF 1387, A 1983, B 4054, C 38, F 1247. Cf. **borneth**.

burthe *n* birth TC 5.209.

buryeles *n pl* catacombs G 186.

busk *n* bush A 2013; **buskes** *pl* A 1579.

but *adv* only PF 54, TC 1.223, A 120, etc.

but *conj* unless BD 1188, TC 3.1483, C 741; except B 431; that . . . not LGW 10; **but as** except that A 4301; **but if, but yf** unless TC 4.1490, 5.124, 877, LGW 13, A 351, 582, B 636, D 2076; provided A 656, 1799.

butiller see **botiller**.

buxom *adj* obedient, yielding, obliging B 1367, E 1287, 1333; gracious B 1432.

buxomly *adv* obediently E 186.

buxumnesse *n* humility Truth 15.

buylden see **bilden**.

by *adv* nearby B 4458; **faste by** near TC 1.117, A 1688, B 3116; **by and by** side by side, in a row A 1011, 4143; one after the other LGW 304.

by *prep* by A 25, etc.; along A 4293, B 1626; at TC 5.1491, G 913; beside BD 388; concerning, with respect to PF 477, 599, TC 3.936, LGW 271, A 2021, D 229, 1922; in comparison with TC 1.889; on A 3929; with D 622; **as by** by C 601; in C 645; considering A 244; according to TC 2.1341; **faste by** near A 1476, F 504; **by the morwe** in the morning TC 2.961, LGW 49, A 334; **by proces** in order TC 5.1491; **by rewe** in a row D 506; **by al weyes** in every respect BD 1271; **be no way** in no wise HF 1258.

byde, bide *v* wait TC 1.1067, A 1576; remain TC 4. 162, 5.496; **bood** *pt s* waited TC 5.29; remained A 4399; **byd, bid** *imp s* TC 2.1519, 3.740.

bye(n), beye *v* buy B 1246, C 845, D 167; **boghte, boughte** *pt s* A 2088, C 293; **boughten, boghte** *pt pl* TC 1.136, B 420; **boght, yboght, ybought** *pp* HF 1752, A 3836, TC 3.1319.

byfor *prep* see **bifore**.

bygyle see **bigyle**.

byheete see **bihote**.

byheste see **biheste**.

byhalve, byhalf *n* behalf TC 2.1458, LGW 497.

byhoveth see **bihove**.

byhynden *prep* behind TC 1.179.

byjaped *pp* ridiculed TC 1.531; deceived A 1585, G 1385, H 145; fooled TC 5.1119.

byldere *adj* used for building PF 176.

byle *n* bill (of bird) B 4051; **biles** *pl* HF 868.

bylyve *adv* quickly, soon TC 2.1513. See **blyve**.

bynde *v* bind A 2414, B 1810; **bond, boond** *pt s* HF 1590, A 4082; **bounde** *pt pl* B 3260; **bonde, bounde, bounden** *pp* Buk 32, TC 1.859, A 1316, B 270; **ibounden, ybounde(n)** PF 268, A 1149, 2151.

byndyng *n* compulsion A 1304.

bynethe *adv* below A 4041, B 4143.

bynethe *prep* beneath D 2142.

bynne *n* bin A 593.

byreve see **bireve**.

byset see **bisette**.

bysynesse see **bisynesse**.

byte(n), bite *v* HF 1044, TC 3.737, A 3745, F 513; eat into A 631; cut into F 158; **boot** *pt s* B 3791; **bitynge** *ppl adj* A 2546.

bytraien see **bitrayen**.

bytrent *3 s* encircles TC 3.1231; goes around TC 4.870.

bytyme *adv* early, soon, promptly TC 2.1093, 4.1105, LGW 452; **bitymes** G 1008.

bywaille, bywayling see **biwaillen**.

bywopen *pp* tear-stained TC 4.916.

by-word *n* proverb TC 4.769.

bywreye see **biwreyen**.

C

caas *n* quiver (for arrows) A 2358. See **cas**.

cacche, cache *v* catch, capture, seize, take HF 404, A 4105; receive, obtain BD 781, 969; **caughte, kaughte** *pt s* BD 681, A 1399, 4273; drew B 1861; **kaught** *pt pl* BD 124; **cache** *imp s* seize TC 2.291; **caught, kaught, ykaught** *pp* BD 395, 838, HF 282, TC 5.703, B 628; **cacche whoso may** catch as catch can D 76.

cadence *n* see note to HF 623.

cake *n* flat loaf A 668, 4094.

calcenyng *part* oxidizing G 771.

calcinacioun *n* oxidation G 804.

calkulyng *n* reckoning, divination TC 1.171, 4.1398.

calle *n*, caul, hairnet, close-fitting cap, esp. for women D 1018; **maken an howve above a c.** engage in double dealing TC 3.775 (see note).

cam see **comen**.

camuse, ka- *adj* flat, pug(-nosed) A 3934, 3974.

can see **conne**.

candele, candle *n* candle TC 3.859, 1141, D 334.

canel-boon *n* collarbone BD 943.

canevas *n* canvas G 939.

canon *n* see note to C 980.

cantel *n* portion A 3008.

cape *3 pl* gape, stare A 3841; **caped** *pt s* A 3473; **capyng** *part* A 3444; **cape after** wish, long for TC 3.558. See **gape**.

capitayn *n* captain B 3741, C 582, H 230.

capon *n* capon D 1839; **capouns** *pl* C 856.

cappe *n* cap A 683; **sette hir aller c.** outwitted them all A 586; cf. A 3143.

capul *n* horse, cart-horse A 4088, 4105, D 2150, H 64; **caples** *pl* D 1554.

carayne see **careyne**.

cardynacle *n* (the Host's mistake for *cardyacle*) palpitation, pain around the heart C 313.

care *n* sorrow, woe, worry TC 5.54, A 1321, etc.

care *v* care, worry, sorrow TC 3.1645, D 329, E 1212; **c. thee noght** don't worry A 3298.

careful *adj* sorrowful A 1565.

careyne, -ayne *n* dead body, carcass PF 177, A 2013, B 3814.

carf see **kerve**.

cariage *n* a feudal obligation to transport goods, payment in lieu of it D 1570 (see note).

carie(n) *v* carry, convey HF 1280, A 130; **carien, carie** *3 pl* TC 5.742, B 1814; **caried** *pt s* G 567; **carieden, caryeden** *pt pl* A 2900, G 1219; **caryinge, cariynge** *part* HF 545, C 875; **caried, ycaried, ycaryed** *pp* A 1021, B 3240, C 791.

carl *n* fellow A 545, 3469, C 717, D 1568. Cf. **cherl**.

carol *n* a song accompanying a round dance; **caroles** *pl* A 1931; **for carole or for daunce** for anything LGW 687.

carole *v* participate in the carol (q.v.) BD 849; **carolynge** *part* G 1345.

carpe *v* joke A 474.

carryk *n* carrack, a large sailing vessel D 1688.

cart(e) *n* chariot HF 943, 956, TC 5.278; cart B 4208, D 1539; **cartes** *pl* PF 102.

carte-hors *n pl* chariot horses HF 944.

carter(e) *n* carter PF 102, A 2022, B 4249, D 1540.

cas, caas *n* something that occurs or happens; an event, occurrence, experience TC 4.420, A 2110, B 3849, 4394, E 316; chance, fortune, misfortune HF 1052, TC 1.568, 2.285, A 844; situation, circumstances BD 725, TC 1.29, A 1411, D 1831; matter, problem TC 4.416, A 2971, F 1514; cause, reason F 1430, H 308; example, supposition TC 2.729;

case at law A 323 (*pl*), B 36, C 163 (*pl*); **in no cas** under any circumstances D 665; **in swich caas** in such a case A 655; **par cas** by chance C 885; **upon cas** perchance, by chance TC 1.271, 4.649, A 3661.

cast *n* throwing TC 2.868; plan, design, plot HF 1178, PF 305, A 3605; occasion B 3477; **castes** *pl* plots, deceits A 2468.

caste(n) *v* throw, cast, *lit. & fig.* (a stone, the eyes, etc.) HF 1048, A 3712, 4386, C 60; leap A 3330; calculate, reckon B 1406; take thought, consider HF 1148, TC 1.749, 2.690, 5.389; **caste 1 s** estimate, conjecture A 2172; **casteth 3 s** BD 212; **casteth hym** applies himself G 738; **caste 3 s** perceives G 1414; **cast of** takes off (clothes) D 783; **caste 3 pl** C 268; **caste** *pt s* TC 2.1259, A 208, etc.; turned TC 5.927; drove (ship) B 508; calculated (astrol.) TC 2.74; considered TC 4.161, A 2854; planned, plotted TC 1.1071, 2.1357, B 406; contrived B 805; determined TC 1.75, 2.1357; resolved TC 4.34; **caste** *pt pl* A 2947, B 1829, C 542; emitted G 244; **casten** *pt pl* considered TC 2.1485, B 212; arranged B 4265; resolved TC 1.88; **cast** *imp pl* lay aside, put away TC 2.222, G 384; **cast, casten, ycast** *pp* BD 185, TC 5.1696, B 1796, G 939; plotted C 880; thrown to the ground TC 2.1389; **casten . . . compace** lay out a plan (?) HF 1170; **japes forth to caste** to make jokes TC 2.1167; **caste to the ground** overturn (a cart) B 4237; **caste up** raise, open TC 1.204, 2.615, D 1249.

casuelly *adv* by chance HF 679, B 4291.

catel *n* property, possessions, chattels, wealth A 373, B 27, C 594, E 1525; goods A 540.

cause *n* cause HF 20, 52, etc.; reason HF 612, 1563; purpose B 4479, D 123; plea TC 5.80; case, condition TC 5.1230; **by the c., by that c.** because TC 4.99, 5.127; to the end that A 2488; **in c. of** responsible for, to blame TC 3.986.

causeles, -lees *adj & adv* without cause or reason HF 667, PF 590, E 1975.

cavillacioun *n* cavilling D 2136.

caytyf, kay- *adj* captive, wretched A 1552, 1946.

caytyf, kai- *n* captive, wretched person TC 4.104, A 3269, C 728; **caytyves** *pl* A 924, 1717.

cedir *n* cedar TC 2.918.

ceint, ceynt *n* girdle A 329, 3235.

celerer *n* cellarer B 3126 (see note).

celle *n* priory or dependent religious house A 172; an individual cell in such a house B 3162; a supposed compartment of the brain A 1376 (see note).

celle *n* floorboard A 3822 (see note).

cementyng *n* fusing by means of heat G 817.

centaure *n* centaury (an herb) B 4153.

ceptre, sc- *n* scepter PF 256, B 3334, 3563.

cercle, se- *n* circle HF 791, 815; sphere Scogan 9; **cercles of his eyen** the iris A 2131.

cerclen *v* encircle TC 3.1767; **cercled** *pp* bounded Rosem 2.

cered *ppl adj* waxed G 808.

cerial *adj* **ook cerial** a species of oak A 2290.

ceriously *adv* in detail B 185.

certes *adv* certainly BD 84, HF 1693, A 875, etc.

certeyn, -ein, -ayn *adj* certain BD 119, HF 1268, TC 2.1548, A 815, 2967, B 149.

certeyn *n* a certain amount: **a c. of gold** G 1024; a certain sum: **a certein of hire owen men** a certain number TC 3.596; A 3193, G 776; (with ellipsis of *of*) **a c. frankes** B 1524; **a c. yeres** B 3367; **in certeyn, in good certayn** certainly HF 426, B 1918, E 1182.

certeyn *adv* certainly HF 363, A 375, 451, etc.

ceruse *n* white lead A 630.

cesse *v* cease TC 2.692, B 1066; put an end to TC 1.445; **cesseth** *3 s* F 257; **cesse** *3 s subj* if it cease TC 2.483, 1388; **cessed** *pt s* G 124, TC 2.849.

cetewale *n* setwall or zedoary (a root) A 3207, B 1951.

ceynt see **ceint**.

chaar, char *n* chariot TC 3.1704, A 2138, 2148, B 3550, F 671.

chaast, chast *adj* chaste C 43, D 1917, etc.

chaastnesse *n* chastity G 88

chace *v* chase, pursue, drive B 1756, E 341; **c. at** rail at, reproach TC 1.908, 3.1801; **chaced** *pp* driven B 366, D 1916.

chaffare *n* trade, business A 4389, B 1530, G 1421; wares, merchandise B 138, 1475, 1518, D 521, E 2438.

chaffare *v* trade, do business B 139.

chalangyng *n* accusation C 264.

chalenge *v* claim D 1200; **chalange** *1 s* F 1324.

chalons *n pl* bedspreads A 4140.

chamberere *n* chambermaid D 300, E 819; **chambereres** *pl* E 977.

chambre *n* room, bedroom BD 258, HF 366, A 1440, B 167; lodging G 1023; **chambres** *pl* A 28, E 263; **grete chaumbre** the great hall of a house or palace TC 2.1712; **c. of paramentz** presence chamber F 269; **c. of Venus** pudendum D 618.

champartie *n* equal power A 1949.

chanoun *n* canon G 573, etc.

chaped *pp* trimmed, mounted A 366.

chapeleyne *n* chaplain A 164.

chapitre *n* chapter (of a book, etc.) B 4255; **chapitres** *pl* PF 32; the body of friars constituting a house D 1945; meeting of the archdeacon's court D 1361.

chapman *n* merchant A 397, B 1444; **chapmen** *pl* B 135, 1416.

chapmanhode *n* business B 143; **chapmanhede** conduct of business B 1428.

charbocle *n* carbuncle B 2061; **carbuncle** HF 1363.

charge *n* burden HF 1439, TC 1.651; anything heavy HF 746; weight BD 893; duty, responsibility PF 507, TC 2.994, C 95, E 163; importance LGW 620, F 359; matter, concern TC 1.444, D 321; consideration A 1284; request, demand TC 4.180; **yeve in c.** request, enjoin B 1622; **no c.** no matter G 749; **it were no c.** it wouldn't matter A 2287; **if it be in his c.** if it is in his power A 733.

charge(n) *v* burden, trouble TC 2.1437; command, enjoin LGW 493, B 802; **charge** *1 s* command, enjoin LGW 548, 551, D 1992, 2026, E 164; **chargeth nought** is not important TC 3.1576; **charged** *pt* ordered, commanded B 209, D 2213, G 287; **charged** *pp* loaded B 3556, D 1539.

char-hors *n pl* chariot-horses TC 5.1018.

charitable *adj* kind, loving LGW 444, TC 5.823; tender-hearted A 143; devoted to good works D 1795, 1940.

charitee *n* Christian love or charity A 532, D 865, 1908; charitable mood A 452, 1623; kindness PF 508; act of justice A 1433; **for seinte c., par c.** for (holy) charity, a mild oath A 1721, B 2081.

chartre *n* charter, deed A 3327; *pl* TC 3.340, E 2173.

chasted *pp* chastised, given an object lesson F 491.

chasteyn *n* chestnut-tree A 2922.

chastise *v* warn, deter B 3695; **chastisynge** *part* punishing C 98; **ben chastised** learn a lesson TC 3.329. See **chasted**.

chaunce *n* unexpected event, accident TC 2.464, 5.1668, A 1752; luck, fortune F 679, G 593, I 20; possibility B 1045; circumstance BD 1113, 1285, G 527; a throw in dice B 125 (see note), C 653; **par c.** by chance C 606.

chaunge *n* change TC 2.22; exchange TC 4.665, F 535.

chaunge(n) *v* change BD 497, A 1637; exchange TC 4.59; **chaunged** *pp* exchanged TC 4.553.

chaungynge *ppl adj* changeable E 996.

chaungyng(e) *n* changing A 1647, F 782; exchanging TC 4.231.

chaunterie *n* chantry A 510 (see note).

chaunteth *3 s* sings A 3367, E 1850.

chayer *n* chair, litter B 3803; rostrum D 1518.

cheere, chere *n* face, countenance LGW 64, TC 3.1356, A 857; look, change of countenance TC 1.312, 3.429; *pl* TC 2.1507; behavior, bearing A 139, 728; mood TC 1.879, E 7; gladness, merriment, mirth TC 3.1710, E 1112; **make(n) c.** be pleasant or agreeable TC 3.1554, 1664; **maked . . . c.** was friendly C 147; showed hospitality D 486; **beele c.** hospitality B 1599.

cheeve *v* succeed; **yvele moot he c.** may he come to a bad end G 1225.

chef, chief *adj* chief BD 910, 973, TC 3.134.

chek *n* check(mate) BD 659.

cheke *n* cheek D 433, 792; cheekbone, jawbone B 3228.

chekker *n* chessboard BD 660.

chek mat *n* checkmate TC 2.754.

chepe *v* buy, bid for D 268.

chep(e), cheep *n* cheapness, bargain D 523; time of low prices HF 1974 **as good chep** as cheaply, as easily TC 3.641.

cherice(n), cheryce *v* cherish TC 1.986, 2.726, LGW 472; bestow favor on B 3710; treat TC 3.175; **cherisseth** *3 s* treats F 1554; **cherisse** *imp s* cherish 1388; **cherisseth** *imp pl* take good care of F 353; **cherisynge** *part* TC 4.1534.

cherl *n* fellow, man TC 1.1024, C 140; **cherles** *gen s* as *adj* vulgar A 3169; **cherles** *gen pl* peasants', rabble's A 2459.

cherlyssh *adj* churlish F 1523.

cherubynnes *n gen* cherub's A 624.

ches *n* chess BD 51, F 900, etc.

chese *n* cheese A 3628, C 448, D 1739, 1747.

chese, cheese v choose PF 146, D 176, 1748; **chese** 3 s subj let him choose A 3177; **chees** imp s A 1595; **ches, chees** pt s BD 791, LGW 146, E 1597, F 1440; **chesynge** part E 162.

cheste n chest D 309, (for books) LGW 510; coffin D 502; **chiste** container TC 5.1368.

cheterynge n chattering TC 2.68. Cf. **chiteren.**

chevalrie see **chivalrie.**

chevyssaunce n loan, usury A 282 (see note), B 1519, 1537, 1581.

chidestere n scolding woman E 1535.

chidynges n chidings, complaints HF 1028.

chieftayn n leader A 2555.

chiertee n fondness, affection B 1526, D 396, F 881.

chiknes n pl chickens A 380.

child n child A 2019, etc; young man A 3325, B 2000, 2007.

childhede n childhood B 1691, 3445.

childly adj childlike, youthful BD 1095.

chilyndre n a kind of sundial B 1396 (see note).

chimeneye, chymenee n fireplace TC 3.1141, A 3776.

chirche, che- n church HF 473, G 546, etc.

chirche dore n church door A 460, D 6.

chirche reves n pl churchwardens D 1307.

chirketh 3 s chirps D 1804.

chirkyng n harsh noise A 2004; **chirkynges** pl creakings HF 1943.

chiste see **cheste.**

chit see **chyde.**

chiteren v chatter G 1394. Cf. **cheterynge.**

chivalrie, che- n knighthood HF 1340, A 45; knightly exploits or distinction A 865, 2184, H 126; body of knights, men-at-arms collectively A 878, B 3871; knightly class B 235.

chivalrous adj doughty TC 5.802.

choppen v strike HF 1824.

chough see **cow.**

choys, chois n choice PF 406, 649, TC 4.971, B 4436, E 154.

chuk n cluck B 4364.

chukketh 3 s cluks B 4372.

chyde, chide v chide, blame BD 937, TC 3.1433, B 1618; **chit** 3 s scolds G 921; **chidde** pt s A 3999, D 223; **chideth** imp pl D 1824; **chidyng** ppl adj D 279.

chymbe n rim of a barrel A 3895.

chymbe v chime A 3896.

chymenee see **chimeneye.**

chyvachee n example of horsemanship H 50; **chyvachie** expedition A 85.

ciprees, cipresse n cypress PF 179, B 2071.

circuit n circumference A 1887.

circumscrive v encompass TC 5.1865.

ciser n strong drink B 3245.

citee n a walled town, city HF 1845, etc.

citezeyn n denizen, inhabitant HF 930.

citole n pear-shaped stringed instrument A 1959.

citrinacioun n assuming a citron color G 816.

citryn adj lemon-colored A 2167.

clamb, clamben see **clymben.**

clappe n clap of thunder HF 1040; idle talk A 3144.

clappeth 3 s knocks D 1581; chatters B 3971; **clappe** 3 pl prate G 964; **clapte** pt s shut quickly or forcibly A 3740, D 1699, E 2159; **clappeth** imp pl clatter, talk noisily E 1200.

claree, clarree n wine flavored with honey and spices A 1471, E 1807, 1843.

claterynge n clattering A 2492, D 1865.

clause n clause, sentence, a few words A 715, E 1431; stipulation TC 2.728.

clawe(n) v scratch TC 4.728, D 940; **clew** pt s scratched HF 1702; **clawed him on the bak** rubbed, patted . . . (complimented him) A 4326; **yclawed** pp clawed D 1731.

clawes n pl claws HF 545, etc.; **clowes** HF 1785.

cled see **clothen.**

cleer(e), clere adj clear, bright, shining A 1062, 1683, B 11, G 201; unclouded, cheerful TC 4.1435; pure C 914; noble PF 77; beautiful B 2048.

cleere, clere adv clearly LGW 139, A 170, 2331, B 1845.

cleernesse n brightness LGW 84, G 403.

clene, cleene adj clean A 133; unsoiled, free from TC 3.257, D 944; chaste G 159; honorable TC 2.580, 3.1229.

clene adv clean, completely BD 423, TC 5.1054, A 367, B 1106, F 626, G 1425.

clennesse n purity, chastity A 506, D 1883, 1910.

clepe(n) v call, name, cry out BD 810, TC 3.317, A 643, F 331; **clepe** 1 s TC 1.8, B 1341; **clepeth** 3 s BD 185; **clepe, clepen** pr pl BD 512, A 620, G 2; **cleped** pt s F 1487; **clepyng** part TC 4.1157; **clepe** imp s A 3432; **cleped, clepid, clept** pp TC 1.66, A 121, B 725, G 863; **ycleped, yclept** pp A 376, G 772; **clepe(n) ayein** recall TC 2.521, 5.914, H 354.

clere v clear TC 2.2, 806; grow light, dawn TC 5.519.

clere adj & adv see **cleere.**

clergeoun n pupil, schoolboy B 1693.

clergial adj learned G 752.

clergye n learning D 1277.

clerk n a member of the clergy or one preparing for the priesthood A 285, B 143; one who can read and write, a learned person E 32, F 1105; **clerkes** gen s A 1163; **clerkes** pl the learned, writers BD 53, LGW 370.

cleve v cleave, split: **cleve** 3 s subj may he cleave TC 3.375; **clefte** pt s BD 72.

clifte n cleft D 2145.

clippe[1] v clip, cut (hair) A 3326, B 3257; **clipped** pp B 3261.

clippe[2] 1 s embrace TC 3.1344; **clippeth** 3 s E 2413.

clobbed adj club-shaped B 3088.

clom interj mum, hush A 3638, 3639.

clomb, clomben see **clymben.**

cloos, clos adj close, concealed TC 2.1534, 3.332, G 1369; shut B 4522, H 37.

clooth, cloth n cloth, woven material PF 273, A 3748; garment D 1633, E 916; robe B 3663; clothing D 238, G 637; clothes pl hangings A 2277, 2281; bed-clothes TC 2.1544; **clooth of gold** A 2158 (see note), 2568, E 1117; **c. of lake** linen B 2048; **cloth of Reynes** linen fabric from Rennes BD 255; **clooth of Tars** A 2160 (see note).

clooth-makyng n weaving A 447.

clos n enclosure B 4550.

closet n small room, bedroom TC 2.599, 3.663, 687; **c. dore** bedroom door TC 3.684.

clote-leef n leaf of the burdock G 577.

clothe(n) v clothe B 1202; wrap, enclose TC 5.1418; **cladde** pt s A 1409; **cladden** pl 2 pl E 864; **clothed** pp A 363; **clad, yclad** pp clothed PF 173, A 103, 3320, G 133; bound A 294; **cled** pp covered BD 252.

clothered pp clotted A 2745.

cloumbe see **clymben.**

clowes see **clawes.**

clowe-gylofre n clove A 1952.

clowt n piece of cloth C 736; **cloutes** pl pieces E 1953; rags C 348.

cloysterer, cloi- n a cloistered person, monk A 259, 3661, B 3129.

cloystre, cloi- n cloister A 181, 185, D 2099, 2102, G 43.

clyket, cli- *n* small key E 2046, 2121, 2123.

clymbe(n) *v* climb HF 1119, A 3625; **clymbeth** *3 s* B 3966; **clamb, clomb** *pt s* HF 1118, B 1987; **clamben, clomben** *pt pl* HF 2151, A 3636; **climbing** *ppl adj* Truth 3; **clombe, cloumbe, clomben** *pp* TC 1.215, B 12, 3592, 4388.

clynke(n) *v* clink, ring B 1186, C 664.

clynkyng *n* clinking B 3984.

coagulat *pp* coagulated, congealed G 811.

cod *n* bag, stomach C 534.

cofre *n* coffer, chest A 298, B 26, 1955; money box F 1571, G 836; coffin PF 177.

coghe, cogheth see **coughen.**

coillons *n pl* testicles C 952.

cok *n* cock PF 350, etc.; **cokkes bones** euphemism for *God's bones* H 9, I 29.

cokenay *n* cockney, weakling A 4208.

cokewold *n* cuckold A 3152, 3226, etc.

cokkel *n* corn cockle (a weed) B 1183.

cokkes see **cok.**

cokkow, cuk- *n* cuckoo PF 358, 498, A 1810.

col-blak *adj* coalblack A 2142, 3240.

colde(n) *v* grow cold PF 145, TC 3.800, 4.362, etc.

col(e) *n* charcoal, coal, fuel TC 2.1332, A 2692, G 1160; **coles** *pl* coals, embers B 3323, G 1114, 1116, etc.

coler *n* collar TC 5.811, A 3239.

colera *n* choler, bile B 4118.

colered *pp* furnished with collars A 2152.

colerik, -yk *adj* irascible A 587; bilious B 4145; inducing passion F 51 (see note).

col-fox *n* a kind of fox with black markings B 4405 (see note).

collacioun *n* conference E 325.

collateral *adj* incidental, of secondary importance TC 1.262.

collect *adj:* **collect yeeris** periods of 20 to 3000 years in the movement of a planet F 1275 (see note).

colour *n* color PF 174; pretence D 399; **colour(e)s** *pl* outward appearances F 511; figures of speech, rhetorical devices HF 859, E 16 (see note to this and prec.), F 39, 726.

colpons *n pl* pieces (cut off) A 2867; shreds, strands A 679.

colt *n* colt A 3263; **a coltes tooth** characteristics of youth, inclination to wantonness A 3888, D 602.

coltissh *adj* colt-like E 1847.

columbyn *adj* dove-like E 2141.

comande(n), comaunde *v* command TC 1.1057, 5.112, D 73, etc.

combre-world *n* an encumbrance to the world TC 4.279.

combust *pp* burnt, burnt up TC 3.717, G 811.

come *n* coming G 343.

comedye *n* cheerful poem or tale TC 5.1788.

come(n) *v* come BD 708, PF 76, etc.; **com, come** *1 s* HF 1906, A 3720; **comest** *2 s* D 246; **cometh, comth** *3 s* HF 71, A 3496; **come** *pl* A 801, G 788; **come** *2 s subj* B 119, H 361; **come, coome** *3 s subj* HF 1786, B 1346; **cam, com, coom** *pt s* BD 78, A 547, G 242; **cam, came, comen, coomen, coome** *pt pl* B 145, 178, 1805, E 752, F 1012, G 1220; **comen** *pt pl subj* TC 4.1522; **com** *imp s* BD 749, A 672; **cometh** *imp pl* A 839; **comynge** *part* A 2128; *as adj* TC 1.378, E 79; **come(n), ycome(n)** *pp* BD 135, HF 1074, LGW 37, A 77; **com(e) of** come on, hurry up PF 494, TC 2.310, A 3728, etc.

comeveden see **commeve.**

comfort see **confort.**

comlynesse *n* comeliness, pleasing appearance or behavior BD 827, 966.

commeve *3 s subj* may move TC 5.1386; **commeveth** *3 s* moves TC 5.1783; **comeveden** *pt 2 pl* instigated TC 3.17.

commune, comune *adj* common, common to all, general, familiar TC 4.392, B 3436, F 107; public E 1583; accustomed BD 812; **in com(m)une, as in c.** in general, generally, commonly A 1251, 2681, B 4190; in the same way HF 1548.

commune *n* common pasturage, etc. E 1313 (see note); common people E 70; **communes** *pl* common people, commons A 2509.

compaignable *adj* sociable A 1194, 4062.

compaignye, companye *n* company HF 1528, A 24, etc.; companionship TC 3.396, 1748, A 2311.

compas *n* craft, cunning HF 462; circle A 1889; large circle HF 798; **a-compas** in a circle LGW 300; **tryne c.** threefold world,—earth, sea, and air, the universe G 45; **compasses** *pl* ingenious figures, images HF 1302.

compassed *pt 3 s* planned B 591.

compassyng *n* contriving, scheming A 1996; **compassinges** *pl* devices, contrivances HF 1188.

compeer *n* comrade, associate A 670, 4419.

compleccioun, complexioun *n* the

combination of the four humors (hot, cold, moist, dry) in the body, from which the temperament of a person resulted; temperament, disposition, complexion A 333, 2475, B 4145, F 782; *pl* temperaments HF 21, TC 5.369, B 4114.

compleet, complet *adj* complete, completed B 4379, A 1893; *as adv* completely TC 5.828.

compleyne *v* complain, lament HF 368, TC 1.415, etc.

compleynt(e) *n* complaint, lament TC 1.541, etc.

compleynyng *n* lament, grief B 929, F 945, etc.

complyn *n* compline, the last canonical hour, the service sung before retiring A 4171.

comporte *v* endure TC 5.1397.

composicioun *n* agreement A 848, 2651; *pl* combinations F 229.

compouned *pp* combined HF 1029, 2108.

comprende *v* contain TC 3.1687.

comyn *n* cumin B 2045.

comyng(e) *n* coming TC 2.1102, 3.196, 921, B 1240, E 912.

conceite, -ceyte *n* idea, conception TC 1.692, 996; *pl* TC 3.804; judgment, opinion G 1078, 1214.

conceyved, -seyved *pp* conceived B 1662, 3675; aroused TC 5.1598.

conclude(n) *v* conclude A 3067, B 14; sum up A 1358, 1895; include G 429; obtain a desired result G 773; **concluded** *pp* reached a conclusion E 1607.

conclusioun, -ion, -yon *n* outcome HF 342; end, purpose TC 1.480, D 115, 430, F 492; desired result G 672; accomplishment F 1263; judgment, decision PF 620, A 1743; *pl* propositions, astrological procedures A 3193; **as in c.** in short B 3824; **as for c.** in conclusion TC 5.765, B 4341; **this my c.** that's all F 889.

concubyn *n* concubine A 650.

condescende *v* get down F 407; **condescended** *pp* agreed, settled (upon) E 1605.

condicioun, -ion *n* state, status A 38, B 99, etc.; manner, disposition A 1431; personal characteristic LGW 40; condition D 2132.

conferme *v* confirm, endorse TC 2.1526, 1589; **confermed** *pp* ratified A 2350.

confiture *n* preparation (of drugs) C 862.

confort, com- *n* comfort A 773, E 1331; encouragement F 1167; relief, remedy TC 4.74; satisfaction, pleasure TC 5.1168; **of good c.** of good cheer TC 1.890.

conforte(n) *v* comfort TC 4.722, E 1918; assuage TC 3.1134; re-assure HF 572, TC 5.263.

confounde *v* ruin B 362; destroy TC 4.245; dismay Rosem 10; **con-founded** *pp* put to shame G 137.

confus *ppl adj* confused, bewildered HF 1517, TC 4.356, A 2230; con-founded G 463.

confusioun *n* destruction, ruin TC 4.123, A 1545, C 499; undoing D 1958; disruption F 869.

congeyen *v* bid good-by, invite to go TC 5.479.

conne, konne *v* be able TC 3.377, 5.1404; know how BD 279, D 1518; learn, learn by heart, know B 1730, 1733; **can, kan** *1 & 3 s* BD 34, 673, HF 15, TC 1.11, A 210, F 786 (understands); **canst, kanst** HF 624, D 904; **kanstow** canst thou TC 4.460, B 1414; **konne, konnen, conne, can, kan** *pl* BD 541, HF 335, PF 333, B 1165, D 980, E 2438, F 3; **konne** *2 & 3 s subj* TC 2.1497, A 4396, F 1591, G 846; **konne** *2 pl subj* A 3118; **couthe, coude, kouthe, kowthe, koude, koud** *pt 1 & 3 s* BD 656, 800, HF 1797, TC 1.984, 2.1582, A 94, 390; **koudest** *pt 2 s* TC 1.622; **koude** *pt pl* BD 235, TC 3.1358, A 4104, D 1008, E 108; **koud, ykoud** *pp* BD 666, 998; **kowthe** *pp* A 14; **koude good** knew what was proper TC 2.1178; **koude his good** knew what was best for him TC 5.106; **koude no good** did not know what to do BD 390.

connyng(e) *n* skill PF 167, 487, 513, TC 2.4, 3.999. See **konnynge.**

conquerynge *n* achievement PF 2.

conscience *n* mind E 1635; qualities of mind, disposition A 142; sense of right and wrong, conscience, scruple TC 1.554, B 1136, C 280, D 1438; tender-heartedness, "sensi-bility" A 150; **nice c.** foolish scruples, compassion A 398; **spiced c.** nice disposition D 435; over-scrupulousness A 526.

consecrat *pp* consecrated B 3207.

conseil, -seyl *n* deliberation, decision A 784; counsel, advice D 82, G 192; plan G 522; body of counselors A 3096, B 204; counselor A 1147; secret(s) C 819, D 538, G 145; confidence(s) A 665, B 1323, D 538, E 243; private affairs B 4478; **in c.** in private D 1437; in confidence E 2431.

conseille, -seyle, counseillen *v*

counsel, advise PF 633, TC 1.648, B 1319, D 66; **conseille** *1 s* B 4135; **conseilest** *2 s* TC 2.1528; **coun-seylled** *pt s* HF 371.

conseillour *n* counseller E 1501.

conseillyng *n* advising D 67.

consentant *adj* consenting C 276.

conserve *v* preserve TC 4.1664, 5.310, A 2329; **conserved** *pp* HF 732, 1160.

conseyte see **conceite.**

consistorie *n* court of justice C 162; council TC 4.65.

constablesse *n* constable's wife B 539.

constance *n* constancy to principle, stability, fortitude E 668, 1000, 1008, 2283.

constellacioun *n* position of the planets TC 4.745, A 1088, D 616, E 1969, F 129, 781.

constreinte, -eynte *n* distress TC 2.776, 4.741.

constreyne *v* compel, force TC 2.476; **constreyneth** *3 s* urge E 800; re-strains TC 3.1761; **constreyne** *2 pl* compel TC 2.1232; **constreyned** *pt s* drove LGW 105; *pp* compelled D 1071.

construe *v* construe, interpret B 1718; explain TC 3.33; **construeth** *imp pl* interpret LGW 152.

contek *n* strife TC 5.1479, A 2003, B 4122.

contemplacioun *n* religious medita-tion HF 34, consideration, regard HF 1710.

contemplaunce *n* contemplation D 1893.

contenaunce, coun-, -ance *n* be-havior, demeanor, bearing E 2205, F 94, 561; composure BD 613, E 1110; appearance A 1916, 4421; countenance, looks BD 1022, A 2010, F 284 (*pl*); **countenaunces** *pl* behavior of one person toward another B 1198; **for a c.** for appear-ance's sake G 1264; **fond his c.** assumed an attitude or appearance TC 3.979.

contene *v* occupy, fill TC 3.502.

contour see **countour.**

contrarie *adj* opposite TC 4.1003.

contrarie, -ye *n* opposite HF 808, TC 1.637, A 3057; *pl* opposites TC 1.645; opposition TC 1.418; adversary A 1859, B 4470; **in c. of** in opposition to G 1477.

contrarie(n) *v* oppose, contradict E 2319, F 705; **contraried** *pt s* opposed, contradicted D 1044, E 1497.

contrarius, -ous *adj* different D 698; contrary 780.

contree *n* land, country HF 196,

TC 2.42, LGW 5; region, district, county A 216, 340, D 1397, 1710.

convenientz *adj* (*pl* form) suitable F 1278.

convers *n:* **in convers** on the other side, behind TC 5.1810 (see note).

converte *v* turn aside C 212; change the opinion TC 1.308, 4.1412; change one's mind TC 2.903; **con-verted** *pp* turned TC 1.999, 1004; converted B 435, 538.

convertible *adj* interchangeable A 4395.

conveyen *v* set on the way E 55; **conveyed** *pt s* escorted A 2737, E 391.

conyes *n pl* rabbits PF 193.

coost, cost *n* coast B 1626, F 995; region D 922.

cop *n* top HF 1166, A 554.

cope *n* cope A 260, B 3139; cape TC 3.724.

coper *n* copper HF 1487, G 829, etc.

coppe *n* cup LGW 647, A 134; **coppes** *pl* A 2949, 3928.

corage *n* heart LGW 397, A 22, B 3857; spirit BD 794, A 2213, E 220; inclination, desire E 905, 1759, H 164; zeal B 1970; courage B 3836.

corbetz *n pl* corbels HF 1304.

cordeth *3 s* accords TC 2.1043.

cordewane *n* Cordovan leather B 1922.

corfew-tyme *n* curfew-time A 3645 (see note).

corn *n* grain, wheat BD 157, LGW 74, B 702, 1183; **cornes** *pl* crops B 3225; **c. of whete** grain of wheat C 863.

cornemuse *n* bagpipe HF 1218.

corniculer *n* a subordinate Roman officer G 367.

corny *adj* (of ale) tasting of corn or malt C 315.

coroned see **corouned.**

coroune, -owne, -one, cr- *n* crown BD 980, Gent 7; wreath or garland for the head LGW 216, A 2290; nuptial garland E 381 (see note); **c. of laurer** laurel wreath A 2875; **c. of lif** eternal reward G 388; representing the highest degree TC 5.547; crown of the head HF 1825, A 4041, B 1499; *pl* HF 1317, TC 2.1735, G 221, etc.

corouned, etc. *pp* crowned HF 1316, LGW 230, A 161, B 3555, etc.; sovereign F 526, Cf. **crouned, ycorouned.**

correccioun *n* correction TC 3.1332, I 56; amendment C 404; punish-ment A 2461, D 1320; fine D 1617; jurisdiction D 1329.

corrected *pp* corrected D 661, F 1274; set right, admonished G 162; reproved D 181.

corrumpable *adj* corruptible A 3010.

corrupcioun, cor- *n* decomposed matter PF 614, A 2754, C 535.

corrupt *adj* corrupt, infected with evil B 519, C 504; rotting E 2252.

cors *n* body, person B 2098, C 304, H 67; corpse TC 5.742, LGW 676, A 3429.

corsednesse *n* cursedness TC 4.994. See **cursednesse**.

corsen *v* curse TC 3.896; **corse** *3 s subj* E 1308; **corsed** *pp* TC 5.1849. See **cursen**.

corseynt *n* saint HF 117.

corven see **kerve**.

costage *n* expense B 1235, E 1126.

cosyn, -in *n* cousin A 1081, etc.; kinsman B 1259, etc.

cosynage *n* kinship B 1226, 1329, 1599.

cote¹ *n* peasant's hut B 4026, E 398; dungeon (?) A 2457.

cote² *n* coat, tunic A 103, etc.

cote-armure, -mour *n* coat-armor, a tunic with heraldic devices, worn over armor TC 5.1651, A 2140; *pl* A 1016.

couche(n) *v* lay G 1152; cower E 1206; **couched(e)** *pt 3 s* laid, arranged PF 216, G 1157; **couched** *pp* laid, arranged A 2933, 3211, G 1200; overlaid, decorated A 2161.

coughen, coghe *v* cough TC 2.254, E 2208; **cougheth, cogheth** *3 s* A 3697, 3788.

counseil, con- *n* secret TC 1.992, D 996, G 145.

countour, con- *n* mathematician BD 435; an official who accounted at the Exchequer for the taxes of a shire A 359 (see note); countinghouse, office BD 436, B 1403.

countour-dore *n* countinghouse door B 1275, 1439.

countour-hous *n* countinghouse, office B 1267.

countrefete, -ter- *v* imitate, reproduce, copy BD 1241, A 139, B 4511, C 447, H 134; imitate successfully, equal C 13, F 554; forge, counterfeit E 743; pretend TC 2.1532, 3.1168; *refl* look or act like HF 1212; **countrefeteth** *3 s* imitates HF 1213; **countrefeted** *pp* counterfeited B 746, 793, E 2121; assumed, pretended BD 869; false, pretentious C 51.

countrepese, contrepeise *v* balance, counterbalance HF 1750, TC 3.1407.

countrepleted *pp* argued against LGW 476.

countretaille *n*: **at the c.** in reply E 1190.

countyng-bord *n* countinghouse table B 1273.

cours *n* movement, passage TC 2.1385, B 3186, F 1066; charge, passage-at-arms A 1694, 2549; nautical course B 4289, E 851; course of a river, planet, etc. TC 2.907, A 8, E 50; procedure B 704; process D 892; course of a meal E 1718, F 66.

court *n* court A 140, etc.; manor house D 2162.

courtepy *n* short coat A 290, D 1382.

court-man *n* courtier E 1492.

couth see **conne**.

covenable *adj* fitting TC 2.1137.

covent *n* body of monks or friars, religious house B 1827, D 1863, G 1007.

coverchief, -chef *n* kerchief B 837, D 590, 1018; veil PF 272; *pl* A 453.

covercle *n* pot-lid HF 792.

covered *adj* hidden TC 3.31.

coveytise, -vei-, covetyse *n* covetousness LGW 136, G 1077, Lak 18.

covyne *n* fraud, deceit A 604.

cow *n* chough D 232; **chough** PF 345.

cowardye *n* cowardice A 2730.

coy *adj* quiet A 119, E 2.

coye *v* quiet, pacify TC 2.801.

cracchynge *n* scratching A 2834.

craft *n* skill D 1468, E 2016; skilful device F 185, 242; wise policy TC 1.747; art PF 1, TC 3.1634; (pseudo-) science G 619; trade, occupation A 401, F 1127; craft gild A 4366; trickery C 84, E 1424; trick TC 4.1458, B 3258; "business" TC 5.90. A given instance may combine two or more meanings.

crafty *n* skilful, skilled BD 439, A 1897; clever G 1290; ingenious G 1253; cunning G 655.

craketh *3 s* croaks E 1850; **craketh boost** blusters, talks loudly A 4001.

crased *pp* cracked G 934; **ycrased** broken, perforated BD 324.

creance *n* faith, belief B 340, 915.

creaunce *v* borrow, obtain credit B 1479; **creaunceth** *3 s* B 1493; **creanced** *pp* B 1556.

crecche *v* snatch, grab TC 3.1375.

credence *n* credence, belief LGW 20, 31, 97, G 415.

creep see **crepen**.

creest *n* top of the helmet B 2096.

crekes *n pl* tricks A 4051.

crepel *n* cripple TC 4.1458.

crepe(n) *v* creep BD 144, HF 2086; **creep** *pt s* A 4226, 4260; **crepte** *pt s* BD 391; **crepte(n)** *pt pl* B 3806, D 1698; **cropen** *pp* TC 3.1011, A 4259, F 1614.

crew see **crowe**.

crie(n), crye(n) *v* cry, cry out, proclaim HF 202, A 3817, F 45; **cridestow** didst thou cry A 1083; **criden** *pt pl* A 949; **crie upon** cry out against F 1496.

crips, crisp(e) *adj* curly HF 1386, A 2165, D 304.

Cristen *adj & n* Christian A 55, etc.

cristenly *adv* in a Christian manner B 1122.

croce *n* staff, stick D 484.

croked *adj* crooked B 560, C 761, Truth 8.

crokes *n pl* hooks LGW 640.

crokke, crowke *n* jug A 4158, Truth 12.

crommes *n pl* crumbs G 60.

crop(e) *n* top (of a tree, etc.) TC 2.348, 5.25, A 1532; **croppes** *pl* BD 424; shoots A 7.

cropen see **crepen**.

croper *n* hind-quarters of a horse G 566.

crosselet *n* crucible G 1117, 1147, 1153, etc.; **crosletz** *pl* G 793.

crouche *1 s* make the sign of the cross A 3479; **croucheth** *3 s* E 1707.

croude, crowde *v* push, press on HF 2095, B 801; **crowdest** *2 s* B 296.

crouned, -ow- *pp* crowned A 161, 1549; *as adj* sovereign F 526.

croupe *n* rump D 1559.

crowdyng *n* driving force B 299.

crowe *v* crow TC 3.1416, B 4523; **crew** *pt s* B 4048, 4387; **crowe, ycrowe** *pp* A 3357, 3687.

crowke see **crokke**.

croys *n* cross A 699, etc.; **crois** TC 5.1843.

crul *adj* curly A 3314; **crulle** *pl* A 81.

cryke *n* harbor, port A 409.

cucurbites *n pl* retorts G 794.

cukkow see **cokkow**.

curacioun *n* cure TC 1.791.

curat *n* parish priest or any member of the clergy having cure of souls A 219, D 2095.

cure *n* care, charge TC 2.741, B 230; responsibility D 1333; care, heed TC 2.283, A 303; **take no c. of** pay no heed to D 138; **with . . . fulle c.** carefully TC 5.1539; intention HF 1298; duty TC 1.369, C 557, E 82 (*pl*); cure, remedy PF 128, TC 1.707, F 1114; **besy c.** diligence, zeal TC 3.1042, B 188; **with bisy c.** diligently A 2853; **dide his besy c.** applied himself diligently PF 369; **diden bisynesse and c.** applied themselves diligently A 1007; **I do no c.** I don't care LGW 152; I make no effort D 1074.

curiosite *n* elaborate or ingenious construction HF 1178.

curious, curyus *adj* careful B 1433; eager HF 29, E 1577; skilful A 577; troublesome, involving much care B 1415; carefully made, elaborate A 196, C 638; recondite F 1120.

curiously *adv* skilfully F 909.

currours *n pl* couriers HF 2128.

curs *n* excommunication A 655, 661; **Cristes curs** damnation A 4349, C 946; excommunication D 1347.

cursednesse *n* wickedness, cursedness B 1821, C 638; shrewishness E 1239.

cursen *v* curse D 1624; excommunicate A 486. See **corsen**.

cursyng *n* excommunication A 660, D 1587.

curteis, -eys *adj* courteous TC 1.81, A 99, etc.

curteisly, -eys- *adv* courteously, graciously B 1281, 1636, etc.; with restraint A 3997.

curteisye, -ie *n* courtesy TC 5.64, A 46, 725; etiquette, courtly behavior A 132.

curtyn *n* sword without a point (?) PF 230 (see note).

cut *n* lot(s) A 835, 845, C 793.

cynamome *n* cinnamon, term of endearment A 3699.

cynk *n* five, a throw in dice B 125, C 653.

D

daf *n* fool A 4208.

dagon *n* piece (of cloth) D 1751.

daliaunce *n* conversation, companionship A 211, D 260; amorous play, intimacies C 66 (*pl*), D 565, Rosem 8; **have your d.** enjoy your conversation or company LGW 356; **doth d.** engages in conversation, is sociable B 1894.

damage *n* a pity LGW 598.

dame *n* mistress of the house, madam A 3956, D 164; mother C 684, D 576, H 317; dam A 3260.

damoysele *n* damsel, young gentlewoman B 4060.

dampne *v* condemn LGW 401; **dampned** *pp* condemned BD 725, A 1175.

dan see **daun**.

dappull gray *adj* dappled grey B 2074.

dar *pr s & pl* dare BD 221, TC 2.1747, C 380; **darst** *2 s* HF 580, etc.; **darstow** darest thou TC 5.1279; **durste, dorste** *pt subj & cond* dared, would dare BD 929, TC 1.27, A 4009; **dorstestow** wouldst thou dare TC 1.767.

dare *3 pl* lie motionless B 1293.

darreyne *v* justify a claim to A 1609, 1853; decide A 1631, 2097.

dart *n* arrow, dart A 1564; spear TC 4.771; (as a prize) D 75; *pl* TC 2.513, 4.44.

daswen *3 pl* are dazed H 31; **daswed** *pp* dazed HF 658.

date *n* period of time G 1411.

daun, dan *n* master, don (title of respect) HF 137, 1623, etc.

daunce *n* dance D 991; **on d.** in a (the) dance TC 5.448; **th'amorouse d.** delights of love TC 4.1431; **the olde d.** the tricks of the game, the ways of love-making A 476, C 79.

daunce(n) *v* dance BD 848, A 2202, etc.

daunger *n* power over a person: **in daunger** in (his) power A 663; power to hinder the lover TC 3. 1321; restraint A 1849; reluctance D 521; distant manner, haughtiness TC 2.384, 1243, 3.399; *pl* dangers, risks A 402.

daungerous *adj* difficult to approach, distant, haughty A 517, D 151, 1090; hard to please B 2129, D 1427; fastidious, dainty A 3338; grudging, reluctant to give D 514.

dauntest *2 s* dost subdue, control PF 114, Truth 13; **daunteth** *3 s* TC 2.399; frightens TC 4.1589; **daunted** *pt s* subdued B 3799; **daunte** *imp s* control Truth 13; **daunted** *pp* frightened D 463.

dawe *v* dawn B 3872, E 1842; **daweth** *3 s* LGW 46, A 1676; **dawe** *3 s subj* A 4249, E 2195; **dawed** *pp* D 353.

dawenynge *n* dawn BD 292, A 4234, B 4072.

dawes *n pl* days F 1180. See **day**.

dawyng *n* dawn TC 3.1466.

day *n* day A 19, etc.; day set, as for payment G 1040; time, lifetime F 1447; **d. natureel** 24 hours F 116; **to-morwe d.** tomorrow morning A 3784; **on a d.** occasionally A 1668; **oft a d.** many a day A 2623; **al d.** continually, constantly HF 386, D 518 (see **alday**).

dayerie *n* milch cows (collectively) A 597; *pl* dairies D 871.

dayesie, -ye *n* daisy LGW 182, A 332, etc.; **daysyes** *pl* LGW 43.

de- *prefix* see **di-**.

debaat, debat *n* strife, contention, war A 1754, B 130; conflict of wills TC 2.753; mental conflict BD 1192; **at d.** in conflict A 3230.

debate *v* fight, contend B 2058, C 412.

debonaire, -ayre *adj* gentle, gracious BD 860, LGW 276, A 2282; **as n** *a* gracious person BD 624, TC 1.214.

debonairly, -ayr- *adv* graciously, politely BD 518, 851, TC 3.156; courteously TC 2.1259; with good grace HF 2013.

debonairte *n* graciousness BD 986.

deceyvable *adj* deceitful E 2058.

declamed *pt pl* discussed TC 2.1247.

declare(n) *v* explain B 1718; state, speak TC 2.1680, E 2437; make known, state A 2356, D 1479, G 719; **declared** *pt 3 s* showed G 331; *pp* told, told about E 1687, G 119.

declination, -yn- *n* distance above or below the equator E 2223, F 1033, 1246 (see note).

decree *n* ordinance A 640; code (of law) B 3667.

dede *n* pestilence TC 3.1301.

dede *v* become dead HF 552; **is deed** died D 1852.

dede see **deed**.

deduyt *n* delight, pleasure A 2177.

deed, ded, dede *adj* dead A 145, 942, B 1423; deadly BD 1211, TC 5.559; deathly A 1578.

deedly, dedly *adj* deadly BD 162, PF 128; deathly, dying A 1082, F 1040.

deedly *adv* in a deadly manner G 476.

deef *adj* deaf TC 1.753, A 446; **deve** *pl* G 286.

deel, del *n* part, bit TC 2.1214, A 3369; share BD 1001; quantity BD 1159; **del** *pl* times HF 1495; **never a de(e)l** not a particle BD 543, HF 331.

deele(n), dele *v* have to do with TC 2.706, A 247; contend, argue TC 2.1749; **delte** *pt s* had to do with; **deled** *pp* divided D 2249.

deer *n* deer D 1370; *pl* animals B 1926.

deerelyng *n* darling A 3793.

deerne *adj* secret A 3200, 3278, 3297.

dees, deys *n* dais, platform HF 1360, A 370, E 1711.

dees *n pl* dice TC 2.1347, B 1494. See also **dys**.

deeth, deth *n* death BD 577, A 964, etc.; plague, pestilence TC 1.483, A 605.

deface *v* deface, spoil TC 4.804, 5.915; obliterate, efface HF 1164, TC 4.1682, E 510.

defame, diffame *n* dishonor B 3738; disgrace C 612; infamy, ill-repute E 540, 730.

defame, diffame *v* defame, slander HF 1581, A 3147; **defamen** *3 pl* TC 2.860; **defamed** *pp* C 415; **diffame** bring dishonor upon TC 4.565.

defaute *n* want, lack BD 5, 25, TC 5.1796; failure, error C 1018,

G 954; failure to follow the scent BD 384; fault F 790, D 1810 (*pl*); offense, wickedness B 3728, C 370.

defence, -se, diff- *n* defense LGW 606; protection PF 273; resistance D 467; prohibition TC 3.138; remedy TC 4.287; **withouten any d.** without remedy, inevitably LGW 279; **at d.** on guard E 1195.

defende(n), deff- *v* defend TC 1.511, B 933; forbid TC 2.413; deny (something) to G 1470; urge against TC 2.1733, C 590; **defended** *pt s* forbade D 60, 1834; *pp* forbidden C 510.

defet *pp* disfigured, wasted away TC 5.618, 1219.

deffie *v* denounce A 3758; **diffye** *1 s* denounce, repudiate A 1604, B 1592, 4316; **deffye** *1 pl* defy LGW 138; **deffie** *imp s* E 1310.

defoulen *v* defile F 1418; *pp* defiled TC 5.1339, F 1396, 1421.

degre(e) *n* step A 1891; *pl* A 1890; rank, status, social or economic position LGW 447, A 40, C 52, D 626, E 1494; state, condition, situation TC 4.1662, LGW 461, A 1841; **in ech d.** at every step D 404; **in his d.** in its proper condition E 263; according to his rank E 957; **after hir d.** according to their rank A 2573, B 1237; **in swich d.** in such a state or condition D 1124; in such a situation H 146; **in my d.** to the extent that I can E 969; **in this d.** in this wise PF 646; **in no d.** in no respect TC 1.437, B 1361, F 198; **at alle degrees** in all respects A 3724.

deignous see **deynous.**

deknes *n pl* deacons G 547.

delay *n* delay, postponement, procrastination TC 3.879, A 2268, G 1220; *pl* TC 2.1744, F 1294.

delaye *1 s* put off, postpone TC 5.1371.

deliberen *v* deliberate, consider TC 4.169; **delibered** *pp* TC 4.211.

delicaat, -cat *adj* delightful E 682, 1646; self-indulgent E 927; fastidious B 3661.

delicasye, -ie *n* voluptuousness PF 359; delight B 3669.

delices *n pl* delights C 547, G 3.

delicious *adj* delightful TC 5.443.

deliciously *adv* delightfully F 79; sumptuously E 2025.

delit, -lyt *n* delight, pleasure A 335, etc.; happiness BD 606; sensual desire HF 309, TC 4.1678, F 1372.

delite, -lyte *v* delight, take pleasure (often reflexive) B 3660, etc.; please PF 27, TC 4.683.

deliverliche see **delyverly.**

delve *v* dig A 536, F 638; **dolven** *pp* buried BD 222.

delytable *adj* delightful LGW 321.

delyvere *adj* agile, athletic A 84.

delyverly, deliverliche *adv* nimbly, deftly TC 2.1088, B 4606.

demaunde *n* question TC 4.1295, B 472, E 1870.

deme(n), deemen *v* judge, decide A 3194, B 1639, D 2236; suppose, consider HF 1746, TC 1.347, A 3161; **deeme, deme** *1 s* decide C 199; suppose F 44; condemn D 2024; **demeth** *imp pl* decide LGW 453, F 1498; **demed** *pp* condemned C 271.

demeyne *n* dominion B 3855.

demeyne *v* manage HF 959.

demonstracioun *n* proof HF 727; **make a d.** prove D 2224.

demonstratif *adj* demonstrable D 2272.

demonyak *n* madman D 2240, 2292.

denye *v* deny LGW 327; refuse TC 2.1489.

depardieux *interj* by God TC 2.1058, B 39, D 1395.

departe(n) *v* separate TC 3.709, A 1134; go away, depart TC 1.78, 2.437; remove TC 4.470; **departe** *1 s subj* break off F 1532; *2 s subj* divide up D 2133; **departe** *imp s* make a distinction TC 3.404; **departed** *pp* separated E 618; parted HF 2068, A 3060; divided C 812; **departen compaignye** part company B 4183.

departynge *n* separation A 2774; departure PF 675, B 260.

depe *adv* deeply A 129, B 4, etc.

depeynted *pp* decorated, adorned with pictures BD 322; depicted A 2027, 2031; stained TC 5.1599; **depeint** stained C 950.

depper *adv* compar. of **deep**; deeper TC 2.485, B 630, G 250.

dere, deere *adv* dearly HF 1752, TC 1.180, C 100.

dere *v* harm, injure TC 1.651, A 1822.

derk *adj* dark BD 912, A 2082, etc.; **dirke** F 1074.

derke *n* darkness BD 609.

derre *adj & adv* more dear, more dearly TC 1.136, 174, A 1448.

des- see **dis-.**

descensories *n pl* retorts G 792.

desclaundred *pp* slandered B 674.

descryve(n), -ive, dys-, dis- *v* describe HF 1105, TC 4.802, E 1737.

desdeyn, -ayn *n* disdain TC 4.1191, A 789; **haveth in d.** be offended at F 700.

deserte *adj* desolate HF 417.

desirous, -us *adj* desirous, eager TC 1.1058, A 1674, F 23.

desolaat, -lat *adj* desolate, abandoned TC 5.540, C 598; empty, completely without B 131, 936; destitute of influence D 703; lonely E 1321.

despence, dis- *n* expenditure, expense HF 260, A 441, B 105, etc.

despit, -yt, dis- *n* contempt, scorn, disdain TC 2.711, 3.1374, D 1876; insult, indignity TC 1.909, A 3752; outrage B 699; malice F 1374; indignation, anger, resentment TC 1.207, 2.1037, B 591, D 481; **have ye d.** do you scorn HF 1716; **hadden d.** scorned F 1395; **in d. of** in spite of HF 1668, PF 281; **in contempt of** TC 3.1705; **in resentment against** TC 4.124; **have in d.** bear a grudge against TC 2.711.

despitous, -us, dis- *adj* contemptuous, disdainful BD 624, A 516; scornful, haughty A 1596, 1777; angry D 761; spiteful, malicious TC 2.435, 3.1458.

despitously, dis- *adv* disdainfully A 1124; scornfully HF 161; cruelly B 605; indignantly B 3785; angrily A 4274, E 535.

desplayeth *3 s* displays A 966.

desteyned *pp* stained, blemished TC 2.840. See **disteyne.**

destourbe(n), -tur-, -tro- *v* agitate, disturb, distract TC 4.573, 4.1403; interfere with TC 4.563, C 340; frustrate, prevent TC 4.934, 1103, 1113; **destourbed** *pp* prevented TC 2.622.

destresse *n* TC 1.439, etc. See **distresse.**

destroubled *pp* disturbed BD 524.

destyne(e), -tin- *n* destiny HF 145, TC 1.520, A 1108, etc.

determinat *adj* definite, exact D 1459.

determyne *v* come to an end TC 3.379; **determynen** *2 pl* end up HF 343.

dette *n* debt LGW 541, A 280, etc.

dettelees *adj* not in debt A 582.

dettour *n* debtor B 1587, D 155, B 1603 (*pl*).

deve see **deef.**

devisynge *n* preparation A 2496.

devoir *n* duty TC 3.1045, A 2598, etc.

devyn *n* priest (of Apollo), soothsayer TC 1.66; **dyvynys** theologians A 1323.

devyn(e), di-, dy- *adj* divine HF 1101, A 122, etc.

devyne(n), di- *v* suspect, infer, imagine, conjecture, guess TC 3.458, 4.389, B 4456, D 26; prophesy PF 182; **devyne** *3 s subj* let him guess HF 14.

devyneresse *n* prophetess TC 5.1522.

devys *n* plan, wish: **at his devys** according to his wish A 816; **at poynt-devys** perfectly HF 917; precisely, carefully F 560; fastidiously A 3689.

devyse(n), di- *v* decide, determine A 1790, 2377, B 1382; order, direct A 1416; suggest, recommend TC 2.388, 5.299; contrive, devise TC 2.1063, A 1254, C 290; construct A 1901; conceive D 999, E 108; conjecture TC 3.458, F 261; consider E 1586; describe, relate, explain, tell BD 901, HF 772, TC 2.1599, A 34, 1844, etc.; **herd d.** heard tell B 613.

dextrer *n* destrier, steed B 2103.

deye *n* dairywoman B 4036.

deye(n) see dye(n).

deyneth *3 s* deigns TC 3.1281; **deigned hire (hym)** she (he) deigned B 3460, 3324.

deynous *adj* proud, scornful A 3941; **deignous** haughty TC 1.290.

deynte(e) *n* pleasure, delight B 139, E 1112, F 681; a delicacy TC 3.609, H 179; *pl* A 346, B 419, H 166; something estimable TC 2.164; **tolde no d. of** had no regard for D 208.

deynte(e) *adj* valuable A 168; good, worthwhile B 1901; pleasant, dainty B 4025; choice, rare TC 5.438, C 520, F 70.

deyntevous *adj* delicious, choice, rare E 265, 1714.

deys see dees.

diffamacioun *n* defamation D 1306.

diffame see defame.

diffence see defence.

diffinicioun *n* explanation D 25.

diffusioun *n* prolixity TC 3.296.

diffyne(n) *v* come to the end of something HF 344; conclude, state in conclusion TC 3.834, 4.390; set forth, state exactly PF 529, TC 5.271.

digestyves *n pl* medicines for absorbing or dissipating melancholy and choler (Curry) B 4151.

dighte *v* appoint, ordain TC 4.1188; prepare E 974; have intercourse, lie with D 767; **dighte** *pt 3 s* lay with D 398; **dight** *pp* lain with H 312; *refl* betake oneself B 3106; **hym dyghte** *pt 3 s* betook himself TC 2.948; **dight** *pp* betaken himself B 3719; **dight, ydight** *pp* furnished A 3205; dressed A 1041; prepared A 1630; **the first in armes dyght** the first one armed TC 3.1773.

digne *adj* worthy HF 1426, TC 1.429, etc.; proud, haughty A 517, 3964.

dignitee *n* worthiness A 4270, B 1169, etc.; high estate B 1646, 3360, E 470.

dilatacioun *n* amplification B 232.

directe *1 s* address, dedicate TC 5.1856; **direct** *pp* addressed B 748.

dirke see derk.

dis- see des-.

disavaunce *v* injure, repel TC 2.511.

disaventure *n* misfortune TC 2.415, 4.297.

disblameth *imp s* excuse TC 2.17.

dis(c)hevele(e) *adj* with the hair loose, unconfined HF 235, A 683.

disclaundre *n* a reproach TC 4.564.

disclaundre *v* disgrace D 2212.

discomfiture *n* defeat in battle A 1008, 2721.

discomfitynge *n* defeat in battle A 2719.

disconfort, -com- *n* discouragement, grief TC 4.311, A 2010; cause of annoyance or distress F 896.

disconforten *v* dishearten A 2704.

discovere *v* reveal, betray TC 1.675, G 1465; *2 s subj* may betray E 1942; **discovered** *pp* revealed G 1468. Cf. **discure**.

discrecioun *n* discernment A 1779, A 4499, C 42; sagacity A 2537, B 4508; discretion, prudence, good sense TC 3.894, D 622, F 685; judgment TC 3.1334; **hath d.** is grown up B 3822.

discryve see descryven.

discure *v* reveal BD 549. Cf. **discovere**.

discussed *pp* settled PF 624.

disese *n* discomfort HF 89, TC 2.987; distress TC 3.884, F 467; trouble B 616, G 747.

disese(n) *v* cause discomfort TC 2.1650; distress TC 1.573, 3.1468; **disesed** *pp* troubled TC 3.443.

disesperat *adj* despairing HF 2015.

disesperaunce *n* despair TC 2.530, 1307.

disfigurat *pp* disfigured, misshapen PF 222.

disfigure *n* disfigurement D 960.

disfigure *v* destroy (one's) attractiveness TC 2.223; **disfigured** *pp* disfigured C 551; altered A 1403.

disherited *pp* deprived, disinherited A 2926.

dishonest *adj* shameful E 876; lewd, immoral H 214.

disjoynt(e) *n* an awkward or difficult situation TC 3.496, A 2962, B 1601.

dismal *n* unlucky days BD 1206 (see note).

disobeysaunt *adj* disobedient PF 429.

disparage *n* dishonor E 908.

disparage *v* dishonor A 4271; **disparaged** *pp* degraded D 1069.

dispence *n* spending, expenditure HF 260, A 441, B 1195, D 1433.

dispende, des- *v* spend B 3500, E 1123; waste F 690; dispense TC 4.921; **despended** *pp* spent A 3983, B 1270; wasted E 1403.

dispeyred, de- *pp* in despair B 3645, F 943, 1084, etc.

dispoillen *v* strip, undress E 374.

disponyth *3 s* disposes TC 4.964; **dispone** *imp s* TC 5.300.

disport, des- *n* amusement, entertainment, pleasure HF 664, TC 4.309, A 775, B 143; joy, delight E 1332; mirth, cheerfulness TC 1.592, A 137; **dooth hym d.** cheer him up E 1924.

disporte(n), des- *v* amuse, entertain, divert HF 571, TC 2.1673, 3.1133, 4.724; *refl* A 3660, F 849; take consolation or cheer TC 5.1398; **disporten** (*3 pl*) **hem** amuse themselves E 2040.

disposed *pt s* decided E 244; *pp* determined E 639; intended E 1067; disposed TC 2.682; liable TC 4.230.

disposicioun *n* situation of a planet as it affects one's horoscope A 1087.

disputisoun, -son *n* dispute, disputation B 4428, E 1474, F 890.

disseveraunce *n* parting, separation TC 3.1424.

dissevere *v* part, part from G 875, Buk 15.

dissimulen *v* dissemble TC 1.322, 3.434; **dissymuleth** *3 s* G 466.

dissymulacioun *n* pretence D 2123.

dissymulynge *n* dissembling G 1073.

distempre *imp s* lose one's temper D 2195.

disteyne, dys- *v* make pale, outshine LGW 255, 262; **desteyned** *pp* stained, blemished TC 2.840.

distresse, des- *n* distress HF 26, etc.; constraint HF 1587.

distreyne, des- *v* oppress, distress TC 3.1528, A 1816; constrain H 161; **distrayneth** *3 s* compresses, grasps PF 337; **destreyneth** *3 s* oppress A 1455, F820; **destrayned** *pt pl* oppressed, occupied TC 1.355; **distreyne** *imp s* constrain TC 5.596.

disturne *v* turn aside TC 3.718.

diurne *adj* daily E 1795.

divinistre *n* diviner A 2811.

divisioun *n* distinction A 1780.

divynynge *n* conjecture A 2521.

doctrine *n* teaching LGW 19, B 1689, 2125; instruction B 4632.

dogge *n* dog B 4573; **d. for the bowe** hunting dog D 1369, E 2014.

doghter, dou-, -tre *n* daughter

HF 391, PF 214, A 2348; **doghter** *gen s* E 608; **doghtren** *pl* B 4019, F 1429.

dok *n* dock (a weed) TC 4.461.

doke *n* duck PF 498, A 3576; **dokes** *pl* B 4580.

dokked *pp* cut short A 590.

dolven see **delve.**

dom see **doom.**

domes day *n* doomsday HF 1284.

domesman *n* judge B 3680.

dominacioun *n* ruling power, sovereignty A 2758, C 560; ascendancy H 57, 181, Lak 16; **in domynacioun** dominant F 352.

dong(e) *n* dung A 530, C 535.

dong-carte *n* dungcart B 4226.

donge *v* spread dung B 4226.

dongeoun *n* dungeon A 1057.

donne *adj* dun, dull brown PF 334, TC 2.908.

doom, dom *n* judgment HF 1905, TC 1.100, etc.; **doomes** *pl* judgments C 163.

doo(n), do(ne) *v* perform, do PF 369, TC 5.903, A 960; act E 493; bring about A 729, 1248; cause, make BD 145, TC 1.692, B 3618, F 46; **dostow** *2 s* dost thou LGW 315; **dooth, doth** *3 s* causes LGW 678, A 2621, B 724; **doon, don** *pl* PF 542, A 268; **dide, did** *pt 1 & 3 s* HF 259, 2132, LGW 134; put B 2047; **didest, dedest** *pt 2 s* HF 1846, TC 3.363; **diden, dide** *pt pl* LGW 150, A 4104, C 967; **dide, did** *pt subj* should do C 746, F 1404; **do** *imp s* cause A 2405, B 662, H 12; **dooth, as dooth** *imp pl* do C 745, E 652, F 458; perform E 568; **do, doo, don, doon, ido, ydoo, ydon, ydoon** *pp* done BD 562, 676, HF 1812; past BD 40; finished BD 539, 1236, PF 542, TC 2.10; **hath doon make, wroght** caused to be made A 1905, E 253, A 1913; **do wey, awey** remove TC 5.1068, A 3287; put away G 487; **did of** doffed BD 516; **dide up** opened A 3801; **dide me colde** chilled me PF 145; **hath doon yow kept** has caused you to be preserved E 1098.

dormant see **table dormant.**

dorste see **dar.**

dortour *n* dormitory D 1855.

dossers *n pl* baskets HF 1940 (see note).

doted *ppl adj* silly, stupid Buk 13.

doten *v* behave foolishly G 983; **dote** *1 s* E 1441.

doublenesse *n* duplicity F 543, 556, G 1300.

doucet *n* dulcet (flute-like instrument) HF 1221.

doumb, domb *adj* dumb, silent HF 656, A 774, B 1055; **dombe** *pl* G 286.

doun *adv* down A 952, etc.; **up so doun** upside down A 1377, G 625; **up and doun** up and down, back and forth, over and over, in every way TC 2.601, 659, D 26, 878, etc. See also **up.**

doutaunce *n* doubt TC 4.963; *pl* uncertainties TC 1.200.

doute *n* fear TC 2.361, F 1096; danger E 1721 (see note); doubt, uncertainty HF 598, etc.

douteles, -lees *adv* without doubt TC 2.414, 494, etc.

doutremer *adj* imported (from beyond the sea) BD 253.

douve, dowve *n* dove PF 341, C 397; *pl* BD 250, HF 137.

dowaire, dowere *n* dowry E 807, 848.

dowe *1 s* give, bequeath TC 5.230.

dradde see **drede.**

draf *n* chaff I 35.

draf-sak *n* sack of refuse A 4206.

drasty *adj* filthy, wretched B 2113, 2120.

drat see **drede.**

draughte *n* quantity drawn off, a drink A 135, 382, 396; a move in chess BD 685; *pl* BD 653; **drawe the same d.** made the same move BD 682.

drawe(n) *v* draw, pull TC 1.224, 833, A 519; draw lots A 842, C 803; move HF 2090; incline E 314; *refl* **drawe hym** betake himself F 355; **drawen** *3 pl* draw (apart) F 252; **drowe** *pt 2 s* Scogan 22; **drow, drough, drew** *pt 3 s* BD 863, PF 490, TC 5.1558; **draweth** *imp pl* TC 3.177, A 835; **drawe, ydrawe** *pp* A 396, B 339; **drawe . . . draughte** made a move (in chess) BD 682.

drecche¹ *v* cause trouble TC 2.1471; **drecched** *pp* troubled (in sleep) B 4077.

drecche² *v* delay, become tiresome TC 2.1264; *2 pl* linger TC 4.1446.

drecchyng *n* delay TC 3.853.

drede *n* fear BD 1211, TC 1.575; anxiety F 455; doubt, uncertainty TC 1.529, 3.1315, B 869; **out of drede** without doubt HF 1142, TC 1.775; **withoute(n) drede** without doubt BD 280, F 1544.

drede *v* fear TC 4.859; **him drede** *refl* be afraid A 660; **dredeth** *3 s* is apprehensive TC 4.574; **drat** *3 s* dreads TC 3.328; **dredde, dradde** *pt 1 & 3 s* feared, dreaded TC 2.874, LGW 199, E 523; was afraid TC

2.482; **dredden** *pt pl* TC 4.56; **dradden** *pt 3 pl subj* feared G 15; **drad, ydred** *pp* TC 3.1775, E 69.

dredeles *adv* without doubt BD 764, TC 1.1034, 5.882.

dredful, drede- *adj* fearful, timid PF 195, TC 5.1331, LGW 109; terrifying, terrible TC 5.590, B 3558.

dredfully *adv* fearfully TC 2.1128.

drem, dreem *n* HF 1, 9, B 804, etc.

drenche(n) *v* drown HF 205, TC 3.1761; **dreinte, dreynte** *pt 3 s* drowned BD 72, TC 1.543; **dreynt** *pp* drowned BD 148, A 3520; **dreynte** *pl* sunk HF 233; **dreynte** *as def adj* BD 195.

drenchyng(e) *n* drowning A 2456, B 485.

dresse *v* prepare, array (often *refl*) TC 5.279, B 1100, E 1049; hold oneself erect TC 2.635; place, mount TC 5.37; address oneself E 1007; direct one's course PF 88, A 3468, G 1271; **dresseth hire** *3 s* prepares B 265; **dresse(n)** *3 pl* arrange A 2594; **(hem) dressen** proceed B 263, F 290; **dressed** *pt 3 s* raised TC 3.71; **dressed hym up** stationed himself A 3358; **dressed** *pp* prepared PF 665; addressed, applied himself to E 2361; **hym dressed** betaken himself E 1820; **ydressed** placed E 381.

dreye see **drye.**

drogges *n pl* drugs A 425.

droghte *n* dryness, drought A 2, 595, F 118.

dronke *adj* drunk, drunken PF 181, A 1261.

dronkelewe *adj* drunken, given to drunkenness C 495, D 2043, E 1533.

dronken *adj* drunken A 3145, C 485, D 246.

drope *n* drop TC 1.23, A 131; **dropes** *pl* A 1496, 2340.

droppyng *adj* leaking D 278.

drugge *v* drudge A 1416.

drye *adj* dry PF 139, A 1362, 3730; **dreye** TC 3.352, A 3024; **drye** *n* A 420; **dreye** PF 380.

drye(n) *v* suffer, endure TC 2.866, 4.154, 5.42; **dryeth forth** continues in, lives through TC 1.1092.

drynke(n) *v* drink A 635, 750, etc.; drank *pt 3 s* B 743, 789; **dronke(n)** *pt pl* A 820, 2714, B 3390; **dronke(n)** *pp* TC 3.674, A 135, C 456. Cf **dronken** *adj.*

dryve(n), -i- *v* drive TC 2.1515, 1535, 5.1179; compel TC 4.1353; press on, rush TC 3.227, D 1694; **dryve forth, awey** spend, endure, cause to pass TC 5.394, B 49, 1421, C 628; **droof, drof** *pt 3 s* TC 3.994,

D 1540; **drif** *imp s* TC 4.1615, 5.359; **dryve(n), driven, ydryven** *pp* PF 682, A 2007, 2727, 4110, F 1230.

duc, duk *n* duke HF 388, A 860, etc.; **dukes** *pl* A 2182.

due *adj* due A 3044, E 1452; incumbent upon LGW 603.

duetee, dewete *n* duty TC 3.970; respect A 3060; amount due D 1352, 1391.

dulcarnoun *n:* at d. completely perplexed TC 3.931 (see note).

dulle(n) *v* grow weary, become bored TC 2.1035, 4.1489; **dulleth** *3 s* depresses G 1093, 1172.

dure(n) *v* last, endure, continue HF 353, PF 616, TC 1.468, etc.

duresse *n* hardship TC 5.399.

durre *v* dare TC 5.840.

durryng *n* daring TC 5.837.

dusked *pt pl* grew dim A 2806.

duszeyne *n* dozen A 578.

dwale *n* sleeping potion A 4161.

dwelle *v* linger, remain, continue BD 217, HF 252, TC 1.144, A 1661, etc.

dyamauntz *n pl* diamonds A 2147.

dyapred *ppl adj* figured A 2158.

dye(n), deye(n) *v* die BD 24, HF 585, A 1109, etc.; **deyde, deyede, dyde** *pt 3 s* HF 106, 374, PF 587, TC 1.56; **dyde** *pt pl* PF 294; **dyde** *pt 3 s subj* would die D 965.

dygneliche *adv* haughtily TC 2.1024.

dyke *v* ditch, dig ditches A 535.

dyne *v* dine TC 2.1163, etc.; **what wol ye dyne?** what will you have for dinner? D 1837.

dyner *n* dinner TC 2.1489, B 1094.

dys *n pl* dice A 1238, 4384. See also **dees.**

dys- see **des-.**

dysordynaunce *n* disturbance HF 27.

dyvynynge *part* guessing, conjecturing A 2515.

dyvynys *n pl* those learned in divinity A 1323.

dyvynytee *n* theology D 1512, 1638; **divinitee** divine being, Godhead G 317, 340.

E

ech *adj & pron* each A 39, 660, etc.; every, everyone TC 5.831, E 413; **ech a** every D 256.

eche *v* increase, add HF 2065, TC 1.887, 3.1509, 5.110; **eche** *3 pl* TC 1.705; **eched** *pp* added TC 3.1329.

echon, -oon *pron* each one BD 335, HF 150, C 349; **echon(e)** all individually BD 695, TC 4.218, C 113.

eek, ek, eke *adv* also BD 339, HF 445, TC 1.630, A 217, etc.

eet see **ete(n).**

effect *n* result, consequence, intent HF 5, LGW 622, A 2989, G 1261; efficacy F 322; point, purpose TC 2.1566, A 1189; purport, substance A 1487, D 1451; significance TC 5.377, B 4325; matter of consequence TC 3.505, 5.1629; **in effect** in reality, in fact TC 1.748, A 319, E 721.

eft *adv* again HF 1072, TC 1.315; at another time BD 41, HF 401, TC 137.

eftsoone(s), -son- *adv* again HF 359, TC 2.1468, B 909, D 1992; another time G 933; soon, soon afterwards TC 4.181, A 3489; immediately D 808; **eftsonys** later TC 2.1651.

egal *adj* equal TC 3.137.

egal *adv* equally TC 4.660.

egge *n* edge TC 4.927.

eggement *n* instigation B 842.

eggyng *n* egging on E 2135.

egle *n* eagle HF 499, etc.

egre *adj* sharp, fierce E 1199.

egremoyne *n* agrimony G 800.

eighe see **eye.**

eighteteene *adj* eighteen A 3223.

eightetethe *adj* eighteenth B 5.

eir see **eyr.**

ek(e) see **eek.**

elaat *adj* lofty, arrogant B 3357.

elde *n* age, old age TC 2.393, A 2447, etc.

elder *adj* older B 1720, 3450.

eldres *n pl* ancestors B 3388, C 364, etc.

eleccioun *n* choice PF 409, 528, Purse 23); favorable time (astrologically) B 312.

element *n* element (fire, air, earth, water) BD 694, TC 5.1810 (see note); celestial sphere HF 975; **elementes** *pl* G 1460; **elementz** TC 3.1753; raw materials D 1506.

elf *n* elf, evil spirit B 754, D 873; **elves** *pl* A 3479, D 864.

elf-queene *n* fairy queen B 1978, 1980, D 860.

ellebor *n* hellebore B 4154.

elles, -is, -ys *adv* otherwise, else BD 74, HF 23, A 375, etc.

elvyssh *adj* abstracted, peevish B 1893; weird, strange, mysterious G 751, 842.

em *n* uncle TC 1.1022, 2.162, 309, etc.; **emes** *gen s* TC 2.466, 472.

embassadrie *n* the work of ambassadors B 233.

embaume *v* embalm LGW 676.

embosed *pp* gone or hidden in the woods BD 353 (see note).

embrace, en- *v* embrace TC 5.224, B 1567; bind, draw to E 412; clasp, enclose H 160; **embraced** *pp* TC 5.1816.

embrouded, en- *pp* embroidered LGW 119, 227, A 89; **enbrowded** HF 1327.

emeraude *n* emerald PF 175, B 1799.

emforth *prep* to the extent of TC 2.243, 3.999, A 2235.

emperice, -isse, -esse *n* empress PF 319, LGW 185, D 1246, F 1048.

empeyre *1 s* harm E 2198.

emplastre *v* plaster over E 2297.

empoysoned *pp* poisoned B 3850; as *adj* D 751.

empoysonyng, -pois- *n* poisoning A 2460, C 891.

emprenteth *imp pl* imprint, impress E 1193; **emprented, en-** *pp* imprinted, impressed E 2117, 2178, F 831.

emprentyng *n* impression F 834.

emprise, -yse *n* undertaking BD 1093, TC 2.73, etc.; **enprise** TC 4.601.

empte(n) *v* empty G 741, 1404.

enbibyng *ppl adj* moistening G 814.

enbrouded see **emb-.**

encens *n* incense TC 5.1466, A 2429.

encense *v* burn incense G 395; cense G 413.

enchesoun *n* reason, cause TC 1.348, 5.632, F 456.

enclyne *v* bow B 3092; be disposed TC 2.674, B 1082; dispose PF 325; **enclyned** *pp* bent down PF 414; disposed BD 991, HF 749.

enclynyng *n* inclination HF 734.

encorporyng *adj* incorporating G 815.

encrees, -cres *n* increase HF 2074, TC 3.1776, A 275, etc.

encresse(n) *v* increase TC 1.443, 2.1337, etc.; **encreessen** E 1808; **encresseth** *3 s* TC 2.1333, A 1315; **encressen** *3 pl* TC 4.579, A 1338; **encresse** *3 s subj* TC 5.1359; **encresede** *pt 3 s* PF 143; **encressed** *pp* B 1271, E 408.

ende *n* end A 15, etc.; destiny A 1844; purpose B 481; decision B 266; agreement A 1865; **this is the e.** this is the end of the matter B 145, G 1471; **demen . . . to the badder e.** put the worst interpretation on the matter F 224.

endelong *adv* from end to end, lengthwise HF 1458, A 1991.

endelong *prep* along, from one end to the other A 2678, F 416, 992.

endere *n* one who ends TC 4.501, A 2776, C 218.

endetted *pp* indebted G 734.

endite(n), -dyte *v* compose (a letter,

poem, etc.) HF 381, TC 1.6, A 95, etc.; write, say A 1209, 2741; tell, express TC 2.886; dictate TC 2.1162; indict, accuse B 3858.

endure(n) *v* continue F 1062; remain A 1185, B 753; last, live A 3018, E 1317; endure, stand TC 2.864, Buk 27; **up endure** bear up TC 2.1518.

enforce *v* reinforce D 340; *1 s refl* attempt TC 4.1016.

engendren *v* beget, procreate B 3148, E 1272; **engendren of** *3 pl* spring from B 4113; **engendred** *pt 3 pl* originated A 421; **engendred** *pp* begotten, produced, brought forth A 4, E 158, etc.

engendrure *n* procreation PF 306, B 3137, D 128.

engendrynge *n* production HF 968.

engyn *n* skill HF 528; imagination G 339; subtlety TC 2.565; contriving TC 3.274; contrivance, machine F 184; catapult HF 1934.

engyned *pp* tortured, racked B 4250.

enhabit *pp* devoted TC 4.443.

enhancen *v* elevate, improve A 1434; **enhaunced** *pp* elevated E 1374; exalted LGW 386, B 3773.

enhorte *v* urge A 2851.

enlumyned *pt 3 s* illuminated, adorned E 33; *pp* brightened TC 5.548.

enlutyng *n* sealing (with lute or clay cement) G 766.

enoynt *pp* anointed A 199, 2961.

enprented see **emprenteth.**

enquere(n) *v* inquire TC 1.123, A 3166, etc.

ensample *n* example BD 911, TC 1.232, A 296, etc.; *pl* B 3188; instances A 2842; *exempla* C 435 (see note).

enseled *pp* sealed up, preserved TC 5.151; finally determined TC 4.559.

enspyre, -ire *v* inspire, move TC 4.187; impart knowledge G 1470; **enspire** *imp s* TC 3.712; **inspired** breathed upon, breathed (life) into A 6.

ensure(n) *v* give assurance HF 2098, C 143.

entecched *pp* imbued with, endowed TC 5.832.

entencioun *n* intention, purpose TC 1.345, C 408; will TC 1.52; **malicious entencion** ill will HF 93; understanding TC 1.211; meaning G 1443.

entende *v* intend, plan D 1479; strive, endeavor B 3498, D 275; incline (to) TC 2.853, F 689; pay attention TC 4.893, F 1097; attend,

devote oneself TC 3.424, D 1478; **entende** *1 s* am aware of TC 4.1649; **entendeth** *3 s* strives D 1114; aims (at) D 275; desires TC 3.27; pays attention F 1097; waits upon, attends E 1900.

entendement *n* understanding HF 983, TC 4.1696.

entent(e) *n* intention, intent TC 5.1630, A 1487, B 324; purpose E 189, F 521; inclination C 88; endeavor, diligence BD 752, TC 5.1110, G 6, HF 1267 (*pl*); mind TC 5.1305, B 1740, F 1178; mood E 186; opinion TC 2.1446, 4.1525; purport F 107; **in hool e.** without reservation E 861; **in . . . pleyne e.** very willingly TC 2.1560; **in good e. with a good e.** with good will B 824, 1902, F 1383; **with glad e.** pleasantly, cheerfully F 1509; **for this e.** in this connection B 942.

ententif *adj* eager, desirous HF 1120, TC 2.838; attentive E 1288.

entewnes *n pl* melodies, harmonies BD 309.

entraille *n* bowels B 1763, E 1188.

entre *v* enter PF 147, 153; **entren** *2 pl* E 1556; **entred** *pp* A 2583, etc.

entrechaungeden *pt pl* exchanged TC 3.1368; **entrechaunged** *pp* reciprocal TC 4.1043.

entrecomunen *v* intercommunicate TC 4.1354.

entree *n* entrance A 1983, 4243; **entrees** *pl* HF 1945.

entremedled *pp* intermingled HF 2124.

entremes *n* a dish served between the courses of an elaborate meal PF 665.

entremeten, -mette *v* meddle D 834; *refl* PF 515; **entremete** *imp s* be concerned (with) TC 1.1026.

entreparten *v* share TC 1.592.

entriketh *3 s* ensnares PF 403.

entune *v* sing TC 4.4; **entuned** *pp* intoned A 123.

envenyme *v* poison BD 641; **envenymed** *pp* poisoned B 3314.

enviroun *adv* roundabout LGW 300.

envoluped *pp* wrapped up C 942.

envye *n* ill-will A 2732, G 1372; enmity TC 5.1479; envy HF 95, TC 3.1805, LGW 356, etc.

envye, envien *v* vie, contend BD 173, HF 1231; strive for D 142; **envie** *imp s* vie with TC 5.1789.

envyned *pp* stocked with wine A 342.

er *adv* before TC 3.763, A 3789.

er *conj* before LGW 107, A 255, etc.; **er that** before A 36, 835, etc. Cf. **or.**

er *prep* before HF 1902, A 1683, C 892, etc.

erchebisshop *n* archbishop D 1502.

erchedeken *n* archdeacon D 1302; **ercedek(e)nes** *gen* A 655, 658, D 1318, 1588.

ere, eere *n* ear BD 182, HF 2044, PF 519, etc.; **eres** *pl* HF 879, PF 500, etc.; also **eris** (TC 2.1022), **erys** (TC 3.1388, A 556), **eeris** (TC 4.817, B 4093).

ere *n* ear (of grain) LGW 76.

ere *v* plow A 886; **eryd** *ppl adj* plowed HF 485.

erme *v* grieve BD 80, C 312.

ernest *adj* serious G 710.

ernest *n* seriousness, earnest TC 2.452, A 3390, E 1594; a serious matter A 3186; **in e.** in earnest TC 2.1529, A 1125; **in e. nor in game, for e. ne for game** under any (no) circumstances TC 4.1465, E 609, E 733 (usually a mere tag).

ernestful *adj* serious TC 2.1727, E 1175.

erratik *adj* wandering; **e. sterres** planets TC 5.1812.

erra(u)nt *adj* wandering, arrant H 224; roving BD 661 (see note).

erre *v* do wrong TC 4.549; **errest** *2 s* dost wander TC 4.302; **erre(n)** *3 pl* are wrong, are mistaken TC 3.1774, G 449; transgress TC 1.1003.

errour, errowr *n* error TC 4.200, 993; false belief, heresy TC 1.1008; anomaly Scogan 7; perplexity PF 146.

ers *n* rump A 3734, D 1690, etc.

erst *adv* before, formerly HF 1496, TC 1.299, A 776, etc.; **at erst(e)** for the first time, at last, finally HF 512, TC 1.842, 4.1321, E 985, G 151; **erst er, erst than** before A 1566, C 662.

eschaunge *n* exchange TC 4.146, 559, A 278; *pl* HF 697.

eschewing *n* avoidance PF 140.

eschu *adj* loath E 1812.

eschue(n) *v* avoid TC 4.389, 1517, G 4; refrain from TC 2.696, E 1451; **eschuwe** *2 pl* avoid TC 2.1255; refrain from TC 1.344; **eschue, eschuw** *imp s* avoid TC 1.634, 2.1018; **eschued, eschewed** *pp* escaped TC 4.1078, B 4528.

ese, eyse *n* ease HF 1256, TC 1.28, D 2101, E 217; comfort, satisfaction TC 3.19, B 4487, E 1643; pleasure D 127, 214; **do(on) e.** please, satisfy A 768, E 664, H 25; **do(on) his, (my, hire, your) herte an e.** relieve one's mind, gratify TC 2.1225, 3.109, 633, 516; **lith in youre e.** is convenient B 1481.

esement *n* redress A 4179, 4186.

ese(n) *v* ease, give comfort to BD 556,

HF 1799, TC 2.1400; make comfortable, entertain A 2194; **esed** accommodated A 29; satisfied A 2670, D 929; comforted, relieved TC 1.249, 4.727.

esily, esilich, esely *adv* easily HF 1929, A 469, F 115; at ease E 423; quietly TC 1.317, A 3764; softly TC 3.156; deliberately, calmly HF 1675, F 388.

espialle *n* body of spies D 1323.

espye *n* spy TC 2.1112, C 755. Cf. **spie.**

espye(n), -ie(n) *v* seek to learn B 180; watch A 1112; look around PF 280, E 1257, 1410; discover, find out HF 706, B 1781; catch sight of, perceive, notice HF 594, 706, TC 4.1224, G 500; **espide** *pt s* noticed PF 250, TC 5.539, G 1230; *pt subj* should see TC 4.1388; **espied** *pp* discovered, perceived LGW 265, G 895. See **spyen.**

est *n* east TC 2.1053, B 493.

est *adj* east TC 5.1109.

est, eest *adv* east BD 88, HF 1680, A 2601, etc.

estat, -taat *n* condition, state, position TC 2.219, 465, A 203; economic or social position, status TC 1.130, 884, A 522, 716; rank PF 550, TC 1.432, LGW 305; term of office D 2018.

estatly, -taat-, estatlich *adj* dignified TC 5.823, A 140, 281; majestic B 3902.

estraunge *adj* strange TC 1.1084.

estres *n pl* the (upper) parts or rooms of a building A 1971, 4295.

esy *adj* easy BD 1008, A 223; gentle PF 382, TC 2.620, G 768; moderate A 441.

ete(n) *v* eat BD 94, TC 2.444, etc.; **eet** *pt 3 s* ate A 2048, B 3362; **ete** *pt pl* ate BD 432, TC 2.1184; **ete(n)** *pp* eaten A 4351, C 355.

eterne *adj* eternal TC 3.11, A 1304; irrevocable A 1109, 1306.

eterne *adv* eternally D 5.

eterne *n* eternity TC 4.978.

ethe *adj* easy TC 5.850.

evel *adv* badly BD 501, 1204. See **yvel(e).**

even *n* evening TC 5.1137, D 750; **evenes** *pl* HF 4.

even(e) *adj* even A 3316; equal A 2588; average, normal A 83; impartial A 1864; **e. herte** even temper E 811.

even(e) *adv* equally D 2249; directly A 1060, G 1200; exactly BD 120, HF 714; quite BD 451, F 1069; fully BD 441; **full even** indeed

BD 1329; **lyche e.** exactly alike HF 10; **bere him evene** restrain himself A 1533.

even-tyde *n* evening B 4262.

ever(e) *adv* forever, always HF 1147, TC 5.418, etc.; **e. in oon** constantly, uniformly TC 5.451, F 417.

ever(e)mo, -moo *adv* evermore, continually BD 81, HF 634, A 1229, etc.

everich *adj* every A 241, etc.

everich *pron* each, each one, every one BD 301, A 2096, B 531, F 762, etc.; **everych oother** each other F 762.

everichon, every- *pron* every one, each one HF 337, TC 1.154, A 31, etc.; all TC 2.1598, B 3345.

everydeel *pron* everything, all F 1288.

everydeel, -del *adv* completely, in every respect BD 222, A 368; **everideel** A 3303.

ew *n* yew tree PF 180, A 2923.

exaltat *pp* exalted F 704 (see note).

exametron *n* the Latin hexameter B 3169.

excepcioun *n* adverse criticism D 86.

excercise *n* physical activity B 4029; discipline E 1156.

excesse *n* intemperance C 514; emotional intemperance, emotion that is excessive to a fault TC 1.626.

exciteth *3 s* causes G 744; **excited** *pt 3 s* exhorted D 1716.

existence *n* reality HF 266.

exorsisacions *n pl* exorcisings HF 1263.

experience *n* first-hand knowledge, experience HF 878, A 3001, D 1; observation D 2057, G 1125; demonstration HF 788; proof TC 3.1283.

expoune, -owne *v* explain, interpret B 3398, G 86; **expowned** *pt 3 s* interpreted B 3346.

expres *adv* expressly C 182, D 27; explicitly stated D 1169.

ey *n* egg B 4035, G 806.

eye, eighe *n* eye A 896, F 1036; **eyen, eighen** *pl* BD 212, TC 1.428, LGW 311, etc.; **at eye** before one's eye, plainly LGW 100. See **yë.**

eyle, aile *v* ail, trouble, afflict A 3424; **ailleth** *3 s* troubles TC 1.766; **what eyleth, aileth** what ails TC 2.211, A 1081, etc.; **eyled** *pt s* afflicted B 4290; troubled F 501.

eyr, eir *n* air A 1246, 2992, etc.; vapor G 767.

eyse see **ese.**

eyryssh *adj* of or belonging to the air HF 932; **ayerissh** HF 965.

F

face see **prime.**

facound *adj* eloquent, authoritative PF 521.

facounde *n* eloquence, way of speaking BD 926, PF 558, C 50.

faculte(e) *n* field of knowledge, subject HF 248; profession, occupation A 244.

fader *n* father HF 168, A 100, etc.; **fader** *gen* HF 943, A 781, etc.

fadme *n* fathom BD 422 (see note), A 2916, F 1060.

faille(n), -ayle- *v* fail HF 297, A 3887, etc.

fair *adj* fair, beautiful BD 484, TC 1.101; fine A 154, 204; proper, desirable A 1523; well D 439; pleasing A 376; *as n* a fine one A 165; a fine thing to do TC 3.850; **the faire** the fair portion F 518.

fair(e), fayr *adv* fairly, well PF 511, TC 2.886, A 94, B 2020; quietly TC 5.347; properly A 539; fortunately LGW 186; firmly, squarely HF 1050.

fairer *adj & adv* fairer E 988, etc.; better TC 5.480, A 4386.

faldyng *n* a coarse woolen cloth A 391, 3212.

falle(n) *v* fall, descend BD 13, HF 1534, A 128; happen TC 3.761, A 1668; befall A 3418; prosper LGW 186; be appropriate or fitting E 259; grow pale BD 564; **fallen forth** engage in TC 5.107; **falleth, falles** (Northern) *3 s* BD 257, A 1669, E 1473; **falle** *3 s subj* A 2555; **faire falle yow** good fortune befall you B 4650; **falle hire faire** good fortune befall her LGW 277; **fil** *pt s* fell BD 128, TC 3.1087, A 845; happened TC 5.842, A 1034, B 176, E 325; befell B 4394; was fitting F 570; **fille(n)** *pt pl* A 949, 2666, B 3183; **fille** *pt s subj* A 131, 2110; **fallyng** *ppl adj* causing to fall, felling TC 2.1382; **falle(n), yfalle(n)** *pp* TC 4.271, A 25, 3231; **was falle** had happened A 2703.

falow, falwe *adj* pale brown HF 1936, A 1364.

fals *adj* false BD 618, etc.

false(n) *v* prove false, betray, deceive BD 1234, TC 3.784, 5.1485; misrepresent A 3174; **falsed** *pt s* TC 5.1053; **falsed** *pp* TC 5.1056; broken F 627.

faltren *3 pl* falter B 772.

falwes *n pl* plowed land D 656.

fame *n* rumor, report B 995, C 111, E 940; reputation, renown HF 305, 1146.

famous *adj* famous HF 1137, 1249; *as n* famous people HF 1233.

famous *adv* famously HF 1780.

famulier *adj* familiar A 215, B 1221; of one's household E 1784.

famyne *n* famine HF 1973; starvation C 451.

fan *n* vane, quintain H 42 (see note).

fanne *n* fan A 3315.

fantasye *n* imaginary experience, illusion, delusion TC 5.261, 1523, A 3840; mood F 844; idea, notion HF 593, TC 3.275, 5.461, D 516; inclination, desire A 3191, D 190; **fantasies** *pl* B 3465.

fantome *n* illusion, delusion HF 11, 493, B 1037.

fare *n* behavior, conduct TC 1.1025, 2.1144, A 1809; **frendes fare** friendly behavior TC 3.605; what goes on, activity, business, fuss, to-do HF 682, TC 1.551, 3.860, A 3999, B 569; condition, state TC 2.1001, 5.1366; **this hoote f.** rash conduct TC 4.1567; eager anticipation, impatience TC 5.507; carrying on A 1809; **loude f.** noise, commotion HF 1065; **strange f.** formality B 1453.

fare-carte *n* cart for produce TC 5.1162.

fare(n) *v* travel TC 5.279; go TC 5.21, A 1395; behave, conduct oneself TC 4.918, 1087; experience good or bad fortune BD 616, PF 698, TC 2.92, A 2435; **yvele fare** fare badly TC 1.626; **farst, farest** *2 s* behavest PF 599, TC 4.463; **faren** *pr pl* A 1261, 3874; **ferde** *pt 1 & 3 s* fared BD 99, 501; **ferde(n)** *pt pl* TC 4.918, A 2117; **fare(n)** *pp* TC 5.466, B 512, F 1169; **lat hym fare wel** let him go, let's forget about him D 501; **wel farynge** *ppl adj* handsome, attractive BD 452, B 3132; **beste farynge** handsomest, most attractive F 932.

farewel *n & interj* good-by B 1510, G 1380; presto! F 1204, G 907, 1384.

farsed *pp* stuffed A 233.

fast *adj* secure D 283.

faste *adv* firmly, closely, tightly TC 5.596, A 2151, 3499; securely B 3260; vigorously A 2359, 2558; faithfully, devoutly G 140; eagerly PF 21, TC 2.144, A 1266, D 520; greatly, heartily B 4277, D 672; steadily TC 2.276, A 1535; quickly BD 140, A 1469; **as f.** very quickly, as quickly as possible TC 2.652, 898, G 1235; **faste** close, near A 1478; **f. by** near A 719, 1476; nearby BD 369, HF 1204, B 3116, D 970.

faste *v* fast B 1405, D 1879; **faste** *pt 3 s* fasted G 139; **fastynge** *part* C 363.

fatte *v* fatten D 1880.

fattyssh *adj* plump, moderately fat BD 954.

faucon, -coun, -koun *n* falcon PF 337, TC 3.1784, F 411; **f. peregryn** F 428 (see note).

faught see **fighte(n).**

fauned *pt 3 s* fawned upon BD 389 (see note).

favour *n* favor A 2682, B 3881; helper HF 519; favorable feeling, partiality TC 2.663; comeliness, grace E 395.

fawe *adj* fain, eager D 220.

fawe *adv* fain, willingly TC 4.887.

fawny *n pl* fauns (collectively) TC 4.1544.

fayerye, fairye *n* fairies (*coll*), the fairy world B 1992, D 859, E 2039, F 201; fairyland E 2227, F 96; enchantment E 1743.

fayn *adj* fain, glad LGW 130, A 2437, etc.

fayn, feyn *adv* gladly, willingly TC 3.222, A 1257, B 222, etc.

faynest *adv* most willingly PF 480.

faynte *v* faint, grow weary BD 488. See **feynte.**

fayr see **fair.**

fayre, faire *n* market, fair TC 5.1840, B 1515, D 221.

fecche(n) *v* fetch, bring TC 3.917, 5.485, E 276; **fecche** *3 s subj* carry off B 1064, D 1544, 1610; **fecche** *imp s* TC 5.322, A 3492. See **fette.**

fecches *n pl* vetches, beans TC 3.936.

fed *pp* fed: **born and f.** born and raised E 397.

fee *n* landed property D 630; **f. symple** unrestricted ownership A 319.

feeblesse *n* feebleness TC 2.863

feend *n* fiend, devil, the Devil A 4288, B 454; **fend** TC 4.437.

feendly, fendly *adj* fiendish, devilish BD 594, B 751, F 868, G 1071; **feendlych** B 783.

feere *n* fire, fireplace TC 3.978 (Kentish form).

feeste see **feste.**

feestlych *adj* given to festivity F 281.

feet *n* feat, art E 429.

feffe *v* enfeoff, grant, bestow upon TC 3.901, 5.1689; **feffed** *pp* enfeoffed E 1698.

feith, feyth *n* faith A 62, etc.; honor, truthfulness BD 632, TC 1.89, E 866; one's given word TC 2.963, A 1622.

feithful *adj* religious, devout B 3081, G 24; reliable, true D 1425; faithful, loyal E 310, 343.

feithfully, fey- *adv* piously, devoutly TC 3.1672, B 461; faithfully TC 2.263, 4.114, 5.1076; sincerely TC 2.1577, E 1111; reassuringly HF 963; assuredly E 1066; truly, indeed HF 853, D 1433.

fel *n* skin TC 1.91, 3.591.

fel, felle *adj* wicked TC 5.50; fierce A 2630, B 3290, D 2002; cruel TC 1.470, 4.44, A 1559; terrible B 2019.

felawe *n* associate, companion, fellow A 395, 648, 1624, C 672; **felawes** *pl* F 1179; **good felawe** rascal A 650.

felaweshipe *n* fellowship, company A 26, 32, 3539; **felawsshyppe** BD 978; companionship TC 2.206, 3.402.

feldefare *n* fieldfare PF 364, TC 3.861 (see note).

fele, feele *adj* many BD 400, HF 1137, TC 4.110, E 917.

fele(n), feele(n) *v* feel TC 3.1697, 4.466, 5.255, LGW 692; perceive, know HF 826, TC 1.808, G 155; find out TC 2.387, 5.1308; understand TC 3.960; **fele** *1 s* perceive LGW 520; **feleth, feeleth** *3 s* feels TC 3.1658, A 1220; **fele(n)** *pr pl* TC 2.1283, 3.11; **felte** *pt s* HF 570, TC 1.306; **felede, feled** *pt s* B 492, G 521; **felte(n)** *pt pl* B 4325, LGW 689; **felt** *pp* TC 1.25, F 586; **feled** *pp* perceived TC 4.984.

felle *v* fell A 1702; **feld** *pp* A 2924.

feloun *adj* angry, sullen TC 5.199.

femele *n* female D 122.

femynynytee *n* the form of a woman B 360.

fen *n* division of a science C 890 (see note).

fenix *n* phoenix BD 982.

fer, ferre *adj* far, distant A 3393, B 658, etc.

fer *adv* far B 508, D 1387, etc.; afar, in the distance TC 5.181.

ferde, fered *n* fear: **for f.** for fear BD 1214, HF 950, TC 1.557.

fere *v* frighten TC 4.1483; **fered** *pp* frightened TC 2.124, B 4576; afraid G 924.

fere, feere *n* fear BD 1209, TC 1.726, A 2344, etc.; peril HF 174.

fere, feere *n* companion TC 1.13, 3.1496, 4.791; mate PF 410, 416; **feres** *pl* fellows TC 1.224.

ferforth *adv* far TC 2.960, 1106; **as f. as** as far as, to the extent that TC 5.866, B 19, 1099; as long as TC 1.121; **so f.** to such an extent PF 377, TC 3.1494, B 572.

ferforthly *adv* completely D 1545; **as f. as** to the extent that TC 3.101; **so f. that** to such an extent that LGW 682, A 960.

ferfulleste *adj* most fearful, timid TC 2.450.

ferly *adj* strange A 4173.

fermacies *n pl* medicines A 2713.

ferme *n* a sum paid for an office or privilege, generally annually A 252a.

fermerer *n* monk or friar in charge of the infirmary D 1859.

fermour *n* farmer, *i.e.* one who pays a lump sum for an office or privilege LGW 378.

fern *adj* former: **ferne yere** last year TC 5.1176.

fern *adv* long ago F 256.

fern-asshen *n pl* fern ashes, ashes of burnt fern F 254; also **asshen of fern** F 255.

ferne *adj pl* distant A 14.

ferre *adj* (*def*) distant A 3393.

ferre *adv*, comp of **fer**: farther HF 600, A 48, 2060; **ferrer** A 835; **fer ne ner** neither farther nor nearer, neither more nor less A 1850.

ferreste *adj pl*, *superlative of* **fer** farthest A 494.

fers *n* queen (in chess) BD 654 (see note), etc.; **ferses** *pl* the pieces in chess or possibly checkers F 723 (see note).

ferthe *adj* fourth HF 1690, B 3, etc.

ferther *adj* farther B 1686, E 2226.

ferther *adv* farther HF 1112, A 36, etc.

ferthyng *n* farthing, a trifle A 255, D 1927; small spot A 134.

fery *adj* fiery TC 3.1600. Cf. **firy**.

fesaunt *n* pheasant PF 357.

fest *n* fist A 4275, D 792; hand C 802, I 35; **fistes** *pl* TC 4.243.

feste, feeste *n* religious festival TC 1.161, 168; feast, banquet, revelry A 883, B 353, D 297; festival, celebration A 2736; rejoicing, joy TC 3.344, 5.524; **maketh (made) feste** makes merry B 1517; makes much of E 1109; welcomes, welcomed TC 5.77, B 1517, 1532; shows respect, pays a compliment BD 638; **make hym . . . moore feste** show more pleasure in seeing TC 2.361; **made swich feestes** was so pleasant TC 5.1429.

festeiynge *part* entertaining, making festivity F 345.

festeyinge *n* festivity, entertainment TC 5.455.

festne *v* fasten A 195.

fether(e) *n* feather A 2144; **fetheres** *pl* HF 1382, PF 334, A 107; wings HF 974.

fethered *pt 3 s* covered with outspread wings, feathered B 4367; *pp* covered with feathers TC 2.926.

fetisly *adv* neatly, handsomely A 273, 3319; agreeably A 3205; carefully D 1742; elegantly A 124.

fette *v* fetch, bring TC 3.609 (to be sought); **fette** *pt s & pl* TC 5.852, LGW 676, B 1483, 2041, D 2159; **fet** *pp* A 819, 2527, B 667, D 217; **yfet** *pp* F 174, G 1116. See **fecche(n)**.

fetys *adj* neat, elegant A 157; shapely, pretty C 478.

fey, fay *n* faith TC 2.1103, A 1126, E 1505, etc.

feyne *v* concoct, invent A 736; practise deception TC 3.1158, F 510; fail an obligation, disappoint TC 2.1558, 3.167; pretend (*refl*) B 351; **feynest** dost pretend TC 5.413; **feyne** *1 pl* assume a disguise D 1507; **feyned, feyned hym (hire)** *pt s* pretended TC 1.354, 5.846, E 1950; **feyned as** pretended that E 513; **feynynge** *part* pretending, inventing HF 1478, D 1378; **feyned** *pp* pretended TC 1.920; **fayned** failed in duty TC 2.997; **feyned** *ppl adj* false, hypocritical, fictitious HF 688, TC 5.1848, A 705; **yfeyned** *pp* shirked E 529.

feynte *1 s* grow faint TC 1.410; **feyntest** *2 s* enfeeblest B 926; **feynte** *3 s subj* would faint G 753. See **faynte**.

feyntyng *n* weariness E 970.

feynyng(e) *n* deception, pretence BD 1100, F 556.

feythed *pp* filled with faith TC 1.1007.

fiers(e) *adj* fierce A 1598; merciless B 300; proud, noble TC 1.226, A 1945.

fifte *adj* fifth HF 1703, TC 5.1205; **fyfte** Scogan 9. Also **fifthe**.

fighte(n) *v* fight TC 4.34, A 1711, etc.; **fyght** *3 s* fights PF 103; **faught** *pt s* A 399, 987; **foghte(n), foughte(n)** *pt pl* A 1178, 1660, 1699, 2655; **fighteth** *imp pl* A 2559; **foughten** *pp* A 62.

figure *n* shape, form B 3412, D 1459, Scogan 27; person B 187, E 1584; image HF 132, TC 1.366, F 831; presentation Buk 25; aphorism A 499; **figures** *pl* shapes, forms C 28, D 1486; apparitions HF 48; rhetorical devices HF 858, E 16 (see note); arrangements of dots (in geomancy) A 2043 (see note); Arabic numerals BD 437; **in f.** symbolically TC 5.1449.

figurynge *n* symbolic meaning; **in f.** symbolically LGW 298, G 96.

fil, fille(n) see **fallen.**

filet *n* fillet, band for the hair A 3243.

first *adj* first C 499; **firste** (*def*) A 831, etc.; original F 711.

firy *adj* fiery A 1493, 1564, etc. Cf. **fery.**

fit *n* experience A 4184; embrace A 4230, D 42; canto B 2078.

fithele *n* fiddle A 296.

fixe *pp* fixed TC 1.298, F 1282; **fix** solid G 779.

flaterynge *adj* flattering, deceitful BD 637, D 1294.

flaterynge *n* flattery BD 639; false promise, exaggeration BD 933; false friendliness B 405.

flatour *n* flatterer B 4515.

flaugh see **fleen**[1].

flaumbe, flaume *n* flame HF 769, PF 250, TC 4.118; **flambes** *pl* B 3353, G 515.

flee(n),[1] **fle** *v* fly HF 2118, TC 3.1263, F 122; **fleeth** *3 s* flies E 119; **flee(n)** *pl* TC 4.1356, B 4132; **flaugh** *pt 2 s* B 4421; **fleigh, fley** *pt 3 s* HF 921, TC 2.194, B 4362; **flowen** *pt pl* B 4581; **fleynge** *part* BD 178; **flowen** *pp* HF 905.

flee(n),[2] **fle** *v* flee BD 584, TC 2.194, A 2993; escape A 1170, G 1081; **fleeth** *3 s* A 1469; **fleen** *3 pt* B 121; **fle** *1 pt subj* TC 2.1564; *imp s* TC 2.1254; **fleigh** *pt 3 s* B 3879; **fledde** *pt 3 s* B 544; **fledden** *pt pl* TC 4.49, A 2930; **fled** *pp* B 541.

fleen *n pl* fleas H 17.

fleigh see **fleen**[1] and **fleen**[2].

flemen *v* banish TC 2.852; **fleemeth** *3 s* puts to flight H 182; **flemed** *pp* banished G 58.

flemere *n* one who drives out or expels B 460.

flemyng *n* banishment TC 3.933.

flessh *n* flesh HF 49, A 2640; meat A 147, 344.

flesshly *adj* fleshy TC 3.1248.

flesshly *adv* carnally B 1775.

flete *v* float, bathe, swim TC 3.1671; **flete, fleete** *1 s* PF 7, A 2397; **fleteth, fleet** *3 s* B 463, 901; **flete** *3 pl* bathe TC 3.1221; **fletynge** *part* HF 133, TC 2.53.

flex *n* flax A 676.

fley see **fleen**[1].

fleynge see **fleen**[1].

flikered *pt s* hovered TC 4.1221; **flikerynge** *part* hovering, fluttering A 1962.

flitted *pp* transferred TC 5.1544.

flo *n* arrow H 264.

flok *n* flock A 824.

flokmeele *adv* in a flock E 86.

flor *n* floor HF 2033; **floor** ground A 3822.

florisshinges *n pl* embellishments HF 1301.

flotery *adj* fluttering, ? wavy A 2883.

flour *n* flower LGW 48, A 4; the choicest kind, a choice example A 3059, 4174, B 1090, E 919; full bloom, prime A 3048, D 113.

floure *3 s subj* may flourish E 120; **floureth** *3 s* flourishes TC 4.1577; **floured** *pt s* C 44.

flourouns, flo-, flow- *n pl* petals, little flowers LGW 217, 220, 529.

floury *adj* flowery BD 398, LGW 174.

flowte *n* flute HF 1223.

floytynge *part* playing the flute A 91.

flyttynge *ppl adj* changeable BD 801.

fneseth *3 s* puffs H 62.

fnorteth *3 s* snores A 4163 (see note), B 790.

fol *adj* foolish PF 505.

folde *v* fold TC 2.1085; clasp TC 3.1201, 4.1230; **folde** *pp* clasped TC 4.1689, 5.1240, 1247; **folden** *pp* TC 4.359.

foled *pp* foaled, born D 1545.

foles *gen s as adj* foolish TC 3.298.

folily *adv* foolishly E 1403, G 428.

foly *adv* foolishly, wantonly BD 874.

fonde *v* test TC 3.1155; strive, endeavor BD 1020, HF 1427, TC 2.273, D 479; try to persuade B 347.

fonne *n* fool A 4089 (Northern).

fontstoon *n* font B 723.

fo(o) *n* foe PF 339, D 751; **foon, fon** *pl* PF 103, TC 5.1866, B 3896.

foom *n* foam A 1659, G 564.

foore *n* track, footsteps D 110, 1935.

foot-hoot, fot-hot *adv* hastily BD 375, B 438.

foot-mantel *n* outer skirt A 472.

for *prep* for A 2142, D 394; before A 3526; in the presence of, beside TC 4.413, B 1927; to F 39; by HF 2136, PF 229, A 3381; because of, on account of LGW 231, C 451, 504; in response to TC 4.1633; tending to C 300; in spite of, notwithstanding TC 4.1462, A 2020, C 129; rather than PF 657, TC 1.928; as being C 141, G 457; **for the nones** for the occasion TC 1.561, A 1423, B 3132 (but sometimes may be a mere rime-tag). See **nones.**

for *conj* because TC 5.460, LGW 362, A 3977; in order that B 478, F 102; **for that** because BD 81, TC 4.998; in order that B 3552.

forage *n* fodder, dry winter food A 3868, E 1422; food, grazing B 1973.

forbeede *v* forbid TC 3.467; **forbede** *1 s* F 1481; **forbedeth, forbet** *3 s* TC 2.717, C 643; **forbede** *3 s subj*

PF 582, A 3508; *imp s* D 519; **forbode** *pp* E 2296, Scogan 17.

forbere *v* endure E 2182; forbear, refrain from A 885, 3168; forgo TC 2.1660; spare D 665; **forbar** *pt s* spared TC 1.437; refrained TC 3.365; **forbereth** *imp pl* bear with LGW 80.

forbise *v* show by examples TC 2.1390.

forbrused *pp* severely bruised B 3804.

forby *prep* past TC 5.563, C 125.

forby *adv* by, past TC 2.658, B 1759, C 668.

force *n* force A 2015, 3912, H 228; **by f.** perforce, of necessity PF 221, A 2554, C 205; **of fyne f.** of sheer necessity TC 5.421; **what f.** what does it matter E 1295; **no f.** no matter TC 5.1616 (elsewhere **no fors,** q.v.).

fordo(on) *v* destroy, ruin TC 4.851, 1681, B 369; abolish TC 1.238; **fordo** *2 pl subj* should destroy B 1317; **fordoon, fordo** *pp* TC 1.74, A 1560, H 290; done for TC 1.525.

fordronke(n) *pp* very drunk A 3120, 4150, C 674.

forgat(e) see **foryeten.**

forgete(n) see **foryeten.**

forgo(n), -goon *v* go without HF 1856, TC 3.1384, 4.479, D 315; give up E 171, H 295; cease from E 2085; lose TC 4.962; **forgoth** *3 s* loses TC 4.713; gives up TC 5.63; **foryede** *pt 3 s* abandoned TC 2.1330; **forgon** *pp* lost TC 3.1442; **forgo** *pp* exhausted from walking HF 115.

forlaft *pp* given up C 83.

forlete *v* yield up B 1848, C 864; **forleten** *pp* abandoned HF 694.

forlore *pp* lost TC 5.23, A 3505; **forlorn** lost F 1557; **forlost** completely lost TC 3.280, 4.756.

forme, fourme *n* shape, form, pattern F 100, 283, 337, 1162; appearance TC 2.1243, F 1161; manner, way TC 4.78, 1579; decorum, formality A 305; beauty TC 5.1854; burrow, lair B 1294; **in swich f.** on such terms TC 3.160; **swiche formes make** assume such shapes D 1471.

formere *n* Creator C 19.

formest *adj* formost BD 890.

forncast *pp* planned TC 3.521; foreseen? B 4407 (see note).

forneys *n* furnace A 202; cauldron A 559.

forpyned *pp* wasted away A 205; tormented A 1453.

fors *n* (the usual spelling of **force** in

the sense of "importance", "something that matters"); **no fors** no matter BD 522, HF 999, TC 2.1477, B 286; **do (make) no f.** take no account of, do not care BD 542, B 4131, D 1234, 1512; **is no f.** it doesn't matter PF 615, TC 4.322, C 303; **what f. were it** what would it matter TC 2.377; Cf. **force.**

forseyd(e) *ppl adj* aforesaid PF 120.

forshapen *pp* metamorphosed TC 2.66.

forshright *pp* worn out with shrieking TC 4.1147.

forslewthen *v* waste in sloth, idle away B 4286.

forster *n* forester A 117.

forstraught *pp* distraught B 1295.

forsweryng(e) *n* perjury HF 153, C 657; *pl* false oaths C 592.

forswor *pt s* purjured HF 389.

forth *adv* forth, forward, on PF 27, B 4498, C 660; away A 2820, B 294; forth, into the open PF 613, B 213, G 312; further, in addition TC 5.196, A 2816, D 1924; hereafter, thereafter TC 4.314, F 1081; continually TC 4.343; **dooth f.** continues E 1015; **drive f.** endure, pass through B 1421; **drof f.** got through TC 5.628.

forthby *adv* away TC 5.537. See **forby.**

forther *adv* further TC 5.1094, A 4117, E 712; **ferther** PF 194, TC 3.281.

forthermoor(e), forther moor *adv* furthermore A 2069, C 357; **forthermo** C 594, D 783.

forther over *adv* moreover TC 4.1027, C 648; **forther over this** furthermore TC 5.963.

fortheryng *n* furtherance PF 384; **furtherynges** *pl* HF 636.

forthre(n) *v* further LGW 71, A 1137; **further** HF 2023; **forthereth** *3 s* TC 2.1368; **furthred** *pp* LGW 413.

forthward *adv* forward B 263, F 1169.

forthy *adv* therefore TC 1.232, 890, A 1841, etc.

forthynke *v* grieve, displease TC 2.1414; **that me forthynketh** I am sorry E 1906.

fortunat, -naat *adj* fortunate, favored by fortune TC 2.280, E 1137, F 25; successful B 3966; characterized by good fortune E 422; favorable, propitious E 1970.

fortunen *v* calculate A 417 (see note); **fortunest** *2 s* givest (good or bad) fortune A 2377; **fortuned** *pt pl* happened BD 288.

forwaked *pp* worn out from staying awake BD 126, B 596.

forward, fore- *n* agreement, promise A 33, 829, etc.

forward *adv* foremost E 2187.

forweped *pp* worn out from weeping BD 126.

for-wery *adj* exhausted PF 93.

for-why, -whi *conj* because BD 461, 793, TC 2.1516, etc.; therefore TC 2.12, 1238; wherefore TC 4.1644; for what reason TC 3.1009.

forwityng *n* foreknowledge B 4433.

forwot, -woot *3 s* has foreknowledge of HF 45, TC 4.1071, B 4424.

forwrapped *pp* wrapped up completely C 718.

foryede see **forgon.**

foryelde *v* requite E 831; *3 s subj* LGW 457.

foryete(n) *v* forget BD 1125, TC 3.55, 4.495; **foryete** *1 s* A 1882; **forgate** *pt 2 s* LGW 540; **foryat** *pt 3 s* TC 5.1535; **foryet(e)** *imp s* TC 4.796, A 2797; **forgete(n)** *pp* BD 410, 413, LGW 125; **foryeten** *pp* A 1914.

foryetful *adj* forgetful E 472.

foryeve, -yive *v* forgive BD 1284, A 743, E 526; give up LGW 458; **foryeve** *1 s* TC 3.1178, LGW 450, A 1818; **foryive, foryyve** *2 s subj* mayst forgive TC 1.937; have mercy TC 5.387; *3 s subj* C 904; **foryeve, foriyve, forgyve** *imp s* BD 525, TC 3.1183, B 1615, D 807.

fostre *v* foster, bring up E 593; feed H 165, 175; **fostreth** *3 s* nourishes E 1387; **fostred** *pt 3 s* took care of E 222; **fostred, yfostred** *pp* A 3946, B 275, E 213, F 500; helped, promoted F 874.

fostryng *n* nourishment D 1845.

fother *n* cartload A 530, 1908.

fouder *n* thunderbolt HF 535.

foul, fowel *n* bird HF 539, A 190; **foules, foweles** *pl* BD 295, A 9.

foul *adj* unclean, defiled A 501; ugly B 764, D 265, E 1209; horrible D 776, E 1095; disgusting C 524, 552; miserable, wretched, poor HF 1642, TC 2.896, B 3273, 4003, F 869; shameful B 1384, D 2049; evil, sinful TC 4.994, B 586, D 485, F 1372; damnable TC 4.275, B 1681; bad D 963; **the foule feend** the devil D 1610, 1639; **foul or fair** good or bad, thick or thin HF 767, 833, B 525, F 121.

foule *adv* miserably, wretchedly, shamefully BD 623, TC 4.1467, D 1069, E 2196, H 40; unfortunately, grievously PF 517, TC 4.1577, D 1312.

founde *v* set the foundation, build TC 1.1065; **founded** *pp* founded, built E 61.

founes, fownes *n pl* bucks in their first year, fawns BD 429, TC 1.465 (see note); fauns A 2928.

fourme see **forme.**

fourtenyght *n* fortnight TC 4.1327, A 929, D 1783.

foyne *3 s subj* let him thrust A 2550; **foyneth** *3 s* thrusts A 2615; **foynen** *3 pl* A 1654.

foyson *n* plenty A 3165, B 504.

frakenes *n pl* freckles A 2169.

frame *v* prepare (timber) for the framework of a building, set in place TC 3.530.

franchise *n* generosity E 1987; courtesy, nobility B 3854, F 1524.

frape *n* troop, pack TC 3.410.

fraught *pp* loaded B 171.

frayneth see **freyne.**

fredom *n* liberality, nobility TC 2.161, A 46, B 168; freedom TC 1.235.

free, fre *adj* generous, noble BD 484, TC 1.1080, B 4104; free, voluntary PF 649, A 852, F 745; unbound, at liberty TC 2.771, A 1292; *as n* the unenslaved TC 1.840; gracious one TC 3.128.

freend, frend *n* friend TC 1.98, A 670, etc.; **frendes** *gen as adj* friendly TC 3.605, 642.

freendlich *adj* friendly A 2680; **freendly, frendly** BD 921, F 274; pleasant TC 2.149.

freendly, frendly *adv* in a friendly manner BD 852, TC 3.130, D 1849.

freendshipe *n* friendship G 1362; **frendshipe** TC 2.240, etc.

freeten see **freten.**

freletee *n* frailty, weakness of the flesh C 78, D 92, E 1160.

fremde *adj* strange TC 2.248; foreign F 429; **fremed and tame** every one TC 3.529.

frenges *n pl* fringes HF 1318; ? bindings D 1383 (see note).

frenetik *adj* frantic TC 5.206.

fressh *adj* fresh HF 1156, A 92, 365, etc.; new LGW 204, C 928; active, vigorous TC 2.157, 3.26, D 508; cheerful, lively BD 483, E 1896.

fresshly *adv* eagerly TC 5.390; **f. newe** with renewed vigor BD 1228, TC 3.143, 5.1010; afresh TC 4.457.

fret *n* cap-like net for the head, caul LGW 215, 225; ? network, garland LGW 228 (see note).

frete(n) eat, devour TC 5.1470, A 2019, B 3294; **freeten, frete** *pp* A 2068, B 475.

freyne *v* ask TC 5.1227; **frayneth** *3 s*

inquires B 1790; **freyned** *pp* asked G 433.

fro *prep & adv* from BD 396, A 44; **to and fro** A 1700.

frote *v* rub TC 3.1115; **froteth** *3 s* A 3747.

frothen *3 pl* froth (at the mouth) A 1659.

fructuous *adj* fruitful I 71.

fructyfye *v* bear fruit Scogan 48.

frutesteres *n pl* female fruit-sellers C 478.

fruyt *n* fruit PF 137, etc.; the best part B 706, D 1373; profit F 74; result C 656; **the firste fruyt** a pun on "first-fruits" D 2277.

ful *adj* full A 233, etc.; satiated, surfeited TC 2.1036, 3.1661; **atte fulle** completely A 651, E 749; squarely TC 1.209.

ful *adv* full, entirely, very A 119, 132, C 25, etc.

fulfille *v* fulfill A 1318; **fulfelle** (Kentish form) finish, complete TC 3.510; **fulfild** *pp* satisfied E 907; **fulfild of, fulfilled of** filled with LGW 54, A 940, B 660, etc.

fullyche *adv* fully HF 428.

fulsomnesse *n* an excessive amount F 405.

fumetere *n* fumitory B 4153 (see note to B 4152).

fumositee *n* vapor rising to the brain C 567 (see note), F 358.

fumygacions *n pl* fumes raised in conn. with incantations HF 1264.

fundement, -da- *n* foundation HF 1132, D 2403; rectum C 950.

furial *adj* furious F 448.

furlong *n* furlong (*as pl*) A 4166, F 1172; **a f. wey** about 2½ minutes, a (little) while B 557 (see note), D 1692, etc.

fustian *n* coarse cloth A 75 (see note).

fyf *adj* five B 3602; usually **fyve.**

fyled *pp* filed, smoothed with a file A 2152.

fyn *adj* fine A 456, etc.; **of fyne force** of sheer necessity TC 5.421.

fyn *n* end, aim TC 1.952, 3.125, etc.; **for f.** finally TC 4.477.

fynch *n* finch; **pulle a f.** cohabit with a woman A 652 (see note).

fynde(n) *v* find BD 102, A 648, C 627, etc.; provide for A 2413, C 537; **fyndeth, fynt** *3 s* A 4071, B 1150, G 218; **fyndes** (Northern) A 4130; **fynden** *3 pl* A 1627; **fond, fownde** *pt 2 s* TC 3.362; **foond** *pt 3 s* found TC 5.1660, A 3440, etc.; **foond hirself** provided for herself B 4019; **fond his contenaunce** assumed an appearance TC 3.979;

foond *pt pl* B 3259; **founde(n)** *pp* TC 2.289, B 243, E 146.

fynder *n* discoverer, inventor BD 1168, TC 2.844.

fyndyng *n* providing A 3220.

fyne *v* finish TC 4.26; cease, stop TC 2.1460, 5.776, D 788, 1136.

fyr *n* firtree PF 179; **firre** A 2921.

fyr *n* fire HF 742, etc.

G

gabbe *1 s* talk idly, lie BD 1075, B 4256; **gabbestow** dost thou talk nonsense TC 4.481; **gabbe** *3 pl* lie, boast TC 3.301.

gadereth *3 s* gathers A 1053; **gadrede, gadered** *pt 3 s* gathered A 824, E 2231; **gadered** *pp* A 2183, 4381.

gaillard *adj* lively, merry A 4367; **gaylard** A 3336.

gaitrys beryis *n pl.* berries of the buckthorn B 4155 (see note to B 4152).

galauntyne *n* kind of sauce Rosem 17 (see note).

gale *v* yelp D 832; *3 s subj* D 1336.

galiones *n* beverages (or medicines) named after Galen C 306.

galle *n* gall TC 4.1137, G 797; bitterness G 58; sore spot D 940.

galoche *n* shoe F 555.

galpyng(e) *part* yawning F 354; *as adj* F 350.

galyngale *n* a spice A 381 (see note).

game *n* amusement B 3740; mirth PF 226, TC 4.1563; happiness TC 5.420; joke, jest A 1806, 3186, D 1279; an amusement, pastime, game, pleasure LGW 33, 489, A 853, 2286; scheme, intrigue A 3405; **in g., in my g.**, in fun, in jest BD 238, HF 822, A 4355; **a-game** in jest TC 3.636, 648, 650.

gamed *pt s impers* it was pleasant A 534.

gan see **gynne**.

ganeth *3 s* yawns H 35.

gape *v* gape, open the mouth B 3924; stare HF 1211; **gapyng** *part* gaping, with mouth open A 2008, B 4232; **gape after** *3 pl* wish, long for TC 5.1133. See **cape**.

gargat *n* throat B 4525.

garleek *n* garlic A 634.

gas see **gon**.

gat see **geten**.

gate *n* gate, door PF 121, D 1581, etc. See **yate**.

gat-tothed *pp* gap-toothed A 468.

gaude *n* trick TC 2.351, C 389.

gaude *adj* yellowish A 2079.

gauded *pp* supplied with gauds or special beads designating the *Paternoster* A 159.

gaure(n) *v* gape, stare TC 2.1157, 5.1153, A 3827, B 912, F 190; **gaureth** *3 s* B 3559.

gay *adj* gay, carefree TC 2.922, A 3254, D 508; wanton A 3769; bright, fancy, ornamented A 111, 3689, D 337; well or elaborately dressed A 74, D 236.

gayler *n* gaoler A 1064, 1470, etc.

gayneth *3 s impers* avails, profits A 1176, 1787, 2755; **gayned** *pt s* profited TC 1.352.

geaunt *n* giant PF 344, TC 5.838, B 1997.

gebet *n* gibbet HF 106.

geen see **gon**.

geery *adj* changeable A 1536. Cf. **gere, gerful**.

geeste *v* narrate, tell a story I 43. Cf. **geste**.

geestours see **gestiours**.

geldyng *n* gelding, eunuch A 691.

general *adj* general A 1663, etc.; comprehending, noble BD 990.

gent *adj* gentle PF 558; graceful A 3234; well-bred B 1905.

genterye, -trye *n* gentility, good-breeding D 1146, 1152; nobility, magnanimity LGW 394.

gentil *adj* well-born, of superior position or quality D 1111; noble, excellent HF 1311, PF 337, A 718, B 2865, D 29; worthy C 304; courteous, polite A 72, 567, 1431; generous, compassionate, gentle PF 196, TC 3.5, A 647, A 1043; **gentile** *as n* one who is well-born, person of rank H 217; **gentils** *pl* gentlefolk A 3113, C 323, D 1209.

gentilesse, -ill- *n* gentility, nobility TC 2.1268, D 1109, F 517; courtesy, kindness, compassion A 920, B 853, E 96; gentle breeding E 593; gracefulness, beauty F 426.

gentilly *adv* courteously TC 1.187, A 3104, B 1471.

gerdon see **guerdon**.

gere¹, geere *n* equipment A 352, 4016; apparel, clothing A 365, E 372; armor TC 2.635, A 2180; trappings A 1016; goods, belongings TC 4.1523, B 800; **geeris** *pl* equipment F 1276.

gere², geere *n* whim, transient mood BD 1257; fits of passion, changeable mood A 1372; **geres** *pl* moods A 1531.

gerful, gere- *adj* changeable TC 4.286, A 1538.

gerl *n* girl A 3769; **girles** *pl* young girls or boys A 664.

gerland, -lond *n* garland HF 135, A 666, 1054, etc.; **gerlandes** *pl* A 2937; **garlondes** PF 259.

gerner *n* garner A 593.

gesse *v* suppose, imagine, think TC 3.984, 5.1616, B 622; *1 s* BD 35, A 82, etc.; **gessyng** *part* intending LGW 363.

gest *n* stranger HF 288, TC 2.1110; company E 338; **gestes** *pl* guests A 3188, B 1214, E 1016.

geste, geeste *n* a story of great deeds or historical fact TC 2.83, B 2123; story, history TC 4.450; **gestes, geestes** *pl* stories, histories HF 1434, 1515, B 1126, D 642, F 211; deeds HF 1737.

gestiours *n pl* reciters of stories, romances, etc. HF 1198; **geestours** minstrels B 2036.

gete(n), gette *v* get, obtain BD 888, HF 1857, B 230; beget E 1437; **gete** *1 s* will get BD 476; **gete** *2 pl* PF 651, E 1945; *3 pl* will catch A 4099; **gat** *pt s* got TC 2.679, A 703; begot B 715; **get** *imp s* A 3465; **gete(n)** *pp* A 291, D 817, 1236; **ygeten** A 3964.

gif *conj* if (Northern) A 4181, 4190.

giggynge *part* fitting (a shield) with an armstrap A 2504.

gilt, gylt *n* offence, fault TC 2.1280, 5.1096, A 1765; **in the g.** in the wrong D 387; **in my g.** through fault of mine PF 434, TC 2.244, 3.1641.

giltif *adj* guilty TC 3.1019, 1049.

gipser *n* purse, pouch A 357.

girdel *n* belt A 358, 3250, B 789, 1921; **girdles** *pl* A 368.

girden *v* strike B 3736.

glade *v* gladden, cheer up BD 563, TC 5.455; **gladeth** *3 s* E 1107; **gladed(e), gladded** *pt s* HF 962, TC 1.116, 5.1184; **gladed** *pp* TC 1.994.

gladere *n* one who makes others glad A 2223.

gladly *adv* willingly, readily BD 754, A 308, F 224; customarily HF 1242, B 4414; **been g. wyse** consider themselves wise F 376.

gladnesse *n* cheerfulness BD 828, G 1287; happiness TC 1.22, 3.6, A 1250; pleasure BD 701.

glareth *3 s* glitters HF 272; **glarynge** *ppl adj* staring A 684.

glas *n* glass BD 322, A 152, F 82, etc.; glass container A 700; mirror A 198.

gledy *adj* glowing, burning LGW 105.

glee *n* music, entertainment TC 2.1036, B 2030; **glees** *pl* musical instruments HF 1209, 1252.

gleede, glede *n* live coal, ember TC 4.337, 5.303, A 1997; *pl* TC 2.538, A 3883.

glente *pt s* glanced TC 4.1223.

gleyre *n* white of an egg G 806.

gliwe *v* glue, fasten HF 1761; **yglewed** *pp* F 182.

glood see **glyde.**

glorie *n* honor A 870, B 3266; glory A 2240, B 3565.

glorifye *v refl* boast, exult HF 1134, TC 2.1593; *intrans* TC 3.186.

glose *n* explanation, interpretation, commentary LGW 328, D 1792, 1919; deceit F 166.

glose(n) *v* explain, interpret TC 4.1410, B 1180, D 26; cajole, beguile, persuade by smooth talking TC 4.1471, B 3330, D 509; mince words E 2351, I 45; **yglosed** *pp* flattered H 34.

glosynge *n* interpretation D 1793 (see note).

glyde, glide *v* glide TC 4.1215, A 1575; **glood** *pt s* B 2094, F 393; **glyden** *pp* E 1887.

glymsyng *n* glimpse E 2383.

glyteren *3 pl* glitter A 977; **glytered** *pt s* shone A 2166; **gliterynge** *ppl adj* shining A 2890.

gnawe *v* gnaw TC 4.621, 5.36; **gnow** *pt s* gnawed B 3638; **gnaw** *imp s* TC 1.509; **gnawynge** *part* champing A 2507.

gnof *n* churl A 3188.

gobet *n* piece A 696.

gold-hewen *pp* made (hewn) of gold A 2500.

goldsmythrye *n* work of goldsmiths A 2498.

gold-ybete *adj* interwoven or embroidered with gold threads TC 2.1229.

golee *n* mouthful PF 556.

gomme *n* gum LGW 121.

go(n), goon *v* go BD 145, LGW 34, A 12, etc.; walk TC 2.1684, A 968, B 3802, etc.; **goost** *2 s* B 1668, D 273; **goth, gooth** *3 s* BD 7, PF 100; **gas** *3 s* (Northern) A 4037; **go(on), gon** *pl* A 769, 1267, B 4042, C 748; **yede** *pt 3 s* went TC 5.843, G 1141; **yeden** *pt pl* TC 2.936; **gooth** *imp pl* A 2560; **go, ygo(n), ygoon** *pp* A 286, B 1402, F 293, G 907; **geen** *pp* (Northern) A 4078; **yede** *as pp* G 1281; **go bet** *imp* go quickly BD 136, C 667.

gonne *n* gun HF 1643; missile LGW 637.

good *adj* good BD 9, etc.; **goode** *pl*, *voc & def form* BD 522, A 74.

good *adv*: **whil yow good list** as long as you please TC 1.119.

good *n* property, goods, wealth TC 3.1108, 4.87, B 1270, D 314; income A 581; **goode myn** my

treasure TC 4.1660; **koude his good** knew what was good for him TC 5.106; **koude no g.** didn't know what to do BD 390.

goodlich *adj* pleasing, beautiful F 623; kind G 1053.

goodly *adj* pleasing BD 919, B 3969; kind TC 1.173; beautiful TC 1.277, 466; excellent B 4010; *as n* pleasing one TC 1.458.

goodly *adv* graciously, patiently BD 1283, TC 3.1035; beautifully TC 5.578; gladly, willingly A 803; well TC 1.253.

goodlyhede *n* goodliness BD 829; **godlyhed(e)** seeming goodness HF 274, 330; **goodlihed(e)** goodness TC 2.842; comeliness TC 3.1730.

gooldes *n pl* marigolds A 1929.

goore *n* gore (of skirt, etc.) A 3237, B 1979.

goosish *adj* goose-like, silly TC 3.584.

goost, gost *n* soul, spirit TC 2.531, C 43, E 926, etc.; ghost HF 186, A 205; person compared to a ghost H 55; mind TC 3.464, LGW 103; conscience Truth 20; Holy Ghost B 1660, G 328.

goostly *adv* spiritually G 109; **gostly for to speke** to tell the truth TC 5.1030.

goot *n* goat A 688, G 886.

goshauk *n* hawk (of an inferior type) PF 335, B 1928.

gossib, -syb *n* woman friend, gossip D 529, 544; relation, acquaintance D 243.

goter *n* gutter TC 3.787.

governaille *n* government, mastery E 1192.

governaunce *n* management, direction, control BD 1008, HF 945, TC 2.1442, A 281; behavior, demeanor TC 3.216, G 989.

gowne-clooth *n* cloth for a gown D 2247, 2252.

grace *n* favor, a favor BD 111, HF 85, LGW 451, A 88; fortune, good fortune BD 810, TC 1.907, D 553; mercy A 3595, C 236; **of g.** through kindness, graciously TC 3.719, A 3080, F 161; **with harde g., with sory g.** bad luck to him C 876, D 2228.

grame *n* sorrow TC 3.1028, G 1403; suffering TC 1.372, 4.529.

grammeere *n* grammar B 1726.

grange *n* an outlying farmhouse (and associated buildings) belonging to a monastery or a secular lord A 3668; **graunges** *pl* B 1256; barns HF 698.

grapenel *n* an instrument with iron claws hurled by a rope LGW 640.

gras *n* grass LGW 118, B 1969; herb

PF 206, F 153; **gres** TC 2.515; **grasses** *pl* blades of grass HF 1353.

graspe *v* grope TC 5.223; **graspeth** *3 s* gropes A 4293.

graunt mercy *excl* gramercy, great thanks BD 560, HF 1874, TC 3.649.

grave(n) *v* dig LGW 678; bury E 681; engrave, scratch TC 3.1462, F 830; carve TC 2.47, C 17; impress, make an impression on TC 2.1241, 4.1377; *3 pl* carve TC 2.47; **grave, ygrave** *pp* buried TC 3.103, D 496; carved BD 164, HF 157.

grece *n* grease A 135, D 487; **greesse** C 60.

gree *n* favor, good-will A 2733; **in g.** favorably, graciously TC 2.529, B 259; without complaint E 1151; **in g. superlatyf** more to be desired E 1375.

greet, gret *adj* great A 84, G 479, etc.; **grete** *def & pl* HF 53, A 879, etc.; **the grete** *as n* the chief part, gist BD 1242, PF 35, TC 5.1036, LGW 574.

greithen *v* prepare B 3784; **greythen** *pp* A 4309.

grene *adj* green A 103, etc.; wan TC 5.243; *as n* grass LGW 282; green leaves or branches A 1512; vegetation F 54.

grenehede *n* unripeness, wantonness B 163.

grete, greete *v* greet TC 3.1556, E 1014; **grette** *pt s* BD 503, TC 5.293; **grete** *imp s* B 1553; **ygret** *pp* BD 517.

gretter *adj compar* TC 1.241, A 197; **grettest(e)** *superl* A 120, D 1310.

grevaunce *n* grievance B 3703; discomfort PF 205.

greve *n* thicket, grove TC 5.1144, A 1478; **greves** *pl* branches BD 417, LGW 227, A 1507; bushes A 1495.

greve *v* annoy, cause discomfort TC 1.1001, B 352; *refl* feel annoyed TC 1.343, A 3859; **greveth** *3 s* B 1362, D 2181; does harm TC 5.783; **greved** *pt s* caused discomfort HF 1119; **greved, ygreved** *pp* injured, harmed LGW 127, A 4181.

grey *adj* gray A 616, D 269; **greye** *pl* gray, hazel (of eyes) A 152, 3317, 3974; *as n* **this olde greye** old graybeard TC 4.127.

greyn, -ayn *n* grain A 596, C 374; a very small amount TC 3.1026; grain of paradise (an aromatic seed) A 3690, B 1852; **greyn of Portyngale** red dye B 4649 (see note); **in g.** in a fast color, in the very fiber F 511. See **scarlet in grayn.**

grief *n* grievance D 2174.

grifphon *n* griffin A 2133.

grisly, grysely *adj* terrible, horrible LGW 637, A 1971, C 708, D 735; very serious TC 2.1700.

grom *n* man HF 206.

grone(n), groone *v* groan HF 338, TC 1.360, B 4076; **gronte** *pt s* B 3899.

gronyng *n* groaning B 4097.

grope *v* probe, test A 644; search D 1817; **gropeth** *3 s* gropes A 4222; **groped** *pt s* groped A 4217; **grope** *imp s* search, feel D 2141, G 1236.

grot *n* particle D 1292.

grote *n* groat, silver coin worth four pence TC 4.586, B 4148, C 945; **grotes** *pl* C 376, D 1964.

ground, -ow- *n* ground A 2427, etc.; foundation TC 2.842; texture A 453.

grounded *pp* grounded, instructed A 414; based TC 4.1672.

groyn *n* grumbling, scolding TC 1.349.

groynynge *n* grumbling, discontent A 2460.

grucche *v* grumble, complain TC 3.643, A 3863, E 170; begrudge, complain about E 354; **gruccheth** *3 s* grumbles A 3045.

grucchyng *n* complaining D 406.

gruf *adv* on the face, face down TC 4.912, A 949, B 1865.

gruwel *n* gruel TC 3.711.

grynde *v* grind A 4032; **grynt** *3 s* HF 1798, D 389; **grounden, ygrounde, i-** *pp* ground A 3991, G 760; ground to a sharp edge TC 4.43, A 2549, B 2073.

grynte *pt 3 s* gnashed D 2161.

grys *adj* gray G 559.

grys *n* fine gray fur, prob. squirrel A 194.

guerdon, -oun, ger- *n* reward HF 619, TC 1.818, B 3820, D 1878, etc.

guerdonynge *n* reward PF 455, TC 2.392.

gunne see **gynne.**

gyde *n* guide A 804, etc.

gyde(n), gide *v* guide, conduct TC 1.183, B 1670, E 776; **gyde** *3 s subj* B 245, 1449.

gye *v* guide, direct, govern HF 943, TC 5.546, E 75; **gye** *3 s subj* A 2786, 2815.

gygges *n pl* squeaking noises HF 1942 (see note).

gyle *n* deceit BD 620, TC 3.777, G 195.

gylour *n* one who practises deceit A 4321.

gyn *n* contrivance, device F 128, 322, G 1165.

gyngebreed *n* preserved ginger B 2044.

gynne *v* begin HF 2004; **gynne** *1 s* TC 2.849; **gynneth** *3 s* TC 1.218, A 4064; **gynnen** *3 pl* TC 5.657, LGW 38; **gan** *pt 3 s* BD 70, TC 1.189; *as auxiliary v* did A 301, C 191, D 1000; **gonne(n), gunne** *pt pl* did HF 2110, TC 5.528, A 1658, etc.

gynnyng(e) *n* beginning HF 66, TC 1.377, 2.671.

gypoun *n* tunic A 75, 2120.

gyse, gise *n* manner, method, way TC 4.1370, F 332, 540; custom TC 5.861, A 993; **at his owene g.** at will A 663, 1789.

gyte *n* long cloak A 3954 (see note); *pl* D 559.

gyterne, gi- *n* a form of guitar A 3333, 3353, 4396, H 268; *pl* C 466.

gyternynge *n* playing on the **gyterne,** q.v. A 3363.

H

haberdasshere *n* dealer in hats and notions (small wares) A 361.

habergeoun, haubergeoun *n* coat of mail A 76, 2119, B 2051.

habit *n* dress TC 1.109, etc.; character A 1378.

habitacles *n pl* niches HF 1194.

habounde *v* abound B 3938, E 1286, Rosem 12.

habundant *adj* abundant B 4115; abounding E 59.

habundantly *adv* abundantly B 870.

habundaunce *n* abundance TC 3.1042, D 1723, E 203.

haches *n pl* hatches LGW 648.

haire *n* haircloth shirt G 133.

halde see **holden.**

hale *v* attract PF 151.

half *n* half TC 3.344, LGW 245; side HF 1136; **halves** *pl* sides A 3481; behalf BD 139; **on my halve** on my part TC 4.945; **a Goddes half(e)** in God's name, for God's sake BD 370, 758, D 50.

haliday *n* holiday A 3309, 3340; **holyday** LGW 35; *pl* LGW 422.

halke *n* corner, nook F 1121; *pl* nooks, hiding places G 311.

hals *n* neck HF 394, PF 458, etc.

halse *1 s* conjure B 1835.

halten *v* limp TC 4.1457; **halt** *3 s* halts, limps BD 622.

halvendel *n* half TC 3.707, 5.335.

halwed *pt s* consecrated G 551; *pp* reverenced TC 3.268.

halwes *n pl* saints B 1060; apostles BD 831; shrines A 14, D 657.

ham *n* home (Northern) A 4032.

han see **have.**

hande-brede *n* handbreadth A 3811.

hap *n* chance, fortune BD 810, TC 3.1246, E 2057; good fortune BD 1039, B 3928, G 1209; favor TC 2.1454; **happes** *pl* happenings BD 1279.

happe(n) *v* happen PF 473, A 585; **happeth** *3 s* PF 10, TC 1.625; **happe(n)** *3 s subj* TC 2.29, LGW 78, D 1401; **happed(e)** *pt s* BD 805, C 606.

hard *adj* HF 118, PF 2, etc.; **of hard** with difficulty TC 2.1236.

hardely, -ily, -yly *adv* assuredly, certainly BD 1043, TC 2.1425, A 156.

hardyment *n* boldness TC 4.533.

hardynesse, -di- *n* boldness, courage TC 1.566, B 939, D 612, E 93.

hardyng *n* tempering F 243.

harlot *n* fellow, rogue, rascal A 647, 4268, D 1754.

harlotrye, -trie *n* ribaldry A 3145, 3184; scurrility, wickedness D 1328, E 2262; *pl* vulgarities, ribaldries A 561.

harm *n* harm, hurt, injury BD 492, HF 99, 577, etc.; sorrow F 586; pity, a pity TC 2.350; **broken harm** ? petty annoyances E 1425 (see note).

harneised *pp* mounted A 114.

harneys, -ays *n* equipment, accouterment A 1613, D 136; armor A 1006, 2140; parts, fittings A 2896, 3762; **harneys** *pl* sets of equipment (arms and armor) A 1630.

harre *n* hinge A 550.

harwed *pt s* harrowed (Hell) A 3512, D 2107.

haryed *pp* dragged A 2726.

hasard *n* gambling with dice C 465, 591, etc.

hasardour *n* gambler at dice C 596, 751; *pl* C 613, 616, 618.

hasardrye *n* gambling at dice C 590, 599.

haselwode *excl* implying skepticism TC 5.505; **haselwodes shaken** for heaven's sake TC 3.890.

haste *n* haste A 3545, etc.; impatience TC 5.1605.

hastif *adj* eager, impatient TC 4.1567, E 1805; **hastif thyng** urgent matter A 3545; **in hastif wyse** without delay E 349.

hastifly *adv* quickly B 688, 1047.

hastily *adv* quickly, soon D 1947, F 471, 839; promptly, without delay A 1714, B 1299, D 1602; hastily C 192.

haten *v* hate TC 5.1079; **hatede** *pt pl* E 731.

haubergeoun see **habergeoun**.

haunche-bon *n* thigh A 3803; *pl* A 3279.

haunt *n* skill A 447.

haunteth *3 s* practises, habitually uses TC 5.1556, A 4392, C 547; **haun-teden** *pt pl* C 464.

hauteyn *adj* haughty, lofty PF 262, C 330.

have, han *v* have TC 3.136, A 224, B 114; **hastow, hastou** hast thou B 676, D 800; **han** *pr pl* have TC 1.199, LGW 458, A 1020; **had, hadde** *pt 1 & 3 s* HF 1156, A 291, 1271; **haddest** *pt 2 s* PF 167; **had, hadde(n)** *pt pl* BD 172, HF 1154, TC 3.870, D 822; **had** *pp* A 4184, etc.

haven *n* haven B 852; **havenes** *pl* harbors A 407.

haven-syde *n* side of a harbor B 4261.

hawberk, hau- *n* hauberk, coat of mail A 2431, B 2053.

hawe¹ *n* yard, enclosure C 855.

hawe² *n* haw (fruit of the hawthorn), something of little value TC 3.854, D 659; *pl* TC 4.1398.

hayis *n pl* hedges TC 3.351.

he, hee *pron* A 1319, 4366; **his, hys, hise** *gen* BD 498, HF 535, A 539; **him, hym** BD 135, 256, A 87, 88; **he . . . he, he . . . hym** *as indef pron* this one . . . that one LGW 643–4, A 2519, 2612–14; **hym** *refl* himself A 87, 703, etc.

hed see **hyde**.

hed(e), heede *n* heed PF 303, TC 1.501, A 303, etc.

hede *v* provide with a head TC 2.1042.

hede, heed, hed, heved *n* head HF 550, TC 2.540, A 198, 1054, etc.; **hedes, heddes** *pl* PF 554, A 2180; **hevedes** *pl* PF 215, B 2032, G 398.

heele, hele *n* health BD 607, B 1540, D 1946; well-being, prosperity BD 1039, TC 2.707, A 1271.

heele(n), hele *v* heal, cure BD 40, E 2372, F 641; **heeleth** *3 s* C 366; **heeled, heled** *pp* TC 3.1212, A 2706.

heep, hep *n* heap, crowd, large number BD 295, TC 4.1281, A 575; **hepe** *dat* HF 2149; **to-hepe** together TC 3.1764.

heer, her *n* hair BD 456, 864, A 589, etc.; **heeres, -is, heres** *pl* hair BD 394, B 4094, E 1085.

heer, here, her *adv* here BD 366, 659, A 1610, etc.

heer-agayns *adv* here against A 3039; **here-ayeins** TC 2.1380.

heere(n), here(n) *v* hear BD 94, HF 879, A 169, 2286; **herist** *2 s*

HF 651; **herestow** hearest thou A 3366; **hereth** *3 s* TC 3.1235; **herde** *pt s* A 221; **herde(n)** *pt pl* B 3974, 4566; **herd** *pp* BD 129, A 849.

heeth *n* heath, uncultivated land A 6, 606; heather A 3262.

hegge *n* hedge TC 5.1144; *pl* TC 3.1236, B 4408.

heigh, high, hy(e) *adj* high HF 914, A 522, etc.; great A 316, 1798; loud HF 1020; grave, weighty A 306; **an (on) heigh (high, hye)** on high, aloft, up high HF 215, 851, 1161, A 1065, 3571; **in heigh and lo(u)gh** in all respects, completely A 817, B 993; **hyer** *compar* higher A 399.

heighe, high(e), hye *adv* high BD 432, HF 106, 921, A 271; proudly TC 2.401; loudly, vociferously BD 183, A 2661.

heighly *adv* strongly TC 2.1733.

helde *v* hold, keep D 272.

helde *pt pl* poured out HF 1686 (OE *hieldan*).

hele *v* conceal D 950; **heled** *pp* hidden B 4245.

heleles *adj* devoid of health or well-being TC 5.1593.

helm *n* helmet TC 2.638, A 2676; **helmes** *pl* A 2500, 2609.

helmed *pp* wearing a helmet TC 2.593, B 3560.

helpe(n) *v* help A 584, 1484, etc.; **heelp** *pt s* A 1651, B 920; **holpe(n)** *pp* helped A 18; cured E 2370.

helply *adj* helpful TC 5.128.

hem see **they**.

hemself *pron* themselves TC 1.922, A 1254, D 761; **hemselve(n)** HF 1215, F 1378.

hemysperie *n* hemisphere TC 3.1439, E 1799.

hende *adj* pleasant, gracious, polite A 3199, D 628, 1286.

henne *adv* hence TC 2.209, A 2356, C 687.

hennes *adv* hence HF 1284, TC 1.572, 5.403.

hennesforth *adv* henceforth HF 782, TC 3.167, F 658.

hente *v* seize, catch, get TC 4.1371, A 299, 2638; **hent** *3 s* catches TC 4.5; **hente** *3 s subj* G 7; **hente** *pt s* seized A 3475, B 1760; captured B 3546; took A 957, 4212, F 1391; **henten** *pt pl* seized A 904; **hent** *imp s* D 1553; **hent, yhent** *pp* seized B 4249; caught TC 1.509, A 1581; taken C 868.

hepe *n* hip (fruit of the wild rose) B 1937.

heped *pp* heaped up TC 4.236.

her see **they**.

herafter, heere- *adv* hereafter TC 4.1562, E 1674.

herafterwardes *adv* hereafter D 1515.

heraud *n* herald A 2533; **heraudes** *pl* HF 1321, A 1017.

heraude *v* herald, proclaim HF 1576.

herbe *n* herb HF 290, TC 1.964, 2.345; **herbes** *pl* TC 1.661, A 2713; herbage B 2104.

herbe yve *n* herb ivy B 4156 (see note to B 4152).

herber *n* arbor, garden TC 2.1705, LGW 203.

herbergage *n* lodging A 4329, B 147, E 201.

herbergeours *n pl* attendants sent ahead to provide lodging B 997.

herberwe *n* harbor A 403 (see note); inn A 765; lodging A 4119; house (astronomical) F 1035.

herberwynge *n* providing lodging A 4332.

herby, heerby *adv* hereby HF 263, D 2204, E 1330.

herde-gromes *n pl* shepherd boys HF 1225.

herdesse *n* shepherdess TC 1.653.

here see **she**.

here and howne all and sundry (?) TC 4.210 (see note).

here-ayeins *adv* here-against TC 2.1380.

herebefore, -forn *adv* herebefore BD 1136, 1304; also spelled **-bifore** (TC 5.26), **-biforn** (TC 5.157), **byforn** (TC 3.302, 4.1248), **heer-biforn** (A 1584, B 613).

heremyte *n* hermit HF 659.

herie *v* praise TC 3.1672; **herye** *1 s* TC 3.951; **heryest** *2 s* worshipest B 3419; **heryeth, -ieth** *3 s* B 1155, 1808; **herye(n)** *3 pl* E 616, G 47; **herying** *part* B 1868; **heryed, iheryed, yheried** *pp* HF 1405, TC 2.973, 3.7, B 872.

heritage *n* inheritance B 366, D 1119; allotment in the next world D 1641.

herken *v* listen (to) TC 2.95, LGW 343; **herke** *imp s* TC 1.1030, B 425, etc.

herknen *v* listen to A 1526; **herkne** *imp s* B 113.

herne *n* nook, corner F 1121; *pl* G 658.

herneys see **harneys**.

herof *adv* hereof PF 502, TC 2.108.

heroner *n* falcon trained to catch herons TC 4.413.

heronsewes *n pl* young herons F 68.

heroun *n* heron HF 346, F 1197.

hert *n* hart BD 351, PF 195, A 1675; **hertes** *pl* F 1191; *gen* A 1681.

herte *n* heart A 150, 229, etc.; sweetheart TC 3.1039, 4.796; **hertes** *gen* s TC 3.1131; **herte** *gen s* heart's TC 2.445, D 471; **herte** *pl* B 4578; **of herte** from the heart B 4493.

hertelees, -les *adj* without spirit, timid TC 5.1594, B 4098.

hert(e)ly *adj* sincere E 176, 502, F 5.

hertely *adv* genuinely, earnestly, heartily BD 85, 1226, A 762, E 1242.

herte-spoon *n* the depression below the breastbone A 2606.

heryinge, -iynge *n* praise, praising TC 3.48, B 1649.

heste, heeste *n* behest, bidding, command TC 3.1157, A 2532, B 1013; commandment A 3588; promise TC 4.1439, F 1064; **hestes, heestes** *pl* commands TC 3.1745; commandments B 284; **Goddes heestes** the Ten Commandments C 640.

het, heete see **hoten.**

hete, heete *n* heat HF 569, C 38, etc.; passion TC 1.978, 4.1583; fever TC 2.942.

heterly *adv* violently, fiercely LGW 638.

hethenesse *n* non-Christian territory A 49, B 1112.

hethyng *n* derision A 4110.

hette *pt 3 s* inflamed PF 145.

heved(es) see **hede.**

heve(n) *v* heave A 550; exert effort TC 2.1289; **haf, haaf** *pt s* heaved A 3470; lifted A 2428; **heve** *imp s* lift, raise TC 5.1159.

heven *n* heaven BD 308, HF 505; **hevenes** *gen s* heaven's HF 988, TC 2.904; **hevene** *gen (descr)* heavenly: **hevene blisse** PF 72, TC 3.704; **hevene kyng** B 1583, E 2407; **on hevene** in the sky TC 5.274.

hevenyssh *adj* heavenly HF 1395, TC 1.104, 5.1813.

hevenysshly *adv* in a heavenly manner A 1055.

hevynesse *n* sorrow, dejection BD 25, HF 2011, TC 1.24, etc.

hewe[1] *n* color PF 354, B 137; complexion BD 497, A 394; appearance D 1622, F 508; **hewes, hewis** *pl* colors, pigments TC 2.21, A 2088; color, complexion TC 2.1258, 3.94.

hewe[2] *n* servant E 1785.

heyne *n* wretch G 1319.

heynous *adj* heinous TC 2.1617.

heyre *adj* made of hair: **heyre clowt** C 736.

heysoge *n* hedge sparrow PF 612.

heythen *adv* hence A 4033.

hider, hy- *adv* hither HF 1872, TC 5.484, A 1797.

hiderward, hy- *adv* in this direction B 1616, 3159.

hidous, hy- *adj* hideous A 1978, 3520, B 4583.

hidously, hy- *adv* hideously, dreadfully HF 1599, A 1701.

hierde, herde *n* cowherd A 603; shepherd TC 3.1235, G 192; **hierdes** *pl* guardians TC 3.619.

highte, hei- *n* height TC 5.827, A 1890; **on (upon) highte** on high, in the air HF 740, A 2607, 2919; in height HF 827; out loud A 1784.

highte see **hoten.**

hipes, hippes *n pl* hips BD 957, A 472; **hypes** B 3904.

hir see **they.**

hire, hyre *n* payment, wages TC 1.125, A 538, D 1973; reward HF 1857; ransom TC 4.506; **quite youre hire** repay you TC 1.334, D 1008; **sette to hyre** farm out, sublet A 507.

hire see **she, they.**

hir(e)self, hir(e)selve(n) *pron* herself TC 2.1223, A 3543, 4142, F 384; **hyrself** B 4062; *as pers pron* TC 4.637.

historial *adj* historical C 156.

hit, hyt, it, yt *pron* it BD 7, 12, 36, 48, etc.; **his** *gen* HF 784, TC 2.42, LGW 125, A 1036, 3006, E 263, etc.; **hym** *acc* it (the philosopher's stone) G 864; **hyt (it) am I** it is I BD 186, TC 1.588, LGW 314.

hit see **hyde.**

hoker *n* scorn A 3965.

holde(n) *v* keep, hold, maintain A 1506, D 1727, F 763; consider TC 1.194; continue TC 1.263; **holde** *1 s* hold B 676, D 572; hold opinion, consider BD 540, D 1186; **holdest** *2 s* hold consider LGW 326; **holdeth, halt** *3 s* BD 621, C 182, F 61; stays in B 721; **holde(n)** *pr pl* B 4403, E 1390, 2021; **holde** *pr subj* TC 5.1339, E 287; **heeld, held** *pt s* PF 372, TC 1.126, A 176; **heelde, helde(n)** *pt pl* A 2517, B 1192, E 426; **helde** *pt s subj* F 916; **hold, hoold, holdeth** *imp pl* PF 521, A 1868, F 1064, H 37; **holde(n), yholde** *pp* kept D 1024; bound BD 1078, TC 5.574, D 135; considered TC 5.703, LGW 489, A 2374; esteemed A 1307; indebted, beholden TC 2.241, 3.1259, 5.966; **halde** (Northern) considered A 4208; **to holde(n) in honde** encourage with false hopes BD 1019, TC 2.477, 3.773, 5.1615; **holdynge hir questioun** carrying on discussion A 2514.

holdynge in hondes leading a lover on with false hope HF 692.

holily, hoo- *adv* holily D 2286; virtuously E 1455, 1507.

holly see **hoolly.**

holm *n* holly PF 178, A 2921.

holour *n* lecher D 254.

holpen see **helpen.**

holt *n* wood, grove A 6; **holtes** *pl* woods TC 3.351.

holwe *adj* hollow A 289, 1363, G 1265; **holowe** HF 1035.

homme *v* hum TC 2.1199.

hond, hand *n* hand A 193, etc.; **beren . . . on honde** make one believe (erroneously) TC 4.1404, D 575; beat down by words or argument D 226, 380; **holden . . . in honde** see holden.

hondred, -hun- *n* hundred A 1851, 2582, etc.

honest *adj* respectable, honorable A 246, C 557; fitting, proper B 1239, C 628, E 2024; virtuous E 333; honest H 75.

honeste(e) *n* good repute TC 4.1576; propriety, decorum B 3902, D 1267; modesty B 3908; virtue, chastity C 77, G 89.

honestetee *n* honor E 422.

honestly *adv* honorably B 1434, G 549; worthily E 2026; fittingly, modestly A 1444.

honge(n), hange *v* hang PF 458, TC 5.1199, A 2410, D 2242; **hongeth, hangeth** *3 s* A 2415, B 1340; **honge** *2 pl subj* remain undecided TC 2.1242; **heng** *pt s* hung BD 122, PF 282, A 160; **hanged** B 1824; **henge** *pt pl* BD 174; **honge** *pt pl* A 2422; **hanged** *pt pl* D 761; **hanged** *pp* hung A 2568, 3837; hanged D 658.

honour *n* honor A 46, etc.; reputation, good name TC 2.480, 4.159, D 821; privilege C 931; rank D 1209, E 1502.

honoure(n) *v* honor HF 1384, TC 3.1262, A 2407; worship TC 1.151.

hony-comb *n* term of endearment A 3698.

hoo *excl as n* ceasing TC 2.1083.

hool *adj* whole, entire BD 554, A 533, etc.; well, in health BD 553, C 357, D 1370; without defect E 1538; **al hool of** recovered from TC 3.1202.

hool, hol *adv* wholly BD 991, TC 1.1053, D 2033; **al hool** completely TC 2.587, 4.1641.

hoold, holde *n* keeping, possession B 4064, D 599, F 167; stronghold, castle B 507; tenement, house D 1607.

hoolly *adv* wholly BD 326, A 599, etc.; **hooly** D 1999; **holly** TC 3.145.

hoolynesse *n* holiness, spirituality A 1158, B 167; religious ceremony E 1708.

hoomlinesse *n* domestic duties E 429 (see note).

hoomly *adj* domestic E 1785, 1792; plain, simple D 1843.

hoomly *adv* unpretentiously A 328, G 608; plainly TC 2.1559.

hoor *adj* white-haired, hoar A 3878, C 743, E 1269; marked by age E 1464; **hoore** *pl* D 2182.

hoord, hord *n* hoard A 3262, 4406, B 1274.

hoost *n* multitude, army A 874, B 3758, etc.

hoost(e) *n* host, innkeeper A 747, 751, etc.

hoot *adj* hot in lit. and fig. senses A 626, 4348, etc.; intense G 887; **hoote, hote** *def* A 394, TC 1.490.

hoote *adv* hotly, fervently A 97, 1737, B 586; intensely TC 3.1650; **hotter** *compar* more hotly LGW 59.

hoppe *v* dance A 4375, 4382; **hoppen** *1 pl* A 3876.

hoppesteres *adj* dancing A 2017 (but see note).

hors *n* horse A 94, etc.; **hors** *pl* HF 952, A 74, B 1823.

horsly *adj* horse-like, as a horse should be F 194.

hose *n* stocking HF 1840, A 3933, G 726; **hosen, hoses** *pl* A 456, 3319, 3955, B 1923.

hostel *n* hostel; **bon hostel** "happy landing" HF 1022.

hostelrye *n* inn, hostelry A 23, 718; lodging house A 3203; **hostelryes** *pl* A 2493.

hostiler, -leer *n* innkeeper A 241, 4360, B 4219.

hoten, hete, highte *v* call, be called or named, command, promise BD 1226, A 1557, D 144. (The normal forms are **hoten**, *pt* **het** or **hight**, *pp* **hote(n)**; other forms are due to leveling.) **hote** *1 s* command HF 1719; **heete** *1 s* promise B 334; assure B 1132; **highte** *1 s* am called A 1558; **hette, hatte** *3 s* is named TC 3.797; **hight(e)** *3 s* is called HF 663, TC 4.790, LGW 417, A 3095, G 550; **hatte, highte(n), hightyn** *3 pl* are called, named HF 1303, 1519, TC 1.788, LGW 423; **heete** *3 s subj* may promise A 2398; **het** *pt 3 s* was called BD 200, 948, HF 1604; **highte, hyghte** *pt 3 s* was named BD 63, A 616, etc.; promised TC 5.1636, Buk 5; **highte(n)** *pt pl* were called A 2920; promised TC 2.1623, E 496; **hoote** *pp* called A 3941; **heet**

pp called, named TC 1.153, F 1388; **hight** *pp* named B 4039; promised TC 2.492, A 2472, D 1024, F 1323; **ihight** called TC 5.541.

hottes *n pl* baskets HF 1940 (see note).

hound *n* dog TC 3.764, B 3292; **houndes** *pl* BD 349, A 146.

houndfyssh *n* dogfish E 1825.

howped *pt 3 pl* whooped B 4590.

hous *n* house A 343, etc.; religious establishment A 252, B 3121; sign of the Zodiac, house (*astrol.*) TC 2.681, B 304, F 672 (see note to each passage); **outer hous** portion of the great hall separated by a traverse TC 3.664; **houses of office** storerooms, kitchens, etc. E 264.

housbondrye, -drie *n* careful management A 4077, B 4018; economy E 1296; housefurnishings, possessions D 288, E 1380.

hove *v* hover TC 3.1427; **hoved** *pt s* remained TC 5.33.

how *adv* however HF 338, TC 3.146, 5.132; **how shal (myghte) I do** what shall (might) I do TC 5.225, 1289.

howgates *adv* how A 4037.

howne ? meaning uncertain TC 4.210 (see note).

howve *n* skullcap, hood: **sette his howve** make him look foolish A 3911; **howve . . . to glaze** mock, delude TC 5.469; **maken an howve above a calle** engage in double dealing TC 3.775.

humanitee *n* benevolence E 92.

humblesse *n* humility HF 630, B 165.

humblynge *n* rumbling HF 1039.

humour *n* humor, bodily fluid A 421, 1375; *pl* B 4115, 4147.

hunte *n* hunter, huntsman B 345, A 1678, 2628; *pl* hunters BD 361, 541.

hurte *v* hurt, injure D 1132, E 1840; **hurt** *3 s, contract. of* hurteth hurts TC 5.350; **herte, hurte** *pt s* BD 883, TC 2.199; **hurt, yhurt** *pp* TC 1.1087, A 2709.

hurtleth *3 s* strikes A 2616; **hurtelen** *3 pl* clash LGW 638.

hust *imper s* hush A 3722; **hust** *pp* hushed, silent TC 2.915, 3.1094, A 2981.

hyde, hide *v* hide HF 1707, A 1477; lie concealed F 141; **hydestow** hidest thou D 308; **hit** *3 s* hides F 512; **hidde, hydde** *pt s* D 745, 955, F 595; **hyd, hid, yhid** *pp* hidden B 103, D 2143, G 317; **hed, yhed** *pp* BD 175, LGW 208; **hidde** *as def adj* TC 1.530.

hyder see **hider**.

hye *n* haste, speed; **in hye** quickly, soon, promptly, speedily TC 2.88, 1712, A 2979, B 210.

hye *v* hurry TC 3.621, F 291; **hiest** *2 s* hastenest TC 3.1441; **hieth** *3 s* TC 4.320; **hied** *pt 3 s* hurried TC 3.157; **hyed** *pt pl* BD 363; **hyed** *pp* TC 3.655.

hye see **heigh**.

hymself, hymselve(n) *pron* himself BD 419, A 219, 739; **himself, himselve** itself TC 1.745, D 1968; *as pers pron* he himself TC 1.256, LGW 13, B 3645.

hyndre *v* hinder A 1135; **hynderest** *2 s* LGW 324.

hyndreste *adj* hindmost A 622.

hyne *n* hind, farm laborer A 603, C 688.

hyt see **hit**.

I

I *pron* I BD 1, etc.; **ich** (Midl. and Southern) occ. before vowels TC 1.678, 3,1818, etc.; **ik** (Northern) only in Reeve's speech A 3867, etc.; **my** *gen* BD 610, 831, etc.; **myn** see separate entry; **me** *dat & acc* A 39, 1646, etc.

i- prefix of *pp*; see **y-**.

iben *pp* been HF 1138. See **ben**.

i-blessed *pp* blessed, praised B 4638.

iblowe *pp* spread abroad TC 1.530, 4.167.

ibounden *pp* bound PF 268.

icched *pp* itched A 3682.

idarted *pp* pierced with a dart TC 4.240.

ido *pp* finished PF 542.

ifounded *pp* based PF 231.

ifourmed *pp* made TC 4.315.

igrounde *pp* ground TC 4.43.

iheryed *pp* praised TC 3.7.

ihight *pp* called TC 5.541. See **hoten**.

ijaped *pp* made sport TC 1.318.

ik see **I**.

iknowe see **yknowe, knowen**.

il, ille *adj* evil A 4045, 4174, 4184.

il-hayl *excl* evil greeting A 4089.

ilke, ylke *adj* same BD 265, HF 37, etc.

illusion *n* illusion, delusion HF 493, TC 3.1041, F 1264; deception, practices intended to deceive F 1134, G 673.

ilost *pp* lost TC 3.896. See **lesen**.

iloved *pp* loved TC 1.594.

ilyke *adv* equally LGW 55.

ilyved *pp* lived TC 5.933.

imaked *pp* made PF 677.

imedled *pp* mingled TC 3.815. See **medle**.

importable *adj* unbearable B 3792; **inportable** intolerable E 1144.

impossible *n* impossibility TC 3.525, D 688; **inpossible** D 2231, F 1009.

impresse(n) *v* impress TC 3.1543; urge, enforce TC 2.1371; *intrans* crowd (upon) E 1578; **impresse** *3 pl* press in, throng about G 1071.

impressioun *n* impression TC 1.298, A 3613; effect F 371; feeling E 1978; *pl* thoughts, emotions HF 39, TC 5.372.

imused *pp* pondered HF 1287.

in *n* lodging, dwelling-place A 2436, 3547, B 1097.

in *prep* in BD 327, etc.; into TC 5.309, A 869; on, upon TC 5.53, A 2529, B 3932, D 768; at D 400; to, within TC 5.716; amid F 292; **in my gylt** throught my fault TC 2.244, F 757; **inne** *as quasi adv at end of line* TC 1.821, 2.6, 851, B 518, etc.

in *adv* in, within, inside A 4037, C 731, G 1164. Cf. **inne**.

in- see **im-**.

incubus *n* evil spirit or creature D 880.

induracioun *n* hardening G 855.

inequal *adj* unequal A 2271 (see note).

infect *pp* invalidated A 320.

in-feere, -fere *adv* together HF 250, TC 2.1266, B 328.

infernal *adj* infernal TC 4.1543, A 2684; **infernals** *pl* TC 5.368.

infortunat *adj* unlucky, inauspicious B 302.

infortune *n* ill fortune, misfortune TC 3.1626, 4.185, B 3591; malevolent influence A 2021.

infortuned *pp* unfortunate, ill-starred TC 4.744.

ingot *n* mold (for molten metal) G 1206, 1209, etc.

inhielde *imp s as pl* pour in TC 3.44.

injure *n* injury TC 3.1018.

in-knette *pt s* contracted TC 3.1088.

inly, ynly *adv* inwardly BD 276, HF 31, TC 1.640, 3.1606.

inne *adv* in, within TC 1.387, A 3907, F 1075; therein TC 2.875.

inned *pp* lodged A 2192.

innocence *n* innocence A 1314, B 363, etc.; blameless character E 1048; simplicity, ignorance TC 2.1048.

innocent *n* innocent creature B 618, 682, D 1983.

inome *pp* taken PF 38. See **nam.**

inportable see **importable.**

inpossible see **impossible.**

inprudent *adj* imprudent B 309.

inspired see **enspyre.**

instaunce *n* urging TC 2.1441, E 1611.

intellect *n* intellect G 339; understanding A 2803.

into *prep* into A 23; to, unto BD 1023, A 692, C 722; on, upon A 3471.

introduccioun *n* introduction: **maketh i.** prepares the way G 1386.

inward *adv* in, inside TC 2.1725, A 4079; on the way in TC 2.1732.

inwardly *adv* closely, intently TC 2.264.

inwith *prep* (MSS often **in with**) within TC 3.1499, 5.1022, B 797, 1794, etc.

ire, yre *n* anger, rage PF 11, A 940, etc.

iren, yren *n* iron PF 149, A 500, etc.

irous *adj* angry, wrathful D 2014, 2016, etc.

ise see **ysee.**

isought *pp* sought TC 3.1317.

issue *n* outlet, vent TC 5.205.

isworn *pp* sworn TC 2.570.

itake *pp* caught TC 3.1198.

ithewed *pp* endowed with virtues PF 47.

itold *pp* told TC 4.141.

iwis see **ywis.**

iwryen *pp* covered, hidden TC 3.1451. See **wrye.**

iyolden *pp as adj* submissive TC 3.96. See **yelden.**

J

Jakke of Dovere *n* a stale or warmed-over pie (?) A 4347.

jalous, jel- *adj* jealous PF 342, TC 3.899, A 1329, etc.

jalousie, jel-, -sye *n* jealousy HF 1971, TC 2.755, 3.987, etc.

jambeaux *n pl* protections for the shins B 2065.

jane *n* small silver coin of Genoa, worth a half-penny B 1925; **deere ynogh a jane** dear at any price E 999.

jangle *v* talk loudly or much TC 2.666; **janglest** *2 s* chatterest B 774; **jangleth** *3 s* talks idly B 4625; **jangle** *3 pl* TC 2.800, F 220, 261.

jangler(e) *n* loud talker or one who talks too freely PF 457, A 560, H 343, 348.

jangleresse *n* noisy talker (female), scold D 638; *pl* great talkers E 2307.

janglerie *n* prating, gossip TC 5.755.

jangles *n pl* idle talk HF 1960, D 1407.

janglyng *n & adj* chattering, idle talk PF 345, F 257, H 350.

jape *n* joke, trick TC 2.130, A 3799, B 1629; folly D 1961; *pl* tricks, deceits A 705, B 4281, D 1440, F 1271; jokes, humorous matters TC 1.911, C 319.

jape(n) *v* joke, jest TC 2.943, B 1883, H 4; trick, mock TC 5.1134; **japedest** *pt 2 s* didst joke TC 1.508, 924; **japed** *pt 3 s* TC 5.509; **japed**

pp tricked A 1729; **ijaped** *pp* made sport (of) TC 1.318.

japer *n* trickster TC 2.340.

japerye *n* joking, mockery E 1656.

jargon *n* chatter E 1848.

jeet *n* jet (mineral) B 4051.

jet *n* device G 1277; style, fashion A 682.

jeupardyes see **jupartie.**

jo *v* TC 3.33 (see note).

jogelour, ju- *n* minstrel, slight-of-hand performer D 1467; *pl* HF 1259, F 219.

jogelrye *n* legerdemain, magic F 1265.

jolif, joly *adj* gay, cheerful, jolly A 3263, B 1399, 4264; amorous A 3355, 3671; fine A 3316, 3931; **jolyer** *compar* brighter, finer F 927.

jolite(e), joliftee *n* cheerfulness, gaity TC 1.559, C 780, H 197; fun, levity A 680; amusement, pleasure PF 226, A 2033, F 344; passion, desire A 1807.

jolynesse *n* pleasure, amusement D 926, F 289.

jompre *imp s* jumble TC 2.1037.

jossa *excl* down here A 4101.

jouken *v* lie at rest TC 5.409.

journee *n* distance traveled in a day A 2738; journey E 783.

jowes *n pl* jaws HF 1786.

joynant *adj* adjoining A 1060.

joyned *pt 3 s* joined BD 393; **joyneden** *pt pl* TC 5.813; *pp* B 3683; in conjunction TC 3.625.

jubbe *n* a large vessel, jug A 3628 (see note), B 1260.

jueles *n pl* jewels E 869, F 341; **jeweles** A 2945.

juge *n* judge PF 101, etc.; **juges** *pl* C 291.

juggement, juge- *n* judgment TC 4.1299, A 778, etc.; **juggementz** *pl* E 439.

juggen *v* judge TC 2.21; conclude 5.1203; **juge** *1 s* decide, rule PF 524, 629; **juggeth** *imp pl* TC 3.1312; **jugged, juged** *pp* HF 357, C 228.

juparten *2 pl* put in jeopardy TC 4.1566.

jupartie, -per- *n* jeopardy, risk TC 3.868, 5.701, 916, F 1495, G 743; **jeupardyes** *pl* problems (chess) BD 666.

jurdones *n pl* physician's flasks C 305.

juste(n) *v* joust A 96, H 42; **jousteth, justeth** *3 s* TC 3.1718, F 1098; **justen** *3 pl* A 2486; **justyng** *part* F 1198.

justes *n pl as s* a justing-match A 2720.

justise, -ice *n* judge A 314, B 664, etc.; justice C 587.

juwise, juyse *n* sentence A 1739; justice B 795.

K

kakelynge *n* cackling PF 562.

kalender *n* guide LGW 542.

kalendes *n pl* the first day of the month; a beginning TC 2.7, 5.1634.

kalkuled *pt 3 s* calculated F 1284.

kamuse see **camuse**.

kan, kanst see **conne**.

kankedort *n* predicament, "pickle" TC 2.1752 (see note).

katapuce *n* a medicine (euphorbium) B 4155 (see note to B 4151).

kaughte, kaught see **cacche**.

kaynard *n* sluggard D 235.

kaytyf see **caytyf**.

kechyl *n* little cake D 1747.

keen *n pl* kine, cows B 4021.

kembe *v* **comb** HF 136; **kembeth** *3 s* A 3374, E 2011; **kembde** *pt s* F 560; **kembd, ykembd** *pp* A 2143, 4369.

kempe *adj* shaggy A 2134.

kene, keene *adj* bold B 3439; sharp A 104, F 57.

kenne, ken *v* know how, be able HF 498, BD 438; **kend** *pp* known BD 787.

kep(e), keep *n* heed, care BD 6, A 398, D 625, etc.; **taak, taken k.** take heed C 360, D 213.

kepe(n) *v* take care, look after, guard TC 5.1048, A 130, C 85; **kepe** *1 s* care, TC 1.676, A 2238; am concerned, intend A 2960; **kepeth** *3 s* E 1133, 1343; **kepen** *pl* HF 1695, F 956; **kepe** *3 s subj* A 4247; **keep(e)**, **kepe** *imp s* preserve A 2302, 2329; stand still A 4101; **kepeth** *imp pl* B 764; **kepte** *pt s* A 415, B 3808; **kept** *pp* A 276, H 144; saved D 1056; guarded E 2129.

kers *n* cress (a worthless thing) A 3756.

kerve *v* cut PF 217, TC 2.325, F 158; **carf** *pt s* carved, cut A 100, B 3647, 3791, E 1773; **kervyng** *part adj* TC 1.631, 632; **korven, corven** *pp* carved, cut HF 1295, PF 425, A 2696, 3318; **ykorven, ycorven, ycorve** *pp* A 2013, B 1801, G 533.

kervyng *n* carving A 1915; *pl* HF 1302. See **kerve**.

kesse, keste see **kisse**.

kevere *v* cover (usually spelled cov-), recover TC 1.917; **kevered** *pp* covered, hidden HF 275, 352.

kid(de) see **kithe**.

kike *v* kick D 941.

kiken *3 pl* gaze A 3841; **kiked** *pp* A 3445.

kisse, kysse *v* kiss PF 378, TC 3.182; **kesse** (Kentish) E 1057; **kisseth, kist** *3 s* kisses TC 5.1287, A 3305; **kiste** *pt 3 s* TC 1.812; **keste** (Kentish) F 350; **kys(se), kis** *imp s*

TC 5.1791, A 3716, B 861; **kist** *pp* A 1759.

kithe *v* show F 748; **kitheth, kytheth** *3 s* shows, makes known LGW 504, F 483; **kithe** *3 s subj* B 636; **kidde** *pt s* TC 1.208; **kith(e)** *imp s* TC 4.538, 619, D 1609; **kithed, kyd** *pp* E 1943, G 1054.

kitte see **kutte**.

knakkes *n pl* tricks BD 1033.

knarre *n* knotty fellow A 549.

knarry *adj* gnarled A 1977.

knave *n* boy B 1500; servant (man or boy) B 474, C 666, E 1302, 2338; one of mean estate D 1190; **knave child** boy B 715, E 444; **knaves** *pl* servants, boys A 2728, B 3087.

knobbes *n pl* lumps, protuberances A 633.

knotte *n* knot TC 3.1732, A 197; main point (of a story) F 401, 407.

knotteles *adj* without a knot TC 5.769.

knowe *n dat s* knee; **sat on knowe** knelt down TC 2.1202; **knowes** *pl* TC 3.1592, B 1719.

knoweliche *n* acquaintance B 1220.

knowe(n) *v* know A 382, B 250, etc.; **knowe(n)** *2 pl* PF 386, LGW 348, A 642, etc.; **knew** *pt 1 & 3 s* A 240, 1227; acknowledged B 3812; **knewe** *pt 1 s subj* might know E 1078; **knewe** *pt 3 pl* A 1017, 2068; **knowe(n), yknowe(n)** *pp* BD 666, HF 1770, A 423, C 156, F 256.

knowlechyng *n* knowledge, ? collaboration G 1432.

knyght *n* knight A 42, etc.; **k. of the shire** member of parliament for the county A 356.

knytte *v* knit (lit. & fig.) I 28, 47; **knette** fasten PF 438; **knyttest thee** joinest thyself B 307; **knetteth** *3 s* TC 3.1748; **knyt** *pp* tied B 3224; bound LGW 89; agreed F 1230; **yknet** knit TC 3.1734.

konne(n) see **conne**.

konnyng(e), kun-, con- *n* ability HF 2056, TC 5.866, B 1099; skill, knowledge PF 167, TC 1.83, F 251, G 653; **of my connynge** by my ability TC 2.4; **of his kunnynge** according to his ability LGW 412.

konnyng(e) *adj* capable TC 5.970; clever, wise TC 1.302.

konnyngeste *adj* cleverest TC 1.331.

konnyngly *adv* skilfully E 1017.

korven see **kerve**.

koude, koud see **conne**.

koudest see **conne**.

kouth(e), kowthe see **conne**.

kouthe *adv* manifestly HF 757.

krone *n* crone, hag B 432.

kultour *n* plowshare A 3763, 3776, 3785, 3812.

kunnynge see **konnyng(e)**.

kutte *v* cut C 954; **kutteth** *3 s* H 342; **kitte** *pt 3 s* B 600, 1761, D 722; **kut** *pp* B 1838.

kymelyn *n* tub, vat A 3548.

kyn *n* kindred, family descent TC 1.90, A 3942, 4038; **som kynnes affray** affray of some kind B 1137. See **alleskynnes**.

kynde, kinde *n* birth, descent D 1101, G 121; natural disposition, instinct B 4386, G 659, H 183; nature BD 16, 56, etc.; condition TC 3.334, A 1401; way, manner G 981; species, type, kind F 608, G 252, 789; **by kynde** by (provision of) nature BD 494; **of (propre) kynde** by (very) nature TC 2.1443, F 610, 768.

kyndely *adj* natural BD 761, HF 730, etc.

kyndely *adv* by nature, naturally BD 778, HF 831, D 402; readily B 1543.

kynrede *n* kindred, family TC 5.979, A 1286, etc.

L

laas *n* cord A 392, G 574; noose, snare LGW 600, A 1817; net A 2389.

labbe *n* blab, idle talker, boaster TC 3.300, A 3509.

labbyng *adj* blabbing E 2428.

laborous *adj* laborious D 1428.

labour *n* labor PF 93, etc.; effort B 1653, E 1765.

laboure(n) *v* work, toil, make an effort A 186, 2408, etc.

lacerte *n* muscle A 2753.

ladde, lad see **leden**.

lade *v* load, pile on TC 2.1544.

lady *n* lady A 912, etc.; lady *gen s* lady's TC 5.1077, A 88, etc.

lafte, laft see **leven**.

lak *n* lack, deficiency BD 958, PF 87, etc.; misdeed E 2199; **lakke** *dat* D 1308, etc.

lake *n* linen B 2048.

lakke(n) *v* disparage TC 1.189; be lacking TC 4.945; **lakken** *1 pl* lack G 672; **lakked(e)** *pt 3 s* A 756, C 41.

lambic *n* alembic TC 4.520. Cf. **alambikes**.

lampe *n* sheet G 764.

langage *n* language HF 861, etc.

lange *adj* long (Northern) A 4175.

langour *n* woeful plight B 3597, F 1101; distress TC 4.844, 5.42.

lappe *n* flap, fold, any part of a garment hanging loose TC 2.448, 3.59, F 441, G 12; piece of cloth E 585.

large *adj* broad A 472, 1956; large A

753, 886; liberal, generous BD 893, B 1621; full-cut, flowing TC 1.109; free F 755; **of tonge l.** free with his tongue TC 5.804.

large *adv* broadly A 734.

large *n* liberty D 322; **at thy (his) l.** at large A 1283, 1327.

largely *adv* fully TC 2.1707, A 1908, 2738.

larges *n* largess, a liberal gift HF 1309.

lasse *adj & n* less TC 3.105, etc.

lasse *adv* less TC 1.651, 2.901, etc.

last *n* load B 1628.

last *adj, adv & n* last A 3430; **atte laste** at last, finally A 707, etc.; **to the laste** in the end, after all TC 2.255.

laste *v* last, continue BD 506, PF 173; **lasteth, last** *3 s* B 499, PF 49; reaches, extends E 266; **laste** *pt s* lasted TC 1.315, B 1826, F 574; *pt pl* BD 177, B 3390.

lat, laten see **leten.**

late *adv* late, lately A 77, 690; **til now l.** until lately BD 45.

lathe *n* barn HF 2140, A 4088.

latoun, -on *n* latten, brass A 699, B 2067, C 350, F 1245.

laude, lawde *n* praise HF 1795, B 1645; what is due a person, deserts D 1353; **laudes** *pl* HF 1322; lauds (the canonical hour) A 3655.

laughe(n) *v* laugh A 474, 3722; **lough** *pt s* laughed TC 1.1037, 2.1592; **loughe** *pt pl* A 3858; **laughynge** *part* BD 633, A 2011; **laughen** *pp* A 3855; **lawghed** *pp* HF 409.

launcegay *n* a kind of lance B 1942, 2011.

launcheth *3 s* thrusts D 2145.

launde *n* glade, clearing in the woods PF 302, A 1691.

laure *n* laurel (tree) HF 1107.

laurer *n* laurel (wreath, tree) PF 182, A 1027, etc.

laurer-crowned *pp* laurel-crowned TC 5.1107.

laus *adj* loose A 4064.

lavendere *n* washerwoman LGW 358.

lavours *n pl* washbasins D 287.

lawe *n* law BD 56, etc.; **lawes** *gen* of faith, of religion B 1754; **lawes** *pl* religions B 221.

lawriol *n* spurge laurel (a laxative) B 4153 (see note to B 4151).

lay *n* law, doctrine, religion TC 1.340, LGW 336, B 376, 572, F 18.

layneres *n pl* thongs A 2504.

layser see **leyser.**

lazar *n* leper, poor or diseased person A 242; **lazars** *pl* A 245.

leche *n* physician TC 1.857, A 3904; **leches** *pl* TC 5.369.

lechecraft *n* medical skill A 2745; remedy TC 4.436.

lede(n) *v* take, carry TC 4.1514; lead D 94, F 744; influence TC 2.1449; govern B 434; **ledeth, let** *3 s* leads TC 2.882, B 1496; **lede** *3 s subj* should bring B 357; **leden** *3 pl* lead F 898; **ladde** *pt s & pl* led LGW 114, D 1678, E 390; carried off B 3338; brought B 442; **lad** *pp* carried LGW 74; led A 2620, B 646, E 2415; **ylad** *pp* carried A 530.

leden(e) *n* language F 435, 436, 478.

leed, led *n* lead HF 739, G 406; cauldron A 202.

leef *n* leaf (of a tree, etc.) TC 3.1200, A 1838, B 1340; (of book) A 3177, D 635; **leves** *pl* BD 418, etc.

leef, lief *adj* dear, agreeable BD 8, A 1837, B 1349, C 760; desirous A 3510; **leve, leeve** *def & pl* dear HF 816, TC 2.251, 4.82, A 1136; **it is me lief** I am glad TC 5.1738; **leef, lief** *as n* something dear or well liked TC 4.1585; sweetheart A 3792, D 431, E 2391; **the . . . leeve** the dear one, sweetheart A 3393; **for lief ne looth** willing or unwilling, willy-nilly B 1322. (See **levere**)

leek, lek *n* leek HF 1708, A 3879, D 572. **lekes** *pl* A 634.

leep see **lepe.**

leere *n* flesh B 2047. See also **lere.**

lees *n* leash G 19.

leeste, leste *adj* least BD 973, A 1701; **atte l.** at least A 3683; **at the (atte) l.** weye at least, leastwise A 1121, G 676.

leet see **leten.**

leeve see **leef.**

leful see **leveful.**

legende *n* legend, tale of martyrdom or suffering B 1335, 4311; legendary, collection of saints' lives LGW 483; a remarkable story A 3141.

leggen see **leye.**

leigh see **lyen.**

lemaille, ly- *n* metal filings G 853, 1162.

lemes *n pl* flames B 4120.

lemes see **lym**[1].

lemman *n* sweetheart A 3278, 3700; lover B 917.

lendes *n pl* loins, buttocks A 3237, 3304.

lene, leene *adj* lean A 287, 591, B 4003, D 1880.

lene *v* lend A 611, B 1209; **lene, leene** *imp s* A 3082, G 1026.

lenger *adj* longer HF 1282, A 330, etc.

lenger *adv* longer BD 656, TC 5.910, F 1462.

lengest *adj* longest TC 1.474.

lengest *adv* longest PF 549.

lengthe *n* length HF 1370, A 1970; height A 83; **upon l.** at length, finally BD 352; **on l., by l.** at length TC 2.262, 5.1491.

lenvoy *n* l'envoy, remarks accompanying a tale E 1176 (rubric).

leonesse *n* lioness D 637.

leonyn *adj* lion-like B 3836.

leopart *n* leopard A 2186; **leopardes** *pl* B 3451.

leos *n* Gk. λεώς people G 103, 106.

leoun, leon *n* lion TC 1.1074, A 1598; **lyoun** TC 3.1780, 4.32.

lepe *v* leap, jump HF 946, TC 2.512, A 4378; **leep** *pt 3 s* leaped A 2687, 4228; **lepte** *pt 3 s* TC 2.1637.

lere, leere *v* teach HF 764, TC 2.1580; learn HF 993, TC 5.161, B 630, C 325; **lere, leere** *3 pl* teach F 104; learn PF 25; **leere** *3 pl subj* learn G 607; **leere** *imp pl* teach TC 2.97; **lered** *pp* learned TC 3.406.

lered *ppl adj* educated, learned PF 46, TC 1.976, C 283.

lerne *v* learn A 308, etc.; teach HF 1235, G 844; **lerned** *pt s* learned F 719; **lerned** *pp* learned B 786, A 613, 640, B 786; taught G 748.

lerned *ppl adj* learned A 480, 575, B 761.

les *n* deceit; **withouten l.** without misrepresentation, truly HF 1464.

lese, leese *n* pasture HF 1768, TC 2.752.

lese(n), leese *v* lose TC 5.381, A 1215, D 2504, E 508; *refl* be lost PF 147; **leseth** *3 s* BD 33; **les** *pt s* lost HF 1414; **leseth** *imp pl* lose B 19; **lorn** *pp* lost BD 1303, LGW 659, A 4073; destroyed BD 565; **lore** *pp* lost BD 1135; **yloren** *pp* LGW 26; **lost, ylost, ilost** *pp* HF 183, TC 3.896, A 2257, 2802.

lessoun *n* lesson TC 3.51, 83, E 1193; "lectio" A 709 (see note).

lest *n* dial. var. (Kentish) of **lust** pleasure, desire, happiness TC 1.330, A 132; desire TC 2.787, E 619; **lestes** *pl* desires HF 1738. See **lust.**

lest *3 s impers* (Kentish form) it pleases TC 1.797, 5.1433, LGW 562, D 854; **leste** *3 s subj* may please A 828; **leste** *pt 3 s* it pleased A 750, E 716; *pers uses:* **leste** *1 s* (I) please TC 1.580; **leste** *3 pl* (they) please E 490; **leste** *pt 3 s* (she) pleased TC 3.542. See **list, lust.**

lesyng(e)[1] *n* losing, loss TC 3.830, A 1707, B 3750.

lesyng(e)[2] *n* falsehood, deceit HF 154, 2089, G 479; **lesynges** *pl* lies HF 676, A 1927.

lete(n), late(n) *v* let, let go TC 1.262, A 3326; leave B 986, D 31, 1276;

give up, forsake PF 391, TC 4. 1556, B 325; **lete** *1 s* leave F 651, 890; **lat, late** *1 & 3 s* let, lets TC 1.133, 4.200, LGW 628; **lat** *3 s subj* B 4622; **leete** *2 pl* give up G 1409; **lette, lete, leet, let** *pt 1 & 3 s* let TC 5.226, A 128, 1206; left A 508; left off, ceased TC 3.473, A 3311, 4214; pretended TC 2.543; considered TC 1.302; *as auxil* caused LGW 676, B 959, 1810, 2064, F 45; **lat** *imp s* let TC 3.740, A 921; leave undone TC 2.1500; **lete, letteth** *imp pl* give up, cease from LGW 411, C 659; **leten** *pp* let HF 1934; **laten** *pp* let, drawn off A 4346.

lette *n* hindrance TC 1.361; delay TC 3.235, 699, 748, 4.41, E 300.

lette-game *n* killjoy TC 3.527.

lette(n) *v* hinder, prevent TC 1.150, A 889, B 3306; interrupt, keep from B 1276; put off, delay B 1117, 4224; cease, desist PF 439, A 1317, D 154; **lettest** *2 s* hinderest LGW 325, D 839; **letteth** *3 s* hinders E 1573; **let** *3 s* hinders, repels PF 151; **lette** *3 pl subj* may hinder F 994; **lette, letted** *pt 3 s* hindered, prevented A 1892, B 4030, E 1904; delayed HF 2070; ceased TC 2.1089, 3.473; **lette** *imp s* hinder TC 3.545, 725; **letteth** *imp pl* be prevented TC 2.1136; **let** *pp* hindered TC 2.94, 3.717; prevented TC 5.1302, B 3788; **lette** *of* keep from E 1677.

lett(e)rure *n* learning B 3486; reading, book-learning B 3686, G 846.

lettre, -ter *n* letter (of alphabet) TC 1.171; (epistle) B 728, etc.; writing B 3398; decree TC 4.560; **letre** study, learning BD 788; **lettres** *pl* PF 19, B 736, etc.

letuarie *n* electuary (a medicine mixed with syrup), remedy TC 5.741, C 307, E 1809; **letuaries** *pl* A 426.

leve, leeve *n* leave, permission A 1064, 1217, B 3136, etc.; **bisyde his (hire) l.** without his (her) permission HF 2105, TC 3.622.

leve¹ *v* believe PF 496, TC 1.688, 2.420, 4.1658, LGW 10, D 319; be believed HF 708, TC 3.308; **leve, leeve** *1 s* BD 1048, HF 1012, E 2205; trust, have faith in BD 691; **leevestow** *2 s* dost thou believe G 212; **leeveth** *3 s* E 1001; **leven** *1 pl* B 1181; **leve** *2 pl* TC 2.1141; **leve** *imp s* BD 1047; **leeveth** *imp nl* A 3088.

leve² *3 s subj* grant: **God leve** may God grant TC 1.597, 2.1212, 4.325, etc.; **leve** *imp s* grant TC 5.959.

leveful *adj* lawful, permissible A 3912,

D 37, E 1448, G 5; **leful** TC 3.1020; **leefful** I 41.

leve(n) *v* leave (allow to remain) BD 1111; leave (depart from), quit HF 431, PF 153, G 714; forsake G 287; cease, desist from TC 1.686, E 250, F 828; **leve** *1 s* TC 4.1205, B 4375; **leveth** *3 s* remains BD 701; **lafte** *pt 3 s* left undone A 492; **lafte(n)** *pt 3 pl* left B 3388; forsook LGW 168; **leef, lef, leve** *imp s* leave A 1614; leave undone TC 2.1008; leave off, cease, desist from TC 4.896, D 2089, Truth 23; give up, forsake TC 4.532, Truth 22; **laft, ylaft** *pp* left A 2746, F 186.

levene *n* lightning D 276.

lever(e) *adj* liefer, more agreeable, rather LGW 191, B 3083, E 444; **hym was levere** he would rather A 293; **levest** HF 87, TC 2.189.

levesel *n* leafy arbor A 4061.

lew(e)d *adj* ignorant A 502, 3455; unlearned A 574, F 221; foolish TC 1.198, E 2275, F 1494, G 1445; low, vulgar A 3145.

lewedeste *adj* vilest, basest H 184.

lewedly *adv* ignorantly, badly G 430, H 59; simply, unskilfully B 47.

lewednesse *n* ignorance PF 520, F 223; simplicity, foolishness B 2111; unintelligent attitude D 1928.

leye, legge(n) *v* lay HF 291, A 3269, 3937; cause to lie, lodge TC 3.659; lay a wager, wager HF 674, 2054, A 4009; **leye** *1 s* lay TC 1.1053, D 1828; wager TC 2.1505; **laye** *1 pl* G 783; **leyn** *3 pl* set H 222; **leyde** *pt s* laid BD 394; **leyden** *pt pl* B 213; **ley(e), lay** *imp s* TC 2.994, A 841, 4085; **leyd, leid** *pp* BD 1036, 1146, PF 554; **laye an ere** listen TC 3.459; **adoun leyde** allayed TC 1034.

leyser, lei-, lay- *n* leisure TC 3.516, A 1188, E 1543; opportunity TC 2.1369, A 3293, D 551; **leyser for** permission of D 1646.

libel *n* written statement of a charge D 1595.

licence *n* license, permission B 1253, D 855.

licenciat *adj* licensed to hear confession A 220 (see note).

licour *n* moisture TC 4.520, A 3; **l. of the vyne** wine C 452.

lifly *adv* in a lifelike manner A 2087. See **lyvely.**

lige *adj* liege LGW 379, C 337, etc.; **liges** *pl as n* LGW 382, B 240.

ligeance *n* allegiance B 895.

ligge(n) *v* lie TC 3.660, 1537, B 2101; **ligge** *2 s subj* TC 5.411; **liggen** *2 pl* TC 3.669; **liggen** *3 pl* TC 3.685,

A 2205; **liggeth** *imp pl* TC 3.948; **liggyng(e)** *part* TC 1.915, A 2390. For other forms see **lye.**

light, lyght *adj* light A 2120, etc.; easy BD 526, PF 553.

lighte¹, lyghte *v* lighten, alleviate HF 467, TC 3.1082; unburden TC 5.634; rejoice F 396; descend HF 508; **lighte** *pt 3 s* alighted B 786, F 169.

lighte² *v* illuminate TC 4.313, A 2426; brighten TC 1.293; light (set fire to) D 334; **lighte** *imp s* illuminate G 71; **lighted** *pp* F 1050; **lyghted** *as adj* HF 769.

lightles *adj* lightless TC 3.550.

lightly, lyghtly *adv* lightly HF 546, F 390; easily TC 2.1647, A 4099; quickly A 1461, B 4129; cheerfully A 1870.

ligne *n* descent A 1551.

ligne aloes *n* lign-aloes, an aromatic wood TC 4.1137.

lik see **lyk.**

like(n), lyke *v* please, be pleasing to HF 860, TC 1.289, 2.1570, etc.; to be liked TC 3.1363; **liketh** *3 s (impers)* PF 165, A 777, etc.; *(pers)* E 1031; **lyke** *3 s subj* LGW 319, 490, D 1278; **liked** *pt s* TC 2.1044, 1266; **likynge** *part* pleasing TC 1.309.

likerous, ly- *adj* lecherous PF 79, D 466, H 189; wanton A 3244; passionate D 752; eager F 1119; luxurious C 540, E 214; tempting A 3345.

likerously *adv* sweetly, wantonly B 3747.

likerousnesse *n* lecherousness D 611; appetite C 84.

likker(e) *adj* more like TC 3.1028, D 1925.

liklihede *n* likelihood B 1786, E 448.

likly *adj* likely TC 3.1270, A 1172; **lykly** suitable Scogan 32.

likne *v* liken D 369; **lykne** *1 s* BD 636; **likned** *pp* likened A 180, B 91.

likyng *n* pleasure, inclination B 3499, C 455, E 320; liking B 767.

liltyng-horn *n* trumpet HF 1223.

lipsed *pt s* lisped A 264.

lisse, lysse *n* alleviation, abatement HF 220, F 1238; peace, joy TC 3.343, 5.550.

lissen, lysse *v* alleviate BD 210, TC 1.702; **lissed, ylissed** *pp* eased, relieved TC 1.1089, F 1170.

list *n* pleasure TC 3.1303; desire D 633. See **lust.**

list, lyst *3 s impers* it pleases A 583, 1127, 1183, etc.; **liste, lyste** *pt 3 s* it pleased BD 962, A 102, B 477; *pers uses:* **list** *3 s* wishes TC 1.398, 857, B 1206. See **lest, lust.**

litarge *n* litharge (protoxide of lead), also white lead A 629, G 775.

lite, lyte *adj* little HF 621, PF 350, A 1193; humble A 494; *as n* LGW 29, B 109, G 699; **a l.** *as adv* BD 249, TC 1.291, A 1334, etc.

litel *adj* little A 87, 298, etc.; **into l.** almost TC 4.884.

lith, lyth *n* limb, joint BD 953, B 4065.

lithe *v* alleviate TC 4.754.

litherly *adv* badly A 3299.

lixt see **lyen.**

liyng *n* lying, telling lies A 3884.

lode *n* load A 2918.

lodemenage *n* piloting, navigation A 403.

lofte *n dat*: **on-lofte, o-lofte, alofte** aloft HF 1726, PF 203, TC 1.950, B 277.

logge *n* lodge B 4043.

logged *pp* lodged B 4186, 4188; **ylogged** B 4181.

loggyng *n* lodging B 4185.

logh see **lowe.**

loke *v* lock D 317; **loken** *pp* B 4065.

loke(n), loo- *v* look HF 964, A 1783, etc.; see, discover B 537; **lookest** *2 s* B 1886; **loketh, lookelh** *3 s* looks A 1499, 1697; appears BD 623; **looked, loked** *pt s* BD 294, B 1884; **lokynge** *part* A 2679; **loked** *pp* looked TC 3.1160; beheld BD 1051; **looke how** just as D 1452; **looke what** whatever F 992; **looketh now wher** wherever A 3073; **looke who** whoever D 1113, F 771.

lokyng, look- *n* look, glance, gaze BD 870, TC 5.1820, F 285; aspect A 2469; **l. of** looking at PF 110.

lokkes *n pl* locks (hair) A 677.

Lollere *n* Lollard B 1173, 1177.

lomb *n* lamb B 617.

lond *n* land A 194, 400, etc.; **upon l.** in the country A 702.

long (on) *adj* on account of G 922; **wheron it was l.** what it was on account of G 930. See **along (on).**

long(e) *adj* long BD 20, A 617, 784, etc.; tall PF 230, A 1424.

longe *adv* long, a long while A 286, 1654, B 3300, etc.

longe(n)¹ *v* long, yearn TC 1.619, 5.597, 690; **longeth** *3 s* E 451; **me longeth** *3 s impers* I long TC 2.312; **longen** *3 pl* A 12; **longed** *pt s* BD 83.

longe(n)² *v* pertains to, belongs (to) TC 2.546, A 2278; **longeth** *3 s* HF 1200, C 109, D 1391, E 285; (for **longen**) TC 2.1346, LGW 151; **longen** *3 pl* A 3885, F 1131.

onges *n pl* lungs A 2752.

longynge (for) *part* pertaining (to) A 3209, F 39.

loone *n* gift, grace D 1861; loan B 1485.

loore, lore *n* teaching G 372; doctrine A 527; advice, counsel TC 1.754, 2.565, B 342; knowledge, learning TC 3.243, B 4540, E 788.

loos *adj* loose, free PF 570, A 4138.

loos *n* repute, fame HF 1620, 1621, G 1368.

looth, loth *adj* loath, reluctant A 486, B 91; distasteful E 491; hateful BD 8; unwanted A 3393; *as adv* unwillingly TC 5.147; **for lief ne looth** willingly or unwillingly B 1322; **be hire lief or looth** whether she liked it or not E 1961; **it be me looth** I regret it B 1574.

lordshipe *n* sovereignity A 1625, B 3430; lordship TC 2.1420; protection, patronage TC 3.76, 79, A 1827.

lore see **lesen.**

lorel *n* rogue, wretch D 273.

lorn see **lesen.**

los *n* loss BD 1138, A 2543; cause of ruin D 720.

losengeour *n* deceiver, flatterer LGW 352, B 4516.

losenges *n pl* lozenges, diamond-shaped ornaments HF 1317.

lother *adj* more displeasing LGW 191.

lothest *adj* most reluctant TC 2.237, F 1313.

lotynge *part* lying hid G 186.

loude *adv* loud, loudly A 171, 2661; aloud TC 1.390; openly, palpably TC 2.1077.

lough see **lowe.**

lous *adj* loose, free HF 1286.

loute *v* bow HF 1704, TC 3.683; bow down B 3352.

love *n* love A 475, etc.; sweetheart BD 91, A 672, D 1066, E 2078; sweetheart, mistress A 2306; lover D 1039.

love-dayes *n pl* reconciliations, agreements HF 695; days fixed for the arbitration of disputes out of court A 258.

love-drury *n* love-making B 895.

love-drynke *n* love-potion D 754.

lovyere *n* lover A 80; elsewhere **lovere.**

lowe *adj* low A 2299, 3696, 4397; humble TC 2.528; **lough** A 522, D 1101; **logh** *as n* B 1142.

lowe *adv* low HF 1121, A 2023, 3677; humbly, inconspicuously A 1405; docilely, obediently E 2013.

lowely *adj* modest in demeanor A 99; humble A 250.

lowely *adv* humbly TC 2.1072, 1122, 5.174, E 421.

lowke *n* accomplice A 4415.

luce *n* pike (fish) A 350.

lucre *n* profit G 1402; **l. of vileynye** wicked gain B 1681.

lufsom *adj* lovesome TC 5.465, 911.

lulleth *3 s* soothes, lulls B 839, E 1823; **lulled** *pt 3 s* E 553.

lunarie *n* honesty (the plant) G 800.

lure *n* a device used to reclaim a hawk (see note to D 1339) H 72.

lussheburghes *n pl* coins of inferior metal from Luxembourg B 3152.

lust *n* pleasure TC 2.844, 3.276, A 192; joy, happiness BD 1038, TC 1.326; desire BD 273, TC 1.407, A 2478; inclination TC 2.476; wish, will TC 3.1690, B 762, E 531; appetite B 925; sensual desire D 736; **lustes** *pl* pleasures, delights BD 581, TC 5.592; desires C 833. See **lest, list.**

lust *3 s* (it) pleases, is pleasing (to) D 78, 820, E 322; **luste** *pt 3 s* it pleased BD 1019, G 1235, 1344. See **lest, list.**

lustier *adj* more joyful G 1345.

lustiheed, -yhede *n* jollity, delight F 288, H 274; pleasure in life BD 27.

lustily, -yly *adv* pleasantly I 21; joyously A 1529; merrily TC 5.568, E 1802.

lustinesse, -y- *n* pleasure A 1939; vigor, enjoyment of life TC 3.177.

lusty *adj* joyful, merry TC 5.393, E 1800; pleasant, agreeable HF 1356, A 2116, E 59, F 52; vigorous, lively A 80, 2111; *as n* vigorous creature TC 3.354.

luxurie *n* lechery B 925, C 484, 897.

lyard *adj* gray, dappled gray D 1563.

lyche see **lyk.**

lyche-wake *n* wake (corpse-watch) A 2958.

lye *n* lie, falsehood A 3015, etc.

lye¹ *v* lie, recline, remain HF 487, PF 279, A 3651; lodge D 1780; **lyest** *2 s* TC 1.797; **listow** liest thou H 276; **lyth, lith** *3 s* A 3023, D 496, 1829; **lyeth noon** exists BD 527; **lay** *pt 1 & 3 s* lay A 538, 679; lodged TC 5.845, A 20, 970, 1023; remained, continued A 937; **lay** *pt 3 s subj* lay, should or would lie TC 4.1560, A 538, 679, 1150; **lay, layen** *pt pl* lay BD 166, TC 3.745, A 3210; **ly** *imp s* lie TC 2.1519. See **liggen.**

lye² *v* blaze D 1142.

lye(n) *v* lie, misrepresent BD 631, TC 2.324, A 763, D 724, etc.; **lye** *1 s* TC 2.300; **lixt** *2 s* liest D 1618, 1761; **leigh** *strong pt 3 s* TC 2.1077; **lyed** *wk pt 3 s* A 659.

lyes *n pl* lees, dregs HF 2130, D 302? (see note).

lyf, lif *n* life BD 64, PF 1, A 71, etc.; age C 72; **lyves** *gen* life's BD 920, E 1036; **lyves, lives** *gen as adj* living HF 1063, TC 3.13, 4.252, 767, A 2395, E 903, 1864; **lyve** *dat* LGW 59; **of lyve** from life TC 5.1559; **his lyve** in his life TC 5.165; **hir lyve** in their life D 392; **on lyve** alive BD 205, TC 2.888, D 5, etc.; **lyves, lives** *pl* BD 58; lifetimes F 233.

lyghter *adj & adv* brighter HF 1289; more easily LGW 410.

lyk, lik *adj* like BD 819, TC 1.103, A 259, etc.; suitable TC 2.1040; likely HF 873; **lyche even** exactly alike HF 10; **it lyche** like it F 62.

lyk, lik *adv* alike TC 2.44; **lyk as** as if HF 1508.

lym[1] *n* limb, organ, part of the body BD 499; **lymes, lymmes** *pl* BD 959, TC 1.282, A 2135, 2714, B 461; **lemes** A 3886

lym[2] *n* lime LGW 649, F 1149, G 806.

lymaille see **lemaille**.

lyme *v* smear with bird lime TC 1.353; **ylymed** *pp* caught D 934.

lymere *n* hound BD 365; **lymeres** *pl* B 362 (see note).

lymrod *n* rod smeared with bird lime B 3574.

lymytour *n* a friar having the exclusive right to beg in a given district A 209, 269, D 874.

lynage *n* lineage, family, descent A 1110, B 999, D 1135, E 71.

lynde *n* lime or linden tree A 2922, E 1211.

lyne *n* line TC 2.1177, 1461; fishing line TC 5.777; **as l. right** directly TC 3.228.

lysse see **lisse, lissen.**

lyst *n* ear D 634.

lystes *n pl* enclosure for tournaments A 63, 2089, F 668, etc.; *construed as sing* A 1713.

lyte see **lite.**

lyth see **lith.**

lythe *adj* easy, soft HF 118.

lyvely *adv* lively BD 905. Cf. **lifly.**

lyvere[1] *n* liver D 1839.

lyvere[2] *n* one who lives B 1024.

lyveree *n* livery A 363.

lyvynge *n* living, way of life TC 1.197, C 97, 847; life G 322; sustenance E 227.

M

maat, mat *adj* downcast A 955; dejected TC 4.342; overcome, vanquished BD 660, LGW 126, B 935.

madde *v* rage TC 1.479; **madde** *2 s subj* be out of thy mind A 3156; madde *3 pl* go mad A 3559.

mafay *excl* upon my faith TC 3.52.

magyk *n* magic B 214, etc.; **m. natureel** natural magic HF 1266, A 416, F 1125, 1155.

maille *n* mail, chain-mail, ring-mail TC 5.1559, E 1202.

maister, may- *n* master, person in authority A 261, 837, etc.; teacher B 3685; title of respect B 1627, 3515, D 1337; one learned in a subject, **maister of dyvynytee** D 1638.

maister *adj* principal A 2902.

maister-tour *n* principal tower F 226.

maistresse *n* mistress BD 797, E 823; object of devotion, sweetheart TC 2.98; governess, maid-servant C 106, F 374, 377; **maistresses** *pl* governesses C 72.

maistrye, -trie *n* skill, ability A 3383, B 3582; evidence of skill HF 1094; mastery, domination, control B 3689, C 58, D 818, F 747; achievement LGW 400; **for the m.** preeminently A 165.

make *n* mate PF 310, E 840, etc.; equal HF 1172; opponent A 2556; mate, wife B 700, 1982; mate, husband D 85; **makes** *pl* PF 389, LGW 158.

makeles *adj* matchless TC 1.172.

make(n) *v* make BD 114, A 384, etc.; **it make** do it, perform your part TC 2.1522; compose (verse, etc.) BD 1160, TC 5.1788, LGW 69, 364; **make** *1 s* make PF 29; **maketh** makes, causes BD 563, B 3149; **make** *2 pl* do F 867; **maken** *3 pl* make A 9; **made** *pt 1 s* BD 96, A 33; **madest** *pt 2 s* didst cause B 368; **made** *pt 3 s* A 387; caused BD 510, B 3257; **maked** *pt 3 s* made A 526, C 147; **made, maden, makeden** *pt pl* made PF 649, TC 4.121, B 433; caused PF 249; **maketh** *imp pl* TC 4.1586; **makynge** *part* A 1366, E 744; **mad, maad, ymaad, maked, ymaked, imaked** *pp* BD 404, PF 677, TC 1.251, A 212, 1247, 2605, G 1149.

makyng *n* composing, writing TC 5.1789, LGW 74, 413, Adam 4.

maladye *n* illness A 419, etc.; **maladyes colde** illnesses due to an excess of cold A 2467 (see note to A 419).

malapert *adj* presumptuous TC 3.87.

male *n* wallet, (traveling) bag A 694, C 920, I 26; **m. tweyfoold** double wallet G 566.

malencolie, -ye *n* black bile B 4123, 4136; sullenness, anger D 252; melancholy TC 5.360, 622; **melancolye** BD 23.

malencolik *adj* pertaining to black bile A 1375.

malisoun *n* curse G 1245.

malt see **melte.**

man *n* man B 159, etc.; **mannes** *gen s as adj* human TC 2.417.

man *indef pron* one BD 892, D 2002, F 553; **men** *pl* people, they TC 3.957, A 169, B 470, C 300; *as sing* BD 30, TC 4.866, A 149, F 1115.

manace *n* menace, threat A 2003, B 3789.

manace *v* threaten E 1752; **manaceth** *3 s* menaces E 122.

manasynge *n* threatening A 2035.

mandement *n* legal summons D 1346, 1360; **mandementz** *pl* D 1284.

maner *n* manor BD 1004.

manere *n* manner LGW 251, A 140; proper behavior BD 1218; usage C 120; way A 876, 3169, B 880, 1385; **of m.** in behavior F 546; **by m. of** by reason of C 264; **manere, maner** (with ellipsis of **of**) kind of HF 1123, PF 54, A 71, etc.; **in which m. wyse** in what way C 279; **in any m. age** in any age whatever D 59; **maners** *pl* manners, ways BD 1013.

manhede *n* manliness H 158; courage A 1285, B 3861.

manhod *n* manliness TC 2.676, 4.1674; firmness TC 3.428; boldness, courage TC 4.529, 5.1476; masculinity A 756.

manly *adv* in a manly way TC 5.30, A 987; boldly TC 4.622.

mannyssh, -ysh *adj* masculine TC 1.284, B 782.

mannyssh *adv* humanly, naturally E 1536 (see note).

mansioun, -syon *n* dwelling-place HF 754, 831, A 1974; as astrol. term see notes to F 49 and 1130.

mansuete *adj* gentle, meek, TC 5.194.

mantelet *n* short cloak A 2163.

many *adj & pron* A 60, etc.; **many oon, many on** many a one A 317, 2118, 2340, E 775, etc.

manye *n* mania A 1374.

many-folde *adv* **ful m.** in great variety, richly BD 260.

mapemounde *n* map of the world Rosem 2.

mapul *n* maple A 2923.

marbul *n* marble A 1893, B 1871, F 500; **marble** TC 1.700.

marc *n* mark (monetary unit = 13s 4d) G 1026, 1030; **mark** *as pl* C 390.

marchal *n* marshall A 752 (see note), E 1930.

marchant *n* merchant A 270, etc.

marcial *adj* martial, warlike, TC 4.1669.

mareys *n* marsh D 970.

mark *n* stamp, image D 619, 696; **merk** image F 880.

market-betere *n* swaggerer A 3936.

markys *n* marquis E 64, 91, etc.; **markys** *gen s* E 994.

markysesse *n* marchioness E 283, 394.

marle-pit *n* marl-pit A 3460 (see note).

martire *n* martyrdom TC 4.818.

martireth *3 s* makes a martyr of, tortures A 1562.

mary *n* marrow C 542.

marybones *n pl* marrowbones A 380.

mased *adj* dazed, bewildered BD 12; **mazed** B 526, 678.

masse peny *n* penny for saying mass D 1749.

masty *adj* fattened, lazy HF 1777.

mat see **maat.**

mateere, -ter(e), -tiere *n* matter, subject-matter BD 43, LGW 365, A 727, etc.; **materes** *pl* materials G 779.

matrimoigne *n* matrimony A 3095, E 1573.

maugre(e), maw- *prep* in spite of BD 1201, HF 461, TC 4.51, A 1169, etc.

maumettrie *n* idolatry B 236.

maunciple, man- *n* manciple A 567 (see note), 4029, etc.

mawe *n* maw, stomach, belly B 486, 1190, 2013.

may *n* maiden B 851; young woman TC 5.1412, 1720.

maydenhed(e) *n* maidenhood, virginity A 2329, B 30, etc.

maydenhod *n* maidenhood, virginity B 3459.

mayme *v* mutilate D 1132.

mayntene *v* maintain A 1441, 1778; **mayntene** *3 s subj* E 1171.

mayster-hunte *n* master huntsman BD 375.

maze *n* delusion, fantasy TC 5.468, B 4283.

maze *2 pl* are bewildered E 2387. Cf. **mased.**

mazednesse *n* bewilderment E 1061.

mazelyn *n* mazer, wooden bowl B 2042.

mede¹, meede *n* meadow LGW 41, A 89, D 861, etc.

mede², meede *n* meed, reward TC 3.415, A 770, Scogan 33; bribery C 133, Lak 6; fulfillment TC 2.423; **to medes** in return TC 2.1201.

mede³ see **meeth.**

medle *v* mix HF 2102; take a hand in, meddle G 1184; **medleth** *imp pl* ~G 1424; **medled, imedled** mingled TC 3.815, 4.329.

meel *n* meal B 466, 4023, D 1774.

meeltide *n* dinner time TC 2.1556.

meeste, meste *adj* highest in rank TC 1.167; *as n* A 2198, E 131; **at the m.** at the most TC 5.947.

meeth *n* mead A 2279, 3261, 3378; **mede** A 2042.

meke, meeke *adj* meek A 69, 3202, etc.

mele *n* meal A 3939, 3995, etc.

melle, mille *n* mill A 3923, 4008, etc.

melodye *n* music BD 314, 569; melody PF 62, HF 1395; sweet music, delight A 3097, H 114; **maken melodie** rejoice TC 3.187.

melte *v* melt TC 3.1445, 4.367; **melte** *3 pl* HF 1648; **malt** *pt 3 s* HF 922, TC 1.582; **molte** *pp* HF 1145, 1149, TC 5.10.

memorie *n* memory G 339; remembrance TC 3.829, 5.583, A 1906, B 3164; **memoyre** remembrance BD 945; **in memorie** conscious A 2698; **drawen to m.** call to mind A 2074, 3112.

men *indef pron* see **man.**

mende *v* mend TC 5.1426; **what mende ye** what do you profit TC 2.329.

mendynantz *n pl* mendicants D 1906, 1912.

mene *adj* average TC 5.806.

mene, meene *n* the mean between extremes TC 1.689; golden mean LGW 165; instrument, means TC 5.104, 1551, E 1671; go-between TC 3.254; **meenes** *pl* go-betweens A 3375; instruments, means B 480, D 1484, F 883.

mene(n) *v* say HF 1104, TC 2.171; signify TC 1.552, B 3941; **mene** *1 s* say G 1424; speak HF 1895; mean TC 3.256, A 793, B 93; **menest** *2 s* art saying BD 743; dost intend TC 3.337; **meneth** *3 s* intends TC 5.1150, A 2287; means TC 2.387; **mene** *3 pl* mean TC 5.364; **mente** *pt 3 s* said TC 4.433; thought TC 1.320; intend TC 4.349; **mente** *pt pl* TC 4.37, F 399, 981; **ment, yment** *pp* intended HF 1742, PF 158.

merciable *adj* merciful LGW 347, 410, B 1878.

mercy *n* mercy A 918, etc.; **graunt mercy** great thanks BD 560, B 1470, 4160.

mere *n* mare A 541; **mare** A 691, 4055, H 78.

merite *n* merit G 33; desert C 277; virtue, righteousness HF 669, 2019.

merk see **mark.**

merlioun *n* merlin, a small type of falcon PF 339, 611.

mersshy *adj* marshy D 1710.

merveille, -aille *n* marvel TC 1.476, 3.189, B 4266; miracle B 502, 677; **merveyle, merveille** wonder, astonishment A 3423, F 87.

merveillous, -vel- *adj* marvelous, astonishing HF 469, B 1643, E 454, F 1206, G 629.

mery see **murye.**

meschaunce *n* bad luck B 602, 914; misfortune, harm TC 4.1561, B 610; calamity, ruin B 964; unfortunate action TC 1.92; misconduct C 80; **meschaunces** *pl* wickedness F 1292; **how m.** confound it! TC 4.1362; **to m.** to the devil TC 2.222; **with m.** a curse upon, bad luck to B 896, D 2215, H 11, 193; **with myschance** D 1334.

meschief, -cheef *n* misfortune, trouble TC 1.755, A 493, B 1318; unfortunate condition TC 3.1622; wrong A 1326, D 2190; **at m.** in difficulty A 2551.

message *n* message TC 4.812, F 99; errand TC 3.401, B 1087; messenger B 144, E 738; **messages** *pl* messengers TC 2.936.

messager, -anger *n* messenger BD 133, HF 1568, A 1491; **messageer** B 724.

messe, masse *n* mass B 1413, A 1826, etc.

messe-dayes *n* feast days B 4042.

mester see **myster.**

mesuage *n* messuage, a house and its pertinences (land and outbuildings) A 3979.

mesurable *adj* moderate, temperate A 435, C 515, F 362.

mesure *n* measure E 256; dimension PF 305; moderation BD 632, 881, B 3489, C 47, E 622; **over m.** beyond measure PF 300.

mete, meete *adj* fitting, suitable BD 316, A 1631, 2291; *as n* equal BD 486.

mete *n* food A 136, 345, etc.; dinner A 348, E 1913; meal (prob. dinner) TC 2.1462; **at mete** at meals A 127.

mete(n) *v* dream BD 118, PF 108, TC 5.251; **meete** *1 s* TC 3.1344; **met** *3 s* dreams PF 104, 105; **mette** *pt s* (*pers*) BD 286, PF 95, TC 1.362, B 3930; **me mette** (*impers*) I dreamed BD 442, 1320, LGW 210, A 3684.

metynge *n* dream, dreaming BD 282.

meve *v* move HF 825, PF 150, TC 1.472; **moveth** *3 s* HF 735, 811; **moeved** *pt 3 s* B 1136; **meved** *pp* moved HF 813; urged LGW 344.

mevynge *n* moving, movement HF 812, TC 1.285, 289; **moevyng** B 295.

meyne(e) *n* household TC 1.127, A 1258, D 2156; retainers, body of followers, company HF 933, E 2436, H 228; **meignee** B 3532.

meyntenaunce *n* demeanor BD 834.

mile way *n* the time needed to walk a mile B 1466.

milnestones *n pl* millstones TC 2.1384.

mirre *n* myrrh A 2938.

misacounted *pp* miscounted TC 5.1185.

misericorde *n* mercy TC 3.1177, D 1910.

mistrusten, mystriste *v* mistrust TC 1.688, C 369; **mystruste(n)** *2 pl* TC 4.1606, E 2343; **mistrust** *imp s* TC 4.1609.

miteyn, -ayn *n* mitten C 372, 373.

mo, moo *adj* more BD 266, HF 121, PF 595, D 992, etc.; besides TC 2.1481, D 894; **tymes mo** more than once E 449.

mo *pron* more, others TC 1.613, 3.1514, D 663; **other mo** more besides A 3183, E 2263; **withouten mo** without others A 2725, G 207; without more ado TC 4.1125, 1641.

mo, moo *adv* never(e) m. BD 1125, A 1352; **never the m.** D 691, E 2089; **everemo(o)** BD 604, A 1345; **forther m.** D 783.

moche see **muche**.

mochel see **muchel**.

mocioun *n* proposal TC 4.1291.

moeble *n* personal property TC 4.1380, 4.1460, 5.300; **moebles** *pl* goods, furnishings E 1314, G 540.

moeved see **meve**.

moevyng see **mevynge**.

mokre *v* hoard TC 3.1375.

mollificacioun *n* softening G 854.

mone¹, moone *n* moan, lament HF 362, TC 1.696, etc.

mone² *n* moon HF 1531, 2116, TC 3.1756 (usually **moone**).

mone *v refl* bemoan, reveal one's sorrow TC 1.98.

moneye, -eie *n* money A 703, B 1478, etc.

monstre *n* monster E 2062; marvel, extraordinary thing F 1344.

montance, moun- *n* amount TC 2.1707, C 863; amount of time LGW 307; value A 1570, H 255.

montayne, -eyne *n* mountain B 3776, 3817, etc.; **montaigne** B 24.

mood *n* mind, feeling C 126; anger A 1760.

mooder, moder *n* mother PF 202, TC 2.50, A 3795, etc.; **moodres** *gen s* B 1783, C 729; **moodres** *pl* C 93.

moorne *v* grieve D 848; **moorne** *1 s*

have a longing A 3704; **moorneth** *3 s* mourns F 819; **moorne** *3 pl* long B 1933.

moornyng(e) *n* mourning A 2968; lamentation B 621; yearning A 3706.

moost, most *adv* most BD 779, HF 847, A 561, etc.

mooste, moste *adj* most, greatest BD 302, 465, TC 1.1080, D 505; **most** HF 2025.

moot, mot *1 s* must PF 469, A 885, 1295; **moost, most** *2 s* TC 1.520, 4.467, B 104, C 215, D 340; **moot, mot** *3 s* may A 738, 1838; must BD 42, PF 408, TC 3.1241, A 732; **moote, mote** *1 pl* must LGW 17, A 1185, B 1427; **moote, mooten, moten, moot** *2 pl* may E 474, F 318; must PF 546, F 164, 316; **mooten, mote, moten** *3 pl* may A 232; must TC 1.846, 847, A 742, D 589; **moote, mote, moot** *1 s subj* may HF 1329, B 2007, 4166; **moote** *2 s subj* mayst B 1626; **moote, mote, mot** *3 s subj* may HF 102, PF 569, LGW 186, D 277, E 557; **moste** *pt 1 s* must, would have to BD 1024, HF 1506, TC 2.799, A 1290; *pt 3 s* must, had to, might HF 187, 2094, TC 1.74, A 712; **moste, mosten** *pt pl* TC 2.894, 1507, LGW 99, B 710, E 1334; **moste** *pt 3 s subj* might B 380, E 550.

moote *n* particle TC 3.1603; **motes** *pl* motes D 868.

mordre *n* murder A 1256, B 1766, 4211.

mordred *pt 2 pl subj* should murder BD 724; *pp* murdered B 4195, D 801, E 728.

mordrour *n* murderer B 4416; **mordrere** E 732; **mortherere** PF 353, 612.

more, moore *adj* more, greater, larger BD 822, HF 907, A 2429, etc.; as *n* B 959, 3433.

more, moore *pron* more TC 1.386, 4.1385, A 2850, 3707, 3725; **namore** no more TC 5.798; **withoute(n) m., withouten any m.** without more ado TC 2.1666, A 1541, 2316, E 1939.

more, moore *adv* more, further BD 190, HF 883, TC 1.406, A 802, etc.; **more and more** TC 4.1345.

more *n* root TC 5.25.

mormal *n* open sore A 386.

morne *adj* morning A 358, 3236.

morsel *n* morsel A 128, B 4025; **morsel breed** morsel of bread B 3624.

morter *n* a bowl of wax or oil with wick, possibly at this date a thick

candle, used as a night light TC 4.1245.

mortifye *v* transform (into a solid) G 1126 (see note), 1431.

mortreux *n* either a thick soup or a hash A 384 (see note).

morwe *n* shortened form of **morwen** morning, morrow BD 22, 1256, PF 489, LGW 49, etc.

morwen *n* morning, morrow TC 2.1555.

morwenynge *n* early morning A 1062, B 4492, F 397; **morwenynges** *pl* D 875.

morwe-song *n* morning-song A 830.

morwe-tyde *n* morning-time, morning B 4206, E 2225, G 588.

mosel *n* muzzle A 2151.

most, moste(n) see **moot**.

most(e) see **moost, mooste**.

mot *n pl* motes, notes on the hunting horn BD 376.

motre *v* mutter TC 2.541.

motyf *n* impression B 628; argument, thought E 1491.

moun see **mowen**.

mous *n* mouse HF 785, A 144, 1261, etc.; **mouses** *gen s* mouse's TC 3.736, D 572.

moustre *n* model BD 912.

mowe *n* grimace TC 4.7; **mowes** *pl* HF 1806.

mowen *v* be able TC 2.1594; **may** *1 s* can BD 31; may A 1232, 1512; **mayst, maist** *2 s* A 1234, 1285; **maistow** mayest thow A 1236; **may** *3 s* can BD 40, A 230, 246; may HF 1563, A 1360; **mowe(n)** *pl* A 3550, B 3151, G 681; **may** *1 pl* HF 1759, A 1268; **mowe(n)** *2 pl* BD 208, TC 4.1330, B 3150, C 932; **may** *2 pl* A 746, 3438; **mowe(n), moun** *3 pl* A 2999, D 1722, F 211, G 510; **may** *3 pl* B 3148, D 1121; **mowe** *1 & 2 s subj* BD 94, HF 804, G 300, 460; **myghte, might** *pt 1 s* BD 44, TC 4.95; **myghtest** *pt 2 s* A 1655; **myghtestow** TC 4.262; **myght(e)** *pt 3 s* BD 506, TC 1.823, A 169; **myghte(n)** *pt 3 pl* TC 1.614, A 568, C 107; **myghte** *pt 1 s subj* E 638.

mowlen *v* grow mouldy B 32; **mowled** *pp* grown mouldy A 3870.

moyst(e) *adj* moist PF 380, A 420; soft, not dried out A 457; new, musty (of ale) B 1954, C 315.

moysty *adj* new, musty (of ale) H 60.

muable *adj* changeable TC 3.822.

mucche *v* munch TC 1.914.

muche, moche *adj* much, great BD 713, HF 147, A 494, etc.; **muche folk, thyng** *collectively as pl* many people, things B 3960, D 1273; *as n* much BD 221, 904.

muche, moche *adv* much, greatly BD 353, HF 500, A 1116, etc.

muche *indef. pron* much TC 3.386, D 2134, G 1124.

muchel, mochel *adj* much, great HF 1138, TC 2.1071, A 870, etc.; **muchel folk, thyng** *collectively as pl* many people, things D 1004; *as n* size, stature BD 454, 861.

muchel, mochel *adv* much, greatly BD 1102, TC 1.386, A 132.

muchel *indef pron* much A 211, 467, E 1241.

mullok *n* rubbish, refuse A 3873, G 938, 940.

murier *adj* merrier, pleasanter B 2024, 4041, E 2322.

murierly *adv* more merrily A 714.

murily, myr- *adv* merrily, pleasantly, without mishap B 1300, 1491, 1743, 4457, etc.; cheerfully D 1192.

mury(e) *adj* merry A 802, 1386, 2562; pleasant E 1348; **myrie** A 757, 3218, B 4158; pleasant, pleasing A 1499, B 4481; **mery** pleasant B 4156.

murye *adv* merrily PF 592, C 843; **myrie** B 126.

muscle *n* mussel D 2100.

muse *v* consider, hesitate over a decision TC 3.563; **mused** *pt 3 s* mused, wondered B 1033; **imused** *pp* pondered HF 1287.

muwe, mewe *n* coop, pen TC 3.602, 1784, A 349; cage F 643, 646; **in muwe** secretly TC 1.381; cooped up 4.496, 1310.

muwe *3 pl* change TC 2.1258.

muwet *adj* mute TC 5.194.

myd *adj* middle BD 660; **in myd** amid HF 923.

myddes *n* middle, midst; **in m. of** in the middle of HF 714.

myght *n* power PF 220, A 538, D 1492, F 133; might A 1607; strength PF 149, TC 5.1438; ability TC 1.33, 3.654, C 468.

myn *poss pron* mine A 1139, 1159; *as n* my own, possession: **my good m., O goodly m.** TC 3.1009, 1473.

mynde *n* mind BD 15, PF 69, etc.; reason BD 511; **forgat hir m.** lost her memory B 527.

myne *v* penetrate TC 2.677; undermine TC 3.767; ? go on TC 4.471 (see note).

mynne *imp s* remember Scogan 48.

mynour *n* miner A 2465.

mynstralcye *n* minstrelsy A 2197, 2524; entertainment A 4394; music E 1718, F 268; musical instrument H 113; *as pl* musical instruments H 267.

myracle, mir- *n* miracle B 636, 683, 1881; wonder A 2675; miraculous power B 477, E 1660; **myracles** *pl* wonderful works PF 11; **pleyes of myracles** *pl* miracle plays, saints' plays, D 558.

myrie see **murye.**

myrthe *n* mirth BD 612; pleasure A 766, B 1508; good time D 399; entertaining story C 319; **murthe** joy E 1123.

myrtheles *adj* mirthless PF 592.

mys *adj* amis, wrong TC 4.1267, 5.1426, G 999.

mysaunter *n* misadventure TC 1.766; **mysaventure** misfortune TC 1.706, B 616; **with m.** a curse upon you D 1334.

mysavyse *3 pl refl* act inadvisedly D 230.

mysboden *pp* insulted A 909.

mysbyleved *pp* misbelieving TC 3.838.

myscarie *v* miscarry, go astray A 513.

mysconstruwe *v* misconstrue TC 1.346.

mysdeme *3 s subj* may misjudge HF 97; **mysdemeth** *3 s* misjudges E 2410; **mysdemen** *3 pl* HF 92.

mysdeparteth *3 s* distributes unjustly B 107.

mysdooth *3 s* mistreats B 3112.

myself, myselven *pron* myself A 1813, F 1362, etc.; *as pers pron* I myself BD 34, TC 2.1201, D 175; *intensive* HF 1878, 1880.

mysfille *pt 3 s impers* went wrong A 2388.

mysforyaf *pt 3 s refl* had misgivings TC 4.1426.

mysgoon, -go(n) *pp* gone amis A 4218, 4252, 4255.

mysgovernaunce *n* misconduct B 3202.

mysgyed *pp* misguided B 3723.

myshappe *3 s subj:* **if that me m.** if I am unfortunate A 1646.

myslay *pt s* lay in an awkward position A 3647.

mysledden *pt pl refl* conducted (themselves) badly TC 4.48.

myslyved *adj* of evil life TC 4.330.

myssat *pt 3 s* was unbecoming BD 941.

mysse *v* fail PF 40, A 3679; lack, be without B 1542; miss, fail to find A 4216, D 1416; **missed** *pt 3 s* was lacking TC 3.445; **missed** *pp* TC 3.537.

mysset *pp* out of place BD 1210.

mysseyest *2 s* speakest falsely, dost slander LGW 323; **mysseyde** *pt 3 s* said wrongly LGW 440; **myssayd, -seyd, missaid** said something better left unsaid BD 528, H 353;

spoken unjustly E 2391.

mysspeke *v* say something wrong A 3139.

mystake *pp* done amiss BD 525.

myster *n* trade, craft A 613; **mester** occupation A 1340; **what myster men** men of what craft, what kind of men A 1710.

mystriste see **mistrusten.**

myswent *pp* gone astray TC 1.633.

myte *n* small copper coin, farthing, anything worthless A 1558, D 1961, G 511.

mytes *n pl* mites, insects D 560.

N

nacioun *n* nation HF 207, B 268, 281; family D 1068; **nacions** *pl* A 53.

nadde *pt s* **ne + hadde,** had not LGW 278, H 51; *pt 3 pl subj* G 879.

naddre *n* adder E 1786; **neddres** *pl* LGW 699.

naille *v* nail, restrain E 1184; **nailynge** *part* nailing A 2503.

naked *adj* naked BD 325, HF 133, etc.; bare BD 978; unfurnished, ill-equipped TC 3.43; **ful n.** completely lacking G 486; Cf. **bely-naked.**

nakers *n pl* kettle-drums, ? trumpets A 2511 (see note).

nale *n* **atte nale,** for **atten ale,** at the alehouse D 1349.

nam *pt s* took G 1297; **nome(n), ynome, inome** *pp* taken PF 38, TC 1.242, 3.606, 5.514.

nam *1 s* **ne + am** am not BD 1188, LGW 47, A 1122, 4289.

name *n* name BD 201, TC 1.99, etc.; good name, reputation TC 4.1581, F 251.

namely *adv* especially TC 1.165, A 1268, etc.

namo *adj & pron* no more A 101, 544; no one else A 1589, B 695.

namo *adv* no more, again F 573.

namoore *adj & pron* no more A 974, 1809, etc.

namoore *adv* no more LGW 551, A 98, 1173, etc.

narwe *adj* narrow B 946; small B 4012.

narwe *adv* closely TC 3.1734, LGW 600, D 1803, E 1988.

nas *pt s* **ne + was** was not A 251, 288, etc.

nat *adv* not BD 20, PF 7, A 246, etc.; **nat but** nothing but A 2722; only C 403; quite G 601.

natal *adj* presiding over nativities TC 3.150.

natheless, -les *adv* none the less, nevertheless BD 32. A 35, etc.

natureel, -el, -al *adj* natural A 416, 2750, etc.; normal HF 28; **day n.** a 24-hour day F 116.

naught *adv* not TC 1.142, A 2068.

nave *n* hub A 2266, 2270.

navele *n* navel A 1957.

navye *n* fleet HF 216.

nay *adv* no BD 558, etc.; *as n.* nay, no A 1667; **it is no n.** it cannot be denied E 817.

ne *adv* not BD 22, 57, 78, etc.; often combined with following word. See **nam, nas, nil,** etc.

ne *conj* nor BD 2, 8, TC 4.1442, A 773, etc.; **ne . . . ne** neither nor BD 22, C 339.

nece *n* niece TC 1.975, etc.; female relation B 1290.

nede, neede *n* need, necessity BD 190, A 304; violence B 3576; **nedes** *pl* necessary things, occupations B 174.

nede *v* be necessary B 871; **nedeth** *3 s impers* is necessary PF 398, TC 2.11; **what nedeth** what is the need of A 849, B 232; **neded(e)** *pt s* was necessary A 4020, B 4024; **neded** *pt 3 s subj* would be necessary TC 4.1344.

nedeles, -lees *adv* unnecessarily TC 2.1527, E 455.

nedely, nedly *adv* of necessity TC 4.970, B 4434, D 968.

nedes *adv* necessarily B 1201, A 1169, 1290, etc.

nedes cost *adv* necessarily A 1477.

nedfully *adv* of necessity TC 4.1004, 1054.

needfulle *adj as n* those in need, the needy B 112.

neen *adj* no (Northern) A 4185, 4187.

neer¹, ner *adv* near BD 134, A 839, B 1888, C 966, etc.; close, intimately A 1439.

neer², ner(e) *adv* nearer BD 450, TC 1.448, A 968; **n. and n.** nearer and nearer A 4304, B 1710; **fer ne ner** farther nor nearer, neither more nor less A 1850; **never the n.** never the nearer BD 38; no better off (nearer to one's purpose) PF 619, G 721. See **neigh.**

neet *n pl* cattle A 597.

neigh, nygh, ny(e) *adj* near, close-by A 3396, 4195; *as n* near one A 3392; *quasi prep* near (to) HF 1047, TC 2.68, F 49.

neigh, negh, nygh, ny(e) *adv* close A 588, 1489; nearly, closely A 732; almost BD 907, A 4400, E 1775; **wel n.** well nigh, almost TC 1.108, A 1330, C 771, etc.

neighen, neghen *v* approach TC 2.1555, LGW 318.

nekke *n* neck BD 939, TC 2.986, etc.

nekke-boon, -bon *n* neckbone, a vertebra at the nape of the neck or the nape of the neck itself B 669,

1839, 4252, D 906.

nempne(n) *v* name, mention B 507, F 318; **nempned** *pt 3 s* mentioned E 609.

nere *pt s subj* were I (it) not, would not be TC 2.409, A 875, B 132; *pt 2 & 3 pl* were not BD 959, LGW 348.

nerf *n* sinew TC 2.642.

nevene *v* name HF 562, TC 1.876; **nevene** *3 pl subj* tell G 1473.

newe *adj* new A 176, etc.; *as n* a new (love) HF 302; **of n.** recently D 1342, E 938.

new(e) *adv* newly, lately LGW 129, A 428, 3221; anew TC 5.1333, 1572, LGW 103, B 171; **al newe** very recently B 4239; **n. and n.** again and again, ever anew TC 3.116, C 929.

newe *v* be renewed TC 3.305; **newed** *pt s* was renewed BD 906.

newefangel *adj* eager for novelty F 618, H 193.

newefangelnesse *n* love of novelty LGW 154, F 610.

nexte *adj* next HF 1107, PF 679, B 1497; nearest TC 1.697, A 1413, B 1814.

nil see **nyl.**

noble *n* gold coin (6*s* 8*d*) A 3256 (see note), G 1037; **nobles** *pl* HF 1315, C 907.

noblesse *n* nobleness TC 1.287, B 185; honor B 3208, D 1167; magnificence, splendor HF 471, TC 5.439, E 782.

nobley(e) *n* high estate E 828; magnificence, splendor HF 1416, F 77; nobles (collect.) G 449.

no fors no matter. See **fors.**

noght, nought *n* nothing HF 765, TC 1.444, A 768; **I am aboute nought** I am acting to no purpose, accomplishing nothing TC 5.100.

noght, nought *adv* not, not at all BD 460, HF 10, A 107.

nolde *pt s & pl* ne + wolde, would not B 311, HF 1780, A 550; did not wish B 1276; **noldest** *2 s* BD 482; **noldestow** TC 3.1264; **nolden** *pt pl* D 1898.

nome(n) *pp* taken TC 3.606, 5.514. See **nam.**

nones *n*: **for the nones** (orig. **for than anes,** *gen of* **an,** one) for the nonce, for the occasion, for that purpose, with more or less specific reference, but often with little explicit meaning so that it sometimes seems to be a mere tag TC 4.428, A 253, 545; **with the n.** on the condition HF 2095.

nonne *n* nun A 118, 163; **nonnes** *gen* B 3999.

nonnerye *n* nunnery A 3946, 3968.

noon *n* noon TC 2.1185, E 1893; the hour of nones (3 P.M.) E 1893.

noon, none *adj & pron* none, no (esp. before vowel) BD 169, A 524, B 87.

noot, not *1 & 3 s* ne + wot, know(s) not BD 29, HF 12, TC 1.426, A 1263; **nost** *2 s* BD 1137; **nostow** knowest thou not HF 1010. See **nyste.**

norice *n* nurse B 4305, D 299.

norissed *pp* brought up E 399; **ynorissed, -sshed** TC 5.821, A 3948.

norissyng(e) *n* nourishment A 437; growth 3017; upbringing E 1040.

noriture *n* nourishment TC 4.768.

nortelrie *n* education A 3967.

nosethirles *n pl* nostrils A 557.

noskynnes *adj* of no kind HF 1794.

not see **noot.**

note¹ *n* work, task A 4068.

note,² noote *n* musical note BD 303; music, melody PF 677, B 1711, 1737; blast on a trumpet HF 1720; tone, quality of voice A 235; **by n.** in unison TC 4.585.

notemuge *n* nutmeg B 1953.

not-heed *n* close-cropped head A 109.

nother, nouther *conj & pron* neither: **nother . . . nor, n. . . . ne** neither . . . nor B 342, 531; **never n.** neither one nor the other LGW 192.

nothyng, no thyng *adv* not at all, in no wise A 1519, 1703, B 575.

notifie *v* take note of TC 2.1591; **notified** *pp* proclaimed B 256.

noumbre, nombre *n* number BD 440, A 716.

noumbre *v* count BD 439; **noumbred** *pp* numbered TC 3.1269.

nouncerteyn *n* uncertainty TC 1.337.

novelrie *n* novelty TC 2.756; **novelries** *pl* new things F 619; quarrels disputes HF 686.

now *adv* now A 573, etc.; **n. and n.** now and again F 430.

nowches *n pl* brooches, ornaments E 382; **nouchis** ornaments, settings (for jewels) HF 1350. Cf. **ouche.**

nowthe *adv* now TC 1.985; **as n.** at this time A 462.

noyous *adj* troublesome HF 574.

noyse *n* noise HF 1058, A 2492, etc.; sound H 300; clamor TC 1.85, A 2534.

nyce *adj* foolish HF 276, TC 1.202, A 398, etc.; stupid TC 4.1625.

nycely *adv* stupidly TC 5.1152.

nycete(e) *n* foolishness PF 572, TC 2.1288, G 463; folly H 152; simplicity A 4046; shyness BD 613; **of n.** through foolishness TC 1.913.

ny(e) see **neigh.**

nyfles *n pl* trifles, fictitious tales D 1760.

nygardye *n* stinginess B 1362.

nyghte *v* grow dark PF 209, TC 5.515.

nyghtertale *n* night-time A 97.

nyght-spel *n* charm or spell against harm at night A 3480.

nyghtyngale *n* nightingale PF 351, TC 2.918, A 98, etc.

nyl, nil *1 & 3 s* **ne** + **wyl,** will not BD 92, 1140, HF 56, TC 1.37, etc.; **nylt** *2 s* TC 2.1000; **nyltow** wilt thou not TC 1.792; **nel** *1 pl* D 941.

nys *3 s* **ne** + **ys,** is not TC 1.203, A 901, etc.

nyste *pt s* **ne** + **wyste, wiste,** knew not BD 272, HF 128, etc.

O

o, oo *adj* one BD 261, TC 3.1026, 5.143, A 304, 738, etc.; only, alone HF 1100. See **oon.**

o *prep* on TC 4.1638.

obeisant *adj* obedient E 66.

obeisaunce, obey- *n* obedience LGW 587, E 24; attentiveness, marks of respect TC 3.478, F 562; **obeisaunces** *pl* marks of respect, attentions LGW 149, F 515.

obeye *v* obey E 1379; yield to TC 2.1490, E 531, F 749; **obeyeth, obeieth** *3 s* LGW 90, E 1961; **obeye** *1 pl* E 194; **obeyed** *pt s* TC 3.581, D 1255.

oblige *v* pledge (myself) TC 4.1414; **obliged** *pp* be under obligation TC 3.1612.

observaunce *n* customary rite or practice TC 2.112, A 1045, 1316; attention, conventional act of respect TC 3.970, E 1564; **observaunces** *pl* A 2264, F 516; obligations E 1548.

observe *v* tolerate B 1821.

occian *n* ocean B 505.

occupie *v* occupy F 64; **occupieth** *3 s* occupies TC 5.1322; takes possession TC 4.836, B 424.

of *prep* of A 55, etc.; according to LGW 412; among E 2278; as E 834; as a result of, because of B 337, C 281, E 723; at TC 2.1639, E 145; by TC 5.1728, A 4341, F 1560; concerning, about B 1323; during A 3415; for B 3388, D 1861; from B 837, 3405; in, in respect to TC 5.1171, E 33, G 979; over F 288, H 128; to F 121; with D 591, G 565; some (partitive use) A 82, 146, 3223.

of *adv* off B 1855, D 783; **com(e) of** come on! TC 2.310, A 3728, D 1602.

of-caste *imp s* cast off PF 132.

offence *n* offence TC 3.137, Scogan 13; injury, wrong A 1083, D 2058, E 922; harm TC 4.199; guilt TC 1.536, B 1138.

offende(n) *v* offend TC 2.244; give pain to E 1756, 1829; annoy E 2164; **offendeth** *3 s* assails TC 1.605; **offended** *pp* injured A 909; assailed A 2394.

offensioun *n* damage A 2416.

offertorie *n* a liturgical chant A 710 (see note).

office *n* duty, task PF 236, TC 3.1436, G 294; obligation D 1137; employment, service A 1418, B 3446, D 1297; secular employment A 292; function D 1144; natural function D 127; religious rite A 2863, 2912; **houses of o.** service buildings (kitchen, etc.) E 264.

offre(n) *n* make an offering C 384, 386; **offre** *imp s* offer up (as a sacrifice) TC 5.306; **offreth** *imp pl* C 910.

of-shawve *v* repel A 3912.

ofte *adj* many, many a A 52, 485, E 226.

ofte *adv* often A 55, B 278; **ful o. a day** many times a day TC 5.689, A 1356; many a day A 2623; **so o.** so many times Adam 5.

ofter *adv* more often TC 1.125, E 215, 620.

of-thowed *pp* melted away HF 1143.

oght, ought *pron* anything BD 158, 459, D 2203, E 595. See **aught.**

oght, ought *adv* at all, in any way TC 2.1019, A 3045, B 1792, G 597. See **aught.**

oghte see **oughte.**

old *n* age A 2142.

o-lofte see **lofte.**

olyveres *n pl* olive trees B 3226.

on *prep* on A 12, etc.; about A 1251; against LGW 625; at TC 5.494, F 225; for TC 5.24, F 784; in D 1695, E 223, F 277; of BD 100, A 3993; to, toward A 2628, E 2150; **on hevene** in the sky TC 5.274; **on shames deeth** by a shameful death B 819.

oned *pp* united D 1968.

ones *adv* once, at one time A 1034, D 543; a single time B 588, 1227; of one mind, agreed C 696; **onis** D 10. See **atones.**

on-lofte see **lofte.**

only *adj* unique TC 4.1668.

on lyve *adv* alive BD 205, A 3039, D 5, etc. Cf. **lyf.**

ook *n* oak tree PF 176, A 1702; **o. cerial** a species of oak (Quercus cerris) A 2290.

oon, on *adj & pron* one, a BD 39, A 148, B 592, etc.; the same TC 3.309, (*modifying a pl*) A 1012; one thing TC 4.1453, F 537; **after o.** alike, by one standard A 1781; of one quality A 341; **al o.** all the same G 847; **evere in o.** invariably, constantly, continually, always in the same way TC 1.816, 4.1602, 5.451, A 1771, D 209; **many o.** many a one A 317, 2509; **o. and o.** one by one A 679. See **aton.**

oonly *adv* only HF 1743, A 1458.

oore *n* favor A 3726.

oost *n* host, army TC 1.80, 4.29, etc. See **hoost.**

ooth *n* oath A 120, etc.; **othes** *pl* A 810.

oother, other *adj* other BD 45, A 113, etc.

oother, other *adv* otherwise TC 1.799, E 2083; **neen other** not otherwise (Northern) A 4187.

ootherweys *adv* otherwise E 1072, 1534.

open *adj* open A 10, etc.; public, visible to all B 636.

opene *v* open BD 872; **opned** *pt 3 s* TC 3.1239; **opened** *pt pl* G 1218; **opened, opned** *pp* HF 1952, TC 3.469.

open-ers *n* medlar tree A 3871.

open-heveded *pp* bareheaded D 645.

opie *n* opium A 1472.

opinion *n* opinion A 183, etc.; **opynyoun** expectation TC 4.1495.

opposen *v* bring against D 1597. See **apposed.**

oppresse *v* suppress, overcome TC 5.398, G 4; violate F 1411; **oppressed** *pp* weighed down TC 3.1089, 5.177; ravished F 1385, 1435.

oppressioun *n* oppression D 1990; wrong TC 2.1418, D 889, Lak 12.

or *conj* ere, before BD 128, HF 101, B 336; **or that** before BD 1032, TC 1.832.

ord *n* point LGW 645. See **word.**

ordal *n* ordeal TC 3.1046.

ordayné *adj* regulated TC 1.892.

ordeyned *pp* arranged B 415; set up A 2553; appointed F 177; equipped G 1277.

ordinaat *adj* well-ordered E 1284.

ordinaunce, orde- *n* arrangement, plan TC 2.510, 3.668, B 805; preparation TC 3.535, B 250, F 903; decree, directive A 3592, B 961, G 445; **in o.** properly E 961.

ordre *n* order, disposition of things A 3003; religious or other constituted body TC 1.336, 4.782, A 214; state (matrimony) E 1347; usage HF 1905; **by o.** in order PF 400, C 645, F 66.

ordure *n* filth, rubbish (nonsense) TC 5.385.

orgon *n* (*as pl*) organ B 4041.

oriental *adj* eastern, superior LGW 221.

orisonte *n* horizon TC 5.276, E 1797, F 1017.

orisoun *n* prayer A 2261, D 1867, F 1026.

orloge *n* clock PF 350

orpyment *n* trisulphide of arsenic G 759, 774, 823.

Osanne *n* hosanna B 642.

other see **oother, outher.**

other(e) *indef pron pl* others HF 23, TC 5.375, A 794, B 3344; **otheres** *gen s* the other's C 476.

ouche *n* necklace, properly a clasp or brooch D 743 (see note). See **nowches.**

oughte (*pt of* **owe** *as auxil v*): 1 *s* ought A 1249; **oughtest** 2 *s* oughtest TC 1.894; **oughtestow** oughtest thou TC 5.545; **oughte, oghte** 3 *s* ought PF 437, A 505; **him oughte, oghte** *impers* he ought LGW 351, B 1097; **ought us** it behooves us, we ought LGW 27; **oughte(n)** *pl* ought TC 2.912, 3.1433.

oules *n pl* (flesh) hooks D 1730. Cf. **al.**

ounces *n pl* small strands A 677; ounces G 756.

oundy *adj* wavy HF 1386.

oure, oures see **we.**

ourselven *pron* ourselves TC 2.1331.

out of *prep* without TC 5.137, A 487, G 46.

out-brynge *v* bring out, speak, say something TC 3.99, 107, 958.

outen *v* set out, expose to view, display E 2438, G 384; **oute** 1 *pl* D 521.

Outhees *n* Outcry, Clamor A 2012.

outher *adj* either A 2556.

outher, other *conj* or BD 810, 1100, PF 46, etc.; **o . . . or** either . . . or TC 2.857, A 1485, B 931.

outrely, outer- *adv* utterly BD 1244, LGW 368; etc.; absolutely TC 2.1004, A 237; emphatically E 768; truly, indeed E 335; plainly A 1154.

outreye *v* go to excess E 643.

outridere *n* an officer in a monastery whose duty it was to look after the manors belonging to it A 166.

out-taken *pp* excepted B 277.

outtreste *adj* uttermost E 787.

out-twyne 2 *pl* give utterance to Rosem 11.

outward *adv* outward HF 281; outside TC 2.1704, E 424.

out-wende *v* issue HF 1645.

over *prep* over BD 67, HF 348, A 1693; above BD 1264; beyond PF 300.

overal, over al *adv* everywhere BD 171, 300, A 216, 547, etc.; on all sides D 264; in every way E 2129; **over al and al** above everything BD 1003.

overbord *adv* overboard LGW 644; **over bord** HF 438.

overbyde *v* outlive D 1260.

overcaste *v* overcloud, darken A 1536.

overeste *adj* overmost, outer A 290.

overgo(n) *v* pass away TC 1.846, 4.424.

over-greet *adj* too great G 648.

overlad *pp* domineered over B 3101.

overlade *v* overload LGW 621.

overloked *pp* looked over BD 232.

over-lippe *n* upper lip A 133.

overmacche *v* be more than a match for E 1220.

overraughte *pt* 3 *s* reached over, encouraged TC 5.1018.

overryden *pp* run over A 2022.

overshake *pp* shaken off PF 681.

overskipte *pt* 1 *s* skipped over BD 1208.

overslope *n* robe, outer garment G 633.

oversprede *v* overspread, cover E 1799; **oversprat** 3 *s* overspreads TC 2.767; **oversprҮadde** *pt* 3 *s* TC 2.769, A 678, 2871.

oversprynge 3 *s subj* may surpass F 1060.

overt *adj* open HF 718.

overthrowe *v* overthrow B 3331; be overthrown HF 1640; *pp* overthrown TC 4.385, 5.1460.

overthwert *adv* sidelong BD 863; **overthwart** opposite TC 3.685.

owe 1 *s* owe D 425; **owest** 2 *s* owest D 1615; **oweth** 3 *s* owns C 361; **owen** 1 *pl* owe D 2106; **oughte** *pt* 3 *s* owed LGW 589. See **oughte** *auxil v.*

owher(e) *adv* anywhere BD 776, A 653, etc.

ownded *adj* wavy, curly TC 4.736.

oynement *n* ointment A 631, Rosem 7.

oynons *n pl* onions A 634.

P

pa see **ba.**

pace, passe(n) *v* go, proceed, move on HF 1355, TC 5.537, A 1602, B 4129; pass by, remain untold B 1124, 1759; travel HF 720; go away, depart HF 239, A 3578, B 205; pass away TC 1.847, A 175; move past or beyond HF 975; pass for, be accepted as TC 1.371; *trans uses:* pass over TC 2.1568; get through HF 2011; surpass A 448, 574; take

precedence over LGW 162, A 3089; exceed E 1417, G 857; exceed (a time limit) HF 392, A 2998; **pace, passe** 1 *s* HF 1112, TC 2.1595; **passeth** 3 *s* PF 300, A 1033; **passen** *pl* B 1199, E 1315; **passed, paste** *pt* 3 *s* TC 2.1260, A 448; **paste** *pt pl* TC 2.658; **passe** *imp s* pass over, disregard B 4452, C 303; **passynge** *part* A 2848; surpassing TC 1.101, E 240; **passed, ypassed** *pp* passed A 464, E 1892; past B 1278.

pacience *n* patience A 1084, etc.

pacient *adj* patient A 484, etc.

pacient *n* patient A 415, etc.

paciently *adv* patiently D 1996.

page *n* boy A 3972; page A 1427, etc.

paillet *n* pallet TC 3.229.

paire, peire *n* pair A 473, 4386; string (of beads) A 159; **a p. plates** a pair of plates A 2121.

pale *n* perpendicular stripe HF 1840.

paleis-ward: to p. toward the palace TC 2.1252.

palestral *adj* athletic, pertaining to the palestra or wrestling-school TC 5.304.

paleys *n* palace A 2199, etc.

palled *adj* incapacitated H 55.

palmeres *n pl* palmers, professional pilgrims A 13.

pan *n* skull A 1165, B 3142.

panade *n* large knife, cutlass A 3929 3960.

panter *n* snare, net LGW 131.

panyer *n* basket E 1568; **panyers** *pl* HF 1939.

papejay *n* popinjay, parrot B 1559, 1957, E 2322; **popynjay** PF 359.

papir *n* paper TC 5.1597, A 4404; papeer G 762.

par, *French prep* by: **p. aventure, p. cas, p. chaunce** by chance A 475, B 1205, C 606, 885; **p. compaignye** for company A 4167; **p. ma fay** by my faith B 2010; **per consequens** as a consequence D 2192.

parage *n* lineage, rank D 250, 1120.

paramour *n* passion E 1450; mistress D 454; loose wench D 1372; love-making A 4372, 4392; **paramours** *pl* lady-loves TC 2.236; **for p.** for love's sake A 3354, B 2033.

paramours *adv* in the manner of a lover TC 5.158, 332, A 1155; ardently, fervently A 2112, B 1933.

paraunter, per- *adv* peradventure, perchance BD 556, HF 792, TC 3.491, etc.

paraventure, per- *adv* peradventure, perchance A 3915, E 234, etc.

parcel *n* part F 852.

parde(e) *excl* par Dieu, by God,

assuredly BD 721, TC 5.142, D 1565; **pardieux** TC 1.197.

pardoun *n* pardon, indulgence(s) A 687, C 906, 917.

paregal *adj* equal TC 5.840.

parementz *n pl* decorated robes A 2501; ornate furnishings (see **chambre de p.**).

parfey, -fay *excl* by my faith HF 938, A 3681, B 110.

parfit *adj* perfect HF 44, PF 568, A 72, etc.

parfitly *adv* perfectly D 111, E 690, 1834.

parfourne *v* perform, carry out B 3137, H 190; **p. up** complete D 2261; **parfournest** *2 s* bringest to pass B 1797; **perfourme out** *imp s* complete TC 3.417; **parfourned** *pp* carried out B 1648; completed D 2104, E 1795.

parisshens *n pl* parishoners A 482, 488.

paritorie *n* pellitory (herb) G 581.

parlement *n* discussion A 2970; decision A 1306; parliament TC 4.143, A 3076.

parodie *n* period, duration TC 5.1548.

part *n* portion A 3006, E 1242; share A 1178, 3498; times, "fold" D 2062; possession A 2792; enjoyment E 650; side A 2185; part of the body PF 397; **parte** party (body of adherents) A 2582; **every p.** all sides A 2446; everywhere TC 3.1331; **on my p.** as far as I am concerned TC 4.181; **the devel have p.** the devil take, a curse on B 1408 (see note).

parte(n) *v* divide, share TC 1.589, LGW 465, E 1630; depart C 649; **parte** *1 s* depart TC 1.5; **partest** *2 s* dost get away C 752; **parteth** *3 s* departs LGW 359; **parted** *pp* divided D 1967; distributed TC 1.960.

particuler *adj* special E 35; out-of-the-way, known to only a few F 1122.

partly *adj* parti-colored A 1053.

party(e) *n* part, portion TC 2.394, LGW 482, B 17, party to a dispute PF 496; partisan A 2657.

Parvys *n* church-porch, esp. of St. Paul's, London A 310.

pas, paas *n* footpace, walk A 825; amble G 575; step TC 3.281; distance TC 5.604; **pas** *pl* paces (yards) A 1890; **a softe p.** quietly, slowly A 3760, B 399; **a ful greet p.** quickly C 164; **a sory p.** sorrowfully A 3741. See **a pas**.

passant *adj* surpassing, outstanding A 2107.

passe(n) see **pace**.

passioun *n* suffering TC 3.1040; anger B 1138; martyrdom G 26; the sufferings of Christ A 3478.

passyng *adj* excellent G 614; extreme E 1225.

pastee *n* meat pie A 4346.

pasture *n* pasture E 1313; act of feeding B 4375.

patente *n* letter patent A 315; licence C 337.

paunche *n* belly PF 610.

paumes *n pl* palms (of the hand) TC 3.1114.

pay *n* satisfaction PF 271; **to p.** satisfactorily PF 474.

paye(n) pay A 806, 4133; reward HF 1549; **payde** *pt 3 s* A 539, 570; **payed, payd, ypayed** *pp* paid A 1802, 4315; satisfied BD 269.

payen *adj* pagan A 2370.

payens *n pl* pagans TC 5.1849, B 534.

payndemayn *n* white bread of the finest quality B 1915.

paynted *adj* highly colored TC 2.424.

pecok, pekok *n* peacock PF 356, TC 1.210, A 3926; *as adj* A 104.

pecunyal *adj* pecuniary D 1314.

peert *adj* pert A 3950.

pees *n* peace BD 615, A 532, etc.

peire see **paire**.

pekke *n* peck A 4010.

pekke *imp s* peck B 4157.

pekok see **pecok**.

pel *n* peel, castle HF 1310.

peler see **piler**.

pelet *n* (stone) cannon-ball HF 1643.

penant *n* penitent, one doing penance B 3124.

penaunce *n* penance A 223; punishment G 446; distress, suffering TC 1.94, A 1315, F 740; injury G 530; sorrow TC 4.342; **penaunces** *pl* sorrows TC 1.201.

pencel *n* token, streamer TC 5.1043.

penner *n* case containing pens E 1879.

penoun *n* pennon A 978.

penyble *adj* painstaking, constant in endeavor D 1846, E 714; indefatigable B 3490.

peple *n* people A 706, etc.

per see **par**.

peraunter see **paraunter**.

peraventure see **paraventure**.

percely *n* parsley A 4350.

perce(n) *v* pierce B 2014, E 1204; **perseth** *3 s* PF 331; perced *pp* A 2, B 1745.

percynge *n* piercing B 2052.

peregryn *adj* foreign, imported: **faucon p.** a species of falcon frequently trained for hawking F 428.

pere-jonette *n* type of early pear A 3248.

perfourme see **parfourne**.

perisse *3 pl subj* perish C 99.

perle *n* pearl LGW 221; **perles, peerles** *pl* A 2161, B 3658.

perled *pp* decorated with beads or drops A 3251.

perree, -ry(e) *n* precious stones, jewels HF 1393, A 2936, B 3495, D 344.

pers *n* blue, bluish gray; cloth of that color A 239, 617.

person, -oun *n* parson A 478, D 1313; **persone** person A 521.

perspectives *n pl* telescopes F 234.

perturbe *v* perturb TC 4.561; **perturben** *2 pl* disturb A 906.

perturbynge *n* disturbance D 2254.

pesen *n pl* peas LGW 648.

pestilence *n* pestilence, plague A 442, C 679; wickedness C 91; a plague (curse) B 4600, D 1264.

peyne *n* pain, suffering, grief BD 587, PF 80, E 1782; penalty D 1314; care C 1398; effort HF 1118; **peynes, paynes** *pl* pains, grief, suffering TC 3.142, 5.864; painful experience B 3976; **bisy p.** attentiveness F 509; **doon my (doost thy) p.** make an effort TC 2.475, H 330; **in the p.** under torture TC 1.674, A 1133; **up p. of** under pain of A 1707, 2543.

peyne *v* inflict pain (upon) B 3794; *refl* put (oneself) to trouble, endeavor B 4495; **peyne me** *1 s* endeavor C 330; **peynest the** *2 s* HF 627; **peyneth hire** *3 s* B 320; **peynen hem** LGW 636; **peyned hire** *pt 3 s* A 139.

peynte(n) *v* paint, depict A 2087, C 15; adorn C 12; **peynted(e)** *pt 3 s* D 692, F 560; **peynted** *pp* adorned with painting A 1970; highly colored TC 2.424.

peyntour *n* painter TC 2.1041.

peynture *n* painting C 33.

peytrel *n* part of a horse's harness covering the breast G 564.

philosophre *n* philosopher, alchemist A 297, B 25, G 837.

phisik *n* medicine TC 2.1038, A 413.

phislyas *n* meaning unknown B 1189.

phitonesses *n pl* witches HF 1261 (see note).

piete(e) *n* pity TC 4.246, 5.1598; devotion: **with p.** dutifully TC 3.1033.

piggesnye *n* name of a flower A 3268 (see note).

pighte *t 3 s* pitched A 2689.

pike¹ *v* peek TC 3.60.

pike² *v* pick TC 2.1274; **pyketh** *3 s* cleanse, preen E 2011; **pyked, ypiked** *pp* picked D 44a; sorted G 941.

pile *v* pluck, rob D 1362; piled, pyled *pp* deprived of hair, bald A 3935, 4306; thin, scanty A 627.

piler, pyler, peler *n* pillar BD 739, HF 1421, A 1993, 2466.

pilours *n pl* pillagers A 1007, 1020.

pilwe, pilowe *n* pillow BD 254, TC 5.224, E 2004.

pilwe-beer *n* pillowcase A 694.

pipe *n* musical instrument HF 773, B 2005.

pipere *n* material for pipe or horn PF 178.

pissemyre *n* ant D 1825.

pistel *n* short lesson D 1021; epistle E 1154.

pit see **putten.**

pitaunce *n* pious donation, an allowance of food A 224.

pitee *n* pity A 920, 1761, etc.; tenderness B 1783.

pith *n* vigor D 475.

pitous *adj* pitiful, sad BD 84, A 955, B 449; deserving pity C 166; sorrowful TC 4.1499; pitying, tenderhearted A 143, 953; *as adv* B 470; **pietous** TC 3.1444, 5.451.

pitously *adv* piteously, pitifully BD 711, A 949, etc.

place *n* place BD 806, A 800; space TC 5.1322, 1629; dwelling-place HF 1053, TC 2.78, D 1768; manor-house (?) B 1910; piece of land B 1463; courtyard (contextually) F 183; battle-field, lists A 2399, 2585; position, rank D 1164.

plages *n pl* regions B 543.

planed *pt 3 s* smoothed D 1758.

plante, plaunte *n* plant TC 4.767, F 1032; slip D 763.

plastres *n pl* plasters F 636.

plat *adj* plain, flat A 1845, B 1865; *as n* F 162.

plat *adv* flatly, plainly TC 1.681, B 886, C 648; fully TC 2.579.

plated *pp* covered with plates HF 1345.

platly *adv* flatly, plainly, bluntly TC 3.786, 881, 4.924.

plaunte *v* plant TC 1.964.

ple *n* plea PF 485; **plees** *pl* cases (law) PF 101.

pledynge *n* lawsuit BD 615; **pletynge** argument PF 495.

pleinte *n* plaint, lament B 66; **pleintes** *pl* B 1068.

plentee *n* plenty B 443, etc.

plentevous *adj* plentiful A 344.

plesaunce *n* pleasure BD 704, B 762, I 41; happiness E 1036; desire PF 389, E 305; that which pleases E 1111; entertainment F 713; favor TC 5.314; pleasant manner F 509; **through p.** willingly BD 767.

plesaunt *adj* pleasant, pleasing A 138, E 1621.

plesynges *adj pl* pleasing B 711.

plete *v* bring suit TC 2.1468.

pletynge see **pledynge.**

pley, play *n* pastime, entertainment BD 50; sport, jest A 1125, 3773, D 1548, E 1030; tricks, devices TC 4.1629; **pleyes palestral** *pl* athletic contests TC 5.304; **playes slye** crafty tricks BD 570; **pleyes of myracles** saints' plays D 558.

pleye(n) *v* play, be merry or sociable, joke BD 239, TC 2.121, A 758; have a good time A 772, B 1249; *refl* amuse onself TC 5.402, A 1503, E 1841; **pleye** *1 s* amuse myself D 245; **pleyeth** *3 s* TC 1.840; plays (a musical instrument) A 3306; **pleye(n)** *pl* perform B 1423, F 219; **pleyde** *pt s* BD 875, A 4068; *pt pl* made merry A 3858; **pleyynge** *part* C 608; **pleyd, played** *pp* BD 618, TC 2.1240.

pleyinge *adj* playful, humorous TC 1.280.

pleyn[1] *adj* open A 988; plain, clear LGW 328; plain, without ornament F 720; **pleyne** *pl* smooth PF 180; **in p.** clearly E 577.

pleyn[2] *adj* full PF 126, A 315, B 324; full, perfect TC 5.1818, A 337; **in p. bataille** in full battle A 988; **in hire pleyne entente** very willingly TC 2.1560.

pleyn[1] *adv* plainly A 790, B 219, 3947.

pleyn[2] *adv* fully A 327, 1464.

pleyne[1] *v* complain, lament HF 231, TC 1.11, LGW 93, A 1320; **pleyne** *1 s* TC 1.409, C 167; **pleyneth** *3 s* A 4114; F 819; **pleyne(n)** *pl* E 97, A 1251; **pleyned** *pt s* D 390, F 1457; **ypleyned** *pp* TC 4.1688.

pleyne[2] *v* explain TC 5.1230.

pleynly[1] *adv* frankly, openly TC 2.1126, A 727; clearly TC 2.272. The meaning is not always clearly distinguishable from that of **pleynly**[2].

pleynly[2] *adv* fully, completely PF 580, TC 2.363, LGW 123.

pleynynge *n* lamentation BD 599.

pleyyng(e), pleynge *n* enjoyment, recreation BD 605, A 1061; amorous play E 1854.

plighte *pt 3 s* pulled, plucked TC 2.1120, B 15; **plyght** *pp* B 3239; plucked, torn D 790.

plighte *1 s* plight, pledge B 1388, F 1537; *pt 3 s* D 1051; **plighten** *pt 2 pl* F 1326; **plight** *imp s* D 1009; **plight, yplight** TC 3.782, 4.1610, C 702.

plit(e), plyt *n* plight PF 294; condition, state TC 3.246, E 2335, G 952; situation TC 3.1377, 1480.

plite *v* fold TC 2.1204; **plited** *pp* folded, turned back and forth TC 2.697.

plogh, plough *n* plow A 887, B 1478.

plye *v* bend, mould E 1169, 1430; **plye** *3 pl* TC 1.732.

poeplissh *adj* vulgar TC 4.1677.

poke *n* bag, sack A 3780, 4278.

poked *pt 3 s* poked A 4169; incited TC 3.116.

pokets *n pl* small bags G 808.

polax, *n* poleax, battle-ax LGW 642, A 2544.

policye *n* administration C 600.

pomely *adj* dappled A 616, G 559.

pompous *adj* magnificent B 3661; arrogant B 3745.

popelote *n* lovable young woman A 3254.

popet *n* poppet B 1891.

poppere *n* dagger A 3931.

poraille *n* poor people A 247.

pore, poore *adj* HF 1532, TC 5.43, LGW 125, 388, See **povre.**

porfurie *n* mortar made of porphyry G 775.

port *n* bearing BD 834, PF 262, A 69.

porthors *n* breviary B 1321, 1325.

portreye, pur- *v* draw, paint BD 783, A 96; **purtreyed** *pt 3 s* pictured E 1600; **purtrayinge** *part* picturing (to oneself) TC 5.716.

portreyour *n* painter A 1899.

portreyture, -ei-, -ay- *n* representation, painting BD 626, HF 131, A 1968; *pl* HF 125, A 1915.

portreyynge *n* painting A 1938.

pose *n* cold in the head H 62; **on the p.** suffering from a cold in the head A 4152.

pose *1 s* put a hypothetical case TC 3.310, 571, A 1162.

positif *adj* positive; **p. lawe** law established by enactment or decree A 1167.

possed *pp* pushed, tossed TC 1.415.

possessioners *n pl* beneficed clergy D 1722.

possessioun *n* possession A 2242; property, endowment TC 2.1419, D 1925, F 686.

post *n* post, support TC 1.1000. A 800; pillar A 214.

potage *n* soup B 3623, C 368.

potente *n* crutch TC 5.1222; staff D 1776.

potestat *n* ruler, magistrate D 2017.

pothecarie *n* apothecary C 852, 859.

pouche *n* purse HF 1349; bag A 3931; *pl* A 368.

poudre *n* powder G 760; dust, ashes

TC 5.309; gunpowder HF 1644; **p. marchant** a spice A 381 (see note).

poune *n* pawn (chess); **p. errant** BD 661 (see note).

poure, powren *v* pore, look closely, stare HF 1121, 1158, A 185; **poure** *2 s subj* D 295; **pouren** *3 pl* G 670; **poured** *pp* gazed TC 1.299.

pous *n* pulse TC 3.1114.

poverte, -tee *n* poverty BD 410, B 99, etc.

povre *adj* poor A 225, 232, etc.

povrely *adv* in a lowly manner, poorly A 1412, 1554; **povreliche** E 213, 1055.

povrest *adj* poorest E 205; **povereste** *def* C 449, 450.

powped *pt 3 pl* pooped, blew B 4589; **pouped** *pp* H 90.

poynaunt *adj* piquant A 352, B 4024.

poynt, point *n* point, detail, essential matter, sharp end (and other modern senses) PF 372, A 114, 2766, etc.; particle TC 3.1509, A 2766; period, full stop G 1480; conclusion, end A 1501, 2965; **poyntes** *pl* laces A 3322; **in this p.** at this point TC 4.658; **in good p.** in good condition A 200; **in p. to, o p. to** on the point of BD 13, HF 2018, TC 4.1153, 1638.

poynt-devys *n*; **at poynt-devys** perfectly HF 917; precisely, carefully F 560; fastidiously A 3689.

poynte *v* describe in detail TC 3.497; **poynted** *pp* pointed TC 2.1034.

poyntel *n* stylus for writing on wax D 1742.

praktike *n* practice, experience D 187; **practyk** D 44d.

praktisour *n* practitioner A 422.

pray(e), prey(e) *n* booty A 2015; prey A 2632, D 1376; victim TC 1.201, D 1455.

preambulacioun *n* making a preamble or introductory discourse D 837.

precept *n* commandment B 3247, D 65.

precious, -ius *adj* valuable, precious B 3333, D 1786, etc.; fastidious D 148; prudish E 1962.

preciously *adv* in a costly manner D 500.

predestyne *n* predestination TC 4.966.

predicacioun *n* preaching, sermon B 1176, C 345, D 2109.

preef *n* proof G 968; issue, result G 1379; **with yvel p.** bad luck to you D 247.

prees, press *n* crowd B 646, D 522; **putte hym forth in pres** put

himself forward, undertook PF 603; **world of p.** busy world B 3327.

preest, prest *n* priest A 501, 503, etc.

preferre *3 s* is considered preferable to D 96.

pregnant *adj* convincing TC 4.1179.

prente *n* print D 604.

prenten *v* print, impress TC 2.900.

prentishood *n* apprenticeship A 4400.

prentys *n* apprentice A 4365, B 1490.

prescience *n* foreknowledge TC 4.987, A 1313.

presence *n* presence A 927, etc.; **in p.** present (in numbers) E 1207; **in heigh p.** in the presence of God B 675; **I have p. of** I have the company of, am present with LGW 51.

present *adv* now PF 423.

presse *n* cupboard, chest A 3212; mould A 81, 263; **leye on p.** put away TC 1.559.

prest *adj* ready PF 307, TC 2.785, 3.485; resourceful TC 5.800; **preste** *pl* swift TC 4.661.

pretende *v* tend toward TC 4.922.

preve, preeve *n* proof HF 878, PF 497, TC 1.470, D 2272; test E 787; experience B 4173; **at p.** by test TC 3.1002, 4.1659; **to p.** to the proof TC 3.307.

preve, preeve *v* prove BD 552, C 169, E 1330; put to the test TC 4.1401, E 699; turn out G 645; **preveth** *3 s* E 2425; **preeve** *3 s subj* test E 1152; **proved** *pt s* proved true A 547; **preved** *pt pl* E 2283; **preved, preeved, ypreved** *pp* HF 874, A 485, 3001.

preye(n), prayen, prey *v* pray, beseech TC 1.17, 48, A 301, B 1146; **prey(e), pray(e)** *1 s* BD 210, 519, PF 383, A 725; **preye** *2 s subj* D 358; **preyeth, prayeth** *3 s* B 866, D 1663; **preyed(e), prayed(e)** *pt 1 & 3 s* BD 131, 771, HF 192, PF 71; **preydest** *pt 2 s* TC 1.917; **preyede(n), preyden, prayed** *pt pl* HF 1815, PF 560, 578, A 811; **preye** *imp s* B 1877, F 1066; **preyed, preied, prayed, yprayed** E 773, G 166; invited TC 2.1549, E 269.

preyneth *3 s* preens E 2011.

preyse, preise(n) *v* praise, commend HF 627, TC 1.189, 3.1662; to be praised C 42; **preise** *1 s* F 674; **preiseth** E 2246; **preyseth** values E 1854; **preyse** *3 s subj* E 1546; **preysen** *2 pl* value, esteem TC 2.95; **preise(n)** *3 pl* praise E 459, 1022, **preysed, preised** *pt 3 pl* C 113; E 1471; **preysed, ypreised** *pp* HF 1577, TC 1.174, D 706; **ypreysed** esteemed TC 5.1473.

preysing(e), preis- *n* praising TC 3.215, LGW 141; praise, commendation TC 2.1589.

prikasour *n* hard rider A 189.

priken *v* spur, goad on TC 4.633; **prike** *1 s* drive, incite PF 389; *2 s subj* ride, spur B 2001; **priketh** *3 s* pierces A 11; spurs, rides hard A 2678, D 656; **pryketh** pains, drives on TC 1.219; **prikke** *2 pl subj* grieve, vex E 1038; **pryked** *pt 3 s* spurred B 1969; **prighte** pricked F 418; **prikynge** *part* riding, hurrying A 2508; **priked** *pp* spurred ridden hard G 561, 584.

prikke *n* dot, point HF 907; point, condition B 119, 1029; point of spear A 2606.

prikyng *n* following the tracks (of a hare) A 191; spurring, riding A 2599; being ridden hard, hurrying B 1965.

prime *adj* first; **at p. face** on first appearance TC 3.919.

pris, prys *n* price A 815; worth, esteem, renown TC 1.375, A 67, B 2087, D 523; praise TC 2.181, E 1026; prize A 237.

prive(e), pryve(e), privy *adj* secret BD 382, TC 3.921, A 3295, B 1991, C 281; confidential E 519; personal, intimate E 192; furtive, sexually intimate HF 285; secretive A 3201; **p. stone** philosopher's (secret) stone G 1452.

privee, pryvee, privy *adv* secretly HF 767, 810; **p. and (or) apert** secretly and (or) openly HF 717, D 1114; under all circumstances D 1136, F 531.

prively, pry- *adv* privately A 609; secretly A 652; unobserved A 1222; alone B 1282.

privete(e), pryv- *n* privacy TC 3.283, 4.1111, A 4334; private affairs A 1411, B 1354, D 531; confidential matter D 542; secret knowledge A 3164; what is hidden, mystery A 3164; secrecy TC 3.283, A 4388; **in p.** confidentially A 3493; secretly A 3623.

proces, -cesse *n* course of events B 3511; matter, affair TC 2.485, 3.334; subject, story, account, discourse TC 2.1615, 3.1739, F 658; **paynted p.** highly-colored story TC 2.424; **in p., by p.** in the course of time or events PF 430, A 2967, F 829; in due course, at length TC 2.678, 5.1491.

procurator *n* proctor, proxy D 1596.

professioun *n* vow D 1925, 2135 (see note); monastic vow B 1345.

profit *n* profit, advantage HF 310, A 249, C 809.

profre *n* offer E 154.

profre *v* offer G 1123; **profrestow** *2 s* dost thou offer TC 3.1461; **profre** *2 s subj* G 489; **prof(e)reth** *3 s* LGW 405, A 1415; **profre** *2 pl* E 848, F 755; **profred** *pt 3 s* A 3289; *pp* E 152.

prohemye *n* proem, introduction E 43.

prolle *2 pl subj* prowl around G 1412.

proporcioneles *n pl* "That which is proportional; a proportionate part" (NED), but see note to F 1277.

propre *adj* personal, one's own TC 2.1487, A 540; inherent HF 43, F 610; special, particular HF 754; suitable D 103; excellent HF 726; good-looking A 3345, 3972; well-proportioned, handsome A 4368, C 309.

proprely *adv* exactly A 729; fittingly A 2787; properly H 209; adequately A 1459; becomingly D 1191; well D 224; finely A 3320.

propretee *n* characteristic B 4142; fitness TC 4.392.

proverbed *pp* taught by a proverb TC 3.293.

provost *n* chief magistrate B 1806.

prow *n* profit, advantage HF 579, TC 1.333, B 4140.

prowesse *n* prowess, valor TC 1.438, 2.632; excellence D 1129.

prye(n), prie *v* look closely TC 2.1710; peer, gaze A 3458, E 2112, G 668.

pryme, prime *n* prime (canonical hour) C 662; a designation for the period of time covering the first quarter of the day from sunrise, sometimes the period from six to nine A.M., sometimes the beginning or end of such a period: sunrise TC 5.15, 472; nine A.M. A 2189, 2576, B 1278, 2015, 4368, D 1476, E 1857; the first hour, beginning TC 1.157; **half-wey p.** about seven-thirty A 3906 (see note).

prymer *n* a small prayer-book used for teaching children to read B 1707 (see note).

prymerole *n* primrose A 3268.

prys see **pris**.

pryvee *n* privy C 527, E 1954.

publiced *pp* disseminated, noised abroad E 415; proclaimed E 749.

pul *n* tug or match (wrestling) PF 164.

pulle(n) *v* pull, draw TC 2.657, E 2353; pluck TC 1.210, 5.1546, A 652; **pulled** *pt s* drew A 1598; plucked H 304; **pulled, ypulled** *pp* plucked A 177, 3245.

pultrye *n* poultry A 598.

punyce *v* punish TC 5.1707; **punysshed, ypunysshed** *pp* made to suffer TC 5.1095, A 657.

purchace(n) *v* purchase, acquire TC 2.713, G 1405; increase one's possessions A 608; **purchace** *3 s subj* may provide B 873; **purchased** *pt 3 s* brought about BD 1122; **yow p.** *imp s* provide yourself TC 2.1125.

purchas *n* profit, acquisition, gain from begging A 256, D 1451, 1530.

purchasour *n* purchaser A 318 (see note).

purchasyng *n* acquisition D 1449.

pure *adj* very BD 1212, TC 4.1620, A 1279; **in p. deth** death itself BD 583.

pure *adv* very, entirely BD 942, 959, 1010.

pured *pp* refined D 143, F 1560.

purely *adv* entirely BD 5; verily BD 843, HF 39.

purfiled *pp* edged, bordered A 193.

purpos *n* purpose, intention A 2542, 3978; question, subject, matter TC 2.897, 5.176; **to p.** pertinent TC 5.1460; **in p.** of the intention A 3978; **was in p. grete** had a great mind to TC 5.1576; **took p.** reached a decision TC 5.1029.

purpre *adj* purple TC 4.869, LGW 654.

purs *n* purse A 656, etc.

pursevantes *n pl* pursuivants HF 1321.

pursuyt(e), -sute *n* suit, entreaty TC 2.959, 1744, D 890.

purtreye see **portreye**.

purveyaunce, -vei- *n* providence, foreknowledge TC 4.961, 5.1446, A 1252, 1665; foresight D 566; preparation TC 3.533; provision A 3566, B 247, D 570, F 904.

purveye *v* provide TC 2.1160, D 917; prepare TC 2.504, E 191; **purveyeth** *3 s* foresees TC 4.1066; **purveye** *imp s* provide TC 2.426; **purveyed** *pp* provided D 591; foreseen TC 4.1006, 1008.

purveyinge *n* providence TC 4.986.

putte(n), put *v* put BD 1332, A 1435, B 801, etc.; **put, putte** *1 s* A 1814, D 1231; **puttest** *2 s* B 3875; **putteth, put** *3 s* LGW 652, A 3802; **putte** *2 pl* G 455; **putte** *pt 3 s* A 987, 3732; **putten** *pt pl* B 3260; **put** *imp s* C 201; **putte** *imp pl* G 1329; **put, yput** *pp* TC 2.613, B 1110, D 1333, G 762; **pit** *pp* A 4088.

pye *n* meat (or fish) pie A 384.

pye, pie *n* magpie PF 345, A 3950, B 1399, D 456; tell-tale bird TC 3.527; **pies** *pl* HF 703.

pyk *n* pike (fish) TC 2.1041, E 1419, Rosem 17.

pykepurs *n* pickpurse A 1998.

pyment *n* sweetened wine A 3378 (see note).

pyn *n* pin A 196, F 127; **hangeth on a joly p.** is lively or merry E 1516.

pynacles *n pl* pinnacles HF 124 (see note), 1193.

pynche(n) *v* find fault (with) A 326, H 74; **pynched** *pp* pleated A 151.

pyne *n* pain, torment, suffering, grief HF 1512, TC 5.268, A 1324; punishment B 3420.

pyne *v* torture A 1746; **pyned** *pp* tortured B 4249.

pype(n), pipe(n) *v* blow in a pipe, whistle HF 1220, A 3876, 3927; **p. in an yvy leef** go whistle TC 5.1433, A 1838.

pyrie *n* pear tree E 2217, 2325.

Q

quaad *adj* bad A 4357; **quade** *pl* B 1628.

quake *v* quake, tremble HF 604, TC 1.871, etc.; **quook** *pt 3 s* TC 3.93, A 1576.

quakke *n* hoarseness: **on the q.** hoarse, had a sore throat A 4152.

qualm *n* plague, death HF 1968, A 2014; croaking TC 5.382.

quappe *v* flutter TC 3.57.

quarter nyght *n* a quarter through the night, about nine o'clock A 3516.

quelle *v* kill B 4580, C 854; *3 s subj* G 705; *3 pl* dash, knock out TC 4.46.

queme *v* please TC 5.695; **queme(n)** *3 pl* TC 2.803, Gent 20.

quenche(n) *v* quench, put an end to TC 3.846, 1058; *3 s subj* TC 3.1456; **queynte** *pt 3 s* was quenched, went out A 2334, 2337; **queynt, yqueynt** quenched, extinguished TC 4.313, 5.543, A 3754.

quene *n* quean, harlot H 18.

querne, queerne *n* handmill HF 1798, B 3264.

queynte *n* pudendum A 3276, D 332.

queynt(e) *adj* strange, curious BD 531, HF 228, etc.; unfamiliar F 726; ingenious, skilful BD 784, A 3605; clever, crafty TC 4.1629, LGW 353, A 4051.

queynte *adv* subtly HF 245.

queynt(e) see **quenchen**.

queyntelych *adv* cunningly HF 1923.

quite(n), quyte *v* repay, give in return TC 4.1663, D 1292, H 293; requite, reward PF 112, TC 1.808, LGW 494; ransom A 1032; satisfy B 354; **quite** *3 s subj* give in return A 770; **quitte, quytte** *pt s & pl* released TC 4.205; paid back D 422; **quit, quyt** *pp* rewarded HF 1614;

quit, freed, released PF 663, F 1363, G 66; paid, satisfied TC 1.334; requited, paid back TC 2.242, D 483.

quitly *adv* freely A 1792.

quod *pt s* quoth BD 109, 136, etc.; **quoth** BD 90.

quoniam *n* pudendum D 608.

quyk *adj* quick F 194; **quyke** *def* alive BD 121, A 1015; **quike** living TC 1.411.

quyke(n), quike *v* quicken TC 3.484; become alive, revive HF 2078, TC 1.295; make live G 481; **quyked** *pt 3 s* came to life A 2335; *pp* enlivened F 1050.

quykkest *adj* busiest F 1502.

quyknesse *n* liveliness BD 26.

quyksilver *n* quicksilver A 629, G 772, etc.

quynyble *n* high treble A 3332.

quyrboilly *n* leather soaked in hot water, shaped, and dried B 2065.

quysshyn, -en *n* cushion TC 2.1229, 3.964.

quyt see **quiten**.

R

raa *n* roe (Northern) A 4086.

Raby *n* rabbi D 2187.

rad, radde see **reden**.

rage *n* madness BD 731; passion LGW 599; grief, distress F 836; violent wind A 1985.

rage *v* carry on, behave wantonly or foolishly A 257, 3273, 3958.

ragerye *n* wantonness D 455, E 1847.

rakel, racle *adj* rash TC 1.1067, 3.429, H 278; **rakle** hasty TC 3.1437.

rakelnesse *n* rashness H 283; **rekelnesse** Scogan 16.

rake-stele *n* rake handle D 949.

raket *n* the game of rackets TC 4.460 (see note).

rakle *v* act rashly TC 3.1642.

rammyssh *adj* ramlike, having a strong smell G 887.

rampeth *3 s* storms, rages B 3094.

ransake *v* ransack A 1005.

rape *n* haste Adam 7.

rape *v* take by force: **rape and renne** snatch and catch G 1422.

rascaille *n* worthless folk, rabble TC 5.1853.

rasour *n* razor HF 690, A 2417, B 3246.

rated *pp* scolded A 3463.

rathe *adv* early, soon HF 2139, TC 2.1088, etc.

rather *adj* earlier, former TC 3.1337, 5.1799.

rather *adv* sooner BD 562, TC 1.835, B 335; earlier C 643; rather, more readily A 487.

raughte see **reche**.

raunson *n* ransom A 1024, 1176; **maad his r.** paid the penalty D 411.

ravyne *n* rapacity PF 323, 336, 527.

ravysshe(n), -vi- *v* carry off by force TC 4.530, 637, 643; *fig* carry away TC 4.1474; **ravysedest** *pt 2 s* drew B 1659; **ravysshed** *pt 3 s* carried off E 2230; **ravysshed** *pp* carried off D 1676; carried away B 4514; enraptured E 1774.

ravysshyng *n* carrying off TC 1.62, 4.548.

rayed *pp* striped BD 252.

rayled *pp* enclosed TC 2.820.

real *adj* royal TC 3.1534, LGW 214, etc.

reawme *n* realm B 797, 1306; **realme** HF 704; **remes** *pl* B 4326.

rebekke *n* a kind of fiddle, used as a contemptuous term for an old woman D 1573.

recche¹, rekke *v pers & impers* care, have concern for PF 593, TC 1.797, E 1994; **recche, rekke** *1 s* A 1398, 2257; **rekkest** *2 s* D 1453; **rekketh** *3 s* LGW 365, D 53, E 2276; **recche** *2 pl* TC 2.1151; **men recche of it but smal** people care little for it F 71; **recche** *3 s subj* may care TC 4.630; **roghte, roughte** *pt s* BD 244, PF 111, TC 1.496; **roughte** *pt 1 s subj* would care TC 1.1039, 2.1428; **rekke** *imp s* B 4004, G 698.

recche² *imp s* interpret B 4086.

recchelees, -les *adj* careless, reckless B 229, 4626; negligent A 179; indifferent HF 668, E 488; **r. of** indifferent to B 4297.

receit(e) *n* recipe G 1353, 1366, 1384.

rechased *pp* chased back, headed back BD 379.

reche *v* reach, hand BD 47; **raughte** *pt 3 s* A 136, 2915; started, proceeded TC 2.447; **reighte** reached HF 1374.

reclayme *v* call back H 72 (see note).

recomaunde *v* commend, commit TC 2.1070, 4.1693; *1 s* TC 5.1414; *2 s subj* TC 1.1056.

recomende *v* commend G 544; *1 s* refer (for authority) B 3909.

recompensacioun *n* recompense HF 665, 1557.

reconforte *v* comfort TC 2.1672; *refl* be comforted A 2852; *2 pl subj* reassure TC 5.1395.

reconyssaunce *n* recognizance, promissory note B 1520.

record(e) *n* proof, supporting argument PF 609; statement BD 934; witness Scogan 22; reputation D 2049; **of r.** recorded D 2117.

recorde *v* call to mind TC 4.1518; remember TC 5.445; declare as a verdict A 1745; *1 s* recall A 829; **r. on** *imp s* think about, reflect on TC 3.1179; **recordynge** *part* rehearsing TC 3.51; recalling TC 5.718.

recours *n* recourse TC 2.1352; **wole have my r.** will return F 75.

recovere(n) *v* gain, obtain TC 3.181, 1406, 4.406; **rekever** *1 s as fut* remedy, make right HF 354; **recovered** *pp* recovered B 27; obtained PF 688; benefited TC 1.383.

recreant *adj* vanquished, faint-hearted TC 1.814.

rede *n* reed, rustic pipe HF 1221.

redely, -ily *adv* promptly, without delay C 667; truly HF 313, 1392, B 1604; in a state of readiness A 2276.

rede(n) *v* think, guess TC 2.129; read LGW 30, A 709, D 685; interpret BD 279, TC 5.1281; counsel, advise TC 1.83, E 1361; **rede** *1 s* speak, speak of HF 77, 1493; advise A 3068, C 793; **redest** *2 s* readest HF 1001; **ret** *3 s* advises TC 2.413; **rede** *3 s subj* may guide or protect HF 1067; **reden, rede** *pl* TC 1.241, E 1154, G 78; **radde, redde** *pt 3 s* TC 2.1085, D 714, 791; **radde, redden** *pt pl* TC 2.1706, 5.737, E 713; **rede, reed** *imp s* B 3769, 4320; **redeth** *imp pl* B 3650, C 586; **rad, red** *pp* read BD 224, A 2595, C 176, D 765.

redere *n* reader TC 5.270.

redoutynge *n* reverence A 2050.

redresse *v* set right, correct TC 3.1008; amend, improve E 431; **redressen hem** *3 pl* raise themselves TC 2.969; **redressed** *pt 3 s* compensated for F 1436.

reed, red, rede *n* counsel, advice BD 105, 1187, PF 586, TC 5.22, C 744; advantage, help, remedy BD 203, 587, A 1216; plan C 146; source of counsel, help A 665; **best to reede** best by way of counsel TC 4.679.

reed *adj* red A 153, etc.; **reede, rede** *def & pl* TC 3.1384, LGW 42, A 90.

reed *n* red LGW 533.

reednesse *n* redness G 1097, 1100.

rees *n* rush TC 4.350.

refere *v* return, revert TC 1.266.

refigurynge *part* reproducing TC 5.473.

refreyde(n) *v* grow cold, cool off TC 2.1343, 5.507, Rosem 21.

refuge *n* protection A 1720.

refus *pp* rejected TC 1.570.

refut *n* refuge, place of refuge TC 2.1014, B 546, 852, G 75.

regard *n* respect; **at r. of** in comparison with HF 1753, PF 58.

registre *n* register, list A 2812.

regne *n* kingdom A 866, etc.; rule, dominion A 1624; **regnes** *pl* kingdoms TC 5.1544, A 2373.

reherce(n), -se(n) *v* rehearse, repeat, say BD 190, 1296, A 732, D 1296; **rehersynge** *part* F 206.

rehersaille *n* enumeration, mention G 852.

rehersyng *n* recital A 1650; *pl* LGW 24.

reighte see **reche.**

rejoie *v refl* rejoice TC 5.395.

rekelnesse see **rakelnesse.**

rekene, rekne *v* reckon A 401, 1933, etc.; **yrekened** *pp* D 367, F 427.

rekenynge *n* reckoning A 600; *pl* A 760.

rekever see **recoveren.**

relayes *n pl* sets of fresh hunting dogs BD 362.

relees *n* remission, cessation; **out of r.** without ceasing G 46.

relente *v* melt G 1278.

relesse *v* release, free from B 1069; **relesse, releesse** *1 s* E 153, F 1613; **relessed** *pt 3 s* B 3367.

releve *v* relieve TC 5.1042; **releved** *pp* given relief A 4182; mitigated LGW 128.

religioun *n* religion A 477; monastic life B 3134, 3144.

relyk *n* relic C 949; sacred image TC 1.153; treasure, ?relict LGW 321 (see note).

remedye *n* remedy A 1216, etc.; effective means TC 4.1623.

remenaunt *n* rest, remainder A 724, 888, etc.

remes see **reawme.**

remeve, -moeven *v* remove TC 1.691, F 1221; **remoeve** *2 pl subj* F 993; **remoeved** *pt pl* moved F 1205; **remoeveth** *imp pl* G 1008; **remewed** *pp* F 181.

remorde *3 s subj* cause remorse TC 4.1491.

remuable *adj* changeable TC 4.1682.

ren *n* run A 4079.

renably *adv* reasonably D 1509.

rende *v* ·tear TC 4.1493; **rent** *3 s* tears LGW 646; **rente** *pt 3 s* tore TC 4.1700, A 990; **rente of** tore away TC 3.1099; **rent, yrent** *pp* torn HF 776, TC 5.1654, B 844.

renegat *n* renegade B 933.

reneye(n) *v* renounce, abjure B 376, 3751, G 268; **reneye** *1 s subj* G 464; **reneyed** *pt pl* B 340; *pp* LGW 336, B 915; **reneye** *imp s* G 459.

renges *n pl* ranks, rows A 2594.

renne(n) run HF 202, PF 247, B 3454;

renne *1 s* LGW 60; **rennest** *2 s* TC 4.1549; **renneth** *3 s* LGW 503, A 1761; **renne(n)** *3 pl* LGW 641, B 4373; **ran** *pt 3 s* A 509; **ran, ronnen** *pt pl* BD 163, A 2925, B 4571; **rennynge** *part* BD 161, HF 2145; **yronne(n)** *pp* TC 2.907, A 8, 2693; **rape and renne** G 1422 (see note).

rennere *n* runner D 1283.

rennyng *n* running A 551.

renomee *n* renown D 1159.

renovelaunces *n pl* renewings HF 693.

rente *n* income TC 4.85, A 373; regular income A 256 (see note); revenue B 3401, 3572; tribute BD 765; what is due D 1821; **to r.** as payment due TC 2.830.

rentynge *n* tearing A 2834.

repair *n* frequenting B 1211, D 1224.

repaire *v* return HF 755, TC 5.1571, F 589; go (repeatedly) TC 3.5, B 4410; **repaireth** *3 s* returns B 967, 3885; **repeireth** F 339; **repeyreth** TC 5.1837; **repeirynge** *part* F 608.

reparacions *n pl* amends, reconciliations HF 688.

repeled *pp* repealed TC 4.294.

repentaunce *n* repentance BD 1114, A 1776; regret, sorrow for what is past TC 3.1308.

repleccioun *n* repletion, surfeit B 4027; *pl* B 4113.

replicacioun *n* reply, rejoiner, rebuttal PF 536; A 1846.

replye *v* reply, answer a charge LGW 343; **repplye agayn** object to E 1609.

reportour *n* reporter A 814.

reprehencioun *n* reproof TC 1.684.

repressioun *n* restraint, control TC 3.1038.

reprevable *adj* deserving of reproof C 632.

repreve, -preeve *n* reproof TC 2.1140, D 16; a reproach C 595; blameworthy matter D 84.

repreve *v* reproach F 1537; *3 s subj* may reproach D 937; **repreeve** *2 pl* D 1177; **repreve** *imp s* TC 1.669.

requere *v* request D 1052; *1 s* TC 2.358, D 1010; **requere(n)** *2 pl* TC 2.473, 5.1600; **required** *pt s* required E 430.

resalgar *n* an arsenic compound (ratsbane) G 814.

rescous, -cus *n* rescue TC 1.478, A 2643.

rescowe *v* rescue, save TC 3.857, 5.231; **rescowed** *pt 3 s* LGW 515.

rese *v* shake A 1986.

resigne *1 s* resign TC 1.432; consign B 780; **resygne** *3 pl* refrain from TC 3.25.

resort *n* source of aid TC 3.134.

resoun *n* reason A 37, etc.; reasoning, argument HF 708, 761; **resons** *pl* opinions A 274; **by r.** with good reason C 458.

resouneth *3 s* resounds A 1278; **resouned** *pt s* resounded F 413.

respect *n* respect; **to r. of** in comparison with TC 4.86, 5.1818.

respit *n* delay TC 5.137, A 948; respite G 543.

respiten *v* grant an extension of time F 1582.

resport *n* regard TC 4.86, 850.

reste *n* rest, repose A 30, 820, etc.; **restes** *pl* TC 2.1722; **at his r.** at its natural resting place F 1212.

reste(n) *v* rest D 1299; remain TC 3.1435, D 1736; set at rest TC 2.1326 3.1281; **reste** *3 s subj* remain quiet PF 514; *2 pl subj* rest F 126.

retenue *n* retinue A 2502, E 270; **at his r.** among his following D 1355.

rethor *n* rhetorician B 4397, F 38.

rethorik(e) *n* rhetoric HF 859, E 32, F 719; **colours of rethoryk** figures of speech, rhetorical devices F 726.

retourne, -torne *v* return TC 5.596, B 986; **retourne** *1 s subj* TC 3.1483; *2 s subj* TC 4.1553; **retorneth** *3 s* TC 4.1003; **retourne** *1 pl subj* let us return E 597; **retourne** *2 pl* TC 5.1351; **retourneth** *imp pl* E 809; **retornyng** *part* turning over (in the mind) TC 5.1023; **retournynge** *as n* A 2095; **retourned, retorned** *pp* TC 3.1534, 4.1143.

reufully *adv* sadly TC 3.65.

reule *n* rule A 173.

reule(n) *v* rule, govern TC 5.758, B 4234; **reulith** *3 s* TC 2.1377; **reuled, ruled** *pp* TC 1.336, A 816; *as adj* marked by self-control LGW 163.

reuthe see **routhe.**

reve *n* reeve A 542, 587, etc.

revel *n* revelry A 2717, 3652; riotous living A 4397; **revels** *pl* revels C 65.

revelour *n* reveler A 4391, D 453.

revelous *adj* pleasure-loving B 1194.

reve(n) *v* take away, deprive TC 1.188, 2.1659, G 376; **reveth** *3 s* takes away PF 86; **rafte, refte** *pt 3 s* D 888, H 305; **raft, yraft, reft** *pp* TC 5.1258, A 2015, F 1017.

reverence *n* respect A 141, B 116; honor, dignity A 312, E 196, 1021; **doon r.** show respect or courtesy TC 3.212, H 142; **at r. of** out of respect for TC 3.40.

revers *n* reverse B 4167, D 2056.

revesten *3 pl* clothe again TC 3.353.

revoken *v* restore to consciousness, bring to TC 3.1118.

reward *n* regard PF 426, TC 5.1736, LGW 375.

rewe *n dat*: **by r., in (on) a r.** in order, successively, in a row HF 1692, A 2866, D 506.

reweful *adj as n* pitiable person B 854.

rewefulleste *adj* most sorrowful A 2886.

rewel boon *n* whalebone, ivory B 2068.

rewe(n) *v* feel sorry, repent TC 5.1070, A 3530, G 729; take pity TC 5.260, A 2382; **rewest** *2 s* B 854; **me reweth** *3 s* I regret A 3462, E 2432; **rewe** *3 s subj* TC 2.789, A 1863; *2 pl subj* TC 4.98; **rewe** *imp s* have pity B 853; **reweth, rueth** *imp pl* TC 4.1501, F 974; **rewed** *pp* TC 4.1141.

rewthelees see **routhelees**.

reye *n* rye D 1746.

reyes *n pl* round dances HF 1236.

reyn, rayn *n* rain A 492, H 301, etc.

reyne *n* rein TC 5.90, A 4083, F 313; **reynes** *pl* HF 951, A 904.

reyne *v* rain TC 3.551, 4.299; **reyneth** *3 s* rains TC 3.562, A 1535; **reyne** *3 pl* TC 4.846, 5.1336; **reyned** *pt 3 s* TC 3.1557; **ron** *pt 3 s* rained TC 3.640, 677.

reysed *pp* campaigned, made a military expedition A 54.

reyse(n), reise *v* raise TC 2.1585; raise, build D 2102; **r. up** collect D 1390; **reysed** *pp* raised BD 1278; **raysed** roused, stirred up TC 5.1471.

ribaudye *n* ribaldry A 3866, C 324.

ribibe *n* a kind of fiddle, used contemptuously for an old woman D 1377.

ribible *n* rebeck, an early type of violin A 4396; **rubible** A 3331.

riche *adj* rich A 479, etc.; expensive, magnificent A 296, 2199; *as n* rich people A 248.

richesse *n* riches, wealth A 1255, D 1110; abundance TC 3.349.

ridyng *n* procession A 4377.

right *adj* right (opp. to left) A 554, 1959; very A 257; **righte** *(def)* correct A 1263; direct B 1130, F 1240; own TC 2.1065, F 1311.

right *adv* very A 288, 1140; directly BD 182; exactly A 535, 661, etc.; also many other uses still current.

right *n* right, privilege TC 1.591, etc.; **of r.** as a right F 1324; **at alle rightes** at all points, in every respect A 1852, 2100.

rightful *adj* righteous PF 55; just A 1719, B 814; rightful PF 639.

rightwisnesse *n* righteousness C 637, D 1909, Gent 8.

rigour *n* harshness, severity F 775.

riot, ryot *n* riotous living, dissipation A 4392, 4395, C 465; wanton revels D 700.

riote *v* riot, dissipate A 4414

riotour *n* reveler, dissolute person C 692, 876; **riotoures** *pl* C 661, 716, 768.

robbour *n* robber B 3818; *pl* G 659.

roche *n* rock HF 1116, TC 3.1497, F 500; *pl* BD 156, HF 1035.

rode *n* complexion A 3317, B 1917.

rode, roode *n* rood, cross BD 923, HF 2, TC 5.1860.

rody *adj* ruddy BD 143, 905, F 384, 394.

roialliche *adv* royally A 378.

rokes *n gen pl* rooks, crows HF 1516.

rollen *v* turn over (in the mind) TC 2.659; **roule** roam, wander D 653; **rolleth** *3 s* rolls A 2614; turns over TC 5.1313, C 838; **rolled** *pt 3 s* D 2217; **rolled** *pp* turned over, discussed TC 5.1061.

rombled *pt 3 s* felt around G 1322; *pt pl* made a tumult B 3725.

romen *v* roam HF 1293, A 1099; **rometh** *3 s* A 1119; **romed** *pt s &* *pl* BD 443, HF 140; **romyng(e)** *part* TC 2.555, A 1071.

ron see **reyne**.

ronges *n pl* rungs A 3625.

roode beem *n* roodbeam, a beam supporting a large cross at the entrance to the choir A 496.

roore *n* uproar TC 5.45.

roore, rore *v* roar HF 1589, B 4078; **roreth** *3 s* TC 4.241, A 2881.

roost *n* roast A 206.

rooste *v* roast A 383; **rosted** *pt 3 s* A 4137; **rosted** *pp* A 147, D 1841.

roote *n* root A 2, etc.; essential part G 1461; foot (of a mountain) E 58; exact moment of birth B 314; **rootes** *pl* astrological data F 1276 (see note); **on r.** well rooted TC 2.1378.

rooteles *adj* rootless TC 4.770.

ropen *pp* reaped LGW 74.

roryng *n* a cry of grief E 2364.

rote[1] *n* musical instrument A 236 (see note).

rote[2] *n* habit, practice; **by r.** by heart A 327, B 1712, C 332.

roten *adj* rotten HF 1778, A 3873.

rotie *3 s subj* corrupt A 4407.

rouketh *3 s* cowers A 1308.

roule see **rollen**.

rouncy *n* a horse of small size, originally a pack horse, often used for riding A 390.

rounded *pt 3 s* assumed a round shape A 263.

roundel *n* roundel, song PF 675 (see note), A 1530; **roundell** small circle HF 791.

rounynges *n pl* whisperings HF 1960.

route *n* company BD 819, HF 1771, A 622, etc.; **rowte** A 3854.

route[1] *v* roar HF 1038, TC 3.743.

route[2] *v* snore BD 172; **routeth, rowteth** *3 s* A 3647, 4167.

route[3] *v* assemble B 540.

routhe, rowthe, reuthe *n* pity BD 592, 1310, PF 427, etc.; sorrow LGW 669, E 562.

routhelees, -les, rew- *adj* without pity PF 613, TC 2.346, B 863.

rowe *n* row HF 1451; line (of verse) HF 448.

rowe *adj* rough G 861.

rowe *adv* angrily TC 1.206.

rowm *adj* large, roomy A 4126.

rowne(n) *v* whisper TC 3.568, B 2025, G 894; **rowned, rouned** *pt 3 s* HF 2044, D 1021; **rownynge** *part* E 2130; **rouned, yrouned** HF 722, 2107.

rowtyng[1] *n* roaring HF 1933.

rowtyng[2] *n* snoring A 4166, 4214.

rubee *n* ruby HF 1362.

rubible see **ribible**.

rubifiyng *n* reddening G 797.

rubriche *n* rubric D 346.

ruddok *n* English robin PF 349.

ruggy *adj* shaggy A 2883.

rumbel, -bul *n* rumbling A 1979; tumult E 997.

rused *pt 3 s* ran to and fro (to obscure its tracks) BD 381.

ryde(n), ride(n) *v* ride BD 371, TC 1.838, A 102, etc.; **riden out** take to the field, go on a military expedition A 45; **ride, ryde** *1 s* A 2252, D 1449; **rydest** *2 s* D 1451; **rydestow** ridest thou D 1386; **ryde** *2 s subj* B 4002; **rideth, rydeth, rit** A 974, 1691, B 375; **ride(n), ryde(n)** *pl* A 780, B 399, D 1274, 1418; **ryde** *2 pl subj* B 1450, C 748; **rood** *pt 3 s* A 169, 390; **riden, ryden** *pt pl* A 825, C 968; **rid, ryd** *imp s* TC 2.1013, 1020; **ryde** *imp pl* B 3117, D 1469; **ridynge** *part* E 777; **riden** *pp* A 48, 57; **ryde or go** ride or walk D 1942.

ryghtwis *adj* righteous LGW 373, 905.

rymeyed *pp* rimed F 711.

rynde *n* hide(?) TC 2.642.

rynge *v* ring A 2359, etc.; **rong** *pt s* A 3215, C 662; **ronge** *pt pl* BD 1164; **ryng** *imp s* proclaim HF 1720; **ronge** *pp* TC 2.805, 5.1062.

rype *adj* mature E 220, 438.

rys *n* branch A 3324.

ryse, rise *v* rise TC 1.278, A 33; **riseth, rist** *3 s* rises A 1493, B 864; arises TC 1.944, 2.812 *(refl)*; **ryse, rise, rysen** A 3768, B 420; **roos** *pt s* rose TC 2.88, A 823; **rys, ris** *imp s* TC 2.944, E 2138; **rysen, risen** A 1065, B 1279.

rysshe *n* rush TC 3.1161.

ryve *v* pierce, stab TC 5.1560, C 828; **rof** *pt 3 s* stabbed HF 373, LGW 661.

ryver(e), river *n* river PF 184, A 3024, etc.; **for r.** beside the river TC 4.413, B 1927.

S

sad *adj* sober PF 578, E 220, 293; constant, steadfast BD 860, E 1047, H 275; trustworthy B 135, H 258; **wexen sadde** have their fill G 877.

sad *adv* quietly E 564.

sadly *adv* firmly D 2264, E 1100; seriously B 1266; deeply B 743.

sadnesse *n* steadfastness E 452, 1591.

saffron *v* color, adorn C 345.

saffroun *n* saffron, yellow B 1920.

sal armonyak *n* sal ammoniac G 798.

sal peter *n* saltpeter, rock-salt G 808.

sal preparat *n* ordinary salt G 810.

sal tartre *n* salt of tartar G 810.

salue, saluwe *v* greet, salute TC 2.1016, 1257, B 1723; **salueth, saleweth** *3 s* A 1492, B 1284; **salwed** *pt 1 s* LGW 315; **salewed** *pp* F 1310.

saluyng *n* saluting, greeting A 1649; **saluynges** *pl* salutations TC 2.1568.

salwes *n pl* willow branches D 655.

samyt *n* samite, a costly silk TC 1.109.

sang *n* song (Northern) A 4170.

sangwyn *adj* ruddy A 333, 2168.

sangwyn *n* cloth of a blood-red (or purple?) color A 439.

sanz *prep* without B 501.

sapience *n* wisdom B 1662, D 1197; **sapiences** *pl* qualities of mind G 338.

sarge *n* serge A 2568.

satiry *n* satyrs (collectively) TC 4.1544.

sauce *n* sauce, gravy A 129, B 4024, C 545.

saucefleem *adj* afflicted with pimples A 625.

sauf *adj* safe B 343, D 1015.

saufly *adv* safely B 4398, D 878, E 870.

saugh, sawgh see **seen.**

saule *n* soul A 4187, 4263.

sautrie, saw- *n* psaltery A 296 (see note), 3305, H 268.

savacioun, sal- *n* salvation D 621, 1618, G 75; safekeeping TC 1.464, 4.1382; preservation HF 208.

save *n* sage (the herb), also the infusion of many herbs A 2713.

save *prep & conj* save, except A 683, 1410, etc.; (followed by nom.) B 627; except that B 1359.

save(n) *v* save, keep, preserve A 3533, 3949, C 200.

savory *adj* pleasant TC 1.405.

savour *n* smell, odor D 2226, G 91, 887; taste, pleasure TC 2.269.

savoure *v* taste D 171; *imp s* have a taste for Truth 5.

savourly *adv* with relish A 3735.

savynge *prep* except A 2838, 3971, B 1486.

sawe *n* saying A 1163, D 660; speech, what one says TC 5.38, G 691, 1441; **al his s.** all that he said A 1526; **sawes** *pl* expressions TC 2.41.

say see **seen.**

sayn(e) see **seyen.**

scabbe *n* mange in sheep C 358.

scalded *pp* burnt A 3853.

scalle *n* skin disease, esp. of the scalp Adam 3.

scalled *adj* scabby A 627.

scape(n) *v* escape A 1107, 3608; **scape** *3 s subj* A 3800; **scaped** *pp* LGW 131, B 1151.

scarlet *n* a rich material, usually (but not always) red A 456.

scarlet in grayn *n* cochineal B 1917 (see note).

scarmuch(e) *n* skirmish TC 2.611, 934, 5.1508.

scarsetee *n* scarcity G 1393.

scarsly, sk- *adv* scarcely BD 283, TC 2.43; economically A 583.

scathe, sk- *n* harm TC 4.207, 5.938; matter for regret, a pity A 446, E 1172.

science *n* learning, knowledge A 316, G 896; art, manifestation of skill B 1666.

sclaundre, sk- *n* reproach, ill-fame HF 1580, B 1373, E 722.

sclaundre *v* defame, reproach G 998; *1 s* G 993; **sclaundrest** *2 s* G 695.

scole *n* school B 1685; fashion A 125, 3329; **in s.** in the schools (universities) B 4427, D 2186; **to the s. is** instructive to thee TC 1.634.

scole-matere *n* matters discussed in the schools D 1272.

scoler *n* scholar A 260, 3190.

scoleward *adv* on the way to school B 1739.

scoleye *v* study, attend school A 302; **scoleiyng** *part* studying, learning D 44f.

scorn *n* contempt A 3388, 4110.

scorne(n) *v* mock TC 1.234, 5.982, G 506; scorn HF 91; **skorneth** *3 s* makes a mockery of BD 625; **scorned** *pt 3 s* derided, mocked BD 927, TC 1.303, B 4277; **scorne** *imp* mock TC 1.576.

scrippe *n* wallet, bag D 1737, 1777; *pl* HF 2123.

scripture *n* posy, inscription on a

ring TC 3.1369; *pl* books, writings A 2044.

scrit *n* writing, deed TC 2.1130, E 1697.

scriveyn *n* copyist, scribe Adam 1.

scryvenysh *adv* in a formal or stilted style TC 2.1026.

seche, seke(n) *v* seek BD 1255, TC 1.707, A 13; search (out) TC 4.943, D 650; pursue PF 340, G 1442; dwell upon TC 1.704; **seke upon** attack D 1494; **seche** *1 s* TC 5.940; **sekestow** seekest thou TC 3.1455; **seketh** *3 s* D 919; **seken, seche(n)** *pr pl* HF 626, TC 2.1068, A 1266, G 863; **soghte** *pt 3 s* searched B 513; **soughte** explored TC 5.1237; **soghte** *pt 3 s subj* should seek C 488; **soghte, soughte(n)** *pt pl* TC 2.937, C 772, G 361; **soght, isought** *pp* HF 626, TC 3.1317.

secree *adj* secret TC 3.286, B 1320; confidential, discreet, able to keep a secret B 4105, E 1909.

secree *n* secrets (collectively) D 1341.

secree *adv* secretly F 1109.

secreely, secrely *adv* secretly E 763, 2006.

secreenesse *n* secrecy B 773.

secte *n* sect, religion F 17; sex E 1171 (see note); **secte saturnyn** the Jewish religion HF 1432.

seculer, -leer *adj* lay as opposed to clerical B 4640, E 1251, 1322.

see *n* seat TC 4.1023; (of government) B 3339; **s. imperiall** throne HF 1361; *pl* seats HF 1210, 1251.

se(e) *n* sea A 276, etc.; **the grete s., Grete See** the Mediterranean BD 140, A 59.

seel *n* prosperity A 4239.

see(n), se(n) *v* see, behold HF 2117, TC 1.569, A 914; look (at) TC 3.359, 5.667; **to sene** seem, appear LGW 224; **fair to seene, semely on to see** pleasant to look at BD 1177, D 1245; **see, se** *1 s* BD 477, 913; **seest** *2 s* A 2232; **sestow** seest thou TC 3.46; **seeth** *3 s* BD 595, B 266; **se(e), seen** *pl* PF 464, 600, TC 2.339; **se(e)** *pr subj* TC 1.997, 2.372; **God yow see** may God watch over you TC 2.85, D 2169; **say, sey, seigh, sigh, sy, saugh, sawgh, saw** *pt 1 & 3 s* BD 500, 806, HF 296, 989, 1162, TC 2.1144, A 3128, G 1381; **say, sey, seye(n), sye(n), sawe** *pt pl* HF 504, TC 2.277, 5.816, E 985, 1114, 1804, G 110; **se** *imp s* TC 1.901, A 1801; **seyn, sayn, seye, yseyn, yseye** *pp* HF 1367, TC 2.168, 3.1060, B 172, D 552; **see for** look out for B 127. See **ysee.**

seeth see sethe.

seigh see seen.

seillynge *part* sailing F 851.

seinte *adj* holy D 1824.

seintuarie *n* box containing relics C 953.

sek, seeke see sik.

selde, seelde *adv* seldom A 1539, E 427; seelde tyme seldom-times E 146.

selve *adj* (*def*) same PF 96, TC 4.1240, A 2584; very B 115.

sely¹ *adj* wonderful HF 513.

sely² *adj* blissful TC 4.503; good, virtuous B 682, 1702; simple, unsophisticated TC 4.1490, D 1906; poor, hapless TC 3.1191, A 3404, D 370; insignificant TC 1.338.

selynesse *n* happiness TC 3.813, 825.

semblable *adj* similar E 1500.

semblant *n* semblance E 928; in semblaunt seemingly F 516.

seme, seeme *v* seem B 1092, C 52, etc.; yow semeth it seems to you F 1497; the peple semed it seemed to the people F 201.

semelieste *adj* (*def*) handsomest H 119.

semely *adj* suitable A 751; comely BD 1177, B 1919.

semely *adv* becomingly A 123, 136.

semy *adj* thin, delicate A 3697, Rosem 11.

semycope *n* short cloak A 262.

sencer *n* censer A 3340.

sendal *n* a kind of thin, rich silk A 440.

sende(n) *v* send A 426, 2976; sendeth, sent 3 s A 2962, E 1151; sente, sende *pt 3 s* TC 2.1734, A 400, 4136; sente *pt 3 s subj* should send B 1091, E 1665; sent, ysent *pp* HF 612, A 2870.

sene *adj* visible BD 498, 941; evident BD 413, LGW 694. Cf. ysene.

senge *v* singe D 349; seynd *pp* broiled B 4035.

sensynge *part* censing A 3341.

sentement *n* sensation, feeling TC 4.1177; sentiment, emotion TC 2.13, 3.43.

sentence *n* opinion PF 530, LGW 381, B 1139; maxim B 113; thought, meaning HF 710, 1100, TC 1.393; substance C 157, G 81; subject B 1753, 4404; insight B 4540; wisdom, moral truth A 798; heigh s. deep insight B 3938.

septemtrioun *n* north B 3657.

serement *n* oath F 1534.

sergeant *n* servant; officer employed in the enforcement of the law E 519, etc.; Sergeant of the Lawe lawyer of the highest rank A 309 (see note).

sermone *v* preach, speak C 879.

sermonyng *n* talking, arguing A 3091, 3597, 3899.

sermoun, -mon *n* sermon D 1789; discourse TC 2.965, 1115, 1299.

servage *n* bondage, servitude A 1946, B 368; service BD 769.

servaunt *n* servant A 1421, etc.; servant of love A 1814.

served *pt 3 s* preserved, kept hidden F 521.

serve(n) *v* serve TC 1.370, A 2380; treat, deal with E 641; served *pt 3 s* A 749; served, yserved *pp* A 963, D 2279.

servitute *n* servitude, restriction E 798.

servysable *adj* useful, serviceable A 99; eager to serve, attentive E 1911; hard-working E 979.

serye *n* succession of points in an argument A 3067.

sese *3 s subj* seize PF 481; sesed *pp* put in possession TC 3.445.

sessiouns *n pl* meetings of the Justices of the Peace A 355.

sethe *v* boil A 383; seeth *pt 3 s* boiled E 227.

sette(n) *v* set, place A 815, etc.; value, care TC 3.900; sette 1 s value A 1570, B 4280; set 3 s sets BD 635, D 1982; sette 2 pl value TC 2.432; 3 pl bedecked E 382; sette *pt 1 & 3 s* A 507, D 215; sette, setten *pt pl* A 4383, B 1118; set, yset *pp* A 132, 666; agreed A 1635; I sette the worste I set up the worst hypothetical case TC 2.367; sette a caas set up an imaginary case TC 2.729.

seur *adv* surely TC 3.1633, 4.421.

seurete, seurte, suretee *n* pledge A 1604, F 528; security, confidence HF 723, TC 2.833, C 937; surety, collateral B 243, F 1581.

sewe, suwe *v* follow TC 1.379, Gent 4; seweth 3 s follows HF 840; sewed *pt 3 s* pursued B 4527; sewynge *part* suitable, proportioned BD 959.

sewes *n pl* broths F 67.

sexte *adj* sixth HF 1727.

sexteyn *n* sacristan B 3126, D 1859.

sey, seye(n) see seen.

seye(n), seyn(e), sayn(e), say *v* say BD 514, 1090, 1194, TC 1.12, A 1268; tell, relate B 1677, D 828, F 715; recite, repeat HF 289, D 1933; seye, sey 1 s A 855, 3153; seist, seyst 2 s A 1605, D 254; seistow, seystow sayest thou A 1125, 3490; seith, seyth, seyeth 3 s HF 360, A 178, 1868; seye(n), seyn, sayn, sygge *pl* TC 4.194, A 1198, 3598, D 945, 1934; sygge we say we TC 4.194; seye 3 s subj C 187, D 119; 3 pl subj TC 2.801;

seyde, sayde, sayede *pt 3 s* BD 215, A 70; told PF 46; reported G 542; seyden *pt pl* B 211; sey, say *imp s* BD 366, A 3905; seyd, ysayd *pp* BD 270, 1145; as who seyth as one may say TC 5.883; was (for) to seye was about, meant A 3605, B 1713.

seyl *n* sail A 696, B 833.

seynd see senge.

shaar *n* plowshare A 3763.

shadde *pt 3 s* fell, poured B 3921.

shadwe *n* shadow B 7, 1199, etc.

shake *v* shake A 1473; shaketh 3 s E 1849; shook *pt 3 s* A 2265; shoken *pt pl* HF 1315; shake *pp* shaken A 406.

shal 1 s owe, owe to TC 3.791, 1649; 1 & 3 s future auxiliary shal, must A 187, etc.; shalt, shul 2 s BD 750, D 1611; shaltow, shaltou shalt thou A 1391, 3565; shal, shul, shulle, shullen *pl* BD 205, A 2356, C 365, D 1331; sholde, shoolde shulde *pt 1 & 3 s* BD 188, LGW 373, A 184, 1380; sholdest, shuldest *pt 2 s* BD 187, A 1137; sholde, sholden *pt pl* TC 5.1825, A 506, B 478, 1542.

shale *n* shell HF 1281.

shalemyes *n pl* shawms (wind instrument) HF 1218.

shame *n* shame D 1393; modesty D 342, 782; embarrassment TC 3.80, D 541; disgrace C 580, D 964; loss of self-esteem BD 617; immorality B 3483; violation of chastity LGW 488, C 214; reproach, insult TC 3.637, LGW 467; injury B 829; shames *gen s as adj* shameful B 819, E 2377; doth . . . s. injure A 1555.

shamefast *adj* modest A 2055, C 55.

shamefastnesse *n* modesty C 55; shyness, bashfulness A 840.

shap *n* shape PF 373, A 1889, etc.

shape(n) *v* arrange, see to it TC 3.196, E 1632; *refl* prepare, arrange TC 5.1211, A 809; shape(n) *pr pl* TC 4.1273, A 772, B 966; shoop, shop *pt 1 & 3 s* determined TC 1.207; planned, arranged E 198, 946; *refl* intended D 1538, 1780; prepared, arranged TC 3.551, LGW 180, F 809; shopen *pt pl* arranged, decided F 897; shapeth *imp p.* TC 4.925, 934; shape(n), yshape *pp* shaped TC 3.411, D 1463; constituted, destined B 3099, E 275; established, ordained TC 2.1092, A 1392, Scogan 8; appointed B 253; determined A 1225, B 142; prepared TC 2.282.

shaply *adj* fit A 372; likely, apt TC 4.1452.

sharpeth *3 s* sharpens A 3763.

shave *v* shave A 3326; **shave, yshave** *pp* shaved A 588, B 1499.

shawe *n* grove, thicket TC 3.720, A 4367, D 1386.

she, shee *pron* BD 83, 90, etc.; **hir, hyr, hire, her** *gen* BD 80, 124, HF 132, TC 1.285; **hires, heres, hyrs** BD 1040, PF 482, TC 1.889; **hir, hire, her, here** *dat & acc* BD 81, 200, HF 1003, A 1052.

sheeld *n* (*as pl*) gold coins with a shield on the reverse, known as *florins d'escu* B 1521; **sheeldes** A 278.

sheene, shene *adj* bright, shining, beautiful TC 2.824, PF 299, A 115, 160.

sheene *adv* brightly TC 4.1239.

shende(n) *v* put to shame, discomfit TC 5.893; ruin TC 4.1496, B 927; injure, damage HF 1016, TC 4.1577; **shende** *1 s* reproach TC 5.1274; **shendeth** *3 s* ruins B 28; **shende** *3 s subj* corrupt A 4410; **shenden** *2 pl* spoil TC 2.590; **shende** *3 pl* destroy D 376; **shente** *pt 1 & 3 s* injured TC 2.357, B 4031; **shent, yshent** *pp* brought to shame, disgraced B 931, H 328; put to shame D 1312; scolded B 1731; ruined E 1320; corrupted A 2754; spoiled TC 2.38.

shenketh *3 s* pours E 1722.

shepne *n* stable, shed A 2000; **shipnes** *pl* cowsheds D 781.

shere, sheere *n* shears A 2417, B 3246; **sheres** *pl* D 722.

shere *v* shear, cut B 3257; **shorn, yshorn, yshore** *pp* shorn TC 4.996, A 589, B 3142; clipped TC 1.222.

sherte *n* shirt TC 3.738, A 1566, etc.

shete, sheete *v* shoot LGW 635, A 3928.

shetere *n as adj* shooter PF 180.

shette(n) *v* shut D 1141, G 517; **shette** *pt 3 s* TC 2.1090; enclosed LGW 677; **shette, shetten** *pt pl* B 3722; shut up TC 1.148; **shette** *imp s* G 1137; **shet, yshette** *pp* BD 335, TC 3.233 (*pl*).

shewe(n) *v* show B 477, 1000; present D 2219; **sheweth** *3 s* B 882; **shewed(e)** *pt 3 s* PF 56, F 1200; **sheweth** *imp pl* C 179; **shewed, yshewed** *pp* H 1095, TC 5.1251.

shifte *v* provide D 104; assign G 278.

shilde *v* protect TC 4.188; **God shilde** *3 s subj* A 3427, B 1356.

shipman *n* ship owner A 388; **shipmen** *pl* sailors HF 2122.

shipnes see shepne.

shirreve *n* sheriff A 359.

shiten *pp* befouled A 504.

shode *n* the part in the hair A 3316; crown of the head A 2007.

shof *pt 3 s* pushed PF 154, TC 3.487; **shove** *pp* TC 3.1026, F 1281.

sholder-boon *n* shoulder blade C 350.

shonde *n* shame HF 88, B 2098.

sho(o) *n* shoe A 253, D 492; **shoon** *pl* B 1922.

shorte *v* shorten TC 5.96, A 791, D 1261; *3 s subj* D 365.

shortly *adv* shortly, briefly A 30; in brief BD 434, D 1077.

short-sholdred *adj* stocky(?) A 549 (see note).

shot *n* arrow A 2544, B 4539; **shotes** *pl* TC 2.58.

shot-wyndowe *n* casement window A 3358, 3695.

shour *n* shower TC 4.751; rain storm A 3520, 3574; assault, encounter TC 4.47; **shoures** *pl* showers A 1; combats, battles TC 1.470, 3.1064.

showvyng *n* shoving H 53.

shredde *pt 3 s* cut up E 227.

shrewe *n* worthless person of either sex, rascal A 3907, C 496, D 505; **shrewes** *pl* rascals G 746.

shrewe *1 s* beshrew, curse B 4616, D 446.

shrewed *adj* cursed D 54; evil, wicked HF 275, 1619.

shrewednesse *n* evil, wickedness HF 1627, TC 2.858; evil disposition D 734.

shrichyng *n* screeching TC 5.382.

shrifte, shryfte *n* absolution BD 1114; confession G 277.

shrifte-fadres *n pl* father-confessors D 1442.

shrighte *pt 3 s* shrieked A 2817, B 4552, F 417; **shright** *pp* TC 5.320.

shryne *n* shrine TC 5.553; casket LGW 672.

shryve *1 s* shrive TC 2.440; **shryven, yshryve(n)** *pp* shriven A 226, C 380, D 2095; absolved (on condition of giving up an evil practice) D 1440; disclosed TC 2.579.

shulder *n* shoulder TC 2.671, A 2163; **shuldres** *pl* BD 952, A 678.

shyne *n* shin A 386; **shynes** *pl* A 1279.

shyne *v* shine TC 4.299; **shyneth** *3 s* is clear, sunny A 1535.

shyvere *n* sliver, thin slice D 1840.

shyveren *3 pl* shiver, break A 2605.

sigh see seen.

signal *n* sign TC 4.818; *pl* HF 459.

signe *n* sign A 2266; evidence A 226; *pl* symptoms C 891.

signifiaunce *n* significance H 17, TC 5.362; sign TC 5.1447.

significavit *n* a writ beginning with the word A 662 (see note).

sik, syk, sek *adj* sick, ill BD 557, HF 1270, A 3993; **sike, seeke** *def & pl* A 18, 245, 424; **the syke** *as n* the sick man PF 104; **for syk** because of illness D 394.

sik, syk *n* sigh TC 2.145, 3.801; *pl* TC 5.646, A 1920.

sike, syke *v* sigh TC 1.192, 5.1006, A 3488; **siketh, syketh** *3 s* PF 404, E 1940; **sighte, siked, syked** *pt 3 s* TC 3.1056, A 2985, E 545; **siked** *pp* TC 5.738.

siker *adj* sure, certain BD 1020, G 934; steady D 2069; safe G 864.

siker *adv* surely, certainly TC 2.991, D 465, G 1047; confidently TC 3.1237.

sikerer *adj* more certain, dependable B 4043.

sikerly *adv* surely, certainly, assuredly HF 1930, A 137, B 1344, E 184.

sikernesse, sy- *n* certainty BD 608; safety TC 3.1243, B 425; security TC 2.773, E 1280.

siklich *adj* sikly TC 2.1528, 1543.

sikly *adv* ill, with ill feeling E 625.

sikynge *n* sighing TC 1.724.

similitude, simy- *n* counterpart F 480; a person of like age or station A 3228; comparison, parable G 431.

singuleer *adj* individual G 997; **synguler** special HF 310.

sire, syre *n* father TC 4.1455; master A 355; man of the house, husband D 713; title of address (Sir) A 837, etc.

sisoures *n pl* scissors HF 690.

sith *conj* since BD 759, TC 1.998, etc.

sith *prep* since TC 2.143, F 1536.

sith, syth, sitthe *adv* afterwards, then LGW 302, B 1238, C 869; since then A 3893.

sithe, sythe *n* (*as pl*) times TC 3.1595, B 733, 1155; **ofte(n) sithe(s)** A 485, 1877, E 233, G 1031.

sithen *conj* since A 2102, E 2307, etc.

sithen *adv* afterwards, then LGW 304, TC 1.833; since then A 2617, B 57; ago TC 1.718, A 1521.

sitte(n) *v* sit A 94, 370, etc.; **sitte** *1 s* D 238; *2 s subj* mayst sit TC 3.1630; **sitteth, sit, syt** *3 s* BD 1108, A 1527, 1599; becomes, is fitting B 1353, E 1277; **sitte** *3 s subj* may sit G 841; **sitte we** *1 pl subj* let us sit G 1195; **sat** *pt 3 s* A 271; **set, seet** (back-formation from *pl*) BD 501, A 2075; **sete** *pt 3 s subj* were to sit BD 436; **it sate her (me)** it were fitting, would befit TC 1.985, 2.117; **sete(n), sate, sat** *pt pl* BD 298, 431, TC 2.81, 1192, C 664; **sit** *imp s* D 2174; **sittynge** *part* resting A 633; **seten** *pp* sat, dwelt A 1452; **sat me sore** was painful to me BD 1220,

TC 3.240; **yvele it sit** it is not fitting E 460.

sittyng *adj* suitable, fitting TC 4.437; **sittyngest** *superl* PF 551.

skile, skille, skylle *n* reason HF 726, TC 2.365, 3.646, B 708; **skiles, skilles** *pl* reasons, arguments HF 867, PF 537, F 205.

skilful, skyl- *adj* reasonable BD 534, TC 2.392; rational B 1038.

skilfully, skyl- *adv* reasonably PF 634, TC 4.1265, G 320.

sklendre, scl- *adj* slender A 587, E 1602; frail, not robust B 3147, E 1198; meager B 4023.

skriked *pt pl* shrieked B 4590.

sky(e) *n* sky F 503; cloud HF 1600.

slake *v* lessen E 802, F 841; end E 137; **s. of** desist from E 705; slight LGW 619; *3 s subj* wane TC 2.291; *2 pl subj* grow slack C 82.

slakke *adj* slack E 1849; slow A 2901; **slakkere** *comp pl* slower B 1603.

slee(n), sle(n) *v* slay A 661, 2556, B 3531, D 1658; **sle** *1 s as fut* will slay B 2002; **sleest** *2 s* TC 4.455; **sle** *2 s subj* A 1615; **sleeth** *3 s* slays A 1118; **sle** *3 s subj* TC 2.459; **sleen, sle** *pl* B 964, F 462; **slow, slough** *pt 1 & 3 s* slew BD 727, A 2466; **quenched** B 3922; **slowe** *pt 2 s* TC 4.506; **slowe** *pt pl* F 1430; **slee, sle** *imp s* A 1721, B 3089; **slawe, yslawe** *pp* slain TC 3.721, A 943; **slayn** mortified, transmuted G 1436; **yslayn** slain A 2708.

sleere *n* slayer A 2005.

sleighly see **slyly**.

sleight(e), -ey- *n* cunning, trickery, craftiness HF 463, A 4050; **slyghte** C 131; **sleght** TC 4.1459; skill, ingenuity TC 5.773, E 1102; trick TC 2.1512, D 1431; **sleightes** *pl* tricks, stratagems TC 4.1451, E 2421; deceits G 976; clever devices G 773.

slepe(n) sleep BD 174, A 3406; **sleepe** *1 s* G 153; **slepestow** *2 s* sleepest thou A 4169; **slepeth** *3 s* HF 74; **slepe** *3 s subj* be asleep TC 2.1636; **slepe(n)** *pl* A 10, E 1928; **slepe(n)** *pl subj* E 118, F 126; **sleep, slep** *pt 1 & 3 s* TC 2.925, A 98; **slepte** *pt 3 s* A 4194, F 367; **slepe(n)** *pt pl* B 166, TC 1.921; **slepte(n)** *pt pl* TC 3.746, D 770; **slepynge** *part* B 21.

slepyng *n* sleep BD 230, B 4202.

slepynge *adj* sleepy BD 162.

slider *adj* slippery LGW 648, A 1264.

slogardye *n* laziness A 1042; sloth, slothfulness C 57, G 17.

slomber *n* slumber A 3816.

slomberynge *n* slumbering TC 2.67; *pl* TC 5.246.

slong *pt 3 s* slung H 306.

sloo *n* sloe, fruit of blackthorn A 3246.

slough *n* mire B 3988, H 64; **slow** D 1565.

slouthe *n* sloth, laxness in one's duty BD 1100, TC 5.1584; tardiness HF 1764.

slowe *adj* slothful HF 1778, B 315, D 1816.

sluttissh *adj* slovenly G 636.

sly, sleigh *adj* sly A 3940; cunning A 3201; secret D 1371; skilful E 1692, G 981; **slye** *pl* crafty BD 570; skilfully contrived F 230; *as n* clever one A 3392.

slyde, slide *v* pass, pass away BD 567, TC 5.351, E 82; **slit** *3 s* slides, passes PF 3, G 682.

slydynge, sli- *adj* slippery, uncertain G 732; unstable TC 5.825.

slyk *adj* sleek D 351.

slyk *adj & pron* such (Northern) A 4130, 4170.

slyly, sli-, sleigh- *adv* craftily D 1994, G 1230; secretly TC 5.83, C 792; cautiously TC 2.462, A 1444.

slyvere *n* sliver, portion TC 3.1013.

smal *adv* little D 592; quietly A 3320, Rosem 11.

smert, smart *adj* brisk G 768; **smerte** *pl* sharp, bitter, painful BD 507, A 2225, 2766.

smert(e) *n* pain BD 555, TC 4.1501, A 3813, G 712.

smerte *adv* smartly, sharply A 149, C 413, E 629.

smerte *v* smart, feel pain, suffer TC 1.1049, D 2092, E 353; **smerteth** *3 s* pains TC 1.667; **smerte** *3 s subj (impers)* it may pain TC 3.146, 5.132, A 230; **smerte** *1 pl subj* may smart, feel pain G 871; **smerte** *pt 3 s* caused pain F 564; felt pain TC 2.930; **him smerte** he suffered TC 5.1224; **smerte** *pt 3 s subj (impers)* might pain A 534; **smerte** *pt pl* B 3903.

smok *n* undergarment, chemise A 3238, D 783, etc.

smoklees *adj* stripped E 875.

smokynge *part* filling with smoke or incense A 2281.

smoterlich *adj* besmirched A 3963.

smyte(n) *v* strike TC 2.1276, 3.81; **smyteth, smyt** *3 s* A 1709, E 122; **smot, smoot** *pt 3 s* smote, struck HF 536, A 1704, D 634; **smyten** *pp* struck BD 1323, TC 2.1145.

smythed *pt 3 s* forged A 3762.

smytted *pp* smutted, sullied TC 5.1545.

snowisshe *adj* snowlike TC 3.1250.

snowte *n* snout, face B 1595, 4095.

snybben *v* rebuke, reprove A 523; **snybbed** *pp* A 4401, F 688.

so *adv* so A 11, etc.; as intensive introducing *imp & subj* (command, wish, etc.) TC 3.1470, 4.1652, B 4256, etc.; **so, so that** as intensive (= how) introducing *excl* PF 171, TC 3.82, 1380, etc. Cf. **as**.

so *conj* so, that, provided BD 29, PF 605, etc.; **so that** provided HF 709, LGW 158, A 1571, etc.

sobre *adj* sober, grave B 97, E 366; temperate D 1902, E 1533; quiet, discreet TC 5.820, Gent 9; earnest TC 3.237.

sobrelich(e) see **sobrely**.

sobrely *adv* gravely, sadly TC 5.81, A 289, B 1445; quietly, seriously TC 3.1616, E 296, F 1585; humbly TC 3.954; **sobrelich(e)** modestly TC 2.648; sadly TC 5.293; gravely TC 5.929.

socour *n* help TC 4.131, A 918.

socouren *v* help TC 3.1264.

socours *n* help TC 2.1354. See **socour**.

sodeyn *adj* sudden B 421, E 316, F 1010; impetuous TC 5.1024.

sodeynly *adv* suddenly BD 272, TC 1.209, etc.; **sodeynliche** TC 3.82, A 1575, etc.

softe *adv* softly, gently, timidly BD 1212, TC 1.195, A 1021, etc.

sojourne, -jorne *v* tarry, delay TC 1.850, 5.598; **sojorneth** *3 s* remains TC 1.326, 5.213; **sojourned** *pp* B 148, 536.

sokene *n* monopoly, privilege A 3987 (see note).

solas, -laas *n* entertainment A 798, 3335; relief, refreshment B 1972; comfort TC 1.31.

solempne *adj* solemn, ceremonious BD 302; imposing, sumptuous E 1125, F 61; important A 209, F 111; distinguished B 387.

solempnely *adv* ceremoniously B 317, F 179; importantly, pompously A 274.

solempnytee *n* pomp, ceremony A 870, 2702, D 629.

soleyn *adj* unique BD 982; solitary, single PF 607, 614.

som *adj & pron* some A 640, 776, 2119; some one G 995; **some, somme** *pl* 192, 233; **som . . . som, somme . . . somme** one . . . another, some . . . others BD 304–5, A 2119–20, G 922–3; **al and some, alle and some** see **al** *pron*.

somdel *adv* somewhat A 174, 446, etc.

somer *n* summer A 394, 1337, etc.; **someres, -is** *gen* BD 821, TC 3.1061.

som kynnes *adj* of some kind B 1137.

somne *v* summon D 1347, 1377; **sompne** D 1577; **somoned** *pp* summoned D 1620.

somonce *n* summons D 1586.

somonour, somn- *n* summoner A 543, 623 (see note); **somonours** *pl* D 1641.

somtyme *adv* for a time, at some time A 65, 1668, etc.

sond, soond *n* sand PF 243, B 509, 4457.

sonde, soonde *n* message TC 3.492, 5.1372; messenger, emissary B 389, G 525; sending, gift, dispensation B 523, 760, 1409.

sonded *pp* covered with sand TC 2.822.

sone, soone *adv* soon BD 66, etc.; promptly, quickly BD 195, TC 5.481, A 1761.

song *n* singing, vocal music BD 297, 472, A 1367; song BD 1182, TC 2.825; poem BD 471, B 1677; **songes** *pl* BD 1171, A 95.

sonne *n* sun A 7, etc.; **sonne** *gen* sun's A 1051; **sonnes** *gen* HF 941, TC 3.1704.

sonne-beem *n* sunbeam D 868.

sonner *adv* sooner TC 2.686.

sonnest *adv* soonest B 3716.

sonnyssh *adj* golden TC 4.736, 816.

soor(e) *n* pain, wound A 2233, 2849; sorrow A 1454.

soor(e) *adj* sore A 2220, 2695, 2804.

soore, sore *adv* sorely A 148, 1115, etc.; bitterly F 1461; violently B 3800.

soot *n* soot TC 3.1194.

soote, sote *adj* sweet PF 296, TC 3.1231, A 1, F 389, etc. See **swete, swote.**

sooth, soth *n* truth LGW 702, B 3154; **the soothe, sothe** BD 35, C 370; **for sothe** A 1093.

sooth, soth *adj* true HF 502, TC 1.239, C 157, etc.

sooth *adv* truly C 636.

sooth- see **soth-.**

soothfastnesse, soth- *n* truth TC 4.1080, B 4518, E 796.

soothly, sothly *adv* truly PF 270, A 117, etc.

soothnesse *n* truth G 261.

sop *n* toasted bread or cake soaked in wine A 334, E 1843.

soper *n* supper A 348, 748, etc.; **sopeer** F 1189.

sophistrye *n* cunning, trickery LGW 137.

sophyme *n* sophism, specious argument E 5; **sophymes** *pl* deceits F 554.

sorer *adv* more sorely LGW 502.

sorest *adv* most sorely PF 504.

sort[1] *n* lot, chance A 844; divination TC 1.76, 3.1047, 4.1401.

sort[2] *n* kind B 4044, 4381; group, company B 141.

sorted *pt 3 s* allotted TC 5.1827.

sorwe, sorowe *n* sorrow BD 10, TC 1.1, etc.; pity F 422; **with s.** may sorrow befall you D 308; **sorwes** *pl* BD 412, A 2419.

sorweful, sorwful(l), sorowful *adj* BD 14, TC 3.1361, A 1070, etc.

sorwefulleste *adj* most sorrowful E 2098.

sorwefully, sorw- *adv* sorrowfully, sadly TC 1.114, A 2978, D 913.

sorwe(n) *v* sorrow, grieve TC 4.394, 1309, 5.325; **sorwest** *2 s* TC 4.640, 1101; **sorweth** *3 s* TC 3.898, A 2652; **sorwen** *3 pl* A 2824; **sorwynge** *part* TC 1.9; **sorwed** *pp* TC 4.883.

sorwynge *n* sorrowing BD 605.

sory *adj* mournful, sad A 2004, 3618, E 1244; wretched, poor B 466, D 746; dismal D 1701; sorry TC 2.94, C 115; **with s. grace** bad luck to him C 876.

soster *n* sister A 3486. See **suster.**

sote see **soote.**

sother *adj* truer G 214.

sothfast *adj* true TC 3.30, 4.870.

sotilly *adv* cunningly E 2003.

sotted *adj* foolish G 1341.

soul *adj* solitary, single E 2080.

soun, sown *n* sound BD 162, TC 2.1118, etc.

soupe(n) *v* sup, have supper TC 2.944, 3.560, F 1217; **soupen** *3 pl* A 4146, F 297.

souple, sowple *adj* pliable, well-fitting A 203; amenable B 3690.

sours *n* swift upward flight, swoop HF 544, D 1938.

soutere *n* shoemaker A 3904.

south lyne *n* meridian I 2.

soutil, sotil *adj* slender A 2030; skilful A 2049, B 888; **sotile** *pl* subtle E 1427.

soutiltee *n* trick, stratagem D 576; skill G 1371. See **subtiltee.**

sovereyn, -ayn, -eigne *adj* supreme, exalted PF 254, F 67; *as n* ruler G 590; **s. lady, lady s.** object of the lover's devotion PF 416, TC 4.316, D 1048.

sovereynly *adv* masterfully, powerfully B 4552.

sowded *pp* made fast B 1769.

sowe *v* sew, ?seal TC 2.1201, 1204; **sowed** *pp* sewed A 685, G 571.

sowen *v* sow B 1182, I 35; **sowe(n), ysowe** *pp* sown TC 1.385, C 375, D 71; **ysowen** broadcast HF 1488.

sowke *v* suck A 4157; extract

A 4416; **soukynge** *part* B 1648; **souked** *pp* E 450.

sowled *pp* animated G 329.

sownde *n* health TC 3.1526.

sowne, soune *v* sound HF 1826, TC 2.573, LGW 91; **sowneth** *3 s* TC 5.678; **sownen** *3 pl* F 270; **sowned** *pt 3 s* sounded HF 1202; **sownynge** *part* BD 926; **best sowned** *pp* best sounding TC 2.1031.

sownen *v* conduce to TC 1.1036; **sowneth, souneth** *3 s* conduces to TC 3.1414; is consonant with B 3157; **sownen** *3 pl* are appropriate F 517; **sowned, souned** *pt 3 s* tended TC 4.1676, B 3348; **sownynge** *part* conducing to A 275; **s. in** reflecting A 307, C 54.

sowre *adv* bitterly B 2012.

sowres *n pl* bucks in their fourth year BD 429.

space *n* extent TC 5.1630; space of time TC 1.505, A 87, E 918; course, custom A 176.

span-newe *adj* like new chips, brand-new TC 3.1665.

sparcle *n* spark B 2095; **sparkles** *pl* signs of fire A 3885.

spare *v* refrain, refrain from PF 699, TC 5.51, A 1396; do without D 1325; economize, save E 1297; show consideration (for) TC 1.435, A 737; **hire s.** be reserved A 3966; **spared** *pt 3 pl* BD 320; **spareth** *imp pl* D 186, 1337; **spared** *pp* restrained TC 5.204; **yspared** *pp* E 2301.

sparre *n* beam A 990, 1076.

sparth *n* battle-axe A 2520.

sparwe *n* sparrow PF 351, A 626, D 1804.

spaynel *n* spaniel D 267.

speces *n pl* species, kinds A 3013.

speche *n* speech, discourse A 307, 517, etc.; language G 1443; **speches** *pl* conversations TC 3.510.

specheles *adj* speechless TC 4.370, 1167.

special *adj* special HF 68; **in s.** especially A 444, C 634, etc.

specially *adv* especially A 15, 4131, etc.

spetacle *n* eyeglass D 1203.

spede, speede *v* succeed TC 1.774, C 134, E 1632; assist HF 78; make haste PF 385; conduct A 4033; *3 s subj* may (God) assist A 769, 2558; **spedde** *pt 1 & 3 s* (often *refl*) hastened LGW 200, A 1217, F 1262; prospered, succeeded TC 1.482, 2.686; advanced, assisted B 3876; **spedde(n)** *pt 3 pl* hastened TC 2.947, 5.501; **sped, speed** *imp s* make haste HF 1595, PF 133, A 3562; **spede** *imp pl* make haste D 1732, E 1927;

sped, ysped *pp* succeeded, fared PF 101, A 4220; carried out A 4205; hastened B 1828.

spedeful *adj* advantageous B 727.

spedily *adv* speedily B 1442, G 1143.

speed *n* success TC 1.17; help TC 2.9; **spede** *dat* profit PF 507; success TC 1.1043.

speere see **spere.**

speke(n) *v* speak A 142, 413, etc.; **speke** *1 s* A 727; **spekest** *2 s* F 676; **spekestow** speakest thou D 837; **speketh** *3 s* HF 931; **speke, speeke** *3 s subj* A 3586, H 325; **speke(n)** *3 pl* A 4146, B 214; **spak** *pt 1 s* LGW 97; **spak** *pt 2 s* C 753, G 494; **spak** *pt 3 s* HF 555; said B 750; **spake** *pt 3 s* TC 3.543; **speke(n), speeke, spake(n)** *pt pl* BD 350, TC 1.565, 2.25, 5.853, F 247; **spek** *imp s* A 3805; **speketh** *imp pl* E 175; **spoke(n), yspoke(n)** *pp* TC 4.1108, A 31, 2972, C 707; **speke . . . shame** reproach LGW 467.

spekyng *n* speaking PF 488, H 335.

spelle *n* discourse, tale B 2083.

spence *n* buttery D 1931.

spende(n) *v* spend A 4135, G 868; **spente** *pt 3 s* A 300; **spent, spended** *pp* A 645, D 1950.

spere, speere *n* sphere TC 3.1495, F 1280.

spered *pp* barred TC 5.531.

sperhauk, spar- *n* sparrowhawk PF 338, 569, B 1957, 4647.

spete *v* spit TC 2.1617; **spitte** *1 s* C 421.

spiced *pp* spiced A 3378; **s. conscience** nice disposition D 435; over-scrupulous nature A 526.

spicerye *n* spices (collectively) A 2935, B 136, 2043.

spie *n* spy TC 5.703; **spies** *pl* HF 704. Cf. **espye.**

spille *v* destroy TC 5.588, D 898, E 503; waste, lose H 153; perish, be destroyed, die B 587, 815, 910; spill, drop TC 5.880; **spille** *1 s* perish A 3278; *1 s subj* B 285; **spilt** *pp* ruined, undone B 857, D 388.

spir *n* shoot TC 2.1335.

spirit *n* soul, spirit TC 4.1620, A 2809, etc.; alchemical substance G 822; **spirites** *pl* spirits BD 489; spiritual agents B 491; substances G 778 (see note), 820.

spitously *adv* spitefully D 223; vigorously A 3476.

spore *n* spur A 2603; **spores** *pl* A 473, 1704; **with spore and yerde** speedily, eagerly TC 2.1427.

sporne, spurne *v* kick F 616, Truth 11; **sporneth** *3 s* kicks TC 2.797;

sporned *pt 3 s* kicked, tripped A 4280.

spot *n* spot TC 5.1815; blemish E 2146.

spousaille *n* marriage E 115; wedding E 180.

spoused *pp* married E 3, 386.

spouted *pp* spewed B 487.

sprede *v* spread B 1767, D 1822; expand TC 1.278; **spredeth** *3 s* expands TC 2.980; **spreden** *3 pl* spread TC 2.970; **spradde** *pt 3 s* E 418, 722; **sprad, ysprad, yspred** *pp* spread LGW 64, A 4140, B 1644; **spradde** *pp pl* wide open TC 4.1422.

spreynd see **springen.**

springen *v* scatter B 1183; **spreynd, yspreynd** *pp* scattered A 2169; sprinkled B 422, 1830.

sprynge(n), spri- *v* spring up LGW 38; rise A 2522, B 4068; dawn A 822, 2491; **spryngeth** *3 s* A 1871; **sprynge(n)** *3 pl* A 2607, F 1147; **sprang, sproong** *pt 3 s* A 3282, B 3234; **spronge** *pp* HF 2079, A 1437.

sprynges *n pl* dances (of a kind not identified) HF 1235.

spyen, spien *v* keep watch D 316, 357; spy, look (for something) TC 3.1454; catch sight of G 314; **spye** *3 s subj* may catch sight of A 3566; **spyed** *pt 3 s* kept watch F 1506. See **espyen, aspye.**

spynne *v* spin B 1907; **spynnynge** *part* E 223; **sponne** *pt pl* spun TC 3.734.

squames *n pl* scales G 759.

squaymous *adj* delicate, modest A 3337.

squier *n* squire A 79, 1410, etc.; **squieres** *pl* A 2502.

squiereth *3 s* squires, accompanies D 305.

sqwirrelles *n pl* squirrels BD 431; **squyrels** PF 196.

squyre *n* carpenter's square D 2090.

staat *n* condition, state A 572. See **estat.**

staf-slynge *n* slingshot B 2019.

stale *adj* old and strong (ale) B 1954.

stalke *n* stalk A 1036; stalk, straw A 3919; **stalkes** *pl* upright shafts of a ladder A 3625.

stalke *v* steal up quietly TC 2.519; **stalketh** *3 s* steals quietly A 1479, 3648; **stalked** *pt s* came up quietly BD 458; went quietly E 525.

stampe *3 pl* pound (in a mortar) C 538.

stant see **stonden.**

stape(n) *adj* advanced B 4011, E 1514.

stare *n* starling PF 348.

starf see **sterven.**

stark *adj* strong E 1458; **starke** *pl* HF 545; hard, severe B 3560.

startlynge *part* prancing A 1502.

statue *n* statue A 2265, B 3349; image, figure A 975, 1955.

stature *n* stature A 83; bodily shape PF 366.

stede *n* place HF 731; **in stede of, in stide of** instead of A 231, 4053.

stedefast, stide- *adj* steadfast B 4558, E 564.

sted(e)fastly *adv* steadfastly D 947; firmly HF 61, E 1094; confidently G 474.

steire, steyre, staire *n* stairs TC 1.215, 2.813, 1705; **steires** *gen* TC 3.205.

stele *n* handle, shank A 3785.

stele(n) *v* steal A 562, 3786; **steleth** *3 s* B 21; **stal, staal** *pt 1 & 3 s* BD 381, 1251, TC 1.81; **stole(n), stoln** *pp* A 2627, 4111, B 744.

stellyfye, -li- *v* make into a star HF 586, 1002, LGW 525.

stemed *pt pl* glowed A 202.

stente(n) see **stinte(n).**

stepe *adj* bright, prominent A 201 (see note), 753.

stere, steere *n* rudder B 833, Purse 12; tiller HF 437; helmsman, pilot TC 3.1291, B 448; **in steere** asterne TC 5.641.

stere[1]**, steere** *v* steer, guide, govern TC 1.228, 3.910, 4.282; **steere** *1 s* TC 2.4.

stere[2]**, stire** *v* stir C 346; urge TC 3.1643; propose TC 4.1451; **stereth** *3 s* stirs HF 817; **stired** *pt 3 s* G 1278; **steryng, stirynge** *part* TC 3.692, 1236, A 3673; **stiryng** *as adj* HF 478.

sterelees, steere- *adj* rudderless TC 1.416, B 439.

sterisman *n* steersman HF 436.

sterlynges *n pl* silver pennies HF 1315, C 907.

sternely, -liche *adv* harshly, severely LGW 239; hard HF 1498, TC 3.677.

sterre *n* star HF 599, PF 300; **sterres** *pl* BD 409, A 268; **sterres seven(e)** the seven planets HF 1376; the Pleiades BD 824.

sterry *adj* starry PF 43.

stert *n* start, sudden movement TC 5.254; **at a sterte** in a moment A 1705.

sterte *v* spring, leap, make a quick, sudden movement TC 5.253, A 1044; go (quickly) TC. 2.1634, 3.949; **sterte, stirte** *pt 3 s* sprang, leaped, started up A 952, 1080, D 163, F 1168; **sterte, stirte(n)** *pt pl* sprang C 705; rushed B 4237, 4567; **stirt, stert** *pp* leaped F 1377; awakened suddenly E 1060.

sterve(n) *v* die BD 1266, TC 1.17, D 1242; sterve *1 s* TC 5.313; *3 s subj* A 1144; starf *pt 3 s* A 933; perished TC 2.449; storven *pt pl* C 888; ystorve *pp* having died A 2014.

sterynge *n* stirring HF 800.

steven(e) *n* voice, sound BD 307, HF 561, A 2562; report TC 3.1723; language F 150; setten s. made an appointment A 4383; at unset s. at an unappointed time, unexpectedly A 1524.

stewe *n* brothel HF 26; stywes *pl* C 465; styves D 1332.

stibourn *adj* stubborn D 456; untamable D 637.

stide see stede.

stidefast see stedefast.

stierne *adj* stern A 2154, E 465; terrible, gruesome A 2610; sterne TC 3.743, 4.94.

stif *adj* strong A 673; taut D 2267.

stiken *v* stick, penetrate TC 1.297; stiketh *3 s* sticks TC 3.1105, A 3877; stiked *3 s* stuck B 509; stabbed B 3897; stak *pt 3 s* stuck TC 3.1372; stikynge *part* piercing C 211; stiked, ystiked *pp* stuck B 2097; stabbed B 430, F 1476; styked swyn stuck pig C 556.

stikke *n* stick G 1265; twig, branch BD 423.

stile, style *n* set of steps in or over a fence B 1988, C 712, F 106.

stillatorie *n* still, retort G 580.

stille, stylle *adv* quietly BD 459, HF 2107; motionless HF 1926, TC 1.723; continually, constantly HF 324, B 720.

stinte(n), stynte(n), stente(n) *v* leave off, cease, stop A 903, 1334, B 3925, F 814; put an end to TC 3.884, A 2442; stynte *1 s* HF 1417, A 2811; stynteth *3 s* TC 3.898; stynte *3 s subj* D 732; *1 pl subj* A 4339; stente, stynte *pt 1 & 3 s* BD 154, 358, 1299; stynte *pt 3 s subj* TC 1.848; stente, stynten *pt pl* TC 1.60, LGW 294; stynt *imp s* TC 2.1242, A 2348, D 1558; stynteth *imp pl* TC 2.1729, A 2674; styntynge *part* halting BD 1213; stynt, ystynt, stynted, stent *pp* A 1368, 2421, 2968, D 390.

stiropes, sty- *n pl* stirrups B 1164, D 1665.

stirt, stirte(n) see sterte.

stok *n* stock A 1551; stokkes *n pl* stumps TC 3.589.

stoke *v* stab A 2546.

stokked *pp* set in the stocks TC 3.380.

stomak *n* stomach TC 1.787; appetite D 1847; tenderheartedness D 1441.

stomblen *3 pl* stumble A 2613.

stonde(n) *v* stand A 88, 745, etc.; stondeth *3 s* TC 2.1146, A 1639; stant *3 s* stands TC 1.602, B 651; stood *pt s* A 354, 555; stode(n) *pt pl* B 176, 678; stondynge *part* B 68; stonden *pp* stood BD 975, E 1494; ystonde TC 5.1612; stonde . . . unto accept the responsibility for A 3830.

stoon, ston *n* stone A 774, 3712, etc.; testicle B 4638; stones *pl* stones, gems BD 979, A 699; stoon of sikernesse rock of security TC 2.843.

stoor *n* store, stock C 365, D 2159; live stock A 598; ne telle . . . no s. set no store by B 4344; I tolde of it no s. I took no account of it D 203.

stoore *v* stock B 1463.

stoore *adj* bold, impudent E 2367.

stordy *adj* sturdy TC 2.1380.

storie *n* story A 1201, etc.; history, legend TC 5.585; *historia*, series of *lectiones* A 709 (see note); stories *pl* stories, histories, books of such TC 5.1044, A 859, D 693.

storyal, -ial *adj* historical, authentic LGW 702, A 3179.

stot *n* horse, prob. a farm horse A 615 (see note); steer (used contemptuously for an old woman) D 1630.

stounde *n* space of time, time, hour, a while TC 1.1086, 3.1695, A 4007; moment A 1212; in a s. in a (short) space of time B 1021; once upon a time A 3992; stoundes *pl* times D 286.

stoundemele *adv* hour by hour, gradually, steadily TC 5.674.

stoupe *v* stoop G 1311; lean forward D 1560; stoupeth *3 s* E 2348; stoupen *pt* TC 2.968; stoupyng *part adj* E 1738.

stoures *n pl* battles B 3560.

strake *v* move, go BD 1312 (see note).

straughte see strecche.

straunge *adj* foreign, strange A 13, 2718, B 178; not of the family TC 2.1660; external D 1161; unknown E 138; surprising TC 5.120; distant PF 584, B 1453; *as n* strangers TC 2.411; made it s. raised difficulties, was reluctant A 3980, F 1223.

straungely *adv* strangely TC 2.1423; coldly, distantly TC 5.955.

strawen *v* strew LGW 207; strawe *2 s subj* F 613; ystrawed *pp* strewn BD 629.

strecche *v* stretch B 4498, C 395; reach TC 1.888; extend G 469, 1087; strecheth *3 s* TC 1.903; streighte *pt 3 s* stretched out HF 1373; straughte *pt pl* A 2916; strecchynge *part* B 4522; long streght (*pp*) stretched out at full length TC 4.1163.

stree *n* straw BD 671, 1237, B 701.

streen *n* lineage E 157.

streght, streighte see strecche.

streight, streght *adj* straight BD 942, 957, A 3316, etc.

streight, streght *adv* straight TC 1.53, A 671, etc.

streit *adj* small A 4122; narrow A 1984; scanty B 4179; strict A 174; streite *pl* limited D 1426.

streite *adj def* drawn B 4547.

streite *adv* tightly TC 4.1689, A 457; strictly E 2129.

strem *n* stream PF 138, A 464; stremes *pl* currents A 402; rays BD 338, C 38.

streng *n* string TC 2.1033, D 2067; strenges *pl* PF 197.

strenger *adj* stronger B 3711, C 825.

strengest *adj & adv* strongest TC 1.243, 1007.

strengthe *n* strength A 84, etc.; force B 3825; with s. with a pack of hunting dogs BD 351.

strepe(n), streepe *v* strip A 1006, E 863, 1958; strepeth *3 s* A 4063; strepen *3 pl* E 1116.

streyne *v* clasp tightly TC 3.1205, 1449, E 1752; afflict TC 3.1071; force, constrain E 144; streyneth *3 s* constrains B 4434; streyne *3 pl* strain C 538.

strif, stryf *n* strife A 1187, 3849, etc.

strike *n* hank A 676.

stronde *n dat* strand: on the s. B 825; doun the s. B 864.

strook, strok *n* stroke HF 779, TC 4.511, A 1701; blow D 636.

strouted *pt 3 s* stuck out A 3315.

stryve *v* strive TC 4.175, A 3040, etc.; stryveth *3 s* TC 3.38; stryve *pl* A 1177; stroff, strof *pt 3 s* strove TC 5.819, A 1038; stryve *imp s* D 1986.

stryvyng *n* striving D 1998; strife C 550.

stubbel goos *n* goose fed on stubble A 4351.

stubbes *n pl* stumps, remains of broken branches A 1978.

studie *n* study A 303, etc.; reverie, meditation TC 2.1180, A 303, 1530.

studie(n) *v* study A 184, etc.; meditate E 8; studieth *imp pl* muse, be abstracted A 841.

sturdinesse *n* harshness E 700.

sturdy *adj* sturdy D 1754; furious D 2162; harsh, cruel E 698, 1049.

stuwe[1] *n* fishpond A 350.

stuwe[2] *n* a small heated room, generally for bathing TC 3.601; **stuwe doore** door to such a room TC 3.698.

stynge *v* sting BD 640, B 406, C 413; **styngeth** *3 s* D 1995; pierces LGW 645; **stongen, ystonge** *pp* stung C 355; pierced A 1079.

stynk *n* stench B 3810, D 2274.

stynketh *3 s* stinks G 1067, H 32; **stynken** *3 pl* G 886; **stank** *pt 3 s* HF 1654, B 3807.

stynte(n) see **stinte(n)**.

styth *n* anvil A 2026.

styward *n* steward B 914, F 291; **stywardes** *pl* A 579.

stywes, styves see **stewe**.

subgit *adj* subject TC 1.231, 5.1790.

subgit *n* subject TC 2.828; **subgitz, subgetz** *pl* D 1990, E 482.

sublymatories *n pl* vessels used for vaporizing solids G 793.

sublymed *pp* sublimated G 774.

sublymyng *n* sublimation, vaporizing G 770.

substance *n* what is essential, essential character HF 1181, TC 4.1505, C 539; basis, foundation B 3993; possessions, wealth TC 4.1513; fixed income A 489; majority TC 4.217.

subtil, -tyl *adj* thin, of fine texture PF 272; subtle B 213, E 459; clever, ingenious A 1054, F 1261; skilful TC 2.257, LGW 672; crafty, cunning B 3890, E 737, 1767; sly F 285; **subtil, subtile** *pl* clever HF 1188, A 3275, F 1141; insidious TC 1.305.

subtilitee, -te *n* subtlety HF 855; intricate matters G 620; **subtilitees** *pl* tricks E 2421. See **soutiltee**.

subtilly *adv* craftily, subtly A 610, B 746, etc.

subtiltee, -te *n* cleverness TC 5.1782, B 4509, D 2290; craftiness G 1091; guile E 691; treachery TC 5.1254, B 3569, F 140; crafty device D 1420; abstract knowledge G 844. Cf. **subtilitee**.

sucre *n* sugar TC 3.1194; **sugre** B 2046, F 614.

sucred *pp* sugared TC 2.384.

suffisaunce *n* sufficiency, enough TC 5.763, A 490; source of satisfaction BD 1038; contentment BD 703, B 4029.

suffisaunt *adj* sufficient LGW 67, A 1631.

suffise, -yse *v* suffice BD 18, TC 3.335; capable of bearing TC 4.258; **suffyce** *imp s* be satisfied Truth 2.

suffrable *adj* patient D 442.

suffraunce *n* patient endurance E 1162; forbearance F 788.

suffraunt *adj* tolerant BD 1010; *as n* patient one TC 4.1584.

suffre(n) *v* allow A 649, 945; endure C 215, E 537; **suffre** *1 s* endure TC 5.40; **suffrest** *2 s* TC 3.1021; **suffreth** *3 s* A 1219; **suffren** *pl* TC 3.1018, 4.1533; **suffre** *2 pl subj* allow TC 3.881; **suffred** *pt 1 s* BD 1183; *pt pl* BD 1292; **suffre** *imp s* allow TC 1.755, E 1377; **suffre to** submit to TC 1.954; **suffred** *pp* BD 37, 1184.

suggestioun *n* accusation B 3607.

supprised *pp* seized, overtaken TC 3.1184.

surcote *n* surcoat A 617 (see note).

suretee see **seurete**.

surmounteth, sour- *3 s* surpasses LGW 123; overcomes TC 3.1038; **surmounted** *pp* surpassed BD 826.

surquidrie *n* pride, arrogance TC 1.213.

sursanure *n* wound superficially healed over F 1113.

surveiaunce *n* surveillance C 95.

suspecious *adj* arousing suspicion E 540.

suspect *adj* arousing suspicion E 541.

suspect *n* suspicion C 263; **in s.** suspicious E 905.

sustene, -teene *v* sustain, bear A 1993, B 847; maintain B 160; support TC 2.1686; **sustened** *pp* maintained B 1680.

suster *n* sister HF 1547, A 871; **soster** A 3486; **sustren** *pl* HF 1401, TC 3.733, A 1019; **sustres** B 4057, 4458.

suwe see **sewe**.

suyte, sute *n* color, pattern A 2873, 3242; **of oo sute** of one color or pattern, matching BD 261.

swa *adv* so A 4040 (Northern).

swal see **swelle**.

swalowe, swolwe *v* swallow HF 1036, H 36; **swelwe** *3 s subj* E 1188.

swalwe, swalowe *n* swallow PF 353, TC 2.64, A 3258.

swap *n* swoop HF 543.

swappe *v* strike E 586; **swapte** *pt 3 s* TC 4.245; **flopped** E 1099; **swap** *imp s* strike G 366.

swartish *adj* dark HF 1647.

sweete *adv* sweetly A 3305, D 1804.

sweigh *n* motion B 296; falling motion TC 2.1383.

swelle *v* swell A 2752, E 2306; **swelleth** *3 s* A 2743; **swelle** *3 s subj* C 354; **swal** *pt 3 s* swelled B 1750, D 967; **swollen** *pp* swollen with rage TC 5.201; puffed up E 950.

swelte *v* die, perish TC 3.347; **swelte** *1 s* grow faint A 3703; **swelte** *pt 3 s* languished A 1356; perished E 1776.

swelwe see **swalowe**.

swere(n) *v* swear A 454, B 663; **swerith, swerth** *3 s* TC 2.654, 5.1430; **swoor, swor** *pt 1 & 3 s* TC 5.127, A 959; **sworen** *pt pl* A 1826; **swore, sworen, sworn, yswore, ysworn, isworn** *pp* HF 1011, TC 2.570, A 810, 1089, 1132, F 325.

swete, sweete *adj* A 5, 265, etc. See **soote, swote**.

swete *n* sweetness PF 161; sweetheart BD 204, 832, TC 1.533, 538, 5.572, F 978.

swete, sweete *v* sweat TC 2.1533, G 522; **swete** *1 s* TC 2.1465, A 3702; *2 pl* TC 2.943, G 1186; **swatte** *pt 3 s* TC 1.1966, G 560.

swetely *adv* sweetly BD 848, A 221.

swetnesse *n* sweetness BD 415, PF 185, TC 3.1219.

sweven *n* dream BD 119, 422, B 3930.

sweynte *adj* lazy HF 1783.

swich *adj & pron* such A 3, 313, etc.; **s. as, s. . . . . as** such as TC 2.207, 3.394, B 1689; **s. oon** such a one F 231.

swogh, swough, swow *n* sough, sound like the rushing wind HF 1031; audible sigh A 3619; swoon TC 3.1120, E 1100; grievous state BD 215.

swoot *n* sweat G 578.

swote, swoote *adj* sweet TC 1.158, LGW 173, A 2860. See **soote, swete**.

swow see **swogh**.

swowne *n* swoon F 1080.

swowne *v* swoon TC 2.574; **swowneth** *3 s* F 430; **swowned, swouned** *pt 3 s* BD 103, A 2943; **swownynge** *part* A 2819; **swowned** *pp* A 913.

swownyng *n* swooning C 246, E 1087.

swymme *v* float A 3550; **swymmen** *3 pl* swim D 1926; are swimming with (full of) PF 188.

swynk *n* labor A 188, 540, G 730.

swynke(n), swinke *v* work HF 16, 1175, A 186; **swynke** *3 pl* A 3491; obtain by labor G 21; **swonken, yswonke** *pp* labored A 4235, H 18.

swynkere *n* worker A 531.

swythe, swithe *adv* quickly HF 538, PF 503; rapidly B 730; **as s.** quickly, immediately PF 623, B637; promptly, without delay G 936, 1030.

swyve *v* have intercourse with A 4178, H 256; **swyved** *pt 3 s* E 2378; *pp* A 3850, 4266, 4317.

sye *v* sink down, fall TC 5.182.

sygge see **seyen.**

syk *n* sickness, illness D 394.

syk see **sik.**

syke see **sike.**

syklatoun *n* light-weight, costly material, generally red B 1924.

symphonye *n* drum B 2005.

syn *conj* since HF 835, PF 64, TC 1.256, etc.

syn *prep* A 1193, 3665, etc.

synge(n), singen *v* sing HF 143, A 236, B 1690; crow A 4233, B 4620; **synge** *1 s* B 1853; **syngestow** singest thou H 244; **syngeth** *3 s* A 3360; **synge** *3 s subj* B 294; **synge(n)** *pl* PF 684, B 642; crow B 4480; **song, soong, sang** *pt 1 & 3* A 122, 710, B 1961; **songe** *pt 2 s* H 294; **songe(n)** *pt pl* D 216, E 1735; **syngeth** *imp pl* B 4510; **syngynge** *part* A 91; **songe(n), ysonge** *pp* sung A 266, 1529, D 1726.

syngyng(e) *n* singing BD 313, B1747; **singynges** *pl* TC 3.1716.

synke(n), sinken *v* sink, cause to sink TC 1.734, 2.560, F 1073; enter into TC 4.1494; **synke** *1 s & 1 s subj* PF 7, TC 4.1554; **synken** *3 pl* G 912; **sonken** *pp* F 892, 1269.

sys *n* six (in dice) B 3851; **sys cynk** six (and) five B 125.

sythe see **sithe.**

T

taas *n* heap A 1005, 1009, 1020.

tabard *n* tabard, smock-like garment A 541.

table *n* table A 100, etc.; tablet HF 142, A 1305; item, commandment C 639; **tables** *pl* tables B 1442; tablets D 1741 (see note); tables for astrological calculations F 1273; the game of backgammon BD 51, F 900.

table dormant *n* a (permanent) table on which food was constantly kept A 353.

tabour *n* drum D 2268.

tabouren *3 pl* drum, beat LGW 354.

taille *n* tally, credit A 570, B 1606 (see note).

taillynge *n* tailing B 1624 (see note).

takel *n* shooting gear, arrow A 106.

take(n) *v* A 34, 3081; seize C 259; take *1 s* A 4052; **me t.** betake myself B 1985; **take** *2 s subj* D 1055; **taketh** *3 s* D 321; **take** *3 s subj* BD 142; take place TC 4.1562; **take** *pl* B 147, 4152; **took** *pt 3 s* A 303; brought BD 48, G 1030; delivered, handed B 1484, 1594; struck D 792; **tooke(n)** *pt pl* A 4309, B 1870; **tak, taak** *imp s* TC 4.617,

A 789; consider TC 1.344; **taak kep** take heed B 3757, C 360; **takestow** *imp s* G 435; **taketh** *imp pl* C 74; **take(n), ytake(n)** *pp* BD 224, A 3353; undertaken TC 5.1765; given B 769; received D 77; **itake** caught TC 3.1198.

tald see **telle(n).**

tale *n* narrative, story, account A 36, 330; talk TC 2.218; something to say BD 536; **tales** *pl* A 792; talks TC 3.224; **took first the tale** spoke first TC 2.1605.

tale(n) *v* talk, converse, tell anecdotes TC 3.231, A 772; speak TC 3.1235.

talent *n* inclination, desire TC 3.145, C 540.

tapes *n pl* tapes, bonnet-strings A 3241.

tapite *v* adorn with tapestry BD 260.

tappestere *n* tapster, barmaid A 241, 3336.

tare *n* tare, weed A 1570, 4000.

targe *n* shield A 471, 975, 2122.

tarie(n), tarye(n) *v* delay A 3409, B 374, F 73; linger A 2820, B 4260; **tarie** *1 s* TC 3.1195; **tarieth** *3 s* TC 5.862; **tarie** *2 pl* delay F 1233; **tariede** *pt 3 s* delayed PF 415; **hem . . . taried** kept them waiting B 3463; **tarie** *imp s* A 3905; **taried** *pp* delayed F 402; *as adj* TC 2.1739.

tariyng, taryinge, taryynge *n* delay TC 5.774; A 821, 3546.

tartre *n* tartar G 813; **oille of t.** cream of tartar A 630.

tast *n* taste, enjoyment PF 160.

taste *imp s* test G 503; **tasted** TC 1.639.

tayl *n* tail B 111, 3224; stalk (of a leek) A 3878.

tecches, techches *n pl* faults, blemishes HF 1778, TC 3.935.

teche(n) *v* teach A 308, 654; direct D 1326; **teche** *1 s* C 440; **techeth** *3 s* F 104; **teche(n)** *3 pl* TC 1.698, H 326; **taughte** *pt 1 & 3 s* A 497, D 1050; taught G 544; **teche** *imp s* D 1418; **taught, ytaught** *pp* A 127, B 224.

techyng *n* teaching A 518; **techynge** *dat* G 93.

telle(n) *v* tell A 38, 73, etc.; reckon BD 440; **telle** *1 s* A 330; **telleth** *3 s* A 797; **telles** (*Northern ending*) BD 73; **telle(n)** *3 pl* A 859, D 948; **tolde** *pt 1 & 3 s* A 1059, B 758; counted HF 1380; accounted B 3676; **tolde(n)** *pt pl* A 3184, D 607; **tel, telle** *imp s* A 808, C 319, D 308; **telleth** *imp pl* BD 555, A 910; **tellyng(e)** *part* TC 1.743, 4.127; **told, toold, ytold, ytoold, itold** *pp* TC 4.141, A 715, 2126, 3109, G 627; **tald** *pp* (*Northern*)

A 4207; **tolde of it no stoor** took no account of it D 203; **tolde no deyntee of** had no regard for, set no value on D 208.

temen *v* bring HF 1744.

temperaunce *n* moderation F 785.

tempest *imp s* disturb violently Truth 8.

temple *n* temple A 928, etc.; the Inner or Middle Temple, one of the Inns of Court A 567 (see note).

tempreth *3 s* mixes G 901; **temprede** *pt 3 s* tempered PF 214; **tempred** *pp* mixed (in proper proportions) G 926.

temps *n* time (expectation) G 875.

tempte *v* tempt D 1661; test E 452, 620; **tempteth** *3 s* E 1153; **tempted** *pp* tested E 621.

tendernesse *n* womanishness B 1154; gentle nature TC 5.242.

tene, teene *n* sorrow, grief TC 2.61, 4.1605; vexation TC 1.814, A 3106.

tenthe *adj* tenth TC 4.1595, etc.; **tenthe som** some ten TC 2.1249.

tentifly *adv* attentively E 334.

tercel *adj* male (applied to birds of the falcon family) PF 393, 449; *as n* PF 405, 415.

tercelet, terslet *n* male falcon PF 529, 533, F 504.

terme *n* period of time BD 79, TC 5.1090; duration A 1029, D 644; appointed time HF 392, TC 5.696; a part of each sign of the Zodiac F 1288 (see note); **termes** *pl* technical terms A 699, E 16; expressions, language A 3917; Year Books A 323 (see note); **in terme** in technical language C 311.

terme-day *n* appointed day BD 730.

termyne *v* reach (or state) a conclusion PF 530.

terrestre *adj* earthly E 1332.

terslet see **tercelet.**

terve *3 s subj* flay G 1274; **terved** *pp* skinned G 1171.

tery *adj* tearful TC 4.821.

testeres *n pl* head-pieces A 2499.

testes *n pl* crucibles G 818.

testif *adj* impetuous TC 5.802; headstrong A 4004.

tete *n* teat A 3704.

text *n* text, a writing, a written work BD 333, B 905; code, a teaching B 45, D 1647; passage in a book F 607; biblical passage A 177, D 1919; **textes** *pl* authorities H 236.

textueel *adj* learned in authorities I 57; book-learned H 235.

teyne *n* rod or flat piece of metal G 1225, 1229, etc.

thakketh *3 s* slaps, pats D 1559; **thakked** *pp* A 3304.

than *adv* then BD 288, TC 1.529, A 42, etc. See **thanne.**

thank, thonk *n* thanks TC 1.803, A 612, E 1801, 2388, H 101; **thankes** *pl* B 1378; good will TC 1.21, 3.1777; **his (hir) thankes** willingly A 1626, 2107, 2114, D 272.

thanke(n), thonke(n), thank *v* thank TC 3.1594, A 3064, 3069, F 557, 1569; **thank(e), thonke** *1 s* BD 561, TC 3.1400, E 830; **thanketh** *3 s* B 383; **thanke** *3 s subj* may reward E 1088; **thanke(n), thonken** *pl* TC 2.1719, E 188, F 354; **thanke we** *1 pl subj* let us thank B 3387; **thanked, thonked** *pt 3 s* A 1876, B 3369; **thanke** *imp s* LGW 454, B 3876; **thankynge** *part* D 1868; **thanked, ythanked, thonked, ythonked** *pp* TC 4.2, A 925, D 5, 2118.

thanne *adv* then HF 368, TC 3.124, A 12, etc. See **than.**

thar *3 s impers* it is necessary or needful: **hym (thee) thar** it is necessary for him (thee) BD 256, D 1365. Cf **thurste.**

that *demons pron* that, the A 102, 113, etc.

that *rel pron* that, which BD 964, A 1131; that which, what HF 1024, PF 163, TC 1.744, 1033, etc.

that *conj* that A 226, 297, etc.; so that BD 566; as that BD 959; as B 979; as well as B 1036; as if TC 4.575.

theatre *n* amphitheater A 1885, 1901, 2091.

thedam *n* thriving: **yvel t.** misfortune B 1595.

theech, theek see **theen.**

thee(n), the *v* thrive, prosper B 4622, D 2232; **so (as) moot I thee(n), so theech** as may I thrive TC 1.341, B 4166, C 309, G 929; **theek** A 3864 (see note). Cf. **ythe.**

theigh *conj* although, though TC 1.677, 3.1630, 4.614.

theme *n* text (of a sermon) C 333, 425.

then *conj* than BD 51, HF 13, 20, 127, LGW 100, 190.

thenche *v* imagine A 3253. See **thynken.**

thenne *adj* thin A 4066.

thenne *adv* thence D 1141.

thennes, thens *adv* thence HF 1038, TC 3.1145, B 308.

ther, there *adv* there TC 1.514, A 43, 827, etc.; *rel adv & conj* where BD 146, TC 5.711, 1220, A 1618; wherever A 3702; whereby D 128; whereas TC 5.1349, A 1272, G 724; whence F 971; *introducing a wish, imprecation, etc.* TC 3.1456, 5.1525, B 602, etc.

ther-agayn, ther-ayeins *adv* thereagainst TC 2.369, D 1488.

theras, ther as *conj* whereas TC 3.1623, D 1177; where A 172, 224, F 307, etc.

therbiforn, ther-biforn *adv* previously, before A 2034, 3997, B 197.

theroute *adv* outside B 3362, G 1136.

ther-while *conj* while TC 3.538.

therwith *adv* therewith A 678, etc.; thereupon BD 500, A 3804, B 862; moreover B 4483, H 123.

thewes *n pl* mental or moral qualities HF 1834, TC 2.723, E 409, 1542; virtues G 101.

they *pers pron* A 81, etc.; **hir, hire, her** *gen* their BD 71, TC 1.162, LGW 485; **hirs** theirs D 1926; **hem** them BD 72, etc.

thider *adv* thither HF 724, A 1263, etc.

thiderward *adv* thither HF 2144, TC 2.1250, A 2530.

thikke *n* thicket BD 418.

thikke *adj* thick HF 1335, A 1056; thick-set A 549; plump A 3973.

thikke *adv* close together TC 2.456, A 3322.

thilke *adj* the same, that same BD 242, 785, A 182, etc.; **thilke, thilk** (before vowel) *pl* those HF 173, PF 61, TC 3.15.

thing, thyng *n* thing A 276, 325, etc.; **thing, thyng** *pl* things BD 349, LGW 11, 99; **thynges** A 175, 759, etc.; **on alle t.** under any circumstance BD 141.

thirled *pp* pierced TC 2.642, A 2710.

this *demon adj & pron* A 269, B 1690, etc.; **this** *pl* PF 473, TC 5.344; **thise** *pl* these A 1452, 1951; those LGW 42; **thise, these** (in the distributive or generalizing sense in which we use *those* and *your*) **thise olde wives** your old women TC 5.379; **thise bokes** those books (that will be written) TC 5.1060; **as thise loveres don** as (your) lovers do TC 5.1572.

this *contr of* **this is** PF 650, TC 2.363, 5.151.

tho, thoo *demon adj & pron* those LGW 153, A 498, 1123, etc.

tho, thoo *adv* then BD 786, 1099, HF 1404, etc.; still BD 1054.

thogh, though *conj* though, although A 68, 727, etc.

thoght, thought *n* BD 4, 524, A 479, etc.; **thoght, bisy t.** anxiety TC 1.579, B 1779.

tholed *pp* suffered D 1546.

thombe *n* thumb A 563, F 83, 148.

thonder *n* thunder HF 534, TC 2.233, A 492.

thonder-dent, -dynt *n* thunderbolt TC 5.1505, D 276; thunderclap A 3807.

thonk, thonken see **thank, thanken.**

thorpes see **throop.**

thorugh-darted *pp* pierced through TC 1.325.

thorugh-girt *pp* pierced through TC 4.627; **thurgh-g.** A 1010.

thorugh-shoten *pp* shot through TC 1.325.

thral *adj* enslaved A 1552.

thral *n* thrall, slave, servant BD 767, B 3343, C 183, etc.

thralle(n) *v* enthrall, enslave TC 1.235, 2.773.

thre, three *adj* three A 164, 639, etc.; **a thre** in three A 2934.

threed, thred *n* thread PF 267, TC 4.1546, A 2030.

threpe *1 pl* assert, maintain G 826.

threshfold *n* threshold A 3482, E 288, 291.

threste *v* thrust A 2612; **thraste, threste, thriste** *pt 3 s* TC 2.1155, 3.1574, E 2003; pierced TC 4.254; **thraste** *pt pl* pushed C 260.

threteth *3 s* threatens TC 4.909.

thretyng *n* threatening G 698.

thrie *adv* three times TC 2.89, 463.

thries, thryes *adv* thrice PF 61, A 63, 463.

thrift *n* prosperity, success TC 2.847, G 1425; **by my t.** a mild oath HF 1847, TC 2.1483, 3.871, A 4049.

thriftiest(e) *adj as n* worthiest TC 1.1081, 2.737.

thriftily *adv* properly A 3131; in a becoming manner TC 3.211, A 105, F 1174.

thrifty *adj* prudent TC 1.275; suitable, profitable B 46, 138; decent, proper D 238.

thringe *v* press TC 4.66; **throng** *pt 3 s* thrust E 2353.

throop *n* village E 199, 208; **thropes, thorpes** *pl* PF 350, D 871.

throstil, thrustel *n* thrush PF 364, B 1963.

throte-bolle *n* Adam's apple A 4273.

throwe *n* short time, little while, moment TC 4.384, 5.1461, B 953, D 1815; **in a t.** quickly, briefly TC 2.1655.

throwes *n pl* throes TC 5.206, 1201.

thrustlecok *n* thrush B 1959.

thurgh *prep* through A 920, etc.

thurghfare *n* thoroughfare A 2847.

thurghout, throughout *prep* through A 1096, C 655; throughout HF 1641, A 1432.

thurste *pt 3 subj impers* it would be needful TC 3.572 (see note). Cf. **thar.**

thwite *v* whittle HF 1938.

thwitel *n* knife A 3933.

thynke, thinke *v* seem TC 1.405, E 908; **thynketh** *3 s impers* it seems TC 1.403, A37; **thoughte, thoghte** *pt 3 s impers* it seemed BD 50, 233.

thynke(n), thenke(n), thinke *v* think BD 100, F 857; imagine, conceive PF 311, E 1341; call to mind, remember HF 387, LGW 379; consider, believe TC 2.1255, E 1503; **thynke, thenke** *1 s* think TC 1.998; have in mind BD 1176, PF 6, D 464; intend TC 1.263, B 1311; **thynkest** TC 2.1506; **thenke** *2 s subj* TC 5.735; **thynk-eth, thenketh** *3 s* TC 1.221, 2.33; **thynke(n), thenken** *pl* think F 537; have regard for A 3701; deem, judge D 2204; **thoghte, thoughte** *pt 1 & 3 s* A 984, 1767, 3453; **thoughte(n)** *pt pl* TC 1.927, D 2030; **thynk, thenk** *imp s* meditate, reflect on A 3478, Scogan 47; remember A 1606, G 59; believe TC 1.1060; consider TC 1.897, E 2165; **thynketh, thenketh** *imp pl* TC 1.26, C 75; **thynkyng, thenk-yng** *part* TC 1.1062, 3.1539; **thought** *pp* TC 4.542.

thyself, thyselven, thi- *refl pron* HF 596, TC 2.1008, E 1385; *as intensive* TC 5.1711, A 1174; *as pers pron* thou thyself TC 3.259, 299.

tidyves see **tydif**.

tigre, tygre *n* tiger A 1657, 2626; **tigres** *gen* HF 1459.

tikel *adj* uncertain A 3428.

til *prep* to TC 1.128, 2.1346, A 180, etc.; into A 2062; until A 1621; **til now late** until recently BD 45; **t. and fra** to and fro A 4039 (Northern).

til *conj* until BD 155, HF 2080, A 698, etc.; **t. into** until TC 4.1516.

tiptoon *n pl* tiptoes B 4497.

tirannye *n* cruelty, imperious behavior A 941, B 165, 696, etc.

tiraunt *n* tyrant A 961.

tiraunt *adj* tyrannical LGW 377.

tiren *3 pl* tear TC 1.787.

titeryng *n* vacillation, hesitation TC 2.1744.

title *n* title, claim B 3512; name TC 1.488.

titlelees *adj* without title, usurping H 223.

to *prep* to A 30, etc.; for D 1791, E 793; of TC 3.1284, LGW 538; against C 416, E 1829; **to respect of** in comparison with TC 5.1818; **to the beste** for the best TC 4.1285.

to *adv* too A 875, B 420, F 525, etc.

tobete *v* beat severely G 405.

tobreke *v* break A 3918; **tobreketh** *3 s* is broken HF 779, G 907; **to-broke** *pp* broken A 4277, D 277; **tobroken** Scogan 1.

tobreste *v* burst or break in two TC 2.608, 4.1546; **tobreste** *3 pl* A 2611; **tobrosten** *pp* shattered A 2691, 2757.

tocleve *v* split in two TC 5.613.

todasshed *pp* battered TC 2.640.

toforn, tofore *prep* before TC 1.1049, 2.1409, F 268.

toft *n* tuft A 555.

toght *adj* taut D 2267.

togidre, togydre *adv* A 824, 2624; **togeder(e)** HF 2109, PF 555; **to-gidres** C 702; **togedres** BD 809.

to-go *pp* dispersed LGW 653.

to-hepe *adv* together TC 3.1764.

tohewen *3 pl* hew to pieces A 2609; **tohewe(n)** *pp* cut to pieces TC 2.638, B 430.

token *n* evidence B 1580; **tokenes** *pl* evidence, proof B 1549, 1593, H 258.

tokenyng *n:* **in tokenyng(e)** in token, as evidence TC 4.779, 870, G 1153, H 302.

to-laugh (for **to-lough**?) laughed TC 2.1108.

tollen *v* take a toll, keep part in payment A 562.

tombe, toumbe *n* tomb B 1871, D 497, F 518.

tombesteres *n pl* female acrobats or dancers C 477.

to-morn *adv* tomorrow D 1245, 1588.

to-morwe, tomorwe *adv* tomorrow TC 1.861, A 780, 1610; **t. day** tomorrow morning, at dawn TC 3.385.

tonge *n* tongue A 265, etc.; language HF 1234, F 711; **tonges** *gen* language's TC 1.395; *pl* languages B 3497.

tonne *n* tun, wine-cask A 3894, E 215; **another t.** something different, a different matter LGW 195, D 170.

tonne-greet *adj* large as a tun A 1994.

to-nyght *adv* tonight A 4253, B 1468; last night B 4116, C 673.

too *n* toe A 2726; **toos** *pl* B 4370, 4521; **toon** *pl* HF 2028, B 4052.

tool *n* sword, weapon B 4106.

toon see **too**.

top *n* top LGW 639, A 2915; head A 3869; hair, top hair A 590, C 255.

torace *3 pl subj* tear to pieces E 572.

torente (torende) *v* tear to pieces B.3451; **torende** *3 pl subj* TC 2.790; **torente** *pt 3 s* B 3251; *pt 3 pl* TC 4.341; **torent** *pp* C 102; tattered PF 432, E 1012.

torment *n* torment, suffering A 1298, 2320; torture B 1818, 3779.

tormente *v* torment, make suffer TC 1.634; **tormenteth** *3 s* A 1314; **tormented** *pp* tortured B 885.

tormentise *n* torture B 3707.

tormentrie *n* torment D 251.

tormentynge *n* torment, suffering E 1038.

torn *n* turn (service) C 815.

torne(n), turne(n), tourne *v* turn BD 256, TC 3.179, A 1488, B 4404; return TC 3.1516, D 988, F 127; **turnest** *2 s* TC 1.196; **torneth, turneth** *3 s* turns BD 644; returns TC 1.324; **torne, turne** *1 pl subj* let us turn TC 2.1709, B 3487; **torne** *2 pl* return TC 5.245; **turnen** *3 pl* turn C 539; **turne, turn** *imp s* HF 925, A 2318; **torned(e), turned** *pt 3 s* TC 3.444, 4.855, B 4200; **torned, turned** *pt pl* TC 2.1347, A 3842; **torned, turned, yturned** *pp* BD 446, TC 3.1400, A 2058; reversed BD 688.

tornyng, turnynge *n* turning HF 182, TC 1.856.

tortuous *adj* ascending obliquely to the horizon B 302 (see note to B 301).

toscatered *pp* scattered about D 1969.

toshrede *3 pl* reduce to shreds A 2609.

to-shyvered *pp* splintered PF 493.

tosterte *v* burst TC 2.980.

totelere *adj* tattling, tale-bearing LGW 353.

totere *3 pl* tear to pieces C 474; **totar** *pt 3 s* B 3801; **totore, totorn** *pp* torn PF 110; tattered G 635; distraught TC 4.358.

toty *adj* dizzy, befuddled A 4253.

tough, towgh *adj* A 1992; difficult BD 531, TC 2.1025; **maketh it ful t.** shows great vigor B 1569; **make it t.** am too forward TC 5.101; **made it t.** behaved haughtily TC 3.87.

toun, town *n* town A 217, B 148, C 796; **of towne** of the town (in contrast to the country) A 3380.

tour *n* tower, stronghold A 1030, etc.; **toures** *pl* A 2464.

touret *n* turret A 1909.

tourettes *n pl* little rings on a dog's collar for attaching a leash A 2152.

tourneiynge, tur- *n* tourneying A 2557; tournament A 2720.

toute, towte *n* rump A 3812, 3853.

tow *n* flax A 3774, D 89.

towaille *n* towel B 3935, 3943.

to-yere, -yeere *adv* this year HF 84, TC 3.241, D 168.

traas, trace *n* path, footsteps Gent 3; train (of persons) LGW 285.

trad see **trede**.

transmewen *v* transmute, change TC 4.467.

trappe *n* trap A 145.

trapped *pp* equipped with trappings A 2157, 2890.

trappe-dore *n* trap door TC 3.759.

trappures *n pl* coverings for horses, trappings A 2499.

traunce *n* trance A 1572; swoon E 1108; dazed state TC 4.341, D 2216; state of suspense TC 2.1306; ecstasy E 1750.

traunce *v* tramp or run about TC 3.690.

travaille, -aile *n* labor BD 602, TC 1.372; laboring A 3646; trouble TC 5.184.

travaille *v* exert oneself, go to any trouble D 1365; **travaillynge** *part* in labor A 2083.

trave *n* enclosure for unruly horse while being shod A 3282.

travers *n* curtain screening off part of a room TC 3.674, E 1817.

trays *n pl* traces TC 1.222, A 2139.

traysen *v* betray TC 4.438; **traysed** *pt 3 s* HF 390.

trayson, traisoun see **tresoun.**

trayterye *n* treachery HF 1812; **traitorie** conduct of a traitor B 781.

traytours *adj* traitorous C 896.

trede *v* tread A 3022; **tret** *3 s* treads TC 2.347, D 2002; **trad** *pt 3 s* trod (copulated with) B 4368; **troden** *pt pl* trod HF 2153; **tredyng** *part* B 3145.

tredefowel *n* treadfowl B 3135.

tree, tre *n* BD 158, 387; wood D 101, E 558; rood tree, cross A 3767, B 456.

tregetour *n* sleight-of-hand performer, magician HF 1277; *pl* HF 1260, F 1141.

trench *n* path through trees or shrubbery F 392.

trenchant *adj* sharp A 3930.

tresor, -our, -oor *n* treasure TC 3.874, B 442, 515, D 204.

tresorere *n* treasurer Purse 18.

tresorye *n* treasury HF 524.

tresoun, trayson, trai- *n* treason TC 1.107; treachery B 4307, D 723, F 139; betrayal BD 1122.

trespace *v* commit an offense against B 3093, E 1828; **trespased** *pp* done wrong C 416.

trespas, -paas *n* offense A 1764, 1818; wrong B 4610.

trespassynge *n* offense LGW 155.

tresse *n* plait A 1049; tresses HF 230; **tresses** *pl* TC 4.816.

tretable *adj* tractable, approachable BD 533; open to appeal LGW 411; inclinable BD 923.

tretee *n* treaty, agreement A 1288, C 619; negotiation HF 453, B 3865, E 1692; discussion F 1219.

trete(n) *v* deal with, negotiate TC 1.975, 4.58; treat, discuss TC 1.686, C 521; tell PF 34, B 3501; be concerned with C 64; behave, treat (a person) TC 4.813, 5.134; **trete(n)** *3 pl* HF 54, TC 1.742, F 220.

tretys, -is *n* treaty, agreement TC 4.64, 136, 670; document, memorandum TC 2.1697; negotiation B 233, E 331.

tretys *adj* slender, well-proportioned A 152.

trewe *n* truce TC 3.1779, 4.58; **trewes** *pl* TC 5.401.

trewe *adj* true TC 1.593, etc.; honest LGW 464, F 537; *as n* true servant TC 3.141; *as n pl* the faithful B 456.

trewe-love *n* herb-paris A 3692 (see note).

treye *n* three (in dice) C 653.

triacle *n* ointment, remedy B 479, C 314.

trice *v* pull, pluck B 3715.

trille *v* turn F 316; *imp s* F 328.

trist *n* trust TC 1.154, 3.1305.

triste *n* appointed place or station in hunting TC 2.1534.

triste *v* trust TC 1.692, 5.1709, LGW 333.

trogh, trough *n* trough A 3548, 3627, 4043.

trompe, trumpe *n* trumpet HF 1240, LGW 635, A 674; **trumpes** *gen s* HF 1642, 1646; **trompes** *as adj* trumpet-like PF 344.

trompours *n pl* trumpeters A 2671.

tronchoun *n* broken shaft of spear A 2615.

trone *n* throne HF 1397, B 3333; **in t.** on a throne A 2529; **t. of God** heaven C 842.

trouble *adj* troubled E 465, H 279.

trouthe *n* troth, pledge BD 936, F 1474; honesty A 4397; faithfulness TC 4.1477.

trowe(n) *v* believe TC 5.327, G 378; **trow(e)** *1 s* BD 269, HF 61; **trowest** *2 s* BD 651; **trowe** *2 s subj* TC 5.331; **troweth** *3 s* TC 4.837; **trowe** *pl* B 222, C 439; **trowed** *pt s & pl* A 2101, E 403; **trowe** *imp s* TC 4.1547, D 1985; **trowed** *pp* TC 4.383, A 1520.

trumpe(n) *v* trumpet HF 1243, 1245; **tromped** *pt 3 s* E 1719.

trussed *pp* packed A 681.

trye *adj* choice, excellent B 2046.

tryne *adj* threefold G 45.

tryp *n* morsel D 1747.

tuel *n* chimney HF 1649.

tukked *pp* belted in A 621.

tulle *v* attract A 4134.

Turkeys *adj* Turkish A 2895.

turneiynge see **tourneiynge.**

turtil, -tel, -tle *n* turtledove PF 355, 577, A 3706; **turtles** *gen s* E 2139.

turves *pl* patches of turf LGW 204, E 2235.

tuwel *n* rectum D 2148.

twelf *adj* twelve B 1674, D 1576, etc.

twelf-month *n* year A 651, D 909.

tweye *adj* two BD 156, TC 5.628, A 704; **t. and t.** two by two A 898.

tweyfoold *adj* double G 566.

tweyne *adj* two, twain TC 2.620, A 1134.

twighte *pt s* pulled TC 4.1185; **twight** *pp* TC 4.572, D 1563.

twiste *n* branch TC 3.1230, E 2349, F 442.

twiste *v* twist, wring TC 4.1129, F 566; **twiste** *pt 1 & 3 s* wrung, tortured TC 4.254, D 494; squeezed E 2005; *pt 3 s subj* TC 3.1769; **twyst** *pp* HF 775.

twyne *3 s subj* twist, spin TC 5.7.

twynes *n gen s* of twine, of cord A 2030.

twynne(n) *v* sever, separate, be parted TC 5.339, B 517; depart TC 5.1662, B 3195; **twynne** *pl* depart A 835, G 182; **twynned, ytwynned** *pp* TC 4.788, 5.679.

twynnyng *n* separating TC 4.1303.

tyde *n* time BD 207, HF 1951, TC 1.954; tide B 510 (see note); hour B 798.

tyden *v* happen, betide B 337; **tydes** *3 s* comes to A 4175 (Northern form); **tit** *3 s* befalls TC 1.333; **tid** *pp* befallen TC 1.907, 2.224, 464.

tydif *n* small bird (not certainly identified) LGW 154; **tidyves** *pl* F 648.

tykelnesse *n* insecurity Truth 3. Cf. **tikel.**

tymber, -bur *n* material, timber HF 1980, TC 3.530, A 3666.

tyme *n* time A 35, etc.; **tymes** *pl* seasons TC 5.376; **by tyme** early LGW 452; **of olde t.** for a long time B 50; **som t.** once, at one time D 527.

tyne *n* tub, vat Rosem 9.

typet, tipet *n* streamer of a hood or sleeve HF 1841, A 233 (see note), 3953.

U

unable *adj* unworthy G 1131.

unavysed *pp* unaware TC 1.378.

unbodye *v* leave the body TC 5.1550.

unbokelen *v* unbuckle F 555; **unbokele** *imp s* C 945; **unbokeled** *pp* A 3115.

unbore *pp* unborn TC 3.269; **unborn** A 2033.

unbounden *pp* unbound, free from marriage E 1226.

unbrent *pp* unburnt B 1658.

unbroiden *pp* unbraided TC 4.817.

uncircumscript *pp* uncircumscribed, unlimited TC 5.1865.

unclose *v* open LGW 65; **unclosed** *pp* LGW 117.

uncommytted *pp* unassigned (*i.e.* not asked for) PF 518.

uncowple *v* let loose B 3692.

uncurteisly *adv* vulgarly E 2363.

under *prep* beneath A 105, 1981.

under *adv* beneath BD 426.

undermeles *n pl* later mornings D 875.

undernoom *pt 3 s* perceived G 243.

underpighte *pt 3 s* propped up B 789.

underspore *v* pry up A 3465.

undertake *v* undertake an enterprise A 405; declare, assert A 3541, E 803; *1 s* declare A 288, D 592.

undigne *adj* unworthy E 359.

undiscreet *adj* indiscreet B 4624; lacking in judgment E 996.

undren *n* "undern," probably 9 A.M. B 4412 (see note), E 260, 981.

unfamous *adj* without fame, fleeting HF 1146.

unfeestlich *adj* unfestive F 366.

unhap *n* mischance TC 1.552; misfortune HF 89; **unhappes** *pl* TC 2.456.

unhardy *adj* cowardly, timid A 4210.

unheele *n* misfortune C 116.

unholsom *adj* corrupt TC 4.330.

unkouth, -couth *adj* strange, unknown HF 1279, 2010, F 284; unusual, marvellous TC 3.1797, A 2497.

unkynde *adj* unnatural B 88; cruel, faithless PF 358, TC 5.1441.

unkyndely *adv* unnaturally C 485; TC 1.617; cruelly HF 295.

unknowe *pp* unknown A 126, 1406; **unknowen** D 1397.

unkonnyng(e) *adj* unskilful A 2393; stupid TC 5.1139.

unlik *adv* in a manner different from TC 2.1656.

unlikly *adj* unsuitable, unpleasing E 2180.

unliklynesse *n* hopelessness TC 1.16.

unloven *v* cease to love TC 5.1698.

unmanhod *n* an unmanly act TC 1.824.

unmerie *adj* gloomy HF 74.

unmyghty *adj* unable TC 2.858.

unneste *v* go out of the nest TC 4.305.

unnethe, unethe *adv* scarcely BD 270, PF 314, TC 1.354.

unnethes *adv* scarcely HF 900, 1140, D 394, E 318.

unpynne *v* unbolt TC 3.698.

unreste *n* disturbed state of mind, distress TC 4.879, 5.1567, D 1104, E 719.

unresty *adj* unquiet TC 5.1355.

unsad *adj* unstable E 995.

unsely, -seely *adj* unhappy TC 1.35, G 468; unlucky A 4210.

unset *adj* unappointed A 1524.

unshette *pt 3 s* opened E 2047; *pp as adj* not shut HF 1953.

unsittynge *adj* not fitting TC 2.307.

unskilful *adj* unreasonable TC 1.790.

unslekked *adj* unslaked G 806.

unstable *adj* subject to the vicissitudes of fortune B 1877.

unswelle *v* become less swollen TC 4.1146, 5.214.

unthank, -thonk *n* blame TC 5.699; bad luck A 4082.

unthrift *n* impropriety TC 4.431.

unthriftily *adv* negligently, poorly G 893.

unthrifty *adj* unprofitable TC 4.1530.

until *prep* until BD 41; unto, to TC 1.354, A 3761.

unto *prep* unto, to A 71, etc.; until B 765.

unto *conj* until PF 647.

untold *pp* uncounted, countless A 3780.

untressed *pp* loose A 2289, E 379.

untrewe *adv* falsely, inaccurately A 735.

untriste *adj* distrustful TC 3.839.

unwar *adj* unaware TC 1.304, 5.1559; unforeseen, unexpected B 427, 3954.

unwar *adv* unexpectedly F 1356; unawares TC 1.549.

unweelde *adj* weak A 3886.

unweeldy *adj* unwieldy H 55.

unwemmed *pp* unblemished, unstained B 924, G 137.

unwist *adj* unknown A 2977; unaware TC 1.93.

unwit *n* imprudence, stupidity G 1085.

unwrye *v* uncover TC 1.858.

unyolden *pp* not having given up A 2642.

up *prep* upon BD 922; **up peril of, up peyne of** A 1707, D 1145.

up *adv* up A 783, 823, etc.; **up and doun** in all directions A 977; back and forth A 1052; from one end to the other A 2054; everywhere A 2587, D 305; without exception D 119; **up so doun** upside down A 1377, G 625. Cf. **doun.**

up-born *pp* respected TC 1.375.

up-bounde *pp* bound up, completed TC 3.517.

upon *prep* upon, on A 111, etc.; about, concerning BD 1023, TC 3.277, B 1805; in A 3359, D 991,
F 925; to A 4006; toward A 2629; **u. lengthe** at last BD 352; **u. lyve** alive TC 2.1030; **u. a rore** into an uproar TC 5.45.

upon *adv* on A 617, D 1382.

upper *adv* farther up, higher HF 884.

upright(e) *adv* face up, upon the back A 4194, B 1506, D 578, 768; **upryght** BD 175; erect BD 622.

uprist *n* rising; **at the sonne upriste** at the rising of the sun A 1051.

uprist see **upryseth.**

upryseth, uprist *3 s* rises TC 4.1443, LGW 49.

urynales *n pl* urinals C 305; glass vessels (in alchemy) G 792.

usage *n* practice, habit A 110, C 899, etc.

usaunce *n* custom, usage PF 674, LGW 586.

usaunt *adj* accustomed A 3940.

use(n) *v* use, practise B 44, D 149, etc.

us self, us selven *pron* ourselves D 812, E 108.

usure *n* usury B 1681, D 1309.

V

vacacioun *n* free time D 683.

vane *n* weathercock E 996.

vanysshe *v* vanish F 328; *1 s* waste away C 732; **vanysshed** *pt 3 s* disappeared F 342, G 216; **vanysshed** *pp* D 996.

vanysshynge *n* disappearance A 2360.

vanyte(e) *n* foolishness A 3835; foolish behavior E 250; foolish ideas, nonsense D 1309, 2208; idle talk TC 4.729; **vanytees** *pl* foolishness B 4281.

vapour *n* vapor F 393; emanation, influence TC 3.11.

variaunce *n* uncertainty, different alternatives TC 4.985.

variaunt *adj* shifty G 1175.

varien *v* be otherwise TC 2.1621; **varye** *1 s* deviate, depart HF 807.

vassellage *n* prowess A 3054.

vavasour *n* baron A 360 (see note).

venerye *n* hunting A 166, 2308.

vengeaunce *n* revenge B 1383; retribution B 923; punishment A 2066, 3506.

venquysseth *3 s* vanquishes F 774; **venquysshed** *pp* B 291, 3782.

ventusynge *n* bloodletting A 2747.

venysoun *n* any beast of chase, esp. deer C 83.

verdegrees *n* verdigris, copper acetate G 790.

verdit *n* verdict PF 503, 525; **voirdit** A 787.

vermyn(e) *n* vermin TC 3.381; objectionable animals C 858, E 1095.

vernycle *n* vernicle A 685 (see note).

vernysshed *pp* varnished; **v. his heed** made himself drunk A 4149.

verraly *adv* verily HF 1729.

verray *adj* true TC 1.913, A 72, D 1204, etc.; faithful E 2285.

verrayment *adv* truly B 1903.

verre *n* glass TC 2.867.

vers *n* verse, line HF 1098; **vers** *pl* verses PF 124, TC 1.7, B 4503.

vertu *n* essential quality TC 4.1491, A 4; faculty HF 550; natural ability A 1436; power, efficacy HF 526, F 146; virtue, goodness E 216.

vertulees *adj* without efficacy TC 2.344.

very *adv* truly, exactly HF 1079. See **verray.**

verye *n* meaning unknown A 3485 (see note).

vessel *n* vessel D 100; (collectively) vessels B 3338, 3494; **vessels** *pl* A 2907.

vestiment *n* vestment, robe F 59; **vestimentz** *pl* A 2948.

vesture *n* garment HF 1325.

veyl *n* veil A 695.

veyn *adj* worthless A 1094, G 497; **veyne glorie** vainglory A 2240, C 411.

veyne-blood *n* bloodletting A 2747.

veze *n* rush of air A 1985.

viage *n* trip, journey A 723, B 259; expedition, undertaking TC 3.732, A 77; voyage B 4274; **viages** *pl* HF 1962.

vicary *n* vicar I 22.

vice *n* vice HF 275, B 364, etc.; fault F 101; blemish D 955; wrong TC 5.1708; wrong-doing D 1578.

vicius, -ious *adj* given to vice D 2048; wicked C 459.

victorie *n* victory A 916; **with v.** victoriously A 872.

vigile *n* vigil, wake TC 5.305; **vigilies** *pl* vigils A 377, D 556.

vileynye, vilanye *n* rudeness of speech or manner, characteristic of a villein A 70, C 740; ill-breeding, bad manners HF 96, TC 5.490, A 726; shame, wrong TC 2.438, E 2310; harm A 4191; disgrace, outrage A 942, 2729, E 2261; reproach TC 4.21, D 34; **lucre of v.** wicked gain B 1681; **in v.** shamefully G 156.

vinolent *adj* full of wine D 1931; under the influence of wine D 467.

violes *n pl* vials G 793.

viritoot *n* meaning unknown A 3770 (see note).

virytrate *n* old woman, trot D 1582.

visage *v* brazen it out D 2273.

visitaciouns *n pl* visits D 555.

vitaille *n* food, foodstuff A 248, 569, 749.

vitremyte *n* hood of glass B 3562 (see note).

vitriole *n* sulphuric acid G 808.

voidë *n* wine, with cakes, etc. taken before retiring TC 3.674.

voide *adj* devoid TC 2.173, LGW 167.

volage *adj* giddy, inconstant H 239.

volatyl *n* wild fowl B 1262.

voluper *n* cap, bonnet A 3241; nightcap A 4303.

vouchesauf *v* vauchsafe TC 5.1341, A 807; **vouchen sauf** TC 5.1858; **vouchsauf** *1 s* TC 2.1083, 4.90; *2 pl subj* TC 5.922.

voyden *v* get rid of, remove A 2751, E 910, 1815; **voyded** *pt 3 pl* made to vanish F 1150; **voyde** *imp s* vacate E 806; send away G 1136; **voyded, yvoyded** *pp* got rid of F 1159; made to vanish F 1195; gone away TC 2.912.

W

waast *n* waist B 1890.

waat see **witen.**

wade(n) *v* go B 3684, E 1684; wade D 2084; enter TC 2.150.

wafereres *n pl* makers and sellers of wafers and cakes C 479.

waget *adj* blue A 3321.

wailen, waille, wayle *v* wail, lament TC 4.399, A 1295, E 1212; **wayle** *1 s* A 931; **wailest** *2 s* TC 1.556; **wayleth, weyleth** *3 s* A 1221, 3618; **wayled** *pt 3 s* B 3811, F 1116; **waillynge** *part* A 1366.

waityng *n* watching H 252.

wake(n) *v* be awake, stay awake BD 236, A 3686, E 1856; keep vigils TC 3.540, D 1847; arouse B 1187; **waketh** *3 s* A 3373; wakes up E 2397; **wake** *3 pl* wake up PF 689; **wook, wok** *pt 3 s* lay awake TC 5.289; was awake B 497; awoke TC 5.928, A 1393; **waketh** *imp pl* watch D 1654.

wake-pleyes *n pl* funeral games A 2960.

waker *adj* vigilant PF 358.

walet *n* bag, knapsack, pilgrim's scrip A 681, 686.

walke(n) *v* walk A 2309, D 448; **walked** *pt 1 & 3 s* A 3458, C 722; **welk** *pt 1 & 3 s* PF 297, TC 2.517, 5.1235; **walked** *pp* A 2368; **I (he) was go walked** I (he) had walked BD 387, D 1778.

walsh-note *n* walnut HF 1281.

walwe *v* wallow TC 1.699; **walweth** *3 s* tosses D 1085; **walwe** *3 pl* A 4278; **walwynge** *part* surging

A 3616; **walwed** *pp* immersed, wallowing Rosem 17, 18.

wanges *n pl* cheek-teeth, molars A 4030.

wang-tooth *n* cheek tooth, molar B 3234.

wanhope *n* despair A 1249.

wante *v* be wanting, be absent LGW 361; **wante** *1 s* lack PF 287; **wanteth** *3 s* is lacking TC 4.1568, H 338.

wantown *adj* wanton E 236, 1846; **wantowne** *as n* person given to pleasure A 208.

wantownesse *n* wantonness A 264 (see note), B 31.

wantrust *n* mistrust TC 1.794; distrust H 281.

wanye, wane *v* wane A 2078, C 23; decrease A 3025.

war *adj* aware PF 218, TC 2.1467, A 157; cautious B 1555; wary A 309; **be war** take warning, beware A 1218, B 3375, 3923.

warde *n* keeping C 201; **on w.** on (my) surety BD 248.

warde-cors *n* bodyguard D 359.

warderere *excl* look behind A 4101.

wardeyn, -dein *n* warden A 3999, 4075; guardian TC 3.665; **warden** TC 5.1177.

wardrobe *n* privy B 1762.

ware *n* wares, merchandise B 140, 1246, D 522.

war(e) *v* (*refl*) beware A 662; *imp pl* B 1889, C 905, D 1903.

warente *v* protect, guarantee C 338; **warante** *1 s* warrant A 3791.

warice *v* cure C 906. Cf. **warisshed.**

warien *v* curse TC 2.1619; **warie, warye** *1 s* TC 5.1378, B 372.

warisshed *pp* cured F 856, 1138, 1162; **warysshed** BD 1104.

warly *adv* carefully, warily TC 3.454.

warne *v* warn HF 1068; *1 s* A 3558; inform E 1073; **warneth** *3 s* HF 46; **warned(e)** *pt 1 & 3 s* informed PF 45, G 590; **warned** *pp* foretold HF 51; informed TC 3.1669.

warnynge *n* information G 593; notice B 4316; invitation, command TC 3.195.

waryangles *n pl* shrikes D 1408.

wasshe *v* wash B 356; **wessh** *pt 3 s* washed A 2283, B 453, 3934; **wesshen** *pt pl* TC 2.1184; **wasshe(n)** *pp* A 3311, C 353.

wast *n* waste C 593, D 500; wastefulness B 1609.

waste *adj* devastated A 1331.

wastel-breed *n* one of the best grades of bread ("cake bread") A 147 (see note).

waste(n) *v* waste PF 283, G 1422; waste away TC 3.348; **wasteth** *3 s* wastes E 1343; wears away A 3023; **wasted** *pp* wasted B 1207; consumed, destroyed A 3020.

water *n* water TC 3.115, A 400, etc.; body of water, stream F 1144; liquid G 1459.

wateryng *n* watering-place A 826.

waterlees *adj* waterless, out of water A 180.

wawe *n* wave B 508; **wawes** *pl* TC 2.1, B 468.

waxe(n), wexe(n) *v* wax, grow, increase BD 415, PF 207, 444, D 28; become TC 2.1578; **waxeth, wexeth** *3 s* TC 1.949, A 3024; **wex, weex, wax** *pt 3 s* BD 1215, B 563, TC 3.242; **wexen** *pt pl* BD 489; **woxe(n), wexen, waxen** *pp* BD 414, HF 1146, 1391, C 71, E 2071.

wayk *adj* weak B 1671; **wayke** *pl & def* A 887, B 932.

wayken *v* weaken, diminish TC 4.1144.

waymentynge *n* lamentation TC 2.65, A 902, 995, 1921.

wayte(n), waiten *v* watch, watch for TC 1.190, F 444, 1263; expect TC 3.491, B 246; **wayte after** expect B 467; **wayteth, waiteth** *3 s* watches B 593, E 708; watches (for an opportunity) A 1222, B 3331; lies in wait B 582, G 9; **wayte** *2 pl subj* A 3295; **wayten** *3 pl* F 88; **wayted** *pt 3 s* watched A 571, F 129; **waited after** looked for A 525; **waited on** observed TC 3.534; **was wayting on** was waiting for TC 5.24; **wayte upon** *imp s* wait for HF 342; **waityng(e)** *part* watching B 4413, D 1376; **wayte what** whatever D 517.

we *pron* A 29, etc.; **oure** *gen* PF 545, TC 4.539; **oures** B 1463, G 786; **us** *dat & acc* BD 1294, A 566.

webbe *n* weaver A 362.

wedde *n* pledge; **to w.** in pawn A 1218; as a pledge B 1613.

wede, weede *n* cloak, garment TC 3.1431; clothing A 1006, E 863.

weder *n* weather TC 2.2, B 873; **wedres** *pl* PF 681.

weel, wel *adj & adv* well A 24, 29, 926, 2123, etc.

weelde(n), welde *v* control B 3452, D 271; have the use of D 1947; **welte, weelded** *pt 3 s* ruled over B 3200, 3855.

weerieth *3 s* wearies G 1304.

weet *adj* wet A 4107; **wete, weete** *pl & def* A 2338, E 2140; **weet, wete** *as n* B 3407, G 1187.

weldy *adj* vigorous TC 2.636.

wele *n* well-being, welfare, prosperity A 895, B 3268, C 115, Truth 4, Buk 27; happiness, good fortune A 1272, E 842.

welfare *n* well-being, prosperity A 3060, B 1529; happiness BD 582; bliss 1040.

wel farynge *adj* handsome, attractive BD 452, B 3132.

welful *adj* blessed B 451.

welked *pp* withered C 738, D 277.

welken *n* sky BD 339, 409; **fro (on) the welkne** from (in) the sky B 3921, E 1124.

welle *n* spring HF 1653, PF 211, A 2283, B 2105; source PF 62, TC 1.873, F 505; pool B 3234; **welles** *pl* springs B 160; small streams F 898.

welle *n* will A 3037.

welle-stremes *n pl* springs PF 187.

welte see **weelden.**

wel-willy *adj* beneficent TC 3.1257.

wem *n* harm F 121.

wemmelees *adj* spotless, without blemish G 47.

wende(n) *v* turn HF 1868; go, go away, leave TC 5.476, A 21; walk B 1683; **wendeth, went** *3 s* goes TC 2.812, D 918; **wende** *2 pl subj* TC 4.1495; **wende** *3 pl* A 16; **wente** *pt 3 s* turned HF 1925; went TC 2.813; went on TC 5.1574; **wente(n)** *pt pl* A 1200, 2490; **went** *pp* gone TC 5.546, E 276.

wendyng *n* departure TC 4.1344, 1436, 1630.

wene *n* doubt TC 4.1593.

wene(n) *v* think, suppose A 1655, G 676; except A 4320; **wene** *1 s* think B 4643; **wenest** *2 s* BD 744; **weneth** *3 s* TC 1.216; **wene(n)** *3 pl* E 1280; consider themselves A 1804; **wende** *pt 1 & 3 s* TC 1.227, LGW 462; **wende(n)** *pt pl* thought, supposed B 3637, D 2029; **wenden** *pt 3 pl subj* should think A 3962; **wend** *pp* TC 5.1682, E 691; **ywent** *pp* weened, supposed TC 5.444.

wente *n* turn TC 2.815, 5.605; twisting and turning TC 2.63; path BD 398, HF 182; passage TC 3.787.

wepe *n* weeping TC 5.1078, F 1480 (but see note).

wepe(n) *v* weep TC 4.912, A 144, etc.; **wepeth** *3 s* A 1221; **wepen** *3 pl* TC 1.7, B 529; **weep, wepte** *pt 3 s* wept TC 5.725, A 148, B 606; **wepten** *pt pl* TC 5.1822; **weep** *imp s* A 2470; **wopen, wepen** *pp* TC 1.941, 5.724, F 523.

werbul *n* tune TC 2.1033.

were[1] *n* state of uncertainty or perplexity HF 979; **withoute w.** without doubt HF 1295.

were[2] *n* trap for fish PF 138, TC 3.35.

were[1] *v* defend A 2550.

were[2] *v* wear B 3562, E 886; **werest** *2 s* HF 1840; **wereth** *3 s* D 1018; **were** *3 s subj* Gent 7, 14, 21; **wered(e)** *pt 3 s* wore A 75, 564; **wered** *pp* worn B 3663.

werk *n* work A 3311, etc.; act, deed A 479, B 930; **werkes** *pl* A 3308; *gen* deeds', labors' B 3286.

werken, werketh see **wirche.**

werkes *3 pl* (Northern) ache A 4030.

werkman *n* workman E 1832.

werkyng, wirkyng *n* working D 698; deed H 210.

werne *v* refuse, deny HF 1797, TC 3.12, 149; forbid D 333; **werne** *1 s* refuse HF 1559; **werned** *pt 3 s* HF 1539.

werre *n* war A 47, 1287, etc.; **of w.** in war TC 1.134.

werre *adv* worse BD 616.

werreye *v* wage war A 1484, B 3522; **werreyest** *2 s* LGW 322; **werreyed** *pt 3 s* F 10; **wereyed** *pp* TC 5.584.

werreyour *n* warrior LGW 597.

wers *adj* worse BD 814, 1118.

wers *adv* worse A 3733; **werse** F 600.

werte *n* wart A 555.

wery *adj* weary TC 2.211, A 4107, etc.; *as pseudo adv with pp* **wery forgo** HF 115; **wery forwaked** B 596 (to the point of weariness).

weste *v* move westward PF 266, LGW 61, 197.

westren *v* move westward TC 2.906.

wete *adv* wet HF 922, TC 4.815.

wete *v* wet HF 1785, TC 3.1115; **wette** *pt 3 s* A 129; **ywet** *pp* A 4155.

wether *n* sheep TC 4.1374, A 3249; **wetheres** *pl* A 3542.

wex *n* wax A 675, E 1430.

wey *n* way A 34; route B 807; **do wey** come, now! TC 2.893; **at the leeste weye** at least E 966; **by no weye** in any way B 590; **weyes** *pl* means BD 1271; **other weyes** otherwise TC 3.1658; **noon other weyes** no other way BD 1272; **any weyes** *gen as adv* in any wise HF 1122.

weyen *v* weigh LGW 398, B 3776; **weyest** *2 s* hast importance B 3423; **weyeth** *3 s* weighs A 1781; **weyed** *pt 3 s* G 1298; **weyeden** *pt pl* A 454.

weylaway *excl* A 938, 4072, 4113; **weylawey** A 3602, 3714; **weilawey** D 216; **wailaway** TC 3.1695.

weyve(n)[1] *v* abandon, forsake, shun D 1176, G 276; turn aside E 2424; **w. from** abandon, forsake E 1483;

weyveth *3 s* TC 4.602, H 178; **weyven** *3 pl* forsake I 33.

weyve(n)² *v* remove, cast aside TC 2.284, 1050; **weyved** *pp* banished B 308.

wezele *n* weasel A 3234.

whan *conj* when A 1, 135, etc.

what *rel pron* what D 1735; who TC 1.765, 862.

what *interrog pro & adj* what A 905, 1029, 3370; **what me is** what is the matter with me BD 31.

what *indef pron* whatever PF 46, TC 1.320, 5.1773; **what so** whatever TC 3.1799, 4.442; whoever A 522; **what . . . so, what . . . that** whatsoever E 157, 160.

what *conj* however, as much as TC 4.35; **what . . . what** both . . . and PF 15.

what *interrog adv* why TC 2.262, A 184, B 374; how BD 1308, TC 2.862, A 1307; **what for, what with** in view of, because of A 865, 1453, 3967.

what *interj* TC 5.904, A 854, 3437, 3666, etc.

wheither *indef pron* whichever A 1856, D 1227; **the w.** which (of two) D 1234.

wheither *interrog adv* (introducing a direct question involving alternatives) A 1125, D 2069. Cf. **wher.**

whelkes *n pl* pimples filled with pus A 632.

whelp *n* puppy, small dog BD 389, A 257; cub A 2627; dog F 491; **whelpes** *pl* dogs B 4122, G 60.

whenne *adv* whence E 588

whennes *adv* whence TC 1.402, C 335, etc.

wher *conj* whether BD 91, HF 890, TC 2.1263, etc.; **wher so** whether TC 1.270, B 294, F 778; wherever BD 977.

wher *interrog adv* (introducing a direct question involving alternatives) HF 1779, TC 4.831, B 3119. Cf. **wheither.**

wher as, where as *adv & conj* where TC 3.516, 5.753; whereas B 3347, E 729.

wherby *conj*: **w. that** by which A 2266; why TC 3.778.

wherof *conj* of what TC 5.1224; for what H 339.

wheston *n* whetstone TC 1.631.

whete *n* wheat A 3988, etc.

whete seed *n* wheat grain D 143.

whette *pp pl* whet, sharpened TC 5.1760.

which *rel pron & adj* which, who, whom BD 96, A 836, 846, C 105, etc.; **which that** who, what B

3205, 3769; **which, whiche** *def adj* D 676, 993; **whiche** *pl* which, what A 2972, E 1445.

which *interrog pron & adj* which, what TC 2.1189, F 1622; *in exclamations* **which a** what a BD 734, TC 1.803, LGW 668; **whiche** *pl* what BD 859, E 2421.

which *indef pron* whichever A 796.

whider *adv* whither HF 602, TC 4.282, E 588; **w. so** whithersoever TC 3.391.

whiderward *adv* whither F 1510.

whielen *v* wheel, carry with the motion of a wheel TC 1.139.

whil *conj* while A 35, 397, etc.

while, whyle *n* time, while A 1437, 3299; time spent, trouble B 584; **in the meene whiles** meanwhile B 668. For *gen s as conj* see **whiles.**

whileer *adv* a while ago G 1328.

whiles, whils *conj* while, whilst BD 177, G 1137, 1139, 1179; **the w.** while, whilst B 151; **that w.** as long as C 439.

whilk *interrog pron & adj* (Northern) which A 4078; **whilk a** what a A 4171.

whilom *adv* at one time, once upon a time A 795, 859, 867, etc.

whippeltree *n* dogwood A 2923.

whistle *n* throat A 4155.

whit, whyt *adj* white A 238, 332, 2178, etc.; blond D 624; **white, whyte** *pl & def* A 90, 976, etc.; specious TC 3.901.

whiten *v* grow light TC 5.276.

who, whoo *interrog pron* who BD 181, A 831, etc.; **whos** *gen* B 1018, E 770; **whom** TC 4.967, 5.235.

who *indef pron* whoever BD 32; one who BD 559.

whos *inter & rel pron* B 642, D 1768; **whom** A 501, 893.

wicchecraft *n* witchcraft D 1305.

wicches *n pl* witches HF 1262.

wight, wyght *n* creature, being, person, fellow BD 244, HF 276, A 71, etc.; **a little (lite) w.** a little bit or while TC 5.927, A 4283.

wight *adj* strong B 3457; fleet A 4086.

wighte *n* weight HF 739, TC 2.1385, A 2145.

wikes see **wyke.**

wikke *adj* wicked, evil HF 349, TC 1.403, A 1087; debased HF 1346; *as n* bad TC 3.1074, 4.840.

wikked *adj* wicked, evil A 3484, D 685.

wilde fyr *n* erysipelas A 4172, E 2252; highly inflammable material, used in warfare D 373 (see note).

wile *n* subtlety PF 215.

wilful *adv* wilfully PF 429.

wilfully *adv* voluntarily B 4557, C 441; intentionally TC 2.284.

wille *v* wish E 721; **willeth, wil** *3 s* wishes HF 447, B 1843. See **wol.**

willynge *n* wish E 319.

wilnen *v* wish A 2114; **wilne** *1 s* HF 1094, TC 3.295; **wilnest** *2 s* A 1609; **wilneth** *3 s* TC 4.615, A 2564; **wilnen** *pl* HF 1312, TC 3.121; **wilned** *pt 1 s* BD 1262, 1267.

wir *n* wire TC 3.1636.

wirche, werken *v* work, do, perform A 779, 3308, 3131, 3430, etc.; **worcheth** *3 s* works, causes BD 815; **werche** *1 pl* G 755; **wroghte, wroughte** *pt 1 & 3 s* TC 1.1071, 3.261, A 497; **wroughte(n)** *pt pl* TC 1.63, 3.1354; **wirk** *imp s* E 1485; **werketh** *imp pl* do TC 3.943, E 504; **wrought, wroght, ywroght** *pp* wrought TC 1.578, A 196, 367.

wirkyng see **werkyng.**

wis, wise see **wys, wyse.**

wisly *adv* certainly, surely HF 1860, PF 117, TC 2.1230, A 1863, etc.

wisse *v* inform, instruct HF 491, D 1415; show the way PF 74; manage TC 1.622; be (my) guide D 1858.

wit, wyt *n* mind BD 505, 751; understanding BD 1095, D 41; intelligence BD 756, 1094, TC 3.216; wisdom C 326; judgment B 10, E 149; opinion TC 4.1425, 5.758; **wittes** *pl* minds, etc. B 202; plans, devices D 1479.

wite *n* blame TC 2.1648, 3.739, G 953.

wite, wyte *v* blame TC 1.825, 2.385, B 3636, D 806; **wyte** *1 s* B 3860; **wytest** *2 s* reproachest B 108; **wyte** *imp s* blame on TC 2.1000, A 3140, E 2177.

wite(n) *v* know BD 112, TC 2.226, LGW 7; **wot, woot** *1 & 3 s* BD 1236, PF 7, A 389; **wost, woost** *2 s* BD 743, A 2301; **wostow** dost thou know LGW 499; **waat** *3 s* (Northern) A 4086; **witen** *pl* A 1260, 1794, D 1890; **woot** *2 pl* BD 16, A 829; **wite** *2 pl* HF 1618; **wiste** *pt 1 & 3 s* A 224, 766; **wystestow** if thou didst know TC 3.1644; **wiste(n)** *pt pl* TC 5.20, B 1820, C 266; **wiste** *pt s subj* BD 262, B 1638, C 370; **witteth** *imp pl* TC 1.687; **wist, wyst** *pp* known B 1072, F 260; come to know G 282.

with *prep* with A 10, 31, etc.; by PF 248, TC 4.1430, A 2018, 2691, 2728, D 594, E 1819; of HF 1306; as to E 1499.

withal, withalle, with-alle, with

alle *adv* withal HF 212, TC 1.288, A 127, 751; besides BD 1205, D 156.

with(h)olde(n) *v* retain TC 4.597; restrain TC 5.76, B 3186; **withholde(n)** *pp* retained G 345; committed to the service of LGW 192; supported A 511.

withoute *adv* outside BD 299, 359, E 332.

withoute(n) *prep* without BD 280, A 343, etc.; without, besides A 461.

withseye, -seyn *v* contradict, deny, oppose A 805, 1140; renounce G 447, 457; refuse LGW 367; **withseyde** *pt 3 s* spoke against TC 4.215.

withstonde *v* oppose, withstand TC 1.839, B 3110; **withstandeth** *3 s* D 1497; **withstonde** *pp* withstood TC 1.253, 4.1298.

witnesse *n* testimony TC 4.741, B 629; witness C 169, 186; **took w. on** took as witness D 382.

witnesse *imp s*: **witnesse on** take or consider as a witness B 4426, C 634, D 951.

witnessyng(e) *n* testimony LGW 299, C 194.

wityng *n* knowledge A 1611, D 649; **wytynge** TC 4.991; **wyttynge** TC 2.236.

wlatsom *adj* loathsome B 3814, 4243.

wo, woo *n* woe A 919, etc.; sorrow, lamentation A 900; **wher me be wo** whether I am unhappy TC 3.66.

wo, woo *adj* unhappy BD 896, 1192, E 753.

wodebynde *n* woodbine TC 3.1231, A 1508.

wodedowve *n* wood pigeon.

wol, wole *1 s* will BD 226, A 723, 1450; wish A 889, B 741; **wolt** *2 s* wilt HF 2099, B 369; wishest A 3511; **wol, wole** *3 s* BD 67, TC 3.1262, A 805, 1042; **wole, wol** *pl* BD 546, TC 2.311, A 816, 3362, D 1117; **wil** *2 pl* F 378; **wolde** *pt 1 s* intended B 4477; *pt 3 s* wished BD 1077, A 3959; *pt 3 pl* intended BD 351, 355; required F 591; **wolde . . . God** would that God grant F 756; **wolde whoso nolde** willy-nilly TC 1.77.

wolle *n* wool A 3249, C 448, 910.

wombe *n* abdomen, belly A 4290, B 3674; stomach B 3627, C 522; womb E 877.

wommanhede *n* womanhood A 1748, B 851; woman's arts TC 4.1462.

wommanliche *adj*: **w. wif** pattern of womanhood TC 3.1296.

wonder, -dre *adj* wonderful BD 233, HF 1083, A 2073; marvellous BD 61; strange TC 1.419.

wonder *adv* wonderfully BD 443, 452, A 483.

wonderly, -lych *adv* wonderfully HF 1173, A 84.

wondermost *adj* most wonderful HF 2059.

wondre(n) *v* wonder F 1514, G 245; show amazement B 1805, E 335; **wondre** *1 s* wonder G 246; **wondreth** *3 s* E 669; **wondren** *3 pl* E 1019, F 258; **wondred** *pt 3 s & pl* A 1445, F 225; **wondreden** *pt 3 pl* F 307; **wondred** *pp* F 236.

wone *n* custom HF 76, TC 2.318, 5.647, A 335.

wone *v* dwell TC 4.474, G 38, 332; **woneth** *3 s* D 1573, G 311; **woned** *pt 3 s* BD 889, D 2163; **woneden** *pt pl* A 2927; **wonynge** *part* A 388; **woned** *pp* BD 150, TC 1.276, B 4406. See **woned** *adj*.

woned, wont *adj* wont, accustomed PF 321, E 339, TC 5.277.

wonger *n* pillow B 2102.

wonyng *n* dwelling, habitation A 606.

wood, wod *adj* mad BD 104, HF 1809, TC 1.499, 2.1554, A 184, etc.; enraged D 664; unreasonable G 450; **woode** *def* TC 2.1355, 5.1213; **for wod** madly HF 1747.

wood *adv* madly, completely A 1456.

woodeth *3 s* rages G 467.

woodly *adv* madly A 1301.

woodnesse, wod- *n* madness TC 3.794, A 2011, C 496.

woon¹ *n* dwelling HF 1166; region B 1991; **wones** *pl* D 2105.

woon², won *n* course, alternative TC 4.1181; abundance BD 475.

wopen see **wepen**.

worcheth see **wirche**.

word *n* properly **ord: word and ende** from beginning to end TC 2.1495, 3.702, 5.1669, B 3911.

world *n* world A 176, etc.; **many a world** ages PF 81 (see note); **worldes** *descriptive gen* worldly PF 53, B 4390.

worm *n* worm PF 326; snake C 355.

worship(e) *n* honor BD 774, 1098, LGW 659, A 1904, F 571; **worshyp** BD 1032; **worshippe** renown, reputation BD 630.

worshipe *v* honor, reverence A 2251, B 1701; respect E 166.

worshipful *adj* honorable A 1435, B 3488.

wort *n* unfermented beer G 813.

wortes *n pl* herbs B 4411, 4464, E 226.

worth *adj* worth A 182, etc.; of value, worthy TC 3.14, H 200; worth while A 785.

worthen *v* be, dwell TC 5.329; **worth** *pt 3 s* got on, mounted B 1941; **worth thow upon** *imp s* get on, mount TC 2.1011; **wo (wel) worth(e)** wo (well) be it (to) HF 53, TC 2.344, 4.747, 5.379.

worthily *adv* worthily TC 2.186, A 2737; deservedly E 1022.

worthy *adj* worthy A 217, D 8, etc.; good, excellent HF 727; distinguished, eminent A 43, 68; proper, just HF 1669; **better w.** more proper, fitting LGW 317.

wot, woot see **witen.**

wowe *v* woo TC 5.791, 1091; **woweth** *3 s* A 3372, B 589.

wowke *n* week TC 4.1278, A 1539, F 1161. Cf. **wyke.**

wrak *n* wreck B 513.

wrak see **wreken.**

wrang *adv* wrong A 4252 (Northern).

wrastle(n) *v* wrestle A 3928, B 3456; **wrastleth** *3 s* A 2961.

wrastlyng(e) *n* wrestling PF 165, A 548, B 1930.

wrath(e), wratthe *n* anger BD 605, TC 5.147, 960; **wrethhe** TC 3.110.

wratthe(n) *v* make angry H 80; be angry with TC 3.174; **wraththed** *pp* angered BD 1151.

wraw *adj* angry H 46.

wrecche *n* exile G 58; wretch, wretched person BD 577, TC 1.777, A 931.

wrecche *adj* wretched B 285, F 1020; **wrechche** HF 919.

wrecchednesse, -chid- *n* wretchedness, misery TC 3.381, A 3897; baseness, meanness PF 601, TC 3.1787, Lak 13; base deed F 1523.

wreche *n* vengeance TC 5.890, B 679, 3403; punishment B 3793; **wrecche** affliction, misfortune, TC 2.784.

wreigh see **wrye.**

wreke(n) *v* avenge TC 1.62, 3.108, A 961; **wrak** *pt 3 s* TC 5.1468; **wrek** *imp s* B 3095; **wreke(n), wroken** *pp* revenged TC 1.88, 207, D 809, 2211, F 784.

wrekere *n* avenger PF 361.

wrenches *n pl* stratagems G 1081.

wreste *v* dispose TC 4.1427.

wrethe *n* wreath A 2145.

wreththe see **wrathe.**

wreye *v* betray, reveal TC 3.284, A 3503, F 944; **wreye** *2 s subj* A 3507.

wrighte *n* craftsman, carpenter A 614; **wrightes** *gen* A 3143.

write *v* write A 96, etc.; **write** *1 s* B 2154; **writest** *2 s* HF 633, E 1733; **writeth, writ** *3 s* HF 1385, B 77, D 709; **writen** *pl* A 1305, B 3438; *3 pl subj* may write A 2814; **wroot,**

wrot *pt 1 & 3 s* TC 1.655, 2.1214, B 725; **writ** *pt 3 s* B 3516, 4313; **write** *pt 1 s subj* should write B 3843; **writen** *pt pl* wrote HF 1441, 1515, F 233; **writeth** *imp pl* TC 5.1399; **write(n), ywrite(n)** *pp* PF 19, A 2350, B 191, 4632.

writhe(n) *v* turn TC 4.9; twist, squirm TC 4.986; **writh** *3 s* twists, winds TC 3.1231.

withyng *n* twisting F 127.

wroken see **wreken.**

wrooth, wroth(e) *adj* wroth, angry A 451, 1840, 4354; **wrooth(e), wrothe** *pl* BD 582, A 1179, E 2350; grieved, sad BD 1294.

wrye *v* cover TC 3.1569, E 887; cover up, conceal TC 1.329; **wrye** *1 s* cover D 1827; **wrien** *3 pl* TC 2.539; **wreigh** *pt 3 s* covered TC 3.1056; **wry** *imp s* wrap TC 2.380; **wrie, iwryen** *pp* covered, hidden TC 3.620, 1451; **ywrien** BD 628; **ywrye** covered, draped A 2904.

wrye(n), wri- *v* turn, change course BD 627, TC 2.906, H 262; **wryed** *pt 3 s* A 3283.

wrynge, wringe *v* wring, squeeze (water from) B 1666; wring the hands HF 299, E 1212; squeeze, force a way HF 2110; **wryngeth** *3 s* presses, pinches E 1553; **wrong, wroong** *pt 3 s* wrung TC 3.1531, 4.738, B 606; pinched D 492.

wyd *adj* wide, broad, extensive A 491, B 3139; **wyde, wide** *def & pl* LGW 289, A 93, 3099; spacious A 28.

wyde, wide *adv* widely TC 1.384, A 2454, E 722.

wyde-wher(e) *adv* widely, everywhere TC 3.404, B 136.

wydwe, widewe *n* widow TC 1.97, A 253, 1171; **wydwes, widewes** *gen* TC 1.109, B 1692; **wydwes** *pl* E 1423.

wyf, wif *n* woman BD 1037, TC 3.1296, C 71, D 998; wife BD 63; **wyves** *gen* B 1631, 3102; *pl* A 374; **to wyve** for wife A 1860.

wyfhod, wif- *n* womanhood LGW 253, B 76, D 149; married life LGW 545.

wyflees *adj* wifeless E 1236, 1248.

wyfly *adj* womanly E 429, 919.

wyke *n* week TC 2.430, B 1461; **wykes, wikes** *pl* TC 5.499, D 1852. Cf. **wowke.**

wyket, wiket *n* wicket, small gate HF 477, E 2045, 2159.

wyle *n* trick BD 673, A 3403, 4047; trickery, subtlety TC 2.271.

wylugh *n* willow A 2922.

wympul *n* wimple A 151 (see note).

wyn *n* wine A 334, etc.; **w. ape** ape-wine H 44 (see note).

wyndas *n* windlass F 184.

wynde *v* pass around, entwine, embrace PF 671, TC 3.1232; wrap E 583, G 42; involve G 980; turn over TC 2.601; bend TC 1.257; **wynde** *1 s* writhe D 1102; *2 s subj* may pass, go TC 3.1440; **wynt** *3 s* turns, directs LGW 85.

wyndmelle *n* windmill HF 1280.

wynke *v* close the eyes TC 3.1537, B 4496; glance F 348; **wynketh** *3 s* shuts (his) eyes B 4621; **wake or w.** wake or sleep PF 482; **loke or w.** look or not look TC 1.301.

wynne(n) *v* win BD 266, A 891; profit, gain TC 1.823, A 427; conquer TC 4.1196; ? complain TC 1.390 (see note); **wynne on** get the better of A 594; **wynnen from** get away from TC 5.1125; **wynne** *1 s* D 1570; *2 & 3 s subj* A 1617, D 414; **wan** *pt s & pl* BD 267, D 1477, F 1401; **wonne(n), ywonne** *pp* TC 2.1236, A 51, 877.

wynnyng *n* profit, gain, advantage A 275, D 416; **wynnynges** *pl* profits, gains HF 1965, B 127.

wynsynge *adj* skittish A 3263.

wynter *n* winter, year B 197; **wynter** *pl* PF 473, B 1216, etc.

wyrdes *n* fates TC 3.617.

wys *adj* wise, prudent A 68, 309, etc.; **wyse, wise** *def & pl* A 1804, 2983; *as n* wise one TC 1.79; wise people LGW 19; **worth to make it wys** worthwhile deliberating on the matter A 785 (see note).

wys, wis *adv* certainly, surely TC 2.474, A 2786; **also wys (as), as wys (as)** as surely as BD 683, TC 3.713, etc.

wyse, wise *n* way, manner TC 1.285, 363, 698; **in w. of** after the fashion of TC 5.64; **in alle w.** by all means B 1251.

wyt see **wit.**

wyte see **wite.**

wyvere *n* viper, snake TC 3.1010.

Y

y- prefix of the past participle and of a few infinitives.

yate *n* gate TC 2.617, E 1013, etc.; **yates** *pl* TC 2.615, 5.603; *gen pl* HF 1301.

ybake *pp* baked A 4312.

ybathed *pp* bathed TC 4.815.

ybe, ybee(n) *pp* been LGW 6, 289, B 4487, E 2401. See **ben.**

ybedded *pp* put to bed TC 5.346.

ybete(n) *pp* beaten TC 1.741, A 3759; **ybet** D 1285. See **gold-ybete.**

yblent *pp* blinded BD 647, A 3808. See **blende.**

yblessed *pp* blessed, praised D 44, H 99.

ybleynt *pp* abstained A 3753.

yblowe *pp* spread abroad HF 1139, TC 1.384.

yboght, ybought *pp* bought TC 1.810, A 3836. See **byen.**

yborn, ybore(n) *pp* born, borne A 378, 1019, E 158, 625.

ybounde(n) *pp* bound A 1149, 2151. See **bynde.**

ybrent, ybrend *pp* burned TC 4.77, A 946, G 318. See **brennen.**

ycheyned *pp* chained Buk 14.

yclenched *pp* bound A 1991.

ycleped, yclept *pp* called A 376, G 772. See **clepen.**

ycorouned *pp* crowned LGW 219.

ycorve(n), ykorven *pp* cut A 2013, B 1801, G 533. See **kerve.**

ycrased *pp* broken, perforated BD 324.

ycrowe *pp* crowed A 3357.

ydel *adj* idle BD 4, A 2505; **in (on) y.** in vain TC 1.955, C 642, F 867.

ydeled *pp* divided D 2249.

ydelly *adv* in vain C 446.

ydight *pp* furnished, supplied A 3205.

ydolastre *n* idolater B 3377, E 2298.

ydon, ydoo(n) *pp* done HF 1812, A 1025; finished BD 1236.

ydrawe *pp* drawn TC 3.853, A 396; gathered A 944.

ydred *pp* dreaded TC 3.1775.

ydressed *pp* placed E 381.

ydropped *pp* sprinkled A 2884.

ye *pron* ye A 780, etc.; **youre** *gen* your A 770, 2598, etc.; yours TC 4.1680, LGW 683; **youres** B 1464, 1474; **yow, you** *dat & acc* HF 547, A 34, 1273; **fro ye** (unstressed) from you TC 1.5.

ye, yee *adv* yea BD 1137, TC 1.77, A 3455, etc.

yë *n* eye BD 184, A 10, etc.; **yën** *pl* eyes TC 1.305, A 152; **at yë** before one's eye, plainly A 3016, E 1168; **I have non other yë** I have no partiality PF 630. See **eye.**

yeddynges *n pl* songs (generally narrative) A 237.

yede(n) see **gon.**

yeer(e), yer(e) *n* year A 347, 1458, B 132; **yeer** *pl* A 82, 601, etc.; **yeres** *pl* A 1521; **yeeris** F 1275; **to-yeere** this year D 168; **yeer by yere** B 1688; **fro yeer to yeer** D 1432.

yeldehalle *n* guildhall A 370.

yelde(n) *v* pay D 130, E 1452; surrender, give up TC 4.212, D 912, E 843; **yelt** *3 s* yields TC 1.385; **yelde** *3 s subj* reward TC 1.1055,

D 1772; **yeld** *imp s* grant C 189; **yeldeth** *imp pl* yield, give in TC 3.1208; **yeldyng** *part* LGW 149; **yolden** *pp* yielded TC 1.801, A 3052; **iyolden** *pp as adj* submissive TC 3.96.

yeldynge *n* yielding A 596.

yelle *v* yell A 2672; **yolleden** *pt 3 pl* yelled B 4579.

yelow *adj & n* yellow A 675, 2166; blond A 1049; **yelowe, yelewe, yelwe** *pl* BD 857, PF 186, A 1929.

yelpe *v* boast A 2238; *3 pl* TC 3.307.

yeman *n* yeoman, attendant, servant A 101, 3270, D 1380, G 562; **yemen** *pl* A 2509, 2728.

yemanly *adv* as a yeoman should A 106.

yerd, yeerd *n* yard, garden TC 2.820, B 4037, 4365.

yerde *n* rod, stick A 149, B 1287; cudgel TC 2.154; wand, caduceus A 1387; yard (length) A 1050.

yerne *adj* eager, lively A 3257.

yerne *adv* eagerly HF 910, PF 21, C 398; quickly PF 3, TC 3.151; soon TC 3.376; **as y.** very soon TC 4.112, 201; very quickly TC 3.151; **late or y.** late or early TC 3.376.

yerne *v* yearn BD 1092; desire TC 3.152; be desired TC 4.198.

yesternyght *adv* last night TC 5.221.

yeve(n), yive *v* give BD 242, HF 2112, A 232; **yeve** *1 s* B 1622; **yevest** *2 s* A 1284; **yeveth** *3 s* LGW 451; **yeve** *2 & 3 s subj* B 602, F 614; **yeve, yive** *pl* BD 695, TC 5.235; **yaf** *pt 1, 2, & 3 s* BD 1269, A 227, B 3641, D 599; **yave** *pt 3 s subj* TC 2.977; **yaf, yave** *pt pl* TC 2.1323, A 302, D 1744; **yif, yef, yeve** *imp s* BD 111, TC 5.308, A 2260; **yeve(n), yive(n)** *pp* BD 765, A 1086, D 401, 771.

yexeth *3 s* hiccups A 4151.

yfalle(n) *pp* fallen, happened A 25, B 3166.

yfare *pp* gone TC 3.577, 4.1169.

yfeere, yfere *adv* together TC 2.152, 910, B 394, etc.

yfet *pp* fetched F 174, G 1116.

yfetered *pp* fettered A 1229.

yfeyned *pp* avoided E 529.

yflatered *pp* flattered D 930, 1970.

yfolowed *pp* followed BD 390.

yforged *pp* forged A 3256.

yformed *pp* formed HF 490, TC 4.451, C 10.

yfostred *pp* fostered, brought up A 3946, E 213; helped, promoted F 874.

yfounded, i- *pp* founded, based BD 922, PF 231.

yfynde *v* find F 470, 1153; **yfounde** *pp* A 1211, B 1152.

ygeten *pp* got A 3564.

yglased *pp* glazed BD 323.

yglewed *pp* glued F 182.

yglosed *pp* flattered H 34.

ygo(n), ygoon *pp* gone B 599, 1402, F 293; attended A 286.

ygraunted *pp* granted C 388.

ygrave *pp* carved D 496; carved, engraved B 164, HF 1136, A 3796.

ygret *pp* greeted BD 517.

ygrounde *pp* ground, sharpened A 2549, B 2073; ground (of grain) A 3991.

ygrounded *pp* founded BD 921.

ygrowen *pp* grown A 3973.

yhalowed *pp* chased with shouts BD 379.

yharded *pp* hardened, tempered F 245.

yhated *pp* hated HF 200.

yhed, yhid *pp* hidden BD 175, G 317.

yheere *v* hear TC 4.1313, A 3176, E 2154.

yhent *pp* taken C 869; caught G 536.

yherd *pp* haired A 3738.

yheried *pp* praised TC 2.973.

yholde *pp* held, kept HF 1286, A 2958, E 1932; considered A 2374, C 602.

yhurt *pp* hurt A 2709.

yif *conj* if BD 1189.

yif see **yeven.**

yifte *n* gift BD 247, D 39, etc.; **yiftes** *pl* TC 4.392, C 148.

yis *adv* yes BD 526, HF 704, etc.

yit *adv* yet PF 10, E 120, F 1577.

yive see **yeven.**

ykaught *pp* caught BD 838. See **cacche.**

ykembd *pp* combed A 4369.

ykist *pp* kissed TC 4.1689.

yknet *pp* knit together TC 3.1734.

yknowe, i- *v* know, recognize HF 1336, D 1370, F 887. See **knowen.**

ykorven see **ycorven.**

ykoud *pp* known BD 666. See **conne.**

ylad *pp* carried A 530. See **leden.**

ylaft *pp* left A 2746, 3862, F 1128.

yle, ile *n* island HF 416, 440, B 68, 545.

ylent *pp* lent G 1406.

yleyd *pp* laid B 1442, 3328; placed A 3568.

yliche, ylyche *adj* like, alike HF 1328, LGW 389.

yliche, ylyche *adv* alike, equally BD 9, 803, A 2526, D 2215.

ylik(e), ylyk *adj* like, alike TC 3.144, A 592, 2734.

ylike *adv* alike, equally D 2230, G 850; **evere y., evere in oon y.** uniformly, constantly TC 3.485, E 602.

ylissed *pp* eased TC 1.1089.

ylke see **ilke.**

ylogged *pp* lodged B 4181.

yloren *pp* lost LGW 26. See **lesen.**

ylost *pp* lost HF 183, 1257, TC 4.1283, A 4314. See **lesen.**

ylymed *pp* caught (as with birdlime) D 934.

ymaad, ymad *pp* made HF 120, 691, LGW 550, C 382, F 218.

ymageries *n pl* carvings HF 1304.

ymages *n pl* images (in astrology or magic) HF 1269.

ymaginatyf *adj* given to imagining F 1094.

ymaginyng *n* plotting A 1995.

ymagynacioun *n* imagination, thoughts BD 14.

ymagynen, -gin- *v* imagine TC 2.836; devise TC 4.1626.

ymaked *pp* made LGW 122, A 2065, 4245.

ymarked *pp* fixed, recorded HF 1103.

ymasked *pp* enmeshed TC 3.1734.

ymel *prep* among (Northern) A 4171.

yment *pp* intended HF 1742.

ymet *pp* met TC 2.586, A 2624; **ymette** *pl* B 1115.

ymeynd *pp* mingled A 2170.

ympes *n pl* shoots B 3146.

ympne *n* hymn, song LGW 422.

ynly see **inly.**

ynogh, ynough, ynow(e) *adj & pron* enough PF 185, A 373, 3178, B 1409, D 1681.

ynogh, ynough, ynow *adv* enough A 888, 3629, F 708.

ynome *pp* taken TC 1.242. See **nam.**

ynorissed, -sshed *pp* brought up TC 5.821, A 3948.

yolden see **yelden.**

yolleden see **yelle.**

yomanrye *n* yeomanry A 3949 (see note).

yong *adj* young A 79, etc.

yore, yoore *adv* formerly, in the past, before TC 5.324, B 174, 1167; long ago PF 476; for a while F 403; **ful y.** for a long time A 3897, 4230; **of tyme y.** for some time F 963; **y. ago(n)** long ago PF 17, TC 5.317, A 1941.

youlyng *n* howling A 1278.

your(e)self, your(e)selven *pron (refl & intensive)* yourself TC 5.881, A 1835, D 1232, E 361; *as pers pron* you yourself (subject) TC 2.131, 3.668, E 1740; (object) TC 3.1005, 1330.

ypassed *pp* passed E 1892.

ypayed *pp* paid A 1802, B 1588, F 1618.

ypiked *pp* sorted G 941.

yplesed *pp* pleased D 930.

ypleyned *pp* lamented TC 4.1688.

ypleynted *pp* full of complaint TC 5.1597.

ypocras *n* a spiced drink, spiced wine C 306, E 1807.

ypocryte, –crite *n* hypocrite F 514, 520.

yprayed *pp* invited E 269.

ypreised, –eys- *pp* praised HF 1577, TC 5.1473.

ypreved *pp* proved A 485.

ypulled *pp* plucked A 3245.

ypunysshed *pp* punished A 657.

yput *pp* put TC 3.275, D 1333, G 762.

yqueynt *pp* quenched A 3754. See **quenchen**.

yquit *pp* acquitted F 673.

yraft *pp* taken away A 2015. See **reven**.

yre see **ire**.

yred *pp* read TC 4.799.

yreke *pp* raked up A 3882.

yrekened *pp* held accountable D 367; considered F 427.

yren see **iren**.

yrent *pp* torn B 844.

yroght *pp* wrought A 196, B 2054. See **wirche**.

yronge *pp* rung, proclaimed HF 1655.

yronne(n) *pp* A 8, 2165, 2693, etc.

yrouned *pp* whispered HF 2107.

ysatled *pp* settled E 2405.

ysayd *pp* said BD 270.

yscalded *pp* scalded A 2020.

yse *n* ice HF 1130.

yse(e), ise *v* see, behold BD 205, HF 804, TC 5.747, LGW 15; gaze TC 2.354; **yseyn, yseye** *pp* seen HF 1367, TC 2.168, 5.448. See **seen**.

ysene, yseene *adj* visible TC 1.700, A 592, F 996; evident TC 5.1607.

ysent *pp* sent HF 984, B 1041.

yserved *pp* served HF 678, TC 5.437, 1721, A 963.

yshadwed *pp* shaded A 607.

yshamed *pp* disgraced HF 356.

yshape(n) *pp* shaped, proportioned

TC 3.411, H 43; decreed TC 3.1240, Scogan 8; prepared B 3420, G 1080; provided A 4179.

yshave *pp* shaved B 1499, 3261.

yshent *pp* put to shame D 1312.

yshette *pp* (*pl*) shut TC 3.233, B 560.

yshewed *pp* showed TC 5.1251.

yshore, yshorn *pp* shorn TC 4.996, A 589.

yshryve(n) *pp* shriven A 226, C 380.

yslayn *pp* slain HF 159, A 2832, B605, F 1365; **yslawe** B 484, C 856.

ysonder *adv* see **asonder**.

ysonge(n) *pp* sung HF 1397, LGW 270, D 1726.

ysounded *pp* sunk, penetrated TC 2.535.

ysowe(n) *pp* sown HF 1488, D 71.

yspared *pp* spared E 2301.

ysped *pp* succeeded, fared A 4220.

ysprad *pp* spread B 1644; **yspred** A 4140.

yspreynd *pp* sprinkled A 2169.

yspronge *pp* spread HF 2081.

ystalled *pp* installed, seated HF 1364.

ystiked *pp* pierced, stabbed A 1565, F 1476.

ystonde *pp* stood TC 5.1612.

ystonge *pp* stung C 355.

ystorve *pp* having died A 2014.

ystrawed *pp* strewn BD 629.

ystynt *pp* stopped, ended D 390.

ysuffred *pp* suffered TC 5.415.

ysweped *pp* swept G 938.

yswonke *pp* labored H 18.

yswore *pp* sworn HF 421, F 325; **ysworn** A 3301, F 1038.

yt see **hit**.

ytake *pp* taken A 3353, B 348, 1858; **ytaken** undertaken TC 5.1765.

ytaught *pp* taught A 127, 755, B 1699, G 267.

yteyd *pp* fastened A 457.

ythanked, ythonked *pp* thanked TC 4.2, D 2118.

ythe *v* thrive TC 2.670, 4.439.

ythrowe *pp* thrown TC 4.6, G 940; cast TC 4.482.

ytoold, ytold *pp* told A 3109, 3913, G 627, I 31.

ytressed *pp* braided TC 5.810.

ytukked *pp* tucked up, belted in D 1737.

yturned *pp* turned BD 446, A 1238.

ytwynned *pp* separated TC 4.788.

yvel *adj & n* evil, ill A 3173, B 1595, etc.; **on y.** amiss TC 5.1625.

yvel(e) *adv* ill A 1127, 3715; **y. avysed** ill advised H 335; **y. apayed** displeased, dissatisfied E 1052, G 921.

yvoyded *pp* got rid of F 1159.

yvoyre, yvory *n* ivory BD 946, B 2066, D 1741.

ywar *adj* watchful, on guard TC 2.398.

ywarned *pp* warned B 4422.

ywaxe *pp* grown BD 1275.

ywedded *pp* wedded A 3098, B 712, D 7.

ywent[1] *pp* gone HF 976.

ywent[2] *pp* weened, supposed TC 5.444.

ywet *pp* wet A 4155.

ywis, iwis *adv* certainly, surely BD 1267, TC 1.415, 3.105, A 3277, etc.

ywonne *pp* won TC 2.1236, A 2659, D 2293; gained TC 3.280.

yworthe *pp* having become BD 579.

ywoxen *pp* grown TC 5.275, 708, E 1462.

ywrite(n) *pp* written B 191, 4632.

ywroght, iwrought *pp* wrought, made BD 327, A 196, B 2054, D117, E 1324; fashioned PF 418.

ywroke(n) *pp* wreaked TC 5.589; revenged Scogan 26.

ywrye, ywrien *pp* covered, hidden BD 628, TC 4.1654; draped A 2904.

ywympled *pp* wearing a wimple A 470.

Z

zeles *n pl* zeal TC 5.1859.